T0398479

# Handbook of Research on Global Hospitality and Tourism Management

Angelo A. Camillo
*Woodbury University, USA*

A volume in the Advances in Hospitality, Tourism, and the Services Industry (AHTSI) Book Series

An Imprint of IGI Global

| | |
|---|---|
| Managing Director: | Lindsay Johnston |
| Managing Editor: | Austin DeMarco |
| Director of Intellectual Property & Contracts: | Jan Travers |
| Acquisitions Editor: | Kayla Wolfe |
| Production Editor: | Christina Henning |
| Development Editor: | Caitlyn Martin |
| Typesetter: | Lisandro Gonzalez |
| Cover Design: | Jason Mull |

Published in the United States of America by
    Business Science Reference (an imprint of IGI Global)
    701 E. Chocolate Avenue
    Hershey PA, USA 17033
    Tel: 717-533-8845
    Fax: 717-533-8661
    E-mail: cust@igi-global.com
    Web site: http://www.igi-global.com

Library of Congress Cataloging-in-Publication Data

Handbook of research on global hospitality and tourism management / Angelo A. Camillo, editor.
    pages cm
 Includes bibliographical references and index.
  ISBN 978-1-4666-8606-9 (hardcover) -- ISBN 978-1-4666-8607-6 (ebook) 1. Tourism--Research--Methodology. 2. Hospitality industry--Research. I. Camillo, Angelo, 1954- editor.
 G155.7.H37 2015
 910.68--dc23
                  2015012015

This book is published in the IGI Global book series Advances in Hospitality, Tourism, and the Services Industry (AHTSI) (ISSN: Pending; eISSN: Pending)

British Cataloguing in Publication Data
A Cataloguing in Publication record for this book is available from the British Library.

For electronic access to this publication, please contact: eresources@igi-global.com.

# Advances in Hospitality, Tourism, and the Services Industry (AHTSI) Book Series

ISSN: Pending
EISSN: Pending

## MISSION

Globally, the hospitality, travel, tourism, and services industries generate a significant percentage of revenue and represent a large portion of the business world. Even in tough economic times, these industries thrive as individuals continue to spend on leisure and recreation activities as well as services.

**The Advances in Hospitality, Tourism, and the Services Industry (AHTSI)** book series offers diverse publications relating to the management, promotion, and profitability of the leisure, recreation, and services industries. Highlighting current research pertaining to various topics within the realm of hospitality, travel, tourism, and services management, the titles found within the AHTSI book series are pertinent to the research and professional needs of managers, business practitioners, researchers, and upper-level students studying in the field.

## COVERAGE

- Cruise Marketing and Sales
- Hotel Management
- Health and Wellness Tourism
- Tourism and the Environment
- Service Training
- Service Design
- Leisure & Business Travel
- Casino Management
- Destination Marketing and Management
- Customer Service Issues

IGI Global is currently accepting manuscripts for publication within this series. To submit a proposal for a volume in this series, please contact our Acquisition Editors at Acquisitions@igi-global.com or visit: http://www.igi-global.com/publish/.

# Titles in this Series

www.igi-global.com

701 E. Chocolate Ave., Hershey, PA 17033
Order online at www.igi-global.com or call 717-533-8845 x100
To place a standing order for titles released in this series, contact: cust@igi-global.com
Mon-Fri 8:00 am - 5:00 pm (est) or fax 24 hours a day 717-533-8661

*To my wife Maggie and my daughters Carolina and Donatella for their love and support in my daily task.*

# List of Contributors

# Table of Contents

# Detailed Table of Contents

>   *Angelo Camillo, Woodbury University, USA*
>   *Angelo Presenza, University G. D'Annunzio of Chieti-Pescara, Italy*
>   *Francesca Di Virgilio, University of Molise, Italy*

This chapter introduces the concept of "Albergo Diffuso" (Diffused Hotel), (AD). A hotel typology that is emerging as a sustainable accommodation with the potential to compete and establish itself as a viable hotel business. To raise awareness about the concept we analyze the scarce literature available and the rather limited publicly available resources provided by the Association of Albergo Diffuso (AAD). We also conducted non-intrusive observations through personal on-location investigative visits of various ADs operations. We present a sample guests' satisfaction ratings of the concept by conducting a web content analysis of the Trip Advisor's website, a hotel rating platform, on the Residenza Sveva, an Albergo Diffuso property located in the city of Termoli, in the Region of Molise in South Central Italy. The data shows that this concept is patronized largely by couples but also by business travelers. The site gives this property a 4.5 / 5 star rating.

>   *Hanafi Hamzah, Universiti Putra, Malaysia*
>   *Shahrim Karim, Universiti Putra, Malaysia*
>   *Angelo Camillo, Woodbury University, USA*
>   *Svetlana Holt, Woodbury University, USA*

In the last decades, the tourism and hospitality industries have increased their awareness toward environmental sustainability and the application of Environmental Management Systems (EMS). However, research into EMS application and its challenges in the hospitality industry has been left out of sight. In fact, it appears that most hospitality and tourism organizations have neglected to adopt and implement EMS and have failed to recognize the benefits EMS can offer. Perhaps this may explain mixed findings on EMS success adoption and implementation to date. This conceptual paper investigates the challenges and opportunities within the concept of sustainability and aims to sum the existing knowledge on EMSs and the opportunities for its successful implementation in tourism and hospitality establishments. The findings will raise awareness of the importance of EMS and stimulate changes in the way management puts its effort toward enhancing the value these establishments put on adoption and implementation of EMS.

**Chapter 3**

    *Angelo Camillo, Woodbury University, USA*
    *Loredana Di Pietro, University of Molise, Italy*

This chapter investigates the determining factors of the popularity of Italian cuisine in mainland China and attitude of restaurant patrons toward Italian cuisine. Published literature suggests that Italian cuisine abroad was first made familiar by Italian national who immigrated to countries in Europe, the Americas and Oceania. The growing popularity of Italian cuisine around the world today continues to shape the global evolution of ethnic cuisines because of its taste and simplicity of food preparation. Chinese patrons support this theory however; they find that Italian restaurants in China have expensively priced menus, and that they doubt the authenticity of Italian food preparation and question originality of Italian ingredients being used. These perceived negative factors identified could hamper this world-renowned cuisine from sustaining its popularity in China. The study used an online survey methodology and applied statistical analysis techniques to determine the factors relative to the popularity of Italian cuisine in mainland China and to the attitude of Chinese restaurant patrons. The results will contribute to the body of knowledge of hospitality marketing and tourism related studies and will help hospitality operators and future investors of new restaurant ventures in the decision making process whether to invest and operate an Italian restaurant in mainland China.

**Chapter 4**

    *Frances Cassidy, University of Southern Queensland, Australia*
    *Margee Hume, Central Queensland University, Australia*

Core and peripheral destinations are very significant to island tourism because of core and peripheral islands. Peripheral locations may be disadvantaged as they are isolated from the core or economic centers and from the main population. This chapter reviews literature on the complexity of core and peripheral destinations, their development, planning, marketing and management together with local resident's perceptions of tourists and the tourist's expectations. The South Pacific is defined and it's Colonial past discussed together with tourist motivations. It is becoming increasingly difficult for all stakeholders to agree on programs and tourism practices and that various South Pacific countries have different ways of collecting statistical data resulting in few generic standards to adhere to.

The aim of this chapter is to study the cooperation between Destination Management Organizations and hospitality stakeholders. The following research questions are addressed in this research: 1. What is the stakeholders' attitude toward cooperation with DMOs in a new destination and in a mass-tourism destination? 2. In DMOs' perspective, what are the most effective strategies to foster cooperation within the destination? 3. What is the level of commitment of hospitality stakeholders with respect to cooperation with DMOs? In order to discuss these points we provide an analysis of two Italian destinations. Specifically we examine an established mass-tourism destination and a new destination. By investigating this relationship we also analyze how cooperation has developed during the years within two destinations, and if actually hospitality stakeholders are interested in cooperating with DMOs, in achieving the destinations' common goals.

Numerous studies have attempted to determine what makes hospitality expatriate executives successful and a large variety of managerial skills have been generated. The rapidly increasing trend toward internationalization of business has fostered an interest in examining important management skills that international hospitality executives should possess. The study findings indicated that there were underlying dimensions that contributed to the success of hospitality expatriate executives on their overseas assignment. National culture and corporate using management skills could influence a successful overseas assignment. However, it was not revealed which one between the two dimensions has more influence towards a successful overseas assignment. Successful expatriates are being profiled as organizations have found that expatriate assignments are an effective, yet expensive, means of developing international qualities in their managers. The increasing globalization of business appears to have led to the emergence of an international business workforce that shares a unique set of cultural beliefs, attitudes, and behaviors. The thrust of this chapter was to examine the influence of national culture and corporate culture of hospitality expatriate executives that led to a successful overseas assignment.

Tourism sector that is increasingly important in the world economy, developing rapidly in Turkey and provides a serious contributions to country's economy because Turkey consistently has a current account deficit, tourism is an important source of income. There are many factors affecting tourism; it is clear that the industry can be affected by changes in macroeconomic variables, just like any other economic focus. In this context, it is possible that the foreign exchange rate and changes in the value of various currencies can affect tourism, especially with regards to the demands of the tourists themselves. By using the Johansen cointegration and Granger causality tests, this chapter focused on identifying the relationship between currency exchange rates and the demand for tourism in Turkey.

# Chapter 8

This chapter analyzes the role of local area resources in the global hospitality market as a way for small and medium enterprises to create a portfolio of distinctive resources to reach a sustainable competitive advantage position in the international markets. After a brief introduction on the tourism industry and its main change factors the chapter adopts a resource base and market-driven approach in order to identify resources role in shaping competitive advantages. The chapter discuss a case-study on a successful example of diffused hotel in Abruzzo, Italy, identifying the core resources and those needed to support them in creating a successful tourism product.

# Chapter 9

Revolutionary development in field of communication and information technology have globally opened new avenue of marketing tourism and hospitality products. Major shift in web usage happened when Napster in 1999 released peer-to-peer share media and then with pioneer social networking websites named 'Six Degrees'. This kind of interactive social web was named as 'Web 2.0'. It would create openness, community and interaction. Web2. is also known as Social media base. Social media is incudes "all the different kinds of content that form social networks: posts on blogs or forums, photos, audio, videos, links, profiles on social networking web sites, status updates and more". It allows people to create; upload post and share content easily and share globally. Social media allows the creation and exchange of user-generated content and experiences online. Thus, social media is any kind of information we share with our social network, using social networking web sites and services.

This chapter analyzes organizational citizenship behavior of permanent versus contingent employees in the Italian hospitality industry. The empirical data were derived from a questionnaire survey conducted in three regions of Southern Italy. Survey respondents were 848 frontline employees from 63 hotels. Findings show that contingent employees exhibited less helping behavior than permanent employees but no difference in their voice behavior. In addition, work status was found to make more of a difference in both helping and voice in less work centrality organizations. Hotel managers are encouraged to focus attention on individual behavior that is discretionary, not directly or explicitly recognized by the formal reward system, and that in the aggregate promotes the effective functioning of the organization. Particularly in Italy, it would be advantageous to develop retention strategies for talented people that exhibit a high degree of organizational citizenship behavior.

# Chapter 11

Luxury hotel and resort spas have been perceived and criticized for their similarities and for not having a true authentic or culturally thematic identity, and for losing their original intention of a spa experience due to rapid commercialization. Empirical research relating to spa management is also limited. The purposes of this chapter are (1) to highlight some of the important global market trends that force all sectors of the travel industry to gear towards a healthy, wellness-minded concept in designing their products and services; (2) to define wellness tourism and the meaning of spa; (3) to address several under-researched variables that account for a crucial role in differentiating or characterizing a spa's identity and customers' preferences or perceived authenticity of a spa. Relevant literature is reviewed. Theories from multiple fields are applied. Future research and managerial implications will also be discussed in the content of this chapter.

# Chapter 12

Hofstede's cultural framework has been very instrumental in furthering an understanding of cross-cultural management and taken center stage as the dominant cultural paradigm to show respect for norms, values, and management styles across cultures. However, resent research on cross-cultural management suggests to go beyond Hofstede's cultural framework and use non-Western, Asian cultural norms which might provide additional insights into the impact of cultural values on service quality dimensions and the resultant implications for customer expectations and satisfaction. This chapter attends to this call and examines the practice of service quality in hospitality sector in the Republic of China (Taiwan) so it may serve as a reference point against which to interpret the fieldwork data of cross-cultural service quality research and its implications for customers' perceptions towards service quality.

Effective tourism strategies of a developing country can create revenue generating opportunities (tax revenues) and provide sustainable employment for semi-skilled or unskilled workers. Such tourism development strategies require systemic thinking and comprehensive investment portfolio strategies regarding the tourism industry as a whole, i.e. going beyond investing in hotels, but also including transportation infrastructure, catering, restaurants, safe water, financial system etc. In other words, the destination countries need to review their tourism value & supply chains and identify structural impediments to the full utilization of their tourism assets and facilities. This chapter shows how Least Developed Countries (LDCs) can define their tourism sector development and suggests a framework which can be used by a LDC to assess its tourism development potential. It can also be used by potential investors interested in investing in an LDC's tourism sector who need to understand the broader context of doing business in LDCs.

# Chapter 14

Managing human resources in the hospitality industry is a challenging task. In today's competitive environment, an increasing number of organizations invest in promoting diversity in the workplace. The concept of diversity as a value is based on the recognition, acceptance, and respect. It implies understanding that each individual is unique and recognizing and valuing the individual differences. Therefore, it is very important to understand "how diversity impacts individual and team processes and outcomes in the workplace". This chapter introduces the notion of diversity in hotel industry: its role, its interrelationship with satisfaction and teamwork. Emphasis is given on the fact that the right to difference and diversity should be incorporated not only in the whole range of processes, strategies, and actions of the company but also within the corporate culture.

# Chapter 15

The search for the right 'pedigree' of innovative menus is endless. As the consumer foodservice markets are converging to one global market, increasingly demand for new menus is evitable. In today's global foodservice markets, the fast changing trend of consumers' preferences and acceptances poses a huge challenge for restaurateurs in managing their new menu innovation. Empirically, little is known the trendsetting in managing menu innovation amid facing market uncertainty. While there are several attributes that have been known to impact menu innovation, this chapter specifically aims to provide empirical evidence of the moderating effect of food trends on the link between innovation orientations and new menu development (NMD) process in a recently concluded research study of chain restaurants in Malaysia.

## Chapter 16

*Sunny Jeong, Wittenberg University, USA*

This chapter examines and compares closely two virtual travel enterprises, Couchsurfing.org (CS, USA) and Gilbut.net (Gilbut, Korea). These platforms allow people to offer free travel resources including information, accommodation and transportation. Both organizations have become a mission driven enterprises similar to a not for profit model, and are run without receiving any advertising funds from the private sector. Their different cultural orientation provides interesting insights that emphasize same core strategies to create a critical mass of highly motivated contributors. At the same time, cultural differences suggest that technical features and core designs should be customized according to the cultural preferences such as the degree of individual visibilities and strong/weak group identity. Comparison of both networks provides an invaluable insight to understand how critical it is to set up strategic online features in order to promote reciprocity and a certain degree of anonymity.

## Chapter 17

*Lichia Yiu, Centre for Socio-EcoNomic Development (CSEND), Switzerland*
*Raymond Saner, Centre for Socio-EcoNomic Development (CSEND), Switzerland*
*Marcus Raphael Lee, Centre for Socio-EcoNomic Development (CSEND), Switzerland*

The objective of this chapter is to map and analyze the available tourism assets and products in the Kingdom of Lesotho. The analysis includes assessments on how to improve performance and sustainability of the tourism industry in Lesotho including greater utilization of existing tourism infrastructure and further development of Lesotho's tourism products. This chapter also addresses the strategic issues of tourism development and how Lesotho could increase the number of its tourists. Tourism development has been identified by the government of Lesotho, the International Monetary Fund as well as the United Nations World Tourism Organization as a sector that can reduce poverty as well as absorb low or semi skilled labor. Boosting the tourism sector in Lesotho would work towards alleviating poverty in the Kingdom overall. This chapter applies a case approach in order to illustrate potential investment opportunities and tourism performance improvements in an existing ski resort in Lesotho.

## Chapter 18

*Raphaël K. Akamavi, The University of Hull, UK*
*Yue Xu, The University of Hull, UK*
*Hrisa Mitreva, The University of Hull, UK*

The global airline industry has currently experienced major changes toward cooperation, where competitive advantages can be built via alliance memberships. The pressure of forming an appropriate alliance strategy is increasing because the airline industry has currently experienced uppermost shifts: intensive rivalry, rapid growth of technological explosion, environmental and terrorist events, etc. Despite positive pre-alliance motivations as recognized in most cases, after certain alliances strategies are formed and implemented, the post-alliance performance is not always satisfactory. Thus, the question of: how do pre-alliance motives and strategies affect post-alliance performance in the airline industry seems under explored. This study therefore looks into the triple relationships among: motives, strategy and performance. This study employs a systematic literature review method for this research topic. The review explores the main factors consisting of each triple dimension and then the linkages between them. Subsequently, it identifies theoretical gaps which indicate areas of further investigations.

# Chapter 19

Learning organizations (LOs) have been identified as an innovative practice essential for global businesses to not only effectively compete in today's dynamic environment but also to achieve and maintain a sustainable competitive advantage and increase overall firm performance. The objective of this chapter is to examine the current body of knowledge on LOs and their impact on sustainability practices in an effort to identify what is being done by organizations, where knowledge is applied, and, how systems are created to influence sustainability practices. In the context of hospitality and tourism businesses, the literature examining LOs is limited though a wealth of studies have been conducted in the mainstream. Using a qualitative approach, a content analysis was conducted to investigate its impact on sustainability practices in hospitality and tourism organizations. The results indicate that destinations in particular have adopted this approach to compete globally and to address triple-bottom line sustainability.

# Chapter 20

This chapter provides an exploration of female sex tourism, or romance tourism, a global consumer phenomenon that has evolved over several decades. Amidst forward strides in their social and economic empowerment, many women in advanced countries still experience marginalizing constraints to their freedom, mobility, and expression in many aspects of life. Yet, scholarly research and anecdotal evidence suggest that some women have utilized sex tourism as a means to escape such domestic constraints and find entrée to myriad social and cultural privileges at certain destinations abroad. Moving beyond tenured, clichéd stereotypes that typically associate sex tourism with male consumers, this chapter brings to light the rationale, justifications, criticisms, and cultural issues pervading this institution. Despite its liberating potential for women, female sex tourism does, at least somewhat, rely upon and reinforce historically entrenched national and cultural demarcations that tend to marginalize the people (partners, families, communities) of targeted destinations in the developing world.

    *Quee-Ling Leong, Universiti Putra Malaysia, Malaysia*
    *Shahrim Karim, Universiti Putra Malaysia, Malaysia*

Malaysia offers a rich potpourri of delicious cuisines from diverse ethnicity. However, not much attention given to promote Malaysian food and the food seems to be ignored in the tourism industry. Furthermore, the concept of utilizing Malaysian food as a marketing means is tenuous. In this chapter, the image dimensions of Malaysian food and the effect of food images on tourists' satisfaction are discussed. Additionally, the influence of socio-demographic factors on tourists' perceived image is deliberated. Univariate and multivariate statistics are used to describe the obtained findings. The results of the study will significantly fill in the gap in the literature about Malaysian food's image and the potential of Malaysia being promoted as a food destination. Additionally, the results would indisputably provide better insight to the tourism and hospitality industry on the perceptions of international tourists towards Malaysian food and Malaysia as a food tourism destination.

    *Maja Šerić, University of Valencia, Spain*
    *Irene Gil-Saura, University of Valencia, Spain*
    *Alejandro Mollá-Descals, University of Valencia, Spain*

The Integrated Marketing Communications (IMC) approach appeared as a response to the need for more sophisticated marketing communication discipline in a confusing tourism marketing environment. This chapter examines the impact of IMC on the hotel brand equity dimensions, i.e. brand image, perceived quality, and brand loyalty. Moreover, it estimates the moderating effect of national culture on the relationships examined. The study is approached from the customer perspective and uses survey methodology to assess guests' perception of IMC and brand equity in the hotel contexts. In particular, 335 hotel guests participated in the empirical investigation while staying in high-quality hotels in Rome, Italy. The findings reveal that IMC exerts a positive impact on hotel brand equity. Furthermore, the inter-relationship exists between the three dimensions of hotel brand equity. In general, national culture does not exert a significant impact within the posited model.

    *Ben Tran, Alliant International University, USA*

Many international hotel chains (IHCs) have sent their employees, their expatriates, overseas to maintain corporate standards, fill skills gaps, and transfer technology and corporate culture in their worldwide properties. The workforce is the backbone of any organization, and IHCs should pay careful attention to trends as well as published research to reduce failures that will ultimately affect its financial state as well as the organization as a whole. This chapter will be on the hotel industry in China. Hence, the focus of this chapter is on the matter that when IHCs are selecting expatriates to send to China, IHRM and IHCs need to identify and assess these expatriates' other characteristics (O). These O characteristics are: (1) desire to prematurely terminate an expatriate's assignment; (2) stable competencies; and (3) intercultural/international business communication.

The principal objective of this paper is to demonstrate the best practices in the rising trend of H2H and Medical Tourism. The concept of "Experience Economy" expedites the merging process of hospitality and hospitals: patients are also travelers now whose needs are not merely commodity type of medical care anymore but a memorable wellbeing experience. Moreover, H2H optimizes the process of realizing excellent care, which serves as the fundamental reason for tourism industry. In the section of "Best Practices in Medical Tourism, Christiana Care Way, Starwood Five Human Truths, and H2H packages in Switzerland are selected to show how patient/guest experience can be made more interactive and less transactional. Therefore, although H2H demands the considerable collaboration from all parties involved in order to ultimately present the excellent care that customers, tourists, and patients want, H2H indeed carries tremendous opportunity for hospitals, hotels, Spa, restaurants, transportation, and more.

The aim of this chapter is to explore how Corporate Social Responsibility (CSR) associations and corporate image influence customers´ behavior. Specifically, a model is proposed in which CSR and corporate image positively condition customer loyalty. It also proposes that the company´ social responsible initiatives influence customer satisfaction. In order to test this model structural equation modelling is employed on a sample of 382 Spanish hotel customers. This study finds that both corporate image and customer satisfaction contribute to achieve customer loyalty, also proving the roles of corporate image as a mediating variable. Additionally, our results show that CSR influences customer satisfaction. Finally, although we did not corroborate that CSR associations increase customer loyalty CSR associations have an indirect effect on loyalty through corporate image. As the results of studies concerning loyalty will depend on the services or products examined other business areas should be considered to find out about the generalization of these results. Second, other relevant variables could be included in further research.

This chapter endeavors to draw attention to staff turnover in the hospitality industry by analyzing a company, which will be referred to as "Crossboarder Hotel Company". The actual name has been disguised to maintain the company's confidentiality. The chapter discusses the causes and effects of employee turnover and ways to prevent turnover. Turnover is divided into three categories: job dissatisfaction, errors in employee selection, and poor management. The common cause of turnover however; is job dissatisfaction which affects employees well-being. A survey instrument that included measures of job satisfaction, and demographic information was used to collect information from hotel employees of an American Hotel Chain we refer to as the "Crossboarder Hotel Company", geographically dispersed in Georgia, Alabama, California, North Carolina, Arizona, Texas, Utah, and Indiana. Data from 78 respondents were collected over a three-year period. The results show that favouritism, nepotism, lack of responsibility and accountability, lack of training and improper communication negatively contributed to job satisfaction.

# Preface

Hospitality and Tourism are truly global in nature. This industry is the second largest employer in the world with one in 11 jobs being related to tourism. According to World Tourism Organization (UNWTO, 2015), over 1 billion tourists have contributed over $1.3 trillion in aggregate exports in 2013. The U.S. Travel Association alone estimates that in 2014 tourism in the U.S. contributes $2.1 trillion in economic impact and about $133.9 billion in taxes. In 2015 the restaurant sector which consist of one million restaurants in the U.S. alone, will generate $1.9 billion daily sales ($709.2 billion annual sales) with 1.5% restaurant industry sales increase in real (inflation-adjusted) terms. It shares 4% sales of the U.S. gross domestic product and 47%: Restaurant industry share of the food dollar. It employees 14 million people and by 2025 it will create 1.7 million new restaurant jobs. Over 10% of the Restaurant workforce as part of the overall U.S. workforce.

The purpose of this book is to contribute to the body of knowledge of Research on Global Hospitality and Tourism Management. It meets the demand for contemporary and futuristic Global Hospitality and Tourism Management learning tool that encompasses knowledge of theory and practice for all stakeholders involved in the Global Hospitality Industry, the largest industry in the world.

This book takes a global view of the challenges and opportunities hospitality and tourism managers face in the global market place. I am pleased to share with you that this book is conceptualized as a scholarly resource, with research articles from four continents. Specifically, the book aims at expanding the concept of "Global Hospitality and Tourism Management" by focusing on what is required to manage modern and ever-challenging hotel enterprises as well as tourism destinations. As the title suggests the book offers valuable discoveries and confirmations based on scientific research and blind peer reviews within the framework of hospitality and future developments in the global market place. The book is based on arduous theoretical and practical development. It is an ideal tool for global hospitality and tourism managers and researchers.

The topics covered include: Business Development / emerging hotel typology, ISO Certification, Strategy, Destination/ marketing management, Organization Behavior, Managerial-Corporate Finance, Global strategy and competitiveness, Social Media-Internet Marketing-Digital Marketing, Organizational citizenship behavior, Global marketing, Wellness trends, Cultural awareness, Tourism development, Food Trends, Innovation, Menu marketing, Strategic Risk Management, Virtual Enterprise, Tourism development, Strategic Alliance, Sustainability, Competitive advantage, Global Sex and Romance Tourism, Integrated marketing, Communication, Medical Tourism, Consumer Behavior and CSR, Strategic Human Resources Management.

In chapter 1, Camillo, Presenza and Di Virgilio discuss the characteristics and dynamic development of an emergent hotel business model in Italy: "Albergo Diffuso" (Diffused Hotel). A hotel typology that is emerging as a sustainable accommodation with the potential to compete and establish itself as a viable hotel business.

In chapter 2 the authors Hamzah, Karim, Camillo and Holt present the challenges in establishing environmental management systems in tourism and hospitality establishments. The conceptual paper investigates the challenges and opportunities within the concept of sustainability to raise awareness of the importance of Environmental Management Systems (EMS) and stimulate changes in the way management puts its effort toward enhancing the value these establishments put on adoption and implementation of EMS.

In chapter 3 Camillo and Di Pietro discuss the findings of an investigation on cultural cuisine of mainland China. Since China opened the doors to international trade, Chinese consumers have been exposed to both Italian cuisine and Italian food and beverage products. The aim of this study is to investigate the factors which contribute to the popularity of Italian cuisine in mainland China and identify implications for restaurant operators. Specifically the study identifies those factors that may or may not contribute to the expansion and sustainability of Italian cuisine in mainland China.

In chapter 4, Cassidy and Hume present the global perspective of tourism by examining core and peripheral destinations which are very significant to the South Pacific Island tourism because of core and peripheral islands. Core and peripheral destinations are very significant to island tourism because of core and peripheral islands. Peripheral locations may be disadvantaged as they are isolated from the core or economic centers and from the main population. This chapter reviews literature on the complexity of core and peripheral destinations, their development, planning, marketing and management together with local resident's perceptions of tourists and the tourist's expectations. The South Pacific is defined and it's Colonial past discussed together with tourist motivations. It is becoming increasingly difficult for all stakeholders to agree on programs and tourism practices and that various South Pacific countries have different ways of collecting statistical data resulting in few generic standards to adhere to.

Moving on to chapter 5, Barbini e Presutti discuss the role of Destination Management Organizations (DMOs) in exploiting global opportunities of tourism destinations. Specifically they examine, compare and contrast an established mass-tourism destination and a new destination. By investigating this relationship they also analyze how cooperation has developed during the years within two destinations, and if actually hospitality stakeholders are interested in cooperating with DMOs, in achieving the destinations' common goals.

The hospitality industry was one the first industries to become global. Within the framework of globalization and management, expatriates play an important role. In chapter 6, Causin and Ngwenya discuss the findings of a study on the influence of national culture and organizational culture on the success of an expatriate overseas assignment. The findings indicate that there were underlying dimensions that contributed to the success of hospitality expatriate executives on their overseas assignment.

Businesses of tourist destinations face the constant challenge of managing foreign currency. Although payments in U.S. dollar is the norm, the actual receipt must be converted in the local currency. The actual exchange rate and dollar multiplier will have an effect on future pricing and decision making by the tourists. In chapter 7 Samirkaş and Samirkaş investigate the foreign exchange rate and changes in the value of various currencies that can affect tourism, especially with regards to the demands of the tourists themselves. By using the Johansen cointegration and Granger causality tests, their study focused on identifying the relationship between currency exchange rates and the demand for tourism in Turkey

Related to chapter 1 is chapter 8. Tani and Papaluca analyze the role of local area resources in the global hospitality market as a way for small and medium enterprises to create a portfolio of distinctive resources to reach a sustainable competitive advantage position in the international markets. The chapter adopts a resource based and market-driven approach to identify the resources' role in shaping competitive advantages. The chapter discuss the example of a successful "Albergo Diffuso" (*diffused hotel*) in the Abruzzi region in Italy which identifies the core resources and those needed to support the strategies in creating a successful tourism product.

The Hospitality and Tourism industry today would not be able to compete and operate without the use of effective and efficient IT infrastructure. Within this context Nadda *et al* discuss in chapter 9 the role of social media in tourism. Websites and social media provide a wealth of information with regards to experiences and review of the destination, property, facilities and restaurants. In fact, social media has added new channels of communication to tourists. Most tourists always use the Internet for destination information seeking to decision-making .The tourism industry value chain starting from countries tourism boards, tourism agents, tour operators, transportations and airline companies, hotel and restaurant operators, destination management companies and local tourism management organization all use social media tools to reach potential customers. Therefore, businesses operating within the industry are compelled to using social media as the main vehicle of marketing exposure to potential customers.

In chapter 10 the authors Di Virgilio, Presenza and Sheehan, raise awareness that human resources are a vital part of the industry. They conducted a field study on the topic of organizational citizenship behavior by using the Italian hospitality industry as an example. They conducted a survey with 848 frontline employees from 63 hotels. The findings show that contingent employees exhibited less helping behavior than permanent employees but no difference in their voice behavior. In addition, work status was found to make more of a difference in both helping and voice in less work centrality organizations. Hotel managers are encouraged to focus attention on individual behavior that is discretionary, not directly or explicitly recognized by the formal reward system, and that in the aggregate promotes the effective functioning of the organization. Particularly in Italy, it would be advantageous to develop retention strategies for talented people that exhibit a high degree of organizational citizenship behavior.

It is true that a hotel operation could not remain viable without food and beverage service and amenities. Luxury properties have expanded their offerings by including all possible products and service a guest can purchase. In chapter 11 Lin discusses the Marketing of Global Luxury Spa and Wellness Trends, Experiences, and Challenges within the industry. She argues that luxury hotel and resort spas have been perceived and criticized for their similarities and for not having a true authentic or culturally thematic identity, and for losing their original intention of a spa experience due to rapid commercialization. Lin highlights some of the important global market trends that force all sectors of the travel industry to gear towards a healthy, wellness-minded concept in designing their products and services, attempts to define wellness tourism and the meaning of spa and addresses several under-researched variables that account for a crucial role in differentiating or characterizing a spa's identity and customers' preferences or perceived authenticity of a spa.

Scholars of hospitality and tourism have researched the effect of culture on customer service however, there is much more to learn at the country level and on the micro level. In chapter 12, Liao, Soltani, and Wang present the results of an investigation on the influence of national culture on customer service experience in China. The chapter attends to these suggestions and examines the practice of service quality in the hospitality sector in the Republic of China (Taiwan) so it may serve as reference point against which to interpret the fieldwork data of cross-cultural service quality research and its implications for customers' (e.g. tourists) perceptions towards service quality. They posit that recent research on the topic has exposed theoretical and methodological weakness of the Hofstede paradigm, thereby raising legitimate concern over the use of the Hofstede paradigm as a theory. It has been suggested to go beyond Hofstede's cultural framework and use Asian cultural norms which might provide additional insight into the impact of cultural values and norms on service quality dimensions and the resultant implications for customer expectations and satisfaction.

Tourism has become a significant source of revenue form many countries. However; many countries, especially those under developed are still in their infancy stage of tourism development. In chapter 13, Saner, Yiu, and Filadoro discuss the challenges and opportunities of tourism development in the least developed countries. They argue that effective tourism strategies of a developing country can create revenue generating opportunities (tax revenues) and provide sustainable employment for semi-skilled or unskilled workers. Such tourism development strategies require systemic thinking and comprehensive investment portfolio strategies regarding the tourism industry as a whole, i.e. going beyond investing in hotels, but also including transportation infrastructure, catering, restaurants, safe water, financial system etc. in other words, the destination countries need to review their tourism value & supply chains and identify structural impediments to the full utilization of their tourism assets and facilities.

In chapter 14, Georgiadou and Iasonos discuss the topic of diversity in hotel industry: satisfaction, retention, teamwork. They introduce the notion of diversity in hotel industry: its role, its interrelationship with productivity, retention and motivation. Hence, the right to difference and diversity should be incorporated not only in the whole range of processes, strategies, and actions of the company but also within the corporate culture. Indeed they confirm that managing human resources in the hospitality industry is a challenging task. In today's competitive environment, an increasing number of organizations invest in promoting diversity in the workplace. Therefore, it is very important to understand "how diversity impacts individual and team processes and outcomes in the workplace".

The globalization of cuisines has inspired hotel and restaurant business to consider important trends in menu innovation. In chapter 15, Mifli, Hashim, and Zainal investigate the impact of food trends on menu innovation analyzing the strategies of the restaurant industry in Malaysia. They determined that the search for the right 'pedigree' of innovative menus is endless. As the consumer foodservice markets are converging to one global market, increasingly demand for new menus is evitable posing a huge challenge for restaurateurs in managing their new menu innovation. Empirically, little is known in managing menu innovation amid facing market uncertainty. While there are several attributes that have been known to impact menu innovation, the chapter specifically aims to provide empirical evidence of the moderating effect of food trends on the link between innovation orientations and new menu development (NMD) process.

In line with chapter 9, Jeong touches on the use of technology by examining Risk Management Strategies and Management Implication of Cultural Difference for a P2P Virtual Enterprise. In chapter 16, the author examines and compares closely two virtual travel enterprises, Couchsurfing.org (CS, USA) and Gilbut.net (Gilbut, Korea). These platforms allow people to offer free travel resources including information, accommodation and transportation. Both organizations have become a mission driven enterprises similar to a not for profit model, and are run without receiving any advertising funds from the private sector. Their different cultural orientation provides interesting insights that emphasize same core strategies to create a critical mass of highly motivated contributors. At the same time, cultural differences suggest that technical features and core designs should be customized according to the cultural preferences such as the degree of individual visibilities and strong/weak group identity. Comparison of both networks provides an invaluable insight to understand how critical it is to set up strategic online features in order to promote reciprocity and a certain degree of anonymity.

Drawing on the investigation highlighted in chapter 13 Yiu, Saner, and Lee, discuss the case of Lesotho as a tourism destination in chapter 17. Specifically they conduct an analysis of Lesotho's current tourism products and potential for growth. The analysis includes assessments on how to improve performance and sustainability of the tourism industry in Lesotho including greater utilization of existing tourism infrastructure and further development of Lesotho's tourism products and how Lesotho could increase the number of its tourists. In 2011, tourism revenues contributed 1.4% to Lesotho´s economy. Tourism development has been identified as a sector that can reduce poverty as well as absorb low or semi-skilled labor. They posit that boosting the tourism sector in the Kingdom of Lesotho would work towards alleviating poverty in the Kingdom overall.

The airline industry flows under the umbrella of the global hospitality industry.

In chapter 18 Akamavi, Xu and Mitreva investigate how pre-alliance motives do and strategies affect post-alliance performance in the airline industry as the base for a future research agenda. They concluded that the global airline industry has currently experienced major changes toward cooperation, where competitive advantages can be built via alliance memberships. The pressure of forming an appropriate alliance strategy is increasing because the airline industry has currently experienced uppermost shifts: intensive rivalry, rapid growth of technological explosion, environmental and terrorist events, etc. Despite positive pre-alliance motivations as recognized in most cases, after certain alliances strategies are formed and implemented, the post-alliance performance is not always satisfactory; indeed an under explored phenomenon. The study therefore, looks into the triple relationships among: motives, strategy and performance and attempts to explore the main factors consisting of each triple dimension and then the linkages between them. Subsequently, it identifies theoretical gaps which indicate areas of further investigations.

In chapter 19, Calhoun and Douglas undertake the task to conduct An Analysis of Hospitality and Tourism Research within the context of Learning Organization's (LO) influence on sustainability practices. They determine that learning organizations (LOs) have been identified as an innovative practice essential for global businesses to not only effectively compete in today's dynamic environment, but also to achieve and maintain a sustainable competitive advantage and increase overall firm performance. In the context of hospitality and tourism businesses, the literature examining LOs is limited though a wealth of studies have been conducted in the mainstream. Using a qualitative approach, they conducted a content analysis to investigate its impact on sustainability practices in hospitality and tourism organizations. The results indicate that destinations in particular have adopted this approach to compete globally and to address triple-bottom line sustainability.

Tourism typology and development have expanded significantly. Among the many form of tourism Smith identified Sex Tourism as a viable typology. In chapter 20 Smith discusses the Privileges and Problems of "Female Sex Tourism" and explores the intersections of culture, commodification, and consumption of foreign romance. Smith determined that a global consumer phenomenon has evolved over several decades. Even with recent strides in their social and economic empowerment, many women in advanced countries still are marginalized by constraints to freedom, mobility, and expression in many aspects of life. However, scholarly and anecdotal evidence suggest that sex tourism (combined travel and compensated sexual experiences abroad) has provided some women escape from such domestic constraints and entrée to a wealth of cultural privileges within their foreign destinations. Blending thought and theory from different disciplines, the chapter examines the obscure history, expansion, and evolution of female sex tourism. While female sex tourism is similar, but not identical, to male sex tourism, each variety is contingent upon a market paradigm that involves intersections of culture, commodification, and consumption of transacted (relations with) marginalized persons in select foreign countries. Thus, despite its liberating possibilities for women, this institution of tourism also relies upon and reinforces social structures that marginalize foreign romantic partners and their communities located predominantly in the developing world. Moving beyond tenured and clichéd stereotypes that overwhelmingly associate sex tourism with male consumers, the chapter brings to light the justifications, criticisms, and cultural debates surrounding this social institution.

In reference to chapters 8, 13, and 17, it is evident that the topic of tourism is one of great interest to hospitality and tourism scholars. In chapter 21, Leong and Karim, they look at the Global Perspective in Tourism Development in the Positioning of Malaysia as a Culinary Destination. Similar to the USA, Malaysia is a melting pot of cultures that includes people with European and Asian origin. Because of their rich cross-cultural heritage, the authors examine the potential of Malaysia as a food tourism destination from the international tourists' perspective. The findings show the potential benefit for Malaysian food's image and the potential of Malaysia being a promoted as a food destination. The results provide an important insight to the tourism and hospitality industry on the perceptions of international tourists towards Malaysian food and Malaysia as a food tourism destination.

In chapter 22, Šerić, Gil-Saura and Mollá-Descals, investigate the impact of integrated marketing communications on hotel brand equity to determine if the national culture really matters? In addition, the study estimates the moderating effect of national culture on the relationships examined. The study is approached from the customer perspective and uses survey methodology to assess guests' perception of IMC and brand equity in the hotel contexts. In particular, 335 hotel guests participated in the empirical investigation while staying in high-quality hotels in Rome, Italy. The findings reveal that IMC exerts a positive impact on hotel brand equity. Furthermore, the inter-relationship exists between the three dimensions of hotel brand equity. In general, national culture does not exert a significant impact within the posited model.

Drawing on the results presented in chapter 6 in the investigation conducted by Causin and Ngwenya, in chapter 23 the author Tran complements the results with his study on expatriate selection and retention and identifying and assessing the other characteristics beyond knowledge, skills, and abilities. Tran, argues that among the workforce which is the backbone of any organization and international hotel companies, management should pay careful attention to trends as well as published research to reduce failures that will ultimately affect its financial state as well as the organization as a whole. The chapter reflects on the on the hotel industry in China. Hence, the focus of the chapter is on the matter that when international hotel companies select expatriates to work at properties in China, they need to identify and assess these expatriates' "other characteristics": (1) desire to prematurely terminate an expatriate's assignment; (2) stable competencies; and (3) intercultural/international business communication.

In chapter 24, Li and DeMicco, investigate and present the Best "Experience" Practices in Medical Tourism. A tourism typology that is gaining dynamic interest across many destinations. Specifically the research id conducted to demonstrate the best practices in the rising trend of "Hotels Bridging Healthcare" (H2H) and Medical Tourism. The concept of "Experience Economy" expedites the merging process of hospitality and hospitals: patients are also travelers now whose needs are not merely commodity type of medical care anymore but a memorable wellbeing experience. Moreover, H2H optimizes the process of realizing excellent care, which serves as the fundamental reason for tourism industry. Although H2H demands the considerable collaboration from all parties involved in order to ultimately present the excellent care customers, tourists, and patients want, it carries tremendous opportunity for hospitals, hotels, Spa, restaurants, transportation, and more.

Chapter 25 is the only research that has contributed to the topic of corporate social responsibility. Martinez and Del Bosque seek to have an in depth understanding of CSR and corporate image by attempting to explain Consumer Behavior in the Hospitality Industry. Specifically, they propose a model in which CSR and corporate image positively condition customer loyalty. It also proposes that the company´ social responsible initiatives influence customer satisfaction. In order to test this model structural equation modelling is employed on a sample of 382 Spanish hotel customers. This study finds that both corporate image and customer satisfaction contribute to achieve customer loyalty, also proving the roles of corporate image as a mediating variable. Additionally, the results show that CSR indeed influences customer satisfaction.

A problem that has concerned both researchers and practitioners for decades is staff turnover. In chapter 26, Camillo, Di Virgilio and Di Pietro conducted a strategic longitudinal study to investigate the unexplainable staff Turnover at the Crossboarder Hotel Company. The authors endeavor to draw attention to staff turnover in the hospitality industry by analyzing a company, which will be referred to as "Crossboarder Hotel Company". The actual name has been disguised to maintain the company's confidentiality. The chapter discusses the causes and effects of employee turnover and ways to prevent turnover. Turnover is divided into three categories: job dissatisfaction, errors in employee selection, and poor management. The common cause of turnover however; is job dissatisfaction which affects employees' well-being. The results of the investigation show that favouritism, nepotism, lack of responsibility and accountability, lack of training and improper communication negatively contributed to job satisfaction.

## SUMMARY

In summary, this book presents a comprehensive view of the Global Hospitality and Tourism Industry and Management from various aspects of hospitality and tourism. As explained earlier, studies included in the book range from Business Development / emerging hotel typology, to Destination marketing and management, to Organization Behavior, Managerial-Corporate Finance, Global strategy and competitiveness, Social Media-Internet Marketing-Digital Marketing, Corporate Social Responsibility and Strategic Human Resources Management, among many others. The cases and articles selected for this book are truly global in nature with research contexts that covered Asia, Europe, and North America. I have considered uniqueness of research methodologies while selecting articles for this book to include ethnographic studies, case studies, research articles, empirical papers, conceptual papers, and review papers.

Finally I want to sincerely thank the authors for patiently working with me in making the necessary revisions following the double blind review process. I am indebted to the invaluable contributions they made to this book. Most importantly, I can't thank enough everyone at IGI – Global but especially Caitlyn Martin, for her incredible patience and guidance she has given me during the last stages of the manuscript completion process.

*Angelo A. Camillo*
*Woodbury University, USA*

## REFERENCE

UNWTO. (2015). *UNWTO tourism highlights.* Retrieved from http://www.e-unwto.org/doi/book/10.18111/9789284416899

# Acknowledgment

I would like to thank the many people at IGI-Global who have helped me make this edited book possible. I am particularly grateful to Caitlyn Martin Development Editor—Book Development Division and Kayla Wolfe, Managing Editor, Acquisitions.

I am especially thankful to the authors who have contributed their chapters with dedication and professionalism. Without them, this book would have not been possible.

I also wish to offer a big thanks to the reviewers for their time and patience especially those who have reviewed multiple chapters. I thank them for their valuable criticism and feed-back during the review process.

Lastly, I like to thank my dear hospitality colleagues from around the world who have recognized the value of scientific research in hospitality. Especially, all my former colleagues from Inter Continental Hotels whom I regularly interact with through ExInternconti.com.

# Chapter 1
# An Analysis of the Characteristics and Dynamic Development of an Emergent Sustainable Hotel Business Model in Italy:
## "Albergo Diffuso" (Diffused Hotel)

**Angelo Camillo**
*Woodbury University, USA*

**Angelo Presenza**
*University G. D'Annunzio of Chieti-Pescara, Italy*

**Francesca Di Virgilio**
*University of Molise, Italy*

## ABSTRACT

*This chapter introduces the concept of "Albergo Diffuso" (Diffused Hotel), (AD). A hotel typology that is emerging as a sustainable accommodation with the potential to compete and establish itself as a viable hotel business. To raise awareness about the concept we analyze the scarce literature available and the rather limited publicly available resources provided by the Association of Albergo Diffuso (AAD). We also conducted non-intrusive observations through personal on-location investigative visits of various ADs operations. We present a sample guests' satisfaction ratings of the concept by conducting a web content analysis of the Trip Advisor's website, a hotel rating platform, on the Residenza Sveva, an Albergo Diffuso property located in the city of Termoli, in the Region of Molise in South Central Italy. The data shows that this concept is patronized largely by couples but also by business travelers. The site gives this property a 4.5 / 5 star rating.*

DOI: 10.4018/978-1-4666-8606-9.ch001

## BACKGROUND

Hotels are part of the hospitality industry and have long been an integral part of travel, whether they are booked for business trips, family vacations, conferences and exhibitions, private functions such as weddings or for other purposes.

The industry's direct contribution of travel and tourism to the global economy from 2016 to 2014 was U.S. $7.58 trillion and in 2014 alone was approximately U.S. $ 2.36 trillion. The European Union makes the largest contribution, closely followed by North America and North East Asia. Due to their less developed tourism industries, regions such as North and Sub Saharan Africa make a much smaller impact. This statistic shows a significant direct economic impact of travel and tourism on the global economy. The direct travel & tourism contribution includes the commodities accommodation, transportation, entertainment and attractions of these industries: Accommodation services, food & beverage services, retail trade, transportation services and cultural, sports & recreational services. The figures for total impact also include indirect and induced contributions (AHLA, 2014)

In Italy, in 2013 alone there were more than 157 thousand tourist accommodation establishments (+0.2% compared with 2012), providing more than 4.7 million of bed-places (-0.7% compared with 2012). Hotels and similar accommodation were more than 33 thousand and offered 2.2 million of bed-places (respectively -1.2% and -0.8% compared with 2012). Other collective accommodation establishments were 124 thousand (+0.6%) with 2.5 million of bed-places (-0.7%). In the year 2013 arrivals at tourist accommodation establishments increased slightly by 0.1 per cent while the number of nights spent decreased by -1.0 per cent, compared with the same period of the previous year. The average length of stay changed from 3.67 nights in 2012 to 3.67 in 2013. In hotels and similar accommodation about 82.6 million of arrivals and 254.8 million of nights spent

(-0.3% compared with 2012) were recorded, and the average length of stay remained substantially unchanged. In other collective accommodation establishments arrivals (21 million) increased by 0.6 per cent, while the number of nights spent (122 million) decreased by 2.5 per cent, thus resulting in a reduction of the average length of stay (-0.18 nights), (ISTAT, 2014). By the end of 2015, the aggregate revenues in Italy are projected to reach approximately 40, 18 billion U.S. dollars, a significant financial impact on the Italian economy.

The data shows that despite cyclical downturns, the hospitality industry as a whole is very dynamic with great growth potential, regardless of the current global political and economic risks and prolonged periods of uncertainty and instability. Hotels are considered complex organizations that create value for consumers and investors. Because of the complexity and direct link to related industries, their performance is always affected by exogenous macroeconomic factors and consumer behavioral trends. Hotel performance is directly linked the parallel sectors such as airlines and travel companies, demand seasonality, product research and development and innovation continuum strategies. As a result, all external variables affect the hotel industry in differing ways. Therefore, with evidence of global – hypercompetition, especially in some of the fastest-emerging tourism destinations in Africa, including Namibia, Zambia and Angola, and the rise of innovative services such as home sharing and vacation rental businesses like *Airbnb* and *HomeAway*, the industry is compelled to improve upon the status quo and find new ways to appeal to travelers. One way is to introduce innovative types of accommodation and overall services.

Given that, travelers' in general and especially tourists' demographics and psychographics are changing across the global tourists' destinations and the emergence of a new tourist typology, operators and new entrepreneurs are compelled to respond to this dynamic phenomenon.

Specifically, a new tourist is emerging in the global tourist markets: the "third-generation" tourist. Historically the "first- generation" tourist was represented by travelers 60 years of age, who had disposable income, and did not demand a specific type of accommodation. The "second-generation" tourist, or the so-called "mass – tourist", represented by tourists of all ages demanded standardized services similar to the comfort he/she enjoyed at home.

This emergent tourist however is experiential in nature and wishes to experience a unique vacation, visit new and diverse places than just the traditional historical-cultural attractions. In addition, this tourist is interested in personalized services, authenticity of local products and lifestyle. This emergent tourist is not solely interested in visiting places, buy keepsakes, take selfies or pictures of local attractions and eat tourist food, instead this tourist wants to experience the life of local residents by blending with their entire way of living.

These unique experiences create personalized relationships for possible return visit. Accordingly, the emergent Albergo Diffuso is able to provide all services and attractions that meet the expectations of the "third-generation tourist" (Dall'Ara & Esposito, 2005; Dall'Ara, 2010; Dall'Ara & Morandi, 2010).

## THE EMERGENT ALBERGO DIFFUSO

The concept of the Albergo Diffuso began to emerge in the late 1980's and continues to expand as a niche form of lodging. It is very similar to a traditional hotel however different from apartment rentals or extended stay, which represent more of a "residence", where typical hotel services and amenities may not offered. It has the characteristics of a typical hotel however it differs from a conventional hotel type in the sense that it has

several distinctive features well defined in the guidelines created by the Italian Association of Albergo Diffusi.

Launched by Giancarlo Dall'Ara, currently President of the Associazione Nazionale Alberghi Diffusi (National Association of Diffused Hotels) the AD concept has had a significant growth since 1998. The Italian definition of "Albergo Diffuso" (AD) can be expressed in English as "horizontal hotel", "multi-building hotel", "integrated hotel" or "diffused hotel". It is a new form of accommodation growing in popularity in Italy and in other parts of Southern Europe. The verb 'diffuse' means, broadly, 'disperse'. From Latin diffus- "poured out", from the verb "diffundere", from dis- "away' + fundere "pour". Within this context, it means "Spread out over a large area; not concentrated" (Oxford Dictionaries, 2014). AD is configured as a niche form of hotel accommodation that is very different from apartment rentals, which represent more of a "residence", where hotel surroundings and services are not offered. It has the typical characteristics of a hotel such as accommodation, assistance, catering, and common spaces and facilities for guests. At the same time, it differs from a conventional hotel because it has several peculiarities that have been formalized in a set of guidelines produced by the Italian Association of Albergo Diffusi. The term "diffuso" (diffused) denotes a structure that is horizontal, and not vertical like the one pertaining to standard hotels which are often not visually appealing. The reception, the rooms and the ancillary services are located in different buildings, although close to each other. The various facilities are housed in existing buildings after a careful process of restoration and conversion, which must comply with the local laws and regulations. The intent is to give guests the opportunity to experience direct contact with the local culture, and experience an authentic representation of resident life in the community.

## THE KEY REQUIREMENTS FOR THE ALBERGO DIFFUSO

- The presence of a living community (usually a small village, with a few hundred inhabitants);
- An owner operated management structure;
- An environment that is "authentic" made of fine homes, completely renovated and furnished;
- A reasonable distance between the guest rooms and common areas (usually no more than 300 meters);
- Non-standard professional management, consistent with the proposal of authenticity of experience, and with roots in the community and region;
- A recognizable style, an identity, a common feel that is identifiable throughout the facility buildings.

## WHO ARE THE GUESTS OF THE ALBERGO DIFFUSO?

Statistical analyses show that guests who patronize these hotel type are foreign customers who represent about 46.4% of the total demand. Most of the clients are couple (54.8%) with kids while seniors account for only 3.2%. Primary interests of the customers are environmental in nature, as well as the food and wine and the typical-unique places. The length of stay in 2012 was 2.9 nights while the average occupancy rate was 68%. Property size ranges from 4 to 73 rooms. Most ADs are family managed and employ about 4.7 associates on average; of these 75.8% are Italian nationals. Mainly Italian locals represent the staff. About 64.2% of the employees live in the immediate vicinity of the hotel operations. Accordingly, hotel guests have a direct contact with the residents in the surrounding areas mainly because the hotel personnel lives nearby. The success of the first operations has led the development of other estab-

lishments now totaling 83 (as of November 2014) throughout Italy with others under development. Although other hotels are promoted as AD and offer exactly the same product and services, they may not be registered members of the Association. Because there is no tracking system, there is not an official national list of all Ads available. It is important to note that these hotels have no affiliation with Italian chains or international chains.

## HOW DO GUESTS RATE THE ALBERGO DIFFUSO CONCEPT?

A "Trip Advisor" web content analysis on the Albergo Diffuso Residenza Sveva, in Termoli, Molise, Italy provided the following results:

Due to space constraints, we introduce only one sample rating listed on the Trip Advisor's website on May 25, 2015. Figure 1 depicts the guests' ratings of the Albergo Diffuso Residenza Sveva, in Termoli, Molise, Italy. Clearly and similarly with most AD's ratings, guests are very satisfied with this emerging concept. The quantitative data shows that this concept is patronized largely by couples but also by business travelers. Together with the positive qualitative comments this property receives a 4.5 / 5 star rating.

## WHAT ARE THE CHARACTERISTICS OF THE ALBERGO DIFFUSO?

An Albergo Diffuso represents a unique development approach, which has no negative impact on the environment. Because buildings consist of old, possible ancient properties there is nothing to be newly constructed; instead, they are restored according to the local cultural and historical backgrounds, and to the existing network.

This type of hotel acts as the most relevant stakeholder of the territory, inspiring entrepreneurs to launch new business ventures based on the increased tourist demand. It promotes and

*Figure 1. Ratings of the Albergo Diffuso Residenza Sveva, in Termoli, Molise, Italy.*
**Source:** *Trip Advisor ratings of Hotel Residenza Sveva, Termoli, Italy*

manages new activities capable of re-positioning the territory on the tourist market, such as events, specific training courses in traditional sectors (local cuisine, local sport events, artisanship, etc.). The dollar multiplier effect is significant. New businesses are created in relationship to this new hospitality concept which offers visitors a unique experience by living the life of "temporary local residents"; something a tourist can never experience in traditional tourist destinations. The authenticity of the local life is fully experienced due to the close range of the structures in regards to the all activities of the local community. This is a contributing factor to the economic turnovers because the tourist does not depend on the seasonality of the destination to book a vacation. Instead the AD concept it "de-seasonalizes" the demand for seasonality vacation travel.

This innovative concept was first tested in the city of Carnia in the Friuli Venezia Giulia, North-East Italy in 1982. The initiative was launched by a local working group whose aim was to recuperate small centers of the city which were destroyed after the 1976 devastating earthquake. The model was the brainchild of Giancarlo Dall'Ara. Accordingly, the initial goal of the Albergo Diffuso was to respond to the need of restoring houses set in historical centers that were not attractive or adaptable as tourist accommodations. This innovative lodging business model received its

first recognition by the Italian Sardegna Region, which provided the first definition of the concept within its regional tourist law. Consequently, other regions have added various definitions to the concept of Albergo Diffuso causing to be officially recognized as a traditional forms of hospitality, such as bed and breakfasts, hotels, rural farmhouses, chalets. Dall'Ara & Esposito, 2005; Dall'Ara, 2010; Dall'Ara & Morandi, 2010).

From the SWOT analysis presented in Table 1, we can posit that the concept of AD does have a fair to strong competitive advantage over other accommodation typology.

According to the promotional strategies of the AD Association (Dall'Ara & Esposito, 2005; Dall'Ara, 2010; Dall'Ara & Morandi, 2010).

- It generates a high quality tourist product, expression of local areas and territories without generating negative environmental impacts (nothing new has to be built, existing houses must be restored and networked).
- It helps to develop and network the local tourist supply.
- It increases sustainable tourist development in internal areas, in villages and hamlets and in historical centers, in the off-beaten tracks areas increasing the supply in the tourist market.

*Table 1. SWOT analysis*

| STRENGTHS | • It is a residence and then a hotel<br>• A strong interaction with the local community<br>• Hospitality in restored structures in historic centers, with modern comfort, no traffic<br>• A new formula of accommodation to answer the need of modern tourists<br>• No real direct competition<br>• Family owned and managed<br>• Human resources coming mainly from the local community | • Capitalize on the authenticity and uniqueness of the product<br>• Take advantage and promote the warmth of the sustainable environments with the mix between old and new<br>• Take advantage of the true essence of the Made in Italy and the Italian way of life<br>• Gain competitive advantage by offering the hospitality of the owner and the local staff | OPPORTUNITIES |
|---|---|---|---|
| WEAKNESSES | • Product difficult to promote and establish a global exposure<br>• Insufficient start-up capital<br>• No management structure<br>• Family ownership may negatively affects management decisions<br>• Hard to compete against well-established local as well as brand or chain owned operations<br>• Lack of resources overall | • Regulatory compliance<br>• Resources from the local community may deplete over time<br>• Substantial initial investment<br>• Relationships with local stakeholders<br>• Large scale expansion may threat the uniqueness and exclusivity of the product<br>• Requires highly skilled management structure | THREATS |

- In contributes to stop the abandoning of the historical centers.

Particularly, it promotes interaction and active participation within the local communities since:

- Everyone becomes aware of the advantages in terms of image, social life, economic returns and of preservation of the resources which it can bring
- The public administration can contribute providing the common spaces (typically a non-productive space) and new services which can increase the demand (such as improving the accessibility of the area or restoring new services such as libraries, congress halls, sport facilities etc.)
- The local associations can increase their activities organizing new events and new personal assistance services.

- The owners of the houses start to look at their patrimony in a different manner; with the "tourist" eyes, they identify problems and common solutions to solve them.
- The local enterprises in the service sectors, in the agro-food and wine sector, in the handicraft sector will participate because they see the Albergo Diffuso as a means to increase their own turnover, because of the induced increase in the demand.

Accordingly, the association posits that an Albergo Diffuso is an innovative form of hospitality that can bring, both during its realization and after its start-up, sustainable development, triggering economic activities and providing opportunities for the balanced utilization of the local resources and tourist potentialities (Dall'Ara & Esposito, 2005; Dall'Ara, 2010; Dall'Ara & Morandi, 2010).

## WHAT ARE THE CONSIDERATIONS TO START AN ALBERGO DIFFUSO?

A hotel start-up is usually subject to local laws and regulations such as various local, regional, state and country governmental agencies such as department of labor, health authorities, fire department, environmental protection agencies, etc., however; the basic concept is somewhat universal.

As experienced in Italy, a successful new AD venture should initially be discussed with the local administration since it involves the restoring of existing buildings that may not be in compliance with current laws. The local business development office, chamber of commerce, banks and other entities may offer insights about the AD venture and the positive effect it may have on the local economy.

Accordingly, the Association proposes that an Albergo Diffuso is usually created if the following conditions are met:

- The idea has been launched within the local community and the residents have learned the advantages that can come from the innovation.
- Therefore local actors are interested in working together.
- A unique management unit can be created and is willing to take most of the entrepreneurial risk. The unit can be either a single entrepreneur, a cooperative, or any other most suitable form of productive association.
- There exists a reasonable number of rooms (minimum 7) located at a reasonable distance from each other (not more than 200 meters or 218 yards), that can be put at disposition of the Albergo Diffuso for a long term (Minimum 9 years).
- The town or village is able to provide minimum services to the guests (existence of a bank, pharmacy, of a food store, a coffee shop, etc.)

- The surroundings of the area should have some appeal (countryside, sea, lake, mountains, archaeological sites etc.
- A lively and welcoming community ready to share experiences with newcomers and to spend quality time with the tourists visiting the town or village.

## START-UP METHODS OF AN ALBERGO DIFFUSO

1.  An investor purchases or rents the apartments and/or the houses and becomes the manager of what effectively is a "hotel which cannot be seen".
2.  A group of local actors creates a consortium and delegates to a private entity (e.g. a cooperative) the management of the structure.

In either cases, the role of the local administration is to "incubate" the project idea to support and incentivize it (e.g. facilitating legal aspect, investing in local infrastructure and/or in urban décor).

The path that leads to the creation of an Albergo Diffuso starts from a feasibility study to determine the existence of the aforementioned conditions, and passes through a promotional phase, which includes entrepreneurial scouting, through a technical phase, aimed at producing a sound business plan, and arrives to the provision of start-up support to the management unit (financial services). In addition, it may be necessary to support local administrations to re-arrange development plans of the towns in order to accommodate the incubation of the project idea and of the new start-up (Dall'Ara & Esposito, 2005; Dall'Ara, 2010; Dall'Ara & Morandi, 2010).

## SUCCESS THROUGH EDUCATION

In 2004, a group of stakeholders created SISAD (International School Specializing in Albergo Diffuso (SISAD, 2015). This school provides business education tailored to the needs of an entrepreneur/ investor who may not have sufficient hospitality business education or work experience.

The objective of SISAD is:

- *To be in charge of training for the national Alberghi Diffusi's association;*
- *Promoted by EBN (European Business Network) and UNDP (United Nations Development Programme) among the 4 related Associations;*
- *Not a typical school, as its costs would be too high compared to income from potential users;*
- *Instead, a series of technical services, created in November 2004, through an agreement with Giancarlo Dall'Ara and the CEOs of 5 alberghi diffusis (litterally translated in "scattered hotels") operating within the Friuli Venezia Giulia region - Italy.*

## VIABILITY OF THE BUSINESS MODEL

The impact of the innovation affects the economy at the local level since an Albergo Diffuso triggers local development where tourism can be a leading business sector if appropriately encouraged and supported by all concerned: local, regional and national governmental authorities which must adopt the criterion of such a model, rendering it possible by lowering the legal, bureaucratic and economic barriers. Laws on tourism must be rewritten in order to formally recognize this new type of hospitality offering giving it the same dignity of traditional hotels and of other models of hospitality. This would facilitate the entrepreneur's pursuit in launching a new venture and the local administrations to adopt this innovation and have access to financial and non-financial services usually dedicated to SMEs and to entrepreneurs. Specific credit schemes and/or public financing

mechanisms could be set-up to support the creation and proliferation of the Albergo Diffuso concept. Their underlying philosophy is to promote local entrepreneurship, restoring historical centers a restoration of historical architecture through the concept of Albergo Diffuso (Dall'Ara & Esposito, 2005; Dall'Ara, 2010; Dall'Ara & Morandi, 2010).

## THE FUTURE OF THE ALBERGO DIFFUSO CONCEPT

1. **Self-Managed and/or Family Owned:** Since there is no binding contract to belong to the association nor there is a universal requirement to operate such a hotel concept the entrepreneur must only comply with the local and regional authorities for necessary permits, taxes and regulatory compliance. Currently, no large hotel chain has invested in an Albgergo Diffuso therefore, there is no set of standard operating procedure each independently owned and/ or operated property must comply with. The number of star ratings assigned to it depends on the standard of service, quality, comfort and other important factors. Therefore, each operation can be designated as a "Boutique" operation, a luxury accommodation, a rural attraction, low budget, etc.

2. **Potential for Cross-Border Expansion:** Since there is no negative environmental impact, and there is nothing to be built this innovative concept can easily be proliferated in other countries contributing to the preservation of underutilized and devalued real estate and to the local economy. Regardless of the political status-quo of the country, the concept has some very appealing characteristics as an entrepreneurial innovation for several reasons. Among these, job creation as well as health and welfare in peripheral areas, which represent fundamental pillars. It also blends a diverse lifestyle orientation

## TRENDS IN HOSPITALITY CONSUMER PSYCHOGRAPHICS AND BEHAVIOR

Current and future trends in consumer behavior will have important implications for the Albergo Diffuso's operators and investors. Therefore, for the AD concept to remain viable, the stakeholders will have to play close attention to the external factors that may affect their competitive posture. These factors include many trends; some are short-lived and some may become standard. The following is a partial list of trends, which AD operators cannot ignore:

1.  **Millennials:** Have become the fasts growing segment in the hospitality and tourism industry. "Millennials want to do things on their own terms: check in virtually, choose to interact with the hosts or to use a virtual concierge, sleep in, have breakfast delivered ordered through the smartphone. Studies show that they want to leave a hotel experience and a destination having had a unique experience, and feeling connected to the stay.
2.  **Technology:** Mobile rooms' reservation represent over 75% of the current bookings. Mobile check-in and check-out is being made available at most hotels which are undergoing technological upgrades.
3.  **Hotels' High-Tech Amenities and Features:** Hotels are also appealing to tech-savvy travelers by offering the latest and greatest amenities to make a stay more convenient for guests. A few examples include:
    a.  In-room touchscreen controls that operate everything from the television and lighting to the curtains and thermostat,
    b.  Free Wi-Fi, complimentary iPads usage for use in the hotel facilities,
    c.  Airline check-in kiosks,
    d.  Keyless Apps to replace electronic room keys,
    e.  Complimentary use of high-tech equipped business centers
    f.  Complimentary digital newspaper and magazine service on any device connected to the hotel's Wi-Fi.
    g.  Texting the hotel for anything, from extra towels to a late check-in
    h.  Option to check in and out via smartphone
    i.  Dedicated social media concierge, who provides recommendations for local activities and accommodates special requests throughout guests' stays
4.  **Focus on Health and Wellness:**
    a.  Fitness-focused programs to help guests maintain their exercise regimen during their stays
    b.  Yoga mats in every room
    c.  Daily exercise classes
    d.  Complimentary use of bicycles
    e.  Rock climbing wall
    f.  Healthy menus for individualized lifestyle programs
    g.  Juice bars

## CONCLUSION AND RECOMMENDATION

This chapter introduces the Italian concept of "Albergo Diffuso" (Diffused Hotel), (AD). A hotel typology that is emerging as a sustainable accommodation with the potential to compete and establish itself as a viable hotel business. Research on this topic is in its infancy since the concept is still exotic and emerging and far from maturation. To raise awareness about the concept we analyzed the scarce literature available and the rather limited publicly available resources provided by the Association of Albergo Diffuso (AAD). We also conducted on non-intrusive observations through personal on location investigative visits of ADs operations in the Molise region in South Central Italy.

## SUGGESTIONS FOR FUTURE RESEARCH

As an emerging type of accommodation, Albergo Diffuso may face challenges in the future however; it may find new opportunities as well, especially if it will gain global recognition. Currently, it has not caught the attention of large hotel chains although some are exhausting their brand extension strategies. However, changes in expansion strategies could happen very rapidly and the concept could become a global phenomenon. To support the effort, more research is needed both, within the industry by the practitioners/ owner – operators and by researchers in academia. Research on this concept is still in its infancy and there is no database system available to track revenues, occupancy and other important information, which are key to financial investment for stakeholders. Possible areas of research include are, but not limited to, entrepreneurship, marketing, franchising, environmental sustainability, innovation, new conversion and concept design, destination management, social interaction between tourists/ travelers, and local community, human resources, family business management, etc.

## REFERENCES

AAD. (2014). Associazione Alberghi Diffusi, Italy. www.alberghidiffusi.it

AHLA. (2014). 2014 LODGING INDUSTRY PROFILE. AHLA Press room Annual Report. Retrieved May 25, 2015 from https://www.ahla.com/press.aspx

Dall'Ara, G. (2010). *Manuale dell'Albergo Diffuso; l'idea, la gestione, il marketing dell'ospitalità. (Albergo Diffuso's practice, idea, management, marketing of hospitality)*. Milano, Italy: Franco Angeli.

Dall'Ara, G., & Esposito, M. (2005). (Il fenomeno degli alberghi diffusi in Italia), Palladino Editor, Campobasso, Italy, 2005.

Dall'Ara, G. & Morandi, F. (2010). *Il turismo nei borghi; la normativa, il marketing e i casi di eccellenza. (Tourism in Hamlets; law, marketing and the best practices)*. Matelica (MC), Italy: Nuova giuridica.

ISTAT. (2014). Capacity and occupancy of tourist accommodation establishments. *Short-term economic statistics*. Directorate of the Italian National Institute of Statistics. Retrieved May 25, 2015 from http://dati.istat.it/?lang=en

SISAD. (2015). International School Specializing in Albergo Diffuso. Retrieved May 25, 2015 from http://www.sisad.it/en/home_page

Trip Advisor. (2015). Reviews and advice on hotels, resorts, flights, vacation rentals, travel packages, and lots more! Retrieved May 25, 2015 from http://www.tripadvisor.com/Hotel_Review-g194930-d633424-Reviews-Residenza_Sveva-Termoli_Province_of_Campobasso_Molise.html

Vignali, C. (2011). L'albergo diffuso da idea-progetto alla concreta realizzazione nella recente legislazione regionale lombarda. The Albergo diffuso: From the idea-project to the carry out into the regional law. *Rivista Italiana di Diritto del Turismo*, 1-2011, pp.159-164.

## ADDITIONAL READING

Berardi, S. (2007). Principi economici ed ecologici per la pianificazione di uno sviluppo turistico sostenibile, Milano 2007.

Eisenhardt, K. M. (1989). Building theories from case study research. *Academy of Management Review*, *14*(4), 532–550.

Kidd, J. (2011). Performing the knowing archive: Heritage performance and authenticity. *International Journal of Heritage Studies*, *17*(1), 22–35. doi:10.1080/13527258.2011.524003

Orlandini, P., Vallone, C., De Toni, A., & Cecchetti, R. (2012). Total quality research of tourism services. Special case: "Albergo Diffuso". In: *15th International Conference on Quality Service Sciences*, Rishon Lezion, Israel, September 3-5, 2012.

Spina, V. (2010). Il turismo sostenibile: opportunità e rischi. The sustainable tourism: Opportunities and risks. In: A.a. V.v. Una breve descrizione della genesi del concetto di turismo sostenibile. (The origin of sustainable tourism concept). Rende Cosenza: Università della Calabria, Italy

Vignali, C. (2010). *L'albergo diffuso: Analisi giuridico-economica di una forma non tradizionale di ospitalità*. Legal and economic analisys of Albergo diffuso. In L. Degrassi & V. Franceschelli (Eds.), *Turismo: Diritto e diritti) (Tourism: Law and rights)*. Milano, Italy: Giuffrè.

## KEY TERMS AND DEFINITIONS

**Albergo Diffuso:** Diffused-dispersed hotel; "a receptive structure, made of 2 or more existent buildings, located in the historical center of a village or of a town, within a hosting existent community. It has a simple management structure, The word Albergo Diffuso was used for the first time in 1982, in the Friuli Venezia Giulia region, for the Conegliano Project "Borgo Maranzanis".

**Arrivals:** The number of Italian and foreign clients hosted in tourist accommodation in the period considered.

**Bed and Breakfast:** Accommodation structures that offer overnight lodging and breakfast for a limited number of rooms and/or beds. These establishments come under the forms of dwelling rented by private people to other private people or to professional agencies, on a temporary basis, as tourism accommodation.

**Bed:** A single bed in holiday and other short-stay accommodation. A double bed is counted as two beds. Space for a tent, roulotte or mobile home is usually considered to represent four beds (unless the actual number is known).

**Hotels and Similar Accommodation Establishments:** Accommodation open to the public, under single management, providing lodging and eventually board and other accessory facilities, in rooms located in one or more buildings or parts of buildings.

**Local Way of Life:** One of the main tourism assets of several little villages as the one which hosts the alberghi diffusi. It requires continuous action in order to become a source of income, new jobs and investments by the local community.

**Post-Industrial Tourism (Tourist):** The guest who is most interested in experiences rather than in products to buy or commodities. He/she demands "customized" activities, knows how to use the Internet, wants a strong local identity and great efficiency, seeks real relationship with inhabitants. It's also known as "3rd generation guest" (Dall'Ara) and follows the industrial-era tourist. He/she is more interested about standard, all-included offers, infrastructures, services dedicated to tourists and holiday.

**Presences:** The number of nights spent by Italian or foreign clients in holiday and other short-stay accommodation.

**Room:** A unit formed of a room or a series of rooms constituting an indivisible unit in holiday and other short-stay accommodation or dwelling. The number of rooms is given by the number which the structure makes available for tourists. Rooms used as permanent residence (for more than one year) are therefore excluded. Bathrooms and toilets are not counted as rooms.

**SISAD:** International School Specializing in the Albergo Diffuso: http://www.sisad.it/en.

# Chapter 2
# ISO14001:
## The Challenges in Establishing Environmental Management Systems in Tourism and Hospitality Establishments

**Hanafi Hamzah**
*Universiti Putra, Malaysia*

**Shahrim Karim**
*Universiti Putra, Malaysia*

**Angelo Camillo**
*Woodbury University, USA*

**Svetlana Holt**
*Woodbury University, USA*

## ABSTRACT

*In the last decades, the tourism and hospitality industries have increased their awareness toward environmental sustainability and the application of Environmental Management Systems (EMS). However, research into EMS application and its challenges in the hospitality industry has been left out of sight. In fact, it appears that most hospitality and tourism organizations have neglected to adopt and implement EMS and have failed to recognize the benefits EMS can offer. Perhaps this may explain mixed findings on EMS success adoption and implementation to date. This conceptual paper investigates the challenges and opportunities within the concept of sustainability and aims to sum the existing knowledge on EMSs and the opportunities for its successful implementation in tourism and hospitality establishments. The findings will raise awareness of the importance of EMS and stimulate changes in the way management puts its effort toward enhancing the value these establishments put on adoption and implementation of EMS.*

DOI: 10.4018/978-1-4666-8606-9.ch002

# 1. INTRODUCTION AND PURPOSE

There is an increasing concern about environmental issues affecting the hospitality industry, particularly in the organizational management and operations. Environmental awareness is turning into a "hot" issue for managers as well as becoming a priority on the agendas of many governments (Alonso & Ogle, 2010).

This awareness is present in many industries, including tourism and hospitality. In fact, it has fostered the adoption and implementation of Environmental Management Systems (EMS), and one of the most popular applied systems is ISO14001. Relevant literature shows that while most large organizations have developed their EMS, others are still standing at the crossroads of making a decision whether to develop and implement the EMS or not. This slow development may be due to factors which include lack of resources, knowledge, and/or readiness of the managers, and other factors, such as cost and return on investment. Based on the mentioned above, we posit that challenges presented earlier could actually motivate the establishments and lead to the implementation of EMS, particularly ISO14001, in their operations – obviously, based on their ability and willingness.

One of the reasons why most tourism and hospitality establishments failed to adapt and implement EMS in their management systems and operations is lack of commitment from the top management and lack of visibility of EMS. Other areas of concern are management turnover, perceptions of costs outweighing benefits of EMS, budget and human capital constraints, insufficient training and recognition of EMS. These are critical elements to improve productivity and efficiency and brand image of the institution. In their study, Chan and Hawkins (2011) outline six EMS implementation activities to take into action for these establishments to identify EMS adoption and implementation. These activities are policy planning; procedures and controls; training and educations; communication; and review and continual improvement. However, despite this level of social responsibility and potential benefits that flow from projecting a positive image to society, the implementation of environmentally friendly initiatives in the tourism and hospitality sectors has had mixed results (Alonso & Ogle, 2005). This paper discusses the existing knowledge on the challenges in establishing environmental management systems in tourism and hospitality and identifies possible gaps in the current efforts.

# 2. THE CONCEPT AND THEORIES

Current literature shows evidence that tourism and hospitality industries have focused their environmental attention toward understanding and motivating and adapting environmental management practices in organizations. Within the scope of EMS implementation, researchers have identified various areas where tourism and hospitality industry could focus and benchmark, and on factors that organizations should consider for successful implementation of ISO14001 (Sambasivan & Fei, 2008). Literature also exists on creative financing techniques in setting up EMS in the organizations (Chan & Ho, 2006), and on barriers, benefits and critical issues in ISO14001 implementation (Chan & Li, 2001).

Many researchers (Chan & Wong, 2006; Chan & Hawkins, 2010; Quazi, Khoo, Tan & Wong, 2001; Lawrence, Andrews, Ralph & France, 2002; Pun, Hui, Lau, Law & Lewis, 2002) agree that the concept of environmental management, which leads to sustainability of the business, is still relatively new for some tourism and hospitality organizations and has a multitude of meanings and connotations. The concept of environmental sustainability has become a very serious and profound topic within the tourism and hospitality arena in the past decade. This is primarily due to the accelerated pace in which customer needs and expectations are changing.

## The Nature of ISO 14001

International ISO 14000 standards are well recognized international voluntary consensus standards, which were developed mainly in response to the proliferation of national EMS standards in various countries. This initiative forced companies to deal with dozens of potentially incompatible systems from each country in which they conducted business (Tibor & Feldman, 1996). The ISO is non-governmental organization established in 1947 to develop worldwide standards to improve international communication and collaboration, and to facilitate the international exchange of goods and services. ISO can be described as a federation of about 100 international standards' bodies which represent 95% of the world's industrial production. Subsequently, 46 years later, in 1993, the ISO established a Technical Committee TC207 comprised of six subcommittees and numerous working groups to develop ISO 14000 series standards in environmental management, in order to develop and produce a set of unified and voluntary standards for environmental management that could be accepted and implemented across countries.

The ISO14000 has been established to assist any company to meet the sustainable development objectives in environmentally friendly ways. The ISO 14000 series standards was developed within 20 environmental standards that are voluntary and process-based (Barnes, 1996). The family includes the following: ISO 14001 – EMS: specifications with guidance to use, ISO14004 – EMS: general guidelines on principles, systems and supporting techniques, ISO 14010 – guidelines for environmental auditing: general principles, ISO 14011 – guidelines for environmental auditing: audit procedures, ISO 14012 – guidelines for environmental auditing: qualification criteria for environmental auditors, ISO 14024 – environmental labeling, ISO14040 – life cycle assessment and ISO 14060 – guide for the inclusion of environmental aspects in product standards. Among these series in the

family, ISO14001 is the one and only environmental management systems standard against which an organization can become certified for EMS.

Figure 1 depicts an EMS model adapted from Ritchie and Hayes (1998), who are well-known among researchers on this topic. Figure 1 shows the EMS framework and the five principles:

- Environmental policy
- Planning
- Implementation and operation
- Checking and corrective action
- Review and improvement

## Relationship between ISO14001 and Hotel Industry

The ISO 14001 standards on environmental management provide a system for tracking, managing, and improving performance regarding environmental requirements. According to Gallagher et al. (2004), the conformance to the ISO standards requires policy commitments to compliance with all regulatory requirements and other mandates, such as pollution prevention and EMS continual improvement, verifiable by external auditors.

Analysis of published literature indicates that a range of environmental management (from basic initiatives to environmental management system certification) has been implemented across the tourism and hospitality sectors. However, the level of environmental management implemented to date depends on various motives, facilitators, and constraints an operation such as a hotel is faced with (Álvarez Gil, Burgos Jimenez & Cespedes Lorente, 2001; Ayuso, 2007; Bohdanowicz, 2005; Bramwell & Alletorp, 2001; Goodman, 2000; Vernon, Essex, Pinder & Curry, 2003). Environmental issues which affect industries across the globe, especially tourism and hospitality, have compelled many organizations to adopt environmental policies. As a result, environmental management has been increasing dynamically across the board. Researchers, nevertheless, have also

*Figure 1. Environmental Management Systems model adapted from Ritchie and Hayes (1998)*

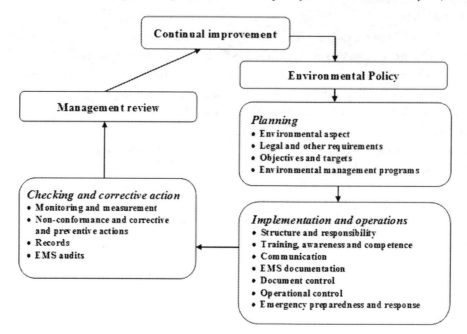

found a certain amount of skepticism with regards to the sincerity of greening efforts (Brown, 1996). The tourism and hospitality industry claims that it doesn't grossly pollute the environment, nor has it consumed vast amounts of non-renewable resources, but it does have a significant effect on global resources in general (Kirk, 1995).

Tourism and hospitality industry has been traditionally considered as one that does not have a great impact on the natural environment compared to industries such as gas and oil, and other consumer product manufacturing industries. However, the hotel industry is largely service based and as such, it is a significant consumer of resources (Bohdanowicz & Martinac, 2003). Hotels operate 24/7 providing a range of services to guests for their comfort and leisure. They are small self-contained cities involving the housing and support of people with associated demands for lodging, food, water and waste management. Managing hotels is a complex undertaking and hotels are not always managed independently but by a management team that runs daily operations. Therefore, the way operations are managed will

have a certain level of impact on the environment as a whole (Revilla, Dodd & Hoover, 2001). Researchers like Houdre (2008) and Brown (2006) have determined that the primary reason for implementing environmental practices is to increase profitability. Nevertheless, Cotton (2007) argues that while the objective of running a business is to make a profit, it is of great concern how many hospitality organizations have yet to adopt green practices in order to drive long-term profitability.

Issues in environmental management and its relationship to sustainability of the industry have long been discussed and debated. Among the most commonly argued issues is the sustainability of waste management in the hotel industry. The application of the systems in the industry depends on the country's policies and infrastructure: for example, it is much more complicated to implement a system in Asia due to rapid industrialization and urbanization and changing waste composition and generation rates (Agamuthu, Fauziah, Khidzir & Noorazamimah Aiza, 2007).

Since the 1990s, voluntary approaches have been considered important initiatives to improve the environmental performance of industries that have direct or indirect effects on the environment from their operations (Paton, 2000). The term voluntary approach means that the initiative is developed and implemented by the organization or sector that causes pollution and is directed at improving their environmental performance (Higley & Convery, 2001). The aim of a firm for adopting voluntary approaches is to integrate the concept of sustainability into their business plans and objectives. Accordingly, there are three types of voluntary approach instruments: Unilateral Initiative/Commitment, Public Voluntary Challenge and Negotiated Agreement (Delmas & Terlaak, 2001). Conversely, Higley and Convery (2001) argue that there are a wide variety of different categories. Within this framework, the tourism and hotel industry has been committed to working toward a sustainable environment since the 1990s by adopting various voluntary initiatives and by using a variety of tools. Ayuso (2006; 2007) states that the most common voluntary instruments used by the hotel industry are codes of conduct, environmental management systems (EMS), best environmental practices, eco-labels and environmental performance indicators. According to Ayuso (2006), eco-labels and EMS are considered the best environmental practices for hotel operations. Ayuso (2006) further states that EMS certification is considered to be the most successful practice in the hotel sector. Having a system in place, including a certification, is beneficial to all stakeholders.

The lodging sector, particularly, is one of the most important in developed and developing countries serving many useful events and functions consuming materials and producing waste out of these events and functions. The hotel sector specifically, has been described as the one of which activities constitute a great impact on the environment (Kasimu, Zaiton & Hassan, 2012). The waste management system is a main contributor to the environmental quality of which the developing countries' hospitality industry is most sensitive

In support of this effort, the hospitality industry as a whole has been 'catalyst' in recycling and source reduction by applying waste management system practices in their operations. To highlight the magnitude of waste, typical urban areas of Asia produce about 760,000 metric tons of municipal solid waste (MSW) per day (World Bank, 1999). In 2025, this figure will increase to 1.8 million tons of waste per day. Even though these estimates are conservative and do not represent the real situations, these numbers could actually turn out to be double the predicted amounts.

# 3. CHALLENGES FOR EMS IMPLEMENTATION IN HOSPITALITY INDUSTRY

After reviewing the various considerations concerning the elements of EMSs, we have identified six core elements affecting the success of implementing environmentally sustainable initiatives in hospitality organizations: policy (Brophy, 1996; Zobel, 2008), planning (ISO, 1996), procedures and controls (Bruner and Burns, 1998; Aboulnaga, 1998), training and education (Dodd, 1997; Hilson and Nayee, 2002), communication (Affisco et al., 1997; Sroufe, 2000), and review and continual improvement (Tribe et al., 2000; Hilson and Nayee, 2002).

Various studies also reveal a number of critical factors that influence (positively or negatively) the implementation of best practice and the relationship between the EMS and the hospitality industry: top management commitment (Penny, 2007; Ronnenberg, Graham & Mahmoodi, 2011), employee and stakeholders involvement (Maxwell et al., 1997), lack of public support (Santos, 2011), insufficient financial resources (Santos, 2011), lack of time (Santos, 2011), poor environmental knowledge (Penny, 2007), and lack of government regulations (Penny, 2007). Therefore, lack of top management support may become a major obstacle according to research in the relationship between the factors involving implementation of environmental management systems and the success level of hospitality environmental management systems.

## 4. IMPLICATIONS, FUTURE CHALLENGES, AND OPPORTUNITIES

Issues of organizational environmental sustainability in the tourism and hospitality industries are expected to gain more attention globally regardless of the size of the operation. Studies determine that certain changes need to be made within the tourism and hospitality industry to achieve environmentally sustainable management practices (Bohdanowics, 2005).

Tourism organizations and hotel establishments need to continue incorporating environmental initiatives in their strategic planning in order to eliminate roadblocks and other EMS implementation challenges. For example, Marriot Hotels International has made EMS part of their strategic planning and aims at becoming the leader in environmental sustainability.

The Zürich Marriott Hotel in Switzerland is an example of Marriott's EMS implementation (Marriott, 2013). Their initiative includes, but not limited to:

- ISO 14001 certification (environmental management system)
- Recycled consumables/Nameplate collection boxes
- Uses only post-consumer paper
- Water saving showers heads in all guest rooms
- Water conserving toilets in all guest rooms
- Motion sensor and timed light switches in all offices and storage rooms
- Water conserving faucets in all public restrooms

- Re-Usable, thermal lunch boxes
- Florescent lighting throughout meeting areas
- Restaurants use whenever possible products supplied by providers of organic products
- Buying of tickets for public transport

Published literature proves it has already been documented that, in the long-run, these activities result in cost savings (UNEP & IH&RA). Nonetheless, to promote even higher environmentally responsible behavior in these industries, it is necessary to demonstrate the cost savings associated with such practices. Bohdanowics (2005) suggests that cost-benefit analyses should be performed across the board and the findings widely disseminated, while new and less expensive technologies should be developed to facilitate the process. Industry representatives and scholars could cooperate in this area of research by preparing successful case studies, offering new ideas, as well as finding solutions by providing answers to close any gap found in available information about the issues discussed.

Governments also should be highly involved by providing incentives for the industry and related/supporting industries such as agriculture and fisheries, to adopt environmentally sound practices both in operations and management.

The opportunities mentioned above could be pursued through EMS. Bohdanowics (2005) proposes suggestions and measurements to address the challenges in EMS applications, such as trade associations and cooperation with environmental organizations. Tourism managers and hotel management companies should develop and offer special promotions and training for all stakeholders in the hospitality sector and educate customers by raising their environmental awareness and creating demand for "green" alternatives and certifications of 'eco-labels'.

# 5. CONCLUSION

In sum, many organizations in the tourism and hospitality industry are now subject to sustainable environment costs and obligations under environmental laws and regulations. Environmental risks are very uncertain, while environmental expenditures are becoming increasingly significant. Currently a series of global environmental standards have been recognized and certified within ISO 14000.

ISO 14001 environmental standards would assist in safe-guarding the organizations in managing their environmental requirements and in ensuring that their environmental policies and practices conform to the vision, mission and objectives of the organizations. Organizations of all sizes and in all industries certainly will be challenged in obtaining ISO 14001 certification.

ISO 14001 environmental standards provide guidelines for the proper implementation of an effective EMS which can be integrated with other managerial functions to assist organizations in achieving environmental and economic goals. ISO 14001 also sets forth standards for conducting environmental auditing and registration to ISO 14001.

ISO 14001 provides organizations with environmental guidelines to assist them in preparing step-by-step implementation plans to adopt an adequate and effective EMS, conduct proper environmental audits, and successfully become registered to ISO 14001 by overcome the challenges.

Based on the challenges and opportunities identified in this investigation, the researchers want to raise awareness and shed some light on the importance of sustainable environment best practices by implementing Environmental Management Systems, and by capitalizing on the benefits the ISO 14001 certification can offer to the tourism and hospitality industries as a whole and to organizations and establishments in developing countries. This study contributes to the body of knowledge within the framework of environmental sustainability policy implantation and the ISO 14001 certification.

# REFERENCES

Aboulnaga, I. A. (1998). Integrating quality and environmental management as competitive business strategy for the twenty-first century. *Environmental Management and Health, 9*(2), 65–71. doi:10.1108/09566169810211168

Affisco, J. F., Nasri, F., & Paknejad, M. J. (1997). Environmental versus quality standards – an overview and comparison. *International Journal of Quality Science, 2*(1), 5–23. doi:10.1108/13598539710159059

Alonso, A. D., & Ogle, A. (2010). Tourism and hospitality small and medium enterprises and environmental sustainability. *Management Research Review, 33*(8), 818–826. doi:10.1108/01409171011065626

Álvarez Gil, M. J., Burgos Jimenez, J., & Cespedes Lorente, J. J. (2001). An analysis of environmental management, organizational context and performance of Spanish hotels. *Omega, 29*(6), 457–471. doi:10.1016/S0305-0483(01)00033-0

Ayuso, S. (2006). Adoption of voluntary environmental tools for sustainable tourism: Analyzing the experience of Spanish hotels. *Environmental Management, 13*, 207–220.

Ayuso, S. (2007). Comparing Voluntary Policy Instruments for Sustainable Tourism: The Experience of the Spanish Hotel Sector. *Journal of Sustainable Tourism, 15*(2), 144–159. doi:10.2167/jost617.0

Barnes, P.E. (1996). Green Standards. *B & E Review, October-December*, 24-28.

Bohdanowicz, P. (2005). European hoteliers' environmental attitudes: Greening the business. *The Cornell Hotel and Restaurant Administration Quarterly, 46*(2), 188–204. doi:10.1177/0010880404273891

Bohdanowicz, P., & Martinac, I. (2003). Attitudes towards sustainability in chain hotels- Results of a European survey. *International conference on smart and sustainable built environment, 19*(21), 1-10.

Bramwell, B., & Alletorp, L. (2001). Attitudes in the Danish tourism industry to the roles of business and government in sustainable tourism. *International Journal of Tourism Research, 3*(2), 91–103. doi:10.1002/jtr.242

Brophy, M. (1996). Environmental policies. In: Chan, E.S.W., & Hawkins, R. (2010), Attitude towards EMSs in an international hotel: and exploratory case study. *International Journal of Hospitality Management, 29*(4), 641–651.

Brown, M. (1996). Environmental policy in the hotel sector; "green" strategy or stratagem? *International Journal of Contemporary Management, 8*(3), 18–23.

Bruner, L. J., & Burns, M. J. (1998). The ISO 14000 Series: Business-friendly environmentalism. *Environmental Regulation and Permitting, 7*(3), 17–19.

Chan, E. S. W., & Hawkins, R. (2010). Attitude towards EMSs in an international hotel: And exploratory case study. *International Journal of Hospitality Management, 29*(4), 641–651. doi:10.1016/j.ijhm.2009.12.002

Chan, E. S. W., & Hawkins, R. (2011). Application of EMSs in a hotel context: A case study. *International Journal of Hospitality Management.*

Cotton, B. (2007). We must find a balance of sustainability. *Caterer & Hotelkeeper, 197*(4498), 32–33.

Delmas, M. A., & Terlaak, A. K. (2001). A framework for analyzing environmental voluntary agreements. *California Management Review, 43*(3), 44–63. doi:10.2307/41166088

Dodd, O. A. (1997). An insight into the development and implementation of the international environmental management system ISO 14001. In R. Hillary (Ed.), *Environmental Management Systems and Cleaner Production.* Toronto, Canada: Wiley.

Gallaghar, D. R., Andrews, R. N. L., Chandracai, A., & Rohitratana, K. (2004). Environmental Management System in US and Thailand. *Greener Management International, 46*(46), 41–56. doi:10.9774/GLEAF.3062.2004.su.00006

Goodman, A. (2000). Implementing sustainability in service operations at Scandic Hotels. *Interfaces, 30*(3), 202–214. doi:10.1287/inte.30.3.202.11653

Higley, C. J., Leveque, F., & Convery, F. (2001). Environmental Voluntary Approaches: Research Insights for policy - makers.

Hilson, G., & Nayee, V. (2002). Environmental management system implementation in the mining industry: A key to achieving cleaner production. *International Journal of Mineral Processing, 64*(1), 19–41. doi:10.1016/S0301-7516(01)00071-0

Houdre, H. (2008). Sustainable Development in the Hotel Industry. *Cornell Industry Perspectives, 2*, 5–20.

Kasimu, A. B., Zaiton, S., & Hassan, H. (2012). Hotels involvement in sustainable tourism practices in Klang Valley, Malaysia. *International Journal of Economics and Management, 6*(1), 21–34.

Kirk, D. (1995). Environmental management in hotels. *International Journal of Contemporary Hospitality Management, 7*(6), 3–8. doi:10.1108/09596119510095325

Lawrence, L., Andrews, D., Ralph, B., & France, C. (2002). Identifying and assessing environmental impacts: Investigating ISO 14001 approaches. *The TQM Magazine, 14*(1), 43–50. doi:10.1108/09544780210413237

Marriott (2013). Green Events, inspired by the environment. Zürich Marriott Hotel, Neumühlequai 42, CH-8001 Zürich.+41 (0)44. 360.7070. Retrieved from: http://www.marriott.com/hotelwebsites/us/z/zrhdt/zrhdt_pdf/zurich_marriott_hotel_green_events.pdf, November 15, 2013.

Penny, W. Y. K. (2007). The use of environmental management as a facilities management tool in the Macao hotel sector. *Emerald Group Publishing Limited, 25*(7/8), 286–295.

Pun, K., Hui, I., Lau, H. C. W., Law, H., & Lewis, W. G. (2002). Development of an EMS planning framework for environmental management practices. *International Journal of Quality & Reliability Management, 19*(6), 688–709. doi:10.1108/02656710210429573

Quazi, H. A., Khoo, Y. K., Tan, C. M., & Wong, P. S. (2001). Motivation for ISO 14000 certification: Development of a predictive model, Omega. *International Journal of Management Sciences, 29*, 525–542.

Revilla, G., Dodd, T. H., & Hoover, C. (2001). Environmental tactics used by hotel companies in Mexico. *International Journal of Hospitality & Tourism Administration, 1*(3), 111–127. doi:10.1300/J149v01n03_07

Ritchie, I., & Hayes, W. (1998). *A guide to implementation of ISO14000 series on environmental management.* Englewood Cliffs, NJ: Prentice-Hall.

Ronnenberg, S. K., Graham, M. E., & Mahmoodi, F. (2011). The important role of change management in environmental management system implementation. *International Journal of Operations & Production Management, 3*(6), 631–647. doi:10.1108/01443571111131971

Sambasivan, M., & Fei, N. Y. (2008). Evaluation of critical success factors of implementation of ISo 14001 using analytic hierarchy process (AHP): A case study from Malaysia. *Journal of Cleaner Production, 16*(13), 1424–1433. doi:10.1016/j.jclepro.2007.08.003

Santos, M. (2011). CSR in SMEs: Strategies, practices, motivations and obstacles. *Social Responsibility Journal, 7*(3), 490–508. doi:10.1108/17471111111154581

Sroufe, R. (2000). Environmental management systems: implications for operations management and firm performance. Ph.D. Dissertation, Michigan State University, Michigan.

Tibor, T., & Feldman, I. (1996). *ISO14000: a guide to the new environmental management standards.* Chicago, IL: Irwin Professional Publishing.

Tilley, F. (1999). The gap between the environmental attitudes and the environmental behavior of small firms. *Business Strategy and the Environment, 8*(4), 238–248. doi:10.1002/(SICI)1099-0836(199907/08)8:4<238::AID-BSE197>3.0.CO;2-M

Tribe, J., Font, X., Griffiths, N., Vickery, R., & Yale, K. (2000). *Environmental Management of Rural Tourism and Recreation.* London, UK: Cassell.

UNEP & IH&RA, (2001). Environmental Good Practice in Hotels in Enz & Siguaw, *Best Hotel Environmental Practices*, 72-7.

Vernon, J., Essex, S., Pinder, D., & Curry, K. (2003). The 'greening' of tourism microbusinesses: Outcomes of focus group investigations in South East Cornwall. *Business Strategy and the Environment, 12*(1), 49–69. doi:10.1002/bse.348

## KEY TERMS AND DEFINITIONS

**EMS Framework:** Consist of five basic principles: Environmental policy, Planning Implementation and operation, Checking and corrective action, Review and improvement.

**Environmental Audit:** Is a general term used to describe the evaluations for environmental compliance and management system implementation.

**Environmental Management Systems (EMS):** A set of processes and practices that enable an organization to reduce its environmental impacts and increase its operating efficiency.

**Environmental Performance Indicators:** Commonly used by businesses, governments and non-governmental organizations they are developed, validated and used to track changes to the quality and condition of the air, water, land, and ecological systems. Performance indicators monitor whether goals and targets will be met or not, and can communicate the need for additional measures.

**ISO 14000:** Is a family of standards related to environmental management that exists to help organizations minimize the negative effect on the environment.

**Sustainability:** The term sustainability derives from the Latin *sustinere* (*tenere*, to hold; *sub*, up). *Sustain* can mean "maintain", "support", or "endure".

**Sustainable Development:** Is a process that deals with human development goals to preserve the natural systems that provides the natural resources and ecosystem services to support human existence.

# Chapter 3
# An Investigation on Cultural Cuisine of Mainland China:
## Management Implications for Restaurant Operators

**Angelo Camillo**
*Woodbury University, USA*

**Loredana Di Pietro**
*University of Molise, Italy*

## ABSTRACT

*This chapter investigates the determining factors of the popularity of Italian cuisine in mainland China and attitude of restaurant patrons toward Italian cuisine. Published literature suggests that Italian cuisine abroad was first made familiar by Italian national who immigrated to countries in Europe, the Americas and Oceania. The growing popularity of Italian cuisine around the world today continues to shape the global evolution of ethnic cuisines because of its taste and simplicity of food preparation. Chinese patrons support this theory however; they find that Italian restaurants in China have expensively priced menus, and that they doubt the authenticity of Italian food preparation and question originality of Italian ingredients being used. These perceived negative factors identified could hamper this world-renowned cuisine from sustaining its popularity in China. The study used an online survey methodology and applied statistical analysis techniques to determine the factors relative to the popularity of Italian cuisine in mainland China and to the attitude of Chinese restaurant patrons. The results will contribute to the body of knowledge of hospitality marketing and tourism related studies and will help hospitality operators and future investors of new restaurant ventures in the decision making process whether to invest and operate an Italian restaurant in mainland China.*

DOI: 10.4018/978-1-4666-8606-9.ch003

## INTRODUCTION

Historical records show that food has always played an important role in the cultural evolution of mankind (Camillo, Kim, Ryan and Moreo, 2005). Eating culture, rituals, and food preferences based on environmental and social conditions emerged steadily over time (Camillo et al., 2005). Societies, in turn, adopted specific food preferences according to taste, environment, and local economy. Foods and drinks have become culturally symbolic and eating habits have evolved to reflect people's own tastes and preferences (Camillo, Connolly & Kim, 2008). Italian food culture based on traditional Italian cooking has evolved into one of the world's most prevalent. Italian cuisine, with its adaptability in preparation, has become the most popular cuisine in the world. Despite rapid changes in international trade and profound lifestyle changes, Italy remains unsurpassed in its culinary traditions and accomplishments. Since China opened the doors to international trade, Chinese consumers have been exposed to both Italian cuisine and Italian food and beverage products. With the onset of mercantilism, restaurants have gained popularity across Asia. Although the concept of globalization was non-existent centuries ago, many indigenous foods and cooking styles, such as Italian were exported from one country to another by merchants (Gernet, 1962; Wang, 1982; West, 1997). Clearly such historical trends have significantly affected people's eating habits. Since the late 1980s a large number of Italian restaurants have opened across mainland China. Italian food and beverage exports to China tripled in just a few years. From 2008 to 2009 alone exports in this sector increased by 18.26% (ISTAT, 2008). This is despite total exports declining by -5% due to the recent global economic downturn (ICE-Istituto del Commercio Estero, 2010). This paper analyzes the popularity of Italian cuisine in mainland China and proposes useful recommendations for hospitality operators and future

restaurateurs regarding ethnic cuisine trends and the evolution of Italian cuisine in mainland China.

## LITERATURE REVIEW

### The Evolution of Italian Cuisine

Italian cuisine, as it is known today, is the result of the culinary evolution born of centuries of cultural, social and political changes. Significant change occurred with the discovery of the New World which helped shape much of what is known as Italian cuisine today with the introduction of items such as potatoes, tomatoes, bell pepper and maize; all central parts of Italian cuisine which were not introduced in scale until the 18th century (Del Conte, 2004). From England and to South America, to Australia and anywhere where Italians emigrated, Italian cuisine eventually became an integral part of the host nations' diet. In the late 1970s and early 1980s, Italian restaurants emerged throughout Europe, the United States, South America and Oceania. Large numbers of Italians had immigrated to these regions following the economic downturn World War II had left behind in Italy. During and after their settlement, Italian immigrants expressed their identity through gastronomic heritage reinforcing their sense of belonging to their native place they left behind (Schlüter, 2011). Concurrently, as U.S. hotel chains expanded around the world, operators benchmarked their success on Italian restaurants and began to integrate Italian style restaurants into their own operations. Chefs from around the world also began to capitalize on the success of Italian cuisine by using local ingredients to promote dishes that did not even exist in Italy. One of the most revolutionary new dishes, "Pasta Primavera," designed for vegetarians, was created at the Italian restaurant Le Cirque in New York; it had no red sauce topping and no meat balls (Maccioni, 2002). The very first Italian restaurant operated outside

Italy was Fior D' Italia, which opened on May 1, 1886 in San Francisco and reopened on the same site after a fire in 2007. This was followed by Tortorici's in 1900 in New Orleans. The first U.S. pizzeria in 1905 New York, Barbetta's restaurant was opened in 1906 in New York City and Frank Grisanti restaurant in Memphis in 1908. The last three decades has seen tremendous changes in food culture, and Italian cuisine has been at centre stage. This has prompted many entrepreneurs around the world to pursue a career in culinary arts and to venture into operating "Italian style" restaurants. Credit must be given to the Americans who have created large restaurant chains such as Pizza Hut and Olive Garden that have been the pioneers in propagating the popularity of Italian cuisine around the world. At what point in time Italian cuisine was introduced to mainland China is not known. However until the late eighties western style restaurants in general were featured mainly in expensive international hotels. Therefore, Italian cuisine in China may have debuted with the establishment of the first international hotels probably in the largest commercial cities. Barolo Ristorante at the Ritz-Carlton Hotel and Prego Ristorante at the Westin Hotel in Beijing are two such examples (The Ritz – Carlton, 2009; The Westin Beijing, 2009). An exact date as to when the first Italian restaurant may have opened in China could also not be established however, an analysis of food-related literature revealed that some of the first free-standing Italian restaurants in mainland China were: Da Marco Ristorante and Pasta Fresca Ristorante both opened in Shanghai in 1990 and 1993 respectively (Da Marco, 2009; Pasta Fresca Da Salvatore, 2009). A number of Italian restaurants opened in locations where Italian ex - patriots would gather which in turn attracted Chinese patrons as well. In the late 1990s when dining out became increasingly popular, many Chinese began to try novelty cuisines and Italian cuisine became increasingly popular among consumers. During the same period Italian-American restaurants like Pizza Hut also debuted

in China. This fast evolution encouraged Asian entrepreneurs to benchmark American restaurant success strategies and to begin to open their own Italian-style restaurants across mainland China. One such originator was a Burger King distributor in Taiwan who opened Gino's Pasta-Cappuccino in Beijing specializing in Italian-style cuisine, premium coffee drinks, and desserts (Capatti & Montanari, 2003; Gino's Pasta, 2009).

## The Popularity of Italian Cuisine in China

Published literature suggests that Italian cuisine has a strong relationship with China's food resources since many spices used in Italian cooking culture were imported to Italy by Marco Polo (Burgan, 2002; Otfinoski, 2003; Yule & Cordier, 1923). However, one cannot infer that this is a contributing factor to the popularity of Italian cuisine in mainland China. Italian cuisine is now becoming more popular in China through marketing sponsored by the Italian Government and organized exporters. E.g.: in an effort to structurally promote Italian cuisine and food products in China, the China-Italy Chamber of Commerce (CICC) was established. The "iFood" initiative is a project of the CICC that informs about current trends in Italian culinary arts in China through interviews, market research, and in-depth analysis. IFood is published quarterly in both the Chinese and Italian languages and is distributed electronically to interested parties. In addition, it is available to all internets for free download (CICC, 2009).

Media promotional activities and articles in trade magazines reveal that over the past decade Italian food has become increasingly popular in China and Italian style restaurants operate in most hotels across China. Also, Italian food ingredients are now available in most major shopping centres in mainland China (Phau & Leng, 2008). The 13th International Exhibition for the Food, Drink, Hospitality, Foodservice, Bakery and Retail Industries took place in Shanghai from 18-20 November 2009 at the Shanghai New International Expo Centre. Organizers scheduled special events that further support the increased popularity of Italian gastronomic representation (FHC China, 2009). Similarly special events were organized during the 20th Shanghai International Hospitality Equipment and Supply Expo which took place from March 29 to April 1st, 2011 (Hotelexpo, 2011). These annually re-occurring events include: The International Culinary Arts Competition, The China Pizza Championship, The Barista Competition, Olive Oil China, and The Great Italian Chefs of Shanghai Gala Lunches. On average, over ninety Italian food and beverage exporters participate in the events and conduct special seminars on pasta, olive oil, cheese, espresso coffee, wine and other beverages, and desserts. As the popularity of Italian cuisine increases and new restaurant venture opportunities present themselves, China has now become home to many chefs who own or manage some of the best restaurants in the world. This trend, among others, has been a precursor to demand for experienced chefs, and contributed to the opening of hundreds of culinary schools worldwide. Many culinary schools now integrate Italian cuisine classes into their curriculum (Culinary Institute of America, 2009). These series of evolutionary events, with the support of mass media campaigns, television cooking shows, and social media networks has strengthened the popularity of Italian cuisine. New trends, such as the "Slow Food" movement which aims mainly at preserving Italian food culture, further support the popularity of Italian cuisine in China (Petrini & Padovani, 2005; Petrini, 2011). Slow Food is a non-profit, eco-gastronomic member-supported organization that was founded in 1989 to counteract fast food and fast life, the disappearance of local food traditions and people's dwindling interest in the food they eat where it comes from, how it tastes and how food choices affect the rest of the world. Its scope is to bring together pleasure, environmental sustainability and responsibility and make them inseparable in the public's mind. The Slow Food movement has over 100,000 members in 132 countries including Japan, South Korea and China (Slowfood, 2011).

## Factors of the Popularity of Italian Cuisine in China

A large number of factors, both intrinsic and extrinsic, may determine the popularity of Italian cuisine in mainland China (Camillo et al., 2005; Camillo et al., 2008). There is scope for further growth in China, as there is still a Chinese market yet to experience Italian cuisine. There is replete literature published explaining customer behavior and attributes impacting cuisine and restaurant choice (Kolpan, Smith & Weiss, 2001; Abdelhamied, 2013). According to The Consumer Psychology in Behavioural Perspective, the most widely-accepted and influential models of consumer behavior derive in large part from cognitive psychology. As a result, consumer choice is usually understood as a problem-solving and decision-making sequence of activities, the outcome of which is determined principally by the buyer's intellectual functioning and processing of information (Foxall, 1990; Huliyeti, Marchesini & Canavari, 2008). Consumer's choice becomes more critical in emerging markets which are usually inundated with novelty products such as ethnic cuisines. Studies on consumer attitude toward specific foods in emerging markets show that traditional consumption patterns can be altered by the availability of new choices (Veeck & Burns, 2005). In addition, menu content and approach to nutritional information on restaurant menus plays an important role in the eyes of the customer (Josiam, Foster & Bahulkar, 2012). In terms of selecting a restaurant by cuisine the consumer is faced with several decisions based on the knowledge acquired about the particular restaurant such as category, cuisines, service, price, and atmosphere (Yurtseven & Kaya, 2011). Studies about Italian cuisine conducted outside China suggest that it is the taste of the ingredients put together and simplicity in which the dishes are prepared, while others argue that the overall cuisine is incomparable to any other. Besides these extrinsic factors many intrinsic factors will affect the consumers' choice in selecting a restaurant. As economic prosperity gives rise to greater purchasing power for a great number of Chinese citizens, along with an increasing number of women working full-time, the propensity to eat meals outside homes becomes greater. If the extrinsic factors mediate the effect Italian cuisine has on the consumer in China, Italian cuisine will eventually mature. It will no longer be an exotic novelty, but simply another choice of cuisine.

## PURPOSE OF STUDY

The aim of this study is to investigate factors contributing to the popularity of Italian cuisine in mainland China and identify implications for restaurant operators. Specifically the authors wanted to identify those factors that may or may not contribute to the expansion and sustainability of Italian cuisine in mainland China. With the evolution of globalization original ingredients can easily be exported from Italy thus preserving the authenticity of Italian restaurants based in overseas markets. It is important to note that all authentic Italian dishes vary by region; however, there are many significant regional dishes that have become both national dishes as well. Different variations for once regionally specific dishes have proliferated across Italy. The traditional meal accompaniments of cheese and wine are also play different roles both regionally and nationally with their many variations and Denominazione di origine controllata (DOC) (regulated appellation) laws. Several researchers maintain that the knowledge of a product's country of origin has a direct influence on product perception (Chambers, Lobb, Butler, Harvey & Traill, 2007; Guerrero et al, 2009; Pieniak, Verbeke, Vanhonacker, Guer-rero & Hersleth 2009). Accordingly many studies

*Table 1. Factors that will influence Italian cuisine in the future, ranked in order of importance*

| Factors |
| --- |
| 1. Taste |
| 2. Simplicity |
| 3. Variety of Italian cuisine, North South |
| 4. Italian style quality ingredients are readily available |
| 5. Italian cuisine is not viewed as exotic, it is no longer a novelty |
| 6. Classic Italian cuisine |
| 7. Expectation of young diners on price, service, quality, convenience |
| 8. Fusion into other cuisines |
| 9. Specialized local food cuisines (e.g. Neapolitan, Piedmontes, Sicilian) |
| 10. Italian "regional" cuisine concept development, e.g. North, Central, Southern |

Camillo et al., (2006)

show that consumers' perception of the country of origin influences their perception of quality, their attitude and their subsequent purchasing intention (Aiello et al., 2008; Teas & Agarwal, 2000). Because of the perishability of specific market fresh products such as fish, seafood and meats, local Chinese ingredients may substitute those used by local chefs in Italy. This exploratory study analyzes if the phenomenon which makes this cuisine appealing to almost anyone can be generalized to include Chinese consumers, regardless of demographic characteristics such as age, ethnicity, education, and gender. Table 1 below shows the results of a previous study conducted in the U.S. which revealed that the top three factors contributing to Italian cuisine popularity are: taste, simplicity, and variety (Camillo at al., 2008).

## SIGNIFICANCE OF THE STUDY

Research pertaining to the popularity of certain cuisines is becoming of wide-ranging academic interest. In eating, humans integrate natural products into culture through cooking practices and eating habits (Meigs, 1997).

The scope of this research is to understand how Italian cuisine is becoming popular in China and if it can sustain its popularity. Changes and shifts in eating habits are spearheaded by new modes of communication, improvements in infrastructure, and new technologies in food production and preparation and distribution channels. Because of globalization many ethnic foods are now available in almost any country and during any season. These evolutionary changes have enabled people to become more educated in developing food consumption preferences according to their cultural identities and social networks (Harris & Ross, 1987).

This study will help understand how the Chinese perceive foreign cuisines such as Italian and, in turn, attempts to identify the determinants that make this cuisine popular now with potential for growth in the future. This research is, therefore, intended to assist future entrepreneurs and current hospitality operators in their marketing and investing in mainland China.

## METHODOLOGY

The basic research design for conducting the analysis was primarily an online survey distributed to Chinese consumers. Owing to the exploratory character of the study and certain resource constraints, a non-probability, convenience sampling method to draw samples was adopted. The following section addresses the methodology used in the data analysis. This study applied qualitative and quantitative methods using an online survey with a self-administered, electronic questionnaire and face-to-face interviews conducted on location during the month of June, 2012.

## Sample

For the online survey a convenience sample included subjects selected on the basis of specific characteristics or qualities (Wimmer & Dominick, 2003). Specifically, the sample includes the people who live in mainland China who have internet access and are members of interest groups under the category of "news, entertainment, lifestyle, cuisine, and sport" in http://www.qq.cn - http://im.qq.com, www.Yahoo.cn and www.Google.cn search engines. This convenience sample is chosen with the understanding that it might represent a specific portion of the population. The sample size is 5,000 and it is made – up of individual group sizes of between 10 and 1,000 members with public access and free membership (The sample for the face-to-face interviews was chosen randomly on location in the cities of Beijing, Guangzhou, and Shenzhen.

## Instruments

The questionnaire used in the online survey was designed to collect information on demographic variables (e.g.: age, education) and consumers' preference of Italian foods and attitude toward Italian cuisine.

About 324 responses were received from the online survey. About 184, or 56.8%, of the respondents were male and 140, or 43.2%, were female. About 42.9% had a high school degree, 49.7% had an undergraduate degree, and 7.4% had a master's degree. Their age ranged from <25 to 65, (see table 2). The Postal Codes provided by respondents indicated that participants' responses came from about 30 different cities.

There were 22 questions in the questionnaire, including yes or no, scaled, multiple choices, closed-ended and open-ended questions. To distribute the web-based questionnaire an online survey website in Chinese languages was set up. The link to the survey was emailed to the recipients in the sample. To administer the online survey the researcher sent an electronic invitation letter to potential participants one week before the survey was launched. The survey was conducted over a 30 day period during the month of June of 2012. The data was collected through a survey

*Table 2. Respondents' demographics*

| Age Range | Frequency | Percent |
|---|---|---|
| <25 | 72 | 22.2 |
| 26-35 | 126 | 38.9 |
| 36-45 | 90 | 27.8 |
| 46-55 | 24 | 7.4 |
| 56-65 | 12 | 3.7 |
| **Total** | **324** | **100.0** |
| | | |
| **Gender** | | |
| Male | 184 | 56.8 |
| Female | 140 | 43.2 |
| **Total** | **324** | **100.0** |
| | | |
| **Education** | | |
| High school | 139 | 42.9 |
| BA or BS | 161 | 49.7 |
| Masters degree | 24 | 7.4 |
| Others | 0 | 0 |
| **Total** | **324** | **100.0** |

website based in the UK. The questionnaire for the face-to-face interviews included questions such as: do you like Italian cuisine and why? What is your opinion about Italian cuisine in respect to authenticity? What dishes do you like most, and what dishes do you dislike? Will you continue to eat Italian cuisine in the future?

## Survey

The estimated target population for the online survey was 5.000. Due to the vast population and a high number of internet users, we expected a high response rate. However, possible constraint factors were considered. We chose not to provide incentives to encourage participation. We considered that if the response rate were to be high it would have been greatly beneficial to the study, however, if the response rate were to be too low we would follow Armstrong and Overton's (1997) recom-

mendation to test non-response bias by comparing the socio-demographic characteristics of the first 10% of early respondents and the last 10% of late respondents (Reynolds, 2007).

## Data Analysis

Literature review was analyzed by applying content analysis techniques such as coding, frequencies, trends, and patterns analysis. Coding was used to identify meaning and significance in relationship to the study.

Quantitative data obtained from the online survey was statistically analyzed using SPSS 17.5 software to determine how the underlying demographic characteristics affect the consumption behaviours and attitudes toward Italian cuisine.

Qualitative data collected from face-to-face interviews was summarized and synthesized to identify and extrapolate the significant factors that have influence on the Chinese consumer.

## Results

A Cronbach's alpha reliability test was performed to assess if the survey results yielded the same measure results on repeated trials. Table 3 below shows that the items measured Cronbach's alphas of .731 which were above recommended .70 thresholds. Overall, the measures are internally consistent.

Table 4 below shows the ranking of the factors that influence the popularity of Italian cuisine presented in order of importance, measured on a scale of 1 to 5; 1 = strongly disagree; 5 = strongly agree. The results show that taste, health related benefits, and accessibility are the top contributing factors to the popularity of Italian cuisine. Factor number 10 is related to the price level of Italian dishes and ranks last as Italian cuisine in mainland China is expensive.

Table 5 presents the summarized results from the literature review and qualitative survey data, in order to understand key differences

*Table 3. Cronbach's test of reliability*

| Items | Mean | Std. Deviation | Cronbach's Alpha |
|---|---|---|---|
| Multi item scale | | | .731 |
| **Italian cuisine popularity factors** | | | |
| 11. "taste" | 3.9259 | .69099 | .715 |
| 12. "simplicity" | 2.9074 | .70210 | .738 |
| 13. "freshness of products used" | 3.5926 | .65417 | .737 |
| 14. "portion size" | 3.2778 | .82717 | .732 |
| 15. "speed of service" | 3.6296 | .91013 | .706 |
| 16. "health related benefits" | 3.3704 | .75385 | .713 |
| 17. "not expensive" | 2.8519 | 1.00907 | .732 |
| 18. "available in every city" | 3.6667 | .84017 | .711 |
| 19. " served in non-Italian restaurants" | 3.3704 | .88949 | .732 |
| 20. "advertising and television shows" | 3.2963 | .85398 | .707 |

Published literature does not provide an exact timeline about how, where, and when the Italian cuisine may have arrived in mainland China and how different factors promote the popularity Italian foods in China today. However, the Italian Government and organized exporters as well as the Chinese–Italian Chamber of Commerce play an important role in the propagation and dissemination of Italian culinary knowledge to-day. Cultural differences, eating habits and taste preferences are important factors that affect the choice to dine at ethnic restaurants. Due to the amount of food products recently introduced to China, it is difficult for Chinese consumers to distinguish between authentic foods and foods not produced in their country of origin i.e. pizza and pasta items imported from the U.S. Also, Italian exporters to China and restaurant owners in

*Table 4. Factors that will influence the decision to appreciate Italian cuisine in the future, ranked in order of importance; N=324*

| Rank | Mean and ranking of popularity factors | |
|---|---|---|
| | **Mean** | **Factor** |
| 1 | 3.9259 | Taste |
| 2 | 3.7037 | Health Related Benefits |
| 3 | 3.6667 | Available In Every City |
| 4 | 3.5925 | Fresh Ingredients |
| 5 | 3.3703 | Non Italian Restaurants Serve Italian Food |
| 6 | 3.3570 | Varied-Everyone Likes It |
| 7 | 3.2962 | Media Exposure |
| 8 | 3.2777 | Portion Size |
| 9 | 2.9074 | Simplicity |
| 10 | 2.5185 | Not Expensive |

*Table 5. Summarized results from literature review and qualitative survey data*

| Summarized results from literature review and the qualitative survey data | |
|---|---|
| **From the literature review** | **From the face-to-face interviews** |
| Italian cuisine was first made popular to non-Italians by Italian immigrants settling abroad | Italian restaurants in China are not really Italian |
| Italian cuisines satisfies everyone's palate | Italian food is more American than Italian |
| International hotel chains may have been the first to introduce Italian cuisine in China | Many dishes are served with lot of tomato sauce, it is not authentic |
| Culinary schools now integrate Italian cooking classes into their curriculum | The food is very varied just like Chinese food |
| Movements, such as "Slow Food" aim at preserving Italian food culture around the world | Italian food in hotel restaurants is very expensive |
| Marketing efforts by Italian Government facilitate the dissemination of knowledge about Italian cuisine | Italian menu items, especially wines, are very expensive |
| New means of communication such as "iFood", help promote Italian cuisine in China | The most delicious dishes are the antipasti and desserts |
| Italian food ingredients are readily available in retail food outlets in China | Italian food is very simple, but tastes very good |
| Educational seminars and culinary competition in China spread the knowledge about Italian cuisine | Italian restaurants are authentic because the chefs are Italian |
| Young curious and adventurous Chinese consumers like to try Italian cuisine | Italian cuisine is very similar to Chinese cuisine |

China fail to translate all Italian products and dish names, making purchasing and ordering difficult for the Chinese consumer. A major distinction is found in the eating habits and eating behavior of Chinese consumers in restaurants. Italians like to consume food slowly with ample breaks between courses. Chinese customers, on the other hand, usually eat different dishes together family style and do not occupy a restaurant table for a long period of time. Chinese consumers, who have travelled abroad and have been to Italy, identify some Italian food sold in China as being of lower quality. Also, there is evidence of product substitution from other countries, and misrepresentation of food preparation. Many dishes served are not authentic and the ingredients do not come from Italy. Many owner operators of several Italian themed restaurants are Chinese entrepreneurs thus; the theory of "Country of Origin" and the perception of authenticity are significant to the Chinese consumer. Restaurants with a chef from

Italy where considered authentic by Chinese patrons. Table 5 highlights some important factors which concern Chinese consumers. There is a perception that Italian food sold in Italian restaurants in China is very expensive and that it is not authentic.

## DISCUSSION AND IMPLICATIONS

Significant factors impact Chinese consumers when selecting an Italian restaurant and appreciating Italian cuisine. There are cultural eating differences and Chinese consumers, do have their own tastes and preferences. Although the Chinese share the same appreciation for fresh food ingredients, Italian dishes are prepared differently. Traditionally, Chinese households don't have the same cooking equipment, and lack baking and roasting ovens and grills. Therefore Italian-specific cooking methods are not easily understood by the Chinese consumer. Some Italian dishes are consequently perceived with scepticism especially when consumed for the first time. A significant finding is that Chinese consumers are not familiar with all Italian raw products such as those for antipasti items and find it hard to distinguish quality products and expensive products from lower quality. This is especially true for those wishing to buy wine to pair with Italian dishes. The authors' visits to several Italian restaurants revealed that many antipasto items are substituted with those from other countries e.g.: Mortadella is substituted with Balloni from the U.S. and prosciutto is substituted with smoked Bavarian ham from Germany. Even though it is not always customary, the Chinese tend to eat everything family style, with all dishes brought to the table at the same time. Italians typically eat food in individually served courses. A concern expressed by consumers during face-to-face interviews was that existing Italian restaurants in China do not translate everything on the menu and this makes it harder for patrons to order. The theory of "Country of Origin" and the perception of authenticity play an important role for the Chinese restaurant consumer. Until the Italian cuisine in mainland China has matured and Chinese consumers are well-educated about Italian food, the scepticism among consumers will continue to persist. There are specific differences in consumption habits between Italians and Chinese; Italians eat slowly and spend lot of time seated at a restaurant. For the traditional Italian restaurant there is no seat turnover contributing to ample time at the table and long conversations. At the traditional Chinese restaurant, customers like to eat quickly and don't like to wait long for food to be served. Compared to the cost of a Chinese meal, consumers in China perceive Italian food to be expensive. Therefore the neophobic Chinese consumers still prefer Chinese cuisine, but younger, adventurous Chinese can appreciate Italian styles and tastes. The most enjoyed Italian food products are wine, pasta,

olive oil and chocolate. Cold meat such as salami and ham also seem to growing in popularity. This study attempts to identify the factors that influence Chinese consumers' decisions to sample new cuisines such as Italian. The preservation of traditional cuisines such as the Italian and its propagation in foreign countries is obviously dependent on positive consumer reviews (Perdrini & Padovani, 2005).

## LIMITATION

There were several constraints in conducting this study. Constraints included the geographical distance, the lack of permanent physical presence of investigators in China, and the logistics involved in conducting such a study with the authors' limited stay in China. The online survey had to be designed in English and then translated in Chinese. However the online survey proved to be, to a certain extent, time-saving, but also cost effective with easy data collection. In terms of quantity it is also more effective than face-to-face interviews which required the authors to be on location for an extended period of time. The face-to-face interviews provided to be a very fruitful source of insight, however. The authors were not proficient in any of Chinese languages such as Mandarin or Cantonese and they relied on an Interpreter.

## CONCLUSION

The results of this study provide stakeholders such as Italian restaurant owners and operators, importers, exporters, and marketers, with useful insights as to why Chinese consumers may or may not appreciate Italian cuisine. Moreover, the results should benefit new restaurant entrepreneurs in their strategy formulation for the opening and operating of an Italian restaurant in mainland

China. The results of this study will also support future research about the popularity of Italian cuisine in China and in other countries and should encourage the research of other popular ethnic cuisines around the world.

## REFERENCES

Abdelhamied, H. H. S. (2013). The Effect of Sales Promotions on Post Promotion Behaviors and Preferences in Fast Food Restaurants. *Tourismos: An International Multidisciplinary Journal of Tourism, 8*(1), 93–113.

Aiello, G., Donvito, R., Godey, B., Pederzoli, D., Wiedman, K., Hennings, N., & Siebels, A. (2008). *Luxury brand and country of origin effect: results of an international empirical study*. Paper presented at the International Congress Marketing Trends, Venezia, Italy.

Armstrong, J. S., & Overton, T. S. (1977). Estimating nonresponse bias in mail surveys. *JMR, Journal of Marketing Research, 14*(3), 396–402. doi:10.2307/3150783

Burgan, M. (2002). *Marco Polo: Marco Polo and the silk road to China*. Mankato: Compass.

Camillo, A., Connolly, D., & Kim, W. G.Woo Gon Kim. (2008). Success and Failure in Northern California. Critical Success Factors for Independent Restaurants. *Cornell Hospitality Quarterly, 49*(4), 363–380. doi:10.1177/1938965508317712

Camillo, A., Kim, W. G., Ryan, B., & Moreo, P. (2005). *Trend Forecasting Model of Ethnic Cuisine in America, Using the Italian Cuisine as an Example*. (Unpublished PhD Thesis). University of Michigan, USA.

Capatti, A., & Montanari, M. (2003). *Italian Cuisine: a Cultural History*. New York: Columbia University Press.

Chambers, S., Lobb, A., Butler, L., Harvey, K., & Traill, W. B. (2007). Local, national and imported foods: A qualitative study. *Appetite, 49*(1), 208–213. doi:10.1016/j.appet.2007.02.003

China, F. H. C. (2009). *13th International Exhibition for the Food, Drink, Hospitality, Foodservice, bakery and Retail Industries*. Retrieved December 18, 2009 from www.fhcchina.com and http://www.fhcchina.com/en/index1_2.asp

*China-Italy Chamber of Commerce CICC.* (2009). Retrieved July 18, 2009 from http://www.cameraitacina.com/

Culinary Institute of America. (2009). *Italian cuisine. An introduction to the principles o planning, preparation, and presentation of the foods of Italy*. Retrieved 14 September 2009 from http://www.ciachef.edu/

*Da Marco Group*. (2009). Retrieved December 17, 2009, from http://www.damarco.com.cn/

Del Conte, A. (2004). *The Concise Gastronomy of Italy*. Barnes and Nobles Books.

Evans, M., Cossi, G., & D'Onghia, P. (2000). *World Food Italy*. London, UK: CA, Lonely Planet Publications Pty Ltd.

Foxall, G. (1990). *Consumer Psychology in Behavioural Perspective*. New York: Rutledge.

Gernet, J. (1962). Daily Life in China on the Eve of the Mongol Invasion. Stanford, CA: Stanford University Press.

*Gino's Pasta*. (2009). Retrieved December 17, 2009 from www.gino.com.cn

Guerrero, L., Guardia, M. D., Xicola, J., Verbeke, W., Vanhonacker, F., & Zakowska, B. S. (2009). Consumer-driven definition of traditional food products and innovation in traditional foods. A qualitative cross-cultural study. *Appetite, 52*(2), 345–354. doi:10.1016/j.appet.2008.11.008

Harris, M., & Ross, E. B. (1987). *Food and Evolution: Toward a Theory of Human Food Habits*. Temple University Press.

Hotelexpo. (2011). *The 20th Shanghai International Hospitality Equipment and Supply Expo*. Retrieved December 17, 2009 from http://www.hotelex.cn/

Huliyeti, H., Marchesini, S., & Canavari, M. (2008). Chinese distribution practitioners' Attitudes towards Italian quality foods. *Journal of Chinese Economic and Foreign Trade Studies, 1*(3), 214–231. doi:10.1108/17544400810912374

Istituto Nazionale di Statistica, I. S. T. A. T. (2008). *Italian Institute of Statistics*. Retrieved July 9, 2019 from www.istat.it

Istituto per il Commercio Estero ICE. (2010). *Italian Foreign Commerce Institute*. Retrieved May 10, 2010, from http://www.ice.it/paesi/asia/cina/index.htm

*Italian Trade Commission ITC*. (2009). Retrieved July 9, 2019 from http://www.ice.it/paesi/asia/cina/ufficio4.htm?sede

Josiam, B.M., Foster, C.R., & Bahulkar, G. (2012). For Whom The Menu Informs: a Market Segmentation Approach to Nutritional Information on Restaurant Menus. *Tourismos: An International Multidisciplinary Journal of Tourism, 7*(2), 237-259.

Kolpan, S., Smith, B. H., & Weiss, M. A. (2001). Exploring Wine: The Culinary Institute of America's Complete Guide to Wines of the World. Wiley, John and Sons, Incorporated.

Maccioni, S. (2002) Pasta primavera, Le Cirque 2000. New York, NY.

Meigs, A. (1997). Food as Cultural Construction. In C. Counihan & P. Van Esterik (Eds.), *Food and Culture: A Reader* (pp. 95–106). London: Routledge.

Otfinoski, S. (2003). *Marco Polo: to China and back*. New York: Benchmark Books.

Pasta Fresca Da Salvatore, P. F. D. S. (2009). *Pasta Fresca Restaurant*. Retrieved 17 December 2009 from http://www.pastafresca.com/AboutUS.html

Petrini, C. (2011). *Slow food and slow fish. Our guiding principles*. Slow Food.

Petrini, C., & Padovani, G. (2005). Slow Food Revolution. Da Arcigola a Terra Madre. Una nuova cultura del cibo e della vita. Milan, Rizzoli Editor, Italy.

Phau, I., & Leng, Y. S. (2008). Attitudes toward domestic and foreign luxury brand apparel, A comparison between status and non status seeking teenagers. *Journal of Fashion Marketing and Management, 12*(1), 68–89. doi:10.1108/13612020810857952

Pieniak, Z., Verbeke, W., Vanhonacker, F., Guerrero, L., & Hersleth, M. (2009). Association between traditional food consumption and motives for food choice in six European countries. *Appetite, 53*(1), 101–108. doi:10.1016/j.appet.2009.05.019

Reynolds, R. A., Woods, R., & Baker, J. D. (2007). *Handbook of research on electronic surveys and measurements*. Hershey, PA: Idea Group Reference/IGI Global. doi:10.4018/978-1-59140-792-8

Schlüter, R. G. (2011). Anthropological Roots of Rural Development: A Culinary Tourism Case Study In Argentina. *Tourismos: An International Multidisciplinary Journal of Tourism, 6*(3), 77–91.

*Slowfood Movement*. (2011). Retrieved July 10, 20111 from http://www.slowfood.com/

Teas, R. K., & Agarwal, S. (2000). The Effects of Extrinsic Product Cues on Consumers' Perceptions of Quality, Sacrifice, and Value. *Journal of the Academy of Marketing Science, 28*(2), 278–290. doi:10.1177/0092070300282008

The Westin Beijing. (2009). *Westin Hotel Beijing*. Retrieved 17 December 2009 from, http://www.starwoodhotels.com/westin/property/area/destinations/overview.html?destination=78andpropertyID=1704

Veeck, A., & Burns, A. C. (2005). Changing tastes: The adoption of new food choices in post- reform China. *Journal of Business Research*, *58*(5), 644–652. doi:10.1016/j.jbusres.2003.08.009

Wang, Z. (1982). *Han Civilization*. New Haven, CT: Yale University Press.

West, S. H. (1997). Playing With Food: Performance, Food, and the Aesthetics of Artificiality in the Sung and Yuan. *Harvard Journal of Asiatic Studies*, *57*(1), 67–106. doi:10.2307/2719361

Wimmer, R. D., & Dominick, J. R. (2003). Mass media research: An introduction. Belmont, CA: Thomson/Wadsworth.

Yule, H., & Cordier, H. (1923). *The Travels of Marco Polo*. Dover Publications.

Yurtseven, R. H., & Kaya, O. (2011). Local Food In Local Menus: The Case Of Gokceada. *Tourismos: An International Multidisciplinary Journal of Tourism*, *6*(2), 263–275.

## KEY TERMS AND DEFINITIONS

**Cognitive Psychology:** Is the branch of psychology that focuses on the way people process information. It looks at how we process information we receive, and how the treatment of this information leads to our responses. In other words, cognitive psychology is interested in what is happening within our minds that links stimulus (input) and response (output).

**Consumer Behaviour:** Is the study of individuals, groups, or organizations and the processes they use to select, secure, use, and dispose of products, services, experiences, or ideas to satisfy needs and the impacts that these processes have on the consumer and society.

**Consumer Choice:** A term usually understood as a problem-solving and decision-making sequence of activities, the outcome of which is determined principally by the buyer's intellectual functioning and processing of information.

**Country of Origin (COO):** Literature suggests that country of origin (COO) can have a 'tremendous influence on the acceptance and success of products'.

**Convenience Sample:** Convenience sampling, as its name suggests, involves selecting sample units that are readily accessible to the researcher. It is also sometimes called accidental sampling and is a form of nonprobability sampling; that is, each member of a population has an unknown and unequal probability of being selected. The advantages of convenience samples are that they are relatively inexpensive and, by definition, easy to access. Sometimes, this form of sampling may be the most efficient way.

**Cultural Identity:** Is the identity or feeling of belonging to, as part of the self-conception and self-perception to nationality, ethnicity, religion, social class, generation, locality and any kind of social group that have its own distinct culture. In this way that cultural identity is both characteristic of the individual but also to the culturally identical group that has its members sharing the same cultural identity.

**Determinants of Cuisine Popularity:** Italian cuisine is characterized by its simplicity, taste and variety. In addition, dishes are prepared with only four to eight ingredients. The main factor is the quality of the ingredients rather than on elaborate preparation. Ingredients and dishes vary by region.

**Food Choice:** Factors that guide food choice include taste preference, sensory attributes, cost, availability, convenience, cognitive restraint, and cultural familiarity. In addition, environmental cues and increased portion sizes play a role in the choice and amount of foods consumed.

**Pasta Primavera:** Is a dish that consists of pasta and fresh vegetables. A meat such as chicken can be added, but the focus of primavera is the vegetables themselves. The dish may contain almost any kind of vegetable, but cooks tend to stick to firm, crisp vegetables, such as broccoli, carrots, peas, onions and green bell peppers, with tomatoes.

# Chapter 4
# Advancing the Global Perspective of Tourism by Examining Core and Peripheral Destinations

**Frances Cassidy**
*University of Southern Queensland, Australia*

**Margee Hume**
*Central Queensland University, Australia*

## ABSTRACT

*Core and peripheral destinations are very significant to island tourism because of core and peripheral islands. Peripheral locations may be disadvantaged as they are isolated from the core or economic centers and from the main population. This chapter reviews literature on the complexity of core and peripheral destinations, their development, planning, marketing and management together with local resident's perceptions of tourists and the tourist's expectations. The South Pacific is defined and it's Colonial past discussed together with tourist motivations. It is becoming increasingly difficult for all stakeholders to agree on programs and tourism practices and that various South Pacific countries have different ways of collecting statistical data resulting in few generic standards to adhere to.*

## INTRODUCTION

This chapter will discuss several issues in relation to core and peripheral destinations using the South Pacific as a case study. Island Tourism (IT) refers to the practice of exploring outer Peripheral Islands while situated in a core destination which may suggest that tourism development inevitably entails exploitation of the periphery by the core

(Chaperon & Bramwell, 2013). This style of tourism has been popularly consumed by tourists yet little research has specifically been conducted to clarify its features and foundations. This work will contribute to the adjectival definitions of tourism and advance a new and exciting stream of research. The chapter will proceed by offering the background and brief overview of island tourism and the core-periphery concept will be

DOI: 10.4018/978-1-4666-8606-9.ch004

introduced and examined. The contribution of this chapter will be in advancing the understanding of the constructs of core and peripheral service in the tourism sector elaborating the notion of Island Tourism as a sub contribution. The chapter will then review the development of tourism in the South Pacific and use this context to examine the foundations of IT. The third section explores the tourist expectations of the tourism experience against those of the indigenous local people while the next section explores the motivation of tourists to visit the South Pacific. It will advance the understanding of the motivations of tourists to the core destination and explore reasons why tourists do not visit the peripheral islands which could enhance their tourism experience. The next section explores how marketers can be proactive in advancing tourism to the periphery islands and finally the areas for implementation considerations and further research will be discussed.

This chapter adopts a case study methodology to identify overall themes and practices and offer a deep understanding of core and peripheral tourism. The case is reflective and retrospective and includes a range of facts related to tourist motivation, island geography and service in the Pacific islands. Exploratory research is a flexible and valuable tool for social science research (Babbie, 1989; Churchill, 1979; Kinnear and Taylor, 1996). The objective of exploratory research is to assist in increasing the researcher's familiarity with a problem and clarifying concepts (Churchill, 1979; Grbich, 2013; Zikmund, Babin, Carr & Griffin, 2013). Exploratory research has limitations. The interpretation of the findings is usually subjective and with small sample cases that cannot be projected to a wider population (Zikmund et. al; Grbich, 2013).

This research conducted a variety of content analysis such as web pages, journal articles and various tourism organisations. Together with in-depth interviews and surveys which were conducted with locals and tourists in Vanuatu. It was found that there is a misalignment between what the tourists feel they would participate in or use in the peripheral destinations to those which the local resident's thought the tourist would use. The contribution is chapter makes towards the global understanding of core and peripheral tourism and destinations will be reflected in the context of Island Tourism (IT).

## BACKGROUND

A number of studies have been undertaken into the development of core and peripheral destinations and tourism in Australia (Schmallegger & Carson 2010) and in islands (Cassidy 2012). In many areas, tourism development in third world countries has come about on an ad hoc basis with little thought given to local society or the expectations of the traveller. Scheyvens and Russell (2012) notes that tourism is not a practice of the indigenous, but of large corporations making as much money as possible in ways which may not be compatible with balanced island development. The large corporations are looking at maximizing profit and this may conflict with traditional island ethics of giving and sharing.

Destinations are a combination of tourism products including, accommodation, transportation, shopping, climate, attractions, culture and tours as well as infrastructure that when combined offer an integrated experience to the traveler. In most instances destinations are regarded as well-defined geographical areas, such as a country, an island or a town (Hall, 2008). According to Qu, Lo and Im (2011) it is now recognized that a destination can also have a 'perceptual concept' which the consumer can interpret subjectively according to their past experiences, cultural background, reason for visit and educational background. Not all destinations can take into consideration the preferences of the consumer of travel and tourism products because of geographical or political barriers that may be imposed and because of the increasing competition among tourism destinations (Mariani & Baggio, 2012).

Peripheral locations can be identified within a global scale, continents, countries and within regions. These peripheral locations may be disadvantaged as they are isolated from economic centers and from the main population base and are often costly to visit needing a sea journey or additional air services (Chaperon & Bramwell, 2013). Hence, the peripheral areas may be disadvantaged economically due to their distance from the core or main islands that are the centers of wealth, local markets and economic leakages (Seetanah, 2011).

The issues of peripheral island tourism can be associated with their relationship with major economic centres or cores. According to the dependency theory, which was developed in the 1960's and 70's these relations may involve domination and exploitation by major developed centres (Scheyvens & Russell, 2012). Traditionally this exploitation occurred through colonial control and it is suggested this continues through international ownership of more profitable businesses and often controlled by transnational corporations so that profits is expatriated (Chaperon & Bramwell, 2013). The dependency theory suggests that this exploitation results in the peripheral islands or countries being actively under-developed, or less developed (Brouder & Eriksson, 2013). For example, in Vanuatu (Refer Figure 1) originally the flights left Australia and landed on the island of Efate where the capital of Port Vila is located. In recent years Air Vanuatu the country's national carrier, fly directly from Brisbane to Luganville on the outer island of Espiritu Santo. Air Vanuatu now also fly directly from Brisbane to Tanna Island. Thus these two latest additions to the airlines schedule will allow for the peripheral island destinations to receive more visitors.

Description: The Political Map of Vanuatu showing names of capital city, towns, states, prov-

Developing such destinations in peripheral regions is a contentious issue which has a number of matters which need to be considered, including cultural differences, infrastructure and the government having pro-tourism policies. These matters alone have created an enormous literature base and have identified many areas of study. However, it appears a central issue to developing the peripheral areas is the readiness of the main local stakeholders to develop a tourism product that can be marketed and the identification of a market for that product. Identifying a shared ground between the two groups (the local residents and the tourists) will involve compromise on the part of the stakeholders rather than the tourists because of the mobile nature of the tourists and immobile nature of much of the tourism product (Cassidy, 2012). Against this background the main issues to be discussed in this chapter are tourism development in peripheral island communities together with the traveller's expectations and the expectations the local residents have on what they think the traveller's want by way of the tourism experience.

The understanding of what a peripheral destination is has changed over time. Initially the term referred to the spatial peripherally, lack of access and the geographical distance from a centre. Now it is widely thought that it also comprises political, economic and social dimensions that sometimes results in a lack of power by stakeholders in the peripheral region (Seetanah, 2011). Tourism management in the peripheral areas can find that there are barriers which could include lack of funding, political support and in some cases a likelihood of conflict within the peripheral community (Albrecht, 2010).

The role of the local stakeholder can be hindered because they are often not in control of the tourism development and management in their area and they tend to work in jobs that are underpaid. They often find that the tourists' experiences are prioritized over those of their own local community

*Figure 1. Map of Vanuatu*
*Source: http://www.ezilon.com/maps/oceania/vanuatu-maps.html*

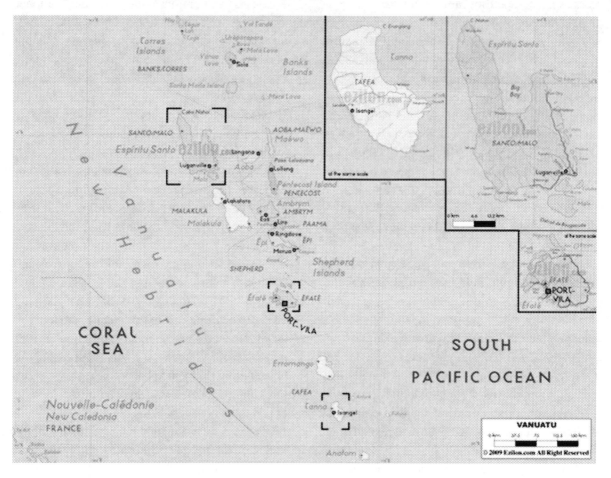

sets are treated as a commodity which strengthens both the actual and perceived marginalization of the local residents. Tourism businesses located in peripheral regions are often micro-scale and prone to issues associated with seasonality and very vulnerable in times of economic hardship (Brouder & Eriksson, 2013).

Whilst there are many peripheral islands in the South Pacific and other destinations, there is no consensus on tourism product development. However, in the core destination arena specialised tourism products are acknowledged to create niche markets for destinations. Chaperon and Bramwell (2013) found that tourists are likely to be attracted to the more remote peripheral rural regions for their traditional rather than novel characteristics.

They explain how it is potentially more profitable to offer a tourism product based on regional characteristics and this should be considered in strategy formulation in particular as local support will be required.

The complexity of destinations, their development, planning, marketing and management is an issue that has intrigued researchers for some time and significant literature has emerged that examines elements of the destination. For example, destination planning and development of facilities has been examined by Ness, Aarstad, Haugland and Gronseth (2014). Other researchers have examined aspects of destination marketing including (Murdy & Pike, 2012). Some research has also been conducted into examining destinations as an experience provided for tourists (Cassidy & Brown, 2010).

While acknowledging that extensive research has been undertaken into many of the central issues that pertain to destination growth and evolution, the development needs of peripheral island regions remains an issue that warrants additional investigation from several perspective's; the views of local stakeholders as to the form and rate of development, and the types of touristic experiences that potential visitors to these regions may wish to experience. Unfortunately, in a buyer's market where the mobility of the tourist is such that there is a wide range of available alternatives, there are significant limitations to the ability of many destinations to dictate the terms of their development, particularly where the wish to target specific markets that may be geographic or life style based.

Thus, for the South Pacific's peripheral island communities tourism development options are subject to a number of constraints that are imposed by remoteness, and resulting difficulty in travel to the destination, as well as a need to make a realistic assessment of markets and who in these markets may be interested in travelling to the destination (Chaperon & Bramwell, 2013). In assessing the wants of particular groups of traveller's who are realistically able to travel to the destination, in this case the peripheral islands, and the development wishes of local stakeholders. There may need to be a series of compromises made to accommodate the needs of a specific market. If the cost of development is perceived to be too high, decisions may be made to impose limitations on development that may preclude otherwise viable development options.

## THE SOUTH PACIFIC

The South Pacific region consists of the following island nations: American Samoa, Cook Islands, and the Federated States of Micronesia;

Fiji Islands, Kiribati, Marshall Islands, Nauru, New Caledonia, Niue, Palau, Papua New Guinea, Samoa, Solomon Islands, Tahiti, Limor Leste, Tonga, Tuvalu and Vanuatu (South Pacific Tourism Organisation, 2014). Features of these island destinations include coral reefs, white sandy beaches and lush forestry contribute to the uniqueness of these aesthetically exotic island nations.

The legacy of the colonial experience in many of these countries underlies the current economic structure and consequently, the characteristics of its tourism industry. All countries are in the Tropics with pristine waters filled with natural and manufactured attractions for diving, including World War II wrecks, coral reefs, lagoons, with volcanic islands and coral atolls. Whilst Papua New Guinea may lay claim to unique fauna and wilderness as part of an ecotourism experience it also as a poor international reputation for law and order which may offset the appeal of the ecotourism market.

As an example, the Fijian Islands are comprised of approximately 330 islands of which Viti Levu and Vanua Levu are the largest, covering a total of 15,985 square kilometres (Fiji Bureau of Statistics 2010). This being the case then there are 328 peripheral islands some of which are not inhabited. Tourism is a major source of income to Fiji and accounted for 35.8% of Fiji's Gross Domestic Profit in 2012, making FJD1.074 billion in 2011 (Ministry of Tourism Fiji, 2012). Fiji's economy is not based exclusively on tourism but also incorporates garment manufacturing, sugar production, gold mining, timber, commercial fishing, kava and coconut produce (Stanley, 2011). To March 2014 the provisional number of tourists to the Fijian Islands was 47,149 with 24,216 being by Australian visitors followed by New Zealanders at 5,234 (Fiji Bureau of Statistics 2014). According to the South Pacific Tourism Organisation, Fiji accounts for around one third of the regional market, while the following seven countries have a combined market share of around fifty percent of the regions arrivals: Papua New Guinea, French

Polynesia, Samoa, Cook Islands, New Caledonia, Palau and Vanuatu (2014).

Papua New Guinea on the other hand had 164,000 visitor arrivals in 2011 which is an increase of 14% over the year 2010. While Australia had the greatest number of visitors to Papua New Guinea 50% of visitors were on business whereas most of the visitors from Japan, America and European markets were on holiday or leisure oriented travel (National Statistical Office of Papua New Guinea, 2014).

Tahiti (French Polynesia) consists of 118 islands with several of the better known ones of Bora Bora, Moorea, Huahine, Taha'a, Raiatea to name just a few. According to the Institut Statistique de Polynesie Francaise (2012) arrivals increased by 3.8% in 2012 over the previous year to attract 169,000 visitors. It is difficult to compare information on the various island countries as the information is fragmented and inconsistent in the data content.

The South Pacific Tourism Organisation (SPTO) (2014) notes that arrivals to the Pacific region have steadily grown over the last five years from 1.49 million arrivals in 2007 to attracting 1.77 million in 2012. The SPTO also advise that the gross value of tourism receipts in the countries noted is estimated to be between US$2.5 billion to US$3.0 billion in 2012.

This context offers an appropriate example of island tourism with tourist spending, as an alternative form of exports is believed to contribute to the balance of payments through foreign exchange earnings and proceeds generated from tourism expansion and can represent significant income for the national economy (Seetanah, 2010). The earnings from foreign exchange on tourism can also be used to produce goods and services, to import capital goods which in turn lead to economic growth. Tourism also provides with economic benefits by way of tax revenues, employment and other sources of income (Belloumi, 2010).

There are several issues which need to be considered when planning for tourism in less developed countries (LDC). Often these countries have narrow resource based economies and are highly dependent on the export of primary produce. They often require large volumes of imports from more developed countries (MDC). As mentioned they are relient on export prices of their coffee, sugar and spices to name a few. There is often weak infrastructure, undeveloped manufacturing sector, high unemployment and diversification. These countries often have a high population growth rate and high proportion of young people (Weaver & Lawton, 2012).

Various countries in the South Pacific are in differing degrees of tourism and destination development. Butler's Sequence (1980) could readily be related to these destinations. For example: the Exploration stage where a destination has small numbers of visitors, the tourism industry does not exist, tourists are adventurous allocentrics (Plog 1974) and tourism makes little impact on the destination. The second stage is the Involvement stage where numbers of tourists noticeably increase and local people begin to provide some services but with very little impact to the destination. The third stage is the Development stage where there is rapid and major changes taking place. There are large numbers of visitors and the local community is overwhelmed by the development and begins to dislike the tourists. Consolidation is the fourth stage where the rate of growth slows but overall visitor numbers remain large. The carrying capacity is many respects begin to be exceeded and visitors tend to by psychocentrics who are the non-adventuresome anxious tourists (Plog 1974). The destination develops crowded high density tourist precincts. Finally, the Stagnation stage where crowding occurs and the whole system is at peak capacity and the glamorous image may be eroded; costs are high and not easy for the tourism industry to make a profit. Once the stagnation stage has been reached, and then the type of management strategy adopted will determine whether the following stages will occur; continued stagnation (which is not good). The decline stage occurs if

*Table 1. Travel characteristics by psychographic types*

| Psychocentric Traveller | Allocentric Traveller |
|---|---|
| Prefer the familiar in travel destinations | Prefer non-touristy areas |
| Like commonplace activities | Enjoy discovery, new experiences, unvisited areas. |
| Prefer sun ' n' fun spots, relaxation | Prefer novel and different destinations |
| Low activity level | High activity level |
| Prefer destinations they can drive to | Prefer flying to destinations |

attempts to recruit new visitors and markets fail and if no attempt is made or there is a failure to upgrade and revitalise the tourism product. The local community resent tourism and makes it an unpleasant place to visit and competitor destinations begin to erode the client base. The third management strategy is one of rejuvenation and this occurs as a result of the efforts of both the public and private organisations for marketing and product development (Weaver & Lawton, 2012).

There is often a link between the development of the destination and the type of tourist who is attracted to that destination. As stated previously the psychocentric tourist tends to be self-inhibited or non-adventuresome, anxious and concerned with the little problems of life. The allocentric tourist on the other hand is classified as self-confident outgoing and adventurous. Whereas the midcentric is just that, between the psychocentric and allocentric tourist (see Table 1).

When relating Plog's (1974) characteristics to the South Pacific region it could be suggested that the psychocentric traveller would be more inclined to travel to the core destination while the allocentric traveller would visit the peripheral islands as they are not as developed for tourism as the core islands and still retain their uniqueness and many original traditions.

## Tourist Expectations vs. Local Resident's Expectations in Island Tourism

Remote Island communities generally face problems in developing sustainable industries (Tao & Wall, 2009). However, these problems are not unsolvable, as shown by successful tourism developments in islands, including Mauritius and Taiwan (Seetanah, 2011), Bali and Fiji (Mistilis & Tolar, 2000), and smaller island nations, including the Maldives (Zubair, Bowen & Elwin, 2011), and Vanuatu (Cassidy, 2012). While Sharpley & Ussi (2014) provides information on the special features of Small Island Developing States (SIDS) which make them vulnerable and highlights the need for special attention for such economies. Factors include; small size, insularity, remoteness, and disaster prone (2004 Boxing Day Indian Ocean tsunami, and the January 2010 Haiti earthquake) together with environmental factors, dependence on foreign sources of finance and demographic factors all need to be considered (Sharpley & Ussi, 2012). This has resulted in difficult economic development for such countries.

This is supported by work done by Larsen & Guiver (2013) in relation to the problems commonly encountered such as, distance and environmental impacts and found that distances between places may hold multiple significances for potential travelers. While lack of infrastructure (Dodds, 2012), unwelcome income distribution consequences (Lacher & Oh, 2012), lack of political and administrative leadership, and a lack of destination knowledge by potential visitors can all have an effect of the traveller's destination choice and expectations. In remote islands, these issues can be seen in different contexts: a core-periphery problem where the political centre of power resides in larger islands and where the main city is the main centre of tourism development, particularly in the early stages (Weaver & Lawton, 2012), or in terms of push-pull demand mechanisms (Dann, 1977; Yang, Gu & Wang, 2011). The impact of both forces shapes development and can be seen in many tourism areas. For example, the main island of Efate in Vanuatu receives more international visitors than the outer islands of Espiritu Santo and Tangoa Island. Hence, considerable public funds are directed towards tourism marketing internationally by core providers but not by the peripherals. This concept has been explored in other contexts such as the arts (Hume, 2008). Further research into the core and peripheral island tourism situation would contribute to the knowledge and development of further island tourism. However, all of this may be to no avail unless the desires and wishes of both visitors and residents are taken into consideration at the planning stage, irritation will continue to rise with long-term disastrous effects to the tourism development (Nunkoo & Ramkisson, 2010).

Several studies have been conducted over recent years in an attempt to analyse the residents' attitudes towards tourism and an indicator of tourism appropriateness by the host population towards tourism (Latkova & Vogt, 2012). In an attempt to give a theoretical base to the study of host perceptions toward tourism several theories have been developed. For example the attribution theory (Juvan & Dolnicar, 2014), dependency theory (Chaperon & Bramwell, 2013), the social representation theory (Moscardo, 2011), together with seminal works of Butler's (1980) destination life cycle, Doxey's (1975) Irridex model, the intrinsic/extrinsic framework (Faulkner & Tideswell, 1997) and the social exchange theory (SET) (Diedrich & Garcia-Buades, 2009). However, the theory which has received the greatest attention by researchers attempting to study community attitudes toward tourism and consequent support for the industry is the SET theory (Diedrich & Garcia-Buades, 2009). The SET theory when applied to tourism would mean that residents benefiting from tourism are likely to perceive the industry as positive and thus, support tourism, while those who perceive themselves not benefiting from tourism development would display negative attitudes towards it there for opposing tourism development (Nunkoo & Ramkisson 2010).

For example, research on the tourist expectations and locals' expectations on what tourists want when they travel to Vanuatu realized a gap in the expectations in several areas. For example, tourists who did go to a peripheral island ranked their responses to activities or facilities that they would use as 1. Going to the beach 2. Going to restaurants and 3. Scuba diving. However, the local residents of the peripheral islands of Espiritu Santo and Tangoa ranked visiting clubs and night clubs as number one followed by visiting a casino when in fact the activities of visiting a casino and night clubs were ranked last followed by fishing. So as can be seen there is a misalignment of expectations (Cassidy 2011).

This study found further misalignment of expectation in relation to accommodation. The research showed the tourists ranked their first three preferences of accommodation as 1. Resort style 2. Hotel and 3. Backpacker and motel ranked the same. Whereas, the local residents ranked the accommodation as 1. Resort style 2. Hotel and 3. Local village. However, the tourists ranked staying in a local village equally last with self-contained apartments and other forms of accommodation.

On one outer island the Village Chief said that he would speak for the whole village and quite strongly suggested that the tourists would:

*'Want to stay in his village and experience the local native accommodation and mix with the local Ni-Vanuatu'.*

Again show casing the misalignment between tourist expectations and local residents' expectation of what the tourist wants to experience.

The study further explored the responses to what were the influencing factors for visiting Vanuatu. Those who visited a peripheral island

*Table 2. Why travelers did not go to a peripheral island.*

| Reasons | Percentage | Rank |
|---|---|---|
| Too expensive | 32.2 | 1 |
| Wanted a stay put holiday | 27.4 | 2 |
| Not enough time | 27.3 | 3 |
| Haven't heard of any outer islands | 15.8 | 4 |
| Did not want to fly in a domestic aircraft | 14.6 | 5 |
| Not recommended at time of booking | 8.9 | 6 |
| Other reasons | 6.2 | 7 |
| Not interested in the outer islands | 2.7 | 8 |

ranked the first three reasons as 1) Climate 2) Reputation as a holiday destination and 3) Local cultural experience. Whereas the local residents ranked 1) Reputation as a holiday destination 2) Local cultural experience and 3) Personal safety. Hence the local residents perceive personal safety as important to visitors when in fact it did not rank in the top three factors.

Whilst there is a disparity between the tourists and the local residents on the peripheral islands as to where they stay, what they do when on the islands and what pulled them to the destination there is strong agreement of the local residents that tourism is good for employment, that more restaurants are required on Espiritu Santo as are more cultural experiences for the tourists (Cassidy, 2011).

In a study conducted by Cassidy (2002) of 185 tourists departing Vanuatu and flying to Australia 164 respondents indicated that they did not go to a peripheral island in Vanuatu and only 21 respondents indicated that they did. Those who

didn't travel to a peripheral island were asked their reasons why and their responses are shown in Table 2.

Interestingly the fact that it was too expensive to fly to a peripheral island was ranked as number one (32%) and that nearly 16% responded that they hadn't heard of the outer islands. The respondents were then asked to advise how much they thought the airfares to various peripheral islands would cost in Australian dollars. The findings are shown in Table 3.

When asked if the respondents knew the applicable airfares 80.8% said that they did know how much the airfares cost. It appears that over 50% actually had the airfares incorrect. Most respondents had the fare cheaper than it actually was with just a minimal percentage overestimating the airfares. At the time of the research all return airfares were between the $200-$299 price range. This could be termed perceptual pricing (PP) by the respondents as the airfares were something each individual put a price on in relation to their

*Table 3. What respondents thought the airfares would be.*

| Islands | Airfares $100-$199 | Airfares $200-$299 | Airfares $300-$399 | Airfares $400-$499 |
|---|---|---|---|---|
| Espiritu Santo | 44.4% | 43.1% | 5.6% | 5.6% |
| Tanna | 44% | 43.7% | 12% | 8% |
| Pentecost | 47.32% | 37.5% | 9.7% | 4.2% |

perception of costs of getting to the peripheral islands.

## Motivations of Tourists

Motivation has often been considered the primary cause of people's thoughts, feelings and actions and refers to an activated state within a person which consists of drive urges, wishes and desires which lead to goal-orientated behavior (Menzies & Nguyen, 2012).

A number of approaches have been posited for understanding tourism motivations (Hsu & Huang, 2008; Goeldner & Ritchie, 2011; Weaver & Lawton, 2012). Some early seminal researchers have discovered the heterogeneous nature of tourist motivation by suggesting tourist typologies which are based on the interrelationship between personality and the activity undertaken by the tourist (Cohen, 1972; Dann, 1977; Plog, 1974). Other researchers suggest tourists have limited motives and that they will change over time with the consumer's lifecycle (Pearce & Butler, 1993). Further, consumer behaviour literature suggests that needs and motivations are interrelated (Lee, Jeon & Kim, 2011), and tourists may intend to take a journey to fulfil their physiological (food, climate and health) and psychological (escape and relaxation) needs (Pearce, 2011).

A review of the literature on tourism motivation shows that people travel because they are 'pushed' into making a travel decision by internal, psychological forces, and `pulled' by the external forces of the destination attributes (Fan & Hsu, 2014; Cohen, 1972; Crompton, 1979; Dann, 1977). The push motivations are related to the tourists' desires, needs and drives while the pull factors or motivations are aligned with the attributes of the destination choice (Cohen, 1974; Crompton, 1979; Dann, 1981; Fan & Hsu. 2014). Put simply the push motivations are related to internal or emotional factors whilst pull motivations are connected to the external, cognitive or situational factors.

Push factors are origin-related and refer to the intangible, intrinsic desires of the individual tourist (Fan & Hsu, 2014)). Early work by Crompton (1979) found that push motivations could be grouped into the following areas: escape, rest and relaxation, prestige, health and fitness, adventure and social interaction, family togetherness and excitement. Tourists may travel to escape the dreariness of their everyday lives and to find authentic experiences and that travel motivations are subject to particular situations and distinctive settings. Recent research has identified similar motivations (Kruger, Saayman & Ellis, 2014).

The pull motivations are attributed to the destination's overall attractiveness, for example, beaches, cultural attractions, natural scenery, shopping, accommodation, and historical resources (Chan & Baum, 2007). Weaver and Lawton (2012) suggest that destination pull factors and be categorised into the following: geographical proximity to markets; accessibility to markets; availability of attractions; cultural links; availability of services; affordability; peace and stability; a positive market image and pro-tourism policies. The destination choice might therefore be reliant on the tourists' assessment of the destination attributes and their perceived value. Several attempts have been made to classify major elements of tourist destinations (Shanka & Phau, 2008). Among these elements are such areas as climate, culture, architecture, catering, transport entertainment, accommodation, cost and so forth. Destination attributes could be many and vary greatly between destinations.

However, these push and pull factors may work together and the destination attributes may stimulate and reinforce inherent push factors (Prayag & Ryan, 2011). Several research studies have been undertaken using both push and pull factors in relation to the destination attributes (Nadeau, Heslop, O'Rielly, & Luk, 2008; Prayag & Ryan, 2011; Shanka & Phau, 2008). For example Nadeau et al. (2008, p. 84) studied the image of a destination and how that image represents the sum of beliefs, attitudes and impressions that a person or group has. The study was based on the destination of Nepal and whilst developing countries may be slightly disadvantaged by negative or less positive images (Kale & Weir, 1986), destination perceptions are usually either positive or negative (Pike, 2002). For Nepal the overall image as a destination was positive which acts as a pull factor for tourists. The research found that the attractive scenery lead to positive perceptions of Nepal based on its natural attractions i.e. mountains, hills and rivers, together with its built environment which showcased cultural attractions of temples and palaces. However, the findings revealed less positive responses in relation to infrastructure issues i.e. ease of getting around, shopping facilities, sport facilities and nightlife and entertainment which also act as pull factors. Nadeau et al. (2008) suggest that Nepal's tourism industry should maintain its message of natural beauty and adventure tourism as their main focus. This creates a positive destination image which will pull the tourist to the destination. This could also be said for the South Pacific islands.

Conversely, the push factors are described as the psychological factors. These push factors are intrinsic and unique to each tourist, as they are determined by the personality and attitude of the individual (Cassidy & Pegg, 2011). For example, once the decision to travel to South Pacific has been made the tourist motivations in relation to push factors could be a combination of rest, escape, prestige or adventure to name just a few.

## Marketing the Peripheral Islands

When undertaking research for this chapter it became very apparent that the region has no uniform system of researching or measuring the quality of their tourism products. Whilst some countries have introduced for example, accommodation standards, they are generally country based and not for the whole region. The Cook Islands has a volunteer system of accreditation with regulations

to support the quality of the product. However, other countries have no formal quality standards. These standards have not necessarily extended to tour operators, coach companies, taxi companies or hospitality providers. Common standards across a region would be beneficial to the consumer albeit difficult to achieve. Hence a conundrum for the marketer, the core islands have the majority of access and infrastructure compared with the peripheral islands and there are no common standards for each country or the region as a whole.

The South Pacific Tourism Organisation through its Pacific Regional Tourism Capacity Building Programme, 2014 (PRTCBP) has highlighted the need to build the SPTO and National Tourism Organisations (NTOs) capacity in Digital Marketing and to develop private sector online presence and capacity in online marketing. They also suggest that synergies should be developed through coordinated regional trade marketing activities.

Destination marketing is a strategic process that is built on competitive advantages, target markets and mixed marketing techniques and appeals to actual and potential tourists. This strategic process involves the matching of the resources of a destination to the opportunities existing in the market. In this way, each destination should seek to differentiate itself by highlighting its unique tangible and intangible products and services in such a way to entice tourists. The highly competitive global market for tourists means that destinations go beyond a onetime visitation to a degree of loyalty which fosters return visitations (Lewis-Cameron & Roberts 2010).

It could be argued that a collective approach to marketing has been heralded as the best way forward for small islands states. By considering this approach there could be larger number of tourists drawn to a region i.e. South Pacific, with using fewer resources. A definition by Wang and Fesenmaier (2007:873): "Tourism marketing alliances are voluntary arrangements between tourism organizations involved in marketing and promoting the destination in a collective way, and can occur as a result of a wide range of motives and goals, take a variety of forms, and occur cross vertical and horizontal boundaries."

## Implementations and Further Research

Most Pacific Islands are busy during the traditional school holidays and festive holiday times and it is the low capacity times which need to be promoted. The SPTO (2014) has recognized that an area for development is emerging markets such as China, India, Brazil, Russia and South Korea. The SPTO realize that they have an important part to play in developing these markets and that they must promote the region as opposed to each island country.

Whilst the SPTO recognise they will take a leading role in coordinating niche marketing activities they will need to be aided by further research into market opportunities and characteristics. Many of the Pacific Island tourism products are niche based, such as ecotourism products and local cultural experiences. Some examples of niche tourism are, fishing, diving, whale watching, weddings and honeymoon packages.

Events could be one way in which niche markets are met. Many destinations have used sustainable tourism and events as a catalyst to enhance visitor numbers and thus economic, social and cultural awareness. There are many types of events such as, special events, mega events, hallmark events, major events, local events, cultural events, sporting events and community events (Weaver & Lawton 2012).

Allen, O'Toole, Harrison & McDonnell (2011) consider a special event to usually be one-off or infrequent by nature. The special event could then be considered as a mega or hallmark event. Getz (2005 p.6) notes that 'mega events, by way of their size or significance, are those that yield extraordinarily high levels of tourism, media coverage, prestige, or economic impact for the host community, venue or organization.'

Ritchie (1984) suggests that a hallmark event is a major one-time or recurring event of limited duration. It is developed primarily as a way to create awareness, appeal and financial gain for the destination in the short or long term. Whereas major events, are events which attract significant visitor numbers, economic benefits and media coverage (Weaver and Lawton 2012). Many sporting events fall into this category e.g. Hyundai Hopman Cup in Perth and Rally Australia.

The event industry understands the importance of all types and classification of events and that it is a growing sector (Hinch & Higham 2011; Ritchie & Adair 2002: Lim & Lee 2006). The tradition of events can be dated back to the ancient Greek Olympics and perhaps beyond. Events can also range in size from local events to mega events but regardless of the size or prominence of the event, all events attract both spectators and participant (Gibson 1998; Jackson & Weed 2003).

This research on core and peripheral islands in the South Pacific could be replicated on Asian destinations and sustainable events could be designed to enhance the nation's economic and socio-cultural benefits.

## CONCLUSION

It is clear that there is still a lot to understand with Island Tourism and the core and peripheral concept. Each destination is different and has different niche products to offer the tourists. However, there are many islands in the South Pacific so the competition is great for the economic dollar. There is a clear need for the local residents, corporations and local stakeholders to encourage 'compatibility tourism (CT) which is both sustainable and culturally sensitive to the local residents and environment in which they operate.

In this age of technological advancements where consumers often book online it is important to develop a standard approach to product i.e. accommodation ratings for the South Pacific. It would also be beneficial for the SPTO and NTOs to build their Digital Marketing capacity and to train and assist the tourism operators in the use of the digital age to enhance the ethical promotion of their products.

# REFERENCES

Albrecht, J. N. (2010). Challenges in tourism strategy implementation in peripheral destinations- The case of Stewart Island, New Zealand. *Tourism and Hospitality Planning & Development*, *7*(2), 91–110. doi:10.1080/14790531003737102

Allen, L., O'Toole, W., Harrison, D., & McDonnell, I. (2011). *Festival & special event management* (5th ed.). Milton, Queensland: John Wiley & Sons, Australia, Ltd.

Babbie, E. (1989). *The practice of social research*. Belmont, CA: Wadsworth.

Belloumi, M. (2010). The relationship between tourism receipts, real effective exchange rate and economic growth in Tunisia. *International Journal of Tourism Research*, *12*, 550–560.

Brouder, P., & Eriksson, R. (2013). Tourism evolution: On the synergies of tourism studies and evolutionary economic geography. *Annals of Tourism Research*, *43*, 370–389. doi:10.1016/j.annals.2013.07.001

Butler, R. (1980). The concept of a tourist area life cycle of evolution: Implications for management of resources. *Canadian Geographer*, *24*(1), 5–12. doi:10.1111/j.1541-0064.1980.tb00970.x

Cassidy, F. (2002). *A Study of the Potential for Future Tourism Development of the Outer Islands of Vanuatu from the Visitor and Resident Perspective*. Ipswich: The University of Queensland.

Cassidy, F. (2012, June 20). *Local Residents' Perceptions on Tourism: An Espiritu Santo and Tangoa Islands, A Vanuatu Study*. Paper presented at the Regional Development: connectedness, business and learning, Springfield, Qld.

Cassidy, F., & Brown, L. (2010). Determinants of small Pacific Island tourism: A Vanuatu study. *Asia Pacific Journal of Tourism Research*, *15*(2), 143–153. doi:10.1080/10941661003629953

Cassidy, F., & Pegg, S. (2011). *The Outer Islands of Vanuatu: Is there a synergy between tourists and locals?* Paper presented at the 4th International Colloquium on Business & Management (ICBM), Bangkok, Thailand.

Chan, J. K. L., & Baum, T. (2007). Motivation factors of ecotourists in ecolodge accommodation: The push and pull factors. *Asia Pacific Journal of Tourism Research*, *12*(4), 349–364. doi:10.1080/10941660701761027

Chaperon, S., & Bramwell, B. (2013). Dependency and agency in peripheral tourism development. *Annals of Tourism Research*, *40*, 132–154. doi:10.1016/j.annals.2012.08.003

Churchill, G. A. (1979). A paradigm for developing better measures of marketing constructs. *JMR, Journal of Marketing Research*, *16*(1), 64–74. doi:10.2307/3150876

Cohen, E. (1972). Towards a sociology of international tourism. *Social Research*, *6*, 164–182.

Crompton, J. (1979). Motivations for pleasure vacation. *Annals of Tourism Research*, *6*(4), 408–424. doi:10.1016/0160-7383(79)90004-5

Dann, G. (1977). Anomie, Ego-enhancement and Tourism. *Annals of Tourism Research*, *4*(4), 184–194. doi:10.1016/0160-7383(77)90037-8

Diedrich, A., & Garcia-Buades, E. (2009). Local perceptions of tourism as indicators of destination decline. *Tourism Management*, *30*(4), 512–521. doi:10.1016/j.tourman.2008.10.009

Dodds, R. (2012). Sustainable tourism: A hope or a necessity? The case of Tofino, British Columbia, Canada. *Journal of Sustainable Development, 5*(5), 54–64. doi:10.5539/jsd.v5n5p54

Doxey, G. (1975, 8-11 September). *A causation theory of visitor-resident irritants: Methodology and Research Inferences.* Paper presented at the Travel and Tourism Research Association Sixth Annual Conference, San Diego, California, U.S.A.

Fan, D., & Hsu, C. (2014). Potential mainland Chinese cruise travellers' expectations, motivations, and intentions. *Journal of Travel & Tourism Marketing, 31*(4), 522–535. doi:10.1080/105484 08.2014.883948

Faulkner, B., & Tideswell, C. (1997). A framework for monitoring community impacts of tourism. *Journal of Sustainable Tourism, 5*(1), 3–28. doi:10.1080/09669589708667273

Fiji Bureau of Statistics. (2011, October 18). 2012.). *Fiji National Census of Population, 2007,* 2014.

Fiji Bureau of Statistics. (2014). Visitor Arrivals: Number by country of residence, 2014

Getz, D. (2008). Event tourism: Definition, evolution, and research. *Tourism Management, 29*(3), 403–428. doi:10.1016/j.tourman.2007.07.017

Gibson, H. (1998). Sport tourism: A critical analysis of research. *Sport Management Review, 1*(1), 45–76. doi:10.1016/S1441-3523(98)70099-3

Goldner, C. R., & Ritchie, J. R. B. (2011). *Tourism: Principles, practices, philosophies* (12th ed.). New York: Wiley.

Grbich, C. (2013). *Qualitative data analysis: An introduction* (2nd ed.). Thousand Oaks, CA: Sage Publication Ltd.

Hall, C. (2008). *Tourism planning: Policies, processes and relationships.* Prentice Hall.

Hinch, T., & Higham, J. (2011). *Sport tourism development* (2nd ed.). Channel View Publications.

Hsu, C. H., & Huang, S. S. (2008). Travel motivation: a critical review of the concept's development. In A. G. Woodside & A. Martin (Eds.), *Tourism Management: Analysis, behaviour and strategy* (pp. 14–27). Wallingford: CABI. doi:10.1079/9781845933234.0014

Hume, M. (2008). Understanding core and peripheral service quality in customer repurchase of the performing arts. *Managing Service Quality, 18*(4), 349–369. doi:10.1108/09604520810885608

Institut Statistique de Polynesie Francaise. (2012). *Visitor arrivals.* Retrieved 05 July 2014, 2014, from http://www.ispf.pf/

Jackson, G. A. M., & Weed, M. E. (2003). The sport tourism interrelationship. In B. Houlihan (Ed.), *Sport in society: A student introduction* (pp. 235–251). London: Sage.

Juvan, E., & Dolnicar, S. (2014). The attitude-behaviour gap in sustainable tourism. *Journal of Tourism Research, 48,* 76–95. doi:10.1016/j.annals.2014.05.012

Kale, S. H., & Weir, K. M. (1986). Marketing third world countries to the western traveller: The case of India. *Journal of Travel Research, 25*(2), 2–7. doi:10.1177/004728758602500201

Kinnear, T. C., & Taylor, J. R. (1996). *Marketing research: an applied approach* (5th ed.). Australia: McGraw-Hill.

Kruger, S., Saayman, M., & Ellis, S. (2014). The influence of travel motives on visitor happiness attending a wedding expo. *Journal of Travel & Tourism Marketing, 31*(5), 649–665. doi:10.108 0/10548408.2014.883955

Lacher, R. G., & Oh, C.-O. (2012). Is tourism a low-income industry? Evidence from three coastal regions. *Journal of Travel Research, 51*(4), 464–472. doi:10.1177/0047287511426342

Larsen, G. R., & Guiver, J. W. (2013). Understanding tourists' perceptions of distance: A key to reducing the environmental impacts of tourism mobility. *Journal of Sustainable Tourism, 21*(7), 968–981. doi:10.1080/09669582.2013.819878

Latkova, P., & Vogt, C. A. (2012). Residents' attitudes towards existing and future tourism development in rural communities. *Journal of Travel Research, 51*(1), 50–67. doi:10.1177/0047287510394193

Lee, S., Jeon, S., & Kim, D. (2011). The impact of tour quality and tourist satisfaction on tourist loyalty: The case of Chinese tourists in Korea. *Tourism Management, 32*(5), 1115–1124. doi:10.1016/j.tourman.2010.09.016

Lewis-Cameron, A., & Roberts, S. (2010). *Marketing Island Destinations: Concepts and Cases.* London, UK: Elsevier.

Lim, S. T., & Lee, J. S. (2006). Host population perceptions of the impact of mega-events. *Asia Pacific Journal of Tourism Research, 11*(4), 407–421. doi:10.1080/10941660600931259

Mariani, M., & Baggio, R. (2012). Special issue: Managing tourism in a changing world: issues and cases. Anatolia. *Journal of Destination Marketing & Management, 2,* 269–272. doi:10.1016/j.jdmm.2013.11.003

Menzies, J. L., & Nguyen, S. N. (2012). An exploration of the motivation to attend for spectators of the Lexmark Indy 300 champ car event, Gold Coast. *Journal of Sport & Tourism, 17*(3), 183–200. doi:10.1080/14775085.2012.734059

Ministry of Tourism Republic of Fiji. (2012). Article. *Tourism Performance, 2012,* 2014.

Mistilis, N., & Tolar, M. (2000). *Impact of Macroeconomic Issues on Fiji's Hidden Paradise.* Paper presented at the Council for Australian University Tourism and Hospitality Education (CAUTHE), Mt. Buller, Australia.

Moscadeo, G. (2011). Exploring social representations of tourism planning: Issues for governance. *Journal of Sustainable Tourism, 19*(4-5), 423–436. doi:10.1080/09669582.2011.558625

Murdy, S., & Pike, S. (2012). Perceptions of visitor relationship marketing opportunities by destination marketers: An importance-performance analysis. *Tourism Management, 33*(5), 1281–1285. doi:10.1016/j.tourman.2011.11.024

Nadeau, J., Heslop, L., O'Rielly, N. O., & Luk, P. (2008). Destination in a country image context. *Annals of Tourism Research, 35*(1), 84–106. doi:10.1016/j.annals.2007.06.012

National Statistical Office of Papua New Guinea. *Visitor Arrivals Summary Papua New Guinea.* Papua New Guinea: Papua New Guinea Tourism Promotion Authority Retrieved from http://www.tpa.papuanewguinea.travel/Papua-New-Guinea-Tourism-Promotions-Authority/Annual-Visitor-Arrivals-Reports_IDL=42_IDT=328_ID=1806_.html

Ness, H., Aarstad, J., Haugland, S., & Gronseth, B. (2013). Destination Development: The role of interdestination bridge ties. *Journal of Travel Research, 53*(2), 183–195. doi:10.1177/0047287513491332

Nunkoo, R., & Ramkissoon, H. (2010). Small island urban tourism: A residents' perspective. *Current Issues in Tourism, 13*(1), 37–60. doi:10.1080/13683500802499414

Pearce, D. G., & Butler, R. (Eds.). (1993). *Fundamentals of Tourist Motivation.* London: Routledge.

Pearce, P. L. (2011). In Y. Wang & A. Pizman (Eds.), *Destination marketing and management: Theories and applications* (pp. 39–52). Wallingford: CABI. doi:10.1079/9781845937621.0039

Pike, S. (2002). Destination image analysis-a review of 142 papers from 1973 to 2000. *Tourism Management, 23*(5), 541–549. doi:10.1016/S0261-5177(02)00005-5

Plog, S. (1974). Why destination areas rise and fall in popularity. *The Cornell Hotel and Restaurant Administration Quarterly, 14*(4), 55–58. doi:10.1177/001088047401400409

Prayag, G., & Ryan, C. (2011). The relationship between the 'push' and 'pull' factors of a tourist destination: The role of nationality - an analytical qualitative research approach. *Current Issues in Tourism, 14*(2), 121–143. doi:10.1080/13683501003623802

Qu, H., Lo, L. H., & Im, H. H. (2011). A model of destination branding: Integrating concepts of branding and destination image. *Tourism Management, 32*(3), 465–476. doi:10.1016/j.tourman.2010.03.014

Ritchie, B., & Adair, D. (2002). The growing recognition of sport tourism. *Current Issues in Tourism, 5*(1), 1–6. doi:10.1080/13683500208667903

Ritchie, J. R. B. (1984). Assessing the impact of hallmark events: Conceptual and research issues. *Journal of Travel Research, 23*(1), 2–11. doi:10.1177/004728758402300101

Scheyvens, R., & Russell, M. (2012). Tourism and poverty alleviation in Fiji: Comparing the impacts of small - and large-scale tourism enterprises. *Journal of Sustainable Tourism, 20*(3), 417–436. doi:10.1080/09669582.2011.629049

Schmallegger, D., & Carson, D. (2010). Is tourism just another staple? A new perspective on tourism in remote regions. *Current Issues in Tourism, 13*(3), 201–221. doi:10.1080/13683500903359152

Seetanah, B. (2011). Assessing the dynamic economic impact of tourism for island economy. *Annals of Tourism Research, 38*(1), 291–308. doi:10.1016/j.annals.2010.08.009

Shanka, T., & Phau, I. Y. (2008). Tourism destination attributes: What the non-visitors say - higher education students' perceptions. *Asia Pacific Journal of Tourism Research, 13*(1), 81–94. doi:10.1080/10941660701883383

Sharpley, R., & Ussi, M. (2014). Tourism and governance in Small Island Developing States (SIDA): The case of Zanzibar. *International Journal of Tourism Research, 16*(1), 87–96. doi:10.1002/jtr.1904

South Pacific Tourism Organisation. (2014). *Pacific Regional Tourism Strategy 2015-2019*. South Pacific Tourism Organisation.

Stanley, D. (2011). *Moon Handbooks Fiji* (9th ed.). Avalon Travel Publishing.

Tao, T., & Wall, G. (2009). A livelihood approach to sustainability. *Asia Pacific Journal of Tourism Research, 14*(2), 137–152. doi:10.1080/10941660902847187

Wang, Y., & Fesenmaier, D. R. (2007). Collaborative destination marketing: A case study of Elkhart County, Indiana. *Tourism Management, 28*(3), 863–875. doi:10.1016/j.tourman.2006.02.007

Weaver, D., & Lawton, L. (2012). *Tourism Management* (4th ed.). Australia: John Wiley & Sons.

Yang, X., Gu, C., & Wang, Q. (2011). Study on the driving force of tourist flows. *Geographical Research, 1*.

Zikmund, W. G., Babin, W. G., Carr, J. C., & Griffin, M. (2013). *Business research methods* (9th ed.). Mason, OH: South-Western Cengage Learning.

Zubair, S., Bowen, D., & Elwin, J. (2011). Not quite paradise: Inadequacies of environmental impact assessment in the Maldives. *Tourism Management, 32*(2), 225–234. doi:10.1016/j.tourman.2009.12.007

## KEY TERMS AND DEFINITIONS

**Core Destination:** A destination that is the primary purpose of the transaction. Eg: the mainland.

**Core Services:** A service that is the primary purpose of the transaction.

**Global Hospitality:** Is the relationship between the guest and the host, or the act or practice of being hospitable in a global context.

**Peripheral Destination:** Destination that are rendered as a corollary to the sale of a tangible product. Eg: outer tourist island, cultural tours.

**Pull Factors:** A pull strategy involves motivating customers to seek out your brand in an active process. "Getting the customer to come to you".

**Push Factors:** Push promotional strategy involves taking the product directly to the customer via whatever means, ensuring the customer is aware of your brand at the point of purchase. "Taking the product to the customer".

**Small Island Developing States (SIDS):** Are low-lying coastal countries that tend to share similar sustainable development challenges, including small but growing populations, limited resources, remoteness, susceptibility to natural disasters, vulnerability to external shocks, excessive dependence on international trade, and fragile environments.

**South Pacific Tourism Organisation (SPTO):** Established in 1983 as the Tourism Council of the South Pacific, the South Pacific Tourism Organisation (SPTO) is the mandated organisation representing Tourism in the region. Its 18 Government members are American Samoa, Cook Islands, Federated States of Micronesia, Fiji, French Polynesia, Kiribati, Nauru, Marshall Islands, New Caledonia, Niue, Papua New Guinea, Samoa, Solomon Islands, Timor Leste, Tonga, Tuvalu, Vanuatu and the People's Republic of China. In addition to government members, the South Pacific Tourism Organisation has about 200 private sector members.

**Supplementary Services:** Services that are rendered as a corollary to the sale of a tangible product.

**Sustainable Tourism:** May be defined as tourism which is developed and maintained in such a manner and scale that it remains viable in the long run and does not degrade the environment in which it exists to such an extent that it prohibits the successful development of other activities.

# Chapter 5
# The Role of Destination Management Organizations in Exploiting Global Opportunities of Tourism Destinations

**Francesco Maria Barbini**
*University of Bologna – Rimini, Italy*

**Manuela Presutti**
*University of Bologna – Rimini, Italy*

## ABSTRACT

*The aim of this chapter is to study the cooperation between Destination Management Organizations and hospitality stakeholders. The following research questions are addressed in this research: 1. What is the stakeholders' attitude toward cooperation with DMOs in a new destination and in a mass-tourism destination? 2. In DMOs' perspective, what are the most effective strategies to foster cooperation within the destination? 3. What is the level of commitment of hospitality stakeholders with respect to cooperation with DMOs? In order to discuss these points we provide an analysis of two Italian destinations. Specifically we examine an established mass-tourism destination and a new destination. By investigating this relationship we also analyze how cooperation has developed during the years within two destinations, and if actually hospitality stakeholders are interested in cooperating with DMOs, in achieving the destinations' common goals.*

## INTRODUCTION

Destination management is an intrinsically cooperative activity. In fact, attractions, tourism enterprises, local businesses, service businesses and residents are called to work together to provide tourists with the best experience. Despite possible benefits, sometimes this kind of cooperation is hindered by the competitive behavior of various players and by the lack of coordination capabilities. Hence, often an ad-hoc organization (Destination Management Organization - DMO) is

DOI: 10.4018/978-1-4666-8606-9.ch005

established to promote cooperation and to manage cooperative relationships among stakeholders. The DMO should then identify governance strategies, promote cooperative behavior and coordinate the activities of the various subjects involved in the delivery of the tourist experience.

Obviously, the sound management of the relationship between the DMO and the local stakeholders is essential to achieve efficiency and to foster the economic development of the destination.

The aim of this contribution is to analyze the cooperative strategies actually implemented by DMOs with respect to their stakeholders. This analysis is carried out by focusing on two Italian destinations, specifically an established mass-tourism destination and a new tourism destination. Furthermore, the stakeholders' commitment and attitude toward cooperation will be investigated.

Therefore the following research questions will be addressed:

1. What is the stakeholders' attitude toward cooperation with DMO in a new destination and in a mass-tourism destination?
2. In DMOs' perspective, what are the most effective strategies to foster cooperation within the destination?
3. What is the level of commitment of hospitality stakeholders with respect to cooperation with DMOs?

The contribution is divided in three main sections. The first section introduces a literature review to systematize the concepts and to propose definitions, the second one deals with methodology and survey results. Finally, the third section proposes a discussion about the results of the survey and the theoretical consequences.

# 1. LITERATURE REVIEW

## 1.1 Destination Management

According to UNWTO (2007), destination management can be defined as *"the co-ordinated management of all the elements that make up a destination"* (p.100). This definition is based on a strategic behavior (the coordinated management) and on a network of relationships between elements, roles, and entities. From an analytical point of view, destination management is composed by five building blocks:

- *Elements of the destination,* such us attractions, enterprises, services, infrastructures, residents;
- *Destination Management Organization,* which is leading and co-ordinating the destination and its tourist offer;
- *Destination marketing,* to inform, promote, and attract tourists;
- *Experience delivery,* i.e. all the activities aimed at delivering value to the visitors, it comprises management of the experience, events development, attractions management;
- *Suitable environment,* which is related to the development of a supportive physical, social and economic environment, it ranges from planning activities to human resources development.

A destination involves many stakeholders, both public and private, who satisfy the composite needs of the tourists: transport providers; attractions, events and cultural organizations; accommodation providers; restaurant, leisure and retail operators; intermediaries (tour operators and travel agencies) and media (Pike, 2004).

Evidently, these stakeholders have to be coordinated through effective mechanisms based on:

- Tourism development and management, linking the development of the competitive strategy and the destination planning and implementation;
- Integrated product development and marketing;
- Integration of all planning activities, including investment planning.

The importance of destination management comes from the very basic features of the tourism industry. In fact, the tourism industry "is an extremely competitive industry and to compete effectively destinations have to deliver excellent value to visitors… It is vital that the various components of the visitor's stay are managed and coordinated to maximize customer value throughout the visit" (WTO, 2007).

Hence, the main tourist attraction (the main reason motivating the tourist journey) is not able, by itself, to control all the relevant aspects influencing the tourist experience (Barbini & Presutti, 2012, 2013).

A useful framework (based on four steps) for implementing a strategy for managing the destination has been suggested by UNWTO (2007). The first step is the situation assessment, in which the most critical tourism challenges, the visitors' expectations gaps, and the opportunities for tourism growth are evaluated. It consists of (a) a macro-environmental analysis, regarding political, economic, social and technological opportunities and threats; (b) a market analysis, including market trends and customers shapes; (c) an audit of internal tourism resources and services; (d) an assessment of ancillary infrastructure and services; and (e) an investigation of the industry structure.

The second step is the actual elaboration of the strategy, in which the strategy is crafted from the outcomes of the situation assessment. It comprises the identification of the vision, of the targets of tourists, the definition of core goals and key actions to accomplish them. In addition, a brand strategy and positioning should be planned (Baggio, Scott, & Cooper, 2011).

Then, the third step is the integrated implementation plan, in which the strategy is operationalized. It is an integrated plan since it is composed by both tourism development and tourism marketing programs. The first category is related to the improvement of infrastructures, development of new products, and development of human resources. The second category is related to the use of the marketing tools, i.e. the marketing mix factors (the 4 Ps).

Finally, the fourth step is the definition of architectures and methods for the governance of the destination. These activities are aimed to develop organizational solutions that are consistent with the strategy and the implementation plan. In addition, it should regulate decision-making processes and the interactions with public and private institutions.

## 1.2. A Model of Destination Competitiveness and Sustainability

After the background of the components and theories of destination management field, we need to sum up everything in a model, in which better understanding the destination management's work.

Ritchie and Crouch (2003) proposed a model to explain the nature of competitiveness among tourism destinations, called "Model of Destination Competitiveness and Sustainability" (Wang & Pizam, 2011). This model was developed basing on a set of qualitative interviews with the DMOs (especially in North America). Two types of competitive advantages are taken into consideration: comparative advantages (e.g. natural and economic resources) and competitive advantages (e.g. efficiency-effectiveness). Together create its overall ability to compete in the tourism marketplace.

Furthermore, this model details the seven components of tourism destinations: (1) *global environment* (macro factors, including economic situation, available technologies, natural environment, political-legal framework, sociocultural and demographic environment); (2) *competitive environment* (micro factors, including customers, suppliers, international interfaces, competitors, destination culture); (3) *core resources and attractors* (such as cultural heritage and history, natural settings, etc.); (4) *supporting factors and resources* (i.e. services related to accessibility, infrastructures, hospitality, etc.); (5) *destination policy, planning and development* (e.g. vision, branding, auditing systems, etc.); (6) *destination management* (i.e. quality of service and experience, marketing, organization, etc.); (7) *qualifying and amplifying determinants* (e.g. awareness and image, carrying capacity, interdependence, etc.).

In conclusion, all these elements explain the competitiveness and the success of a sustainable tourism destination (Lockwood & Medlik, 2001).

## 1.3. New Challenges and Opportunities for Destination Management

The micro and macro environment of a destination is continuously changing, for example because of crisis, competition among destinations, innovations and changes in tourist behavior (Laws, Richins, Agrusa, & Scott, 2011).

In order to deal with this problem, Fyall proposed a framework, the '15 Cs Framework' (Wang & Pizam, 2011), which details and explains the success factors for a tourism destination.

The first factor is C*omplexity and control* of a tourism destination. Complexity is imposed by external subjects, such as visitors (who often change expectations and preferences) and by internal stakeholders (who have multiple preferences and contrasting points of view about tourism development). On the other hand, control is related to the

composite nature of the tourism destination, which conditions its goals and its path of development. In the future, according to Fyall, destinations should be managed in a flexible and innovative way to anticipate and promptly react to new tourist's needs and to technological innovations.

The second element is the consideration of the *destination community*, both hosts and residents. In fact, the local community is often a critical success factor for the visitor experience, since many community members implement initiatives like festivals and events within the destination. Destination management should consider not only community as revenue of local taxes, but also as an attraction able to play an integral role in destination marketing and management.

The third element is *change*. With respect to the external environment, destinations should adapt to changes in visitor behaviors and in the macroeconomic and social environment. Nevertheless, all these reasons impose to manage the destination towards closest market, markets less subject to risks and support the local community (Jamal & Getz, 1995).

Fourth element is *crisis and the fear of crisis*. They are been presented in tourism industry in the last decades, and safety is an issue for all markets. Unfortunately, old markets are rather vulnerable, so that destinations adopt every possible effort to overtake that fear. A coming opportunity consist in develop and markets destinations as secure destination and hence create competitive advantage in tourism markets. Moreover, regarding crises, destination management could adopt a 'holistic approach', in which implement crisis management in its destination strategies.

Fifth element is *complacency*. Crisis, climate changes and events run as 'diluter' of complacency of destinations, restricted by traditional custom. In fact, in these current years, destinations are oversensitive to highly price-sensitive markets with low destination's fidelity. But actually, markets are constantly changing and destinations should be incorporate flexibility in own plans, in order to reply to future market changes and turbulences (Novelli, Schmitz, & Spencer, 2006)

Sixth element concerns *customers, co-creation and the visitor experience* in an experiential marketing context. On this way, several destinations get in touch with new customers, reducing emphasis on destination itself and creating identities and sense of loyalty by means of consumption. Furthermore, service delivery into destination are evident and personal meets of experiences, and where visitors have active participant, ensuring value to brand and destination development.

Seventh element is *culture*. It is a crucial issue between public and private sectors in tourism, which acts a barrier for progress in many countries. One solution could be through a change in organizational culture, and specifically by means of the quality of employees. In addition, rather than adopts this change, many destinations develop nice tourism strategies with a strong cultural essence

Eighth element is *competition* among destinations that is growing at highly rate. This phenomenon is grown thanks to low-cost airlines, that has led inaccessible destinations to a mass tourism and growth in second homes tourism across countries. Even though all, low-cost airlines are developed around the world, their low-cost focus depends on the degree of preserve their found markets or lose them due to competitive and financial threats of many airlines companies. Anyhow tourism destinations must show a better positioning and a more clear proposition in the markets.

Ninth element is *commodification*. It means that since competition is quite powerful, more and more destination become substitutable and strive to adopt differentiation in crowded markets. This also is a consequence of internet technology, the adoption of 'me too' strategies, that leads to share in the markets identical 'selling points'. A opportunity consists in adopting experiential marketing, focus on niche tourism, low focus on old markets and development of original brand identity (Sharpley, 2009).

Tenth element is *creativity*. Still through some element this characteristic comes up, and especially represent a mean of challenge in destination substitution issue and old branding approach. Unfortunately branding and managing destination brands is not a simple task due to influence of political environment, low budgets and not quick decision-making. A newest opportunity is television and film-induced tourism that leads a highly cost-effective approach to the branding in small destinations with a few resources (Edgell & Swanson, 2013; Bornhorst, Ritchie, & Sheehan, 2010).

Eleventh element is *communication*. The growing of Web 2.0, tourist blogs and social network is taking place on the last years. Although more destinations use even traditional means of communication such as brochures, the new web forms of communication are becoming established. Moreover, it offers a highly cost effective than traditional forms, even if there is not an actual study on the real advantages and disadvantages on destination branding context.

Twelfth element is *distribution channels* It is a mean with which destinations can get competitive advantage in the own markets. The new means in distribution destination products use technology, in order to control better markets and represent a great opportunity for both big and small destinations.

Thirteenth element is *cyberspace*. It means that the use of Internet and social network are changed the customer-centric orientation of some destinations and has stimulate the 'conservative' tourists.

Fourteenth element is *consolidation*. It is related to polarization issue, that is the creation of small number of large international corporations and, at the same time, small enterprises that carry on to rule the customer's experiences. A suggestion ought to be managing a destination by scale, through the development of consolidated corporations with following benefits of budgets, technology and supremacy of private sector, crushing the smaller and overcoming the balance of power.

Fifteenth and last element is *collaboration*. It is seen as a mean with which the dominance of corporations can be engaged and, in general, every element of the framework function as catalyst for collaboration. Developing and implementing stakeholders' collaboration becomes essential to survive in the competition and environmental challenges, and as a component that help DMOs to better manage destination both for marketing tasks and delivery destination's perspectives.

In conclusion, all of the individual components of the 15 Cs offer considerable opportunity for future, but the collaboration remains the 'glue' that bonds all other components together. This remains the key element within a touristic destination.

## 2. HOSPITALITY SECTOR

### 2.1 Overall of Tourism Demand

In these last years, global economy was going to have a decrease in term of economic indicators. As highlighted by International Monetary Fund, the 2013 projections point out a decrease respect 2012 (IMF, 2013). In fact, whatever markets both advanced and emerged are stressing a light downturn, in term of world output and world trade volume, because of the current Recession that has hit all the world economies.

Tourism represents 9% of world GDP, 1.3 trillion of dollar in exports and stands for 6% of global exports (UNWTO, 2013). International tourist arrivals overtook 1 billion for the first time in 2012, exactly 1,035 million of tourists, respect to 995 million in 2011, hence increasing in 4%. Europe just grew in 3.4%, Asia and the Pacific got a large growth in 7% increasing in arrivals, then Africa up 6% and the Americas up 5%. Moreover, the purpose of visit is mainly leisure and holidays for 52%, followed by 27% for religion and health and 14% for business.

As regard the receipts, international tourism

ing a new record of 1,075 billion of dollars. Europe just grew in 2% in receipts, Asia and the Pacific recorded 6.2%, then the Americas up 5.9% and Africa up 5.8%. Anyway Europe remains the main large share market both in arrivals and receipts, although Asia and Americas as components of emerging economies are expanding always more. In conclusion, even in periods of economic crisis and natural events, tourism however leads to positive impacts on economic indicators. Moreover, it represents a safe investment in development of countries, and improving economy worldwide.

### 2.2 Hospitality Industry

Every industry has different structural and dynamic traits and hospitality is not excluded from in this approach. So, it presents different peculiarities that can be point out below (Rispoli & Tamma, 1996):

- *Model of territorial presence*, about the possibility that a hotel is placed in a specific area with attractive factors for the touristic demand;
- *Dimension of operative units and technical concentration*, referred to size of the firms in this sector, rather varied;
- *Dimension of firms and economic concentration*, referred to different branches of that firm, that obviously depends from different countries around the world;
- *Economies of scale*, that is the decrease of unit costs of production when the firm dimension increases;
- *Economies of scope or size*, namely cost advantages linked to production diversification in several sectors;
- *High entry barriers*, that is limits when a firm would like entry in a market or sector;
- *Degree of segmentation of demand and supply differentiation*, obviously present in this sector with its variety of supply and

- *Composition of social capital and enterprise legal form,* running from individual form to more complex forms like limited company;
- *Rate of capital and job,* for example labour-intensive trait that it is characterized;
- *Kind of utilized manpower,* with high experience on the field, rather than high education request.

Furthermore, according to business dimension, the kind of supply in this sector can be:

- *Small family firm single-unit,* managed by a single person;
- *Small entrepreneurial firm single-unit,* characterized by familiar form and entrepreneurial management;
- *Managerial firm single-unit,* with mid-large size and managerial administration;
- *Middle multi-unit firm or small chain,* composed by a limited number of hotel that are controlled by only one;
- *Multi-unit firm or proprietary chain,* that represents a large size of proprietary chain;
- *Hotel group or multi-chain,* composed by more hotel chains;
- *Aggregation of hotels or brand-chain,* that is more hotels that are controlled by several hotels linked to collaboration agreements;
- *Chain of international brand,* like Hilton or Leading Hotels of the World;
- *Franchising chain,* namely collaboration agreements through franchising contracts;
- *Chain founded on management contract,* that is collaboration among hotel firms and other firms, that just have the purpose of buy the buildings rather than management hotels.
- *Private multi-sectorial aggregation,* that consists in collaboration among businesses that produce goods and services (restaurants, hospitality, recreation activities, event,…) in order to provide the possibility to sell a unique package to own customers.
- *Public-private multi-sectorial aggregation,* that has the aim of developing a particular area with the help of whatever operator placed in that area

Basically, beyond this classification, hospitality firms can be gathered both hotels and no-hotel accommodations, which are more different in term of facilities provided to customers. Hotels usually provide several facilities as reception, restaurant, room service, and so on; while, no-hotel accommodation offer less facilities but correlated to specific customer interests. In this category can be found agritourism, bed & breakfast, holiday house, camping, and so on.

Considering not-known structures, the major part of tourism movement uses holiday houses owned or rental. The utilization of rental holiday houses are in decrease, while owned house are increased (Federalberghi, 2010).

Agritourism and bed & breakfast are actually real hotels, but with less organizational-operative restrictions and low internal costs. So, there is highlighted a problem in term of competition among firms, that sometimes is faithless, producing a disadvantage to more facilities firms as hotels.

For this reason can be stated that against the extension of hospitality's typology should be identified the firms that offer a hotel service. Unfortunately, even markets and the international classification, that not evaluating the diversity typology existed in the various countries, follow own standard including in the number of firms and rooms also residence, holiday villages, and so on, with a type of management that include reception, housekeeping and restaurant.

Currently, we can frequently hear resorts or holiday villages as a combination of hospitality structures, from camping to village, integrating accommodation option as theatre, wellness centre, tennis, sail, diving and so on. This phenomenon regards both Europe for its sea and mountain trait, and Extra-Europe destinations.

Finally, tourism market, both international and domestic, is influenced by outgoing and not by incoming, as known from intermediated operator, that is holiday agents that mainly work on line. However, the Internet diffusion is determining a new logic market through the incoming's re-valuation rather than outgoing. From this point of view, web technology is fixing a new market opportunity, since hospitality and productive chain can arrive inside the tourist's houses, providing itineraries or personalising package, according own preferences. With the continuous evolution, web 2.0 has really represented a better means of communication through social network and revolutionising the 'word of mouth', conveying it more neutral and informed.

## 3. COOPERATION

### 3.1 Cooperation: A Background

Cooperation is a fundamental building block of any tourism destinations. Cooperation is "*the action or process of working together to the same end*" (Oxford Dictionary). This definition is supported by classical literature of Organization Studies. For instance, Simon (1947) stated that a collective behavior may be qualified as cooperative when the involved subjects prefer the same set of consequences, i.e. share (deliberately or not) a common goal. The fundamental characteristic of any cooperation is its common finalization (Maggi 2003). More in detail, subjects start to cooperate when they cannot achieve their personal goals independently, because of physical, biological, and/or cognitive limitations (Barnard 1938). Obviously, for every participant, the objective of the cooperation is instrumental to the attainment of his own goals. According to such classical literature, in order to achieve a satisficing effective-ness, every cooperative behavior is (consciously

on unconsciously) coordinated (Maggi 2003): every subject involved in the cooperation needs to have information and to develop expectations about the current and future behavior of the others (Simon 1947).

From different perspectives, many other theoretical approaches state the importance of cooperation. For instance, Resource dependence theory relates the joint behavior of partner to the need to control critical resources and the the same time, to accesso other subjects' resources. Transaction cost theory see cooperation as a strategy for lowering transaction costs (thanks to recurrent transactions, the development of shared communication channels, the development of a trust and reputation, etc.). Functionalist theories deem cooperation as a necessary strategy for achieving, at the same time, flexibility and adaptability to the market's need and a strong focalization on core competencies. Even subjectivist theories consider cooperation as a way for enacting shared realities and as an arena for power-dependance games.

According to Beritelli (2011), three occurrences reinforce the need for cooperation within a tourism destination. First phenomenon is 'tragedy of commons', which includes the no stimulus by government in preventing an overuse of natural resources within a tourism destination, and the absence of pricing upon that public good since a missing in ownership rights. Second phenomenon is 'prisoner's dilemma', in which stakeholders, with limited information and having just single round available, avoid to cooperate together, even if they could have a better pay-off in case of cooperation. Third phenomenon is 'challenge of collective action', in which there is an increasing in not understanding of importance of public goods, due to missing of institutions that stimulate collective actions.

According to Barbini and Presutti (2014), a tourism destination can arise through two different development paths: planned development or emergent development.

*Figure 1. DMO Framework*

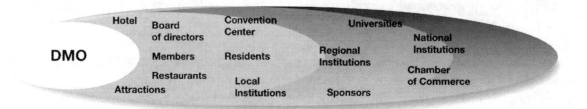

The planned development implies the preliminary recognition of all the subjects involved, the definition of the tasks to be carried out, the allocation of authority and responsibility, the detailed definition of coordination procedures (Presutti, Boari, & Fratocchi, 2007).

On the other hand, emergent development implies an absolute lack of intentionality: the various stakeholders working within and around a tourist attraction start to interact and, while reiterating these interactions, they develop a social network (which becomes the tourism destination).

Actually, Barbini and Presutti (2014) propose a different process of development: the various subjects involved in the delivery of the tourist experience start an informal cooperation, based on recurrent interaction. When the scale and scope of this informal network become relevant and complex the involved partners try to develop formal rules for coordinating their behavior (in order to limit coordination costs and to enhance the efficiency of the collective behavior). The DMO is usually established in this last step of the process, to allow smoother and more efficient internal coordination.

## 3.2 Understanding Importance of Stakeholders

Stakeholder was defined by Sheehan and Brent Ritchie (2005), as "'any group or individual who can affect, or is affected by, the achievement of a corporation's purpose" (p. 12). From this definition, the concept of stakeholder can be referred to both an individual or a group that is affected from others or that affect others. Sheehan and Brent Ritchie (2005) identified the main stakeholders of a tourism destination and analyzed their salience with respect to the perceptions of the DMO, providing a framework which we have elaborated in *Figure 1*.

The authors stated that the more a stakeholder is relevant for the performance of the destination the more the distance between such stakeholder and the DMO will decrease. The result was that *hotels* are the most important stakeholders, and this could be explained basing on the importance of their role in attracting visitors, in promoting attractions and amenities, in managing the tourist experience.

On the other hand, Bornhorst, Ritchie and Sheehan (2010) adopted the stakeholders' perspective to explain the success of destination management strategies. According to stakeholders, the most critical success factors of a destination are *product and service offerings, location or accessibility of the destination, quality of the tourist experience and community support*. Furthermore, the effectiveness od the DMO depends on *its ability in developing and managing internal relations with all the stakeholders and in effectively panning and managing the strategy*.

Overall, stakeholders focus on *community support*, *marketing activities* and *performance management*.

Volgger and Pechlaner (2014) proposed an extension of the study of Bornhorst et al. and, by means of a regression analysis, they provided a more general framework. The first findings was that success of the destination is directly linked to success of the DMO, and that this latter variable is influenced by four factors, namely networking capability, transparency of performance, available resources, and professionalism. In addition, they found that power and dependence relationships mediate the effect of networking capability toward the success of the DMO.

Together, these theories stress the importance for the DMO to manage the relationships with stakeholders in order to enable the achievement of sustainable competitive advantages.

## 3.3. Public-Private Partnership

Partnership is a relationship that implicates the sharing of authority, work, and information to achieve mutual goals or benefits among the involved partners. Evidently, partnerships can be interpreted as a form of cooperation. Moreover, according to subjects involved, it can be qualified as public-public / private-private / public-private partnership.

UNWTO (2000b) pointed out that public-private partnership/cooperation has four main purposes in a tourism destination:

- Improvement of the attractiveness of a destination;
- Improvement on destination marketing's efficiency;
- Improvement on destination's productivity;
- Improvement on the quality of tourism-related activities.

Moreover, according to UNWTO (2003), the roles of both parts do not includes the same ben-

efits. In fact, from the public side, a partnership is useful to access new capitals, to share the cost of infrastructures, to share risks, to access additional resources or competences and, eventually, to enhance social well-being. From the private side, a partnerships with public sector would allow to enter new markets, to expand products and services, to enhance reputation and, eventually, to enlarge the profits.

The most critical success factors impacting on public-private partnerships are (UNWTO):

- The definition of a well-balanced structure with clear roles and responsibilities;
- The identification of shared decision-making processes;
- The recognition of the needs and the motives driving the behaviour of all the members;
- The common agreement on general values, such as on the sustainability of tourism strategies;
- The long-term commitment through the combination of strategic vision and plans for ensuring the consistency of short-term, medium-term, and long-term goals;
- The definition of detailed procedures of evaluating the efficiency of each member;
- The establishment of an effective information system to allow communications among members.

Franco and Estevao (2010) analyzed the elements mentioned above to specify how partnership actually works in a tourism destination. We elaborated this framework in *figure 2*.

Specifically, the objectives of the partnership are related to products, infrastructures and human resources, marketing and promotion, as well as funds; the, its critical success factors are related to the formalization of agreements, to clear definitions of goals, organizational structure, and authority systems, to the flexibility, efficiency and effectiveness of the cooperation. The authors

*Figure 2. Elaborated framework*

contend that the coherent management of these relationships and variables would improve the probabilities of success for the partnership, which in turn will entail a continuous development of the tourism destination.

## 3.4 Understanding Asymmetric Stakeholders Interdependencies among City, Hotels, and DMO

Sheehan et al. (2007) studied the relationship between DMO and two important stakeholders within a destination, namely city government and hotels, and explained the singular relations that connect each other.

They proposed a framework based on a triad of asymmetrically-interdependent relationships, as shown in *Figure 3*.

The city (playing the role of public stakeholder in the partnership) should provide the DMO with financial resources and should define a vision and

a strategy for the local tourism development; it should also invest on infrastructures and in accessibility services.

Hotels (as private stakeholders) should support DMO by providing peculiar resources, 'in-kind resources', such as discounts for rooms, information about tourists, and by showing a continuous commitment toward the expansion of its activities.

Finally, the DMO (as the leading partner) plays the role of coordinator of the triad, so providing organizational resources and managing the relationships. In particular, the DMO has two main tasks to fulfill, one internal and one external.

Internally, DMO has to communicate and interact with its stakeholders, in order to identify strengths and weaknesses of the destination, has to propose a competitive strategy, and has to mobilize resources and commitments toward the actual implementation of the strategy.

Externally, DMO has to understand market trends, to promote the destination, and to man-

*Figure 3. Proposed framework*

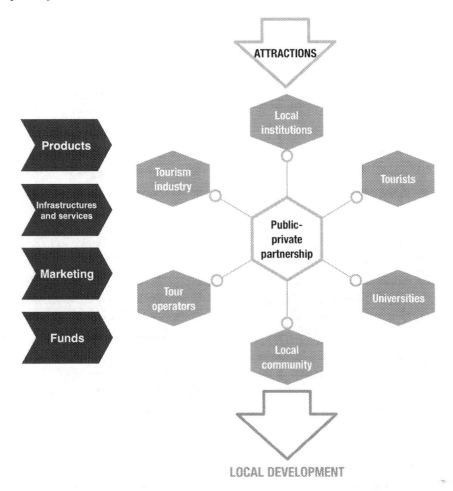

age the relationships with potential tourists and professional operators, trying to exploit all the opportunities.

## 3.5 Reinforcing Stakeholder Cooperation in Hospitality Industry

Pechlaner and Volgger (2012) studied cooperation in hotel sector. In particular, they investigated the methods for promoting local and regional cooperation and they identified four types of enabling factors

First of all, there are the organizational factors: they establish the framework upon which cooperation cooperation can be implemented. Second,

they affirmed that the establishment of a DMO for managing the network relationships would boost cooperation. Third, cooperation can be enabled by social conditions and psychological commitment of actors. Moreover, the research comes up two dimensions in cooperation among stakeholders, that is firstly legitimacy (as degree of trust), and secondly efficiency. Finally, cooperation can be stimulated by carefully balancing the degree of trust among the stakeholders and the efficiency in achieving the common goals.

Wang and Krakover (2008) studied the stakeholders of tourism destinations to understand the types of relationships emerging among them when planning destination marketing activities;

in particular, the two scholars were interested in understanding the relationship between cooperation and competition from the point of view of stakeholders. They found that, while implementing a destination marketing initiative, the stakeholders develop three types of behavior: competitive, cooperative and, occasionally, coopetitive.

The cooperative relations among stakeholders can take different forms, on the basis of different degrees of formalization, integration, and structural complexity of the marketing projects:

- *Affiliation,* i.e. the most informal relationship, it is based on informal exchange of information and personal contacts;
- *Coordination,* i.e. many stakeholders communicate and synchronize their activities;
- *Collaboration,* stakeholders work together, sharing common strategies;
- *Strategic networks*, where stakeholders agree on a common vision, develop group objectives and apply integrated strategy and coordination.

With respect to the factors impacting on the choice of the cooperative form, they identified: strategic thinking, maturity of destination marketing approach, distance of the marketing campaign, and leadership of the local DMO. Obviously, cooperation requires higher level of commitment, high maturity of marketing campaign, a close distance of marketing campaign and a strong leadership of local DMOs. On the other hand, competition requires the opposite of cooperation, whereas 'coopetition' requires intermediate positions of these factors.

## 4. METHODOLOGY

The aim of this research is to explore tourism cooperation between DMOs and hospitality stakeholders, oriented to achieve specific goals within tourism destination. In order to conduct this analysis, a quantitative research method was applied, through a descriptive statistical analysis based on the comparison of two different samples in two opposite destinations: a mass-tourism destination, that is Rimini, and a new destination, that is Trapani. The research focuses on both strategic level as DMOs' viewpoint and operative level as hospitality stakeholders' viewpoint.

A data collection method was conducted using 'face to face' interviews to local DMOs, through specific open questions with the aim to understand the possible mechanisms of cooperation with the most representative stakeholder within that destination, namely hospitality stakeholders.

On the other hand, a data collection method was conducted using anonymous questionnaires to twenty hospitality stakeholders in both destinations. The questionnaire is divided in three sections. The first one deals with the characteristics of the hospitality firms, proposing questions like number of stars and typology of hospitality firm, seasonality, types of customers and ownership. The second section focus on the management of the firm, providing such as education, tools in looking for new customers, tools in customer's satisfaction and how they determine the fixing price. Finally, the third section deals with the core phenomenon studied, that is cooperation. This section evaluates different aspects of cooperation, ranging from the awareness of the meaning of cooperation among stakeholders and its potential, to previous cooperation experiences and the willingness to enter new cooperative ventures.

Regarding the proposed interviews, these have highlighted that due to the composition of hospitality supply within Trapani, the casual samples covers a major share in complementary hospitality firms (mainly B&Bs), rather than hotels. Besides, it will be also underlined in the further Trapani's background. On the other hand, because of the composition of hospitality supply within Rimini, then revealed to be a mass-tourism destination,

*Table 1. Stakeholders*

| Place | DMOs' perspective (through 'face to face' interviews) | Hospitality stakeholders' perspective |
|---|---|---|
| *Rimini* | • Municipality of Rimini – Tourism Department;<br>• *Riminireservation* (as a DMC-Destination Management Company);<br>• Promozione Alberghiera (cooperative company) | *20 interviews according to casual samples, through administration of questionnaires* |
| *Trapani* | • *TrapaniWelcome;*<br>• *Camera di Commercio di Trapani;*<br>• *Province of Trapani - Tourism Department;*<br>• *'Turismo & Territorio' Association.* | *20 interviews according to casual samples, through administration of questionnaires* |

the casual samples shows instead a major share in hotel firms (mainly three and four stars hotels), rather than complementary hospitality firms.

Then, in order to clarify the organizations and stakeholders involved in this thesis, they are pointed out in the underlying framework (see Table 1).

Finally, before answering to research questions in findings section, a background about both destinations is provided. In this background's analysis is showed a brief description of both destinations and then a description about their tourism demands, and their hospitality supplies.

## 4.1 The Case of Rimini

Rimini is placed in the northern part of Italy, in Emilia-Romagna Region, and is a leader tourism destination in Europe since July 1843, when was inaugurated the first privileged bath called "Bagno", that represented the beginning of Italian and international tourism's industry. About 170 years later, Rimini is still the more famous beach in Europe and one of the most popular destinations, desired by Italian and foreign tourists (mainly Russian, Japanese and German). It was able to capture visitors during the years, often supplying before their wishes, and that has made hospitality's culture a core value.

The success of Rimini has to be found not only in the classical formula and a seaside tourism's winning for all types of tourists, through family hotels, good food, beach and warm hospitality of residents; but also in the ability of the residents, throughout continually reproducing creativity and new ideas. Nowadays Rimini offers more than three hundred hotels with annual opening, ready to receive managers and business people engaged to follow trade fairs or international conferences in a new dedicated area, close to city centre. Moreover, for amateurs of wellness and active holidays, Riviera of Rimini represents also a right choice for their wishes.

The city offers even heritage sites, i.e. Roman monuments that disclose Middle Ages and Renaissance buildings. Thanks to the powerful of Malatesta's dominion has been built more monuments like 'Malatesta Temple' and 'Castel Sismondo', now location of prestigious exhibitions of international standings. In addition, in Rimini was born "Federico Fellini", a movie director that carried on his movies the essence of Rimini.

These different values - cultural, seaside, business and congress, warm hospitality and wellness - confirmed Rimini as 'beach of Europe', in a place in which know people; a destination in which going willingly, feeling like at home; and a city in which always discover new tourism ideas such as "Pink Night", "Molo Street Parade", "Rimini Wellness", and so on.

## Hospitality Sector in Rimini

As regards tourism demand in Rimini (or hospitality demand), it seems to be quantified in 9,234,020 visitors in 2012, obtained from *tab.3* in statistics section (Province of Rimini, 2012). Moreover, tourism demand had a little decrease in minus 0.2% respect 2011.

Rimini is preferred mainly by Italian tourists that represent 69% of tourism demand in 2012, decreasing in minus 1.1% in term of arrivals and minus 5.8% in term of presences respect 2011. Foreigners represent 31% of tourism demand in 2012, increasing in 10.3% in term of arrivals and plus 6.9% in term of presences respect 2011. In addition, in 2012, the tourism demand is concentrated for about 97.5% in hotels, and for 2.5% in complementary firms. Hotels increased own demand in 2.3% in term of arrivals, and decreased in minus 2.2% in presences respect 2011; while complementary firms decreased in demand in minus 11.5% in term of arrivals, and minus 1.8% in presences respect 2011.

As regards the length of stay, in *tab.* 4, Italians prefer to stay on average 4.52 days, whereas foreigners prefer to stay little bit more in about 5.02 days.

In sum, in Rimini, the tourism demand in 2012 decreased a little bit respect 2011 (-0.2%); Italian tourists represent the main tourism demand, even if foreigners increase in arrivals and presences in 2012 respect 2011; tourists basically prefer to stay in hotels rather than complementary firms, that have had a decrease both in arrivals and presences; and the length of stay generally is generally between 4.5 and 5 days for both type of tourists.

On the other hand, hospitality supply in Rimini is characterized in a major number of hotels in 2012, that represent 92.8% of the hospitality supply; whereas complementary firms represent 7.2% of hospitality supply Evaluating hospitality supply

in term of beds in 2012, hotels provided 93.8% of the hospitality supply, whereas complementary firms represent 7.2% of hospitality supply.

Regarding hotels firms, they were composed in 1,118 firms in 2012, about which 759 seasonal opening hotels, providing 68% of the total of hotels, and 359 annual opening hotels, providing 32% of the total of hotels.

In sum, hospitality supply in Rimini was composed mainly by hotel firms in 2012 (92.8% in term of firms and 93.8% in term of beds); two and three stars hotels represent the main categories in hotels supply, both in term of firms and beds; hotels highlight a seasonal opening; complementary firms are in minority. Moreover, after this discussion about tourism demand and hospitality supply, Rimini can be seen as a mass tourism destination, since the arrivals and presences overtake deeply the residents, surely lower than 9,2 million of tourists.

## 4.2 The Case of Trapani

Trapani is a tourism destination placed in the southern part of Italy, specifically in Sicily Region. The territory is characterized for its richness in resources, natural resources represented by pictorial landscapes, cultural resources born with the links of antique cultures during the years, and environmental resources derived from reserves, animals and plants that it hosts.

The economy is mainly focussed on tourism and trade, as well as fishing. As regards tourism, Trapani has been developed in the last year, around 2005, when after the hosting an act of 32th American's cup event, residents and local government understood the importance of tourism in own economy. From that year, the main stakeholders, both public and private, within destination started to invest in tourism development through several initiatives, that include marketing efforts to tourism markets both international and national, airport management with the institution of new destination through Ryanair low cost flight company, cruises hosting through agreements with international cruise companies, funds to hospitality sector in order to incentive the openings of hospitality firms, and the use of regional and European funds to improve the infrastructures within territory, such as the requalification of the harbour.

During these last years, Trapani has invested basically in events on fields according to own territorial features, that is in food events, in wine events, in sport and sail events, in cultural events, in entertainment events and summer events.

After this brief background of Trapani, it can be seen as a new destination, since, as argued later on, hospitality capacity and touristic flow are not completely in stagnation, but highlight a gradual trend in growth. Moreover, this pillar can be favourite because the destination development has been started rather close to current year of this thesis.

## Hospitality Sector in Trapani

As regards tourism demand in Trapani (or hospitality demand), it seems to be quantified in 275,413 visitors in 2012, obtained from *tab. 6* in statistics section (Province of Trapani, 2013). Moreover, analysing it, tourism demand increased respect 2011, getting 23,393 more tourists with a plus 9.3%.

Trapani is preferred mainly by Italian tourists that represent 53.7% of tourism demand in 2012, increasing in 30.5% respect 2011; and for 42.3% by foreigners, decreasing in minus 21.2% respect 2011. In addition, in 2012, the tourism demand is concentrated for 54.4% in complementary firms, and for 45.6% in hotels. Complementary firms increased own demand in 28.1% respect 2011; while hotels decreased in demand in minus 7.01% respect 2011.

As regards the length of stay, Italians prefer to stay on average in 2.7 days, obtaining a plus 10.5% respect 2011; whereas foreigners prefer to stay little bit less in about 2.5 days, obtaining a negative impact in minus 14.3% respect 2011.

In sum, in Trapani, the tourism demand in 2012 increased respect 2011; Italian tourists increased and foreigners have had a decrease in 2012 respect 2011; tourists basically prefer to stay in complementary firms rather than hotels; and the length of stay generally decreased in minus 1.5%.

On the other hand, hospitality supply in Trapani is characterized in a major number in complementary firms in 2012, that represent 92% of the hospitality supply; whereas hotels represent 8% of hospitality supply (*see tab. 7 in statistics section*). Evaluating hospitality supply for beds in 2012, complementary firms provided about 65% of the hospitality supply, whereas hotels represent about 35% of hospitality supply.

In sum, hospitality supply in Trapani was composed mainly by complementary firms in 2012 (92% in term of firms and 65% in term of beds), that came under an optimal increase, especially for bed & breakfasts and rental houses; whereas hotels remained the same, but increased beds a little bit.

## 5. EMPIRICAL RESULTS

First of all, the empirical research has been aimed to compare the different degree of cooperation from the hospitality stakeholders' perspective in a new destination and in a mass-tourism destination. Several questions have been elaborated with this aim as you can see in the figure 4 where you can also distinguish the different answers according to both Rimini and Trapani destination. Focusing on Rimini, the obtained answers show that: 50% of hospitality stakeholders know the meaning of cooperation among stakeholders in a tourism destination; 65% of hospitality stakeholders is involved in cooperation, mainly through achieving destination strategy (46%), and then politics of occupation rate (31%) and marketing (23%); 85% of hospitality stakeholders did not started cooperation as 'first player'; and 95% of the sample know that the cooperation could produce concrete results, as improvement of the image, a major vision as

*Figure 4. Benefits from cooperation: The stakeholders' perspective*

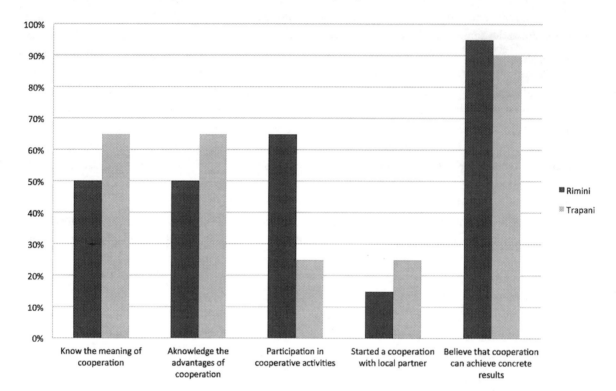

an integrated system for public-private planning, an improvement of delivery on the ground; and a major competitive advantage; but it cannot lead to economies of scale.

In the case of Trapani, we obtained these results: 65% of hospitality stakeholders know the meaning of cooperation among stakeholders in a tourism destination; 25% of hospitality stakeholders is involved in cooperation, mainly through achieving occupational rate (80%), and then destination strategy (20%); 75% of hospitality stakeholders did not started cooperation as 'first player';and 90% of the sample know that the cooperation could produce concrete results, as mainly an improvement of delivery on the ground (27%); economies of scale (24%); and then a major competitive advantage, an improvement of the image, and a major vision as an integrated system for public-private planning.

Second, the research is interested in verifying *how the hospitality cooperation has been developed during the last years according to the DMOs' perspective* (Figure 5). If we analyse Rimini, that is a mass-tourism destination, unfortunately direct interviews did not find any initiative or action by DMOs, as public part in the destination. On the other hand, the research found two important subjects that more or less cover part of DMO's tasks, and that were also come up from the hospitality stakeholders' interviews by means of questionnaires. These are a cooperative company, thus as private part, that is 'Promozione Alberghiera' and a DMC, that is 'Rimini Reservation', which is controlled for 61% by the first one, so a public-private partnership. 'Promozione Alberghiera', later on 'P.A.', is a cooperative company in Rimini since 1968, that connects 200 selected hotels of whatever category, from Grand Hotel of Rimini to hotel chains, and also family hotels. Moreover, it

*Figure 5. Participation in cooperative activities*

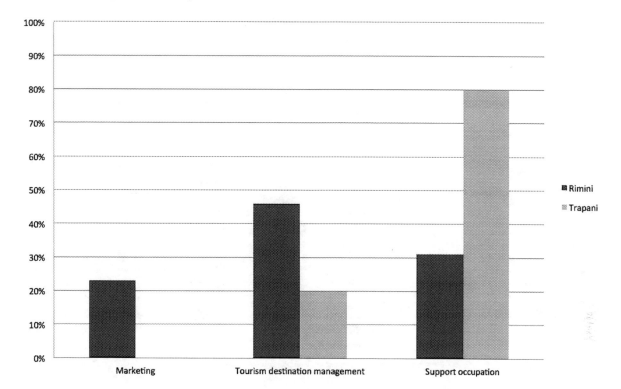

is the biggest hotel cooperative company in Italy, that deals to provide promotional, formative and management tools to own members. Its 'motto' is "*protection of the host*", with which they always host tourists into destination Rimini trying to offer a quality product and distinctive services, in order to satisfy whatever wishes. The philosophy of the cooperative company is to use the action of competitive cooperation among hotel members. It means also to compete for a common objective, where each member conserves own peculiarities and drawing together these to system, in order to improve the competition of the destination Rimini. Instead, 'Rimini Reservation', later on 'R.R.', is a DMC composed in a private and public partnership, as supposed from the regional law n. 7 in 2003, between 'P.A.' and Municipality of Rimini,

that it is respectively divided in 61% and 39% of the corporation stock. Usually, a Destination Management Company –DMC- provides just in the destination facilities for individual visitors or in group. These services include meetings planners, arrange local events and logistics such as transportation or accommodation, and other activities.

The philosophy of 'R.R.' is to integrate reception and hospitality, between public and private sector. Moreover, as the cornerstone of its activity, it employs IAT offices, that is offices for information and touristic reception, that allow the union between tourism demand and destination supply.

In sum, both subjects are not properly DMOs, but they work carrying out activities as a DMO. Moreover, they promote a large cooperation within Rimini, where there is not an exclusively coop-

*Figure 6. Stakeholders' interest in cooperating with DMOs*

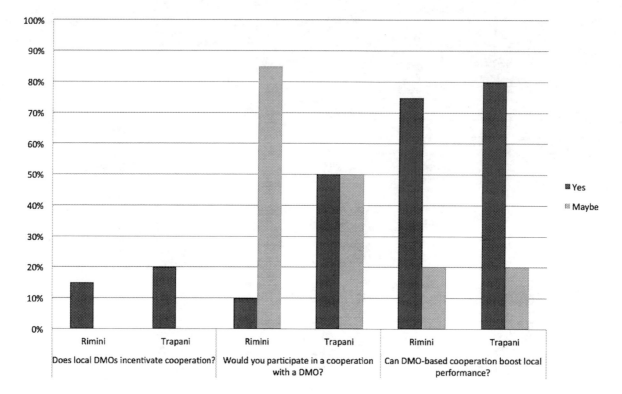

eration's relation towards hospitality sector, but they are a part of the cooperation system created by them, and Rimini HD is the main example.

On the other hand, investigating toward this research question in Trapani, that is a new destination, unfortunately direct interviews to did not find any initiative or action by DMOs, as public part in the destination; and also no-one association on cooperation's purpose exists or works on this field. In fact, in the precedent research question's answer, the sample showed that the degree of cooperation was low (25% of the sample) and then it regarded mainly occupational rate among politics of swap of customer's surplus among B&Bs.

The third aim is to verify the different level of interest by the *hospitality stakeholders to cooperate with DMOs*. We use different questions to verify this point as you can verify in the Figures

6 and 7 where you can also verify the different answers according to two specific different destinations. In sum, in Rimini, the results show that: 85% of the sample did not receive any incentive in cooperation by DMO; 85% of the sample is insure to be part in cooperation with DMO; and 75% of the sample believes that cooperation could 'relaunch' destination to obtain a better competitive advantage in tourism markets.

On the other hand, examining Trapani, that is a new destination, 80% of the sample did not receive any incentive in cooperation by DMO; 50% of the sample would like to be part in cooperation with DMO and 50% of the sample is uncertain; and 80% of the sample believes that cooperation could 'relaunch' destination to obtain a better competitive advantage in tourism markets, and no-one was in dissonance.

*Figure 7. Perceived benefits from cooperation*

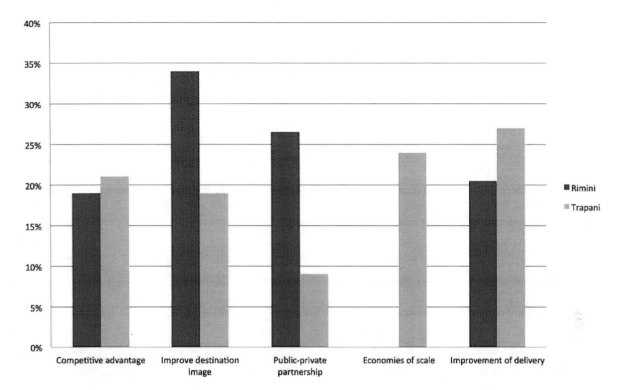

## 6. DISCUSSION

### Comparing the Degrees of Cooperation in Hospitality Stakeholders' Perspective

According to the results show in the four different graphs based on the comparison among the degree of cooperation in hospitality stakeholders' perspective in both destinations, the research comes up basically three things.

First, the knowing of cooperation among stakeholders within a destination is quite known in both destinations, even if in Trapani it is known mainly than in Rimini. Moreover, a better involvement in cooperation seems to be placed in Rimini, where stakeholders are involved in aspects that regard destination strategy, occupational rate and marketing. Whereas, in Trapani it is rather low

and involves just occupational rate among B&Bs through the swap of customer's surplus.

Second, the large share in both destinations highlights that hospitality stakeholders did not start cooperation as 'first player', but waits for other part of the cooperation. Maybe it can be associated to *game theory*'s aspects.

Third, a large share of the sample is aware that cooperation can have concrete results within destinations. Nevertheless, in Rimini were underlined as major results mainly improvement of the destination image and major vision as an integrated system for public-private planning; instead in Trapani were underlined mainly an improvement of delivery on the ground and economies of scale. On the other hand, within visible results, hospitality stakeholders in Rimini did not believe that cooperation can lead to economies of scale, as on the opposite in Trapani.

Finally, in a mass tourism destination as Rimini the degree of cooperation for hospitality stakeholder's position seems to be stronger than in a new destination as Trapani. This process could be justified due to the fact that a mass tourism has shaped own stakeholder's relations during the years.

## Comparing Cooperation in DMOs' Perspectives

Comparing the findings in cooperation in DMOs' perspective in both destination, the research comes up basically two things.

First, in both destinations, DMOs do not implement cooperation with hospitality stakeholders.

Second, in Rimini, a private cooperative company and a DMC, owned by the first one, implement cooperation through own activities or synergic initiative in stakeholders' cooperation (as Rimini HD), even if not exclusively with hospitality sector and carrying out activities as a DMO. Instead in Trapani, no-one association as private part in tourism never worked on this field, leaving this important element as unexplored.

Hence, even if not properly DMOs take care cooperation in Rimini, other subjects implement it, caused also from the regional reform in tourism through law n.7/2013 with the creation of public-private partnership in tourism as Rimini Reservation, leading to join in cooperation a large part of hospitality stakeholders. Instead in Trapani, perhaps for the type of destination, cooperation is not involved among hospitality stakeholders. Moreover, the unique initiative of cooperation from hospitality stakeholders' perspective consists in swapping customer's surplus among B&Bs. Surely, it is not useful for the development of tourism in Trapani, since a large part of hospitality stakeholders interviewed in Trapani shared the healthy effect of cooperation.

## Comparing Interests of Hospitality Stakeholders in Future Cooperation with DMOs

Finally, we compare the findings in interests of hospitality stakeholders in a future cooperation with DMOs in both the two destinations. First, in Rimini, a large share of interviewed hospitality stakeholders showed a insure feeling toward a future cooperation with DMOs, but also a large share understood that cooperation could relaunch the destination to obtain advantage in tourism markets.

Second, in Trapani, half sample of interviewed hospitality stakeholders showed propensity toward a future cooperation with DMOs, but the other half was insure in future cooperation with DMOs. Moreover, as for Rimini, a large share of the interviewed hospitality stakeholders understood that cooperation could re-launch the destination to obtain advantage in tourism markets.

So, this result lead to affirm that hospitality stakeholders in Trapani are more favorable in future cooperation with DMOs than in Rimini, showing more confidence toward local DMOs.

In a general viewpoint, on the one hand Rimini seems to implement several aspect about cooperation, on the other hand it exhibits some shortcomings.

On the positive aspects, firstly, Rimini shows a private-public partnership between Municipality of Rimini (as DMO) and 'Promozione Alberghiera', creating a DMC called Rimini Reservation', that carries out some DMO's tasks. Secondly, 'Promozione Alberghiera' creates a network together with Rimini Reservation for developing cooperation among hospitality actors.

On the negative aspects, firstly, Municipality of Rimini (as local DMO) should care the task of cooperation as first person involved and not through the DMC, where could verify organizational problems in destination planning like confusion in tourism decision-making. Secondly, public-private partnership work rather well, even if this relation is going to be limited due to the coming close of Province of Rimini, that will lead to a reduction in public grants into this relationship. Thirdly, hospitality stakeholders' perspective highlighted a low level of trust in cooperation towards DMOs, which means that there is a low level of legitimacy or degree of trust in cooperation relationship because of insecurity expressed.

Although Rimini is already a known destination and is a tourism-based destination since a lot of years, it could perfect oneself about some shortcomings that are come-up from this research.

On the other hand, Trapani shows an opposite condition, since anyway none association or DMOs took care about cooperation. This could be justify due to the fact that it is a new-destination with not more experience in tourism as Rimini; but also there is a precarious relationships among hospitality stakeholders, which showed in the end of the interview several problems in personal relationships mainly linked to attitude of the stakeholders in the destination.

However, the result in Trapani leads to a high level of future cooperation toward DMO, so hospitality stakeholders know that cooperation could be important in their destination; as well as a high level of legitimacy and trust, and probably efficiency in cooperation. From this point, hopefully, a cooperation starting step ought to be started, that could lead to re-launch the destination Trapani to an high level of tourism visitors and becoming more competitive, even if the problem in stakeholders' attitude is not simple to manage.

## CONCLUSION

The aim of this paper is to study cooperation between destination management and hospitality stakeholders. In order to achieve this, an analysis of two Italian destinations is provided, specifically

examining a mass-tourism destination and a new destination. Moreover, within this relationship, this paper would also analyse how cooperation has been developed during the years within two destinations, and if actually hospitality stakeholders are interesting in cooperation with DMOs, achieving destination's goals.

A literature review divided in three main concepts as destination management, hospitality industry and stakeholders' cooperation within tourism destinations was discussed, in order to support the quantitative analysis of the two cases study. The realized analysis highlighted that in a mass tourism destination as Rimini the degree of cooperation from the hospitality stakeholder's perspective seems to be higher than in a new destination as Trapani. In addition, because of new regulation in the tourism sector in Rimini, the DMOs do not take care cooperation, but two subject as private part in tourism implement stakeholders' cooperation through some DMO's typical actions; whereas in Trapani any subject supports cooperation with local hospitality industry. Lastly, hospitality stakeholders in Trapani are more favorable in future cooperation with DMOs than in Rimini, showing more confidence toward local DMOs.

As suggested by the literature review, cooperation among stakeholders can lead to obtain more competiveness for a destination and determinate success, but obviously also major competiveness among them, also for destinations less developed. In our opinion, for this reason, each destination should invest in a more intensive cooperation and to develop itself a coordinated and cooperated system network of stakeholders. Moreover, hospitality stakeholders in this field are the most useful stakeholders in building cooperation within a tourism destination, so DMOs should implement primary relations with them.

As a final point, future researches could aim to a better filling of the gap in cooperation' literature exclusively between DMOs and hospitality stake-

building cooperation within a destination; an investigation through game theory on the relations among stakeholders in adopting cooperation as 'first player'; and lastly, perhaps as more important aspect in future research, toward an investigation in which variables influence the relation between both subjects achieving mutual cooperation

## REFERENCES

Baggio, R., Scott, N., & Cooper, C. (2011). Design of Tourism Governance Networks. In E. Laws (Ed.), *Tourist Destination Governance: practice, theory and issues* (pp. 159–172). CABI Publishing. doi:10.1079/9781845937942.0159

Barbini, F. M., & Presutti, M. (2013). Tourist experience as an enabler for the development of tourism destinations. In Skills and Tools and Cultural Heritage and Cultural Tourism Management (pp. 59-74). Edizioni D'Errico.

Barbini, F. M., & Presutti, M. (2014). Transforming a peripheral area in an emerging tourism destination. *Tourism Geographies, An International Journal of Tourism Space. Place and Environment, 16*(2), 190–206.

Barnard, C. J. (1938). *The functions of the executive*. Cambridge: Harvard University Press.

Beritelli, P. (2011). Cooperation among prominent actors in a tourist destination. *Annals of Tourism Research, 38*(2), 607–629. doi:10.1016/j.annals.2010.11.015

Bornhorst, T., Brent Ritchie, J. R., & Sheehan, L. (2010). Determinants of tourism success for DMOs & destinations: An empirical examination of stakeholders' perspectives. *Tourism Management, 31*(5), 572–589. doi:10.1016/j.tourman.2009.06.008

Edgell, D. L., & Swanson, J. R. (2013). *Tourism policy and planning: yesterday, today and tomorrow* (2nd ed.). New York: Routledge.

Federalberghi. (2010). *Sesto rapporto sul sistema alberghiero in Italia 2010*. Roma: Edizioni Ista.

Federalberghi. (2013a). *Relazione sull'attività di Federalberghi nell'anno 2012*. Roma: Edizioni Ista.

Federalberghi. (2013b). *Datatour 2013: Trend e statistiche sull'economia del turismo*. Roma: Edizioni Ista.

Franco, M., & Estevao, C. (2010). The role of tourism public-private partnerships in regional development: a conceptual model proposal. *Cadernos EBAPE.Br, 8*(4), 600-612.

IMF. (2013). *World Economic Outlook: a survey by the staff of the International Monetary Fund*. International Monetary Fund Publications Services.

Jamal, T. B., & Getz, D. (1995). Collaboration theory and community tourism planning. *Annals of Tourism Research, 22*(1), 186–204. doi:10.1016/0160-7383(94)00067-3

Laws, E., Richins, H., Agrusa, J. F., & Scott, N. (2011). *Tourist Destination Governance: Practice, Theory and Issues*. CABI International Publishing. doi:10.1079/9781845937942.0000

Lockwood, A., & Medlik, S. (2001). *Tourism and Hospitality in the 21ˢᵗ Centhury*. Oxford: Elsevier.

Maggi, B. (2003). *De l'agir organisationnel. Un point de vue sur le travail, le bien-etre, l'apprentissage*. Toulouse: Octarès Editions.

Novelli, M., Schmitz, B., & Spencer, T. (2006). Networks, clusters and innovation in tourism: A UK experience. *Tourism Management, 27*(6), 1141–1152. doi:10.1016/j.tourman.2005.11.011

Pechlaner, H., & Volgger, M. (2012). How to promote cooperation in the hospitality industry. *International Journal of Contemporary Hospitality Management, 24*(6), 925–945. doi:10.1108/09596111211247245

Pike, S. (2004). *Destination Marketing Organizations*. Amsterdam: Elsevier.

Presutti, M., Boari, C., & Fratocchi, L. (2007). Knowledge acquisition and the foreign development of high-tech start-ups: A social capital approach. *International Business Review, 16*(1), 23–46. doi:10.1016/j.ibusrev.2006.12.004

Province of Rimini. (2012). *Osservatorio sul turismo*. Retrieved from http://www.provincia.rimini.it/informa/statistiche/turismo/2012_report/index.html

Province of Trapani. (2013). *Rapporto sul turismo nella Provincia di Trapani periodo 2012/2013*. Retrieved from: http://www.provincia.trapani.it/Sito/servizi/Avvisi/doc/report%202012.pdf

Province of Trento. (2005). *Destination management*. Retrieved from http://www.turismo.provincia.tn.it/binary/pat_turismo_new/presentazioni_materiale_interni/Marketing_territoriale_e_destination_management_13_03_05_.1203518817.pdf

Rispoli, M., & Tamma, M. (1996). *Le imprese alberghiere nell'industria dei viaggi e del turismo*. Padova: CEDAM.

Ritchie, J. R. B., & Crouch, G. I. (2003). *The Competitive Destination: A Sustainable Tourism Perspective*. Wallingford: CABI Publishing. doi:10.1079/9780851996646.0000

Sharpley, R. (2009). *Tourism Development and the Environment: Beyond Sustainability*. London: Earthscan.

Sheehan, L., Brent Ritchie, J. R., & Hudson, S. (2007). The Destination Promotion Triad: Understanding Asymmetric Stakeholder Interdependencies Among the City, Hotels, and DMO. *Journal of Travel Research, 46*(1), 64–74. doi:10.1177/0047287507302383

Sheehan, L. R., & Brent Ritchie, J. R. (2005). Destination Stakeholders: Exploring Identity and Salience. *Annals of Tourism Research, 32*(3), 711–734. doi:10.1016/j.annals.2004.10.013

Simon, H. A. (1947). *Administrative behavior*. New York: MacMillan.

UNTWO. (2003). *Cooperation and partnerships in tourism: a global perspective*. Madrid: World Tourism Organization.

UNWTO. (2000a). *Millennium Development Goals*. Retrieved from http://www.unmillenniumproject.org/goals/

UNWTO. (2000b). *Public-Private Sector Cooperation: Enhancing Tourism Competiveness*. Madrid: World Tourism Organization.

UNWTO. (2007). *A practical guide to tourism destination management*. Madrid: World Tourism Organization.

UNWTO. (2013). *Tourism Highlights 2013 Edition*. Madrid: World Tourism Organization.

Volgger, M., & Pechlaner, H. (2014). Requirements for destination management organizations in destination governance: Understanding DMO success. *Tourism Management, 41*(9), 64–75. doi:10.1016/j.tourman.2013.09.001

Wang, Y., & Krakover, S. (2008). Destination marketing: Competition, cooperation or coopetition? *International Journal of Contemporary Hospitality Management, 20*(2), 126–141. doi:10.1108/09596110810852122

Wang, Y., & Pizam, A. (2011). *Destination marketing and management: theories and applications*. CABI International Publishing. doi:10.1079/9781845937621.0000

## KEY TERMS AND DEFINITIONS

**Cooperation:** The action or process of working together to the same end.

**Destination Management:** Co-ordinated management of all the elements that make up a destination.

**Destination Management:** Is composed by: Elements of the destination, Destination Management Organization, Destination marketing, Experience delivery, Suitable environment.

**Partnership:** Is a relationship that implicates the sharing of authority, work, and information to achieve mutual goals or benefits among the involved partners.

**Stakeholder:** Any group or individual who can affect, or is affected by, the achievement of a corporation's purpose.

**The Emergent Development:** The various stakeholders working within and around a tourist attraction start to interact and, while reiterating these interactions, they develop a social network.

**The Planned Development:** Implies the preliminary recognition of all the subjects involved, the definition of the tasks to be carried out, the allocation of authority and responsibility, the detailed definition of coordination procedures.

# Chapter 6
# The Influence of National Culture and Organizational Culture on the Success of an Expatriate Overseas Assignment

**Gina Fe G. Causin**
*Stephen F. Austin State University, USA*

**Charito G. Ngwenya**
*BE Meeting Services, Philippines*

## ABSTRACT

*Numerous studies have attempted to determine what makes hospitality expatriate executives successful and a large variety of managerial skills have been generated. The rapidly increasing trend toward internationalization of business has fostered an interest in examining important management skills that international hospitality executives should possess. The study findings indicated that there were underlying dimensions that contributed to the success of hospitality expatriate executives on their overseas assignment. National culture and corporate using management skills could influence a successful overseas assignment. However, it was not revealed which one between the two dimensions has more influence towards a successful overseas assignment. Successful expatriates are being profiled as organizations have found that expatriate assignments are an effective, yet expensive, means of developing international qualities in their managers. The increasing globalization of business appears to have led to the emergence of an international business workforce that shares a unique set of cultural beliefs, attitudes, and behaviors. The thrust of this chapter was to examine the influence of national culture and corporate culture of hospitality expatriate executives that led to a successful overseas assignment.*

## INTRODUCTION

An expatriate is defined as an employee who has spent at least once of his/her career working on temporary, short-term, long-term and/or semi-permanent assignments in overseas locations (Adapted from Heizman et al., 1990; quoted in Gliatis, 1992). In addition, an expatriate is

DOI: 10.4018/978-1-4666-8606-9.ch006

a person who was not born in the country the hotel is located; does not hold the nationality of the country the hotel is located and who is hired on the expatriate status (Li, 1995). Expatriates often have detailed knowledge of the managerial systems used by a company and have an important part to play in the solidity of an organization's corporate culture in distant locations (Causin, 2007). A major driving force behind the expansion and utilization of expatriates is the growing demand for labor in the international hospitality industry combined with a major labor shortage in some Asian countries (Barber & Pittaway, 2000; Burns, 1997). The predicted employment requirements of the international hospitality industry are quite staggering and are forecasted to rise from 255 million in 1996 to 385 million by 2006 (The Economist, 1997; Barber & Pittaway, 2000). Expatriates were required to support this growth at many operational and managerial levels. The management of expatriate labor in the future became more important to hotel companies and would cover many aspects of hotel labor as well as managerial and professional positions (Barber & Pittaway, 2000).

Why use expatriates instead of host-country managers and/or domestically-based international managers? According to numerous authors (Causin, 2007; Barber and Pittaway, 2000), expatriates running foreign operations are more likely to be familiar with the corporate culture and control systems of headquarters than are host-country managers, which results in more effective communication and coordination with the corporation. Second, expatriates provide managerial talent in developing countries where there is limited local talent. Third, the use of expatriates enhances the global mind-set of the organization. Expatriates are also a better option than domestic international managers when short-term international visits are insufficient for successfully growing a business in the target country. When expatriates are sent for an overseas assignment, they possessed both

national culture and corporate or organizational culture. Theories provided tools for understanding the make-up of culture. As seen, divergent traditions have understood culture as values, codes, narratives, pathologies, discourses, and common sense as well as in many other ways. Each of these understandings has its own repercussions for interpreting the ways that culture works and how everyone should study it (Causin, 2007).

Here theory is concerned with offering models of the influence that culture exerts on social structure and social life. Theorists attempt to explain the role of culture in providing stability, solidarity, and opportunity or in sustaining conflict, power, and inequality. Cultural theory also suggests divergent mechanisms through which this influence is channeled, ranging from individual-level socialization through to macro-level institutions and social systems (Causin, 2007). The most critical issue concerns the ways in which culture shapes human action. Some thinkers stress the constraining nature of culture, while others point to its ability to enable action. Issues relating to the cultural construction of the self, motivation, and identity are fundamental to both sets of arguments (Causin, 2007).

The careless application of theories of organizational psychology across cultures is fraught with danger because research has found that, while there are similarities, the differences between organizations operating in distinct cultural and societal settings are significant (Causin, 2007). The similarities tend to be consistent for the same types of business and organizational structure, though there can be considerable variance between organizations operating as similar organizational types but in different societies in such areas as employee-management relations, communication within organization, and staff involvement in decision making (Causin, 2007; Maurice, Sorge & Warner, 1980).

Even though the role of a manager is generally consistent across organizations and cultures, managerial styles can vary substantially. While the evidence available from research on managerial styles in different cultures is limited, distinct social systems can have a considerable impact on management systems, which, in turn, affects managerial styles. Further, research in international settings has clearly shown that management techniques developed in and for a particular culture or country do not always produce the same results in other cultures (Causin, 2007; Adler, 1997).

The effectiveness of a manager is, in part, based on the values that the manager holds and his or her ability to motivate employees. Values are influenced by both the nationality of the manager and the business environment within which the individual manages (Causin, 2007; Adler & Bartholomew, 1992). These values guide the selection and evaluation of managerial behaviors such as techniques for motivating subordinates and enhancing employee job satisfaction (Causin, 2007). Style of organizational leadership has also been shown to be a relevant variable in the implementation of management practices. The norms established by the leader and by the organizational culture allow employees to make sense of their organizational world; if that world makes sense to them, they are likely to be more productive and more satisfied with their jobs.

Organizations in Western cultures have embraced the idea of organizational-development interventions designed to enhance organizational effectiveness at the individual and organizational levels. However, organizational-development interventions can be influenced by culture, resulting in reduced, negative, or nonexistent change outcomes. This suggests that in multinational companies some adaptation of organizational-development interventions is necessary. The primary and recurring issue is whether a subsidiary is influenced more by the parent-company culture or the local culture. A comparison of American, Japanese, European, and Hongkong Chinese multinational companies indicated that organizational-development interventions differ by country, primarily as a function of the organization's home-country culture. American and European organizations are most likely to use both at home and in subsidiaries, organizational-development interventions than Asian companies. Chinese firms have been found to be less open to individual-level interventions and more open to system-level changes, given their long-term orientation. Evidence indicated that organizational-development interventions that take place at a system level can be used independently of culture, while individual-level interventions are more affected by cultural differences and are, therefore, more likely to need to be adapted to local-culture needs (Causin, 2007).

Anyone who has visited other countries knew that differences existed in language, mannerisms, dress, and customs. But in addition, there are hidden differences that are less obvious. Being able to speak the language can help highlight these differences, but Americans are often at a disadvantage in this regard, since being fluent in another language is the exception rather than the rule for most nonimmigrants in the United States. However, culture and the perception of cultural differences are hard to define and explain, and it must be remembered that while culture suggests similarities and uniformity within a society, there is also a wide range of individual differences (Causin, 2007). The purpose of this study is to determine the influence of national culture and corporate or organizational culture on the success of an expatriate's overseas assignment. For this particular study expatriates referred to the executives, managers or the heads of various departments within a hospitality and tourism facility located outside of his/her native country. Figure 1 showed that national culture and corporate culture influenced successful overseas assignment using management skills.

*Figure 1. Conceptual Framework*

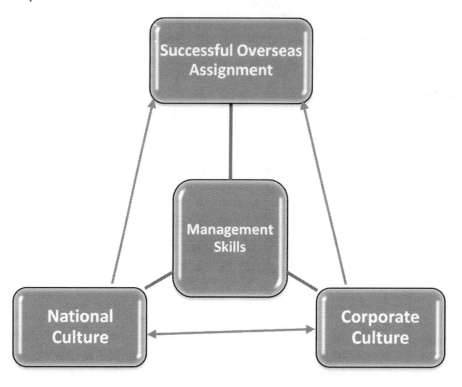

## BACKGROUND

### Introduction

This generation had entered the Global Age. More and more people are global, they shared many global values and practices, and a huge number of individuals worked for global organizations. Globalization caused a converging of economic and social forces, of interests and commitments, of values and tastes, of challenges and opportunities. One can easily communicate with people 10,000 miles away because of a shared global language (English) and a global medium for communications such as computers and the Internet (Black, Gregersen, Mendenhall, & Stroh, 1999). Four main forces have quickly brought about this global age: technology, travel, trade, and television. These four T's have laid the groundwork for a more collective experience for people everywhere. An increasing number of people share common tastes in foods

(hamburgers, pizza, tacos), fashion (denim jeans), and fun (Disney, rock music, television). Nearly 2 billion passengers fly the world's airways each year. People watched the same movies, read the same magazines, and danced the same dances from Boston to Bangkok to Buenos Aires (Mendenhall, 2000).

Ever more people speak English – now spoken by more than 1.5 billion people in over 130 countries (often as a second, third, or fourth language). The English language, like all languages, carries with it implicit and explicit cultural and social values (e.g., precision, individualism, active control, clarity). It became the global language of the airlines, the media, computers, business, and the global marketplace (Marquardt, 1999). The global marketplace created the need for global corporations. These organizations, in turn, created an even more-global marketplace. The growing similarity of what customers wished to purchase, including quality and value, spurred both tremendous opportunities and incredible pressures for businesses becoming global. To a great extent companies, regardless of size or age, recognized that the only choice was between becoming global or becoming extinct (Schwandt & Marquardt, 2000; Marquardt, 1999).

Global organizations were companies that function as if the entire world were a single entity. They were fully integrated so that all of their activities link, leverage, and compete on a worldwide scale (Marquardt & Snyder, 1997). Global firms emphasized global operations over national or multinational operations. They used global sourcing of human resources, capital, technology, facilities, resources, and raw materials. They believed cultural sensitivity to employees and customers were critical to the success of the organization (Adler, 1991). The global economy created a level of complexity that most organizations were not prepared to understand, let alone deal with. Organizations must relate to the ever-growing complexity of multiple relations in their environments – foreign markets, partnerships, and growing and failing economies, to mention a few (Schwandt & Marquardt, 2000).

## Theoretical Background

### Globalization

Globalization is the process by which the world is becoming more and more interconnected, with existing political, cultural, and economic boundaries being superseded. Many discussions of post-modernity of cultural theory involved some discussion of globalization. A major reason for this was the social forces associated with the postmodernization of culture (e.g. the media, consumerism, tourism, the transnational corporation) also played a core role in generating a world that is growingly interconnected. Globalization can be thought of as a process involving three key dimensions (Causin, 2007). These were as follows:

- Economic globalization is associated with the rise of world finance markets and free-trade zones, the global exchange of goods and services, and the rapid growth of transnational corporations.
- Political globalization is about the way that the nation-state is being superseded by international organizations (e.g. the United Nations, the European Union) and the rise of global politics.
- Cultural globalization is about the flow of information, signs, and symbols around the world and reactions to that flow.

While discussion of globalization took off in social science during the 1980s, it is important to remember that the process has been going on for millennia. The movement from small-scale hunting and gathering societies toward the modernist nation state, for example, can be seen as a step toward a global society. For this reason much orthodox social and cultural theory can be understood as relating to the issue. The theories of Durkheim, Marx and Weber (year) provided diverse accounts of ways that forms of social organization extending over ever larger regions of time and space followed one another during the broader span of history. Notwithstanding the fact that people can reconstruct past theoretical traditions in this way, most attention in research on globalization is focused on contemporary settings. In the field of cultural globalization, in particular, themes relating to capitalism, commodities, time/space distanciation, and information flows lead to an inevitable convergence between globalization, postmodernization, and postmodernism literatures (Causin, 2007).

The best-known theory in this tradition was George Ritzer's (1996) concept of McDonaldization, which draws on the work of Marx and Weber. The idea here was that the principles of fastfood organizations were engulfing to a greater extent sectors of society and areas of the world (Causin,

2007). These principles can be summed up as efficiency, calculability, predictability, and control. A model emerged which stressed the incredibly complex interplay of the global and the local. Global refers to the spatially extensive social and cultural forces associated with globalization (e.g. consumerism, satellite communications, culture industries, migration), while local refers to small-scale, geographically confined traditions and ways of life (e.g. ethnic traditions, language, religion). This pointed to the way that processes of globalization have seen global and local cultures brought into contact with each other. These collisions have brought about hybridization. Hybridization can arise from the mixing of cultures and lifestyles. A major theme here can be the way that global forces and products and adapted or modified by local conditions (Causin, 2007).

## Globalization in Business

It has been argued by many scholars and business observers that people – not plans, systems, or strategies – were the key to obtaining a global competitive advantage for a company in any given industry (Mendenhall, 2000). What skill sets or competencies make up the repertoire of an expatriate executive? The following list were the determinants of expatriate adjustment from the research literature: self-efficacy, resilience, behavioral flexibility, curiosity, extroversion, broad category width, flexible attributes, open-mindedness, high tolerance for ambiguity, empathy/respect for others, non-verbal communication, relationship skills, willingness to communication, spouse adjustment, family adjustment, social/logistical support, culture novelty, organization culture novelty, role conflict, role novelty, role discretion, goal orientation, technical competence, reinforcement substitution, and stress reduction program (Mendenhall, 2000). These skill sets or competencies influenced expatriate adjustment which correlated to success in international assignments. The field of expatriate adjustment was

well developed and the majority of scholars in this field would agree that each of the variables listed has been empirically or theoretically demonstrated to positively influence expatriate adjustment (Mendenhall, 2000; Black et al., 1999).

## Organizational Culture Theory

According to West and Turner (2004), Pacanowsky and O'Donnell-Trujillo were instrumental in directing researchers' attention toward an expansive understanding of organizations. The theoretical principles of the theory emphasize that organizational life is complex and that researchers must take into consideration not only the members of the organization but their behaviors, activities, and stories. By looking at organizational culture in this aspect would enable researchers to appreciate the importance of connecting with the people and their performances in an organization.

## Culture

Culture refers to the cumulative deposit of knowledge, experience, beliefs, values, attitudes, meanings, hierarchies, religion, notions of time, roles, spatial relations, concepts of the universe, and material objects and possessions acquired by a group of people in the course of generations through individual and group striving. Culture is the systems of knowledge shared by a relatively large group of people. In its broadest sense, it is cultivated behavior; that is the totality of a person's accumulated experience which is socially transmitted, or more briefly, behavior through social learning. It is symbolic communication. Some of its symbols include a group's skills, knowledge, attitudes, values, and motives. The meanings of the symbols are learned and deliberately perpetuated in a society through its institutions. It consists of patterns, explicit and implicit, of and for behavior acquired and transmitted by symbols, constituting the distinctive achievement of human groups, including their embodiments in artifacts;

the essential core of culture consists of traditional ideas and especially their attached values; culture systems may, on the one hand, be considered as products of action, on the other hand, as conditioning influences upon further action (Watkins, 2013). Furthermore, it is the sum of total of the learned behavior of a group of people that are generally considered to be the tradition of that people and are transmitted from generation to generation. Culture is a collective programming of the mind that distinguishes the members of one group or category of people from another (Kotter, 2012).

## National Culture

One of the most significant studies to look at the role of cultures within a single organization operating across many parts of the world was conducted by the Dutch researcher Geert Hofstede (1984). His research played a significant role in generating interest and additional research in multicultural settings, and it is important to discuss the influence of his studies and theoretical framework on cross-cultural research and controversy it has generated (Causin, 2007; Hofstede & Bond, 1984).

Specifically, Hofstede & Bond (1984) looked at the work-related attitudes and values of comparable groups of managers working in a multinational company that operated in forty countries. The research began in 1967 and continued between 1971 and 1973, when surveys completed by over one hundred thousand IBM employees in different countries were tabulated and analyzed. To help in maintaining the comparability of the groups, only employees from the marketing and servicing divisions of the company were included in the sample. The data were collected using questionnaires, and the answers from those surveyed were averaged for each country. Then scores were developed for each country and these scores were analyzed using a factor-analysis technique designed to isolate the key factors that account for the majority of the variation in the employees' responses. Based on this analysis, Hofstede (1984) theorized that

cultural differences could be usefully described by using four bipolar dimensions: power distance, individualism-collectivism, masculinity-femininity, and uncertainty-avoidance (Causin, 2007; Hofstede, 1984).

## Power Distance

The bipolar ends of this dimension are high and low, and it measures the level of inequality between people that is considered normal in the culture. The concept of power distance implies that in a hierarchical organization, people in power will try to maintain their power, keeping power distance high. The level of power distance helps to define who has the power in the organization to make decisions in general and specific types of decisions in particular, as well as to help prescribe rules and procedures within the organization. In high-power-distance cultures, such as Malaysia, subordinates accept their status and respect formal hierarchical authority. Cultures low in power distance, such as Israel, will have the organizations in which managers are willing to share authority (Causin, 2007; Hofstede, 1984).

## Individualism-Collectivism

This dimension is the degree to which people prefer to work as individuals rather than as group members. Cultures high in individualism, such as the United States, respects and values personal achievement, autonomy, and innovation. Concern is for oneself as an individual rather than the group to which one belongs, and people tend to classify one another on the basis of individual characteristics rather than group membership. On the other hand, cultures high in collectivism, such as Taiwan, emphasize group harmony, social order, loyalty, and personal relationships. Individual contributions are not valued if they work against group goals or interests. In order to maintain harmony in a collectivist culture, it is often necessary to be conservative and cautious

The majority of countries are collectivist, where group membership dictates a person's loyalty and identification and the interests of the group take precedence over the interests of the individual (Causin, 2007; Hofstede, 1984).

## Masculinity-Femininity

This dimension is the degree to which perceived typical masculine attributes (e.g. assertiveness, success, and competition) prevail over perceived typically feminine attributes (e.g. sensitivity and concern for others). Cultures high in masculinity, such as Japan, are more likely to be male dominated, especially in management, whereas cultures high in femininity, such as Sweden, are more likely to have women in managerial and professional positions. In addition, masculine societies are more likely to define occupations by gender, whereas in feminine cultures women and men can do any job and are not restricted by gender-role stereotypes (Causin, 2007; Hofstede, 1984).

## Uncertainty-Avoidance

The bipolar ends of this dimension are high and low, and it measures the degree to which individuals prefer structure to a lack of structure. The concept of uncertainty avoidance suggests that countries high in this dimension have high stress levels and design rules and norms to reduce uncertainty or ambiguity to the greatest extent possible. Cultures high in uncertainty avoidance tend to be uncomfortable or insecure with risks, disorganization, and unstructured situations and will try to control their environments by creating laws, rules, and institutions. This is manifested in lifetime-employment practices in countries such as Japan and Greece. Cultures low in uncertainty-avoidance are more likely to accept differences in society, and people in these cultures are more curious about discovering and trying new things. The result is more job mobility, as seen in countries such as the United States

and Denmark. Uncertainty can be due to human behavior or the nature of the environment, and it shapes the organizational mechanisms that are used to control and coordinate activities (Causin, 2007; Hofstede, 1984).

## Corporate Culture

For this particular study, corporate and organizational culture are synonymous and interchangeable. One of the most important building blocks for a highly successful organization and an extraordinary workplace is corporate culture, the values and behaviors that contribute to the unique social and psychological environment of an organization. According to Needle (2004), corporate culture represents the collective values, beliefs and principles of organizational members and is a product of such factors as history, product, market, technology, and strategy, type of employees, management style, and national cultures and so on. It includes an organization's expectations, experiences, philosophy, and values that hold it together, and is expressed in its self-image, inner workings, interactions with the outside world, and future expectations. In addition, it is the behavior of humans who are part of an organization and the meanings that the people attach to their actions. It affects the way people and groups interact with each other, with clients, and with stakeholders. Furthermore, Ravasi and Schultz (2006) added that corporate culture is a set of shared mental assumptions that guide interpretation and action in organizations by defining appropriate behavior for various situations.

## What is Expatriation?

For most of business history the term international sufficed; its meaning was clear – outside the home country of the organization. An international executive, for the most part, was an expatriate, someone who lived and worked overseas. According to McCall & Hollenbeck (2002), the responsibilities of those early expatriates were not too different from how companies use expatriates today. They were charged with control, making sure that the provinces operated according to Roman law and sent in their taxes. These early expats were also responsible for knowledge transfer, bringing the province new administrative and technical skills, and in those days, perhaps, new gods, language and culture. Accomplishing those duties required that some knowledgeable and trustworthy executive go there to live and work in another country – building a set of skills, accumulating wealth, getting one's ticket punched for a promotion, escaping a bad situation, or perhaps just for the adventure itself (McCall & Hollenbeck, 2002). As communication and transportation evolved and became global, traveling between continents became a convenience. The apparent ease of travel between countries enabled these executives to fly out from headquarters and manage overseas operations on short-term or long term basis (Schwandt & Marquardt, 2000). Since then, the word global has been used interchangeably with transnational in describing an organization characterized by working across borders. As with crossing borders became easier and faster, organizations had increasingly followed their markets outside of their borders. What forms these organizations have taken and what types of executives they needed have depended, ideally at least, on what tasks had to be performed across borders (McCall & Hollenbeck, 2002).

## The Expatriate Executive

Expatriates are defined as the non-citizens of the countries where they work (Daniels and Radebaugh, 1993). Frith (1981) defined an expatriate as one who works for a company in an overseas location for a contracted period of time, usually an excess of one year (Li, 1995). Simply put, expatriate executives are those who do global work. With so many kinds of global work, again depending on the mix of business and cultural

crossings involved, there is clearly no one type of global executive. Executives, as well as positions, are more or less global depending upon the roles they play, their responsibilities, what they must get done, and the extent to which they cross borders (Schwandt & Marquardt, 2000).

The terms international executives and global executives have been used interchangeably here. Both terms, as descriptors of both executives and jobs, involve "more or less" rather than absolutes (McCall & Hollenbeck, 2002). All global executives must have the ability to create trusting relationships across boundaries, to do so quickly, and to maintain them (Dotlich & Noel, 1998). Therefore, an expatriate is any individual who works outside their country of birth but does not immigrate to the country where they work. This included staff employed across all aspects of a hotel's operation and all work roles (Barber & Pittaway, 2000).

## Importance of Expatriate Management in Business

As the world economy became more globalized, the labor forces worldwide became more mobile. To develop a management cadre with a global perspective and a familiarity with the company's interests in overseas operation (Li, 1995; Deresky, 1994), multinational firms are using expatriate managers to fill overseas managerial positions. As the need of international management grows, the use of expatriates to run foreign operations is increasing as well (Scullion, 1991). Daniels and Radebaugh (1994) summarized the three major reasons for using expatriates: 1) technical competence; 2) management development; and 3) control. The need for technical competence is reflected in the tendency for companies to use expatriates in countries where management talents are not available.

The second reason for using expatriates is for the purpose of management development. Expatriation is part of the career development process since multinational experience can reinforce the international perspectives of upward moving managers. It can also enhance manager's ability to work in a variety of social systems and is therefore considered valuable training for ultimate corporate responsibility (Schwandt & Marquardt, 2000). The third reason for using expatriate executives is to have close control of foreign operations. Expatriates are considered to be more familiar with the corporate culture of a company, which results in more effective communications and coordination. Therefore, as companies are developing international expansion strategies, the need to use more expatriates for control purposes grows (Daniel & Radebaugh, 1994).

Despite the important role that the expatriate managers can play, many executives have not realized their potential contributions and have a narrow and myopic view of how they can be used and who should be involved with them (Black, Gregersen & Mendehall, 1992). Historically, firms have sent managers and professionals overseas to fill positions on a seemingly ad hoc basis; they have paid little attention either to their selection and training or to the role they could play in the overall organization (Boyacigiller, 1990). This approach created inherent problems. Individuals sent overseas without adequate training often failed, which incurs substantial costs to these companies (Li, 1995).

## Expatriates in the Hospitality Industry

In the hospitality industry, expatriate management is becoming very crucial as more hotel chains are now seeking expansion into overseas markets. Ruddy (1991) conducted a study on career development of general managers in Pacific Asia and found that 68% of hotel managers were from Europe and North America. As more multinational hotel chains are setting their sights on Pacific Asia, the opportunities for expatriates working in that part of the world had increased. As the need for international management in hospitality grows,

the use of expatriates to run foreign operations is increasing as well (Li, 1995; Scullion, 1991). However, despite the important role that expatriate managers can play, many executives have paid little attention either to their selection and training or the role they could play in the overall organization (Li, 1995; Boyacigiller, 1990). Expatriates sent overseas without adequate training often cannot adjust to the work life overseas which could affect the management of the business.

International expansion brings to the hotel chains many unique problems in the management of human resources, the most fundamental of which is the necessity for managers to play bicultural or multicultural roles (Robock and Simmonds, 1983). With international transfers becoming more frequent, hotel chains have to determine new policies and procedures to ensure that such moves are successfully administered. Powers (1992) indicated that multinational lodging firms had to hire expatriates to work in hospitality operations at overseas locations because some countries do not have qualified managers. Boyacigiller (1990) indicated that multinational companies must view expatriation as a strategic tool to develop future managers with a global orientation and to manage key organizational and country linkages.

## Management Skills

The most fundamental management skills are technical, interpersonal, conceptual, diagnostic, communication, decision-making and time-management skills. Technical skills are the skills necessary to accomplish or understand the specific kind of work being done in an organization. Technical skills are especially important for first-line managers. These managers spend much of their time training subordinates and answering questions about work-related problems. They must know how to perform the tasks assigned to those they supervise if they are to be effective managers (Griffin, 2005).

Managers spend considerable time interacting with people both inside and outside the organization. The manager also needs interpersonal skills – the ability to communicate with, understand, and motivate both individuals and groups. As a manager climbs the organizational ladder, she must be able to get along with subordinates, peers, and those at higher levels of the organization. Although some managers have succeeded with poor interpersonal skills, a manager who has good interpersonal skills is likely to be more successful (Griffin, 2005). Conceptual skills depend on the manager's ability to think in the abstract. Managers need the mental capacity to understand the overall workings of the organization and its environment, to grasp how all the parts of the organization fit together, and to view the organization in a holistic manner. This allows them to think strategically, to see the big picture, and to make broad-based decisions that serve the overall organization (Griffin, 2005).

Successful managers also possess diagnostic skills, or skills that enable a manager to visualize the most appropriate response to a situation. A physician diagnoses a patient's illness by analyzing symptoms and determining their probable cause. Similarly, a manager can diagnose and analyze a problem in the organization by studying its symptoms and then developing a solution (Griffin, 2005). Communication skills refer to the manager's abilities both to effectively convey ideas and information to others and to effectively receive ideas and information from others. These skills enable a manager to transmit ideas to subordinates so that they work well together properly, and to keep higher-level managers informed about what is going on. In addition, they help the manager listen to what others say to understand the real meaning behind letters, reports, and other written communication (Griffin, 2005).

For this particular study, management skills were determined using the following variables: Grasps on how all the parts of the organization fit together; Has the mental capacity to understand

the overall workings of the organization and its environment; International negotiation skills; Get along with subordinates, peers, and those at higher levels of the organization; Views the organization in a holistic manner; Understanding international marketing; Understanding international finance; Ability to work in international teams; Effectively receive ideas and information from others; and Effectively convey ideas and information to others.

## MAIN FOCUS OF THE CHAPTER

### Issues, Controversies, Problems

The time and costs invested in providing expatriates and their families with such cultural awareness briefings that would reduce their difficulties in adjusting in both business and social forum would certainly contribute to minimizing the risk of early returns of expatriates and the potentially more damaging cultural offense and alienation of local employees and business partners (Hutchings, 2003). In general, expatriates are sent overseas to fill job assignments when qualified local country nationals cannot be found to fulfill the needed requirements (Dowling, Schuler & Welch, 1994). Any position where local country personnel lack the expertise or knowledge to adequately perform the required functions may serve as a potential expatriate assignment (Geber, 1992). Expatriates usually originate from the organizational headquarters where such expertise either currently exists or is recruited (Kobrin, 1984; Parker, Heira, Hatem, 1996). Early termination of an expatriate assignment is considered a failure that could significantly impact the organization (Tung, 1984; Tung, 1987). Thus, staffing positions with expatriates should meet a critical business need to ensure the greatest benefit to the organizations (Tung, 1988). Potential benefits of expatriate assignments include developing local country personnel, establishing high level contacts with host country governments, serving key clients on a global basis, and developing a cadre of internationally competent managers (Handy & Barham, 1990; Harvey, 1997). While the benefits of strategically implemented expatriate staffing can be numerous, the costs associated with expatriate assignments are high (Handy & Barham, 1990).

In 1979, the direct costs (training, travel, salary, and relocation expenses) attributed to early termination of an expatriate assignment have been estimated between $55,000 and $80,000 depending on the exchange rate and location of the assignment (Misa & Fabricatore, 1979). According to Ioannou (1995), the cost of bringing the failed manager and his family home is estimated at $250,000. In March 1996, Foster-Higgins Inc. conducted a privately funded survey of 500 organizations and 500 expatriates associated with these organizations (Aschkenasy, 1997). Responses were received from 190 human resource departments and 171 expatriates. The findings indicate that expatriate compensation and benefits packages were at least two and a half times as expensive as hiring local country nationals to fill the same positions. In some countries, organizations are investing over five times as much to employ expatriate staff as they would hire their local country counterparts. Expatriate assignments are an expensive business solution and many organizations are reducing the number of expatriates they employ. Additionally, there are hidden costs involved in expatriate failure that reach far beyond the direct costs associated with compensation and benefits (Nelson, 1999; Aschkenasy, 1997).

Costs associated with losing key client contacts, jeopardizing government relations, affecting host country employee morale, and sagging productivity are difficult to measure. While overseas, the expatriate may also suffer from a loss of self-esteem, self-confidence, and prestige among peers (Mendenhall & Oddou, 1978; Mendenhall & Oddou, 1985). Additionally, measuring expatriate performance has proved to be extremely difficult, costly, and often neglected by organizations (Schuler, Fulkerson & Dowling,

1991; Harvey, 1997; Nelson, 1999). This lack of performance assessment data has made it difficult to reintegrate expatriates into their home country organizations (Harvey, 1997). Naturally, this situation has led to great dissatisfaction among returning expatriates resulting in high turnover of repatriated personnel. These addition hidden costs arising out of expatriate failure may lead to a loss in market share. Thus, organizations have a vested financial interest in ensuring expatriate success. A number of studies have been conducted to profile successful expatriates. These profiles can be broken down into three major categories including: reasons for expatriate failure, predictors of expatriate success, and profiles of successful expatriates.

Tung (1981) found that among American companies surveyed the reasons for expatriate failure were cited to be (in descending order of importance) inability of the spouse to adjust, manager's inability of the spouse to adjust, manager's inability to adjust, other family reasons, manager's personal or emotional maturity, and inability to cope with the larger overseas responsibility. Interestingly, in repeating this element of the study with the Japanese organizations, the reasons were ranked in almost exact opposite order of the American organizations. Among European organizations, the only reason for expatriate failure that respondents consistently marked was the inability of the spouse to adjust. Similar studies have been conducted with Japanese (Allen, 1988), British (Hamill, 1987), and Australian expatriates (Dowling & Welch, 1988; Welch, 1990). These findings from studies conducted with non-American expatriates serve to underscore that the reasons for American expatriate failure are uniquely different from other cultures. Failure rates among American expatriates are particularly high when compared to other cultures (Tung, 1987; Hendry, 1994). In fact, nearly 50% of American expatriates fail to complete the full length of their overseas assignment (Ioannou, 1995). Adding to this staggering figure is the fact that nearly 25% of American expatriates returning to their U.S. organizations leave the organization within one year (McFarland, 1995; McFarland 1997). Researchers point out that there are two factors organizations can control that directly influence expatriate success: improved selection practices for overseas assignments and improved preparation of expatriates through cross-cultural training (Mendenhall & Oddou, 1985; Harris & Moran, 1996).

The relatively poor success rate of American expatriates, coupled with the high costs associated with expatriate and repatriate failure has led U.S. organizations to spend considerable effort in examining the characteristics that help to predict expatriate success for overseas staffing purposes (Nelson, 1999). The purpose of this chapter is reveal the demographic and professional background of hospitality expatriate executives; determine the important management skills of successful hospitality expatriate executives; determine whether the expatriate executives' management skills vary by national culture, and examine whether the expatriate executives' management skills vary according to the parent company's corporate culture.

## SOLUTIONS AND RECOMMENDATIONS

### Background of the Respondents

Simple descriptive statistics were used to determine the respondents' demographic and professional background. Table 1 showed the demographic information of the respondents. This revealed that the respondents' age varied widely. Nine percent were between 20 to 30 years old; twenty-seven percent were between 31 to 40 years; twenty-one percent were between the ages of 41 to 50 years old; thirty percent (30%) were between the ages of 51 to 60 years old and eleven percent (11%) of these executives was from 61 years old and above. Most (73%) of the respondents were male and twenty-four (24%) were female. An

overwhelming sixty one (61%) of the respondents was married; twenty seven percent (27%) were never married; three percent (3%) were widowed; and nine percent (9%) did not provide an answer.

In terms of the highest educational level obtained or achieved, three percent (3%) had attended

*Table 1. Demographic Information of the Respondents (n = 66)*

| Variables | Mean | Frequency | Percent |
|---|---|---|---|
| Age Group | 4.15 | | |
| 20-30 years old | | 6 | 9.1 |
| 31-40 years old | | 18 | 27.3 |
| 41-50 years old | | 14 | 21.2 |
| 51-60 years old | | 20 | 30.3 |
| 61 years old and above | | 7 | 10.6 |
| No Answer | | 1 | 1.5 |
| | | | |
| Gender | 1.75 | | |
| Female | | 16 | 24.2 |
| Male | | 48 | 72.7 |
| No Answer | | 2 | 3.0 |
| | | | |
| Current marital status | 1.70 | | |
| Married | | 40 | 60.6 |
| Never been married | | 18 | 27.3 |
| Widowed | | 2 | 3.0 |
| No Answer | | 6 | 9.1 |
| | | | |
| Highest educational level obtained/achieved | 5.45 | | |
| Some College | | 2 | 3.0 |
| College Degree (hospitality undergraduate degree) | | 4 | 6.1 |
| College Degree (other undergraduate degrees) | | 8 | 12.1 |
| Some Graduate School | | 2 | 3.0 |
| Graduate School Degree | | 36 | 54.5 |
| Other | | 6 | 9.1 |
| No Answer | | 8 | 12.1 |

on some college; six percent (6%) obtained a college degree particularly hospitality undergraduate degree; twelve percent (12%) achieved a college degree or other undergraduate degrees; three percent (3%) acquired some graduate school; a vast fifty five percent (55%) obtained a graduate school degree; six percent (6%) had other degrees and eight percent (8%) had no answer.

Ninety-seven percent of the respondents had prior overseas experience or they had experience working outside of their home countries. Only 3% did not provide an answer. The number of months the respondents worked as an expatriate executive in the host country varied. Sixteen percent (16%) worked for less than six months; eight percent (8%) worked for 7 to 12 months; another eight percent (8%) worked for 13 to 14 months; ten percent (10%) worked for 25 to 36 months; none of the respondents worked between the 37 to 48 months; eight percent worked for 49 to 60 months; another eight percent worked for 61 months and beyond; and eight percent did not provide any answer regarding the number of months they worked as expatriates.

Regarding the job title, two percent (2%) of the respondents served as consultant, twenty seven percent (27%) were directors or managers, five percent were educators and twenty eight percent (28%) were top executives. In terms of the number of months of hospitality experience the respondents had, seven percent (7%) just worked for less than six months; five percent (5%) worked at most twenty four months; six percent (6%) worked in the industry between 25 to 36 months; three percent (3%) were in the hospitality industry for four years (37–48 months); six percent (6%) were involved in the hospitality industry for sixty months and below; and an overwhelming 73% of the respondents had been with the hospitality industry for more than sixty one months.

These respondents had worked in different departments of the hospitality industry. Six percent (6%) were assigned in the personnel department; nine percent were detailed in marketing or sales;

twelve percent (12%) were responsible of the food and beverage department; fifteen percent (15%) were delegated in the general management area; few (6%) were appointed in the front office; and some (8%) were delegated for financial control. The largest percentage (22%) of the respondents served in other departments of their property which included human resources, training, event management, and research and development. The information on other departments was provided by the respondents in an open-ended question, *question number 11 other*.

The respondents worked in different hotel categories. Six percent (6%) were in a mid-priced property; twenty one percent (21%) managed a boutique hotel and thirty nine percent (39%) worked in a luxury hotel property. One third (33%) of the respondents did not indicate the category of the property where they worked. The level of the self-reported success of the respondents' overseas experience differed. For this particular question, four scales were used: 1= not successful, 2= somewhat successful, 3=successful and 4=extremely successful. Three percent (3%) were not successful; fifteen percent (15%) were somewhat successful; forty six percent (46%) were successful and twenty four percent (24) were extremely successful. In general, the expatriate executives indicated that they viewed themselves as being successful in their assignments to the host country (mean=3.03, successful). Table 2 provided a complete frequency distribution of this background information.

## Important Management Skills International Hospitality Executives Should Possess

Respondents indicated in Table 3 that there were important management skills hospitality expatriate executives should possess. The variable with the highest to lowest means were as follows: grasps on how all the parts of the organization fit together (mean=3.59); has the mental capacity to under-

*Table 2. Professional Background of the Respondents (n = 66)*

| Variables | Mean | Frequency | Percent |
|---|---|---|---|
| Overseas experience prior to present job | 2.00 | | |
| Yes | | 64 | 97.0 |
| Missing/No Answer | | 2 | 3.0 |
| Number of months as an expatriate executive in the host country | 3.45 | | |
| Less than 6 months | | 16 | 24.2 |
| 7-12 months | | 8 | 12.1 |
| 13-24 months | | 8 | 12.1 |
| 25-36 months | | 10 | 15.2 |
| 37-48 months | | 0 | 0.0 |
| 49-60 months | | 8 | 12.1 |
| 61 months and above | | 8 | 12.1 |
| Missing/No Answer | | 8 | 12.1 |
| Job Title | 2.95 | | |
| Consultant | | 2 | 3.0 |
| Director/Manager | | 27 | 40.9 |
| Educator | | 5 | 7.6 |
| Top Executive | | 28 | 42.4 |
| Number of months of hospitality experience | 6.06 | | |
| Less than 6 months | | 5 | 7.6 |
| 13-24 months | | 3 | 4.5 |
| 25-36 months | | 4 | 6.1 |
| 37-48 months | | 2 | 3.0 |
| 49-60 months | | 4 | 6.1 |
| 61 months and above | | 48 | 72.7 |
| Department in which the respondents worked/are working | 5.58 | | |
| Personnel | | 4 | 6.1 |
| Marketing/Sales | | 6 | 9.1 |
| Food & Beverages | | 8 | 12.1 |
| General Management | | 10 | 15.2 |
| Front Office | | 4 | 6.1 |
| Financial Control | | 8 | 12.1 |
| Other | | 22 | 33.3 |
| Hotel category | 3.50 | | |
| Mid-priced Hotel | | 4 | 6.1 |
| Boutique Hotel | | 14 | 21.2 |
| Luxury Hotel | | 26 | 39.4 |
| No Answer | | 22 | 33.3 |
| Level of success as an expatriate executive | 3.03 | | |

*Table continued on following page*

*Table 2. continued*

| Variables | Mean | Frequency | Percent |
|---|---|---|---|
| Not Successful | | 2 | 3.0 |
| Somewhat Successful | | 10 | 15.2 |
| Successful | | 30 | 45.5 |
| Extremely Successful | | 16 | 24.2 |
| No Answer | | 8 | 12.1 |

stand the overall workings of the organization and its environment (mean=3.58); international negotiation skills (mean=3.44); get along with subordinates, peers, and those at higher levels of the organization (mean=3.32); views the organization in a holistic manner (mean=3.30); understanding international marketing (mean=3.26); understanding international finance (mean=3.24); ability to work in international teams (mean=3.19); effectively receive ideas and information from others (mean=3.15); and effectively convey ideas and information to others (mean=3.10).

## Do Expatriates Management Skills Vary by National Culture?

The "Sig" column gives the probability (p) value of the F test. Since the p value is very highly significant, the researcher concludes that management skills did vary by the respondents' national culture as shown in Table 4. The F test indicates that national culture is significantly related to effectively convey ideas and information to others due to difference in the mean and variance of effectively convey ideas and information to others in the twelve categories of national culture. However, it did not show the structural differences among the twelve categories. This is revealed by pairwise multiple comparisons. To get the pairwise comparisons, post hoc tests should be conducted for the variables that were statistically significant.

For this study the variables that were statistically significant were: understanding international marketing (p=0.038); ability to work in international teams (p=0.027); grasps on how all the

parts of the organization fit together (p=0.045); and views the organization in a holistic manner (p=0.004). Note, however, that post hoc tests were not performed for the following significant variables: Understanding international marketing; Ability to work in international teams; Grasps on how all the parts of the organization fit together; and Views the organization in a holistic manner because at least one group has fewer than two cases.

## Do Hospitality Expatriates' Management Skills Vary According to the Parent Company's Corporate Culture?

One-way analysis of variance as indicated in Table 5, was used to examine the relationship between the following management skills (dependent variables): effectively convey ideas and information to others, effectively receive ideas and information from others, understanding international finance, international negotiation skills, understanding international marketing, ability to work in international teams, get along with subordinates, peers, and those at higher levels of the organization, has the mental capacity to understand the overall workings of the organization and its environment, grasps on how all the parts of the organization fit together, views the organization in a holistic manner and the factor or independent variable, location of the parent company.

The "Sig" column gives the probability (p) value of the F test. Since the p value is very highly significant for four dependent variables (management skills), the researcher concludes

*Table 3. Descriptive Frequency Distribution of the Most Important Management Skills that Hospitality Expatriate Executives should Possessed (n = 66)*

| Variables | Frequency | Mean | Standard Deviation |
|---|---|---|---|
| Grasps on how all the parts of the organization fit together | 44 | 3.59 | 1.386 |
| Has the mental capacity to understand the overall workings of the organization and its environment | 52 | 3.58 | 1.513 |
| International negotiation skills | 36 | 3.44 | 1.362 |
| Get along with subordinates, peers, and those at higher levels of the organization | 56 | 3.32 | 1.574 |
| Views the organization in a holistic manner | 40 | 3.30 | 1.604 |
| Understanding international marketing | 38 | 3.26 | 1.349 |
| Understanding international finance | 34 | 3.24 | 1.362 |
| Ability to work in international teams | 54 | 3.19 | 1.555 |
| Effectively receive ideas and information from others | 52 | 3.15 | 1.500 |
| Effectively convey ideas and information to others | 58 | 3.10 | 1.575 |

that understanding international finance (p=.000), international negotiation skills (p=.002), has the mental capacity to understand the overall workings of the organization and its environment (p=.027), and grasps on how all the parts of the organization fit together (p=.018) vary by the respondents' location of the parent company. The F test indicates that location of the parent company is significantly related to the dependent variables mentioned above. Therefore, there is a significant difference between Australian, Chinese, Indian, Middle Eastern, Switzerland, Thailand and United States parent company's location on their level of: understanding international finance, international negotiation skills, understand the overall workings

*Table 4. Relationship between Management Skills of Expatriates and Country of Origin (*denotes significance at p<.05; n = 66)*

| Dependent Variables (Management Skills) | F | Sig. |
|---|---|---|
| Effectively convey ideas and information to others | 1.133 | .386 |
| Effectively receive ideas and information from others | 1.246 | .330 |
| Understanding international finance | 2.400 | .064 |
| International negotiation skills | 1.970 | .117 |
| Understanding international marketing | 2.784 | *.038 |
| Ability to work in international teams | 3.051 | *.027 |
| Get along with subordinates, peers, and those at higher levels of the organization | 2.193 | .085 |
| Has the mental capacity to understand the overall workings of the organization and its environment | 2.389 | .065 |
| Grasps on how all the parts of the organization fit together | 2.650 | *.045 |
| Views the organization in a holistic manner | 4.753 | *.004 |
| Factor or Independent Variable: National Culture (Australia, Canada, China, India, Korea, Malaysia, Switzerland, Taiwan, Thailand, Turkey, United Kingdom and United States) | | |

*Table 5. Relationship between Management Skills of Expatriates and Location of the Parent Company (* denotes significance at p≤.05)*

| Dependent Variables (Management Skills) | F | Sig. |
|---|---|---|
| Effectively convey ideas and information to others | 1.612 | .198 |
| Effectively receive ideas and information from others | 2.409 | .067 |
| Understanding international finance | 23.264 | *.000 |
| International negotiation skills | 5.629 | *.002 |
| Understanding international marketing | 2.214 | .087 |
| Ability to work in international teams | 2.273 | .080 |
| Get along with subordinates, peers, and those at higher levels of the organization | 2.441 | .064 |
| Has the mental capacity to understand the overall workings of the organization and its environment | 3.103 | *.027 |
| Grasps on how all the parts of the organization fit together | 3.433 | *.018 |
| Views the organization in a holistic manner | 2.575 | .054 |
| Factor or Independent Variable: Parent Company's Corporate Culture (Australia, China, India, Middle East, Switzerland, Thailand and United States). | | |

of the organization and its environment and how all the parts of the organization fit together.

This significant relationship was due to difference in the mean and variance of understanding international finance, international negotiation skills, mental capacity to understand the overall workings of the organization and its environment, and grasps on how all the parts of the organization fit together in the seven categories of corporate culture.

However, ANOVA did not show the structural differences among these categories. The structural difference was revealed by pairwise multiple comparisons. To obtain the pairwise multiple comparisons, post hoc tests were conducted. Note, however that post hoc test was only conducted for the variables that were statistically significant. Tukey's HSD (Honestly Significantly Different) was the post hoc test used to determine which category of the parent company's corporate culture was significant. The Tukey's HSD multiple comparisons revealed that on the variable, understanding international finance, Australia, China, India, Middle East, Switzerland, Thailand and the United States were significantly different from each other. And the variable international

negotiation skills, Switzerland is significantly different from China, India, and the Middle East.

The findings of this study would have a great impact to the following entities: hospitality expatriate executives, Human Resource professionals, and higher education. This section is divided into three parts:

## Recommendations to Hospitality Expatriate Executives

1. Executives and managers should build knowledge and skills in gathering information on international business. Information gathering skills appear to be critical on a variety of levels. At a very basic level all managers and executives should learn how to gather information on the global marketplace. Country-and-market-specific informational gathering skills should also be developed over the course of a career. Managers and executives holding international positions should work on improving cross-cultural skills to improve information gathering and personal interaction skills. Managers should begin to try to develop

these skills long before they take an international position, thereby ensuring a maximum potential for success when assigned such a position. Executives, in particular, should focus on being aware of cultural differences that could affect strategy formulation and personal business interactions.

2. Executives may wish to consider taking extended business trips in order to foster personal contacts with foreign country managers. Such trips could help to improve strategy formulation on the part of executives, as well as, to develop cross-cultural and global information gathering skills. Additionally, executives may want to focus on imparting business development strategies to help develop foreign country managers during these extended trips.

3. Executives and managers having difficulty progressing in all areas should be provided opportunities for developing the areas they are lacking in. In fact, such opportunities could be provided for managers of all levels to develop a variety of international behaviors. This would help to ensure that a substantial cadre of managers is being developed for future executive level staff positions. In particular, training on gathering global information and implementing international strategy should be provided early in the careers of junior executives and middle managers to ensure that these behaviors are firmly instilled for later access at higher levels. Junior-level executives should also be given opportunities to practice strategy development, as these skills will be required when they reach the senior ranks.

## Recommendations to Human Resources Department Professionals

1. Human Resource Development professionals should be especially cognizant of identifying

elements for selecting such high-potential managers slated for executive positions. One tool that appears to be quite promising in developing international behaviors among managers and executives appears to be taking part in expatriate assignments.

2. Opportunities for taking part in expatriate assignments should be provided to all high potential managers to solidify the career background of such individuals. Expatriate experiences appear to be particularly effective in developing some of the personal traits and characteristics required of executives managing in multinational organizations. However, such assignments need to be more systematically implemented by Human Resource Department (HRD) professionals. Indeed, a method for systematically implementing expatriate assignments as a tool for building international competencies for a broad variety of managers needs to be developed. However, HRD professionals should be careful in how they go about offering expatriate assignments to prospective managers.

3. The offer of an expatriate assignment could very well be a test for personal and professional flexibility. It should be made clear that expatriate assignments are a mandatory requirement for promotion to the highest levels of multinational organizations. However, the decision to take part in such a developmental experience should not be forced onto prospective managers. Allowing managers to self-select with very little or no pressure could help to screen out individuals who are not as flexible. In this manner, self-selection could serve as a simple, yet effective, screening mechanism. Finally, expatriate experiences should not be unique experiences for those lucky enough to attain in international assignment.

4. Expatriate assignments should be a tool

international competencies among the cadre of managers earmarked for promotion to the highest levels of organization. Expatriate assignments could become a programmatic intervention for the development of upper-level managers within the multinational organization. Having international experience would be the norm for promotion into the highest levels of American multinational organizations. Indeed, it could be argued that a system providing opportunities for all managers to obtain international competencies should be developed.

5. Managers of all levels should be exposed early in their careers to provide sufficient time to develop as many of the behaviors as possible. This may prove to be impractical in large multinational companies where managerial positions exist that never interface with international operations. However, international competencies such as gathering global intelligence and improving cross-cultural could be developed in all managers. Providing cross-cultural training for all managers in the multinational corporation could be linked to diversity initiatives which have been found to be similar in learning outcomes as cross-cultural training interventions (Nelson, 1999; Wentling & Palma-Rivas, 1997). Such cross-cultural learning experiences should be provided early in a manager's career so that these critical behaviors are firmly instilled for later access at higher levels. Executives at the highest levels will need to be evaluated for their international expertise, as well.

6. Senior-level executives should be evaluated for their people-oriented skills. In particular, focusing on developing and maintaining close personal contacts with foreign area managers appears to be critical to success. These front-line contacts also appear to aid senior-level executive in developing and evaluating international business strategy.

As such, senior-level executives should be encouraged to visit field operations to keep abreast of the feasibility of implementing business strategies. Extended business trips to foreign operations help senior-level managers to stay in touch with the inner workings of the organization and may help to ensure growth within the executive corps. Additionally, such visits could develop competencies among foreign managerial staff.

7. Managers hired into foreign locations by American organizations have traditionally been provided with very few developmental interventions (Caudron, 1997). In many cases foreign managers are the products of exceptional educational experiences, often holding degrees from English speaking countries, rather than an internal development plan. These managers frequently represent the educational elite of their country and are hired purely because of their international educational experiences by a variety of multinational organizations, including American multinational enterprises (Caudron, 1997). Senior-level executives could help to develop these managers through frequent visits focusing on business development strategies.

8. Such foreign country managers could be rotated into U.S.-based headquarters positions for purposes of improving the international competencies of both the foreign country manager and the U.S.-based managerial staff. Such developmental interventions could lead help in the process of building multinational team and could represent an interesting developmental strategy for hospitality expatriate executives.

## Recommendations to Higher Education

1. Educational programs preparing students for work in international business should strive to expose students to all of the behavioral aspects of international business identified

in this study. However, such educational programs should strive to provide sound business fundamentals for all functional disciplines as technical/functional expertise is the basis of managerial success. Internationally-focused education personnel should strive to develop the knowledge and skill components of international business, especially helping students in learning to gather global information. Students should be given opportunities to practice strategic planning on international basis.

2. Perhaps a capstone course in strategic planning could serve to instill the importance of strategy formulation into students. Similarly, supervised internships with international corporations could be made available to students to begin to learn tactical applications of strategic plans. Such internships could also be beneficial in developing personal communication skills required to top managers. Cross-cultural knowledge and skills could be provided in a classroom setting and then applied through internationally focused internships. Such internships may prove difficult to obtain; however, the benefits of preparing appropriately and adequately prepared international managers would appear to be quite substantial to U.S. business. Internships would also help students to understand the importance of personal traits and characteristics in international business. While the importance of flexibility and receptiveness to new ideas and thoughts can be taught in a classroom setting, students cannot truly appreciate the importance of these areas unless they experience at least one international assignment.

## FUTURE RESEARCH DIRECTIONS

The following are future research opportunities about globalization or internationalization:

1. The current research focus into international success criteria appears indicative of managerial practice. The emphasis being given to cross-cultural knowledge, skills, attitudes, and traits should be continued as these types of behaviors appear very important to success in international business. Further explanation of the types of personal traits and characteristics that contribute the most to success would be helpful in selecting and developing U.S.-based internationally active managers.

2. A model for implementing expatriate assignments as a systematic managerial developmental tool needs to be developed. Research into the types of expatriate assignments that most efficiently or most effectively develop the behaviors described in this study would enable Human Resource Development professionals to customize such assignments for each potential manager.

3. This study used exploratory factor analysis. Another recommendation for further research is to use confirmatory factor analysis, and use bigger population and use chain hospitality companies as the research frame.

4. Additional recommendation for research is to explore leadership qualities of executives and managers from different cultural backgrounds. Hofstede (1980) suggested that there should be differences in executives and leadership styles that are attributable to cultural aspects. The focus of the study would be to develop a set of recommendations for hospitality industry based on the differences found among these global executives.

5. Research regarding national culture and organizational culture and its influences on the success of hospitality expatriate executives must be explored.

# CONCLUSION

## Background and Demographics

Senior-level executives and non-senior level managers that had experienced working at least once in their careers outside of their home country were included in this study. Respondents' email addresses were selected from the online directory of the International Hotel and Restaurant Association (IHRA). The majority of the respondents were between the ages of 51 to 60 years old, male, married and highly educated (most of them had graduate degree). They had prior overseas experience, had worked in the host country for six months and they worked in luxury hotel properties. A high percentage of no answer on the hotel category had been noted.

A reason for this may be that these respondents were consultants of several hotel properties. This is evident on the high education obtained. There was a broad variation in professional backgrounds, years of international experience, and expatriate assignments across the 70 respondents. The participants included in this study derived from a broad spectrum of functional backgrounds including general managers, consultants, Human Resources generalists, marketing managers, training and development specialists, food and beverage directors, front office directors, financial controllers, event managers, and scientists. It seemed that success in international assignments can be obtained through a variety of different career paths and functional disciplines.

## Important Management Skills

Respondents indicated that there were important management skills hospitality expatriate executives should possess. These important management skills were: Grasps on how all the parts of the organization fit together; Has the mental capacity to understand the overall workings of the organization and its environment; International negotiation skills; Get along with subordinates, peers, and those at higher levels of the organization; Views the organization in a holistic manner; Understanding international marketing; understanding international finance; Ability to work in international teams; Effectively receive ideas and information from others; and Effectively convey ideas and information to others. These suggest that expatriate executives should possess these skills in order for them to be successful in international settings or locations.

## Management Skills and National Culture

Management skills vary by the respondents' country of origin or national culture: For this study the variables that were statistically significant were: understanding international marketing; ability to work in international teams; grasps on how all the parts of the organization fit together; and views the organization in a holistic manner. This indicates that the ethnicity of an individual influences their management skills. The time is now ripe for considering new approaches to cross-cultural management. Well-known researchers in the field, notably Hofstede (2003), and his followers who undertook a global study on leadership, have developed cultural dimensions and typologies for classifying and differentiating countries across the globe. The functional value of such research efforts tends to get diluted by their extensive global sweep. If countries are indeed culturally distinguishable, can they usually compared against each other? Or are apples being compared to oranges? In other words, countries with high power distance scores can be so different from countries with low power distance scores that managers from the first type may not be able to work in the latter type and vice versa (Jacob, 2005).

There is a second problem associated with global sweep studies. A country with a high power index score comprises individuals who may have low scores as well. The rule may suggest that individuals from that country have high power distance scores. But a larger number of exceptions to that rule may exist. If exceptions to the rule are as numerous as the rule itself, can meaningful predictions based on that rule be made about individual managerial behavior? The answer is likely to be a resounding no (Littrell & Salas, 2007).

What needs to be done is to see the complex interplay between culture and management in terms of a constantly evolving dynamic, because both are constantly evolving. Others work with their emphasis on typologies and dimensions provide us with a static snapshot of a country's orientation. But how does it help to know that managers in Mexico have high power distance scores? Does it render them unfit to work in Sweden? Can the archetypical Chinese corporation CEO with his long-term orientation, be able to function effectively in a culturally antithetical country like America? The evidence is that he can. In which case, he is not a slave of his own cultural orientation as some typologies would have others believe. The orange is not an orange and the apple is not quite the apple after all (Littrell & Salas, 2007). Thus cultural boundaries need to be construed as permeable, rather than as walls which differentiate and segregate. Centuries ago, Alexander Pope had cautioned scholars that a little learning was a dangerous thing. To counter the damage that can be wrought by a little learning, researchers today should employ more robust methodology. Such methodology should resort to different approaches done at varying levels of analyses. Extensive individual surveys can be bolstered by organizational surveys, and then reinforces by case-studies. Most cross-cultural studies of note and repute have contended themselves with a single assessment approach.

Since there is no such thing as cultural purity, what needs to be emphasized is that countries have different cultural mixes and people tend to be hybrids who simultaneously hold membership in different cultural groups. Hence, what is of

the essence is that hybridization of management practices becomes more widespread. Hybrid management practices explicitly reflect the culturally heterogeneous context of countries. Thus, effective Swiss management practices may actually combine with the best features of Swiss-French and Swiss-Italian management. The actual combination will depend on the exigencies of the situation (Jacob, 2005).

## Management Skills and Corporate Culture

Management skills vary according to the culture of the parent company. This means that there is a difference on the management skills of executives based on the cultural practices of the parent company. The researcher concludes that understanding international finance; international negotiation skills; has the mental capacity to understand the overall workings of the organization and its environment; and grasps on how all the parts of the organization fit together vary by the respondents' location of the parent company which means that Australia, China, India, Middle East, Switzerland, Thailand and United States differ on their level of: understanding international finance, international negotiation skills, understand the overall workings of the organization and its environment and how all the parts of the organization fit together. This suggests that parent companies follow their own organizational culture and they want their child companies to adhere to this.

## REFERENCES

Adler, N. J. (1997a). Global leaders: A dialogue with future history. *International Management, 1*(2), 21–33.

Adler, N. J., & Bartholomew, S. (1992). Managing globally competent people. *The Academy of Management Executive, 6*(3), 52–65. doi:10.5465/AME.1992.4274189

Allen, L. (1988). Working better with Japanese managers. *Academy of Management Review*, 77(11), 32–49.

Aschkenasy, J. (1997). Culture shock: Expatriate benefits are getting squeezed as companies tighten their belts. *International business, 10*(2), 20-27.

Barber, N., & Pittaway, L. (2000). Expatriate recruitment in South East Asia: Dilemma or opportunity? *International Journal of Contemporary Hospitality, 12*(6), 352–359. doi:10.1108/09596110010343530

Black, J. S., Gregersen, H. B., & Mendenhall, M. (1992b). Toward a theoretical framework of repatriation adjustment. *Journal of International Business Studies, 23*(4), 737–760. doi:10.1057/palgrave.jibs.8490286

Black, J. S., Gregersen, H. B., & Mendenhall, M. E. (1992a). *Global assignments: Successfully expatriating and repatriating international managers.* San Francisco, CA: Jossey-Bass.

Black, J. S., Gregersen, H. B., Mendenhall, M. E., & Stroh, L. K. (1999). *Globalizing people through international assignments.* New York, NY: Addison-Wesley Longman.

Boyacigiller, N. (1990). The role of expatriates in the management of interdependence, complexity and risk in multinational corporations. *Journal of International Business Studies, 21*(3), 357–381. doi:10.1057/palgrave.jibs.8490825

Burns, P. M. (1997). Tourism's workforce: Characteristics and inter-cultural perspectives. *Tourism Recreation Research, 22*(1), 48–54. doi:10.1080/02508281.1997.11014785

Caudron, S. (1997). World-class execs. *Industry Week, 246*(22), 60–66.

Causin, G. G. (2007). *A Study to Examine the Preparation and Training of Hospitality Expatriate Executives.* Oklahoma State University. DAI Theses and Dissertations. Retrieved from http://dc.library.okstate.edu/utils/getfile/collection/Dissert/id/73340/filename/74031.pdf

Daniels, J. D., & Radebaugh, L. H. (1994). *International Business: Environments and operations.* Reading, MA: Addison-Wesley Publishing Company.

Deresky, H. (1994). *International management: Managing across borders and cultures.* New York: Harper Collins College Publishers.

Dotlich, D. L., & Noel, J. L. (1998). *Action learning: How the world's top companies are recreating their leaders and themselves.* San Francisco: Jossey-Bass.

Dowling, P., Schuler, R., & Welch, D. (1994). *International dimensions of human resources management* (2nd ed.). Belmont, CA: Wadsworth.

Dowling, P., & Welch, D. (1988). International human resource management: An Australian perspective. *Asia Pacific Journal of Management, 6*(1), 39–65. doi:10.1007/BF01732250

Frith, S. W. (1981). *The expatriate dilemma.* Chicago, IL: Nelson-Hall, Inc.

Geber, B. (1992). The care and breeding of global managers. *Training (New York, N.Y.), 29*(7), 32–37.

Gertsen, M. (1990). Intercultural competence and expatriates. *International Journal of Human Resource Management, 1*(3), 341–362. doi:10.1080/09585199000000054

Gliatis, N. (1992*). The management of expatriate executives in international hotel companies.* Doctoral dissertation. University of Surrey, Guildford.

Griffin, R. W. (2005). *Management* (8th ed.). New York: Houghton Mifflin Company.

Handy, L., & Barham, K. (1990). International management development in the 1990's. *Journal of European Industrial Training, 14*(6), 28–31.

Harris, W., & Moran, R. (1996). *Managing cultural differences: Leadership strategies for a new world* (4th ed.). Houston, TX: Gulf Publishing.

Harvey, M. (1997). Focusing the international personnel performance appraisal process. *Human Resource Development Quarterly, 8*(1), 41–62. doi:10.1002/hrdq.3920080106

Hendry, C. (1994). *Human resource strategies for international growth*. London: Routledge.

Hofstede, G. (1980). *Culture's consequences: International differences in work-related values*. Beverly Hills, CA: Sage.

Hofstede, G. (1991). *Cultures and organizations: Software of the mind*. London: McGraw-Hill.

Hofstede, G., & Bond, M. (1984). Hofstede's cultural dimensions: An independent validation using Rokeach's value survey. *Journal of Cross-Cultural Psychology, 15*(4), 417–433. doi:10.1177/0022002184015004003

Ioannou, L. (1995). Unnatural selection. *International Business, 8*(7), 53–57.

Jacob, N. (2005). Cross-cultural investigations: Emerging concepts. *Journal of Organizational Change Management, 18*(5), 514–528. doi:10.1108/09534810510614986

Kotter, J. (2012). *The key to changing organizational culture*. Retrieved from http://www.forbes.com/johnkotter/2012/09/27/the-key-to-changing-organizational-culture/

Li, L. (1995). *Antecedents and consequences of expatriate satisfaction: An empirical investigation of hotel managers in Pacific Asian countries*. (Doctoral dissertation). Virginia Polytechnic Institute and State University, USA.

Littrell, L. N., & Salas, E. (2005). A review of cross-cultural training: Best practices, guidelines, and research needs. *Human Resource Development Review, 4*(3), 305–334. doi:10.1177/1534484305278348

Marquardt, M. (1999). *The global advantage: How to improve performance through globalization*. Houston, TX: Gulf Publishing.

Marquardt, M., & Snyder, N. (1997). How companies go global: The role of the global integrators and the global mindset. *International Journal of Training and Development, 1*(2), 104–117. doi:10.1111/1468-2419.00011

McCall, M. W., & Hollenbeck, G. P. (2002). *Developing global executives: The lessons of international experience*. Boston, MA: Harvard Business School Press.

McGrath-Champ, S., & Yang, X. (2002). Cross cultural training, expatriate quality of life and venture performance. *Management Research News, 25*(8-10), 135.

Mendenhall, M. E. (1999). On the need for paradigmatic integration in international human resource management. *Management International Review, 39*(2), 1–23.

Mendenhall, M. E. (2000). New perspectives on expatriate adjustment and its relationship to global leadership development. In M. E. Mendenhall, T. M. Kuhlmann, & G. K. Stahl (Eds.), *Developing global leaders: Policies, processes, and innovations*. Westport, CT: Quorum Books.

Mendenhall, M. E., & Oddou, G. R. (1985). The dimensions of expatriate acculturation: A review. *Academy of Management Review, 10*, 39–47.

Nelson, E. M. (1999). *Internationally-focused managerial behaviors of executives working in large U.S. multinational corporations*. (Doctoral dissertation). University of Illinois at Urbana-Champaign.

Parker, B., Zeira, Y., & Hatem, T. (1996). International joint venture managers: Factors affecting personal success and organizational performance. *Journal of International Management, 2*(1), 1–29.

Powers, T. F. (1992). Managing international hospitality. *FIU Hospitality Journal, 2*, 25–34.

Robock, S. H., & Simmonds, K. (1983). *International business and multinational enterprises.* Homewood, IL: Richard D. Irwin, Inc.

Rothwell, W., & Kazanas, H. (1992). *Mastering the instructional design process: A systematic approach.* San Francisco: Jossey-Bass.

Ruddy, J. (1991). Patterns of hotel management development in South East Asia. *Hospitality Research Journal, 3*, 349–361.

Schuler, R., Fulkerson, J., & Dowling, P. (1992). An integrative framework of strategic international human resource management. *Human Resource Management, 30*(3), 365–392. doi:10.1002/hrm.3930300305

Schwandt, D. R., & Marquardt, M. J. (2000). *Organizational learning from world-class theories to global best practices.* Washington, D. C.: St. Lucie Press.

Scullion, H. (1991). Why companies prefer to use expatriates. *Human Resource Management, 23*, 41–44.

The Economist. (1997). The world in figures: The world in 1998. *Economist Publications*, 95-98.

Tung, R. L. (1981). Selection and training of personnel for overseas assignments. *The Columbia Journal of World Business, 16*, 68–78.

Tung, R. L. (1984). Strategic management of human resources in the multi-national enterprise. *Human Resource Management, 23*(2), 129–144. doi:10.1002/hrm.3930230204

Tung, R. L. (1987). Expatriate assignments: Enhancing success and minimizing failure. *The Academy of Management Executive, 1*(2), 117–125. doi:10.5465/AME.1987.4275826

Tung, R. L. (1988). *The new expatriates: Managing human resources abroad.* Cambridge, MA: Ballinger.

Watkins, M. (2013). *What is organizational culture?* Retrieved from http://blogs.hbr.org/2013/05/what-is-organizational-culture?

Welch, D. (1990). *The personnel variable in international business operations: A study of expatriate management in Australian companies.* (Doctoral dissertation). Monash University, Melbourne, Australia.

Wentling, R., & Palma-Rivas, N. (1997). *Diversity in the workplace series report #2: Current status and future trends of diversity initiatives in the workplace: Diversity expert's perspective.* Berkeley, CA: National Center for Research in Vocational Education.

West, R., & Turner, L. H. (2004). *Introducing communication theory: Analysis and application* (2nd ed.). USA: McGraw-Hill Companies.

## ADDITIONAL READING

Bennett, R., Aston, A., & Colquhoun, T. (2000). Cross-cultural training: A critical step in ensuring the success of international assignments. *Human Resource Management, 39*(2&3), 239–250. doi:10.1002/1099-050X(200022/23)39:2/3<239::AID-HRM12>3.0.CO;2-J

Bentley, R. (2007, January). It pays to be a cross-cultural vulture. *Personnel Today*, 28.

Causin, G. G., & Ayoun, B. (2011). Packing for the trip: A model of competencies for successful expatriate hospitality assignment. *International Journal of Hospitality Management, 30*(4), 795–802. doi:10.1016/j.ijhm.2010.12.011

Causin, G. G., Ayoun, B., & Moreo, P. J. (2011). Expatriation in the hotel industry: An exploratory study of management skills and cultural training. *International Journal of Contemporary Hospitality Management, 23*(7), 885–901. doi:10.1108/09596111111167515

Celaya, L., & Swift, J. S. (2006). Pre-departure cultural training: US managers in Mexico. *Cross Cultural Management: An International Journal, 13*(3), 230–243. doi:10.1108/13527600610683372

Chang, K., & Lu, L. (2007). Characteristics of organizational culture, stressors and wellbeing. *Journal of Managerial Psychology, 22*(6), 549–568. doi:10.1108/02683940710778431

Delle, E., & Mensah, M. E. (2013). The influence of national culture on expatriate work adjustment, intention to leave and organizational commitment. *European Journal of Business and Management, 5*(19), 62–68.

Friedman, P. A., Dyke, L. S., & Murphy, S. A. (2009). Expatriate adjustment from the inside out: An autoethnographic account. *International Journal of Human Resource Management, 20*(2), 252–268. doi:10.1080/09585190802670524

Gudmundsdottir, S. (2012). The influence of prior living and working experience of Nordic expatriates on cultural adjustment in the United States. *International Journal of Humanities and Social Science, 2*(19), 87–92.

Halsberger, A., & Brewster, C. (2009). Capital gains: Expatriate adjustment and the psychological contract in international careers. *Human Resource Management, 18*(3), 379–397.

Heijden, J. A. V., Engen, M. L., & Paauwe, J. (2009). Expatriate career support: Predicting turnover and performance. *International Journal of Human Resource Management, 20*(4), 831–845. doi:10.1080/09585190902770745

Hofstede, G. (1997). *Cultures and Organizations: Software of the mind*. New York: McGraw Hill.

Hu, B., Cai, L. A., & Kavanaugh, R. R. (2001). Chinese and British hotels: Cultural differences and management. *FIU Hospitality Journal*, 37-54.

Joshua-Gojer, A. E. (2012). Cross-cultural training and success versus failure of expatriates. *Learning and Performance Quarterly, 1*(2), 47–62.

Kriegl, U. (2000, April). International hospitality management: Identifying important skills and effective training. *The Cornell Hotel and Restaurant Administration Quarterly, 41*(2), 64–71. doi:10.1177/001088040004100218

Li, J., & Karakowsky, L.Li & Karakowsky. (2001). Do We See Eye-to-Eye? Implications of Cultural Differences for Cross-Cultural Management Research and Practice. *The Journal of Psychology, 135*(5), 501–517. doi:10.1080/00223980109603715

Littrell, L. N., Salas, E., Hess, K. P., Paley, M., & Riedel, S. (2007). Expatriate preparation: A critical analysis of 25 years of cross-cultural training research. *Human Resource Development Review, 5*(3), 355–388. doi:10.1177/1534484306290106

Liu, C. H., & Lee, H. W. (2008). A proposed model of expatriates in multinational corporations. *Cross Cultural Management, 15*(2), 176–193. doi:10.1108/13527600810870615

Lu, L. T. (2006). The influence of cultural factors on international human resource issues and international joint venture performance. *Journal of American Academy of Business, 10*(1), 192.

Muenjohn, N., & Armstrong, A. (2007). Transformational leadership: The influence of culture on the leadership behaviours of expatriate managers. *International Journal of Business and Information*, *2*(2), 265–283.

Osman-Gani, A. M., & Rockstuhl, T. (2009). Cross-cultural training, expatriate self-efficacy, and adjustments to overseas assignments: An empirical investigation of managers in Asia. *International Journal of Intercultural Relations*, *33*(4), 277–290. doi:10.1016/j.ijintrel.2009.02.003

Schaffer, R. A., & Rhee, J. H. (2005). Consider cost and strategy when choosing between expatriate and host - national managers. *Journal of Business and Management*, *11*(1), 59–71.

Selmer, J. (2007). Which is easier, adjusting to a similar or to a dissimilar culture? *International Journal of Cross Cultural Management*, *7*(2), 185–201. doi:10.1177/1470595807079385

Shay, J. P., & Baack, S. A. (2004). Expatriate assignment, adjustment and effectiveness: An empirical examination of the big picture. *Journal of International Business Studies*, *35*(3), 216–232. doi:10.1057/palgrave.jibs.8400081

Shay, J. P., & Baack, S. A. (2006). An empirical investigation of the relationships between modes and degree of expatriate adjustment and multiple measures of performance. *International Journal of Cross Cultural Management*, *6*(3), 225. doi:10.1177/1470595806070634

## KEY TERMS AND DEFINITIONS

**Collectivism:** A cultural value that places emphasis on the collective or group over the individual.

**Corporate Culture:** Refers to the shared values, attitudes, standards, and beliefs that characterize members of an organization and define its nature.

**Culture:** Is a way of life of a group of people--their behaviors, beliefs, values, and symbols that they accept and live by that are passed along by communication and imitation from one generation to the next.

**Expatriate:** An expatriate is defined as an employee who has spent at least once of his/her career working on temporary, short-term, long-term and/or semi-permanent assignments in overseas locations. It is a person who was not born in the country where he/she is working and does not hold the nationality of the country of his/her work environment. For this particular study expatriate referred to the executives, managers or the heads of various departments within a hotel facility located outside of his/her native country.

**Host Country:** The country that allows expatriate workers.

**Individualism:** A cultural value that places emphasis on the individual over the group.

**Management Skills:** Expertise of an expatriate executive in order to be successful to their host community or country. Examples are language skills and interpersonal skills.

**National Culture:** The set of norms, behaviors, beliefs and customs that exist within the population of a sovereign nation.

**Skills:** The ability of a person to do something well.

# Chapter 7
# The Impact of Exchange Rate on Tourism Industry:
## The Case of Turkey

**Meryem Samirkaş**
*Yuzuncuyil University, Turkey*

**Mustafa Can Samirkaş**
*Mersin University, Turkey*

## ABSTRACT

*Tourism sector that is increasingly important in the world economy, developing rapidly in Turkey and provides a serious contributions to country's economy because Turkey consistently has a current account deficit, tourism is an important source of income. There are many factors affecting tourism; it is clear that the industry can be affected by changes in macroeconomic variables, just like any other economic focus. In this context, it is possible that the foreign exchange rate and changes in the value of various currencies can affect tourism, especially with regards to the demands of the tourists themselves. By using the Johansen cointegration and Granger causality tests, this chapter focused on identifying the relationship between currency exchange rates and the demand for tourism in Turkey.*

## INTRODUCTION

Tourism, with the generating of commercial airline industry after the World War II and with the using of the technologies of jet aircraft which highly accelerates transportation in 1950s, has gained speed and grown up significantly. As of 1990s, it has become a vast sector that provides employment at most in the world. At present time, international tourism, both in terms of providing new occupation opportunities and being basis

of the exchange income in many countries, has become one of the primary points. From the 20th century, tourism sector with telecomunication and information technologies has become one of the most expanding sectors in the world economy. Moreover, it is, after the petrochemistry, the second largest sectors in the west and it is also among the first large three sectors in the world (Pınar, 2005).

According to the World Travel and Tourism Council (WTTC), tourism is one of the largest sectors in the world not only in the sense of gross

DOI: 10.4018/978-1-4666-8606-9.ch007

production scope, employment, tax contribution but also capital investment and value-added (Aslan, 2008). While the world tourism revenue was $2.1 billion in 1950, it increased to $1.075 billion in 2012. It was also same for the number of tourists. Whereas 25.3 million people participated in tourism circulation in 1950, this number reached to 1.035 million people in 2012 (UNWTO, 2013).

Although the tourism industry has several important dimensions—historical, social and cultural—it is foremost a social activity which is most important when considered as an economic variable. From the economic perspective, the tourism industry's foreign exchange earnings, encouragement of foreign capital investment, employment, and economic growth and development effects make it one of the most important industries for any country. Particularly, the development of international tourism has some advantages for developing countries in terms of needed foreign currency (foreign exchange) and increasing revenues. Tourism is a constantly growing source of commerce, and the market is relatively less stable or reliable when compared other major industries such as manufacturing or the production of basic commodities. In addition, the tourism market necessarily requires that consumers themselves must travel to the source of the goods or services they wish to consume: the products of or utility derived from the act of partaking in tourism cannot be delivered to the customer. Therefore, it is a more effective import substitution. Finally, for many countries, a strong tourist sector means both diversification of the economy and a reduction of the dependence on traditional exports (Samırkaş & Bahar, 2013).

The tourism sector in Turkey demonstrated rapid development, especially after the 1980s. One of the most powerful steps taken to foster this growth was the introduction of "Tourism Incentive Law No. 2634," which came into force in 1982 (Tosun, 1999). The law incentivised investments made in the country's tourism sector and was an important step for the development of the industry in Turkey.

In 1980 a total of 778 facilities were registered as certified tourism businesses, with 42,011 rooms and 82,332 beds available to guests. By the year 2012, investment had raised those numbers 3,830 facilities, 463,039 rooms, and 979,896 beds. As a direct result of these developments, the country has seen a dramatic rise in the number of visitors and associated tourist revenue. In 1970, only 754 thousand tourists came to Turkey. In contrast, 1.2 million visited in 1980 and 35 million visited in 2013. Alongside these increased visitor numbers, tourist revenues of 1970 measuring US$51.6 million rose to US$326.7 million in 1980—an increase of approximately six and a half times—and had become US$32 billion by 2013 (Ministry of Tourism, 2013). These Tables demonstrate that the tourist market in Turkey continued to grow even after 1980.

In Turkey, which suffers a constant negative balance of trade, tourist revenue assumes a very important role in eliminating the trade deficit—in other words, ensuring the current account balance. As seen in Table 1, the deficit in Turkey's balance of international payments has been a problem for many years. At the beginning of planned development period, Turkey aimed to reduce the deficit in the country's balance of payments through growth in tourist revenues and tourism development.

Factors affecting the number of visitors to the country can be generally sorted into the following categories: number of available tourist facilities, global economic development, prices of tourist-oriented products and services, and exchange rates. Currency exchange rates in particular have significance due to their ability to represent tourist-oriented product and service prices for foreign tourists visiting the country (Uğuz & Topbaş, 2011). The ability of any improvement in the exchange rates to be effective in stimulating tourism depends on the capacity of that country to compete in the global tourism market.

*Table 1. Foreign Trade Deficit of Turkey's Tourism Revenue Share in Closure*

| Years | Balance of Trade (Million $) | Tourism (Million $) | Foreign Trade Deficit Share of Tourism in Closure (%) |
|---|---|---|---|
| 1985 | -2,976 | 770 | 25.9 |
| 1990 | -9,448 | 2,705 | 28.6 |
| 1995 | -13,152 | 4,046 | 30.8 |
| 2000 | -21,959 | 5,925 | 27.0 |
| 2001 | -4,543 | 8,328 | 183.3 |
| 2002 | -7,283 | 10,021 | 137.5 |
| 2003 | -14,010 | 11,090 | 79.2 |
| 2004 | -23,878 | 13,364 | 56.0 |
| 2005 | -33,530 | 15,83 | 46.0 |
| 2006 | -40,941 | 14,109 | 34.4 |
| 2007 | -46,661 | 15,227 | 33.0 |
| 2008 | -63,429 | 18,405 | 29.0 |
| 2009 | -38,730 | 17,103 | 44.1 |
| 2010 | -71,661 | 16,083 | 22.4 |
| 2011 | -105,934 | 18,044 | 17.0 |
| 2012 | -84,066 | 24,414 | 29.0 |
| 2013 | -99,843 | 27,078 | 27.1 |

Source: turizm.gov.tr; tuik.gov.tr

Turkey readily demonstrates its ability to meet the demands of this market; in response to any fall in exchange rates, the number of foreigners visiting the country climbs—and so does the demand for tourist services. The competitiveness of Turkey's tourist sector stems from the reality that there are a number of national, natural, geographical, and cultural characteristics that cannot be substituted with or provided by other countries. These features provide Turkey with a significant competitive advantage compared with other countries seeking tourist revenues (Demirel et al., 2008).

This chapter examines the impact that transformations in real exchange rates have on the number of tourists visiting Turkey. The chapter is described in four sections. Following the introduction is a literature review. The third section contains the model used to study the phenomena at hand and includes all the relevant data gathered. This section also introduces and analyses these results. The final section of the paper summarizes and evaluates the results.

## LITERATURE REVIEW

Principal studies that examine the relationship between exchange rates and tourist statistics that are utilized in this chapter can be summarized briefly as follows: first, Crouch (1994) relates a study which finds that the exchange rate can either positively or negatively affect tourism and that the exchange rate can be used to estimate the demand for tourism in a given country. Sinclair & Stabler (1997) suggest tourists take the exchange rate into account when choosing which locations to visit and that an enforced low exchange rate regime could promote the growth of tourism even when information about relative money values is limited.

Eugenio-Martin & Morales (2004) attempted to explain the relationship between economic growth and tourism revenues between 1985 and 1998 in Latin America with Panel Data Analysis. Their study proposes that there is little connection between tourist revenues, foreign exchange rates, and purchasing power parity.

Gallego et al. (2007), examine the exchange rates effects on international tourism. Covering ten years, from the beginning of 1995 to the end of 2004, Gallego et al. consider important tourism destinations in a total of sixty countries—thirty of which are OECD countries—and attempt to construct a weighted conventional (gravity) model using tourism and exchange data. They find that less flexible exchange rates serve to stimulate tourism mobility and that a fixed exchange rate has a positive impact on tourism.

Demirel, Bozdağ & İnci (2008) analysed the impact of fluctuations in exchange rates on the number of tourists visiting Turkey from the United States of America, Germany, France, and the United Kingdom. According to the results of their study, the increase or decrease in the number of tourists in response to fluctuations in currency exchange rates is quite high. When analysing the effect of a change in the real value of foreign currencies against the Turkish Lira, they find that there is a delayed effect on the number of tourists visiting from the United States, no effect on the number of tourists visiting from Germany, and an immediate and significant effect on the number of tourists arriving from Britain and France. A change in the real exchange rate has a negative impact on the number of tourists visiting. With the exception of France, there is no evidence that uncertainty itself about the real exchange rate has any effect on the number of tourists entering the country.

Uğuz & Topbaş (2011) examine the relationship between the exchange rate and the tourism industry in Turkey, referencing monthly tourist arrivals and exchange rate data for the twenty years between 1990 and 2010. The study highlights that the monthly exchange rate volatility for the period was identified with the use of EGARCH model, and that exchange rate volatility and tourism demand was studied within the framework of a Johansen cointegration analysis. According to the findings, there is a statistically significant relationship between tourist demand and the exchange rate volatility, in the long term.

Yap (2012) uses the multivariate conditional volatility regression model to examine the effect that the exchange rate volatility had on the number of tourists entering Australia. In this chapter covering January 1991 to January 2011, Yap measured tourist numbers for visitors to the country coming from China, India, Japan, Malaysia, New Zealand, Singapore, South Korea, the United Kingdom, and the United States of America, and several others. According to the findings, Malaysia New Zealand are more sensitive than others to fluctuations in exchange rates. However, a change in the value of the dollar in Australia does not adversely affect the Australian tourist industry in the long term.

## DATA, METHOD, AND ANALYSIS

As evidenced by many studies, tourist revenues are a source of support to economic development for Turkey (Bahar, 2006; Çetintaş & Bektaş, 2008; Alper, 2008). As a result, it can be said that the industry is very important for developing countries like Turkey. Many countries implement various tourism policies with the intent of stimulating tourism income by increasing tourist demand. Undoubtedly, there are many factors affecting the demand for these services. Primary factors can include the country's tourism potential as well as tastes, desires, and preferences of the visitors themselves. It is also possible that foreign exchange rates and fluctuations in the value of any given currency can affect the demand for tourism. It is a reasonable assumption that most tourists are aware of exchange rates when making travel decisions and that they therefore make travel decisions based on the movement of currencies. This assumption has led to exchange rates becoming one of the prime determinants used for estimating international tourism demand (Yap, 2012). In this chapter, we try to determine if there actually is a significant relationship between tourism demand and rate of currency exchange.

A time series data is used to define a relationship between exchange rate and tourism demand. Many macroeconomic time series contain unit roots dominated by stochastic trends developed by Nelson & Plosser (1982). Unit roots are important in examining the stationary of a time series because a non-stationary regressor invalidates many standard empirical results (Dritsakis, 2008). If standard regression techniques are applied to non-stationary data, the end result could be a regression that looks good under standard measures (significant coefficient estimates and high $R^2$), but which is ultimately valueless. Such a model would be termed a "spurious regression" (Brooks, 2008). The presence of a stochastic trend is determined by testing the presence of unit roots in time series data. In this chapter, Augmented Dickey-Fuller (ADF) and Phillips-Perron unit root test are used for testing to the series' stationarity. According to the unit root tests results, we tried to find cointegration relations for the non-stationary series groups which are stationary after first difference.

The notion of cointegration was first introduced by Granger (1981) and Granger & Weiss (1983). It was further extended and formalised by Engle & Granger (1987). Cointegration describes the existence of an equilibrium or stationary relationship among two or more time series, each of which is individually non-stationary. The advantage of the co-integration approach is that it allows integration of the long-run and short-run relationships between variables within a unified framework (Narayan, 2003). If the time series (variables) are non-stationary in their levels, they can be integrated with integration of order 1

when their first differences are stationary. These variables can be cointegrated as well, if there are one or more linear combinations among the variables that are stationary. If these variables are being cointegrated, then there is a constant long-run linear relationship among them (Dritsakis, 2008). We use Johansen's maximum eigenvalue and trace tests to defining cointegration relation between foreign exchange and tourism demand for the integrated order one (I(1)) series. Johansen's procedure builds cointegrated variables directly on maximum likelihood estimation instead of relying on OLS estimation. This procedure relies heavily on the relationship between the rank of a matrix and its characteristic roots. Johansen derived the maximum likelihood estimation using sequential tests for determining the number of cointegrating vectors. We use this procedure to test for the existence of cointegrating relationships between series group.

Cointegration analysis gives an account of whether there is a long-run relationship or not; however, it does not explain the direction of the relationship. Granger causality developed by Engle & Granger (1987), based on error correction model, enables us to explain the direction of the relationship. We used the Granger causality test for explaining the direct relationship between foreign exchange rate and tourism demand.

We examine the relationship between tourism and foreign exchange rates in two stages. First we define the association between tourists' expenditure abroad and exchange rate. We have chosen the average tourism revenue per tourist (PERT) and real effective exchange rate index (REX) as data for the 2003Q1 - 2013Q4 period. The data on exchange rates was obtained from Central Bank of the Republic of Turkey and average tourism revenue per tourist was obtained from Turkish Statistical Institute. During the second stage we tried to find relationship between the foreign currency exchange rate and demand for tourism. We have created three basic groups according to major currencies for the January 2003 - December 2013

*Table 2. Unit Root Tests Results*

| Variables | Level/ First Difference | Augmented Dickey-Fuller (ADF) Test Statistic | | | | Result |
|---|---|---|---|---|---|---|
| | | Intercept | Prob | Trend and Intercept | Prob | |
| REX | Level | -2.935557 | 0.0497** | -2.607801 | 0.2790 | **I(1)** |
| | First Difference | -6.743114 | 0.0000* | -5.803222 | 0.0002* | I(0) |
| PERT | Level | -2.016610 | 0.2788 | -1.975042 | 0.5958 | **I(1)** |
| | First Difference | 0.0136 | 0.0136** | -3.626205 | 0.0407** | I(0) |

*Significant at the 5% level. **Significant at the 10% level.

period. Selected as data were the United States Dollar and tourist arrivals from USA, the Euro (EURO) and tourist arrivals from Germany, the British Pound (GBP) and tourist arrivals from United Kingdom. Tourist numbers was obtained from Turkish Statistical Institute. Series are seasonally adjusted. All rates are expressed in real terms using the equation 1.

$$REX = NEX \left( \frac{CPI_f}{CPI_d} \right) \qquad (1)$$

REX express real exchange rate, $CPI_f$ is foreign country's consumer price index; $CPI_d$ is Turkey's consumer price index, and NEX is nominal exchange rate.

Relationship between Foreign Exchange Rate (REX) and Revenue per Tourist (PERT)

The first order of business is to investigate whether the REX and PERT series are stationary. ADF unit root test is used to test a series'

stationarity. The findings of the unit root tests can be found in Table 2. The series in Table 2 are checked based on intercept, intercept and trend, and the results vary according to the implications of these characteristics for the choice of intercept and trend in the unit root test regression. Neither series is stationary at level, but for the model of the first difference, the series is stationary.

If the time series are nonstationary in their levels, they can be integrated with integration of order one (I(1)), when their first differences are stationary. These variables can be cointegrated and it is possible for them to exhibit a long-run linear relationship. Since it has been determined that the variables under examination are integrated of order one (I(1)), the cointegration test is performed. The testing hypothesis is the null of non-cointegration against the alternative that is the existence of cointegration. Johansen cointegration test is used for testing series' cointegration relation.

The finding of the cointegration test is that cointegration exists between real exchange rate

*Table 3. Johansen Cointegration Results*

| Null Hypothesis | Trace Test | Prob | Result | Null Hypothesis | Maximal Eigenvalue Test | Prob. | Result |
|---|---|---|---|---|---|---|---|
| $r \leq 0$ | 20.11119 | 0.0094 | Reject $H_0$ | $r=0$ | 14.78320 | 0.0414 | Reject $H_0$ |
| $r \leq 1$ | 5.327981 | 0.0210 | Reject $H_0$ | $r=0$ | 5.327981 | 0.0210 | Reject $H_0$ |

**Note**: $r$ is the number of the cointegrating vectors. * Indicates that at 5% level of significance, the null hypothesis, saying that there is no cointegration relationship between variables is not accepted. Critical values vary based on trend, intercept. A lag of r=1 for VAR was selected before Johansen cointegration test.

*Table 4. Granger Causality Test Results*

| | | F-Sta. | Prob. | Result |
|---|---|---|---|---|
| $H_0$ Hypothesis | PERT does not Granger Cause REX. | 5.08211 | 0.0299 | Rejected |
| Alternative Hypothesis | PERT does Granger Cause REX. | | | Accepted |
| $H_0$ Hypothesis | REX does not Granger Cause PERT. | 0.49733 | 0.4849 | Accepted |
| Alternative Hypothesis | REX does Granger Cause PERT. | | | Rejected |

* A lag of r=1 for VAR was selected before Granger Causality Test.

and tourism revenue per tourist. It means that there is significant long-run relation between the two variables. To explain the direction of this relation, we used the Granger causality test, and the results are presented in Table 4.

According to Granger causality test results, although real exchange rate does not affect tourism revenue per tourist, tourism revenue per tourist is affected by the real exchange rate of Turkey.

## RELATIONSHIP BETWEEN FOREIGN EXCHANGE RATE AND TOURISM DEMAND

We sought to discover whether there was a relationship between the foreign exchange rate and tourism demand by analysing our data through with a Johansen cointegration test and a Granger causality test. We created three basic groups according to major currency for the January 2002

- December 2013 period. Selected as data were the United States Dollar and tourist arrivals from USA, the Euro (EURO) and tourist arrivals from Germany, the British Pound (GBP) and tourist arrivals from United Kingdom (see Table 5).

First we examined whether all of the groups' series were stationary. An ADF unit root test is used for testing series' stationarity. The findings of the unit root tests can be found in Table 6.

The series in Table 5 are checked based on intercept, intercept and trend, and the results vary according to the implications of these characteristics for the choice of intercept and intercept and trend in the unit root test regression. The unit root test result shows that Germany and USD series are stationary at level and the other series are not stationary at level, but for the model of the first difference, the series is stationary. For cointegration using Johansen methods, all the series have to be integrated of the same order as (I(1)). Thus, we search cointegration relation

*Table 5.*

| | Variable | Description |
|---|---|---|
| Group 1 | GERMANY | Tourist number arrive from Germany to Turkey |
| | EURO | Real Exchange rate of Euro (Turkish Lira/Euro) |
| Group 2 | UK | Tourist number arrive from the UK to Turkey |
| | GBP | Real Exchange rate of British Pound (Turkish Lira/GBP) |
| Group 3 | USA | Tourist number arrive from the USA to Turkey |
| | USD | Real Exchange rate of USD (Turkish Lira/USD) |

*Table 6. ADF Unit Root Tests Results*

| Variables | Level/First Difference | Augmented Dickey-Fuller (ADF) test statistic | | | | |
|---|---|---|---|---|---|---|
| | | Intercept | Prob | Trend and Intercept | Prob | Result |
| GERMANY | Level | -4.070329 | 0.0015* | -4.053770 | 0.0091* | I(0) |
| | First Difference | - | - | - | - | - |
| EURO | Level | -2.376140 | 0.1503 | -2.322787 | 0.4186 | **I(1)** |
| | First Difference | -10.68180 | 0.0000* | -10.67837 | 0.0000* | I(0) |
| UK | Level | -1.637715 | 0.4607 | -1.545223 | 0.8092 | **I(1)** |
| | First Difference | -13.27932 | 0.0000* | -13.34425 | 0.0000* | I(0) |
| GBP | Level | -2.138640 | 0.2301 | -2.810538 | 0.1961 | **I(1)** |
| | First Difference | -8.924613 | 0.0000* | -8.932037 | 0.0000* | I(0) |
| USA | Level | -1.285234 | 0.6354 | -4.182122 | 0.0061* | **I(1)** |
| | First Difference | -10.52484 | 0.0000* | -10.51703 | 0.0000* | I(0) |
| USD | Level | -3.502667 | 0.0093* | -3.532581 | 0.0397** | I(0) |
| | First Difference | - | - | - | - | - |

*Significant at the 5% level. **Significant at the 10% level.

only for Group 2 (UK and GBP). The results of Group 2 Johansen cointegration test results are summarized in Table 7.

Trace and Max-eigenvalue test indicates one cointegrating vector at the 5% level of significance. The finding of the cointegration test is that cointegration exists among GBP exchange rate and the number of tourists arriving from the United Kingdom. It means that there is significant long-run relation between the two variables. To explain the direction of this relation, we used the Granger causality test. The results of this test can be found in Table 8.

According to the Granger causality test results, the exchange rate of TL to GBP is not affected by the number of tourists from the United Kingdom that visit Turkey. However, the number of tourists from the United Kingdom who visit Turkey is affected by the exchange rate of TL to GBP.

We also use Granger causality test for the other groups, which are not integrated at the same level, after making them stationary. The results of these tests are summarized in Table 9.

The Granger Causality tests of $H_0$ hypothesises are accepted for Group 1 and Group 3. It means there is no relationship between the exchange rate of the Euro to TL and the number of tourists from Germany who arrive in Turkey as well as there being no relationship between exchange rate of USD to TL and the number of tourists from the United States of America who arrive in Turkey.

## CONCLUSION

Based on the results of previous studies, it is assumed that tourism revenue supports to economic development for Turkey (Bahar, 2006; Çetintaş & Bektaş, 2008; Alper, 2008). Many countries implement various tourism policies with the intent of stimulating tourism income by increasing tourist demand. Undoubtedly there are many factors affecting the demand for these services. Primary factors can include the country's tourism potential as well as tastes, desires, and preferences of the visitors themselves. It is also possible that foreign

*Table 7. Johansen Cointegration Results for UK and GBP*

| Null Hypothesis | Trace Test | Prob. | Result | Null Hypothesis | Maximal Eigenvalue Test | Prob. | Result |
|---|---|---|---|---|---|---|---|
| $r \leq 0$ | 17.96695 | 0.0208 | Reject $H_0$ | $r=0$ | 15.23468 | 0.0350 | Reject $H_0$ |
| $r \leq 1$ | 0.0208 | 0.0983 | Not Reject $H_0$ | $r=1$ | 2.732266 | 0.0983 | Not Reject $H_0$ |

**Note**: $r$ is the number of the cointegrating vectors. * Indicates that at 5% level of significance, the null hypothesis, saying that there is no cointegration relationship between variables, is not accepted. Critical values vary based on trend and intercept. A lag of r=2 for VAR was selected before Johansen cointegration test.

*Table 8. Granger Causality Test Results for UK and GBP*

| | | F-Sta. | Prob. | Result |
|---|---|---|---|---|
| $H_0$ Hypothesis | UK does not Granger Cause GBP | 3.77391 | 0.0254 | Rejected |
| Alternative Hypothesis | UK does Granger Cause GBP | | | Accepted |
| $H_0$ Hypothesis | GBP does not Granger Cause UK | 0.96608 | 0.3831 | Accepted |
| Alternative Hypothesis | GBP does Granger Cause UK | | | Rejected |

* Lag length chosen using an SC information criterion as 2 before Granger Causality Test.

*Table 9. Granger Causality Test Results for Group 1 (GERMANY and EURO) and Group 3 (USA and USD)*

| | | | F-Sta. | Prob. | Result |
|---|---|---|---|---|---|
| Group 1 | $H_0$ Hypothesis | GERMANY does not Granger Cause EURO | 0.73062 | 0.5355 | Accepted |
| | Alternative Hypothesis | GERMANY does Granger Cause EURO | | | Rejected |
| | $H_0$ Hypothesis | EURO does not Granger Cause GERMANY | 0.24046 | 0.8680 | Accepted |
| | Alternative Hypothesis | EURO does Granger Cause GERMANY | | | Rejected |
| Group 3 | $H_0$ Hypothesis | USA does not Granger Cause USD | 0.00382 | 0.9508 | Accepted |
| | Alternative Hypothesis | USA does Granger Cause USD | | | Rejected |
| | $H_0$ Hypothesis | USD does not Granger Cause USA | 0.18661 | 0.6664 | Accepted |
| | Alternative Hypothesis | USD does Granger Cause USA | | | Rejected |

* Lag length 3 for group 1, 1 for group 2. Chosen by using an SC and HQ information criterions.

exchange rates and fluctuations in the value of any given currency can affect the demand for tourism.

This chapter focused on real exchange rates and tourist numbers, which represent tourism demand. Initially we attempted to answer the question about whether there is any relationship between real currency exchange rates and tourism revenue per tourist by using Johansen Cointegration and Granger causality tests. Results showed that revenue per tourist and real exchange rates have significant cointegrate relationship in the long-run. They also have a causal relation; real currency exchange rates have an effect upon where visitors arriving in Turkey originate. Our tests show that tourism revenue per person can be one of the determinants of exchange rate policy for Turkey.

As well, this chapter answers the question of whether the real exchange rates have an impact on the number of tourists arriving in Turkey from the United States of America, Germany and the United Kingdom. According to our analysis, there is no significant relation between exchange rate of Euro and number of tourists arriving from Germany and exchange rate of USD and number of tourist arriving from United States of America. However, there is significant cointagrate relation between exchange rate of GBP and number of tourists arriving from United Kingdom. In addition, there is a causal relation: the exchange rate of GBP and TL has affected the number of tourists from the United Kingdom who visit Turkey.

Thus we have demonstrated that there is no significant relationship between the number of tourists from Germany and the United States of America visiting Turkey and the real exchange rate between these tourists' own currency and that of Turkey. There may possibly be many other determinants—such as quality of the products and services provided in Turkey and overall tourist satisfaction with these services—that affect the choice of the tourists from the aforementioned countries visiting Turkey.

While this may also be true for British tourists, British tourist numbers are definitely affected by the real exchange rate of their currency to ours. Test results show the real exchange rate affected both tourist revenue per tourist earned from British visitors and British tourist numbers themselves. This means that the number of British visitors and the money they bring to Turkey during their visits can be used as determinants of exchange rate policies for Turkey. This information should encourage additional policies aimed at increasing tourism demand in Turkey.

Tourism demand must be analyzed in detail to supplement further contribution to countries' economical welfare, to use sources in an efficient and productive way and to rise the income and the share of getting by tourism. The finding of the tourism demand and the factors affecting the demand make easier the preparation of further plans and policies. That's why, the tourism demand, especially in developing countries such as Turkey, is one of the paramount factors which provides an economical development and improvement. Main factor affecting the tourism demand with regards to economical perspective can be summarized as follows: one's level of income, level of price at destination, exchange rates and transportation cost. In this chapter, only the shifts in reel exchange on the effect of the tourism demand was analyzed. It's possible to enhance this chapter providing contribution to further studies by taking into consideration the other factors that impress the tourism demand and the changes in exchange rates.

# REFERENCES

Alper, A. (2008). Türkiye'de Ekonomik Büyüme ve Turizm İlişkisi Üzerine Ekonometrik Analiz. *Sosyal Bilimler Enstitüsü Dergisi, 24*, 1–11.

Aslan, A. (2008). Türkiye' de Ekonomik Büyüme ve Turizm İlişkisi Üzerine Ekonometrik Analiz. *Sosyal Bilimler Enstitüsü Dergisi,* Say:24 Yıl:2008/1, 1-11.

Bahar, O. (2006). Turizm Sektörünün Türkiye'nin Ekonomik Büyümesi Üzerindeki Etkisi: VAR Analizi Yaklaşımı. *C.B.Ü. Yönetim ve Ekonomi Dergisi, 13*(2), 137–150.

Brooks, C. (2008). *Introductory Econometrics for Finance* (2nd ed.). Cambridge, UK: Cambridge University Press. doi:10.1017/CBO9780511841644

*Central Bank of Turkish Republic.* (n.d.). Retrieved from http://www.tcmb.gov.tr

Çetintaş, H., & Bektaş, Ç. (2008). Türkiye'de Turizm ve Ekonomik Büyüme Arasındaki Kısa ve Uzun Dönemli İlişkiler. *Anatolia, 19*(1), 1–8.

Crouch, G. I. (1994). The Study of International Tourism Demand: A Review of Findings. *Journal of Travel Research, 33*(1), 12–23. doi:10.1177/004728759403300102

Demirel, B., Bozdağ, E. G., & Inci, A. G. (2008). *Döviz Kurlarındaki Dalgalanmaların Gelen Turist Sayısına Etkisi: Türkiye Örnegi.* Retrieved from: http://www.deu.edu.tr/userweb/iibf_kongre/dosyalar/demirel.pdf

Dritsakis, N. (2008). Immigration and Economic Growth: Further Evidence for Greece. *Applied Economics and Policy Analysis, 2*(1), 207–213.

Eugenio-Martin, J. L., Morales, N. M., & Scarpa, R. (2004). Tourism and Economic Growth in Latin American Countries: A Panel Data Approach. *Nota di Lavoro, 26.*

Gallego, M. S., Ledesma-Rodriguez, F. J., & Perez- Rodriguez, J. V. (2007). *On the Impact of Exchange Rate Regimes on Tourism.* Retrieved from: http://www.aeefi.com/RePEc/pdf/defi07-07-final

Narayan, P. K. (2003). Tourism Demand Modelling: Some Issues Regarding Unit Roots, Cointegration and Diagnostic Tests. *International Journal of Tourism Research, 5*(5), 369–380. doi:10.1002/jtr.440

Pınar, İ. (2005). İzmir İli İçin Turizmin Yeri ve Geliştirme Örneği. *Yönetim ve Ekonomi, 12*(1), 47–60.

*Republic Of Turkey Ministry Of Culture And Tourism.* (n.d.). Retrieved from http: //www.turizm.gov.tr

Samırkaş, M., & Bahar, O. (2013). *Turizm, Yoksulluk ve Bölgesel Gelişmişlik Farklılıkları.* Ankara, Turkey: Detay Yayıncılık.

Tosun, C. (1999). An Analysis of the Economic Contribution of Inbound International Tourism in Turkey. *Tourism Economics, 5*(3), 217–250.

*Turkish Statistical Institute.* (n.d.). Retrieved from http://www.tuik.gov.tr

Uğuz, S. Ç., & Topbaş, F. (2011). *Döviz Kuru Oynaklığı Turizm Talebi İlişkisi: 1990-2010 Türkiye Örneği.* Paper presented at EconAnadolu 2011: Anadolu International Conference in Economics II, Eskisehir, Turkey.

UNWTO. (2013). *Tourism Highlights.* Madrid, Spain: UNWTO.

Yap, G. C. L. (2012). An Examination of the Effects of Exchange Rates on Australia's Inbound Tourism Growth: A Multivariate Conditional Volatility Approach. *International Journal of Business Studies, 20*(1), 111-132.

## KEY TERMS AND DEFINITIONS

**Balance of Trade:** The difference between a country's imports and its exports.

**Causality:** Causality is the relation between a cause and its effect or between regularly correlated events or phenomena.

**Cointegration:** Is an econometric technique for testing the correlation between non-stationary time series variables.

**Exchange Rate:** The price of one currency expressed in terms of another currency.

**Real Exchange Rate:** The nominal exchange rate adjusted for inflation.

**Tourism Demand:** Tourism demand is defined as the number of people that plan to buy tourism products supported by sufficient purchasing power and spare time in order to meet tourism needs of people.

**Tourism:** Tourism is a travel and accommodation event that is made as a consumer in order to meet tourists' needs in relation to the relaxation, entertainment, culture in a place outside the permanent inhabitation.

**Turkey:** Turkey is a developing country. Turkey, officially the Republic of Turkey, is located in Western Asia with the portion of Eastern Thrace in South-eastern.

# Chapter 8

# Local Resources to Compete in the Global Business:
## The Case of Sextantio Hotels

**Mario Tani**
*University of Naples Federico II, Italy*

**Ornella Papaluca**
*University of Naples Federico II, Italy*

## ABSTRACT

*This chapter analyzes the role of local area resources in the global hospitality market as a way for small and medium enterprises to create a portfolio of distinctive resources to reach a sustainable competitive advantage position in the international markets. After a brief introduction on the tourism industry and its main change factors the chapter adopts a resource base and market-driven approach in order to identify resources role in shaping competitive advantages. The chapter discuss a case-study on a successful example of diffused hotel in Abruzzo, Italy, identifying the core resources and those needed to support them in creating a successful tourism product.*

## INTRODUCTION

Today new technologies, not only web-based ones, have driven several markets to go global.

Tourism has been affected from this trend for several reasons. On one side the new transportation systems have made possible for tourists to travel easily, and cheaply too, all over the globe making even far away locations as viable *tourist destinations*; on the other hand, they can more easily access information on distant areas, and their attractions, and so tourists can satisfy their

crave to reach them in their journeys creating new opportunities for hospitality enterprises. Moreover as the culture becomes more global, the tourists needs across the world become more similar and hospitality services can be successful in attracting them.

On the other hand playing in a global markets makes the competition more dynamic and more intense as new players from all over the world can appear in the competitive landscape creating new, valuable offers for appealing the global tourist. So hospitality business have to continuously re-

DOI: 10.4018/978-1-4666-8606-9.ch008

invent their services in order to re-buff these new sources of competition and to be more appealing to these more volatile tourists' flows.

Another viable strategy these enterprises can try to exploit is to displace competitors leveraging the specific resources from their own local area, mainly traditional and cultural resources, that other enterprises in the other destination cannot easily copy. Building their strategies on these kind of resources helps hospitality businesses in succeeding in separating themselves from other similar services creating new market bubbles where the competitors potential of being a threat is very limited. This approach is coherent with a resource-based vision of the tourism product as these enterprises can exploit some valuable, rare inimitable and not easily substitutable resources as the source of their strategies' sustained competitive advantage.

One successful example of this different way to compete in the global markets can be found in the way Daniele Kihlgren has created Sextantio Hotels using a *process of sustainable development* in S. Stefano di Sessanio in Abruzzo (Italy) and leveraging it as a way to get a sustainable competitive advantage in the global market. Sextantio Hotels is a case of *diffused hotel*, a way to re-define hospitality services in small villages full of cultural and historical resources. In these villages hospitality entrepreneurs do not design their services in a single location but they embed them in various traditional buildings that are converted to rooms and flats.

We start this chapter with a presentation of tourism in the global market not only looking at his economic side but focusing on its social effects as well, later we present globalization and ICT as two of the main factors driving change in tourism industry and how they impact on the relationship between the local and the global resources in creating a tourism product.

The role of resources has been presented using a Resource-Based Theory perspective with the complementary approach of the Market-Driven Management as a way to identify those resources the enterprise needs to support the value creation processes.

In this chapter the case of Sextantio Hotels has been analyzed looking at it from the eyes of the main entrepreneurial actor, the founder Daniele Kihlgren, as a way to show how hospitality entrepreneurs can exploit local area inimitable, and difficult to substitute, resources as a way to build a successful offer in the global tourism markets that can be a source of a *sustainable development process* as well.

## BACKGROUND

This chapter theoretical background starts with the tourism and later focuses on strategic management literature.

### Tourism as an Economic and Social Phenomenon

Over the decades, tourism has become an industry characterized by continuous growth and an ever increasing, strong, diversification. As the concept of globalization has gone mainstream there have been several effects. On one side as ever growing number of locations, even those previously unknown or just ignored by tourist, have been considered as *tourist destinations*, or potential ones, on the other globalization has contributed to erode places *territorial identity* leading to a service standardization process that have aligned the different products, both sold and demanded (Seaton & Alford, 2005). Today tourism is closely linked to the society development processes and it is becoming fast one of the key factors in driving each nation's socio-economic progresses on a global scale (World Tourism Organization [UNWTO], 2014).

Today, tourism is valued as an ever more polycentric and wide-ranging activity. The pervasiveness of its manifestations, ranging from environment to culture, from arts to religions, along with several operators actively engaged in the travel and tourism industry have also helped to conceptualize tourism as a complex phenomenon (Rispoli & Tamma, 1996, Middleton, 2001; Della Corte, 2009), highlighting its dual nature: on one hand it is seen as an economic activity in terms of the "tourism industry", on the other one it is considered a social phenomenon (Desbiolles-Higgins, 2006), a part of the life's experiences (Pine & Gilmore, 1998).

Intending tourism as an economic activity (Saarinen, Rogerson, & Manwa, 2011) means above all to recognize how much it contributes to the growth of a society's economy. Tourism strongly influences diffusion of welfare practices and economic development in several countries (Candela & Figini, 2003). Moreover, traveling has been more and more considered as a consumption model by itself (Hazari & Sgro, 1995) occupying a prominent position among the purchasing decisions of most people, especially for those living in the most developed countries. The demand for holidays has been shaped in increasingly differentiated patterns of behavior in which the tastes of the tourists have a leading role in defining and customizing the various tourism products sold so that they can meet, and hopefully satisfy, tourists needs (Moutinho, 2011). The ability of businesses, organizations and territories to interact with the changing expectations in society and in the market, in fact, becomes a real competitive edge that can have a value precisely because of the importance of the tourism sector for the economy (Martini, 2013).

As reported by the UNWTO (2014), in fact, the international tourism expenditure has got a threefold increase the last twenty years making a significant contribution to world economy. According to the data of recent years, the tourism industry turnover in 2010 had been estimated at 9.1% of world GDP (corresponding to 5.657 billion U.S. dollars), employing a total of nearly 216 million workers all over the world (7.4% of

global workers employed) (Body, 2012; Vellas, 2012; World Travel & Tourism Council [WTTC], 2012). Even in 2013 tourism sector has grown ever more getting the record level of 1,087 million arrivals, a growth of 5% over the data found in the previous year (UNWTO, 2014) and employing a total of 12 to 14 million workers, of whom more than 2.3 million in the hospitality industry (Martini, 2013).

Besides having a profound economic connotation, tourism, however, is first and foremost a social phenomenon touching social life in many ways, such as division of labor, division of powers, migrations, habits and customs but even arts and traditions. Recent years trends have shown a wide variety of connotations - even if they are often still gathered in official statistical data under the label "other types of tourism" (Weaver, 2001) - accounting for several social processes that are at the origin of the practice, of the spatial transformations, of the many historical, cultural and social factors that it causes, without considering the various processes of regulation and government needed to manage them at the local area governmental level (Leotta, 2005).

Tourism, in fact, manifests itself primarily as a phenomenon of masses traveling and it is an event where different cultures meets, and sometimes merge (Gretzel, 2011). The motivation behind the choice of visiting a place for the tourist is often the desire to rediscover their authentic locations, values, and historical evidence (Pearce, 1982). Since no other type of economic phenomenon has the ability to affect so deeply and so wide-ranging society, much of the literature on the subject (Rojas & Turner, 2011; Giordana, 2004; Nash & Smith, 1991; Nunez, 1989) does not neglect the anthropological aspect of tourism, identifying it with the study of man and his behavior away from his daily environment (Smith, 2012). Tourism as a fact and a social force (Desbiolles-Higgins, 2006) is to assume such importance not only as a mirror of the society in which we live, but also as an indicator of the major changes that are so curring in it. This process helps to bring out the differences between the generations, between men and women, between members of the same family, formalizing innovative attitudes and behaviors, often motivated by the desire to define and assert their identity and distinguish it from that of others (Apostolopoulos, Leivadi, & Yiannakis, 2013). This perspective sees the journey as a research process going beyond mere observation - and, in this sense, it becomes a real life experience (Pine & Gilmore, 1998) - and that the formation of new social values is determined in the emergence of new fashions and trends (Uriely, 2005).

## EVOLUTIONARY PROCESSES IN THE MODERN GLOBAL TOURISM MARKETS

Beyond the evolutionary changes dictated primarily by the momentary trends (as, for example, the preference for exotic *destinations*), and by the habits of tourists (such as, for example, the growth of the short - break type of holidays) (Murphy, 2014), tourism industry, both on the demand and the supply sides, has also been changed by several structural forces linked to new technologies development, and diffusion, and by the emergence of the phenomenon also known as globalization (Martini, 2013).

The emergence of Internet and the development and dissemination of more and more pervasive technologies and the increase of their performance, have had far-reaching consequences on the evolutionary dynamics of the tourism industry. These forces has helped its growth in terms of quantity and has become themselves growth factors making a better tourists trip experience thanks to several new services he/she could be provided with to ensure more positive results for the travel (Stipanuk, 1993). With these tools, the most innovative tourism businesses have been able to redefine theirs organizational structure and their relationships with partners (Fesenmaier, Leppers,

& O'Leary 1999), achieving, at the same time, efficiency and effectiveness (Poon, 1993). However, if on the one hand the technologies and the development of the Internet channel has allowed the major tourism organizations to implement strategies for promotion, communication and low-cost distribution due to a continuous presence on the web (Martini, 2000), on the other hand they have driven the market behavior to change (Mills & Law, 2013), facilitating in fact only certain categories of actors in the field and benefiting the weakest part in the market: the tourist.

Internet, and the related mobile technologies, have contributed to change the destination search and selection processes by the user / traveler / navigator (Gursoy & McCleary, 2004), supporting the incessant birth of new do-it-on-your-own solutions and driving to a steep development of the On Line Travel Agencies at the expense of the more traditional tour packages assembled and sold by tour operators and travel agencies (Bonel, 2011).

Internet as a distribution channel and the use of the new technologies have brought about significant changes in terms of information availability and access (Della Corte & Sciarelli, 2003). The emergence of social networks (as Facebook, Twitter, but even the specialized ones as LinkedIn), coupled with the search engine advanced features and ease of use (see Google or Bing travel searches), and the development of tourism portals (TriVaGo, TripAdvisor or Booking.com) together with the widespread dissemination of smartphones, tablets, and other technological devices, are responding to that need for information that a tourist has when he chooses a destination or when he, or she, buys a specific tourist product (Feng & Cai, 2013). For example today tourists have the opportunity to go online to read other tourists reviews of the very same services and facilities they are looking for, they have the power to post and share their experiences, creating a virtuous circle representing a significant source of information and driving to create brand awareness and trust in a company (Di Vittorio, 2003).

ICT devices, however, not only allow easy access and dissemination of information on *tourist destinations* and services but they can be helpful to tourists in several phases of their holidays organization processes: the typical user / navigator can exploit these services to compare the different proposals, paying attention to the quality / price ratio of the products he is evaluating. The average user can look for getting, at the same time a good variety of choice and the best price. Upstream and downstream tourist products purchasing processes, when you factor in the effects of new technologies, are made easier on the web as the user can get access to a richer and more varied set of products and these technologies increase the number of reachable *destinations* more than ever before (and today the effect is strengthened by low cost travel companies), and for the greater autonomy of the user in building their own tourism package and the increasing willingness to transact online (Collesei, Casarin, & Vescovi, 2001).

If the development of technology and the diffusion of Internet have favored the disintermediation of the tourism industry making tourists and local tourist services providers nearer and nearer; on the other hand, the process of globalization has engaged global populations in a systematic and relentless way contributing to the broadening the scope of tourism and pushing millions of people to discover and explore more and more distant *destinations* (Hjalager, 2007; Wahab & Cooper, 2005). Though the two phenomena - the spread of the Internet and globalization - can be considered independently one from the other, in reality they interact and reinforce each other (Buhalis & Law, 2008). Globalization has had strong, and diversified, effects on the social, cultural, political, and economic life of the people around the globe and, like the spread of the Internet and information technology, is a phenomenon that has profoundly changed the structure of the tourism industry, bringing in positive and negative consequences.

Removing market barriers between countries and giving tourists the opportunity to find indi-

vidual deals for those *destinations* that were previously inaccessible without a specialized travel agent or tour operator, if considered together with the increased mobility of people, helped popularize the sense of adventure and quest of the unknown that was previously only present in some types of tourists (Plog, 1987), makes one feel as close to what in reality it is not (Dall'Ara, 2010).

At the same time, globalization has fostered the development of some sectors of the economy - first of all transport - encouraging investments in the creation of roads, railway lines and connections airports even in countries that previously lacked it by strengthening the process of making the various countries and populations nearer and easier to reach for.

Globalization, however, has also been the result of an unprecedented process of homogenization of behavior, tastes, fashions and trends (Yip, 1992; Whitla, Walters, & Davies, 2007) that has resulted in the reduction, if not the outright elimination of the differences between the various cultures. Globalization has often meant a gradual loss of national identities, traditions and culture resulting in a collapse of the cultural and social ties in different communities.

Globalization, finally, has stimulated a distinct change even in the competitive rules of the tourism market in the world in at least two different points of view (Cooper & Wahab, 2005). Above all the phenomenon of globalization has been a further boost to the business combination between the companies, despite this trend was already present and already strongly felt by organizations due to the characteristics of the specific fund. In the tourism sector, in fact, the strong degree of complementarity between the services composing a given tourism package, drive the organizations to continuously create relationships between different firms (Della Corte, 2000) in order to co-produce a global tourist package (Rispoli & Tamma, 1996) which, according to an *overlapping logic* (Casarin, 1996), can be used to identify the tourism package with the overall tourist experience (Pine & Gilmore, 1998). Moreover as in the large global markets business have to grow in order to stay competitive, cooperation has become a tool tour operators may use to face competition (Sciarelli, 2007) exploiting a greater critical mass (Bharwani & Butt, 2012; Burns, 2006), maintaining at the same time, adequate levels flexibility (Sciarelli, 1996).

Secondly, the removal of barriers between markets and the resulting increase in competition have led companies to focus on specialization in services. Tourism businesses are aware of the general weakening of their supply systems and they have become more attentive to changes in the market and they are asked to be ready to react quickly. Knowledge, reputation, brands, and, especially, human skills and organizational capabilities (the so-called intangibles) have become one of the main factors firms invest into in order to stay competitive in the market (Vidal Gonzàlez, 2008). For this reason modern tourism enterprises direct their efforts on training human resources in order to prepare and make available new skills compatible with the most innovative sectors of tourism and to activate the resources they can get access to - mainly those firm-specific - and trying to appear, from the point of view of the intangibles, more attractive than their competitors.

## GLOBAL AND LOCAL FACTORS IN TOURISM

Although the process of globalization in fact contributes more and more to erode the *cultural identity* of specific places and to homogenize the tourism products to appeal a broader audience (Ferrari & Adam, 2011) till they are often completely global without specific location based characteristics, tourism, in the more general sense, remains an activity that is based on the discovery and pursuit of what is different. The main pivots on which it rests, therefore, are always the authenticity of places, seen in their particular identity, and

the ability of the populations of those places to preserve and protect the existing elements of their cultural authenticity (Al Sayyad, 2013; Salazar, 2005; Kearney, 1995). This is also true if we consider a global market perspective. The global competition, in fact, must always be considered on at least two levels: at the first level we have the target and then we have the level of local operators. If it is true that all the players are competing on the same global chessboard and that the typical user / browser makes their own choices in order to minimize the trade - off between the quality and price of services he is looking for, it is also true that his rational assessments - of course within the limits of expenditure that he is willing to sacrifice and security levels he considers appropriate - may give rise to more instinctive buying decisions when, in the research phase, is particularly struck by the beauty of a place and the particularity that it offers or that he perceives, in a specific destination, a place where he, or she, can completely disconnect from everyday life.

Already the new types of tourism - often enclosed under the label of sustainable and responsible tourism - strongly support the search for authenticity and guidelines with a view to its protection, rejecting mass tourism and relying on offering differentiated and protected places (Becken & Job, 2014). But the tendency to preserve localism is not only seen as a niche market. The organization of local areas suitable for exploiting the reconstruction of traditional activities - such as those for artisanship promotion (e.g. that of Ceramics of Vietri, the San Gregorio in Naples or to Matera), or those to creating market-places for characteristic, distinctive local products, are found more and more often even in large cities (such as, for example, the Boqueria Market in Barcelona, the San Miguel one in Madrid or Portobello Road and Camden Lock in London), or for the attractions based upon showing how local area products are created (such as the Guinness Storehouse in Dublin) - and the spread of local traditions - by country festivals (such as that of the Queen of Holland, the Bull Run in Pamplona, the Piedigrotta Festival in Naples), religious festivals (such as that of St. Agatha in Catania), or other events aimed at promoting local food culture (such as the Oktoberfest in Munich of Bavaria, Eurochocolate in Perugia or the Festa del Peperoncino in Calabria Region). These local cultural elements help in creating an offer linked to the territory that, in addition to architectural, landscape resources also provides for the recovery of what history has left (farms, old houses, ancient villages, etc..) and may become, at least in some cases, the instrument for the preservation and continuity of a tourist destination (Ferrari & Adam, 2011) being a competitive lever on which to focus for the affirmation or the revival of a town and, in general, a way to attract tourist flows even not in the summer holidays (Yúdice, 2003; Nuryanti, 1996).

## LOCAL AREA RESOURCES IN STRATEGIC MANAGEMENT LITERATURE

As shown in the previous sections tourism is today a well-developed industry spanning the globe. Tourism players have to operate in a more turbulent market than just a few years ago for several reasons linked to the new opportunities coming out of new technologies and globalization.

As new technologies help operators to reach for tourists interested in their products cutting out the other value chain players and help them to create a more deep relationship they can become a valuable strategic asset in order to create a sustainable competitive advantage out of these ties, but they can become the vehicle for a more intense competition as other operators with similar set of resources, even from other *destinations*, enter the market and start competing for the same tourists.

These similar, but opposite, forces are stronger for those tourism operators dealing in the incoming side of tourism market as they are tightly linked to

the local area they operate into depending, at least partially, on these out-of-control resources to create tourism products that tourists will value more than the one delivered by their global competitors.

Tourism operators have to compete in this more turbulent markets using their knowledge and competences to operate on resources, both firm specific and diffused in the local area, in order to create a bundle of product and services that its customers will deem as superior (Vargo & Lusch, 2004). Using this perspective in looking at the tourism service is coherent with a service dominant logic where resources are seen as static potential sources of competitive advantage, called operand resources, that become valuable only when they are leveraged using the right set of competences and capabilities, the operant resources (Constantin & Lusch, 1994).

Using a strategic management approach we can study the tight link between the resources a firm can exploit in its processes and the related competitive advantage using the lens of the stream of research known as Resource-Based Theory (RBT). This stream of research builds on Edith Penrose's (1959) definition of the enterprise as "a bundle of productive resources that falls under the direction of an entrepreneur for the purpose of supplying goods and services to the economy" (p.15), RBT is a theory of the firm (Foss, 1996) that focuses to explain enterprises' competitive advantage looking at how managers are able to leverage a given set of resources in order to reach, and sustain over time, a competitive position in the market that is different from the any of its competitors can easily attain (Wernerfelt, 1984; Rumelt, 1984).

Given the theory focus on enterprise's own resources, some authors have focused their studies on some specific type of resources ending up creating several branches of research (see, among the others, the competence-based competition theory by Prahalad and Hamel (1990); the knowledge-based theory by Grant (1996); the dynamic capabilities perspective by Pisano

Shuen and Teece (1997); and the relational view by Dyer and Singh (1998)). Other authors (Barney, 2007) argue that all the different resources will contribute, at least partially, to the competitive advantage so it is better to speak of resources in general terms as a way to include all the different strategic factors that managers can use in defining, and later implementing, strategic paths.

On the other side Amit and Schoemaker (1993) argue that scholars should, at the very least, divide the resources in two main classes if they want to comprehend how a sustainable competitive advantage can be attained. The first class, called resources, will consist of all the various production factors that the enterprise can get access to, while the second one, under the label of capabilities, is used to address all the different knowledge and organizational capabilities that a given firm will use to operate on the resources in order to reach for its own goals.

Common to all the different branches is the main idea that firms can reach, and sustain over time, a competitive advantage only when they can create its product/services from a different set of resources than those its competitors can use (Barney, 1991). According to Barney (1986a) heterogeneity in resources portfolios between enterprises operating in the same industry is usually the result of an imperfect knowledge of the resource value between all the involved parties, it can even be the results of pure luck in accumulation processes that end up creating resources more valuable than expected. Instead Peteraf (1993) held that heterogeneous resource portfolio were possible only when valuable resources were available, at least for some short period of time, only in a quantity lower than what was needed to satisfy the requests of all the interested parties.

In literature various authors have defined three main ways for firms in a given market to get an heterogeneous set of resources. The first way is to develop internally the set of resources through one or more different accumulation processes that increase the stock of valuable resources the firm

owns (Dierickx & Cool, 1989). A second path is to get these resources from external vendors that have developed them earlier (Barney, 1986a). Last, but not least, firms can get access to the needed resources through their partners (Dyer & Singh, 1998).

Each one of these processes needs some external condition for creating a potentially profitable heterogeneous set of resources. Amit and Schoemaker (1993) stated that managers will be able to successfully extract value out of a resource development process only when it is built starting from a different interpretation of the market's evolution leading to a different vision of the future embedded in the managerial vision or they can be the consequence of different decision making processes; and, last but not least, the heterogeneous set of resources can be the result of a different approach to change embedded in the culture of a given organization. Using a more holistic approach, Hamel and Prahalad (1994) classified several different processes that managers can exploit to increase the value a given resource focusing on the different interactions between the newly developed resources and the effects they'll have on all the other resources the enterprise already has access to taking into account even the various resources that the firm's managers think they will be able to develop in the near future.

In Resource-Based Theory getting to a heterogeneous set of resources is only the tip of the Sustainable Competitive Advantage iceberg as firms will be able to reach a favorable position in the market only when four main conditions have been met (Peteraf, 1993). Resource heterogeneity is indeed the first one (Peteraf, 1993). In order to reach a favorable position enterprises should benefit from ex-ante limits to competition enabling them to acquire the other resources needed to leverage the ones they already have at a cost lower than their real value; these limits have to be strengthened by an imperfect mobility in the strategic factors market, and, last but not least the firm need to benefit from ex-post limits to the competition to avoid that competitors can successfully leverage a similar set of resources to close the gap with the firm product / services and to make the competitive advantage only a temporary one.

Barney (1991) identified two main way expost limits to competition can manifest. The first way encloses all those factors effectively limiting competitors in exploiting the observation of firms processes to use them as a guidance to implement more effective accumulation processes on their resources' portfolios in order to close, or at least reduce, the competitive gap with the firm. On the other side Barney defines the *barriers to substitution* as all the factors that will support the enterprise's competitive advantage by hindering the competitors attempts in using a different set of resources to offer customers similar or better services.

A first form of these barriers is linked to exploiting, in the enterprise processes, socially complex resources. The main characteristic of these sets of resources is that they can be successfully used in value creation processes only when different actors do interact between themselves (Barney, 1986b; Amit & Schoemaker, 1993). A similar form of barrier is called causal ambiguity (Reed & DeFilippi, 1990). This barrier is created when the resources that are effectively used in creating the competitive advantage are not clearly defined, and often even utterly unknown, mostly as they are linked to a tightly interconnected, complex, set of resources. The limiting factor in this latter type of barriers as a way to sustain an heterogeneous portfolio of resources is tied to the fact that sometimes even the very same firm does not really know they are in place.

Sometimes competitors will not be able to easily get access to a similar set of resources as the firm's resources have been developed over a long time span and so competitors are really limited by the choices their managers did in previous periods (*path-dependence*, see Dierickx & Cool, 1989) and sometimes they are even linked to some

specific favorable condition that are no more in place so the newcomers have to pay dearly for getting access to the same set of resources, or a similar one (*time-compression diseconomy*, see Barney, 1991).

Finally, another form of barrier comes out of the capability to sustain over time a continuous innovation process (*Dynamic Competitive Process*, see Johannessen, Olsen, & Olaisen, 1997) to enhance the perceived value of the product before that competitors are able to close the gap.

Barney developed the VRIO Framework (Barney, 1996) as a more general framework to evaluate if a strategy built on a given portfolio of resource can attain a sustainable competitive advantage. According to this framework a given firm can successfully reach a sustainable competitive advantage only when its own strategies are created to fully exploit in the Organization processes those resources that are Valuable, Rare, Inimitable and not easily substituted.

Even if Barney (1996) shuns the differentiation between the various classes of resources the VRIO Framework appears to be consistent with the Amit and Schoemaker (1993) classification of resources and capabilities as the first three questions deal with the potential competitive value of the resources, knowledge and / or competences the enterprise can get access to, while the fourth question has been designed to help managers in organizing the enterprise portfolio of resources in a coherent whole.

According to the VRIO Framework managers should always design their strategies around valuable resources in order to avoid being in a competitive disadvantage situation. Barney (1991) gave a first, general, definition of valuable resources as those that will help the enterprise in getting more efficient and more effective strategic paths. Some years later, Barney (1996) held that resources are valuable only when they help the enterprise in catching an opportunity or in avoiding a threat. Later on, Peteraf and Barney (2003) defined valuable resources in a more customer oriented way

They argued that a resource can be considered as a valuable one only if it is able to broaden the gap between the perceived value of the benefits consumers' will get from the product/service and the economic cost to produce/provide them.

Another way to drive the actions of management towards exploiting their portfolio of resources as a leverage in creating customer value as a way to secure a sustainable competitive advantage as been addressed in the stream of research on the Market-Driven Management (MDM). MDM is a theory of the firm (Kohli & Jaworsky, 1990; Deshpandé & Webster, 1989) rooted in Drucker's idea that the main goal of managers' action are to innovate and create relationship with other market players in order to satisfy customer's needs (Drucker, 1954). Drucker (1954) stated that to satisfy customer's needs is not only about selling more products but it comes out of the conscious managerial activities of focusing on the customers' perception of the enterprise products/services in order to develop market knowledge to later exploit in analyzing market evolution and rebuild accordingly the organizational processes.

Sciarelli (2008) found a link between MDM and RBT in both theories main idea that managers should focus on resources portfolios (Hult & Ketchen, 2001) leveraging knowledge and competences they can reach through their own relationships in product/services creation processes (Lambin, 2007) that some class of high-value customers will perceive as more valuable than competitors' ones (Day, 1994; Jaworski & Kohli, 1993; Kohli & Jaworski, 1990).

At the same time MDM does advise managers against being customer-led (Narver & Slater, 1995) and to search more advantageous positions implementing processes to redefine market structure (Jaworski, Kohli & Sahay, 2000) as a consequence a market-driven enterprise should excel at having a good market orientation (Webb, Webster, & Krepapa, 2000; Lambin, 2000).

An enterprise will be able to develop a good market orientation only when its managers suc-

ceed in creating, and diffusing in the organization a participative entrepreneurial culture, a coherent set of processes and competences (*organizational climate*, see Narver & Slater, 1995), leading all the various parts of the organization to coordinate themselves in marketing a bundle of product and services aimed at satisfying customers' needs (Shapiro, 1988).

The organizational climate includes the processes needed to understand how the customers, and their needs, do relate with those of the other market players (Vorhies & Harker, 2000). In this way the enterprise should be able to foresee the market evolution and to identify the still latent customers' needs (Brondoni, 2007) thus helping the enterprise in being competitive in the long run (Deshpandé, Farley, & Webster, 1993). In a similar way to RBT the relationships the enterprise will be able to create with the other players in the market it operate into will become a vehicle to create the foundations for a continuous learning process that will help the enterprise in leveraging their portfolio of resources in new, more valuable ways, thus helping them in reaching a sustainable competitive advantage position (Van de Ven & Polley, 1992).

Milfelner, Gabrijan, and Snoj, (2008) held that a similar entrepreneurial climate should be considered as a competence by itself.

In MDM, as in service dominant logic and RBT, the spotlight is on the central role of knowledge and capabilities more than on the one played by assets (Hooley, Greenley, & Cadogan, 2005). The authors classified the enterprise resources in two main classes. The first one, labeled as market-based resources, includes all those resources that can promptly be used to reach a sustainable competitive advantage and it is mostly composed of intangible resources as human resources and their ability to manage relationships linking the enterprise with its own customers, or the brand and the related enterprise reputation and, more generally, all the capabilities linked to innovation. In the other one, labeled marketing support resources, the authors include all those resources needed to support those in the first class. Entrepreneurial culture and related managerial processes do belong to this second class.

Focusing on the external environment the enterprise is in relationship with other market players, factoring in relationships with customers and with competitors as well, as the main vehicle to the resources needed to drive strategic definition processes, to support their later implementation and to protect the resulting advantageous positions is a central point in MDM (Jaworsky & Kohli, 1993; Day, 1994).

Managers should focus in creating new relationships within the market and to later diffuse the knowledge into the organization as a whole.

Creating new relationships has several long run positive effects according to MDM. Above all it will help the enterprise in getting a more central role in its own relationship network while helping it to create a more favorable reputation as a valuable partner to be related to (Kogut, Shan & Walker, 1992) this virtuous circle is strengthened by the development of a specific set of capabilities that follows the continuous, and conscious, interaction with the external environment (Gulati, 2007; Kale, Dyer, & Singh, 2002).

On the other hand, in order to increase the absorptive capacity (Cohen & Levintal, 1990; Levintal & March, 1993) of these new knowledge, the organizational culture should favor the existence of different levels of interactions along the same relationships (Jaworsky & Kohli, 1993) with the further advantage that diffusing a given knowledge to a greater audience, potentially the whole organization, will help to increase its own *generativity* (Donald, 1993) and, consequently, its value (Moran & Ghoshal, 1999; Conner & Prahalad, 1996).

The capability to leverage external knowledge in the organization processes is particularly important in the modern turbulent markets as the increased competition intensity asks managers to be more pro-active in their strategies (Brondoni, 2007).

## CASE STUDY AND METHODOLOGY

The analysis of global tourism industry has shown that in the modern context tourism has become a complex phenomenon with both economical, social, and experiential sides in it (Rispoli & Tamma, 1995; Pine & Gilmore, 1998; Middleton, 2001; Higgins-Desbiolles, 2006). In this industry firms will succeed only marketing products aimed at satisfying the needs of one or more specific class of customers. According to Martini (2013), tourism businesses have to evolve their offer in order to leverage their own experience in marketing tailor-suited bundles of services and goods. In the last few years several different niches, often in the official statistics grouped all together under the label "other tourisms" label (Weaver, 2001), have been developed in order to market tourism services more keen to local area specific, and distinctive, characteristics that tourists will decide to experience in order to get a grasp on those local area values and traditions that are, oftentimes, really different from their own and felt as a truer approach at local area culture (Giordana, 2004; Rojas & Turner, 2011).

These tourism products, more linked to local area resources, can today be more easily brought to the market thanks to two different factors that have strongly influences tourism market dynamics: ICTs and Globalization.

The related effects do strengthen each other as while globalization creates a fertile ground where the interest in different cultures can grow ICTs let the various tourists find an offer nearer to their own desires. On the negative side ICTs help market competition to become more intense as more and more of them do compete against each other as, at the same time, tourism services become less differentiated as the various global markets do merge (Collesei, Casarin, & Vescovi, 2001, Eade, 2003).

At the same time this factors have led to an easier access to information by the tourists so they can share opinions and evaluations of their travel experiences. Accordingly tourism enterprises need to be more honest and truer in their communication processes (Di Vittorio, 2003).

At the same time literature on strategic management have shown that firms can exploit external resources in their strategies in order to secure a competitive advantage over time (Barney, 1991) and this is really important in tourism as the specific characteristics of a given destination in terms of specific cultural and traditional resources, have been often considered as a solid foundation of a differentiation strategy (Salazar, 2005; Kearney, 1995).

In particular, using the perspective of RBT, local area distinctive resources can be considered as rare and not easily imitable resources (Barney, 1997) so, in order to get a sustainable competitive advantage out of them, the enterprise must be able to focus their own strategies on those resources that customers can consider valuable (Peteraf & Barney, 2003) and later they should be able to define the organization in order to extract the highest value out of them.

In order to identify these resources managers should focus on the value that they can create with the specific classes of tourists that can really value the experience linked to the local area and its resources (Vargo & Lush, 1996).

But according to market-driven management the managerial action should not be limited in creating what tourists asks (Slater & Narver 1995). Instead they should interact with customers (Jaworsky & Kholi, 1993) without forgetting the needs of the other market players (Vorhies & Harker, 2000) and, in particular, they should try to cooperate with the other local actors as a way to create a coherent portfolio of resources to use at the roots of their own services (Hamel & Prahalad, 1990).

Moreover managers should involve the various parts of the organization in value creation activities, according to their know-how (Jaworsky & Kholi, 1993), and should broaden their vision to enclose the marketing-support resources (Hooley, Greenley, & Cadogan, 2005) in order to create a portfolio of resources that can help managers in continuously developing a set of products able to satisfy tourists' needs and their evolution over time (Deshpandé, Farley, & Webster, 1993; Gulati, 2007; Brondoni, 2007).

In this chapter we focus on a single case study: Sextantio Hotels [SH].

Following Yin (2001), the main reason to use case study research as a way to understand the way a given phenomenon do happens, we have chosen to study SH as we feel it is a good example to understand how an entrepreneur have shaped an hotel around the main strategic idea to market, in the global tourism industry, a bundle of products and services that are rooted in a strong set of local area resources tightly linked to the specific culture and traditions of the local area so to leverage them in a tourism service that can be sold all over the world.

In order to carry on this study we have gathered information both from primary sources and from secondary ones. The secondary data sources we have considered come out of the various news articles (in newspaper and on the Internet as well) that have started describing the idea behind SH and the related results they have reached in the last ten years.

The primary data sources have been several interview with the entrepreneur himself in the last few months on the motivation behind the creation of SH on the main steps of the *diffused hotel* creation and on the results they have attained.

## THE CASE OF SEXTANTIO HOTELS

The Sextantio Hotels project is the result of an initiative by an Italian-Swedish entrepreneur and inspired by a trip to Abruzzo: Daniele Kihlgren. Mr Khilgren decided to pave the way for a redevelopment project of a medieval fortified village, Santo Stefano di Sessanio, located in the Abruzzean Apennines, within the National Park Gran Sasso-Monti of Laga.

At the time of his first visit to the village mr. Kihlgren found out two main elements that could be the foundation of a successful entrepreneurial project. First, unlike many other historic villages in Abruzzo, that had been restored using a foreign Tyrolean style during the economic boom years Santo Stefano di Sessanio architecture had retained the cultural-integrity of its historical buildings and even the surrounding landscape was the expression of a specific, and unique, *identity* strongly linked to the local area territory's characteristic: the local historical structures were, in fact, the frame of a typical medieval village built with the traditional mix of wood and stone. Moreover they had not been restored to a more modern, and not linked to the specific local area, style.

At the same time, however, the village suffered the consequences of a strong emigration which, while it helped the local craft tradition to survive the years untouched by modern technologies they still lead to a slow, but progressive, village depopulation (it went from 7000 residents of the half on nineties to 70 inhabitants in 2004). Above all the emigration led to an inexorable process of decay of the place and, as a consequence, to a collapse of real-estate assets prices (of which approximately 75.5% is still completely unused) and the almost total absence of traces of tourism development.

The intuition that prompted Mr. Kihlgren to start-up a complex project as Sextantio Hotels, was centered around his vision of the medieval village in the semi-abandoned state as a way to address a specific market niche and as a way to answer at a still unsatisfied tourism demand, the one looking for an approach to cultural tourism as a way to experience the authenticity of historic village

product in Santo Stefano di Sessanio targeted at those tourists with a higher spending capacity. The aim of the project was, therefore, to start a process to revitalize the medieval village in respect of its local culture and to promote local area historical heritage recovery to start a wide-ranging economic process rooted in the specificity of the area itself and of its local traditions.

The project, funded by the entrepreneur recurring to a subsidized loan, was focused on restoring the village first. The entrepreneurial groups proceeded, in fact, to purchase 11500 square feet in several, different, properties to give way to one of the first examples in the world of *diffused hotel*, Sextantio Hotel, and was centered around a big structure restoration process as a way to rent them or to sell them in order to finance the project as a whole.

The project has restored each single building to its original structure, and its example has been followed by several other entrepreneurs. Today there are quite 20 hospitality structures in Santo Stefano di Sessanio and in order to be created none of them has built a single square feet of new real estates. They have created a coherent, and rare, product that has become quite known.

The village redevelopment was, in fact, carried out without altering the typical architectural and historical - cultural heritage of the existing structures and only the intended use of some of the houses was changed, but, even in those rare cases, the restoration process was designed to ensure that tourists could get a genuine contact with the life and historical traditions of the village.

The restoration was designed without losing sight of the global vision behind the project so technology related facilities (i.e. Wi-Fi access points) have been concealed from sight and all the architectural material used have been chosen taking into account the local traditions. This protective approach has been enhanced using local plasters and respecting the local traditional styles in choosing, and acquiring, the rooms furniture

Sometimes the entrepreneur asked local artisans to use the antique wooden frames to produce handmade quilts. These elements were often created from scratch, under the guidance of the elderly memory collected using specific research activities commissioned by competent authorities and by the Sextantio Hotels itself. For those elements necessary for contemporary living not existing in the past, for example health-care materials, the choice was to use a minimalist design approach trying to exploit their shape simplicity as a way to let them merge in the rooms without altering the visitors' perception.

To ensure compliance with the historical characteristics of housing units and those that were the subject of restoration has been used in specialized personnel, were initiated public - private research activities involving the locals and involving several research institutions (as the Museum of the people of Abruzzo) and the University of Chieti Gabriele D'Annunzio. The search for the link with the territory is also favored guided tours and excursions to cultural resources throughout the area.

Today Santo Stefano di Sessanio benefited from the positive effects of the revitalization process at all the levels (social, environmental and economic as well), increasing its appeal both as a tourism destination and as a place where to live. Beyond the regeneration of the resource portfolio in the area and the preservation of the place traditions place and the housing, the project has encouraged the creation of new jobs, the recovery of old jobs and creating new entrepreneurship in compliance with the local traditions indigenous cultural. This led to a slow recovery of the village and surrounding areas and a significant increase of the price of real estate not intended for the reception of tourists from the data analysis of the agency's territory, it is clear that in only two years 2006 - 2008 there was an increase of about 90% of the value of the property. Finally, the village now receives around 7300 visitors per year, even in winter. The number of hotels in the area has increased from 3 to 20, and the local tourism

market, measured by the rate of room occupancy, has grown about 30 times since project start. Of these, Sextantio Hotels represents about 30% of the market.

In light of the results obtained, the redevelopment project is implemented, it can be considered as a role model for the recovery of other villages in the southern Italy.

## CASE DISCUSSION AND FINDINGS

We have chosen the case of Sextantio Hotels as it shows clearly how a small hospitality enterprise can leverage the local area distinctive resources to create a valuable tourism product that is difficult to imitate by its competitors.

Above all we have to factor in that the main idea behind the Sextantio entrepreneurial idea is tightly linked to the personal experiences by Daniele Kihlgren himself. Daniele Kihlgren has been amazed by the beauty of this isolated land and by the state of preservation of the Santo Stefano di Sessanio village since his first visit in the area; he acknowledged that the local area and its portfolio of heritage and natural resources, coupled with a strong tradition and local area peasants' culture, could be stacked together as a good set of resources to leverage in creating a global tourism product that could be used to fuel a *sustainable development process*.

Kihlgren designed the project behind the *diffused hotel* Sextantio Hotels starting from the consideration that in the world there were many tourists that wanted to experience the real Italian traditions and that were tired of the typical mainstream visit in the main cities of Italy (mostly visited in organized tours touching Rome, Venice and Florence).

The main resource in Sextantio Hotel operation in Santo Stefano di Sessanio is its strong link with the local area resources. The hotel has been developed around a medieval village that has been inserted between the most beautiful in Italy. In particular the village distinctive historical structures, from the Medici's tower and its Captain's house, now in ruins after the L'Aquila's earthquake of 2009, to its three main churches (Santa Maria in Ruvo, Santo Stefano, and Santa Maria of Grazie). And the village can be particularly interesting for the foreign tourist as most of its buildings have not been touched by modern construction techniques so the tourists have the opportunity to see, and visit, the Abruzzo medieval houses still in their original state.

In the surrounding area tourists can visit the Rocca Calascio, a walled fortress used in the medieval age as watchtower, and the near Santa Maria of Pietà.

So tourists coming to Sextantio Hotels can experience a good portfolio of historical resources and, if they want, they can benefit from being in the Gran Sasso and Monti of Laga National Park to experience several naturalistic excursions.

As for most of the isolated area in the Apennines the inhabitants of Santo Stefano di Sessanio developed their own specific foods and, in particular, the local area is famous for a specific variety of lentils and the related recipes. These lentils have always been organically grown so they are particularly apt to be served to nature-conscious tourists and Sextantio Hotels have complemented them with several other local area organic products that are used in the food they serve to the tourists.

The relative isolation of the village during the middle ages, and in the later periods as well, has led the inhabitants to develop their own traditions in carpentry and weaving with specific designs leading to a distinctive, and coherent experience with the room furnitures, mostly furniture and wool blankets.

So the set of local area resources could be used by Daniele Kihlgren in building a coherent portfolio of resource, a real bundle of resources in the RBT's terms, to exploit in its own project as a way to get a competitive advantage but, in order for this advantage to be sustainable he had

to identify a set of barrier to imitation in order to create the ex-post limits to competition defined by Peteraf (1993).

The main barrier to imitation is the composed effect of two different forces, that strengthen each other, the progressive fall of inhabitants coupled with the isolation of the village itself. These forces have helped in preserving local area resources from a standardization process creating an unique example of the lesser known Italian cultural tradition that can be marketed as a product really different from the more mundane Italian cities. At the same time the isolation has helped to preserve the traditional carpentry of the local area buildings making them even more distinctive from those tourists can find in other, more easily reachable, villages that have been restored using the Tyrolean style.

On the other side the sparse population and the relatively high number of uninhabited buildings has created the opportunity to acquire a vast amount of structures, in strategic locations in the village as well, without breaking the bank and giving the whole project a kind of strategic flexibility that its followers could not have.

Using RBT these barriers to imitation can be considered as a kind of time-compression diseconomy (Barney, 1991) as the positive conditions in Santo Stefano of Sessanio have been, at least partially, changed by the creation of a *sustainable development process* after the Sextantio Hotels operation itself. At the same time the changes the tourism players have brought in other similar areas create a barrier to imitation that could be considered as a path-dependence one (Barney, 1991) as standardizing their offer to a more common, and known to the tourists, model they have slowly undermined the foundation of a set of distinctive competences.

In order to get a sustainable competitive advantage out of this positive situation, considering both the portfolio of resources and the related barriers to imitation, Sextantio Hotels' projects had to be designed in order to exploit them. Kihlgren developed three main foundation to Sextantio Hotels market placement strategy.

The first one was to focus on a real-estate investment in order to get the ownership of a large base of buildings to restore in order to reach two different goals:

- Become the owner of some structure to resell in order to finance the later stages of the restoration process
- Get the control on the village restoration process in order to preserve the local area characteristics in the village.

The second reason was the really meaningful one as it was needed to avoid that the village become an incoherent mess of different styles eroding the barrier to imitation that he had already identified.

A second root was identified in focusing the whole tourist experience on the local area using the idea of the *diffused hotel* as a way to help tourists to live the village having to travel through it in order to use the various services of the hotel structure. In this way the whole village became a distinctive resource embedded in the tourism product sold by Sextantio Hotels. At the same time the model of the *diffused hotel* helped the whole Sextantio Hotels project feasibility as the enterprise have been able to restore only some of the buildings before starting up and it was able to use the related revenues, from its own operations, to pay for the restoration of other rooms.

The third foundation of Sextantio Hotels Strategy has been to decide to sell its tourism products ossssssnly to a specific niche of the tourism market those that are more interested in knowing the usually never experienced side of the Italian culture and those that prefer to shun the crowded tourism locations. These choices rest, according to Daniele Khilgren himself, on three main drivers. The first one was that Daniele Khilgren himself do belong to the niche of tourists that

likes to experience the local, less known, traditions of the Apennines' villages so he could see the potential of Santo Stefano di Sessanio and use his own past experiences as a driver in designing the Sextantio Hotels distinctive characteristics. The second factor is related to the opportunity to target the Sextantio Hotels' product to a niche with very specific needs, and, as a consequence, a really loyal one if the enterprise was able to reach for them. Moreover having a well-defined target was essential to identify which feedback from the customers was really relevant in order not to make unneeded, if not dangerous, changes to the product.

As a third factor the entrepreneur vision was that the chosen niche was way bigger than what Sextantio Hotels could really provide so they do not needed to standardize their product in order to increase the appeal of the product for a bigger target market.

The combined effect of the opportunity to offer a product targeted at still unsatisfied needs and a strong set of barriers to imitation had been considered by the entrepreneur as a set of circumstances that could help Sextantio Hotels to be successful.

But in order to exploit this entrepreneurial idea Sextantio Hotels had to develop several resources that went far beyond the structures restoration in order to complement, and leverage on, the ones in the local area and helping him to create a plausible tourism product. In particular Daniele Kihlgren decided to work with an anthropologist and to define several research activities to discover the other local area resources that were still unknown as the local area designs in the wool and in the linen to use in the rooms. In this research activities the entrepreneur involved the village elders in order to find the real traditions and he later appointed as director of the hotel the very same researcher that had carried on the interviews as a way to help in creating a richer experience for the tourist.

Using an anthropologist in creating the bundle of resources used in the *diffused hotel* experience,

Daniele Kihlgren was able to follow two different principles of Market-Driven Management. Above all he was able to create a complementary set of marketing support resources to enhance the value tourists can give to the portfolio of market-based resources he got from the local area and its start-up investments. At the same time appointing a managerial position to those involved in the researches he was able to exploit these competences at the point of contact with the tourist increasing the perceived value of the product following the main idea of market-driven management that in each single point of contact with customers the personnel, being managers or operatives, with the specific set of competences needed should be able to enter in direct connection with the customer.

Last but not least the very same idea of using the *diffused hotel* as a way to start a *sustainable development process* through restoration of the medieval village has been useful in helping Sextantio Hotels to create a link with customers. The project as a whole, and sometimes even some of its main operative details, have been covered by national and international press both related to tourism, to natural resources, and to Italian traditions.

In this way the clear cut idea of preserving the lesser known local area tradition that Sextantio Hotels has been developed onto has been communicated to the potential customers helping the hotel in the start-up phase and helping the entrepreneurial actor to build the *specific identity* he needed to market Sextantio Hotels the way he had designed it.

## CONCLUSION AND FUTURE RESEARCH DIRECTIONS

The data we have collected on Sextantio Hotels show that this successful entrepreneurial activity has been indeed designed as a way to leverage a specific set of distinctive resources to get a sustainable competitive advantage in the global market.

The cornerstone in the idea has been to identify that the tourism product had to be designed preserving the already known local area resources and to define a complementary set of resources as a way to make the tourist experience truer and nearer to the local area traditions.

Looking at the start-up process, we have find out that Daniele Kihlgren was able to follow several of the principles of market-driven management leveraging a resource-based approach. This approach to start-up has been later replicated at the Sassi in Matera where Sextantio Hotels has created a new experience of *diffused hotel* following the same principles.

We have still to acknowledge that the data in this case study could be richer if we were able to include the vision of the other local area stakeholders, paying particular attention to the difference between the perception of those loyal tourists that use the *diffused hotel's* services for several weeks each year and those of the more traditional short-break customers.

Still we think that this case study shows clearly that small, and even new hospitality enterprises, can become a global players when they are successful on leveraging a distinctive set of resources in its products and in targeting them at those customers that value them most.

## REFERENCES

AlSayyad, N. (Ed.). (2013). *Consuming tradition, manufacturing heritage: global norms and urban forms in the age of tourism*. Routledge.

Amit, R., & Schoemaker, P. J. (1993). Strategic assets and organizational rent. *Strategic Management Journal*, *14*(1), 33–46. doi:10.1002/smj.4250140105

Apostolopoulos, Y., Leivadi, S., & Yiannakis, A. (Eds.). (2013). *The sociology of tourism: theoretical and empirical investigations, 1*. Routledge.

Barney, J. B. (1986a). Strategic factor markets: Expectations, luck, and business strategy. *Management Science, 32*(10), 1231–1241. doi:10.1287/mnsc.32.10.1231

Barney, J. B. (1986b). Organizational culture: Can it be a source of sustained competitive advantage? *Academy of Management Review, 11*(3), 656–665. doi:10.5465/AMR.1986.4306261

Barney, J. B. (1991). Firm resources and sustained competitive advantage. *Journal of Management, 17*(1), 99–120. doi:10.1177/014920639101700108

Barney, J. B. (1996). *Gaining And Sustaining Competitive Advantage*. Reading, MA: Addison Wesley Publishing Company.

Barney, J. B. (2007). *Gaining And Sustaining Competitive Advantage* (3rd ed.). Upper Saddle River: Prentice-Hall.

Becken, S., & Job, H. (2014). Protected areas in an era of global–local change. *Journal of Sustainable Tourism, 22*(4), 507–527. doi:10.1080/09669582.2013.877913

Bharwani, S., & Butt, N. (2012). Challenges for the global hospitality industry: An HR perspective. *Worldwide Hospitality and Tourism Themes, 4*(2), 150–162. doi:10.1108/17554211211217325

Body, W. D. S. (2012). *Annual Report*. Retrieved November, 17, 2011, from www.wto.org

Bonel, E. (2011). La vendita di prodotti turistici: Internet versus agenzia? Un'analisi dal punto di vista della domanda. *Sinergie rivista di studi e ricerche, 5*(66), 213-236.

Brondoni, S. M. (2007). Prefazione. In S. M. Brondoni (Ed.), *Market-Driven Management, concorrenza e mercati globali* (pp. XI–XIV). Torino: Giappichelli.

Buhalis, D., & Law, R. (2008). Progress in information technology and tourism management: 20 years on and 10 years after the Internet - The state of e-Tourism research. *Tourism Management, 29*(4), 609–623. doi:10.1016/j.tourman.2008.01.005

Burns, P.M. (2006). Innovation, creativity and competitiveness. *Tourism Management Dynamics-trends, management and tools*, 97-107.

Candela, G., & Figini, P. (2003). *Economia del turismo: principi micro e macro economici.* McGraw-Hill.

Casarin, F. (1996). *Il marketing dei prodotti turistici. Specificità e varietà.* Torino: Giappichelli.

Cohen, W. M., & Levinthal, D. A. (1990). Absorptive capacity: A new perspective on learning and innovation. *Administrative Science Quarterly, 35*(1), 128–152. doi:10.2307/2393553

Collesei, U., Casarin, F., & Vescovi, T. (2001). Internet e i cambiamenti nei comportamenti di acquisto del consumatore. *Micro and Macro marketing, 10*(1), 33-50.

Conner, K. R., & Prahalad, C. K. (1996). A resource-based theory of the firm: Knowledge versus opportunism. *Organization Science, 7*(5), 477–501. doi:10.1287/orsc.7.5.477

Constantin, J. A., & Lusch, R. F. (1994). *Understanding resource management: How to deploy your people, products, and processes for maximum productivity.* Oxford, OH: Planning Forum.

Cooper, C., & Wahab, S. (Eds.). (2005). *Tourism in the Age of Globalisation.* Routledge.

Dall'Ara, G. (Ed.). (2010). *PMI nel turismo. Un'opportunità per lo sviluppo.* Milano: Franco Angeli.

Davison, L., & Ryley, T. (2010). Tourism destination preferences of low-cost airline users in the East Midlands. *Journal of Transport Geography, 18*(3), 458–465. doi:10.1016/j.jtrangeo.2009.07.004

Day, G. S. (1994). The Capabilities of Market-Driven Organizations. *Journal of Marketing, 58*(4), 37–52. doi:10.2307/1251915

Della Corte, V. (2000). *La gestione dei sistemi locali di offerta turistica.* Padova: Cedam.

Della Corte, V. (2009). *Imprese e Sistemi Turistici. Il management.* Milano: Egea.

Della Corte, V., & Sciarelli, M. (2003). Evoluzione del marketing nella filiera turistica: Il ruolo dell'Information and Communication Technology. Proceedings of Congresso Internazionale "Le tendenze del marketing 2003, 11, 28-29.

Deshpandé, R., Farley, J. U., & Webster, F. E. Jr. (1993). Corporate Culture, Customer Orientation, and Innovativeness in Japanese Firms: A Quadrad Analysis. *Journal of Marketing, 57*(1), 23–37. doi:10.2307/1252055

Deshpandé, R., & Webster, F. E. Jr. (1989). Organizational Culture and Marketing: Defining the Research Agenda. *Journal of Marketing, 53*(1), 3–15. doi:10.2307/1251521

Di Vittorio, A. (2003). E-Tourism. Le nuove forme di comunicazione nel settore turistico. *Micro and Macro Marketing, 12*(1), 59–84.

Dierickx, I., & Cool, K. (1989). Asset stock accumulation and sustainability of competitive advantage. *Management Science, 35*(12), 1504–1511. doi:10.1287/mnsc.35.12.1504

Donald, M. (1993). *Origins of the modern mind: Three Stages in the Evolution of Culture and Cognition.* Boston: Harvard University Press.

Drucker, P. F. (1954). *The Practice of Management.* New York: Harper and Row Publishers.

Dyer, J. H., & Singh, H. (1998). The relational view: Cooperative strategy and sources of inter-organizational competitive advantage. *Academy of Management Review, 23*(4), 660–679.

Eade, J. (Ed.). (2003). *Living the global city: Globalization as local process.* Routledge.

Feng, R., & Cai, L. A. (2013). Information Search Behavior and Tourist Characteristics: The Internet vis-à-vis. Other Information Sources. In J. E. Mills & R. Law (Eds.), *Handbook of Consumer Behavior Tourism and the Internet.* Routledge.

Ferrari, S., & Adamo, G.E. (2011). Autenticità e risorse locali come attrattive turistiche: il caso della Calabria. *Sinergie rivista di studi e ricerche, 5*(66), 79-112.

Fesenmaier D.R., Leppers A.W., & O'Leary J.T. (1999). Developing a Knowledge-Based Tourism Marketing Information System. *Information Technology and Tourism, 2*(1).

Foss, N. J. (1996). Knowledge-based approaches to the theory of the firm: Some critical comments. *Organization Science, 7*(5), 470–476. doi:10.1287/orsc.7.5.470

Giordana, F. (2004). *La comunicazione del turismo tra immagine, immaginario e immaginazione, 42.* Milano: Franco Angeli.

Grant, R. M. (1996). Toward a Knowledge-Based Theory of the firm. *Strategic Management Journal, 17*(S2), 109–122. doi:10.1002/smj.4250171110

Gretzel, U. (2011). Intelligent systems in tourism: A social science perspective. *Annals of Tourism Research, 38*(3), 757–779. doi:10.1016/j.annals.2011.04.014

Gulati, R. (2007). *Managing network resources: alliances, affiliations and other relational assets.* Oxford: Oxford University Press.

Gursoy, D., & McCleary, K. W. (2004). An integrative model of tourists' information search behavior. *Annals of Tourism Research, 31*(2), 353–373. doi:10.1016/j.annals.2003.12.004

Hamel, G., & Prahalad, C. K. (1994). *Competing for the Future*. Boston: Harvard Business School Press.

Hazari, B. R., & Sgro, P. M. (1995). Tourism and growth in a dynamic model of trade. *The Journal of International Trade & Economic Development*, *4*(2), 143–252.

Higgins-Desbiolles, F. (2006). More than an "industry": The forgotten power of tourism as a social force. *Tourism Management*, *27*(6), 1192–1208. doi:10.1016/j.tourman.2005.05.020

Hjalager, A. M. (2007). Stages in the economic globalization of tourism. *Annals of Tourism Research*, *34*(2), 437–457. doi:10.1016/j.annals.2006.10.006

Hooley, G. J., Greenley, G. E., Cadogan, J. W., & Fahy, J. (2005). The performance impact of marketing resources. *Journal of Business Research*, *58*(1), 18–27. doi:10.1016/S0148-2963(03)00109-7

Hult, G. T. M., & Ketchen, D. J. Jr. (2001). Does Market Orientation Matter?: A Test of the Relationship between Positional Advantage and Performance. *Strategic Management Journal*, *22*(9), 899–906. doi:10.1002/smj.197

Jaworski, B., Kohli, A. K., & Sahay, A. (2000). Market-Driven Versus Driving Markets. *Journal of the Academy of Marketing Science*, *28*(1), 45–54. doi:10.1177/0092070300281005

Jaworski, B. J., & Kohli, A. K. (1993). Market Orientation: Antecedents and Consequences. *Journal of Marketing*, *57*(3), 53–70. doi:10.2307/1251854

Johannessen, J. A., Olsen, B., & Olaisen, J. (1997). Organizing for innovation. *Long Range Planning*, *30*(1), 96–109. doi:10.1016/S0024-6301(96)00101-X

Kale, P., Dyer, J. H., & Singh, H. (2002). Alliance capability, stock market response, and long-term alliance success: The role of the alliance function. *Strategic Management Journal*, *23*(8), 747–767. doi:10.1002/smj.248

Kearney, M. (1995). The local and the global: The anthropology of globalization and transnationalism. *Annual Review of Anthropology*, *24*(1), 547–565. doi:10.1146/annurev.an.24.100195.002555

Kogut, B., Shan, W., & Walker, G. (1992). The make-or-cooperate decision in the context of an industry network. In N. Nohria & R. Eccles (Eds.), *Networks and Organizations: Structure, Form and Action* (pp. 348–365). Boston: Harvard Business School Press.

Kohli, A. K., & Jaworski, B. J. (1990). Market orientation: The construct, research propositions, and managerial implications. *Journal of Marketing*, *54*(2), 1–18. doi:10.2307/1251866

Lambin, J. J. (2000). *Market-Driven Management*. London: McMillan Business.

Lambin, J. J. (2007). La nuova complessità del mercato globale. In S. M. Brondoni (Ed.), *Market-Driven Management concorrenza e mercati globali* (pp. 65–86). Torino: Giappichelli.

Leotta, N. (2005). *Approcci visuali di turismo urbano: il tempo del viaggio, il tempo dello sguardo*. Milano: Hoepli.

Levinthal, D. A., & March, J. G. (1993). The myopia of learning. *Strategic Management Journal*, *14*(S2), 95–112. doi:10.1002/smj.4250141009

Martini, U. (2000), L'impatto di Internet sulla struttura del mercato turistico *leisure*. *Technical Report DISA, 36*.

Martini, U. (2013). Introduzione. Approccio alla sostenibilità, *governance* e competitività delle destinazioni turistiche: stato dell'arte e prospettive. In M. Franch & U. Martini (Eds.), *Management per la sostenibilità dello sviluppo turistico e la competitività delle destinazioni* (pp. 17–63). Bologna: Il Mulino.

Middleton, V. T. C. (2001). *Marketing in travel and Tourism* (3rd ed.). Oxford: Butterworth – Heinemann.

Milfelner, B., Gabrijan, V., & Snoj, B. (2008). Can Marketing resources contribute to company performance? *Organizacija*, *41*(2), 3–13.

Mills, J. E., & Law, R. (Eds.). (2013). *Handbook of Consumer Behavior Tourism and the Internet*. Routledge.

Moran, P., & Ghoshal, S. (1999). Markets, firms, and the process of economic development. *Academy of Management Review*, *24*(3), 390–412.

Moutinho, L. (Ed.). (2011). *Strategic management in tourism*. New York: CABI Publishing. doi:10.1079/9781845935887.0000

Murphy, P. (2014). Potential Synergies for the Short-Break Holiday and Rural Tourism Markets: Evidence from a National Australian Survey. *Tourism Planning and Development*, 1-14.

Nash, D., & Smith, V. L. (1991). Anthropology and tourism. *Annals of Tourism Research*, *18*(1), 12–25. doi:10.1016/0160-7383(91)90036-B

Nunez, T. (1989). Touristic studies in anthropological perspective. *Hosts and guests: The anthropology of tourism, 2*, 265-279.

Nuryanti, W. (1996). Heritage and postmodern tourism. *Annals of Tourism Research*, *23*(2), 249–260. doi:10.1016/0160-7383(95)00062-3

Pearce, P. L. (1982). *The social psychology of tourist behavior*. Pergamon Press.

Penrose, E. T. (1959). *The Theory of the Growth of the Firm*. Oxford: Oxford University Press.

Peteraf, M. A. (1993). The cornerstones of competitive advantage: A resource-based view. *Strategic Management Journal*, *14*(3), 179–191. doi:10.1002/smj.4250140303

Peteraf, M. A., & Barney, J. B. (2003). Unraveling the Resource-based tangle. *Managerial and Decision Economics*, *24*(4), 309–323. doi:10.1002/mde.1126

Peteraf, M. A., & Bergen, M. E. (2003). Scanning dynamic competitive landscapes: A market-based and resource-based framework. *Strategic Management Journal*, *24*(10), 1027–1041. doi:10.1002/smj.325

Pine, J., & Gilmore, J. H. (1998). Welcome to the Experience Economy. *Harvard Business Review*, *76*, 97–106. PMID:10181589

Pisano, G., Shuen, A., & Teece, D. (1997). Dynamic capabilities and strategic management. *Strategic Management Journal*, *18*(7), 509–533. doi:10.1002/(SICI)1097-0266(199708)18:7<509::AID-SMJ882>3.0.CO;2-Z

Plog, S. C. (1987). Understanding psychographics in tourism research. In J. R. B. Ritchie & C. R. Goeldner (Eds.), *Travel, tourism, and hospitality research. A handbook for managers and researchers* (pp. 203–213). New York: Wiley.

Poon, A. (1993). *Tourism, Technology and Competitive Strategies*. UK: CAB International.

Prahalad, C., & Hamel, G. (1990). The Core Competence of the Corporation. *Harvard Business Review*, *68*(3), 79–91.

Reed, R., & De Fillippi, R. J. (1990). Causal ambiguity, barriers to imitation, and sustainable competitive advantage. *Academy of Management Review*, *15*(1), 88–102.

Rispoli, M., & Tamma, M. (1995). *Risposte strategiche alla complessità: le forme di offerta dei prodotti alberghieri*. Torino: Giappichelli.

Rojas, D. S., & Turner, E. (2011). Spam and Pop-Tarts? Joint Response to Anthropology and Tourism. *Anthropology News, 52*(3), 4–4. doi:10.1111/j.1556-3502.2011.52304.x

Rumelt, R. P. (1984). Towards a Strategic Theory of the Firm. In R.B. Lamb (Ed.), Competitive Strategic Management (pp. 556-570). Englewood Cliffs, NJ: Prentice-Hall.

Saarinen, J., Rogerson, C., & Manwa, H. (2011). *Tourism and Millennium Development Goals: tourism for global development?* Routledge.

Salazar, N. B. (2005). Tourism and glocalization "local" tour guiding. *Annals of Tourism Research, 32*(3), 628–646. doi:10.1016/j.annals.2004.10.012

Sciarelli, M. (1996). *Processo decisionale e valutazione strategica, la formulazione degli accordi tra imprese*. Padova: Cedam.

Sciarelli, M. (2008). Resource-Based Theory e Market-Driven Management. *Symphonya, 2*.

Sciarelli, S. (2007). *Il management dei sistemi turistici locali. Strategie e strumenti per la governance*. Torino: Giappichelli.

Seaton, A. V., & Alford, P. (2005). The effects of globalisation on tourism promotion. In C. Cooper & S. Wahab (Eds.), *Tourism in the Age of Globalisation* (pp. 97–122). Routledge.

Shapiro, B. P. (1988). What the Hell Is 'Market Oriented'? *Harvard Business Review, 66*(6), 119–125.

Slater, S. F., & Narver, J. C. (1995). Market Orientation and the Learning Organisation. *Journal of Marketing, 59*(3), 63–74. doi:10.2307/1252120

Smith, V. L. (Ed.). (2012). *Hosts and guests: The anthropology of tourism*. University of Pennsylvania Press.

Stipanuk, D. M. (1993). Tourism and technology: Interactions and implications. *Tourism Management, 14*(4), 267–278. doi:10.1016/0261-5177(93)90061-O

Uriely, N. (2005). The tourist experience: Conceptual developments. *Annals of Tourism Research, 32*(1), 199–216. doi:10.1016/j.annals.2004.07.008

Van de Ven, A. H., & Polley, D. (1992). Learning While Innovating. *Organization Science, 3*(1), 92–116. doi:10.1287/orsc.3.1.92

Vargo, S. L., & Lusch, R. F. (2004). Evolving to a new dominant logic for marketing. *Journal of Marketing, 68*(1), 1–17. doi:10.1509/jmkg.68.1.1.24036

Vellas, F. (2012), *The indirect impact of tourism: an economic analysis*. Retrieved April, 23, 2012, from www2.unwto.org/agora/indirect-impact-tourism-economic-analysis

Vidal González, M. (2008). Intangible heritage tourism and identity. *Tourism Management, 29*(4), 807–810. doi:10.1016/j.tourman.2007.07.003

Vorhies, D. W., & Harker, M. (2000). The Capabilities and Performance Advantages of Market-Driven Firms: An Empirical Investigation. *Australian Journal of Management, 25*(2), 145–173. doi:10.1177/031289620002500203

Weaver, D. B. (2001). Ecotourism in the Context of Other Tourism Types. In D. B. Weaver (Ed.), *The encyclopedia of ecotourism* (pp. 73–84). New York: CABI Publishing.

Webb, D., Webster, C., & Krepapa, A. (2000). An Exploration of The Meaning and Outcomes of a Customer-Defined Market Orientation. *Journal of Business Research, 48*(2), 101–112. doi:10.1016/S0148-2963(98)00114-3

Wernerfelt, B. (1984). A resource-based view of the firm. *Strategic Management Journal, 5*(2), 171–180. doi:10.1002/smj.4250050207

Whitla, P., Walters, P. G., & Davies, H. (2007). Global strategies in the international hotel industry. *International Journal of Hospitality Management*, *26*(4), 777–792. doi:10.1016/j.ijhm.2006.08.001

World Tourism Organization. (2014), *World Tourism Barometer, 12*. Madrid: UNWTO, Retrieved Dicember, 2014 from www.unwto.org/facts/eng/barometer.htm

World Travel & Tourism Council. (2012), *Travel and Tourism Economic Impact*. London: WTTC. Retrieved from www.wttc.org/site_media/uploads/downloads/world2012.pdf

Yin, R. K. (1994). *Case Study Research. Design and Methods*. Newbury Park, CA: Sage Publications.

Yip, G. S. (1992). *Total global strategy: Managing for worldwide competitive advantage*. Englewood Cliffs, NJ: Prentice Hall.

Yúdice, G. (2003). *The expediency of culture: Uses of culture in the global era*. Duke University Press.

## KEY TERMS AND DEFINITIONS

**Barriers to Substitution:** The limits to competitors capability of substituting part of the resources used in a given tourist product without compromising their products competitively.

**Cultural Identity:** The common cultural characteristics defining the people living in a given area as a community.

**Diffused Hotel:** A single hotel which rooms are located in separated, but near, buildings as a way to restore and valorize towns and villages lacking bigger structures.

**Knowledge Generativity:** Knowledge resources capability to increase their value the more they are combined with more other resources.

**Overlapping Logic:** The process of designing tourist products starting from the perspective of the tourist trying to defining it as a system and not as a simple bundle of services.

**Sustainable Development Process:** A process of development aimed to help current generations to satisfy their needs without compromising the future generations ones.

**Tourist Destinations:** A location that is able to generate tourist inflows by itself, thanks to some local tourism attractions helped by local area services and accommodations.

# Chapter 9
# Role of Social Media in Tourism

**Vipin K Nadda**
*University of Sunderland – London, UK*

**Sumesh Singh Dadwal**
*Glyndwr University, UK*

**Dirisa Mulindwa**
*University of Sunderland, UK*

**Rubina Vieira**
*University of Sunderland – London, UK*

## ABSTRACT

*Revolutionary development in field of communication and information technology have globally opened new avenue of marketing tourism and hospitality products. Major shift in web usage happened when Napster in 1999 released peer-to-peer share media and then with pioneer social networking websites named 'Six Degrees'. This kind of interactive social web was named as 'Web 2.0'. It would create openness, community and interaction. Web2. is also known as Social media base. Social media is incudes "all the different kinds of content that form social networks: posts on blogs or forums, photos, audio, videos, links, profiles on social networking web sites, status updates and more". It allows people to create; upload post and share content easily and share globally. Social media allows the creation and exchange of user-generated content and experiences online. Thus, social media is any kind of information we share with our social network, using social networking web sites and services.*

## INTRODUCTION

In the tourism industry, websites and social media provide a wealth of information with regards to experiences and review of the destination, property, facilities and restaurants (Manap KhairulHilmi A., 2013). Social media has added new channels of communication to tourists. Most tourists always use the Internet for destination information seeking to decision-making .The tourism industry value chain starting from countries Tourism boards, tourism agents, tour operators, transportations and airline companies, hotel and restaurant operators, destination management companies and

DOI: 10.4018/978-1-4666-8606-9.ch009

*Figure 1. UGC Value Chain of Internet*
Source: (The Equity Kicker, 2012)

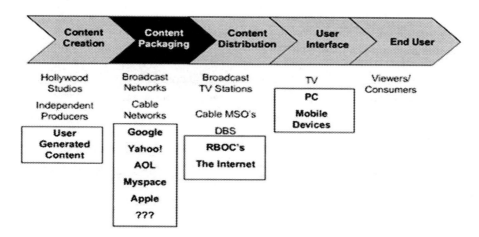

local tourism management organisation all use social media tools to reach potential customers (Ernestad V., 2010).

The social media marketing generates more business exposure, increased traffic and improved search, generating leads and improved sales at lower cost (Stelzner, 2011).Social media or web 2.0 is changing the methods by which tourists search, find, evaluate, trust and collaboratively produce information about tourism suppliers and other members of the value chain. Consequently tourists are becoming consumers who not only participate in production but also marketing of tourist's products. Using social media, travellers become co-producers, co-marketiers, co-consumers by creating user generated content (UGC) and social intelligence. (Manap KhairulHilmi A., 2013).This user generated contents of the online comments, profiles, and photographs a mixture of facts and opinions shared by tourists is trustworthy for new users .UGC have AIDA effect on travellers by creating attention, interest, desire and action (Sigala M.,Christou E.,Gretzel U.,2012),),sources of information and its evaluation, channels used for booking and buying travel products including travel itineraries and reservations and also disseminating experiences through word of mouth

after the trip. The UGC content it can be in the form of any comments on Amazon, Facebook or YouTube. Nielsen (2009) argues that Internet is the mass medium used for social media marketing. However, Kessler et al. (2007) argue that social media is still in competition with traditional marketing techniques. User generated content value chain of Internet is shown below.

Consumer behaviour in tourism has always been influenced by information and communication technologies.

## THEORETICAL MODELS OF SOCIAL MEDIA

Research indicates that there can be multiple reasons of why people want to share online content using offline or online medias. These motivations may be narcissism, social and hedonistic reasons, pursuit of personal identity as a gratifications,, status seeking self-concept, social support, selflessness, fame, having fun and passing time etc. on the other hand reasons for not sharing information may be a desire to remain anonymous due to issues of privacy, security time constraints, and anxiety, laziness, and shyness, vengeance, and anxiety (Manap KhairulHilmi A., 2013). Various theories (Pan B., 2011) have been discussed as basis of this such as discussed below :

## Micro Theories

*Word of mouth and psychological ownership theory:* This theory postulates that loyal customers would express their loyalty and sense of ownership by expressing their views to others. Psychological ownership theory explains why tourists are motivated to talk through word of mouth due to the fact that tourist start identifying with company or destination and start feeling it as their own. Another reasons may be that they feel in control and get feelings of efficacy, intrinsic pleasure, and extrinsic satisfaction in providing such an advice. The information communicated by friends is considered as more credible, honest, and trustworthy than that generated by marketers (Pan B., 2011).

*Social exchange theory:* this theory uses a cost-benefit framework and comparison of alternatives to explain how and why tourists wish to share information. They will engage of benefit such as such as opportunity, prestige, conformity, approval, or acceptance are more than costs of sharing and reciprocity (Pan B., 2011).

*Social penetration theory:* states that as the relationship progresses, a person would start to with public, visible, and superficial information, such as gender, clothing preferences, and ethnicity; and then will penetrated deeper layers of self and slowly start sharing feelings; at the deepest level,, goals, ambitions, and beliefs (Pan B., 2011).

## Macro-Theories

*Social network analysis:* Social network theory views the community of individuals as connected actors or nodes that are connected by commination edged at multiple levels of hierarchy from individual people, to families, communities, and nations . This theory uses mathematical models to study its structure, development, inter-prelateship and evolution (Pan B., 2011).

*McLuhan's Media Theory:* theory postulated media is message and the media itself, rather than its actual content, will transform people and society. Theoretically one can perform all the Twitter functions through a blog service. However, limited 140 words itself made Twitter more successful.

## SOCIAL MEDIA MARKETING

Marketers can create and implement marketing campaigns through use of social media that is an inexpensive way of marketing. Marketers' major focus during use of social media is to create such content that can generate attention. Moreover, the marketers focus on creation of such content that can offer motivational incentive to individuals. Mahnomen and Runnel (2008) argue that user motivations, user loyalty and user participation are the keys to success of social media. Establishment of social networks, collaborative content creation, and user centred content and flexible design facilitation is the major factors that can make social media attractive to the users.

Eely and Tilley (2009) argue that social media enables the individuals to share their experiences with others even if they have no knowledge of web development or coding. It can be done through status updates, profiles on social networking websites, links, videos, audio, photos, posts on blogs or forums.. Weber (2009) points out numerous opportunities provided by social media that help the organisations in expanding and strengthening the relationships with the customers. Some of the opportunities highlighted by him include targeted brand building that can be done through microsites, executive blogs and podcasts.

In spite of many opportunities provided by social media, there are certain challenges for marketers as well. As reported by Weber (2009), marketers using social media have to adopt many techniques that they do not need to adapt while using traditional marketing techniques. A clear understanding of opportunities and challenges arising due to social media marketing is extremely important to stay competitive. Moreover, marketers should be fully aware of the potential gains and risks and it should be done through comparisons with traditional marketing channels as hinted by Hearn et al. (2009).

In business context, engaging people is the major purpose of social media marketing. People can be engaged using four different ways. These ways include communication, collaboration, education and entertainment. All these attributes can change over time and this result in desired action or outcome.

## SOCIAL MEDIA IN DECISION MAKING PROCESS

Decision making process include stages such as need identification, information search, evaluation of alternatives and selection, purchasing, and post purchase behaviour. Social media is useful for tourists during each stage and also for businesses at corresponding value chain of tourism and hospitality industry; tourist product planning and development, product production and consumption, tourist product marketing and logistics, post purchase support to the consumers. The consumer decision-making models guide that, buying behaviour results from consumer involvement and engagement in multistage problem solving tasks. The stages are: need recognition, information search, evaluation of alternatives (evoked set), evaluation result and when buying, post-purchase evaluation (Schiffman & Kanuk, 2009). Marketing communication using social platforms provides consumers information, so they become able to support the learning process by which they acquire the purchase and consumption knowledge. Consumers' learning, attitude and motivation can change due to any newly acquired knowledge gained from reading, observation, dis-

cussions and virtual or actual experience. Social platform can effect consumer perception about evaluating the desired and actual state, and can drive active or latent 'problem recognition' and also offer solution to the problem. During second stage of 'the information search', social platform can aid in learning process by helping to search either internal or external memory sources. The evaluation of alternative stage is conditioned by the type of consumer's choice and discussion on social platform can aid by influencing consumers' learning, motivation and attitudes with help of augmented reality experiences. In last stage of consumer decision-making process-post-purchase evaluation, the consumer compares the product real performance with his expectations, and right discussions and word of mouth on platforms is useful in setting right levels expectations at well above consumers' minimum noticeable threshold levels and by reducing any uncertainty in offerings or services. Right evaluation not only sets evokes set and helps in making choice of brand offerings or destination but also, can create positive word of mouth, customer loyalty, feedback and cross product buying.

The social platforms can provide conditions for high level of customer involvement and engagements with the product or the services. Level of customer involvement in buying process means amount of psychophysical energy spent by consumer in the buying process. Higher levels of involvement are associated with greater use of affective and cognitive decision making strategies across different cultures (Edgett & Cullen, 1993). During buying or consuming highly involved individuals compared to lower involved individuals will use more criteria search for more information, accept fewer alternative, process relevant information in detail, and will form attitudes that are more resistant to change. Involvement levels, therefore, can have an impact on the information processing decision-making and responses to advertising. Lack of proper management of touch points / customer encounters can cause a churn among

*Figure 2. Purchasing process*
Source: (Turner and Shah, 2011)

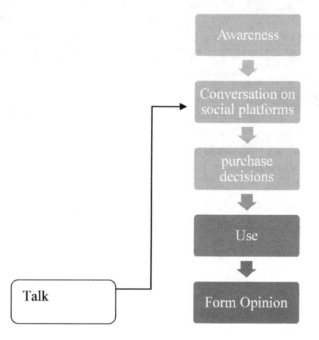

the firm's existing customers. Social platform not only increases customer relations but also enhances loyalty, satisfactions through customer's involvement and encounter management, socially, emotionally, visually, auditory and kinaesthetically. The social media marketing platforms are useful for businesses to spread a positive word of mouth through which they could influence them and exchange information. These platforms also provide an opportunity to clear any mis- understanding that could have become the hindrance in the purchasing decisions of customers. Singh et al (2008) states that because of the sharing of instant information the developed societies have got in the habit of creating awareness, sharing it on the Internet on social platforms and then making purchasing decisions.

The above diagram clearly shows that when people use a product, they then share their experiences on the internet with others on the conversation on social media platforms and this makes others to revise their purchasing decisions. A business can effectively take the advantage of such a platform and interact with its customers in order to help them satisfy their needs through addressing their issues promptly. (Turner and Shah, 2011)

It has also been noticed that social media also plays a pivotal role in the launching of the product. A wealth of word of mouth information regarding the brands and products, on social platforms leads to its use as a new channel that has features of search engines, review sites, and price comparison. It directly act as least two marketing mix place and promotion and aids in other 2 Ps Price and product strategies (Bolotaeva, 2011).

Like any other media, social platform also offers challenges to the business. Challenges such as invasion of user privacy, aggressive advertising, lack of e-commerce abilities, lack of brand controls, and certain legal pitfalls, can be major disruptions to social platforms. The consumers don't like intrusive advertisements and communications and they are not ready to share their privacy that can be pervaded in an online platform.

## SOCIAL MEDIA IN TOURISM INDUSTRY

Social Media is a group of Internet-based applications that contribute towards building of ideological and technological foundations of Web 2.0. Marketing via Social Media is trendy method market communication using different tools of Social Media; Facebook, LinkedIn, YouTube, Twitter, Blogs. YouTube, social bookmarking, forums, group on etc. (Stelzner, 2011). Other type of tools include; email marking, search engine optimisation, event marketing, press releases, online adds St. Google ad word, direct mail, print display ads, sponsorships, webinars and other ads. .There are many tools or platforms of social media marketing (Ernestad V., 2010).

Social networking platforms develop virtual communities, or social networks, for individuals, who have similar Attitude, interests, education, opinion and lifestyles, thus creating communities of practices. Bolotaeva, (2011) defines social networking platform as: "… a loose affiliation of people who interact, communicate and share contents through the platforms building relationships among communities. The companies have to mange a social platform management in order to development, deployment, use it for customer services. A social platform' empowers customers in, posting, editing, sorting, co-creating and sharing a variety of contents. Thus it enables in communication implicitly or explicitly with specific person or broadcast to all. More features are used in adding friends into the network, setting privacy controls etc (Leonardi, 2013). In technological dimension, a social platform consists of dimensions of social mark-up language for creating native applications,

an application programming interface (API) for third party application integration and a back-end admin console for managing the entire user base and preferences, etc. It provides continuous visibility and persistence to people and content.

## INFORMATION TECHNOLOGY AND TOURISM

Tourism as a global industry is one of the biggest job providers and technology has seen a development that brought fundamental changes in the industry. Besides improving communications, ICTs are increasing the competitiveness of tourism organisations and destinations.

Travellers use technologies to plan their journeys, access reliable information and to make reservations, while tourism organisations have become more efficient and effective. Buhalis and Law (2008) believe that ICTs have benefited the new tourist who is sophisticated and more demanding. This means that package tours are losing their appeal as tourists prefer to organise independently organised trips to explore their personal and professional interests.

Technological progress and tourism have been going hand in hand for years. Developments in ICTs have changed business practices as well as strategies and the structure of the industry. In the 1970s, Computer Reservation Systems were establishment and in the late 80's was the time for Global Distribution Systems, followed by the development of the Internet in the 1990's.

Technology has been the focus of the last 20 years and since 2000 communication technologies have brought new developments and tools that facilitate international interactions between the different stakeholders.

Travellers have now more access to information provided by the different tourism organisations, can book flights and accommodation and as a results most tourism organisations have embraced internet technologies as part of their marketing strategy (Buhalis and Law, 2008).

As a consequence, consumers have an active role in co-creating the product design as well as promotional messages. Consumers use digital media not only to research products but also to engage with the companies and other consumers.

In a new social media-driven business model which is dominated by customers' connectivity and interactivity, content goes hand in hand with technology in the form of social networks and blogs that enable individuals to create, share and recommend a product (Hanna, Rohm and Crittenden, 2011).

Mobile devices will be used to access these platforms but it is not easy to classify the different types of social media. Facebook, YouTube, Blogger, Twitter, MySpace and Flickr are characterised as social networks, social networking and social media.

Marketers are using several of the major platforms and interactive digital marketing platforms are changing the marketing landscape by empowering consumers to connect, share and collaborate and to create spheres of influence (Hanna, Rohm and Crittenden, 2011).

This means that traditional media cannot be the solely tool to capture the attention of consumers. The focus cannot be in reaching the customers but on continuing attention via engagement that involves traditional and social media.

Social media is seen as a development of digital media where communities share and discuss information. It has been defined as the evolution of digital media based on the notion of discussing and sharing information between the social community's online users (Serlen, 2013). The word refers to the development of audio, videos, pictures and words by integrating social interactions, telecommunications and technology (Corstjens and Umblijs, 2012).

On one hand, social media connects individuals of different nationalities, religion and cultural background and messages are spread internationally very easily (Bertrand, 2013). On the other hand, social media is an effective tool for marketers to develop brand awareness and loyalty, increase sales and to improve customer service. It is a tool which can be used by large corporations as well as small businesses (Schlinke and Crain, 2013).

Although the benefits and impacts of social media have yet to be understood, social media turns passive consumers into active consumers through what people share in networks (Corstjens and Umblijs, 2012). Clients feel they are valuable and have more control and responsibility, while tourism companies end up spending less time and money on promotion (Seth, 2012).

Historically, companies could control the information available about them by placing press announcements and using public relations managers. Thus, today firms have been relegated as mere observers having neither the knowledge, chance or the right to change publicly posted comments that customers provide. The current trend toward social media can be seen as an evolution, making the internet a platform to facilitate information exchange between users (Kaplan and Haenlein, 2010).

User Generated Content is the sum of all ways in which people use social media. The terms is applied to describe content that is publicly available and created by end-users. According to Kaplan and Haenlein, social media is *«a group of Internet-based applications that build on the ideological and technological foundations of Web 2.0, and that allow the creation and exchange of User Generated Content, pp. 61»*

In terms of types of social media and the opportunities they bring, there are the 'Collaborative projects' that enable the creation of content by end-users. The main goal is the joint effort of different people to a better outcome and the fact that they are becoming the main source of information for many consumers. An example would be Wikipedia.

Blogs represent one of the earliest forms of Social Media. They are personal web pages and are normally managed by one person but provide the possibility of interaction with others through the addition of comments.

Content communities are another social media that share media content between users including text, photos, videos, PowerPoint presentations, etc.

Social networking sites are applications that enable users to connect by creating personal information profiles and the information can include photos, videos, audio files, etc. Facebook and Myspace are examples of social networking sites.

Creating customer awareness about a product is one of the main reasons tourism companies may use social media. Thus, the company business strategy should contemplate a strategy for the use of social media (Manap, 2013/Schlinke and Crain, 2013) and these can help the company to find out what customers want and how do they behave and what do they purchase.

Dewey (2013) wrote in the 'Business Journal' that as mobile device users increase, traveller's reliance on app and online resources for tourism and travel planning is also increasing. The use of online resources has grown, with more consumers reading travel blogs and destination reviews, as well as photos and videos.

In relation to mobile phones, 53% of travellers are using apps and 29% of travellers have used mobile apps to search for flight deals and 30% to find hotel deals.

Because of the increased use of the Internet and apps, social media are more important than ever to travellers' purchase decision, even if 'word of mouth' is of online strangers. Companies are trying to establish relationships with consumers and some managers respond to comments and complaints. Some large corporations even have a full-time social media person who read and respond to reviews (Dewey, 2013).

## ELECTRONIC WORD-OF-MOUTH

Consumers have the ability to develop powerful influences upon each other and virtual interactions have spread with electronic technologies. A good example is the website tripadvisor.com where consumers share their hospitality and tourism opinions.

With more than 2 million reviews and being updated every minute, hospitality and tourism marketers realised its importance do to the intangibility of the goods they sell. Tourism products are cannot be evaluated before consumption and are seen as high-risk purchases. Therefore, more studies should be developed to understand what kind of information consumers seek online and how they actually use information acquired online from other consumers to make their travel and hospitality decisions (Litvin, Goldsmith, Pan, 2007).

Interpersonal experiences and influences flows from opinion leaders to followers and among followers. Thus, favourable word-of-mouth (WOM) increases the probability of purchase while negative WOM has the opposite effect. The low-cost access to information exchange can create new dynamics in the market and greater control over format and communication types.

Travellers are using search engines to locate travel information and as a consequence this brings changes to the structure of travel information, to travellers knowledge and perception of travel products.

e-WOW strategies will be informal and revenue generating. Marketers will use the online feedback left by customers to enhance visitors satisfaction, improve the product, solving visitor problems and monitor companies reputation and image (Litvin, Goldsmith, Pan, 2007).

Social media constitute part of the online tourism domain and play an important role. However, they do not consume all places on search result pages and leave room open for marketers to compete with social media for customers attention (Xiang, Gretzel, 2010).

## DIGITAL DIVIDE AND ITS IMPACTS

Innovation technologies are critical for the management and marketing of tourism organisations and destinations. Consumer behaviour is affected from product search to consumption and memories and the web allows users to compare products and prices and to build personalised itineraries (Minghetti and Buhalis, 2010).

Thus, disparities exist in access, skills, use of ICTs and services. Not everybody has the opportunity to benefit from internet opportunities and digital divide can lead to digital and social exclusion. For tourists and destinations, this means being unable to participate in the emerging electronic market and benefit from its opportunities.

The global digital divide is caused but differences in GDP and income, human capital and digital skills, telecommunications infrastructure and connectivity, policy and regulatory mechanisms.

The geographical evolution of tourism is followed by a similar development of the digital divide. More than 50% of the international tourism flows and receipts are concentrated in the developed areas of the world where (with the exception of China) are also included within the high-opportunity digital access economies. Not all ICT users will use technology wisely or effectively. Some people lack the knowledge, trust, literacy or language skills.

As for destinations, ICT-Skilled tourism companies and destination marketing organisations will increase their visibility on the marked and to strengthen their competitiveness. On the contrary, tourism companies with low ICT use are often cut off from electronic distribution channels and e-commerce and may risk in becoming invisible for a share of the market (Minghetti and Buhalis, 2010). Tourists and destinations suffer from a multiplicity of technological divides which lead to different levels of digital exclusion.

## SOCIAL MEDIA TOOLS/PLATFORMS AND USER BEHAVIOURS

Thus a social platform enables in creating social media websites and services with complete social media network along with technical, user specific and social functionality. These are second generation (Web 2.) websites/ platforms that provide users the ability and tools to create and publish their own mini web sites or web pages using the "bottom up"—using a many-to-many model. Such platforms provide features such as; user created contents, high degree of user participation in communities of practice and ability to integrate with multiple sites or networks (Campbell, 2010). Thus a social platform include things like social networking (Facebook, Google+ MySpace, twitter, LinkedIn); photo and video sharing sites (Flickr, Vimio and YouTube); blogs (such as Blogger, WordPress, Typepad), social bookmarking (Delicious, Stumble Upon) news sharing (Digg, Yahoo! Buzz) (Campbell, 2010). The social networked platforms can attract traffic by managing touches of 4Ps; Personal, Participatory, Physical, Plausible (Clemons, 2009. cited in Bolotaeva, 2011).

The companies have used social platforms for internal and external communication and marketing . Its increasing use can be attributed to demand side factors (the fact that social media give us that we can't get offline and let us meet our social needs) and supply side factors (websites such as Facebook, Twitter, and LinkedIn have more than 1.2 billion users and account for almost 25 per cent of Internet use). To get full advantaged of social media, companies need to develop and harness their social strategy (Piskorski, 2014).

Over 1.7 billion people use social platforms on the Internet. Different platforms have certain distinctive features or USP. For instant platforms, such as Twitter, MeetUp and eHarmony, enable "strangers" to connect. eHarmony let meet people to meet up for marriages. LinkedIn helps one expand business relationships. Other platforms, like Facebook or Renren in China, creates more relationships with other "known" peoples. In fact, Facebook boasts staggering 750 million users, and valuation in excess of $100 billion (Piskorski, 2014). Different platforms have different levels of restrictions to users' choices and uses . Platforms like e-Harmoney (dating site), Whatsup (social one to one texting on phone), headhunting (recruitment) etc., are successful even with restrictive access and a user fee. On the other hand platforms like Facebook (social networking), Monster (job hunting), Lastminute.com (travel and tourism), YouTube etc. that offers unlimited free access are also successful. The understanding becomes more complex when even platforms with middle grounds on access like twitter (limited in words with unlimited in access to network) and LinkedIn etc. are also growing. Thus, It can be argued that the value of participating in a social platform often depends on the number of choices offered, and a platform offering unrestricted access (yet in user's control) could quickly displace a platform that restricts choice or provides restricted access.

## SOCIAL MEDIA SEGMENTS

Social platforms has been ranked by comprehensively average of integrating rankings from others ranking evaluators (Alexa Global Traffic, compete and Quantcast) (EbizMBA, 2014). In 2013, the studies have found that users segments of different platforms are distinct and sometime duplicate. Facebook is preferred by diverse mix of demographic segments and who also visit site daily many times. Pinterest has four times high appeal to female users, LinkedIn has more college graduates with higher income households. On the other hands the segments of Twitter and Instagram are overlapping with younger adults,

urban dwellers, and non-whites (Duggan, 2013). Further 90% of Twitter users, 93% of instagram and 83% of linkedin users also use users also use Facebook. A small number of users use only one type of plateform; 8% use only LinkedIn, 4% use only Pinterest, and 2% Instagram or Twitter only (Duggan, 2013). This pattern shows high level of similarities between user needs to visit social platforms on one hand and also put forward a question that why people visit many platform if one platform can meet their social needs! Do people have different motives at each platform or do they have different network of connections at each of the platform or they want to exhibit different personalities and roles at different platforms. Marketers can also target users as Word of Mouth marketer, according to their characteristics or social media preferences there can be seven kinds of social media users. The 'Deal Seekers' are always hunting for bargain or value deals from the marketers, so companies should always offer them deals along with a request to refer more friends to the brand; the 'Unhappy Customer' can cause harm to a company by creating stream of negative words of mouth (-WOM), so company should solve their problems immediately; the 'Loyal Fans' are useful to spread positive word of mouth (+WOM) and even defends their brand, so the company should reward their behaviour; a 'Quiet Follower' is neutral and is just there because his friends are there, so the company should put effort them to engage them as active users; the 'Cheerleaders' are top-class fans of the brand and likes everything a company does, hence the company should keep them updated and inspiring; and lastly the 'Ranters' can fight virtually due to their strong opinions about everything, so the company should react cautiously and very selectively to their opinioins (SEOPressor, 2012). Hence in overall the company should have a customised social platform strategy and the contents of the messages should be engaging with a sense of community, inclusive in action, newsworthy, and contents from all followers be allowed and recognised.

## SOCIAL MEDIA STRATEGIES

Piskorski, (2012) argued that companies that simply ported their digital strategies onto the social environments, 'maximising number of followers', and merely trying to broadcast their commercial information to customers, do not succeed on social platforms. Social strategies should be gradually unfolded in stages. At stage one, advises business to build better relationships between people and provide incentives if people undertake corporate tasks for free. At second stage the company should make non-intrusive attempt to build relationship between companies and consumers. A social strategist will create social presences of 'many to many interaction'. For example the Nike Plus platform, that allows its 5 million customers of Nike's digital products to interact with their friends; has contributed up to the 30% increase in sales. Similarly Cisco's social platform is not only protecting the company from aggressive moves of Chinese giant Huawei but also it has enabled engineers to interact with each other, achieve a number of certifications and become more effective on their jobs (Olensky, 2014).

Piskorski, (2014) supports three kinds of social stargic pardigms The first pardigm is, 'the pipes view', it conciders social networks are conduits which transfer trustworthy information about exchange opportunities between interested prties. The second vparadigm is 'prisms view' and posits that a platform offers a network tie between two parties, it has implications not only for the parties but also for third-parties not involved in the exchange. A third pardigm is 'networks as cover', that assumes that interactions with friends and acquaintances give actors an excuse to engage in other kind of prying activities, while still maintaining plausible deniability that they are not engaging

in such behaviors. For instant, LinkedIn allows users who are currently employed to go on the job market without apearing that they are on the job hunt, and facebook networks can allow people to look for new parteners without others realising this explicitly. Similaraly on social networking sites people can peek into privace areas that social norms may not allow in physical world. The study found that, only 50 per cent of profile and picture views are of friends, the remaining 50 per cent is of strangers (Piskorski, 2012).

A well thought out social strategy is usefull in toursim sector. following section sections details main social startgic actions using different social media tools .

## VARIETY OF SOCIAL MEDIA TOOLS

### 1. Social Networking

Social networking sites- Facebook, Google Plus, Cafe Mom, Gather, Fitsugaretc allows users to connect and share with people who have similar interests and backgrounds. The most famous example of social networking is Facebook, Twitter, and LinkedIn etc. That enables the tourists to efficiently communicate and interact with other members of social network like friends, family and co-workers and world at large. For using Facebook as a tool The business need to develop their brand profile through creating a Facebook page and share interesting, and newsworthy information with consumers. The company needs to help consumer meet their social needs and let them fulfil each other needs. Do not intrude or be pushy like salesman, and act as facilitator for creating social presence. Depending upon kind of users they can offer customised communications. Foe example does offer incentives or recognitions for new needs for deal seekers. Do respond to comments from complainers or fans and weave into your comments and posts to continually extend this. They can also create discussion forums to have feedback about their products and services. (Treadway and Smith, 2010). Another social platform is Linkedin. LinkedIn has 225 million registered users and on the average 110 million unique monthly visitors. Remember to follow effective communication principle of AIDA – attention-interest- desire and action. Request cheerleaders and opinion leaders for testimonials. Promote company through 'follow' button and remember to link your other social media accounts to your LinkedIn Company Page. Make the information engaging and varied but also remember pictures speak more than words.

## 2. Micro-Blogging Sites

Twitter, Tumblr, Posterous etc allow the users to submit short written entries, which can include links to product and service sites, as well as links to other social media sites. Twitter is very popular micro blogging site amongst the celebrities and Politicians, due to which it attracts a wide variety of fans of such personalities from around the globe. It provides an excellent opportunity to businesses to market there offerings through celebrates or by themselves. The message or tweet can be personal thoughts, quotes, news and picture links, brand, and product and service links, thus creating interest and buzz. Invite friends or brand cheer leaders and follow opinion leaders or media channels that are of interest to your customers & followers. Your followers are following you as role models or reference groups or your brand leadership due to power, authority, rank, expertise, referrals, coercive etc. ensure that you continuously perform your role. Tweet yourself and retweet from higher ups in industry, media, consumer groups, government reports and news channels etc.

## 3. Blog

Web log, is a web page that serves as a publically accessible personal journal for an tourists (Blood 2002 in (Ernested V., 2010)). A blog is power-

ful and inexpensive tool to can convey different types activities, interests and opinions such as political, commercial, public and personal word of mouth. They are also known as Publishing tools; like WordPress, Blogger, Squarespace etc. allows users engage in conversations by posting and responding to community message. Blogs can be updated on a frequent basis. Blogs can also be regularly developed for a variety of different marketing and branding campaigns. They are an active source of promoting products and services and spreading information (Khare, 2012). There are many different blogs that cover and attract people from specific industry. Marketers generally develop their profile and carry on updating them so that the fans and connected users are kept well informed.

## 4. Multimedia or Video Sharing

It enables sharing of multimedia content, for example Flickr (photographs) and YouTube (videos) are used by Millions of people exchange information and interests. Video sharing sites- YouTube, Vimeo, Viddler; etc.allow users to share different types of media, such as pictures and video. YouTube has more than 1 billion registered users at which videos are viewed 4 billion times per day is largest media sharing site in the world. Once registered a business can upgrade with a fee to get YouTube's 'branded channel' option. The business can increase traffic by using SEO keys and tags that are in line with interests of your consumer segment and your brand. Business should stay current and follow the rules of movie making and education. People like seeing more than reading but it must be something for them (SEOPressor, 2012).

## 5. Collaboration Tools

Wikipedia, WikiTravel, WikiBooks; etc are Apps or software based social platforms where users can work together (synchronously or asynchronously) to create, modify and manage content (Decidedlysocial, 2012; SEOPressor, 2012; About.com 2014).

## 6. Rating/Review Sites

Amazon ratings, Angie's List; Kind of platforms allow reviews to be posted about people, businesses, products, or services. It is a social strategy tool professionally designed and written to maximize conversions sales. (Decidedlysocial, 2012; SEOPressor, 2012; About.com 2014)

## 7. Photo Sharing Sites

Flickr, Instagram, Pinterest; etc. enable users to upload, transform edit, publish and share pictures and videos etc (Decidedlysocial, 2012; SEOPressor, 2012; About.com 2014). Instagram is very popular photos and videos sharing platform and recently purchased by Facebook. It has 130 million active monthly users. The business can upload photos or videos of brands or other issues of interests and can link with other social platforms and invite people to click for favourite ones. To keep always in the trend continuously upload new actions photos about your actions that would be of interest to users. That addresses their social, rational, emotional and epistemic needs. (SEOPressor, 2012).

## 8. Personal Broadcasting Tools

Blog Talk radio, Ustream, Livestream, tumbler are platforms that offers a way of participatory journalism and synonyms to personal publishing.

## 9. Platforms like Virtual Worlds

Second Life, World of Warcraft, and Farmville Are 3D computer based online community environment in which users are represented on screen as themselves or as made-up characters and interact in real time with other users using texts, or 2D or 3D models, knows as Avatars (Decidedlysocial, 2012; SEOPressor, 2012; About.com 2014).

## 10. Location based Services

Check-ins, Facebook Places, Foursquare, and Yelp etc are Apps on gadgets and mobiles that uses geographical position (GPS) and link it with information, entertainment, or social media service that is available nearby location. E.g. gas prices and services or restaurants near your location (Decidedlysocial, 2012; SEOPressor, 2012; About.com 2014).

## 11. Widgets

Profile badges, Like buttons etc are sets of small helpful software program or Apps, which gives extra power an control to the user when embedded directly into a web page. These can be used to add features like, weather, clock, local news, Twitter widget, Mailing list, gossips and joke of the day etc (Decidedlysocial, 2012; SEOPressor, 2012; About.com 2014).

## 12. Group Buying Sites

Groupon, Living Social, Wowcer, Crowdsavings etc are latest trend in money saving, with the power to pull in big discounts(Decidedlysocial, 2012; SEOPressor, 2012; About.com 2014).

## 13. Social Bookmarking and News Aggregation

Digg, Delicious, StumbleUpon and son on allow users to save and organize links to any number of online resources and websites(Decidedlysocial, 2012; SEOPressor, 2012; About.com 2014). Social bookmarking such as StumbleUpon discovery engine has 25 million registered users. It searches and recommends web pages to its users and can also be shared by others to 'like it'. This also recommends users other related sites or sites that your network has liked or submit industry related sites and blogs or create a stumble upon channel (SEOPressor, 2012).

## 14. Email Marketing

Sending emails to exiting or potential tourists is one of the most effective Internet marketing .

## 15. Search Engine

*Like Google, bing, yahoo etc are* used by tourist to find the company or destination information and search engine optimisation can bring a particular site at top search position (Ernestad V., 2010).

## MEASURING SOCIAL MEDIA PERFORMANCE AND EFFECTIVENESS IN TOURISM

Social media marketing has become a critical success factor that is driving the success of many businesses today. However as more and more tourism organisations investing money into their social media strategy questions are now emerging on whether this spending on social media result in better performance for the whole business. Unfortunately there is no clear answer to this question at the moment. Social media marketing is still in its infancy stages for many tourism businesses, this makes it difficult to measure its performance. Managers and marketers responsible for promoting the use of social media continue to find it challenging to demonstrate the value of their investment on Facebook, Twitter and other bring to their business. Hoffman and Fodor (2010) noted that business in general and their marketing departments in particular are still searching for the right way to measure the impacts of their social media strategy because most of the models used are primarily by 'reach and frequency'.

Business Metrics provide a feedback mecha-

improvement. Organisations just like working with metrics, the CEO and department managers need a number to measure the performance of their investment; this is because orient people towards a goal, help them to focus and measure success. It is believed that activities that are not measured they often do not get done. However, much as the numbers have their advantages if they are note well managed they may bring problematic behaviour and ultimately detract from broader organisational goals. Therefore, without a reliable measurement it may be difficult to judge whether goals have been successfully achieved (Demopolous, Futch and Pisello 2008). Thus measuring the impacts of social media on the organisations is likely to guide investment on the right networks to use, though this poses other questions 'what is to measure?'; what key metrics can help the organisation to understand the influence of social media in the context of their own industries, size, and geographies? And lastly how should the organisation interpret these metrics?

One would wonder if organisations can realistically specify bottom line benefits that result directly from the use of social media as a marketing strategy. Much as Social media starts with ideation and creativity, differs from any other marketing tool, because it is a science that revolves around big data, statistics and numbers. It is also much more than just posting or sharing or number of likes or followers. Tourism organisations need to measure not only its influence on the overall performance of the business but also to justify the time and money invested in social media. Organisations that fail to scrutinise the deep data generated by social networks they use data are doomed to fail in their social media marketing. Tourism organisation should note that social media bears many of the core principles of measuring other marketing tools and also apply them to social media. For instance, marketers and managers are still interested in understanding how big is their audience on the social media? The rate at which

well as, the extent of the traffic generated to their business from the social media networks.

When measuring the influence of social media to the business performance, there are two main aspects to consider: impacts and Return on Investment (ROI). Regarding impacts of social media, the business has to find answers to the following questions:-

The impact of social media on a business performance can vary significantly from one organisation to another, and between industries and sectors, the size of the organisation as well as the geographical region. Thus making it difficult to measure and determine whether the investment on social media provide the desired effect to the business. However, it is now accepted by many business managers and marketers that a well-designed social media strategy can provide a competitive advantage. Measuring a business social media influence has become important as more and more people use these networks to seek for advice from their peers on the products and services about what they think, say and by (Elderman 2007). Online social networks produce information every minute, whenever, someone posts something on Facebook, Twitter or Pinterest, they create a digital footprint. Similarly, every time someone reads the post on any of the social networks or watch a video on Vimeo or YouTube they add to their digital trail. But how does a business identify these opportunities and justify its investment on social media channels that will deliver the best return?

Social media measurement is not straight forward process as it has various areas numbers may not provide the real insights on its impacts to the business. One of the problem of measuring social media's ROI is that the organisation is trying to convert non quantifiable elements such as people's interactions and conversations into numeric quantities. Organisation that try to measure the impact of social media on the business often rely on the number of followers but, it is difficult to measure the number of tweets a

day or to determine the worth of 1000 followers on Facebook.

Some commentators have argued that much as it may not be easy to measure social media, there are ways this can be done but the managers have decide what could be regarded as 'return' (Bitzer, 2012). This is so because the social media metrics such as the number of likes or followers cannot be relied on when measuring the revenue generated to the tourism business from social media though other social metrics such as customers' sentiments of the business and feedback can provide valuable insights that can help the business to improve.

On the other hand without a proper framework for measuring, there is no way of knowing how an activity is performing. Therefore the number of tweets a day or followers provides the initial basis it is not enough to give the true picture of social media strategy success. Organisations need to be able to identify and develop a criteria as well as metrics that can enable them not only to understand the landscape of their social media strategy but also its impact on it operations and audiences. Tourism managers and marketers using social media need to understand that it is not the destination; it is just a vehicle. They need to ask themselves question such as 'what is the ROI of social media?'; what is the ROI of the particular activities that the organisation engage in using the social media?. Answering these question will help organisation to focus on measuring only the right things instead of wasting resources measuring each and every activity

The market as well as the internet is full of tools to measure social media as well as numerous metrics, measurement gurus making it extremely difficult for tourism managers and marketers to wade through this maze of options to choose the right one that will help them. However, there are models that can help the managers to understand the value of their efforts on social media, for example Etlinger (2011) developed a the Altimeter's social measurement compass framework and identified six main organisation goals that

*Figure 3. The seven steps to social media measurement*
*Source: Paine (2011)*

| | |
|---|---|
| 1. | Define the "R" — Define the expected results? |
| 2. | Understand your audiences and what motivates them |
| 3. | Define the "I" -- What's the investment? |
| 4. | Determine what you are benchmarking against |
| 5. | Define the metrics (what you want to become) |
| 6. | Pick a tool and undertake research |
| 7. | Analyze results and glean insight, take action, measure again |

social media can help influence including *brand health, marketing optimisation, revenue generation, operational savings, customer experience,* and *innovation.*

Paine (2011) argued that measurement of social media should always be linked to the business objectives and goals and provides the following framework that can also be used by tourism and hospitality managers.

As Table 1 above indicates this framework is made up of seven steps that can be summarised as business objectives, audience, and cost of social media management, benchmarking, KPIs, data collection tools, and action. In this chapter we will outline these steps because they are not exclusive to social media but instead provide a basis for measuring the other business strategies.

Moreover these steps are familiar to most managers and marketers as they are not knew instead Paine used the same steps marketers have been using for a long a time. The purpose of Paine's framework is to provide a models that can help managers prove that social media is working and be able to use the results to plan for future performances.

Firstly, social media should be treated like any investment a tourism organisation undertake to achieve its business objectives. For example a hotel may have one of its objective as 'increase occupancy by X% by the end of December 2014. By having such a specific objective it helps the business to focus their social media campaigns. This way the business can claim that the time spent on updating their Facebook page and competitions they hosted there in the past 2 months

*Table 1. Impact on social media*

| Impacts | ROI |
|---|---|
| | Did sales, revenue and profit increase due to the business' activities on the social media |
| How the messages were communicated? | Did the business get the right type of customers |
| Did the relationship improve? | Did the relationship with the customers and other businesses change |
| Did the business get the exposure it was looking for? | Did the customers' behaviour change |

have helped to drive the business to achieving its objective. Focussing the social media strategy on the business objectives may also lead to creating sub-objectives or tasks that social media should meet in order to achieve the business objectives. For instance, if the business objective is to increase hotel occupancy b X% by the end of the year then what should be the social media strategy? In this case the strategy may use short term campaigns such as time-limited offers lasting a fortnight, a month or two and then measure their impact on the main business objective. On the other hand the strategy may be to increase brand awareness, in this case viral campaigns targeting potential customers may be initiated by using general awareness messages. The bottom line is that when a business link its objectives to their social media strategy it is able to measure the success of individual tasks and determine its impacts on how the business achieved its objective or objectives.

The second step on Paine (2011) model is the identification of the audience. That is who is the business talking to? This question will help the tourism business identify the people associated with their brand and then the next questions are 'how will the business know that thy have reached their audience?' When identified and reached, 'what is it that they business want them to do?' and lastly, how will this help the business to achieve its objectives? For a tourism business such as a hotel or restaurant the target audience is most likely to be varied. For instance for a hotel the audience could be business or leisure customers of varied age, geographical locations and cultures. All these groups may be on different social media channels, therefore, whilst the hotel message may be seen by all the people on that channel, the hotel has to make it clear as to which message is intended for business or leisure customers and the actions expected from them intended audience. Note that the messages for each audience group is different as each group has different needs and requirements.

The next step for the hotel would be to attach a value to each of these audience groups, this will to determine if the business audience group picking up on the message is more valuable than the leisure audience. Just like in the 1st step the business need to relate its social media activities to its objectives such as 'increase leisure customer engagement, because the recent analysis of the business showed that games and competitions on Facebook led to more leisure guests bookings in the past'. In this case, the business measure of social media could be to count the number of leisure customers following the hotel brand and to monitor the number of reviews they produce about the brand.

Thirdly the business has to determine the cost of running the social media campaign in terms of the money invested and the number of hours put in the campaign to be able not only to put a monetary value to the cost but also to be able to determine the opportunity cost. This is Delahaye Paines model is referred to as the 'I' in ROI (Paine, 2011).

The fourth step is to determine some benchmark to help the business to compare against something, this could be the business past performance and/ or a competitor. The business need to set up baseline numbers to compare to in order to measure change. This is just like if a hotel's objective is to increase occupancy by X% by the end of the year, what was the occupancy last year? Then how has the use of social media led to his increase. Benchmarking can also be based on the other marketing campaigns to measure its influence or effectiveness compared to the other ways the business is promoting itself. For instance in terms of the Facebook what could be the worth of a 'page view' as compared to for example the cost of a click in pay per view campaign. Comparing with other marketing campaigns or past performance can help the business to measure the success or social media campaign in achieving its business objectives.

Following determination of the business objectives and identification of the audience, as well as establishing benchmarks the fifth step of measurement detail is to determine the criterial for success or the Key Performance Indicators [KPIs] (Lovett, 2011). These are the outcome metrics that focus on the different objectives of the business social media strategy which may be for example increase leisure customer followers on Twitter. In this case the audience is leisure customers while the benchmark is the current number of followers, therefore the KPI would be how many follower have been signed up among leisure and business customers, this could be classifying the customers in their audience groups and carry out a head count.

Analysis of KPIs may be an important tool for determining the effectiveness of the social media marketing strategy. KPIs can be measured by deterring both the pre and post- campaign periods, this will allow the business to have a clear understanding of the success or failure of the social media strategy. KPIs analysis also help the business to be able to produce quantified metrics that may lead to making informed decision as well as producing qualitative data that may provide the analysis for future social media trends. Qualitative data such as feedback expressed by the customers on social media platforms can help organisations to improve the product or service.

The sixth step involves selecting tool to measure data gathered. On the social media such as Facebook the business may put their main focus on three key areas likes, shares and links and comment on post, this is because when someone likes the business' page it will know that its audience is listening. While a comment made by a follower on the business post means a two way conversation is taking place and the customer is engaged; and when the customer share the hotel's post with their friends on Facebook, it is a sign that the audience has expanded. Likewise the process of gathering data and analysing it for social media may differ depending on the type of data the business gather. Today, there is a great number of data collection tools available each of them produce a different

kind of data. What is to be noted is that there is not a single tool that can measure all the nuances of social media by itself, though each tool may be used to gather data on a particular aspect and the sum of all the data gather by each tool may provide a better understanding of the effectiveness of social media strategy. For data involving sentiments, messaging or conversations content analysis is the best tool to use, whereas measuring perceptions, awareness or relationships survey research would the tool to use. However, when the data to be measured involves making predictions or correlations then web analytic tool such as google analytics would provide better outcomes

Lastly, Paine (2011) noted that measuring social media is an iteration process that involves doing something, measure the results and act or make changes where necessary, which will eventually lead to new results. At this point the business may ask questions such did we meet our business objectives? Then based on the results go through the process may be with some changes for improved results. The whole process is ongoing aimed at optimisation or continuous improvement.

As has been noted in this discussion social media is the way of marketing a tourism related business. Paine's seven steps are of measuring social media performance are grounded in the fundamentals, they are not different from the way other business performances are measured. Failure to relate social media to the underlying business fundamentals chances of understanding the business performance from the social media may be futile.

## REFERENCES

Anjum, A. (2011). *Social Media Marketing*. GRIN.

Barefoot, D., & Szabo, J. (2010). *Friends with Benefits: A Social Media Marketing*. Handbook, California: No Starch Press Inc.

Bitzer, M. (2012). *Social Media ROI and Why Your Hotel May Be Focussing on the Wrong Turn.* Available at http://www.bluemagnetinteractive. com/blog/117-social-media-roi-and-why-your-hotel-may-be-focusing-on-the-wrong-return.html

Bolotaeva, V. A. (2011). Marketing Opportunities with Social Networks. *Journal of Internet Social Networking and Virtual Communities.*

Borgan, C. (2010). *Social Media 101.* New Jersey: John Wiley and Sons. doi:10.1002/9781118256138

Bryan, D. (2013). *Small business advertising and brand promotion using Facebook Ads.* Retrieved June 20, 2014 from Opace Web: http://www.opace. co.uk/blog/social-media-ppc-facebook-ads-vs-linkedin-ads-vs-google-adwords-which-would-you-choose

Buhalis, D., & Law, R. (2008). Progress in information technology and tourism management: 20 years on and 10 years after the Internet – The state of e-Tourism research. *Tourism Management, 29*(4), 609–623. doi:10.1016/j.tourman.2008.01.005

Campbell, A. (2010, Jan 21). *Social Media — A Definition.* Retrieved June 16, 2014 from Amy Cambell's Web log: https://blogs.law.harvard. edu/amy/2010/01/21/social-media-a-definition/

Conrad, J. (2010). *Guerrilla Social Media Marketing.* Entrepreneur Media Inc.

Corstjens, M, & Umblijs, A. (2012). The Power of Evil: The Damage of Negative Social Media Strongly Outweigh Positive Contributions. *Journal of Advertising Research, 52*(4), 433-449.

Decidedlysocial. (2012). *13 Types of Social Media Platforms and Counting.* Retrieved June 20, 2014 from Decidedlysocial: http://decidedlysocial. com/13-types-of-social-media-platforms-and-counting/

Deighton, J. K. (2007, Sept 26). *Digital Interactivity: Unanticipated Consequences for Markets, Marketing, and Consumers.* Retrieved June 20, 2014 from HBS.edu: http://www.hbs.edu/faculty/Publication%20Files/08-017_1903b556-786c-49fb-8e95-ab9976da8b4b.pdf

Demopoulos, P., Futch, J., & Pisello, T. (2008). *The Importance of measuring ROI: the Indicators of Business and IT performance.* An Alinean White Paper.

Dewey, C. (2013). Tourism goes mobile and social. The Business Newspaper, 31(18).

Duggan, M. S. (2013, Dec 30). *Social Media Update 2013.* Retrieved June 25, 2014 from Pew Internet Reserch: http://www.pewinternet. org/2013/12/30/social-media-update-2013/

EbizMBA. (2014, June). *Top 15 Most Popular Social Networking Sites | June 2014.* Retrieved June 25, 2014 from EbizMBA: http://www.ebizmba.com/articles/social-networking-websites

Edelman, J. B. (2007). *Distributed Influence: Quantifying the Impacts of Social Media.* Available at http://technobabble2dot0.files.wordpress. com/2008/01/edelman-white-paper-distributed-influence-quantifying-the-impact-of-social-media.pdf

Ernestad V., H. R. (2010). *Social media marketing from a bottom-up perspective - the social media transition.* Retrieved March 28, 2014 from http://www.carphonewarehouse.com

Etlinger, S. (2011). *A Framework for Social Analytics: Six Use Cases for Social media Measurement.* Altimeter Group Publication.

Evans, D. (2012). *Social Media Marketing* (2nd ed.). Indiana: Wiley Publshing.

Evans, D., & McKee, J. (2010). *Social Media Marketing.* Indiana: Wiley Publishing.

Gunelius, S. (2011). *30 Minute Social Media Marketing*. Ontario: McGraw Hill.

Hajir, K. (2012). *Your Social Media Marketing Plan*. Available at: http://yoursocialmediamarketingplan.com/

Halligan, B., & Shah, D. (2010). Inbound Marketing. New Jersey: Wiley Publishing.

Hanna, R., Rohm, A., & Crittenden, V. L. (2011). *We're all connected: The power of the social media ecosystem Kelley School of Business, 54* (pp. 265–273). Elsevier.

Hendricks, J. (2010). *The 21ˢᵗ Century Media Industry*. Lexington Books.

Hoffman, D. L., & Fodor, M. (2010). Can you measure the ROI of your social media marketing? *MIT Sloan Management Review, 52*(1), 41–49.

Jaoker, A., Jacobs, B., & Moore, A. (2009). *Social Media Marketing*. Future Text.

Kabani, S., & Brogan, C. (2010). *The Zen of Social Media Marketing*. Dallas, TX: Barbell Books.

Kaplan, A. M., & Haenlein, M. (2010). *'Users of the world, unite! The challenges and opportunities of Social Media', Kelley School of Business, 53* (pp. 59–68). Elsevier.

Khare, P. (2012). *Social Media Marketing Elearing Kit for Dummies*. New Jersey: John Wiley and Sons.

Kimbarovsky, R. (2009). *10 Small Business Social Media Marketing Tips*. Available at: http://mashable.com/2009/10/28/small-business-marketing/

Leonardi, M. H., Huysman, M., & Steinfield, C. (2013). Enterprise Social Media: Definition, History, and Prospects for the Study of Social Technologies in Organizations. *Journal of Computer-Mediated Communication, 19*(1), 1–19. doi:10.1111/jcc4.12029

Litvin, S. W., Goldsmith, R. E., & Pan, B. (2008). Electronic word-of-mouth in hospitality and tourism management. *Tourism Management, 29*(3), 458–468. doi:10.1016/j.tourman.2007.05.011

Lovett, J. (2011). *Social Media Metrics Secrets*. Indianapolis: John Wiley and Sons.

Manap, K. A. (2013). The Role of User Generated Content (UGC) in Social Media for Tourism Sector. *International Academic Conference Proceedings*, 11-78.

Manap KhairulHilmi, A. A. N. (2013). *The Role of User Generated Content (UGC) in Social Media for Tourism Sector*. Retrieved March 28, 2014 from http://www.westeastinstitute.com/wp-content/uploads/2013/07/Khairul-Hilmi-A-Manap.pdf

Minghetti, V., & Buhalis, D. (2010). Digital divide in Tourism. *Journal of Travel Research, 49*(3), 267–281.

Olensky, S. (2014, March 3). *Social Media And Branding: A One On One With A Harvard Business Professor*. Retrieved June 24, 2014 from Forbes: http://www.forbes.com/sites/steveolenski/2014/03/17/social-media-and-branding-a-one-on-one-with-a-harvard-business-professor/

Paine, K. D. (2011). *Measuring What matters: online Tools for Understanding Customers, Social Media, Engagement and Key Relationships*. Indianapolis: John Wiley and Sons.

Pan, B. C. J. (2011). *Theoretical Models of Social Media, Marketing Implications, and Future Research Directions*. Retrieved March 25, 2014 from Theoretical Models of Social Media, Marketing Implications, and Future Research Directions: https://www.google.co.uk/search?q=Theoretical+Models+of+Social+Media%2C+Marketing+Implications%2C+and+Future+Research+Directions&rlz=1C5CHFA_enGB513GB513&oq=Theoretical+Models+of+Social+Media%2C+Marketing+Implications%2C+and+Future+Research+Directions&aqs=chrome.69i57j0.1765j0j4&sourceid=chrome&espv=2&es_sm=91&ie=UTF-8

Piskorski, M. (2012). *Networks as covers: Evidence from business and social on-line networks.* Retrieved June 20, 2014 from HBS. Edu: http://www.people.hbs.edu/mpiskorski/papers/FA-Platforms.pdf

Piskorski, M. (2014). *A Social Strategy: How We Profit from Social Media.* http://www.amazon.com/Social-Strategy-How-Profit-Media/dp/0691153396

Safko, L. (2010). *The Social Media Bible.* New Jersey: John Wiley and Sons.

Schlinke, J., & Crain, S. (2013). Social Media from an Integrated Marketing and Compliance Perspective. *Journal of Financial Service Professionals, 67*(2), 85-92.

SEOPressor. (2012). *Social Media Marketing.* Retrieved June 20, 2014 from Seopressor: http://seopressor.com/social-media-marketing/

Singh, S. (2008). *Social Media Marketing for Dummies.* John Wiley and Sons.

Stelzner, M. (2011). *2011 Social Media Marketing Industry Report How Marketers Are Using Social Media To Grow Their Businesses.* Retrieved March 16, 2014 From 2011 Social Media Marketing Industry Report: http://www.socialmediaexaminer.com/SocialMediaMarketingReport2011.pdf

Sterne, J. (2010). Social Media Metrics. New Jersey: John Wiley and Sons

Taylor, E., & Riklan, D. (2009). *Mastering the world of Marketing.* New Jersey: Wiley and Sons.

The Equity Kicker. (2012). *More on the future of TV.* Retrieved March 20, 2014 from http://www.carphonewarehouse.com

Thomases, H. (2010). *Twitter Marketing: An Hour a Day.* Indiana: Wiley Publishing Inc.

Treadway, C., & Smith, M. (2010). *Facebook Marketing: An hour a Day.* Indiana: Wiley Publishing.

Turner, J., & Shah, R. (2011). *How to Make Money with Social Media.* New Jersey: FT Press.

Tuten, T. (2008). *Advertising 2.0: Social Media Marketing.* Westport: Greenwood Publishing.

Xiang, Z., & Gretzel, U. (2010). *'Role of social media in online travel information search', Tourism Management, 31* (pp. 179–188). Elsevier.

Zarrella, D. (2009). *The Social Media Marketing Book.* Sebastopol, CA: O`Reilly Books.

Zimmerman, J., & Sahlin, D. (2010). *Social Media Marketing for Dummies.* New Jersey: Wiley Publishing. doi:10.1002/9781118257661

# Chapter 10
# Organizational Citizenship Behavior:
## A Field Study in the Italian Hospitality Industry

**Francesca Di Virgilio**
*University of Molise, Italy*

**Angelo Presenza**
*University G. D'Annunzio of Chieti-Pescara, Italy*

**Lorn Sheehan**
*Dalhousie University, Canada*

## ABSTRACT

*This chapter analyzes organizational citizenship behavior of permanent versus contingent employees in the Italian hospitality industry. The empirical data were derived from a questionnaire survey conducted in three regions of Southern Italy. Survey respondents were 848 frontline employees from 63 hotels. Findings show that contingent employees exhibited less helping behavior than permanent employees but no difference in their voice behavior. In addition, work status was found to make more of a difference in both helping and voice in less work centrality organizations. Hotel managers are encouraged to focus attention on individual behavior that is discretionary, not directly or explicitly recognized by the formal reward system, and that in the aggregate promotes the effective functioning of the organization. Particularly in Italy, it would be advantageous to develop retention strategies for talented people that exhibit a high degree of organizational citizenship behavior.*

## INTRODUCTION

The hotel industry is a significant contributor to the global service economy. The contemporary hospitality industry is usually characterized by a high number of contingent employees, with low and unstable wages (Krakover, 2000; Bernhardt, Dresser, & Hatton, 2003), a requirement to provide high levels of customer service to all guests

DOI: 10.4018/978-1-4666-8606-9.ch010

for continual business (Lashley, 2001; Grandey, 2003), and an environment where employees often serve as the single point of contact with customers, representing the entire service provision. How employees interact with customers determines to a great extent how customers perceive the service quality. Individual employee uniqueness in terms of personality, attitudes and skills, means that the quality of service that they deliver is very often inconsistent. Additionally, hotel service is a highly interactive process, and both employees' and customers' physical well-being and moods influence the service experience. Thus, the mix of the workforce (i.e., replacing permanent employees with contingent employees) significantly influences customer evaluations, overall customer satisfaction, and customer perceptions of the organization's service quality (Johnson & Ashforth, 2008).

In the present study, contingent employees includes those who are employed under various forms of contractual arrangements. Traditionally in the tourism industry contingent work is used to meet short-run labor needs, so contingent employees are employed on the basis of an explicit and implicit contract that the work relationship will be for a specific and finite duration (Gallagher & McLean Parks, 2001; Connelly & Gallagher, 2004; Ismert & Petrick, 2004). Shortages of traditional, permanent employees have caused many organizations to increase their dependence on contingent employees (Connelly & Gallagher, 2004; Buonocore, 2010).

These trends in workforce recomposition, however, may have unintended, negative consequences on employee behaviors (especially discretionary behaviors) which may offset the benefits associated with reduced labor costs. To date, the comparison of contingent and permanent employees has focused on differences in job related attitudes such as satisfaction and commitment, without examining job behaviors, despite calls for research on potential differences in behavior

(Barling & Gallagher, 1996; Gallagher & McLean Parks, 2001).

The present research is based on Social Exchange Theory (Blau, 1964), which claims that individuals are likely to participate in an exchange with others if they believe that they are likely to gain benefits without incurring unacceptable costs. This approach views social situations economically, as people compare alternatives and choose that which they perceive to have the most value (Emerson, 1976). Social exchange involves behaviors that are dependent on rewards from others, and results in mutually beneficial relationships (Cropanzano & Mitchell, 2005).

The workplace organization forms an important part of the core social support system for its employees (He, Lai, & Lu, 2011). It follows that when employees feel that their workplace organization is acknowledging their contributions, meeting their socio-emotional needs, and taking their well-being into consideration, they will feel obligated to care about the organization's welfare and to help the organization reach its objectives because of the norm of reciprocity (Rhoades & Eisenberger, 2002).

This chapter analyzes this structural relationship, specifically highlighting the similarities and differences in helping and voice in relation to the role of work status and work centrality among frontline employees.

The norm of reciprocity further explains the positive relationship between Organizational Citizenship Behavior (OCB) and professional development. Ackfeldt and Coote (2005) conclude that professional development positively affects frontline employees' OCB, especially in those who are young. In addition, professional development has been found to be positively related to job attitudes (Hart et al., 2000). Employees are more inclined to reward their company with extra-role behavior when they are provided with learning opportunities. From an organizational perspective, professional development may considered an investment in the human capital which not only

*Figure 1. Research model*

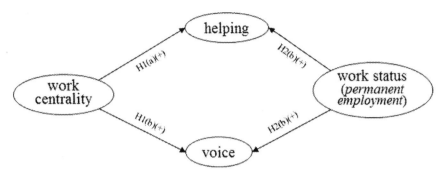

encourages OCB but also leads to the development of social skills and technical skills important to the delivery of quality service in the hospitality and tourism industry (Karatepe, Beirami, Bouzari & Safavi, 2014).

Achieving OCB can be challenging in the hospitality and tourism industry where front-line workers have a heavy workload, work long hours and receive relatively low wages (Baum, 2006). However, when frontline employees feel encouraged and well-equipped to cope with customer service, it is more likely that they will engage in OCB. In particular, employees tend to spend more time and effort in helping others (e.g., new employees, or temporarily overburdened ones) when they believe their managers are trustworthy (Yoon & Suh, 2003).

This leads us to hypothesize that contingent employees will display a lower level of organizational citizenship behavior (discretionary behavior that is not a required part of the job) than those that have permanent positions (Figure 1). In addition, we propose that work centrality (low versus high) moderates this relationship.

A questionnaire survey was conducted in three regions of Southern Italy which may be differentiated from Northern Italy in that they are almost exclusively organized around tourism product based on "Sun, Sea and Sand". The result is a concentration of tourism demand mainly in the summer period (OECD, 2011).

The respondents for this study are 848 frontline employees across 63 hotels. Stratified random sampling was employed based on the number of hotels in each category (luxury, midrange, economy, etc.).

Hotel frontline employees were selected for three reasons:

(1) service sector positions make up an increasingly large percentage of the total jobs in the Italy economy;
(2) most service-oriented organizations employ a large number of contingent workers who perform the same jobs as permanent employees (Kalleberg & Schmidt, 1996); and
(3) there is a relatively small amount of research on Italian hotel employees.

This chapter is organized as follows: in the first section, we discuss the structure of tourism and hospitality and the factors influencing OCB and describe the relevant literature. Following that, present a theoretical approach for explaining the role of work status and work centrality among service employees in typical customer-contact positions facilitating OCB in the Italian hospitality industry. We conclude with a discussion of the practical implications regarding organizational citizenship behavior in general as well as specific suggestions for the hospitality industry, and potential new paths of investigation for researchers.

## CHALLENGES FACING THE HOSPITALITY INDUSTRY

### Frontline Employees in the Hospitality Sector

Tourism has become a major economic activity as expectations with regard to the use of our leisure time have evolved, attributing greater meaning to our free time. Hotels are a fundamental element of the tourism product. Not only it is "the largest and most ubiquitous subsector within the tourism economy" (Cooper, Fletcher, Wanhill, Gilbert, & Shepherd, 1998, p. 313), typically accounting for around one-third of total trip expenditure, but it is also an essential ingredient of the tourism experience (Goss-Turner, 1996). Among the specific characteristics of the hotel industry that make it different from other service activities is the regular classification of hotels to indicate quality (Orfila-Sintes, Crespì-Cladera & Martìnez-Ros, 2005). The "stars" categorization that goes from 1 star to 5 stars signifies the type, number and quality of services provided.

Even though the official stars classification might be considered a good indicator of quality, it is not comprehensive because it does not reflect a range of factors related to the generally intangible nature of the final product (Núñez-Serrano, Turrión, & Velázquez, 2014). It follows that a more holistic approach is required to reinforce the customer attractiveness and satisfaction.

A more comprehensive analysis of hotel quality must take into account that the actual complexity of the product of hospitality comes from the cohesion of multiple services with different physical characteristics and intangible factors. Even when viewed entirely as a service, the hotel business is characterized by the coexistence of a number of factors such as: the intangibility and the immateriality of the service, the simultaneity of the stages of production and supply, the non-homogeneity of production, the heterogeneity of perception by tourists, the direct involvement of the tourist in the process of production and distribution as well as the importance and the significant contribution of human resources (Kandampully, 2003).

Given the importance of intangible factors, a quality hospitality experience depends on the ability to valorize the human resources. Hence the need for staff members with a variety of knowledge, skills, and experience that can provide products and services that are marketable and desirable to consumers (Hayes & Ninemeier, 2009). Furthermore, service in the hospitality industry is characterised by frequent interaction between employees and customers. It follows that the professionalism and friendliness of the employees are factors that have a significant impact on the overall perception of the hotel (Nickson, 2007; Torres & Kline, 2013). Because front-line employees are so critical to the tourist's experience, the hospitality industry is highly reliant on the talent of their employees. This reality has led many to conclude that the hospitality industry is more heavily dependent on its employees, and that they need to be different and have specific characteristics as compared to the employees in other industries.

Workers in hotels can be classified as frontline or backline (sometimes referred to as back-of-the-house) employees. Frontline employees are those who have direct contact with customers while backline employees seldom have contact with customers. In this study, the focus is on frontline hotel employees due their important role connecting the organization and its customers. Because of this boundary-spanning role, frontline employees differ from other employees in the organization. Frontline employees represent their organization to outsiders (customers), enhance the image of the organization, and improve the organization's legitimacy through advocacy. Because frontline employees are the interface between customers and the organization, and thus represent the organization, they are expected to express emotions that are aligned with how the organization wishes the quality of its services to be perceived (Karatepe et al., 2014). Ideally, frontline employees should enjoy serving customers, giving personalized attention to customers, and be capable of delivering the intended services to customers.

Such employees also routinely have to deal with numerous customer requests and complaints while adhering to the service standards set by the organization (Karatepe et al., 2014). Frontline service jobs require employees to deal with these various customer requests and problems and meet customer expectations. Therefore, astute hotel managers empower their employees to solve customer problems on the spot. This gives them a high degree of personal responsibility. Under these circumstances, frontline employees tend to invest more time and energy to meet challenging demands, because they see these demands as challenging, meaningful, and an opportunity for learning, development, and growth. As a result, such employees feel invigorated, have a sense of effective connection with their work, and experience a sense of personal accomplishment.

## The Italian Context

Italy has long been a renowned and appreciated global tourist destination, noted for its unique art cities, extensive history and cultural heritage, outstanding natural landscape, as well as shopping opportunities and food and wine tours. Among the world's top tourism destinations, Italy ranks fifth in arrivals (46 million) and sixth in receipts (US$ 41 billion) (UNWTO, 2013).

Tourism plays a very important role for the Italian economy. In 2011 Italy's tourist industry overall turnover was about € 136.1 billion, contributing to over 8.6% of GDP with more than 1.1 million employees. In 2012, the total contribution of Travel & Tourism to employment, including jobs indirectly supported by the industry, was 11.7% of total employment (WTTC Travel & Tourism Economic Impact, 2013) spread across more than 153,000 firms (Italian Institute of Statistics, 2014). The tourist industry is essentially composed of the accommodation system, a complex of structures

and services aimed at welcoming tourists and other travellers. The total number of accommodation facilities in Italy (Invitalia, 2014) is over 153,000 accommodation facilities that may be further described as:

- almost 34,000 hotels (from five-star luxury to one star)
- almost 4,6 million bed spaces (in all types of accommodation) over 2,2 million bed spaces (in hotels)

The sector is composed primarily of small businesses where the vast majority (90%) have less than 10 employees and 8% with between 10 and 49 employees (UnionCamere, 2013). Over the years there has been a process of rationalization and upgrading of the Italian system of accommodation (Federalberghi, 2010). The result is a relatively stable number of accommodation facilities and an expansion of actual accommodation capacity (in terms of rooms and, consequently, in terms of beds available). In addition to the restructuring process just outlined, since the nineties the accommodation sector has underwent an upgrading of facilities. The result has been a reduction of the number of structures of the lower quality category (1 and 2 stars), and a commensurate increase in the number of structures in the higher quality categories. Despite this positive quality shift, the highest quality group of structures still remains in the minority so the Italian accommodation system continues to be characterized by hotels of medium-low quality with 51.9% of structures in the 3-star category (representing 53.3% of beds and 52.5% of rooms). Based on employment, hotels are the largest group, accounting for 75.9% of companies and 82.2% of employees.

The accommodation sector is greatly influenced by seasonal demand, leading many businesses to stay open only during certain periods of the year. In addition to depressing the profitability of enterprises, this concentration leads to several

in unemployment. This also creates higher training costs as each season begins.

## THEORETICAL FRAMEWORK

### Organizational Citizenship Behavior

One of the most widely studied topics in organizational behavior research is Organizational Citizenship Behavior (OCB) (Podsakoff, MacKenzie, Paine & Bachrach, 2000; Hannam & Jimmieson, 2002). The concept was introduced by Bateman and Organ (1983) and later refined and strengthened by number of researchers such as Podsakoff, Ahearne and MacKenzie (1997).

Organizational Citizenship Behaviors are defined as those individual behaviors that are beneficial to the organization and are discretionary, not directly or explicitly recognized by the formal reward system or individual behavior that is discretionary, not directly or explicitly recognized by the formal reward system, and that in the aggregate promotes the effective functioning of the organization (Organ, 1988).

Although researchers hold different views regarding the specific dimensions of OCB, they generally agree that OCB is a multidimensional construct (Graham, 1989; Moorman & Blakely, 1995; Organ, 1988; Podsakoff, MacKenzie, Moorman & Fetter, 1990; LePine, Erez & Johnson, 2002). However, perspectives on the dimensionality of OCB have diverged.

To date, researchers have proposed a variety of specific dimensions of OCB including altruism, conscientiousness, sportsmanship, courtesy, civic virtue, obedience, loyalty, advocacy participation, social participation, functional participation (Van Dyne, Graham, & Dienesch, 1994), helping and voice (Van Dyne, Cummings, & McLean Parks, 1995; Van Dyne & LePine, 1998), as well as organization-focused and interpersonal-focused behavior (Williams & Anderson, 1991).

Research that focuses on the targets of OCB is more limited, but dates to the establishment of the construct. Smith et al. (1983) conducted a factor analysis on the attributes of OCBs, and generated two factors: altruism and generalized compliance. Williams and Anderson (1991) further classified the two factors as (1) OCB-O, which refers to OCBs that benefit the organization in general and (2) OCB-I, which refers to OCBs that pertain primarily to individuals (employees) within the organization. Although different, these two ways of categorization are inter-correlated. The framework of OCB-O, for example, includes the Conscientiousness, Sportsmanship and Civic Virtue dimensions of Organ's (1988) framework, while OCB-I includes the remaining Altruism and Courtesy dimensions.

In our chapter we chose to focus on OCBs that pertain primarily to individuals (employees) within the organization and in particular two specific behaviors (helping and voice) because they form an interesting, theoretically-based contrast that we hypothesized would be important in service settings. We began empirical analysis of the typology by examining two promotive behaviors: helping (affiliative-promotive) and voice (challenging-promotive). In the hospitality and tourism industry, frontline employees play a critical role in affecting service encounters. In marketing literature, frontline employees are considered an integral part of hospitality and tourism products. Because service interactions between frontline employees and customers are numerous, frontline employees have more opportunities to perform OCB. Thus, empirical research provides strong evidence that OCB has a direct and positive relationship with service encounter practices (Gonzalez & Garazo, 2006). Therefore, it is sensible to assert that the success of the service encounters will be affected by frontline employees' OCB.

This study suggests that helping is particularly important in service jobs where fluctuating demand increases the benefits derived from cooperation. Specifically, employees have direct customer contact and often must balance competing demands for their time and attention. When work-flow is uneven, cooperative behavior can enhance customer interaction and quality service delivery.

Helping co-workers thus has the potential to enhance customer satisfaction in ways that cannot be specified in advance while simultaneously having important implications for overall service firm success.

In contrast, challenging promotive behavior emphasizes ideas that are change oriented. An example is speaking up and making recommendations for change and innovation. We suggest that expressing constructive suggestions (voice) is especially important in situations where consumers value high quality and novelty. In hospitality settings, employees are close to the service delivery process and often in the best position to generate ideas that can directly affect service quality and customer satisfaction.

Although helping and voice each have the potential to contribute positively to organizational success, these two forms of discretionary behavior differ fundamentally because helping is affiliative and voice is challenging. Helping promotes cooperation and positive interpersonal relationships. In contrast, voice focuses on change to the status quo (Van Dyne & LePine1998).

Helping and voice have evolved separately in the literature, and no empirical research has examined the extent to which these behaviors are distinct but related. According to the typologies in the literature (Van Dyne et al., 1995), helping and voice are similar not only because they are proactively promotive, but also because individuals who engage in helping and voice can be described as generally satisfied with their organizations.

## Helping Behavior

For over 50 years, scholars have recognized the importance of behavior that goes beyond normal

role expectations or job requirements that benefits or is intended to benefit the organization (Barnard, 1938; George & Brief, 1992; Katz & Kahn, 1978). Over the last decade research interest in these discretionary or extra-role behaviors has increased; however, the primary focus has been on affiliative behaviors (e.g., helping) associated with "organizational citizenship" (Organ, 1988) and "contextual performance" (Motowidlo & Van Scotter, 1994). Although this research has led to a great deal of insight, other types of extra-role behavior have received far less attention (Graham, 1991; Van Dyne, Cummings, & McLean Parks, 1995).

According to Van Dyne and colleagues (1995), helping is cooperative behavior that is noncontroversial. It is directly and obviously affiliative; it builds and preserves relationships; and it emphasizes interpersonal harmony. Helping is important for the organizations when roles are interdependent and employee cooperation facilitates overall performance.

Podsakoff et al. (2000) labeled the dimension helping behavior and defined it as voluntarily helping others with work related problems. While other researchers have addressed this category of behavior in a number of ways, all are similar to Williams and Anderson's (1991) definition of OCB-I.

The notion of behavioral exchange is a fundamental aspect of organizations, and has provided a theoretical foundation for understanding organizational life from a variety of perspectives, including psychology and social psychology (Adams, 1965), sociology (Blau, 1964; Gouldner, 1960), economics (Rappaport & Chammah, 1965; Williamson, 1981), and evolutionary biology (Axelrod, 1984). Exchange in the form of pay is a defining aspect of the employment relationship, although there has been increasing interest recently in examining non-monetary aspects of employment relationships, especially those rooted social in exchange concepts (Blau, 1964).

Gouldner (1960) argues that reciprocity helps to maintain social systems particularly in situations where there is no clear authority structure, and thus no formal definition of obligations. This is often the case among coworkers, who may each report to someone else but not each other. Absent formal or contractual obligations for reciprocity, coworkers are likely to rely on norms of reciprocity to govern interactions and maintain the stability of the social group (Gouldner, 1960).

This may be especially the case related to the helping dimension of OCB. Helping behaviors in organizations are defined as voluntary behaviors that promote interpersonal harmony and help coworkers solve or avoid work-related problems (Podsakoff et al., 2000). These include employee acts of altruism, peacekeeping, cheerleading, courtesy and other small demonstrations of consideration and cooperation (Podsakoff et al., 1997; Podsakoff et al., 2000; Van Dyne et al., 1995; Van Scotter & Motowidlo, 1996), all of which have been shown empirically to load on the single "helping behavior" factor of OCB (Podsakoff et al., 2000). Thus, when an individual feels helped by the work group, the norm of reciprocity and social exchange suggest that s/he will reciprocate by exhibiting OCB directed toward helping others in the work group.

In summary, we argue that an important factor in explaining how much helping behavior an individual will exhibit in organizations is how much help the individual has received from coworkers.

## Voice Behavior

The notion of voice stems from the idea that employees recognize some source of dissatisfaction or opportunity for improving their own and/or their organization's well-being (Hirschman, 1970).

Speaking up in such situations can feel risky because they involve pointing out need for improvement in a program or policy to those who may have devised, be responsible for, or feel personally attached to the status quo. Given this, along with

the reality that voice cannot be coerced or readily designed into the in-role requirements of a job (Van Dyne & LePine, 1998), an initial motivation to speak up is likely to manifest in behavior only when the net perceived benefits outweigh potential costs. Perceived potential benefits of speaking up include getting the problem solved as well as formal (e.g., money or promotion) or informal (e.g., recognition or status) rewards that might be associated with having one's ideas be well received and possibly implemented. Conversely, potential costs include "existence losses" (e.g., demotion or termination) and "relatedness losses" (e.g., humiliation or loss of social standing) (Maslow, 1943). In short, the decision to speak up results from an affect-laden expectancy-like calculus (Ashford, Rothbard, Piderit, & Dutton, 1998; Milliken, Morrison, & Hewlin, 2003; Withey & Cooper, 1989).

Although scholars have acknowledged the contributions that voice and change-oriented behavior can make to organizational effectiveness (Katz & Kahn, 1978; Nemeth & Staw, 1989; Schein, 1968), voice is particularly important today given the emphasis on flexibility, innovation, and continuous improvement (Howard, 1995).

Van Dyne et al. (1995) reviewed the literature on extra-role behavior and proposed a two dimensional typology and nomological network. On one dimension, their typology contrasts promotive and prohibitive behavior (encouraging something to happen vs. encouraging something to cease). On the other dimension, their typology contrasts affiliative and challenging behavior (interpersonal behavior that promotes cooperation and strengthens relationships vs. change-oriented behavior that focuses on ideas and issues). Using this typology, Van Dyne and her colleagues distinguished between several forms of extra-role behavior.

Voice, defined as non required behavior that emphasizes expression of constructive challenge with an intent to improve rather than merely criticize (Van Dyne & LePine, 1998, p. 109), falls clearly in the promotive-challenging cell of the

Van Dyne et al. (1995) typology. Voice is distinct from affiliative behavior (e.g., helping) normally associated with organizational citizenship (Smith, Organ, & Near, 1983) or contextual performance (Motowidlo & Van Scotter, 1994; Van Scotter & Motowidlo,1996) because affiliative behavior (e.g., helping) is meant to preserve or improve relationships, whereas voice is challenging and may upset interpersonal relationships.

Voice is also distinct from prohibitive behaviors such as whistle-blowing (Near & Miceli, 1987; Miceli & Near, 1992). Whistle-blowing is critical and meant to stop some activity as opposed to being constructive and meant to change (improve) some activity.

From a theoretical and definitional perspective, given the definition of voice above, it is possible to further distinguish voice from other related behaviors. For example, we do not consider principled organizational dissent (Graham, 1986) to be voice because principled organizational dissent focuses on objections based on conscientious or moral principles rather than suggesting more effective ways of doing things. Voice behavior is also distinct from complaining. Complaints reflect expression of dissatisfaction and do not necessarily include suggestions for change (Kowalski, 1996). Because we define voice as a behavior, our use of the term does not refer to the availability of grievance procedures or perceptions of access to grievance procedures. Finally, voice is distinct from normal role or in-role behavior when the expression of constructive challenge is not specified in formal job requirements or descriptions. That is, constructive suggestions made by consultants or other change agents in the context of their job requirements are not voice as defined here. One example of voice as we define it is when a group member makes an innovative suggestion for change to a standard operating procedure in order to improve the context of their job requirements are not voice as defined here. One example of voice as we define it is when a group member makes an innovative suggestion for change to a standard operating procedure in

order to improve work flow, even when such a suggestion might upset others.

Voice is making innovative suggestions for change and recommending modifications to standard procedures even when others disagree. Voice is important when an organization's environment is dynamic and new ideas facilitate continuous improvement (Nemeth & Staw, 1989).

## Work Centrality and Work Status

Researchers suggest that OCB is a complex behavior that can be influenced by demographic factors (Ford & Richardson, 1994), personality traits (Konovsky & Organ, 1996; Elanain, 2007) and contextual factors (Chonko & Hunt, 2000; Baker, Hunt & Andrews, 2005). Of the many factors that have been investigated, social exchange has been repeatedly found to be an important motivator for employees' OCBs (Cho & Johanson, 2008; Podsakoff, et al., 2000).

The social exchange theory grew out of the disciplines of economics, psychology and sociology (Homans, 1958). In his seminal writing on social exchange, Homans (1958, p. 606) noted that:

"Social behavior is an exchange of goods, material goods but also non-material ones, such as the symbols of approval or prestige. Persons that give much to others try to get much from them, and persons that get much from others are under pressure to give much to them."

Blau (1986) further defined social exchange as voluntary actions of individuals that are motivated by the returns they are expected to derive from others, as well as social exchanges from relationships. Similar to economic exchange, social exchange generates an expectation of some future return for contributions; however, unlike economic exchange, the exact nature of that return is unspecified.

Social exchange theory has been used to explain the various phenomena and processes that occur in organizations, including OCBs (Tsui, Pearce, Porter & Tripoli, 1997; Tsui & Wu, 2005; Van

Dyne & Ang, 1998). For example, social exchange theory has been used to explain the relationship between employees and the organization (Tsui et al., 1997; Van Dyne & Ang, 1998). Employers utilizing the social exchange approach seek a long-term relationship with employees and show concern about employees' well-being and career development, and expect the concern and commitment to be reciprocated. From the social exchange perspective, if an employee is treated with respect they would be more likely to engage in OCBs (Cho & Johanson, 2008). Researchers also found that leaders' and supervisors' support can lead to employee citizenship behavior because a social exchange relationship is developed between employees and their supervisors (Organ, 1988; Podsakoff, et al., 2000). Similar findings have also emerged in the context of coworkers' social exchange (Ilies, Nahrgang & Morgeson, 2007; Rhodes & Eisenberger, 2002).

To date, most research on organizational citizenship has focused primarily on individual level predictors and has focused less on contextual factors (Cappelli & Sherer, 1991; Mowday & Sutton, 1993). The focus of this chapter is on work centrality as a key contextual characteristic.

Work centrality suggests that work plays a central role in employees' lives. It resembles the concepts of "job involvement" (Lodahl & Kejner, 1965) and "central life interest" (Dubin, Champoux, & Porter, 1975), but these were considered properties of individuals and not of the social system.

Despite its widespread use, both Brown (1996) and Paullay, Alliger, and Stone-Romero (1994) have argued that this measure is conceptually flawed because it confounds job involvement with work centrality. However, work centrality, refers to the extent to which individuals view work as a main component in their life. Work centrality is broader in scope than job involvement insofar as it reflects a belief in the importance that work should take in one's life. Thus, a person could report a low level of work centrality, indicating

that work is not one of the most important things in his/her life. An item from the job involvement scale reflecting work centrality (Lodahl & Kejner, 1965) is as follows: "most things that happen to me involve my work". This item clearly reflects an implicit assessment of the relative importance of work compared to other aspects of individuals' lives, rather than how immersed people are in their present job.

Given the fact that work centrality and job involvement represent different constructs, the use of measures confounding the two is inappropriate and may have contributed to the non significant relationship with performance reported (Brown, 1996). Recognizing this dilemma, factorially distinct measures of job involvement and work centrality have been developed (Paullay et al., 1994). Although Paullay et al.'s work separated the measurement of the two constructs, it did not provide criterion-related evidence for their distinctiveness. Our prediction is that work centrality has positive impacts on helping and voice.

Social exchange is different from economic exchange (Blau, 1964). Economic exchange is based on quid pro quo transactions, such as when employees receive pay for contributing their performance to the organization. In social exchange relationships, however, the details of the exchange are not specified in advance and monitoring inducements and contributions is less relevant. Instead, relational trust leads individuals in social exchange relationships (Rousseau & Tijoriwala, 1998) to believe that if they exercise initiative and contribute above minimum expectations, they will receive some forms of reciprocity from the organization at an unspecified future date (Gouldner, 1960).

Extending social exchange theory to help explain differences in contingent versus permanent work status suggests that contingent employees are more likely to develop economic rather than social exchange relationships with their employers (Rousseau, 1989; Tsui, Pearce, Porter, & Tripoli, 1997; McLean Parks, Kidder, & Gallagher,

1998). Contingent employees generally receive less from their organization, they perceive few if any rewards for their performance, they are not routinely considered for promotions, they do not have a steady work schedule (Van Dyne & Ang, 1998), and rarely receive benefits, training, and advancement from the organization as compared to permanent workers (Hipple, 1998).

Human capital theory (Becker, 1964) suggests that organizations invest in employees (especially in training and other less tangible benefits) when they can expect a return on their investment. When employees work more hours, the organization is more likely to accrue a higher return. In contrast, when employees work fewer hours, the potential return to the organization is less. Thus, employers are less likely to provide extra inducements to contingent employees. Given fewer inducements, contingent employees have less reason to perform tasks that require effort beyond that specified in their job descriptions (e.g., discretionary behaviors like helping and voice).

In summary, these arguments suggest that differences in the exchange relationships experienced by contingent versus permanent employees based on their work status will influence their behavior at work. Specifically, we expect that work status will influence voice and helping. In particular, contingent employees will exhibit less discretionary behavior than permanent workers due to the more economic nature of their employment relationship and the organization's emphasis on tangible (rather than both tangible and intangible) inducements.

## Research Model

The mediating role of work centrality and work status on OCB is presented in figure 1. In particular, the research model proposes the positive relationships that are expected to exist between work centrality and helping and voice, and between permanent employment and helping and voice.

Therefore, the research model introduces the following hypotheses:

*Hypothesis 1 (H1):* High levels of work centrality lead to increased helping behavior; and (*H1a*) high levels of work centrality lead to increased voice behavior (*H1b*).

*Hypothesis 2 (H2):* Permanent employees will exhibit more helping behavior than contingent employees; and (*H2a*) Permanent employees will exhibit more voice behavior than contingent employees. (*H2b*).

## METHODOLOGY

### Instrument Development: Structure of the Questionnaire

A structured questionnaire was used to gather data regarding OCB. The questionnaire consisted of three sections. The first section asked for information relating to the hotel characteristics (such as number of employees, ownership, etc.). The second section consisted of questions related to employee characteristics (such as gender, age, and contract type). The last section listed a set of 28 statements (explained in the next sections) to which respondents were asked to indicate their level of agreement on a 5-point Likert scale. Response choices were: 1 (strongly disagree), 2 (disagree), 3 (neither disagree nor agree), 4 (agree), and 5 (strongly agree).

Direct surveys are a method used to gain information by contacting respondents personally and surveying them face-to-face. For this research, all respondents were assured of confidentiality. This method usually gets a good response rate and information is more reliable and accurate (Singh and Mangat, 1996). A pilot study was conducted in one hotel on a total of four employees. The employees were interviewed to make sure that questions were clearly worded, properly phrased, and interpreted in a manner consistent with the intended meaning.

## Measurement Validation

Helping behavior was measured with a previously developed and validated 5-item scale (Podsakoff et al., 1990). Sample helping items included "Helps others who have been absent", and "Helps orient other employees even though it is not required" (Cronbach's alpha = 0.87).

Voice was measured with a previously developed and validated 8-item scale (Van Dyne, 1994). Items included "Frequently makes creative suggestions to coworkers" and "Encourages others to speak up at meetings" (Cronbach's alpha = 0.79).

Work centrality was measured using a previously developed and validated 12-item scale (Paullay et al., 1994) (Cronbach's alpha = 0.62).

Several control variables were included in the model since previous researchers demonstrated that attitudes of individuals at work may be influenced by demographic factors. These variables are: age (0= young (18-40) and 1= senior (>40)); gender (0 = male, 1 = female); work status (0= contingent employee, 1= permanent employee).

Other variables measured are directly relate to the hotel's characteristics, and are: quality (number of stars: 0= <4, 1= ≥4); size (number of employees: 0= ≤20, 1= >20); ownership (0= family business, 1= corporate).

## Sampling and Data Collection

The empirical research has been conducted in a geographic area consisting of three bordering and contiguous regions (Abruzzo, Molise, and Puglia), representing the Southern Italian Adriatic coast. The three regions have been selected on the basis of their accessibility. The main assumption associated with this convenience sampling is that the members of this sample are representative of the larger population of Southern Italy and reflect the "Sun, Sea, and Sand" tourism product.

Data collection was conducted during the months from October, 2012 to April 2013. After seven months of field study, 63 hotels were visited and 848 customer contact employees interviewed, representing a response rate of 94.2%. Descriptive statistics, correlations and regression (reported next) were performed by using SPSS 17.0.

## FINDINGS

### Demographic Profile of Participants and Hotel-Related Information

The demographic profile and work-related information of the hotel employees who responded to the survey (Table 1) indicate a fairly even split between men (47.17 percent) and women (52.83 percent). The sample was relatively youthful with

*Table 1. Participants' profile*

| | | Total (N = 848) | |
|---|---|---|---|
| | | N | Percentage |
| Gender | Men | 400 | 47.17 |
| | Women | 448 | 52.83 |
| Age | 18-40 years old | 655 | 77.24 |
| | 40 years old and above | 193 | 22.76 |
| Work status | permanent | 373 | 43.99 |
| | contingent | 475 | 56.01 |

*Table 2. Profile of hotels*

| | | Total (N = 63) | |
|---|---|---|---|
| | | Respondents | Percentage |
| Quality (star rating) | 1 to 3 stars | 352 | 41.51% |
| | 4 and 5 stars | 496 | 58.49% |
| Size (employees) | 20 employees or less | 316 | 37.26% |
| | more than 20 employees | 532 | 62.74% |
| Ownership | family business | 553 | 65.21% |
| | corporate | 295 | 34.79% |

people less than 40 years of age comprising 77.24 percent of the respondents.

Among permanent employees, (373) (45.58 percent) were women and 54.42 percent were men. Among contingent employees, 475 (58.53 percent) were women and 41.47 percent were men.

A profile of the 63 hotels (Table 2) revealed that the majority (58.49 percent) have either a 4 or 5 star rating, while the balance (41.51 percent) have a three star or lower rating. Examining size reveals that 62.74 percent of the hotels have more

than 20 employees and 37.26 percent have less than 20. The analysis of ownership reveals that 65.21 percent are family owned while 34.79 percent are corporate owned.

**Tests of Hypotheses**

Descriptive statistics and correlations for regular and contingent employees are reported in Table 3. On average workers reported higher levels of helping (4.30) and voice (4.13) than of work

*Table 3. Descriptive statistics and correlations*

| | Mean | SD | 1 | 2 | 3 | 4 | 5 | 6 | 7 | 8 | 9 |
|---|---|---|---|---|---|---|---|---|---|---|---|
| 1. Helping | 4.30 | 0.51 | 0.87** | | | | | | | | |
| 2. Voice | 4.13 | 0.54 | 0.58* | 0.79 | | | | | | | |
| 3. Workcentrality | 2.95 | 0.53 | 0.09* | 0.03 | 0.62 | | | | | | |
| 4. Gender[a] | 0.53 | 0.50 | -0.06 | 0.02 | -0.06 | - | | | | | |
| 5. Age[b] | 0.23 | 0.42 | 0.07* | 0.07* | 0.01 | -0.09* | - | | | | |
| 6. Work status [c] | 0.44 | 0.50 | 0.00 | 0.04 | 0.03 | -0.12* | 0.33* | - | | | |
| 7. Hotel quality [d] | 0.67 | 0.85 | -0.03 | 0.1* | -0.24* | 0.08* | 0.01 | -0.06 | - | | |
| 8. Hotel size [e] | 0.63 | 0.48 | -0.04 | -0.01 | -0.12* | -0.07* | 0.04 | 0.09* | 0.27* | - | |
| 9. Hotel property [f] | 0.35 | 0.48 | 0.01 | 0.01 | -0.47* | -0.01 | -0.02 | 0.01 | 0.06 | 0.31* | - |

* p < 0.05.
** Cronbach's coefficients are reported in bold
[a] 0= male; 1= female
[b] 0= young (18-40); 1= senior (>40)
[c] 0= seasonal employee; 1= permanent employee
[d] 0= <4; 1= ≥4
[e] 0= ≤20; 1= >20

*Table 4. Regression results*

| Independent variable | Dependent variable | |
|---|---|---|
| | Helping | Voice |
| Intercept | 3.99*** (0.13) | 3.82*** (0.14) |
| Work centrality | 0.11*** (0.04) | 0.08** (0.04) |
| Gender | -0.06* (0.04) | 0.03 (0.04) |
| Age | 0.10** (0.04) | 0.09* (0.05) |
| Work status | -0.03 (0.04) | 0.03 (0.04) |
| Hotel quality | 0.01 (0.02) | 0.08*** (0.02) |
| Hotel size | -0.06* (0.04) | -0.07* (0.04) |
| Hotel property | 0.09** (0.04) | 0.06 (0.05) |
| F (7, 839) | 2.69 | 2.79 |
| Prob > F | 0.01 | 0.01 |
| Adj R-squared | 0.01 | 0.01 |
| Number of obs | 847 | 847 |

*Significance at 10%; ** 5%; *** 1%. Standard errors in parenthesis.

centrality (2.95). Work centrality was positively related to voice.

The regression results (Table 4) support hypotheses 1a and 1b, that high levels of work centrality lead to increase in helping (0.11) and voice (0.08).

The results indicate that the relationships between work status (seasonal employee vs permanent employee) and helping and voice are not significant. However, there is a positive (yet not significant) relationship between work status and voice and a negative (yet not significant) relationship between work status and helping.

Both age and gender were found to be significantly related to helping, with gender being more significant. However, only age has a statistically significant effect on voice.

## CONCLUSION

This study proposed and tested a research model that examines the influence of work centrality and work status on Organizational Citizenship

Behaviour, in particular helping and voice. Data gathered from both permanent and contingent frontline hotel workers, were used to test four hypothesis.

The results show support for the hypotheses that high levels of work centrality are related to higher levels of helping and voice. In other words, the importance of work centrality is related to the demonstration of OCB by employees.

Conversely, the findings do not support the hypotheses concerning the effect of work status (permanent vs contingent employment). Work status was not significantly related to helping and voice. It follows that work status does not lead to significant differences in the two forms of OCB specifically examined - helping and voice.

Finally, while not hypothesized apriori, age and gender were both found to have a significant relationship to helping behaviour. Also unhypothesized, was the finding that age has a significant positive relationship with voice behaviour.

Implementing fairness and equality in human resource practices may, in fact, provide employees with a strong sense of psychological alignment with the corporate or family owner and may even reduce the perception of unfair treatment (Corbetta & Salvato, 2004; Pierce, Kostova, & Dirks, 2001). Human resource practices have been found (Barnett & Kellermanns, 2006) to have a mediating role between the influence of the family over the business and the perception of fairness and positively influence the overall level of organizational performance.

## THEORETICAL AND MANAGERIAL IMPLICATIONS

The current research contributes to the organizational citizenship behavior (OCB) literature in several important ways. First, this study confirms that work centrality is a potentially important determinant of individual behavior. Second, it demonstrates that work centrality is a useful predictor of OCB. Specifically two dimensions of OCB, helping (cooperative behavior) and voice (innovative suggestions for change), were shown to be directly related to work centrality. It also contributes to a better understanding of OCB in the hospitality literature by bringing an organizational behavioral perspective to the analysis of work centrality.

Due to its restricted geographic scope in the context of the hotel industry of Southern Italy, the present research might most appropriately be considered a pilot study. However, the results have interesting implications for management. The study has provided a valuable perspective on the importance of good human resource practices in this context. Due to the peculiar characteristics of the hospitality industry, it is clear that much of the success of the hotel in providing a high quality of service depends on the ability of the employer to find, retain, and valorize employees with high OCB. It follows that human resource management practices have to become an essential component

of the competitive strategy for hotels, irrespective of the structure, the size, and the market served.

## LIMITATIONS AND FUTURE RESEARCH DIRECTIONS

Generalizations from these findings, strictly speaking, are limited by industry (accommodation) and geography (the South Adriatic Coast of Italy). Second, the research has analyzed only two aspects of the employment relationship that may mediate the relationship between work status and OCB. In this regard, future research could examine various, other factors such as employee feelings of perceived organizational support (Eisenberger et al., 1986; Settoon et al., 1996; Shore & Tetrick, 1991) as key link between work status and OCB. Other mediating processes may include characteristics of the manager-employee relationship such as the quality of vertical dyadic relationships (Graen, 1976) and employee feelings of fairness (Moorman, 1991).

Further research might document the implications that both training and compensation have on specific dimensions of citizenship behaviors (Nasurdin, Ahmad, & Tan, 2014) in the accommodation sector. Other efforts could be made to examine human resource practices in other types of accommodation, and especially in small family businesses that are traditionally under-investigated despite their significant presence in the Italian tourism economy.

## REFERENCES

Ackfeldt, A. L., & Coote, L. V. (2005). A study of organizational citizenship behavior in a retail setting. *Journal of Business Research*, *58*(2), 151–159. doi:10.1016/S0148-2963(03)00110-3

Adams, J. S. (1965). *Inequity in Social Exchange.* In L. Berkowitz (Ed.), Advances in Experimental Social Psychology (Vol. 2, pp. 267–299). Academic Press.

Ashford, S. J., Rothbard, N. P., Piderit, S. K., & Dutton, J. E. (1998). Out on a limb: The role of context and impression management in selling gender-equity issues. *Administrative Science Quarterly, 43*(1), 23–57. doi:10.2307/2393590

Axelrod, R. (1984). *The Evolution of Cooperation.* New York: Basic Books.

Baker, T. L., Hunt, T. G., & Andrews, M. C. (2005). Promoting ethical behavior and organizational citizenship behaviors: The influence of corporate ethical values. *Journal of Business Research, 59*(7), 849–857. doi:10.1016/j.jbusres.2006.02.004

Barling, J., & Gallagher, D. G. (1996). Part-time employment. In C. L. Cooper & I. T. Robertson (Eds.), *International Review of Industrial and Organizational Psychology* (Vol. 11, pp. 241–277). Chichester: Wiley.

Barnard, C. I. (1938). *The functions of the executive.* Cambridge, MA: Harvard University Press.

Barnett, T., & Kellermanns, F. W. (2006). Are we Family and are we treated as Family? Non-family employees' perception of justice in the Family Firm. *Entrepreneurship Theory and Practice, 30*(6), 837–854. doi:10.1111/j.1540-6520.2006.00155.x

Bateman, T. S., & Organ, D. W. (1983). Job satisfaction and the good soldier: The relationship between affect and employee citizenship. *Academy of Management Journal, 26*(4), 587–595. doi:10.2307/255908

Baum, T. (2006). *Human resource management for tourism, hospitality and leisure: an international perspective.* London: Thomson.

Becker, G. S. (1964). *Human capital.* New York: Columbia University Press.

Bernhardt, A. L., Dresser, & Hatton, E. (2003). The coffee pot wars: Unions and firm restructuring in the hotel industry. In E. Appelbaum, A. Bernhardt, & R. Murnane, (Eds.), Low-wage America: How Employers are Reshaping Opportunity in the Workplace. New York: Russell Sage Foundation

Blau, P. M. (1964). *Exchange and Power in Social Life.* New York: John Wiley & Sons.

Blau, P. M. (1986). *Exchange and Power in Social Life.* New Brunswick, NJ: Wiley & Sons, Inc.

Brown, S. P. (1996). A meta-analysis and review of organizational research on job involvement. *Psychological Bulletin, 120*(2), 235–255. doi:10.1037/0033-2909.120.2.235

Buonocore, F. (2010). Contingent work in the hospitality industry: A mediating model of organizational attitudes. *Tourism Management, 31*(3), 378–385. doi:10.1016/j.tourman.2009.04.005

Cappelli, P., & Sherer, P. D. (1991). The missing role of context in OB: The need for a meso-level approach. *Research in Organizational Behavior, 13*, 55–110.

Cho, S., & Johanson, M. (2008). Organizational citizenship behavior and employee performance: Moderating effect of work status in restaurant employees. *Journal of Hospitality & Tourism Research (Washington, D.C.), 32*(3), 307–326. doi:10.1177/1096348008317390

Chonko, L. B., & Hunt, S. D. (1985). Ethics and marketing management: An empirical examination. *Journal of Business Research, 13*(4), 339–359. doi:10.1016/0148-2963(85)90006-2

Connelly, C. E., & Gallagher, D. G. (2004). Emerging trends in contingent work research. *Journal of Management, 30*(6), 959–983. doi:10.1016/j.jm.2004.06.008

Cooper, C. J., Fletcher, S., Wanhill, Gilbert, D., & Shepherd, R. (1998). Tourism Principles and Practice. Essex, UK: Pearson Education.

Corbetta, G., & Salvato, C. A. (2004). The board of director in family firms: One size fits all? *Family Business Review, 17*(2), 119–134. doi:10.1111/j.1741-6248.2004.00008.x

Cropanzano, R., & Mitchell, M. S. (2005). Social exchange theory: An interdisciplinary review. *Journal of Management, 31*(6), 874–900. doi:10.1177/0149206305279602

Dubin, R., Champoux, J. E., & Porter, L. W. (1975). Central Life Interests and Organizational Commitment of Blue Collar and Clerical Workers. *Administrative Science Quarterly, 20*(3), 411–421. doi:10.2307/2392000

Eisenberger, R., Huntington, R., Hutchinson, S., & Sowa, D. (1986). Perceived organizational support. *The Journal of Applied Psychology, 71*(3), 500–507. doi:10.1037/0021-9010.71.3.500

Elanain, H. M. A. (2007, Summer). The Five-factor model of personality and organizational citizenship behavior in United Arab Emirates. *SAM Advanced Management Journal.*

Emerson, R. M. (1976). Social exchange theory. *Annual Review of Sociology, 2*(1), 335–362. doi:10.1146/annurev.so.02.080176.002003

Federalberghi. (2010). *Report about the Italian hotel system.* Available at http://www.federalberghicatania.it/allegati/allegato%20circ125.pdf

Ford, R. C., & Richardson, W. D. (1994). Ethical decision making: A review of the empirical Literature. *Journal of Business Ethics, 13*(3), 205–221. doi:10.1007/BF02074820

Gallagher, D. G., & McLean Parks, J. (2001). I pledge thee my troth contingently. Commitment and the contingent work relationship. *Human Resource Management Review, 11*(3), 181–208. doi:10.1016/S1053-4822(00)00048-6

George, J. M., & Brief, A. P. (1992). Feeling good-doing good: A conceptual analysis of the mood at work organizational spontaneity relationship. *Psychological Bulletin, 112*(2), 310–329. doi:10.1037/0033-2909.112.2.310 PMID:1454897

Gonzalez, J. V., & Garazo, T. G. (2006). Structural relationships between organizational service orientation, contact employee job satisfaction and citizenship behavior. *International Journal of Service Industry Management, 17*(1), 23–50. doi:10.1108/09564230610651561

Goss-Turner, S. (1996). The accommodation sector. In P. Jones (Ed.), *Introduction to Hospitality Operations* (pp. 21–35). London: Cassell.

Gouldner, A. W. (1960). The norm of reciprocity: A preliminary statement. *American Sociological Review, 25*(2), 161–178. doi:10.2307/2092623

Graen, G. (1976). Role-making processes within complex organizations. In M. D. Dunnette (Ed.), *Handbook of Industrial/Organizational Psychology* (pp. 1210–1259). Chicago: Rand McNally.

Graham, J. W. (1986). Principled organizational dissent: A theoretical essay. In B. M. Staw & L. L. Cummings (Eds.), *Research in organizational behavior* (Vol. 8, pp. 1–52). Greenwich, CT: JAI Press.

Graham, J. W. (1989). *Organizational Citizenship Behavior: Construct redefinition, operationalization, and validation.* Unpublished working paper, Loyola University of Chicago.

Graham, J. W. (1991). An essay on organizational citizenship behavior. *Employee Responsibilities and Rights Journal, 4*(4), 249–270. doi:10.1007/BF01385031

Grandey, A. A. (2003). When the show must go on: Surface acting and deep acting as determinants of emotional exhaustion and peer-rated service delivery. *Academy of Management Journal, 46*(1), 86–96. doi:10.2307/30040678

Hannam, R., & Jimmieson, N. (2002). *The relationship between extra-role behaviors and job burnout for primary school teachers: A Preliminary model and development of an OCB scale.* Retrieved 19 September 2007 from http://www.aare.edu.au/02pap/han02173.htm

Hart, P. M., Wearing, A. J., Conn, M., Carter, N. L., & Dingle, R. K. (2000). Development of the school organizational health questionnaire: A measure for assessing teacher morale and school organizational climate. *Brain Education Psychology, 70,* 211–228. PMID:10900779

Hayes, D. K., & Ninemeier, J. D. (2009). *Study Guide To Accompany Human Resources Management in the Hospitality Industry.* New Jersey: John Wiley & Sons.

He, Y., Lai, K. K., & Lu, Y. (2011). Linking organizational support to employee commitment: Evidence from hotel industry of China. *International Journal of Human Resource Management, 22*(1), 197–217. doi:10.1080/09585192.2011.538983

Hipple, S. (1998). Contingent work: Results from the second survey. *Monthly Labor Review, 121*(11), 22–35.

Hirschman, A. O. (1970). *Exit, voice, and loyalty: Responses to decline in firms, organizations, and states.* Cambridge, MA: Harvard University Press.

Homans, G. (1958). *Social Exchange Theory.* Retrieved from http://www.fsc.yorku.ca/york/istheory/wiki/index.php/Social_exchange_theory

Ilies, R., Nahrgang, J. D., & Morgeson, F. P. (2007). Leader-member exchange and citizenship behaviors: A meta-analysis. *The Journal of Applied Psychology, 92*(1), 269–277. doi:10.1037/0021-9010.92.1.269 PMID:17227168

*Invitalia.* (2014). Retrieved from http://www.invitalia.it/site/eng/home/investment-opportunities/tourism/what.html

Ismert, M., & Petrick, F. (2004). Indicators and standards of quality related to contingent employment in the ski industry. *Journal of Travel Research, 43*(1), 46–56. doi:10.1177/0047287504265512

Italian National Institute of Statistics - Istat. (2014). *Viaggi e vacanze in Italia e all'estero (Travel and Vacations in Italy and abroad).* Available at http://www.istat.it/it/archivio/turismo

Johnson, A. S., & Ashforth, E. B. (2008). Externalization of employment in a service environment: The role of organizational and customer identification. *Journal of Organizational Behavior, 29*(3), 287–309. doi:10.1002/job.477

Kalleberg, A. L., & Schmidt, K. (1996). Contingent Employment in Organizations: Part-Time, Temporary, and Subcontracting Relations. In A. L. Kalleberg, D. Knoke, P. Marsden, & J. L. Spaeth (Eds.), *Organizations in America; Analyzing Their Structures and Human Resource Practices* (pp. 253–275). Thousand Oaks, CA: Sage Publications.

Kandampully, J. A. (2003). Services Management: the new paradigm in hospitality. Prentice Hall.

Karatepe, O. E., Beirami, E., Bouzari, M., & Safavi, H. P. (2014). Does work engagement mediate the effects of challenge stressors on job outcomes? Evidence from the hotel industry. *International Journal of Hospitality Management, 36,* 14–22. doi:10.1016/j.ijhm.2013.08.003

Katz, D., & Kahn, R. L. (1978). *The social psychology of organizations.* New York: Wiley.

Konovsky, M. A., & Organ, D. W. (1996). Dispositional and contextual determinants of organizational citizenship behavior. *Journal of Organizational Behavior, 17*(3), 253–266. doi:10.1002/(SICI)1099-1379(199605)17:3<253::AID-JOB747>3.0.CO;2-Q

Kowalski, R. M. (1996). Complaints and complaining: Functions, antecedents, and consequences. *Psychological Bulletin, 119*(2), 179–196. doi:10.1037/0033-2909.119.2.179 PMID:8851274

Krakover, S. (2000). Partitioning contingent employment in the hospitality industry. *Tourism Management, 21*(5), 461–471. doi:10.1016/S0261-5177(99)00101-6

Lashley, C. (2001). *Empowerment: HR strategies for service excellence.* Oxford: Butterworth-Heinemann.

LePine, J. A., Erez, A., & Johnson, D. E. (2002). The nature and dimensionality of organizational citizenship behavior: A critical review and meta-analysis. *The Journal of Applied Psychology, 87*(1), 52–65. doi:10.1037/0021-9010.87.1.52 PMID:11916216

LePine, J. A., & Van Dyne, L. (1998). Predicting voice behavior in work groups. *The Journal of Applied Psychology, 83*(6), 853–868. doi:10.1037/0021-9010.83.6.853

Lodahl, T. M., & Kejner, M. (1965). The definition and measurement of job involvement. *The Journal of Applied Psychology, 49*(1), 24–33. doi:10.1037/h0021692 PMID:14279757

Maslow, A. H. (1943). A theory of human motivation. *Psychological Review, 50*(4), 370–396. doi:10.1037/h0054346

McLean Parks, J., Kidder, D. L., & Gallagher, D. G. (1998). Fitting Square Pegs into round holes: Mapping the Domain of Contingent Work Arrangements onto the psychological contract. *Journal of Organizational Behavior, 19*(S1), 697–730. doi:10.1002/(SICI)1099-1379(1998)19:1+<697::AID-JOB974>3.0.CO;2-I

Miceli, M. E., & Near, J. E. (1992). *Blowing the whistle: The organizational and legal implications for companies and employees.* New York: Lexington Books.

Milliken, F. J., Morrison, E. W., & Hewlin, P. F. (2003). An exploratory study of employee silence: Issues that employees don't communicate upward and why. *Journal of Management Studies, 40*(6), 1453–1476. doi:10.1111/1467-6486.00387

Moorman, R. H. (1991). Relationship between organizational justice and organizational citizenship behaviors: Do fairness perceptions influence employee citizenship? *The Journal of Applied Psychology, 76*(6), 845–855. doi:10.1037/0021-9010.76.6.845

Moorman, R. H., & Blakely, G. L. (1995). Individualism collectivism as an individual difference predictor of organizational citizenship behavior. *Journal of Organizational Behavior, 16*(2), 127–142. doi:10.1002/job.4030160204

Motowidlo, S. J., & Van Scooter, J. R. (1994). Evidence that Task Performance should be Distinguished from Contextual Performance. *The Journal of Applied Psychology, 79*(4), 475–480. doi:10.1037/0021-9010.79.4.475

Mowday, R. T., & Sutton, R. I. (1993). Organizational behavior: Linking individuals and groups to organizational contexts. *Annual Review of Psychology, 44*(1), 195–229. doi:10.1146/annurev.ps.44.020193.001211 PMID:19090760

Nasurdin, A. M., Ahmad, N. H., & Tan, C. L. (2014). *Cultivating service-oriented citizenship behavior among hotel employees: the instrumental roles of training and compensation.* Springer.

Near, J. E., & Miceli, M. E. (1996). Whistle-blowing: Myth and reality. *Journal of Management, 22*(3), 507–526. doi:10.1177/014920639602200306

Nemeth, C. J., & Staw, B. M. (1989). *The tradeo Vs of social control and innovation in small groups and organizations.* In L. Berkowitz (Ed.), Advances in experimental social psychology (Vol. 22, pp. 175–210). New York: Academic Press.

Nickson, D. (2007). *Human Resource Management for the Hospitality and Tourism Industries.* Oxford, UK: Elsevier.

Núñez-Serrano, J. A., Turrión, J., & Velázquez, F. J. (2014). Are stars a good indicator of hotel quality? Assymetric information and regulatory heterogeneity in Spain. *Tourism Management, 42,* 77–87. doi:10.1016/j.tourman.2013.10.004

OECD. (2011). *Studies on Tourism. Italy: Review Of Issues And Policies.* OECD Publishing. doi:10.1787/9789264114258-en

Orfila-Sintes, F., Crespi-Cladera, R., & Martinez-Ros, E. (2005). Innovation activity in the hotel industry: Evidence from Balearic Islands. *Tourism Management, 26*(6), 851–865. doi:10.1016/j.tourman.2004.05.005

Organ, D. W. (1988). *Organizational Citizenship Behavior: The good soldier syndrome.* Lexington, MA: Lexington Books.

Paullay, I. M., Alliger, G. M., & Stone-Romero, E. F. (1994). Construct validation of two instruments designed to measure job involvement and work centrality. *The Journal of Applied Psychology, 79*(2), 224–228. doi:10.1037/0021-9010.79.2.224

Pierce, J. L., Kostova, T., & Dirks, K. T. (2001). Toward a theory of psychological ownership. *Academy of Management Review, 26*(2), 298–310.

Podsakoff, P. M., Ahearne, M., & MacKenzie, S. B. (1997). Organizational Citizenship Behavior and the Quantity and Quality of Work Group Performance. *The Journal of Applied Psychology, 82*(2), 262–270. doi:10.1037/0021-9010.82.2.262 PMID:9109284

Podsakoff, P. M., MacKenzie, S. B., Moorman, R. H., & Fetter, R. (1990). Transformational leader behaviors and their effects on followers' trust in leader, satisfaction, and organizational citizenship behaviors. *The Leadership Quarterly, 1*(2), 107–142. doi:10.1016/1048-9843(90)90009-7

Podsakoff, P. M., MacKenzie, S. B., Paine, J. B., & Bachrach, D. G. (2000). Organizational citizenship behaviors: A critical review of the theoretical and empirical literature and suggestions for future research. *Journal of Management, 26*(3), 513–563. doi:10.1177/014920630002600307

Rappaport, A., & Chammah, A. M. (1965). *Prisoner's Dilemma.* Ann Arbor: University of Michigan Press.

Rhodes, L., & Eisenberger, R. (2002). Perceived organizational support: A review of the literature. *The Journal of Applied Psychology, 87*(4), 698–714. doi:10.1037/0021-9010.87.4.698 PMID:12184574

Rousseau, D. M. (1989). Psychological and implied contracts in organizations. *Employee Responsibilities and Rights Journal, 2*(2), 121–139. doi:10.1007/BF01384942

Rousseau, D. M., & Tijoriwala, S. A. (1998). Assessing Psychological Contracts: Issues, Alternatives and Measures. *Journal of Organizational Behavior, 19*(S1), 679–695. doi:10.1002/(SICI)1099-1379(1998)19:1+<679::AID-JOB971>3.0.CO;2-N

Schein, E. H. (1968). Organizational socialization and the profession of management. *Industrial Management Review, 9,* 1–16.

Settoon, R. P., Bennett, N., & Liden, R. C. (1996). Social exchange in organizations: Perceived organizational support, leader-member exchange, and employee reciprocity. *The Journal of Applied Psychology, 81*(3), 219–227. doi:10.1037/0021-9010.81.3.219

Shore, L. M., & Tetrick, L. E. (1991). A construct validity study of the survey of perceived organizational support. *The Journal of Applied Psychology, 76*(5), 637–643. doi:10.1037/0021-9010.76.5.637

Singh, R., & Mangat, N. S. (1996). *Elements of Survey Sampling*. Dordrecht, The Netherlands: Kluwer Academic Publishers. doi:10.1007/978-94-017-1404-4

Smith, C. A., Organ, D. W., & Near, J. P. (1983). Organizational citizenship behavior: Its nature and antecedents. *The Journal of Applied Psychology, 68*(4), 653–663. doi:10.1037/0021-9010.68.4.653

Torres, E. N., & Kline, S. (2013). From customer satisfaction to customer delight: Creating a new standard of service for the hotel industry. *International Journal of Contemporary Hospitality Management, 25*(5), 642–659. doi:10.1108/IJCHM-Dec-2011-0228

Tsui, A. S., Pearce, J. L., Porter, L. W., & Tripoli, A. M. (1997). Alternative approaches to the employee-organization relationship: Does investment in employees pay off? *Academy of Management Journal, 40*(5), 1089–1121. doi:10.2307/256928

Tsui, A. S., & Wu, J. B. (2005). The employment relationship versus the mutual investment approach: Implications for human resource management. *Human Resource Management, 44*(2), 115–121. doi:10.1002/hrm.20052

UnionCamere. (2013). *Impresa Turismo, Report about tourism economy in Italy*. Available at http://www.ontit.it/opencms/export/sites/default/ont/it/riservativip/files/impresa_turismo_2013.pdf

UNWTO. (2013). *Tourism Highlights*. Available at www.unwto.org

Van Dyne, L., Cummings, L., & McLean Parks, J. (1995). Extra-role behaviors: In pursuit of construct and definitional clarity (a bridge over muddied waters). *Research in Organizational Behavior, 17*, 215–285.

Van Dyne, L., Graham, J. W., & Dienesch, R. M. (1994). Organizational citizenship behavior: Construct redefinition, measurement, and validation. *Academy of Management Journal, 37*(4), 765–802. doi:10.2307/256600

Van Dyne, L., & LePine, J. A. (1998). Helping and voice extra-role behavior: Evidence of construct and predictive validity. *Academy of Management Journal, 41*(1), 108–119. doi:10.2307/256902

Van Scotter, J. R., & Motowidlo, S. J. (1996). Interpersonal Facilitation and Job Dedication as Separate Facets of Contextual Performance. *The Journal of Applied Psychology, 81*(5), 525–531. doi:10.1037/0021-9010.81.5.525

Williams, L. J., & Anderson, S. E. (1991). Job satisfaction and organizational commitment as predictors of organizational citizenship and in-role behaviors. *Journal of Management, 17*(3), 601–617. doi:10.1177/014920639101700305

Williamson, O. E. (1981). The Economics of Organization: The Transaction Cost Approach. *American Journal of Sociology, 87*(3), 548–577. doi:10.1086/227496

Withey, M. J., & Cooper, W. H. (1989). Predicting exit, voice, loyalty, and neglect. *Administrative Science Quarterly, 34*(4), 521–539. doi:10.2307/2393565

World Travel & Tourism Council (WTTC). (2013). *Travel & Tourism Economic Impact 2013 – Italy*. Available at http://www.ontit.it/opencms/export/sites/default/ont/it/documenti/files/ONT_2013-07-12_02986.pdf

Yoon, M. H., & Suh, J. (2003). Organizational citizenship behaviours and service quality as external effectiveness of contact employees. *Journal of Business Research*, 56(8), 597–611. doi:10.1016/S0148-2963(01)00290-9

## KEY TERMS AND DEFINITIONS

**Frontline Employee:** Are those who have direct contact with customers.

**Helping Behavior:** Is cooperative behavior that is noncontroversial. It builds and preserves relationships and it emphasizes interpersonal harmony.

**Hospitality Industry:** Is a broad category of fields within the service industry that includes lodging, event planning, theme parks, transportation, cruise line, and additional fields within the tourism industry.

**Organizational Citizenship Behavior:** Is defined as those individual behaviors that are beneficial to the organization and are discretionary, not directly or explicitly recognized by the formal reward system, and that in the aggregate promotes the effective functioning of the organization.

**Social Exchange Theory:** Which claims that individuals are likely to participate in an exchange with others if they believe that they are likely to gain benefits without incurring unacceptable costs.

**Voice Behavior:** Defined as non required behavior that emphasizes expression of constructive challenge with an intent to improve rather than merely criticize.

**Work Centrality:** Suggests that work plays a central role in employees' lives.

**Work Status:** The legal status and classification of someone in employment as either an employee or working on their own account (self-employed).

# Chapter 11
# Marketing Global Luxury Spa and Wellness Trends, Experiences, and Challenges

**Ingrid Y. Lin**
*University of Hawaii – Manoa, USA*

## ABSTRACT

*Luxury hotel and resort spas have been perceived and criticized for their similarities and for not having a true authentic or culturally thematic identity, and for losing their original intention of a spa experience due to rapid commercialization. Empirical research relating to spa management is also limited. The purposes of this chapter are (1) to highlight some of the important global market trends that force all sectors of the travel industry to gear towards a healthy, wellness-minded concept in designing their products and services; (2) to define wellness tourism and the meaning of spa; (3) to address several under-researched variables that account for a crucial role in differentiating or characterizing a spa's identity and customers' preferences or perceived authenticity of a spa. Relevant literature is reviewed. Theories from multiple fields are applied. Future research and managerial implications will also be discussed in the content of this chapter.*

## INTRODUCTION

The global spa and wellness industry has moved from its infancy to the growing stage. It has much potential for continuous growth as the aging population is increasing worldwide and as people are becoming more health-conscious, wellness-minded, and interested in sustaining a good quality of life. Spa is a core business within wellness tourism and it accounts for a significant portion (about 41 percent) of wellness tourism economy (Yeung, Johnston, & Chan, 2014). Currently, there is a spa service establishment in just about all the luxury hotels or resorts in the world. The growing demand for healthier travel will increase 9 percent annually through 2017. This growth is 50 percent faster than tourism in general ("Health Hotels 2.0," 2014). As the spa industry continues to grow, sophisticated consumers also want things that are authentic rather than

DOI: 10.4018/978-1-4666-8606-9.ch011

homogenized. This chapter begins by defining the basic terminologies of wellness tourism and the meaning of spa followed by some highlights of the macro-environmental trends in the travel, spa and wellness industry.

## WELLNESS TOURISM

The essence of wellness refers to the balance and harmony of health, body, mind, spirit, quality of life, and well-being. Health includes nutrition and diets; mind relates to mental activity or education; body refers to physical fitness and beauty care; spirit associates with meditation and relaxation; well-being directs attention to individual self-responsibility of all components of wellness attributes. Wellness tourism has developed rapidly as a component of health tourism since the 1970s (CBI Ministry of Foreign Affairs, 2014). Today, spa tourism also emerges as a component of wellness tourism and the terms "wellness" and "spa" can even be used interchangeably as long as the goal of the individual's spa experience is geared towards maintaining and improving health ("Spa Finder's Top Ten European Spa Trends," 2006). Sheldon and Bushell (2009) define wellness tourism as "…a holistic mode of travel that integrates a quest for physical health, beauty, or longevity, and/or a heightening of consciousness or spiritual awareness, and a connection with community, nature, or the divine mystery; it encompasses a range of tourism experiences in destinations with wellness products, appropriate infrastructures, facilities, and natural and wellness resources" (p. 11).

## THE MEANING OF "SPA"

"Spa" or "health through water" includes various meanings from different countries, cultures, and languages. The word spa derives from the influence of the Belgian town called Spa, where a thermal spring was discovered in the 14th century (Tubergen & Van der Linden, 2002). Some of its various meanings from Latin are "espa," meaning fountain (Tubergen & Van der Linden, 2002), "spagere" (to scatter, sprinkle, moisten), and "Sanitas per aquas" (health through water) (Tubergen & Van der Linden, 2002, p. 273). Johnson and Redman (2008) postulate that the underpinning substance of spa lies in the forms that water brings into existence (i.e., ice, cold, cool, hot, warm, steam, etc.). De Vierville (2003) claimed that

*Regardless of the spa type, the true purpose of a spa is to provide, through some form of the waters, helpful health services and treatments that are relaxing, restful, regenerating and socially re-creative… A spa is an eco-sociocultural learning community that attempts to bring together and truthfully integrate all the dynamic dimensions of time and space, temperatures, touch and therapeutic treatments within a supporting context of goodness, beauty, harmony and wholeness of nature. (p. 23).*

Today's luxury spas are criticized for losing the essence of the spa experience and a lack of authenticity and over-commercialization. O'Dell (2010) argues that the original intentions for a spa are often lost because many spas fail to act upon and connect these elements with culture and nature or humanity and earth, or soul and cosmos. Customers continue to expect spas to take the lead and guide them towards holistic wellness—body, mind, and spirit (Tabacchi, 2010). Spa consumption is not a necessity for survival; usually, customers have specific motivational factors or purposes in mind (Mak, Wong, & Chang, 2009). Luxury spas help individuals strike a balance among physical, mental, emotional, and spiritual wellness. Rather than focusing on the money given up, some consumers emphasize the benefits and all components (money, time, and effort) they receive from a service or product as the most important, making it even more relevant for luxury spas to demonstrate quality core competencies, personal customization, culture, and authenticity. Culture and authenticity will be further discussed.

## GLOBAL MARKET TRENDS

### Economic Trends

Research from the Global Wellness Tourism Economy (Yeung et al., 2014) reported that wellness tourism represent about 6 percent ($524.4 million) of all domestic and international trips and wellness tourism accounts for about 14 percent ($438.6 billion) of all domestic and international tourism expenditures (Yeung et al., 2014). "Wellness tourism economy is all expenditures made by tourists who seek to improve or maintain their well-being during or as a result of their trip; those who seek to maintain wellness while traveling represent 87 percent of wellness tourism trips and 86 percent expenditures" (Yeung et al., 2014, p. 6).

Asia is considered the world's fastest growing economic region (Foster, 2014). Asia encompasses 51 countries and 60 plus percent of the earth's population (Foster, 2014). The emerging countries of Asia include China, India, Thailand, and Indonesia, are expected to have great potential regarding spa investments. As for the newly industrialized countries in Asia--Taiwan, Singapore, Hong Kong, and South Korea; consumers from these countries have and will continue to have great spending power for consuming spas (Foster, 2014). For countries such as Australia, due to currency fluctuations, consumers will likely be driven to other more affordable and exotic spa destinations (e.g., Bali, Indonesia) (Foster, 2014).

### Social/Demographic Trends

There is a shift to an era of gender equilibrium. This means there are more reversed roles in households and fewer gender specific brands ("Landers

Top 10 Brands Trends for 2014," 2014). Females are experiencing higher levels of stress due to the balance between work and family; this provides one of the reasons why the majority of spa customers are female. However, recent global socio-demographic trends show that men like spas as much as women. Forty-seven percent of the total spa-going population in the U.S. consists of men (Who's the Average Male Spa-Goer," 2014). The average age of the typical male spa-goer is between 25 to 44, with an average household income of over US$50,000. Male spa-goers look for treatments to relieve sore muscles, expertise/credentials of therapists/staff, and quality of products used ("Who's the Average Male Spa-Goer," 2014). The top spa treatments among the male spa-goer are massage, followed by fitness classes, and pedicure ("Who's the Average Male Spa-Goer," 2014). The major barriers for male spa-goers to visit a spa is too costly, followed by do not see any perceived benefits, and not familiar with a spa environment and/or spa etiquette ("Who's the Average Male Spa-Goer," 2014). Men are considered another group of potential targeted customers for many countries and for many spas worldwide.

The aging baby boomers (born between 1943 and 1960) worldwide yearn for anti-aging wellness or spa products and services, healthy eating, and quality of lifestyle (Hilton Hotels and Resorts, 2012). Generation Xers (born between 1961 and 1981) are tech savvy, knowledgeable about spa trends, and environmentally conscious (Hilton Hotels & Resorts, 2012). They are highly dependent on the Internet and they blog, review and comment about buying experiences. Social responsibility from organizations becomes a vital influential attribute in their consumption decision-making (Hilton Hotels & Resorts, 2012). The Millennials (born between 1982 and 2000) are highly aware of trends, technology, and spas; they are known as trendsetters (Hilton Hotels & Resorts, 2012). The Millennials want almost everything instantly; they view spas as a necessity and expect immediate results (Hilton hotels & Resorts, 2012). Among all age groups, people within the age bracket of 18 to 34 want the most support in living a healthier lifestyle (Hilton Hotels & Resorts, 2012); the Millennials will be the most important consumers in the category of luxury brands by 2016 ("Landor's Top 10 Brand Trends for 2014," 2014).

## Technological Trends

Social media, mobile phones, and photo sharing have become part of people's lifestyles. The market for mobile health-device technology was worth $2 billion in 2011 and is projected to reach $6 billion by 2016 ("Landor's Top 10 Brand Trends for 2014," 2014). The power of mobile applications and social media force service providers to have to adapt to new marketing strategies such as utilizing non-traditional promotional media—social network and mobile phones — in order to capture the tech savvy Gen X and Millennial markets. Technology also helps advance cosmetology with the innovation of machines for facials and treatments without any surgical intervention; this will attract more spa customers, especially those from the West rather than the East (Loh, 2008). Spas in the West focus on delivering wellness through aesthetics, medical approaches and holistic modalities (Loh, 2008). The West depends highly on high-tech equipment and techniques. In contrast, spas in the East focus on high-touch and low-tech" (Loh, 2008). The East depends highly on human touch and the traditional modalities and rituals. In addition, technological advancements are already forcing hospitality and tourism service providers to change their marketing strategies in that more Internet and social media will be used to market products and services than the traditional television and magazine medias.

## Political Trends

Despite the tremendous growth in health and wellness tourism, many countries such as Brazil, Canada, and China are known for health and well-ness tourism that is either lacking standards or lacking government support (Manacap-Johnson, 2014). Many other nations are enforcing policies, laws and regulations that gear towards making wellness and healthy behaviors mandatory for their citizens ("2014 Trends Report: Top 10 Global Spa and Wellness Trends Forecast," 2014). In the U.S., Obamacare provides opportunities for consumers to enhance their healthy lifestyle ("Landor's Top 10 Brand Trends for 2014," 2014). In light of the U.S. health care reform, people will be more interested in eating healthy. However, health care expenditure in the U.S. is expected to increase due to the aging population; hence, the outbound medical tourism is likely to increase due to the high price of health care procedures in the U.S. (Manacap-Johnson, 2014). Global economists also present another challenge in that more governments will not be able to afford health care for their populations in the near future ("2014 Trends Report: Top 10 Global Spa and Wellness Trends Forecast," 2014).

## Ecological/Natural Environmental Trends

The issue of global warming and unusual weather patterns sent warning signals to businesses and consumers to become more aware of social responsibility and sustainability practices. Protecting the environment is no longer a choice; it is mandatory for all. In order for any organization to be competitive, green or sustainable practices and social responsibility should be part of its corporate culture. Consumers today not only choose organizations that implement green practices, but they also demand organic and sustainable products and services. Six Senses Resorts and Spas is a good example of taking the lead of incorporating sustainability into its corporate mission: "To create innovative and enriching experiences in a sustainable environment" ("About Six Senses-Six Senses Hotels Resorts Spas-Luxury Resorts," n.d.). Banyan Tree is also another luxury resort company that not only positions itself as a company that embraces environmental conservation and responsible tourism but also as a company that can inspire its employees, partners, and the community to create sustainability developments (Banyantree Global Foundation, 2014). The passion and the care that Banyan Tree has for the natural environment, communities, and society at large has helped the company build a differentiating brand within the luxury resorts.

## GLOBAL WELLNESS TRAVEL TRENDS

Despite the tremendous growth in wellness tourism, travel has not always been compatible with wellness. Richards and Rundle (2011) studied business travelers and found that frequent and extensive travel can increase cardiovascular risk factors such as obesity, high blood pressure, and high cholesterol. Yeung, Johnston, and Chan (2014) studied leisure travelers and found that "85 percent of travelers return from a vacation less rejuvenated and well than when they left" (p. 3). For these reasons, different global hospitality and tourism service sectors around the world (i.e., hotels, airlines, airports, and spas in Asia, Europe, and the U.S.) are beginning to take notice of healthy concepts and have tried to find ways to meet the wellness-minded customers' expectations and satisfaction and at the same time, make their travel journey as comfortable as possible. For example, travelers in Singapore airport have access to spas, gyms, yoga rooms, rooftop swimming pool; in Hong Kong a golf course; in New Delhi airport, affordable soundproof napping pods, and in Dubai airport a Snoozecube. Airport food and beverage establishments have also started to offer healthier selections than before (i.e., fresh juice bars) ("2014 Trends Report: Top 10 Global Spa and Wellness Trends Forecast," 2014).

Airlines (e.g., Air Asia, Malaysia Airlines) offer kid free seating zones so the majority of passengers can rest or sleep without the disturbance of crying or screaming children ("Healthy Hotels 2.0", 2014). Singapore Airlines and Emirates Airlines also offer private rooms for their first class passengers. Many airlines (i.e., Cathay Pacific and China Airlines) offer a wide variety of complimentary special meals for all passengers to choose from with options that range from gluten free meals to different religious or ethnic food selections.

The hotel industry is also quickly catching up and shifting gear to fuel the wellness-minded customers' health conscious wants and needs, including healthier food and sleep, more engaging fitness, and overall care for their health. For example, many luxury hotels are starting to keep gyms and spas open around the clock, to encourage people to explore cities on foot or by bike and they pack healthy lunches for their guests, and to help guests improve the vitality of sleep, fitness, and healthy eating ("Healthy Hotels 2.0", 2014). Hotel guest rooms are beginning to implement wellness designs where in-room workout equipment (e.g., treadmills), air and water purification, hypoallergenic sleep-enhancing lighting, sleep-inducing massages, aromatherapy, sleep-aiding snacks, a menu of a variety of different types of pillow selections are available for guests ("Healthy Hotels 2.0", 2014). Food and beverage offerings within resorts and hotels have also repositioned themselves to offer more convenient, nutritious, farm-sourced or farm-to-table food and beverage; customized foods and more expansive gluten free, vegan and vegetarian restaurant menus and room service; workout kits, and juice bars to fulfill wellness-minded customers' healthier, faster, diet-customized expectations ("Healthy Hotels 2.0", 2014).

## GLOBAL SPA INDUSTRY TRENDS

Globally, spa destinations such as Argentina, Brazil, Puerto Rico, and Russia, have gained increasing attention across the globe (Manacap-Johnson, 2014). There are three major trends shaping Argentina's spa industry: the growing integrative health or wellness concept; strong demand for men's skin care, and growth of the corporate segment demanding spa services within and outside their work offices. Local spa-goers go to day spas for skin care and treatments and foreign guests book spa treatments in hotel resorts or locations that offer a regional thematic experience (i.e., therapies with grapes, yerba mate and muds) (Manacap-Johnson, 2014).

According to the Brazilian Ministry of Health, data in the last three years shows that more than 180,000 international travelers went to Brazil seeking treatments and surgeries. "People are becoming more conscious about their health and investing more time to take care of it. Wellness tourism in Brazil has become one of the fastest growing segments with more men and women taking preventive actions to live longer and enjoy meaningful lives (Manacap-Johnson, 2014). However, consumers are more cautious about spending due to Brazil's economic crisis this year. Nevertheless, Brazil has much potential in the growth of medical tourism. Another interesting country that shows an arising trend in regards to male spa consumers is Puerto Rico. Male consumers in Puerto Rico are demanding for more organic and anti-aging products without losing their masculinity focus. The popularity of consumers questing for online discounting websites, like LivingSocial, is another growing trend (Manacap-Johnson, 2014).

The latest statistics and trends in the U.S. spa industry showed that there are 19,960 spa establishments as of January 2014 (Mcilheney, 2014). Day spas continue to dominate the spa market and they remain the industry's mainstay (78.9 percent) of the total, followed by medical spas (8.8 percent), resort/hotels (8.7 percent), and club spas (2.9 percent) (Mcilheney, 2014). Total spa revenue is up 4.7 percent, at US$14 billion (Mcilheney, 2014). In the U.S., "The total number of visits to spa establishments hit record high since 1999 ($69 million); it is estimated to have risen from 160 million in 2012 to 164 million in 2013" (ISPA, 2014, p. 13).

There is a growing interest in aesthetic medical treatments that offer quick results (i.e., Botox, fraxel, and facial peeling treatments) in Russia. As the trend is developing, the spa industry can benefit from guests who start to demand a more natural look without signs of strong invasive treatments and pay more attention to preparations before and rehabilitation after medical treatments. There is also a shift toward treatments that embrace Russia's national healing traditions—"Russian banya, amber-therapy, honey and buckwheat massage, hay wraps and even shaman energy healing are coming forward" (Manacap-Johnson, 2014, p. 40).

Asia is the home to the world's oldest healing cultures—e.g., Indian, Chinese, Tibetan (Foster, 2014). These healing cultures derived from several influences: Hinduism, Buddhism, Taoism, Confucianism, Islam, Communism, and Colonization. Each of these influence help foster and shape spa's products and services. For example, Yoga, holistic philosophy, and yoga derived from Hinduism (Foster, 2014). Buddhism exerts spiritual practices and meditation. Taoism promotes yin-yang, herbs, diets, life force, Feng shui (Foster, 2014). Confucianism speaks for social harmony, obedience, and relationships. Islam introduces the *hammam* or the Turkish bath. Communism enforces the importance of visible status and appearance (Foster, 2014). Last but not the least, Colonization nourishes good language skills and service culture (Foster, 2014). The integration of each of these beliefs emphasizes the importance of luxury and traditional spa culture, etiquette, products and services. In general, Asian consumers have high expectations of service quality and top end service rituals (Foster, 2014). However, international spa guests often experience language barrier when they encounter with the spa staff in Asia (Foster, 2014).

Euro-American health tourists and emerging middle class have become an integral process of

Ayurvedic health life without changing their lifestyle; "Ayurveda has become part of the process of 'new age orientalization' and the 'commodified' version of Ayurveda has been developed in the west as part of the wellness and spa culture" (Islam, 2012, p. 220). Ayurveda has also become a wellness therapy instead of a means to restore health (Islam, 2012).

The different global market trends described above show that the future outlook of the international spa market looks promising; spas from different countries, regions, and segments have many opportunities to take advantage of to gain competitive advantages. In the following sections, the possible factors that may create spa guests' perceived authenticity, preferences, or evaluation of a holistic luxury spa experience will be discussed. Sections focusing on future research and future challenges will wrap up the chapter.

## LUXURY SPA EXPERIENCE

There are several different types of spas within the spa industry. In this chapter, luxury hotel or resort spas will be the primary focus. A luxury hotel or resort is a place for leisure, pleasure, or an escape; for recreational activities or business meetings or conferences; in short, for well-being purposes to enhance an individual's lifestyle (Monteson & Singer, 2004). It is rare to find a luxury hotel or resort without a spa establishment; spas are a mandatory feature for most resorts and upscale properties. Some spas epitomize thematic spa design (e.g., The Hotel Hershey). Luxury resort spa offerings are geared to target those who are physically well and just want relaxation, pampering, and luxury (Kelly & Smith, 2009). The meaning of luxury includes extravagance (Yeoman & McMahon-Beatie, 2006), exclusivity, high quality (Phau & Prendergast, 2000), authenticity,

aspects of physical and mental wellness (Yeoman & McMahon-Beattie, 2006), extraordinary experience, and high price (Mandhachitara & Lockshin, 2004).

The idea of "experience" has been suggested as an alternative to "commoditization". Hotel, resort, and spa managers are exhorted to provide a memorable and lasting experience for each guest (Gilmore & Pine, 2002). The way to create memorable experiences for guests is to use "'services as the stage and goods as props to engage individual customers in an inherently personal way'" (Gilmore & Pine 2002, p. 88). However, in the case of luxury spa experience, spa operators are expected to go to a greater extent by not only educating customers but also transforming them. One of the current trends in today's luxury experience includes feeling emotionally content and healthy and looking physically beautiful and fit (Bakker, 2005); luxury spa products and services serve those purposes. It is no longer enough to simply provide excellent services. Sophisticated customers today want to know about the product ingredients that spa therapists use on them for treatments; customers want immediate results and non-invasive treatments, and they want to learn how to take better care of themselves (i.e., their skin, or how to cook a healthy and balanced meal) after they leave the spa establishment. It is imperative for luxury spa professionals to focus not only on creating a memorable experience for customers with personalized products and services, but also on creating a specific theme that is unique or authentic about their business, and guiding customers to fulfill their aspirations or change some dimension of self (Gilmore & Pine II, 2007). To create a life-transforming experience requires "the customization of experience that is designed to be exactly what an individual needs at an exact moment in time" (Gilmore & Pine, 2007, p. 47). Luxury spas have to move from a service economy to a transformation economy in order to define the spa operators' unique authenticity and identity.

## THEORETICAL FRAMEWORK

To understand the notion of a holistic luxury spa experience, three prominent theories have been widely cited within the environmental psychology, marketing and servicescape literature: Stimulus-Organism-Response (S-O-R) theory (Mehrabian & Russell, 1974), cue utilization theory (Reimer & Kuehn, 2005), and Gestalt theory (Carmer & Rouzer, 1974; Schiffman, 2001). The three theories can be incorporated in future research developments of spa management. The S-O-R model suggests that individuals represent the (O) in the model. (S) refers to environmental stimuli where they will induce the individual to respond (R) either emotionally, cognitively, or behaviorally. This model has been widely cited and tested in the servicescape literature to explain that specific environmental attributes or sensory cues (i.e., touch, scent, color, artifact, etc.) can stimulate individuals' positive or negative emotional responses (i.e., pleasure or displeasure). The individual's total quality experience encompasses numerous factors and elements such as human senses, feelings, thoughts, actions, and relationships (Schmitt, 1999), similar concepts and S-O-R paradigm can also be applied to examine customers' responses in the context of luxury resort spas.

Cue utilization theory can also be implemented to examine customer evaluation and perceived authenticity of the spa establishment. Cue utilization theory describes products or services as consisting of a number of cues that help consumers evaluate the quality of product and service offerings (Reimer & Kuehn, 2005). In the case of manufactured products, physical attributes or product such as size or shape serve as intrinsic cues, while extrinsic cues include brand names and price. In the case of services, because of simultaneous production and consumption, the only intrinsic cues available are in the servicescape or interior décor and ambience itself. The theory is used to model an individual's information search process and consequent behavior in a consumption setting (Namasivayam & Lin, 2008). The role of servicescape as an influence on the information search processes is thus modeled using the perspective of cue utilization theory. Likewise, cues related to our sensation and perception no doubt serve as important attributes and as the basis of our evaluation of a spa experience.

The concept of Gestalt should also be introduced and incorporated to aid in the understanding of individuals' perceptual formation of authenticity and the overall, holistic experiential value of the spa experience (Lin & Worthley, 2012). It emphasizes the holistic approach (Schiffman, 2001). Gestalt psychology is grounded in assumptions about how living organisms relate to their environment (Carmer & Rouzer, 1974). According to Gestalt theory, individuals subconsciously evaluate particular stimuli such as color and music (Lin, 2010) or scent and music (Mattila & Wirtz, 2000) together with the environment itself (e.g., spa treatment room), creating a holistic impression of the physical environment. The Gestalt concept emphasizes that the whole is greater than the sum of various parts (Schiffman, 2001). A luxury resort spa environment entails not only the servicescape, but also the natural landscape and the interactive relationship between the spa service agents and the customers, as well as between customers. As such, an individual's perception cannot be meaningfully deconstructed into its individual components (i.e., sensations); the Gestalt approach also emphasizes the relationship between components of the stimuli in producing perceptual organization (Schiffman, 2001).

## FUTURE RESEARCH

In this section, three important topics of research are recommended for future research developments relating to spas and consumer behavior. Spa experience is physically removed from outside distractions and it is a very private and sensual experience. First, there have been limited empirical studies done on the importance of sensory marketing as it applies to the human five senses in the context of spas. Second, it is necessary to better understand the conceptualization of customers' perceived spa authenticity in order for a spa to differentiate itself from its competitors and limit the possibility of price wars. Third, culture and rituals, and inter-cultural service encounters are the core of the spa experience. The topic of culture is broad; the combination of culture and spa offerings can help enrich the spa literature.

### Sensation and Perception

Our senses serve as our sole detecting mechanism for the energy and chemistry evolving from the environment (Schiffman, 2001). Sensation is concerned with the initial contact between the person and his or her environment. Schiffman (2001) defined sensation as the initial process of detecting and encoding environmental energy. It refers to certain immediate and direct experiences to the conscious awareness of qualities or attributes linked to the physical environment. Sensation is biochemical and neurological in nature (Schiffman 2001). Spa guests react immediately and subconsciously to sensory inputs (i.e., the therapeutic touch, the scent of herbal oil, the sound of music, the taste of herbal tea, the dim lighting of the treatment room). The five senses can serve as powerful marketing tools to establish a spa's brand, identity, character, or signature (Krishna, 2010).

Perception is the awareness or understanding of sensory information. It is the process of organizing and interpreting sensations into meaningful experiences (Schiffman, 2001). Perception is

the result of psychological processes in which meaning, context, judgment, past experience, and memories are invoked (Schiffman, 2001). Even though there is a clear distinction in defining the terms of sensation and perception, Schiffman (2001) argues that sensation and perception are unified, inseparable processes. Sensation and perception are stages of processing of the senses.

The total awareness of the reality of our environment derives from our senses and perception. All sensory modalities contribute to a holistic spa experience. Making sense of the individual's sense and sensibilities of a luxury spa experience is imperative. A holistic luxury spa experience encompasses numerous elements and all human senses (e.g., touch, visual, auditory, olfactory, and taste). Spa services can evoke feelings of intense enjoyment or relaxation in multiple ways and through multiple sensory modalities in physical, social, and cultural contexts. Researchers should take multisensory modalities into account in terms of their interactive effects on an individual's perception and emotions. It is also worthwhile to investigate how one sensory modality can contribute to another sensory effect.

### Spa Authenticity/ Customer Preferences

Scholars from different disciplinary areas have viewed authenticity from different perspectives. There is no one clear definition of authenticity. The importance of defining the spa establishment's authenticity is to bridge the gap between the rapid developments of luxury spas and to limit the perception of commercialization while enhancing its core competencies and differentiation in order to gain competitive advantage. The notion of authenticity is suggested by previous literature; common themes of authenticity include original, heritage, true, real, self-identity, individuality, and meaning-making. Only one's own direct experience yields truth (May 1953; Rogers, 1961).

Applying the theory of Gestalt, the integrated factors that may contribute to an individual's luxury spa authenticity include the following: (1) the natural surrounding environment of the spa location (i.e, natural hot spring and natural landscape); (2) the servicescape or the man-made environment and ambience within a service organization; it includes color, lighting, scent, music, spatial layout and design; (3) service encounters depend heavily on the personal attributes of employees (i.e., attitude, professionalism, appropriate speed of delivery; friendliness, etc.); (4) the cultural component that includes the rituals of cultures, human history, and shared memories and longings; (5) well-being—for example, Canyon Ranch Spa and Resort provides private consultations, hands-on workshops, lectures, and cooking demos to educate the guests about healthy cooking techniques and enhance their nutritional knowledge. Many luxury spas also offer yoga, Pilates, and a zero gravity floating experience to help relax the mind, body and spirit. Further, in a recent trend, spa establishments serve as a unique crossroads where medical spa and traditional spa treatments meet. "'Clients today are better educated about the health benefits of relaxation therapies and will often schedule a massage, facial or spa pedicure and to see a medical director for injectables or laser treatments'" (Manacap-Johnson and Menrisky, 2014, p. 33). The above factors can be empirically examined to see what factor or factors account for most in an individual's perceived authenticity or preferences; at the same time, help spa establishments determine what factors will contribute most to enhance their brand, uniqueness and or authenticity.

## Culture and Rituals

The notion of culture is complex and difficult to define. Culture is the link between human beings and the means they have of interacting with others (Hall, 1966). "Culture is man's medium; there is not one aspect of human life that is not touched and altered by culture" (Hall, 1966, p. 16). Swedish spas actually organize themselves materially and spatially to impress themselves upon the bodies, sense, and emotions of their guests. Rituals and representational treatments which spas engage in are highly important in framing the spa experience. Each culture devises its own internally consistent set of rules. It is important for spa professionals to understand the system of rules and the assumptions that guide the private and social behaviors of people in the local as well as international culture. For example, due to the nature of a luxury spa setting, the facilities include both public and communal space (Jacuzzi, hot spring communal bathing area) and private or personal space (massage treatment room; private hot spring bathing room). Culture can be dissected into different layers. Researchers can study the effects of the following on customers' evaluation of their overall spa experience: culture and spa rituals and treatments, spa establishment's organization, its indigenous local culture, and customers' cultural background. In order to best meet the international customers' comfort level and to meet their satisfaction, it is important for researchers to investigate more in depth regarding different cultures around the world and compare and contrast the different cultural spa etiquette, rituals, and social behaviors in order to bridge the gap between the norms that international guests are accustomed to and what the local culture where the spa is located has to offer.

## Inter-Cultural Service Encounters

Inter-cultural service encounters are defined as the service exchanges or interactions of two or more parties from two different cultural backgrounds (Strauss & Mang, 1999; Zhao & Lin, 2014). For example, in the context of luxury spa service, if the spa guests in Indonesia are Americans and the spa therapists are Indonesian, when the American guests and the Indonesian spa therapists interact, it is an inter-cultural service encounter. Inter-cultural service encounters have long been an important subject of academic research in management. However, this topic has not been investigated in the context of spa industry; it is essential for spa professionals to understand inter-cultural service encounters in order to enhance service quality, reduce cultural misunderstandings that may unintentionally cause service failures, and more importantly, enhance international customer satisfaction.

## GLOBAL CHALLENGES AND MANAGERIAL IMPLICATIONS

As the future travel, spa and wellness trends evolve, some challenges may also arise. First, referring to the social and demographic trends, Generation Xers and the Millenials are known to be environmentally conscious and tech savvy groups of potential luxury spa consumers. However, according to an in-depth interview with a spa director in the U.S., she admitted that "We are reliant on so many different factors to run the business. I don't think we can be considered as sustainable at the moment; I don't think it is something that we are 100% aware of it" (L. Amasio, personal communication, January 24, 2014). Some countries are much better at practicing sustainability than others. However, it is not too late for those who did not practice sustainability to catch this bandwagon in order to gain a competitive advantage. The major barrier of practicing sustainability needs to be resolved in order for spas to win over the business of Generation Xers and the Millenials in the future. Perhaps more educational training relating to sustainability is needed for spa professionals.

Another challenge relates to the fast technological advancements and marketing and promotion in the spa industry. Spa managers not only need to understand the different high tech media but also how their target customers include technology as part of their lifestyle. The technological

to sway from the more traditional promotional media such as television and magazines to fill the schedule; nowadays, spa directors tend to invest more marketing dollars on social media such as Facebook, Twitter, and Groupon. However, some spa directors may disagree with the strategy of relying on social media to promote their spa in the U.S. Based on a face-to-face personal interview, one spa director in the U.S. states: "We are not involved with social media promotion because you have to offer 50 percent off your regular price to the consumer. Of that 50 percent you collect, Groupon or Living Social will take 50 Percent of it. Now you are only collecting 25 percent but after you pay your therapists, you are making nothing" (T. Kono, personal communication, Nov. 1, 2013). Despite the popularity of social media, striking the balance between attracting new customers and managing the revenue and profit can be a dilemma for spa managers. However, it is reasonable for luxury spas to be cautious about implementing promotions on social media, as the intention and message for using some of these social media (e.g., Groupon) is supposed introduce and lure new customers to the spa in the hope that they will return and pay full price. Unfortunately, it is the experience of many luxury resort spa directors that customers who use Groupon or Living Social may not be exactly their target market for luxury spas; they are only looking for deals so they are not willing to come back and pay full price later.

Technological advancements and cultural differences together pose another future challenge. Technology helps advance cosmetology with the innovation of machines for facials and treatments without any surgical intervention; according to Loh (2008), this will surely attract more spa customers from the West than the East. The West depends highly on high-tech equipment and the East depends highly on human touch and low-tech (Loh, 2008). While we are not sure whether Loh's assumption is true or not, one obvious future challenge relates to the understanding of cultural differences and inter-cultural service encounters between the spa service agents and international spa guests. As the world becomes smaller and globalized, cultural etiquette and rituals are usually part of the spa establishment to create the thematic and authentic identity. If not managed well, cultural misunderstanding can easily cause service failures.

Another challenge in the spa industry relates to lack of upper-level managers/leaders and labor shortages. Take Thailand as an example. As Thailand cooperates with the Asean Economic Community (AEC) in 2015, Thailand might stimulate a huge migration of Thai therapists to work abroad; this may create a therapist shortage in Thailand (Grant, 2014). In some developing countries such as Brazil and China, there is a lack of government support and regulations over spas and little standardized development (Grant, 2014). Even for developing country such as Canada, government provides little support for developing budgets for marketing, education, and building awareness of spa and wellness (Grant, 2014). Perhaps spa providers need to work together and be proactive in taking initiatives of more corporate social responsibility in order to earn the support from their governments.

In the U.S., health care expenditure is expected to increase; consequently, outbound medical tourism will likely increase due to the high price of health-care procedures (Grant, 2014). As more players are entering the medical tourism category in India and as 3-star hotels will begin offering spas as a key component of the hotel's products and services in France, there definitely will be a challenge of increased competition and the difficulties of differentiating luxury spa products and services. As such, constant value sales growth could be hampered by discounting and price promotions; hence, it is necessary for spa professionals to clearly define the spa's unique identity, thematic culture, and understand how customers compose and perceive authenticity. With such an understanding, spa professionals will be able to design holistic spa products and service offerings

that integrate wellness (body, mind, and spirit), culture, and aesthetics. In addition, more health care and spa collaboration is needed to train and develop spa professionals to have basic knowledge about medicine since spas will serve as a middle player between health care (traditional medicine) and illness prevention (alternative medicine). Well-trained spa professionals will definitely help spa establishments prepare for and accommodate the upcoming fast growing segment of the wellness industry, such as spa tourism and medical tourism. Educational institutions should also offer courses relating to spa management within the hospitality and tourism curriculum.

Asia was once a destination for outbound Europeans and a source of inspiration for treatments (Foster, 2014). Asian customers admire western 'science' for diagnostics, medical and holistic therapies. European prestige brands are still aspirational, but there is a growing movement to organic and natural products (Foster, 2014). Asian spa guests must have instant results and they are willing to try new products (e.g., snail facials). Korea is famous for cosmetic procedures. In the future, Asia will become a great source of inbound tourism and investment (Foster, 2014). It is a huge new market with money to spend (Foster, 2014). However, spas in Asia will experience an operational challenge of staff retention and hiring issues due to social stigma and job-hopping norm (Foster, 2014). Spas in Asia have much to improve despite the prosperous growth; spas need to partner with governments to set policies and regulations to better standardize and regulate spa operations. Spa operators need to be more willing to invest in employee training in order to retain their best employees.

Spa branding is definitely a challenge in a global environment. "Even a powerful brand will have trouble sustaining growth with a different image in every country" (Dev, 2012, p. 14). Global spa providers should take great advantage of sensory marketing to create signature branding (Krishna, 2010) and use sensory cues to market their spa establishments. Spa providers need to create a brand that is global and locally indigenous and relevant. "A brand with both high strength and high stature is a leadership brand that enjoys customer commitment" (Dev, 2012, p. 14). In order to build a reputable global spa brand, spa providers not only have to communicate a specific unique image, positioning, and character of its organization, it also must promise a set of benefits. The essence of a good brand differentiation entails a supportive community, efficiency, trust, and love in its brand message in order to sustain a strong differentiation among its competitors and to limit price wars.

## CONCLUSION

As discussed throughout this chapter, there are many factors that can influence customers' evaluation of their spa experience and there are infinite elements that spa providers can incorporate to differentiate themselves or to form a thematic or authentic identity. The evaluation of each individual's spa experience can be idiosyncratic. It is the idiosyncratic perception of spas within sophisticated customers' individual preferences that make spa research interesting and at the same time, extra challenging.

Spa experiences are inherently personal; as a result, no two people can have the same experience.

To improve research in the area of spa management and consumer experience, research relating to spas calls for more qualitative as well as quantitative research in order to thoroughly understands the phenomenon of the holistic spa experience.

Global spa, health and wellness tourism are on a continuous rise. This chapter also discussed several key factors that may help conceptualize an individual's perceived authenticity of a luxury spa experience that can be empirically tested across different countries. Further, exactly how spa consumption or spa treatments affect an individual's mind, body, and spirit and how we can connect spa

elements with nature or humanity and earth, or soul and cosmos definitely deserve more attention and investigation through multi-disciplinary research (i.e., neurobiology, neurophysiology) especially when sensation is regarded as biochemical- and neurologically-related in nature (Schiffman, 2001) and that spa experiences are highly sensual.

As the global market demands for healthy living increase, different sectors of the hospitality and tourism service providers must be proactive and wellness-minded in order to win the hearts of the growing health-conscious and wellness-minded customers; this means marketing global luxury resort spas and wellness should revolve around health and wellness concepts because consumers globally are leading very hectic lives so relaxation and stress relief remain key drivers for spa treatments or health and wellness tourism (Manacap-Johnson, 2014). It is also obvious that without the health concept design, hospitality and tourism providers will no longer be able to sustain or gain competitive advantage in this competitive global environment.

## REFERENCES

*About Six Senses-Six Senses Hotels Resorts Spas-Luxury Resorts*. (n.d.). Retrieved May 20, 2014, from http://www.sixsenses.com/about-us/about-us

Bakker, M. (2005). Luxury and tailor-made holidays. *Journal of Travel and Tourism Analyst, 20*, 1–47.

*Banyantree Global Foundation*. (2014). Retrieved May 5, 2014, from http://www.banyantreeglobal-foundation.com/about_us/CSRPublications

Carmer, J. C., & Rouzer, D. L. (1974). Healthy functioning from the Gestalt perspective. *The Counseling Psychologist, 4*(4), 20–23. doi:10.1177/001100007400400408

CBI Ministry of Foreign Affairs. (2014). *CBI product factsheet: Wellness tourism from France, Germany, Italy and the UK to Latin America.* Retrieved on June 1, 2014, from http://www.cbi. eu/system/files/marketintel_documents/2014_ pfs_wellness_tourism_from_france_germany_italy_and_the_uk_to_latin_america_0.pdf

Cohen, M., & Bodeker, G. (2008). *Understanding the global spa industry.* New York, NY: Routledge.

De Vierville, J. P. (2003). Spa industry, culture and evolution: Time, temperature, touch and truth. *Massage and Bodywork, 18,* 20–31.

Dev, C. S. (2012). *Hospitality branding.* Ithaca, NY: Cornell University Press.

Foster, S. (2014). *Spa business trends in Asia and their impact on the global spa industry.* Bangkok, Thailand: Destination Spa Management Ltd. Retrieved June 30, 2014, from http:// www.itb-kongress.de/media/itbk/itbk_media/ itbk_pdf/praesentationen_2014/wellness_forum/ Spa_Business_Trends_in_Asia-ITB-2014.pdf

Gilmore, J. H., & Pine, I. I. J. II. (2002). Customer experience places: The new offering frontier. *Strategy and Leadership, 30*(4), 4–11. doi:10.1108/10878570210435306

Gilmore, J. H., & Pine, I. I. J. (2007). *Authenticity.* Boston, MA: Harvard Business Press.

Grant, M. (2014). The road to health and wellness tourism: Trends and prospects across the globe. *The Pulse of the Montana State Nurses' Association, 24*(3), 26–31.

Hall, E. (1966). *The hidden dimension.* New York, NY: Anchor Books.

Hilton Hotel and Resorts Blue Paper. (2012). *Emerging global spa trends.* Retrieved May 22, 2014, from http://news.hilton.com

International Spa Association (ISPA). (2014). *Spa industry reports.* Lexington, KY: ISPA.

Islam, N. (2012). New age orientalism: Ayurvedic 'wellness and spa culture'. *Health Sociology Review, 21*(2), 220–231. doi:10.5172/ hesr.2012.21.2.220

Johnson, E. M., & Redman, B. M. (2008). *Spa: a comprehensive introduction.* Lexington, Kentucky: International SPA Association Foundation and American Hotel and Lodging Educational Institute.

Kelly, C., & Smith, M. (2009). Holistic tourism: integrating body, mind, spirit. In R. Bushell & P. S. Sheldon (Eds.), *Wellness and tourism: Mind, body, spirit, place* (pp. 127–143). New York, NY: Cognizant Communication Corporation.

Krishna, A. (2010). *Sensory marketing.* New York, NY: Routledge Taylor and Francis Group.

Landor's top 10 brand trends for 2014. (2014, January). *Marketing News,* p. 4.

Lin, I. Y. (2010). The interactive effect of Gestalt situations and arousal seeking tendency on customers' emotional responses: Matching color and music to specific servicescapes. *Journal of Services Marketing, 24*(4), 294–304. doi:10.1108/08876041011053006

Lin, I. Y., & Worthley, R. (2012). Servicescape moderation on personality traits, emotions, satisfaction, and behaviors. *International Journal of Hospitality Management, 31*(1), 31–42. doi:10.1016/j.ijhm.2011.05.009

Loh, M. (2008). The spa industry in Asia. In M. Cohen & G. Bodeker (Eds.), *Understanding the global spa industry: Spa management* (pp. 41–52). New York, NY: Routledge. doi:10.1016/B978-0-7506-8464-4.00003-5

Mak, A. H. N., Wong, K. F., & Chang, R. C. Y. (2009). Health or self-indulgence? The motivations and characteristics of spa-goers. *International Journal of Tourism Research, 11*(2), 185–199. doi:10.1002/jtr.703

Manacap-Johnson, M. (2014, May). A snapshot of spa destinations across the globe. *The Pulse of the Montana State Nurses' Association*, 36–40.

Manacap-Johnson, M., & Menrisky, A. (2014, May). Medical spa: Leading tourists at the crossroads between medical spa and wellness. *The Pulse of the Montana State Nurses' Association*, 32–34.

Mandhachitara, R., & Lockshin, L. (2004). Fast moving luxury goods: Positioning strategies for scotch whisky in Thai department stores. *International Journal of Retail & Distribution Management*, *32*(6), 312–319. doi:10.1108/09590550410538015

Mattila, A. S., & Wirtz, J. (2001). Congruency of scent and music as a driver for in-store evaluations and behavior. *Journal of Retailing*, *77*(2), 273–389. doi:10.1016/S0022-4359(01)00042-2

Mcilheney, C. (2013, September). U.S. spa industry returns to growth. *The Pulse of the Montana State Nurses' Association*, 32–35.

Mehrabian, A., & Russell, J. (1974). *An approach to environmental psychology*. Cambridge, MA: MIT Press.

Monteson, P. A., & Singer, J. (2004). Marketing a resort-based spa. *Journal of Vacation Marketing*, *10*(3), 282–287. doi:10.1177/135676670401000307

Namasivayam, K., & Lin, I. Y. (2008). The servicescape. In P. Jones & A. Pizam (Eds.), *Handbook of hospitality operations and IT* (pp. 43–62). Burlington, MA: Butterworth-Heinemann. doi:10.1016/B978-0-7506-8753-9.50007-X

O'Dell, T. (2010). *Spas: the cultural economy of hospitality, magic and the senses*. Sweden: Nordic Academic Press.

Reimer, A., & Kuehn, R. (2005). The impact of servicescape on quality perception. *European Journal of Marketing*, *38*(7/8), 785–808. doi:10.1108/03090560510601761

Research reveals how the world views wellness and health. (2014, January/February). *Pulse*, 12.

Richards, C. A., & Rundle, A. G. (2011). Business travel and self-rated health, obesity, and cardiovascular disease risk factors. *Journal of Occupational and Environmental Medicine*, *53*(4), 358–363. doi:10.1097/JOM.0b013e3182143e77 PMID:21436731

Schiffman, H. R. (2001). *Sensation and perception*. New York, NY: Wiley & Sons.

Schmitt, B. (1999). *Experiential marketing*. New York, NY: The Free Press.

Sheldon, P. S., & Bushell, R. (2009). Introduction to wellness and tourism. In R. Bushell & P. Sheldon (Eds.), *Wellness and tourism: Mind, body, spirit, place* (pp. 3–18). New York, NY: Cognizant Communication Corporation.

Spa Finder Wellness 365. (2014). *2014 trends report: Top 10 global spa and wellness trends forecast*. Retrieved May 5, 2014, from http://www.spafinder.com/trends2014.htm

Spa Finder Wellness 365. (2014). *Healthy hotels 2.0*. Retrieved May 5, 2014, from http://www.spafinder.com/trends/2014/healthy-hotels.htm

*Spa Finder's Top Ten European Spa Trends*. (2006, August 27). Retrieved June 20, 2014, from http://www.americanspacom/spa-news/spa-finders-top-ten-european-spa-trends.

Strauss, B., & Mang, P. (1999). Culture shocks in inter-cultural service encounters*? Journal of Services Marketing*, *13*(3/4), 329–346. doi:10.1108/08876049910282583

Tabacchi, M. H. (2010). Current research and events in the spa industry. *Cornell Hospitality Quarterly*, *51*(1), 102–117. doi:10.1177/1938965509356684

Tubergen, A. V., & Van der Linden, S. (2001). A brief history of spa therapy. *Annals of the Rheumatic Diseases, 61*(3), 273–275. doi:10.1136/ard.61.3.273 PMID:11830439

Voigt, C., Brown, G., & Howat, G. (2011). Wellness tourists: In search of transformation. *Tourism Review, 66*(1/2), 16–30. doi:10.1108/16605371111127206

Who's the average male spa-goer? (2014, January/February). *Pulse*, 36-37.

Yeoman, I., & McMahon-Beattie, U. (2006). Luxury markets and premium pricing. *Journal of Revenue and Pricing Management, 4*(4), 319–328. doi:10.1057/palgrave.rpm.5170155

Yeung, O., Johnston, K., & Chan, N. (2014). *The global wellness tourism economy 2013*. New York, NY: Global Wellness Institute.

Zhao, D., & Lin, I. Y. (2014). Understanding tourists' perception and evaluation of inter-cultural service encounters: A holistic mental model process. *International Journal of Culture, Tourism, and Hospitality Research.*

## ADDITIONAL READING

Areni, C. S., & Kim, D. (1993). The influence of in-store lighting on consumers' examination of merchandise in a wine store. *International Journal of Research in Marketing, 11*(2), 117–125. doi:10.1016/0167-8116(94)90023-X

Bitner, M. J. (1992). Servicescapes: The impact of physical surroundings on customers and employees. *Journal of Marketing, 54*, 69–82. doi:10.2307/1251871

Chambers, E. (2009). From authenticity to significance: Tourism on the frontier of culture and place. *Futures, 41*(6), 353–359. doi:10.1016/j.futures.2008.11.003

Cooper, M. (2009). Health and wellness spa tourism environment. In P. Erfurt-Cooper & M. Cooper (Eds.), *Health and Wellness Tourism* (pp. 156–180). Bristol: Channel View Publications.

Demoulin, N. (2011). Music congruency in a service setting: The mediating role of emotional and cognitive responses. *Journal of Retailing and Consumer Services, 18*(1), 10–18. doi:10.1016/j.jretconser.2010.08.007

Dong, P., & Siu, N. Y. (2013). Servicescape elements, customer predispositions and service experience: The case of thee park visitors. *Tourism Management, 36*, 541–551. doi:10.1016/j.tourman.2012.09.004

Hughes, G. (1995). Authenticity in tourism. *Annals of Tourism Research, 22*(4), 781–803. doi:10.1016/0160-7383(95)00020-X

Kelley, S. (1992). Developing customer orientation among service employees. *Journal of the Academy of Marketing Science, 20*(1), 27–36. doi:10.1007/BF02723473

Lin, I. Y. (2010). The combined effect of color and music on customer satisfaction in hotel bars. *Journal of Hospitality Marketing and Management, 19*(1), 22–37. doi:10.1080/19368620903327675

Lin, I. Y., & Mattila, A. S. (2010). Restaurant servicescape, service encounter, and perceived congruency on customers' emotions and satisfaction. *Journal of Hospitality Marketing and Management, 19*(8), 819–841. doi:10.1080/19368623.2010.514547

Mattila, A. S., & Enz, C. (2002). The role of emotions in service encounters. *Journal of Service Research, 4*(4), 268–277. doi:10.1177/1094670502004004004

McCabe, C., Rolls, E. T., Bilderbeck, A., & Mc-Glone, F. (2008). Cognitive influences on the affective representation of touch and the sight of touch in the human brain. *Social Cognitive and Affective Neuroscience, 3*(2), 97–108. doi:10.1093/scan/nsn005 PMID:19015100

Mkono, M. (2012). A netnographic examination of constructive authenticity in Victoria Falls tourist restaurant experiences. *International Journal of Hospitality Management, 31*(2), 387–394. doi:10.1016/j.ijhm.2011.06.013

Mueller, H., & Kaufmann, E. L. (2001). Wellness tourism: Market analysis of a special health tourism segment and implications for the hotel industry. *Journal of Vacation Marketing, 7*(1), 5–17. doi:10.1177/135676670100700101

Namasivayam, K., & Mattila, A. S. (2007). Accounting for the joint effects of the servicescape and service exchange on consumers' satisfaction evaluations. *Journal of Hospitality & Tourism Research (Washington, D.C.), 31*(1), 3–18. doi:10.1177/1096348006292996

Oliver, R. L. (1981). Measurement and evaluation of satisfaction process in retail setting. *Journal of Retailing, 57*(3), 25–48.

Oliver, R. L. (1997). *Satisfaction.* New York, NY: McGraw-Hill.

Orth, U. R., Heinrich, F., & Malkewitz, K. (2012). Servicescape interior design and consumers' personality impressions. *Journal of Services Marketing, 26*(3), 194–203. doi:10.1108/08876041211223997

Pearce, P. L. (1983). Fundamentals of tourist motivation. In D. W. Pearce & R. W. Butler (Eds.), *Tourism Research: Critiques and Challenges* (pp. 113–134). London, UK: Routledge.

Peterson, R. A. (2005). In search of authenticity. *Journal of Management Studies, 42*(5), 1086. doi:10.1111/j.1467-6486.2005.00533.x

Pine, B. J. II, & Gilmore, J. H. (1998). Welcome to the experience economy. *Harvard Business Review,* (July-August): 97–105. PMID:10181589

Pons, P. (2003). Being-on-holiday: Tourist dwelling, bodies and place. *Tourist Studies, 3*(1), 47–66. doi:10.1177/1468797603040530

Steiner, C., & Reisinger, Y. (2005). Understanding existential authenticity. *Annals of Tourism Research, 33*(2), 200–318.

Turley, L. W., & Milliman, R. E. (2000). Atmospherics on shopping behavior: A review of the experimental evidence. *Journal of Business Research, 49,* 193–211. doi:10.1016/S0148-2963(99)00010-7

Wang, C. Y., & Mattila, A. S. (2013). The impact of servicescape cues on consumer prepurchase authenticity assessment and patronage intentions to ethnic restaurants. *Journal of Hospitality & Tourism Research (Washington, D.C.), 2013,* 1906348013491600.

Wang, N. (1999). Rethinking authenticity in tourism experience. *Annals of Tourism Research, 26*(2), 349–370. doi:10.1016/S0160-7383(98)00103-0

## KEY TERMS AND DEFINITIONS

**Authentic:** Original, trustworthy, unique, different, not false or copied.

**Brand:** A name or a log that has its distinctive identity, character, or positioning.

**Competitive Advantages:** Benefits or means specially favorable to success over competitors-- offering customers greater value (e.g., lower prices or providing more benefits that justify higher price).

**Core Competencies:** Something that the company is best at doing or offering that distinguishes the company from its competitors.

**Differentiation:** Separation. If a company has a distinct differentiation: that means a company has unique characteristic that separates itself from among its competitors. What separates the company from its competitors?

**Experience:** The process of personally encountering or interacting with a thing, a person, or the overall environment of a particular place that occur in the course of time; it is the totality of the cognitions given by perception and affection given by sensation; all that is perceived, learned, understood, and remembered.

**Luxury:** A hedonic pleasure out of the ordinary allowed to oneself; a material or an expensive product or service conducive to sumptuous living, usually a delicacy, elegance, or refinement of living rather than a necessity.

**Market Trends:** External macro-environmental impacts that an organization has very little or no control over and are likely to affect the marketing in which a company operates.

**Servicescape:** A servicescape is composed of numerous elements such as the color, music, scent, and layout and design and is the physical environment of a service organization where customers experience the service.

**Spa:** "Health through water"; fountain. Water and the form it takes is the core foundation.

**Wellness:** An approach to healthcare that emphasizes preventing illness and prolonging life: the balance and harmony of health, body, mind, spirit, quality of life, and well-being.

**Well-Being:** A good or satisfactory condition of existence; a state characterized by health, happiness, prosperity and welfare.

# Chapter 12
# The Influence of National Culture on Customer Service Experience:
## Case of China

**Ying Ying Liao**
*Hamdan Bin Mohammed Smart University, UAE*

**Ebrahim Soltani**
*Hamdan Bin Mohammed Smart University, UAE*

**Wei-Yuan Wang**
*Shih-Chien University, Taiwan*

## ABSTRACT

*Hofstede's cultural framework has been very instrumental in furthering an understanding of cross-cultural management and taken center stage as the dominant cultural paradigm to show respect for norms, values, and management styles across cultures. However, resent research on cross-cultural management suggests to go beyond Hofstede's cultural framework and use non-Western, Asian cultural norms which might provide additional insights into the impact of cultural values on service quality dimensions and the resultant implications for customer expectations and satisfaction. This chapter attends to this call and examines the practice of service quality in hospitality sector in the Republic of China (Taiwan) so it may serve as a reference point against which to interpret the fieldwork data of cross-cultural service quality research and its implications for customers' perceptions towards service quality.*

## INTRODUCTION

Due to the current role and contribution of service sector in general and hospitality industry in particular to the economy and rapid pace of internationalization of service companies, it is difficult for hospitality practitioners to establish a universal marketing strategy which can be effectively used across a complex of diverse national cultures. This also poses a challenge to academics

DOI: 10.4018/978-1-4666-8606-9.ch012

to propose a 'vanilla, one size fits all' approach or the existing Western-driven theoretical cultural models to offer prescriptions for organizational success and survival in the competitive global business environment of hospitality sector. To a considerable extent these challenges are attributed to the broad economic reach of the hospitality industry, global community of its customers, and more specifically their cultural differences. So focusing on the generic service quality gap models (e.g. SERVQUAL – see Parasuraman et al., 1985, 1988; Zeithaml et al., 1990), although valid instruments for explaining a great deal of customers' expectations and perceptions towards service quality offerings and the resulting quality gaps, cannot, in itself, serve as the only point of reference for delighting and retaining customers.

Analysis of cross-cultural customer behavior issues, drawing upon the global nature of the hospitality industry and its diverse constituents (e.g. workforce, guests, shareholders, owners), has come to the fore in the service quality management research over the past two decades (Lockyer & Tsai, 2004; Furrer et al., 2000; Mattila, 1999; Wang et al., 2008; Winsted, 1997; Soltani & Wilkinson, 2010; De Mooij & Hofstede, 2011; Camillo & Di Pietro, 2014). These scholars argue that customer behavior is largely 'culture-bound' and stress the importance of understanding cultural components of customer behavior, if an organization is to survive and succeed in the competitive global business environment (De Mooij & Hofstede, 2011, pp. 181). In this respect, the Hofstede (1980) dimensional model of national culture (i.e. individualism-collectivism, uncertainty avoidance, power distance, masculinity-femininity, & long- versus short-term orientation) has led the way with its hypothesized connection between national cultural norms and associated differences in customer behavior over the past three decades. However, this chapter draws upon non-Western, more specific cultural values as a theoretical lens to further interpret a customer's behavior dynamics in the global hospitality industry.

More specifically, it gains insight from Chinese cultural values of *Gunaxi* (關係), *Mien-tzu* (面子), and *Hé* (和) to both enhance the theoretical base of cross-cultural service quality research and to help practicing hospitality managers delight their customers. Given the role of China and its consumers in the global economy, the substantial (in)direct contribution of hospitality sector to the country's GDP (with a faster growth rate than the total economy) (see WTTC, 2013) and previous call for more cross-cultural consumer behavior research (see Camillo, 2014), this study brings new insights into the long-standing debate on service quality and culture.

More specifically, the primary aim of this chapter is to examine the influence of Chinese cultural values on expectations of service quality. In doing so, it poses a challenge to the marketing and service research scholars in terms of applicability of Western-dominated cultural frameworks to study customer expectations of more specific cultural contexts. Overall, this chapter makes a contribution to the advancement of Asian management research by diverting its emphasis from primarily Western-dominated service management research context to the more unique context of the Asian region so as to explore and examine the peculiarities of Chinese cultural norms and values and its implications for customer expectations and perceptions of service quality. For comparative purposes and in an attempt to unravel the practice of culture-bound behaviors of customers, we focus on the results of a recently conducted survey research on 'service quality and culture' in the context of hospitality sector in the Republic of China (Taiwan). In comparison to other economic sectors in the mainland China, Hong Kong and Taiwan, the hospitality sector has significantly contributed to GDP and created competitive employment opportunities for local, regional and international businesses (see National Statistical, 2009).

This chapter is divided into four sections. The first discusses the nature, characteristics and significance of services and the determinants of service quality. Second, it presents an overview of hospitality industry in terms of definition, function, importance as well as the challenges facing hospitality industry practitioners. Third, it examines the current conceptual modeling of customer behavior across different cultures in hospitality industry. A particular focus of this section will be on the application of Hofstede dimensional model of national culture and the need for utilizing non-Western, more specific cultural norms to explain and differentiate between customer behaviors across culture. This section also offers an overview of Chinese cultural values of Gunaxi (關係), Mien-tzu (面子), and Hé (和) and their influence on customer buying behavior. The final section presents the concluding remarks and discusses the implications for hospitality industry practitioners and cross-cultural customer behavior scholars.

## SERVICE QUALITY: NATURE, SIGNIFICANCE, AND DETERMINANTS

Whilst the world's economy reliance on manufacturing sector was evident until early 1990s, the economy now follows the service path. Integral to the dominant service economy is the increased importance of the service sector in both developing and industrialized economies as well as the relative importance of services in a product offering (i.e. the servitization of products). In the light of the rise of global service economy, a key tendency appears to be the increased emphasis upon the 'quality of services' (or service quality) and the need to tailor the service offerings to meet customer's individual needs. The importance attached to the need for more effective management of services and delivering superior service quality stems from the unique characteristics of services. In contrast to the production and marketing of physical products, services are highly perishable, intangible, variable due to the

involvement of the human element, inseparable, and finally the consumer does not secure ownership of the service. These characteristics in turn give rise to special problems for the management of service organizations to define and measure the quality of service offerings and set out standards and delivery systems which drive best value and optimized service levels for the customers (see Soltani et al., 2008, 2012).

Accordingly, there has been an upsurge of interest in the factors that (in)directly influence the quality of service offerings (i.e. service quality performance). A key factor which might be expected to play a major part in the service quality performance is the 'quality of the service provider' – i.e. people who provide the service. The hypothesized relationship between the quality of service provider and the service quality performance has led the way for service management scholars to further study those forces or factors that could influence a service firm's approach and orientation towards quality. A review of the extant literature on the determinants of service quality at firm level highlights several internal/organizational and external/environmental forces which play a part in the service firm's approach to the quality of service offerings. Table 1 presents both a firm- and individual-level analysis of potential forces that shape and determine the quality of service offerings.

A close analysis of Table 1 reveals quite clearly that these factors differ in their relative importance and impact on service quality performance and that whilst some of these forces are deemed to be core to the formulation of a firm's service quality strategy, the relative importance and impact of the others could be peripheral to a service firm's decision to plan and implement its service quality strategy. At the (individual) customer level of analysis of service quality –i.e. people who receive the service/customers – customers compare their expectations of service quality with their perceptions of the services they receive. The clearest expression of this position is found in

*Table 1. Factors influencing the quality of services offerings: firm- vs. customer-level analysis level*

| | Firm-Level Determinant of Service Quality | | (Individual) Customer-Level Determinants of Service Quality |
|---|---|---|---|
| | **Internal Forces** | **External Forces** | |
| Service quality | • Management style<br>• Organizational culture<br>• Organizational approach to employee training | • National cultural values<br>• Economic status<br>• The degree of political stability<br>• The extent of competition across the sector | • Product ownership & usage (personal needs of the customer),<br>• The customer's own pre-purchase beliefs, knowledge, and experiences with a service or a product<br>• Word-of-mouth communication<br>• Brand loyalty<br>• Learning from advertisements<br>• Media usage<br>• Complaining behavior |

**Sources:** Parasuraman et al. (1985); Zeithaml et al. (1990); Winsted, K. F. (1997); Ramaseshan et al. (2006); Parasuraman et al. (1988); Mattila (1999); Furrer et al. (2000); Donthu & Yoo (1998).

Parasuraman et al.'s (1985) discussion of service quality gap model (referred to as 'SERVQUAL' in the extant literature on services and services marketing management). The SERVQUAL model offers a direct comparison between a customer's service expectations and perceived performance based upon the five service quality dimensions of reliability, assurance, tangibles, empathy, and responsiveness (which create the acronym 'RATER') (see also Parasuraman et al., 1988; Zeithaml et al., 1990). As Table 1 serves to emphasize, customers' expectations towards service quality is also shaped by and built upon complex considerations (see Zeithaml, Bitner, & Gremler, 2006). Of these many are uncontrollable factors which in turn make it even harder for service provider to anticipate, meet and manage customers' expectations. Personal needs of the customer, the customer's own pre-purchase beliefs, the customers' knowledge of a product or service, the customer's previous experiences with a service, learning from advertisements, and word-of-mouth communication (to name but a few) have been often-cited and used in the extant literature to characterize the nature of a customer's expectation towards service quality and as standards against which performance is delivered.

In addition to the aforementioned individual- and firm-level factors, more recently the primary determinant of service quality and customer satisfaction has revolved around the idea of improving service quality by diagnosing and understanding national cultural norms and their influence on customer behavior (see Hofstede, 2001; De Mooij, 2004; De Mooij & Hofstede, 2002; Adler, 2007). This is the position taken by the advocates of cross-cultural consumer behavior studies who suggest the potential of gaining competitive service value through identifying the cultural components of customer behavior. According to this view, "most aspects of consumer behavior are culture-bound" (De Mooij & Hofstede, 2011, pp. 181). Despite the substantial contributions of cross-cultural studies of customer behavior, they have been criticized on two fronts. First, the primary focus of cross-cultural studies of customer behavior represents the dominant Western cultural values –thereby devoid of critical analysis of managing service quality in non-Western organizational contexts with dominant local cultural norms and values affecting buying behavior of consumers. Second, the Hofstede dimensional model of national culture has been used as the primary theoretical lens of cross-cultural customer behavior – thereby devoid of the characteristics of culture specific manifestations of non-Western, local cultural norms and values.

As is evident from the above summary of research on service quality, there is a need for further research in under-researched context of non-Western, emerging and developing markets to diagnose and understand their cultural orientations and the ramifications for the local and international businesses and customers. There is also a need on the part of cross-cultural management scholars to go beyond Hofstede's cultural framework (Fang, 2010) and use more specific (e.g. Asian) cultural norms which might provide additional insight into the impact of cultural values and norms on service quality dimensions and the resultant implications for customer expectations and satisfaction (Reimann et al., 2008, pp.70). This remainder of this chapter attends to these suggestions and examines the practice of service quality in hospitality sector in the Republic of China so it may serve as reference point against which to interpret the fieldwork data of cross-cultural service quality research and its implications for customers' (e.g. tourists) perceptions towards service quality. The focus on Chinese culture, customers, and service providers is timely not least because of China's emergence as the second largest economy in the world and the fact that Chinese customers constitute one of the most important sources of growth for the global economy. The paramount importance of research in the wider Asian Pacific context (as opposed to Western-dominated research) has also been highlighted by White (2002), Meyer (2006), Fang (2010), and Ahlstrom (2010) in a sense that "there is a need to move beyond the Hofstede paradigm (as he explored, among other things, the general characteristics of Asian management as opposed to management elsewhere) if today's borderless and wireless cross-cultural management has a chance to be understood and theorized" (Fang 2010, p.156).

## HOSPITALITY INDUSTRY: DEFINITION, FUNCTION, AND IMPORTANCE

In a manner similar to other business management concepts, the term hospitality has also been open to organisational scholar scrutiny over the past years. A useful review of the term and its key elements has been presented by Brotherton (2002; 1999) and Brotherton and Wood (2008, pp.38-39). As their review indicates, despite the widespread adoption of the term, hospitality, its use to describe the activities of the industry, and its meaning are still elusive (Bright & Johnson 1985). Therefore, in the study of hospitality in general, and hospitality management in particular, defining the term is rather problematic not least because of a lack of general agreement as to what hospitality is. Oxford Dictionaries Online (2010) defines hospitality as 'friendly and generous reception and entertainment of guests or strangers'. For Tideman (1983), hospitality can be defined as 'the method of production by which the needs of the proposed guest are satisfied to the utmost and that means a supply of goods and services in a quantity and quality desired by the guest and at a price that is acceptable to him or her so that he or she feels that the product is worth the price'. Jones (1996) argues that hospitality is made up of two distinct services: one relates to the provision of overnight accommodation for people staying away from home, and the other refers to the provision of sustenance for people eating away from home. Cassee (1983) takes a more holistic approach to defining the term and views hospitality as a harmonious mixture of tangible and intangible components –i.e. food, beverages, beds, ambience and environment, and staff behaviour (see also Brotherton, 2002; 1999, pp.168; Brotherton &Wood, 2008; Cassee & Reuland, 1983, pp.144). Based upon a review of past definitions of the term, Morrison and O'Gorman (2006, p.3) view hospitality as a multi-faceted activity which represents a host's cordial reception, welcome and entertainment of guests or strangers of diverse social backgrounds and cultures charitably, socially or commercially with kind and generous liberality, into one's space to dine and/or lodge temporarily (see Brotherton, 2002; 1999; Brotherton & Wood, 2008, pp.38-39, for further details).

Despite some similarities and differences in focus between the aforementioned definitions and perspectives towards the term, one thing is clear-cut: given different circumstances and contexts and their unique characteristics, the degree to which the hospitality offering is conditional or unconditional may vary from one context to another one, and from one circumstance to the other. In addition, when people's living standards are improving they are able to spend more on leisure activities including dining away from home as well as other hospitality-related services – an indication of the fact that foodservices have now become a generally accepted part of people's lifestyles. Hence as Brotherton and Wood (2008) have rightly commented, it is not uncommon to see that people everywhere purchase food while they work, travel and engage in leisure activities. This in turn implies that the provision of food and beverage (by hospitality industry in general and restaurants or food service providers in multitudes of form in particular) to customers as a key business activity has played a long and important role in society.

In addition to the nature of hospitality term, the hospitality industry is deemed essential for both developing and developed economies. This is primarily because hospitality is responsible for providing good quality services (such as accommodation, food, attractions, leisure activities, and entertainment) to the public where each individual consumer has his or her unique and different preferences, expectations and tastes. Given such broad mission, hospitality is viewed as the umbrella industry under which the foodservice segment provided by restaurants in its multitude of forms

(as the research sites for the current study) operates. The foodservice industry is often classified into two primary segments: (i) the commercial segment and, (ii) the onsite/non-commercial segment on a global scale (Barrows, 2008). Whilst the former refers to most types of foodservice operations such as quick-service, fine-dining, pubs, and family restaurants, the latter segment covers those foodservice outlets that serve a larger entity such as a business/ industry, university, hospital and the like. The commercial sector is the largest and most dominant on both a regional and global scale (Barrows, 2008). According to Barrows' (2008) review of the existing statistics on hospitality industry turnover and extent of operations in global marketplace, the commercial sector is approximately ten times larger than the on-site/ non-commercial sector. As part of the commercial segment, restaurants are generally categorized into two main types: (i) full-service restaurants and (ii) limited-service restaurants (Barrows, 2008). The full-service restaurant category is composed of any operations in which the customers receive complete table service such as dinner houses (including themed restaurants), family restaurants, and fine-dining. Here customers seem to spend more time to get served as, for example, once they have arrived they have to wait to be seated, order a meal, interact with restaurant staff, and sit for a relatively longer time. The implication of the customers' (guests') long stay at the restaurants is that the management of restaurant needs to provide a comfortable dining environment (and of course high quality food) to the customers and pay sufficient attention to such service components of physical setting and dinning environment. As Barrows (2008) has pointed out, this is because each of these service components would highly likely influence customer satisfaction and his or her subsequent behavioral responses. The limited service category (e.g. fast-food restaurants), on the other hand, refers to any operations where the customer is an integral part of the service delivery system. Quick-service, cafeterias, buffets, coffee shops, and pubs are some examples of limited service restaurants (Sulek & Hensley, 2004). In short, foodservice (including both food and beverage) industry is a part of the larger hospitality sector. In the context of foodservice industry, various components of service delivery (both tangible and intangible) would clearly influence, form and shape customers dining experiences and therefore both need to be managed and delivered effectively by the service provider. The current chapter makes an attempt to assess customers (guests) experience with dinning in both hotel chain restaurants and local Chinese chain restaurants operating in Taiwan.

## HOSPITALITY INDUSTRY IN TAIWAN

According to the recent statistics (Domestic Statistic, 2010), the entire unit number of industrial and commercial enterprises accounted for 1,105,102 in Taiwan during 2001-2006 – an increase of 18.15% within the past five years. The breakdown of such statistics in terms of economic sectors was as follows: service sector 79.55% and industrial sector 20.45%. In reference to hospitality sector in Taiwan, there was an increase of 42.33 percent in food/beverage and accommodation services (e.g. hotels, guest house) over the past five years – putting the sector in the first position in 2007. Indeed, the major source of revenue of hospitality sector came from accommodation and foodservices. At a macro level, the service sector had also attracted the greatest number of working population –i.e. 4,309,646 which accounted for 57.08% of working population. Because of continuous development of tourism and travelling and more importantly changes in people's life style, hospitality industry has been viewed as a major contributor to Taiwan's economy (Domestic Statistic, 2010).

Across the hospitality industry and in particular food and accommodation services, chain system has become the mainstream of commercial development as it makes most use of collective

purchase and marketing activities. This in turn has resulted in two separate but related developments: first, higher flexibility of small-scale enterprises, and (ii) achieving economy of scale for large-scale enterprises. With regard to the current study, a chain restaurant is a set of related restaurants with the same brand name in more than one location across the country that are managed either under common ownership or franchising agreements (Converse, 1921). Currently, there are some 284 chain hospitality industries, engaged in various activities such as restaurants and hotels, with over 4800 franchised stores in Taiwan. Each chain restaurant has 11.8 franchised stores and each chain beverage industry has 20.8 franchised stores. In terms of service quality, it is expected that all service providers, both the parent company and its franchisees, provide the same level of service quality to the customers (guests) across the country and be consistent in their service quality measures. This issue is of paramount importance not least because if one franchised outlet (e.g. store, restaurant, and hotel) causes service failure, the other franchised outlets' businesses will also be adversely affected. Nielsen Global Online Survey (2009) of Taiwanese consumers reveals that 1 in 7 Taiwanese eats out every day or more than once a day. National statistics for family income and expenditure in 2008 report that personal and household consumption expenditure in food is regarded as the most highest expense than any other household expenses. Indeed, more recent evidence confirms that dinging-out rate has reached 34.8 percentage of household food expenditure in 2008 – an increase of 7.6 percent compared to that of 1998 (National Statistical 2009). Whilst food consumption has an important and indispensable role in Taiwanese life as well as in other nations, the key issue and one related to the current study is that consumption style of dining-out in a range of different restaurants (both modern 5-start hotel chain restaurants and more traditional chain family-owned restaurants) is very common and emphasized in Taiwanese society. So food provided and served in restaurants reflects the nature of Taiwan's colourful cultural background and norms. For instance, food can be integrated using Chinese ingredient styles from mainland and Japanese taste which emphasizes healthy diet. As a result of such cultural tendency towards other nations' dietary habits, Taiwanese people are more open-minded and try to embrace and accept other foreign foods. Thus, various foods from different countries can be found easily in Taiwan and are served along with local dishes. It is therefore not uncommon to see that people in Taiwan spend more money on dining-out. Indeed, dining out seems to be the preferred option than cooking at home for several reasons, namely, economical (cheaper), social (interaction with others), and quality wise issues. With regard to the latter, it should be noted that dining-out is not only a common and preferred economic choice for Taiwanese but also it is rather easy to find good quality restaurants with diverse dishes everywhere in the country.

## CONCEPTUAL MODELING OF CUSTOMER BEHAVIOR

Conceptual modeling of customer behavior in services and marketing management literature has a rich heritage. However, the research base of this genre is of doubtful quality not least because of the origin and source of the proposed models. The dominant approach to conceptualizing hospitality customer behavior has been to pursue basic cross-cultural differences as a platform to explain differences in customer behavior across cultures and countries and to assist practicing marketing managers to design effective marketing, branding and advertising strategies which are customer-driven and entail a strong cultural fit (Storey, 1992, pp. 32).

Of different cross-cultural customer behavior frameworks, Hofstede dimensional model of national culture is the most widely cited in existence (Bond, 2002; Hofstede, 1997; Jones,

2007). Five dimensions which characterize a national culture express the essence of Hofstede's cultural framework: power distance, uncertainty avoidance, individualism/collectivism, masculinity/femininity, and long-term orientation. Power distance Index (PDI) 'is the extent to which the less powerful members of organizations and institutions (like the family) accept and expect that power is distributed unequally'. Individualism (IDV) connotes "the degree to which individuals are integrated into groups'. Uncertainty avoidance index (UAI) refers to 'a society's tolerance for uncertainty and ambiguity'. Masculinity (MAS) signals 'the distribution of emotional roles between the genders'. Long-term orientation (LTO) (also referred to as 'Confucian dynamism') describes societies' time horizon.

The emphasis arising from Hofstede's cultural framework emerges from the 'cultural values' and 'customer buying behavior' lineage (see De Mooij & Hofstede, 2011; Kirkman et al., 2006). It connotes the compelling idea of 'cultural fit' to better understand consumer buying behavior. As Hofstede (2001) has pointed out, familiarity with different cultures and their influence on customer behavior is to be integral to the core performance objective of the marketing managers not least because it has the potential to reduce the level of concern and frustration on the part of both local and specifically international managers who wish to operate beyond their own local and national boundaries.

Increased recognition of the importance of understanding cultural norms as a prerequisite for delivering high quality services to diverse range of customers with different cultural patterns, coupled with wider concerns about 'brand', have pushed the notion of 'cultural fit' into centre-stage on the research agenda in services, marketing and international management. The emphasis arising from this strand of research has been to assist local and international businesses by explaining cultural differences in consumer behavior and to develop marketing strategies that effectively target customers across culture (De Mooij & Hofstede, 2011, pp. 190). A brief review of the cross-cultural research on service quality and customer satisfaction constitutes the focus of next section.

## CROSS-CULTURAL ANALYSIS OF HOSPITALITY CUSTOMER BEHAVIOR: HOFSTEDE'S CULTURAL DIMENSIONS

There are several cultural models within the field of cross-cultural and cross-national consumer behavior which have been advanced to help compare, contrast and explain consumer behavior across culture (e.g. Hall's high- and low-context cultures; Hofstede model). In this chapter, the focus of the review will only be on those studies which have utilized Hofstede's cultural dimensions not least because it has been the predominant model in cross-cultural service research (see Donthu & Yoo, 1998; Furrer et al., 2000; Malhorta et al., 2005; Keillor et al., 2004; Voss et al., 2004; Liu et al., 2001; Hui & Au, 2001; Wong, 2004; Patterson & Smith, 2003; Mattila & Patterson, 2004). Overall, a review of these studies seems to suggest three broad categories of cross-cultural service research: culture and service expectations, culture and service evaluation and culture and reactions to services (Zhang et al., 2008). In other words, the primary theme of cross-cultural service research has been on the process of service experience (i.e. from 'expectations' to 'evaluation' of the service quality performance to the follow-up 'behavioral reactions' to service quality performance). For example, Donthu and Yoo (1998) adopted Hofstede's cultural framework and SERVQUAL scale to conduct a cross-country survey in Canada, Great Britain, India, and the United States in terms of how customers' cultural orientations could impact on their service quality expectations. Of the 25 possible relationships between the five cultural dimensions, they limited their focus to 6 items

SERVQUAL dimensions. Their main conclusions were that customers with high scores in power distance, uncertainty avoidance, and individualism had higher service quality expectations than customers with low respective scores. With regard to individual service dimensions, customers with high power distance scores had lower expectations of responsiveness and reliability than those with low power distance customers. In addition, high uncertainty avoidance customers placed more importance on tangibles than low uncertainty avoidance customers. Finally, individualistic customers appeared to have higher expectations of empathy and assurance than collectivistic customers. Despite various strengths of the study, one crucial limitation, similar to that of the studies of Winsted (1997) and Mattila (1999), was that they failed to take into account the contingency variables. Although they used the power distance dimension, their study did not make a distinction between powerful and weak customers; while they used the masculinity dimension their study did not differentiate between services provided by male or female employees; and finally, although they used the uncertainty avoidance dimension they ignored or undermined the difference between frequent and infrequent service situations (see Furrer et al., 2000 for further detail).

In another study, Mattila (1999) chose the environment of luxury hotels in order to investigate the impact of culture on customer evaluation of complex services. Her primary objective was to understand the trade-off between the personalized service and pleasant physical environment of the luxury hotels from the points of view of two different types of customers: Western and Asian hotel guests. To this end, she initially developed a framework to depict the cultural differences between Western and Asian customers in terms of individualism versus collectivism, power distance (see Hofstede 1980, 1991), and high- versus low-context communication (see Hall, 1976). It should be noted that she did not control for

three categories: Westerners, Asian Chinese, and Asian Indian. She also related these three groups of customer to only a reduced set of service dimensions (e.g. physical environment, personal service components, and hedonic dimension). Her main findings were that customers with Western cultural backgrounds were more likely to rely on the tangible cues from the physical environment than their Asian counterparts and that the hedonic dimension of the consumption experience could be more important for Western consumers than for their Chinese Asian counterparts.

Using Hofstede's cultural dimensions, Furrer et al. (2000) empirically analysed customers' perceptions towards service quality across several different cultural groups. In doing so, they initially mapped the relationship between service quality perceptions and cultural dimension positions. One of their research aims was to show that SERVQUAL dimensions were closely correlated with Hofstede's cultural dimensions. Furthermore, in order to enhance the level of their interpretation of the relationship between cultural dimensions and service quality perceptions, they chose the individual level rather than national level as the unit or focus of their analysis. Given such assumptions, their main findings were as follows: culture with a large power distance was characterized by differences between more powerful and less powerful people. The level of difference between people was found to be dependent on social class, education level, and occupation (Hofstede, 1991). In some situations, for example, the power of the service provider came from their expertise, professional knowledge, or skills. However, in the context of other service activities such as hotels, restaurants, and retailers, it was seen that service employees were of low status (see Mattila, 1999). In addition, masculine cultures were distinguished by social gender roles. It emphasized different characteristics between female and male service employees. In a culture with uncertainty avoidance, it was defined in frequent and infrequent service situations as it related to risks and uncertainties. With reference to individualism and long-term orientation, they were defined on the basis of Hofstede's explanation (see Furrer et al., 2000). Furrer et al. (2000) proved the existence of a significant positive correlation between power distance and tangibles and assurance; significant negative correlation between power distance and empathy, responsiveness, and reliability; significant positive correlation between individualism and responsiveness, reliability, tangibles, and empathy; significant positive correlations between uncertainty avoidance and responsiveness, assurance, empathy and reliability; significant negative correlation between uncertainty avoidance and tangibles; significant positive correlation between long-term orientation and responsiveness and reliability; and finally significant negative correlation between long-term orientation and tangibles and assurance.

In a similar vein, Tsoukatos and Rand (2007) explored and analyzed the influence of Hofstede's cultural dimensions on service quality dimensions in the context of Greek retail insurance. In a manner consistent with Furrer et al. (2000), they adopted the definition of cultural dimensions at individual level as a basis for their analysis. Their results showed that tangibles and empathy had no significant correlation with any of the cultural dimensions; and that individualism had no significant correlation with any of the service quality dimensions. Moreover, while both responsiveness and assurance had negative correlations with power distance and masculinity, they had positive relationships with uncertainty avoidance. Finally, although reliability was found to have negative correlation with power distance and masculinity, it had a positive correlation with uncertainty avoidance and long-term orientation.

Taking a more cross-country approach, Dash et al. (2009) investigated the relationship between Canadian and Indian consumers' national cultural orientations and banking service quality expectations. Their study employed Hofstede's power distance and individualism dimensions, and five dimensions of service quality from Parasuraman et al. (1988) to explore the relationship between cultural factors and service quality dimensions. The findings of this study revealed the two cultural dimensions of power distance and individualism to significantly impact on the five service quality dimensions (SERVQUAL). At national level, it was found that the two Hofstede's cultural values had impact on tangibles and reliability; nevertheless, there was no significant effect on responsiveness, empathy, and assurance. At individual level, consumers with low power distance had higher service expectations of responsiveness and reliability, whilst those with high power distance highly expected tangible service attributes. On the other hand, consumers with high individualism expected lower empathy and assurance service attributes. In addition, Indian consumers were found to attach more importance to tangible cues when evaluating service quality, whereas Canadian showed service reliability to be of more importance. However, differences in overall service quality expectations were not significantly different across the two countries.

Smith and Reynolds (2009) explored consumers' service evaluation from both cognitive and affective perspectives. Their primary aim was to examine the relationship between service evaluation and behavioural intentions and how this might differ across individualist and collectivist cultures. To this end, three groups, namely, African, Chinese, and English higher education students were selected as participants to assess service quality of retail banking, customer satisfaction, affect (emotions/feelings), and customers' behavioural intentions. With reference to the determinants of consumers' service evaluation, assurance was found to be a determinant of overall positive affect/emotion for both African and Chinese respondents under collectivist cultures. However, responsiveness was a significant factor only for English consumers under individualist cultures. In addition, service quality, satisfaction, and affect/ emotion were found to have significant positive relationships with customers' behavioural intentions (e.g. consumer loyalty) for all three groups.

In summary, the aforementioned studies (which were mainly built upon or adopted Hoftsede's (1991) cultural dimensions and Parasuraman et al.'s (1988) service quality dimensions as the bases for their research design, analysis and interpretation) strongly confirm the dynamics of customer behavior and importance of cultural values and service quality dimensions. In other words, it is evident that cultural values have significant implications for and influence over service quality dimensions. However, the applicability and generalisability of Hofstede's cultural framework have received further scrutiny in the extant cross-cultural services and marketing management literature – an indication of the need for more novel and specific cultural model for explaining differences in customer behavior across culture and country.

This in turn suggests a need on the part of organizational scholars to utilize more specific cultural values and norms and understand peculiarities of other rules of social behavior in order to reflect the reality of their dynamics and interconnections (see Reisinger & Turner, 2002). Batonda and Perry (2003) assert that there are common beliefs among mainland Chinese and the overseas Chinese diasporas including Taiwan, Hong Kong, and Singapore, which are different from Western culture. Reisinger and Turner (2002) argue that using specific cultural values can reflect the reality of social behavior of a society. Such lack of research on culture and its implications for service quality dimensions in the context of Asian cultures may provide different views of explaining the relationship between cultural values, service quality, and customer satisfaction (see Reimann et al., 2008). To further explore the influence of specific cultural values, the following section will introduce Chinese Culture and its influence on customers' service experiences.

## BEYOND HOFSTEDE: ANALYSIS OF HOSPITALITY CUSTOMER BEHAVIOR THROUGH THE LENS OF CHINESE CULTURAL VALUES

Due to the heterogeneous socio-economic, religious, political, and historical context of the Far East region which is deeply embedded in its people's way of doing things in daily life, and more importantly personal beliefs and values, it is not uncommon to argue that Chinese cultural values to be different from those of the Western societies in many ways (see Chen & Francesco, 2000; Child & Lu, 1996). Chinese cultural norms and values have been evolved, shaped and established largely from interpersonal relationship and social orientation of the Chinese community. Chinese culture has its roots in and derived from specifically works of Confucius, whose firm religious convictions have made up the vital pillars of Chinese life and their ways of doing things (Qian et al., 2007). Given the underlying precepts of Confucianism and other influential ethical and religious philosophies such as Taoism which have established the norms for a series of common individual beliefs among Chinese, Chinese culture is believed to have a strong focus on a preference for tightly-knit social networks, the expectation that in-group members will support each other (Ramaseshan et al., 2006), and a strong urge to maintain social *hé* and interdependence within the in-group members (Lee & Dawes, 2005). Based upon such shared preferences among Chinese, most current studies on Chinese national culture have commonly revealed three core rituals which can be regarded as the main representations of Chinese cultural values (see Mente, 2000; Alon, 2003). These are: *Mien-tzu* (face), *Guanxi* (personal connection), and *Hé* (harmony).

*Hé* as the axis of the wheel of Chinese behavioural norms is supported by two spokes: *guanxi* and *mien-tzu*. Guanxi forms the structural pattern of the Chinese social fabric and mien-tzu is the operational mechanism that connects the nodes of guanxi network (Chen, 2001). In Chinese society, individuals must deal regularly with a variety of public officials, agencies, associations, and commercial operations for personal as well as business reasons. These connections should include a number of people who are in positions that can be useful to them (e.g. from hotel staff and restaurant managers to businesspeople and government officials in the ministries, and agencies concerned with their areas of business). If they do not have their own guanxi within these organizations, their chances of getting whatever they need or want are greatly diminished and often zero. Indeed, the whole of Chinese community whether socially, economically and politically, runs on personal connections i.e. on guanxi. People therefore spend a great deal of time, energy, creativity and money on developing and nurturing connections. All interactions, whether major or minor, are treated as matters of considerable importance. Consequently, maintaining an acceptable balance with personal relationships is a subtle and sometimes mysterious challenge for Chinese community (Mente, 2000).

According to Melendez (2007), while 'mien-tzu' is the fuel that makes the Chinese business engine turn over, 'Guanxi' is the "personalized glue" that makes it all stick together as a working dynamic. So corollary to mien-tzu, as Melendez's review of Chinese culture suggests, is the inseparable concept of Guanxi (relations) (Melendez, 2007). That is, mien-tzu and guanxi work hand-in-hand. While one without the other renders useless, it is the dynamic of these two concepts which collectively work together. Also, Chinese often endeavour to establish guanxi and give mien-tzu to others in order to avoid confrontation and conflict. If conflict is unavoidable, harmony is still the goal for reducing the negative impact of conflict by searching for any possible guanxi or saving face between the two parties. This kind of indirect communication pattern provides the Chinese with an opportunity for not saying no and not showing aggressive behaviours in public. This is because both saying no and showing aggression will lead to losing face and are detrimental to hé (Chen, 2001).

Alon (2003) also emphasizes the importance of these three Chinese cultural values in Chinese society and Chinese people's daily life. For example, a person's ability and strength can be described through how he/she uses his/her guanxi with him/her to gain special offer/discount from a five-star hotel restaurant. The person needs to know somebody through guanxi to gain this offer. So, it is a matter of mien-tzu as to whether or not the person would respond to this request. Denying such a request would result in a loss of 'mien-tzu' for those who unsuccessfully request this favour. Conversely, it is given 'mien-tzu' when the request has been approved. With each favour granted, there would accrue renqing (human sentiment) and the potential requirement for a return favour at sometime in the future. When an individual is interacting with others in the network, all in-group members may evaluate his or her mien-tzu in terms of either performance or morality to maintain interpersonal hé (Hwang, 1987). Hé is viewed as the end rather than the means of human interaction in which people try to adapt and relocate themselves in the dynamic process of interdependence and cooperation by a sincere display of whole hearted concern between each other (Chen, 1993). This applies to the maintenance of interpersonal harmony within a group, implying that integrity is deemed essential in Chinese society.

As the three core and prominent elements of Chinese culture, guanxi, mien-tzu, and hé have strong implications for interpersonal dynamics (Chen, 1997; Child & Lu, 1996; Lai, 2006; Tung & Worm, 2001). At the heart of guanxi is the national cultural value of collectivism. The concept of guanxi indicates the primacy of relations over rules (Alon, 2003). It is therefore an inseparable part of the Chinese business environment. Given the paramount importance of interpersonal relations in effective management of today's busi-

nesses both at national and more importantly at international levels, developing good guanxi seems to permeate every level of Chinese business environment. The positive implications of an effective guanxi-based business practices are many. For example, establishing good and long-term guanxi with both local and international business partners can result in, among others, reduction in uncertainty, decrease in transaction costs, providing usable resources, and a sense of connectedness (Chen & Peng, 2008; Wellman et al., 2002). Mien-tzu also is an equally important concept in Chinese culture. In a manner similar to that of guanxi's root and origin, mien-tzu has its roots in the unequivocal ideological precepts of Confucianism. In Chinese culture, it is not only important to maintain good relationships but also it is vital to protect a person's mien-tzu or dignity and prestige. By definition, mien-tzu resembles to the notion of 'reputation' which can be established through one's good personal/individual and team/organizational relationship. Since reputation can be achieved through networking with others, the concept of mien-tzu is believed to be inseparable from the concept of guanxi or 'relations'. So the dynamic of these two concepts collectively work together (Melendez, 2007) or as Sherriff et al. (1999) put it, "mien-tzu is a key component in the dynamics of guanxi (personal relationship)." For others, the concept of mien-tzu can be used as a mechanism for realization of human relationships which in turn constitute the social hé (Jia, 1997-8; Lee et al., 2001). Hé (Harmony), on the other hand, is one of the primordial values of Chinese culture. Chinese consider hé as the universal path which we all should pursue. So guanxi forms the structural pattern of the Chinese social fabric; mien-tzu is the operational mechanism that connects the nodes of guanxi network; and both concepts of guanxi and mien-tzu are natural products of the emphasis of hé on the Chinese society. They also function to keep the wheel of hé in good repair (Chen & Starosta, 1998, pp. 6-7).

## CHINESE CULTURE AND CUSTOMER SERVICE EXPERIENCE: A REVIEW OF EMPIRICAL RESEARCH

As seen in the previous sections, differences in cultural values across different countries were evident, thereby differences in customer's view towards a specific service category and its dimensions. While this implies that there is a need on the part of the service provider to get to know the dominant cultural values of its marketplace, it is also imperative to elucidate the peculiarities of each specific culture. This elucidation of cultural values in the context of Republic of China (a representative of Chinese culture) is timely largely due to China's growing role in the world economy and the rise in the purchasing power of Chinese consumers. In doing so, this section makes an attempt to revisit the past research to further explain the influence of Chinese cultural values on customer service experience.

In an attempt to conceptualize a comprehensive model at the business-to-business level, Armstrong and Seng (2000) used guanxi (i.e. relationship) in the context of the Asian banking industry. Interestingly, they found that a business relationship which connoted by good guanxi was also closely associated with higher expectations in services of the service providers. Taking a different service context, Lockyer and Tsai (2004) analysed Chinese cultural values in respect of dining experiences, restaurant attributes and customer satisfaction in a five-star international hotel in Taiwan. Their main findings were as follows: Taiwanese guests had higher expectations of service quality in a sense that cleanliness, good quality food, and good attitude of staff were considered as mien-tzu giving by the guests; the concept of mien-tzu giving, social status and hé with people were seen to strongly influence dining experience of the guests; and mien-tzu giving and social status were seen to be strongly correlated; in respect of the staff and guest interaction, 'mien-tzu giving'

meant to carry a sense of high status for guests, which was seen to be formed by increasing the social distance with service providers; social status could be demonstrated by dining in a five-star hotel as a symbol of social position; due to the nature of hé, guests were unwilling to complain about the service when even they were dissatisfied. In short, Lockyer and Tsai's study highlights the paramount importance of understanding of what Chinese guests want in the course of a customer service provider relationship.

Similarly, in Hoare and Butcher's (2008, p.156) study, the authors examined the antecedent roles of the Chinese cultural values of "mien-tzu" and "hé" in influencing customer satisfaction/loyalty, and the service quality dimensions that were most salient to the context of Chinese diners. In other words, they made an attempt to answer the question of "Do Chinese cultural values affect customer satisfaction/loyalty?" In doing so, a self-administered survey was conducted for a convenience sample of Chinese diners (from China, Taiwan, and Hong Kong) in Australia. Despite the limitation of the study in that the choice of student sample tended to limit the generalizability of the findings to a wider population, the authors used factor analysis and the following conclusions were drawn from their study: the findings identified three service quality dimensions, namely, interaction quality (e.g. service personnel's reception and farewell manners, politeness, friendliness, promptness, and food service skills), food appeal (e.g. freshness, taste, variety and price of food), and performance comparison (customers' expectations of food quality and service quality, their impression of meal experience and their standard of food hygiene). Further regression equations analysis of the data revealed that both cultural factors and the three quality dimensions were significantly and positively correlated to both customer satisfaction and customer loyalty. Furthermore, "mien-tzu" was shown to have an influence on customer satisfaction, while food appeal and performance comparison were found to influence both customer satisfaction and loyalty. In another study, but in a different context, Wang et al. (2008) assessed Chinese tourists' perceptions of the UK hotel service quality and analysed the role of Chinese culture in influencing their expectations and perceptions. Their findings indicated that Chinese tourists had high expectations of the UK hotel service quality, preferred customized and personalized services (empathy dimension), expected employees not only to be consistently courteous but also to have the ability and knowledge to help the customers (assurance dimension), strongly believed in reliable service from employees who had to be ready to help with enthusiasm (reliability and responsiveness dimension), and finally expected UK hotels to have similar and adequate facilities (tangible dimension). Particularly, the Chinese tourists perceived the three service dimensions of empathy, reliability, and tangible to be the most important factors influencing their service experiences.

As mentioned earlier, a plethora of previous and existing research evidence suggests quite clearly that Hofstede's cultural dimensions provide a widely used instrument for the study of the impact of culture on service quality dimensions, thereby understanding the customers' perceptions of service quality. Despite sufficient commonality in the current evidence about the applicability of Hofstede's cultural dimensions for the study of culture and service quality dimensions, a key contention of this chapter is to use Chinese cultural values as a new means of exploring the research phenomenon. In more accurate language, this chapter proposes three Chinese cultural values of mien-tzu, guanxi and hé for examining the relationship between cultural values and service quality dimensions and the resultant implications for the customers. In short, both guanxi and mien-tzu are prevalently used and are regarded as integral ingredients of any business partnership taken place in the context of Chinese spoken countries (see Gilbert & Tsao, 2000; Hwang, 1998; Wang et al., 2008). Hé emphasizes on and encourages in-group

members to create a harmonious atmosphere. More specifically, with regard to service quality dimensions, guanxi appears to have a close association with reliability, responsiveness, assurance, and empathy of service quality, whereas mien-tzu seems to have a close link with all service quality dimensions. In addition, hé appears to have a link with reliability dimension. So, it can be argued that Chinese cultural values affect service assessment and that 'mien-tzu', 'guanxi' and 'Hé' are all closely linked with customer expectations of service quality.

## CHINESE CULTURE AND CUSTOMER SERVICE EXPERIENCE: EVIDENCE FROM THE TAIWAN HOSPITALITY INDUSTRY

In order to empirically unravel the influence of Chinese cultural values of 'mien-tzu', 'guanxi' and 'Hé' on hospitality customer behavior, a survey strategy was employed so as to target Taiwan hospitality sector and collect appropriate empirical data from customers of two types of restaurant: (i) five star hotel chain restaurants, and (ii) local chain restaurants. Overall, the data collection lasted some five months (Mid-September 2009 to Mid-February 2010). During a two-stage process, the data were collected from the customers of the five star hotel chain restaurants and local chain restaurants who were residing across three regions of Taiwan –i.e. North region (Taipei), Middle region (Taichung), and South region (Kaohsiung). More importantly, they were different in terms of several demographical variables such as gender, age, marital status, education, occupation, and salary (see APPENDIX 1: demographic profile of respondents to the survey).

In stage 1 which lasted 2 months, some 227 questionnaires were collected from the customers of both restaurant settings. Given our initial target of a minimum of 500 questionnaires and low re-

were collected during stage 2 which lasted over 3 months (N = 525). In short, the overall response rate across both restaurant settings was comparable to previous similar studies where the average response rate ranged from 17% to 30% (e.g. Smith et al., 1999; Andaleeb & Conway, 2006; Smith & Bolton, 1998, 2002; Atkinson, 1988; Bowen & Chen, 2001; Wolak et al., 1998; Caruana, 2002). Indeed our response rate was quite higher than a majority of self-administered survey instruments of past similar research in restaurant and food services in both Taiwan and elsewhere. This was largely attributed to the adopted approach to survey administration and initial briefing of the potential respondents by the research team.

In order to empirically test the working hypotheses and analyse the relationships between the associated research variables, a questionnaire survey was utilised as the major data collection instrument. Despite its limitations in terms of depth of information where respondents can not provide more detail information and instead they only can provide standardised answers, it was found to be the most appropriate method of data collection instruments for several reasons, namely, accommodating the large sample chosen for the study, time constraints, and more importantly, allowing the researchers to provide questions that could rigorously be analysed. More specifically, a paper-and-pencil questionnaire administration, where the researcher was available, was adopted. Although this is similar to a face-to-face questionnaire administration, none of the questions were presented orally by the researcher. Instead, the researcher only handed in the questionnaire, responded to any questions on the part of the respondents, and finally collected the completed questionnaires from the cashier counter of the restaurants. In designing various sections of the questionnaire (i.e. individual background information, service expectations, Chinese cultural values, and service quality) and format of the questionnaire, the insights of a panel of experts were sought ensued by a pilot test, purification of the questionnaire,

and therefore a questionnaire with high reliability was designed. Using the final version of the questionnaire, the data were then collected from customers in the five-star hotel chain restaurants and local chain restaurants, resulting in response rates of 31% and 42% accordingly. The collected data were finally analysed by SPSS and LISREL software using descriptive and inferential statistics methods. The remainder of this book chapter is devoted to a review and analysis of the research findings.

Overall, the results are rather mixed and limited and that such impact appears to be different across the five star hotel chain and local chain restaurants. Whilst mien-tzu has positive link with service expectations of assurance in the five star hotel chain restaurants, it appears to positively impact on tangible dimensions (tangible and food quality) of service quality in the local chain restaurants. This finding implies that customers of five star hotel chain restaurants place a heavy emphasis on staff's expertise/skills/knowledge (i.e. greeting customers, cooking skills, familiarity with various methods of serving, courtesy, ability to convey trust and confidence), and consequently expect that dining in these luxurious restaurants to bring them special feelings and esteem – an indication of the importance of mien-tzu giving and the willingness of people to avoid being humiliated in the presence of others in a social encounter such as dining out in prestigious restaurants (see Goffman, 1955, pp.213). In respect of the local chain restaurants where mien-tzu is positively linked to tangible and food quality dimensions of service quality, mien-tzu giving hinges on attributes such as authenticity in Chinese cuisine coupled with Chinese red interior design and good staff attitudes. Clearly, dining in such atmosphere which represents both favorite authentic Chinese cuisine and ancient Chinese dining activities (e.g. live music and dance performances) results in the diners' positive social value by the staff during dining out as an important social encounter in Chinese society. These findings have close affinity with Lockyer and Tsai's (2004) study in a sense that mien-tzu giving is associated with restaurant attributes of cleanliness, good quality food and good attitude of staff of five star hotel restaurants. Lockyer and Tsai's (2004) study views cleanliness and good quality food as tangible dimensions and observes good attitude of staff to be met and expected in all kinds of restaurants.

In respect of the second element of Chinese cultural values –i.e. guanxi – the results seem to be different across the two settings of five star hotel chain and local chain restaurants. In the five star setting, the relationship between guanxi and service expectations is insignificant. One explanation is that the customers' (guests') impression of five start hotel restaurants is that hotel restaurants are expected to offer delicious food in spectacular surroundings by staff who are well-trained and disciplined. Regardless of the type of the guests or whether a guest is familiar with the staff, there exists a set of common code of practices for the staff in terms of how to serve the guests. So a certain level of service quality is expected, no matter who the guest is. Guanxi as a central cultural norm in Chinese society describes the personalized networks of influence, and refers to a guest's social or business network. Given the hotel staff well-established code of practice and existence of in-house regulations where each member of staff has to closely follow their defined responsibilities and abide by the rules, having guanxi does not necessarily bring about any extra attention and offer to the guests. In other words, having guanxi does not affect the way a guest is served in the five star hotel chain restaurants not least because a member of staff is more concerned to follow the pre-defined rules and regulations than to go beyond the rules to favor a guest at the price of ignoring the rules or disfavoring other guests. However, guanxi has positive influence on service expectations of responsiveness in the local chain restaurants. One primary reason is that it is easier to know a member of staff in the local restaurants and benefit from such prior acquain

tance. In the presence of such (prior) guanxi, it is rather common to see a guest expects prompt response and more willingness to help on the part of the staff whom s/he knows. In the same vein, it is also expected that staff are more willing to help the guests of their acquaintance for enhancing and further maintaining guanxi. Clearly, such personal connections between the guests and the staff where one is able to prevail upon another to offer extra services and personal care could result in the frequency of visits to gradually grow and generate more sales. As a result of such network of contacts between the guests and staff at the local chain restaurants, some 70 percent of the respondents of local chain restaurants are repeat customers – compared to less than 40 percent at the five star hotel chain restaurants. These findings are consistent with Furrer et al.'s (2000) argument that in cultures with a long-term orientation, long-term relationships with service providers are expected. More specifically, service quality dimensions of reliability and responsiveness are found to be positively linked to long-term orientation. Similar results are also reported by Donthu and Yoo (1998).

In regard to the third Chinese cultural values – i.e. hé – there is clear evidence that hé is highly stressed and observed in Chinese community. As a result, it is not surprising to see that the relationship between hé and service expectations of reliability is not deemed essential. This implies that customers can tolerate staff's unintentional mistakes so as to maintain a harmonious environment in particular when they dine in a group of several individuals. Similarity, Lockyer and Tsai (2004) also found that guests were unwilling to complain about the service when even they were dissatisfied because of the nature of hé – an indication of the paramount importance of the collective interest and its priority over that of the individual. Hence it is not uncommon to see individual diners are reluctant to complain in order to serve the needs of and be in harmony with the whole group. These findings conform to past research evince (e.g. Donthu & Yoo, 1998) which suggest that collectivist customers place a heavy focus on 'we' rather than 'I' – an indication of easy conformance to or even being tolerant of poor services to maintain group harmony (i.e. good relationship between the customer, the service provider, and more importantly between the members of the same group). Thus, as Donthu and Yoo (1998) have observed, collectivist customers do not have high level of service quality expectations not least because they prepare themselves to conform to whatever level of service is provided. Consistent with deep-seated social belief of long-term orientations of Chinese people, Chinese customers are expected to be more tolerant of things that may go wrong unintentionally or seem unclear. Poor service delivery is likely to be accepted among long-term oriented customers. In line with high power distance culture of Chinese society, customers seem to have lower reliability expectations – an indication that they are more tolerant of reliability shortcomings compared to customers in lower power distance cultures (see Donthu & Yoo, 1998; Furrer et al., 2000; Dash et al., 2009).

## CONCLUSION

The chapter on cross-cultural customer behaviour makes an attempt to highlight the contingent nature of customer behaviour to make a particularly crucial point which has generally not been given the attention it serves in cross-cultural service research, namely, to go beyond Hofstede's cultural model and use Asian cultural norms which might provide additional insight into the variance between various consumer behaviours across cultures. Whilst the chapter offers some secondary and primary analysis on the nature and direction of cross-cultural hospitality service research, it would be imperative to further validate the results by examining other research contexts such Main-

land China, Hong Kong, Singapore or any other Chinese-spoken countries to reveal the similarities and differences. A similar line of enquiry into the research phenomena in other service-oriented organizations could prove beneficial to further explore the influence of culture on customer expectations and perceptions towards services.

## REFERENCES

Adler, R. P. (2007). *Next-generation media: The global shift*. Aspen Institute. Retrieved March 10, 2014, from http: www.aspeninstitute.org/atf/cf/%7BDEB6F227-659B-4EC8-8F84 8DF23CA704F5%7D/NEXTGENERATION.PDF

Ahlstrom, D. (2010). Publishing in the Asia Pacific Journal of Management. *Asia Pacific Journal of Management*, *27*(1), 1–8. doi:10.1007/s10490-009-9181-0

Alon, I. (Ed.). (2003). *Chinese Culture, organizational behavior, and international business management*. Westport, Connecticut: Praeger Publishers.

Andaleeb, S. S., & Conway, C. (2006). Customer satisfaction in the restaurant industry: An examination of the transaction-specific model. *Journal of Services Marketing*, *20*(1), 3–11. doi:10.1108/08876040610646536

Armstrong, R. W., & Seng, T. B. (2000). Corporate-Customer satisfaction in the banking industry of Singapore. *International Journal of Bank Marketing*, *18*(2/3), 97–111. doi:10.1108/02652320010339617

Atkinson, A. (1988). Answering the eternal question: What does the customer want? *The Cornell Hotel and Restaurant Administration Quarterly*, *29*(2), 12–13. doi:10.1177/001088048802900209

Barrows, C. W. (2008). Food and beverage management. In R. C. Wood & B. Brotherton (Eds.), *The SAGE handbook of hospitality management*. London: Sage. doi:10.4135/9781849200417.n20

Batonda, G., & Perry, C. (2003). Influence of culture on relationship development processes in overseas Chinese/Australian networks. *European Journal of Marketing*, 37(11/12), 1548–1574. doi:10.1108/03090560310495357

Bond, M. H. (2002). Reclaiming the individual from Hofstede's ecological analysis: a 20-year odyssey: Comment on Oyserman et al. (2002). *Psychological Bulletin*, 128(1), 73–77. doi:10.1037/0033-2909.128.1.73 PMID:11843548

Bowen, J. T., & Chen, S. L. (2001). The relationship between customer loyalty and customer satisfaction. *International Journal of Contemporary Hospitality Management*, 13(5), 213–217. doi:10.1108/09596110110395893

Bright, S., & Johnson, K. (1985). Training for hospitality. *Journal of European Industrial Training*, 9(7), 27–31. doi:10.1108/eb014229

Brotherton, B. (1999). Towards a definitive view of the nature of hospitality and hospitality management. *International Journal of Contemporary Hospitality Management*, 11(4), 165–173. doi:10.1108/09596119910263568

Brotherton, B. (2002). Finding the hospitality industry (A response to Paul Slattery). *Journal of Hospitality, Sport, and Tourism Education*, 1(2), 75–77.

Brotherton, B., & Wood, R. C. (2008). The nature and meanings of hospitality. In R. C. Wood & B. Brotherton (Eds.), *The SAGE handbook of hospitality management*. London: Sage. doi:10.4135/9781849200417.n2

Camillo, A. A., & Di Pietro, L. (2014). An investigation on cultural cuisine of mainland China. Management implications for restaurant operators. In A. A. Camillo (Ed.), Handbook of Research on Global Hospitality and Tourism Management. IGI Global.

Caruana, A. (2002). Service loyalty: The effects of service quality and the mediating role of customer satisfaction. *European Journal of Marketing*, 36(7/8), 811–828. doi:10.1108/03090560210430818

Cassee, E. H., & Reuland, R. (1983). Hospitality in hospitals. In E. H. Cassee & R. Reuland (Eds.), *The Management of hospitality*. Oxford: Pergamon.

Chen, G. M. (1993). *A Chinese perspective of communication competence*. Paper presented at the annual convention of the Speech Communication Association, San Antonio, Texas.

Chen, G.-M. (1997). *An examination of PRC business negotiating behaviors. Chicago ERIC Document reproduction service* (No. ED422594). Paper presented at the annual meeting of the national communication association.

Chen, G.-M. (2001, July 11). From Sorry to Apology: Understanding the Chinese. *Chinese Community Forum*, 27.

Chen, G.-M., & Starosta, W. J. (1998). Chinese conflict management and resolution: Overview and implications. *Intercultural Communication Studies*, 7(1), 1–16.

Chen, X. P., & Peng, S. (2008). Guanxi dynamics: Shiftsi N the Closeness of Ties between Chinese Coworkers. *Management and Organization Review*, 4(1), 63–80. doi:10.1111/j.1740-8784.2007.00078.x

Chen, Z. X., & Francesco, A. M. (2000). Employee demography, organizational commitment, and turnover intentions in China: Do cultural differences matter? *Human Relations, 53*(6), 869–887. doi:10.1177/0018726700536005

Child, J., & Lu, Y. (1996). Introduction: China and international enterprise. In J. Child & L. Yuan (Eds.), *Management issues in China: International enterprises.* London: Routledge. doi:10.1093/0198236255.003.0001

Converse, P. D. (1921). *Marketing methods and politics.* New York: Prentice Hall.

Dash, S., Bruning, E., & Acharya, M. (2009). The effect of power distance and individualism on service quality expectations in banking. *International Journal of Bank Marketing, 27*(5), 336–358. doi:10.1108/02652320910979870

De Mooij, M. (2004). *Consumer behavior and culture: Consequences for global marketing and advertising.* Thousand Oaks, CA: Sage.

De Mooij, M., & Hofstede, G. (2002). Convergence and divergence in consumer behavior: Implications for international retailing. *Journal of Retailing, 78*(1), 61–69. doi:10.1016/S0022-4359(01)00067-7

De Mooij, M., & Hofstede, G. (2011). Cross-cultural consumer behavior: A review of research findings. *Journal of International Consumer Marketing, 23*(3-4), 181–192.

Domestic Statistic. (2010). *Trade and food services activity.* Taiwan: Department of Statistics, Ministry of Economic Affairs.

Donthu, N., & Yoo, B. (1998). Cultural influences on service quality expectations. *Journal of Service Research, 1*(2), 178–186. doi:10.1177/109467059800100207

Fang, T. (2010). Asian management research needs more self-confidence: Reflection on Hofstede (2007) and beyond. *Asia Pacific Journal of Management, 27*(1), 155–170. doi:10.1007/s10490-009-9134-7

Furrer, O., Liu, B. S.-C., & Sudharshan, D. (2000). The relationships between culture and service quality perceptions: Basis for cross-cultural market segmentation and resource allocation. *Journal of Service Research, 2*(4), 355–371. doi:10.1177/109467050024004

Gilbert, D., & Tsao, J. (2000). Exploring Chinese cultural influences and hospitality marketing relationships. *International Journal of Contemporary Hospitality Management, 12*(1), 45–53. doi:10.1108/09596110010305037

Goffman, E. (1955). On facework. *Psychiatry, 18*, 213–231. PMID:13254953

Hall, E. T. (1976). *Beyond culture.* Garden City, New York: Doubleday.

Hoare, R. J., & Butcher, K. (2008). Do Chinese cultural values affect customer satisfaction/loyalty? *International Journal of Contemporary Hospitality Management, 20*(2), 156–171. doi:10.1108/09596110810852140

Hofstede, G. (1980). *Culture's consequences: International differences in work related values.* Beverly Hills, CA: Sage.

Hofstede, G. (1991). *Cultures and organizations: software of the mind.* London: McGraw-Hill.

Hofstede, G. (1997). The Archimedes effect. Working at the interface of cultures: 18 lives in social science (pp.47-61). M.H. Bond. London: Routledge.

Hofstede, G. (2001). *Culture's consequences: Comparing values, behaviors, institutions, and organisations across nations.* CA: Sage Publications.

Hui, M. K., & Au, K. (2001). Justice Perceptions of Complaints-Handling: A Cross-Cultural Comparison between PRC and Canadian Customers. *Journal of Business Research, 52*(2), 161–173. doi:10.1016/S0148-2963(99)00068-5

Hwang, K. K. (1987). Face and favor: The Chinese power game. *American Journal of Sociology, 92*(4), 944–974. doi:10.1086/228588

Hwang, K.-K. (1998). Guanxi and Mientze: Conflict resolution in Chinese society. *Intercultural Communication Studies, 7*(1), 17–39.

Jia, W. (1997-8). Facework as a Chinese conflict-preventive mechanism- a cultural/discourse analysis. *Intercultural Communication Studies, 7*, 43-58.

Jones, M. L. (2007). *Hofstede- culturally questionable?* Retrieved March 3, 2014, from Http: http://ro.uow.edu.au/cgi/viewcontent.cgi?article=1389&context=commpapers

Jones, P. (1996). The hospitality industry. In P. Jones (Ed.), *Introduction to hospitality operations.* London: Cassell.

Keillor, B. D., Hult, G. T. M., & Kandemir, D. (2004). A study of the service encounter in eight countries. *Journal of International Marketing, 12*(1), 9–35. doi:10.1509/jimk.12.1.9.25649

Kirkman, B. L., Lowe, K. B., & Gibson, C. B. (2006). A quarter century of "Culture's Consequences": A review of empirical research incorporating Hofstede's cultural values framework. *Journal of International Business Studies, 37*(3), 285–320. doi:10.1057/palgrave.jibs.8400202

Lai, K. (2006). *Learning from Chinese philosophies: Ethics of interdependent and contextualised self.* Hampshire: Ashgate.

Lee, D.-J., Pae, J. H., & Wong, Y. H. (2001). A model of close business relationships in China (Guanxi). *European Journal of Marketing, 35*(1/2), 51–69. doi:10.1108/03090560110363346

Lee, D. Y., & Dawes, P. L. (2005). Guanxi, trust and long-term in orientations in Chinese business markets. *Journal of International Marketing, 13*(2), 30–56. doi:10.1509/jimk.13.2.28.64860

Liu, B. S.-C., Furrer, O., & Sudharshan, D. (2001). The relationships between culture and behavioral intentions toward services. *Journal of Service Research, 4*(2), 118–129. doi:10.1177/109467050142004

Lockyer, T., & Tsai, M. (2004). Dimensions of Chinese culture values in relation to the hotel dining experience. *Journal of Hospitality and Tourism Management, 11*(1), 13–29.

Malhotra, N. K., Ulgado, F. M., Agarwal, J., & Lan Wu, S. (2005). Dimensions of service quality in developed and developing economies: Multi-country cross-cultural comparisons. *International Marketing Review, 22*(3), 256–278. doi:10.1108/02651330510602204

Mattila, A. S. (1999). The role of culture in the service evaluation process. *Journal of Service Research, 1*(3), 250–261. doi:10.1177/109467059913006

Mattila, A. S., & Patterson, P. G. (2004). The impact of culture on consumers' perceptions of service recovery efforts. *Journal of Retailing, 80*(3), 196–206. doi:10.1016/j.jretai.2004.08.001

Melendez, J. (2007). *The concept of 'Face' in Chinese culture.* Retrieved April 15, 2010, from http://www4.associatedcontent.com/article/391443/the_concept_of_face_in_chinese_culture.html?cat=9 10/6/2009

Mente, B. D. (2000). *The Chinese have a word for it: The complete guide to Chinese thought and culture.* Lincolnwood, IL: McGraw-Hill Professional.

Meyer, K. E. (2006). Asian management research needs more self-confidence. *Asia Pacific Journal of Management, 23*(2), 119–137. doi:10.1007/s10490-006-7160-2

Morrison, A., & O'Gorman, K. (2006). Hospitality studies: Liberating the power of the mind. In P. A. Whitelaw & O. G. Barry (Eds.), *CAUTHE 2006: To the city and beyond* (pp. 453–465). Footscray, Vic.: Victoria University, School of Hospitality, Tourism and Marketing.

National Statistical. (2009). *National statistics, Republic of China (Taiwan)*. Retrieved March 9, 2009, from http://eng.stat.gov.tw/mp.asp?mp=5

Nielsen Global Online Survey. (2009). *Global diners want familiar foods and fair prices*. Retrieved July 7, 2010, from http://tw.en.nielsen.com/site/news20090409e.shmtl.shtml

Oxford Dictionaries Online. (2010). In *Oxford Dictionaries Online: English dictionary and language reference*. Retrieved August 3, 2010, from http://oxforddictionaries.com/?attempted=true

Parasuraman, A., Zeithaml, V. A., & Berry, L. L. (1985). A conceptual model of service quality and its implication. *Journal of Marketing, 49*(Fall), 41–50. doi:10.2307/1251430

Parasuraman, A., Zeithaml, V. A., & Berry, L. L. (1988). SERVQUAL: A multiple-item scale for measuring consumer perceptions of service quality. *Journal of Retailing, 64*(1), 12–40.

Patterson, P. G., & Smith, T. (2003). A cross-cultural study of switching barriers and propensity to stay with service providers. *Journal of Retailing, 79*(2), 107–120. doi:10.1016/S0022-4359(03)00009-5

Qian, W., Razzaque, M. A., & Keng, K. A. (2007). Chinese cultural values and gift-giving behavior. *Journal of Consumer Marketing, 24*(4), 214–228. doi:10.1108/07363760710756002

Ramaseshan, B., Yip, L. S., & Pae, J. H. (2006). Power, satisfaction and relationship commitment in Chinese store-tenant relationship and their impact on performance. *Journal of Retailing, 82*(1), 63–70. doi:10.1016/j.jretai.2005.11.004

Reimann, M., Lunemann, U. F., & Chase, R. B. (2008). Uncertainty avoidance as a moderator of the relationship between perceived service quality and customer satisfaction. *Journal of Service Research, 11*(1), 63–73. doi:10.1177/1094670508319093

Reisinger, Y., & Turner, L. W. (2002). Cultural differences between Asian tourist markets and Australian hosts: Part 1. *Journal of Travel Research, 40*(3), 295–315. doi:10.1177/0047287502040003008

Sherriff, T. K., Lorna, F., & Stephen, C. Y. (1999). Managing direct selling activities in China - A cultural explanation. *Journal of Business Research, 45*(3), 257–266. doi:10.1016/S0148-2963(97)00237-3

Smith, A., & Reynolds, N. (2009). Affect and cognition as predictors of behavioral intentions towards services. *International Marketing Review, 26*(6), 580–600. doi:10.1108/02651330911001305

Smith, A. K., & Bolton, R. N. (1998). An experimental investigation of service failure and recovery: Paradox or peril? *Journal of Service Research, 1*(1), 65–81. doi:10.1177/109467059800100106

Smith, A. K., & Bolton, R. N. (2002). The effect of customers' emotional responses to service failures on their recovery effort evaluations and satisfaction judgments. *Journal of the Academy of Marketing Science, 30*(1), 5–23. doi:10.1177/03079450094298

Smith, A. K., Bolton, R. N., & Wagner, J. (1999). A model of customer satisfaction with service encounters involving failure and recovery. *JMR, Journal of Marketing Research, 34*(August), 356–372. doi:10.2307/3152082

Soltani, E., & Wilkinson, A. (2010). Stuck in the middle with you: The effects of incongruency of senior and middle managers' orientations on TQM programmes. *International Journal of Operations & Production Management, 30*(4), 365–397. doi:10.1108/01443571011029976

Storey, J. (1992). *Developments in the management of human resources*. Cambridge, MA: Blackwell Publications.

Sulek, J. M., & Hensley, R. L. (2004). The relative importance of food, atmosphere, and fairness of wait: The case of a full-service restaurant. *The Cornell Hotel and Restaurant Administration Quarterly, 45*(3), 235–247. doi:10.1177/0010880404265345

Tideman, M. C. (1983). External influences on the hospitality industry. In E. H. Cassee & E. Reuland (Eds.), *The management of hospitality*. Oxford: Pergamon.

Tsoukatos, E., & Rand, G. K. (2007). Cultural influences on service quality and customer satisfaction: Evidence from Greek insurance. *Managing Service Quality, 17*(4), 467–485. doi:10.1108/09604520710760571

Tung, R. L., & Worm, V. (2001). Network capitalism: The role of human Resources in penetrating the China market. *International Journal of Human Resource Management, 12*(4), 517–534. doi:10.1080/713769653

Voss, C. A., Roth, A. V., Rosenzweig, E. D., Blackmon, K., & Chase, R. B. (2004). A tale of two countries' conservatism, service quality and feedback on customer satisfaction. *Journal of Service Research, 6*(3), 212–230. doi:10.1177/1094670503260120

Wang, Y., Vela, M. R., & Tyler, K. (2008). Cultural perspectives: Chinese perceptions of UK hotel service quality. *International Journal of Culture. Tourism and Hospitality Research, 2*(4), 312–329.

Wellman, B., Chen, W., & Dong, W. (2002). Networking Guanxi. In T. Gold, D. Guthrie, & D. Wank (Eds.), *Social connections in China: Institutions, culture, and the changing nature of Guanxi*. Cambridge: Cambridge University Press. doi:10.1017/CBO9780511499579.013

White, S. (2002). Rigor and relevance in avian management research: Where are we and where can we go? *Asia Pacific Journal of Management, 19*(2/3), 287–352. doi:10.1023/A:1016295803623

Winsted, K. F. (1997). The service experience in two cultures: A behavioral perspective. *Journal of Retailing, 73*(3), 337–360. doi:10.1016/S0022-4359(97)90022-1

Wolak, R., Kalafatis, S., & Harris, P. (1998). An investigation into four characteristics of services. *Journal of Empirical Generalizations in Marketing Science, 3*, 22–43.

Wong, N. Y. (2004). The role of culture in the perception of service recovery. *Journal of Business Research, 57*(9), 957–963. doi:10.1016/S0148-2963(03)00002-X

WTTC. (2013). *China-World Travel & Tourism Council*. Retrieved March 15 2014, from http: http://www.google.com.hk/url?sa=t&rct=j&q=&esrc=s&source=web&cd=1&ved=0CB0QFjAA&url=http%3A%2F%2Fwww.wttc.org%2F~%2Fmedia%2Ffiles%2Freports%2Fbenchmark%2520reports%2Fcountry%2520results%2Fchina%2520benchmarking%25202013.ashx&ei=CL5oVPCMHtCxacKEgsgE&usg=AFQjCNGIvcWEUvLOoPAdAqzJ3gX_7xo5wA

Zeithaml, V. A., Bitner, M. J., & Gremler, D. D. (2006). *Services marketing: integrating customer focus across the firm*. New York: McGrawhill.

Zeithaml, V. A., Parasuraman, A., & Berry, L. L. (1990). *Delivering Quality Service; Balancing Customer Perceptions and Expectations*. New York: Free Press.

Zhang, J., Beatty, S. E., & Walsh, G. (2008). Review and future directions of cross-cultural consumer services research. *Journal of Business Research, 61*(3), 211–224. doi:10.1016/j.jbusres.2007.06.003

## KEY TERMS AND DEFINITIONS

**Chinese Cultural Values:** Values and norms that are unique to the Chinese community and characterize the peculiarities of Chinese cultural beliefs and traditions.

**Guanxi:** Personal connection. Knowing or being familiar with someone who works in the restaurant.

**Hé:** A customer's preferences to maintain a harmonious atmosphere in the restaurant during dining.

**Hofstede's Cultural Model:** The cultural model developed by Geert Hofstede incorporates five dimensions including power distance, individualism, uncertainty avoidance, masculinity and long term orientation. It is widely used to analyse culture-related studies.

**Mien-Tzu:** A situation where customers feel free to demonstrate themselves in front of others and get respect as well as individual requests from staff of restaurants.

**Service Quality:** It refers to the difference between service expectations and service perceptions.

**SERVQUAL:** Service quality measurement scale. It includes five elements, reliability, responsiveness, tangible, empathy, assurance.

## APPENDIX

*Table 2. Demographic profile of respondents to the survey*

| | Five star chain hotel restaurant | | Local Chain restaurant | | Total |
|---|---|---|---|---|---|
| **Area** | | | | | |
| | **Frequency** | **%** | **Frequency** | **%** | |
| Northern (Taipei) | 128 | 49.8% | 115 | 43.1% | 243 |
| Middle (Taichung) | 84 | 32.7% | 90 | 33.7% | 174 |
| Southern (Kaohsiung) | 45 | 17.5% | 62 | 23.2% | 107 |
| Total · | 257 | | 267 | | 524 |
| **Education** | | | | | |
| | **Frequency** | **%** | **Frequency** | **%** | |
| Elementary school | 0 | 0% | 5 | 1.9% | 5 |
| Junior high school | 5 | 1.9% | 8 | 3% | 13 |
| Senior high school | 29 | 11.3% | 74 | 27.7% | 103 |
| College/University | 154 | 59.9% | 133 | 49.8% | 287 |
| University (post-graduate) or above | 69 | 26.8% | 47 | 17.6% | 116 |
| **Gender** | | | | | |
| | **Frequency** | **%** | **Frequency** | **%** | |
| Male | 109 | 42.4% | 102 | 38.2% | 211 |
| Female | 148 | 57.6% | 165 | 61.8% | 313 |
| **Age** | | | | | |
| | **Frequency** | **%** | **Frequency** | **%** | |
| 20-29 | 27 | 10.5% | 83 | 31.1% | 110 |
| 30-39 | 73 | 28.4% | 81 | 30.3% | 154 |
| 40-49 | 65 | 25.3% | 81 | 30.3% | 146 |
| 50-59 | 64 | 24.9% | 19 | 7.1% | 83 |
| 60-65 | 19 | 7.4% | 3 | 1.1% | 22 |
| > 66 | 9 | 3.5% | 0 | 0% | 9 |
| **Marital status** | | | | | |
| | **Frequency** | **%** | **Frequency** | **%** | |
| Married | 182 | 71.9% | 81 | 30.4% | 263 |
| Single | 75 | 29.1% | 186 | 69.6% | 261 |
| **Occupations** | | | | | |
| | **Frequency** | **%** | **Frequency** | **%** | |
| Executive/ manager | 59 | 23% | 3 | 1.1% | 62 |
| Self-employed | 65 | 25.3% | 4 | 1.5% | 69 |
| White collar | 53 | 20.6% | 57 | 21.3% | 110 |
| Blue collar | 9 | 3.5% | 14 | 5.2% | 23 |

*continued on following page*

*Table 2. Continued*

|  | Five star chain hotel restaurant | | Local Chain restaurant | | Total |
|---|---|---|---|---|---|
| Professional | 23 | 8.9% | 43 | 16.1% | 66 |
| Civil servant | 24 | 9.3% | 44 | 16.5% | 68 |
| Retired/ unemployed | 11 | 4.3% | 37 | 13.9% | 48 |
| Others | 13 | 5.1% | 65 | 24.3% | 78 |
| **Income (monthly)** | | | | | |
|  | **Frequency** | **%** | **Frequency** | **%** | |
| < NT$17,280 | 9 | 3.5% | 43 | 16.1% | 52 |
| NT$17,280-NT$ 29,999 | 14 | 5.4% | 57 | 21.3% | 71 |
| NT$30,000-NT$59,999. | 123 | 47.9% | 132 | 49.4% | 255 |
| NT$60,000-NT$99,999. | 66 | 25.7% | 23 | 8.6% | 89 |
| >=100,000 | 45 | 17.5% | 12 | 4.5% | 57 |

# Chapter 13
# Tourism Development in Least Developed Countries:
## Challenges and Opportunities

**Raymond Saner**
*Centre for Socio-EcoNomic Development (CSEND), Switzerland*

**Lichia Yiu**
*Centre for Socio-EcoNomic Development (CSEND), Switzerland*

**Mario Filadoro**
*Centre for Socio-EcoNomic Development (CSEND), Switzerland*

## ABSTRACT

*Effective tourism strategies of a developing country can create revenue generating opportunities (tax revenues) and provide sustainable employment for semi-skilled or unskilled workers. Such tourism development strategies require systemic thinking and comprehensive investment portfolio strategies regarding the tourism industry as a whole, i.e. going beyond investing in hotels, but also including transportation infrastructure, catering, restaurants, safe water, financial system etc. In other words, the destination countries need to review their tourism value & supply chains and identify structural impediments to the full utilization of their tourism assets and facilities. This chapter shows how Least Developed Countries (LDCs) can define their tourism sector development and suggests a framework which can be used by a LDC to assess its tourism development potential. It can also be used by potential investors interested in investing in an LDC's tourism sector who need to understand the broader context of doing business in LDCs.*

## INTRODUCTION

Effective pro-business tourism strategies can create income generating business opportunities for the tourism industry while, at the same time, provide employment needed to absorb large numbers of semi-skilled or unskilled workers in developing and in Least Development Countries (LDCs). A government's coherent cross-sector tourism strategy offers investment incentives to

DOI: 10.4018/978-1-4666-8606-9.ch013

foreign tour operators and provides local service providers ample opportunities to link up to with the supply and value chains and to develop possibilities to integrate with the global tourism industry.

Tourism development strategies require investments in the tourism infrastructure itself, i.e. good road and transportation conditions, access to safe water, control of law and order, provision of trained and motivated work force, availability of efficient banking facilities etc. All these physical and social infrastructure factors, as well as a sustainability approaches to business, should be part of a holistic tourism development strategy of a developing country.

The objective of this chapter is twofold. On one hand, this chapter aims to help an LDC country answer the question: How to put in place a proper policy framework that attracts investments by foreign tourism operators while, at the same time ensures that benefits of these foreign direct investments have a positive sustainable impact on its population development? On the other hand, this chapter intends to help tourism operators from developed countries understand the concerns, needs and strategic objectives that an LDC host country has which by definition are not the same as the strategies of a private sector tourism operator from a developed country. Finally, this chapter provides guidance for both private sector tourism operators and LDC governments to achieve mutually beneficial agreement when negotiating an in-bound investment deal.

## GLOBAL HOSPITALITY AND TOURISM BUSINESS LANDSCAPE

*Main message: Tourism is an important contributor to GDP, employment and international appreciation of a country and its culture – regardless of its level of development. Tourism can also serve as driver for increased demands for other products and services in the countries and trigger quality improvement and upgrading of their supply chain and related value creation. Tourism creates opportunities for both, the destination country, especially the LDCs and private sector tourism operators/investors of developed countries.*

## Impact of Global Hospitality and Tourism Industry

Services account for an increasing share in global trade, in particular if measured in value added terms. In particular, hospitality and tourism emerged as one of the most dynamic and fastest growing industries worldwide representing about 6% of international trade in goods and service and accounting for 30% of the world's export of commercial services. Globally, tourism also ranks fourth as an export category, after fuels, chemicals and automotive products (United Nations World Tourism Organization, 2010).

Travel & Tourism's direct contribution to world GDP and employment in 2012 was US$ 2.1 trillion (2012 prices) and 101 million jobs (World Travel and Tourism Council, 2013). Taking account of its combined direct, indirect and induced impacts, the total economic contribution in 2012 was US$ 6.6 trillion in GDP (2012 prices). This represented 260 million jobs, US$ 760 billion in investment (2012 prices) and US$ 1.2 trillion in exports (2012 prices). This total contribution represents 9% of total economy GDP in 2012, 1 in 11 jobs, 5% of total economy investment and 5% of world exports.

Overall, global travel & tourism direct contribution to GDP grew by a 3.2% in 2012, faster than growth of the world economy as whole, which was 2.3% for this period. In terms of employment, including those working in the industry's supply chain and supported by the spending of their employees, the industry increased by 4.0 million jobs in 2012.

It is worthwhile noting that while travel & tourism GDP growth slowed throughout 2012 and was weaker than forecast one year ago, visitor exports exceeded expectations, rising 4.7% year on year. Asia, Latin America and Sub-Saharan Africa were, in percentage growth terms, amongst the fastest growing destination markets in 2012.

Besides its important economic impact, the tourism industry has strong untapped potential. According to the World Travel and Tourism Council, it is projected that the contribution of travel & tourism to GDP globally will rise from 9.2% (US $5,751 billion) in 2010 to 9.6% (US $11,151 billion) by 2020. The contribution of the travel & tourism economy to employment is also expected to rise from 8.1%, or 235,758,000 jobs across the world in 2010, to 9.2%, or 303,019,000 jobs, by 2020 (World Travel and Tourism Council, 2010). By 2023, the industry´s total economic contribution is forecast to rise to US$ 10.5 trillion in GDP (2012 prices), almost 340 million in jobs, over US$ 1.3 trillion in investment (2012 prices) and almost US$ 2.0 trillion in exports (2012 prices).

The growing importance of the industry in the global economy means that by 2023, the total contribution will account for 10.0% of GDP and 1 in 10 jobs globally. Similarly, employment is forecasted to increase by over 70 million jobs over the next decade, with two-thirds of the additional jobs in Asia. If LDC governments are able to design and implement effective tourism development strategies and successfully attract investments by tour operators, they will be able to materialize this potential.

## Opportunity for LDCs

Recent reports from different agencies have highlighted the importance of tourism for LDCs. A flourishing tourism sector can contribute to LDCs´ development through its linkages with other economic sectors and through the inclusion of local communities, as well as through job reaction and reduction of poverty.

The Istanbul Programme of Action called to *"(s)upport the Least Developed Countries' efforts to develop a sustainable tourism sector,*

*capital development, increased access to finance and enhanced access to global tourism networks and distribution channels..."* (United Nations, 2011, p.12)

Sustainable tourism development has been identified by the New Partnership for Africa's Development (NEPAD) as an important vehicle to address the current development challenges facing Africa. Finally, the United Nations Economic Commission for Africa (UNECA) Report on *"Sustainable Development Report on Africa"* highlights the approval of a Tourism Action Plan in 2004. Its main objective is to *"provide an engine for growth and integration, and to contribute to poverty eradication. Most African governments have included tourism in their national development strategies. Countries have also started adopting policies that unlock opportunities for the poor to gain employment through tourism development. Additionally, countries have adopted the Global Code of Ethics for Tourism and have reported on implementation progress."* (United Nations Economic Commission for Africa, 2008, p.17)

Countries across Africa specifically cite travel and tourism as a key pillar for economic growth and have allocated government funds to promote tourism. From a government perspective point of view, the main constraints that the tourism sector in Africa faces have to do with leakages and limited linkages to the local economy. Hence the challenge for sustainable tourism development is to *"overcome these risk factors; ensure effective market place value, quality of service products and meaningful community-private-public partnerships, supported by policies that influence flows to the poor."* (United Nations Economic Commission for Africa, 2008, p.18)

Furthermore, UNECA noted that the tourism industry *"is still very fragmented, and coordination is required, particularly for small and micro tourism firms. Traditionally, the focus of national governments has been at macro level (international promotion, attracting investors for major hotel master planning). Regulations, economic incentives, fiscal measures, resources and institutions to promote and disseminate good practices and in general, the policy space for tourism to respond to sustainability issues is inadequate, if not lacking in most cases."* (United Nations Economic Commission for Africa, 2008, p. 60)

Tourism is an economic sector offering key comparative advantages for countries in Africa due to its natural endowments, low cost labour and abundance of land. Governments need to find ways to transform these potentials into practices. Productivity improvement and better connections to and among markets are the basis for reaping the benefits of recent trends of tourism uptake. As mentioned by the World Economic Forum, *"key ingredients to this success are governance and infrastructure, and the deployment of a combined strategy of spatial and economic development called growth poles."* (World Economic Forum, 2013, pp. 104-105)

In this global context of expansion and potential of the hospitability and tourism, the industry experiences sub-optimal performance and business constraints in LDC countries. In most of these countries, the tourism sector has not lived up to its full potential. The tourism industry grew from a mere US$ 6.8 billion in international tourist receipts beginning in the 1960s to US $ 941 billion by 2008 before falling to US $ 852 billion in 2009. The geographical distribution of tourist receipts for 2009 reflects that of the indicated total: 48.5% went to Europe, 23.9% to Asia and the Pacific, 19.4% to the Americas, 4.8% to the Middle East and only 3.4% to Africa (United Nations World Tourism Organization, 2010). Africa's share of tourist receipts has since grown as well albeit slowly.

Africa, however, is emerging as a key target market for international hotel investors and operators, particularly, the sub-Saharan Africa. According to a recent study published by Ernst & Young (2014), *"approximately 30 sizable hotel groups operate in Africa, representing more*

*than 60 brands. From a geographic standpoint, approximately 47% of existing hotel rooms are in sub-Saharan Africa... In 2013, the development pipeline in sub-Saharan Africa increased 23% over the previous year, with about 80 hotels in various stages of development."* (pp. 20-21)

In particular, two LDCs are currently seen as hot spots for hotel investment and development. On the one hand, travel to Ghana increased due to extensive public investments in the country's infrastructure, notably in the Kotoka International Airport). On the other side of the African continent, coastal Tanzania is drawing international attention, relying on leisure tourists, offering guests pristine beach resorts and extensive nature reserves for safaris. As in the case of Ghana, Tanzania´s government has recently increased its efforts to promote domestic and international tourism to the country, particularly China, India and Russia. (Ernst & Young, 2014)

Tourism is an economic sector offering key comparative advantages for countries in Africa. Governments need to find ways to develop this industry in a competitive way. In order to do so, they need to improve productivity and connections to and among markets and reap the benefits of recent trends toward regional integration. As mentioned by the World Economic Forum, *"key ingredients to this success are governance and infrastructure, and the deployment of a combined strategy of spatial and economic development called growth poles."* (World Economic Forum, 2013, pp. 104-105)

If LDCs manage to overcome these constraints, they could offer new products for the hospitality and tourism industry, generating benefits for both parties. Greater tourist receipts could be generated, if the domestic business environment and international trading potentials could be better aligned and harnessed. Sound tourism development strategies and well coordinated implementation plans could enable the LDCs to achieve greater value creation without compromising national tourism assets. LDCs need to develop and more fully exploit their tourism resources in a sustainable manner to achieve their midterm poverty reduction objectives.

## TOURISM A KEY ECONOMIC SECTOR IN LDCS

*Main message: Tourism is an industry with great potential and has strong links with economic growth and development. Local people living in LDCs could benefit in multifaceted manner from tourism investments. Tourism also provides LDCs opportunities for economic diversification and skills upgrading. Finally, tourism can support protection of environmental and cultural assets. LDCs have many unexploited tourism assets which could be offered as a very different tourism experience, rarely found in more commercialized destinations.*

### Great Development Potential and Strong Links with Economic Growth and Development

According to empirical studies by the World Bank, there is a causal relationship between tourism development and economic growth. Furthermore, the IMF found that an increase of one standard deviation in the share of tourism exports leads to about 0.5 percentage point in additional annual growth, everything else being constant (Arezki, Cherif & Piotrowski, 2009). Hence, investing in its tourism industry represents an opportunity for LDC governments to stimulate growth over the long term and to enabling the poor to share in economic gains.

*Livelihood.* As put by the World Bank (2011), tourism is an industry *"where the 'good' or 'service' is consumed at the site of production."* Local people are both at an advantage for benefiting from it, but also at risk from exclusion (or even suffering the negative impacts that it can generate, e.g. mass tourism). This is the main reason why governments

need to implement a strategic approach to tourism to create attractive investment conditions while at the same time ensuring long term benefits of their tourism potential. Following the World Bank, *"[a] well planned, regulated and responsible tourism can be an excellent mechanism of channeling resources from rich to poor - even at the large scale. Commercial tourism activities provide an opportunity for local people to participate in direct employment, in providing goods and services to tourism businesses through the supply chain, but also in direct interaction with the tourist (for example: crafts, excursions, food and beverage). The generation of earnings amongst those local people directly involved with the industry in turn stimulates indirect spend (of wages) in the local economy."* (World Bank, 2011 October 27)

*Opportunities for economic diversification and skills upgrading.* LDCs could use tourism to support local business in developing new products for exports. In this sense, the tourism industry could provide a means for the local business to experiment with new products and test them in their home country before exporting them. While quality standards can be difficult to reach in the short-term, fully established quality standards lead to growth and improvement over time.

*Potential for sustainable protection of environmental and cultural assets.* LDCs often own a variety of natural and cultural tourism assets which need to be preserved in order to ensure the sustainable benefits of tourism products. LDC governments do not have the financial resources to ensure the preservation of natural areas. The revenue generated from tourism could be one solution to this problem, provided tourism is regulated and managed in a responsible manner and taxes are being collected from tour operators.

*Alternative market opportunities for the tourism industry.* LDCs are endowed with natural tourism assets and distinctive cultural heritage and historical sites. Some are designated UNESCO World Heritage Sites, representing a variety of unexploited tourism assets which can be turned into tourism products. LDCs´ could offer a very different tourism experience, rarely found in more commercialized tourism destinations such as natural beauty, rich flora and fauna, and prehistoric and cultural heritage. Likewise, mountains, valleys, and rivers provide memorable scenery for tourists, if international standards of tourism services and infrastructure are implemented.

For instance, tourism holds great potential for Lesotho because of its natural beauty and cultural heritage. A number of strategic objectives were implemented by the government to unleash this potential and increase the sector's contribution to growth and development. The government seeks to develop new tourism products and circuits while, at the same time, protecting, conserving and managing cultural heritage resources. In order to do so, the government of Lesotho aims at improving the quality and standards of services by implementing accommodation star grading system and facilitating the provision of appropriate training to improve the skills of services providers. In addition, a different branding is envisaged to improve its marketability and visibility as a tourist destination (Central Bank of Lesotho, 2012).

## Sub-Optimal Performance and Business Constraints in LDC Countries

In most of LDCs, the tourism sector has not lived up to its full potential. The tourism industry grew from a mere US$ 6.8 billion in international tourist receipts beginning in the 1960s to US $ 941 billion by 2008 before falling to US $ 852 billion in 2009. The geographical distribution of tourist receipts for 2009 reflects that of the indicated total: 48.5% went to Europe, 23.9% to Asia and the Pacific, 19.4% to the Americas, 4.8% to the Middle East and only 3.4% to Africa (United Nations World Tourism Organization, 2010). Africa's share of tourist receipts has since grown as well albeit slowly.

Unfortunately, long-standing business risks and barriers persist in Africa. The most important limitation to the expansion of tourism is the poor transportation infrastructure, restricting the connectivity of the sub-Saharan region. Air travel is also limited and is generally expensive compared to other developing markets, such as the Middle East, mostly due to costly and unreliable supply of utilities. The road infrastructure is fragmented requiring official documentation (e.g., licenses, customs) result often in construction delays (Ernst & Young 2014). In spite of these constraints, the undersupply of hotel rooms in sub-Saharan Africa gained the attention of investors. At the end of 2013, *"a major hotel brand announced its intention to acquire one of Africa's leading hotel groups, whose assets encompass a portfolio of nearly 120 hotels with more than 10,000 rooms. This acquisition would not only double the brand's footprint in Africa, it would further circumvent market entry barriers and result in gaining a significant competitive advantage on the continent."* (Ernst & Young, 2014, p. 21)

The lack of infrastructure also hampers greater productivity of the tourism sector in LDCs. In many cases, the scale of investment needed to improve the existing infrastructure often exceeds the potential of LDCs.

Tourism is a people driven industry. In countries such as LDCs, where most of the people work in the informal economy, the chance of escaping poverty trap is slim. Advanced and productive tourism services would offer opportunities to many people to be engaged in gainful employment. Other enabling conditions which address managerial skill shortage and/or capital scarcity would make sense. Effective tourism strategies can create sustainable income generating opportunities and provide employment needed to absorb large numbers of semi-skilled or unskilled workers. However, little progress has been made concerning the free movement of persons and the right of commercial presence which is raising real costs for the tourism sector (United Nations Economic Commission for Africa, 2008, p. 39).

## REQUSITES FOR TOURISM BECOMING KEY DRIVER FOR SUSTAINABLE DEVELOPMENT IN THE LDCS

*Main message: LDCs need to attract investments while at the same time promoting the public interest. This approach requires a general macro framework for economic development covering a wide range of issues such as economic growth & regional development; poverty, inequality & polarization; unemployment, health & education; environment & climate change; infrastructure; quality standards; and business environment. Based on these general objectives, an LDC government can design sector-specific development plans for selected industries, such as tourism in order to establish the right conditions for the industry to operate efficiently. This requires in turn interaction between different areas, namely: infrastructure, education, health, agriculture, etc.*

### Pillars for Sustainable Development

In order to attract tourism investment, LDC governments need to establish a sector-specific strategy which should be aligned with the country´s general strategic framework for development. Any general strategic framework for development conceives, at least, four major macro intervention pillars: political, economic, social and environmental. These pillars are very relevant for the tourism industry because they provide the basics for the implementation of the enabling conditions and for the establishment of clear regulatory frameworks.

The figure below shows the different pillars of a national economic development strategy and their link to sustainability.

The *political pillar* aims at stabilizing the political process in the LDC as well as ensuring

peace and security. The economic pillar focuses on the country´s integration into the global/regional markets, the economic reforms needed to accelerate structural transformation and on the diversification of the economy. The social pillar strengthens the social sectors of education and employment and promotes poverty reduction efforts and promotes the reduction of regional inequalities. Lastly, the environmental pillar includes the "green dimension" in different actions and promotes sustainable development. Each intervention pillar requires clear result-based framework which identifies strategic objectives, strategic challenges, and problems impeding the achievement of strategic objectives, and expected long-term outcomes.

National development strategies encompass the activities of different sectors such as agriculture, education, housing, tourism and provide a general framework for the country's development. Within a national development strategy, the tourism sectors specific strategy and objectives should, as identified by the International Union for Conservation of Nature (IUCN) *"define a general methodological framework, the macro-economic parameters within which tourism will develop, sectoral policy guidelines, and goals that public investment must attain in this sector. The overall development plan of a country should recognize that tourism can play an important role in national development, especially at the regional (sub-country) level, due to its ability to generate employment and foreign exchange, and on account of the opportunities it provides for the recreation and education of the domestic population."* (International Union for Conservation of Nature website)

Planning tourism at all levels is essential for achieving successful tourism development and for preventing of suffering from environmental and social problems resulting in marketing difficulties and decreasing economic benefits.

LDC governments need to establish a development strategy linked to the overall economic development of the country. They include a set

*Figure 1: Pillars of a national economic development strategy (Authors own elaboration)*

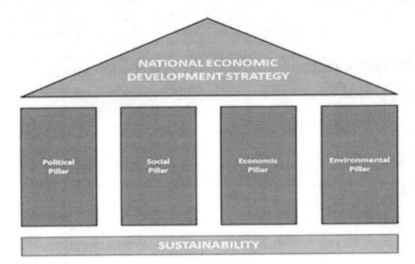

of national strategic objectives as well as priority areas (such as tourism) where it envisages an opportunity for national development. These objectives are included in a national strategy which establishes the actions required to accomplish these objectives. Normally, these are cross-sectoral issues that require coordination among different government agencies and consultations with civil society and the private sector. For instance, the following are general objectives that an LDC government has:[1]

- *"Employment creating economic growth*
- *Promotion of peace, democracy, good governance and effective institutions*
- *Development of infrastructure (minimum infrastructure platform)*
- *Transformation of skills development institutions and improvement of skills and innovation base*
- *Reversal of environmental degradation and adaptation to climate change*
- *Improve health, combat HIV and AIDS and reduce social vulnerability"*

Overall, a general macro framework for economic development covers a wide range of issues.

Some of the most important objectives are briefly discussed below.[2]

## Conditions for Economic growth and Regional Development in LDCs

The main objective of an LDC government is to create conditions for accelerated growth and job creation to ensure regional balance and inclusive development. In doing so, the government needs to ensure the creation of (higher value added) jobs and on the reduction of regional disparities. Persistent dependence of the economy on low-cost production and export sectors with low value added make it uncompetitive and vulnerable. LDC governments focus both on enhancing the business climate and improving public service delivery and access to employment in disadvantaged regions. In particular, regional trade agreements enabled LDCs to reach important milestones regarding liberalization and integration.

*Poverty, inequality & polarization.* The government needs to reduce socio-economic disparities as a way to cope with social challenges. In doing so, it must focus on poverty alleviation and food security. Social policies based on direct and indirect transfers (food and energy subsidies) aim at promoting inclusive growth-driven development. Likewise, economic growth is needed to reduce poverty in rural and urban areas and improving health and education indicators.

*Unemployment, health & education.* Structural unemployment as well as informal employment are key objectives for the economic development of LDCs. The government needs to implement the right policies to address a quantitative (between higher education and private sector needs) and qualitative (graduates lacking the required skills to enter the labor market) mismatch. Health risks are a major challenge for LDC governments.

*Environment & climate change.* Management of environmental issues is for LDC governments a key way to preserve their natural assets. In many cases, the environmental degradation is related to the difficulties encountered by the government in applying the law

*Infrastructure.* This is a crucial element for both the government as well as for the private sector tourism operators. Infrastructure development support requires the formulation and/or implementation of (public and private) investment programmes and strategies to improve the business environment at the national level and in the regions and to back the sophistication of the economy. Continuous infrastructure development is required for economic transformation.

*Quality standards.* High quality services standards need to be in place in the LDCs in order to attract investments in tourism. LDC governments focus on improving standards through different actions such as formulation of manpower training policies, establishing national curriculums and train-the-trainer programmes and organizing modalities for management training.

*Business environment.* Whether sectors are open or not to foreign investment, and requests for prior authorization are limiting factors of tourism development. LDC governments must overcome the main challenges for private sector tourism development such as insecurity, corruption, human resources, infrastructure, administrative procedures and systems, etc.

Once these general objectives have been reached, the government should design sector-specific development plans for selected industries, such as tourism.[3] The establishment of the right conditions for the tourism industry to operate efficiently requires the interaction between different areas such as infrastructure, education, health, agriculture, etc. For example, LDC governments need to ensure the occurrence of the following factors for the hospitality and tourism industry: sustainable waste management; local supply of food and other inputs; roads to get to tourism assets; hotel infrastructure; tourism specific skills training; energy provision.

The main goal for an LDC to promote tourism development is to increase the number of tourist arrivals and spending in the country. Many LDCs identified tourism as one of the key sectors to drive growth and employment because of it is labor-intensive and it has a potential to raise income in rural areas. For this specific objective, LDC governments need to find ways to develop tourism industry and encourage further private sector participation.[4]

As mentioned before, infrastructure remains the biggest challenge for tourism development in LDCs. A key specific objective for the LDC governments should be to ensure that existing accommodation facilities and attractions are linked and that the basic infrastructure is in place on sites that have been identified for tourism investment. In some cases LDC governments, such as Lesotho, design a national tourism marketing strategy that identifies the country's unique selling-point and creates a distinctive brand to attract tourists in a number of niche areas (for instance, exploring traditional culture, pony-trekking, off-road biking, etc.).

LDC governments also need to protect their cultural assets. Limited protection of the rich cultural heritage from destruction threatens their existence for future generations. Efforts in packaging cultural products also limit the use of the product for viable tourism exploitation.

In closing, LDC governments have the objective of developing tourism products to their full potential while, at the same time, they have to protect their cultural heritages, improve quality and service standard, improve the marketability and visibility of the country as a destination of choice and, most importantly, improve the institutional framework and regulations. Strategic components to improve LDC´s competitiveness need to be put in place by the government. As highlighted by Tanzania´s Tourism Master Plan, these include:[5]

- *"knowledge and 'know-how' strategy – improving range and quality of information on customers, distribution channels, suppliers, etc.*
- *investment strategy – attracting direct foreign and local investment*
- *product strategy – expanding and improving the tourism product*
- *infrastructure strategy – improving roads, utilities, etc.*
- *access strategy – improving air and ground access transport*
- *human resource development – improving skills and service standards*
- *marketing and communications strategy – creating greater awareness in marketplace*
- *capacity building strategy – strengthening tourism institutions*
- *security awareness strategy"*

LDC governments can also reach their tourism specific objectives by making commitments in the framework of the General Agreement on Trade and Services (GATS). Such commitments could establish the conditions for foreign tour operators to invest and operate in the LDC market. GATS commitments can be an important part of improving the business climate, by increasing regulatory transparency and predictability.

Tourism is one of the sectors where many LDCs have taken commitments in the context of the GATS and several countries within then group have included tourism as a priority sector under their poverty reduction strategic plans and programmes. According to Honeck, *"LDCs often lack internationally credible mechanisms for making commitments, which contributes to their evident difficulty in attracting the more employment-generating types of investment that could bring greater opportunities for poverty alleviation. Considering that most LDCs, under domestic laws, have already opened a wide range of services sectors to foreign direct investment (FDI), there may be an opportunity to enhance the international consistency and credibility of LDC investment promotion efforts by making GATS commitments, while preserving substantial "policy space" with regard to the actual status quo."* (2011, p. 2)

In this sense, GATS commitments, can be used by LDC governments to establish investment priorities in services (such as attracting new businesses, encouraging joint ventures and technology transfer, etc.), and make them legally binding internationally.

For example, as depicted in the WTO website, Mali´ GATS schedule of commitments establishes that "Hotel and restaurant services" are liberalized, with no limitations in GATS modes 2, 3 and 4 (consumption abroad; commercial presence; and presence of natural persons). Hence, foreign services suppliers in this sector face no limitations to: -offer their services to Mali citizens who travel to foreign countries concerned (mode 2); -establish a "commercial presence" in Mali by which the service is supplied by setting up a business or professional establishment, such as a subsidiary corporation or a branch or representative office (mode 3); and -allow natural persons to enter to Mali´s national territory to deliver services (mode 4) (e.g. ICT experts specialized in sophisticated booking and administrative software).

Finally, some LDCs are members of major regional trade agreements (RTAs).[6] These agreements contain provisions on different subjects which are very relevant for the tourism industry ranging from common standards, to joint marketing, to establishing training institutions.[7] All such agreed initiatives should be implemented with immediacy to foster greater regional integration in both supply and value chains in accordance with respective comparative advantages of each member country of a RTA. Active use of RTAs could enhance tourism sector competitiveness and the attractiveness of its products.

## Reducing Revenue Leakages through Government Measures and Strategy

"Leakage" refers to the negative economic impacts of tourism in the local economy. For instance, LDC governments are not able to reap the benefits of tourism due to large-scale transfer of tourism revenues out of the host country and due to the exclusion of local businesses and tourism products.

According to the United Nations Environment Programme (UNEP) website, *"[i]n most all-inclusive package tours, about 80% of travelers' expenditures go to the airlines, hotels and other international companies (who often have their headquarters in the travelers' home countries), and not to local businesses or workers. In addition, significant amounts of income actually retained at destination level can leave again through leakage... Of each US$ 100 spent on a vacation tour by a tourist from a developed country, only around US$ 5 actually stays in a developing-country destination's economy."* The figure below shows how leakages occur.

Two main forms of leakages are identified. The "import leakage" occurs when *"tourists demand standards of equipment, food, and other products that the host country cannot supply. Especially in less-developed countries, food and drinks must often be imported, since local products are not up to*

*the hotel's (i.e. tourist's) standards or the country simply doesn't have a supplying industry. Much of the income from tourism expenditures leaves the country again to pay for these imports. The average import-related leakage for most developing countries today is between 40% and 50% of gross tourism earnings for small economies and between 10% and 20% for most advanced and diversified economies."* (United Nations Environment Programme website)

On the other hand, the "export leakage" relates to multinational corporations and large foreign businesses having a substantial share in the import leakage. Often, especially in LDCs, the foreign tourism operators are the only ones that possess the necessary capital to invest in the construction of tourism infrastructure and facilities. As a consequence, an export leakage occurs when overseas investors who finance the resorts and hotels repatriate their profits back to their country of origin.

Finally, there are other negative economic impacts of tourism that LDC governments must prevent. These negative impacts can result in tensions between LDC governments and foreign tourism investors. One has to do with the high costs of tourism development infrastructure for local governments and local taxpayers. As put by UNEP, *"developers may want the government to improve the airport, roads and other infrastructure, and possibly to provide tax breaks and other financial advantages, which are costly activities for the government. Public resources spent on subsidized infrastructure or tax breaks may reduce government investment in other critical areas such as education and health."* (United Nations Environment Programme website)

Tourism development often results in a rise in real estate demand which can dramatically increase building costs and land values. This makes it more difficult for local people to meet their basic daily needs, especially in LDCs. But it can also result in a dominance by outsiders in land markets and in-migration that erodes economic opportunities for

*Figure 2: Tourism leakages (United Nations Environment Programme website)*

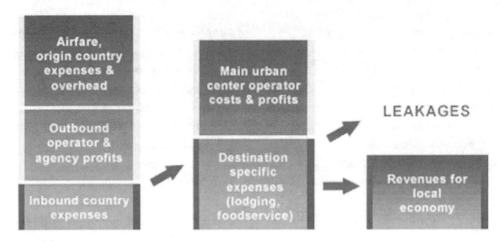

the locals, eventually disempowering residents. As identified by UNEP, long-term *"tourists living in second homes, and the so-called amenity migrants (wealthy or retired people and liberal professionals moving to attractive destinations in order to enjoy the atmosphere and peaceful rhythms of life) cause price hikes in their new homes if their numbers attain a certain critical mass."* (United Nations Environment Programme website)

LDC governments need to keep a balance between tourism development and their overall economic diversification strategy. An extreme economic dependence of the local community on tourism can put major stress upon this industry as well as the people involved to perform well. *According to UNEP, the "[o]ver-reliance on tourism, especially mass tourism, carries significant risks to tourism-dependent economies. Economic recession and the impacts of natural disasters such as tropical storms and cyclones as well as changing tourism patterns can have a devastating effect on the local tourism sector."* (United Nations Environment Programme website)

And last but not least, the seasonal character of jobs created by tourism development can create economic problems. These problems include: *"job (and therefore income) insecurity, usually with no guarantee of employment from one season to the next, difficulties in getting training, employment-*

*related medical benefits, and recognition of their experience, and unsatisfactory housing and working conditions."* (United Nations Environment Programme website)

LDC governments need to ensure a positive and sustainable impact of the tourism industry on the local economy. Partnerships are certainly an option to do so and can cover a variety of issues such as *"waste management, water use, energy supplies, development of local craft markets, local guiding services, improvement of local enterprises and services, seafront development, creation of pedestrian streets and local restaurants and cafes, management of attractions and development of new ones, management of begging, traffic control, control of sex tourism and policing of crime, as well as festivals for local people and tourists to enjoy together."* (United Nations Environment Programme website)

Partnerships between tourism operators and local communities can help enrich an LDC´s destination by offering the opportunity to local entrepreneurs to sell their products and services to tourists and by benefitting from enhancement of public spaces, parks, gardens, promenades and pedestrian streets. Effective local partnerships between government, hoteliers and local communities could also help to reduce hassle of tourists and feelings of risk to health or safety.

## VALUE AND SUPPLY CHAIN: SYSTEM PERSPECTIVE FOR TOURISM DEVELOPMENT IN LEAST DEVELOPED COUNTRIES

*Main message: LDC governments seek to attract tourism investments. In order to do so they put in place, sector-specific strategies that are embedded in the general macro framework strategy for development. One of the key components to facilitate the efficient operation of the tourism industry is the adoption of a value and supply chain approach.*

LDC governments seek to attract tourism investments. In order to do so, they put in place, sector-specific strategies that are embedded in the general macro framework strategy for development. One of the key elements to facilitate the efficient operation of the tourism industry is the adoption of the value and supply chain system perspective.

A value chain describes *"the full range of activities that are required to bring a product or service from conception, through the intermediary phases of production (...), delivery to final consumers, and final disposal after use."* (Kaplinsky, 2004, p. 76)

On the other hand, according to The Travel Foundation, the benefits for business from adopting a tourism supply chain management include *"retention of clients, as they increasingly expect responsible behavior even from those not willing to pay for it; increased revenue; reduced costs and improved operational efficiency, remaining competitive to assess and respond to risks and opportunities in the market; management of risks and staying ahead of legislative requirements; enhanced staff performance, achievement of better recruitment and staff retention, as satisfied staff are a key asset; protection of the core assets of the business (environment and culture); and enhanced brand value, reputation and market share, protecting image and status, particularly for companies publicly quoted on stock markets."* (The Travel Foundation, 2002, p. 1)

It is worth mentioning that in regard to tourism supply chains, tourists travel to tourism destinations that have particularly high service component, involving a high proportion of people in the immediate production of tourism (The Travel Foundation, 2002, p. 3). Supply chain activities refer to activities, inputs and support services relevant to the tourism products to be offered. As mentioned before, supply side constraints are inadequate infrastructure, low productivity, untapped economies of scale, and lack of support services.

The value chain analysis complements the supply chain can result in diversification and industrial economic development. Activities that add value are the crucial first step in moving up the value chain. However, these capacities need to be augmented with appropriate quality standards and practices in order to gain access to important global markets and to satisfy consumers in an increasingly competitive marketplace. Along with appropriate infrastructure, the value addition process can be upgraded by the creation of environmentally sustainable production capacities, distribution systems, business linkages and investment regimes. This requires suitable national policies, adequate institutional support and extensive enterprise development involving the private sector.[8]

A value and supply chain perspective is useful to identify both the needs of the hospitality and tourism industry, and the strengths and weaknesses that an LDC has in terms of enabling conditions for business. It can also support greater value creation of the countries' tourism industry and economy.

A government's coherent cross-sector tourism strategy offers investment incentives to foreign tour operators and provides local service providers opportunities to better link up to with the supply and value chains and backward linkages of the global tourism industry. Effective tourism strategies require investment in the tourism industry itself, i.e., hotels, transportation, catering and restaurants, but also entail investments to strengthen forward linkages to value chains and backward linkages to supply chains. The absence of integrated development approaches such as project investments ranging from infrastructures to game parks impedes the higher rates of return that would otherwise be possible.

A joint study prepared by the World Trade Organization, the United Nations World Tourism Organization and the Organization for Economic Cooperation and Development (2013, pp. 10-11) showed that the quality of the general business environment and adequate access to finance play an important role when it comes to allowing suppliers in LDCs to operate effectively and to connect to global value chains. One of the main elements for the success of local suppliers of services is adequate levels of labor skills. However, other inter-linkages are equally relevant such as sourcing food from the local economy, offering other leisure services or selling local products to travelers.

The figure below shows the complexity of a typical tourism value chain illustrating the activities that take place in the outbound country (i.e. the tourists' country of residence) and those taking place in the inbound country (i.e. the tourists' destination country). As it can be seen from this figure, there are activities that are a direct part of the tourism sector, while others that are indirectly linked. LDCs that manage to exploit these linkages in an optimal way will maximize the development potential of tourism.

Without such a systemic approach to tourism development for example, health and hygiene or transportation, international tourists might be deterred and going instead to countries with much higher level of tourism development and product sophistication. In turn, if investments made in hotels and other facilities show disappointing returns and if adequate attention is not been paid to the rest of the supply chain, such as guarantee sufficient supply of fresh foods, or convenience

of access; or the value chain such as service quality, construction standard just to name a few. The above-mentioned phenomenon of "leakage" in the tourism sector has often been the consequence of these neglects.

Examples of backward and forward linkages of the tourism industry are: transport, hotel & facilities, health and hygiene, quality standard, investment, education & training services, and local agricultural inputs. For example, Zambia is an LDC that has adopted a value and supply chain system orientation and addressed fully these business linkages in the key development instruments such as the country´s Diagnostic Trade Integration Study and Poverty Reduction Strategy Paper (CSEND, 2011, p. 46).

## TOURISM DEVELOPMENT STRATEGY AND PARTNERSHIPS

*Main message: Developing a strategic tourism framework requires a lot of inter-sectoral work among government ministers and agencies. Tourism is a cross-sectoral activity and, as such, it requires the interaction of different policy areas. While the Ministry of Tourism is a critical component for tourism development, other ministries are very relevant as well. In addition, government to industry consultation is critical for the design and implementation of an effective tourism development strategy.*

A lack of policy coherence often leads to suboptimal government responses and ineffective policy design. Inter-Ministerial Policy Coordination (IMC) is a must each time a country faces complex and interconnected cross-sector challenges like climate change, migration, financial instability, refugees, conflicts, unemployment, and job perspectives for the youth which affect trade policy directly and/or indirectly. Effective inter-ministerial policy co-ordination is based on achieving three targets namely eliminating redundancy of policy and projects; achieving policy

*Figure 3: Tourism value chain (World Trade Organization, United Nations World Tourism Organization & Organization for Economic Cooperation and Development, 2013, p. 23)*

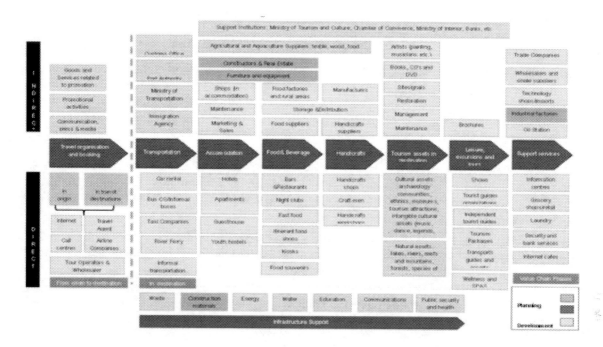

coherence and reducing fragmentation resulting from cross-cutting issues; and integrating numerous tourism development initiatives in a coherent manner (Saner, 2010).

Different levels of intra-governmental coordination are identified in the figure below. This typology defines the different types of mechanism for government´s coordination in terms of country´s governance orientation (along the centralization / decentralization continuum). This typology provides a tool for LDC governments in determining the appropriate coordination structure for the design and implementation of tourism development strategies.

Through improved IMC mechanisms, developing countries and LDCs could achieve more effective tourism development strategies. However, without broader policy consultation with economic and social partners, IMC alone cannot achieve national consensus on trade policy objectives. IMC and stakeholder consultation processes

are complementary and need to be conducted in during all stages of policy making namely: 1) initiation; 2) formulation; 3) implementation; 4) evaluation; 5) monitoring.

Improving on existing coordination and consultation practices requires a well designed and functioning monitoring system. LDCs need process monitoring systems to keep abreast of current practice which in turn provides them with the possibility to continuously improve institutional performance and organizational learning.

IMC and stakeholder consultation are key issues in the process of mainstreaming tourism development in a coherent manner with the LDCs general economic development strategies. The development of a strategic framework requires a lot of inter-sectoral coordination among different government agencies. Tourism is a cross-sectoral issue and, as such, it also involves the interaction between different issue areas in order to establish a sector specific strategy. High performance in

*Figure 4: Levels of intra-governmental coordination (CSEND, 2010)*

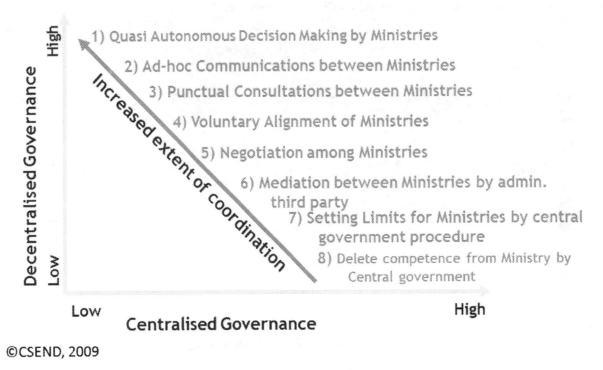

©CSEND, 2009

the tourism sector requires a well coordinated development strategy to ensure quality inputs such as transportation, hotel accommodations, restaurants, sightseeing, sports and entertainment. Other business conditions are equally important in making a tourist feel comfortable and secure. This involves health and hygiene, variety of food choices, banking services, electricity and water supply just to name a few. Provision of the above requires cross-sector cooperation and setting investment priorities. Without proper governance mechanisms for policy making and implementation, it would not be easy to develop a well configured and diversified tourism product.

Coordination can be utilized to eliminate tourism development objectives that are redundant or are duplicating certain activities. Coordination is also a necessary element to manage tourism-related cross-cutting issues, when different client groups should be provided with services and programmes that are comprehensive and integrated. Furthermore, the effective functioning of

coordination can ensure greater internal policy coherence in government as well as collaboration in implementation of tourism development strategies.

The Ministry of Tourism is an important component for tourism development but other ministries and public agencies are also equally relevant as well as tourism business associations and other industry stakeholders. In the case of LDCs, some ministries have mandates which include other issues than tourism: Burundi´s government has a Ministry of Trade, Industry and Tourism (http://www.commerceetindustrie.gov.bi/) while Benin´s government has a Ministry of Culture, Traditional Crafts, and Tourism (http://www.cotonou-benin.com/mcat.html).

The role and function of a Ministry of Tourism is to act as nodal agency for the formulation of national tourism policies and programmes and for the coordination of activities. The Ministry plays a crucial role in coordinating efforts with other policy areas. For example, Tanzania´s Ministry of Natural Resources and Tourism is the ministry responsible for the sustainable conservation of natural and cultural resources and development of responsible tourism. The Tourism Division of the Ministry is responsible for the sectoral policy, planning, research, manpower, training, statistics, licensing and quality control of tourist agents. The Division is responsible for formulation and enhancement of sectoral policy and regulatory functions and its major objective is to ensure the implementation of the National Tourism Policy as well as regulatory functions. The main objective of National Tourism Policy is to promote the economy and livelihood of the people, essentially poverty alleviation by encouraging the development of sustainable and quality tourism that is culturally and socially acceptable, ecologically friendly, environmentally sustainable and economically viable.

The main functions of the Tourism Division are reproduced in the box below.

In addition to the Ministry of Tourism, there are other government agencies which are very important for the design and implementation of a tourism development strategy. The presence of governance mechanisms pertaining to tourism development is crucial for the development of an effective strategy and for ensuring effective communication between government and industry. In this sense, LDCs domestic institutions such as an Inter-Ministerial Policy Coordination Mechanism, a Government to Industry Policy Consultation Mechanism, and Tourism Industry Organizations, play a critical role in ensuring the enabling conditions for the tourism industry.

Many LDCs have a National Tourism Board for consultation with the business sector. Such Boards often do not have a clear mandate with cross-ministry coordination function and power. For example, the Madagascar National Tourism Board (http://www.madagascar-tourisme.com/en/terms-and-conditions) is an independent agency working to promote the destination and preserving the natural and cultural environment. It has the

following functions: ensure the dialogue and consultation with the private sector; contribute to the development, coordination and implementation of tourism policy both nationally and internationally; perform actions contributing to the promotion of the "Madagascar" destination in foreign markets; represent the private tourism sector in relations with international donors; provide facilities and information for tourists; coordinate the activities of various private partners in tourism development in Madagascar; coordinate the organization of training identified; among other issues.

Another example is Lesotho´s Tourism Development Corporation which has the following functions:

- *"To promote and generate sustainable and profitable tourism projects which demonstrate a high absorptive capacity for labor.*
  - *-Mobilization of requisite resources to meet the demand for financial and infrastructural requirement from the local and international donor/financial institutions and the private sector.*
  - *-To market and promote Lesotho as a preferred destination for tourists (increased market share of global tourist traffic) in such a manner that will contribute to generation of additional foreign exchange, improved balance of payments and creation of employment.*
  - *-To promote and increase the flow of domestic tourism by marketing internally the unique selling points of Lesotho with particular accent on appreciation of heritage, traditional and cultural endowments and responsible use of environment." (Lesotho Tourism Development Corporation website)*

*Box 1: Main functions of the Tourism Division of Tanzania´s Ministry of Natural Resources and Tourism (http://www.mnrt.go.tz/sectors/category/tourism)*

- Sectoral planning and budgeting
- Formulating and reviewing legislation
- Monitoring and evaluation of the sector
- Manpower planning and human resource development
- Researching, training and curriculum development
- Licensing and control of tourist agency business.
- International co-operation and collaboration
- Identification of tourist attractions and diversification of tourism activities.
- Undertaking impact assessment on cultural and social-economic activities
- Setting and reviewing license fees and monitoring their issuance
- Controlling quality of tourism facilities & services by carrying out inspection, classification and grading
- Taking legal actions
- Appraising investment proposals
- Undertaking resource mobilization
- Developing and promoting domestic tourism

Finally, national tourism websites are often made available online by LDC governments promoting different tourist destinations and attractions in the country. These websites are useful for the tourism investors to identify the current and tourism products.

Based on information available from the Diagnostic Trade Integration Studies and Poverty Reduction Strategy Papers, it can be observed that the majority of LDC governments have not established formal IMC mechanisms linked to tourism policies. Furthermore, institutional reinforcement of Ministries of Tourism in terms of capacities and budget (mainly) is needed and hence has been proposed in several of these instruments. (CSEND, 2011, p. 21) Inter-ministerial coordination and private sector consultations have not been sufficiently formalized with clear guidelines and monitoring mechanisms. In many LDCs there seems to be no clear designation of policy leadership in regard to tourism development where inter-sectoral cooperation is necessary and unavoidable. Better coordinated and consulted tourism policies with cross-sector commitment and engagement by the private sector would also ensure better returns of investment directly or indirectly of tourism development.

## CONVERGENT AND DIVERGENT INTERESTS OF GOVERNMENT AND BUSINESS

*Main message: There are convergent and divergent interests between LDC governments and tourism operators of developed countries. These are defined by the different roles played by each actor. The government needs to attract sustainable investment and the investors need to maximize their profits and, hence expect business friendly conditions from governments. Sustainability is the most important convergent interest. Partnership and collaboration between LDC governments and private sector can leverage convergent interests.*

Host country's governments need to ensure a proper business landscape for the operation of the global hospitality and tourism industry. An effective tourism development strategy, from the perspective of a host LDC must create attractive investment conditions (and make effective use of development aid) while at the same time ensuring long term sovereign rights of their tourism potential. The United Nations World Tourism Organization has identified a set of LDC government´s interests when ensuring the benefits of tourism for the poor:

- *"employment of the poor in tourism enterprises;*
- *supply of goods and services to tourism enterprises by the poor or by enterprises employing the poor;*
- *direct sales of goods and services to visitors by the poor (informal economy);*
- *establishment and running of tourism enterprises by the poor - e.g. micro, small and medium sized enterprises or community based enterprises (formal economy);*
- *tax or levy on tourism income or profits with proceeds benefiting the poor;*
- *voluntary giving/support by tourism enterprises and tourists; and*
- *investment in infrastructure stimulated by tourism also benefiting the poor in the locality, directly or through support to other sectors."* (United Nations World Tourism Organization website)

The overall objective of government interventions in tourism development is to enhance the positive impacts that tourism can have on poor people by removing barriers that prevent poor people from entering the tourism industry; enhancing the terms on which they work; and improving the knock-on effects that tourism operations have on surrounding communities (Ashley Mitchell & Spenceley, 2008). It is a major responsibility for the LDC governments to minimize the adverse impact of tourism. This is a major political concern that governments have but companies do not necessarily have to have.

On the other hand, there are different elements required by global tourism operators without which they might not be willing to invest in an LDC. [9] Travel and tourism industry´s main interest is to be given top priority by the LDC government in the creation of a competitive business environment. The industry expects the tax burden to be reduced on air travel to boost tourism. Its main interest is to ensure that taxation of the sector does not hinder the development of travel and tourism

The industry seeks to encourage greater freedom of travel overcoming political demands for strict immigration controls. Investing and cooperating in regional visa integration is envisaged as an initiative which can offer enormous economic returns. The industry hence often requests smarter visa procedures. Strategies for visa facilitation include investments in more streamlined processes, improved delivery of information, development of technological solutions (such as e-visa programmes), and cooperation and collaboration with neighbouring regions.

Tourism investors need to avoid human resources shortages, which could limit its ability to provide the necessary levels of services to travellers. A growing industry should also have the appropriate and sustainable physical infrastructure to support its growth (rail, airport and other facilities to enable the industry to grow).

Other issues demanded by the tourism industry are related to the question as to who implements the tourism development strategy. According to Ernst & Young, tourism enterprises *"today look for private sector leaders, such as senior executives with direct hospitality experience, rather than political appointees to carry out a destination's marketing strategy. Tourism enterprises that seek top talent in the private sector often outperform their public counterparts, given their ability to function free of political interference and familiarity with an incentive- and goals-driven operating model."* (2014, pp. 18-19)

Global tour operators often have everything in place to start a new business but a destination is missing. This creates an opportunity for the LDCs. Table 1 below identifies different issues needed by the government and the business sector. If both parties are engaged, they have many things to offer for the benefit of the other.

LDC governments and tourism operators have convergent interests which can help them to reinforce the mutual partnership and collaboration. For example, both actors aim to transform national tourism assets (resources) into tourism "capital" to be offered as mew destinations or experiences. Both LDC governments and industry share the objective of increasing of tourism receipts.

Sustainability is another convergent interest. It is an important aspect of an effective tourism development strategy (both for LDC governments and for the tourism investors) and for the better use and conservation of national tourism assets. Lack of oversight of sustainability in today's context of climate change and environmental vulnerability could mean accelerated deterioration of a country natural environment, a key element of LDCs tourism assets. From a socio-economic perspective, environmental vulnerability also diminishes the country's policy potential in achieving greater job creation and improved standard of living.

Sustainability is not only important for LDC governments. Many developed countries such as Italy have already started to implement measures to ensure the natural environmental sustainability of their tourism destinations. Indeed, a remarkable competitive sustainability advantage is available in natural environments without factories, with a local economy based on agriculture, with nuclear-free zones, only a few airports in the region. A recent study shows that the quality of the environment, its uniqueness and integrity are of greatest satisfaction and are key to maintaining tourist satisfaction (Camillo, Minguzzi, Presenza & Holt in press).

Conversely, there are other issues where government and tourism industry are likely to have divergent interests. These divergent interests are a natural consequence of the logic with which the government and the industry operate: while the government must promote the public interest, the industry must focus on the maximization of benefits and return on tourism investments.

For instance, in terms of a more conducive investment environment, both actors have divergent views. Tourism investors normally ask governments to reduce market entry requirements while LDC governments might need to maintain them at a certain level in order to ensure that the

benefits of those investments remain in the country (limitation of profit leakages).

A similar situation occurs when a country attempts to promote diversification of its tourism products. LDC governments might face certain difficulties with big global tour who request an exclusive market presence in the country. It is in the interest of the government to prevent tour operators from gaining monopolistic dominance which is also not useful for a foreign tour operator as it can slow down productivity improvements and more sustainable tourism practices.

Partnership and collaboration between LDC governments and private sector can leverage convergent interests. For example, tour operators can provide support to help LDC governments make better use of their tourism assets and potentials. Sometimes, government officials and experts from international organizations approach tourism development from a theoretical point of view and experience difficulties in regard to product specification and market development. What can very much be missing is a business development plan and tourism operational perspective seen from a tourism operator with regional commercial presence.

Partnership and collaboration also require competitors to work with each other, and different sectors to cooperate with each other. Economies of scale can be gained by businesses working together and transparent partnership approach can help engage all stakeholders with the support of government.

## CONCLUSION AND RECOMMENDATIONS

Tourism is an opportunity for both LDC governments and for tourism operators. This is confirmed by the recent trends in tourism development showing the increase of tourists travelling around the world. As a sector with potential, tourism is an opportunity for LDC governments to create jobs,

*Table 1: Business and Government needs and offers (Authors own elaboration)*

| | **What are their needs?** | **What can they offer?** |
|---|---|---|
| **Tourism Operators** | -A predicable investment environment with clear rules<br>-Basic infrastructure (roads, etc.)<br>-High quality standards<br>-Low transaction costs<br>-Revenues and profits | -Jobs<br>-Economic dynamism<br>-Creation of local suppliers<br>-Spillover effect on other economic sectors<br>-Know how<br>-Foreign investments<br>-Tax revenues |
| **Government** | -Economic growth<br>-Create sustainable jobs<br>-Reduce poverty<br>-Ensure that benefits from FDI are re-distributed<br>-Ensure consumers´ access to goods and services | -Tourism assets (new markets)<br>-Competitive enabling environment for investment<br>-Support for SMEs willing to link up the tourism value and supply chain<br>-Provision of specific skills required by industry<br>-Infrastructure for improving the movement of travelers from the airport to tourist attractions<br>-stable and safe environment |

reduce poverty and foster economic growth. At the same time, the unexploited potential of tourism in non-traditional destinations can create opportunities for tourism operators searching for new markets and offering new tourism products.

Performance of the tourism industry depends on many different factors, ranging from infrastructure, local attractions, security, health conditions and the quality of services. To get all these factors right for the tourism industry, the role of government in setting the policy environment, investment conditions and market conditions in general is critical for the effective operation of tourism industry. Incoherence or fragmentation in regard to governmental vision, strategy, policies and actions can however become barriers which prevent LDCs from achieving sustained and successful tourism development. A minimum coherence among the various policy instruments and complementarity is needed to foster a more comprehensive development of the sector.

In order to improve the economic performance of the tourism industry in LDCs, greater efforts are needed to improve tourism infrastructure including physical (roads, transportation) as well as other soft and human factors (e.g. managerial competence, service quality, food security and hygiene). Equally important is the development

of cultural and creative industries. Strengthening these different elements requires an overarching strategic plan, concerted investments and political leadership; otherwise countries risk an increase in fragmentation and ineffectiveness in their tourism plans.

Tourism strategies require intense coordination among ministries including those with mandates not directly related to tourism, but which nevertheless govern policies that impact the tourism industry.[10] None of the countries assessed in the authors´ recent study showed evidence of an institutionalized Inter-Ministerial Coordination (IMC) process (Saner, 2010)[11], whether in terms of mechanisms, procedures and guidelines for institutional leadership. LDCs need process monitoring systems to keep abreast of current practice which in turn provides them with the possibility to continuously improve institutional performance and organizational learning.

In order to maximize the benefits of tourism investments, the LDC governments should design and implement sector specific strategies which define objectives to be met because governments need to provide the right conditions for business to operate efficiently while, at the same time, ensure that the benefits of the tourism investments reach a large part of their population. In other words,

LDC governments need to provide enabling conditions for business, reduce profit leakage and externalities, and ensure that tourism investments create jobs and opportunities for the local communities. The role of the public sector in tourism development should encompass infrastructural investment; registration, grading and inspection; development planning; manpower planning and training; destination marketing; enterprise development; and security awareness.

When a company invests in an LDC, negotiations are not simple business-to-business negotiations but instead consist of business-to-government and government-to-business negotiations. Both parties need to obtain negotiated agreements that are mutually beneficial and sustainable. Information on decision making at the government level is crucial for tourism operators and investors. In many cases, in countries such as LDCs, it is not clear who the focal point is in the government administration nor which is the area or ministry with which a company needs to interact in order to channel its demands and ensure an effective access to the market.

Understanding an LDC government´s tourism strategy is equally important for tourism operators and investors in order to reach better outcomes when negotiating with the government on the conditions to operate in the local tourism market. Regular monitoring can support gathering useful information needed to maintain factual reflections with an LDC government. Gathering information about an LDC national development strategy establishing the general framework and the sector-specific strategy highlighting the governments´ objectives are of utmost importance for tourism operators. A well informed business investor can certainly increase the chances of getting a better outcome from the interactions and negotiations with the government.

Relationships between the public and private sectors need to be based on partnership and collaboration, especially when capital is involved to improve infrastructure. Partnership and collaboration between LDC governments and private sector can leverage convergent interests and help both actors to find mutual positions around divergent interests.

## Recommendation for Tourism Operators and Investors in Tourism in LDCs

- Given the aforementioned challenges, hotel operators and investors entering the market need to effectively collaborate with strong local partners and advisors to mitigate risks. Yet such collaboration needs to observe the established international norms and conventions such as the Organization for Economic Cooperation and Development (OECD) Guidelines for Multinational Enterprises. This is of particular importance as greater transparency and scrutiny by the public for "unethical" or "irresponsible" business conducts.

- Promote joint activities and knowledge exchanges such as workshops to help LDC governments to identify potential tourism assets for future development and to share information on the business requirement for making investment decisions.

- Partnering with other local and global competitors to support the creation of national chambers of commerce for tourism in order to identify common needs and advocating comprehensive tourism development strategy and soft and hard infrastructure investments. Furthermore, such chambers can also support the upgrading of skills, quality standards and deployment of best practices.

- Establishing proper business-to-government channels to ensure that the tour operators´ requests and needs are heard and considered by the government. On the other hand a two way communication and exchange could also facilitate innovation and new business models in developing this sector.

## Recommendation for LDC governments

- Promoting partnership and collaboration with the local tourism industry and foreign tour operators. Inclusive collaboration needs to involve non-business stakeholders in the process in order to ensure the long term interests of the investor and local communities and small businesses will be addressed and sustainability achieved.
- Mobilizing alternative resources including domestic private investors to support the development of transport networks and physical connectivity essential to tourism flows. For the landlocked countries, transport networks with neighboring countries would be essential to increase the number of incoming tourists and the shares of revenue per tourist in the destination country. Reducing financial leakage and negotiating better conditions from foreign investments can also help finance some of the essential infrastructure investment. Private-Public Partnerships can also be considered if the government has the "maturity" to manage and regulate such modalities.
- Supporting a forum for the tourism sector to work more closely with other sectors vital to tourism industry. Consultation can improve the service or product provisions by the connected sectors which increase the value of tourism investment such as hotels, game parks and other tourist attractions.
- Implementing structural reforms to reduce bureaucracy and red tapes and to prevent corruptions and other self-destructive practices such as the conflicting requirements of different government offices. The latter is essential to achieve coherent public investment programmes to ensure sustainable development of the tourism industry.

- Strengthening linkages of the national tourism industry with other sectors of the national economy. Tourism creates demands in its own right for diverse products and service inputs. It also provides spin-off business opportunities for other secondary services, from health services, banking to training and other cultural and festive programmes and activities. Hence, strong links would facilitate greater dynamism of the sector and higher turnover and circulation of financial benefits.
- Improving the quality infrastructure of the country, including the provision of laboratory testing services for product safety and skill development, which is essential to safeguard health conditions, sanitation and food safety on the one hand, meeting performance standards on the other.

## REFERENCES

African Development Bank. (2014). *Tunisia Country Strategy Paper: General Framework for Development*. Retrieved May 7 from http://www.afdb.org/fileadmin/uploads/afdb/Documents/Project-and-Operations/2014-2015_-_Tunisia_Interim_Country_Strategy_Paper.pdf

Arezki, R., Cherif, R., & Piotrowski, J. (2009). Tourism Specialization and Economic Development: Evidence from the UNESCO World Heritage List. *IMF Working Paper 176*

Ashley, C., De Brine, P., Lehr, A., & Wilde, H. (2007). The Role of Tourism Sector in Expanding Economic Opportunity. *Economic Opportunity Series*, John F. Kennedy School of Government, Overseas Development Institute and International Business Leaders Forum. Retrieved May 7, 2014, from http://www.hks.harvard.edu/m-rcbg/CSRI/publications/report_23_EO%20Tourism%20Final.pdf

Camillo, A., Minguzzi, A., Presenza, A., & Holt, S. (in press). Natural Environmental Sustainability and Micro-Tourism Destinations. *The Case of Southern Italy.*

Central Bank of Lesotho. (2012). *CBL Economic Review.* May, No.142. Retrieved May 7, 2014, from http://www.centralbank.org.ls/publications/MonthlyEconomicReviews/2012/May%20 2012%20ER.pdf

CSEND. (2010). *Inter-ministerial Coordination and Stakeholder Consultation of Trade Policy Making.* Presented at CSEND-CUTS Book Vernissage, Geneva. Retrieved May 7, 2014, from http://www.csend.org/images/articles/files/20100730-PresentationBookVernissage7.pdf

CSEND. (2011). Mainstreaming Tourism Development in Least Developed Countries: Coherence and Complimentarity of Policy Instruments. *CSEND Policy Study.* Retrieved May 7, 2014, from http://www.csend.org/images/articles/files/2011%2008%2029_Mainstreaming%20 Tourism%20Development_Full%20Report.pdf

Ernst & Young. (2014). Effectively implementing your tourism strategy. *Global Hospitality Insights: Top Thoughts for 2014.* Retrieved May 7, 2014, from http://www.ey.com/Publication/vwLUAssets/EY_-_Global_hospitality_insights_2014/$FILE/EY-Global-hospitality-insights-2014.pdf

Government of Lesotho. (2012). *Growth and Development Strategic Framework "Towards an accelerated and sustainable economic and social transformation,* pp. 88-91. Retrieved May 7, 2014, from http://www.gov.ls/documents/NSDP%20 FINAL%20PRINT%20VERSION%2013%20 01%202013[1].pdf

Honeck, D. (2011). ΄Expect the Unexpected΄? LDC GATS Commitments as Internationally Credible Policy Indicators? The Example of Mali., *WTO Staff Working Paper,* ERSD-2011-07. Retrieved May 7, 2014, from http://www.wto.org/english/res_e/reser_e/ersd201107_e.pdf, International Union for Conservation of Nature website. Retrieved May 7, 2014, from http://data.iucn.org/dbtw-wpd/html/tourism/section7.html

Kaplinsky, R. (2004). Spreading the gains from globalization: What can be learnt from value-chain analysis. *Problems of Economic Transition, 47*(2), 74–115.

Lesotho Tourism Development Corporation website. Retrieved May 7, 2014, from, http://www.ltdc.org.ls/organisation.php

Molapo, M. (2013). *Mainstreaming IPoA into National Development Strategies: The Case of Lesotho.* Presented at the Ministry of Development Planning, Lesotho. Retrieved May 7 from http://unohrlls.org/custom-content/uploads/2013/11/Lesotho-Presentation.pdf

PWC website. Retrieved from, http://www.pwc.com/us/en/asset-management/hospitality-leisure/travel-and-tourism.jhtml

Saner, R. (2010). *Trade Policy Governance through Inter-Ministerial Coordination: A Source Book for Trade Officials and Development Experts.* Dordrecht: Republic of Letters Publishing.

Tanzania's Ministry of natrual Resources and Tourism (2012). *Tourism Master Plan – Strategy and Actions,* p.68. Retrieved May 7, 2014, from http://www.tzonline.org/pdf/tourismmasterplan.pdf

The Travel Foundation. (2002). *Tourism supply chains.* Retrieved May 7, 2014, from, http://www.thetravelfoundation.org.uk/images/media/5._Tourism_supply_chains.pdf

United Nations Economic Commission for Africa. (2008). *Sustainable Development Report on Africa*. Retrieved May 7, 2014, from http://www.uneca.org/eca_resources/publications/books/sdra/SDRAfull.pdf

United Nations Environment Programme website. Retrieved from http://www.unep.org/resourceefficiency/Business/SectoralActivities/Tourism/FactsandFiguresaboutTourism/ImpactsofTourism/EconomicImpactsofTourism/NegativeEconomicImpactsofTourism/tabid/78784/Default.aspx

United Nations World Tourism Organization. (2010). *Tourism Highlights*. Retrieved May 7, 2014, from http://www.unwto.org/facts/eng/pdf/highlights/UNWTO_Highlights10_en_HR.pdf

United Nations World Tourism Organization website. Sustainable Tourism – Eliminating Poverty (ST-EP) Programme Retrieved May 7, 2014, from http://www.unwtostep.org/

World Economic Forum. (2013). *The Africa Competitiveness Report*. Retrieved May 7, 2014, from http://www3.weforum.org/docs/WEF_Africa_Competitiveness_Report_2013.pdf

World Trade Organization. United Nations World Tourism Organization & Organization for Economic Cooperation and Development (2013). *Aid for Trade and Value Chains in Tourism*. Retrieved May 7, 2014, from http://www.wto.org/english/tratop_e/devel_e/a4t_e/global_review13prog_e/tourism_28june.pdf, World Bank (2011, October 27). Should we be promoting tourism sector investment? [Web log comment]. Retrieved May 7, 2014, from http://blogs.worldbank.org/psd/should-we-be-promoting-tourism-sector-investment

World Travel and Tourism Council. (2010). *Progress and Priorities Report*. Retrieved May 7, 2014, from http://www.wttc.org/bin/pdf/original_pdf_file/pandp_final2_low_res.pdf

World Travel and Tourism Council. (2013). *Travel & Tourism Economic Impact*. Retrieved May 7, 2014, from http://www.wttc.org/site_media/uploads/downloads/world2013_1.pdf

## ADDITIONAL READING

Adesina, K. I., & Ngozi, E. (2013). Hospitality Business Vs Environmental Sustainability: A Study of Soarak Hotel and Casino Lagos. *International Journal of Science and Research (IJSR)*, India Online ISSN: 2319-7064. Retrieved May 7, 2014, from http://www.ijsr.net/archive/v2i9/MTAwOTEzMDM=.pdf

Sidibé, D., & Saner, R. (2012). Intersection between States and Multinationals in emerging markets, in Amjad Hadjikhani, A., Elg, U. & Ghauri P. (Eds) International Business and Management; Vol 28; Business, Society and Politics. Emerald Group Publishing Ltd.

United Nations. (2011). *Programme of Action for the Least Developed Countries for the Decade 2011-2020*. Presented at the Fourth United Nations Conference on the Least Developed Countries, Istanbul. Retrieved May 7, 2014, from http://ldc4istanbul.org/uploads/IPoA.pdf

World Economic Forum. (2013). *World Travel and Tourism Competitiveness Report*. Retrieved May 7, 2014, from http://www3.weforum.org/docs/WEF_TT_Competitiveness_Report_2013.pdf

## KEY TERMS AND DEFINITIONS

**Business Strategy:** Means by which it sets out to achieve its desired objectives). It can simply be described as a long-term business planning.

**Inter-Ministerial Coordination:** Co-ordination and co-operation among ministries and numerous policy actors. It is crucial to ensure coherence and complementarity in trade policy making and implemention.

**Investment:** Action or process of investing money for profit.

**Leakage:** Negative economic impacts of tourism in the local economy

**Least Developed Countries:** Countries that, according to the United Nations, exhibit the lowest indicators of socioeconomic development, with the lowest Human Development Index ratings of all countries in the world.

**Supply Chain:** Sequence of processes involved in the production and distribution of a commodity.

**Tourism Backward and Forward Linkages:** Intersectional forward and backward relationships between tourism sector and the non- tourism industries.

**Tourism Development:** Planning and implementation of strategies with the objective to develop the tourism sector.

**Value Chain:** Process or activities by which a company adds value to an article, including production, marketing, and the provision of after-sales services

## ENDNOTES

[1]   Adapted from Lesotho (Molapo, 2013).

[2]   Adapted from Tunisia´s Country Strategy (African Development Bank, 2014).

[3]   These sector-specific objectives were adapted, as an example, from Lesotho´s National Strategic Development Plan 2012-2017. These objectives are similar to those of any other LDC government.

[4]   Adapted from Lesotho´s tourism specific objectives (Government of Lesotho, 2012).

[5]   Adapted from Tanzania´s Tourism Master Plan. (Tanzania´s Ministry of natrual Resources and Tourism, 2012).

[6]   East African Community (EAC), Commission de la Communauté Economique et Monétaire de l´Afrique Centrale (CEMAC), Economic Community Of West African States (ECOWAS) and Common Market for Eastern and Southern Africa (COMESA).

[7]   Details of these RTAs containing specific elements to tourism include the following: integrate environmental management and conservation measures in a all developmental activities; standardize hotel classifications, harmonize professional standards of agents in the tourism and travel industry within the community; coordination of marketing of quality tourism into and within the community, joint promotion of products portraying natural and socio cultural values of the region; facilitate movement of travelers; framework for tourism statistics; promote establishment of efficient tourism enterprises; and establish training institutions.

[8]   For an analysis on the value chain in LDCs, see Saner, R., Yiu L. & Bhatia, A. (2009). *Commodity Development Strategies in the Integrated Framework*. UNDP Study, p11. Retrieved May 7, 2014, from http://www.undp.org/content/dam/aplaws/publication/en/publications/poverty-reduction/poverty-website/commodities/commodity-development-strategies-full/Commodities%20in%20the%20IF%20Study%20UNDP.pdf

[9]   Global The International Briefing website (2012), "Countries should understand the huge economic benefits of travel and tourism", http://www.global-briefing.org/2012/10/countries-should-understand-the-huge-economic-benefits-of-travel-and-tourism/

[10]  For concrete recommendations for LDC governments to develop the tourism industry, see the CSEND document adopted by the Sub- Committee on LDCs and Council for Trade in Services (WT/COMTD/LDC/18, S/C/W/328), available from http://docsonline.wto.org/GEN_viewer-window.asp?http://docsonline.wto.org:80/DDFDocuments/t/WT/COMTD/LDC18.

doc. For more information on IMC and tourism development see information and documents of two Round Tables organized by CSEND in 2010 and 2011 respectively, available from the following links: http://www.csend.org/announcements/whats-new/256-round-table-at-wto-on-sustainable-tourism and http://www.csend.org/related-information/280-2nd-round-table-on-tourism

[11] See also CSEND (2009). Inter-Ministerial Coordination in Trade Policy Making, November 2011, *Policy Brief no. 6.* Retrieved May 7, 2014, from http://www.csend.org/images/articles/files/20111130rev-Policy_Note_IMC-Tourism_UNCTAD_DOHA_2012_LSY_RS.pdf

# Chapter 14
# Diversity in Hotel Industry:
## Satisfaction, Teamwork

**Andri Georgiadou**
*University of Hertfordshire, UK*

**Chryso Iasonos**
*London South Bank University, UK*

## ABSTRACT

*Managing human resources in the hospitality industry is a challenging task. In today's competitive environment, an increasing number of organizations invest in promoting diversity in the workplace. The concept of diversity as a value is based on the recognition, acceptance, and respect. It implies understanding that each individual is unique and recognizing and valuing the individual differences. Therefore, it is very important to understand "how diversity impacts individual and team processes and outcomes in the workplace". This chapter introduces the notion of diversity in hotel industry: its role, its interrelationship with satisfaction and teamwork. Emphasis is given on the fact that the right to difference and diversity should be incorporated not only in the whole range of processes, strategies, and actions of the company but also within the corporate culture.*

## INTRODUCTION

The prevailing competitive environment stimulates the need for establishing a business strategy in which each stakeholder is involved, not only those who hold leading positions in a company (Brown, Squire & Lewis, 2010). Research indicates that by investing in the development of an effective human resource management mechanism, a significant positive contribution to the performance the organization is generated (Caulkin, 2001;

Nicu, 2012). Managing human resources in the hospitality industry is conditioned by specific characteristics, including labor and customer's diversity and formation of dissimilar groups of professionals. These has led researchers to endeavour to fill the gap in existing knowledge, based on the assumption that organizations can only achieve their strategic objectives if they fully utilize the potential of their working groups (Dreachlin, 1999, 2007). However, there is ample evidence supporting the idea that group members do not

DOI: 10.4018/978-1-4666-8606-9.ch014

realise and perceive teamwork similarly, hence causing effective human resource management to be even more challenging (Doran, 2003).

In light of this, in this chapter we introduce the notion of diversity in hotel industry: its role, its interrelationship with satisfaction and teamwork, whereas we conclude emphasizing that the right to difference and diversity should be incorporated not only in the whole range of processes, strategies, and actions of the company but also within the corporate culture.

## DIVERSITY IN HOTEL INDUSTRY

In today's competitive environment, an increasing number of organizations invest in promoting diversity in the workplace. Therefore, it is very important to understand *"how diversity impacts individual and team processes and outcomes in the workplace"* (Harrison & Sin, 2006, pp. 191). The role of diversity in workplaces has been widely discussed in the field of organizational studies. Diversity has been claimed to impact team effectiveness (Harrison & Sin, 2006), whilst diverse work teams were found to attain high value to organizations. Literature highlights that diversity provides benefits that increase success. Given the multicultural and globalised perspective of the hospitality industry (Korjala, 2012), diversity management practices can offer organizations advantages in facilitating transactions with customers (Hicks-Clarke & Iles, 2000), and by committing to diversity, businesses' reputation and corporate image can be effectively enhanced (Roberson & Park, 2007).

Hospitality plays an important role in the economy of a country– often constitutes its backbone. According to Reisinger (2009), hospitality and tourism organizations operate in a very complex multicultural tourism environment and thus they cannot afford to neglect understanding and capturing individuals' perception on culture nor underestimate the role of the national cul-

ture. While most managers recognize the value and importance of culture, they find it difficult, if not impossible, to successfully link culture to diversity so that it becomes viable and leads to the achievement of the strategic objectives. Literature highlights that traditional organisational cultures and systems include factors that create significant barriers and constraints to successful diversity management. In general however, the organizational competitiveness lies significantly on the ability to manage cultural diversity in a workplace and communicate effectively across cultures (Okoro & Washington, 2012, pp.58).

Carbery, Garavan, O'Brien and McDonnell (2003), state that a combination of demographic, human capital and psychological attributes contributes to employees' job satisfaction and retention. Nevertheless, changes in workplace demographics have played a major role on stimulating scholar's interest to investigate diversity within the hotel industry and especially its impact on employees' satisfaction. As Franek and Vecera (2008) state, employees' satisfaction is subject to the diversification of employees' aspirations and needs; it fluctuates when one group of employees starts to desire differently from what another group is seeking.

## Individuals and Diversity in the Hotel Industry

Individuals provide organizations with an identity since they maintain and support the company's subsistence. By the same token, the effectiveness of the organization is a function of the knowledge and diverse characteristics of its workforce. When employees are actively engaged in the decision making process, then their sense of belonging is enhanced resulting in a more natural immersion in the corporate culture. Researchers have argued persuasively that the latter facilitates the significant increase of employees' productivity and satisfaction.

The diverse nature of the workforce requires the elimination of any form of discrimination that can find fertile ground within a working environment. Diversity, equality and inclusion are necessary for the competitiveness of contemporary organisations, whereas their benefits are distinct at each operational level. Ensuring a diverse human capital and the provision of equal opportunities, can only benefit the hospitality and tourism organization when and if the requisite conditions that promote diversity and equal treatment of employees within this environment are ensured. The configuration of a corporate culture from which any form of discrimination is absent requires the active participation of the human resources department and the design of a respective strategy that enhances and safeguards equality within the company.

Companies, whose organisational culture and climate promote and embrace diversity, identify numerous prospects for escalating their services. The literature reveals a number of promotional campaigns designed to gain market share through covering new market segments and conventionally underrepresented cultural groups. A number of these initiatives were designed to increase access to and awareness of existing services to these groups. Under the umbrella of the increasing social responsibility awareness, such initiatives are not only motivated by the objective to augment profitability, but are also considered as a means to improve the corporate image by promoting social inclusion, diversity and equality within the workplace.

The concept of diversity has been interpreted and presented in a variety of ways and has been the subject of the research agenda for many scholars. Jackson (1996) argued that the term diversity was used as an umbrella to highlight the presence of different characteristics between groups' members and to illustrate the changing demographic characteristics in the workforce. Diversity may be defined as the set of all the dimensions where the employee is differentiated with respect to the role, function-

ing and personality. Managing diversity refers to the utilization of people of different genders, ages, skills and cultural backgrounds, ultimately aiming to develop genuine relationships between different people in the workplace. If diversity contributes to maximizing a competitive advantage as these researches assert, a significant issue for research is the creation of a positive diversity climate to enhance the operational strategy, using the various policies and procedures of human resource management as the main tools.

When a group is formed, its members are likely to have elements and attributes that differentiate one member from another. There are several classifications for the source of diversity within team members. Therefore, individual differences may be divided into the directly recognizable differences (surface features) such as age, ethnicity and gender, (Bowers et al., 2000). Following are the less obvious characteristics (deeper features) such as personality, knowledge, skills and abilities, values and beliefs, then the job oriented differences such as knowledge and skills, experience and seniority in the company and finally, are the differences related to human relations (less job oriented) such as some personality traits. It is evident that these attributes cannot be exclusively categorized in a single category. The superficial characteristics are the ones that are immediately shown during the formation of a team. For example, we know that the team consists of two men and three women. On the other hand, the deeper traits appear throughout the long-term behavior of each individual and via its interactions with other members.

Harrison, Price, Gavin and Florey (2002) claimed that as cooperation among team members develops, the more any negative effects of surface characteristics are reduced, while the effects, either positive or negative, of the underlying characteristics are increased. This implies that it is likely that at first distrust among members of different sexes or nationalities could arise, but as members start to know each other and become more familiar, these differences disappear. Nevertheless, when some negative personality features come up, then as time passes the problems will grow, since personality is relatively stable in the human life and thus it is difficult to change. They also revealed that the surface traits have no influence in forming an opinion on the deeper features. For instance, nationality will have no impact on the members' ability to draw conclusions about the beliefs or competencies of an individual. Of course, this might be questioned, because on many occasions we tend to treat some people stereotypically, thus drawing hasty conclusions regarding them only because they belong to a particular category.

Differences in deeper characteristics like personality, knowledge and skills, if properly managed, can constitute a competitive advantage for the team, since it will allow the best utilization of each member' contribution (Roberson and Park, 2007). The surface features, if not overcome, are likely to lead to low cohesion of the group, frequent replacement of members, social isolation, and lack of identification of members with the group and therefore miscommunication and poor dedication, which will eventually result in poor performance.

## DIVERSITY MANAGEMENT, SATISFACTION, AND TEAMWORK

In business terms, diversity can be described as "a set of differences of individual traits including socio demographic variables and professional variables, which can be found in an organisation's various levels." (Panaccio and Waxin, 2010, p.54).

A perusal of the literature indicates that, there are still hospitality and tourism organizations that cannot understand the significance and rationale of considering diversity. The most common and typical answer to this could be that discrimination is an erroneous tactic to follow, both morally and legally. Other than this perspective, currently another concept appears to be gaining more ground; the business case for diversity. A plethora of scholars argues that a diverse workforce can increase the

effectiveness of the company towards achieving its goals and accomplishing its mission. The effective management of diversity can provide a greater access to new market segments, promote morale, and enhance job satisfaction and productivity.

Considering diversity has progressed since the 1980s, when the term was mainly used as a reference to employed women and minorities (Ely and Thomas, 2001). Back then, it was common for the upper echelons to consider diversity in the workplace as a way to pay greater attention to gender, national and cultural representation in the recruitment and retention of people coming from underrepresented social groups. As Cook and Glass (2009) revealed, "the similarity attraction model builds on social identity theory to suggest that in-group preferences often lead to evaluation bias. In work organisations, implicit preferences often lead to homophile in which individuals promote those most similar to themselves in terms of demographic characteristics and cultural and social background" (Cook and Glass, 2009, p. 395). In 1964, the U.S. Government based on constitutional amendments, requested businesses to employ more women and people that were considered as minorities, while giving them greater opportunities to ascend the organisational hierarchical ladder. In 2010, the Equality Act ensured that no individual could be discriminated against within their potential or current working environment, with regard to their age, belief, gender, race or sexuality (Equality Act, 2010; Gittinger and Fisher, 2004).

In light of this, experts on issues of diversity began to express doubts on the effectiveness and role of the proposed affirmative action. They observed that it was often used only within the HR department and was not applied to the entire organisational environment, nor did it consist of an integral part of the organisational culture. At first, they were establishing some very creative recruitment methods towards changing the human medley in organisations. However, the flow of labour renewal was often peculiarly high and actually, minority groups and women were not given the opportunity for professional development, as originally planned. They were often stigmatized by colleagues and superiors in the workplace as unsuitable candidates for promotion. The dominant group of white Anglo-Saxon men perceived diversity management as a disguised form of invalid discreet discrimination. Any training and educational programs of diversity management and equal opportunities in companies were therefore abandoned or abolished.

The necessity for moving and establishing diversity policies beyond the strict boundaries of the human resource department is manifest in a study conducted by the European Commission (2003, p. 3), under the name "Costs and Benefits of Diversity". As stated in this study, companies that establish and promote diversity policies enjoy a number of important benefits, including reinforcing the company's cultural values, enhancing their corporate image and helping to recruit and retain highly talented people. By the same token, they provide their employees with greater incentives, and thus produce higher productivity and performance, whilst also enhancing innovation and creativity among employees. The most important aspect of the aforementioned reimbursements that companies have embraced is that they consider the company as an entity and not just one part of it.

As globalization has generally elicited diversity and unambiguously cultural diversity as an integral part the daily business functions and operations, none organization can be justified if ignoring it. The gap that could be noticed among the customs, cultural values, perceptions and ways of communicating the feelings of the hotel's employees, could have an impact on the performance, the establishment of effective communication channels and the team's coherence. Therefore, it is crucial for scholars to develop and identify the method by which hotels will be able to manage the inevitable presence of diversity, in order for the team to remain united and in total alignment with the core values of the organization (Shapiro, Young Von Glinow & Cheng, 2005).

## Job Satisfaction

One of the major issues that hotel managers are called to address is to measure the satisfaction of both customers and employees. Perusal to the literature (Khalilzadeh, Chiappa, Jafari, & Borujeni, 2013), selecting the ideal instrument for measuring employee satisfaction in a business can be a debilitating process, since although there are a number of available measurement tools, they all have limitations in size, properties, and usage. Hence, there is no simple answer to the questions of researchers seeking the best tool for measuring satisfaction; obviously, it depends on the individual, on how the researcher wants to determine the measurement, and unsurprisingly on the aim underpinning the investigation.

Job satisfaction is usually determined by surveying upon the feelings of employees towards their work using questionnaires and interviews. In this way, employees are given the opportunity to indicate whether they are satisfied or not by their working environment. Using several scales in the questionnaire the degree of satisfaction can be calculated and thus the job satisfaction and workplace morale can be estimated.

There are several definitions for the concept of job satisfaction. In particular, according to Wright and Davis (2003) job satisfaction is the pleasant or positive state, which derives from the job evaluation, appraisal or simply by the job experience. Previously, scholars argued that job satisfaction reflects an interactive process between employees and their working environment, which results in a positive or negative effect, depending on the degree of fulfilling their expectations. Moreover, researchers classified satisfaction into two main categories, internal and external. Internal satisfaction, derives from the opportunity of enhancing employees' capacities, respecting their feelings and recognizing their effort; whereas external satisfaction is related with the corporate culture, promotion schemes, wages, remuneration and bonuses.

By and large, increased employee satisfaction motivates employees to participate more actively in the business and therefore they are more likely to take actions that will result in increased customer satisfaction and profitability. Research has shown that the most satisfied employees better meet the needs of individual visitors, which increase the overall level of satisfaction of the guests. So customers will recognize the excellent services provided attributable to high job satisfaction (Spinelli & Canavos, 2000).

## Teamwork

Many theories derived from the field of psychology, sociology, psychoanalysis and anthropology, are trying to describe and explain the phenomena of teams. Each theory approaches the issue through a different perspective; still none appears to effectively explain it all, and none can be regarded as absolutely correct and objective. Each theoretical approach contributes in its own way and through its own principles and perspectives in the common assumption of knowledge and in the interpretation of teams and of phenomena taking place within them.

Group Dynamics concerns a thorough analysis and study of the developmental trail of a team by examining the forces that are deployed both internally and externally and contribute either positively or negatively towards the achievement of its objectives. Through the recording of data and information, Group Dynamics enables us to foresee the potential trail of different groups in different contexts and situations. However, predictability is relevant insofar as minor alterations within the team are able to have serious impacts on its progress and its effectiveness.

Within a team, members are provided with a number of stimuli either through their colleagues

or the methods, the techniques and the materials with which the team is working, but also by the external environment. These stimuli are either addressed to one or more of the members of the team – for example an encouragement message to a specific individual.

A team can encourage or discourage an individual, can stimulate or suppress it, can induce or prevent it from specific acts. It can even inspire a particular behavior by providing reinforcing stimuli, fees and rewards. The team, however, can indirectly influence the behavior of its members, influencing the formation of their attitudes and beliefs.

Focusing attention on the teamwork, being the ability to effectively work and cooperate within groups, where the result is considered to be more than just the sum of the efforts of the individual members, it can be considered as the most crucial contribution towards the achievement of the overall business mission and vision of the hotel. By and large, effective teamwork promotes communication, a sense of belonging, loyalty and commitment, whilst it provides learning opportunities, thus increasing creativity, innovation, engagement and satisfaction.

According to Kinlaw (1991), teamwork is the way in which people must work and cooperate together in order to produce services that could not be produced by a single individual. To this end, teams appear to have a synergy effect, which implies that the total outcome that is produced by the team is by far more than the equivalent result which the sum of the team's part would have had. By and large, the formation of groups is very useful for the organization and its members, because they perform important tasks. Johnson, Kikora and Kantner (1990) support the rationale of forming groups through the following arguments:

1. Individuals within the team know each other well, thus deploying confidence and trust, which results in cooperation and support.

2. Teamwork promotes and establishes effective communications channels within the members of the team.

Daft (1996) considers the formation of teams as critical and immense for the effectual elaboration of a task, since teams:

1. Encourage and promote creativity and innovation.
2. Are more effective problem solving devices as opposed to individuals.
3. Enhance the dedication and commitment needed to implement the decisions
4. Provide greater opportunities for interaction and
5. Increase the coherence within their members.

When an employee changes position within a company, he or she ultimately changes ways of thinking, in accordance with the effects of the new position and his or her moods change until they come closer to the norms of the new team. Various groups within a company, serve different work-related and personal-related functions. A group gives its members the opportunity to fulfill the security needs, social needs, and the needs of self-fulfillment and self-esteem they may have. Namely, participation in the group gives the person a sense of security and safety, the ability to create friendships and prove their skills, gain recognition and acceptance, which might not otherwise have. On the other hand, a group can potentially experience conflicts, disagreements that may lead to strain and poor performance.

According to Steiner (1972), team performance depends on the nature of the ongoing project whereas he even advocated that the actual performance of a group is usually lower than the potential performance. The potential performance of a group depends on the available human resources and the requirements of the project to be executed. The difference between the potential and actual performance lead to procedural losses,

which may be due to loss of coordination, lack of proper organization of individual efforts, loss of motivation; that is failure of members in the group to pay sufficient effort.

When employees predispose positive feelings towards their work, then they tend to accept its norms and values and are influenced by them. Conversely, when the person is disappointed and nourishes negative experiences and feelings, then he or she generally opposes to work and the organization.

## CONCLUSION

The concept of diversity as a value is based on the recognition, acceptance, and respect. It implies understanding that each individual is unique and recognizing and valuing the individual differences. These can be developed around different personality dimensions related to race, ethnicity, gender, sexual orientation, socioeconomic status, age, natural and physical abilities, language, religious and political beliefs, or other ideologies. Diversity as a value is aligned with the exploration, recognition, and coexistence of these differences in a safe, positive, and supportive environment, particularly in the context of a continuous social coexistence, interaction, and cooperation, such as a contemporary hotel unit.

Today's hotels operate in a complex and constantly changing business environment. The market is now globalised and competitive, profoundly affected by the socio-economical-political environment. Considering that a hotel can attract customers from all over the world, services must be adapted to the needs and desires of a broad range of different people. This development turns to be a bottleneck for companies whose cultures are not inclusive. It compels them to be open to new messages and challenges, requires them to utilize prior knowledge, and in a way obliges them to introduce innovative ideas and strategies. While the phenomenon of multiculturalism in the workplace intensifies, the recruitment policy, standards and attitudes of businesses are still adapted to homogeneous groups of workers. The informal systems often determine choices, decisions, and collaborations. Nowadays many skills and knowledge are lost because people either are excluded from the labor market, or are not exploited to the extent or way they should.

Diversity is inevitable within the hotel industry, but if managed properly it can constitute a significant competitive advantage against rivals. The results of course are contradictory when evaluating various practices in diversity management. This probably implies that there is no one-size-fits-all approach for effectively managing diversity and its impact varies depending on various conditions. This philosophy however, is a valuable tool towards the development of an innovative culture and the improvement of the organizational dynamic. Diversity management broadens the access to markets, attracts new customer groups, and increases productivity. In addition, indirectly, a company that promotes the principle of diversity can improve its image and to reduce the costs for promotion through advertising; the notion of social corporate responsibility.

Recognizing the right to difference and diversity should be incorporated not only in the whole range of processes, strategies, and actions of the company but also within the corporate culture. Systematic respect of these principles helps to cultivate an open and productive working environment, where employees are innovative, responsible, active, energetic, motivated, pioneers, and motivating. Horwitz (2005) concludes that diversity may provide the hotel with a valuable competitive advantage if the different features available to its members are combined correctly when forming the subgroups. Perusal the literature, it is evident that a business must have the potential to be inclusive and coherent, but also differentiated through diversity.

The truth is that it is not easy to analyze and understand the dynamic processes that occur

within a group. Complications always occur as well as and constantly mutating interactions and relationships between the different members of the group over time. In light of this, it is easy to see the need for establishing clear and realistic goals, but also a dynamic leadership that will not be afraid to decisively tackle the difficulties that will arise, nor will hesitate to collide with established perceptions and attitudes. Instead, it will seek to draw lessons that will fortify the hotel with faith and prudence for the future by ensuring a stable gait in the unstable international economic environment.

Besides, the ability to manage diversity in the workplace is not just desired or desirable, but rather a necessary condition for the successful operation and growth of a business. The harmonization of individuals to the modern multicultural reality marks the functionality of the group to achieve goals and exceed obstacles.

## REFERENCES

Act, E. (2010). *Equality Act 2010.* The Equality Act.

Bowers, C., Pharmer, J. A., & Salas, E. (2000). When member homogeneity is needed in work teams: A meta-analysis. *Small Group Research, 31*(3), 305–327. doi:10.1177/104649640003100303

Brown, S., Squire, B., & Lewis, M. (2010). The impact of inclusive and fragmented operations strategy processes on operational performance. *International Journal of Production Research, 48*(14), 4179–4198. doi:10.1080/00207540902942883

Carbery, R., Garavan, T., O'Brien, F., & McDonnell, J. (2003). Predicting hotel managers' turnover cognitions. *Journal of Managerial Psychology, 18*(7), 649–679. doi:10.1108/02683940310502377

Caulkin, S. (2001). The Time is Now. *People Management, 7*(17), 32–34.

Cook, A., & Glass, C. (2009). Between a rock and a hard place: Managing diversity in a shareholder society. *Human Resource Management Journal, 19*(4), 393–412. doi:10.1111/j.1748-8583.2009.00100.x

Daft, R. (1996). *Organizational performance.* New York: Wiley.

Doran, D. M. (2003). *Nursing-Sensitive Outcomes: State of the Science.* Sudbury, MA: Jones and Bartlett.

Dreachlin, J. L., Hunt, P. L., & Sprainer, E. (1999). Communication patterns and group composition: Implications for patient-centred care team effectiveness. *Journal of Healthcare Management, 44*(4), 252–268. PMID:10539199

Dreachslin, J. L. (2007). Diversity Management and Cultural Competence: Research, Practice, and the Business Case. *Journal of Healthcare Management, 52*(2), 79–86. PMID:17447535

Ely, R. J., & Thomas, D. A. (2001). Cultural diversity at work: The effects of diversity perspectives on work group processes and outcomes. *Administrative Science Quarterly, 46*(2), 229–273. doi:10.2307/2667087

European Commission. (2003). *The costs and benefits of the costs and benefits of diversity. A study on methods and indicators a study on methods and indicators to measure the cost-effectiveness to measure the cost-effectiveness of diversity policies in enterprises of diversity policies in enterprises.* [Online]. Available at: http://ec.europa.eu/social/BlobServlet?docId=1440&langId=en (Accessed: 16 May 2014).

Franek, M., & Vecera, J. (2008). Personal characteristics and job satisfaction. *E+M Ekonomie A Management, 4*, 63-75.

Gittinger, T., & Fisher, A. (2004). LBJ champions the Civil Rights Act of 1964. *Prologue-Quarterly Of The National Archives And Records Administration, 36*(2), 10–19.

Harrison, D. A., Price, K. H., Gavin, J. H., & Florey, A. T. (2002). Time, teams, and task performance: Changing effects of surface-and deep-level diversity on group functioning. *Academy of Management Journal, 45*(5), 1029–1045. doi:10.2307/3069328

Harrison, D. A., & Sin, H. S. (2006). What is diversity and how should it be measured? In A. M. Konrad, P. Prasad, & J. K. Pringle (Eds.), *Handbook of workplace diversity* (pp. 191–216). Newbury Park, CA: Sage Publications. doi:10.4135/9781848608092.n9

Hicks-Clarke, D., & Iles, P. (2000). Climate for diversity and its effects on career and organisational attitudes and perceptions. *Personnel Review, 29*(3), 324–345. doi:10.1108/00483480010324689

Horwitz, S. K. (2005). The compositional impact of team diversity on performance: Theoretical consideration. *Human Resource Development Review, 4*(2), 219–245. doi:10.1177/1534484305275847

Jackson, S. E. (1996). The consequences of diversity in multidisciplinary work teams. In M. A. West (Ed.), *Handbook of Work Group Psychology* (pp. 53–76). Chichester, UK: Wiley.

Johnson, P., Kikora, R., & Kantner, M. (1990). *TQM Team- Building and Problem Solving.* Southfield, MI: Perry Johnson, Inc.

Khalilzadeh, J., Chiappa, G. D., Jafari, J., & Borujeni, H. Z. (2013). Methodological approaches to job satisfaction measurement in hospitality firms. *International Journal of Contemporary Hospitality Management, 25*(6), 865–882. doi:10.1108/IJCHM-05-2012-0067

Kinlaw, D. (1991). *Developing Superior Work teams: building quality and the competitive edge.* Lexington, MA: Lexington Books.

Korjala, V. (2012). *Cultural Diversity In Hospitality Management. How to improve cultural diversity workforce* (Bachelor's thesis). Turku University of Applied Science, Finland.

Nicu, I. E. (2012). Human resources motivation - an important factor in the development of business performance. *Annals of the University of Oradea. Economic Science Series, 21*(1), 1039–1045.

Okoro, E., & Washington, M. (2012). Workforce diversity and organizational communication: Analysis of human capital performance and productivity. *Journal of Diversity Management, 7*(1), 57–62.

Panaccio, A. J., & Waxin, M. F. (2010). HRM case study: diversity management: facilitating diversity through the recruitment, selection and integration of diverse employees in a Quebec bank. *Journal of the International Academy for Case Studies, 16*(4), 53–66.

Reisinger, Y. (2009). *International Tourism: Cultures and Behaviors*. New York: Butterworth-Heinemann.

Roberson, Q. M., & Park, H. J.Hyeon Jeong Park. (2007). Examining the link between diversity and performance: The effects of diversity reputation and leader racial diversity. *Group & Organization Management, 32*(5), 548–568. doi:10.1177/1059601106291124

Shapiro, D. L., Young Von Glinow, M. A., & Cheng, J. L. C. (2005). *Managing multinational teams: global perspectives*. Oxford: Elsevier.

Spinelli, M. A., & Canavos, G. C. (2000). Investigating the Relationship between Employee Satisfaction and Guest Satisfaction. *The Cornell Hotel and Restaurant Administration Quarterly, 41*(6), 29–33.

Steiner, D. (1972). *Group process and productivity*. New York: Academic Press.

Wright, B. E., & Davis, B. S. (2003). Job satisfaction in the public sector – the role of the work environment. *American Review of Public Administration, 33*(1), 70–90. doi:10.1177/0275074002250254

## KEY TERMS AND DEFINITIONS

**Diversity:** The set of all the dimensions where the employee is differentiated with respect to the role, functioning and personality.

**Job Satisfaction:** The degree to which individuals are content with their job, or aspects of their job.

**Teamwork:** The ability to effectively work and cooperate within groups.

# Chapter 15
# The Impact of Food Trends on Menu Innovation

**Mazalan Mifli**
*Universiti Malaysia Sabah, Malaysia*

**Rahmat Hashim**
*Universiti Teknologi MARA, Malaysia*

**Artinah Zainal**
*Universiti Teknologi MARA, Malaysia*

## ABSTRACT

*The search for the right 'pedigree' of innovative menus is endless. As the consumer foodservice markets are converging to one global market, increasingly demand for new menus is evitable. In today's global foodservice markets, the fast changing trend of consumers' preferences and acceptances poses a huge challenge for restaurateurs in managing their new menu innovation. Empirically, little is known the trendsetting in managing menu innovation amid facing market uncertainty. While there are several attributes that have been known to impact menu innovation, this chapter specifically aims to provide empirical evidence of the moderating effect of food trends on the link between innovation orientations and new menu development (NMD) process in a recently concluded research study of chain restaurants in Malaysia.*

## INTRODUCTION

Over the years, restaurateurs had managed to tap into trendy menus. In recent years, however, the waves of food trends have been increasingly unpredictable. This poses a great challenge for restaurateurs and chefs to be equipped with latest innovation 'know-how' in managing their new menus innovation. This is because, as globaliza- tion enters a borderless world, diverse trends in global consumer food preferences and acceptances become apparent, and such trends create wider menus repertoires. Yet, innovating what are 'hot' and 'trendy' food items is not an easy business, as nowadays, global consumers are increasingly becoming well-traveled and affluent from a palette standpoint. This issue of concerns poses challenges for menu planners to stay afloat in their business.

DOI: 10.4018/978-1-4666-8606-9.ch015

Simply put, exiting menus that able to capture of today's consumers' preferences may have to be rejuvenate likely unable to sustain longer in the market as new rival competitors with similar menu concept joined the fray (Thompson & Strickland, 1996). Thereby, what is known to be a lucrative menu has turned to a mundane one as the act of 'copy-cat' saturates the consumer market (Jones & Wan, 1992). Such a scenario has led to fierce competition amongst restaurateurs along with new entrants, battling to gain market shares, which in turn make the consumer market reaches its saturation point even quicker. A point that marks the end of the product life cycle in the consumer market largely due to abandon supplies of similar products (Hashimoto, 2003). Strategically, in shaping competition, innovation is widely used to resurrect the curve of the product life cycle upwards (Cobbenhagen, 2000).

Generally, innovation management to new product development (NPD) falls either being driven by radical or incremental orientations. Notably, these two product innovation orientations are widely used across different industries in shaping the NPD process. Theoretically, such a relationship between innovation orientations and NPD process is deemed inseparable as innovation orientation spurs the outcome of the NPD in the marketplace (Drucker, 1985). However, to which innovation orientations to be integrated in shaping the NPD process is also dependent on menu planners' adaptations to the surrounding environmental factors (Ettlie & Subramaniam, 2004). Technological innovations have been widely used across different restaurant sectors in shaping NMD to be more effective and efficient in term of speed, frequency, standardization and consistency (Reid & Sandler, 1992; Nerker & Roberts, 2004). While the use of technological innovations in managing menu innovation has been long incorporated in production of new menus in many ways (Porter, 1985), another external factor that is equally important is the rapid changing trends of global food consumptions.

This chapter then put forward a discussion of the impact of global food trends and its implication for restaurant management. The objective of this chapter is to provide empirical evidence on the impact of food trends, as a moderator, between the links of innovation orientations and NPD process in chain restaurants based on a recently concluded research study in the region of Klang Valley, Selangor, Malaysia. In this chapter, trends of food acceptances, preferences and habits highlighted in literature were qualitatively analyzed, adopting a content analysis method, to identify the emerging themes of global food trends. Seven types of food trends emerged from this analysis, which is shown in Table 1[1], which then used as a framework for the respondents to describe its influences in their recent engagement of menu innovation and development process. In order to accurately assess the moderating effect of food trends on managing menu innovation, in this chapter, Partial Least Square (PLS-SEM) path modeling (or component-based structural equation modeling) was used to estimate the interaction effect and the reflective hierarchical model of NMD process as this would achieve more theoretical parsimony and less model complexity (Chin, 2010; Wetzels, Schoder & Oppen, 2009; Edward, 2001; Mackenzie, Podsakoff & Podsakoff, 2005).

In line with the main objective of this chapter that is to ascertain the impact of food trends when menu planners engage in managing menu innovation, a structural theory is drawn in Figure 1. The inclusion of the moderating variable of food trends, as moderator, on the relationship between the exogenous variables (product innovation orientations) and endogenous variables (concept development) is expected to unveil to what extent has food trends played a role in influencing menu planners when they engage in menu innovation. This chapter is structured in the following manners: the first section discusses on the general perspective of managing menu innovation leading to the theoretical development of the study. It follows then to the trends of food development across the

*Table 1. Data Analysis Map*

| 3. Themes: | Asian flavors | Healthy foods | Freshness and quality | Mediterranean flavors | Build on customer favorites and taste preferences | Experience new and different taste | Something new but have a familiar taste |
|---|---|---|---|---|---|---|---|
| 2. Categories: | Thai Indian Chinese Japanese Malay Korean | Low carbohydrate Low fat Low cholesterol | Consistency Simplicity | Western cuisines | Foreign tourists food preferences and acceptances | Bold flavors Fusion foods | Contrasting flavors Comfort foods |
| | Spicy flavors | Health conscious groups | | Spicy flavors | | | |
| 1. Open codes: Sources: Yee (2002a, 2002b); Bertagnoli (2000); Josaim and Monteiro (2004); Spark et. al (2003); Jones (2002); Harnet (2005); Grest (2004); Euromonitor (2004, 2006; 2012). | | | | | | | |

Note: The numbers at the far left represent the three stages of analysis, moving upwards from the bottom of the figure

globe. The next section is about research method, analysis and results, and ends with the discussion and its implication to management practices.

## MANAGING MENU INNOVATION

Generally, all new menus would undergo some forms of development process either through a structured or unstructured approach. Conceptually, although both approaches are managed differently, they are in fact shared a common goal that is to innovate a new menu that is competitively sustainable in the marketplace and able to gain larger market shares. The notion of these approaches is closely linked to the company's strategic direction along with the adopted innovation orientations in shaping the development of the new menu (Miller, 1985). There are several terminologies, such as proactive, reactive, reaction, rationality, assertiveness and bounded rationality, that are used to denote strategic management orientations, and each of them are carried out differently (Wood & Robertson, 1997; Porter, 1980, 1985; Miller & Friesen, 1984; Cyert & March, 1963). Miles and Snow's (1978) typology of strategic

types, four archetypes – prospectors, analyzers, defenders and reactors – are also known to have closely related to managerial orientations and/ or individual decision-making behaviors toward product-market development.

The notion of these strategic management orientations shed some lights of different managerial orientations in pursing organizations/or individual destiny. In light of this, the decision-making process, depending on which types of managerial orientations being adopted, is influenced by the surrounding external environmental factors, which causes the degrees of 'riskiness' in managing menu innovation differently from one company to another (Abernathy & Clark, 1985; Ettlie & Subramaniam, 2004).

Therefore, in this chapter, models of product innovation and NMD are synthesized. Both of these models posit a two-stage approach, and although, a three-stage model of product innovation model has been hypothesized, the two-stage model is considered theoretical parsimony and widely cited in innovation literature. Furthermore, the application of this two-stage model of product innovation is conceptually similar to NPD model of which the first-stage, which is called concept

*Figure 1. Theoretical Framework*

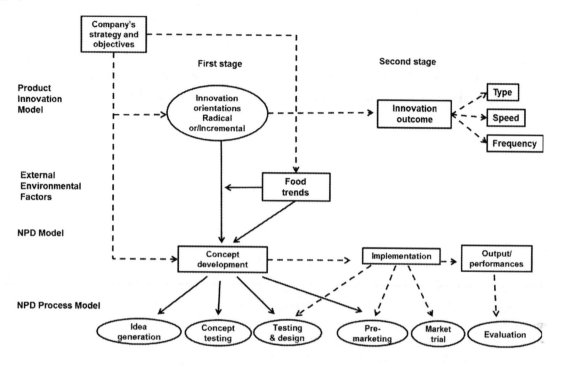

Note: Solid lines represent the relationships that are examined in this study

development, involves the activities of innovation idea generations whilst, the later stage is about the implementations of those selected ideas that have been undergone in several process stages.

In Figure 1, both models of product innovation and NPD are placed parallel along with the NPD process model, which involved various stages. However, the number of stages in NPD process models that are advocated in the literature appear to be unstandardized (e.g. Booz, Allen & Hamilton, 1982; Fuller, 1994; Graf & Saguy, 1991; MacFie, 1994; Kotler & Armstrong, 1991; Urban & Houser, 1993; Feltenstein, 1986; Jones, 1996; Mifli, 2004; Ottenbacher & Harrington, 2007, 2008). Yet, we firmly believe that, since most companies, if not all, face varying degrees of competitions and environmental hostilities, which then responded differently by one firm to another due to adoption of different managerial orientations, variations of stage approaches to NPD process is inevitable.

In theory, the impact of external environmental factors on new product innovation occurs at the first stage where innovation generations are screened and final selection is made along the concept lead time, which is also termed as a 'window of opportunity'. Once the window of opportunity is closed, additional inputs of innovation generations are no longer accepted as the development of the new product enters into the implementation stages. Nevertheless, other theories of NPD, such as the compression, integrative and concurrent models, incorporated the elements of flexibility as opposed to rigid sequential NPD process. In light of this, it is posited that overlapping of activities in-between the two stages is foreseeable. Therefore, in this study, the pre-marketing stage commonly associated with marketing activities in the implementation stage is also added in the first stage of the NPD process. With this proposed structural model, we believe that this new theoretical linkage of food trends, as moderators, on the linear relationship between innovation orientations and concept development, which has never been done empirically, should shed some valuable contributions to knowledge in managing menu innovation and its implication to the industrial practices.

## TRENDS IN MENU DEVELOPMENT

Historically, food development on cross ethnic cuisines has been around since the Middle-Ages. Back then, the Roman nobilities were known to have used different types of spices in their cooking. Importation of food supplies, such as exotic condiments and spices from the Middle East and Asian regions to European nations, had been regarded by many food historians to have high levels of acceptance and recognition in gastronomic perfections (Melis, 1999). Today, as the hype of the new millennium is fastly forgotten, globalization and travelling to a borderless world have since taken over, and cross ethnic cuisines have become even more apparent in consumers' food preferences and acceptances. The flood of ethnic restaurants, such as Thai, Indian, Chinese and Japanese in most major cities in the world 'speak for itself'. The reflection of 'hot and spicy' flavors on restaurants' menus shows that this trend is well receptive across the globe. The flavor of the Mediterranean and other warmer regional areas, such as South America, the Caribbean and Mexico is immensely well-known for its regional cuisines that feature hot and spicy cooking, and known to have been well accepted in other parts of the world (Josaim & Monteiro, 2004). This trend seems to be in line of Spark, Bowen and Klag's (2003) study when they found that many top restaurants in New York, Melbourne and Sydney had their menus with a concept of simplicity by combining both Asian and Mediterranean flavors. It appears that such a menu concept played a key

role in luring tourists to these cities in a pretext of indulging gastronomic perfections.

The trend of healthy foods that started in United State of America (USA) in the 80s also made a profound impact on menu development as health conscious awareness begun to disseminate of its important in the general public minds (Robichaud & Khan, 1988). In the new millennium, the trend of healthy foods begun apparent in food productions as the society across the globe started to perceive of its benefits (Jones, 2002). Development of new menus selections to low fats and cholesterols, such as salads, pasta and chicken options that are perceived as being 'light' and 'healthy' were some of the notable ones undertaken by many major foodservice chains in the United Kingdom (UK) (Bertagnoli, 2000). Review in food journal reveals that the trend towards quality food that is perceived 'fresh' is what drives customers to this menu. Apparently, menus that come with the concept of 'lightness' and 'freshness' that gained a huge momentum in the early years of the millennium were known to resurrect old menus back its popularity (Yee, 2002a). Strategically, according to Yee (2002a), it is to boost existing menu items back to demand as these menus are familiar in the eyes of the consumers, especially to the health conscious groups. This notion of resurrecting old menus by making them look healthy is perhaps could be argued that consumers are likely to feel intimidated when confronting with unfamiliar foods, which may lead to difficulty in food selections (Mifli, 2004).

Thirdly, the uprising comfort foods in the local markets that relates to personal or regional identifications in the local society, inheriting a closed-bond customary of food acceptances and habits. This strong bond of relationships has always been in menu planner's repertoires with a distinctive characteristic of what the customer 'feel-good' to dine as Yee (2002b) states 'comfort food is highly personal, based on customer and generational culinary memories'. Yet, as the local consumers market becomes more diverse, changes in preferences and acceptances of comfort foods begin to follow as well. The apparent changes in demographic patterns in many urban areas across the globe have raised a diverse taste of consumer acceptances for comfort foods in many ways. This, to large extent, poses great challenges for restaurateurs to strategize and differentiate their comfort food definitions. Analogy that states what seems to be today's favorite or customary comfort foods are less likely not be in the near future as the lifestyle of the society become more vibrant. Whilst, some restaurateurs may be able to innovate their comfort food in line to this changing lifestyles, future generation, which is likely to be more educated, well-travelled and even more affluent lifestyles, may again alter the definitions of comfort foods.

Fourthly, recent food development indicated that the sales growth of Asian flavors is significantly gained momentum. It shows that foods from the melting-pot of ethnics Asia-Pacific regions are becoming more 'exotic' (Hartnett, 2005). According to Yee (2002b), ethnic cuisines, such as Thai, Indian, Chinese and Japanese immensely played a big part in global foodservice markets. Yet, Yee (2002b) argues that as consumers become sophisticated, trends towards the concept of 'experience new and different things' become apparent in today's perspective as the global markets are increasingly affluent in palate point of view, gearing for new concepts of exotic flavors. A concept that Hartnett (2005) referred to as a blended of Asian and Mediterranean flavors, which is also known by many as fusion foods. In light of this, it is quite apparent that global food trends toward foods ethnicity has shifted to fusion foods. Hartnett argues that such a trend is seemingly indicated that global foodservice markets, nowadays, also prefer for occasion solutions, and not ethnicity.

Indeed, the wave of food trends is increasingly unpredictable, shifting from one direction to another. Undeniably, restaurant patrons do not just want fresh food on their plates; they want fresh

popular chain restaurants revealed in Restaurants & Institutions that state: "We look at trends, but we also want to make sure the food tastes good…We serve food that appeals to people who watching calories, carbohydrates, fat and cholesterol, and to people who want to indulge on occasion" Such a trend continues that "some innovations incorporate the latest food trends, while others caters to customers' diet and health concerns, or beef up perceived weaknesses in the existing menu…in all cases, the goal is to lure new customers and keep old ones coming back" (Grest, 2004). .

In this chapter, the focus of inquiry of the research study is in Malaysia. Foreign tourist arrivals in this country, to a large extent, have played a key role in diversifying the food repertoires. The overwhelming influx of foreign tourists, mainly from Arab nations, Koreans and other selected Asian countries saw an amalgam of different cuisines that are offered mainly in the region of Klang valley markets. Recent evident suggests that the numbers of foodservice outlets of the Middle Eastern and Latin American concepts have reached to an unprecedented growth in both the full-service restaurants (FSR) and fast food outlets (Euromonitor, 2012). "These foodservice outlets received strong consumer response, attribute to…demand from the increasing number of international travelers…changing local tastes and an increased readiness to explore new cuisines" (Euromonitor, 2004: 8).

## METHODOLOGY

In this study, a new set of questionnaire for food trends and concept development constructs was designed. Existing literature that deemed relevant to the focus of inquiry were synthesized and characteristics of variables suspected to be closely related to represent the respective understudied constructs were put forward, which can be seen in Table 2.

*Table 2. Total of Scale Items Used from Various Relevant Sources*

| Constructs | Characteristics | No. of Items | Sources |
|---|---|---|---|
| Innovation orientations* | Original source | 9 items | Single source |
| Food Trends° | • Asian flavors<br>• Mediterranean flavors<br>• Healthy foods<br>• Freshness and quality<br>• Experience new and different taste<br>• Something new but have a familiar taste<br>• Building on customer favorite and taste preferences | 7 items | Multiple[1] sources |
| Concept development° | **Idea generations**<br>• Culinary magazine<br>• Cooking books<br>• Competitors<br>• Personal experiences<br>• In-house market research<br>• Customer comments/suggestions<br>• Interdepartmental/group meetings<br>**Concept testing**<br>• Customer survey<br>• Focus group<br>• Pre-testing in selected markets<br>**Business analysis**<br>• Recent competition actions amongst rival competitors<br>• Changes in economic conditions<br>• New legislation<br>• Changing demographic patterns<br>• Past and current restaurants' success and failure<br>**Product testing and design**<br>• To convert the concept into an operational entity, testing and re-design are required.<br>• Testing and design of new products are performed by in-house specialists' team.<br>• If in-house specialists are lacking, new ones will be hired or outside consultant is sought.<br>• By introducing new products, design of new production process is required.<br>• By introducing new products, installing new equipment is required.<br>**Preliminary marketing**<br>• In-house panel<br>• Focus group<br>• Market survey<br>• Food testing<br>**Market trials**<br>• Place-card on dining table<br>• Blackboard menu<br>• Promotional campaigns-flyers, trade magazine, etc.<br>• Pre-determined market areas<br>**Customer feedback**<br>• Quality<br>• Price<br>• Value perception<br>• Intent to repurchase<br>• Regularity of patronage | 7 items<br>3 items<br>5 items<br>5 items<br>4 items<br>4 items<br>5 items | Multiple[2] sources |

*Questionnaires were adapted from existing measures in the literature (Salavou & Lioukas, 2003).

°Newly developed variables adopted/extracted from various sources and subjected to appropriate measures of purifications.

[1]Yee, (2002), Yee (2000b), Grest (2004), Bertagnoli (2000), Josaim & Monteiro (2004), Harnet (2005), Spark et al. (2003), Euromonitor (2004, 2006, 2010, 2012).

[2]Feltenstein (1986), Mooney (1994), Jones (1996), Ottenbacher & Harrington (2007, 2008)

To ensure a complete clarity and readiness, a pre-test was conducted by a selected panel of experts who reviewed and revised the draft version of these questionnaires for several times to enhance its content validity. As for the construct of innovation orientations, we replicated Salavou and Lioukas' (2003) by-polar semantic differential measurement scale with minimal adjustment made for the purpose of this study. This type of scale instrument has been used in previous empirical study on product innovation orientation (Abernathy & Clark, 1985), where the characteristics of both incremental and radical orientations were paired side by side, using a 7-point scale.

The research instrument was then piloted, adopting a judgement sampling technique that was deemed appropriated for this pilot study to obtain information from the 'expert' personnel (Sekaran, 2000). A total of 205 established foodservice companies were identified and arrangements for a survey interviewer-completed method were made to interview the expert personnel that directly involved in managing the company's new menu development. 50 companies agreed to participate and a total of 33 companies were successfully interviewed and rests were simply not interested along the process. In accordance to Hair, Black, Babin and Anderson's (2010) exploratory factor analysis (EFA) guidelines, the piloted data was then purified, using Statistical Package for Social Science (SPSS Ver. 19), to enhance and determine its reliability and structural factor of these newly developed five-point measurement scales. All of the multi-item scales measuring variables were factor-analyzed to assess the factorial validity and internal consistency, which is also a form of construct validity (Allen & Yen, 1979).

In Table 3, the results of the EFA that considered significant with value of Kaiser-Meyer-Okin (KMO) statistic at 6.0 and based on factor loadings of the variables at or greater than 0.5 and anti-image correlation matrix cut-off value of 0.5 were retained (Kline, 2005; Tabachinck & Fidell, 2001; Comrey & Lee, 1992; Nunnally, 1978; Malhotra

1996). In addition, raw scores of individual items pertaining to factors extracted, using Principle component analysis (PCA) method, were summed in each dimension/construct to arrive at overall measures along with the minimum acceptable Cronbach's Alpha values of 0.60 (Nunnaly, 1978).

The final research instrument comprised of five parts. First, the original version of Salavou and Lioukas' (2003) by-polar semantic differential seven-point scale was adopted with minimal adjustment to denote respondents' product innovation orientations. Second, the five themes of food trends that were retained, using a five-point Likert scale ranging from 'greatly influenced' to 'hardly any influenced' and 'greatly influenced' to 'not at all' respectively. Third, the stage-approach to NPD construct was measured using a five-point Likert scale ranging from 'very often' to 'never' for the dimensions of idea generation and pre-marketing, and 'very important' to 'not at all important' and 'strongly agree' to strongly disagree' were used for the dimensions of product concept testing and product testing and design respectively. Finally, the demographic variables of the subjects, such as gender, age groups, education levels, etc, and business information, such as business tenure, restaurant type, etc. were measured.

At the time of final data collection, there were nearly four thousand chained outlets in operated across major cities in Malaysia by 112 local and international chained companies (Euromonitor, 2010). Notably, most of these chained outlets, particularly in the fast food sector, are internationally brand ownerships that made possible through franchising agreements. In terms of brand names and numbers of outlets, the full-service restaurant (FSR) sector dominated the most with 86 brands and more than 1200 outlets followed by fast food (21/1000+), café's/bars (7/160), street stalls/kiosks (2/108) and 100% home delivery/takeaway (1/19). Out of these 112 chained companies, a total of 71 data was successfully collected that took almost a year to complete.

*Table 3. Results of Preliminary Statistical Purifications*

| Construct: Food Trends | | | |
|---|---|---|---|
| | | | Loading |
| Healthy foods | | | .544 |
| Freshness and quality | | | .664 |
| Experience new and different taste | | | .611 |
| Something new but have a familiar taste | | | .755 |
| Building on customers favorites and taste preferences | | | .811 |
| | | | |
| % of total variance explained | | | 46.76 |
| Coefficient alpha | | | .65 |
| Number of items | | | 5 |
| Table 3a. Extraction method: Principle component analysis (PCA) | | | |

| Construct: Concept development | Pattern Matrix[a] | | | |
|---|---|---|---|---|
| (Coefficient Alpha for scale:0.69) | F1 | F2 | F3 | F4 |
| Factor 1: Idea generation | | | | |
| Culinary magazines | .653 | | | |
| Cooking books | .751 | | | |
| Meeting to discuss market trends | .870 | | | |
| Value perception | .693 | | | |
| Factor 2: Concept testing | | | | |
| Competitors | | .903 | | |
| Testing and design are performed by in-house specialist team | | .772 | | |
| Food testing | | .677 | | |
| Regular customer | | .747 | | |
| Factor 3: Product testing and design | | | | |
| To convert the concept into operational entity, testing & design is required | | | .868 | |
| By introducing new product, design of new production process is required | | | .901 | |
| Factor 4: Pre-marketing | | | | |
| Customer survey | | | | .873 |
| In-house panel | | | | .641 |
| Place-card on dining table | | | | .723 |
| | | | | |
| % of total variance explained | 29.99 | 15.09 | 15.00 | 12.38 |
| Cumulative variance (%) | 29.99 | 45.07 | 60.10 | 72.45 |
| Coefficient alpha | .76 | .78 | .90 | .62 |
| Number of items | 4 | 4 | 2 | 3 |

Extraction method: Principle component analysis (PCA)

Rotation method: Promax with Kaiser Normalization

[a]Rotation converged in 8 iterations

*Figure 2. Concept Development as a Hierarchical Model (Adopted from Chin, 2010)*

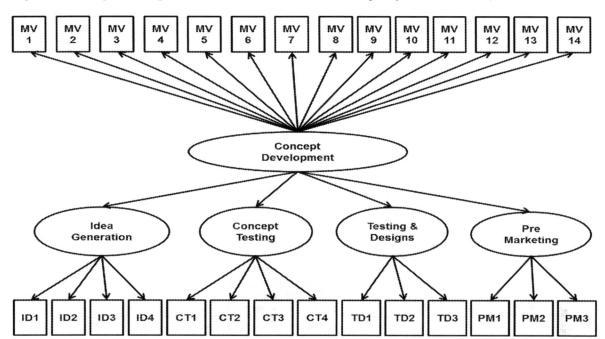

## ANALYSIS AND RESULTS

In specifying concept development as a higher-order construct (HOC), Partial Least Square (PLS) path modeling (or component-based structural equation modeling), using Smart-PLS Version 2.0 M3, was used to estimate the HOC of concept development by adopting repeated use of manifest variables (Lohmoller, 1989). As can be seen in Figure 2, the scores of lower-order latent variables of idea generation, concept testing, product testing and design and pre-marketing determinate in PLS path analysis were subsequently used as manifest variables for the HOC of concept development. This method allows for estimating the hierarchical model to achieve more theoretical parsimony and less model complexity (Chin, 2010; Mckenzie et al. 2005). HOC, which is also known as hierarchical construct, refers to a construct that has more than one dimension, where each dimension captures some portion of the overall latent variable (Wetzels et al. 2009).

Smart-PLS was used to assess the hierarchical model of concept development in order to estimate the parameters in the outer and inner structural theories. The application of nonparametric bootstrapping (Chin, 1988; Tenenhous, Vinzi, Chatelin & Lauro, 2005; Wetzels et al. 2009) was then applied with 5000 replications (Hair, Hult, Ringle & Sarstedt, 2014) to obtain the $\tau$ value and standard errors (*se*). In assessing the structural outer model, all the structural links among constructs were drawn and path weighting scheme was set in the PLS algorithm settings (Chin, 2010). The preliminary evaluation of the reflective outer models is shown in Table 4.

Diagonals (in Bold) represent the average variance extracted (AVE) while the other entries represent the squared correlations

Subsequently, the structural outer model was reassessed of its goodness of measures. Loadings and cross loadings of the respective outer models were compared and all the items measuring each

*Table 4. Results of Preliminary Evaluation of the Reflective Outer Models*

| Constructs/ Latent Variables | Original Items | | | Label Items | Loadings | Deleted Items |
|---|---|---|---|---|---|---|
| *Innovation orientations* | Less new product | 1-7 | More new products | IO1 | 0.598 | |
| | Changes in menu products have been mostly of minor nature | 1-7 | Changes in menu products have usually been radical | IO2 | 0.371 | Deleted |
| | There is a strong emphasis on marketing of true and tried menu products | 1-7 | There exists a very strong emphasis on the development of new and innovative products | IO3 | 0.419 | |
| | There is a strong proclivity for low risk NPD with normal and certain rates of return | 1-7 | There is a strong proclivity for high risk NPD with changes of very high return | IO4 | -0.253 | Deleted |
| | Owing to the nature of the environment (saturated), it is best to explore gradually via cautious, incremental behavior | 1-7 | Owing to the nature of the environment (saturated),wide-ranging acts are necessary to achieve the restaurant's objective | IO5 | -0.029 | Deleted |
| | Typically we adopt a cautious, wait & see posture in order to minimize the probability of making costly decision | 1-7 | Typically we adopt a bold, aggressive posture in order to maximize the probability of exploiting potential opportunities | IO6 | 0.262 | Deleted |
| | Typically we respond to action which competitors initiate | 1-7 | Typically we initiate action to which competitors then respond | IO7 | -0.324 | Deleted |
| | We are very seldom the first business to introduce new products | 1-7 | Very often we are the first business to introduce new products | IO8 | 0.541 | |
| | We typically seek to avoid competitive clashes, preferring a 'live-&-let live' posture | 1-7 | We typically adopt a very competitive, undo-the-competitors' posture | IO9 | 0.641 | |
| *Food trends* | Healthy foods | | | FT1 | 0.004 | Deleted |
| | Freshness and quality | | | FT2 | 0.437 | |
| | Experience new and different taste | | | FT3 | 0.784 | |
| | Something new but have a familiar taste | | | FT4 | 0.917 | |
| | Building on customer favorites and taste preferences | | | FT5 | 0.518 | |
| *Idea generations* | Culinary magazines | | | ID1 | 0.880 | |
| | Cooking books | | | ID2 | 0.915 | |
| | Meeting to discuss market trends | | | ID3 | 0.373 | Deleted |
| | Value perception | | | ID4 | 0.623 | |
| *Concept testing* | Competitors | | | CT1 | 0.857 | |
| | Testing and design are performed by in-house specialist team | | | CT2 | 0.898 | |
| | Food testing | | | CT3 | 0.601 | |
| | Regular customers | | | CT4 | 0.835 | |
| *Testing & Design* | To convert the concept into operational entity, testing and design is required | | | TD1 | 0.959 | |
| | By introducing new product, design of new production process is required | | | TD2 | 0.950 | |
| *Pre-marketing* | Customer survey | | | PM1 | 0.745 | |
| | In-house panel | | | PM2 | 0.892 | |
| | Place-card on dining tables | | | PM3 | 0.088 | Deleted |

Items with lower loading value below 0.4 were deleted in accordance to Hulland's (1999) cut-off value at 0.40 in exploratory studies.

*Table 5. Psychometric Properties of the Outer Models*

| Constructs/ Latent Variables | Measurement Items | Loadings | Se[ii] | τ2 | CR | AVE |
|---|---|---|---|---|---|---|
| Innovation orientations | IO1 | 0.786 | 0.168 | 4.683 | 0.811 | 0.523 |
| | IO3 | 0.523 | 0.219 | 2.387 | | |
| | IO8 | 0.782 | 0.215 | 3.638 | | |
| | IO9 | 0.769 | 0.164 | 4.680 | | |
| Food trends | FT2 | 0.457 | 0.114 | 4.015 | 0.788 | 0.50 |
| | FT3 | 0.802 | 0.051 | 15.762 | | |
| | FT4 | 0.910 | 0.029 | 31.601 | | |
| | FT5 | 0.560 | 0.124 | 4.496 | | |
| Idea generation | ID1 | 0.898 | 0.022 | 40.257 | 0.852 | 0.666 |
| | ID2 | 0.927 | 0.015 | 61.205 | | |
| | ID4 | 0.576 | 0.127 | 4.541 | | |
| Concept testing | CT1 | 0.861 | 0.076 | 11.342 | 0.879 | 0.649 |
| | CT2 | 0.899 | 0.062 | 14.445 | | |
| | CT3 | 0.593 | 0.166 | 3.572 | | |
| | CT4 | 0.833 | 0.136 | 6.128 | | |
| Testing & design | TD1 | 0.958 | 0.012 | 78.217 | 0.953 | 0.911 |
| | TD2 | 0.950 | 0.021 | 44.642 | | |
| Pre-marketing | PM1 | 0.804 | 0.081 | 9.935 | 0.841 | 0.726 |
| | PM2 | 0.894 | 0.031 | 29.031 | | |

*Significant at $\rho < 0.10$; the rest of the $\tau$ values were significant at $\rho < 0.01$.

of the respective constructs and latent variables loaded highly and loaded lower on the opposite thus confirming construct validity. Additionally, the structural outer model was also assessed of its convergent validity and discriminant validity. The results, which is shown in Table 5, saw the measures of the constructs/latent variables were theoretically related where most items loading values were higher than the cut-off value of 0.7 (Hulland, 1999; Hair et al. 2010) and significant at $\rho < 0.01$. In addition, the Average Variance Extracted (AVEs) and Composite Reliability (CRs) values for all the constructs and latent variables of concept development were also found exceeded the threshold values of 0.5 and 0.7 respectively (Bagozzi & Yi, 1988; Hair et al. 2010) thus confirming strong evident of convergent valid-

ity. Comparison between the AVE values and the squared correlations among constructs/latent variables was also used to measure the constructs discriminant validity and found each of the constructs was highly related to its own measures than with others, which can be seen in Table 6). With these results, the structural outer models, therefore, can be validly and reliably confirmed of its theoretical relationships.

The second-order construct of concept development was measured by modeling each of the latent variable (i.e. idea generations, concept testing, product testing & design and pre-marketing) coefficients to the second-order construct (concept development) (Chin, 2010). Accordingly, these latent variables, representing 11 (3x4x2x2) indicators (manifest variables) were pulled together

*Table 6. Discriminant Validity of Constructs*

| Constructs/ Latent Variables | 1 | 2 | 3 | 4 | 5 | 6 | 7 |
|---|---|---|---|---|---|---|---|
| 1. Innovation Orientations | **0.523** | | | | | | |
| 2. Food Trends | 0.186 | **0.50** | | | | | |
| 3. Market Saturation | 0.004 | 0.015 | **0.630** | | | | |
| 4. Idea Generation | 0.505 | 0.407 | 0.052 | **0.666** | | | |
| 5. Concept Testing | 0.000 | 0.181 | 0.069 | 0.182 | **0.649** | | |
| 6. Testing & Design | 0.069 | 0.138 | 0.099 | 0.278 | 0.242 | **0.911** | |
| 7. Pre-Marketing | 0.026 | 0.031 | 0.045 | 0.135 | 0.121 | 0.175 | **0.726** |

as the reflective measure of concept development in Smart-PLS for statistical model and the results can be seen in Table 7.

As shown in Table 7, all the standardized path coefficients ($\beta$) found to be significant at $\rho<0.01$. In term of coefficient of determination ($R^2$), a measure commonly used in model predictive accuracy (Hair et al. 2014), latent variables of idea generations, concept testing and product testing and designs were found to be nearly at 70% of the threshold value of high predictive accuracy, whilst pre-marketing found to be at moderate level with 32% explained variance based on Hair's et al. (2010) assessment of $R^2$ values of 0.20 (weak), 0.50 (moderate) and 0.75 (substantial).

Next, in order to appropriately measure the structural theory, the predictive power of the linear structural model was carried out first, excluding the moderating variable of food trends. The results of the PLS algorithm analysis, a statistical measurement tool that emphasis on predictive accuracy of

explained variance (Hair et al. 2014), indicated that an $R$ square value of 0.151 was obtained for concept development. Hence, categorically, in term of its predictive accuracy, the structural model of this linear relationship was found to be at slightly below weak level based on Hair et al. (2010) assessment of $R^2$ values as only 15% explained variance yielded. On the other hand, a negative standardized coefficient value was obtained at 99% significance level ($\beta=-0.388$, $\tau=2.382$, $\rho<0.01$).

Finally, with the inclusion of the moderating variable of food trends in the structural theory, the result shows that the value of the $R^2$ for concept development has gone up to 0.644, which increases the structural model's predictive accuracy by almost 50% to a moderate level. The analysis of the interaction path estimates, which is highlighted in Figure 3, also found the coefficient value was significant ($\beta=-0.198$, $\tau=1.803$, $\rho<0.05$) at 95% significance level based on a single tailed test. A

*Table 7. Results of Higher-Order Construct and It Associations with First-Order Latent Variables*

| Relationships | Mean | *Se* | $\beta$ | $R^2$ | $\tau$ |
|---|---|---|---|---|---|
| Concept development $\rightarrow$ Idea generations | 0.796 | 0.052 | 0.785 | 0.616 | 15.193 |
| Concept development $\rightarrow$ Concept testing | 0.792 | 0.091 | 0.799 | 0.639 | 8.775 |
| Concept development $\rightarrow$ Testing & design | 0.811 | 0.055 | 0.806 | 0.650 | 14.734 |
| Concept development $\rightarrow$ Pre-marketing | 0.670 | 0.051 | 0.609 | 0.317 | 11.877 |

Note: $\tau$ values were all found significant at $\rho<0.01$

*Figure 3. Results of Structural Model*

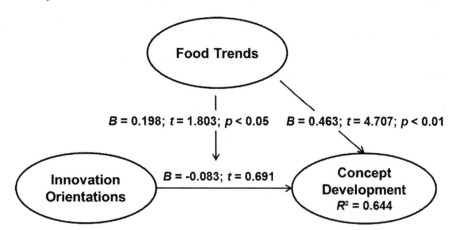

summary of this result along with the other paths estimate are shown in Table 8.

Following this result, the $f^2$ effect size was undertaken to determine the effect size of the food trends as a moderator between the linked of innovation orientations and concept development. Effect size $f^2$ is defined where $R^2_{included}$ model and $R^2_{excluded}$ model are the $R$ squares provided on the endogenous (dependent) latent variable when the predictor latent variable is used or omitted in the structural equation respectively (Chin, 2010). Reporting effect size $f^2$ has been long advocated in research literature as indispensable when presenting empirical research findings since it facilitates the interpretation of substantive, as opposed to the statistical, significance of the research result (Cohen, 1988). Hence, the change in $R^2$ value was

used to estimate the impact of the moderator on the relationship between the exogenous variables and endogenous variables based on Cohen's (1988) assessment of $f^2$ effect size of 0.02 (small), 0.15 (medium) and 0.35 (large). The result is presented below along with the computation formula of $f^2$. A value of 0.635 was obtained, indicating a support of a large effect size.

$$f^2_{\text{Innovation orientations*Food trends} \rightarrow \text{Concept development}} = \frac{R_i^2 - R_e^2}{1 - R_i^2} = \frac{0.644 - 0.418}{1 - 0.356} = 0.635$$

Finally, the predictive relevance $Q^2$ was also carried out to ascertain the predictive relevance of the interaction effect on concept development. Stone-Geisser's $Q^2$ refers to predictive sample

*Table 8. Results of Path Coefficients, Standard Errors and τ - Statistics*

| Interaction Path in Moderating Research Model | Path coefficients (β) | Standard errors (se) | τ - statistics | ρ value |
|---|---|---|---|---|
| Innovation orientations*Food trends → Concept development | 0.198 | 0.110 | 1.803 | 0.038** |
| Paths in Research Model | | | | |
| Innovation orientations → Concept development | -0.083 | 0.121 | 0.691 | 0.491[NS] |
| Food trends → Concept development | 0.463 | 0.098 | 4.707 | 0.000* |

[NS]Not Significant; *significant at ρ < 0.01; **significant at ρ < 0.05 based on a single tailed test

Note: A nonparametric bootstrapping applying 5000 replications as recommended by Hair et al. (2014) was performed to obtain the τ

reuse technique developed by Stone (1974) and Geisser (1975), using blindfolding procedures (Tenenhaus et al. 2005), to obtain the cross-validated redundancy (CV-Red) and cross-validated Communality (CV-Com) that is readily available in SmartPLS. Stone-Geisser's $Q^2$ has been widely used to provide a prediction of the endogenous latent variable's indicators in a structural model, represents a synthesis of function fitting and cross validation, which fits the PLS-SEM path modeling approach 'like hand in glove' (Wold, 1982).

Following the blindfolding procedure set in SmartPLS, an omission distance was specified in accordance to guideline of which should not be the division of the number of observation used in the model estimation and the distance must be an integer (Hair et al. 2014). Hence, with 71 observation obtained in this study, an omission distance of $D = 5$ was chosen, and the endogenous construct of concept development was specified to be analyzed in blindfolding. Based on the blindfolding algorithm analysis performed in SmartPLS, the predictive relevance $Q^2$ of innovation orientations and food trends (as direct exogenous variables) along with the moderator (as indirect latent variable) on concept development, a value of 0.252 was obtained, indicating above zero, thus providing support of predictive relevance in regards to the respective path models.

## DISCUSSION AND CONCLUSION

Model of menu innovation process in the foodservice industry was first proposed in the mid-1980s (Feltenstein, 1986), and such a proposition, after almost a decade, resurfaced in hospitality literature in the mid-1990s (Mooney, 1994; Jones, 1996). These early models of menu innovation process are conducted in a stage-approach, which in fact has been long used in the manufacturing and engineering industries (e.g. Booz et al. 1963, 1983; Kotler & Amstrong, 1991; Graf & Saguy, 1991; Urban & Hauser, 1993; MacFie, 1994; Fuller,

1994). Recent research findings seem to confirm that this stage-approach to menu innovation process remains steadfast in the industry apart from the number of stages, which vary from one to another (Mifli 2004; Ottenbacher & Harrington, 2007, 2008). Logically, this is not surprising as most business landscapes, if not all, have different levels of market uncertainty and being managed in difference philosophy of managerial orientations. Therefore, one can argue that one model to another is likely to be differed in terms of it stages level and the activities at each stage.

In this chapter, the structural theory of managing menu innovation is put forward along with the moderating variable of food trends. The main objective is to ascertain the moderating effects of these food trends when restaurateurs' engage in new menu innovation. Unlike previous studies (Jones, 1996; Mifli, 2004; Ottenbacher & Harrington, 2007, 2008), which used qualitative method to frame the stages of the menu innovation process, this study has successfully structured concept development with appropriate validation estimates as a second-order hierarchical construct, showing all four dimensions significantly associate to concept development. However, in the EFA analysis, the results show that none of the indicators for business analysis were found to be significantly important predictors. This discovery appears to suggest that business analysis, one of the stages of menu innovation process advocated strongly in literature (Feltenstein, 1986; Mooney, 1994; Jonas, 1996), did not play a critical role along the NPD process.

Innovation orientations, either radically or incrementally driven, are strongly correlated to product innovation process. Previous findings have all came to a conclusion that most NPD are incrementally driven (Booz et al. 1983; Abernathy & Clark, 1985, Jones & Wan, 1992; Mifli, 2004). On the other hand, radical product development, which is commonly associated with transforming new knowledge to the development process, is rarely implemented (Booz et al. 1983; Jones &

Wan, 1992). However, other researchers argue that relying on incremental product development, which is also referred to those products being developed based on responsive market orientation, is less competitive advantage due constant changes in consumers' preferences and acceptances. Hence, proactive market orientation, which is synonymous to radical orientations of product innovation, is called upon (Narver, Slater & Maclachlan 2004). A recent study by Salavou and Lioukas (2003) on entrepreneurship indicate that there is a significant evidence of risk taking undertaken by managers in their decision making process. This finding suggests that, while most new products are developed incrementally, such engagement of riskiness in NPD appeared to support radical product orientation.

In this study, the initial result of the linear relationships appears to confirm a support of radical orientation adopted by chain restaurants in Malaysia when engage in new menu innovation. A negative path coefficient value of 0.388 with a $\tau$ value at 2.382 and significant at $\rho < 0.01$ confirmed a radical product orientation was being used in shaping their new menu development in a business landscape that is hypothetically no interference from external environmental forces. However, in reality, most business landscapes, if not all, are surrounded by different elements of external forces that may or may not be taken into consideration in decision making process (Enz, 2009). Hence, to accurately ascertain this proposition, a simultaneous assessment was undertaken with the inclusion of food trends dimension in the structural theory, as a moderator. Iacobucci and Dunhachek (2003) argue that when two or more natures of forces come into effect along the decision making process, a simultaneous analysis is essential in order to accurately draw the conclusion. Recently, Helm, Eggert and Garnefeld (2010) have also recommended using this method because of superior results to other existing methods. Therefore, a simultaneous analysis was performed in order to accurately hypothesize

the moderator's influences on radical innovation orientation in shaping the outcome of the new menu development. The notion of managing menu innovation along the first-stage of the process is that the external forces (as in this case is the food trends) are generally played a part in moderating decision making process (Iansiti, 1995; Eisenhardt & Tabrizi, 1995; Cooper, 1988; Cunha & Gomes, 2003).

Past studies have examined the direct effect of environmental turbulence, a generic terminology commonly used to denote market uncertainty/unpredictable market, on NPD and found significantly correlated (Montoya-Weiss & Calantone (1994), Iansiti (1995), Calantone, Garcia & Dröge (2003), Dess & Davis (1984), Miller (1987), Glaser & Weiss (1993), Chalravarthy (1997). While such direct relationships testing are consistently yielded significance findings, in this study, the identified themes of food trends depicted from across the global perspective would shed some lights of which one or a combination of them that have implications to decision-making process.

Indeed, one of the challenges for restaurateurs in menu management is innovating new menus that are in line with consumers' food preferences and acceptances. Seven co-integrated themes with multidimensional scale concerning food trends that include Asian flavors, Mediterranean flavors, healthy foods, freshness and quality, experience new and different taste, something new but have a familiar taste and building on customer favorite and taste preference' emerged based on previous literature. To assess the internal consistency of the entire seven themes, the consistency coefficient or Cronbach's alpha become the right choice in hand. As can be seen in Table 3, out of seven themes, only five themes were taken into account that yielded high consistency value of 0.7. This indicates that (with the exception of Asian and Mediterranean flavors) the five themes that are taken in accont obtained a high single measurement of one-dimensional latent or hidden structure of the food trends strategy among the restaurateurs. Simply put, the higher the internal consistency values the higher the inter-item correlation across all items. With this result, the Asian and Mediterranean flavors had to be excluded in the next analysis since it did not show obvious multidimensional pattern among the entire themes as opposed to what had been cited of its immense acceptances in other part of the world (Harnett, 2004; Yee, 2002b; Josaim & Monteiro, 2004; Spark et al.2003).

To further verify the impact of these five themes, the path model of food trends was then linked to concept development in the structural theory of this study in order to access its measurement model[3] in SmartPLS. The result shows that all the coefficient loadings values of the themes (except themes labeled FT1-Healthy foods) were higher from the threshold value of 0.4 (Hulland, 1999) and significant at $p<0.01$. Among those four themes, experience new and different taste (theme labeled 3) and something new but have a familiar taste (themes labeled 4) were found to be the main predictors of food trends used by menu planners when engage in NMD with loading values at 0.784 and 0.917 respectively. However, theme labeled FT1-Healthy foods that had a loading value of 0.004 was almost completely ignored by menu planners, and therefore excluded from the structural model. A reasonable explanation to this could be that the consumers in Malaysia, particularly in the region of Klang valley are not health conscious in their daily dietary intakes as opposed to those that do in developed country, such as in the UK and USA, where this source of literature depicted. Nevertheless, theme labeled 2-freshness and quality seemed to play a key part in shaping NMD, which tells us that menu planners did use the elements of freshness and quality in their menus to entice customers that may perceive them healthy, which support Yee's (2002a) proposition of the growing trends by resurrecting old menus back to popular demand by simply make them look 'fresh'.

Finally, in Figure 3 and Table 8, the results of the moderation analysis show that there was

a support of moderating effect of food trends on the relationship between innovation orientations and concept development. Earlier, we presented the linear relationships between the predictor and criterion variable, excluding the moderator, and found a negative sign of $\beta$ value (-0.388) and significant at $p<0.01$ ($\tau=2.382$), indicating a radical innovation orientation was adopted by restaurant chains in managing their new menu innovation. Nevertheless, in the moderation analysis, the negative sign of the $\beta$ value of innovation orientation (radical) on concept development has decreased drastically to -0.083 and found no longer significant. Correspondingly, the path coefficient of the interaction effect ($p =0.038$) found to be significant at 95% significance level based on a single-tailed test. This finding confirmed that there was a support of moderating effect of food trends on the relationship between innovation orientation and concept development. To further confirm this, testing of its $f^2$ effect size was performed, and an $f^2$ value of 0.635 was obtained, confirming a large degree of moderating effect based on Cohen's (1988) assessments of $f^2$ effect size. Simply put, this explained the dropped of the coefficient path value from being significant at $p <0.01$(without moderator) to not significant (with moderator), indicating that the practice of radical menu innovation is no longer imminent due to the presence of food trends.

However, the results of the $q^2$ effect size ($q^2=0.01$), which is summarized in Table 9, indicated that there was no predictive relevancy of the food trends on the interaction to innovation orientation. Hence, although there was a support of significant moderating effect of food trends on the relationship between innovation orientations and concept development, its predictive interaction effects was found not relevant. This result come no surprise to us since most restaurant chains, if not all, have their own concept menus. Therefore, we argue that changing existing products to something new based on contemporary food preferences is less likely to happen. Yet, with the

*Table 9. Results of the $q^2$ Effect Size*

| Interaction Path in Moderating Research Model | β | $Q^2_{included}$ | $Q^2_{excluded}$ | $q^2$ | Effect[+] Size |
|---|---|---|---|---|---|
| Innovation orientations*Food trends → Concept development | 0.198 | 0.252 | 0.245 | 0.01 | No effect |
| Paths in Research Model | | | | | |
| Innovation orientations → Concept development | -0.083 | 0.252 | 0.193 | 0.08 | Small |
| Food trends → Concept development | 0.463 | 0.252 | 0.169 | 0.08 | Small |

[+]In accordance toCohen's (1988)$f^2$ effect size assessments of 0.02(small), 0.15(medium) and 0.35(large)

In order to ascertain the effect size of the path models, $q^2$ effect size was also being assessed. The base formula for the calculation is similar to $f^2$ deployed earlier, where, instead of the $R^2$ values, the CV-Red $Q^2$ values of the predictive relevance were used as inputs. The summary of the results based on the computations are shown in Table 9.

evident of radical product innovation adoption is still noticeable (β =-0.083) though not significant and had a small negative path coefficient value, enquiring new knowledge related to these four trendy food themes is still being incorporated in their new menus but very minimal. Hence, it can be concluded based on this research finding, these four food trends are not totally embraced by restaurant chains in relation to their menu innovation orientation.

Yet, another school of thought argues that product innovations are also judged on its competitiveness and impact in the marketplace as opposed to which types of innovation orientations that lead to product supremacy (Ettlie & Subramaniam, 2004; Cooper & Kleinschmidt, 2000). Earlier, we have discussion some of the characteristics of radical and incremental approaches to product development and its realism. Correspondingly, in these study's findings, managing menu innovation is less likely dependent on innovation orientation in shaping the innovation process; rather the execution of what to develop is discreetly done within the concept development stages. In Figure 3, it shows that the path coefficient of food trends to concept development had a 99% significance level, whereas the interaction path coefficient had only 95% significance level. Thus, based on these findings, it can be summed up that the impact of the four food trends is in fact directly felt at the stages of the concept development. Hence, it

is reasonable to argue that the theory of radical versus incremental innovation orientations that is known to spur NPD and claimed to be inseparable (Drucker, 1985) could now be challenged as both innovation orientations may come in force later after the decision of what product to innovate/develop is made. Likewise, the theory of incremental innovation orientation that has been previously found as the dominant strategy in engineering and manufacturing industries in shaping NPD (Booz et al. 1985; Abernathy & Clark, 1985) appear not supported in the context of this study.

This chapter sheds some lights of what possibly be the actual engagement of menu innovation in the context of chain restaurants in Malaysia. The forces of food trends found to have significantly moderated the radical menu innovation to a point that is no longer significant, and yet, not strong enough to change to incremental orientation. A possible explanation to this is that the restaurateurs are in fact still incorporating new knowledge but minimal due to maintain the existing status qua of their menus that are likely related to the chain's brand image. Another word, existing dishes are maintained but minimal refinements are done based on new knowledge (radical) as opposed to improving the dishes based on current knowledge (incremental).

Additionally, this chapter can also be viewed as the expansion of theoretical reconceptualization. Our structural theory has successfully illustrated an empirical evident by developing a second-order hierarchical reflective model of concept development, the first-stage of NPD process, using existing models in the literature (Feinstein, 1986; Mooney, 1994; Jones, 1996: Mifli, 2004; Ottenbacher & Harrington, 2007; 2008). In line with the strength of PLS in explaining complex relationships (Hair et al. 2014; Chin, 2010), the use of PLS path modeling in this case has made it possible to advance the theoretical contribution of this study. As readily available in SmartPLS, estimating the higher-order latent variables with the use repeated indicators method (as manifest variables), both measurement and structural theory for this research model shows confirmed of adequate results. Hence, we firmly believe, with this second-order hierarchical model of NPD process put forward in a statistical perspective and empirically tested in this structural theory, the findings presented in this book may provide some useful insights both in theoretical and practical perspectives.

Finally, as most research works, if not all, do have limitations, and this study has no exception either as the observation of the respondents did not represent the whole spectrums of the restaurant sectors that existed in Malaysia. Out of the five restaurant sectors, only full-service restaurant (FSR) and café and bar were successfully interviewed in this study. Therefore, the fast food chains, which have the highest number of outlets and known to have standardized and consistent product development, were not in this study due strict company policy, which prevented us to include them in this research study. The others two chain companies are street stalls/kiosks and 100% home delivery/takeaways but their total population is quite small, and therefore, their absent in this study is not an issue.

Secondly, some of the respondents participated in this study were international chain based companies, such as Starbucks, Pizza Hut, Shakey's, Sushi King, Dave's Deli, Four Season, Coffee Bean & Tea Leaf, Gloria Jean's, and Dome to name a few.

Although, some local companies hold the right of being the master franchisors for some brands here in Malaysia, we believe that their NPD or product innovation management, to a large extent, is still being developed at the corporate headquarters overseas. Therefore, if there are some changes undertaken here in regional offices there are likely to be minimal and such changes may likely link to the changes in socio-cultural food preferences, acceptances and habits, as compliance to the brand image of the chains' ownership is indeed to be obliged. Thus, the findings presented in this chapter should be used with caution and not be generalized as universally acceptable paradigm.

We strongly recommend for future researchers to replicate our structural model and do some cross comparisons between international and local brand ownerships or within the restaurant sectors as these would provide interesting findings and meaningful to theoretical build up and practical implications. Equally, it would be a great achievement if academia in a similar field, especially in the USA, to replicate this study since most main headquarters of established chain companies are based there and this definitely will be a good opportunity to approach them in finding out about menu innovation.

# REFERENCES

Abernathy, W. J., & Clark, K. B. (1985). Innovation: Mapping the winds of creative destruction. *Research Policy*, *14*(1), 3–22. doi:10.1016/0048-7333(85)90021-6

Allen, M. J., & Yen, W. M. (1979). *Introduction to Measurement Theory*. Long Grave, IL: Waveland Press.

Bagozzi, R. P., & Yi, Y. (1988). On the evaluation of structural equation models. *Journal of the Academy of Marketing Science*, *16*(1), 74–94. doi:10.1007/BF02723327

Bertagnoli, L. (2000). Goin' green. *Restaurants & Institutions, 110*(19), 45–48.

Booz, Allen, & Hamilton. (1968). *Management of new product*. New York, NY: Booz, Allen and Hamilton Inc.

Booz, Allen, & Hamilton. (1982). *New product management for the 1980s*. New York, NY: Booz, Allen and Hamilton Inc.

Calantone, R., Garcia, R., & Dröge, C. (2003). The effects of environmental turbulence on new product development strategy planning. *Journal of Product Innovation Management, 20*(2), 90–103. doi:10.1111/1540-5885.2002003

Chakravarthy, B. A. (1997). A new strategy framework for coping with turbulence. *Sloan Management Review, 38*(2), 69–82.

Chin, W. (1988). The partial least squares approach for structural equation modeling. In G. A. Marcoulides (Ed.), *Modern methods for business research* (pp. 295–336). New Jersey, NJ: Lawrence Erlbaum Associates.

Chin, W. W. (2010). How to write up and report PLS analyses. In V. Esposito Vinzi, W. W. Chin, J. Henseler, & H. Wang (Eds.), *Handbook of partial least squares: Concepts, methods and applications in marketing and related fields* (pp. 645–689). New York, NY: Springer. doi:10.1007/978-3-540-32827-8_29

Cobbenhagen, J. (2000). *Successful innovation: Towards a new theory for the management of small and medium-sized enterprises*. Cheltenham, UK: Edward Elgar Publishing Limited.

Cohen, J. (1988). *Statistical power analysis for the behavioral sciences* (2nd ed.). Hillsdale, NJ: Lawrence Erlbaum Associates.

Comrey, A. L., & Lee, H. B. (1992). *A first course in factor analysis* (2nd ed.). Hillsdale, NJ: Lawrence Eribaum.

Cooper, R. G. (1988). The new product process: A decision guide for management. *Journal of Marketing Management, 3*(3), 238–255. doi:10.1080/0267257X.1988.9964044

Cooper, R. G., & Kleinschmidt, E. (2000). New product performance: What distinguishes the star products. *Australian. Journal of Management, 25*(1), 17–45.

Cunha, M. P., & Gomes, J. F. (2003). Order and disorder in product innovation models. *Creativity and Innovation Management, 12*(3), 174–187. doi:10.1111/1467-8691.00280

Cyert, R., & March, J. G. (1963). *A behavioral theory of the firm*. Englewood Cliffs, NJ: Prentice-Hall.

Daft, R. L. (2001). *Organization theory and design* (7th ed.). Cincinnati, Ohio: South Western College Publishing.

Dess, G. G., & Davis, P. S. (1984). Porter's generic strategies as determinants of strategic group membership and organizational performance. *Academy of Management Journal, 27*(3), 467–488. doi:10.2307/256040

Drucker, P. (1954). *The practice of management*. New York, NY: Harper & Brothers.

Enz, C. A. (2010). *Hospitality strategic management: concepts and cases* (2nd ed.). New York, NY: Wileys.

Ettlie, J. E., Bridges, W. P., & O'Keefe, R. D. (1984). Organization strategy and structural differences for radical versus incremental innovation. *Management Science, 30*(6), 682–695. doi:10.1287/mnsc.30.6.682

Ettlie, J. E., & Subramaniam, M. (2004). Changing strategies and tactics for new product development. *Journal of Product Innovation Management, 21*(2), 95–109. doi:10.1111/j.0737-6782.2004.00060.x

Euromonitor International. (2004). *Consumer food service industry in Malaysia*. Chicago, IL: Euromonitor International.

Euromonitor International. (2006). *Consumer food service industry in Malaysia*. Chicago, IL: Euromonitor International.

Euromonitor International. (2010). *Consumer food service industry in Malaysia*. Chicago, IL: Euromonitor International.

Euromonitor International. (2012). *Consumer food service industry in Malaysia*. Chicago, IL: Euromonitor International.

Feltenstein, T. (1986). New-product development in food service: A structured approach. *The Cornell Hotel and Restaurant Administration Quarterly*, 27(3), 63–71. doi:10.1177/001088048602700314

Fuller, W. G. (1994). *New food product development from concept to the market place*. Boca Rotan, FL: CRC Press.

Glaser, R., & Weiss, A. M. (1993). Marketing in turbulence environments: Decision processes and the time-sensitivity of information. *JMR, Journal of Marketing Research*, 30(4), 431–453.

Graf, E., & Saguy, S. L. (1991). *Food product development from concept to the market place*. London, UK: Chapman and Hull.

Grest, V. (2004). Mass customization: Consumer trends drive menu innovation at top 400 chains. *Restaurants & Institutions*, 112(15), 26–38.

Hair, J. F., Black, W. C., Babin, B. J., & Anderson, R. E. (2010). *Multivariate data analysis* (7th ed.). Englewood Cliffs, NJ: Prentice Hall.

Hair, J.F., Hult, G.T., & Ringle, C.M. & Sarstedt. (2014). *A primer on partial least squares structural equation modeling (PLS-SEM)*. Thousand Oaks, CA. *Sage (Atlanta, Ga.)*.

Hair, J. F., Sarstedt, M., Ringle, C. M., & Mena, J. A. (2012). An assessment of the use of partial least squares structural equation modelling in marketing research. *Journal of the Academy of Marketing Science*, 40(3), 414–433. doi:10.1007/s11747-011-0261-6

Harnett, M. (2005). Exotic tastes becoming favorites. *Frozen Food Age*, 53(8), 24–28.

Hashimoto, K. (2003). Product life cycle theory: A quantitative application for casino courses in higher education. *International Journal of Hospitality Management*, 22(2), 177–195. doi:10.1016/S0278-4319(03)00017-3

Helm, S., Eggert, A., & Garnefeld, I. (2010). Modeling the impact of corporate reputation on customer satisfaction and loyalty using partial least squares. In Vinzi V.E, Chin, W.W., Henseler, J., & Wang, H. (Eds.). Handbook of partial least squares. Concepts, methods and applications in marketing and related fields (pp. 515-534). New York, NY: Springer. doi:10.1007/978-3-540-32827-8_23

Hulland, J. (1999). Use of partial least squares (PLS) in strategic management research: A review of four recent studies. *Strategic Management Journal*, 20(2), 195–204. doi:10.1002/(SICI)1097-0266(199902)20:2<195::AID-SMJ13>3.0.CO;2-7

Iacobucci, D., & Duhachek, A. (2003). Mediation analysis. Paper presented at the round table at the *Association for Consumer Research Conference (ACR)*, Toronto, Canada.

Iansiti, M. (1995). Shooting the rapids: Managing product development in turbulent environment. *California Management Review*, 38(1), 37–58. doi:10.2307/41165820

Jones, P. (1996). Managing hospitality innovation. *The Cornell Hotel and Restaurant Administration Quarterly*, 37(5), 86–95. doi:10.1177/001088049603700528

Jones, P., & Wan, L. (1992). Innovation in the UK food-service industry. *International Journal of Contemporary Hospitality Management*, *4*(4), 1–3.

Josiam, B. M., & Monteiro, P. A. (2004). Tandoori tastes: Perceptions of Indian restaurants in America. *International Journal of Contemporary Hospitality Management*, *16*(1), 18–26. doi:10.1108/09596110410516525

Kline, R. B. (2005). *Principles and practice of structural equation modelling* (2nd ed.). New York, NY: The Guilford Press.

Kotler, P., & Armstrong, G. (1996). *Principles of marketing* (8th ed.). Englewood Cliffs, NJ: Prentice-Hall.

Lohmöller, J. B. (1989). *Latent variable path modeling with partial least squares*. Heidelberg, Germany: Physica-Verlag. doi:10.1007/978-3-642-52512-4

MacFie, H. (1994). Computer assisted product development. *World of Ingredient*, *8*, 45–49.

MacKenzie, S. B., Podsakoff, P. M., & Podsakoff, N. P. (2011). Construct measurement and validation procedures in MIS and behavioral research: Integrating new and existing techniques. *Management Information Systems Quarterly*, *35*(2), 293–334.

Malhotra, N. K. (1996). *Marketing research: An applied orientation*. Upper Saddle River, NJ: Prentice Hall.

March, S. J. (1991). Exploration and exploitation in organizational learning. *Organization Science*, *2*(1), 71–87. doi:10.1287/orsc.2.1.71

Melis, A. R. (1991). Society, food, and feudalism. In J. L. Flandrin, M. Montanari, & A. Sonnenfeld (Eds.), *Food: A culinary history from antiquity to the present* (pp. 251–267). New York, NY: Columbia University Press.

Mifli, M. (2004). Managing menu innovation. Paper presented at the 3rd Asia- Pacific Forum for Graduate Student Research in Tourism, Beijing, China.

Miles, R. E., & Snow, C. C. (1978). *Organizational strategy, structure and process*. New York, NY: McGraw-Hill.

Miller, D., & Friesen, P. H. (1982). Innovation in conservative and entrepreneurial firms: Two models of strategic momentum. *Strategic Management Journal*, *3*(1), 1–25. doi:10.1002/smj.4250030102

Montoya-Wess, M. M., & Calantone, R. J. (1994). Determinant of new product performance: A review and meta-analysis. *Journal of Product Innovation Management*, *11*(5), 397–417. doi:10.1016/0737-6782(94)90029-9

Mooney, S. (1994). Planning and designing the menu. In P. Jones & P. Merricks (Eds.), *The management of foodservice operations* (pp. 45–58). London, UK: Cassell.

Narver, J. C., Slater, S. F., & Maclachlan, D. L. (2004). Responsive and proactive market orientation and new-product success. *Journal of Product Innovation Management*, *21*(5), 334–347. doi:10.1111/j.0737-6782.2004.00086.x

Nerker, A., & Roberts, P. W. (2004). Technological and product-market experience and the success of new product introductions in the pharmaceutical industry. *Strategic Management Journal*, *25*(89), 779–799. doi:10.1002/smj.417

Nunnally, J. C. (1978). *Psychometric Theory* (2nd ed.). New York, NY: McGraw-Hill.

Ottenbacher, M. C., & Harrington, R. J. (2007). The Innovation development process of michelin-starred chefs. *International Journal of Contemporary Hospitality Management*, *19*(6), 444–460. doi:10.1108/09596110710775110

Ottenbacher, M. C., & Harrington, R. J. (2008). The product innovation process of quick-service restaurant chains. *International Journal of Contemporary Hospitality Management, 21*(5), 523–541. doi:10.1108/09596110910967782

Porter, M. E. (1980). *Competitive strategy: Techniques for analyzing industries and competitors.* New York, NY: John Wiley & Sons, Inc.

Porter, M. E. (1985). Technology and competitive advantage. *The Journal of Business Strategy, 5*(3), 60–79. doi:10.1108/eb039075

Porter, M. E. (Ed.). (1986). *Competition in global industries.* Boston, MA: Harvard Business School Press.

Reid, R. D., & Sandler, M. (1992). The use of technology to improve service quality. *Cornell Hotel and Restaurant Quarterly, 33*(3), 68–73. doi:10.1016/0010-8804(92)90123-M

Robichaud, R., & Khan, M. A. (1988). Responding to market changes: The fast-food experience. *The Cornell Hotel and Restaurant Administration Quarterly, 29*(3), 46–49. doi:10.1177/001088048802900315

Salavou, H., & Lioukas, S. (2003). Radical product innovations in SMEs: The dominance of entrepreneurial orientation. *Creativity and Innovation Management, 12*(2), 94–108. doi:10.1111/1467-8691.00272

Sekaran, U. (2000). *Research methods for business: A skill -building approach* (3rd ed.). New York, NY: John Wiley & Sons, Inc.

Spark, B., Bowen, J., & Klag, S. (2003). Restaurant and the tourist market. *International Journal of Contemporary Hospitality Management, 15*(1), 6–13. doi:10.1108/09596110310458936

Stone, M. (1974). Cross-validatory choice and assessment of statistical predictions. *Journal of the Royal Statistical Society. Series A (General), 36*(2), 111–147.

Tabachnick, B. G., & Fidell, L. S. (2001). *Using multivariate statistics* (4th ed.). Boston, MA: Allyn and Bacon.

Tenenhaus, M., Vinzi, V. E., Chatelin, Y.-M., & Lauro, C. (2005). PLS path modeling. *Computational Statistics & Data Analysis, 48*(1), 159–205. doi:10.1016/j.csda.2004.03.005

Thompson, A. A., & Strickland, A. J. (1996). *Strategic management: concepts and cases* (9th ed.). Chicago, IL: Irwin Truss.

Urban, G. L., & Hauser, J. R. (1993). *Design and marketing of new products* (2nd ed.). New Jersey, NJ: Prentice Hall.

Wetzels, M., Schroder, G. O., & Oppen, V. C. (2009). Using PLS path modeling for assessing hierarchical construct models: Guidelines and empirical illustration. *Management Information Systems Quarterly, 33*(1), 177–195.

Wold, H. (1982). Soft modeling: The basic design and some extensions. In K. G. Jöreskog & H. Wold (Eds.), *Systems under indirect observation: Causality, structure, prediction* (Vol. 2, pp. 1–54). Amsterdam, Holland: North Holland.

Wood, V. R., & Robertson, K. R. (1997). Strategic orientation and export success: An empirical study. *International Marketing Review, 14*(6), 424–444. doi:10.1108/02651339710192975

Yee, L. (2002a). Stepping up. *Restaurants & Institutions, 112*(16), 28–34.

Yee, L. (2002b). Tailoring trends. *Restaurants & Institutions, 112*(21), 26–44.

## ADDITIONAL READING

Castagna, N. G. (1997). To market, to market. *Restaurants & Institutions, 107*(20), 89–98.

Charles, B. (1996). Big burgers for big people. *Restaurants & Institutions, 106*(17), 26–30.

Cooper, R. G. (1999). The invisible success factors in product innovation. *Journal of Product Innovation Management, 16*(2), 115–133. doi:10.1016/S0737-6782(98)00061-7

Cooper, R. G., & Edgett, S. J. (2003). *Best practices in product innovation: What distinguishes top performers (American Productivity & Quality Center Study).* Ancaster, Ontario, Canada: Product Development Institute Inc.

Cooper, R. G., & Kleinschmidt, E. (2000). New product performance: What distinguishes the star products. A*ustralian. Journal of Management, 25*(1), 17–45.

Crawford, C. M. (1994). *New product development* (4th ed.). Chicago, IL: Irwin Truss.

Cyert, R., & March, J. G. (1963). *A behavioral theory of the firm.* Englewood Cliffs, NJ: Prentice-Hall.

DeLuca, M. (1996). Growing your way. *Restaurant Hospitality, 80*(3), 77–81.

Dewar, R. D., & Dutton, I. E. (1986). The adoption of radical and incremental innovations: An empirical analysis. *Management Science, 32*(11), 1422–1433. doi:10.1287/mnsc.32.11.1422

Dickson, P. R., & Giglierano, J. J. (1986). Missing the boat and sinking the boat: A conceptual model of entrepreneurial risk. *Journal of Marketing, 50*(3), 58–70. doi:10.2307/1251585

Flandrin, J. L., Montanari, M., & Sonnenfeld, A. (1999). (Eds). Food: A culinary history from antiquity to the present. New York. NY: Columbia University Press.

Flynn, M., Dooley, L., O'Sullivan, D., & Cormican, K. (2003). Idea management for organizational innovation. *International Journal of Innovation Management, 7*(4), 417–442. doi:10.1142/S1363919603000878

Frambach, R. T., & Schillewaert, N. (2002). Organizational *Innovation Adoption*: A multi-level framework of determinants and opportunities for future research. *Journal of Business Research, 55*(2), 163–176. doi:10.1016/S0148-2963(00)00152-1

Fuller, J., & Waller, K. (1991). *The menu food & profit.* London, UK: Stanley Thornes.

Gillespie, C. H. (1994). Gastrosophy and nouvelle cuisine: Entrepreneurial fashion and fiction. *British Food Journal, 96*(10), 19–23. doi:10.1108/00070709410072472

Goldenberg, J., & Mazursky, D. (1999). The voice of the product: Templates of new product emergence. *Journal of Creativity and Innovation Management, 8*(3), 157–164. doi:10.1111/1467-8691.00132

Goldman, K. L. (1993). Which comes first, the location or the concept? *The Cornell Hotel and Restaurant Administration Quarterly, 34*(6), 59–72. doi:10.1177/001088049303400612

Grest, V. (2004). Mass customization: Consumer trends drive menu innovation. *Restaurants & Institutions, 29*(3), 26–36.

Gruenwald, G. (1985). *New product development: What really works.* Illinois, IL: NTC Business Books.

Hume, S. (2003). The difference maker. *Restaurants & Institutions, 113*(15), 30–40.

Jones, P., & Mifli, M. (2001). Menu Development and Analysis in UK Restaurant Chains. *Tourism and Hospitality Research, 3*(1), 61–71.

March, S. J. (1991). Exploration and exploitation in organizational learning. *Organization Science, 2*(1), 71–87. doi:10.1287/orsc.2.1.71

Margaret, L. (1996). Capturing the casual market. *Restaurants & Institutions, 106*(17), 72–78.

Margaret, S. (2001). The old order changes. *Restaurants & Institutions*, *111*(18), 85–90.

Matsumoto, J. (1998). Drumming up new ideas. *Restaurants & Institutions*, *108*(5), 16–21.

Ottenbacher, M. C., & Gnoth, J. (2007). How to develop successful hospitality innovation. *The Cornell Hotel and Restaurant Administration Quarterly*, *46*(2), 205–222. doi:10.1177/0010880404271097

Roger, S. (2006). Innovation in food service technology and its strategic role. *Hospital Management*, *20*, 899–912.

## KEY TERMS AND DEFINITIONS

**Concept Development:** The first-stage of NPD model that encompasses all the activities of idea generations undertaken within the concept lead-time. It is also known as the 'window of opportunity', a generic term used by others to denote the period that is opened for ideas generation.

**First-Order Constructs:** Constructs that have only one dimension.

**Incremental Innovation Orientation:** A new knowledge is acquired and embedded in the existing innovation activities as a mean to improve, refine or modify current practices.

**New Menu Development:** A new menu item is invented/or developed either through modifications or improvements of an existing recipe or a combination of both approaches or development of a new recipe but not new to the market or a very new recipe in the market.

**New Product Development (NPD) Model:** A model that is divided into two stages that includes concept development and implementation. In between these stages, a concept freeze point is drawn to segregate the activities of the two stages.

**New Product Development (NPD) Process Model:** A process model that is generally contained these four main stages namely formulation, development, testing and design and evaluation. At each stage, discreet activities are underlined and deployed in a sequential manner.

**Product Innovation Model:** A model that is generally being deployed in a two-stage approach where the first stage mainly involves all sorts of innovation generations before proceeding to the implementation stage.

**Radical Innovation Orientation:** A new knowledge is acquired and transformed in the innovation activities replacing the old ones.

**Second-Order Constructs:** Constructs that have multiple dimension also known as higher-order constructs or hierarchical constructs.

## ENDNOTES

[1]  In Figure 1, levels 1 and 2 denote open codes ad conceptual categories in the initial review of the secondary data. The bottom row, called open codes, indicates the initial set of codes (variables) which were identified from the secondary data. These codes were reviewed, compared and contrasted to identify the common features among them in order to cluster them into 'conceptual categories'. Level 2 contains those identified categories. For example, all those ethnics flavors identified in the initial stage previously were subsumed under the category of ethnic or cooking origin. Although the approach of this analytic process was 'grounded', initial construction for these codes or researchers interpretation actually started early in the process. Thereby, this to some extents shed the doubt on the notion that the ultimate approach was totally 'grounded'. Nevertheless, as the nature of this

method incurred in social science study, the researcher is often a relative insider in the field, studying a topic that she/or he already knows quite well (Harry et. al, 2005). Thus, it would be naïve to think that preconceived beliefs and perspectives will not be brought to bear on the data.

2    A nonparametric bootstrapping (Chin, 1988; Tenenhous et al. 2005; Wetzels et al. 2009) applying with 5000 replications (Hair et al. 2014) was performed to obtain the empirical $\tau$ and *se* values.

3    Testing a measurement model in PLS-SEM is equivalent to the method of Confirmatory Factor Analysis (CFA) performed in Covariance based-Structural Equation Modeling (CB-SEM) that is used to confirm (reject) theories. Whilst, PLS-SEM, a variance based-Structural Equation Modeling, is primarily used to develop theories.

# Chapter 16

# Risk Management Strategies and Management Implication of Cultural Difference for a P2P Virtual Enterprise

**Sunny Jeong**
*Wittenberg University, USA*

## ABSTRACT

*This chapter examines and compares closely two virtual travel enterprises, Couchsurfing.org (CS, USA) and Gilbut.net (Gilbut, Korea). These platforms allow people to offer free travel resources including information, accommodation and transportation. Both organizations have become a mission driven enterprises similar to a not for profit model, and are run without receiving any advertising funds from the private sector. Their different cultural orientation provides interesting insights that emphasize same core strategies to create a critical mass of highly motivated contributors. At the same time, cultural differences suggest that technical features and core designs should be customized according to the cultural preferences such as the degree of individual visibilities and strong/weak group identity. Comparison of both networks provides an invaluable insight to understand how critical it is to set up strategic online features in order to promote reciprocity and a certain degree of anonymity.*

## INTRODUCTION

Recent developments in online commerce and social media have made sharing travel services easier and affordable, leading to new business models involving peer-to-peer (P2P) options. Forbes estimates that the revenue flowing through the share economy directly into people's wallets will surpass $3.5 billion this year, with growth exceeding 25% (Geron, 2013), and World Travel Market Global Trend Report made by Euromonitor International (2014) indicates that P2P travel services are recording strong growth in European markets. P2P is a gateway to allow complete strangers to rent out their homes to travelers (e.g. Airbnb.com, HouseTrip.com, Homeaway. com, Gilbut.net, Couchsurfing.org) to lend their vehicles (e.g. Blablacar.com & Avis bought car

DOI: 10.4018/978-1-4666-8606-9.ch016

sharing company Zipcar for US$500 million in 2013), to lead guided tours (e.g. Vayable.com), and to meet out-of-towners for meals (e.g. Couchsurfing.org), all set up via the Internet.

Despite growing popularity, the P2P industry is experiencing growing pains. Feedback given by P2P users often include negative aspects of virtual organizations. Problems range from vandalism, defrauding and scamming users, illegal behavior, extreme cases of rape or inappropriate sexual conduct, gross violations of privacy, and residents' rights, to difficulty of any real appeals or dispute resolution process, violation of local tax payment and short-term rental laws, etc. This study is particularly intrigued by the emerging strategies of P2P ventures to manage the risk and gain legitimacy of its operation and financial transactions. In a traditional hospitality industry, hotels and service providers seek a permit for business operation from the government, which provides legitimacies of its operation to customers. All transactions are made formally under the law, and responsibilities of service providers are clear. Conflicts between the customers and service providers are often mediated by 3rd parties such as Customer Council or Hotel Association etc. However, P2P business has emerged in an informal economy. Service matching websites connect travelers to individuals who can offer their houses or cars for a short term for extra income. Transactions are often made in cash. Most service providers, therefore, are not legitimized and regulated by the industry or commerce laws. P2P service matching websites or customers themselves need to find ways to build trust, legitimacy and manage uncertainties and risk. As such, there is a managerial and theoretical need for a more in-depth understanding of P2P venture management.

In order to understand the nature of the collective crowds in the P2P travel trend, this chapter focuses two salient risk management strategies: traceability and visibility management, in addition

to the suggestion of cross-cultural management implication. By illustrating each strategy, this chapter addresses the following questions. What aspects of ICT allow a P2P venture to gain, keep, and grow customers where high risks are involved in delivering, using, and sharing services between strangers? Is it possible to create a safe environment to sustain users that encompass different nations, cultures, values, and norms? What are some contextual and technological strategies to improve the experiences of P2P online ventures?

This chapter examines and compares closely two virtual travel enterprises, Couchsurfing.org (CS, USA) and Gilbut.net (Gilbut, Korea) that I have studied over many years by active participations, observations, interviews and content analysis. Couchsurfing is a global online network of travelers that originated in the USA, and Gilbut is a national network started in South Korea where people offer free travel resources including information, accommodation and transportation. Both organizations have become a mission driven organization similar to a not for profit model, and are run without receiving any advertising funds from the private sector. Their different cultural orientation provides interesting insights that emphasize same core strategies to create a critical mass of highly motivated contributors. At the same time, cultural differences suggest that technical features and core designs should be customized according to the cultural preferences such as the degree of individual visibilities and strong/weak group identity. Comparison of both networks provides an invaluable insight to understand how critical it is to set up strategic online features in order to promote reciprocity and a certain degree of anonymity.

## COUCHSURFING AND GILBUT

Couchsurfing was started by an internet entrepreneur, Casey Fenton, 27, in Anchorage, Alaska.

When he turned 25, he described himself as having a 'quarter-life crisis,' which prompted him to travel all around the world, and he got the idea of starting Couchsurfing after a trip to Iceland. He said "I spammed 1,500 students at the University of Iceland and in 24 hours I had between 50 and 100 people saying, Yeah, come stay with me! At that point I had the opposite problem. Who should I stay with?" He wound up staying at the home of an Icelandic rhythm-and-blues singer and this positive experience inspired him to start the CouchSurfing Project. Though Fenton registered the Couchsurfing.com domain name in 1999, it was not until January of 2004 that he was able to bring his non-profit idea to life. Within 3 years of opening, 38,000 members have successfully couchsurfed. Currently, nearly 7 million members populate CouchSurfing, which represents 100,000 cities across the world. To overcome the language barrier, the English-language site can be translated into 13 other languages, including French, Spanish, and Chinese. Members' average age is 29, but some are as young as 18 (the minimum age), and as old as 78. Couchsurfing is a variation on the old home-swapping idea, except that the owner is there and visitors do not necessarily need to reciprocate. The largest national group of members of Couchsurfing are from the USA (21%), and 85% of members are from Europe and America. Only 1% of members are from Asia. Since the market share of tourism in Asia is about 20%, vs 16% in the USA, what possibly explains the imbalance of regional participation in Couchsurfing when membership is open to the world? Do the organizational and technological settings of the online network have anything to do with cultural distance between the West and the East? These questions will be addressed in findings when the different social context and attributes of computer mediated communication are taken into consideration.

Another national online network, Gilbut.net is examined and compared with CouchSurfing. Members share their travel information, photos, travel essays, and journals, and provide travel resources. Similarly, members of Gilbut made their homes available to others and shared their cars with anonymous members "for free" through web boards. The founders of Gilbut were two men in their early 30s who were seeking a way to share experiences, information, relationships, and knowledge they gained through their numerous travels. They opened the Gilbut online community with the help of one patron (both have jobs in computer science) who was willing to provide a free online 'home' (server) for this community.

The Gilbut network (www.gilbut.net) which means 'friends on the road (of travel)' opened to the public in March 2001. Over the years, this site has been nominated as number one among virtual travel communities by several web search engines, such as Naver, Dreamwiz, and Yahoo in Korea. Gilbut reached 15,000 in 2003 and 500 visitors every day. According to secondary data, a Gilbut member survey done by Gilbut staff in 2003, user groups of Gilbut are predominantly in their early 30s for men and late 20s for women. Their marital status is mostly single, with 3% married people. As far as occupations, more than half are working (65%), and most others are students (35%), according to one interviewee, Yun, a core member of Gilbut in Seoul (Yun, personal communication, April 9, 2003). Six officers and a founder who major in web design, computer programming, and information science moderate Gilbut's system.

Both Gilbut and CS experienced crises at one point of their lives differently and evolved to become a model of failure and success respectively. Gilbut network does not exist any longer since early 2008 while CS continues to thrive and grow further through several crises.

On the day of June 29, 2006, a crisis message from the founder of CS, Casey, announcing a database crash, was sent out to members. He wrote:

*Dear CouchSurfers,*

*Two days ago CouchSurfing experienced what could be described as the perfect storm. The database administrators we hired made two critical mistakes. First, we had a major, avoidable hard drive crash. Secondly, the incremental back-ups weren't executed in the correct manner, and twelve of our most important data files didn't survive... CouchSurfing as we knew it doesn't exist anymore.....I have devoted the last three years of my life to CouchSurfing. I have literally poured every cent I have into the site. I've sacrificed my health, my time, and my own ability to travel and meet people. In many ways I've put my life and wanderlust on hold to build this network. I'm not complaining; it's been a fantastic ride. As devastating as it is to consider, it looks like the ride is over.... We all own a piece of the CouchSurfing flame, it's up to us to keep the fire going and light the world. So let's do it, let's light the world! What will you do with your flame? Goodnight, Couch-Surfing. May our flames burn bright.*

*I love you,*

*Casey*

*If you wish to send your thoughts, encouragement or positive messages, contact us at shunyata@ couchsurfing.com <mailto:shunyata@couchsurfing.com>*

Approximately 48 hours after the crash happened, he posted a note of "miracle happened":

*What happened next was unbelievable. Within the following 24 hours we received more than 2,000 emails of support from members express-*

*of CouchSurfing, they wanted to help bring it back, and would have no problem re-entering their profile information. Many users expressed that they didn't mind if the databases were zeroed out and the community completely started from scratch. I was reminded that the CS community is not about the data, or about the furniture, it is about the network and the friendships that have already been created. The data was dead, but the community was alive...It was clear that CS could not die...We decided that it would be worth it to continue to develop CouchSurfing.com if the community would be willing to participate in an even deeper way and take on the majority of the workload. It was apparent that I just couldn't do all of the work myself. The plan was to gather as much data as we could and re-launch the site as soon as possible. CS collective was organized around the world.*

On July 11, 2006, twelve days after the report of crash, CS announced the launch of a new/better version of CS. More organized human power, which was comprised of skilled individuals scattered around the world, showed their capacity to get together and strengthen the CS community in a better fashion. Version 2.0 was re-designed, re-built, and re-organized through the Montreal Collective 2006 and remote CouchSurfers around the world. In addition to having improved backup plans, and more ways to get involved including ambassadorship and a renewed focus in the mission, the strength of weak ties was systemized by having collectives. All the collectives are supported by all other members of CS with donations of cash, food, garbage bags, lamps, chairs, and tables. Donations for the Montreal collective only reached over $8,000, so that the core group of skilled people can get together to improve the CS project:

CouchSurfing Collectives are gatherings of dedicated members who work on building this project. These collectives meet for as little as a few

New Zealand, Austria, and Canada. Indeed, crisis became an opportunity to improve systems by collective actions and strengthen the capacity of community for CS. The transition toward a new phase of organizational development is always accompanied by a crisis. Founders and leaders of CS should reflect the entrepreneurial culture of the revolutionary idea they brought into reality and continuously revitalize them to keep CS as a living organism.

In contrast, Gilbut became inactive over time. It lost its rigorous interest in growth and finally stopped the service since 2008. No discussion and communication with members were made as if it confirms that Gilbut is a founder's personal project. What can explain this totally different life path of P2P hospitality networks?

## Method

This study uses qualitative methods guided by a grounded theory (Corbin & Strauss, 1990). Distinct from other qualitative methods, grounded theory dictates that data emerge from the experiences of participants (Taylor & Bogdan, 1998), and the analysis begins as soon as the first bit of data is collected (Corbin & Strauss, 1990). All seemingly relevant issues must be incorporated into the next set of interviews and observations. This process is a major source of the effectiveness of the grounded theory approach in particular of this study's nature of years of participation in two online communities. Repeating concepts present in interviews, documents, and observations in one form or another are the basic units of analysis, and categories group these concepts to develop theory. This is why the research method is one of discovery, and one which grounds a theory in reality (Glaser & Strauss, 1967). In this study, core categories are identified and saturated into two risk management strategies: visibility and traceability. Each strategy is strengthened, sustained or limited by organizational and technical strategies chosen differently by Gilbut network than by Couchsurf-

ing. Organizational and technical strategies are further investigated by their cultural orientation.

## Data

The data in this study come from various sources. Data collection procedures involve interviews and participant observations, as well as examination of documents, newspapers, and emails. The preliminary investigation was done through several interviews and participant observations between April 2003 and August 2005 for Gilbut. Participant observation of six year of membership in Gilbut (2003-2008) and CS (2006-2010) and actual trips with members from both communities (2002 with Gilbut members and 2006 with CS members) were taken into account for the analysis. Analysis of documents related to CS and Gilbut during those years, such as email newsletters, newspaper articles, online testimonials, blog writings, and email communication with members of CS were conducted. When observation and participation took place, I recorded non-verbal behaviors on the field notes as they occurred. In-depth qualitative interviews were conducted on August 2005 with 10 Gilbut members and on December 2006 with 5 CS members to deeply explore the respondent's point of view, feelings and perspectives about their motivations to join and retain their contributions to each community. Open-ended questions were asked such as "What motivated you to participate in Gilbut?," "What aspects of this online travel community have you liked or disliked the most?" and "How would you describe your experience in hosting strangers at your home, if you ever hosted?" Although semi structured questions were prepared before the interviews, the order of questions and specific wording of questions were left flexible. The flow of the conversation dictated the questions asked and the order of the questions, so that the smooth transition from one topic to the next was ensured. In general, each interview took about one to three hours. The responses were recorded with an audio tape and transcribed. The researcher's immediate views and analysis after the interview were written in a separate note and put together with related interviews later when transcriptions were done. Testimonies from 335 CS participants were collected on August 2007 and analyzed to find common themes and concepts. Content analysis techniques (Snyder and Omoto, 2000) were used for the quantitative description of the contents of communications and text.

# RISK MANAGEMENT STRATEGIES

## Visibility vs. Anonymity

Building trust is key for online communities to allow people to build friendships from them. An important step in creating trust and building a trustworthy identity is providing personal information to other members. In contrast to Gilbut's lack of technical support for members' personal pages, using a personal profile page for each member and encouraging its use are one of the best strategies to build trust in CS. This page includes pictures, some self-description including motto, dreams, interests, languages, and links to other resources relevant to the member's professional and personal life, which they wish to share in addition to their occupation, age, and gender. These profiles help members get a better concept of the other person's expertise and interests. Links to other relevant resources from a profile can extend the notion of sharing expertise without having to ask and wait for an answer. Also, this profile helps one to find like-minded people to create sub-communities inside of CS.

Personal pages also help to lessen the fear of posting by newcomers. Arcichvili et al. (2003) shows that online participants were afraid that what they post might not be important (might not deserve to be posted), or might not be completely accurate, or might not be relevant to a specific discussion. There was an obvious fear of 'losing face' in this sense and letting colleagues down

or misleading them. However, upon reading a couple of profiles, people found it easy to post one of their own and even be more creative and fun in describing themselves.

On the other hand, a certain degree of anonymity was found to positively connect members through online interactions The anonymity of P2P networks creates inflated positive images of an individual's identity. It helps people to establish initial contact with others quicker in a virtual environment than the real world. This aspect was found in both online communities of CS and Gilbut. On the other hand, since the success of an online network lies in the enrichment of offline meetings (staying together, traveling together, showing guests around), validity of personal identifications inflated online is complemented by offline meetings. Because of that, total anonymity such as giving no clue of each other's expectation of their meetings can be detrimental to the trust building process and the sustainability of online network. System of Gilbut adopted total anonymity with no registration process. It initially worked to recruit members to try out at the first time but failed to retain repetitive contributors. The possibility of misrepresentation of some members in an online hospitality network is attributed to two reasons. First, leaving negative feedback toward volunteers in good faith to host strangers with no cost are strongly discouraged, although not explicitly. In other words, leaving only positive feedbacks are enforced and positive experiences are widely promoted to the public. Secondly, when users are leaving negative feedback to anyone, they take the same risk of receiving negative feedback in return. P2P allows loose boundaries between service providers and customers, and people do not like to take a risk to receive a negative or unfair feedback from others.

CS requires the registration of individual pages which release a certain degree of members' identities including nationality, gender, appearance, race and ethnicity. It provides cues for members to determine who they can trust and like to in teract with so that their interaction with other members is not too far from their expectation. In sum, allowing a certain degree of anonymity is one critical factor that P2P hospitality networks are more successfully connecting world than real world networks. However, it is necessary to set up systems to control mistrust possibly caused by total anonymity.

In line with a positive effect of visible online contributions in CS, concepts of stigmergy (Susi & Ziemke, 2001), collective intelligence (Heylighen, 1999, 2007) and the simulation of swarming behavior (Bonabeau, Dorigo & Theraulaz, 1999) are particularly relevant in this study. The basic idea is that a termite initially drops a little bit of mud in a random place, but that the heaps that are formed in this way stimulate other termites to add to them (rather than start a heap of their own), thus making them grow higher until they touch other similarly constructed columns. Stigmergy is more than blind variation and natural selection, though: the visible traces of the work performed previously function as a mediator system (Heylighen, 2007), storing, and (indirectly) communicating information for the community. In that way, the mediator coordinates further activity, directing it towards the tasks where it is most likely to be fruitful. This requires a shared workspace accessible to all contributors (similar to what in AI is called a "blackboard system"). Likewise, successful stories of online users contribute to generating a strong trail of their following collective actions. Community reinforces norms of reciprocity (Blanchard & Horan, 1998) because small acts of helping can be more easily viewed by the entire group, and might create the perception of a strong norm of reciprocity within an entire online community.

Findings of this study confirm that in order to desgintechnological settings effective, features of online community should makecontributions visible, identifiable and interactive. By doing this, further contributions are induced andcritical mass can be successfully reached. However, a culture which values humility and modesty may not favor this setting of high visibility of contributions and initial participations can be hesitated because of this. Visualizing contributions without releasing personal identities have been observed in Gilbut Korean community.

## Traceability

The flip side of trust in this type of online community is insecurity and a lack of safety. As identified by the first surfers, the issue of security is the biggest obstacle for participating in hosting or being hosted by CS and Gilbut. Trust, safety, and security issues seem to have been well taken care of by technological settings of online communities. In CS, an optional verification system basically ensures that a member is who he says he is and lives where he says he lives by checking their credit card information. On the other hand, the vouching system in CS also functions as the verification system. Verified small numbers of members (founders and their initial friends) can vouch for their friends and only vouched-for members can further verify others. Members can vouch for other members through postings, which can be found on a member's profile page under the heading 'Friends.' Thinking of it as positive word-of-mouth and networking among friends and friends of friends, most of them are somehow linked to other CS members, which makes people feel safe about participating, assuming that someone they know in this community knows the other person they are contacting.

As stated earlier, one of the technical strategies incorporated into the psychological aspect of participating in the online community is an inflated positive image of other members. In some cases, only positive confirmation of identification gained by face-to-face (FtF) meetings are visually displayed while negative experiences after FtF meetings in foreign places tend not to be widely shared. The lack of physical cues in online communities and the positively inflated image of other members are fostering possible meetings and interactions in both Gilbut and CS. Members of electronic groups inflate their perceptions of their partners, and group members even report that their partners are more attractive over computer mediated communications than they are in F-t-F or telephone interactions (Blanchard & Horan, 1998). In Gilbut, the lack of physical cues of age, appearance, and class induces people to agree to be a travel partner imagining he or she might be the right one to travel with. One interviewee (Oh, Gilbut member, male, 35) answered the question about the motivation of providing free transportation or free accommodation with, "you don't know who you will be end up for traveling with for hours or even days together…it gives me an excitement, high expectation and anticipation to meet a new person that I never interacted although I don't know whether he or she might be the right travel partner for me…I prefer waiting to know the person until I meet."

CS keeps a lower degree of anonymity than Gilbut since personal pages in CS include gender, nationality, race, ethnicity and appearance. It is worth noting that age and social class are not manifest elements of identification in CS. Positively inflated images of other members in both communities are constructed from two factors. People who upload information and images about themselves choose which part of themselves they wish to portray. Second, negative feedback about each other seldom happens, considering no one likes to be seen as a 'bad person' who spreads bad experiences or negative feelings directly toward others. Rather, people with negative experiences will stop their participation and leave the community. Several interviews taken from both communities show negative experiences about meetings and information about these experiences are not shared with the majority of other members on community sites but some serious complaints and legal actions were taken outside of online communities. One woman interviewee (31, Seoul, Gilbut) said that one trip she initiated with other members was cancelled after the first

meeting because of different expectations about each other. "He (guy she met online) does not want to pursue trips that I initiated once he knows that I have a boyfriend with me at the meeting… no potential dating means no trip for him and I was very disappointed." Similar examples were provided by another interviewee in CS (34, USA, CS) who visited Mexico. She recalled:

*When I arrived to the airport, I was told to give a call to the guy that I met through CS and who offered me a coffee or city tour…When I finally gave him a call to explain where I was and we arranged how to meet…My male friend was talking next to me at that time and suddenly the guy over the phone asked me "Is your friend you are with a girl or boy?"…Once I said it's a guy, he suddenly changed his mind and said it might be better for us to explore without him…I felt very uncomfortable and unhappy about that…I don't know why he only received positive feedbacks…I did not leave any feedback for him though (Sophia, 34, USA, CS).*

There have been serious complaints followed by legal actions about hosts of CS but no additional policy changes or formal responses were at least officially made by Couchsurfing.

*Still, the online service ignores complaints from women and LGBTQ travelers who have been attacked, drugged, raped, molested, and harassed by hosts…CouchSurfing denies responsibility with the pat response that victims should more vigorously vet potential hosts and report illegal behavior to the proper authorities in the country in which they're traveling…"CouchSurfing should be shut down," says Ulto. "It's a menace to women, and allowing sexual predators to continue to prey on them is irresponsible, especially in this economy, when young travelers are looking for cheaper accommodations." Harvard University agrees that the risk outweighs the benefit: it recently*

*ing (retrieved on December 10, 2010 from http://
news.change.org/stories/couchsurfing-ignores-
harassment-and-assault).*

*One of the most disconcerting things about Couch-
Surfing is the pressure to hang out with people
when you would not otherwise want to do so. Not
in a positive way as in talking to people you would
not normally talk to and gaining new insight, but
rather a pressure for people who simply don't
get along to pretend they like and are interested
in learning more about each other (retrieved on
November 30, 2010 from http://allthatiswrong.
wordpress.com/2010/01/24/a-criticism-of-couch-
surfing-and-review-of-alternatives/)*

One interviewee in Gilbut who is one of the
dedicated administrators mentioned:

*There are events not visible, publicized, or shared
among other members which can be detrimental
for sustaining this type of online community.
There is always a certain level of unsuccessful or
unhappy stories involving even robbery or feelings
of being ripped off, etc...but nobody knows except
oneself, and administrators are very careful not to
let things like this be heard by other members...
This type of information is only released when we
feel it can be prevented by announcing it or suggesting a couple of strategies to prevent negative
experiences (Ho, 38, Seoul, Gilbut).*

Sometimes, the excitement to meet with new
people contains a certain degree of risk and danger,
including possible negative outcomes. Members
in CS live all around the world, and across borders
of diverse cultures and languages. Because people
meeting over CS are from many different cultures,
languages, and places in the world, CS sets several
safeguards for members, while Gilbut seems to be
less sensitive to the safety issue in terms of hosting
and traveling with strangers. This difference might
be attributed to the homogenous nature of Gilbut
members (all Korean). The relatively denser and

closer network of Korean society makes it easier
to track down a host who violates the norms and
values set for this community. Another explanation
might be the nature of online networks in Korea,
extension of offline relations to online as major
motivations of online users. Core members of
Gilbut are all good friends and they move their
offline relationships into online spaces. Safety issues appear to be their main concern, but they are
not wary enough to change their technical settings
to make participation and identification of persons
visible. In addition, the nature of the voluntary
organization does not handle any criticism well
because volunteers invest their time and energy
in exchange of appreciation and recognition of
their efforts. However, not taking criticism into
account for improvements will degenerate the
system in the long run.

*It is important to note that many CouchSurfing
members cannot handle any criticism of the project
at all. They have a lot of love for their community
and oppose anyone who would ask questions or
demand answers. This is a shame, as most of the
time these people raise valid points and just get attacked by the more rabid members. It is yet another
example of supreme close-mindedness...(retrieved
on December 10, 2011 from http://allthatiswrong.
wordpress.com/2010/01/24/a-criticism-of-couch-
surfing-and-review-of-alternatives/)*

Technological strategies of visibility as a basis
for reputation and identification are very critical
factors of CS's success. When someone hosts
others in CS, this contribution must be tracked
with positive feedback from guests so that there
is accountability, i.e., the actor can be adequately
credited with the cost or benefit of the contribution.
As simple as having a tracking system, making
sure everyone must log in with a username and
password before contributing and keeping a log-
file, and incorporating highly complex rating and
reputation systems, both leave the stigmergic trails
to reinforce and increase contributions from others.

The bigger an online community becomes, the more it needs a better system of members' identification authentication. Due to the nature of the cosmopolitan community of CS, where members are citizens of the world, controlling anonymity of members' identification is widely debated in regard to the safety and trust issues. On the positive side, the CS community reaps the benefits of a heterogeneous crowding effect through the world-wide members it recruits: retention of active participants and talented volunteers. However, the system should evolve as an organization grows. Sophisticated authentication and verification processes of member identifications become more critical once an organization passes the pioneering phase or the organizational scope expands to be global in order to address anonymity issues and trust building.

## MANAGEMENT OF CULTURAL DIFFERENCE

### Distributed Authority and Ownership of Community Rules

Organizations exist to establish a certain degree of procedural and institutional authority (Steinmueller, 2002, Mateos Garcia & Steinmueller, 2003). Procedural authority consists of incentives, social norms, and power that define how decisions about practices, routines, and procedures should be taken within an organization. Institutional authority concerns the recruitment of members to an organization, assignment of roles, and the government of membership conditions and expression. Both founders of CS and Gilbut exercised strong institutional authority to set up the mission and membership conditions of online community. They were governed by strong-headed founders and their associates. However, CS evolved to have their procedural authority flexible and flat to be shared. Personal pages are all that a user needs and administrators' roles to moderate contents posted

from users are minimal to non-existent. All communication between members is mediated by the system which leaves logs to each other's personal page and at the same time sends automatic email to both parties involved without any intervention by founders or staff. Personal contact information is never released to the public. On the contrary, many procedures in Gilbut, specifically the main contents of the home page and user communications are governed by core members and founders of Gilbut. They are 'not open' and hence, reserved for administrators (i.e., experienced and trusted users/developers) to delete, edit or change. Users can only participate in the discussion about categories and topics decided and generated by administrators. Connections among members are made by postings with their contact information available to the public via the designated online forum of "Free Accommodation". There is no registration required in order to participate and all postings are anonymous. Administrators in Gilbut exercise a strong degree of institutional authority. They can ban certain IP addresses and permanently delete pages and their histories of participations if they think postings are harmful, irrelevant or detrimental to the mission of Gilbut. Such actions are undertaken when specific users are responsible for postings not relevant to the categorized topics administrators initiated. One of speculations is that the hierarchic culture of Korean society might be associated with the rigidity of the system and an unwillingness to share authority with members. Sharing management authority with members instead of strong central governance contributed to the success of the CS online community. Devising their own rules resulted in processes that allowed social norms to evolve and thereby increase the probability of individuals better cooperating and actively participating in online community.

Distributed authority or ownership of community rules, and smart systems which require minimum human intervention for members' participation, are critical factors to grow and sustain the online community. In addition, different orgnizational structures define one's role in a network. CS started from 2 founders and became structurally similar to a nonprofit organization with 6 board members and 5 divisions: Member Experience, Technology, Operation, Project Management, and Volunteer Teams. Their 5 teams are organized to address different tasks at hand and therefore, actual tasks of an organization define individual roles in a community. However, the more rigid structure of Gilbut resembles a traditional organizational structure with a president, vice president, treasurer, and PR manager. Positions in Gilbut broadly defined individual roles, which often confused who was responsible for what tasks. People in these positions felt that they were expected and forced to make sacrifices for an organization due to their abstract yet grand titles, and frustration was built up to the point of their discontinued participation.

## Individual Recognition

Building fame and reputation often appeared among several motivations that participants offer services online. One interviewee (Kim, 37, Gwangju regional chapter, Gilbut) confessed that the main reason for him to host people from other cities was to give them an opportunity to appreciate "Gwangju, my city." Building self-identity related to their home town, city, and region was clearly one of the main factors to induce online contributions in the Gilbut network. When asked about factors and reasons to be voluntarily hosting strangers at their homes, several interviewees noted a regional identity. One said, "I noticed that people from my region do not host as many people from other regions and it motivated me to host.... I want people to know that Junla province also has a lot of nice people... " (Kim, 35, Soonchun regional chapter, Gilbut). As stated, hosting other members at one's home is considered as producing "good will" at their own cost, and building a credit in this case is not only for creating positive self-identity, but also strengthening social identity

associated with pride of place and belonging to the geographically-defined community or region. Put differently, positive group identity of the local chapter is believed to be built by having many 'good people' who are willing to host others. This also can strengthen positive self-identity. Below is another example of how an online participant is embracing the online community as a part of his/her life. By dedicating part of their home for the CS community, James and Pamela embrace CS into their daily lives.

*I wanna surf with... James and Pamela! These guys are dedicating one of the rooms in their Tennessee house to CouchSurfing. They want to outfit the space with donations from members, got a surfboard they could hang on the wall or turn into a headboard for the bed? How about some special trinket from your corner of the globe? Send them a postcard from your travels and it they will display it with pride. These two are making CS a big part of their home, and surfers a part of their family. (Newsletter, March 26 of 2006, Vol 1. No 1)*

Self-education and improvement are other psychological motivations to participate actively online, although these motives are not directly related to bringing first-time users, rather they work to retain existing members in the CS network. About 65 persons out of 335 testimonies that I analyzed mentioned that they saw changes in their lives that allowed them to understand themselves better, make friends, travel around the world, and live daily lives with a richer experience:

*... Ok. Couchsurfing has been changing my life in 360 degrees....great, discovering hidden values about others and myself... (Testimony from Foxbaz, Portugal on Nov. 11. 2006)*

*CouchSurfing has changed my life. I am constantly learning about myself, other cultures and on how to be a better communicator, a better friend, a better stranger, a better person…I have become a citizen of the World. (Cosmic Girl, Canada on Oct 21, 2005, CS)*

Ninety-three members out of 335 noted a rich experience through using CS, even so far as gaining further education:

*Since joining the experience has been absorbing. Now I have the bug and want everyone to allow me to Host. It's a wonderful experience meeting and learning so much from around the world. After all we are getting educated all the time and I just love it. (Reggief, UK, November 16, 2006)*

*CS is without a doubt the best thing on the internet since Google!! Search and you will find. It's the Holy Grail of globe-trotters; free accommodation, fantastic friends as you travel, and really get to know the place you visit. If not, then right home you can have the world come to you - practice languages, meet all cultures under the sun, and make some friends for life without leaving your house! So what are you waiting for?? The more the merrier:-) (Irishpolyglot, Spain, November 8, 2005)*

Altruism and feeling useful to others are other psychological motive for CS participants. The following testimony shows that being helpful and feeling good about it are obvious motives for their participations:

*This system brings peace, generosity, friendships to people around … My involvement in CS future is going through major inputs I can add with others during the collective. Here is the chance for us all to be part of it, to feel even more useful!! (Superyami, France on February 17, 2006, CS)*

Interestingly, personal identity, such as being known as 'a nice person', is a psychological motive found more prominently in CS than in Gilbut. By the same token, group identity is often promoted by Gilbut members: typically stating that 'folks in this region seem to be nice' is more important contributor of their participation than individual recognition of being considered 'a nice person.'

Stories like "CS is my extended family" or "CS defines me" are hardly found in Gilbut, yet the regional/ national identity common in Gilbut is almost never mentioned by CS members. The concern about CS's group identity or regional/ national identity is seldom seen among CS members, nor promoted. Members in CS are apparently not hosting others to make sure people have a positive impression about a certain state, country, or ethnic group. Therefore, group identity or belongingness is not a main factor to ensure active contribution in CS compared to Gilbut. The variance can be attributed to the different cultural dimension of group versus individual orientation. Korea is categorized into a collectivistic society by Hofstede's study (2010).

The technical settings of CS allow high visibility of personal contributions to the organization so the individuals receive credit and feedback about their participation from others. However, Gilbut's settings make it hard to leave any feedback to specific members since no place is designated toward individuals and most postings are anonymous. It might be something to explore further if the humility and modesty value of Asian society might restrain members from making their contributions visible and individually recognized. Wasko (2009) found in his research of collective action in electronic network of practice that online communities which incorporate technology that supports identities of individuals may be more likely succeed than networks where participation is anonymous. It is partly true more for cases based on western culture, such as CS, where incorporating technical features to make members' identity and contributions visible and accessible by other members is essential. However, members in Gilbut much preferred anonymous participations with no personal information posted on the site. Instead, they use alternative identification with fake ID and avatars. Members address other members by their online ID not by their actual names.

## Organizational Identity

CS and Gilbut adopted different strategies to develop their core organizational identities. Both organizations populated new social projects initiated by members. As Müller (1999) and Rheingold (1993, 2003) indicate, most relationships that are created online are continued in a physical space, thus creating new forms of offline and online involvement. It was found that the extension of relationships to external communities did not take place in Gilbut, while a couple of projects in CS are linked to members' personal relationships in work, projects, and friendships. Members in Gilbut rarely incorporate Gilbut relationships into their other communities. Rather, they tend to participate in more community engagement activities within Gilbut. Gilbut's philosophy of appreciating travel to spread peace and harmony helps them to organize more activities within its limited social mission?. This aspect confirms the finding of Pigg and Crank's (2004) research showing that participation is limited to social network members, rather than carried out with outsiders. There are several social and political activities organized by the Gilbut executive board members. Travel packages and Gilbut t-shirts that help the poor and people in North Korea are examples of Gilbut's focus on social activism. On the other hand, the CS collective makes a profit out of selling their T-shirts and other gifts for the further development of CS.

*C-ch-ch-check him out. I wanna surf with... MJ! This guy is creating an ecological community/ utopian tribe on a remote island in Fiji. He's got some big ideas and that same CouchSurfing ambition to make the world a smaller, more peaceful place. Both CS founder Dan and myself dig the concept and have joined the tribe. Find out more*

*about him and the project in his profile. In the mean time, surf with him in his home island of England (Newsletter, Vol 1, Issue 2, April 19, 2006)*

The mission of connecting the world into a small place and promoting peace through travel is extended to other projects like the one cited above. The connection of a personal project of one member with other community members can be made easily, and it develops into the community's common project. Another case like this is the publication of a book called "The Great Deluge" based on interactions with CS members. The story is found in a newsletter on July 21 of 2006 (Vol 1. Issue 3):

*In the aftermath of Hurricane Katrina, Emma surfed and hosted with her friend Douglas Brinkley (author and historian) who lives in New Orleans. She and a couple of her family members went to Houston and worked on the relief effort, and while there, hosted other surfers who were volunteering. The second day she was there Douglas said he'd write a book about it if she helped him. The book, "The Great Deluge" came out in May and the author gives a great nod to CouchSurfing, the compassionate surfers he met through Emma, and their work on Katrina relief. Rock it like a rocket, Emma!*

CS shared initiations by only connecting members with members of interest without centrally organizing any offline events or meetings for them or adding them into their mission. Therefore, new initiatives never change or divert core activities or identities of the organization. Gilbut, on the other hand, has taken these new initiatives as an organizational mission to diversify their activities, which in turn weakens their core mission. Again, online networks in South Korea are often used to extend off-line social relations to online to complement or deepen their off line relations. In this line, new initiatives raised by Gilbut members online became another opportunity for offline relations, while members' new projects in CS become means to connect one with others online.

This study challenges the premise of club theory that an association efficiently providing excludible goods is bound in size. This study finds that the crowding effect is not likely to hinder the development of a community, but will attract heterogeneous members and is beneficial. When the Couchsurfing community faced the database crash examined earlier, a great deal of efficiency, reliability, and quality were provided, due to the vast number of individuals who checked lines of code, fixed bugs, and provided every release with a detailed explanation in Couchsurfing wiki pages. It is worth mentioning that, as has shown true for every kind of online community, cyberspace remarkably enlarges the boundaries of a location in which to find individuals with certain desirable characteristics. In sum, crowding is interpreted as massive participation, which is a desirable factor in online communities, especially if heterogeneous.

It is more critical to keep the core identity of an organization to survive and utilize heterogeneity. The heterogeneous nature of CS, which is composed of 7 million people from 245 countries might mandate one core value as the only way to bring everyone together and sustain weak ties. Other relational opportunities and projects to link members are shared and encouraged but this should never become the new mission of an organization. Gilbut started with a homogenous group of people from one country and core members were linked by strong friendship ties. They seemed to take new projects as a way to recruit heterogeneous members and create weak ties. Divergence from the core mission weakens organizational values and contributes to organizational failure. Regardless of culture, guarding the core values and mission of an organization is critical to its success in an online community.

## BALANCED RECIPROCITY

Another significant contributor to the sustainability of P2P hospitality networks concerns reciprocity. As the French anthropologist Marcel Mauss has pointed out, a 'gift' is never free or it should not be free in order to sustain any relation in the long run; the receiver is always obligated in one way or another to reciprocate. It is important to understand 1) the context of when and how the reciprocal interaction takes place with the temporality of relation made through online network, and 2) different reciprocity required to sustain voluntary users (host) and voluntary operators of online mediation system. Two concepts of balanced and generalized reciprocity were interrogated.

The context of reciprocity between the host and the guest is a direct exchange of favors in some sense. The host provides free accommodation and possibly showing around the parts that tourist tend to miss out in exchange of enriched life experiences with new perspectives and cultures the guest brings in. In this regard, the cosmopolitan nature of CS has an advantage to reciprocate favors over Gilbut, since a Gilbut host does not enjoy new cultural perspectives in return for hosting homogenous groups of people in a nation. Although some reciprocities take place only virtually as members exchange information and knowledge of travel destinations, sustaining the network is indebted to the deeper reciprocity, which takes place when actual visits are made. Mode of reciprocity and how the reciprocity takes place provide an interesting insight. Physical interactions on top of online interactions play a more important role in building a strong and positive sense of reciprocity and explaining the sustainability of an online network than online reciprocity alone can do.

The superior difference between CS and Gilbut to foster balanced reciprocity is that the CS system allows symmetric reciprocity more easily than Gilbut. In other words, individual user pages of CS make it easy for the host to request any others including his or her guests to host him or her, while Gilbut has a rigid system that allows only a handful of individuals who sign up on the designated host bulletin board to receive requests. Number of requests easily overwhelms those volunteers over time. Reciprocating a gift (hosting) with a similar gift in kind (being hosted) in other time is possible in CS, as a balanced reciprocity explains.

Technical attributes of personal pages in CS allow larger groups of individuals to scour larger groups of resources in search of materials, projects, collaborations, and combinations. While Gilbut sets up 'many to one' service model of a handful voluntary providers listed for free accommodation, Couchsurfing allows 'many to many' role exchanges between host and guest through personal pages, so that anyone with personal page set up in CS can host and visit other members. Average number of hosting in CS is 1/2 to one (one member either hosts or visits one other member) while Gilbut is 50 to one (one member hosts 50+ members) Unbalanced reciprocity prohibits the community from retaining members and growing. Gilbut's posting system onlylisted handful volunteers whoare willing to host. Those who want to request free accommodations are individually contacting host. Therefore, free accommodation requests are intensively made toward handful volunteers in Gilbut which overwhelmed most host. There is no way to see profiles of service requesters and no easy way to become a host unless you post your name and contact openly to the public bulletin board. Often, these good-willed volunteers in Gilbut decided to stop their participations after imbalanced reciprocity overwhelmed them.

The collective action resides at the opposite side of self-interest theory (refer to early rational choice theorist Homans, 1961). According to the collective action theory, actions by individuals seem counter to the economic self-interest of the individual (Marwell & Oliver, 1993). However,

through the work of Olson (1965) and others (Goetze, 1994; Heckathorn, 1993; Taylor & Singleton, 1993), sociologists and economists have developed a theory that illustrates these "altruistic" behaviors as still based on self-interest and exchanges of a different kind. Reciprocities do not just contain financial or material benefits in exchange for producing collective goods (Olson, 1965; Axelrod, 1984). As one major reconceptualization of collective action theory put forth by Marwell & Oliver (1993), a balanced, serial (Ulrich, 1998) and generalized reciprocity (Ekeh, 1974) extend exchange theory (Homans, 1961, 1964; Blau, 1964; Emerson, 1972) to a broader context. A balanced reciprocity explains that exchange occurs not between two particular individuals, but with anyone in a group, so that a balance might occur within a group as a whole, rather than only between giver and taker. What makes this interaction "reciprocal" is the sense of satisfaction the giver feels, and the social closeness that the gift fosters.

Voluntary participations in P2P network help others contribute to the self-interest of the individual at the end, due to interactions between giver and taker, which consists of the exchange of items or values such as reputation, self-esteem, education, joy, and making friends (Jeong, 2004).

As Heckathorn (1993) notes, it is necessary to have a critical mass of strongly motivated individuals and their willingness to absorb organizational costs in order to allow collective action to begin. To the contrary of the researcher's expectation that saving money should be a strong motivation for people to participate in Gilbut and CS, instrumental motivation like saving money is mentioned as a secondary benefit after the primary benefits of nourishment, education, and joy are made possible by their participation. Participants contributing to P2P networks receive many psychological benefits as an exchange for their services. However, it is worth mentioning that one of the predominant motives to "initiate" their participation in both Gilbut and CS is "saving money" as written, shown and advertised in many news articles and testimonies of members for both networks. This paper argues that instrumental motivation is necessary to build a critical mass at the initial stage of the project, while other motivations or incentives follow instrumental motivation and they help sustain membership and increase contributions instead of driving initial participations:

*Besides the obvious benefit of not having to pay for accommodation, CouchSurfing allows travelers to experience a country and its culture from within, instead of just as an observer. (Thesavagefiles, Australia, 2005)*

*This site has gone much beyond simply saving money! The wealth of knowledge I have already acquired is unbelievable! (TheScientist, Canada, June 8, 2005)*

*The great part about couch surfing is that you're not just saving 50 bucks by not going to a hotel, but you get a real taste of the lifestyle and culture of the area you're visiting. (Djomino, USA, December 27, 2004)*

*When I first heard about couchsurfing, I thought, hey cool. I'm going to save a ton of money. Though this did happen, haha, I gained soooo much more from my experiences...(Naomi, USA, May 29, 2006)*

*i'm travelling around the world, just depending on couchsurfing, and it works. you meet people everywhere, get to know their life and culture, experience weird, funny, amazing, lovely things and besides save a lot of money. (Ruthio, Germany, January 12, 2006)*

*CouchSurfing Project does not only save money on traveling, but also gives you a unique opportunity to discover the face of everyday life, performed regularly by all those local people with local ideas,*

*local activities and local customs they live by. (Christie987, Japan, November 29, 2005)*

Another aspect of instrumental motive is that better and more articulated plans for travel are made possible by local host:

*Taking a part in CS I received...much much better and interesting planning than just use offers from travel agencies...(Bigbrother, Estonia, November 10, 2006)*

*We were in Mexico (and we knew nothing about life there ; but we were lucky 'cause a couchsurfer picked us up at the airport and gave us the possibility to stay in Mexico City for four days; he was amazing, always at disposal, friendly and kind; he cooked, he took us seeing the pyramids on Saturday. (Elena_Mike, Italy, September 23, 2006)*

*The experience one get from couchsurfing is like a dream come true...in couchsurfing you are treated to a new activity everyday, people are discovering more and more tip of traveling everyday. (Thevillagechief, Kenya October 8, 2006)*

Gilbut's technical aspects confirm and strengthen the instrumental motivation of users to search for trustworthy travel information. Gilbut uses software tools that better support two-way transactions for communication to allow rich and valid information storage and retrieval. It supplies the function of interactive database storage involving "broadcast-reception-response-reception." This information function of supporting communication is qualitatively different from personal email exchanges.

It is noteworthy to state that instrumental motivations such as 'saving money' or 'finding a new job' might work to attract new members, and help establish critical mass at the initial stage of an organizational development. Such instrumental motives seem to precede other motives or manifest

communities reach critical mass, other relational and psychological motivations become major factors to retain members and grow further. As every organization evolves in different phases, follow up research on the link of each motivation to a specific organizational form (instrumental to pioneering phase then relational/ psychological ones to the next phase) might be needed to prove if this observation is valid.

Concerning reciprocity between operational volunteers and the others is not clear, though. Most often, founders and leaders of online hospitality networks are sacrificing their individual lives to provide public services in exchange of benefits of receiving recognition, fame and appreciation by members. When volunteers invest hundreds hours to sustain and improve the system, recognition and appreciation do not seem to be satisfactory incentives to retain them. Many volunteers who resigned their ambassadorship in CS reflected how poorly volunteers were managed. In this regard, generalized reciprocity of sharing goods or labor with others without expecting anything in return will sustain short lives if it works once or twice. Should we ask, then, how to retain dedicated volunteers and how to fix asymmetrical reciprocity? I think we should ask more fundamental questions about the voluntary nature of the online hospitality network. Is asking for repetitive voluntary contributions, as is the case in non-for-profit organizations, for the operation and management of organization ever sustainable? I would like to shed a different light onto covering the operational costs of online community and suggest a new organizational identity of online hospitality networks: social business.

Recently, serial comments of resigned volunteers of CS system and unsatisfied users were made on several blogs. Problems range from defrauding and scamming users, illegal behavior, and extreme cases of rape or inappropriate sexual conduct, to gross violations of privacy, a complete lack of any real appeals or dispute resolution process and censorship, dishonesty of organizational legal status, transparency of financial transactions, and nepotism in operation and volunteer managements. Volunteers do not trust the intuition of the founder any longer, and user complaints increase and can't be handled substantially anymore. However, most problems are operational issues which are common in the transitional stage of organizational growth. Therefore, the success of transitioning to the next phase of organizational development can be determined by an operational decision of how to reform the organizational identity to allow reliable management and legitimate operation. I speculate that most problems are attributed to the voluntary nature of this organization and its operational positioning of non-for-profit organizational status. When the majority of the operation is managed by random or temporary volunteers, evolution of the system can't catch up with the increasing rate of participants and their new requests. The voluntary nature of online hospitality networks raises the important question about the sustainability of online communities. Volunteers can run the project successfully as long as it is a short term project basis with specific tasks at hand, or involves a small scale of heterogeneity in participants. The longer and bigger the organization scales up, operation costs grow beyond what volunteers can handle.

As was examined in detail in my findings, the nature of voluntary participation of generalized reciprocity escalates an unwillingness of taking constructive criticism to lead to changes in the organization. Targeting volunteers who sacrifice their time for others is a tough call. There is nothing wrong with making profits from the profile verification process in CS that users are willing to pay for, as long as CS makes it clear that what they are doing is exactly what they said they would do. If verification is nothing more than the process of seeking mandatory donations of small amounts (or profit making to cover operation costs), CS should say we collect donations to cover operational costs instead of claiming it a verification system, which has been widely criticized as scam and fraud. A solution to this type of management issues should be sought not in finding quick remedies of a current crises but to transform completely into new organization with reframed model of social venture. This new form of social venture makes profit making legitimate and necessary as long as it carries out social missions. Non for profit status, regardless of the fact that CS is incorporated successfully or not, puts CS in a constrained position where members continuously evaluate the legality issue of non for profit management, such as the organizational structure of board and CEO, the proportion of donation money to be used in volunteers' rent, food and travel instead of evaluating the successful accomplishment of its missions.

## CONCLUSION

The examination of two cases of online tourism communities from USA and Korea explains that there are both common threads beyond their differences to explain initial popularity and different attributes of P2P networks to manage risks. Visibility of contributions and participations in addition to the validity of members' identity are necessary to build trust and sustain a P2P network. Initially, a certain degree of anonymity was found positively related to connect members to interact with others online until members feel comfortable enough to release their identities and visible contributions. Anonymity helps people to establish initial contact with others more quickly in a virtual environment than in the real world. However, in the long run, visibility of members' participation and contribution on top of valid identification became necessary to build a sustainable enterprise. Concepts of stigmergy explains the positive effect of visible and traceable contributions of members to encourage more participations of others and reach a critical mass. In addition, balanced reciprocity is introduced to explain a P2P network's success. The context of reciprocity between the host and the guest is based on the exchange of favors in

some sense. The host provides free accommodation, transportation, and local tour guide service in exchange for making new friends, joys, and educational benefit brought by the guest. The superior difference of CS to Gilbut is that the CS system allows symmetric reciprocity more easily than Gilbut. The individual user pages of CS make it easy for the host to request any others, including his or her guests to host him or her, while Gilbut has a rigid system that only handful individuals who sign up on designated host bulletin board will receive requests. Number of requests easily overwhelms those volunteers over time. Reciprocating a gift (hosting) with a similar gift in kind (being hosted) in other time is possible in CS and it fosters a balanced reciprocity that promotes sustainability.

On the other hand, cultural differences between CS and Gilbut show different preferences on visibility of members' identities and contributions. Members in Gilbut prefer anonymity of their identities and participations. On top of this, culture of collectivism attributes to the different participation pattern such as joining online community as a group due to the strong off-line group affiliation. A good portion of Gilbut members joined the P2P network through their close friends, family members, companies, and other social associations. Implication of this cultural difference can be made such as adjusting marketing strategies of P2P network to identity market segments based on groups of people. Thus, this chapter addresses both a managerial and theoretical need for a more in-depth understanding P2P hospitality networks.

## REFERENCES

Ardichvili, A., Page, V., & Wentling, T. (2003). Motivation and barriers to participation in virtual knowledge-sharing communities of practice. *Journal of Knowledge Management*, 7(1), 64–77. doi:10.1108/13673270310463626

Axelrod, R. (1984). *The evolution or cooperation.* New York: Basic Books.

Blanchard, A., & Horan, T. (1998). Social capital and virtual communities. *Social Science Computer Review, 16,* 293–307. doi:10.1177/089443939801600306

Blau, P. M. (1964). *Exchange and power in social life.* New York: Wiley.

Bonabeau, E., Dorigo, M., & Theraulaz, G. (1999). *Swarm intelligence: From natural to artificial Systems.* New York, NY: Oxford University Press.

Ciffolilli, A. (2003). Phantom authority, self–selective recruitment and retention of members in virtual communities: The case of Wikipedia. *First Monday, 8*(12[REMOVED HYPERLINK FIELD]). doi:10.5210/fm.v8i12.1108

Corbin, J., & Strauss, A. (1990). Grounded theory research: Procedures, canons, and evaluative criteria. *Qualitative Sociology, 13*(1), 3–21. doi:10.1007/BF00988593

Ekeh, P. P. (1974). *Social exchange theory: The two traditions.* Cambridge, MA: Harvard University Press.

Emerson, R. M. (1972). Exchange Theory: Part II: exchange relations and networks. In J. Berger, M. Zelditch, & B. Anderson (Eds.), Sociological theories in progress (vol. 2, pp. 58-87). Boston: Houghton Mifflin.

Euromonitor International. (2013). *World Travel Market Global Trend Report.* Retrieved from http://www.wtmlondon.com/files/wtm_global_trends_2013.pdf

Geron, T. (2013). Airbnb and the unstoppable rise of the share economy. *Forbes, 11*(Feb). Retrieved from http://www.forbes.com/sites/tomiogeron/2013/01/23/airbnb-and-the-unstoppable-rise-of-the-share-economy/

Glaser, B., & Strauss, A. (1967). *The discovery of grounded theory.* Chicago: Aldine.

Goetze, D. (1994). Comparing prisoner's dilemma, commons dilemma, and public goods. provision in the laboratory. *The Journal of Conflict Resolution, 38*(1), 56–86. doi:10.1177/0022002794038001004

Heckathorn, D. (1993). Collective action and group heterogeneity: Voluntary provision versus selective incentives. *American Sociological Review, 58*(3), 329–350. doi:10.2307/2095904

Heylighen, F. (1999). Collective intelligence and its implementation on the web: Algorithms to develop a collective mental map. *Computational & Mathematical Organization Theory, 5*(3), 253–280. doi:10.1023/A:1009690407292

Heylighen, F. (2007). Why is open access development so successful? Stigmergic organization and the economics of Information. In B. Lutterbeck, M. Bärwolff, & R. A. Gehring (Eds.), *Open source.* Lehmanns Media.

Hofstede, G., Hofstede, G. J., & Minkov, M. (2010). *Cultures and organizations: Software of the mind* (3rd ed.). McGraw-Hill.

Homans, G. (1961). *Social behavior: Its elementary forms.* New York: Harcourt, Brace & World.

Homans, G. (1964). Bringing men back in. *American Sociological Review, 29*(6), 809–818. doi:10.2307/2090864

Jeong, S. (2004). Sharing information and cultivating knowledge in virtual setting: Increasing social capital in online community of tourism. *e-Review of Tourism Research, 2*(3). Retrieved from http://ertr.tamu.edu/pdfs/a-64.pdf

Marwell, G., & Oliver, P. (1993). *The critical mass in collective action: A micro-social theory.* Cambridge, UK: Cambridge University Press. doi:10.1017/CBO9780511663765

Mateos-Garcia, J., & Steinmueller, W. E. (2003). *Dynamic features of open source development communities and community processes*. Open Source Movement Research INK Working paper no. 3. Brighton: SPRU-Science and Technology Policy Studies

Müller, C. (1999). Networks of 'personal communities' and 'group communities' in different online communication services. In *Proceedings of the Exploring Cyber Society: Social, Political, Economic and Cultural Issues* (Vol. 2). Newcastle, UK: University of Northumberland. Retrieved from: http://www.soz.unibe.ch/ii/virt/newcastle.html

Olson, M. (1965). *The logic of collective action*. Cambridge, MA: Harvard University Press.

Pigg, K. E., & Crank, L. D. (2004). Building community social capital: The potential and promise of information and communications technologies. *The Journal of Community Informatics, 1*(1), 58–73.

Rheingold, H. (1993). *The online community: Homesteading on the electronic frontier*. New York: Harper Perennial.

Rheingold, H. (2003). *Smart mobs: the next social revolution*. Cambridge, MA: Basic Books.

Steinmueller, W. 2002. Virtual communities and the new economy. In: R. Mansell (Ed.), Inside the communication revolution: Evolving patterns of social and technical interaction. Oxford: Oxford University Press doi:10.1093/acprof:oso/9780198296553.003.0002

Susi, T., & Ziemke, T. (2001). Social cognition, artifacts, and stigmergy. *Cognitive Systems Research, 2*(4), 273–290. doi:10.1016/S1389-0417(01)00053-5

Taylor, M., & Singleton, S. G. (1993). The communalresource: Transaction costs and the solution ofcollective action problems. *Political Science (Wellington, N.Z.), 21*, 95–215.

Taylor, S. J., & Bogdan, R. (1998). *Introduction to qualitative research methods: A guidebook and resource*. New York: Wiley.

Ulrich, D. 1998. Six practices for creating communities of value, not proximity. In F. Hesselbein, M. Goldsmith, R. Beckhard, & R. Schubert (Eds.), The community of the future. San Francisco, CA: Jossey-Bass Publishers.

Wasko, M. M., Teigland, R., & Faraj, S. (2009). The provision of online public goods: Examining social structure in an electronic network of practice. *Decision Support Systems, 47*(3), 254–265. doi:10.1016/j.dss.2009.02.012

# Chapter 17
# Lesotho, a Tourism Destination:
## An Analysis of Lesotho's Current Tourism Products and Potential for Growth

**Lichia Yiu**
*Centre for Socio-EcoNomic Development (CSEND), Switzerland*

**Raymond Saner**
*Centre for Socio-EcoNomic Development (CSEND), Switzerland*

**Marcus Raphael Lee**
*Centre for Socio-EcoNomic Development (CSEND), Switzerland*

## ABSTRACT

*The objective of this chapter is to map and analyze the available tourism assets and products in the Kingdom of Lesotho. The analysis includes assessments on how to improve performance and sustainability of the tourism industry in Lesotho including greater utilization of existing tourism infrastructure and further development of Lesotho's tourism products. This chapter also addresses the strategic issues of tourism development and how Lesotho could increase the number of its tourists. Tourism development has been identified by the government of Lesotho, the International Monetary Fund as well as the United Nations World Tourism Organization as a sector that can reduce poverty as well as absorb low or semi skilled labor. Boosting the tourism sector in Lesotho would work towards alleviating poverty in the Kingdom overall. This chapter applies a case approach in order to illustrate potential investment opportunities and tourism performance improvements in an existing ski resort in Lesotho.*

## INTRODUCTION: MAPPING THE TOURISM LANDSCAPE OF LESOTHO

The United Nation's World Tourism Organization (UNWTO) reports that tourist arrivals surpassed 1 billion for the first time in 2012. Despite occasional shocks, international tourist arrivals have enjoyed virtually uninterrupted growth – from 277 million in 1980 to 528 million in 1995, and 1.035 billion in 2012. Developing countries are playing an increasingly prominent role in this growing sector. Tourism is one of the top three exports for the majority of developing counties and for at least

DOI: 10.4018/978-1-4666-8606-9.ch017

22 Least Developed Countries (LDCs) (including Lesotho) (World Trade Organization, 2013).

As of 2012, according to the World Economic Forum, the Tourism industry in Lesotho is worth USD152.3million, almost 7% of the country's economy (World Economic Forum 2013). The industry is slated to grow 4.4% in value during the time period 2013 – 2022. It currently employs 34,000 Lesotho natives representing 6% of the workforce. With the expected growth of the international tourism industry, Lesotho should take the opportunity to use the tourism sector as a primary driver for their national economy.

Aside from the pure economic benefit, tourism has many other social benefits that are intangible according to UNWTO's Secretary-General Taleb Rifai (2013), including:

1.  Jobs
    ◦   Especially for young people smooth and soft entry into the labour market.
    ◦   People don't have to move. Jobs are where they are/grew up.
    ◦   For every 1 Tourism job, 1.4 extra jobs are created in parallel sectors – multiplier effect. A hotel employing 100 persons creates 250 indirect jobs (International Labour Organization, 2010).
2.  Infrastructure Development
    ◦   Roads and other forms of transit are usually built or improved upon with the onset of tourism operations. While this facilitates the tourists who visit, it also directly benefits the local community who now have access to these public goods. Additionally, more often than not, tourism in LDCs tends to be in rural areas – meaning rural areas would benefit from infrastructure development not otherwise extended to them.

Tourism development has been identified by the Lesotho government, International Monetary Fund as well as the United Nations World Tourism Organization as a sector that will reduce poverty as well as absorb many low or semi skilled labor (Rifai, 2013). Boosting the tourism sector in the Kingdom will alleviate poverty in the Kingdom overall. If developed well, tourism could effectively lead an LDC country like Lesotho out of poverty like it did for Cape Verde, a small chain of islands off the west coast of Africa who graduated from LDC status in 2007.

Mobility and accommodations are two fundamental factors in determining the volume, costs and eligibility of tourism. As a result, these basic infrastructures affect the attractiveness of tourist operations and investment from abroad. A detail analysis of the macro picture including the border entry, existing hospitality establishment and other facilities is presented here.

## POINTS AND MEANS OF TOURIST ENTRY INTO LESOTHO

Lesotho is a landlocked country completely surrounded by the Republic of South Africa. One of the biggest challenges facing many international tourists planning a trip to Lesotho is how to get to the Kingdom. The follow section will review the entry points tourists can make use in order to gain entry into the Kingdom and related transport service provision.

### Moshoeshoe I International Airport (IATA Code: MSU)

The Moshoeshoe I International Airport is the main airport in Leosotho serving the capital city, Maseru. The airport complex has one terminal building and is located about 10 km away from downtown Maseru. The only runway at the airport

*Table 1. Arrivals by Purpose of Visit and Port of Entry, January – December 2011 (Lesotho Department of Research and Development, 2012)*

| Purpose | Port of Entry | | | | | | | | | | |
|---|---|---|---|---|---|---|---|---|---|---|---|
| | Caledon | Makhaleng | Maputsoe | Maseru | Airport | Peka | Qacha | Sani | Tele | Vanrooy | Total |
| Business | 7,325 | 116 | 7,620 | 25,439 | 6,277 | 481 | 0 | 158 | 358 | 3,021 | **50,795** |
| Employment | 454 | 5 | 310 | 714 | 138 | 15 | 0 | 4 | 52 | 116 | **1,808** |
| Holyday | 40,396 | 971 | 22,266 | 30,288 | 1,372 | 1,555 | 0 | 10,989 | 2,329 | 8,369 | **116,535** |
| Returning | 295 | 1 | 532 | 346 | 60 | 8 | 0 | 0 | 18 | 92 | **1,352** |
| School | 65 | 0 | 190 | 183 | 29 | 1 | 0 | 30 | 14 | 36 | **548** |
| Others | 21,955 | 758 | 94,586 | 74,325 | 3,885 | 1,711 | 10 | 1,068 | 6,474 | 21,907 | **226,679** |
| No response | 64 | 6 | 147 | 133 | 23 | 2 | 0 | 4 | 8 | 45 | **432** |
| **Total** | **70,554** | **1,857** | **123,651** | **131,428** | **11,784** | **3,773** | **10** | **12,253** | **9,253** | **33,586** | **398,149** |

is 10498 ft (3199.79 m) long. A Boeing 747-400 (the most commonly flown B747 model by commercial airlines) requires 3,490m of runway for take off and 2,134m to land. It would however be suitable to support the take off and landings of a standard Boeing 737 model aircraft that requires 1,676m to take off and 1,207m to land.[1]

SA Link is the only airline that currently serves Lesotho via the Moshoeshoe I International Airport. SA Link provides three daily departures and arrivals connecting Maseru with Johannesburg. SA Link is a privately owned airline based in Johannesburg that links smaller towns, regional centers and hubs throughout South Africa. South African Airways has a codeshare agreement with SA Link into and out of Moshoeshoe - which is the country's main link to the world outside of South Africa. SA Link is also part of the leading global Star Alliance network. Via the Star Alliance network, Lesotho (and the Moshoeshoe I International Airport) is technically connected via air to 195 destination countries and 1,329 destination airports.[2]

## Road Points of Entry

Travel into the country is easiest through the road connection with the highway system of South Africa. Amongst these individual border crossings,

the Maseru Crossing was the most frequented with a total of 131,428 entries in 2011 (Lesotho Department of Research and Development, 2011). The Maputsoe border crossing was a close second with 123,651 entries in that same year. The Caledon crossing rounded off the top 3 points of entry with 70,554 crossings in 2011. The Moshoeshoe I International Airport by contrast accounted for only 11,784 arrivals in 2011. By comparison, the Sani Pass, which requires travelers to use a four-wheel drive vehicle to pass through accounted for 12,253 of the arrivals into Lesotho in the year 2011. Table 1 illustrates the arrivals by the different ports and the purpose of the individual arrivals as documented in the arrival documents collected at immigration.

Out of all 398,149 international tourist arrivals in 2011, only 3% arrived via air travel. The overwhelming majority – 97% arrived via road. The majority of business travelers arrived by air however. This statistic could be attributed to the fact that over 93% of all international tourists arrivals came from South Africa and only about 5% of all arrivals were from outside the African continent (Lesotho Department of Research and Development, 2011).

The Lesotho Department of Research and Development[3] attributes this statistic to the fact that that the majority of all tourist arrivals comes from South Africa who visit Lesotho for business or personal reasons including visiting relatives or maintaining their second homes. Additionally the most populous towns in Lesotho, including the capital Maseru share the western border with South Africa and that's where the majority of arrivals come from – the Maseru Crossing and Maputsoe border crossing. Major roads in South Africa like the N8 link these major border crossings into Lesotho, which could be a reason why they are most used.

## Maseru Branch Railway

The Maseru Branch Railway (a form of mass public transit) also enters Lesotho via the Maseru Crossing into the capital city and is Lesotho's connection to the rest of the South African Railway network with the connection at Marseilles, Free State.

Overall, Lesotho does have the basic infrastructure – international airport and functioning border crossings. The potential is there for Lesotho to receive more than the almost 400,000 tourist arrivals it received in 2011 based on the infrastructure already on the ground.

The two major border crossings of Maseru and Maputsoe are already operating at 24 hours a day 7 days a week while the Moshoeshoe I International Airport is currently underutilized at less than 50% utilization level with only 2 inbound and 2 outbound flights a day. SA Link would almost certainly increase the number of inbound and outbound flights if there were a demand for additional flights.

Other rival African airlines would also almost certainly add the Moshoeshoe I International Airport to its routes if there were sufficient demand for air travel from the airports they currently serve. One way to do this is to increase arrivals from other cities and create new airlinks to Maseru on a seasonal basis. Travel into Lesotho increases

steadily during the months of November and December annually – the southern hemisphere summer months – and there could therefore be summer season flights (from new destinations) established to capitalize on the demand for Lesotho during the summer time and bring even more tourists in. (Lesotho Department of Research and Development, 2012)

The Moshoeshoe I International Airport is operating currently at less than 50% utilization level with only two outbound and inbound flights a day and this is evident with the airport closing for periods during the day when there are no scheduled arrivals or departures. There is therefore no immediate need to expand the transportation infrastructure of Lesotho to support any additional tourist arrivals and the focus should instead be turned instead to how to bring these additional tourist numbers to fully utilize the infrastructure that is already in place.

## ACCOMMODATION PRODUCTS IN LESOTHO

According to the Lesotho Tourism Development Corporation there are almost 70 different accommodation products in Lesotho. These accommodation options are concentrated in the major tourist regions of Maseru (the Capital), the Berea District, the Leribe District, the Butha-Buthe District (Skiing), the Mokhotlong District, the Thaba Tseka District, the Mafeteng District, the Mohale's Hoek District, the Quthing District and the Qacha's Nek District. The variety of accommodations that are available in Lesotho range from the luxury Lesotho Sun Hotel and Casino in Maseru to smaller lodges and beds and breakfasts sprinkled all over the country. There is also one ski resort the Afriski Ski and one Mountain Resort in Butha-Buthe.

## Current Market Details

*Hotels:* There are 21 registered hotels in the country offering over 1,400 beds, of which 75% are in Maseru (the Capital). The quality of hotels is varied with, by international standards, 2 three-to four-star hotels, the rest ranging from 2 stars to no stars. All hotels are registered and licensed by the Lesotho government (World Bank, 2013).

*Guest Houses/Bed and Breakfast/Lodges:* There are 17 guesthouses and bed and breakfasts around the Kingdom and there are 16 lodges (all registered), several of which are of relatively good quality (World Bank, 2013).

*Home stays:* Several have been set up by in the Highlands; Malealea Lodge works with home stays in several of the villages around Mafeteng which it uses for guests who take their overnight treks; and in Quthing there are at least 10 home stays in villages set up with the help of the German DeD and the Quthing Wildlife Trust.

*Campsites:* Many of the lodges allow camping on their grounds. There are 14 organized camp-sites although visitors can camp anywhere in the country as long as they inform the 'chief' of the area for security purposes.

*Average Length of stay:* 2.82 Nights (World Bank, 2013)

## Industry Price Range

(Highest Value Double Room)
M700> (or USD70) = 7 Properties or 10% of the market
M350-700 (or USD35-70) = 19 Properties or 27% of the market
M<350 (or USD35) = 45 Properties or 63% of the market

As derived from the market details above, the average length of stay as determined by the World Bank (2013) is 2.82 nights. Additionally, Lesotho overnight accommodation rates are priced fairly low compared to its neighboring Republic of South Africa. The Kingdom only has 7 properties priced over USD 100 per night for a double occupancy room. The majority of properties, 63%, are priced less than USD 50 per night in double occupancy room. This raises two observations, on one hand it could be argued that the accommodation options in Lesotho are competitively priced relative to its other competitors in Southern Africa but it also projects to the potential traveler a sense of a cheap lodging industry offering inferior, wanting products. That being said, the prices are right to attract a large number of young, adventurous travelers looking for a different Southern Africa experience.

In 2007, a group of World Bank economists and surveyors visited and surveyed a total of 82 accommodation enterprises in Lesotho between December 22, 2006 and January 11, 2007 (McKeeman & Rozga, 2007). Through a combination of the two scores, each of the establishments was classified into one of three categories: MARKET READY, NEARLY MARKET READY, and NOT MARKET READY. Market Ready product is product that is globally competitive product and is ready to be listed and sold to the international marketplace today. Nearly Market Ready product is product that is close to being market ready with just a few capacity building issues to be addressed. Not Market Ready product is product that does not meet international standards for offering, management or product quality and will take a much more intensive improvement before reaching Market Ready status. As found and classified by the group, 37.5% of the accommodation facilities in Lesotho are considered Market Ready, while 23.75% are almost market ready and 38.75% are not market ready. The high percentage of accommodation products that do not fall into the market ready segment – 62.5% is a worrisome statistic for a country trying to grow and develop their tourism industry. Accordingly, the existing hotels in Lesotho in 2007 were classified as described in Table 2 below:

*Table 2. Classification of accommodation infrastructure in Lesotho (McKeeman & Rozga, 2007)*

| Market Ready Accommodations | Nearly Market Ready | Not Market Ready |
|---|---|---|
| Afri-Ski Leisure Kingdom Aloes Guesthouse<br>• Black Swan Guest House<br>• Durham Link and Maseru Backpackers<br>• Foothills Guest House<br>• Golden Hotel<br>• Hotel Mount Maluti<br>• Khali Hotel<br>• Lancer's Inn Hotel<br>• Lesotho Sun Hotel<br>• Malealea Lodge, Adventure & Pony Trek Centre<br>• Maseru Sun Hotel<br>• Mmelesi Lodge<br>• Mohale Lodge<br>• Molengoane Lodge<br>• Moorosi Chalets<br>• Morija Guest House & Tours<br>• Mountainside Hotel<br>• Mpilo Lodge<br>• New Oxbow Lodge<br>• Palace Hotel<br>• Phokeng Gardens B&B<br>• Phomolo Self Catering Guest House<br>• Ramabanta Trading Post Adventures<br>• Sani Top Chalet<br>• Semonkong Lodge<br>• The Mamohase Guest House<br>• The Trading Post Guest House<br>• Tribute Guest House<br>• Victoria Hotel | Anna's B&B<br>• Blue Mountain Inn Hotel<br>• Boikhutsong B&B<br>• Catholic Training Centre<br>• J&E Cyaara B&B<br>• Ka Pitseng Guest House<br>• Khotsong Lodge<br>• Lapeng B&B<br>• Letloepe Lodge<br>• Likileng Lodge<br>• Mafeteng Hotel<br>• Maly's B&B<br>• Marakabei Guest House<br>• Mashai Lodge<br>• Molumong Guest Housel<br>• Mountain View Hotel Nthatwoa Hotel<br>• Sekekete Cazi Brothers Hotel<br>• Senqu Hotel<br>• Tloung B&B | Boikhethelo Guest House<br>• Butha-Buthe Youth Hostel<br>• Chock's Centre B&B<br>• Cindi Lodge<br>• Crocodile Inn Hotel<br>• Crown Lodge<br>• DR Guest House<br>• Fuleng B&B<br>• Granny & 4 Sisters<br>• Katse Lodge<br>• Lakeside Hotel<br>• Lenonyeling Guest House<br>• Liphofung Cave Heritage and Cultural Center<br>• Mabela Guest House<br>• Mabotle Guest House<br>• Mahloenyeng Lodge<br>• Maluti Guest House<br>• Mokhotlong Hotel<br>• Monateng Lodge<br>• Mountain Delight<br>• Mountain Star Guest House<br>• New Central Guest House Ntina Guest House<br>• Orange River Lodge<br>• Pyramid Gardens B&B<br>• Sehlabathebe Lodge<br>• Seilatsatsi B&B<br>• St James Lodge<br>• Thimo B&B<br>• Ts'ehlanyane Nature Reserve<br>• Umbrella B&B |

## The Kingdom's Problem of Low Occupancy

While the Lesotho Sun Resort and Casino remains relatively successful according to Sun International's Annual Financial Statements, the rest of the accommodations and lodging industry in Lesotho has continued to struggle to maintain a decent occupancy rate. The average occupancy rate for the quarter across the Kingdom is 19.4% and even in the popular market section – lodge accommodations in Mafeteng, it struggles to hit 40%. By contrast, neighboring Republic of South Africa managed 53% National Occupancy Rate for the Financial Year 2011, see figure 3 below. The American Hotel and Lodging Association reports the national occupancy rate in 2011 to be 60%.[4] While the American national rate is hardly comparable to Lesotho, due to the different level of developments experienced by both countries, the occupancy rate of the Republic of South Africa would be a better indicator given its close geographical proximity and the economic dependence Lesotho has on the Republic. Additionally,

*Table 3. Bed Occupancy Rates by Type of Establishment and District, Quarter 4, 2011 (Lesotho Tourism Development Corporation, 2011)*

| District | Hotel | Lodge | Other | Total |
|---|---|---|---|---|
| Berea | 15.2 | - | 4.1 | **13.2** |
| Botha Bothe | 14.4 | 11.9 | 2.6 | **10.6** |
| Leribe | 32.2 | 28.8 | 15.9 | **26.0** |
| Mafeteng | 31.2 | 36.4 | 9.0 | **22.8** |
| Maseru | 32.7 | 15.7 | 19.7 | **23.1** |
| Mohale's Hoek | 15.6 | - | 13.9 | **15.1** |
| Mokhotlong | 22.6 | - | 12.9 | **17.6** |
| Qacha's Nek | 25.9 | 22.2 | 12.7 | **16.2** |
| Quthing | 16.8 | 5.4 | 4.9 | **6.8** |
| Thaba Tseka | 9.0 | 12.5 | 14.3 | **13.2** |
| Total | 25.9 | 18.9 | 14.6 | **19.4** |

according to figure 3 below, the occupancy rate in South Africa is slated to grow to up to 70% by 2017.

Lesotho has the opportunity to latch on to this upward trend of its neighbor if it employs the right strategies and tactics moving forward since most of its inbound tourists are coming from South Africa as an additional side visit site. Accordingly, the attached table of the revenue generated by area and type of lodging accommodation shows the capital, Maseru, generating the most revenue in the hotel sector (M11million in the 4th quarter), most likely benefitted from the effects of being home to the Lesotho Sun Hotel and Casino.

Tables 3 and 4 below show the bed occupancy rate for the 4th quarter of 2011, it is segregated into the district the accommodation is located in as well as the type of accommodation (Lesotho's Tourism Development Corporation reports the data by bed occupancy rates, international standards report findings based on Room Occupancy rates).

## Detrimental Factors in the Accommodations Sector

Before the Lesotho Tourism Development Corporation can move forward with new strategies for improving the number of inbound tourists, certain factors that currently exist within the accomodations sector have to be addressed. In their report about accomodation products in Lesotho after their 2007 visit, World Bank economists led by Jodi McKeeman & Zachary Rozga found that the following impediments that exist in the industry: *"Low-levels of understanding of tourism and essentials like Hospitality & Customer Care - One of the biggest issues and common findings is that there is a very low understanding of "What is tourism?" in the hotels, both at a management and staff level. The employees at these enterprises see the tourist as a burden and simply go through the motions of servicing them. Customer service or customer care is nearly nonexistent. In general there is very little tourism awareness among tourism industry employees and very little understanding of the great levels of service that are involved to create a welcoming environment. The tourism employees have very little sensitivities to the needs of leisure tourists; on the whole, they have no concept of what leisure tourists want to do or why leisure tourists are in Lesotho, how important leisure tourists are to the country (bringing in foreign currency), nor how important their role is in the promotion of tourism."*. (2007, pp. 10-11)

Another problem McKeeman & Rozga (2007, p.11) found was that a lot of the accommodation statistics were skewed in that the Kingdom's government contracts a vast majority of these hotel and lodging facilities for government workshops and conferences. In some hotel's cases their business is 90-95% generated from government contracts. While this government created demand might be good for revenues of the individual lodging accom-

*Table 4. Revenue Accrued from Accommodation by Type of Establishment and District, Quarter 4 2011 (Lesotho Tourism Development Corporation, 2011)*

| District | Hotel | Lodge | Other | Total | % Share |
|---|---|---|---|---|---|
| Berea | 1 334 132 | - | 74 580 | 1 408 712 | 4.0 |
| Botha Bothe | 460 774 | 559 576 | 29 460 | 1 049 810 | 3.0 |
| Leribe | 6 027 571 | 263 826 | 1 331 164 | 7 622 561 | 21.4 |
| Mafeteng | 1 045 627 | 788 468 | 158 590 | 1 992 685 | 5.6 |
| Maseru | 11 115 475 | 1 269 386 | 4 072 465 | 16 457 326 | 46.3 |
| Mohale's Hoek | 1 662 281 | - | 196 950 | 1 859 231 | 5.2 |
| Mokhotlong | 965 544 | 0 | 458 480 | 1 424 024 | 4.0 |
| Qacha's Nek | 401 019 | 253 359 | 500 550 | 1 154 927 | 3.2 |
| Quthing | 178 260 | 87 730 | 575 416 | 841 406 | 2.4 |
| Thaba Tseka | 423 035 | 282 900 | 1 055 230 | 1 761 165 | 5.0 |
| Total | 23 613 717 | 3 505 245 | 8 452 885 | 35 571 847 | 100.0 |
| % Share | 66.4 | 9.9 | 23.8 | 100.0 | |

modations that were lucky enough to benefit from earning a government contract, the negatives are that *"this form of business has created an environment of stagnation."* McKeeman & Rozga have found on their visits to such establishments that, *"...apathy in employees and management is rife in these properties because there is no need to apply customer service practices because the workshop attendees, in general, are easily pleased and do not have high service demands. Also government workshop attendees are not looking for tourist activities such as curio shopping, site-seeing or cultural activities, so the accommodations have not developed them or do not know of their existence."* (2007, p.11)

This government inflated demand for hotel accommodation does not bode well for an industry struggling to find its feet. In this instance, government driven demand might be helpful to nurture a tourism industry at its infancy. However in the mid-term horizon, the critical task is to increase the number of arrival by creating greater customer values and branding as an attractive destination.

## Lesotho's Tourism Products That Do Not Meet Standards

Tourism is about selling experiences and meeting tourist expectations. One of the detrimental activities a destination can do for its image is to not meet the tourist expectations of the place they are visiting. McKeeman & Rozga's World Bank report illustrates this point through specific encounters during their 2007 trip to the Kingdom to survey the tourism products available. Below are examples of tourism products that don't meet tourist expectations for a whole variety of reasons (McKeeman & Rozga, 2007, p. 12).

*"Katse Dam – Advertising Product that Doesn't Exist*

*While interviewing the manager of the Katse Lodge he lamented that he has many international clients that have booked for three nights but end up leaving after staying only one day because there is nothing to do in the area besides the dam tour and the botanical garden. However, in printed national marketing material and on signposts on major roads there are advertisements of pony trekking, rock climbing, canoeing, trekking, and fly-fishing."*

*"Ts'ehlanyane National Park – Product Deterioration*

*The park is a beautiful gem with massive potential, but the existing infrastructure is deteriorating. The bridge to the rondavels and tent sites has been washed away, so travelers must forge a dangerous river. The tent sites are totally derelict and not useable. The rondavels are threatened to be destroyed by erosion. One of the cottages has been stripped of its furniture and the other has broken furniture in it. The ranger who was interviewed said that most guests who have booked to stay overnight end up returning to town without staying."*

*"Dinosaur Footprints – Mismanagement Destroying the Product*

*One of the proclaimed tourist attractions in Quthing is the Dinosaur Footprints yet there is very little to actually see or experience. The manager was not there at the time of our visit and his son had been put in charge. The boys had very little information to tell us about the footprints nor did they speak much English nor was there any significant written information about the site inside the structure. The footprints are completely exposed to the weather and therefore very faded and growing more and more difficult for anyone to actually see. We were not required to sign the visitor's log yet we were asked to pay the visitation fee which is supposed to go towards site protection and enhancement. In addition, there was a young boy begging outside of the site and the "managers" did nothing to curb it."*

The danger of Lesotho continuing to have tourism products that do not meet tourist expectations

is that they will lose an entire market segment – return customers. Returning visitors is vital for the tourism industry – hotels and specific tourist attractions including National Parks, Theme Parks, Zoos and Aquariums. It is more difficult to convince a brand new individual to visit or stay at a place for the first time but it is easier to have your guest come back if they enjoyed the experience.

## Areas within the Tourism Industry That Needs Immediate Improvement

After an analysis of the current situation of the lodging and accommodation facilities industry, the following areas have been identified as areas that need to be immediately addressed and improved in order to bring about a significant improvement on the current tourism products on offering.

1. *Tourism Awareness Training* – As the UNWTO reports (2006) have noted there is a general lack of understanding of the tourism industry. This point was illustrated strongly by the McKeeman and Rozga World Bank report (2007) when managers interviewed by the team did not understand the terms seasonality or occupancy rates.

2. *Market Access and commission system* – In 74% of the lodging and accommodation establishments in Lesotho, there are not an established system of commissions for bookings (McKeeman & Rozga, 2007, p. 13). The tourism industry is built on commissions and it is essential for the growth of the destination that the individual properties learn the basics of market access and start to source business of their own – one way to do it is via commissions – rather than remain reliant on government sector demand for the bulk of their business.

3. *Customer Service/Customer Care* – This issue has been identified as a major constraint for growth of the tourism industry in Lesotho. *"Good customer service is not*

just missing in the accommodations sector but in the service industry as a whole in Lesotho." (McKeeman & Rozga, 2007, p. 13) Customer service must be addressed at a national level and radically transform the industry if it´s done right.

4.  Hospitality Business Management – Evident from the McKeeman & Rozga World Bank report (2007) is the lack of adequate hospitality and management training of the top managers in the majority of Lesotho's tourism accommodations, with the exception of the Lesotho Sun Hotel and Casino. This is evident not only in Lesotho but on the African continent in general where the general lack of hospitality education and training continues to impede the growth of the local communities and their access to the possible and potential benefits of the growing tourism sector. In 2006, The Lesotho Sun Hotel and Casino provided raining for some small accommodation providers in Maseru. The training was a two-week course covering hospitality, customer service, housekeeping and food & bar service. It was provided by Lesotho Sun at no charge and only a handful of establishments were involved. Lesotho Sun has however not provided this service since. The market awaits a entrepreneurial education provider or professional services training provider – possibly from South Africa or internationally – to fill this training and education gap in the domestic Lesotho market.

## BUSINESS OPPORTUNITIES

The following are a list of the Unique Selling Points that the World Bank team (McKeeman & Rozga, 2007, p. 15) noticed while touring the country in the southern hemisphere summer of 2006 - 2007:

- Lesotho is a true Mountain Environment in Africa
- Lesotho does receive regular snowfall
- The highlands culture is authentic and unique to other African cultures
- Water is in abundance
- Recreational activity development is in its infancy
- A large and viable demand market on its doorstep

## Lesotho Sun Hotel and Casino: the Jewel in the Kingdom's Crown

The Lesotho Sun Hotel and Casino is a 4-star hotel and casino destination situated on a hillside overlooking Maseru, the capital of Lesotho. Regarded as one of the best places to stay in Lesotho by Discovery Travel and Living Magazine, this elegant, modern sandstone building is designed to offer guests beautiful views of both the city and the Drakensberg Mountains in the background.

The resort is located on Hilton Road and can easily be accessed from the capital city of Maseru via principal highway A2 heading southeast. The resort also offers a variety of transportation options from The Moshoeshoe I International Airport for their international guests and arrangements can be accommodated at reservation.

Fully operational as of November 2009, Lesotho Sun is equipped with premium comforts and facilities. Its 158 bedrooms and suites are decorated to give an elegant chic feel. While the definition of a 4-star hotel varies slightly between American and European standards, The European Hotelstars Union defines a 4-star level accommodation to be one that has the following services and amenities as a basic requirement:

- Reception opened 18 hours, accessible by phone 24 hours from inside and outside
- Lobby with seats and beverage service
- Breakfast buffet or breakfast menu card via room service

- Minibar or 24 hours beverages via room service
- Upholstered chair/couch with side table
- Bath robe and slippers on demand
- Cosmetic products (e.g. shower cap, nail file, cotton swabs, vanity mirror, tray of a large scale in the bathroom)
- Internet Access and internet terminal
- "À la carte" restaurant

The Lesotho Sun Hotel and Casino does not have its 4-satr designation awarded by the European Hotel Stars Union[5] but follows these guidelines carefully and has each and every one of the basic requirements met. The Lesotho Sun Hotel and Casino also has a sizeable Conference and Events space on site. 58 former guests of the hotel have given it an average of 3.5 Stars out of 5 on the popular travel website, TripAdvisor.com and it has the highest ratings of any hotel in Lesotho.[6] A worrying statistic for Lesotho's premier hotel is that the majority of respondents rates the Lesotho Sun as an 'average' hotel under TripAdvisor's 5 categories of Excellent, Very Good, Average, Poor, Terrible. The Cape Grace Hotel in the neighboring Republic of South Africa, benchmarking hotel, was voted as the top hotel in South Africa by the same website, TripAdvisor.com, and received a 5 star rating from 661 reviewers with a majority 583 of reviewers giving the hotel the 'excellent' rating.

If Lesotho wants to latch onto South Africa's booming tourism economy and becoming either an alternative tourism destination to South Africa or an accompanying destination, its top hotels need to be of a closer standard to the its top rivals in South Africa, and by accounts of guests at both hotels the current disparity is clear.

The average daily rate (ADR) at the Lesotho Sun Hotel varies by season with the ADR during the winter months hovering around M 2,800 (Lesotho Loti) (Conversion = USD281) and M 2,955 (USD296).

## Afriski Ski and Mountain Resort

AfriSki is the only skiing resort in Lesotho, located 3222 m above sea-level in the Maluti Mountains, near the northern border of Lesotho and South Africa. The resort is 4.5 hours' drive from Johannesburg, or Pretoria South Africa via the Moteng pass and the Mahlasela pass; it sits along Highway A1.

The ski resort is open from June through September annually, during the southern hemisphere winter months and has about 1.4km of ski slopes combined over a main slope and a beginner slope. There are also four dedicated ski lifts to serve patrons. Daily lift tickets at the resort go for about ZAR 350 or £25.[7] In addition to ski facilities, Afriski operates similar to most international ski resorts like Kolsters or Aspen in that it has food and beverage facilities in the form of The Sky Restaurant for a full service meal and the Gondola Café for more self serve options. Afriski also has the capabilities to host conferences and has continually hosted the Kings Cup Ski Championships in July and the Quiksilver sponsored SA National Snowboarding Championships in August. These two events attract significant participation within the African skiing community during the southern hemisphere winter months.

In the summer months, from November to March, the resort stays open to host mountain adventure sports. Summer activites at Afriski include guided quad bike and motorbike trails, abseiling, fly fishing and hiking.

Afriski, shares the distinction of being one of only two ski resorts outside North Africa with the Tiffindell Ski Resort in South Africa`s Eastern Cape. Afriski`s elevation is siglightly higher than Tifindell and its slopes are 0.1km longer than Tiffindell`s.[8] Afriski`s strength in the African ski industry (if it exists) is that it is one of the only few premier options avaliable to skiers who want to ski in Africa. Given the differences in climate between Northern Africa and Southern Africa, the ski resorts in Lesotho and South Africa are the only viable ski options for skiers and boarders who wish to hit the slopes during the months of June – September, the Southern Hemisphere winter. This leaves Tiffindell as Afriski`s principal rival in the African skiing market. Afriski has been operational for 8 ski seasons now and the fact that the older Tifindell Resort recently embarked on a 150 million rand expansion indicates that Afriski is gaining monentum and getting successful enough to challenge the old standard bearer.

*Target Audience.* Afriski has a unique niche market it can tap on going forward – rich, young customers who are interested in coming for practice skis in preparation for the more serious winter skiing months in Europe or North America. If Afriski successfully markets itself to this young, rich, Aspen and Kolsters goers, Afriski would be having many more successful ski seasons to come.

*Lodging Accomodations.* The lodging accommodation at the resort sleeps about 250 people. The lodging accomodations on the resort are mainly 8 person lodges which can be rented out as a whole for big parties wanting to have complete privacy in the lodges or it can function like a hostel/dormitary style accomodation where indidvidal borders are placed together in a 8 person lodge with shared common facilities like bathrooms and kitchen areas. The average rate per person as quoted on the Afriski website is between R513 – R 1150 (between USD 50-100) for both the summer and winter months. A 10-sleeper surprior Chalet, the most luxurious accomodation opetion at Afriski goes for R12,375 (USD 1,200) a night during the winter peak season. Comparably, The St. Mortiz Lodge and Condominiums in Aspen, Colorado – deemed the affordable option by most visitors – charges USD 48 for a hostel style shared room during the non peak season to USD 498 for a 2 bedroom condominum that sleeps up to 6 during the peak Christmas – New Year's period. Afriski's direct rival, Tiffindell in South Africa does not publish its accomodation

rates online. Occupancy rates in the Botha-Bothe region (where Afriski is located) remained around the 12.5% mark through 2011 (Lesotho Tourism Development Corporation, 2011). One inference drawn from this could be that most of the visitors to Afriski be it in the summer or winter months are day tourists from neighboring South Africa. These day tourists come in for either the half day or full day ski lift tickets and return home at the end of the day, indicating that very few skiiers at Afriski are actually from abroad.

## Tour Operating

The tour operating and tour-guiding sector of the tourism industry has been growing rapidly in the last 5 years with the onset of increased tourist arrivals to the Kingdom (Lesotho Department of Research and Development, 2012). Presently, the country depends very heavily on South African based tour operators to manage and coordinate tour packages and organize trips in Lesotho. These same South African based tour operators are also responsible for the majority of tour groups entering the Kingdom (Lesotho Review, 2013). There is therefore the possibility and opportunity to develop a credible tour operation business within Lesotho rather than remain dependent on the South African tour operators. Local tour operators would be able to better collaborate with local attractions and gives the traveler a more authentic local experience.

The main observation from the McKeeman & Rozga World Bank report (2007, p. 21) about the local Lesotho tour operators are that they are "indeed weak", and "do not operate like a professional tour operation businesses" of international standard. Additionally they do not have connections into the regional or international market place. The number one complaint of the operators is that South African companies come into Lesotho with their guests and then leave without ever interacting with the local Lesotho companies, completely bypassing them. One of

operators is that *"there is no formal training process or accreditation to become an operator or a guide, which causes a lack of confidence in them as operators."* (McKeeman & Rozga, 2007, p. 21)

With the previous Lesotho Tourism Board (LTB) there was no role in the economy for tour operators, *"because the LTB had a monopoly on tour operation."* (McKeeman & Rozga, 2007, p. 21) As with any new industry there needs to be a start somewhere and there are growing pains to be endured. In order to facilitate an environment where tour operation can get off the ground, a national guide program and a national guide school is needed – something that the Lesotho Tourism Development Corporation could look into. This process will legitimize the tour operators by giving them local knowledge that their South African counterparts will not be privy to and thus establish for the local Lesotho tour operators a niche and competitive advantage, and at the same time give them the accreditation they need in order to interact with the international market.

## RECOMMENDATIONS

### Expanding Afriski and Turning Lesotho into a Winter Wonderland

Given Afriski`s location on the slope of the Drakensberg Mountains in southern Africa and the fact that there are currently only two developed slopes in the facility, there is potential room for significant expansion. Expansion, however, should only happen if Afriski reaches its full capacity during the ski seasons. Currently, Afriski sees about 5000 skiiers during the winter months and is not yet reliably profitable (Peng, 2008). Should maximum capacity be reached during the coming years with the right marketing strategy, Afriski`s owners and potential investors could look at expanding the number of slopes avalible at the resort. The limitation would be that any additional slopes added to the resort would not be significantly higher or steeper than the current trails given the elevation of the Drakensberg. The Drakensberg Mountains are not tall by Alpine standards rising to about 3000m above sea level. Fortunately for Afriski, its prinicipal rival Tiffindell is located on the same mountain with similar elevations meaning any Tiffindell expansion would probably also be in number of slopes and expanding lodging and dining facilities rather than steeper and more challenging courses.

Afriski's future expansion plans – should it happen – should be modelled closely to that of Nashoba Valley in Westford, Massachusetts, USA. Nashoba Valley, like Afriski is set on a relatively small area, is not of an apline standard and like Afriski is surrounded by several bigger industry players. Yet Nashoba Valley has held its own all these years, in part attributed to the right business strategies. The Nashoba Valley Ski Resort is set on an elevation of 422ft in the Nashoba Valley in Western Massachusetts. The elevation of 422ft is the equalivent of 128m, the Drakensberg Mountains that Afriski is set on is over 3000m above sea level and dwarfs Nashoba Valley. Afriski's longest run is more than twice the length Nashoba has to offer but Nashoba does have 17 different trails for skiiers to experience.[9]

While Nashoba Valley cannot compete with the ski resorts in the neighboring White Mountains in New Hampshire, it has managed to hold its own since 1964. Nashoba's longevity is attributed to its cleverly designed ski courses. The Nashoba Valley Ski Resot despite its low elevation has 5 Black Diamond trails, Afriski on the other hand has none. Given the higerh elevation of the Drakensberg Mountains, it is definitely possible to pencil in a black diamond trial in future expansions. Black diamond trails would be the key to attracting top level international skiiers to consider Afriski as a destination for skiing during the southern hemisphere winter months. The Tomahawk Trail and the Nashoba Trail are interestingly designed course because of their meandering ways on the far right and left side of the park. With innovative designs,

Afriski would be able to pencil in trails that would meander and weave making them more thrilling and challenging to be skiing on. If Afriski were to adopt similar courses to Nashoba's two outer trails, given its elevations, it would most definitely be able to create trails as long and as challenging at those at premier alpine locations.

Additonally, Afriski is presently somewhat inacessible by the local population. While it has a decent community outreach program by offering skiing lessons to both adults and children, many in Lesotho are unable to reach or do not consider Afriski as a viable recreation destination during the winter months. Most of Afiski's cliente are instead wealthier South Africans or other African and international skiiers. What Afriski and the Lesotho government can collaborate on is to make the only ski resort in the country more accessible to the local population by offering discount life tickets for locals as well as heavily discounted ski lessons for the local population. This way skiing would be promoted as an activity on the national level and Afriski stands to benefit from the increased number of skiiers frequenting the resort, Lesotho though small has a population of over 2 million, meaning an additional market of 2million.

Access to the ski resort should also be expanded by implementing a shuttle bus system that runs once a day in the morning taking skiiers from major cities like Maseru to Afriski, with a return bus taking the skiiers back in the evening. Nashoba Valley operates a similar system by running a daily bus service from major cities in the area like Boston, Manchester and Springfield.

## Lesotho: High Performance Sports Acclimitaztion Ground

The natural geography of Lesotho allows it to be a premier sport destination by virtue of its high elevation and rugged terrain. In the 2010-2011 government budget, M177million (USD 15million) was set aside for the Ministry of Gender and

Youth, Sport and Recreation for sports development. Provisional plans have been drawn up by the Sport Ministry to develop a High Atitude Sports Center in Mohale. This should be followed through and international consultants should be involved in the development process. There is real potential here for Lesotho being the next destination for High Altitude Sport training, given its high elevation and rugged terrain. Altitude training usually takes place at elevations of 2,400m above sea level and higher where the oxygen levels are lower than the usual sea-level average of 20% (West, 1996). While the Swiss have an Olympic Training Base in St. Moritz at over 1,800m elevation many countries without this natural georgraphic endowment have to do their altitude training somewhere else. If Lesotho follows through with this development right, it would be in a prime position to capitalize on this niche market popularized by the 1968 Olympic Games held in Mexico City (West, 1996).

With the plans for the premier high altitude sports center should come the question of financing. Financing of sports facilities today could be easily and chaeply be accomplished by the selling of naming rights of the facility as well as selling the access rights. One way the Ministry of Gender and Youth, Sport and Recreation could be to source a financial backer for the project – usually a major corporate brand who wish to have their brands associated with the development. Similar recent developments include the Emirates Stadium in London, England and the Allianz Arena in München, Deutschland. Additionally, Ministry of Gender and Youth, Sport and Recreation could also look at partnering with other national sports bodies or selling the access rights of the facility. Many national sports bodies would appreciate the opportunity to engage their top flight atheletes in high performance altitidue training especially during a lead up to a major sports event like the Olympics, Commonwealth Games, World Championships or FIFA Soccer World Cup. Many countries find access to high altitude training

requirements for such a facility to come into being. These countries at times tend to be rich countries too (oil-rich Gulf states, developed East and South East Asian countries) who crave sporting suceess to compete with the traditionally dominant OECD countries. These countries would pay to have access to such a training facility or even partner the Ministry to build it to their unique specifications. Lesotho should capitalize on their natural geographic endowments and they could yet turn this into a very successful venture.

## High Performance Sports Academies

Building on the high altitude training facilities, the Ministry of Gender and Youth, Sport and Recreation could develop the diea further and turn Lesotho into a training academy for some sports that would be doable in Lesotho year round. The idea would come off the State of Florida in the United States – which is internationally renowed for its premier tennis academies like the Nick Bollettieri Tennis Academy which produced tennis greats like the Williams sisters, Maria Sharapova and Andre Aggassi. The reason for Florida being a successful place to host these premier tennis academies is its sunny and warm tropical climate. Lesotho should make use of its high altitude, rugged terrain and constantly cooler temperatures, even in the summer – which makes sporting activities more comfortable and minimizes the risk of heat exhaustions and other heat related conditions. As it stands, Lesotho is being viewed as an ideal destination for motocross and dirt bike racing because of its terrain.

The Kingdom of Lesotho has been host to the premier international motocross race, The Roof of Africa, for the last decade. *Dirt Bike Magazine* calls The Roof of Africa „the mother of all real hard enduro racing. Motocross News says of the race, *"...without question, there are certainly numerous offroad races on the planet, including difficult, brutal races, but there are not many hard-core events of the calibre of the Roof of Africa Rally."* (Dirtibike Magazine, 2008)

Every year over 200 top riders gather in Lesotho to compete at what is considered the most important off road event in southern Africa (Dirtibike Magazine, 2008). The Roof, as it is fondly known as by motocross enthusaists offers every element a daredevil rider could ask for, from brutal heat and dust right up to continous, unforgiving rain which proves challenging when riders have to cross impassable rivers. The rally also passes through the 3000m high Maluti Mountains which can be bitterly cold. Depending on the climatic conditions during the race, "the drop out rate can average 90%" with the most common cause being physical exhaustion (Dirtibike Magazine, 2008).

The success of the Roof of Africa rally has been noted by both organizers and the Lesotho government with the Lesotho Off-Road Assocation (LORA) announcing in 2011 that it is launching a revised version of the event which will see the traditional off-road spectacle divided into five editions in response to the increased calls for participation from both spectators and racers alike. From 2012, the LORA will host the Quad Roof of Africa in February, the Junior Roof of Africa (for both motorcycles and quad bikes) in April, the Enduro 5 Roof of Africa in July, the Roof of Africa Cars in August and the old Roof of Africa (for motorcycles) in November (Lesotho Review, 2013). This is a clear indicator of the success of the original Roof of Africa event to warrant such an expansion in scale and scope.

If Lesotho could team this up with the building of premier academies for motocross and dirt bike sports it would capitalize on the fact that there is now a Junior Roof of Africa – which would encourage more participantion in the sport from adolsecents. Many of the participants in the Roof of Africa are South Africans and other international racers, meaning the demographic of the junior version would probably be similarly international. These international motocross enthusiats are generally well heeled and can afford the send their children to academies to further hone their skills at the sport. While many South Africans would prefer to train within South Africa, Lesotho could provide competition to that by being more price competitive and offering an all-inclusive option that a training academy(with room and board) would.

## Upgrading Lesotho's Existing Accommodation Facilities

As seen from earlier in the report, the Kingdom is still home to many accommodation facilities that are nearing or do not meet the minimum standards of being inhabitable by international guests. (More than half of all available accommodation in the Kingdom falls in this category) These accommodation facilities, which include a wide variety from hotels, bed and breakfasts to lodges, are detrimental to the development of tourism as a whole for Lesotho. The image of Lesotho right now is that of cheap, low quality accommodation – save for the Lesotho Sun Hotel and Casino. While revamping all these accommodation options to bring them up to international standards would be extremely costly and difficult for the Department of Tourism to finance – Ministry should turn towards looking at micro-financing which has grown tremendously over the last 5 years. Individual micro-finance deals could go towards the upgrading of the accommodation products in Lesotho and bring them up to the international standards necessary to attract international visitors, who have the spending power to continue the momentum of the growing tourism industry in Lesotho.

Another alternative would be for the Ministry of Tourism to actively source international hotel chains that might be interested in setting up international standard hotels in Lesotho. The draw of Lesotho for many international hotel chains is that due to the relatively under-developed state of the tourism industry, whichever chain enters the Lesotho hotel market would enjoy the much sought after first-mover advantage and the chance to dominate the market in the future. In order to draw these international hotel chains in, the

Ministry would have to embark on a series of liberalization policies that would make Lesotho extremely conducive and attractive for foreign hotel firms to enter (Centre for Socio-EcoNomic Development, 2011, p. 58). Tax breaks and tax relief as well as preferable star-up policies should be considered. According to the policy paper, *Mainstreaming Tourism Development in Least Developed Countries* by The Centre for Socio-Economic Development in Geneva, Lesotho's current government policies are not conducive for encouraging foreign direct investment in the country which also applies to getting foreign hotel chains to set up shop in Lesotho. The paper found that among other inhibitions, *"Foreign investors do not have direct access to land title. Under Lesotho's leasehold land title system only Lesotho citizens and commercial entities majority controlled by Lesotho citizens may lease land. Foreign citizens and investors may only sub-lease from Sesotho-owned entities. All transactions in leases and sub-leases, including issue, transfer and mortgages require Ministerial approval."* (Centre for Socio-EcoNomic Development, 2011, p. 58) Land ownership is one of the key components of hotel ownership and if this primary facet of ownership is made impossible for foreigners, it would be extremely challenging, almost impossible for quality foreign hotel chains to enter and improve the market. Additionally, the current fiscal regime *"does not encourage investment in the non-manufacturing sectors – in particular in tourism, property development and mining that require more competitive arrangements to attract investment, especially FDI."* (Centre for Socio-EcoNomic Development, 2011, p. 58) Lesotho should instead look to its African neighbor, Cape Verde for parallels in liberalizing the tourism industry to make it favorable for foreign investors. The Cape Verde government has used this very successfully to attract international hotel chains (including Melià Hotels International) to enter the market to complement the local offerings.

## STRUCTURAL GOVERNMENT IMPROVEMENT PROJECTS THAT WOULD AID TOURISM GROWTH

*Ineffective Investment Promotion for Tourism Related Infrastructure.* Lesotho Tourism Development Corporation, according to the Tourism Act of 2002, *"is responsible to steer tourism promotion for Lesotho."* A 2010 paper written by Masters students at Paris' Sciences Po University outlines the possibilities and direction the Lesotho government and in particular the Lesotho Tourism Development Corporation needs to work on to be more effective with attracting investment for tourism infrastructure. The report states that the *"Government agency needs to gear up its capacity to drive the promotion strategy, such as the development of a comprehensive annual promotion program; a promotion performance measurement framework; as well as a reliable and sustainable tourism statistic database."* (Baweh, Lo, Snow & Werner, 2011) Tourism Related Infrastructure (TRI) investment promotion and facilitation is essential to enable private investment decision of both foreign and local investors to participate in TRI development. Without accurate and accessible data, for example, investors would be more difficult to evaluate the investment risk and profitability of the TRI projects, as these projects usually incur high initial capital input and longer duration for return on investment.

*Official Tourism Data Are Not Accurate and Sufficient to Facilitate Private Investors' Decision.* One fundamental piece of information that can influence the investment decision of private sectors is the official tourism data, which enables investors' assessment of business opportunities and risks related to investment in TRI. According to the same Sciences Po paper, under the current arrangement, the Lesotho Tourism Development Corporation releases the Visitors' Arrival Statistics Report on an annual basis to keep track of inbound tourism activities in Lesotho (Baweh, Lo, Snow & Werner, 2011). *"The analysis focuses on the profile of visitors, the nature and characteristics of visits as well as the trends of visitor flow over years. According to the LTDC, the empirical data are collected, by the Department of Immigration of the Ministry of Home Affairs (MHA), via the use of entry and departure cards visitors submitted before entering or leaving the country at the nine border ports. The Bureau of Statistics (BOS), together with LTDC, conducts the data analysis on a periodic basis. On the other hand, entry form data of citizens of Lesotho are not processed. According to the Lesotho Statistics Yearbook, a portion of tourism statistics before 2003 were not available, and the data set was not complete in 2004 and 2005. A complete set of official tourism data from the Government of Lesotho is only available from 2006 onwards."* (Baweh, Lo, Snow & Werner, 2011, p. 79) This lack of tourism data can therefore impede potential investor's decisions to making tourism investments in the Kingdom and should proper tourism entry data and records should be kept from hereon forth to eliminate this questionable data situation facing potential investors.

*Expanding air links to Lesotho.* Lesotho's Tourism Ministry and the Tourism Development Corporation should look at expanding air links into Lesotho to encourage more international travelers to come to the Kingdom. Currently, only one entry point by air exists – from Johannesburg to Maseru via SA Link. New airlinks should be created first on a seasonal basis, before being expanded to permanent links. These links should reach northern African cities as well as European cities if the aim is to bring it more international tourists to Lesotho for skiing or for sporting pursuits. The Moshoeshoe I International Airport is operating currently at less than 50% utilization level with only two outbound and inbound flights a day and this is evident with the airport closing for periods during the day when there are no scheduled arrivals or departures. There is therefore no immediate need to expand the airport facilities even if the number of inbound and outbound flights increases as a result of new connections.

## Sustainable Tourism in Lesotho

"Sustainable Tourism" is the IT word in the 21$^{st}$ century for marketing tourism products and destinations around the world. As the size of the global middle class continues to grow and with them comes and increasingly educated population with disposable income to spend on vacations. These groups of travelers are increasingly conscious of their environment and the impact of climate change. Their disposable incomes allow them to exercise decisions that they feel would positively impact the environment and preserve it for future generations.

Many tourism products have acknowledged this trend and have set policies and products catered specifically towards this group of travelers including sustainable hotels, carbon footprint offsetting credits for air travelers and sustainable leisure activities like sustainable golfing or whale watching.

Lesotho's relatively under-developed tourism industry puts it in an ideal position to capitalize on this market segment with low transition costs since not much in terms of infrastructure has been solidly put in place yet. What the Lesotho Tourism Development Corporation has to be wary off is that marketing the destination as a a sustainable tourism destination or as an ecological tourism destination brings about the burdens of actually following through with the marketing statement. Tourist who visit so-called eco-tourism or sustainable tourism sites but realize its nothing more than a marketing ploy do not tend to return and Lesotho has to depend very much in the future for repeat tourists if it wants to sustain a high number of tourist arrivals every year and not just for a year or two.

The Lesotho Tourism Development Corporation should focus on dedicated eco-tours showing casing the unique natural flora and fauna that is native to Lesotho and its high altitudes. There could be dedicated tours that specifically showcase Lesotho's natural beauties. This would be a good source of employment for many locals who are very familiar with Lesotho's natural landscape and would require minimal additional content training.

## CONCLUSION

In conclusion, it can be stated that Lesotho has a relatively undeveloped tourism sector, even by African standards, compared to its neighbors South Africa and other premier African destinations like Tanzania, Morocco or Egypt. Lesotho has many unique selling points like its high elevation and rugged terrain. Many of the tourism products remain underdeveloped and service standards remain appalling by international standards. These factors contribute to the already negative image placed on African countries as tourist destinations and perpetuate the cyclical situation making it unfavorable for international travelers who are not just looking for a cheap, low quality destination, to consider Lesotho as their next vacation destination.

The government and its relevant tourism agencies like the Lesotho Development Corporation should invest heavily on ensuring the tourism products in the country are of international standard and that service standards are up to par before marketing the country as an attractive tourist destination to the world.

Successfully marketing alone would do nothing if visitors are unconvinced upon their first visit that Lesotho is a quality leisure destination worth visiting again. Or worse, if visitors are let down on their initial visit by sub-standard products and service. Word of mouth is a powerful tool in tourism and if negative words get associated with Lesotho's tourism industry it would be harder to rectify that reputation.

# REFERENCES

African Development Bank. (2012). *Lesotho Economic Outlook*. Retrieved April 23, 2014, from http://www.africanexonomicoutlook.org

*Afriski Ski and Mountain Resort website*. (n.d.). Retrieved July 17, 2013, from http://www.afriski.net

*American Hotel and Lodging Association website*. (n.d.). Retrieved July 16, 2013, from http://www.ahla.com/content.aspx?id=34706

*Boeing Company website*. (n.d.). Retrieved June 28, 2013, from http://www.boeing.com

Centre for Socio-EcoNomic Development. (2011). Mainstreaming Tourism Development in Least Developed Countries: Coherence and Complimentarity of Policy Instruments. *CSEND Policy Study*, Geneva. Retrieved April 23, 2014, from http://www.csend.org/publications/csend-policy/studies

Magazine, D. (2008 November 19). *Roof of Africa Rally*. Ezilon Maps website. Retrieved July 17, 2013, from http://www.ezilon.com/maps/africa/lesotho-maps.html

Hein, W. (1997). *Tourism and Sustainable Development*. Hamburg.

Baweh, I. A., Lo, C., Snow, B., & Werner, J. (2011). *An analysis of the policy framework for investment in infrastructure of the Kingdom of Lesotho and its impact on tourism-related infrastructure*. (Unpublished Master Thesis). Sciences Po, Paris.

International Labour Organization. (2010). Developments and challenges in the hospitality and tourism sector. *Issues paper for discussion at the Global Dialogue Forum for the Hotels, Catering, Tourism Sector*. Retrieved April 23, 2014, from http://www.ilo.org/wcmsp5/groups/public/---ed_dialogue/---sector/documents/meetingdocument/wcms_162202.pdf

Lesotho Department of Research and Development. (2011). *Arrival Statistical Report*. Maseru.

Lesotho's Ministry of Finance and Development Planning. (2010). *Lesotho Statistical Yearbook*, Maseru. Retrieved April 23, 2014, from http://liportal.giz.de/fileadmin/user_upload/oeffentlich/Lesotho/10_ueberblick/Statistical_Yearbook_2010.pdf

Review, L. (2013). *Tourism*. Maseru: Wade Publications, n.d. Retrieved April 23, 2014, from http://www.lesothoreview.com/tourism.htm

*Lesotho Tourism Development Corporation*. (2011). Maseru: Lesotho Accommodation Statistics.

McKeeman, J., & Zachary, R. (2007). *Private Sector Competitiveness Project*. Washington: World Bank.

Motocross News blog. (2008, May 7). *Motocross* [Web log comment] Retrieved July 16, 2013, from http://www.mxnewsfeed.com/article.php?artid=2164

*Nashoba Valley Ski Resort website*. (n.d.). Retrieved July 17, 2013, from http//www.skinashoba.com

Peng, M. W. (2008). *Global Strategy*. Dallas: University of Texas.

PriceWaterhouseCoopers. (2013), *Hospitality Outlook*. Retrieved July 17, 2013, from http://www.pwc.co.za/en_ZA/za/assets/pdf/hospitality-outlook-june-2013.pdf

Rifai, T. (2013), *Tourism and Value Chains*. Presentation at, Aid for Trade 4th Annual Review, 8th July, Geneva. Star Alliance website. Retrieved June 30, 2013, from http//www.staralliance.com

*Tifindell Ski Resort website*. (n.d.). Retrieved July 17, 2013, from http://www.tiffindell.co.za

United Nations World Tourism Organization. (2006). *Support to Institutional and Capacity Strengthen of the Tourism Sector*. Madrid.

West, J. B. (1996). Prediction of barometric pressures at high altitude with the use of model atmospheres. *Journal of Applied Physiology (Bethesda, Md.), 81*(4), 1850–1854. Retrieved from http://www.ncbi.nlm.nih.gov/pubmed/8904608 PMID:8904608

*World Bank website*. (n.d.). Retrieved July 16, 2013, from http://siteresources.worldbank.org

World Economic Forum. (2013). *The Travel & Tourism Competitiveness Report 2013*. Geneva: Author.

World Trade Organization. (2013). *Aid for Trade 4th Annual Review Programme*. Retrieved July 17, 2013, from http://www.wto.org/english/tratop_e/devel_e/a4t_e/aid4trade_e.htm

World Trade Organization, United Nations World Tourism Organization and Organization for Economic Cooperation and Development. (2013). Tourism and Value Chains. *Aid for Trade 4th Annual Review*. Retrieved July 17, 2013, from http://www.wto.org/english/tratop_e/devel_e/a4t_e/global_review13prog_e/tourism_28june.pdf

## KEY TERMS AND DEFINITIONS

**Competitiveness:** Ability and performance of a firm, sub-sector or country to sell and supply goods and services in a given market, in relation to the ability and performance of other firms, subsectors or countries in the same market.

**Hotel Management:** Professional management techniques used in the hospitality sector, including hotel administration, accounts, marketing, housekeeping, front office or front of house, food and beverage management, catering and maintenance.

**Infrastructure:** Basic physical and organizational structures and facilities (e.g. buildings, roads, and power supplies) needed for the operation of a society or enterprise.

**Supply Chain:** Sequence of processes involved in the production and distribution of a commodity.

**Tourism Development:** Planning and implementation of strategies with the objective to develop the tourism sector.

**Tourism Products:** Anything that can be offered for attraction, acquisition or consumption. It includes physical objects, services, personalities, places, organizations and ideas.

**Value Chain:** Process or activities by which a company adds value to an article, including production, marketing, and the provision of after-sales services.

## ENDNOTES

[1] Boeing Company website. Retrieved July 16, 2013, from http://www.boeing.com

[2] Star Alliance website. Retrieved July 16, 2013, from http://www.staralliance.com

[3] Lesotho Department of Research and Development website. Retrieved July 16, 2013, from http://www.bos.gov.is

[4] American Hotel and Lodging Association website. Retrieved July 16, 2013 from http://www.ahla.com/content.aspx?id=34706

[5] European Hotel Stars Union website. Retrieved July 16, 2013, from http://www.hotelstars.eu

[6] TripAdvisor website. Retrieved July 16, 2013, from http://www.tripadvisor.com/Hotel_Review-g293803-d305110-Reviews-Lesotho_Sun_Hotel-Maseru_Maseru_District.html

[7] Afriski Ski and Mountain Resort website. Retrieved July 16, 2013, from http://www.afriski.net

[8] Tifindell Ski Resort website. Retrieved July 16, 2013, from http://www.tiffindell.co.za

[9] Nashoba Valley Ski Resort website. Retrieved July 16, 2013, from http://www.skinashoba.com

# Chapter 18

# How Do Pre–Alliance Motives and Strategies Affect Post–Alliance Performance in the Airline Industry?
## A Future Research Agenda

**Raphaël K. Akamavi**
*The University of Hull, UK*

**Yue Xu**
*The University of Hull, UK*

**Hrisa Mitreva**
*The University of Hull, UK*

## ABSTRACT

*The global airline industry has currently experienced major changes toward cooperation, where competitive advantages can be built via alliance memberships. The pressure of forming an appropriate alliance strategy is increasing because the airline industry has currently experienced uppermost shifts: intensive rivalry, rapid growth of technological explosion, environmental and terrorist events, etc. Despite positive pre-alliance motivations as recognized in most cases, after certain alliances strategies are formed and implemented, the post-alliance performance is not always satisfactory. Thus, the question of: how do pre-alliance motives and strategies affect post-alliance performance in the airline industry seems under explored. This study therefore looks into the triple relationships among: motives, strategy and performance. This study employs a systematic literature review method for this research topic. The review explores the main factors consisting of each triple dimension and then the linkages between them. Subsequently, it identifies theoretical gaps which indicate areas of further investigations.*

DOI: 10.4018/978-1-4666-8606-9.ch018

# INTRODUCTION

The global airline industry has currently experienced uppermost changes such as an intensive rivalry, a rapid growth of technological explosion, environmental and terrorist events, regulations, new entrants etc. These forces have shaken the airline industry. Hence, airline corporations have to sustain their competitive advantages and performance that can be built through alliance memberships. The pressure of forming appropriate alliance strategy is increasing due to the above forces. In fact, there are three major global airline alliances. The largest one is Star alliance, which in 2011 hold 26% of the market measured by available seat kilometers; the second is Skyteam with 15%; the third one is Oneworld with 14% (Centreforaviation.com). In summary, each alliance demonstrates that pre-alliance motives, strategies and performance are inter-related.

In the last two decades, the growing body in the literature has explored relationships in the inter-firm alliances and their impact on the firms' performance (Baum, Calabrese, & Silverman, 2000; McEvily & Zaheer, 1999; Rowley, Behrens, & Krackhardt, 2000). For example, several scholars also apply theoretical arguments to the airline alliances to understanding how to improve performance as indicated by consumers' welfare and perceptions (Brueckner, 2001; J. Park, 1997), fares, passenger volume and traffic output (Brueckner & Whalen, 2000; Oum, Park, & Zhang, 1996; J. Park, Park, & Zhang, 2003). Despite positive pre-alliance motivations as recognized in most cases, after certain alliances strategies are formed and implemented, the post-alliance performance is not always satisfactory. Therefore, the question of: how do pre-alliance motives and strategies affect post-alliance performance in the airline industry seems under-researched. This study thus explores the triple relationships among: motives, strategies and performance.

The first element of triple relationships is the motives of alliance. Firms may have variety of incentives to engage in an international alliance such as building a global network, seeking entry opportunities of foreign markets, and reducing cost (Gudmundsson & Rhoades, 2001). These motives provide only part of the story. Additional reasons can be institutional conditions such as regulations and norms that shape the growth of this particular industry (Luo, 2007). Strategic partnerships provide airlines a platform to share risks and collectively respond to institutional restrictions (Amankwah-Amoah & Debrah, 2011). When two or more airlines join the membership of strategic alliances, they can better access to scarce resources (Oum, Park, Kim, & Yu, 2004), transfer knowledge (Inkpen, 1995), and operational cost reductions (J. Park, Zhang, & Zhang, 2001). Therefore, alliances may arguably enhance firm's competitive advantage which influences firms' performance. This debate has not been well established in the airline industry.

The second element of the triple relationships is firms' alliance strategies. The types of alliances range from a full integration of different firms to a simple market exchange between airlines (Z. Chen & Ross, 2003). One of the most often adopted alliances is code-share agreements, by which partners acquire and exchange strategic information (Min & Mitsuhashi, 2012; Weber, 2005). Revenue sharing is another form of airline alliances. It can be defined as a joint activity of share revenues between two or more airlines (Gudmundsson & Rhoades, 2001). Joint ventures are also popular by firms' joint development and collaboration to pool resources in order to benefit from operational synergies (Dussauge & Garrette, 1995). In addition, Lazzarini (2007:346) suggests constellations are the "alliances among multiple autonomous firms, such that these groups compete against each other in the same or similar industries for both clients and members". Frequent flyer programs offer alliances that can be defined as an extension to the marketing agreements (Yang & Liu, 2003), for covering complementary itineraries, or transferring passengers to partners at a transit point. This practice is apparent in the airline industry but scholars overlook this phenomenon. All these examples suggest that forming an appropriate alliance strategy, i.e. the form of alliance is subject to motives, hence sometimes is not straightforward.

The last element of the triple relationships is the firm's performance. Performance can be distinguished between financial measures (e.g. traditional accounting metrics) and operational performance. Financial performance has focused on accounting-based financial measures which indicate the financial health of airlines (Cappel, Pearson, & Romero, 2003). The financial performance has received its criticism: undervalue/overvalue airline's assets, manipulation of revenues and expenditures, differences from international standard international accounting conventions, and lack of standardized international accounting practices etc. This performance financial performance relies heavily on historical indicators of the balance sheet which the senior management levels fundamentally weight up at the end of the financial year. As a result, it can be risky for airlines to solely evaluate financial performance metrics which do not generally consider operational performance. Conversely, operational performance has various strengths which mirror risk adjusted performance of airlines. Consequently, it is crucial that airlines' management has an understanding of operational performance measures which may lead to financial growth and sustainable competitive advantages. Operational performance is measured by the airline's level of activity, service quality, taking physical and monetary elements into account (Assaf & Josiassen, 2012). Operational performance can also be viewed from the perspective of relational management whereby partners and customer relationships with the airlines are crucial performance indicators. The

existing literature suggests that the alliance formation affects airlines' performance outcomes such as: air fares, passengers volume, market share and consumer surplus (J. Park & Zhang, 2000), profitability (Brueckner, 2001) and welfare (Czerny, 2009), fares, passenger volume and traffic output (Brueckner & Whalen, 2000; Oum et al., 1996; J. Park et al., 2003). However, these studies have not sufficiently addressed the relationships between alliances' motives, alliances' strategies and alliances performance outcomes in the airline sector. Hence, the extant literature is nascent. Thus, this study attempts to achieve the following objectives. Firstly, it examines systematically the key studies in this arena. Secondly, it provides a thorough content analysis of theoretical development in the airline industry.

As a result, this study employed a systematic literature review method for this research topic. The review focuses on exploring the main factors consisting of each triple dimension and then the linkages between them. This research method aims to identify key knowledge contributions to a particular field and to minimize bias by adopting a replicable, scientific and transparent process of exhaustive literature search (Tranfield, Denyer, & Smart, 2003). In total 68 studies from top tier journals to form our data source.

As a result of the above findings from the systematic literature review, this study proposes a comprehensive conceptual framework which reveals complex links between motives, strategies and performance outcomes Firstly, the key antecedents, which influence the airline firms' decisions to join an alliance, are revealed. Secondly, it outlines different types the airline alliances and how each type relates to the measure of airline performance. Thirdly, it highlights certain important performance measures have been less addressed such as the duration, survival, divorce of alliance. Finally, it highlights the crucial role of the institutions in maintaining fair competition, which leads to increased customer welfare.

*Table 1. Systematic review criteria*

| Criteria | Inclusion | Exclusion |
|---|---|---|
| Language | English | Non-English |
| Journal scope | ABS ranked 2, 3 and 4 stars journals | ABS 1 star ranked journals |
| Research focus | Airline alliances, drivers, firm performance | Other factors |
| Industry | Airline | Other industries |

# SYSTEMATIC LITERATURE REVIEW AND EMERGED THEORETICAL FACTORS

## Systematic Literature Review Method

The current research area consists of three sub-areas: motives, alliance types, and performance. Given the variety of possible elements in each sub-area, the research aims to explore the complexity and define the relationships between all the elements involved. This systematic review is limited to articles published in top tier journals, because they can be considered as academic knowledge and are likely to have highest impact in studied area (Podsakoff, MacKenzie, Bachrach, & Podsakoff, 2005). Although there is no perfect method for an evaluation and assessment of journal quality, the Association of Business School (ABS – UK) presents a comprehensive ranking guide of academic journal quality (Morris, Harvey, & Kelly, 2009:1442). The ABS Ranking is used as a basis for journals' assessment. As a result, two, three, and four stars journals have been included in this work. The reason for inclusion of two stars papers is based on the authors' motivation to not miss any good papers that may have impact on the studied field. By examination of peer-reviewed studies in the ABS' journals, this work examines what has been done and what needs to be explored in the future studies concerning the linkages among factors identified from each sub-literature domain.

The paper selection criteria are based on several elements. The search was conducted in English via databases and abstracts, with hit search numbers recorded. The three searched-databases' protocols are shown in Appendix 1. The next phase is related to the inclusion and exclusion criteria which are formed, and ultimately narrowed down. The inclusion and exclusion criteria are shown in Table 1.

The time span of examined peer-reviewed papers is between 1990 and 2013. This study presents an opportunity to gradually collect and examine changes in the practices and motives of airlines to form an alliance and airlines' performance indicators. As a number of studies significantly increased after the year 2001, the interesting trend can be noticed, which can be attributed to a certain degree on the profound effect of the changes in the industry followed by the 09/11/2011 act in the USA. One could argue that some of the articles published in the 2002, were actually started prior to the latter event, based on the methodology issues such as data collection. However, the trend of increase of the researchers' interest is apparent and in the years 2002-2013, 47 published papers were found relevant in the context of this study. The analysis based on the year of publication is shown in Figure 1.

Another tendency in this research field is the methodological ones. The largest number of studies (29) used empirical data for an econometric analysis. It has been observed a significant role of purely theoretical studies (22), and those based on the case studies (8). The case studies can be defined as a useful method to get in-depth insights into a new phenomenon and to explore neglected part from previous studies factors (Eisenhardt & Graebner, 2007; R. Yin, 2003). Finally, the descriptive analysis is presented in nine articles.

*Figure 1. Papers by year of publication*

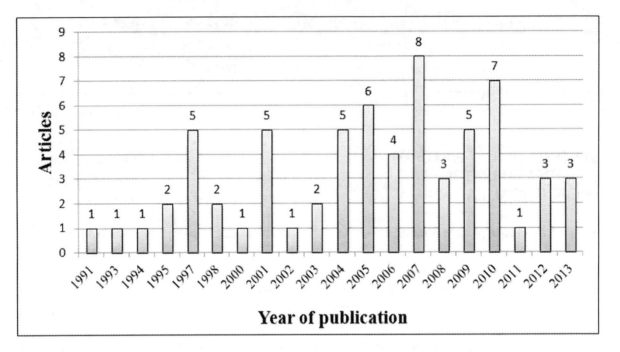

North American scholars produced more relevant published papers in the air travel market. This study found 20 papers from Canadian and American scholars. Cairns and Galbraith (1990) share a similar line of viewpoint and note that deregulations in Canada and the United States' air travel market present a fertile ground and magnet for scholars to conduct investigations of the airline industry. Europe (15 papers) is the next region that captures academics' interests. Indeed, the European Union three packages brought some necessary changes into the union's legislation related to the airline industry. We also found 8 papers that examined Asia. Surprisingly, Africa was under-researched and hardly investigated (1 paper), while South America is not presented in the review, as not even a single paper emerged to study the airline alliances and performance. The airline industry's structure, competition and regulations of latter regions remain under-explored. Consequently, academic writers should expand their research activities and investigations in these regions.

We also include studies based on different level of observations analysis. As it is expected, the majority of articles (55 papers) focused their analysis on the alliances and their different forms. However, firm-based analysis is presented as well in the review (11 papers) researching the particular context. This methodological approach found four papers that have studied alliances from industry level of analysis. Furthermore, two papers have looked at the airline alliances from team level and examined the effect of the intra-organizational and inter-organizational relationships and their impact on the alliances performance (Bruch & Sattelberger, 2001; Carrig, 1997). Our systematic search shows that the airline industry has experienced profound changes due to the liberalization of the markets, first in the USA, and later on in Europe and other regions. A weakened power and influence of national carriers, can lead to increased market entry from other players, such as the low-cost companies. However, in the current systematic review this trend cannot be sufficiently evidenced. The largest share of papers (46 out 68 papers) examined mainstream companies, which inevitably show that such types of carriers are the main players in the industry's partnership and consolidation. Nine papers have studied include in their samples other types of airlines such low-cost carriers (Fan, 2009). Therefore, this study can induce its results only to large airlines, but not to low-cost carriers. Nine papers have focused on other types of players such as the low cost carriers low-cost carriers (Fan, 2009).

## Emerged Theoretical Factors

The systematical examination of the particular literature field is impossible without an analytical review scheme (Ginsberg & Venkatraman, 1985). A thorough analysis of the airline alliances literature revealed three broad categories: alliance motives, alliance strategies/types, and alliance performance. The next section discusses key factors of each sub-areas emerged from the literature review.

## Motives of Alliances

Motives or drivers of alliances could be defined as the antecedents of the process of strategic partnership involvement. Several motives emerged from the literature review. First, institutional regulations are likely to influence the decision of airlines to form variety of alliances. On one side, airline partners are also likely to be supported by institutions. For example, airline partners can be given the right of antitrust immunity (the right to coordinate prices for interline trips) (Bilotkach, 2007a). On the other side, as Amankwah-Amoah and Debrah (2011) have argued that airlines are motivated to form alliance in response to restrictive regulations from the institutions (Amankwah-Amoah & Debrah, 2011; Barla & Constantatos, 2006). In other words, by forming alliances, airlines could escape from various bilateral agreements between countries. Furthermore, even when restriction onts to be lifted, airlines still wish to form the

strategic partnerships as a mean of avoiding the remained limitations (Brueckner, 2001). Specific regulations (e.g. bilateral agreements between particular countries) may also limit the market entry of new carriers on routes between particular countries (Brueckner, 2001).

Therefore, the second motivation behind alliance participation can be entry into international markets (market entry). For example, Gudmundsson and Rhoades (2001) have highlighted that by engaging in alliances, airlines gained entry and could serve new markets, without the requisite need to obtain the rights of doing so through complex countries negotiations. Alliances provide opportunities for airlines to expand their reach by relying on partner to provide service, where otherwise they have no route authority (Brueckner, 2001).

Third, the decision to join alliances could be attributed to the economies of scale effect. As explained by Mak and Go (1995) the airline industry has a capital-intensive character, with costs that are rising rapidly. Hence, carriers aim on cost reductions, by pooling similar assets, skills and knowledge (Gudmundsson & Rhoades, 2001; Wassmer, Dussauge, & Planellas, 2010). For example, alliance members may benefit from a joint purchase of fuel and aircrafts, and engineering services or parts (Amankwah-Amoah & Debrah, 2011). The economies of scale may include economies of traffic density, which emerge when an alliance participation adds more flights or seats into an airline network, which result in lower 'per seat' costs (Tretheway, 1990). More recently, alliances and their members, have started to implement ''consortia-led-e-marketplaces' that should serve as mediators to aggregate demand and facilitate transactions'' (Wagner, Huber, Sweeney, & Smyth, 2005). The latter can be considered as an important factor to reduce costs and thus leading to economies of scales for the parties involved.

Fourth, the access to resource is amongst the most important drivers to be involved in alliances. Firms are motivated to become part of alliances because of a need to obtain resources (Das & Teng, 2002) in order to generate synergies (Jones, 2002). According to Evans (2001), a firm's specific resource imbalance or inadequacy can be overcome by a collaboration with alliance partners that possess different sets of such resources. The partnerships help the airlines to obtain access and transfer resources (e.g. knowledge) from partners (Amankwah-Amoah & Debrah, 2011; Wassmer et al., 2010). Moreover, as asserted by Amankwah-Amoah and Debrah (2011) combined resources of allied firms become competitive advantages that can enhance a competitive position of each firm in a particular alliance.

Fifth, airlines tend to participate in alliances in order to build global networks (Gudmundsson & Rhoades, 2001). J. Park (1997) explained that through strategic alliances, major carriers have enhanced the reach of their networks, which otherwise may not be possible. To achieve that objective, alliances engaged in hub and spoke networks. In such network system services from smaller airports are directed into a larger central hub and then the hubs are linked by direct flights (Hamill, 1993). By doing this, the network leads to a consolidation of connecting passengers and thus affecting the density of traffic along each hub (Nero, 1996; Wang, Evans, & Turner, 2004). In addition, such networks present customers with reduced travel time, larger number of online connections and availability to participate in improved frequent flyer programs (Tretheway & Oum, 1992).

Sixth, competitive dynamics and risk diversification are another factor that influences the motivation of airlines to form alliances. Prior research on competitive dynamics stated that partnerships between rival firms are often dangerous, because the fierce competition encourages an opportunism and appropriation of capabilities (Kogut, 1989; S. Park & Russo, 1996). However, Gimeno (2004) has argued that countervailing alliances with rivals' partners could be set up to duplicate rivals' benefits. Moreover, a possible

reason that stems from competitive dynamics to form an alliance is to overcome competition from a third party (Gimeno, 2004). Furthermore, Ku and Fan (2009) have explained that airlines use alliances in order to increase their competitiveness in service quality.

## Strategies of Alliances

Global strategic alliances are defined as "inter-firm cooperative arrangements, involving cross-border flows and linkages that utilize resources and/or governance structures from autonomous organizations headquartered in two or more countries, for the joint accomplishment of individual goals linked to the corporate mission of each sponsoring firm" (Parkhe, 1993:94). This study has revealed six forms of strategic alliances.

First, one of the most often adopted types of alliance is code-share agreements (F. Chen & Chen, 2003), which are "an integral part strategic airline alliances" (Weber, 2005:258). By code-share agreement, partners acquire and exchange strategic information (Min & Mitsuhashi, 2012). The US Department of transportation defined code-sharing as the process in which at least two airlines share airline designation codes (Oum & Park, 1997). Oum and Park (1997) note that code-share agreements help to identify airlines on computer and passenger reservation tickets and airport information boards. This type of alliance is also likely to involve a joint coordination of a flow of passengers and baggage (Lazzarini, 2007). In other words, this makes each airline network naturally connected with their route systems. As a result, it provides 'seamless' service and makes passengers feel as if traveling in a single airline (Brueckner, 2001).

The literature distinguishes three main types of code-sharing agreements:

I.    Complementary code-sharing refer to the case where carriers link up their networks and setting up a new complimentary network (J. Park, 1997);

II. Single-carrier virtual codesharing agreement, in which although a passenger stays on a single carrier plane for the whole round-trip, the ticket was marketed and sold by a partner (Gayle, 2008);

III. Interline mixed virtual codeshare, where a passenger travels on an interline connecting itinerary, but the sole ticketing airline for the whole trip is not an operating airline (Gayle, 2008).

Secondly, an alliance can be referred as joint ventures. Based on joint development and collaboration, joint venture partners pool their resources together in order to benefit from synergies (Dussauge & Garrette, 1995; Wang et al., 2004). In addition, an equity stake partnership has been implemented by some alliances, which refers to bilateral system agreements of coordination of routing, joint fares, shared reservations and databases decisions (Wang et al., 2004). We also observed another type of an alliance, where two or more airlines swap stock and/or set up a joint governance structure (Gudmundsson & Rhoades, 2001).

Third, this study finds that constellations offer an additional alliance format. According to Lazzarini (2007:346) constellations are "alliances among multiple autonomous firms, such that these groups compete against each other in the same or similar industries for both clients and members". Instead of competition each other, constellation requires a cooperation between firms. A membership in such alliance types enables carriers to capture externalities from other companies (e.g. direct or indirect traffic flows).

Fourth, a common form of strategic alliances is marketing agreements. One type of marketing agreements, or franchising, refers to the rent of the brand name of one airline to another carrier for the purpose of offering flight service, but supplies its own aircraft or staff (Gudmundsson

& Rhoades, 2001). In similar direction, brand alliances can be a type of marketing partnerships as network branding (Woisetschläger, Michaelis, & Backhaus, 2007). Moreover, partners may implement frequent flyer programs based on an extension of the marketing agreements (Yang & Liu, 2003). They are designed to push passengers to book more frequently with a particular carrier, which leads to loyal customer base (Mak & Go, 1995; Yang & Liu, 2003).

Fifth, alliances may exist in the form of block space (Gudmundsson & Rhoades, 2001). A block space agreement exists when one airline allocates to another airline seats to sell on its flight (Gudmundsson & Rhoades, 2001; J. Park, 1997). For example, KLM and Northwest have formed such agreements (Man, Roijakkers, & Graauw, 2010).

Sixth, alliance agreement can be based on a joint service defined as combined flight service between airlines (Gudmundsson & Rhoades, 2001; J. Park, 1997). For example, maintenance services or facilities sharing take place when one airline contracts with another to provide services, personnel or facilities at particular sites.

As a result, airlines may set up various types of alliances for different motives in order to shape their market position through collaborative networks and cost leaderships which consequently enhance their performance. It is arguable that the bottom line of any airline alliance is to improve an airline's performance in the short or long run.

## Performance of Alliances

It is difficult task to evaluate the alliance performance due to the complex objectives of many of these partnerships (Evans, 2001). This study found each firm's performance in the alliance is affected by two types of forces: factors outside of a firm's control (e.g. weather); and such that are under its control (e.g. inefficiency) (Marín, 1998). It is noted that performance is generally viewed from two main directions: financial performance and operational performance

First, financial performance is a category that provides data about performance of the airlines and margins on its activities (Cappel et al., 2003). In term of financial performance two broad factors are found which affect on allied firms' performance. Airlines' profitability is one of the most important performance indicators. The term profit has attracted scholars' attention for many decades. Some scholars have shown that a participation in an airline alliance has serious impact on the firm's profit (Adler & Smilowitz, 2007; Bilotkach, 2005; J. Park, 1997). Other writers have pointed out that a type of the alliance is also likely to affect profitability (Oum et al., 2004; Yan & Chen, 2008; Zhang & Zhang, 2006). For example, Hassin and Shy (2004) have studied how codeshare agreements determine airlines' profitability. Furthermore, a network size also has been studied as an important factor that affects airlines performance in terms of profitability (Lin, 2008). In fact, practitioners, managers and other stakeholders look at this key indicator at the end of each financial year to determine their airline's survival and growth.

Performance indicators which are very sensitive to indirect factors such as pricing strategy, also attract scholars' attention (Bilotkach, 2007b; Brueckner, 2001). For example, a pricing element is presented by Czerny (2009), who asserted that fares depend on total demand of interline and non-interline customers. Therefore, a change of the pricing strategy would affect revenue. In addition, some authors have studied how an alliance partnership and competition affect revenues and their management (Man et al., 2010; Netessine & Shumsky, 2005). When airlines participate in alliances, they engage in revenue sharing, which can be defined as a joint activity of share revenues between two or more airlines (Gudmundsson & Rhoades, 2001). A variety of measures are used to assess financial performance: return on assets; operating income, net results, and net profit margin (Casanueva, Gallego, & Sancho, 2013).

Second, operational performance is an alternative way of measuring airline performance, which is based on its level of activities that include physical as well as economy criteria in consideration (Assaf & Josiassen, 2012). In addition, operational performance is measure by productivity (Oum et al., 2004). Because firms generally use multiple inputs to produce multiple outputs, they used total factor productivity in order to measure firm productivity. total factor productivity is based on the use of multiple inputs to produce multiple outputs (Oum et al., 2004). Moreover, a passenger load is also an indicator of operational performance, which measures aircraft capacity utilization (Lazzarini, 2007).

In term of operational performance, the economies of traffic density to a large degree affect airlines' performance either positively or negatively (Brueckner, 2001; J. Park, 1997). Moreover, it is shown that an alliance participation affects a load factor, or an aircraft seat utilization (F. Chen & Chen, 2003; Lazzarini, 2007), and traffic levels for the airlines in alliances (Gayle, 2008). The operational revenue by passenger kilometer or other (Barros & Peypoch, 2009). indicators such as: a total number of passengers transported by an airline in a particular period; a total number of passengers transported in a aircraft by kilometer flown; tons of cargo transported per kilometer flown; a total revenue obtained by each carrier (Casanueva et al., 2013).

Third, performance of airlines in alliances is also likely to be moderated by relationships between factors such as service quality and customer satisfaction. Literature distinguished a clear relationship between the level of airline service quality and customer satisfaction (Olaisen & Revang, 1991; Steven, Dong, & Dresner, 2012). On one side, authors have examined the service quality throughout the prism of service failures of alliance partners and its impact over the firm's participation in strategic alliances (Weber & Sparks, 2009). One the other side, Steven et al. (2012) observe that customer complaints determine customer satisfaction. It is debatable that customer complaints can be considered as a useful barometer for an airline's service quality and customer satisfaction level. Furthermore, consumer perceptions are also an important factor that contributes to an airline performance in alliances. The consumers' evaluation of airlines that enter or quit alliance is found to have an effect on both economic (financial) and non-economic (operational) performance (Woisetschläger et al., 2007).

In relation to service quality, welfare, which is a non-economic indicator, is also likely to be considered in performance measurement. Literature suggests that different types of alliances (e.g. scheduling and pricing, codeshare agreements, network integration) may affect their customer welfare through factors such as service quality and costs (Bilotkach, 2007b; Brueckner, 2001; Hassin & Shy, 2004; J. Park, 1997; Reggiani, Nijkamp, & Cento, 2010; Sadi & Henderson, 2000; Zhang & Zhang, 2006).

## MAIN FINDINGS

### Relationships of Alliance Motives, Strategies, and Performance

Most studies reveal certain type of relationship among alliance motives, type of alliances and performance measures. Moreover in some cases, motives and alliances strategies determine several performance indicators at the same time, which makes difficult to distinguish specific connections.

The first set of studies has analyzed the link between motives, alliances types and performance outcomes. As argued by Bilotkach (2007b:428) ''the most noticeable feature of the consolidating efforts between airlines is uniting of the parents' network, referred to as codesharing''. Therefore, it is not surprising that the largest share of studies has linked motives with particular type of alliance (codesharing) and performance outcomes. It is

noted that advantages and drawbacks of each type is viewed for its relationships with performance. For example, J. Park (1997) differentiates global service networks through complementary and parallel alliances. He went to analyze the effect of alliances on multiple performance factors linking to both types of alliance and found three main performance issues.

I.     In term of operational performance, scholars have found a positive impact on alliance membership (Lazzarini, 2007; J. Park et al., 2001). For example Wang et al. (2004) have tested the impact of five types of alliances on airlines' performance. They have also found that an alliance membership enhances an airline in tits strives to gain economies of density, by increasing flights' number and frequency, a number of passengers per flight and an overall number of passengers. In other words, operational performance of alliance firms is improved, because of this membership. On the other side, it can be seen that alliances may result in possible drawbacks for airlines' operational performance. For example, in order to enlarge their networks by alliance formation or membership, partners improved their services, which attract high volume of passengers (Flores-Fillol, 2010; Gayle, 2008; Youssef & Hansen, 1994). Therefore, alliance participation may lead airlines to internalize their partner's congestion. The literature also has paid particular attention on the alliance impact on operational performance in codesharing alliance. J. Park et al. (2001) explained that an increased traffic between partner airlines may results in a high load factor in their flights on local routes, which may lead to lower operating costs and subsequently lower prices for local consumers. A high load factor and lower operating costs also can be seen as improved operational performance. As argued by F. Chen and Chen (2003), the extended reach of the global network, increased demand may create higher load factor for both parallel and complimentary alliances. However, a load factor increases differently, while a complimentary alliance needs to increase a seat supply, a parallel alliance can supply fewer seats than its counterpart by conducting risk management with alliance partners.

II. Literature also examines airline alliances in term of financial performance. The airlines partnership allowed firms to gain larger market and network route share, in compare with carriers that stayed out of alliances (Wang et al., 2004). In term of a complementary alliance, it is observed increased partners' flights frequencies, which resulted in higher market share (Wen & Hsu, 2006). Similarly, a membership of complimentary partnerships offers a crucial advantage to allied partners, by allowing them to commit to greater outputs based on 'within alliance complementarities and cross-alliance substitutability (Zhang & Zhang, 2006). As a result, a complementary alliance leads to increase in profitability, and prevents market entry from new competitors. In addition, rivalry between such types of alliances result in a higher level of alliances is associated with greater outputs and an improved economic welfare. In contrast, when each airline sells seats on the partner' flights, but both airlines are unwilling to coordinate their yield management decision, hence the code-share partnership can result in competition (Netessine & Shumsky, 2005). In other words, in such case, carriers lose revenues, which directly affect their financial performance. In term of parallel alliances, it is revealed that partners may decrease their productivity when their market shares are lower (Wen & Hsu, 2006).

III. The literature on airline alliances also evaluates customer satisfaction and welfare as performance indicator. Steven et al. (2012) analyzed concentrated markets characterized with less competition and dominated by alliances. They found that the partners' airlines increased their profitability, but customer satisfaction decreased. For example, Youssef and Hansen (1994) analyzed SAS-Swissair strategic alliance. They found increased fares can be attributed to the increased concentration. In other words, reduced competition due to a high-level of concentration in a particular airline market deters airlines to focus on satisfying their customers. Thus it could be observed a trend of increasing alliance partners' profitability tends to come alone with decreased customers' welfare. On the other side, Netessine and Shumsky (2005) have argued that competition tend to push airline companies to improve their service to different groups of passengers including high-fare passengers under horizontal competition, and low-fare passengers under vertical competition become better-off

In term of codeshare type of alliance, existing studies have analyzed alliances in term of performance factors such as quality of services and consumer welfare (Brueckner, 2001; Hassin & Shy, 2004; J. Park, 1997; J. Park et al., 2001). In term of a complementary partnership, it is shown that this collaboration improves the quality of connecting services, which leads to decrease in fares, making customers better off (J. Park, 1997; J. Park et al., 2001). Similarly, Hassin and Shy (2004) explained that because of code-share agreements between airlines, none of the passengers is worse off, with some passengers become better off. Furthermore, a decision to join partner airlines' network through a codeshare partnership leads to a substantial impact on the consumers' welfare, measured by decreased interline fares (Bilotkach, 2007b; Brueckner, 2001).

Negative effects of code-share alliance on consumer welfare are also evidenced in literature. For example, (Brueckner, 2001), indicated a possible drawback of codesharing, which is the lack of competition in the inter-hub market that connects partners' hub cities, which tends to raise fares and producing countervailing effects (raise fares). In other words, it affects consumer welfare as a performance indicator. Similarly, in parallel alliance market fares increased, which leads to losses in consumer surplus (J. Park, 1997). Moreover, Gayle (2008) examines single-carrier virtual codesharing, where a customer remains on a particular airline plane for the entire trip, but the ticket is sold by a partner airline. He can observe a price increase, which could be explained by collusive behaviors. Implications for airlines and alliances that they form in this case could be institutional restrictions based on this collusion as well as customers left worse off because of the higher fares.

The second set of literature has focused on the link between institutional factors (as a motive), alliance strategies and performance outcomes. Institutional factors such as a market's liberalization and consequent bilateral agreements between particular countries are shown to have positive impact on airlines' efficiency and productivity as performance indicators (Marín, 1998). In addition, Li, Lam, Wong, and Fu (2010) have argued that the competition leads to decreased fare and consumer surplus, and thus affects social welfare. Moreover, removing entry barriers always increase consumers' welfare and industry profits (Gillen, Harris, & Oum, 2002). It is found that institutions may have negative impact on the alliance participation and performance. For example, Amankwah-Amoah and Debrah (2011) concluded that the institutional hindrances (e.g. stated ownership), insufficient market reforms and route networks are the main factors contributing to the relative isolation of these airlines from current trend to alliance membership. Bilotkach (2007b) also found that antitrust immunity has no significant effect on interline trips' pricing.

Bilotkach (2007a) further argued that coordination in both scheduling and pricing (antitrust immunity) resulted in lower fares and a higher quality product. Lower fares and higher quality product emerge because coordination in scheduling results in less stop-over delay. For example, Lufthansa network integration into the Star Alliance positively affects consumers because they can use more connections, which shorter their travels (Reggiani et al., 2010). In other words, if the airlines are given the antitrust immunity, partners in the alliance, are likely to coordinate pricing and scheduling strategies, which result in passengers being better off.

The third set of studies deal with the relationship between revenues' share management in an alliance and its impact on airline performance. Wright, Groenevelt, and Shumsky (2010) highlighted that each a revenue management decision of each alliance members may result in suboptimal revenues for the whole alliance. Therefore, they formulate a multiperiod Markov game model of two airline partners in alliance. They asserted that "no Markovian transfer-price scheme can guarantee optimal revenues because of sharing of interline revenues cannot directly affect acceptance decisions for intraline itineraries" (Wright et al., 2010:33). In another study Kimms and Cetiner (2012) have argued that despite the obvious advantages that stem from an airline membership in alliances, there is an important issue how to share revenues from selling tickets among the allied airlines in a fair way. Moreover, such fair allocation is likely to have a crucial importance on the alliance stability in a long-term. Kimms and Cetiner (2012) suggested the use of revenue proration scheme based on a theoretical model of the nucleolus as a revenue share mechanism. Hu, Caldentey, and Vulcano (2013) used two-stage approach that combines cooperative and non-cooperative game theory in order to tackle a revenue share issue within alliances. Their theoretical approach is useful in term of the support that provide to the use of simple fixed proration rates as revenue share rule.

The fourth set of studies, concerns the effect of the alliance size over the airline performance

On one side, in term of financial performance, Chua, Kew, and Yong (2005) have argued that large codeshare alliances lead to economies of scale, thus reducing costs, while small alliances tend to increased cost for the partners in the alliance. On other side, Lazzarini (2007) has studied multilateral alliances formed by large players that shared a common organizational structure. Additionally, he asserts that these airlines can use a 'multilateral nature of explicit constellations instead of complex bilateral connections, and thus increase their operational performance.

The fifth set of studies has focused on relationship between alliance governance structure and duration or termination of alliances that are likely to impact on the overall airline performance. For example, Man et al. (2010) have pointed out on internal changes such as a change of other alliance members' strategy, or a position change of key managers in alliances that may affect the partnership. Moreover, other causes that may lead to change in an alliance and its governance structure include success or failure of an alliance business, relationship building, and tensions that need to be managed. In other words, an impossibility to manage all these factors may lead to decreased relevance of such strategic partnerships, which inevitably will affect each aspect of an airline's performance.

A duration or termination of alliances as performance characteristics is also found in some of the studies reviewed. On one side, alliance types such as code-sharing, marketing and frequent flyer programs, pooling and joint purchases or procurements and block-space have a lower risk of termination (Gudmundsson & Rhoades, 2001). On other side, equity alliances with their complexity are among alliances with highest risks of termination (Gudmundsson & Rhoades, 2001). Furthermore, Wassmer et al. (2010) have explored an overlap between newly formed alliance' product or market scope and existing partner's operations. This overlap may result in higher conflict resolution costs and even termination of the existing

alliance as a reaction to a new alliance formation, by existing partners.

The sixth set of studies deals with the link between consumers' perceptions, alliance and performance. For example Weber (2005) has argued that passengers from both hemispheres have different perceptions. Hence, these passengers should be targeted as different market segments. She has also asserted that marketing communications and a choice between right or wrong strategy are crucial to ensure a profitability of allied airlines. Furthermore, consumer perceptions in a case of failure's alliance services have been studied through a prism of high and low identification groups (Weber & Sparks, 2006). They found that the passengers from high identification group felt stronger dissatisfaction than the passengers from low identification group . The analysis of the consumers' perceptions revealed that both groups do not want to associate with a particular alliance in the future. Moreover, Woisetschläger et al. (2007) have revealed that the airline decision to enter strong brand's network have a substantial positive influence on consumers' perceptions, while exit from alliance has a negative effect on their perceptions.

## Solutions and Recommendations

The focus of the current systematic review is on the drivers that motivated the alliance formation in the airline industry and how these factors affect airline's performance. The 68 studies that hit back the systematic search offered wide range of analyses, discussions and conclusions. The main findings entirely revealed the interwoven connections and relationships between the three pillars.

First, global network building becomes a key motive for airlines to form new, or join existing alliances. Scholars have shown that passengers prefer to fly larger network carriers, thus reduce their travel time and increase their online connections (Bilotkach, 2007a; Gayle, 2008; Gillen et al., 2002; Hassin & Shy, 2004). In a fast-paced environment nowadays, in order to attract more customers, airlines must engage in different forms of partnerships. The globalization and the rapid growth of the emerging market' countries expanded a global map for doing business and travel, which pushed the airlines industry to enhance cooperation's between the carriers.

Second, competitive dynamics push firm to be more strategic in choosing the route of joining alliances. For example, Lazzarini (2007) has pointed out that competitive advantages can be gained from a membership of the airline alliances because of competition has changed from airlines to constellations, and firm's performance could depend on alliances' choice. Therefore, it is necessary to become a member of group and then to compete with rival groups. Moreover, an airline firm can be seen as an isolated actor on the worldwide airline scene, and not only its competitive power, but its survival is likely to depend upon a selection of alliances' decision. Adler and Smilowitz (2007) have suggested a strategic model that airlines can use in order to analyze potential alliances. In addition, airlines also can use this model to evaluate anti-trust problems.

In addition, it is evidenced an importance of economies of scale and density as key drivers for alliance memberships, and their impact over the firm's performance (Brueckner, 2001; Chua et al., 2005; J. Park, 1997; Wang et al., 2004). A positive outcome from an alliance membership is revealed to impact on costs reductions: an increased number of flights and frequency, and gain a larger share of passengers. On one side, these advantages that stem from partnerships in alliance affect both financial and operational performance, as well as on consumers' welfare. On other side, they may result in an increased traffic, congestions and service failures. Therefore, they may directly affect the consumers' welfare and perceptions toward airlines and their alliances.

Fourth, the literature reviewed has shown that service quality and service failure are closely linked with firm's performance. Service qual-

ity and service failure need to be addressed by airlines, in order to implement (choose) right alliance strategy. For example, a review of the airlines alliances revealed two kinds of airlines, one with a volume orientation control, and other with a service orientation (Weber & Sparks, 2009). Thus, airlines should join alliances with similar service philosophy about service quality and service failure resolutions (Weber & Sparks, 2009). Moreover, as highlighted by Bilotkach (2007a) improved schedule coordination is one of the examples for a higher quality product that come with alliance participation. He introduced a model, which shows that if allied airlines are allowed by regulators to coordinate schedules, they will position connecting flights closer compared with airlines that lack institutional approval to coordinate their actions. In other words, it is not only important to integrate operational and financial concerns, but also in the decision-making process to join alliance, is crucial to evaluate the potential partners' service practices. Literature revealed a strong connection between high service quality and customer satisfaction, which is not surprising. Furthermore, it is found even more important linkage between service failures and a negative image formed by customers. Moreover, when airlines cooperate in alliances, a partner's mistake or negligence is likely to impact on the other partners, who have not done anything wrong. Hence, the question of right partners' selection gains momentum.

Fifth, although the ambition to engage in alliance may affects different aspect of airline firm's performance, the alliance itself should not be perceived as a static condition. Various environmental changes such as institutional regulations, new technologies, or shifted competition, may cause tensions in the alliances. For example, institutions (e.g. regulations, bilateral agreements. etc.) contributed to the current trend to alliance formation (Li et al., 2010; Marín, 1998). For example, the airline deregulation act in the USA at the end

transport lead to waves of cooperation agreements within the industry. However, although many of the bilateral agreements between countries have been removed, existing agreements present limits to new entrants in order to serve particular routes. Bilotkach (2005) has suggested that despite drawbacks of an antitrust immunity policy (e.g. welfare decreasing), an airline may not be willing to join an alliance without such immunity. A decision to not join alliances is because of the likelihood of decreasing profits. Furthermore, partner's strategy change, or new top management team on board may also influence a change in alliances (Man et al., 2010). The latter fact reveals a complexity of partners' relationship.

Sixth, it is noted a significant presence of a code-share type of alliances in this systematic review. In term of airline financial performance (profitability), complementary alliance is one of the reasonable types of partnership that leads to increased profitability, which in addition restrict competitions from new market entries. Furthermore, it is shown that a complementary alliance results in an improved quality of connecting services and lower fares for the customer, thus resulting in better customers' welfare. It is also found that a codesharing strategy supports carriers in their ambition to build a larger network. However, a negative effect of the code-share alliances in term of higher fares due to collusion between the partners is reported in some of the studies. A possibility of collusive behaviors must be carefully evaluated and controlled by regulators, and thus to protect passengers' welfare. Besides, while the institutional frames of the European Union and North America are well established and effectively working, it cannot be said the same for an experiencing high growth emerging countries such as BRICS (Brazil, Russia, India, China and South Africa) and other economical over-performing countries around the world. Most of these countries are leaping forward in their economic development, but their institutional and legislative frames are still not well developed. The rapidly growing middle class in those countries offers an excellent opportunity to airlines and alliances to gain a market share, which should happen only in condition to respect regulations and consumer rights in those countries.

## FUTURE RESEARCH DIRECTIONS

Several main theories have been identified in this systematic literature review, they are: resource-based view, network resources perspective, alliance portfolio approach, alliance constellation theory, and social identity theory.

First, resource-based view (RBV), has asserted that a main motivation behind the firm's alliance engagements is to obtain resources and capabilities (Das & Teng, 2000). Therefore, resource-seeking is seen as explanation why airlines choose particular alliance partners. Various benefits such as financial, technological, and knowledge resources and skills are drawn from the carriers, because of their memberships in alliances. For example, KLM increased equity stakes in Northwest, when the American airline experienced financial in 1993 (Man et al., 2010). The combinations of all these resources enhanced carrier's competitive advantages, and subsequently build airlines' competitive edge.

Second, an analysis of the theories that have been used in the literature revealed connections between RBV and network theory. This terminology is the so-called network resources theory (Casanueva et al., 2013). It combines elements from both theories and postulates that "network resources are assets that are owned by the firms' partners, but can potentially be accessed by the firm through its ties to those partners" (Lavie, 2008:548). Thus, the network resources theory emphasizes a network-specific nature of a resource-seeking decision, and provides a basis to explain an airline choice of strategic alliances.

Third, closely related to RBV and network resource theory is alliance portfolio approach.

This theoretical approach starts gain researcher's interest (e.g. Casanueva et al., 2013; Wassmer et al., 2010). It is "situated around the confluence of the RBV with network theory" (Casanueva et al., 2013:442). The alliance portfolio approach examines how an individual firm manages its relations with the other parties in alliances. Hence, the focus of an analysis is shifted from alliances to firm as the units of analysis, and from a complex and complete network to an egocentric focal network firm (Casanueva et al., 2013). Studies based on such approach to large degree match the aim of this systematic review to reveal the complex linkages between drivers, alliances and firm's performance outcomes.

Fourth, alliance constellation perspective has focused on the alliances between multiple firms. A participation in such alliances offers firms with "possibility to internalize positive externalities emanating from the presence of other firms in the group" (Lazzarini, 2007:346). An alliance constellation is a valuable perspective that can determine the impact of an alliance membership on the firm's performance.

Fifth, the crucial role that customers have played in the carrier's performance can be evaluated by the social identity theory. According to this theory, there is no need for people to interact or to have strong interpersonal ties to perceive themselves as group members (Weber & Sparks, 2006). Thus, a service quality or service failure of alliances' members can be easily echoed by passengers, which may lead to positive or negative image of carriers as a performance outcome.

Factors that motivate an alliance formation in the airline industry, and how this process influence firm's performance have been studied more than 20 years. Research shifts from studying alliances and their impact to consumers in the North American market (Tretheway, 1990), to the impact of the liberalisation in the UAE airline sector on the indigenous airlines' economic performance (Squalli, 2013). Moreover, Tretheway (1990) paper

of liberalisation in the airline industry, characterized with a democracy and legislation supremacy. Squalli (2013) study concerns newly emerged country, with still a long way in its development. These examples are indicative about the complex world of alliance formations, the rationale behind them and multiple effects on the member firm's performance deserve more research.

First, as shown, the largest share of studies in this literature review has been focused on North America and Europe. Furthermore, as Amankwah-Amoah and Debrah (2011) highlighted, more research is needed to explore how institutions (e.g. government) in developing countries affect (support or restrict) airlines' involvement in a constellation. This study agrees with this point and adds that particularly great attention is needed toward rapidly economic growing emerging markets. An inherent characteristic of emerging countries is their institutional context (environment), which has a great impact on businesses.

Second, a promising direction for future research is examination of consumer evaluations and behaviours in case of alliance members' service failure, to extend current findings (e.g. Weber & Sparks, 2009). In other words, future studies would benefit if analysed other than Western world context. For example, emerging countries get a large number of their population moving to middle class and beyond, which results in more people being able to use airlines as a mean of transport. Therefore, it is needed to examine emerging markets consumers' perceptions of an airline failure, because an informal cultural background is likely to has an impact on consumers' perception in these countries. Furthermore, it would be interesting to examine whether brand loyalty, and a particular airline alliance entrance, and/or alliance exit have a significant impact on emerging market consumers' perceptions. Finally, as suggested by Weber and Sparks (2009) communication literature might prove useful to shed further light on the service recovery process.

Third, except the case of service failure, future research should carefully examine the link between service quality, customer satisfaction and airline performance. Future studies need to consider highly competitive markets, where customer expectations are likely to be too high and affect their perception of what is a 'good' service quality.

Fourth, a possible direction for future research is within the domain of alliance portfolio approach. As highlighted by Casanueva et al. (2013) it is necessary to study temporal effects on the endowments of network resources, and on relations between social capital and airline's performance (financial and operational). Furthermore, it would be interesting to study linkages between network resources, social capital and alliance portfolio on the particular airline sector (e.g. flag carriers, low cost, and freight transport).

Fifth, the relationship between regulators, customer welfare and operational performance, future research is also necessary. For example, Li et al. (2010) suggested a multilevel hierarchical system of interactions between regulators, airlines and passengers that aims to optimize additional routes allocation in a liberalising airline market. However, future studies may want to shift their focus from regulators to airport authorities as an institution that directly allocates additional routes and airport slots. In their theoretical study Flores-Fillol (2010) proposed that because of alliances, airlines internalize their partner's airport congestions. Therefore, an empirical study would be welcomed to explore if a similar link between alliances' partners and airport congestion exists.

Sixth, a fruitful direction for future research is the revenue management issue in alliances. Although several papers have studied a revenue share among airlines in alliances, there are still possibilities for future contributions in this area. For example, Hu et al. (2013) approach lacks of focus on the contractual stage' negotiation process between partners, which a process can be studied through the prism of bargaining theory. Moreover,

as they argue static proration rules are easy to implement, but it would be important to use dynamic proration rules, because they may result in increased revenues. In term of a nucleolus-based revenue share (e.g. Kimms & Cetiner, 2012), a promising future direction is to include, additional costs such as an airline's operating costs that stem from alliances' participation.

Seventh, in term of alliance governance structure, it would be interesting if future studies could expand on elements of a robust governance form as suggested by Man et al. (2010) in other alliance contexts. Moreover, it would worth if future studies examine governance structures and their effects on brokerage persistence (e.g. X. Yin, Wu, & Tsai, 2012).

Finally, future research can also extends (Reggiani et al., 2010:457) findings about complex aviation networks (e.g. concentration, topology and connectivity) and focus on "the structure and driving forces of the demand side" i.e. types of customers.

## CONCLUSION

This study determines factors that influence airlines in their decision to join alliances, and performance outcomes because of this choice. It employs systematic literature review, which is efficient research methodology that can examine what have been done in the related literature in this field and offers the possibility to systemize and reduce huge volume of information into reasonable pieces. Given the vast literature body, it would not be appropriate to be said that this systematic review offers completeness. However, the précised, structured and thorough work that have been done, suggest representativeness of the findings. This systematic review resulted in 68 studies that are spread between two, three and four stars categories of the ABS Ranking. This study revealed six important findings.

First, it indicated a complex link between antecedents, alliance strategy and performance outcomes. It also evidenced that network building is key motive for alliance participation. Moreover, the largest number of studies has researched particular type of alliance i.e. codesharing. The airline performance can be seen from three perspectives: operational, financial, and customer satisfaction and welfare. In term of *operational performance*, it found positive effect from alliance membership on airline performance. Alliance membership benefits airlines in term of increasing flights number, frequency of flights, number of passengers per flight, and overall number of passengers. Furthermore, when codeshare alliance is taken into account, it is characterized with increased traffic between partners, which is followed by high load factor and results in lower fares.

In term of *financial performance* airlines also benefit from alliance membership. The partnership allows the carriers to gain a larger market and network route share, in compare with those carriers are outside of alliance. In addition, it found that a complementary alliance results in improved profitability for its members. It also prevents from a market entry of new competitors.

In term of *customer satisfaction and welfare* as a performance indicator which is seen a strong positive effect from membership in complementary codeshare alliance. A complementary collaboration improves the quality connecting services, thus it will decrease fares and makes customers better off. In contrast, it can be noted that in concentrated markets with less competition and dominated by alliances, customer satisfaction decreases.

Second, this study found a link between institutional antecedents, alliances and performance outcomes. Institutional elements such as market liberalization, bilateral agreements, and antitrust immunity are likely to have positive effect on airline performance. For example, airlines' market liberalization brings a rivalry that leads to a traffic growth and consequent decreases fares and con-

sumer surplus. In addition, based on an antitrust immunity, partners in alliance can coordinate pricing and scheduling activities, thus resulting in lower fares and better quality products.

Third, a revenue share management in alliance is found to have significant impact on airline performance. The literature has pointed in the fact that each revenue management decisions may result in suboptimal revenues for the entire alliance. Therefore, it has been suggested the use of proration taxes as revenue rules.

Fourth, this study found that the size of an alliance also has effect on the airline performance. In term of financial performance, the large alliance size is likely to result in economies of scale and cost reductions. In term of operational performance's multilateral partnerships set up by large carriers sharing a common organizational structure are likely to increase their performance.

Fifth, it has been highlighted the link between a governance structure, and duration and termination of airline alliances. Factors such as internal alliances changes (e.g. alliance members; strategy, and key managers' position change) are likely to affect the alliance and its structure. On one side, code-sharing, marketing and frequent flyer programs, pooling and joint purchasing, and block-space face a lower risk of termination. On other side, equity alliances that are characterized with a complexity are likely to face the highest risk of termination.

Sixth, this study found a link between consumers' perceptions, alliance and performance. It is crucial to mention that the literature has noted different perceptions of consumers in different regions. Therefore, it is important to implement a proper marketing communication strategy, in order to ensure a profitability of allied airlines. Furthermore, consumers' perceptions related to service failure of alliances have been studied through a prism of high and low identification groups. Results have shown that both groups do not want to associate with a particular alliance in the future. Moreover, an airline decision to enter strong brand's network has a substantial positive influence on the consumers' perceptions, while exit from the alliance has a negative effect on their perceptions.

This study offers some implications for managers and policy-makers. Firstly, from the managerial point of view, the question of a precise partner's choice is crucial for alliances' duration and survival. In the globalised world, an airline joins an alliance or forms new one, is likely to face with problems such as cultural differences and trust issues. It may be vital for a carrier to engage in a partnership, with only those partners that follow similar philosophies not only toward its business, but to its customers as well. Secondly, with scarce resources, firms must expand their networks in their search for resources, skills and capabilities. By joining larger networks, managers could internalize external resources in order gain a competitive edge.

Thirdly, developing and emerging countries are excellent opportunities for Western airlines that need to focus on building robust links with emerging markets airlines. Moreover, through establishing of new or joining existing alliances both parties (e.g. Western and emerging carriers) will expand their networks and build a robust presence and relationships. They need to start gaining a share in such markets, characterized with a rapidly increasing middle-class and a purchasing power, and explore opportunities that these markets offer.

From the policy perspective, the key issue is to monitor a fair competition between carriers and alliances. Regulation bodies must ensure that consumers will not be hurt by collusive agreements, and to implement measures to secure their welfare. In addition, institutions should make more steps to remove existing bilateral agreements, and thus to contribute to 'market openness', which most likely will allow new players to enter markets and enhance the competition. Again, it will result on the increased customers' welfare.

The main limitation of this review is the fact that it revealed trends and makes conclusions mostly over the studies based on either North America or Europe. Although, those two regions look representative, the small number of studies that examined Asia and Africa, and the lack of research on other regions such as Latin America causes concerns. Future research should make attempts to reveal factors that influence an alliance formation and performance outcomes from such move among carriers in South America, Australia, Asia, Africa and other regions that are not presenting in this review.

Another drawback of this work can be found in the fact that code-share alliances are over-represented in our sample papers. Therefore, our conclusions to a large degree are based on this particular alliance type. Future research should be directed to explore in-depth other types of cooperation and their influence over the firm's performance. Although this systematic review revealed number of drivers that influence alliance formation decisions, other studies might be dedicated to find addition motives. A larger scale of studies could employ more extensive set of keywords, and thus to result in more antecedents of alliance formation.

# REFERENCES

Adler, N., & Smilowitz, K. (2007). Hub-and-Spoke Network Alliances and Mergers: Price-Location Competition in the Airline Industry. *Transportation Research: Part B: Methodological, 41*(4), 394-409. Retrieved from http://www.elsevier.com/wps/find/journaldescription.cws_home/548/description#description

Amankwah-Amoah, J., & Debrah, Y. A. (2011). The evolution of alliances in the global airline industry: A review of the African experience. *Thunderbird International Business Review, 53*(1), 37–50. doi:10.1002/tie.20388

Assaf, A. G., & Josiassen, A. (2012). European vs. U.S. airlines: Performance comparison in a dynamic market. *Tourism Management, 33*(2), 317–326. doi:10.1016/j.tourman.2011.03.012

Barla, P., & Constantatos, C. (2006). On the Choice between Strategic Alliance and Merger in the Airline Sector: The Role of Strategic Effects. *Journal of Transport Economics and Policy, 40*(3), 409–424.

Barros, C. P., & Peypoch, N. (2009). An evaluation of European airlines' operational performance. *International Journal of Production Economics, 122*(2), 525–533. doi:10.1016/j.ijpe.2009.04.016

Baum, J. A. C., Calabrese, T., & Silverman, B. S. (2000). Don't go it alone: Alliance network composition and startups' performance in Canadian biotechnology. *Strategic Management Journal, 21*(3), 267–294. doi:10.1002/(SICI)1097-0266(200003)21:3<267::AID-SMJ89>3.0.CO;2-8

Bilotkach, V. (2005). Price competition between international airline alliances. *Journal of Transport Economics and Policy, 39*(2), 167–189.

Bilotkach, V. (2007a). Airline Partnerships and Schedule Coordination. *Journal of Transport Economics and Policy, 41*(3), 413.

Bilotkach, V. (2007b). Price effects of airline consolidation: Evidence from a sample of transatlantic markets. *Empirical Economics, 33*(3), 427–448. doi:10.1007/s00181-006-0108-z

Bruch, H., & Sattelberger, T. (2001). Lufthansa's transformation marathon: Process of liberating and focusing change energy. *Human Resource Management, 40*(3), 249–259. doi:10.1002/hrm.1015

Brueckner, J. (2001). The economics of international codesharing: An analysis of airline alliances. *International Journal of Industrial Organization, 19*(10), 1475–1498. doi:10.1016/S0167-7187(00)00068-0

Brueckner, J., & Whalen, T. (2000). The Price Effects of International Airline Alliances. *The Journal of Law & Economics, 43*(2), 503–546. doi:10.1086/467464

Cairns, R. D., & Galbraith, J. W. (1990). Artificial Compatibility, Barriers to Entry, and Frequent-Flyer Programs. *The Canadian Journal of Economics. Revue Canadienne d'Economique, 23*(4), 807–816. doi:10.2307/135563

Cappel, S. D., Pearson, T. R., & Romero, E. J. (2003). Strategic group performance in the commercial airline industry. *Journal of Management Research, 3*(2), 53–60.

Carrig, K. (1997). Reshaping Human Resources for the Next Century: Lessons from a High Flying Airline. *Human Resource Management, 36*(2), 277–289. doi:10.1002/(SICI)1099-050X(199722)36:2<277::AID-HRM8>3.0.CO;2-U

Casanueva, C., Gallego, Á., & Sancho, M. (2013). Network resources and social capital in airline alliance portfolios. *Tourism Management, 36*, 441–453. doi:10.1016/j.tourman.2012.09.014

Chen, F., & Chen, C. (2003). The effects of strategic alliances and risk pooling on the load factors of international airline operations. *Transportation Research Part E, Logistics and Transportation Review, 39*(1), 19–34. doi:10.1016/S1366-5545(02)00025-X

Chen, Z., & Ross, T. (2003). Cooperating upstream while competing downstream: A theory of input joint ventures. *International Journal of Industrial Organization, 21*(3), 381–397. doi:10.1016/S0167-7187(02)00058-9

Chua, C. L., Kew, H., & Yong, J. (2005). Airline Code-Share Alliances and Costs: Imposing Concavity on Translog Cost Function Estimation. *Review of Industrial Organization, 26*(4), 461-487. doi: http://www.springerlink.com/link.asp?id=100336

Czerny, A. I. (2009). Code-Sharing, Price Discrimination and Welfare Losses. [doi: http://www.bath.ac.uk/e-journals/jtep/]. *Journal of Transport Economics and Policy, 43*(2), 193–212.

Das, T. K., & Teng, B.-S. (2000). A Resource-Based Theory of Strategic Alliances. *Journal of Management, 26*(1), 31–61. doi:10.1177/014920630002600105

Das, T. K., & Teng, B.-S. (2002). Alliance Constellations: A Social Exchange Perspective. *Academy of Management Review, 27*(3), 445–456. doi:10.2307/4134389

Dussauge, P., & Garrette, B. (1995). Determinants of Success in International Strategic Alliances: Evidence from the Global Aerospace Industry. *Journal of International Business Studies, 26*(3), 505–530. doi:10.1057/palgrave.jibs.8490848

Eisenhardt, K. M., & Graebner, M. E. (2007). Theory Building from Cases: Opportunities and challenges. *Academy of Management Journal, 50*(1), 25–32. doi:10.5465/AMJ.2007.24160888

Evans, N. (2001). Collaborative strategy: An analysis of the changing world of international airline alliances. *Tourism Management, 22*(3), 229–243. doi:10.1016/S0261-5177(01)00024-3

Fan, T. P. C. (2009). Determinants of de novo new entrant survival in the liberalized intra-European scheduled passenger airline industry. *Transportation Research Part E, Logistics and Transportation Review, 45*(2), 293–306. doi:10.1016/j.tre.2008.09.009

Flores-Fillol, R. (2010). Congested Hubs. *Transportation Research: Part B: Methodological, 44*(3), 358-370. doi: http://www.elsevier.com/wps/find/journaldescription.cws_home/548/description#description

Gayle, P. G. (2008). An empirical analysis of the competitive effects of the Delta/Continental/Northwest code-share alliance. *The Journal of Law & Economics, 51*(4), 743–775. doi:10.1086/595865

Gillen, D., Harris, R., & Oum, T. (2002). Measuring the economic effects of bilateral liberalization air transport. *Transportation Research Part E, Logistics and Transportation Review, 38*(3–4), 155–174. doi:10.1016/S1366-5545(02)00003-0

Gimeno, J. (2004). Competition within and between Networks: The Contingent Effect of Competitive Embeddedness on Alliance Formation. *Academy of Management Journal, 47*(6), 820–842. doi:10.2307/20159625

Ginsberg, A., & Venkatraman, N. (1985). Contingency Perspectives of Organizational Strategy: A Critical Review of the Empirical Research. *Academy of Management Review, 10*(3), 421–434. doi:10.2307/258125

Gudmundsson, S. V., & Rhoades, D. L. (2001). Airline alliance survival analysis: Typology, strategy and duration. *Transport Policy, 8*(3), 209–218. doi:10.1016/S0967-070X(01)00016-6

Hamill, J. (1993). Competitive strategies in the world airline industry. *European Management Journal, 11*(3), 332–341. doi:10.1016/0263-2373(93)90059-Q

Hassin, O., & Shy, O. (2004). Code-sharing agreements and interconnections in markets for international flights. *Review of International Economics, 12*(3), 337–352. doi:10.1111/j.1467-9396.2004.00453.x

Hu, X., Caldentey, R., & Vulcano, G. (2013). Revenue sharing in airline alliances. *Management Science, 59*(5), 1177–1195. doi:10.1287/mnsc.1120.1591

Inkpen, A. C. (1995). *The Management of International Joint Ventures: An Organizational Learning Perspective.* London: Routledge.

Jones, M. T. (2002). Globalization and organizational restructuring: A strategic perspective. *Thunderbird International Business Review, 44*(3), 325–351. doi:10.1002/tie.10024

Kimms, A., & Cetiner, D. (2012). Approximate nucleolus-based revenue sharing in airline alliances. *European Journal of Operational Research, 220*(2), 510–521. doi:10.1016/j.ejor.2012.01.057

Kogut, B. (1989). The Stability of Joint Ventures: Reciprocity and Competitive Rivalry. *The Journal of Industrial Economics, 38*(2), 183–198. doi:10.2307/2098529

Ku, E. C. S., & Fan, Y. W. (2009). Knowledge sharing and customer relationship management in the travel service alliances. *Total Quality Management & Business Excellence, 20*(12), 1407–1421. doi:10.1080/14783360903248880

Lavie, D. (2008). Network Resources: Toward a New Social Network Perspective. *Academy of Management Review, 33*(2), 546–550. doi:10.5465/AMR.2008.31193585

Lazzarini, S. (2007). The impact of membership in competing alliance constellations: Evidence on the operational performance of global airlines. *Strategic Management Journal, 28*(4), 345–368. doi:10.1002/smj.587

Li, Z.-C., Lam, W. H. K., Wong, S. C., & Fu, X. (2010). Optimal route allocation in a liberalizing airline market. *Transportation Research Part B: Methodological, 44*(7), 886–902. doi:10.1016/j.trb.2009.12.013

Lin, M. H. (2008). Airline alliances and entry deterrence. *Transportation Research Part E, Logistics and Transportation Review, 44*(4), 637–652. doi:10.1016/j.tre.2007.05.003

Luo, Y. (2007). A coopetition perspective of global competition. *Journal of World Business, 42*(2), 129–144. doi:10.1016/j.jwb.2006.08.007

Mak, B., & Go, F. (1995). Matching global competition: Cooperation among Asian airlines. *Tourism Management, 16*(1), 61–65. doi:10.1016/0261-5177(94)00008-X

Man, A.-P., Roijakkers, N., & Graauw, H. (2010). Managing dynamics through robust alliance governance structures: The case of KLM and Northwest Airlines. *European Management Journal, 28*(3), 171–181. doi:10.1016/j.emj.2009.11.001

Marín, P. L. (1998). Productivity differences in the airline industry: Partial deregulation versus short run protection. *International Journal of Industrial Organization, 16*(4), 395–414. doi:10.1016/S0167-7187(96)01058-2

McEvily, B., & Zaheer, A. (1999). Bridging ties: A source of firm heterogeneity in competitive capabilities. *Strategic Management Journal, 20*(12), 1133–1156. doi:10.1002/(SICI)1097-0266(199912)20:12<1133::AID-SMJ74>3.0.CO;2-7

Min, J., & Mitsuhashi, H. (2012). Dynamics of Unclosed Triangles in Alliance Networks: Disappearance of Brokerage Positions and Performance Consequences. *Journal of Management Studies, 49*(6), 1078–1108. doi:10.1111/j.1467-6486.2011.01035.x

Morris, H., Harvey, C., & Kelly, A. (2009). Journal rankings and the ABS journal quality guide. *Management Decision, 47*(9), 1441–1451. doi:10.1108/00251740910995648

Nero, G. (1996). A structural model of intra European Union duopoly airline competition. *Journal of Transport Economics and Policy, 30*(2), 137.

Netessine, S., & Shumsky, R. A. (2005). Revenue management games: Horizontal and vertical competition. *Management Science, 51*(5), 813–831. doi:10.1287/mnsc.1040.0356

Olaisen, J., & Revang, Ø. (1991). Information management as the main component in the strategy for the 1990s in Scandinavian airline system (SAS). *International Journal of Information Management, 11*(3), 185–202. doi:10.1016/0268-4012(91)90032-8

Oum, T., & Park, J.-H. (1997). Airline alliances: Current status, policy issues, and future directions. *Journal of Air Transport Management, 3*(3), 133–144. doi:10.1016/S0969-6997(97)00021-5

Oum, T., Park, J.-H., Kim, K., & Yu, C. (2004). The effect of horizontal alliances on firm productivity and profitability: Evidence from the global airline industry. *Journal of Business Research, 57*(8), 844–853. doi:10.1016/S0148-2963(02)00484-8

Oum, T., Park, J.-H., & Zhang, A. (1996). The effects of airline code sharing agreements on firm conduct and international air fares. *Journal of Transport Economics and Policy, 30*, 187–202.

Park, J. (1997). The effects of airline alliances on markets and economic welfare. *Transportation Research Part E, Logistics and Transportation Review, 33*(3), 181–195. doi:10.1016/S1366-5545(97)00013-6

Park, J., Park, N., & Zhang, A. (2003). The impact of international alliances on rival firm value: A study of the British Airways/USAir Alliance. *Transportation Research Part E, Logistics and Transportation Review, 39*(1), 1–18. doi:10.1016/S1366-5545(02)00023-6

Park, J., & Zhang, A. (2000). An Empirical Analysis of Global Airline Alliances: Cases in North Atlantic Markets. *Review of Industrial Organization, 16*(4), 367–384. doi:10.1023/A:1007888821999

Park, J., Zhang, A., & Zhang, Y. (2001). Analytical models of international alliances in the airline industry. *Transportation Research Part B: Methodological, 35*(9), 865–886. doi:10.1016/S0191-2615(00)00027-8

Park, S., & Russo, M. (1996). When Competition Eclipses Cooperation: An Event History Analysis of Joint Venture Failure. *Management Science, 42*(6), 875–890. doi:10.1287/mnsc.42.6.875

Parkhe, A. (1993). Strategic Alliance Structuring: A Game Theoretic and Transaction Cost Examination of Interfirm Cooperation. *Academy of Management Journal, 36*(4), 794–829. doi:10.2307/256759

Podsakoff, P. M., MacKenzie, S. B., Bachrach, D. G., & Podsakoff, N. P. (2005). The influence of management journals in the 1980s and 1990s. *Strategic Management Journal, 26*(5), 473–488. doi:10.1002/smj.454

Reggiani, A., Nijkamp, P., & Cento, A. (2010). Connectivity and concentration in airline networks: A complexity analysis of Lufthansa's network. *European Journal of Information Systems, 19*(4), 449–461. doi:10.1057/ejis.2010.11

Rowley, T., Behrens, D., & Krackhardt, D. (2000). Redundant governance structures: An analysis of structural and relational embeddedness in the steel and semiconductor industries. *Strategic Management Journal, 21*(3), 369–386. doi:10.1002/(SICI)1097-0266(200003)21:3<369::AID-SMJ93>3.0.CO;2-M

Sadi, M. A., & Henderson, J. C. (2000). The Asian economic crisis and the aviation industry: Impacts and response strategies. *Transport Reviews, 20*(3), 347–367. doi:10.1080/014416400412841

Squalli, J. (2013). Airline Passenger Traffic Openness and the Performance of Emirates Airline. *The Quarterly Review of Economics and Finance*, (0). doi:10.1016/j.qref.2013.07.010

Steven, A. B., Dong, Y., & Dresner, M. (2012). Linkages between customer service, customer satisfaction and performance in the airline industry: Investigation of non-linearities and moderating effects. *Transportation Research Part E, Logistics and Transportation Review*, *48*(4), 743–754. doi:10.1016/j.tre.2011.12.006

Tranfield, D., Denyer, D., & Smart, P. (2003). Towards a Methodology for Developing Evidence-Informed Management Knowledge by Means of Systematic Review. *British Journal of Management*, *14*(3), 207–222. doi:10.1111/1467-8551.00375

Tretheway, M. (1990). Globalization of the Airline Industry and Implications for Canada. *Logistics and Transportation Review*, *26*(4), 357.

Tretheway, M., & Oum, T. (1992). *Airline Economics: Foundations for Strategy and Policy*. Vancouver: University of British Columbia.

Wagner, C. M., Huber, B., Sweeney, E., & Smyth, A. (2005). B2B e-marketplaces in the airline industry: Process drivers and performance indicators. *International Journal of Logistics: Research & Applications*, *8*(4), 283–297. doi:10.1080/13675560500407390

Wang, Z. H., Evans, M., & Turner, L. (2004). Effects of strategic airline alliances on air transport market competition: An empirical analysis. *Tourism Economics*, *10*(1), 23–44. doi:10.5367/000000004773166501

Wassmer, U., Dussauge, P., & Planellas, M. (2010). How to Manage Alliances Better Than One at a Time. *MIT Sloan Management Review*, *51*(3), 77–84.

Weber, K. (2005). Travelers' Perceptions of Airline Alliance Benefits and Performance. *Journal of Travel Research*, *43*(3), 257–265. doi:10.1177/0047287504272029

Weber, K., & Sparks, B. (2009). The effect of preconsumption mood and service recovery measures on customer evaluations and behavior in a strategic alliance setting. *Journal of Hospitality & Tourism Research (Washington, D.C.)*, *33*(1), 106–125. doi:10.1177/1096348008329863

Weber, K., & Sparks, B. A. (2006). Social Identity's Impact on Service Recovery Evaluations in Alliances. *Annals of Tourism Research*, *33*(3), 859–863. doi:10.1016/j.annals.2006.03.003

Wen, Y.-H., & Hsu, C.-I. (2006). Interactive multiobjective programming in airline network design for international airline code-share alliance. *European Journal of Operational Research*, *174*(1), 404–426. doi:10.1016/j.ejor.2005.02.040

Woisetschläger, D. M., Michaelis, M., & Backhaus, C. (2007). The "Dark Side" of Brand Alliances: How the Exit of Alliance Members Affects Consumer Perceptions. *Advances in Consumer Research. Association for Consumer Research (U. S.)*, *35*, 483.

Wright, C. P., Groenevelt, H., & Shumsky, R. A. (2010). Dynamic revenue management in airline alliances. *Transportation Science*, *44*(1), 15–37. doi:10.1287/trsc.1090.0300

Yan, S., & Chen, C.-. (2008). Optimal flight scheduling models for cargo airlines under alliances. *Journal of Scheduling*, *11*(3), 175–186. doi:10.1007/s10951-007-0020-1

Yang, J.-Y., & Liu, A. (2003). Frequent Flyer Program: A case study of China airline's marketing initiative—Dynasty Flyer Program. *Tourism Management*, *24*(5), 587–595. doi:10.1016/S0261-5177(03)00007-4

Yin, R. (2003). *Case Study Research: Design and Methods*. SAGE Publications.

Yin, X., Wu, J., & Tsai, W. (2012). When Unconnected Others Connect: Does Degree of Brokerage Persist After the Formation of a Multipartner Alliance? *Organization Science, 23*(6), 1682–1699. doi:10.1287/orsc.1110.0711

Youssef, W., & Hansen, M. (1994). Consequences of strategic alliances between international airlines: The case of Swissair and SAS. *Transportation Research Part A, Policy and Practice, 28*(5), 415–431. doi:10.1016/0965-8564(94)90024-8

Zhang, A., & Zhang, Y. (2006). Rivalry between strategic alliances. *International Journal of Industrial Organization, 24*(2), 287–301. doi:10.1016/j.ijindorg.2005.04.005

## KEY TERMS AND DEFINITIONS

**Airline Industry:** The air transportation business carries passengers and consignment using air means of transportation (e.g. airplanes and helicopters).

**Airline Performance:** Assessment of financial measures (e.g. profit, ROI, revenues etc) and operational performance (e.g. productivity, passengers' satisfaction level etc).

**Alliance Motives:** Drivers of alliances as antecedents of the process of strategic partnership involvement (e.g. economies of scale effect, access to resource, development of global networks etc).

**Complementary Code-Sharing:** A case where two or more carriers link up their networks and setting up a new complimentary network.

**Interline Mixed Virtual Code-Share:** An agreement which permits a passenger travels on interline connecting itinerary, but the sole ticketing airline for the whole trip is not an operating airline.

**Single-Carrier Virtual Code-Sharing:** An agreement that allows a passenger stays on a single carrier plane for the whole round-trip but her / she ticket was marketed and sold by a partner.

**Strategic Alliance:** An inter-firm cooperative arrangement, involving cross-border flows and linkages for the use of common resources.

## APPENDIX

## Databases Searching Protocols

### Protocol for Searching in EBSCO

EBSCO database' search protocol offers the justified search process, and follows next steps. This protocol provides the choice decision and the rationale behind.

Step1. For [search option] area:

- In case it is necessary the truncation (*) is used following the key word string list as shown in Appendix 3.1;
- Keyword strings are connected with Boolean operators [AND];
- In [select a field (optional)] it was chosen [Abstract] for all strings.

Step3. For [limit your results] area:

- In [document type] choose [Article];
- In [publication type] choose [Academic journal];
- In [limit your results] choose [Scholarly (Peer Reviewed) Journals];
- All other options left unchecked;
- EBSCO automatically removed all duplicated files.

### Protocol for Searching in Science Direct.

Searching protocol for Science Direct database consists of several steps. This protocol provides the choice decision and the rationale behind.

Step1. For [search] area:

- Where it is necessary the truncation (*) is used following the key word string list as shown in Appendix 3.1;
- Boolean operators [AND] were used to connect key words strings;
- Select [Journals] and choose [Abstract, Title, Keywords] for all strings;
- Leave other options unchecked.

### Protocol for Searching in Proquest

Searching protocol for ProQuest database consists of several steps. This protocol provides the choice decision and the rationale behind.

Step1. For [Advanced search] area:

- Where it is necessary the truncation (*) is used following the key word string list as shown in Appendix3.1;

- Boolean operators [AND] were used to connect key words strings;
- Select [Abstract] for all streams;
- In [Source type] choose [Scholarly Journals];
- Leave other options unchecked.

Step2. For [limit your results] area:

- In [document type] choose [Article];
- In [publication type] choose [Academic journal];
- In [limit your results] choose [Scholarly (Peer Reviewed) Journals];
- All other options left unchecked;
- EBSCO automatically removed all duplicated files.

## Protocol for Searching in Science Direct.

Searching protocol for Science Direct database consists of several steps. This protocol provides the choice decision and the rationale behind.

Step1. For [search] area:

- Where it is necessary the truncation (*) is used following the key word string list as shown in Appendix 3.1;
- Boolean operators [AND] were used to connect key words strings;
- Select [Journals] and choose [Abstract, Title, Keywords] for all strings;
- Leave other options unchecked.

## Protocol for Searching in Proquest

Searching protocol for ProQuest database consists of several steps. This protocol provides the choice decision and the rationale behind.

Step1. For [Advanced search] area:

- Where it is necessary the truncation (*) is used following the key word string list as shown in Appendix3.1;
- Boolean operators [AND] were used to connect key words strings;
- Select [Abstract] for all streams;
- In [Source type] choose [Scholarly Journals];
- Leave other options unchecked.

Chapter 19

# An Analysis of Hospitality and Tourism Research:
## Learning Organization's (LO) Influence on Sustainability Practices

**Jennifer Calhoun**
*Auburn University, USA*

**Alecia Douglas**
*Auburn University, USA*

## ABSTRACT

*Learning organizations (LOs) have been identified as an innovative practice essential for global businesses to not only effectively compete in today's dynamic environment but also to achieve and maintain a sustainable competitive advantage and increase overall firm performance. The objective of this chapter is to examine the current body of knowledge on LOs and their impact on sustainability practices in an effort to identify what is being done by organizations, where knowledge is applied, and, how systems are created to influence sustainability practices. In the context of hospitality and tourism businesses, the literature examining LOs is limited though a wealth of studies have been conducted in the mainstream. Using a qualitative approach, a content analysis was conducted to investigate its impact on sustainability practices in hospitality and tourism organizations. The results indicate that destinations in particular have adopted this approach to compete globally and to address triple-bottom line sustainability.*

## INTRODUCTION

Increased competition and globalization of the hospitality and tourism industries have forced operators to become more efficient through the practice of environmental sustainability in their organizations (Dunlap, Gallup, & Gallup, 1993;

Smith 2003; & Salzmann, O., Ionescu-Somers, A., & Steger, U. 2005). Sustainability is viewed as transitional and a continuous learning process (Farrell & Twining-Ward, 2005), as well as treated as a dynamic goal (Lee, 2001). Organizational leaders have viewed learning as a key element in developing and maintaining a competitive

DOI: 10.4018/978-1-4666-8606-9.ch019

advantage (Armstrong & Foley, 2003) but more importantly, achieving a sustainable competitive advantage. This view shared by Nevis, DiBella and Gould (1995) and Jashapara (2003) is considered vital for organizations to thrive in the global business arena and is dependent upon their capacity to learn and react to emergent forces driving change. Given the dynamic nature of today's hospitality and tourism industry where mergers, acquisitions, and competition for market share are top strategic priorities, practitioners are seeking new knowledge to enable them to be more competitive.

One innovative approach that could be used to achieve a sustainable competitive advantage is that of a Learning Organization (LO), a concept proposed by Peter Senge in 1990 where organizations learn quickly from, and adapt to, changes taking place in their internal and external micro- and macro-environments. What emerges is a hospitality company or tourism destination with new skills and capabilities to compete in a constantly changing business environment. Such an organization would be driven by individuals who would also embrace the concept of continuous learning and it would foster or enhance the ability for its employees to adapt as a necessary ingredient for organizational success. With these new skills and capabilities the hospitality company or tourism destination is able to compete in the new business environment. In this environment, the organization is able to create its own future by using various techniques, systems, and approaches to achieve sustainable results.

The objective of this chapter is to examine the current body of knowledge on learning organizations and their impact on sustainability practices in an effort to identify what is being done by organizations, where knowledge is applied, and, how systems are created to influence sustainability practices. To achieve this objective, a content analysis of prior literature based on LO was conducted to investigate its impact on sustainability practices. While not a new approach, content analysis has been used liberally by researchers

such as Jogaratnam, McCleary, Mena, and Yoo (2005), Rivera and Upchurch (2008), Law, Leung, and Cheung (2012) among others to analyze prior hospitality and tourism research in an effort to enhance the current body of knowledge and inform readers about general issues and emerging trends in hospitality and tourism. On the basis of the evaluation of prior studies, several important factors were identified. These factors that will be discussed are definitions and dimensions of LO, theoretical approaches to LO, LO and the tourism and hospitality industry, LO and sustainable competitive advantage, and LO and innovation.

## BACKGROUND

### Definitions and Dimensions of Learning Organizations

There are many definitions of LOs. However, the most frequently used definition is that of Senge's (1990, p. 3) who defines the term as "organizations where people continually expand their capacity to create the results they truly desire, where new and expansive patterns of thinking are nurtured, where collective aspiration is set free, and where people are continually learning how to learn together." This definition highlights a systems approach to LOs that incorporates five disciplines (Yang, Watkins, & Marsick, 2004, pp 6) namely:

1.  Team learning - emphasizes the learning activities of the group rather than on the development of team process;
2.  Shared visions - ability to unearth shared "pictures of the future" that foster genuine commitment and enrollment rather than compliance;
3.  Mental models - deeply held internal images of how the world works;
4.  Personal mastery - continually clarifying and deepening personal vision, focusing

energies, developing patience, and seeing reality objectively;

5.   System thinking - ability to see interrelationships rather than linear cause-effect chains.

Flood (1999) and Senge, Kleiner, Roberts, Ross, Roth, and Smith (1999), expanded this definition to include "their capacity to create their own future." Garvin's (1993, p. 80) definition took a more strategic approach by suggesting that LO should be defined in terms of "creating, acquiring, and transferring knowledge, while modifying its behavior to reflect new knowledge and insights." Pedler, Burgoyne, and Boydell (1991), suggested a definition that incorporates eleven elements by which LOs facilitates learning of all its members and continuously transforms itself to achieve organizational goals. At the heart of their philosophy is the belief that all employees possess an untapped potential that, if effectively developed and harnessed, results in a high performing organization. Second to performance is the promotion of a learning culture within the organization that is supported by the employees, or community of learners, empowered to work cohesively toward achieving organizational goals and objectives. In this instance, core values identified in LOs include valuing differences among what is currently known and how learning occurs in the community while developing leadership and creative thinking throughout the organization (Shabbir, 2009).

Several other researchers have also emphasized that a definition of LO should highlight the power of intentional learning, a practice that would systemically transform the organization's future direction (Calvert, Mobley, & Marshall, 1994; Campbell & Cairns, 1994; Coopey, 1995; Daft & Marcic, 1998; Jashapara, 1993; McGill, Slocum, & Lei, 1993; Loermans, 2002; and Sankar, 2003). Though not discounting the later interpretations of the term, it is Senge's (1990a, p. 3) original definition that still articulates the best stating that "LOs allows people to continually expand their

capacity to create results, examine new patterns of thinking and where collective aspiration is set free, and people are continually learning how to learn together."

Some researchers have argued that from a practical perspective it has been very difficult to identify and recognize when an organization has become a LO. This is perhaps due to the intricate process that is involved. As Pedler (1995) aptly puts it, a learning company is more of a journey than a destination with very few solid examples or cases about how an organization actually acquires this status; majorly, it is a "way of life" that is organically developed from within to fit the unique mix of peoples and business processes. Garvin, Edmondson and Gino (2008) contends that the difficulty lies deeper with managers who do not understand the precise steps for creating a LO and are not equipped with the necessary assessment tools to determine whether or not learning has been achieved and if so, how. Therefore, what becomes integral to the success of any LO (Aksu & Özdemir, 2005) is its ability to: (1) change the current applications and the views of organizational members, (2) embrace changes in order to improve and innovate, (3) ensure or facilitate the ease with which learning of all members is achieved, (4) direct the future of the organization, and (5) encourage the input of all members. Therefore it is important to examine the theoretical approaches in an effort to make LO more explicit.

However, before delving into the theoretical foundations of the learning organization, it is important to first differentiate the concept from that of organizational learning as both terminologies have been used interchangeably though differences are evident from the literature. The most basic differentiator between the two is that organizational learning is used to refer to the process of learning while LO refers to a type of organization rather than a process (Yeo, 2003). Fiol & Lyles (1985) clarifies this difference by suggesting that organizational learning answers the question of "how" learning is developed within an organization. The process of organizational learning includes but is not limited to individual development and organizational adaptation and is seen as a core competence of the LO (Edmondson & Moingeon, 1998). Yang et al. (2004) further distinguishes between the two terminologies by suggesting that LOs either display or work to instill continuous learning and adaptive characteristics whereas organizational learning is the acquisition of knowledge and the development of skills resulting from the learning experiences of the whole. Members thus acquire knowledge from data-driven observations which are then used to alter behavior in order to promote adaptation of the organization as it responds to external changes (Edmondson & Moingeon, 1998).

## Theoretical Approaches to Learning Organization

Given the complexity of the discussion surrounding LOs there are various approaches in literature used to describe a LO, but the most common recurring theme is that the LO has the capacity to learn, and this ability is used to achieve a sustained competitive advantage. An understanding of the various approaches to LOs will allow scholars and practitioners to identify the attributes and qualities of a LO, the paradoxical views used to describe LOs, the systems, policies, and processes used within LOs, and the measurement and assessment tools used within LOs.

Ronald (1996), suggest a theory of the learning organization which posits that if individuals learn specific skills on a continuous basis, then their performance and ultimately their organization will be favorably impacted; although some might argue that the occurrence of two independent events does not necessarily prove a causal relationship. He further argues that in the LO, when individuals learn and apply their knowledge, skills and expertise to situations then organizational performance is enhanced. Managers within the LO must therefore play a leadership role where he/she assumes the

role of a planner, instructor, and overseer thereby enabling them to gain consensus, build a shared vision, and challenge the status quo so that their employees are continually expanding their capabilities to the benefit of the organization. Senge (1990) suggest a systems theory approach to LO which is the ability to comprehend and address the whole by examining the interrelationship between the parts. His approach suggests five main activities of LO namely: (1) systematic problem solving, (2) experimentation with new ideas and solutions, (3) learning from experience and history, (4) learning from the best practices of others, and (5) transferring knowledge efficiently and quickly throughout the organization.

In several papers by Ortenblad (2002, 2004), the researcher uses a typology that incorporates four distinct perspectives about LOs. These include: (1) *"organizational learning"* which is focused on knowledge retention (2) *"learning at work"* where employees learn in the workplace, (3) *"learning climate"* where the organization fosters an environment for individuals to learn, and (4) *"learning structure"* where the organization is perceived as a flexible entity with a less hierarchical structures that facilitates information exchange. Organizations that implement all four aspects were referred to as a LO, while those that implemented only one aspect were called a partial LO. These four perspectives were used by both scholars and practitioners to describe LOs, and as such, may provide consensus.

In an earlier study, Watkins and Marsick (1993) proposed an integrative theoretical framework for a LO that includes seven dimensions, four on an individual level and three on a structural level. The four dimensions at the individual level seek to: (1) create continuous learning opportunities, (2) promote inquiry and dialogue, (3) encourage collaboration and team learning, and (4) empower people toward a collective vision. The three dimensions on the structural level are designed to: (1) connect the organization to its environment, (2) establish systems to capture and share learning, and (3) provide strategic leadership for learning. In this research, prior literature and case studies were examined and a diagnostic tool developed. This tool was used to measure changes in organizational learning practices, culture and performance. The seven dimensions were also tested in a structural equation model by Yang et. al (2004) as antecedents to organizational knowledge and organizational financial performance. In another study, Altman and Iles (1998) suggest that there are four theoretical streams of influence that shaped the concept of LO. The first is strategic management (Barnes, 1991), the second, systems theory, the third, psychological learning theory (Swieringa & Wierdsma, 1992), and the fourth, the study of organizational context.

From a marketing perspective, Slater and Narver (1995) identified five critical components anchored by two key elements: culture and climate. The culture of a LO is expressed in the terms of entrepreneurship and market orientation while the LO's climate is based on organic structure, facilitative leadership, and decentralized strategic planning. These five components are directly influenced by the challenging external business environment and impact strategic organizational goals in the areas of customer satisfaction, new product success, sales growth, and profitability. In their more recent study, Garvin et. al (2008) proposed a framework for a LO consisting of three distinctive building blocks: (1) *"a supportive learning environment"* where employees would feel free to disagree with others, recognize the value of opposing ideas, take risks and explore the unknown, (2) *"concrete learning processes"* were formal procedures have been established to generate, collect, interpret and disseminate information; experiment with new offerings, gather intelligence on competitors, customers and technological trends, identify and solve problems and develop employees' skills and, lastly, (3) *"leadership that reinforces learning"* where the organization's leaders demonstrate willingness to entertain alternative viewpoints, engage in ac-

tive questioning and listening and devote time to problem identification, knowledge transfer and reflection.

The discussion on the LO's theoretical foundation has unearthed some of the core traits or characteristics of these organizations. Among these traits are "cultural values, leadership commitment and empowerment, communication, knowledge transfer, employee characteristics and performance upgrading" (Sudharatna & Li, 2004; pp 164). Focusing on the impact of these organizations on the workforce, Confessore (1997) recognize three core characteristics of LOs as one where: (1) individuals have opportunities to exploit their work environment to increase their individual knowledge bases, (2) the creation of new knowledge is encouraged through collaboration and sharing of knowledge amongst individual members, and (3) mechanisms are in place to integrate and encourage the practice of these behaviors on a daily basis. Confessore's (1997) perspective also supports that of Shabbir (2009) who states that employees in a learning organization are "fully awakened" individuals willing to take risks in order to learn and understand how to solve enduring problems instead of chasing a quick fix.

Pedler et. al (1991) on the other hand take a more strategic approach to identifying the characteristics of a LO such as: taking a learning approach to strategy, incorporating participative policy-making among the workforce, enabling "flexible" structures across departments, appointing boundary workers as environmental scanners, and co-learning or inter-company learning with customers and suppliers. Shabbir (2009) also sees the LO as one that is a "no hostile, empowering culture" where the continued development of the organization's competences are shared amongst all three levels of the organization: leadership, management and the workforce. Regardless of the different perspectives, Porth, McCall and Bausch (1999) found three key common characteristics; those of: employee development and continuous learning within the organization, information sharing and meaningful collaboration, and team building and shared purpose/vision.

## Research on Learning Organizations in Tourism and Hospitality

Researchers have argued that when a LO is applied to the tourism industry, it is mainly used for strategic destination planning and impact prediction. Holling (1978) proposed an adaptive management approach that explored the structure and dynamics of tourism systems. In another study, Van den Bergh (1991) examined sustainable economic development factors of tourism using an integrated dynamic modeling approach. A third study by Walker, Greiner, McDonald, and Lyne (1999), took a systems approach that incorporated elements of society, the economy, the environment, and tourist behaviors. In a later study, Wiranatha,'s (2001) also applied a systems model approach of sustainable development for regional planning in Bali, Indonesia. The introduction of System Dynamics Modeling (SDM), a technology based methodology that supports system thinking, is used today for strategic planning and to test mid- and long-term policy implications at tourism destinations (Sterman, 2000; Meadows *et al.*, 2004; Van den Belt, 2004). These studies suggest that LOs, when used in sustainable tourism development should incorporate assets such as information, knowledge, and human capital in order to achieve sustained competitiveness.

Farrell and Twining-Ward (2005), like Holling (1978), viewed tourism as a complex adaptive system integrated with many sub-systems compounded by human activities. Under this system, tourism and change is examined; primarily, in the areas of politics, policy, development, conservation, and human-environmental relations over a period of 30 years. They further suggest that sustainability is affected by changes in these areas, and this leads to the realization that the current approaches to tourism is not adequately providing an explanation of what is occurring.

They acknowledged that human activity within ecosystems is regarded as a complex system of people, land and ideas and that sustainability concepts are evolving and adapting to unique conditions that should not be regarded as universal. They suggest that instead of managing tourism through maintaining stability, one must acquire new insights guided by close observations of reality. Three threads of understanding are proposed; namely, (1) revised ecosystem ecology thread, (2) sustainability transition, and (3) non-linear tourism thread. The researchers also presented seven introductory steps to greater understanding of sustainable tourism in the context of complex system dynamics.

McLennan et al. (2012), suggests that tourism has been changing and transforming the world economies. However, the economic transformation has been problematic to quantify due to poor leadership, lack of decision making tools and funding, these issues have limited the ability of governments to develop sustainable destinations (Kelly, 2002; Sorenson & Eps, 2003). They suggest applying transformation theory, a systems approach, which may be used to better understand the dynamic interactions between the structure of the industry and the collective human actions that are occurring when a system undergoes change. Transformation is defined as long-run structural shifts that result from institutional change (Geels & Kemp, 2007; Seliger, 2002). Under this premise, tourism destination's structure is defined by the triple bottom line (Carter, 2004; Faulkner, 2002; & Prideaux, 2000), which they suggest is the only viable strategy for capturing tourism growth (Popesku & Hall, 2004). This theory incorporates four interrelated dimensions of: time, space, structure, and institutions. This theory has been applied by tourism destinations to explain, the evolution of its social dimensions, the transformation of individual products (Zhong et al., 2007), logistics systems (Mrnjavac & Ivanovic, 2007; Ivanovic & Baldigara, 2007), destination and regional products (Gartner, 2004; Nepal,

2007; Pavlovich, 2003; Saarinen, 2004; Saarinen & Kask, 2008; Sorenson & Epps, 2003), as well as,the transformation that occurrs within countries (Kotlinski, 2004; Sergeyev & Moscardini, 2006; Taylor, H L. & McGlynn, 2009).

From a hospitality perspective, there have been very few research studies about LOs, with the exceptions of hotels in Turkey (Bayraktaroglu & Kutanis, 2003), in which researchers examined LOs as a model for sustainable development of the Turkish tourism sector, and in Taiwan (Yang, 2004), where two hotels were examined to determine how they captured knowledge. The study examined both individual knowledge, defined as the "comprehensive interpretations and syntheses of information being gathered," and "organizational knowledge," defined as "knowledge by individuals interpreted in the organizational context" (Bhatt 2000, p. 18). The results of this study indicate that to achieve organizational competitiveness, individual learning needs must be enhanced in order to foster organizational learning. By and large, where hospitality researchers, and to an extent tourism researchers, fall short of investigating the application of LO, the literature is rife with investigations of organizational learning and knowledge management research, for example, Yang (2004). Aksu and Özdemir (2005), Hallin and Marnburg (2008) and Yang (2010).

## Learning Organizations as a Sustainable Competitive Advantage Strategy

Sackmann, Eggenhofer-Rehart, and Friesl (2009), suggest that globalization and competition can impact a company's competitive advantage and suggest that organizations must be willing to adapt quickly to changes within the dynamic environments. The longitudinal study sought to identify and explain the strategic changes occurring within the ABA trading company in Germany. Their investigation was based on a lack of understanding about the dynamics involved in strategic change

within an organization and as such, examined the problem over a four-year period through longitudinal research in an effort to achieve a better understanding of the phenomenon. They had three research questions that included:

(1) How does strategic change unfold over time, including the role of managers' conception of change, change supporting activities, and organization members' attitudes toward change?

(2) Which role does employees' trust in their supervisors and management play in a change effort?

(3) Which factors influence the sustainability of change from the stage of its initiation to its implementation and institutionalization?

Findings from their study suggested that strategic change is usually accompanied by planned changes in organizational structures and processes, management systems, emerging changes in leadership, organization members' attitudes and behaviors, and was supported by management's development activities. The results indicate that there were enablers of change and factors that sustain change within the organization. Some enablers of change include the culture, level of trust between superiors and subordinates, employees' affective organizational commitment, and managers' ability to critically reflect on their role. These results were consistent with existing research and found that the alignment, availability, and proper use of management instruments represent important sustaining conditions of a strategic change process.

Ramirez (2012), posits that prior research has cast a gloomy view about the sustainable practices of companies, and that most of the problems with sustainability concerns are that a new approach is needed to address it. The paradox view was proposed, in which every aspect of reality was seen to have opposing forces that create, confront and conflict with each other, and this view was needed in order to address complex issues relating to sustainability. This process leads to new forces that will retain some of the characteristics of the original situation and produce *"path-dependent features."* The theoretical framework is based on the theory of organizational learning and managerial cybernetics posed by Beer, (1979). Under this paradigm, "human organizations includes the global society and share some essential features that are inseparably, undissolvable in totality and coupled to a complex, recursive network of a configured environment." The paper suggests that managerial cybernetics, and holistic approaches are needed to promote sustainability issues and can contribute to a better understanding of such issues. This study can provide information for governments, international agencies and multinational business about the paradoxal view to understanding the complexity of sustainability. This includes applying epistemological and analytical methods should be applied in the research. The researchers suggest that at the organizational levels, it is necessary to harness tensions that emerge from natural paradoxical situations and this can enhance sustainable oriented decision-making. The paper was a complex discourse about the implications of societal learning on sustainability and emerging ideas in a rapidly changing environment.

In the study by Johnson & Vanetti (2005), the researchers examined expansion strategies used by international hotel operators in five countries to achieve sustained competitive advantage. The results of the study showed that knowledge about guest requirements and proprietary reservation systems were extremely important and consistent with previous studies, but more importantly, planning was perceived as an important advantage, especially by North American chains. In addition, they discovered that the size and nature of the city in which the hotels were located, the infrastructure and the perception of the regions, whether it was attractive for business or not, were important factors for sustained competitive advantage.

In Kozak's study (2002), the researcher used a qualitative case study approach to examine the

sentiments of tourists in Mallorca and Turkey. The purpose of the research was to identify and highlight the importance of tourist satisfaction within the destinations and to encourage improvement to these European destinations in order to remain competitive. The researcher applied benchmarking techniques to data obtained from tourists visiting the two areas. This data was later used to measure destination performance between the two areas. Chen and Hsiang (2007) studied emphasized e-learning and suggested that the development of a knowledge community through e-learning is an important strategy for implementing a knowledge management policy within LOs. They defined e-learning as, "the use of Internet technologies to deliver a broad array of solutions that enhance knowledge and performance" (Rosenberg, 2001, p. 28). They suggest that for corporate success, LOs plan and organize its use of technology, procedure, and personnel so that the company could expand its e-learning systems into a *"knowledge community-based e-learning system"*. As a result of this approach, LOs studied achieved positive results in finance, customer satisfaction, improvements in internal procedures, and organizational learning.

In the article by Kearney et al. (2012), the researchers extended the LO concept to include community sustainability through Lifelong Learning. They suggest that this approach is beneficial, especially to disadvantaged communities such as, the Samoan Community in Logan City, Australia. The study examined how leaders in this migrant community achieved positive change in their personal, professional, team, and community learning levels. This was achieved through a participatory action learning and action research (PALAR) framework. The researchers utilized a qualitative case study approach that allowed them to identify key characteristics of the sustainable learning community and combined the PALAR learning system and the Global University for Lifelong Learning (GULL) and were able to use this framework for the study. The use of the framework designed by

GULL was primarily for developing countries. However, this proved to be an effective system for achieving personal and organizational learning in this disadvantaged community. Their findings suggest that a lack of cultural understanding by government agencies may have contributed to many socio-economic disadvantages within the community; such as high unemployment, high crime rates, under-achievement in education, and exclusion from higher education. The researchers suggest that the study provided new insights for evaluating and tracking learning outcomes in a community by applying the GULL system. This was used to develop a conceptual model that enhanced the understanding of the key principles and processes in LO projects used for sustainable development within a learning community.

## INNOVATION AND THE LEARNING ORGANIZATION

The definition of innovation in the literature has many interpretations based upon the context in which it is used. The underlying theme in the literature is that in order to achieve innovation, knowledge must be applied in a tradable way (Landau, 1991). Hjalager (1997) suggest that innovation is divided into five different types. These include: product, process, and process of handling information, management, and institutional innovations.

When applied to the tourism industry, innovation was regarded as a defensive strategy resulting from innovative efforts in other sectors, which ultimately impacts the industry and forces change (Hjalager, 1997), and can lead to new products, services, or processes. Other researchers have suggested that innovative organizations have certain attributes such as creativity, involvement, responsibility, flexibility, and learning (Vigoda-Gadot, Shoam, Schwabsky, & Ruvio, 2008; Fard, Rostamy, & Taghiloo, 2009).

Pomykalski (2001) suggest that innovation be regarded as a process, which generates creativity and results in improved solutions in techniques, technology, organization, and social life. This eventually leads to new or improved products, processes, and or services. Wodecka-Hyjek (2013) research examined a process management approach within the public sector. The research revealed how the organization can achieve efficiency and improved performance within the LO. The researcher focused on the role of organizational learning and how it was used to shape the culture of learning within the organization. This culture allowed for an innovative operation and the implementation of innovative solutions.

According to Nieves and Haller (2014), knowledge is the most distinctive and inimitable strategic asset available to firms. They suggest that a discussion about knowledge must be framed in light of the resource-based view (RBV) of a firm, in which knowledge and a dynamic capabilities approach is used to provide an important framework for understanding how a firm's resources are used to achieve or maintain sustainable competitive advantages. (Ambrosini & Bowman, 2009; Augier & Teece, 2009; Cavusgil, Seggie, & Talai, 2007). They suggest that knowledge can reside within an individual, a group, or be distributed throughout the organization (Yang & Wan, 2004).

Organizational knowledge was defined by Akgun, Dayan, and Di Benedetto (2008) as declarative or procedural. Declarative organizational knowledge is more general and refers to the knowledge of concepts, facts or events, making it applicable to a wide range of situations (Kyriakopoulos, 2011). Procedural organizational knowledge is associated with domain-specific skills and refers to knowledge about routines, processes and procedures (Tippins & Sohi, 2003).

Other researchers have argued that organizational knowledge is a separate entity from that of the sum of individual knowledge possessed by members of the organization (Brown & Duguid, 1991; Nahapiet & Ghoshal, 1998). In this argument, knowledge is an attribute of the firm and it is not limited to the knowledge of an individual. Nelson and Winter (1982) also suggest that knowledge is an attribute of the firm and represent an aggregation of the various competences and capabilities held by employees, equipment or installations of the organization.

Nieves and Haller (2014) study is supported by prior literature, in which firms knowledge-based resources were seen to influence the achievement of dynamic capabilities within the firm. (Verona & Ravasi, 2003; Wang & Ahmed, 2007; Zollo & Winter, 2002). Thus a firm's knowledge influences the overall organizational learning process, which in turn forms the basis of generating dynamic capabilities (Ambrosini, Bowman, & Collier, 2009; Lichtenthaler, 2009; Prieto, Revilla, & Rodríguez-Prado, 2009). According to Ipe (2003) for this to be realized, individuals must be carefully recruited, selected, establish trust, and be willing to share their knowledge. Nieves & Haller (2014), suggest that within the concept of the LO, this is achieved through three stages, namely (1) knowledge acquisition, (2) knowledge sharing, and (3) knowledge utilization (Dibella, Nevis, & Gould, 1996). Within the LO, individual knowledge and expertise are shared with other idividuals both within and outside the organization and used to create a sustainable competitive advantage. Therefore, LOs place great emphasis on learning through sharing, which is at the core of knowledge management and extremely important for developing LOs.

Chan and Huang (2004) posit that the concept of think globally, act locally and plan regionally of sustainable development is about planning a sustainable community in terms of systems thinking. The researchers used the sensitivity model (SM) as a systems tool to build a model of the development of the community of Ping-Ding, located adjacent to the Yang-Ming-Shan National Park in Taiwan. The issue with the development of Ping-Ding was that there were conflicts between environmental conservation and the development of the local tourism industry that was a major attraction for residents of Taipei metropolitan during weekends and leisure time.

The researcher collaborated with local residents, planners, and interest groups, and developed a system model of 26 variables that identify characteristics of Ping-Ding through pattern recognition. Two scenarios concerning the sustainable development of Ping-Ding were simulated with interlinked feedbacks from variables. The method incorporated the 26 variables into a Criteria Matrix of 18 criteria used to analyze and interpret the data. This Matrix tested the system completeness in relation to four categories; namely, sectors of life, the physical category, the dynamic category, and the system relationship. The results of the analysis indicated that the development of Ping-Ding would be better served by planning for the agricultural and the tourism industries.

Prior research in this area had shown sustainability indicators for local development (Huang et al., 1998). However, by themselves, these indicators only partially explained community development. Applying the sensitivity model (SM), which is a systems approach developed by Vester and Hesler (1982), this planning tool was used to deal with development issues in the Ping-Ding village. The system thinking was an integrated approach and the researchers were able to apply it to deal with the sustainability issues of local development. This approach had its foundations in systems thinking and bio-cybernetic rules. That provides a convenient tool for assessing the sustainability of a local community by identifying the pertinent characteristics of a community, and, by simulating its development in scenarios using semi-quantitative data. The definition of a sustainable community was seen to include economic, environmental, and social interest. Therefore a long-term, integrated, and systems approach was needed to address the economic, environmental, and social issues of that community.

They suggest that there are two strategies for analyzing a community system, namely the micro and macro viewpoints. The micro perspectives focus on individual features of a community such as population growth, industry or transportation issues. Whereas, the macro view sees the community as a total holistic system, in which elements of the community are interlinked and individual contributions are not taken into account. By using a systematic approach, they were able to identify and describe the interactions between system components.

The SM perspective incorporates the General System Theory, which includes systems thinking, fuzziness, and simulation of semi-quantitative data. This approach emphasizes pattern recognition and the theory of feedback mechanism. This makes the analysis of complex systems possible by using the approach of fuzzy logic, which is regarded as a new systematic way of thinking about complex systems with accuracy. Key inputs are obtained from group discussions and consultation to discover the process of model construction, pattern recognition, and system simulation. These discussions were carried out with residents, industries, government, environmental groups, and community groups. The SM applies a top-down approach to dealing with complex system problems and uses nine steps in the operation of these SM tools. These are divided into three phases namely: system definition, pattern recognition, and system simulation and evaluation.

The results indicate that the application of SM to the community development in Ping-Ding was a very positive experience and provided planners with an effective tool for getting the public's participation, building consensus, and policy formulation. The simulation of partial scenarios suggests that the community should be carefully controlled to avoid the negative impacts caused by tourist pollution. This semi-quantitative approach provided a practical solution for dealing with the complicated relations within the community.

A practical application that supports these findings is by Schianetz et al. (2009), in which researchers utilized a Learning Tourism Destination (LTD) framework (Schianetz et al, 2007) with the case study of Ningaloo Coast region in Western Australia. This framework supported tourism planning, collaboration, and collective learning among various stakeholders within the coastal region and provided a shared vision for tourism development.

## METHOD AND ANALYSIS

A qualitative content analysis approach was used to examine research articles published in journals relating to LO. Only main articles were content analyzed. Comments, research notes, book reviews, and conference proceeding issues were not included. The data were obtained online via an academic university library and through the use of Google Scholar with the population sample drawn from three major publishing databases. Various keywords such as: learning organization, learning tourism destinations, learning communities, systems thinking, innovations, organizational learning, sustained competitive advantage, collaboration, and sustainability were used to identify articles. Data were analyzed by both authors so that a consistent grouping of the articles could be made according to selected criteria, i.e. focus of the articles, adapted from Baloglu & Assante's (1999) study, which was adapted from Chon et al. (1989) and Crawford-Welch and McCleary (1992) studies.

Two hundred and sixty-seven articles published in 1978 to 2014, a period that encompassed 76 journals were identified. The data were counted, screened, and themes manually determined. The first coding produced 17 research themes, with the most prevalent research field related to the organization, and the least researched area was leadership. Themes were adapted from Baloglu

*Table 1. Themes of the Learning Organization/Learning Destination*

| Articles | Themes | Premise | Method | Research Sample |
|---|---|---|---|---|
| 8. Kearney (2012) | Community sustainability through lifelong learning | Adapted from Senge's (1990) LO, Collectively learning within a community, where people interact as equals, express ideas and challenge themselves to achieve shared goals. | Qualitative Case Study Approach [Leadership Development Program (LDP) and Participatory Action Learning and Action Research (PALAR) Framework] | Disadvantaged Samoan Community in Logan City Australia |
| 9. Sackmann (2009) | Globalization and competition on a company's competitive advantage | The ability of LO to adapt and utilize knowledge as a source of sustainable competitive advantage | Mixed method Approach- Case study and quantitative analysis | Employees of 14 Service Centers of ABA company in Germany |
| 10. Ramirez (2012) | Paradoxes of societal learning on sustainability and emerging ideas | In every single aspect of reality there are opposing forces (confronting and developing new opposing forces, while conserving some of the characteristics of the original situation) that will display path- dependent features | Conceptual Approach: Prior literature and Application of Theoretical Framework (theories of Organizational Learning & Managerial Cybernetics) | Paradoxes – based on views and theories built around them (Quinn, 1988; Chae and Bloodgood, 2006; Dittrich et al., 2006; Smith and Lewis, 2011) |
| 11. Chan and Huang (2004) | Sustainable communities through system's thinking | A community is a complex system of humans and natural environment, it is necessary to deal with it from a comprehensive and systematic viewpoint | Semi-quantitative Approach: • Community Group discussions • Application of Sensitivity Model (SM) – Systems Tool & Bio-cybernetics Simulation (Vester & Hesler, 1975, 1982) • Bio-cybernetic assessment | Ping-Ding, a small village in northern Taipei |
| 12. Farrell & Ward (2005) | Adaptive systems using tourism and change | Developing people who learn to see as systems thinkers and learn how to surface and restructure mental models collaboratively (Senge 1990) | Conceptual paper based on prior literature about sustainability and adaptive systems | Literature based upon politics, policy, development, conservation, human-environmental relations, and the convergence of these areas over 30 years |
| 13. Schianetz, et al.,(2007). | The Learning Tourism Destinations (LTD) | Proposes a framework for a Learning Tourism Destination (LTD) based on the concept of the LO (Senge, 1990), which uses systems thinking and system dynamics modeling (SDM) approaches to implement and foster collective learning processes. | Qualitative paper about SDM case studies analyzed in the context of the LTD | Six Cases: (1) Obergurgl/Austria (1974–1984): Environmental assessment in Austria; (2) Sporades Islands/Greece (1990–1993): Experiment in policy options; (3) Bali/Indonesia (1998–2000): strategic sustainability; (4) Douglas Shire/Australia (1998–2004; Management policy on rainforest (5) Ping Ding/Taiwan (2003–2005): A sensitivity model; and (6) Guilin/Mainland China (1998–2000): A systems model |
| 14. Leana Reinl, Felicity Kelliher (2014) | the social dynamics that influence learning within a micro-firm tourism learning community | the social dynamics of micro-firm learning and participation in an independent learning network | A longitudinal interpretive case study conducted over a four-year period | An evolving learning community (ELC) in Ireland's south west region |

and Assante's (1999) study and provided 17 subjects areas.

These include: theory, service quality, knowledge and innovation, dimensions and systems, models, leadership and culture, change, education and research, tourism, other industries and/countries, operations management, organization, measuring, Small and Medium Enterprises (SEMS), sustainability, human resources and others, which included articles that did not fit into any category, such as governance and bureaucracy, public sector, etc. The second coding provided seven (7) articles that were found to focus specifically on LO and sustainability. Table I shows the themes and the underlying premise of these articles. These seven (7) articles were published in six (6) journals and became the focus of the analysis. The data were also analyzed for collection method, data type, nature of the study, (qualitative or quantitative) data analysis method, sample, findings, and type of journal (shown in Tables 2 & 3).

## Themes

The predominant themes related mainly to tourism and included community sustainability through lifelong learning, globalization and competition, sustainable communities through systems thinking, adaptive systems using tourism and change, the Learning Tourism Destination (LTD), and the social dynamics that influence learning in microfirms tourism learning community. The theme that mainly related to hospitality was the paradoxes of societal learning on sustainability and emerging ideas. The results suggest that gaps exist within LO, and there is a need for more research specific to hospitality, as well as tourism in the area of LO and sustainability. The findings highlighted that hospitality organizations may not be as involved

in this area as they ought to be. Even though there are obvious benefits to this approach as evidence by Sackman's (2009) research where it was proposed that the ability of LO to adapt and utilize knowledge can be a source of sustainable competitive advantage. With the hospitality and tourism industries competing for market share, LO may be a viable option to ensure sustainability. Schianetz, et al.'s (2007) study also posits that systemic awareness can be brought about by utilizing system dynamics modeling (SDM) as a tool for implementing and enhancing collective learning. In this research SDM were incorporated into the LTD and contributed to creating a tourism organization which was adaptive to change and able to continuously learn and be more sustainable. In Reinl & Kelliher (2014) study, the researchers suggested that a single tourism operator will not be as successful without a socially supported learning environment. Their research examined micro-firm's, which was defined as "a firm that employs no more than ten fulltime employees and possesses a turnover of less than two hundred and fifty thousand euro" (European Commission, 2010). This is particularly true for many tourism

*Table 2. Data Analysis & Results*

| Articles | Research Questions/Hypotheses | Data Analysis | Results |
|---|---|---|---|
| Kearney (2012) | How to develop a sustainable learning community? | Evaluations of participants using predetermined guidelines | 1. Developed a conceptual model of new ways of doing, knowing, and being in a learning community. 2. Provided an effective system for achieving personal and organizational learning in a disadvantaged community in Australia |
| Sackmann (2009) | Organizational members' perceptions of change may vary and develop as the change process unfolds over time Employees ' trust in their direct supervisors plays an important role for achieving change Leader-member exchange, organizational commitment, change-oriented organizational citizenship behavior, and attitudes toward change are important | Observations, interviews and surveys; Descriptive statistics and ANOVA | The availability and proper use of change aligned with management instruments may help in sustaining change over time and institutionalized it as part of work |

371

*Table 2. Data Analysis & Results (cont'd)*

| Articles | Research Questions/Hypotheses | Data Analysis | Results |
|---|---|---|---|
| Ramirez (2012) | What are the Paradoxes in managerial and organizational learning processes? | Conceptual exploration and discussion of societal learning on sustainability based on the paradox view of management | Shows relevance of the paradox view to management's understanding of the complexity of sustainability Demonstrates that at organizational levels, harnessing tensions that emerge from natural paradoxical situations enhances sustainable oriented decision-making |
| Chan and Huang (2004) | None | Fuzzy Logic (Jorgensen, 1997) and System Simulations – nine steps conducted in three phases and the use of a Criteria Matrix (18 criteria) | The development of Ping-Ding would be better served by planning of agriculture and the tourism industry Raises the awareness of local residents and interest groups to development policy for their community |
| Farrell, B., & Twining-Ward, L. (2005) | None | An analysis of prior literature based upon the seven steps of understanding sustainable tourism in the context of complex system dynamics | A contextual foundation for understanding sustainability |
| Schianetz, et al.,(2007). | None | Observation, note taking and the use NVivo software to code and create themes | The results reveal that SDM is capable of promoting communication between stakeholders and stimulating organizational learning |
| Leana Reinl, & Felicity Kelliher (2014) | None | Team observations, in-depth interviews, internal documentary review, field notes and reflective diaries . Data analysis was with NVivo software. A longitudinal case study conducted over a four-year period | Observations confirmed that there were varying levels of ELC participation and demonstrated the complexity associated with creating and sustaining a social learning infrastructure. |

*Table 3. Research Design and Journals*

| Articles | Applied | Conceptual | Journal |
|---|---|---|---|
| Kearney (2012) | √ | | Learning Organization |
| Sackmann (2009) | √ | | Journal of Applied Behavioral Science (JAB) |
| Ramirez (2012) | | √ | Learning Organization |
| Chan and Huang (2004) | √ | | *Journal of Environmental Management* |
| Farrell & Ward (2005) | | √ | Journal of Sustainable Tourism |
| Schianetz, et al.,(2007). | | √ | Annals of Tourism (AT) |
| Leana Reinl, & Felicity Kelliher (2014) | | √ | Tourism Management (TM) |

and hospitality business environments, which often depend heavily on this sector where small businesses make up the bulk of the business sector (Kozak & Rimmington 1998; Morrison & Teixeira 2004).

These studies support the argument that sustainability is impacted when LO strategies are incorporated and relies on the collaboration of all stakeholders. This suggests that sustainability will not occur in a vacuum. In addition, for organizations to truly say that they are a LO, learning must be a continuous process at the individual level, as well as at the organizational level. This premise can also be applied to the LTD, as well as for learning communities. However, when applied to learning communities a systems management approach would be applicable.

## Research Questions/Hypotheses and Methods Section

There were three research questions proposed of the seven articles reviewed for this analysis. This was very surprising because research question(s) is an extremely important step in both quantitative and qualitative studies. These questions allow the researcher to narrow the research objective, as well as and the purpose of the research, in order to address pertinent issues in their studies (Johnson & Christensen, 2004; Creswell, 2005). This is even more important in the mixed methods studies where complex research design and systems were used.

There were more applied research geared toward solving real problems within organizations and destinations. The conceptual research articles provided new approaches and framework for addressing concerns about LO and sustainability, as well as generated new knowledge. This could be seen in Farrell & Ward's (2005) research, in which people are seen as system thinkers who "collaborate and learn to restructure their mental models" in an adaptive learning tourism environment.

## Data Analysis and Results

Data analyses for all the studies (shown in Table 2) were very detailed and included prior literature that either confirmed and or disconfirm the outcomes of the studies. Some approaches were very complex, such as Fuzzy Logic and System Simulations (Chan and Huang 2004), which included nine steps and a Criteria Matrix of 18 criteria. This could be a challenge for researchers trying to replicate the research at other destinations, partly because of the large possibility for design, analytical and interpretational errors that might occur.

Table 3 shows that there were more conceptual research that applied research and that most articles were published in various journals that include Journal of Sustainable Tourism, Annals of Tourism (AT), Journal of Applied Behavioral Science (JAB), Journal of Environmental Management, Tourism Management (TM) and Learning Organization. Despite the research articles significant contributions to the development of knowledge, the quality of the range of journals could potentially hinder their overall value. Since these studies rely on materials extracted from various publication channels, it is therefore unknown whether the journals are all of comparable quality.

## DISCUSSION AND IMPLICATIONS

The results of this study are mainly exploratory and provide insightful information about what knowledge exists in the areas of LO and sustainability. Globalization and competition have made it imperative for destinations and operations to address triple-bottom line sustainability. This has been the focus of the concept of Learning Organizations (LO), in which destinations/organizations have the capacity to anticipate environmental changes and economic opportunities and adapt accordingly. The results indicate that there are various models for operationalizing LO and even though differences exist in the approaches to LO there are also similarities. Most scholars agree that LO provides continuous learning at systems level and that knowledge is generated and shared within the system. People are required to apply systemic thinking and they must be willing to participate fully in the activities of the organization. We recognize that organizational learning is a dynamic process and must be carefully managed, especially within LO. Therefore, managers must carefully recruit and select employees so that they are acculturated into the culture of the organization.

We identified gaps that can provide new areas of research. Especially, using mixed methods or quantitative data analyses. This study is important because the tourism and hospitality industries are challenged by stakeholder's demands for environmentally conscious business practices, while still maintaining profitability and increased market share (Edwards, 2005; Freeman, Pierce, & Dodd, 2000). A collaborative approach is needed that incorporates learning at the micro and macro levels at the organizational, as well as destination or regional levels. Learning at the destination level employs systems thinking and system dynamics modeling (SDM) approaches to implement and foster collective learning that address all stakeholders concerns and needs and ensure that sustainable development issues are incorporated.

## CHALLENGES, LIMITATIONS, ASSUMPTIONS

There has been much debate about the core concepts associated with LO. For example, many definitions of LO exist, some argue that it is difficult to identify the theory(ies) that explains it, how to identify when an organization becomes a learning organization, and what characteristics and outcomes can be expected from the LO. This study's approach in conducting an in-depth analysis provided an opportunity to examine the literature and provide some insights about LO. This analysis created large amounts of data that took much time to screen and analyze. The main limitations are that the data were limited to keywords selected by the researchers and this might have limited the search parameters of the research even though three large databases were utilized. In addition, the researcher's interpretations of the selected themes and articles could be construed as being biased. Another limitation is that the counting method used in the research did not assess the quality of the published articles.

## CONCLUSION

One emerging trend in sustainability is the importance of corporate social responsibility (CSR); defined as an overall ethic or vision that implies the need for businesses to contribute back to the communities and markets that have made them successful (Smith, 2003). This has been difficult to quantify in the past. However, by using the TBL approach the hospitality and tourism sectors have been able to quantify organizations' contributions. This was evident in the study by McGehee et al. (2012), about the Gulf Coast Hurricane season of 2005. Another trend that is impacting the industry is the adoption of technology, in which biometrics is used in front office systems by guests, to check in/out, access guest areas, and make payments, as well as improve security and control employee attendance (Morosan, 2010). Such adoption is seen as critical for sustained competitive advantage.

The implications for scholars include more opportunities for research in areas of LO and sustainability. Specifically, more applied research articles that have practical applications to the hospitality and tourism industry. Researchers should include research questions and or hypotheses and provide an explanation of the research design and methodologies. These features are important for methodological rigor and a systematic approach required for such research.

Various systems were examined relating to LO, such as SM and Bio-Cybernetics Simulation and adaptive systems, in which people were seen to be system thinkers. These provided options for analyzing complex relationships and the dynamics of LO and LTD and implication for sustainability. We hope that the insights into LO and sustainability presented in the study may stimulate more in-depth discussions about how companies and destinations are achieving sustainability in the context of LO.

# REFERENCES

Akgun, E., Dayan, M., & Di Benedetto, A. (2008). New product development team intelligence: Antecedents and consequences. *Information & Management*, *45*(4), 221–226. doi:10.1016/j.im.2008.02.004

Aksu, & Özdemir. (2005). Individual learning and organization culture in learning organizations. Five star hotels in the Antalya region of Turkey. *Managerial Auditing Journal*, *20*(4), 422–441.

Altman, Y., & Iles, P. (1998). Learning, leadership, teams: Corporate learning and organizational change. *Journal of Management Development*, *17*(1), 44–55. doi:10.1108/02621719810368682

Ambrosini, V., & Bowman, C. (2009). What are dynamic capabilities and are they a useful construct in strategic management? *International Journal of Management Reviews*, *11*(1), 29–49. doi:10.1111/j.1468-2370.2008.00251.x

Ambrosini, V., Bowman, C., & Collier, N. (2009). Dynamic capabilities: An exploration of how firms renew their resource base. *British Journal of Management*, *20*(1), 9–24. doi:10.1111/j.1467-8551.2008.00610.x

Armstrong, A., & Foley, P. (2003). Foundations of a learning organization: Organization learning mechanisms. *The Learning Organization*, *10*(2), 74–82. doi:10.1108/09696470910462085

Augier, M., & Teece, D. J. (2009). Dynamic capabilities and the role of managers in business strategy and economic performance. *Organization Science*, *20*(4), 410–421. doi:10.1287/orsc.1090.0424

Baloglu, S., & Assante, L. M. (1999). A content analysis of subject areas and research methods used in five hospitality management journals. *Journal of Hospitality & Tourism Research (Washington, D.C.)*, *23*(1), 53–70. doi:10.1177/109634809902300105

Barnes, J. (1991). From resources and sustained competitive advantage. *Journal of Management*, *17*(1), 99–120. doi:10.1177/014920639101700108

Bayraktaroglu, S., & Kutanis, R. O. (2003). Transforming hotels into learning organizations: A new strategy for going global. *Tourism Management*, *24*(2), 149–154. doi:10.1016/S0261-5177(02)00061-4

Beer, S. (1979). *The Heart of Enterprise*. New York, NY: Wiley.

Bhatt, G. D. (2000). Organizing knowledge in the knowledge development cycle. *Journal of Knowledge Management*, *4*(1), 15–26. doi:10.1108/13673270010315371

Brown, J. S., & Duguid, P. (1991). Organizational learning and communities of practice: Toward a unified view of working, learning and innovation. *Organization Science*, *2*(1), 40–57. doi:10.1287/orsc.2.1.40

Calvert, G., Mobley, S., & Marshall, L. (1994). Grasping the learning organization. *Training & Development*, *48*(6), 38–43.

Campbell, T., & Cairns, H. (1994). Developing and measuring the learning organization: From buzz words to behaviors. *Industrial and Commercial Training*, *26*(7), 10–15. doi:10.1108/00197859410064583

Carter, R. W. (2004). Implications of sporadic tourism growth: Extrapolation from the case of Boracay Island, The Philippines. *Asia Pacific Journal of Tourism Research, 9*, 383–404. doi:10.1080/10941660042000311264

Cavusgil, E., Seggie, S. H., & Talai, M. B. (2007). Dynamic capabilities view: Foundations and research agenda. *Journal of Marketing Theory and Practice, 15*(2), 159–166. doi:10.2753/MTP1069-6679150205

Chan, S.-L., & Huang, S.-L. (2004). A systems approach for the development of a sustainable community - the application of the sensitivity model (SM). *Journal of Environmental Management, 72*(3), 133–147. doi:10.1016/j.jenvman.2004.04.003 PMID:15251220

Chen, R.-S., & Hsiang, C.-H. (2007). A study on the critical success factors for corporations embarking on knowledge community-based e-learning. *Information Sciences, 177*(2), 570–586. doi:10.1016/j.ins.2006.06.005

Confessore, S. J. (1997). Building a learning organization: Communities of practice, self-directed learning, and continuing medical education. *The Journal of Continuing Education in the Health Professions, 17*(1), 5–11. doi:10.1002/chp.4750170101

Coopey, J. P. (1995). The learning organization: Power, politics, and ideology. *Management Learning, 26*(2), 193–213. doi:10.1177/135050769502600204

Crawford-Welch, S., & McCleary, K. W. (1992). An identification of the subject areas and research techniques used in five hospitality-related journals. *International Journal of Hospitality Management, 11*(2), 155–167. doi:10.1016/0278-4319(92)90008-J

Creswell, J. W. (2005). *Educational research: Planning, conducting, and evaluating quantitative and qualitative research* (2nd ed.). Upper Saddle River, NJ: Pearson Education.

Daft, R., & Marcic, D. (1998). *Understanding management*. Forth Worth, TX: Dryden Press.

Dunlap, R. E., Gallup, G. H. Jr, & Gallup, A. M. (1993). Of global concern: Results of the health of the planet survey. *Environment, 35*(9), 7–15, 33–40. doi:10.1080/00139157.1993.9929122

Edmondson, A., & Moingeon, B. (1998). From organizational learning to the learning organization. *Management Learning, 29*(1), 5–20. doi:10.1177/1350507698291001

Edwards, A. (2005). *The sustainability revolution*. Gabriola Island, BC, Canada: New Society.

European Commission. (2010). *Small and medium sized enterprises- craft and micro enterprises.* Available at: http://ec.europa.eu/enterprise/policies/sme/promoting-entrepreneurship/crafts-micro-enterprises/

Farrell, B., & Twining-Ward, L. (2005). Seven steps towards sustainability: Tourism in the context of new knowledge. *Journal of Sustainable Tourism, 13*(2), 109–122. doi:10.1080/09669580508668481

Faulkner, B. (2002). Rejuvenating the Gold Coast. *Current Issues in Tourism, 5*, 472–520. doi:10.1080/13683500208667938

Fiol, M. C., & Lyles, M. A. (1985). Organizational learning. *Academy of Management Review, 10*(4), 803–813.

Freeman, R. E., Pierce, J., & Dodd, R. (2000). *Environmentalism and the new logic of business: How firms can be profitable and leave our children a living planet.* New York, NY: Oxford University Press.

Gartner, W. (2004). Rural tourism development in the USA. *International Journal of Tourism Research, 6*(3), 151–164. doi:10.1002/jtr.481

Garvin, D. A. (1993). Building learning organizations. *Harvard Business Review, 71*, 78–91. PMID:10127041

Garvin, D. A., Edmondson, A. C., & Gino, F. (2008). Is yours a learning organization? *Harvard Business Review*, 1–11. PMID:18411968

Geels, F. W., & Kemp, R. (2007). Dynamics in socio-technical systems: Typology of change processes and contrasting case studies. *Technology in Society*, 29(4), 441–455. doi:10.1016/j.techsoc.2007.08.009

Hallin, C. A., & Marnburg, E. (2008). Knowledge management in the hospitality industry: A review of empirical research. *Tourism Management*, 29(2), 366–381. doi:10.1016/j.tourman.2007.02.019

Hjalager, A. (1997). Innovation patterns in sustainable tourism: An analytical typology. *Tourism Management*, 18(1), 35–41. doi:10.1016/S0261-5177(96)00096-9

Holling, C. S. (Ed.). (1978). *Adaptive environmental assessment and management*. Chichester, UK: Wiley.

Huang, S.-L., Wong, J.-H., & Chen, T.-C. (1998). A framework of indicator system for measuring Taipei's urban sustainability. *Landscape and Urban Planning*, 42(1), 15–27. doi:10.1016/S0169-2046(98)00054-1

Ivanovic, Z., & Baldigara, T. (2007). Logistics processes in a tourism destination. *Tourism and Hospitality Management*, 13, 595–606.

Jashapara, A. (1993). The competitive learning organization: A quest for the Holy Grail. *Management Decision*, 31(8), 52–62. doi:10.1108/00251749310047160

Jashapara, A. (2003). Cognition, Culture and Competition: An Empirical Test of the Learning Organisation. *The Learning Organization*, 10(1), 31–50. doi:10.1108/09696470310457487

Jogaratnam, G., McCleary, K. W., Mena, M., & Yoo, J. J. (2005). An analysis of hospitality and tourism research: Institutional contributions. *Journal of Hospitality & Tourism Research (Washington, D.C.)*, 29(3), 356–370. doi:10.1177/1096348005276929

Johnson, C., & Vanetti, M. (2005). Locational strategies of international hotel chains. *Annals of Tourism Research*, 32(4), 1077–1099. doi:10.1016/j.annals.2005.03.003

Johnson, R. B., & Christensen, L. B. (2004). *Educational research: Quantitative, qualitative, and mixed approaches*. Boston: Allyn and Bacon.

Jorgensen, S. (1997). *Integration of Ecosystem Theories: A Pattern, 2nd*. London: Kluwer Academic Publisher. doi:10.1007/978-94-011-5748-3

Kearney, J., & Zuber-Skerritt, O. (2012). From learning organization to learning community sustainability through lifelong learning. *The Learning Organization*, 19(5), 400–413. doi:10.1108/09696471211239703

Kelly, I. (2002). Australian regional tourism handbook; industry solutions, 2002.

Kotlinski, W. (2004). The government's role in stimulating national tourism development: The case of Poland. In D. Hall (Ed.), *Tourism and transition: Governance, transformation and development* (pp. 65–72). Wallingford, CT: CABI. doi:10.1079/9780851997483.0065

Kozak, M. (2002). Destination benchmarking. *Annals of Tourism Research*, 29(2), 497–519. doi:10.1016/S0160-7383(01)00072-X

Kozak, M., & Rimmington, M. (1998). Benchmarking: Destination attractiveness and small hospitality business performance. *International Journal of Contemporary Hospitality Management*, 10(5), 184–188. doi:10.1108/09596119810227767

Kyriakopoulos, K. (2011). Improvisation in product innovation: The contingent role of market information sources and memory types. *Organization Studies*, *32*(8), 1051–1078. doi:10.1177/0170840611410833

Landau, R. (1991). How competitiveness can be achieved: fostering economic growth and productivity. In R. Landau (Ed.), *Technology and economics: papers commemorating Ralph Landau's service to the National Academy of Engineering*. Washington: National Academy Press.

Law, R., Leung, D., & Cheung, C. (2012). A Systematic Review, Analysis, and Evaluation of Research Articles in the *Cornell Hospitality Quarterly*. *Cornell Hospitality Quarterly*, *5*(4), 365–382. doi:10.1177/1938965512457458

Lee, K. F. (2001). Sustainable tourism destinations: The importance of cleaner production. *Journal of Cleaner Production*, *9*(4), 313–323. doi:10.1016/S0959-6526(00)00071-8

Lichtenthaler, U. (2009). Absorptive capacity, environmental turbulence, and the complementarity of organizational learning processes. *Academy of Management Journal*, *52*(4), 822–846. doi:10.5465/AMJ.2009.43670902

Loermans, J. (2002). Synergizing the learning organization and knowledge management. *Journal of Knowledge Management*, *6*(3), 285–294. doi:10.1108/13673270210434386

McGehee, N., & Wattanakamolchai, S. (2009). Corporate Social Responsibility within the U.S. Lodging Industry: An Exploratory Study. *Journal of Hospitality & Tourism Research (Washington, D.C.)*, *33*(3), 417–437. doi:10.1177/1096348009338532

McGill, M. E., Slocum, J. W. Jr, & Lei, D. (1992). Management practices in learning organizations. *Organizational Dynamics*, *21*(1), 5–17. doi:10.1016/0090-2616(92)90082-X

McLennan, C., Ruhanen, L., Ritchie, B., & Pham, T. (2012). Dynamics of destination development: Investigating the application of transformation theory. *Journal of Hospitality & Tourism Research (Washington, D.C.)*, *36*(2), 164–190. doi:10.1177/1096348010390816

Meadows, D. H., Randers, J., & Meadows, D. L. (2004). *The Limits to Growth: The 30-Year Update*. Chelsea Green: White River Junction, VT. Saarinen, J. (2004). Destinations in change: The transformation process of tourist destinations. *Tourist Studies*, *4*, 161–179.

Morosan, C. (2012). Theoretical and Empirical Considerations of Guests' Perceptions of Biometric Systems in Hotels: Extending the Technology Acceptance Model. *Journal of Hospitality & Tourism Research (Washington, D.C.)*, *36*(1), 52–84. doi:10.1177/1096348010380601

Morrison, A., & Teixeira, R. (2004). Small business performance: A tourism sector focus. *Journal of Small Business and Enterprise Development*, *11*(2), 166–173. doi:10.1108/14626000410537100

Mrnjavac, E., & Ivanovic, S. (2007). Logistics and logistics processes in a tourism destination. *Tourism and Hospitality Management*, *13*, 531–546.

Nahapiet, J., & Ghoshal, S. (1998). Social capital, intellectual capital, and the organizational advantage. *Academy of Management Review*, *23*(2), 242–266.

Nelson, R. R., & Winter, S. G. (1982). *An evolutionary theory of economic changes*. Cambridge: Belknap Press of Harvard University Press.

Nepal, S. K. (2007). Tourism and rural settlements: Nepal's Annapurna region. *Annals of Tourism Research*, *34*(4), 855–875. doi:10.1016/j.annals.2007.03.012

Nevis, E. C., DiBella, A. J., & Gould, J. M. (1995). Understanding Organizations as Learning Systems. *Sloan Management Review*, *36*(2), 73–85.

Nieves, J. A., & Haller, S. (2014). Building dynamic capabilities through knowledge resources. *Tourism Management, 40,* 224–232. doi:10.1016/j.tourman.2013.06.010

Ortenblad, A. (2002). A typology of the idea of learning organization. *Management Learning, 33*(2), 213–230. doi:10.1177/1350507602332004

Ortenblad, A. (2004). The learning organization: Towards an integrated model. *The Learning Organization, 11*(2), 129–144. doi:10.1108/09696470410521592

Pavlovich, K. (2003). The evolution and transformation of a tourism destination network: The Waitomo caves, New Zealand. *Tourism Management, 24*(2), 203–216. doi:10.1016/S0261-5177(02)00056-0

Pedler, M., Burgoyne, J., & Boydell, T. (1991). *The learning company: A strategy for sustainable development.* New York: McGraw-Hill.

Pomykalski, A. (2001). *Zarządzanie innowacjami.* Warszawa, Łódź: Wydawnictwo Naukowe PWN.

Popesku, J., & Hall, D. (2004). Sustainability as the basis for future tourism development in Serbia. In D. Hall (Ed.), *Tourism and transition: Governance, transformation and development* (pp. 95–104). Wallingford, CT: CABI. doi:10.1079/9780851997483.0095

Porth, S., McCall, J., & Bausch, T. A. (1999). Spiritual themes of the learning organization. *Journal of Organizational Change Management, 12*(3), 211–220. doi:10.1108/09534819910273883

Prideaux, B. (2000). The resort development spectrum: A new approach to modelling resort development. *Tourism Management, 21*(3), 225–240. doi:10.1016/S0261-5177(99)00055-2

Prieto, I. M., Revilla, E., & Rodríguez-Prado, B. (2009). Building dynamic capabilities in product development: How do contextual antecedents matter? *Scandinavian Journal of Management, 25*(3), 313–326. doi:10.1016/j.scaman.2009.05.005

Ramirez, G. A. (2012). Sustainable development: Paradoxes, misunderstandings and learning organizations. *The Learning Organization, 19*(1), 58–76. doi:10.1108/09696471211190365

Reinl, L., & Kelliher, F. (2014). The social dynamics of micro-firm learning in an evolving learning community. *Tourism Management, 40,* 117–125. doi:10.1016/j.tourman.2013.05.012

Rivera, M. A., & Upchurch, R. (2008). The role of research in the hospitality industry: A content analysis of the IJHM between 2000 and 2005. *International Journal of Hospitality Management, 27*(4), 632–640. doi:10.1016/j.ijhm.2007.08.008

Ronald, J. L. (1996). Impressions bout the Learning Organization: Looking to see what is behind the curtain. *Human Resource Development Quarterly, 6*(2), 119–122.

Rosenberg, M. J. (2001). *E-learning: Strategies for Delivering Knowledge in the Digital Age.* New York: McGraw-Hill.

Saarinen, J., & Kask, T. (2008). Transforming tourism spaces in changing socio-political contexts: The case of Parnu, Estonia, as a tourist destination. *Tourism Geographies, 10*(4), 452–473. doi:10.1080/14616680802434072

Sackmann, S. A., Eggenhofer-Rehart, P. M., & Friesl, M. (2009). Sustainable change: Long-term efforts toward developing a learning organization. *The Journal of Applied Behavioral Science, 45*(4), 521–549. doi:10.1177/0021886309346001

Salzmann, O., Ionescu-Somers, A., & Steger, U. (2005). The business case for corporate sustainability: Literature review and research options. *European Management Journal, 23*(1), 27–36. doi:10.1016/j.emj.2004.12.007

Sankar, Y. (2003). Designing the learning organization as an information-processing system: Some design principles from the systems paradigm and cybernetics. *International Journal of Organization Theory and Behavior, 6*(4), 501–521.

Schianetz, K., Jones, T., Kavanagh, L., Walker, P. A., Lockington, D., & Wood, D. (2009). The practicalities of a learning tourism destination: A case study of the Ningaloo Coast. *International Journal of Tourism Research, 11*(6), 567–581. doi:10.1002/jtr.729

Schianetz, K., Kavanagh, L., & Lockington, D. (2007). The learning tourism destination: The potential of a learning organisation approach for improving the sustainability of tourism destinations. *Tourism Management, 28*(6), 1485–1496. doi:10.1016/j.tourman.2007.01.012

Schianetz, K., Kavanagh, L., & Lockington, D. (2007). The Learning Tourism Destination: The potential of a learning organisation approach for improving the sustainability of tourism destinations. *Tourism Management, 28*(6), 1485–1496. doi:10.1016/j.tourman.2007.01.012

Seliger, B. (2002). Toward a more general theory of transformation. *Eastern European Economics, 40*, 36–62.

Senge, P. M. (1990). *The fifth discipline: The art and practice of the learning organization.* New York: Currency Doubleday.

Senge, P. M., Kleiner, A., Roberts, C., Ross, R. B., Roth, G., & Smith, B. S. (1999). *The dance of change: The challenge of sustaining momentum in learning organizations.* New York: Currency Doubleday.

Sergeyev, A., & Moscardini, A. (2006). Governance of economic transitions: A case study of Ukraine. *Kybernetes, 35*(1/2), 90–107. doi:10.1108/03684920610640254

Shabbir, S. (2009). Supportive learning environment – a basic ingredient of learning organization. *Proceedings from the 2nd CBRC Conference,* Lahore, Pakistan.

Slater, S. F., & Narver, J. C. (1995). Marketing orientation and the learning organization. *Journal of Marketing, 59*(3), 63–74. doi:10.2307/1252120

Smith, N. C. (2003). The new corporate philanthropy. In Harvard Business School Press (Eds.), Harvard Business Review on corporate social responsibility (pp. 157-188). Boston: Harvard Business School Press.

Sorenson, T., & Epps, R. (2003). The role of tourism in the economic transformation of the Central West Queensland Economy. *The Australian Geographer, 34*(1), 73–89. doi:10.1080/00049180320000066164

Sterman, J. D. (2000). *Business Dynamics: Systems Thinking and Modeling for a Complex World.* Boston: Irwin McGraw-Hill.

Sudharatna, Y., & Li, L. (2004). Learning organization characteristics contributed to its readiness-to-change: A study of the mobile phone service industry. *Managing Global Transitions, 2*(2), 163–178.

Swieringa, J., & Wierdsma, A. (1992). *Becoming a learning organization: Beyond the learning curve.* Reading, MA: Addison-Wesley.

Taylor, H. L. Jr, & McGlynn, L. (2009). International tourism in Cuba: Can capitalism be used to save socialism? *Futures, 41*(6), 405–413. doi:10.1016/j.futures.2008.11.018

Tippins, M. J., & Sohi, R. S. (2003). IT competency and firm performance: Is organizational learning a missing link? *Strategic Management Journal, 24*(8), 745–761. doi:10.1002/smj.337

Van den Belt, M. (2004). *Mediated Modeling: A System Dynamics Approach to Environmental Consensus Building.* Washington, DC: Island Press.

Van den Bergh, J. C. J. M. (1991). *Dynamic models for sustainable development.* Amsterdam: Thesis Tinbergen Institute.

Verona, G., & Ravasi, D. (2003). Unbundling dynamic capabilities: An exploratory study of continuous product innovation. *Industrial and Corporate Change, 12*(3), 577–606. doi:10.1093/icc/12.3.577

Vester, F., & Hesler, A. (1982). *Sensitivity Model.* Frankfurt: Main, Umlandverband Frankfurt.

Vigoda–Gadot, E., Shoam, A., Schwabsky, N., & Ruvio, A. (2008). Public Sector Innovation for Europe: A Multinational Eight–Country Exploration of Citizens' Perspectives. *Public Administration, 2*(2), 307–329. doi:10.1111/j.1467-9299.2008.00731.x

Walker, P. A., Greiner, R., McDonald, D., & Lyne, V. (1999). The tourism futures simulator: A systems thinking approach. *Environmental Modelling & Software, 14*(1), 59–67. doi:10.1016/S1364-8152(98)00033-4

Wang, C. L., & Ahmed, P. K. (2007). Dynamic capabilities: A review and research agenda. *International Journal of Management Reviews, 9*(1), 31–51. doi:10.1111/j.1468-2370.2007.00201.x

Watkins, K. E., & Marsick, V. J. (1993). *Sculpting the Learning Organization.* San Francisco: Jossey-Bass.

Wiranatha, A. S. (2001). *A systems model for regional planning towards sustainable development in Bali, Indonesia.* (Unpublished Ph.D. thesis). University of Queensland, St. Lucia, Australia.

Wodecka-Hyjek, A. (2014). A learning public organization as the condition for innovations Adaptation. *Procedia: Social and Behavioral Sciences, 110*(24), 148–155. doi:10.1016/j.sbspro.2013.12.857

Yang, B., Watkins, K. E., & Marsick, V. J. (2004). The construct of the learning organization: Dimensions, measurement, and validation. *Human Resource Development Quarterly, 15*(1), 31–55. doi:10.1002/hrdq.1086

Yang, J. T. (2004). Qualitative knowledge capturing and organizational learning: Two case studies in Taiwan hotels. *Tourism Management, 25*(4), 421–428. doi:10.1016/S0261-5177(03)00114-6

Yang, J. T. (2010). Antecedents and consequences of knowledge sharing in international tourist hotels. *International Journal of Hospitality Management, 29*(1), 42–52. doi:10.1016/j.ijhm.2009.05.004

Yang, J. T., & Wan, C. (2004). Advancing organizational effectiveness and knowledge management implementation. *Tourism Management, 25*(5), 593–601. doi:10.1016/j.tourman.2003.08.002

Yeo, R. K. (2006). Learning Institution to Learning Organization: Kudos to reflective Practitioners. *ICFAI Journal of European Industrial Training, 30*(5), 396–419. doi:10.1108/03090590610677944

Zhong, L., Deng, J., & Xiang, B. (2007). Tourism development and the tourism area life-cycle model: A case study of Zhangjiajie National Forest Park, China. *Tourism Management, 29*(5), 841–856. doi:10.1016/j.tourman.2007.10.002

Zollo, M., & Winter, S. G. (2002). Deliberate learning and the evolution of dynamics capabilities. *Organization Science, 13*(3), 339–351. doi:10.1287/orsc.13.3.339.2780

# Chapter 20

# Privileges and Problems of Female Sex Tourism:
## Exploring Intersections of Culture, Commodification, and Consumption of Foreign Romance

**Brent Smith**
*Saint Joseph's University, USA*

## ABSTRACT

*This chapter provides an exploration of female sex tourism, or romance tourism, a global consumer phenomenon that has evolved over several decades. Amidst forward strides in their social and economic empowerment, many women in advanced countries still experience marginalizing constraints to their freedom, mobility, and expression in many aspects of life. Yet, scholarly research and anecdotal evidence suggest that some women have utilized sex tourism as a means to escape such domestic constraints and find entrée to myriad social and cultural privileges at certain destinations abroad. Moving beyond tenured, clichéd stereotypes that typically associate sex tourism with male consumers, this chapter brings to light the rationale, justifications, criticisms, and cultural issues pervading this institution. Despite its liberating potential for women, female sex tourism does, at least somewhat, rely upon and reinforce historically entrenched national and cultural demarcations that tend to marginalize the people (partners, families, communities) of targeted destinations in the developing world.*

*I know you don't know but that's why you came here. So stop pretending you just came here just to get a nice tan. I mean, think of those cute boys. They are a dime a dozen. Take your pick. […] If you are too shy to pay them, just give them gifts. – Ellen, Heading South (2005, directed by Laurent Cantet)*

*… there's a denial of the power that money brings to the relationship that creates a culture of dependency and exploitation. – Chris Beddoe, Director, ECPAT UK*

DOI: 10.4018/978-1-4666-8606-9.ch020

# INTRODUCTION

Thinking globally and acting locally represents a common paradigm for people to understand the terms of survival and prosperity in our dynamically integrating world community. For some people, signs of globalization are knotted with the multinational corporate investments, currency exchanges, and value-added supply chain networks that define today's most advanced formal economies. However, evidence of globalization (and its precursor internationalization) has been inconspicuously evident for many decades in the form of sex tourism, one of the world's most conspicuous systems involving transactions between people for people. Overwhelmingly, such systems have flourished without pause, tying together haves and have-nots, respectively coming from once-colonizing nations and once-colonized nations. In the case of female sex tourism, exchange partners – foreign buyers and local sellers – find one another by the gravity of potential relationships that offer access, opportunity, and mobility not necessarily possible within the confines of their respective home communities. Jacobs (2009) offers an interesting description of the female sex tourist in one study: "They are travelling independently of their families, taking a highly visible place in a culturally male public space, being the major wage-earner in a relationship and selecting and proposing to a partner who might be significantly younger than them" (p. 54).

Indeed, evidence of globalization can be observed in the informal, but established exchanges and economies of sex tourism. Whether in times of world peace or conflict, prosperity or recession, the "market" in sex tourism has seldom, if ever, relented. One significant feature of the globalization process is cultural influence. Regarding such influence, Appadurai (1996) notes that communities affect and are affected by myriad influences, which can be understood in the form of "scapes" — *ethnoscapes* (e.g., movement people across borders), *financescapes* (e.g., money, currency), *technoscapes* (e.g., internet, transportation), *mediascapes* (e.g., information dissemination, constructions of one's imagined world), and *ideoscapes* (e.g., lifestyle, worldview) — that enable and affect interactions and influences between people across geographies. Indeed, female sex tourism exhibits aspects of these scapes:

- international travelers and local romantic partners (ethnoscapes);
- exchange of money or gifts for sexual experiences (financescapes);
- internet sites for recommending destination hotspots (technoscapes/ mediascapes); and
- and female sex tourists "recourse to perhaps their most important 'masculine' privilege – their mobility" (Jacobs, 2009) (ideoscapes)

Sex tourism is a significant global, cultural phenomenon. Historically, the majority of sex tourists have been males from the United States, Europe, and Australia; and, there also have been significant flows of sex tourists within Asia. Given its exchange oriented nature and transaction style features, sex tourism occasionally has been linked to prostitution (Enloe, 1989), where a buyer provides some form of consideration (e.g., money, gifts, meals) to an anonymous seller (e.g., prostitute, gigolo, companion) with the anticipation of a sexual experience or romantic companionship free of personal commitments (Karch, 1981).

While the study of male sex tourism has received the overwhelming majority of scholarly and media attention (Jacobs, 2009), female sex tourism has gone largely understudied and underreported as a phenomenon that taps the global intersections of culture, commodification, and consumption. Much of the scholarly research conducted on the subject has dealt with "ethnosexual relationships" (Nagel, 2003), focusing on Western tourist women who favor destinations in the Caribbean, Central America, and Africa

Anecdotes and memoirs have also been added to discourse. For example, Jeanette Belliveau, author of *Romance on the Road* (2006), a compilation of memoirs and interviews on the topic, notes that female sex tourism has existed for over 150 years and been practiced by nearly 600,000 women from 1980 to 2005. At the time of the book's writing, one in seven of these women was married or in committed relationships with boyfriends. Three in five visited Jamaica frequently to find native male lovers. One in 1,000 was expected to contract human immunodeficiency virus (HIV).

Definitions of sex tourism are many (see Enloe, 1989; Jeffreys, 1998) and not without debate, particularly because they have pre-supposed exclusively male tourists and applications of male patriarchal power (Sanchez Taylor, 2001). Thus, sex tourism is defined here simply as a vacation oriented experience where consumers travel to foreign destinations with the expectation that part or all of their vacation will involve a paid/compensated sexual experience. It involves pay-for-hire transactions, such as enlisting escorts, visiting strippers, or engaging in sexual experiences (Evans et al., 2000). The very nature and scope of sex tourism include both international and cross-cultural contexts (See Figure 1). While sex tourism does occur domestically, Bishop and Robinson (1999) note that it is practiced largely by international tourists visiting and moving about within the borders of developing countries, most of which are clustered around Latin America (e.g., Brazil), the Caribbean (e.g., Jamaica, Dominican Republic), and Southeast Asia (e.g., Thailand, Vietnam). Beyond these destinations, sex tourism also has been linked to parts of Eastern Europe, East Africa, and West Africa.

## Sex Tourism: Perpetuating Cultural Discourse between Different Worlds

*Women enjoy casual sex and prostitution, too, but with far more hypocrisy. They help themselves to men in the developing world, kidding themselves that it's a 'holiday romance' that has nothing to do with the money they spend. Go to any Jamaican beach and you'll find handsome 'rent-a-dreads', who get by servicing Western women – lots from Britain. I've seen similar things in Goa.– Nirpal Dhaliwal, author of Tourism*

In light of scholars' focus on male sex tourists, Phillips (1999) poses an important question regarding female sex tourists, "Are they or aren't they like male sex tourists?" (p. 183). Others have also made similar inquiries. Pruitt and La Font (1995) contend that female tourists bring an emotional element, suggesting that "romance tourism" would be a better term than "sex tourism." That view is not without its detractors who find that some Western females, like their male counterparts, possess the means, motive, and opportunity to participate in sex tourism while abroad. For example, in a survey of 104 women, O'Connell Davidson and Sanchez Taylor (1999) concluded that female sex tourists "employ fantasies of Otherness not just to legitimate obtaining sexual access to the kind of young, fit, handsome bodies that would otherwise be denied to them [and] also to obtain a sense of power and control themselves and others as engendered, sexual beings, and to affirm their own privilege as Westerners" (p. 49).

In 2012, audiences at the Cannes Film Festival were exposed to Ulrich Seidl's "Paradise: Love," a film depicting the European female sex tourist and the Kenya male partner/sex worker (Seidl, 2012). Of the story presented in the film, lead actress Margarethe Tiesel stated summarily, "The exploited begin to exploit in a place where they have power. I don't judge these women, I understand them and I understand completely what they struggle with." While international business experts are typically concerned about a liability of foreignness, Tiesel's remark underscores the fact the European women can become enriched when they engage with contrastingly marginalized foreign countries *and* their men.

*Figure 1. World map of countries involved in sex tourism\**
*\* Countries appearing in gray indicate typical home countries of female sex tourists.*
*Countries appearing in black indicate typical destination countries for female sex tourists.*
*Sources: Belliveau (2006), Clark (2007), Miller (2011), Nagel (2003), Omondi (2003), Pruitt and Lafont (1995), Ryan and Hall (2001), and others.*

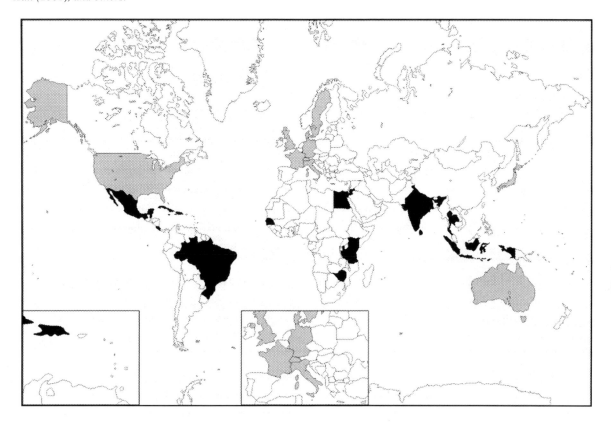

\* Countries appearing in gray indicate typical home countries of female sex tourists.
  Countries appearing in black indicate typical destination countries for female sex tourists.

Sources: Abu-Nasr (1998), Belliveau (2006), Clark (2007), Miller (2011), Nagel (2003), Omondi (2003), Pruitt and Lafont (1995), Ryan and Hall (2001), and others.

The transnational, transracial, and transcultural characteristics of female sex tourism underscore critical contextual issues (Phillips, 1999) that kindle not only romance, but also stir up long-standing status differences in the global community. Weichselbaumer (2012) disagrees, suggesting that many female sex tourism encounters are *carnivalesque* – situational, brief, and having little effect on racial discourses. Specifically, given that many female sex tourists originate from predominantly White western countries and visit

once-colonized nations, such as the Caribbean or East Africa, Tate (2011) finds, "the romance is a deeply colonial, heteronormative text. Thus, 'conventional romance formulas' [are inappropriate] because neither the sexual violence of slavery nor ideology of imperialism can be written out of understanding romance" (p. 46).

Tourism provides substantial economic benefits for popular destination countries, particularly those frequented by male and female tourists from developed countries of the so-called First World

According to the World Tourism Organization (1999), nearly 30% of all international tourist arrivals occurred in the Third World by the close of the 20th Century. Adams (1984) and Reimer (1990) note that the First World accounts for the majority of tourism promoters and tourism consumers interested in the Third World. In a review of Third World tourism marketing, Echtner and Prasad (2003) find that relationships between the First and Third Worlds remain asymmetric in nature, favoring the former over the latter.

Given the inherent historical ties between these worlds, it is important to consider how tourism has supported and characterized these ties over time. With regard to First World generated tourism of the Third World, postcolonial theorists (Ashcroft, Griffiths, & Tiffin, 1998, 1995; Ghandi, 1998; and others) assert that colonialism has continued to exert compelling influences on Western interpretations and engagements of people from comparatively different, exotic, and non-Western cultures. From the postcolonial perspective, sex tourism contextualizes (and reproduces) the economically and socially uneven statuses of people from the First and Third Worlds (Prasad & Prasad, 2002).

This perspective is informative since human rights advocates and public policy leaders have often linked sex tourism to the poverty of particular countries or individual prostitutes themselves. That is, sex tourism generally involves consumers from wealthier, developed countries and prostitutes from poorer, developing destination countries. Hence, sex tourism, regardless of whether males or females are its consumers, thrive in climates where poverty precipitates limits and costs for some people (e.g., prostitutes, companions) as well as mobility and benefits for others. So then, sex tourism simultaneously signals and corroborates evidence for the postcolonial view that First World exploits and engages the Third World on asymmetric bases.

Hannum (2002) notes that as travel opportunities became more accessible to growing Western middle classes during the mid-19th century, sex tourism, as it were, became a relatively common activity. The Western world's wealth, interests, and cultural power were augmented by their military conquests abroad. For example, British, Spanish, French, and United States military installations and outposts in the Caribbean, Africa, Latin America, Central Asia, and East Asia, drew a proliferation of nearby, readily accessible prostitution venues. In the 1940s and 1950s, before the US embargo of Fidel Castro's Cuba in response to the missile crisis, Cuba was a popular sex tourism destination of US men (Hannum, 2002). As the above evidence suggests, Western interest in sexual experiences in faraway lands has an established history. As will be shown in this paper, that history is still expanding.

Like diamonds, coffees, and metals, sex tourism is an industry that generates benefits for many players, including, but not limited to sex tourists and their romantic partners. Hannum (2002) finds that it "supports an international workforce estimated to number in the millions. Employees benefiting from the sex tourism industry include female and male sex workers as well as directly or indirectly members of the entire travel and tourism sectors, from taxi drivers to airline, hotel, and restaurant employees." Enloe (2002) asserts similar contentions about the web of interlinked stakeholders involved. Chutikul (n.d.), an advisor in Thailand's Office of the Prime Minister, reports that international sex tourists often pursue sexual experiences abroad that would have grim consequences in their home country.

Given its exchange-based transactions, sex tourism is a market whose transactions occur because they are permitted by social and political institutions (Fish, 1984; Richter, 1998). Despite the illegality of prostitution and sex tourism, social perspectives and evaluations regarding sex-for-sale between consenting adults has by no means approached consensus. For example, while Western governments lead the charge against prostitution, the fact remains that Westerners account for significant consumption of sex-related services beyond their home countries. This suggests that international sex tourists may opt for a "bracketed morality" that frees them of guilt or other reservations about paying/gifting a local for sex. Personally held sexual values and practices are rather complex, and, hence, can be challenging to evaluate in light of freedom, privacy, consent, personal beliefs, and human rights. However, in the context of social and business ethics, it is possible and appropriate to explore factors that underlie sex-for-sale practices, especially with regard to the cross-national and cross-cultural settings that characterize them. As with male sex tourism, the relationships associated sex-for-sale transactions in female sex tourism can be linked to the objectification and commodification of other people's bodies (Ryan & Hall, 2001).

Within the context of female sex tourism, or romance tourism, this chapter addresses how sex-for-sale exchanges reflect and reproduce power/status divides between the developed and developing worlds. Advancing the current knowledge on sex tourism, which to date has focused largely on foreign male consumers and local female companions, this chapter examines the evolution of and rationale for the commodification and consumption of foreign romance that define female sex tourism. It details, in part, how marketing practices, such as segmentation and targeting can be observed in tourists' preferences for certain kinds of destination countries and companions. The content presented here aims to provide a strong foundation for understanding how culture, sex, romance, power, and tourism have intersected to sustain sex-for-sale institutions abroad and draw the continual interests of female consumers from the developing world.

## Female Sex Tourism: Socially Veiled but with Growing Notoriety

*A woman is never going to walk into a brothel ...*

*essentially they are paying for sex the same way men do.—Jacqueline Sanchez-Taylor*

Despite the notoriety of prostitution as the "oldest profession in the world," the global case of sex tourism "remains a fairly obscure and unknown activity to the general public, academia, and helping professions" (Bender & Furman, 2004). While research suggests that the majority of known sex tourism consumers are male (Abu-Nassr, 1998), characterizations like "obscure" and "unknown" seem particularly appropriate in describing the history and growth of female sex tourism, a phenomenon which has largely eluded scholarly or media attention, despite its existence since the 19th Century (Belliveau, 2006).

## Romance Tourism: Obscure and Unknown Existence

For most of its long history, female sex tourism "has been veiled in secrecy – a reluctance to publicize their sexual dalliances is one reason women choose to indulge overseas in the first place" (McCombs, 2007, p. 72). Possibly further veiling the institution, some stakeholders and observers have applied terminology that may not clearly describe it. The term *romance tourism*, for example, represents a euphemism for female sex tourism, which has arguably obscured the nature and scope of its existence. Rhetorically, the prefix *romance* intimates one's pursuit of a relationship oriented encounter (re: feminine) as opposed to a one-time, instrumental encounter (re: masculine). Dr. Joan Phillips, a researcher of sex tourism in Barbados, suggests that although "beach boys" receive consideration (e.g., meals, drinks, clothing, electronics, plane tickets) for their companionship, romance tourism is "not like the traditional prostitution we know" (McCombs, 2007), since female sex tourists generally engage in more courtship with their companions during their stays than do male sex tourists. Pruitt and LaFont (1995), in a Jamaican study, also suggested that female tourists and their companions generally view their relationship in terms of courtship and romance, *terms* contrary to those typically associated with sex tourism or prostitution.

Regardless of which term may be applied, female sex tourism, or romance tourism, refers to the social practice of women who travel with the specific intent of seeking out, engaging, and remunerating native companions, prostitutes, or gigolos for sexually oriented experiences as part of the tourism experience. Female sex tourists are typically from Western, developed countries who travel abroad, engaging male companions in Asia, the Caribbean, Latin America, and Africa (See Table 1).

Research of sex-for-sale phenomena has seldom contemplated a framework that portrays female consumers and males companions, particularly when the female is empowered disproportionately over the male. Yet, in today's era of globalization, given the long-standing socioeconomic divides between the developed and developing worlds, scholars may appreciate the fact that many traveling female tourists possess, exploit, and transact for sex with greater power than their male companions, particularly those native to countries of the developing world (see Table 2). On this point, Jones (2009) notes, "Women are able to 'lose themselves' yet stay in control because of their access to greater economic and cultural capital" (p. 55).

Countries like Jamaica and Kenya have long been choice tourism destinations for their natural climate, aesthetic scenery, and lively music. Additionally, these same countries have earned reputations among more Western women for their value-added draw of native men who will entertain the sexual interests of female tourists. For example, regarding the practice of older rich women visiting Kenya to have sex with young Kenyan men, Jakes Grieves-Cook, chairman of

*Table 1. Male and Female Sex Tourism Home and Destination Countries*

| Male Sex Tourists | | Female Sex Tourists | |
|---|---|---|---|
| Home Countries | Destination Countries | Home Countries | Destination Countries |
| Australia | Brazil | Australia | Bahamas |
| England | Czech Republic | Denmark | Barbados |
| France | Costa Rica | England | Belize |
| Germany | Cuba | France | Brazil |
| Italy | Dominican Republic | Germany | Costa Rica |
| Japan | Egypt | Italy | Cuba |
| Switzerland | Kenya | Japan | Dominican Republic |
| United States | Morocco | Sweden | Egypt |
| | Philippines | Switzerland | Fiji |
| | Vietnam | United States | Gambia |
| | Thailand | | Haiti |
| | | | India |
| | | | Indonesia |
| | | | Jamaica |
| | | | Jordan |
| | | | Kenya |
| | | | Mexico |
| | | | Nepal |
| | | | Sri Lanka |
| | | | Tanzania |
| | | | Thailand |
| | | | Trinidad and Tobago |
| | | | Zimbabwe |

Sources: Belliveau (2006), Clark (2007), Miller (2011), Nagel (2003), Omondi (2003), Pruitt and Lafont (1995), Ryan and Hall (2001), and others.

the Kenya Tourist Board states "It's not evil ... but it's certainly something we frown upon" (Clark, *Reuters*, 26 November 2007).

Female sex tourism has evolved and expanded over time as more women have entered the middle class or started traveling on their own internationally. The social institution has also become quite diverse, such that it now "encompasses women for every class, race, and age, and a whole range of travelers from seasoned veterans of the foreign sex scene to dabblers" (McCombs, 2007, p. 70-71). Belliveau (2006) also attributes much of the expansion trend of female sex tourism to mounting publication of many novels, films, personal mem-

*Table 2. Profiles of Female Sex Tourism: Home Countries and Destination Countries*

| | PDI[1] | IDV[1] | MAS[1] | PPP ($)[2*] | Age at First Marriage[3*] | | Years Life Expectancy[4*] | | HIV Adult Prevalence[4*] | |
|---|---|---|---|---|---|---|---|---|---|---|
| | | | | | M | F | M | F | % | Rank |
| **Home Countries (HC)** | | | | | | | | | | |
| Australia | 36 | 90 | 61 | 37,299 | 29.2 | 27.0 | 79 | 84 | .20 | 109 |
| Denmark | 18 | 74 | 16 | 37,266 | 27.7 | 25.0 | 76 | 81 | .20 | 103 |
| Germany | 35 | 67 | 66 | 35,442 | 31.8 | 29.0 | 76 | 82 | .10 | 123 |
| Italy | 50 | 76 | 70 | 30,581 | 29.3 | 26.1 | 77 | 83 | .40 | 82 |
| Japan | 54 | 46 | 95 | 34,100 | 30.3 | 26.9 | 79 | 86 | .10 | 153 |
| Sweden | 31 | 71 | 5 | 37,245 | 34.0 | 31.8 | 79 | 83 | .10 | 125 |
| Switzerland | 34 | 68 | 70 | 42,783 | 26.0 | 22.4 | 78 | 83 | .60 | 69 |
| United Kingdom | 35 | 89 | 66 | 36,523 | 28.4 | 26.4 | 77 | 82 | .20 | 95 |
| United States | 40 | 91 | 66 | 46,859 | 28.7 | 26.0 | 76 | 81 | .60 | 68 |
| **Destination Countries (DC)** | | | | | | | | | | |
| Caribbean | 45 | 39 | 68 | 7,766 | 34.6 | 33.1 | 72 | 75 | 1.60 | 41 |
| East Africa | 64 | 27 | 41 | 1,713 | 26.3 | 21.7 | 57 | 58 | 6.70 | 10 |
| West Africa | 77 | 20 | 46 | 1,520 | 26.2 | 20.5 | 59 | 60 | 1.90 | 33 |
| India | 77 | 48 | 56 | 2,762 | 23.9 | 19.3 | 67 | 73 | .30 | 89 |
| **HC's Mean** | 37 | 75 | 57 | 37,586 | 29.5 | 26.7 | 77 | 83 | .28 | 103 |
| **DC's Mean** | 66 | 34 | 53 | 3,440 | 27.8 | 23.7 | 64 | 67 | 2.63 | 43 |
| **Difference** | (29) | 41 | 4 | 34,146 | 1.7 | 3.0 | 13 | 16 | (2.35) | 60 |
| **World Average** | 55 | 64 | 50 | 10,400 | n/a | n/a | 65 | 69 | .80 | - |

Source(s): [1] Hofstede (2009); [2] International Monetary Fund (2008); [3] UN Populations Division (2000); [4] CIA World Factbook (2009);
* Estimates from Jamaica (Caribbean), Kenya (East Africa), and Ghana (West Africa).

oirs, and collection of autobiographical narratives on the topic. For example, there is the cult classic French film, Laurent Cantet's *Heading South* (*Vers Le Sud*) (2006) which depicts French women on holiday in 1970s Haiti romantically engaging young native men and boys in exchange for money, gifts, and meals. Books such as *The Nomad: The Diaries of Isabelle Eberhardt* (Eberhardt, 2003), *Women on the Verge: Japanese Women, Western Dreams* (Kelsky, 2001), and *How Stella Got Her Groove Back* (McMillan, 1996), which was later produced in a commercially successful film, have also fascinated and captivated the interests of many new and veteran female tourists alike.

# Have Empowerment Will Travel: Female Consumers and Male Companions

As more women have entered the middle classes of their respective First World societies, some have realized that tourism provides a means for them to realize their economic opportunity and social mobility. In fact, Belliveau (2006) suggests that it may be "a leading indicator of the state of feminism and real increases in female power" (p. 6). While female sex tourists account for lesser numbers than their male counterparts, they share some similar tendencies and exert comparable influences in their cultural discourse with their companions in Third World destination countries. Reflective of postcolonial ideology, these female tourists, native to the First World, interact with males, native to the Third World, in exchanges defined by First World/Third World boundaries and power structures.

Realizing the power that they derive from the wealth, mobility, and postcolonial dominance of their home countries, more First World women have expanded the cohort of globetrotting consumers looking for sexually oriented or romantic experiences. Gender "remains a fundamental social, psychological, and cultural category" (Schroeder & Zwick, 2004, p. 27). This tends to hold true with regard to work, social, and relationship settings. In the developed world, females still face gender inequalities marginalize them relative to their male counterparts, especially in more traditional of patriarchal societies. Yet, the relative wealth, mobility, and power of female sex tourists from these same societies (see Table 1) enable them to produce situations where they can experience an unfamiliar parity with or dominance over male companions, albeit in foreign countries. Ironically, the "reversal of fortune" that favors the foreign female sex tourist also reveals how sex-for-hire with male companions may subordinate the males in professionally, socially, and relationally.

## Cultural Exploration and Commodification of Men

*Our idea of a male prostitute is like Richard Gere and that wasn't what this was at all. This was really a poor African man who lived in a shack and had a miserable life and had to [expletive] women to make a living. — Heidi Postelwait, co-author Emergency Sex and Other Desperate Measures (2005)*

Perspectives vary about the desire of prostitutes, or companions, to enter and remain in their profession, particularly when they are males. Whether male prostitutes living in the developing world willfully adopt or are drawn into their "profession," they are by practice subject themselves to the demands, whims, and wishes of female sex tourists who enjoy greater economic wealth, social freedom, and personal mobility (Ryan & Hall, 2001). Consequently, for some young men prostitution reflects an attempt to mitigate challenging socioeconomic circumstances that define their limited mobility in the developing world. Male prostitution in service of international female sex tourists may represent for these men the chance for freedom or retreat, however ephemeral or permanent, from everyday reminders of these bleak circumstances.

## Segmenting, Targeting, and Consuming Companions

Belliveau (2006) notes, "White women from Europe, especially Scandinavia, and North America, as well as Japanese women, use travel as a chance to explore black men" (p. 95). With regard to the Caribbean, which represents much of the Black African Diaspora, research has shown that international female tourists have determined their own sets of preferred destination countries. For example, British women have targeted Barbados (Phillips, 1999), African American women have staked out Jamaica (O'Connell et al., 1999), and other females have preferred Belize (Gorry, 1999) and the Dominican Republic (Herold, 2001). According to *Reuters*, one in five single women from wealthy Western countries comes to Kenya in search of sexual experiences with native "beach boys." Despite the prevalence of HIV/AIDS in Kenya, many female sex tourists prefer not to use condoms, seeing them as too "businesslike" for satisfying their sexual fantasies (Clark, *Reuters*, 26 November 2007).

The above evidence of racial segmentation and targeting suggests that sex tourism has objectified black males as commodities for sale and consumption, much like their predecessors of the former African slave trade sans shackles and plantations. Consumption in the context of sex tourism especially underscores the view that it involves more than just the mere acquisition of goods and services. For example, regarding the commodification of human identity, Schroeder and Zwick (2004) suggest, "consumption plays a major role in the construction, maintenance, and representation of male bodies" (p. 21). The female sex tourist's preference for and pursuit of chances to "explore" black men, as if on safari, would tend to support this view. Compounding this desire for exploration, the female sex tourism community has branded male companions across the developed with myriad pet names. For example, in their consumer shopping lexicon, Jamaican companions have been collectively referred to as *rent-a-dreads*, *rent-a-rastas*, *restitutes*, or the *Foreign Service*; Costa Ricans as *sharks*; Balinese as *cowboys*; Gambians as *bumsters*; Dominicans as *sanky pankies*.

Regarding the interface of wealthier Western women and poorer African males prostitutes, Omondi (2003) states that "European women imagine Black men (or men of color) to be stronger and active in bed compared to the men back in their home countries" (p. 5). In 2002, it was estimated that 5% of European women, principally from Germany and Switzerland, visit Kenya with intention to participate in sex tourism (*New York Times*, 14 February 2002). Many of these women seek something "nouveau" with a different race (Omondi, 2003). In an article prepared by *Reuters*, Julia Davidson, a sex tourism researcher from the University of Nottingham, states, "This is what is sold to tourist by tourism companies —— a kind of return to a colonial past, where white women are served, serviced, and pampered by black minions" (Clark, *Reuters*, 26 November 2007).

## Conspicuous Cultural Consumption of Companions in the Developing World

In contemporary materialistic societies, such as those of North America, Europe, and Australia, consumption is one of the most meaningful routines in a woman's life. In a study of female identity and cultural consumption (Fung, 2002), asserts that women "articulate their culture and narrate their identities through the consumption of necessities [as well as] products for leisure, relaxation, and personal satisfaction" (p. 322). Inheriting and expanding aspects of the own social empowerment, contemporary women from the developed world have assumed greater roles in shaping consumption. For example, Solomon (2004) noted that today's era of young mainstream female achievers represents a historically unique global cohort that is larger than its male equivalent. Here, female sex tourism represents an opportunity for this global cohort of contemporary women from materialistic societies to articulate and narrate part of their modern identities through leisure, personal satisfaction, and sexual experiences provided by their purchase and consumption of "romance" from foreign male companions.

The gradual socioeconomic empowerment of females has included greater means, abilities, and freedoms to make personal consumption choices. As shown in this chapter, results of such empowerment occur within the very social institution of sex tourism (Hannum, 2002; Enloe, 2002). In his model of social behavior, Walter Goldschmidt (1990), noted cultural analyst and scholar, contends that individuals are regularly driven by an "affect hunger" which when sated help one attain self-worth, status, and prestige. From a social perspective, individuals are often motivated to attain these through acquisitions, associations, or display of status-oriented symbols. In the context of shopping for a human companion, societies have made use of negative, but instrumentally charged such as "trophy wife" or "sugar daddy". Many veteran female sex tourists have shared their own stories and market data about romantic encounters with Caribbean, African, and Asian men, thus signaling a similar sentiments of status, worth, and prestige for having scored prized ethnicities of male companions Belliveau (2006).

Goldschmidt (1990) asserts that social institutions ultimately aim to keep their social structures intact. He expounds further stating, "the essential fact about social institutions is that they are self-maintenance mechanisms serving to preserve the state of equilibrium" (p. 18). Despite its historical obscurity, the mere survival and expansion of female sex tourism over the last 150 years confirms its role as a social institution that has helped reproduce and maintain the familiar "equilibrium" between the First and Third Worlds. Whether carried out at beach resorts, bars, clubs, or restaurants, sex tourism's consumers and companions maintain this equilibrium in market-style fashion by engaging one another in "imagined spaces that are designed for a specific purpose of set of objectives" (p. 298). The climate of these spaces is fueled by market-driven "servicescape fantasies" that suggest where customers will be served and feel important and cared for (Fitchett 2004).

Traveling internationally and participating in sex tourism signals the ability of First World females to project their gains in status, worth, and prestige on domestic and global fronts. In their home countries, females have struggled to achieve status and power equal to men. However, their residency in the First World and their ability to travel internationally suggests that they probably, indeed, have greater status and power than women or men in the destination countries. Hence, despite the patina of romance, Dr. Joan Phillips notes that sex tourism "is empowering for women in the sense that they have the opportunity to do something that men have always done since travel

began. But it's empowering because it's not an equal relationship." (McCombs, 2007).

The situation of First World females consuming sex-for-sale from Third World males also manifests an intersection of postcolonial thought and Veblen's (1902) notion of conspicuous consumption. That is, the contemporary "jane," or female sex consumer, from the First World has become an opportunistic participant in an established market system that distinguishes herself and her First World above and apart from her companion and his Third World. With and despite these stratifying distinctions, this market system does provide some recursive profits between the female sex tourist and her companion. For not only are female sex tourists and their male companions exotic to one another, they both derive mutual benefits from their engagement. For example, some female tourists "reacting to mate shortage at home or perhaps feeling sexually invisible in their own countries due to age or body type, get a much-needed ego boost" (McCombs, 2007, p. 73). Dr. Joan Phillips, a sex tourism researcher, highlights the benefit, as it were, to male "beach boys" in Barbados: "Engaging in relationships with white tourist women offered them money. It also gave them an opportunity that they wouldn't have with Barbadian society – which was to have sexual relationships with white women – and it gave them some sort of power" (McCombs, 2007, p. 73). These sentiments reflect a significant interplay between the notions of conspicuous consumption (Veblen, 1902), "affect-hunger" (Goldschmidt, 1990), and maintenance of the structural equilibrium within social institutions (Goldschmidt, 1990).

The idea of "romance" can flow across cultures and conjure mutual interests between the parties involved. For example, Mangaliso (2001) suggests that human identity for men in Sub-Saharan African cultures can be understood in terms of *umntu ngumntu ngabanye*, or "a person is a person through others" (p. 24). Therefore, it is possible that romantic companions in developed countries find some "affect fulfillment" in receiving special considerations (e.g., money, gifts, affiliation, social access) channeled by foreign female sex tourists. An alternative view from the African cultural scholars suggests that "the African's individual response to overpowering foreign influences has been and remains derived from the personal strategy he uses for survival... Therefore, the large world, like his family and communal milieu, present the African individual with an equally formidable set of circumstances and requirements her is conditioned not to challenge, is dependent on, and from which he cannot escape" (Lassiter, 2000, p. 1). Together, these views suggest that some tourists' local young, male companions may be affected by their relatively high power distance, or acceptance of social inequalities (Hofstede, 1997) (see Table 2).

The market scheme through which female sex tourist seeks out countries and companions also reflects the "marking" property of goods advanced by Douglas and Isherwood ([1979] 1982): "Treat the goods then as markers, the visible bit of the iceberg which is the whole social process" (p. 74). Hence, consistent with the findings of Hannum (2002), the ability to travel the world as female sex tourists, affords certain women the ability to narrate their identities in ways that bond them to a global cultural cohort serviced by subordinate companions (re: power distance), while also distinguishing them from female outsiders unaware of or uninvolved in sex tourism.

Able to exploit their First World affiliations, female sex tourists who specifically target male companions of Third World reflect not only informed consumption choices, but also the intention or willingness to maintain asymmetric power present in sex-for-sale relationships. Therefore, as alluded by Phillips, while female sex tourism creates intercultural exchanges, at the same time it inherently exploits and reproduces inequalities between the haves of the First World and have-nots of the Third World. The intentional

targeting of particular kinds of companions and destination countries supports the contention of Schroeder and Zwick (2004) that "as long as the structural dialectic of class (labor-capital), race (black-white), or gender (female-male) remain intact, no change can occur because it is exactly this system of classification that orders what is thought, practiced, and represented" (p. 28). Therefore, female sex tourism thrives in situations where the female tourist is advantageously empowered by structural social inequalities (re: Hofstede's notion of power distance) that are historically established and intrinsically sustained by the sex-for-sale market itself (see Tate, 2011).

Aside from the structural differences present within the sex-for-hire transaction, female sex tourism can create harmful market externalities that affect the societies of their destination countries. For example, Kam Williams, in his review of the "Rent-a-Rasta" practice in Jamaica states "Sex tourism is not merely the harmless indulgence of horny white women gone wild, but a burgeoning trend which continues to wreak havoc on a Caribbean culture and a family culture already in crisis" (McQueen, *Edmonton Sun*, Tue, Mar 6, 2007). Williams notes that many "beach boys" are married men with families who use their monetary profits from prostitution to provide for their families.

## Discerning the Rationale and Values of Female Sex Tourism

*Increased female incomes gave women, especially those single and divorced, the ability to travel. It's no surprise that today unmarried women make up an estimate half of adventure travelers. In time, these traveling women joined in the heretofore male activity of taking foreign lovers and in some cases paying for sex. And feminism led to altered sex roles and ultimately a dating war that made exotic foreign men seems appealing than domestic brands.*—Belliveau, Romance on the Road (2006)

Inspired, in part, by postcolonial theory, this chapter examines how female sex tourism reflects the developed world's interpretation and engagement of the developing world. Though the First and Third worlds share centuries of mutual interaction, that interaction has often reflected that the two are lopsided bedfellows. Here, this chapter presents the multifaceted rationale for female participation in the social institution of sex tourism. Additionally, it considers how this rationale reflects the underlying culture that female sex tourist bring to the institution. In doing so, it helps broaden the typical discussions of First World interactions with the Third World.

The historically disproportionate focus on male sex tourism versus female sex tourism (Abu Nasr, 1998), though important, has somewhat obscured general knowledge about sex tourism and sex tourists (Gorry, 1999; Thomas, 2000; Belliveau, 2006). However, given the strides made in the socioeconomic empowerment of females around the world, and particularly in developed countries, it is necessary to scrutinize sex tourism beyond its clichéd masculine attributions.

## Reasons for Becoming a Female Sex Tourist

*Cultural processes, such as consumption and the subsequent identity formation are by definition ideological in the way that the world is made to appear in a society tends to coincide with the interests of certain dominant or powerful classes and group in society. – Fung (2002)*

Researchers of female sex tourism and female sex tourists themselves have provided an array of reasons to explain why females get involved in the institution. These reasons traverse a broad spectrum of psychological, demographic, and cultural domains, which also suggests both similarities and differences between female sex tourists and male sex tourists. Among the reasons cited and distilled are:

1. Men have done it and continue to do it.
   - Men have set a standard for sex-for-sale and sex tourism.
   - Men have more freedom to do as they please, especially when traveling.

*"It is empowering for women in the sense that they have the opportunity to do something that men have always done since travel began." - Dr. Joan Phillips (McCombs, 2007)*

2. Shortage of available, attracted, and interested men in the female's home country
   - Older women experience difficulty finding relationship companions at home.
   - Trend of vacation liaisons has created a "take your pick" atmosphere across the Caribbean islands.

*"After about five minutes on the beach, I felt like [supermodel] Naomi Campbell.... You see women melting in front of these guys and I can completely understand why." – Tanika Gupta, playwright, Sugar Mummies (Martin, The Observer, Sunday, 23 July 2006)*

3. Identity loss and social anonymity
   - Tourists enjoy certain releases provided by anonymity, which allow them to "lose their identity" and free them from restraints on behavior that may be illegal, frown upon, or simply monitored in the home countries (Omondi, 2003).
4. Opportunity to develop self-identity
   - Sex-for-sale frees buyer from indemnification after transaction.

*Some Japanese women have pursued foreign travel romances as escapes from confines of traditional home culture and opportunities to forge their own social identity (Kelsky, 2001).*

5.   Pursuit of empowerment

   ◦   Sex-for-sale frees buyer from indem-nification after transaction.

*"Making sex available as a commodity, something that is bought and sold subject to market forces, at a stoke give almost any salaried Western woman options for short-term, no-obligations companion-ship – if she travels abroad." (Belliveau, 2006, p. 85)*

*Furthermore, (Bonsu, 2009) alludes that the physical and psychological distance between tourists and Africans provides assurances to foreign target consumers that their developing world companions are "confined to well-defined socio-geographic areas" (p. 13).*

*Therefore, the geographical, sociological, and psychological distances between sex tourists and their partners in targeted destinations – Jamaica, Kenya, Tanzania, Zimbabwe, and others – appar-ently satisfy the "confined" and "exotic" criteria.*

6.   Deeper cultural exploration

   ◦   "Enclave tourism" at resorts limits possibility for true cultural exposure.
   ◦   Companionship with local men offers of few means for cultural exploration.

*"The vast majority of non-sex tourists have a difficult time getting below the surface of the Caribbean. Many tourists stay in a gated resort community with guest-only beaches, where no islanders circulate except staff." (Belliveau, 2006, p. 82)*

*"... exoticism commodifies the African experi-ence, making it readily available to anyone who is willing and able to pay for it" (Bonsu, p. 13).*

7.   Commodification of foreign men and sex abroad are amoral

   ◦   Sex-for-sale frees buyer from indem-nification after transaction.

*"Making sex available as a commodity, something that is bought and sold subject to market forces, at a stoke give almost any salaried Western woman options for short-term, no-obligations companion-ship – if she travels abroad." (Belliveau, 2006, p. 85)*

*"I see nothing immoral about it. I regard it as a temporary love affair. He tells me what all the things I want to hear, and I guess in return I pay for everything – meals, accommodation, transport, tours – and buy him gifts. But that is because I have much more money than he does. It is mutually beneficial." – Jackie, a 38 year-old single woman from London (Martin, The Observer, Sunday, 23 July 2006)*

8.   Freedom from rules regarding "off-limits" practices at home; liberty to act on cultural curiosities and variety-seeking behavior, whilst avoiding social stigma

   ◦   Geographically distant destination countries are free from the stigma that would typically inhibit or preclude sex-for-sale practices (Chutikul, n.d.).
   ◦   Women tend to engage in more pro-miscuous behavior than they would at home, taking one or more different companions over a few days, paying for "romantic services," and prioritiz-ing male appearance and reputations over other typical mate selection cri-teria (Gorry, 1999).
   ◦   Women demonstrate strong prefer-ences towards dark skinned Caribbean men whom they describe as "manly," "exotic," "primitive," and "taboo." (Gorry, 1999)
   ◦   Women attribute their behaviors to the influences of the novel, exotic

for temporary sex-for-sale relationships is available and their indulgence will have minimal, short-term impact on how they are viewed by others. (Gorry, 1999)

9.   Mutual interest and reciprocated benefit
     ◦   Some native men actively pursue foreign female tourists

*"...in the Caribbean, female tourists can find male companionship options ranging from polished gigolos in resorts to freelancers almost everywhere" (Belliveau, 2006, p. 154).*

*While interviewed by Reuters at a dance club, "Joseph" -- a 22-year-old African local male -- attests to having slept with over 100 white women who are typically 30 years his senior:*

*"When I go into the clubs, those are the only women I look for now, I get to live like the rich mzungus (white people) who come here from rich countries, staying in the best hotels and just having my fun."*

*Interviewed for Reuters on the same evening and at the same club, "Bethan" -- a Western woman – admits:*

*"It's not love, obviously. I didn't come here looking for a husband. It's a social arrangement. I buy him a nice shirt and we go out for dinner. For as long as he stays with me he doesn't pay for anything, and I get what I want — a good time. How is that different from a man buying a young girl dinner?"*

The above reasons suggest that the rationale sustaining the evolution of female sex tourists is multifaceted. The reasons do show that some First World females view sex tourism as a way to minimize their power gaps with their males of that same world. Moreover, female sex tourism provides a means for females to achieve self-discovery and affirmation through foreign romances. It also provides for empowerment through the ability to manage those encounters by commodifying them.

Having cited perspectives from a diverse sample of key informants, these reasons also reveal divisions among females about whether female sex tourism should be associated with prostitution, deemed exploitive, evaluated as immoral, or even defended. These divisions are particularly significant in light of the various justifications on its behalf leveraged by citations on the history and scale of male sex tourism. Regardless of the reasons provided or the divisions they bring to light, the facts remain that female sex tourists are almost exclusively from the developed world (e.g., North America, Europe, Australia, and Japan) and their male companions are almost exclusively from the developing world (e.g., the Caribbean, Africa, South Asia, Southeast Asia) (See Table 2). These facts make way for considering how cultural values may be manifest in social exchange connecting the consumers and companions of female sex tourism.

As a social institution that has brought together parties from two very different worlds, female sex tourism provides an insightful vantage for understanding how consumers and companions have typically related to one another on asymmetric terms. While wealth is an important factor in setting the terms of this institution, other factors are at work as well. Beyond just "romance," the interaction between the sex tourist and her companion embodies service experience and, thus, "a social relation determined by both economic and cultural factors" (Fitchett, 2004, p. 298).

## Culture Matters

*No matter how hard man tries, it is impossible for him to divest himself of his own culture, for it has penetrated to the roots of his nervous system and determines how he perceives the world ... people cannot act or interact in any meaningful way except through the medium of culture (Hall, 1966, p.177).*

While there are myriad opinions about how to make sense of the general choices that people make, scholars have generally supported the view that culture matters (Bourdieu, 1984, Hall, 1976; Hofstede, 1980, 1997; Malinowski, 1939/1944; Meade, 1953; Schwartz, 1994; and others). Described as the "software of the mind" (Hofstede, 1997), culture provides good insight into understanding what people tend to value and how their practices reflect that tendency.

Why might culture be useful in helping understanding the female sex tourism phenomenon? First, culture is transmitted through various form of exchange and consumption (Appadurai, 1996; Appadurai, 1988; Fung, 2002). Hence, in the present research context, culture provides an insightful basis for understanding how female sex tourists transmit their interpretations and perceptions of their destinations countries and companions (see Table 1 and Table 2). Second, although wealth may enable females to tour the world, it does not programmatically dictate that females become sex tourists or seek out romantic companions in targeted destination countries. Culture, as a medium, can illuminate the meaning transmitted by female sex tourists through their commodification and consumption of foreign romance. Third, sex tourism has most commonly been associated with male tourists *and* masculine values. Yet, as more female sex tourists have joined the existing male cohort, questions ensue about whether these females are enacting masculine behaviors or opportunistically exploiting social inequalities that enable their consumption choices.

It is beyond the scope and purpose of this paper to apply culture taxonomically as a factor that exhaustively explains why First World females participate in sex tourism or seek out intercultural experiences with men from the developing world. Rather, the intention here is consider whether female sex tourism reflects any values rooted in national or societal culture. Here, the focus is on two dimensions of cultural values — masculin-

(1997). It should be noted, however, that masculine values are discussed in terms that include the perspective of scholars other than Hofstede. These perspectives are relevant to the consumption aspects of sex tourism.

## Consumption Reflecting Culture: 'Masculine' Values or Unveiled Feminine Values?

*They behave much the same as men do," says [Jeannette] Belliveau. "'I want to pay for a relationship, because I want you to go away at the end of it.' — Interview with Ann Marie McQueen, Edmonton Sun, 06 March 2007*

*Old white guys have always come for the younger girls and boys, preying on their poverty ... But these old women followed ... they never push the legal age limits, they seem happy just doing what is sneered at in their countries. — Store manager in Kenya in interview with Jeremy Clark Reuters, 26 November 2007*

Aside from the debate about what actually leads females to sex tourism, there is some inquiry about whether females are simply following the example of their male predecessors, instrumentally espousing masculine values towards tourism and sex, merely expressing their own consumption tastes, or some combination of these. This inquiry is itself multifaceted, given the diverse rationale cited above for the existence and expansion of female sex tourism. Prior to the advent of the Passenger Jet Age, very few females were able to participate in tourism, an activity dominated by, and hence, associated with First World males. With increasing wealth, mobility, and independence, more First World females have gradually established their presence and participation in tourism and other cultural institutions.

Only recently, female tourists have begun to create and narrate their own personal accounts of

ration (such as Jeanette Belliveau's *Romance on the Road* and Terry McMillan's *How Stella Got Her Groove Back*). Accordingly, many would-be female travelers, tourists, and romance tourists can now learn of these female accounts through memoirs, films, novels, and plays authored by the sentiments of their own First World sisters. The creation and consumption of these narratives illustrates a "for us by us" theme of empowerment not necessarily available to past generations.

Returning to the discussion of terminology, the distinctions between *romance tourism* and *sex tourism* may represent, at one level, a tension of semantics, and on another level, an earnest proclamation of seeing different kinds of values. Whether females are directly imitating the established behaviors of male sex tourists or initiating their own improvisations cannot be clearly determined at this time. Advocates of "romance tourism" may interpret the service encounter on as one where the female consumer feels valued, courted, and charmed by foreign companions. By contrast, those who contend that no distinctions exist between the terms may interpret the service encounter as one that is implicitly transactional, leveraged by the commodification of "romance" and the males who provide it for meals, gifts, or other non-cash consideration.

Argument about whether distinctions exist between the terms sex tourism and romance tourism reveals, in part, that consumption in this realm reflects underlying cultural values of the tourists. Are those females who choose to look abroad for specific international, intercultural, and interclass romantic experiences reflecting the masculine and individualistic values described by Hofstede (1997)? That is, are such female consumers utilizing this market context as an opportunity to harness independence, project power, reinforce "ego", and be catered to by erstwhile companions who compete to fulfill their tastes and preferences? Furthermore, are these females more tolerant of the social inequalities they observe and experience abroad versus those the witness in their home countries

(re: power distance)? That is to say, while they come from cultures that generally reject the idea of a fated "lot in life" (i.e., low power distance) are they not deriving benefits from a market that structurally and economically subordinates their companions abroad (i.e., high power distance)? Echoing the insights of Goldschmidt (1990), are social institutions like female sex tourism not protracting the already inequitable social equilibrium at work between the developed and developing worlds (i.e., high power distance)?

Depending on the social context, people tend to cherry-pick the masculine and feminine personality traits that are/have been/should be associated with an activity (Caldwell, Kleppe, & Henry, 2007). Yet, Solomon (2004) contends that contemporary women enact feminine and masculine gender roles in their social life. Of the latter, some scholars suggest that capitalist-based commodities arguably symbolize the traditional knowledge and worldviews that are grounded genealogically in masculine values (Moore, 1991; Stacey, 1994). Accordingly, it may be fair to declare that female sex tourists do espouse masculine cultural values (based on currently predominant views on what actually constitutes masculine values). The consumption of romance (re: feminine) as a commodity embodies the rationalized, asserted determination (re: masculine) of the economic value of other individuals (e.g., sex tourist determining what form and amount of consideration to give her companion). This commodification has empowered economically superior consumers who can exert their power (of purchase) over their subordinated, willing companions (re: power distance). Hence, female sex tourism, if perceived as an adjunct to the larger cohort of male sex tourism, arguably diminishes female values and "produces and reproduces the identity associated with male values" (Fung, 2002, p. 322). As alluded by Appadurai (1996, 1988) and Belk (1988), the culture of appropriating value and meaning to commodities (e.g., romance companions) enable consumers (i.e., female sex tourists) to fulfill and sustain their own aims and motivations (re: power distance; re: *Reasons for Becoming a Female Sex Tourist*).

Each era of females participating in sex tourism has increasingly traversed socially defined gender spaces (Ahuvia, 20005) —— international tourism (re: more masculine activity) and consumption (re: more feminine activity). Furthermore, this traversing of gender spaces also traverses cultural ones. As Chutikul (n.d.) and Omondi (2003) note, females from the developed world leave their home countries to experience romantic encounters, especially interracial ones, in order to escape social stigmas and judgments. Accordingly, female may make conscious choices to eschew domestic brothels or prostitutes, so that they can avoid any negative sanctions drawn by enacting cross-sex behavior (i.e., traditionally associated with males) (Ahuvia, 20005). These facts hint that the relationship oriented term *romance tourism* (re: feminine) may be a well-intentioned euphemism that might, by chance, elude the negative sanctions levied against the more transaction-geared term *sex tourism* (re: masculine).

As shown, female sex tourism has been justified *and* criticized on the basis that it signals "advancements" by females who do what males have done for generations. Female sex tourism has evolved in commodifying, segmenting, and targeting foreign romance for consumption. As a result, it draws inquiry about whether it bears any resemblances to prostitution, an institution with which male tourists (e.g., businesspersons traveling to Thailand) have been inextricably associated.

## Capturing Culture: Caveats and Constraints

*Hofstede's work became a dominant influence and set a fruitful agenda. There is perhaps no other contemporary framework in the general field of 'culture and business' that is so general, so broad, so alluring (Chapman, 1997, p. 18–19).*

Female sex tourism does manifest elements of culture at the level of consumption. Arguably, it also reflects and reproduces tenured cultural paradigms for the First World's engagement and consumption of the Third World. Yet, while culture certainly frames much of the climate surrounding female sex tourism, it cannot fully explain the roles or actions of sex tourists or romantic companions. At present, anthropologists and social scientists still debate what culture really means by definition, concept, and construct. Fueling all sides of the debate is a plethora of nuanced definitions and myriad manifestations of culture (Kroeber & Kluckhohn, 1952). These facts underscore the need to carefully (re)consider the actual utility of discussing Hofstede's cultural dimensions in relation to female sex tourism, or even tourism in general. Given their origins in the national contexts of multinational management, Hofstede's dimensions reflect interpretations of culture and cultural values that are not necessarily congruent with those of tourism. To his credit, Hofstede (2001) does acknowledge that extensive use of his cultural dimensions can have disadvantages, stating, "Some carry the concepts further than I consider wise. At times, my supporters worry me more than my critics" (p. 73). Hence, Hofstede's taxonomy and other related perspectives on culture (Hall, 1976; House et. al, 2004) may be better fit as tools for cross-cultural management research, but not as universal instruments to characterize all forms of cross-cultural engagement.

Unfortunately, the cultural research styled by Hofstede and others does not necessarily lend itself to capturing unique concepts of culture within non-Western societies (Lassiter, 2000). After all, Hofstede developed his definition and dimensions of national culture based on analysis of IBM employees representing just 40 countries, leading some scholars to question whether nations, developed or developing, actually have clearly identifiable cultures (McSweeney, 2002). Wallerstein (1990) is "skeptical that we can op-

that enables us to use it for statements that are more than trivial" (p. 34). Even with its characteristic dimensional and index approach, this approach to cultural research has still produced little knowledge about the cultural profiles of developing countries, particularly those sought out by international tourists. Furthermore, aside from the debate about what constitutes culture, Tayeb (2001) cautions that "by putting culture into neat, sometimes unconnected, little boxes we are in danger of losing sight of the big picture" (p. 93). Hence, this chapter focuses on how culture *can be* expressed through the commodification and consumption of romance. Moreover, it also considers how culture *can be* expressed through the commodification and sale of romance. As evidenced in this research, romantic commodification represents an exceptional context through which scholarship can reveal more knowledge about cross-cultural exchanges linking the developed and developing worlds. While nations may be "imagined communities" (Anderson, 1991), these two worlds and their distinctions are quite compelling.

## Implications for Stakeholders

Tourism provides an especially relevant context to understand enduring linkages between the developed and developing worlds. It also represents a significant pipeline and lifeline for the small, less diversified economies of developing countries. Thus, stakeholders in government and hospitality have keen interests in maintaining a steady, unobstructed flow of tourists and tourism revenues. In recent years, that flow has increased considerably thanks to greater financial and social mobility of European and American women.

From the empires of Egypt and Rome to the present day, the sex trade has thrived in social inequalities and facilitated an unseemly, but accepted comingling of society's powerful and marginalized classes. While this trade can provide benefits to its sellers, buyers, and intermediaries, it can impose

costs that, in present times, require more careful evaluation. For example, government agencies, medical professionals, and wives of male sex workers must be concerned about public health issues (e.g., sexually transmitted infections) (Bauer, 2014). Additionally, tourism officials, hospitality investors, and business managers risk becoming mired by marketing myopia. Diversification of market offerings is vital. Thus, these stakeholders should coordinate planning and efforts to protect their countries from becoming fettered as pigeon-holed, flavor-of-the-month, and narrowly diversified sex tourism destinations. Given that the market tends to provide solutions, history suggests that sex tourism may be here to stay. After all, sex tourism tends to *accentuate* disparities between sex workers and their first-world clients (McPhee, 2014). As government and hospitality leaders in Brazil and Kenya work to diminish their reputations as preferred sex tourism destinations, business scholars and tourism professionals should actively consider a timely review of sex tourism's sustainability, social costs, and impact on the "nation brand" (Anholt, 2006, 2009). Should it be maintained, promoted, or discouraged? Should it be formalized and taxed per the example of state-approved providers in Rome or the US State of Nevada? Should it be accompanied with a public health program (e.g., safer sex education, regular STI testing for sex workers)?

In the current era of globalization, these and other topics are particularly salient because they reflect the myriad connections that now bind people together across race, gender, class, and status.

## CONCLUSION AND DISCUSSION

Female sex tourism represents a global social institution and cultural phenomenon whose obscure existence has evolved over more than 150 years. As females have made advances in education, employment, and social mobility, so too have they made advances in tourism. Whether it embodies an independent sign of progress and/or an imitation of male sex tourism, female sex tourism has met a mix of justifications and criticisms. Separate and apart from this debate, the romance-for-sale market involved in female sex tourism seems to reproduce the historical social stratifications dividing the ever-connected First and Third worlds. While the institution may serve well-justified motivations of First World female tourists, it does effect the ongoing subordination of their companions from the Third World.

This chapter has contributed a meaningful foundation for understanding the evolution and commodification of foreign romance for consumption by female tourists. It has provided a thorough review of the rationale supporting the justifications for and criticisms of female sex tourism. The research presented here has also expanded current knowledge about how romance, sex, and tourism sustain a market that can be associated with and distinguished from prostitution. Having leveraged this point, the chapter also illustrates how the semantics of *romance tourism* versus *sex tourism* may reflect actual and euphemistic differences between female and male consumers.

Looking forward, future research should more investigate what factors enable or encourage females to participate in sex tourism. At present, sex tourists have been associated exclusively with First World origins. Clearly, differences in economic wealth set the basis for many demarcations between the developed and developing worlds. Wealth does financially enable First World females to travel and secure romantic companions in exchange for money, gifts, or meals; however, it does not programmatically predispose all females to commodify or consume foreign romance abroad. Perhaps, researchers should consider whether cultural orientation, personality, or other psychological factors play a role in determines whether females decide to become sex tourists or prefer certain destination countries. Concern-ing culture, however, care must be taken when

applying popular taxonomies of culture (Hall, 1976, Hofstede, 1980, 1997; Donthu & Yoo, 1998; Lewis, 2006; and others) to interpersonal, cross-cultural consumption. Aside from performing such applications at the correct level of analysis (e.g., individual, country), scholars must also heed the "big picture" admonitions of Tayeb (2001).

Future directions should also explore the debate about whether female sex tourists are espousing masculine values or unveiling historically obscured feminine values. The related inquiry posed here echoed Eckert and McConnell-Ginet (2003) who declare: "Gendered performances are available to everyone, but with them come constraints of who can perform which personae with impunity" (p. 10). Thus, further inquiry and exploration could be useful in understanding the evolution of perceptions about female identity, consumption, and community.

# REFERENCES

Ahuvia, A. C. (2005). Beyond extended self: Loved objects and consumers' role identity narratives. *The Journal of Consumer Research*, *32*(June), 171–184. doi:10.1086/429607

Ajiferuke, M., & Boddewyn, J. J. (1970). Culture and other explanatory variables in comparative management studies. *Academy of Management Journal*, *13*(2), 153–163. doi:10.2307/255102

Anholt, S. (2006). *Competitive identity: The new brand management for nations, cities, and regions*. Palgrave Macmillan. doi:10.1057/9780230627727

Anholt, S. (2009). *Places: Identity, image, and reputation*. Great Britain: Palgrave Macmillan. doi:10.1057/9780230251281

Appadurai, A. (1988). *The social life of things. Commodities in cultural perspective*. Cambridge: Cambridge University Press.

Appadurai, A. (1996). *Modernity al large: cultural dimensions of globalization* (Vol. 1). U of Minnesota Press.

Bauer, I. L. (2014). Romance tourism or female sex tourism? *Travel Medicine and Infectious Disease, 12*(1), 20–28. doi:10.1016/j.tmaid.2013.09.003 PMID:24332659

Belk, R. W. (1988). Possessions and the extended self. *The Journal of Consumer Research, 15*(September), 139–167. doi:10.1086/209154

Belliveau, J. (2006). *Romance on the road.* Baltimore: Beau Monde.

Bender, K., & Furman, R. (2004). The implications of sex tourism on men's social, psychological, and physical health. *Qualitative Report, 9*(2), 176–191.

Bishop, R., & Robinson, L. S. (1998). *Night market: Sexual cultures and the Thai economic miracle.* London, New York: Routledge.

Bonsu, S. K. (2009). Colonial images in global times: Consumer interpretations of Africa and Africans in advertising. *Consumption Markets & Culture, 12*(1), 1–25. doi:10.1080/10253860802560789

Chapman, M. (1997). Preface: Social anthropology, business studies, and cultural issues. *International Studies of Management & Organization, 26*(4), 3–29.

Chutikul, S. (n.d.) *Who are the clients: The exploiters?* http://www.cwa.tnet.co.th/Vol12-1&2/Saisuree.htm

CIA. (2009). *The world factbook.* Retrieved from http://www.cia.gov/cia/publications/factbook

Clark, J. (November 26, 2007). Older white women join Kenya's sex tourists. *Reuters.* Retrieved March 20, 2012 from http://www.reuters.com/articlePrint?articleId=USN2638979720071126

D'Andrade, R. G. (1984). Cultural meaning systems. In R. A. Shweder & R. A. LeVine (Eds.), *Cultural theory: Essays on mind, self, and emotion* (pp. 88–119). Cambridge: Cambridge University Press.

Dhaliwal, N. S. (2006). *Tourism.* Vintage Books.

Donthu, N., & Yoo, B. (1998). Cultural influences on service quality expectations. *Journal of Service Research, 1*(2), 178–186. doi:10.1177/109467059800100207

Enloe, C. (2002). *Maneuvers: the international politics of militarising women's lives.* Los Angeles: University of California Press.

Enloe, C. (2014). *Bananas, beaches and bases: Making feminist sense of international politics.* London: Pandora.

Fish, M. (1984). Controlling sex sales to tourists: Commenting on Graburn and Cohen. *Annals of Tourism Research, 11*(4), 615–617. doi:10.1016/0160-7383(84)90055-0

Fitchett, J. A. (2004). The fantasies, orders and roles of sadistic consumption: Game shows and the service encounter. *Consumption Markets & Culture, 7*(4), 285–306. doi:10.1080/1025386042000316298

Fung, A. (2002). Women's magazines: Construction of identities and cultural consumption in Hong Kong. *Consumption Markets & Culture, 5*(4), 321–336. doi:10.1080/1025386022000001460

Hall, E. T. (1966). *The hidden dimension: Man's use of space in public and private.* London: Bodley Head. Hall, E. T. (1976). *Beyond culture.* Garden City: Anchor Press/Doubleday.

Hannum, A. B. (2002). Sex tourism in Latin America. *ReVista: Harvard Review of Latin America.* Winter. Retrieved March 25, 2014 from http://revista.drclas.harvard.edu/book/sex-tourism-latin-america

Hofstede, G. (1980). *Culture's consequences: International differences in work-related values.* Newbury Park: Sage Publications.

Hofstede, G. (1997). *Culture and organizations: Software of the mind.* New York: The McGraw Hill Companies, Inc.

Hofstede, G. (2001). *Culture's consequences: Comparing values, behaviors, institutions and organizations across nations* (2nd ed.). Thousand Oaks, CA: Sage.

Hofstede, G. 2009. *Geert Hofstede Cultural Dimensions.* Retrieved July 14, 2009 from http://www.geert-hofstede.com/hofstede_dimensions.php

Jeffreys, S. (1998). Child versus adult prostitution: A false distinction. In S. Jeffreys (Ed.), *Fight against child sex tourism: Participants' speeches and contributions* (pp. 65–71). Brussels: European Commission.

Lassiter, J. E. (2000). African culture and personality: Bad social science, effective social activism, or a call to reinvent ethnology. *African Studies Quarterly, 3*(3), 1–20.

Malinowski, B. (1939/1944). The functional theory. In *A scientific theory of culture and other essays.* Chapel Hill, NC: University of North Carolina Press.

Mangaliso, M. P. (2001). Building competitive advantage from Ubuntu: Management lessons from South Africa. *The Academy of Management Executive, 15*(3), 23–33. doi:10.5465/AME.2001.5229453

Martin, L. (July 23, 2006). Sex, sand, and sugar mummies in a Caribbean beach fantasy. *The Guardian.* Retrieved August 11, 2013 from http://www.theguardian.com/travel/2006/jul/23/jamaica.theatre.theobserver

McCombs, E. (1988). Ticket to ride. *BUST,* April/May, 70-73.

McCracken, G. (1988). *Culture and consumption: New approaches to the symbolic character of consumer goods and activities.* Indianapolis, IN: University Press.

McPhee, D. (2014). Sex offending and sex tourism: Problems, policy and challenges. *Responding to Sexual Offending: Perceptions, Risk Management and Public Protection,* 93.

Mcsweeney, B. (2002). Hofstede's model of national cultural differences and their consequences: A triumph of faith – a failure of analysis. *Human Relations, 55*(1), 89–118. doi:10.1177/0018726702055001602

Mead, M. (1953). *Cultural patterns and technical change.* New York, NY: UNESCO.

Miller, J. (2011). Beach boys or sexually exploited children? Competing narratives of sex tourism and their impact on young men in Sri Lanka's informal tourist economy. *Crime, Law, and Social Change, 56*(5), 485–508. doi:10.1007/s10611-011-9330-5

Nagel, J. (2003). *Race, ethnicity, and sexuality: Intimate intersections, forbidden frontiers.* New York: Oxford University Press.

O'Connell Davidson, J., & Sanchez Taylor, J. (1999). Fantasy islands: Exploring the demand for sex tourism. *Sun, sex, and gold: Tourism and sex work in the Caribbean,* 37-54.

Omondi, R. K. (2003). Gender and the political economy of sex tourism in Kenya's coastal resorts. Paper presented at International Symposium/Doctorial Course on Feminist Perspective on Global Economic and Political Systems and Women's Struggle for Global Justice, September 24-26 2003, in Tromso, Norway.

Phillip, J. L. (1999). Tourist-oriented prostitution in Barbados: The case of the beach boy and the white female tourist. In K. Kempadoo (Ed.), *Sun, sex and gold – Tourism and sex work in the Caribbean* (pp. 183–200). Lanham, MD: Rowman and Littlefield.

Pruitt, D., & La Font, S. (1995). For love and money: Romance tourism in Jamaica. *Annals of Tourism Research*, *22*(2), 419–440. doi:10.1016/0160-7383(94)00084-0

Richter, L. K. (1998). Exploring the political role of gender in tourism research. In W. F. Theobald (Ed.), *Global tourism in the next decade*. Oxford, Woburn: Butterworth Heinemann.

Ryan, C., & Hall, C. M. (2001). *Sex tourism: Marginal people and liminalities*. London, New York: Routledge.

Schwartz, S. H. (1992). In M. P. Zanna (Ed.), *Universals in the content and structure of values: Theoretical advances and empirical tests in 20 countries* (pp. 1–65). Advances in Experimental Social Psychology San Diego: Academic Press, Inc.

Seidl, U. (2012). *Paradies: Liebe* [Paradise: Love]. Austria: Ulrich Seidl Filmproduktion.

Sherzer, D. (1996). Race matters and matters of race: Interracial relationships in colonial and postcolonial films. *Cinema, Colonialism, Postcolonialism: Perspectives from the French and Francophone World*, 229-248.

Solomon, M. (2004). *Consumer behavior: Buying, having and being* (6th ed.). Upper Saddle River, NJ: Prentice-Hall.

Tate, S. (2011). Heading South: Love/Sex, necropolitics, and decolonial romance. *Small Axe*, *15*(2), 43–58. doi:10.1215/07990537-1334230

Tayeb, M. (2001). Conducting research across cultures: Overcoming drawbacks and obstacles. *International Journal of Cross Cultural Management*, *1*(1), 91–108. doi:10.1177/147059580111009

Taylor, J. S. (2001). Dollars are a girl's best friend? Female tourists' sexual behaviour in the Caribbean. *Sociology*, *35*(3), 749–764. doi:10.1177/S0038038501000384

Thomas, M. (2000). Exploring the contexts and meanings of women's experiences of sexual intercourse on holiday. In Tourism and sex: Culture, commerce and coercion (pp. 45-66). New York: Pinter.

United Nations. (2000). *World marriage patterns 2000*. Retrieved February 26, 2012 from http://www.un.org/esa/population/publications/world-marriage/worldmarriagepatterns2000.pdf

Veblen, T. (1902). *The theory of the leisure class: An economic study of institutions*. New York: Macmillan.

Wallerstein, I. (1990). Culture as the ideological battleground of the modern world-system. *Theory, Culture & Society*, *7*(2-3), 31–55. doi:10.1177/026327690007002003

Weichselbaumer, D. (2012). Sex, romance and the carnivalesque between female tourists and Caribbean men. *Tourism Management*, *33*(5), 1220–1229. doi:10.1016/j.tourman.2011.11.009

## KEY TERMS AND DEFINITIONS

**Commodification:** A process of transforming a non-commercial item (e.g., idea, person) into a saleable or marketable commodity (e.g., good, service).

**Consideration:** In the context of female sex tourism, any form of compensation, remuneration, or reward to initiate or sustain a romantic courtship.

It may take various forms, such as meals, drinks, clothing, electronics, or plane tickets.

**Culture:** A set of values and principles, or collective programming, which characterizes a group of people and distinguishes it from another group of people.

**Flows/Scapes:** Means by which intercultural influences are transmitted within a society and between societies around the world. Flows may involve finance, media, movement of people, finance, etc.

**Prostitution:** The illegal practice of providing sexual relations for money.

**Romance Tourism:** A term that typically refers to female sex tourism rather than male sex tourism.

**Sex Tourism:** A vacation experience where consumers travel to foreign destinations with the expectation that part or all of their vacation will involve paying for (e.g., money, gifts) a sexual experience with a local resident.

# Chapter 21
# Global Perspective in Tourism Development:
## Positioning Malaysia as a Culinary Destination

**Quee-Ling Leong**
*Universiti Putra Malaysia, Malaysia*

**Shahrim Karim**
*Universiti Putra Malaysia, Malaysia*

## ABSTRACT

*Malaysia offers a rich potpourri of delicious cuisines from diverse ethnicity. However, not much attention given to promote Malaysian food and the food seems to be ignored in the tourism industry. Furthermore, the concept of utilizing Malaysian food as a marketing means is tenuous. In this chapter, the image dimensions of Malaysian food and the effect of food images on tourists' satisfaction are discussed. Additionally, the influence of socio-demographic factors on tourists' perceived image is deliberated. Univariate and multivariate statistics are used to describe the obtained findings. The results of the study will significantly fill in the gap in the literature about Malaysian food's image and the potential of Malaysia being promoted as a food destination. Additionally, the results would indisputably provide better insight to the tourism and hospitality industry on the perceptions of international tourists towards Malaysian food and Malaysia as a food tourism destination.*

## INTRODUCTION

The Malay Peninsula (now Peninsula Malaysia) was known as the Golden Khersonese to the ancient Greeks (Hutton, 2005) and the land was inhabited by the Malays who originally lived along the coasts and the rivers (Ryan, 1976). Some came during the glorious Melaka Sultanate era while others who settled down in the Malay Peninsula were the *Bugis* from the Celebes and the *Minangkabau* from Sumatra (Ryan, 1976). Soon after, in 1963, the peninsula coalesced with Sabah and Sarawak

DOI: 10.4018/978-1-4666-8606-9.ch021

or the Borneo States to form Federation of Malaysia (National Institute of Public Administration [INTAN], 2003; Hutton, 2005).

As time faded changes in Malaya's social structure occurred; from singular to a plural society. Chinese immigrants were brought into the flourishing land via the Straits Settlements to work in the tin mines (Ryan, 1976; INTAN, 2003). Eventually, Indian immigrants joined the labor force for the then booming rubber plantation activities (Ryan, 1976; INTAN, 2003). Intermarriage took place between the immigrants and the locals. The intermarriage between the Chinese immigrants and the local Malay women enriched the social structure with another group of ethnicity which is the *Peranakan* community or the Straits Chinese; where males are called *Baba* and females are *Nyonya* (Ryan, 1976). Since the migration of the Chinese and Indians, the cultural and social structure of the country had enormously altered as well as the eating habits (Hutton, 2005). People, regardless of ethnicity had cross-culturally borrowed the cooking styles of others and this has led to the creation of a number of distinctive Malaysian dishes (Hutton, 2005). Since then, assimilation of cultures transpired and Malaysia is seen as an exciting and rich potpourri that offers variety of cuisines from different ethnics.

Gastronomy tourism, culinary tourism and food tourism are tourism activities related to food and cuisines in a destination. With the advancement of technology and global networking, people or even culture travelled beyond boundaries. Restaurants selling ethnic cuisines from other countries can be easily found. Despite the convenience of enjoying different ethnic food in a person's local setting, today's travelers' would seek to experience ethnic cuisine in the original setting of the cuisine. At potential tourist destinations, food is usually presented as an attraction by strategizing the promotion of different ethnic food of unfamiliar people and the culture of a country (Cohen & Avieli, 2004).

When travelling across Malaysia, it is not surprising to find regional styles of cuisine. The northern Malaysian states such as Perlis, Kedah and Kelantan have considerable influences from Thailand as these states are situated at the border of the neighbor country (Hutton, 2005). Meanwhile, Terengganu and Pahang which share the border with Kelantan also portray Thai influences in their cuisine (Hutton, 2005). *Nasi ulam* and *Nasi Kerabu* are popular dishes in Kelantan. *Nasi kerabu* is cooked using the juice of butterfly pea flower that gives a natural bright indigo blue color and a tinge of sweet-scented flower aroma to the rice. Meanwhile *Nasi ulam* (rice salad with fresh herbs) is commonly cooked with *pandanus* leaves, galangal, lemongrass and kaffir lime leaves (Hutton, 2005). Both dishes are usually served with a combination of fresh herbs such as cilantro, dill, fennel leaves, parsley, sprig mint leaves, lemon balm leaves, wild ginger bud, and fresh ginger (Hutton, 2005); however the combination of herbs is subject to own preference. Not forgetting the accompanying condiments which is a must to the dishes are *sambal belacan* (chili shrimp paste) and *budu* (fermented fish sauce).

In the state of Pahang, fresh and luscious seafood are definite items to savor and being abundance in seafood, the state is also popular for its salted fish especially in the capital; Kuantan (Hutton, 2005). Traditional dishes such as *Puding Raja* (king's pudding) and *Ayam Golek* (rolling chicken) are famous in royal weddings in Pahang (Saw, 2009). At times, these dishes are also popular among the masses in festive celebrations. Alternatively, bean sprouts is to be boasted in Perak due to its minerals wealth in the underground water especially in Buntong region that produces big, fat and juicy bean sprouts (Saw, 2009). Ipoh *Nga Choi Kai* or Ipoh bean sprout chicken that is famous in Perak is well-liked among Malaysians.

Whereas in Selangor and Kuala Lumpur (the capital of Malaysia), abundance of supreme restaurants are available to cater to individual's needs.

However hawker or food stalls that do a boisterous trade selling food of local favorites like *Bak Kut Teh* (herbal meat soup) and *Hokkien Mee* (Hokkien noodles) should not be overlooked (Saw, 2009). Further to the south of Peninsula Malaysia, such as Negeri Sembilan is famous for its *Rendang Rembau* or *Rendang Minangkabau* and *Lemang* (bamboo glutinous rice roll) (Saw, 2009). In addition to being popular in Negeri Sembilan, these dishes are definite dishes served during *Hari Raya Aidilfitri* celebration among the Muslims (Saw, 2009). The food in Negeri Sembilan is strongly influenced by the *Minangkabau* from West Sumatra which was reflected in the history in which migration occurred in the past from Indonesia to this promising land (Hutton, 2005). On the other hand, Johor which is at the end of southern Peninsula Malaysia carries the influence of Javanese cuisine (Hutton, 2005). Dishes that are famous in Johor are *Laksa* Johor and *Nasi Beriyani Gam*. *Laksa* Johor is a unique noodle dish and it differs from other types of *Laksa* by having coconut milk in the dish (Saw, 2009).

Melaka and Penang, on the contrary have a similar influence which is the *Peranakan* community. The term *Peranakan* was described as "referring to the Chinese who settled in Southeast Asia up till the late 19th century, who married the local Malays, and practiced a localized way of life" (Khor, 2006; p. 4). However, being geographically separated, the cuisines of both states demonstrate some different qualities resulted from regional and past colonial influence (Khor, 2006). The common ingredients in the *Peranakan* cuisine are spices, edible roots, coconut cream, a variety of local herbs and chilies (Khor, 2006). However, the *Peranakans* in Penang has incorporated Thai influences in their culinary practices such as the love for spicy and sour food; and hence contributing to a much more diverse food choice in Penang (Hutton, 2005; Khor 2006).

Despite being the earliest *Peranakan* settlement in the west coast of Peninsula Malaysia, Melaka portrays not only the *Peranakan* influence but also the Portuguese and Dutch as the land was under Portuguese and Dutch colonial in 1511 and 1641 respectively (INTAN, 2003; Khor, 2006). The cuisine in Melaka contains typical Chinese ingredients such as soy sauce, tofu and dried mushrooms but with a touch of Malay herbs and spices. Given that the *Peranakans* are non-Muslims, pork dishes cooked in Malay style such as *Babi Chin* (stewed pork belly with spices) is among the famous dishes to the *Babas* and *Nyonyas*. In addition, the *Peranakan* is also famous with their mouth-watering and eye-catching sweetmeats and cakes. A few example of the delicious *Peranakan* cakes and desserts are *Kow Chan Kuih* (nine layer cake), *Kuih Kosui* (steamed rice puddings), *Rempah Udang* (spiced glutinous rice rolls), *Huat Kuih* (sweet rice cake), *Bubur Cha-Cha* (sweet potato and taro medley in a light coconut sauce), and *Bee Koh Moy* (black glutinous rice broth). Meanwhile, popular Eurasian dishes are such as Devil's Curry which is an altered version of Goanese *Vindaloo* in which the main ingredients are chilies, spices and vinegar (Hutton, 2005).

On the other side of the coin, in the Borneo states of Malaysia (Sabah and Sarawak), fresh and succulent seafood is easily accessible with low prices as both of the states are in nature located along the South China Sea. One of the favorites among the locals in Sarawak is *Bubur Pedas* (spicy porridge) which is cooked using spices, turmeric, lemon grass, galangal, chilies, ginger, coconut milk and shallots (Saw, 2009). Another signature dish of Sarawak is *Kolok Mee*, which is commonly found in the state. The dish is made of egg noodle which is served in light sauce with shredded beef. Fried noodles is a common dish to Malaysians, however *Mee Goreng* Tuaran (Tuaran fried noodles) is a special fried noodles that is named after one of the district in Sabah. Egg yolk and flour are the essence that contributes to the noodles texture and aroma when fried.

Malaysian cuisine can be describe as a kaleidoscope of appetizing tastes, interesting colors that exist in different forms and textures which stimulates and delights the palate. In addition to being attractive and enticing, Malaysian food is more than satisfying hunger but also contains nutritional and medicinal values according to traditional beliefs (McArthur, 1962; Wilson 1970 as cited in Manderson, 1981). Generally, Malaysians are not restricted to cultural food except for several food that are constrained by religious taboos such as pork for the Muslims, beef for Hindus and Buddhists and any kind of meat for Vegetarianism (Manderson, 1981). An additional restriction to the Muslims is the way food is sourced and prepared; especially meat products are of main concern proviso the slaughtering procedures adhere to the halal rules and regulations (Riaz & Chaudry, 2004)

Traditional food beliefs in Malaysia, regardless of ethnicity, categorized food in hot and cold properties which are believed to have effect on human's body (Manderson, 1981). Ingredients used in Malaysian cooking especially herbs and spices are food categorized as having 'hot' properties. Food with 'hot' properties is best to consume especially during rainy and cold weather to counter flu, flatulence and colds; for example ginger, lemongrass, chilies, pepper, galangal and turmeric. In contrast, food with 'cold' properties such as spinach, papaya, mangoesteen and cucumber is generally used to reduce body heat during hot and sunny weather (Manderson, 1981).

In addition to the traditional food beliefs that formed today's culinary practices in Malaysia, food-related cultures and events also play an important role in shaping Malaysian gastronomic experience (Jalis, Zahari, Izzat & Othman, 2009). Festivals or religious celebrations are the connotations of food-related cultures and events in Malaysia; for example *Hari Raya Aidilfitri*, Chinese New Year, *Deepavali*, *Hari Gawai* and Mid-Autumn festival are significant events in Malaysia in which arrays of delicious food in conjunction with the celebrations are served for feast. Being blessed with cultural and culinary diversity, Malaysia will

surely serve as a food paradise to cater for food lovers with a tinge of fusion taste.

Ryan (1997) claimed that food exploration in destinations is considered as one of the most pleasurable activity to be undertaken. Malaysia, a country built on multiculturalism has plenty to offer and Malaysian food or gastronomy was claimed to be the most pertinent product in the tourism market (Jalis et al., 2009). Yet, there are a few key issues related to food in the tourism industry remain unanswered or perplexing. The issues are: do demographic factors have influence on a tourist's perceived image of Malaysian food?; what are the core characteristics that define and describe Malaysian food?; are the tourists satisfied with Malaysian food?; what is the outcome of tourist's satisfaction level? Hence, this study aimed to uncover the image dimensions of Malaysian food and examine the effect of food images on tourists' satisfaction. Additionally, the influence of socio-demographic factors on tourists' perceived image were also studied. The research objectives of this study are as follows:

- To investigate the influence of tourists' demographic factors on their perceived image towards Malaysian food
- To uncover the underlying factors of Malaysian food image
- To determine the relationship between tourists' perceived image and tourists' satisfaction towards Malaysian food

## LITERATURE REVIEW

Malaysia is built on diversity which comprises *Bumiputera* (Malay constitutes 50% and the aborigines are 12%), Chinese (23%), Indians (7%), and 1% of several other ethnicities with relatively small population in the country (Department of Statistics Malaysia, 2013). Every ethnicity inherits norms, culture, mother language and not forgetting culinary heritage from own ancestors which is still being practices up till today. Due to time factor, the ethnics began to assimilate among themselves to form a unique Malaysian culture – 'multiculturalism'. This is also true to the distinctive cuisine of Malaysia where Hutton (2005) described Malaysian cuisine as "Asia's greatest cuisines meet and mingle" (p. 5). Cultures in Malaysia have played an important role in forming and shaping the dishes which are apparently accepted by people from all walks of life in the country. Culinary practices had gradually changed in due course of time and respect to each other cultural and religious sensitivity. People started to incorporate other culture's culinary practices into their own. For instance, the usage of Malay and Indian spices in Chinese food and the creation of halal version of Chinese food that is consumable to all races. This had significantly contributed to the variety of distinct cuisine in Malaysia.

Various festivals are celebrated throughout the year; each of the festival is related to the unique and diverse cultures and traditions in Malaysia. Traditional cuisine and gracious hospitality are the strength and positive encounter that Malaysians possessed. Hand in hand, mouth-watering cuisine and warmth hospitality will definitely produce a positive image to tourists. These strengths should be capitalized as a source suggesting images that can portray the true Malaysia. It has been generally accepted that image plays an imperative role in influencing an individual's perceived image, choice of destination, satisfaction and behavioral intention (Chon, 1991; Bigné, Sánchez & Sánchez, 2001; Echtner & Ritchie, 1993; Gallarza, Saura & García, 2002; Lee, Lee & Lee, 2005). Therefore, to facilitate a memorable food experience for tourists, a well-bound set of characteristics reflecting precise Malaysian food image should be projected to attract tourists. Images that meet tourists expectation will definitely satisfy them and in turn repeat visitation and the likelihood of recommendation to friends and family will

increase (Chen & Tsai, 2007; Lee, Yoon, & Lee, 2007; González, Comesaña, & Brea, 2007).

Local food is part of a destination's intangible heritage and through consumption of local food, tourists are able to gain an authentic cultural experience (Okumus, Okumus & McKercher, 2007). Moreover, tasting novel food was claimed to be an exciting activity that can induce excitement, curiosity and expectation in individuals (Rust & Oliver, 2000). However, the process of food selection for consumption is a multifaceted function that comprised of sensory attributes and non-sensory attributes which includes food expectations, price, ethical and taboo concerns, nutritional values and mood (Shepherd, 1989; Vickers, 1993; Rogers, 1996; Rozin, 1996, McFarlane & Pliner, 1997; Prescott, Young, O'Neill, Yau & Stevens, 2002).

Hunt (1975), among the pioneers in destination image research, concluded that image is a significant factor in a destination's success as the perceived image held by potential visitors about a destination may have impact upon the feasibility of that place as an attraction to tourists. Since then, there was a wide agreement among the tourism researchers and the conclusion that image was critical to a destination's success was strengthened. Echtner and Ritchie (1993) had further examined the concept of destination image and suggested a conceptual framework that consists of three continuums: attribute-holistic; functional-psychological; and common-unique axes. On the contrary, Gartner (1993, 1996) contributed to the destination image literature by illustrated that the images of a destination are developed by three interrelated components which are cognitive, affective and conative. Alternatively, Gallarza et al. (2002) proposed a model based on four features: complex, multiple, relativistic, and dynamic. While the existing literature has conceptualized the dimensions of destination image extensively, a gap was identified – a lack of understanding on the food image dimensions particularly from the Malaysian food perspective. Consequently, this research aimed at determining the dimensions of Malaysian food image and examining the effect of food images on tourists' satisfaction and revisit intention.

Despite the fact that food disbursement of an average tourist covered approximately 34% of their overall expenditures (Meler & Cerović, 2003), food was viewed as merely an element of an entire destination image and research on food image has been ignored (Scarpato, 2002; Quan & Wang, 2004). Additionally, Hjalager and Corigliano (2000) argued that research on relationship between food image and a tourist destination was incomplete and nebulous. Correspondingly, Selwood (2003) said that "food is very much overlooked and unsung component of the tourism literature" (p. 178), although cuisine is increasingly having the potential to enhance a destination's image, satisfaction and repeat visitation (Kivela & Crotts, 2006; Henderson, 2009). Furthermore, food was claimed to be an influential tool for differentiation and imparting impact on tourists' emotion (Henderson, 2009).

Malaysia is renowned for its natural blessings such as beaches, forests, islands and highlands. In addition, PETRONAS Twin Towers and Kuala Lumpur Tower are famous symbols of Malaysia's skyscrapers which are located in the country's capital. Although a variety of delicious food is being offered in Malaysia, local food is deficient of serious promotional efforts and image projection. The image association of Malaysia as a culinary destination is unclear and this has led to confusion and ambiguity among tourists (Anonymous, 2009).

To date, very few studies have conceptually and empirically investigated this relatively new concept of food image in Malaysia. Therefore, to address this problem, this study aimed at uncovering the image dimensions of Malaysian food, tourist's satisfaction and revisit intention. In addition, the influence of demographic factors on tourist's perceived image was also inspected. This study differs from previous studies by looking from the

perspective of functional, symbolic and experiential values association used by scholars in the area of products, destinations and wineries marketing (Park, Jaworski & MacInnis, 1986; Keller, 1993; Gnoth, 2002; Hankinson, 2004; Orth & Marchi, 2007). Functional image is the product-related features or characteristics; meanwhile symbolic image is linked to the emotional values that could satisfy a person's self-expression needs. On the other hand, experiential image is associated with the feelings of using a product or service; for example sensory pleasure resulted from food tasting experience (Keller, 1993; Bhat & Reddy, 1998).

## The Relationship between Food, Wine, and Tourism

Various studies were carried out in the area of food, wine and tourism in the past. Scholars have been emphasizing the significant link between these industries (food, wine and tourism) in a way to sustain future tourism activities in destinations as nature-based destinations will be uncompetitive when the nature conservation began to deplete (Kivela & Crotts, 2006). In addition, Gross and Brown (2008) argued that food and wine can be very influential on feelings of involvement and place connection. Studies conducted on food, wine and tourism are summarized in Table 1.

Past studies have researched on the concepts of tourist behavior and tourist satisfaction to assist in the explanation of the influence of destination's food culture on tourists' satisfaction and tourists' revisit intention. However, these studies were focusing on tourists' general experience of physical attachment to a destination's food culture and the influence of tourists' experience on their behavioral intention. The analysis of the literature revealed that although studies on gastronomy and tourism are increasing, previous studies have limitations in uncovering the dimensions of food image and the effect of food images on tourists' satisfaction. To be a successful tourist destina-tion, image plays an important role (Bigné, et al.

2001; Chen & Tsai, 2007); therefore the image of a destination's gastronomy is hypothesized as an essential factor to promise the success of the food tourism market.

## Destination Image

Destination image is gaining attention from destination marketers and image was claimed to be a focus in destination research because image was believed to have impact on a person's behavior (Bigne et al., 2001; Chen & Tsai, 2007) and the levels of satisfaction (Chon, 1992; Chen & Tsai, 2007). Destination image was argued to be the subset of a general image dimension (Echtner & Ritchie, 2003). From the psychological perspective, image consign a visual illustration; meanwhile from the marketing perspective, image composed of attributes that underlie it and image is believed to be interrelated with consumer behavior (Jenkins, 1999).

Gartner (1993) described destination image as a combination of cognitive, affective, and conative components which are hierarchically interrelated. Cognitive constituent is related to attributes of objects; affective component is linked with individual's motivations; and conative element is an action element which is associated with behavior (Gartner, 1993). On the other hand, Echtner and Ritchie (1993; 2003) exemplified that destination image comprised of three dimensions: functional-psychological, common-unique and attributes-holistic dimensions. Functional characteristics depict tangible aspects while the psychological characteristics describe the intangible aspects of a destination. Additionally, image can ranged from common traits to unique traits to illustrate a destination; and destination image also encompassed perceptions that span from individual attributes to a holistic impression of the destination (Echtner & Ritchie, 2003). The most prominent definition on destination image was suggested by Crompton (1979), who defined destination image as "the sum of beliefs, ideas and impressions that a person has of a destination" (p. 18).

The aptitude of image as a powerful marketing tool has been agreed upon by past scholars. However, by judging or examining the superficial changes of image upon consumer behavior and satisfaction level is not sufficient to understand the consumer market. Brokaw (1990) claimed that it is crucial for marketers to understand the factors that manipulate an image before the image can be utilized to influence consumer behavior. Correspondingly, Goodall (1990) affirmed that considering the influential factors on image would aid in identifying and matching the right image for the right target market.

Studies on destination image were criticized due to lacking of conceptual framework (Fakeye & Crompton, 1991; Echtner & Ritchie, 1993; Gartner, 1996). Nevertheless, Gallarza et al. (2002) commented that among the studies on destination image, Baloglu and McCleary (1999) has contributed significantly in the literature with a more inclusive conceptual model for the understanding of tourism destination image.

Baloglu and McCleary (1999) illustrated that destination image is influenced by three main determinants although without actual or prior visitation experience. The determinants are tourism motivations, socio-demographic factors and information sources; where motivations and socio-demographic factors represent consumer characteristics or personal factors while information sources embody the stimulus variables.

Gender, age, education, income, occupation and marital status are the socio-demographic factors included in most destination selection studies, in which these factors were assumed to have influence on perceptions of objects, products and destinations (Sheth, 1983; Friedmann & Lessig, 1986; Woodside & Lysonski, 1989; Stabler, 1990; Um & Crompton, 1990). Among the socio-demographic factors, age and education emerged to be the main determinants of image (Baloglu & McCleary, 1999).

*Table 1. Summary of past studies on food, wine and tourism*

| Authors | Research Aim | Results |
|---|---|---|
| Telfer & Wall (1996) | The purpose of the study was to investigate the connection between the local food sectors and the tourism industry by using a case study of Lombok Island, Indonesia. | Findings showed that the tourism industry and local food sectors were collaborating well and special programs were designed to cater for training and anticipated to increase employment of local people. |
| Hjalager & Corigliano (2000) | The study compared the food culture qualities and images of food between Denmark and Italy. | Local food produce is a major economic activity in Denmark and this had compromised the country's image as a food destination. Contrary, the policies and traditions in Italy that prefer the quality of freshness had permitted the consumers to experience the gastronomic culture comprehensively as compared to Denmark. The paper suggested further enhancement of the food heritage especially in Denmark should be considered in addition to probable changes in food policies. |
| Au & Law (2002) | The study examined the potential of using rough set theory into mixed data relationship modelling in the Hong Kong dining market. | A model of dining information technology was developed using a rough set theory and important information on travelers spending patterns was constructed. |
| Meler & Cerović (2003) | The study was about food marketing in the function of tourist product development in the Republic of Croatia. | The authors proposed solutions in the field of food marketing that would be in the function of tourist product development. |
| Cohen & Avieli (2004) | The purpose of the study was to discuss local food as an attraction as well as a factor of impediment to a destination in tourist market. However, the authors focused more on food as an impediment in tourism. | The authors discussed the role and meaning of food in tourism from the sociological perspective. The article included a discussion of the various food limitation faced by Western tourists in Third World countries such as cleanliness and health. |
| Hwang, van Westering & Chen (2004) | The aim of the study was to understand the diverse ways in which gastronomy and heritage are related and how this specifically applies to tourism in the city of Tainan and their traditional snack food. | The findings revealed four issues which were the concept on traditional food, the modifications in the method of food productions, the role of traditional food within society, and historical inheritance through mass media promotion. |
| Quan & Wang (2004) | The study aimed at providing a conceptual framework that explains the multiple components that contribute to tourists' experience in a destination. | A structural equation model was developed to explain different aspects of travelers' food experience. In addition, the relationship between food consumption and tourist experience was also examined. Managerial implications were discussed and recommendations for future research were provided. |
| Getz & Brown (2006) | The study covered wine-related travel habits and preferences of wine consumers. | The findings divulged the core wine-related characteristics, in relationship to general destination appeal and cultural products. |
| Ryu & Jang (2006) | The main purpose of the study was to examine the validity of a modified version of the theory of reasoned action and to predict tourist behavioral intentions. | The authors' proposed model of modified theory of reasoned action was found to have strong predictive ability for tourist intentions to experience local cuisine. |
| Kivela & Crotts (2006) | The purpose of the study was to determine the influence of gastronomy on tourists' experience at a destination. | The authors affirmed that motivation to travel for gastronomy reasons was a valid construct. The results also revealed that gastronomy was crucial in influencing the way tourists experience a destination and indicated that some tourists would return to the same destination to savor its gastronomy products. |
| Fox (2007) | The study aspired to explore a new, exciting gastronomic identity of Croatian tourist destinations | The author outlined approaches applicable to the reinvention of gastronomic identity of Croatian tourist destinations. |

*continued on following page*

*Table 1. Continued*

| Authors | Research Aim | Results |
|---|---|---|
| Okumus et al. (2007) | The study's aim was to compare and contrast the use of food in the marketing of Hong Kong and Turkey. | A case study approach using content analysis was adopted. The authors found that when using food in destination marketing, expertise and knowledge are essential not only in marketing destinations but also in local and international cuisines as well as in socio-cultural characteristics of potential tourists. |
| Sparks (2007) | The study aimed to investigate the potential wine tourists' intentions to take a wine-based vacation. | Structural equation modelling was employed to test the developed model based on Theory Planned Behavior (TPB) to predict tourist intentions. The findings revealed that the model based on TPB have relatively good predictive validity of tourists' intention to visit wine-based destinations. |
| Tikkanen (2007) | The purpose of the study was to explore the sectors of food tourism in Finland by using Maslow's hierarchy of needs in the classification. | The findings introduced five sectors of food tourism where the needs and motivations are linked with Maslow's hierarchy of needs. |
| Galloway, Mitchell, Getz, Crouch & Ong (2008) | This study aim to examine the predictive ability of the personality variable in predicting wine tourists' attitudes and behaviors | The results revealed that the personality variable of sensation seeking was found to be significant in predicting the differences in various attitudes and behaviors of wine tourists by controlling the demographic variable. |
| Henderson (2009) | The purpose of the study was to review the contribution of food to tourism. The importance of food tourism and its critical success factors were also discussed. | The findings revealed that food plays a primary or supporting role in destination has good prospects and is already practiced widely. Additionally food was found to be a common theme in marketing by businesses and destination authorities. |
| Jalis et al. (2009) | This study investigated the acceptance of western tourists towards Malaysian gastronomy products | The results revealed that Malaysia was perceived as having great choices of food, snacks and beverages of good tastes besides encompasses a unique food culture and identity. |
| Kim, Eves & Scarles (2009) | The study examines the factors influencing consumption of local food and beverages in destinations. | A conceptual model of local food consumption at a holiday destination was proposed. The model comprised of motivational factors, demographic factors and physiological factors that were claimed by the authors have influence on local food consumption. |
| de la Barre & Brouder (2013) | The study examines the emerging food tourism trends in the Circumpolar North. | The paper presented on the food tourism trends and underlined how food impacted the tourists in the Arctic tourism industry. |

According to a study conducted by Walmsley and Jenkins (1993), tourists' perceptions towards several resorts in North Coast of New South Wales, Australia were significantly different due to gender and age factors. On the other hand, Baloglu (1997) studied the destination image variations of the United States based on socio-demographic factors, found that image among the West German tourists varied due to age, marital status and occupation.

A survey was carried out by Husbands (1989) to investigate the perceptions of Livingstone, Zambia local residents towards the world-famous Victoria Falls. The findings revealed important differences in residents' perceptions towards destination tourism and the differences were related to residents' social status and social class cleavages. Further, the findings demonstrated significant differences among the Livingstone, Zambia locals based on age and education factors (Husbands, 1989). Based on the review of past literature, socio-demographic variables were included into the theoretical framework of this study and it is hypothesized that socio-demographic variables have significant influence on food images.

Several scholars defined motivations as socio-psychological factors that influence an individual to partake in a touristic activity (Crandall, 1980; Beard & Raghep, 1983; Iso-Ahola, 1982). In addition, motivations were said to have formed in a conscious or unconscious manner (Moutinho, 1987) in which motivations could influence destination choice and destination image formation (Mayo & Jarvis, 1981; Stabler, 1990; Um & Crompton, 1990; Um, 1993). On the other hand, motivation was argued to be the key factor in understanding destination selection behavior, as motivation is the pushing and pulling factors in the wake of tourists' actions in destination choice process (Crompton, 1979; Iso-Ahola, 1982; Uysal & Hagan, 1993; Weaver, McCleary, Lepisto & Damonte 1994).

The image of a destination is highly related to the motivations that tourists seek and tourists will compare the image of a destination before and after a visit to a particular place (Mill & Morrison 1992). Further, several authors suggested that motivations have significant influence on tourists emotions (affective element) while selecting a potential vacation destination (Gartner, 1993; Walmsley & Jenkins, 1993; Dann, 1996; Baloglu & McCleary, 1999). Whereas other information sources such as promotional materials are influential to an individual's perceptions formation and information sources will be discuss in the following section.

Information sources were emphasized in several studies as a powerful factor that influences the construction of perceptions or the cognitive evaluations of a destination image (Burgess, 1978; Holbrook, 1978; Woodside & Lysonski, 1989; Um & Crompton, 1990; Fakeye & Crompton, 1991; Um, 1993). According to Burgess (1978) the type of image developed depended on the type, quality and quantity of information received by an individual. Correspondingly, Holbrook (1978) has empirically proven that information sources have

influence on the cognitive element of image, in which the image attributes formed will ultimately manipulate an individual's emotions. Similarly, Woodside and Lysonski (1989) also found that information sources have influence on perceptions or image attributes evaluations formation.

On the other hand, the perceptions of destination image attributes were claimed to have formed by symbolic stimuli such as the information sources through media and social stimuli such as recommendations from friends and family (Um & Crompton, 1990). Whereas Gartner (1993) denoted that the perceptions of a destination developed is a result of the amount and type of information sources that a tourist received. The followings section will give an overview of the influence of image on tourists' evaluation (satisfaction levels and revisit intention) of a destination.

Satisfaction was claimed as an outcome of pre-consumption expectation and post-consumption experience (Parker & Mathews, 2001). On the other hand, it was argued that, in predicting satisfaction, perceptions and experiences related to a product or service are important factors for satisfaction assessment (Cronin & Taylor, 1992; Halstead, Hartman & Schmidt, 1994). The perceptions on a product or service in fact, involve the benefits received for the prices, and studies have empirically proven that perceptions have positive impact on both satisfactions and consumer's behavioral intention (Chen & Tsai, 2007).

Crompton (1979) defined destination image as the psychological representation of perceptions and feelings of a destination. In addition to being a mental illustration, destination image was claimed by past scholars to have influence on human behavior such as decision-making process, evaluation of destination during on-site experience, and future behavioral intention (Ashworth & Goodall, 1988; Bigné et al., 2001; Lee et al., 2005). The gap between pre-visit perceptions and the actual visit experience was described as satisfaction (Chen & Tsai, 2007) and generally,

*Figure 1. Conceptual framework of the study*

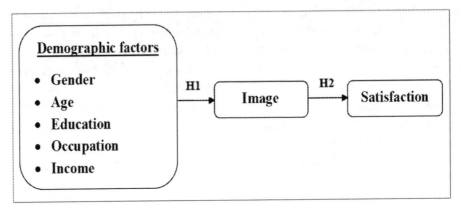

tourists' evaluation will be positive and this will lead to inner satisfaction (Lee et al., 2005). Hence measuring factors that influence satisfaction should not be taken for granted as the success of a travel destination is directly related to tourists' satisfaction (Haber & Lerner, 1998).

Chen and Tsai (2007) employed exploratory factor analysis using principal component method with varimax rotation to examine the dimensionalities and psychometric characteristics of Kengtin region, a famous coastal destination in southern Taiwan. Subsequently structural equation modelling (SEM) was used to determine the relationships of destination image, evaluative factors (trip quality and satisfaction) and behavioral intention. On the other hand, Kozak and Rimmington (2000) used exploratory factor analysis for data reduction and regression procedures to examine the relationship between a destination's image and tourists' satisfaction. Past studies have confirmed the relationship between destination image and tourists' satisfaction. However, to date, the relationship between food image and satisfaction is still questionable. Few studies have initiated research to determine the possible effect of food image on tourists' satisfaction. Hence, by adopting destination image theory, the present study hypothesized that tourists' who have favorable food image of a destination will be more satisfy with the destination's gastronomic products.

## Theoretical Framework of the Study

Orthodox branding theory has focused heavily on consumer products (de Chernatony & Segal-Horn, 2001) however evolution has taken place that creating a brand image is equally important in other sectors such as destination branding and food image branding. Branding was claimed to be a way of marketing in destinations that can boost awareness and develop destination image of a particular tourism place (Scott, 2002). In addition to advertisement, the brand image of food or gastronomy in tourist destinations could be enhance by strong associations of the food with certain positive symbols, slogans, tangible and intangible characteristics that could appeal to human senses and emotions (Keller, 1993; Scott, 2002).

Competitive situation has forced the branding strategies to be applied in various conditions in order to be different from others and maintain irreplaceable. This issue had encouraged many scholars to study on branding strategies in the food and tourism industry (Mowle & Merrilees, 2005), as food was claimed to be one of the key sources in generating revenue for the tourism industry besides inducing tourist influx (Telfer & Wall, 1996; Kivela & Crotts, 2006). A combination of theories such as destination image and branding were adopted and used to design the conceptual framework of this study. The study's conceptual framework is shown in Figure 1.

Motivations, socio-demographic factors and information sources were proven to have impact on the formation on image. However, this study was narrowed down to examine the effect of demographic factors on food image only. Socio-demographic factors were widely used and have been incorporated in numerous image studies (Husbands, 1989; Woodside & Lysonski, 1989; Stabler, 1990; Um & Crompton, 1990; Stern & Krakover, 1993; Walmsley & Jenkins, 1993; Baloglu, 1997; Baloglu & McCleary, 1999; Beerli & Martin, 2004). Hence, the following hypotheses were proposed:

H1: There is a significant mean difference in Malaysian food image with regard to demographic factors.

H1a: There is a significant mean difference in gender on image of Malaysian food.

H1b: There is a significant mean difference in age categories on image of Malaysian food.

H1c: There is a significant mean difference in education level on image of Malaysian food.

H1d: There is a significant mean difference in occupation on image of Malaysian food.

H1e: There is a significant mean difference in annual income on image of Malaysian food.

The theory of brand image was incorporated in this study to determine tourist satisfaction and tourist's behavioral intention. This study adopted brand associations from Keller's (1993) conceptual framework to determine the image of Malaysian food. Keller (1993) claimed that brand benefits which comprises of functional, symbolic and experiential associations are personal values that consumers attach to a product or service characteristics. This study adopted the functional, symbolic and experiential dimensions as an exploratory step to distinguish Malaysian food image. Empirical studies showed that image has a significant relationship with tourists' satisfaction towards a particular destination (Chen & Tsai, 2007; Lee et al., 2007; González et al., 2007).

As argued by past scholars, image was said to be an essential component that abet in developing destination brand (Jensen & Korneliussen, 2002; Kotler et al., 2003). Brand benefits association was used by past scholars to position and market positive images of consumer products, tourist destinations and wineries to build a significant brand image (Clarke, 2000; Gnoth, 2002; Hankinson, 2005; Mowle & Merrilees, 2005; Orth & De Marchi, 2007). Therefore the following hypothesis was suggested:

H2: The image of Malaysian food will significantly influence their satisfaction level towards Malaysian food.

## METHODOLOGY

Four focus groups were conducted with a total of 31 informants provided ideas on the development of multi-item scales capturing various aspects of Malaysian food image. Individuals participating in the focus group sessions were drawn from various professional backgrounds and of multi-races with age ranged from 24 to 53. The informants were selected through purposive sampling (Jankowicz, 2000) and snowballing method (Tellström et al., 2006) where initial informants were requested to propose associates whom could provide more details about the discussion matter. Table 2 shows the profile of the focus group's informants.

Subsequent to conducting the focus group, the survey instrument was developed and a cross-sectional survey was administered to uncover the image of Malaysian food and to determine tourists' satisfaction towards Malaysian food. The targeted population of this study was the visitors stopping at two airports in Malaysia during a five days period in between April and May. The target sample was tourists who visited Malaysia within 24 hours to less than 12 months of duration (Mill & Morrison, 1985; Choi, Chan & Wu, 1999). Respondents were approached using systematic

*Table 2. Focus group informant's profile*

| No | Gender | Race | Age | Occupation |
|----|--------|------|-----|------------|
| 1 | M | Chinese | 26 | Application Engineer |
| 2 | F | Chinese | 26 | Marketing Executive |
| 3 | M | Malay | 44 | Postgraduate |
| 4 | F | Malay | 28 | Project Manager |
| 5 | M | Indian | 31 | Fitness Trainer |
| 6 | F | Bidayuh | 33 | Postgraduate |
| 7 | F | Chinese | 25 | Underwriting Officer |
| 8 | F | Malay | 24 | Postgraduate |
| 9 | M | Indian | 33 | Engineer |
| 10 | F | Chinese | 24 | Accounts Manager |
| 11 | F | Chinese | 26 | Human Resources Executive |
| 12 | M | Malay | 36 | Procurement Manager |
| 13 | F | Chinese | 24 | Postgraduate |
| 14 | F | Malay | 36 | Senior Management Executive |
| 15 | M | Malay | 27 | University Tutor |
| 16 | F | Chinese | 31 | Lecturer/Researcher |
| 17 | M | Indian | 50 | Chef Trainer |
| 18 | F | Malay | 49 | Executive Chef |
| 19 | M | Malay | 53 | Professional Chef |
| 20 | M | Malay | 48 | Executive Chef |
| 21 | M | Malay | 39 | Cost Controller |
| 22 | M | Malay | 27 | University Tutor |
| 23 | M | Malay | 45 | Executive Chef |
| 24 | M | Malay | 46 | Executive Chef |
| 25 | M | Malay | 39 | Offshore Catering Owner |
| 26 | M | Malay | 39 | Executive Chef |
| 27 | M | Malay | 43 | Executive Chef |
| 28 | M | Indian | 44 | Director of Culinary School |
| 29 | M | Malay | 36 | Executive Sous Chef |
| 30 | M | Malay | 38 | Food Blogger |
| 31 | M | Malay | 44 | In-Flight Operation Culinary Manager |

sampling method in the Kuala Lumpur International Airport (KLIA) and the Low Cost Carrier Terminal (LCCT). Voluntary respondents had to satisfy a screening question prior to be qualified to participate in the survey. The screening questions were whether the respondent was a resident in Malaysia and whether they had prior experience of tasting Malaysian food. Malaysian residents and tourists who had no prior experience of Malaysian food were excluded from the survey.

## FINDINGS

A total of 433 survey questionnaires were distributed to tourists who were departing from two major airport in Malaysia when the survey was conducted. Out of the total figure, 339 questionnaires were usable out of the 392 completed questionnaires. Fifty three sets of questionnaires were unusable due to the significant amount of missing values.

## Respondents' Demographic Profile

The proportion of male (63.1%) and female (36.6%) was not equally distributed as male tourists were more responsive in participating in this survey (Table 3). Majority of the respondents were from age group of 21 – 30 (30.7%), followed by the age group of 31 – 40 with a frequency of 96 (28.3%). Approximately 36.9% of the respondents had a bachelor degree followed by postgraduate (28.6%) and diploma / certificate with 19.4%. Nearly half of the respondents held executive / managerial / professional position (41.9%) and was followed by the student's group (9.4%). This result is consistent with previous studies which found that the frequencies of travelling are higher among people with higher disposable income as compared to people with lower disposable income (Yuan & Mcdonald, 1990; Basala & Klenosky, 2001).

Approximately 24.8% of the respondents had annual income above 80,000 US Dollar. On the contrary, 18.6% had income equal to or below 30,000 US Dollar. Nearly 8.8% (33) of the respondents refused to reveal the range of their annual income because income was considered as a private and confidential matter. A significant percentage of the respondents were Europeans (36.3%) followed by Asians (29.2%), Oceania (18.9%), Americas (10.6%) and a minority came from Africa with a percentage of 2.9%. The arrangement of the findings was almost similar to the statistics provided by the Malaysian Tourism

Promotion Board except that Asia was reported as the biggest market and Europe was the second that contributed to Malaysia tourism. A significant percentage (93.5%) of the respondents had tasted Malaysian food more than once whereas a small number (5.6%) of the respondents tried Malaysian food for only once. Respondents who had tasted Malaysian food for multiple times could indicate the likelihood of higher satisfaction level towards Malaysian food.

## Respondents' Travel and Dining Characteristics

Based on the statistics provided by Malaysian Tourism Promotional Board (MTPB), tourist's average length of stay was approximately 6 nights. The findings in this study revealed that a significant percentage (27.1%) of the respondents stayed in Malaysia for 3-6 days which was approximate to the average length of stay reported by MTPB. Almost 9.1% of the respondents stayed in Malaysia less than 24 hours; these respondents were those on transit to another destination. Several respondents indicated they went out of the airport to savor some local delicacies before their next flight whereas several others savored Malaysian food inside the airport's outlet. Half of the respondents (51.3%) visited Malaysia for holiday/pleasure purpose and 25.7% came to Malaysia for business/meeting purpose. Interestingly 1.5% indicated they came to Malaysia just to explore the local food and this could be a good indicator of the rising interest in food tourism in Malaysia.

Majority (74.6%) of the tourists visited local food outlet or restaurant. This was followed by night markets / hawker stalls / street food with a percentage of 57.5% which accounted more than half of the respondents in the survey. This could be a good indicator that tourists who visited Malaysia were curious to try new food and might have the tendency of food neophilic where food neophilia was claimed to be a key factor for food tourism and globalization of a destination's cuisine

*Table 3. Respondents' demographic profile*

| Characteristics | Frequency | Percentage (%) |
|---|---|---|
| *Gender* | | |
| Male | 214 | 63.1 |
| Female | 124 | 36.6 |
| Total | 338 | 99.7 |
| Missing | 1 | 0.3 |
| Total | 339 | 100 |
| *Age* | | |
| 20 and below | 13 | 3.8 |
| 21-30 | 104 | 30.7 |
| 31-40 | 96 | 28.3 |
| 41-50 | 58 | 17.1 |
| 51-60 | 45 | 13.3 |
| Above 60 | 22 | 6.5 |
| Total | 338 | 99.7 |
| Missing | 1 | 0.3 |
| Total | 339 | 100 |
| *Education* | | |
| Primary school | 1 | 0.3 |
| Lower secondary school | 4 | 1.2 |
| Higher secondary school | 38 | 11.2 |
| Diploma / certificate | 66 | 19.4 |
| Bachelor degree | 125 | 36.9 |
| Postgraduate | 97 | 28.6 |
| Others | 5 | 1.5 |
| Total | 336 | 99.1 |
| Missing | 3 | 0.9 |
| Total | 339 | 100 |
| *Occupation* | | |
| Student | 32 | 9.4 |
| Homemaker | 12 | 3.5 |
| Production/clerical/administrative | 16 | 4.7 |
| Technical/sales | 25 | 7.4 |
| Executive/managerial/professional | 142 | 41.9 |
| Academician/educator | 29 | 8.6 |
| Self-employed | 31 | 9.1 |
| Retired/unemployed | 20 | 5.9 |
| Others | 31 | 9.1 |
| Total | 338 | 99.7 |

*continued on following page*

*Table 3. Continued*

| Characteristics | Frequency | Percentage (%) |
|---|---|---|
| Missing | 1 | 0.3 |
| Total | 339 | 100 |
| *Annual Income* | | |
| 30,000 USD and below | 63 | 18.6 |
| 31,000 – 40,000 USD | 45 | 13.3 |
| 41,000 – 50,000 USD | 36 | 10.6 |
| 51,000 – 60,000 USD | 43 | 12.7 |
| 61,000 – 70,000 USD | 23 | 6.8 |
| 71,000 – 80,000 USD | 15 | 4.4 |
| Above 80,000 USD | 84 | 24.8 |
| Total | 309 | 91.2 |
| Missing | 30 | 8.8 |
| Total | 339 | 100 |
| *Nationality according to region* | | |
| Africa | 10 | 2.9 |
| Americas | 36 | 10.6 |
| Asia | 99 | 29.2 |
| Europe | 123 | 36.3 |
| Oceania | 64 | 18.9 |
| Total | 332 | 97.9 |
| Missing | 7 | 2.1 |
| Total | 339 | 100 |
| | | |
| *Tasted Malaysian food more than once* | | |
| Yes | 317 | 93.5 |
| No | 19 | 5.6 |
| Total | 336 | 99.1 |
| Missing | 3 | 0.9 |
| Total | 339 | 100 |
| | | |

(Bell & Valentine, 1997). Whereas 55.5% of the respondents' noted they took their meals mostly in hotel's restaurant or upscale dining outlet; they could be people under the category of who dislike tasting unfamiliar food which was suggested by Tuorila, Meiselman, Bell, Cardello and Johnson (1994) as food neophobic. Moreover as noted by Cohen and Avieli (2004) tourists would tend to worry and take extra precautions about the palatability of unfamiliar food and beverage, food hygiene, culturally unacceptable food and also food related to religious dietary laws (kosher for

Jewish and halal for Muslims). Hence, dining in hotel's restaurant or familiar upscale dining outlet would ease the tourists' off their worries.

More than half (54.6%) of the respondents said they made ad hoc decision on where to dine in Malaysia whereas 47.8% dine in places recommended by their friends and family. 30.7% respondents were attracted to eat in local outlets advertising Malaysian food. Approximately 53 respondents (15.6%) said they would dine in a local food outlet only if there were a lot of local people dining in that particular outlet. Additionally price was also a major concern in their decision making of where to dine for Malaysian food. Approximately 18.9% of the respondents have searched for food information from travel guide such as Lonely Planet magazine/website before they travel to Malaysia. A handful percentage (15.6%) of the respondents ticked 'others'; respondents in this category noted that they dine at friends or relatives house during their stay in Malaysia. Almost 14.7% went back to the restaurants they are familiar with and this designated that this particular group of respondents had repeat visitation to Malaysia and were familiar with the local food.

## Respondents' Knowledge and Perceptions on Malaysian Food

Two open-ended questions were included in the first section of the questionnaire to identify respondents' knowledge and perceptions on Malaysian food. The top five favorites rated by the tourists were the *Mamak* (Indian Muslim) style fried rice, *Nasi Lemak* (coconut fragrant rice), *Satay* (Malaysian style skewered meat), *Roti Canai* (Malaysian style grilled flatbread) and curry dishes. Fascinatingly, most of the foods elicited by the respondents were among the 100 food items listed as Malaysian national heritage which was announced by the Ministry of Unity, Culture, Arts and Heritage (Elis, 2009). Most of the respondents spelled the name of the food correctly, hence this signified the respondents

remembered the Malaysian food that they have tasted during their stay in the destination.

Majority of the respondents characterized Malaysian food as hot and spicy. However, there were several respondents who thought oppositely whereby they felt that Malaysian food was mild. Based on the nationality profile, respondents who elicited Malaysian food as mild were respondents who came from countries such as Thailand, Indonesia, India and South Africa (Cape Town) whereby the people in these countries savor chilies and spices as well. The second mostly rated characteristic associated to Malaysian food was good value for money. A global survey carried out by FutureBrand, a leading global brand consultancy firm concluded that Malaysia was placed 7th for 'Best Country Brand for Value for Money' (MTPB, 2009). With all the good values that Malaysia as a destination accumulated over the years, the country won 'Best Family Destination Award 2014' by Lonely Planet Magazine (Bernama, 2014).

## The Image of Malaysian Food

The descriptive statistics of mean scores and standard deviations for the image of Malaysian food are shown in Table 4. The images were grouped under functional, symbolic and experiential associations. Functional associations of Malaysian food focused on the food's tangible or more abstract characteristics. The spiciness of Malaysian food was rated moderately on the scale (Table 4) and this was relatively contradicted with the result in the previous section of respondent's perceptions towards Malaysia food, where 'hot and spicy' comprised the highest percentage of votes. This might indicate that respondents' initial or implanted image of Malaysian food was 'hot and spicy'. Though, after trying Malaysian food this attribute did not stay true for all Malaysian food. The major strengths of Malaysian food in terms of functionality focused more on food price, flavors, services and variety. On the other hand the

*Table 4. Descriptive analysis of the image of Malaysian food*

| Attributes | Mean | Std. Deviation |
|---|---|---|
| *Functional Dimension* | | |
| Reasonable prices | 4.12 | 0.88 |
| Rich in flavors | 3.97 | 0.89 |
| High availability of food | 3.87 | 0.99 |
| Food providers are friendly | 3.85 | 0.85 |
| Contain a lot of herbs and spices | 3.82 | 0.85 |
| Variety of local specialties | 3.71 | 0.84 |
| Appealing to human senses | 3.70 | 0.88 |
| Services by food providers are good | 3.66 | 0.91 |
| Food spots are located in convenient places | 3.61 | 0.89 |
| Hot and spicy | 3.51 | 0.97 |
| Clean and safe to consume | 3.43 | 0.96 |
| Well presented | 3.43 | 0.99 |
| Uses variety of cooking methods | 3.41 | 0.99 |
| Comfortable eating surroundings | 3.32 | 0.92 |
| Various information guide on local food | 2.92 | 0.96 |
| *Symbolic Dimension* | | |
| Herbs and spices | 3.92 | 2.33 |
| Convenience | 3.87 | 0.90 |
| Cultural diversity in Malaysia | 3.85 | 0.90 |
| Food with multicultural influence | 3.83 | 0.92 |
| Street food / hawker stalls | 3.74 | 0.97 |
| Cultural food | 3.74 | 0.88 |
| Harmony | 3.68 | 0.90 |
| Authentic | 3.61 | 0.88 |
| Fascinating ethnic food | 3.60 | 0.88 |
| Togetherness | 3.60 | 0.97 |
| Chilies | 3.57 | 0.90 |
| Unique and distinctive | 3.56 | 0.87 |
| Malaysian heritage | 3.52 | 0.92 |
| Traditional food with contemporary features | 3.49 | 0.85 |
| *Experiential Dimension* | | |
| Enjoying variety of food from different ethnic groups | 3.85 | 0.89 |
| Opportunity to taste local street food | 3.85 | 1.00 |
| Experiencing a full range of taste from mild to spicy | 3.83 | 0.90 |
| Experiencing the richness of herbs and spices in food | 3.78 | 0.83 |
| Experiencing warm and friendly hospitality | 3.78 | 0.89 |
| An exciting experience to be shared with friends and family | 3.75 | 0.95 |

*continued on following page*

*Table 4. Continued*

| Attributes | Mean | Std. Deviation |
|---|---|---|
| Authentic dining experience | 3.68 | 0.88 |
| Experiencing alfresco dining | 3.67 | 1.01 |
| Eating Malaysian food is simply a food adventure | 3.62 | 0.94 |
| Exploring Malaysian cultures | 3.58 | 0.92 |
| Experiencing Malaysian lifestyles | 3.56 | 0.89 |
| Experiencing food in different cooking methods | 3.48 | 0.91 |
| Unique dining experience | 3.47 | 0.86 |
| Learning about Malaysian culture through the food | 3.38 | 0.94 |
| Note:<br>Scale: 1 = Strongly disagree; 5 = Strongly agree | | |

respondents did not perceive strongly on attributes such as 'clean and safe to consume' (3.43), 'well presented' (3.43), 'variety of cooking methods used on Malaysian food' (3.43), 'comfortable eating surroundings' (3.41) and 'various information guide on local food' (2.92). Seeing that respondents had rated relatively poor on food hygiene, food presentations and accessibility of local food information, it is suggested that food providers should be more attentive to these attributes in order to attract tourists and confer a positive image of Malaysian food and hospitality. Food outlets should have menus provided with descriptions of local food such as the ingredients used and the level of food spiciness. This will surely help tourists to make a wise choice according to their preference besides educating them on Malaysian food culture.

Malaysian food symbolic images had higher mean scores on ingredients used and cultural diversity in the country. Most of the respondents have associated Malaysian food with the symbol of 'herbs and spice' (3.92) and 'convenience' (3.87) in which food is available at all times with great choices to pick such as in Alor Street situated in Kuala Lumpur which is a hot spot for tourists in Malaysia. The respondents also rated relatively high on terms symbolizing 'cultural diversity in Malaysia' (3.85), 'food with multicultural influ-

ence' (3.83), 'street food / hawker stalls' (3.74), and 'cultural food' (3.74). Malaysian food was also denoted as being 'harmony' (3.68) because every ethnic in Malaysia have some common culinary practices and lived in harmony for decades although each ethnicity has own distinct food culture. All the attributes under symbolic dimension were rated fairly above moderate score and this indicated that respondents seemed to agree with these attributes listed.

Experiential dimension of the food image association comprised of the multifaceted Malaysian qualities; for example, a few attributes with higher mean scores were 'enjoying variety of food from different ethnic groups' (3.85), 'opportunity to taste local street food' (3.85), 'experiencing a full range of taste from mild to spicy' (3.83), 'experiencing the richness of herbs and spices in food' (3.78), 'experiencing warm and friendly hospitality' (3.78), 'an exciting experience to be shared with friends and family' (3.75), 'authentic dining experience' (3.68), 'experiencing alfresco dining' (3.67) and 'eating Malaysian food is simply a food adventure' (3.62). Attributes in experiential dimension with lower mean scores were 'exploring Malaysian cultures' (3.58), 'experiencing Malaysian lifestyles' (3.56), 'experiencing food in different cooking methods' (3.48), 'unique dining experience' (3.47) and 'learning about

*Table 5. Descriptive analysis of tourists' overall evaluation towards Malaysian food*

| Attributes | Mean | Std. Deviation |
|---|---|---|
| *Tourists' Satisfaction* | | |
| Malaysian food contributes to the quality of my visiting experience | 3.89 | 0.96 |
| Malaysian food contributes to my eating pleasure | 3.84 | 0.90 |
| Eating Malaysian food adds to my visiting enjoyment | 3.81 | 0.97 |
| The food experience in Malaysia meets my expectation | 3.70 | 0.94 |
| I experienced the culture of Malaysia through Malaysian food | 3.46 | 0.92 |
| | | |
| Note:<br>Scale: 1 = Strongly disagree; 5 = Strongly agree | | |

Malaysian culture through the food' (3.38). The mean scores show that even though respondents symbolized Malaysian food as 'culturally diverse food', respondents seemed to be relatively neutral on whether they have experienced Malaysian cultures and lifestyles through Malaysian food. The findings might indicate that the respondents did not have much understanding about Malaysian culture and lifestyle through local food. Therefore, it is suggested that more information be provided to tourists regarding Malaysian food and the cultures behind the food in Malaysian airports and tourists' information booth. Even the local food providers should be well-versed about Malaysian food when asked by tourists in order to create consistent information made available for access. Information provided prior to tourists experiencing Malaysian food will definitely enhance tourists' experience and be more memorable to them. This might in turn creates positive impact on recommendations to their friends and family.

## Tourists' Overall Evaluation towards Malaysian Food

Overall, respondents' satisfaction was fairly skewed to the positive side. Attributes with highest mean score was 'Malaysian food contributes to the quality of my visiting experience' (3.89). This was followed by 'Malaysian food contributes to my eating pleasure' (3.84), 'eating Malaysian food adds to my visiting enjoyment' (3.81) and 'the food experience in Malaysia meets my expectation' (3.70). The result indicated that Malaysian food played an important role to impart memorable and positive image of Malaysia as a tourism destination as tourists' were deemed to be agreeable that Malaysian food added values to their vacation experience in Malaysia. However, the attribute 'I experienced the culture of Malaysia through Malaysian food' was rated slightly lower (3.46) as compared to other attributes mentioned. The result was consistent with the mean scores for attributes that measure tourists' perceptions on learning cultures and lifestyles through Malaysian food (Table 5). This implied that tourists' did not perceive there was enough information to educate them about Malaysian lifestyles and food cultures. Therefore, this perception was reflected in the mean score of the respondents' satisfaction towards whether they experienced the culture of Malaysia through Malaysian food. Consequently, more advertising materials such as websites, brochures and even promotional booths should be made available for tourists to access information on Malaysian food and culture. This would definitely in turn, construct a possible opportunity for Malaysian food to penetrate the global market in the tourism sector.

## The Influence of Demographic Variables on Tourist's Perceived Food Image

Independent-samples T test was used to examine the differences of image mean scores between male and female (Table 6). Whereas one-way ANOVA was performed to determine the differences of image mean scores in age, education, occupation and annual income (Table 7). Levene's test was used to check the assumption of homogeneity of variance for both independent-samples T test and one-way ANOVA.

Based on the value of t-test for equality of means, it was found that the significant p-value ($t =$ -0.64, $p = .52$) was larger than .05. As a result, the null hypothesis was supported which meant there was no significant mean difference in image mean score between male and female respondents. The finding was found to be consistent with previous study done on destination image (Baloglu, 1997), in which gender does not have any influence on tourist's perceived image.

The findings in Table 7 shows that the significant p-values for age, occupation and annual income were larger than .05; therefore the null hypotheses were supported. These implied that there were no significant means difference in image across age, occupation and annual income groups. However, the significant p-value for education groups was found to be significant,

$F (5,329) = 3.00$, $p = .01$, $\eta^2 = 0.04$. Hence the null hypothesis was rejected. This indicates that there was a significant mean difference in image mean score across the education groups. Baloglu and McCleary (1999) averred that among the socio-demographic variables, age and education emerged to be the main determinants of image. However, the findings of this research revealed that food image differed across education levels only and the findings was found to be in congruence with several studies on destination image in which image was found to differ due to education levels (Baloglu & McCleary, 1999; Rittichainuwat, Ou & Brown, 2001).

The effect size ($\eta^2$) of the mean difference for groups in education level was 0.04. Comparing this eta-squared value ($\eta^2 = 0.04$) to Cohen's (1988) criteria, it was obvious that the effect size obtained was considered to be small and this denoted that the mean difference is very small. Groups under education variable were analyzed further in post hoc tests. Hochberg's GT2 procedure was chosen for the post hoc tests comparison because the sample sizes among the groups of education variable were unequal (Field, 2005). The findings from the post hoc test show that there was difference between respondents with diploma / certificate and respondents with bachelor degree with a significant p-value of .003 ($p \leq .05$).

## The Underlying Dimensions of Malaysian Food Image

Principal component analysis with orthogonal (VARIMAX) rotations was used to uncover the

*Table 6. Differences of image based on gender*

| Attributes | Male | | Female | | Mean Difference | *t* value | Sig. (2-tailed) | 95% Confidence Interval | |
|---|---|---|---|---|---|---|---|---|---|
| | Mean | SD | Mean | SD | | | | Lower | Upper |
| Image | 3.65 | 0.53 | 3.69 | 0.51 | -0.04 | -0.64 | .52 | -0.15 | 0.08 |

Note: The mean difference is significant at .05 level

Levene's Statistics: 0.75

*Table 7. Differences of image based on age, education, occupation and annual income*

| | | Sum of squares | df | Mean square | F | Sig. | Levene statistic | Sig. |
|---|---|---|---|---|---|---|---|---|
| **Differences of Image across Age** | | | | | | | | |
| Image | Between groups | 1.61 | 5 | 0.32 | 1.18 | .32 | .93 | .46 |
| | Within groups | 90.42 | 332 | 0.27 | | | | |
| | Total | 92.03 | 337 | | | | | |
| | | | | | | | | |
| **Differences of Image across Education Level** | | | | | | | | |
| Image | Between groups | 3.91 | 5 | 0.78 | 3.00 | **.01** | .38 | .87 |
| | Within groups | 85.83 | 329 | 0.26 | | | | |
| | Total | 89.74 | 334 | | | | | |
| | | | | | | | | |
| **Differences of Image across Occupation** | | | | | | | | |
| Image | Between groups | 2.47 | 8 | 0.31 | 1.14 | .34 | .71 | .69 |
| | Within groups | 89.58 | 329 | 0.27 | | | | |
| | Total | 92.05 | 337 | | | | | |
| | | | | | | | | |
| **Differences of Image across Annual Income** | | | | | | | | |
| Image | Between groups | 2.69 | 6 | 0.45 | 1.62 | .14 | .80 | .57 |
| | Within groups | 83.54 | 302 | 0.28 | | | | |
| | Total | 86.23 | 308 | | | | | |
| | | | | | | | | |
| Note: The mean difference is significant at .05 level | | | | | | | | |

underlying dimensions of Malaysian food image. Several assumptions suggested by Coakes, Steed & Price (2008) were taken into consideration, such as sample size, normality, linearity, outliers, and factorability of the correlation matrix. The factorability of the correlation matrix was examined through visual inspection, Bartlett's test of sphericity and Kaiser-Meyer-Olkin measure of sampling adequacy (KMO). Bartlett's Test of Sphericity should have a significant value in which $p \leq .05$ (Hair, Anderson, Tatham & Black, 2006); while

KMO value should be above .60 in order to meet the criterion of measure of sampling adequacy (Field, 2005). The percentage of variance and scree test criterion were used for factor extraction on each construct. In determining significant factor loadings for interpretation, factor loadings of $\pm$ .40 are considered to have met the minimal level for interpretation of structure (Hair et al., 2006).

The result of Barlett's Test of sphericity (Table 8) was significant ($\chi^2 = 4897.115$, $p = .000$) and the value of KMO was .884 which was above the

*Table 8. Kaiser-Meyer-Olkin and Bartlett's Test*

| | |
|---|---|
| Kaiser-Meyer-Olkin Measure of Sampling Adequacy | **.884** |
| Bartlett's Test of Sphericity | |
| Approx. Chi-Square | 4897.115 |
| df | 630 |
| Sig. | **.000** |

recommended threshold of sampling adequacy at the minimum of .60 (Field, 2005). These two values indicated that the dataset is suitable for an exploratory factor analysis. A total of ten factors were extracted based on the eigenvalue, the percentage of variance criterion and scree plot criterion. Only factors with eigenvalue greater than one were chosen and the cumulative percentage of variance indicated the ten-factor solution explained 66.89% of the total variance.

Hair et al. (2006) suggested that, when variables do not load on any factor due to loadings less than .40, with unacceptable communalities or have cross-loadings, these variables can opt for possible deletion. Cross-loadings means the loadings of an item is found in two factors. Small communalities show that a significant percentage of the variable's variance is not accounted for by the factors and .40 was used as the cut-off-point in this study (Hair et al., 2006). Among the 43 food image attributes, seven items were deleted due to cross-loadings, and loadings less than .40. The variables are 'hot and spicy', 'food with multicultural influence', 'exploring Malaysian cultures', 'experiencing Malaysian lifestyles', 'experiencing food in different cooking methods', 'experiencing the richness of herbs and spices in Malaysian food', and 'unique dining experience'. The deletion of these items increases the total variance explained approximately 2.89% (from 64% to 66.89%). The results of the principle component analysis with orthogonal (VARIMAX) rotations are shown in Table 9.

Each factor in the ten-factor solution was tested for internal consistency by assessing the Cronbach's alpha value. The results showed that the alpha coefficients for the ten factors ranged from .62 to .82. Cronbach's alpha with a value of .70 is recommended as the lower limit for assessing scale's reliability. However alpha coefficient with a value of .60 is acceptable for exploratory research (Robinson, Shaver & Wrightsman, 1991, as cited in Hair et al., 2006). The factors in the ten-factor solution were labelled based on items with greater weight on the factor, in other words items with higher loadings. Based on the ten-factor solution, it was found that 4 factors were functionality-related features, 3 factors indicated the symbolic dimension of food images, and 3 factors comprised of experiential-related attributes.

The factors that were denoting functional images of Malaysian food were Factor 1 (food and dining information), Factor 7 (food characteristic), Factor 8 (essence of Malaysian food), and Factor 9 (accessibility and value-for-money). Individually, these factors explained approximately 8.32%, 6.29%, 5.86% and 5.54% respectively out of the total variance explained in Malaysian food image; meanwhile in collective, the functional dimension was accounted for 26.01% of the total variance explained in Malaysian food image.

Factors that represented the symbolic dimension were Factor 3 (facet of attraction), Factor 4 (food originality) and Factor 10 (symbols of heritage). These factors which embodied the symbolic dimension accounted for 19.80% collectively, out of the total variance explained in food image. On the other hand, the experiential dimension comprised of 3 factors namely 'exotic culinary experience' (Factor 2), 'lifestyles and

*Table 9. The underlying factors of Malaysian food image*

| Factor | Factor Loadings | | | | | | | | | | Communality |
|---|---|---|---|---|---|---|---|---|---|---|---|
| **Factor 1: Food and Dining Information** | F1 | F2 | F3 | F4 | F5 | F6 | F7 | F8 | F9 | F10 | |
| Comfortable eating surroundings | .76 | | | | | | | | | | .66 |
| Well presented | .70 | | | | | | | | | | .63 |
| Various information guide on local food | .66 | | | | | | | | | | .67 |
| Clean and safe to consume | .60 | | | | | | | | | | .55 |
| **Factor 2: Exotic Culinary Experience** | | | | | | | | | | | |
| Opportunity to taste local street food | | .79 | | | | | | | | | .72 |
| Experiencing alfresco dining | | .78 | | | | | | | | | .72 |
| Street food / hawker stalls | | .73 | | | | | | | | | .68 |
| Authentic dining experience | | .49 | | | | | | | | | .67 |
| **Factor 3: Facet of Attraction** | | | | | | | | | | | |
| Togetherness | | | .81 | | | | | | | | .76 |
| Harmony | | | .78 | | | | | | | | .74 |
| Convenience | | | .63 | | | | | | | | .67 |
| Traditional food with contemporary features | | | .49 | | | | | | | | .63 |
| Cultural diversity in Malaysia | | | .45 | | | | | | | | .59 |
| **Factor 4: Food Originality** | | | | | | | | | | | |
| Unique and distinctive | | | | .72 | | | | | | | .68 |
| Authentic | | | | .62 | | | | | | | .66 |
| Fascinating ethnic food | | | | .61 | | | | | | | .64 |
| **Factor 5: Lifestyles and Cultures** | | | | | | | | | | | |
| Learning about Malaysian culture through the food | | | | | .73 | | | | | | .73 |
| Experiencing a full range of taste from mild to spicy | | | | | .65 | | | | | | .74 |
| Eating Malaysian food is simply a food adventure | | | | | .57 | | | | | | .58 |
| An exciting experience to be shared with friends and family | | | | | .50 | | | | | | .65 |
| **Factor 6: Food Service and Hospitality** | | | | | | | | | | | |
| Food providers are friendly | | | | | | .83 | | | | | .82 |
| Services by food providers are good | | | | | | .75 | | | | | .74 |
| Experiencing warm and friendly hospitality | | | | | | .66 | | | | | .74 |
| **Factor 7: Food Characteristic** | | | | | | | | | | | |
| Herbs and spices | | | | | | | .78 | | | | .74 |
| Contain a lot of herbs and spices | | | | | | | .76 | | | | .72 |
| Chilies | | | | | | | .65 | | | | .60 |
| **Factor 8: Essence of Malaysian Food** | | | | | | | | | | | |
| Appealing to human senses | | | | | | | | .74 | | | .68 |
| Rich in flavors | | | | | | | | .71 | | | .67 |
| Variety of local specialties | | | | | | | | .51 | | | .58 |

*continued on following page*

*Table 9. Continued*

| Factor | Factor Loadings | | | | | | | | | | Communality |
|---|---|---|---|---|---|---|---|---|---|---|---|
| Uses variety of cooking methods | | | | | | | | .44 | | | .55 |
| **Factor 9: Accessibility and Value-for-money** | | | | | | | | | | | |
| High availability | | | | | | | | | .79 | | .74 |
| Reasonable prices | | | | | | | | | .73 | | .71 |
| Food spots are located in convenient places | | | | | | | | | .45 | | .58 |
| **Factor 10: Symbols of Heritage** | | | | | | | | | | | |
| Cultural food | | | | | | | | | | .77 | .68 |
| Malaysian heritage | | | | | | | | | | .65 | .63 |
| Enjoying variety of food from different ethnic groups | | | | | | | | | | .43 | .53 |
| **Eigenvalue** | 10.74 | 2.34 | 2.01 | 1.69 | 1.44 | 1.37 | 1.22 | 1.16 | 1.10 | 1.01 | |
| **Variance (%)** | 8.32 | 7.85 | 7.70 | 6.74 | 6.69 | 6.54 | 6.29 | 5.86 | 5.54 | 5.36 | |
| **Cumulative Variance (%)** | 8.32 | 16.17 | 23.87 | 30.61 | 37.30 | 43.84 | 50.13 | 55.97 | 61.53 | 66.89 | |
| **Cronbach's Alpha** | .73 | .77 | .82 | .76 | .78 | .80 | .73 | .73 | .68 | .62 | |

Extraction Method : Principal Component Analysis
Rotation Method : Varimax with Kaiser Normalization
a. Rotation converged in 8 iterations

cultures' (Factor 5), 'food service and hospitality' (Factor 6). These factors were accounted for 21.08% when the percentage of variance for each individual factor was combined.

## Tourists' Satisfaction towards Malaysian Food

A multiple linear regression analysis was used to approximate the coefficient of the linear equation that involved ten independent variables (factors derived from Table 9) that best predicts the value of the dependent variable (tourists' satisfaction towards Malaysian food). Table 10 showed a significant regression model had existed [$F(10, 328) = 37.294, p = .000$]. The result of the regression model suggested that the null hypothesis of H2 to be rejected and this indicates that food image has significantly contributed to tourists' satisfaction towards Malaysian food. The R squared ($R^2$) value illustrated that food image could explain roughly 53.2% of the total variance in tourists' satisfaction.

There was a positive and high correlation between food image and tourists' satisfaction.

Among the ten factors analyzed, three factors were found to have significantly contributed to tourists' satisfaction on Malaysian food. Factors that were found to have a significant-p value are 'exotic culinary experience' (Factor 2), 'lifestyles and cultures' (Factor 5), and 'essence of Malaysian food' (Factor 8). The findings revealed that functional (Factor 8) and experiential (Factor 2 and Factor 5) image associations have significant effect on tourists' satisfaction towards Malaysian food. Factors comprising the symbolic-related image were found to be insignificant in predicting tourists' satisfaction.

Standardized coefficient (Beta) was examined across the three factors to determine the level of importance in each of the independent variable on tourists' satisfaction. The findings revealed that Factor 8 has the highest standardized coefficient value (.287) followed by Factor 2 (.254) and Factor 5 with a value of .211. These figures implied

*Table 10. Regression model of food image attributes*

| Model Summary[b] | | | | | |
|---|---|---|---|---|---|
| Model | R | R² | Adjusted R² | Std. Error of the Estimate | Durbin – Watson |
| 1 | .729[a] | .532 | .518 | .547 | 1.925 |

| ANOVA[b] | | | | | | |
|---|---|---|---|---|---|---|
| Model | | Sum of Squares | df | Mean Square | F | Sig. |
| 1 | Regression | 111.626 | 10 | 11.163 | 37.294 | .000[a] |
| | Residual | 98.176 | 328 | .299 | | |
| | Total | 209.802 | 338 | | | |

| Coefficients[a] | | | | | | | |
|---|---|---|---|---|---|---|---|
| Model | Unstandardized Coefficients | | Standardized Coefficients | t | Sig. | Collinearity Statistics | |
| | B | Std. Error | Beta | | | Tolerance | VIF |
| 1 (Constant) | -.065 | .224 | | -.292 | .771 | | |
| Factor 1 | .059 | .054 | .053 | 1.101 | .272 | .606 | 1.649 |
| **Factor 2** | .269 | .052 | **.254** | 5.220 | **.000** | .601 | 1.665 |
| Factor 3 | .116 | .062 | .102 | 1.883 | .061 | .490 | 2.040 |
| Factor 4 | .055 | .056 | .050 | .967 | .334 | .536 | 1.865 |
| **Factor 5** | .230 | .059 | **.211** | 3.905 | **.000** | .490 | 2.042 |
| Factor 6 | -.046 | .051 | -.043 | -.904 | .366 | .617 | 1.621 |
| Factor 7 | -.011 | .032 | -.014 | -.340 | .734 | .828 | 1.207 |
| **Factor 8** | .337 | .062 | **.287** | 5.450 | **.000** | .515 | 1.941 |
| Factor 9 | -.018 | .053 | -.017 | -.345 | .731 | .615 | 1.627 |
| Factor 10 | .049 | .057 | .042 | .863 | .389 | .597 | 1.675 |

a. Predictors: (Constant), Factor 1, Factor 2, Factor 3, Factor 4, Factor 5, Factor 6, Factor 7, Factor 8, Factor 9, Factor 10
b. Dependent Variable: Satisfaction

that for any one unit increase in the perceived image of 'essence of Malaysian food', tourists' satisfaction will increase by .287 units; while for any one unit increase in the perceived image of 'exotic culinary experience', tourists' satisfaction will increase by .254 units. Additionally, for any one unit increase in the perceived image of 'lifestyles and cultures', tourists' satisfaction will increase by .211 units. This indicates that the senses pleasure while savoring Malaysian food has direct effect on tourists' satisfaction besides being the most influential facet among the three significant factors.

## DISCUSSION AND CONCLUSION

The study aimed to determine the dimensions of Malaysian food image, in addition to empirically predicting tourists' satisfaction towards Malaysian food. The first contribution of the present study lies in identifying ten dimensions of food image in relation to Malaysian food. The findings revealed evidence that food image is multidimensional in relation to a destination. The identified dimensions may enrich the literature and provide better understanding of the image associated with Malaysian food.

Previous studies often adopt either quantitative or qualitative research method to elicit tourists' perceptions on food tourism. This study has gone the extra mile to employ mixed methodology to examine the effect of food image on tourists' satisfaction. Focus group was conducted to gather insights on the image associated with Malaysian food which subsequently formed the design of the survey instrument. The methodology used provides researchers in the food and tourism area an example of the application of mixed method approach which to date has not been widely employed in Malaysia. In terms of the contribution to the image studies, this study is particularly important because it propounds the employment of qualitative research method to gain more detailed insights into the understanding of food image and subsequently developing a scale measuring on food image in particular.

The findings revealed that tourists favored the outdoor/alfresco dining experience in Malaysia such as *Mamak* stalls and the hawker/street food. This image was perceived to portray the uniqueness of Malaysian gastronomic features. Therefore, this distinct image of Malaysia from the food perspective should be preserved as one of Malaysia selling points. Furthermore, the food characteristics are crucial to all citizens and may form a conversant basis for Malaysians to communicate the same characteristics of Malaysian food while introducing Malaysian food culture to others. This is in another way to aid in synchronization of the image of Malaysian food.

Secondly, the findings of the study showed a positive inclination to travel agencies in which a new target market has emerged in the tourism industry. Hence, travel agencies should take proactive action to incorporate gastronomic activities or food events in existing tour packages as a means of attracting food tourists. This will amicably increase tourist arrivals in Malaysia when there are more exciting tour packages that could cater to individual needs. In addition to increasing tourist arrivals, foreign exchange currency and employment in Malaysia will as well ascend.

Finally, in addition to other contributions mentioned, the findings may contribute to the Ministry of Tourism while drafting policies related to destination development in Malaysia. Past scholars have confirmed that images are critical to destinations development (Hunt, 1975; Echtner & Ritchie, 1993) and correspondingly the present study also confirmed that food images are as critical as the images of a destination as a whole. The findings revealed that food images have significant influence on tourists' satisfaction and high level of satisfaction will end with the intention to revisit a destination. Therefore, it is crucial for the Ministry of Tourism in Malaysia to bear the fact that another niche market has emerged and it is important for destination stakeholders to investigate the effectiveness of the projected food images through determining the number of tourists with repeat visitation periodically using cross-sectional survey. Ultimately, destination stakeholders can assess the viability of the projected food images through tourists' influx and hence, marketing strategies may be adapted and tailored to the current situation of the food tourist market. Sufficient capital can be assigned in constructing, promoting and maintaining culinary tourism as an important niche market in Malaysia tourism industry.

The present study was conducted by gathering information from focus groups to facilitate the design of survey instrument. Notwithstanding that this study has conferred valuable findings to the determination of Malaysian food image; several recommendations are suggested for future studies to further contribute to the body of knowledge.

First, future studies may attempt to recruit expatriates in Malaysia to participate in focus group. This may aid in the examination of Malaysian food image from an alternative perspective besides helping to validate the findings in this study. In addition, future researchers are suggested to collaborate with tour agencies in search for participation in the focus group from specific market; for example, Asians, Europeans, Americans and Africans. In due course, findings can be contrasted across markets to understand the needs and expectation of different target markets and marketing strategies can be planned conscientiously to promote Malaysian food.

Motivational factors, demographic factors and information sources can be examined across these regions to identify the factors that have influenced on their perceived image. Eventually the information will be valuable to enhance better understanding of each market and serve the potential markets accordingly. Finally, this study can be replicated in the future to determine the perceptions of tourists from different regions of the world on the image of Malaysian. This will aid in validating the survey instrument of the present study and provide a comparison on perceptions due to time changes. Investigating tourist's perceptions and the image of Malaysian food are crucial because image and perceptions are dynamic elements that changes according to time and other factors. Finally, the survey instrument is suggested to be produced in different languages as possible, in order to avoid language barrier faced by certain respondents' who are not familiar with English.

# REFERENCES

Ashworth, G., & Goodall, B. (1988). Tourist images: Marketing considerations. In B. Goodall & G. Ashworth (Eds.), *Marketing in the tourism industry: The promotion of destination regions* (pp. 213–238). USA: Croom Helm.

Au, L., & Law, R. (2002). Categorical classification of tourism dining. *Annals of Tourism Research*, 29(3), 819–833. doi:10.1016/S0160-7383(01)00078-0

Baloglu, S. (1997). The relationship between destination images and sociodemographic and trip characteristics of international travelers. *Journal of Vacation Marketing*, 3(3), 221–233. doi:10.1177/135676679700300304

Baloglu, S., & McCleary, K. W. (1999). A model of destination image formation. *Annals of Tourism Research*, 26(4), 868–897. doi:10.1016/S0160-7383(99)00030-4

Basala, L. S., & Klenosky, D. B. (2001). Travel style preferences for visiting a novel destination: A conjoint investigation across the novelty familiarity continuum. *Journal of Travel Research*, 40(16), 172–182. doi:10.1177/004728750104000208

Beard, J. G., & Raghep, M. G. (1983). Measuring leisure motivation. *Journal of Leisure Research*, 15(3), 219–228.

Beerli, A., & Martin, J. D. (2004). Factors influencing destination image. *Annals of Tourism Research*, 31(3), 657–681. doi:10.1016/j.annals.2004.01.010

Bell, D., & Valentine, G. (1997). *Consuming Geographies: We Are Where We Eat*. London: Routledge.

Bernama (2014, June 14). Malaysia bags destination award. *The Star*, Nation, pp. 20.

Bhat, S., & Reddy, S. K. (1998). Symbolic and functional positioning of brands. *The Journal of Consumer Marketing, Santa Barbara*, 15(1), 32–43. doi:10.1108/07363769810202664

Bigné, J. E., Sánchez, M. I., & Sánchez, J. (2001). Tourism image, evaluation variables and after purchase behavior: Inter-relationship. *Tourism Management*, 22(6), 607–616. doi:10.1016/S0261-5177(01)00035-8

Brokaw, S. C. (1990). *An Investigation of Jewellery Store Image Structure*. Unpublished doctoral dissertation, Florida State University: Tallahassee.

Burgess, J. A. (1978). *Image and Identity* (Occasional Papers in Geography, 23). Hull, UK: University of Hull Publication.

Chen, C.-F., & Tsai, D. C. (2007). How destination image and evaluative factors affect behavioral intentions? *Tourism Management, 28*(4), 1115–1122. doi:10.1016/j.tourman.2006.07.007

Choi, W. M., Chan, A., & Wu, J. (1999). A qualitative and quantitative assessment of Hong Kong's image as a tourist destination. *Tourism Management, 20*(3), 361–365. doi:10.1016/S0261-5177(98)00116-2

Chon, K. S. (1991). Tourism destination modification process: Marketing implications. *Tourism Management, 12*(1), 68–72. doi:10.1016/0261-5177(91)90030-W

Chon, K. S. (1992). The role of destination image in tourism: An extension. *The Tourist Review, 47*(1), 2–8. doi:10.1108/eb058086

Clarke, J. (2000). Tourism brands: An exploratory study of the brands box model. *Journal of Vacation Marketing, 6*(4), 329–345. doi:10.1177/135676670000600404

Coakes, S. J., Steed, L., & Price, J. (2008). *SPSS Version 15.0 for Windows: Analysis without Anguish.* Australia: John Wiley & Sons.

Cohen, E., & Avieli, N. (2004). Food in tourism (Attraction and Impediment). *Annals of Tourism Research, 31*(4), 755–778. doi:10.1016/j.annals.2004.02.003

Cohen, J. (1988). *Statistical power analysis for behavioral sciences.* Hillsdale: Erlbaum.

Crandall, R. (1980). Motivations for leisure. *Journal of Leisure Research, 12*(1), 45–54.

Crompton, J. L. (1979). An assessment of the image of Mexico as a vacation destination and the influence of geographical location upon the image. *Journal of Travel Research, 18*(4), 18–23. doi:10.1177/004728757901700404

Cronin, J. J., & Taylor, S. A. (1992). Measuring service quality: A re-examination and extension. *Journal of Marketing, 56*(3), 55–68. doi:10.2307/1252296

Dann, G. (1996). *The language of tourism: A sociolinguistic perspective.* Oxford: CAB International.

de Chernatony, L., & Segal-Horn, S. (2001). Building on services' characteristics to develop successful services brands. *Journal of Marketing Management, 17*(7-8), 645–670. doi:10.1362/026725701323366773

de la Barre, S., & Brouder, P. (2013). Consuming stories: Placing food in the Arctic tourism experience. *Journal of Heritage Tourism, 8*(2-3), 213–223. doi:10.1080/1743873X.2013.767811

Department of Statistics Malaysia. (2013). *Population projection, Malaysia 2010-2040.* Retrieved from Department of Statistics Malaysia website: http://www.statistics.gov.my/portal/images/stories/files/LatestReleases/population/Ringkasan_Penemuan-Summary_Findings_2010-2040.pdf

Echtner, C. M., & Ritchie, J. R. B. (1993). The measurement of destination image: An empirical assessment. *Journal of Travel Research, 31*(3), 3–13. doi:10.1177/004728759303100402

Echtner, C. M., & Ritchie, J. R. B. (2003). The meaning and measurement of destination image. *Journal of Tourism Studies, 14*(1), 37–48.

Elis, S. (2009, February 15). Our rich 'food' heritage. *New Straits Times.*

Fakeye, P. C., & Crompton, J. L. (1991). Image differences between prospective, first-time and repeat visitors to the Lower Rio Grande Valley. *Journal of Travel Research, 30*(2), 10–16. doi:10.1177/004728759103000202

Field, A. (2005). *Discovering statistics using SPSS: and sex, drugs and rock 'n' roll* (2nd ed.). London: Sage.

Food and Tourism is Interrelated. (2009, December 19). *Nan Yang Press*, pp. A12.

Fox, R. (2007). Reinventing the gastronomic identity of Croatian tourist destinations. *Hospital Management*, *26*(3), 546–559. doi:10.1016/j.ijhm.2006.03.001

Friedmann, R., & Lessig, V. P. (1986). A framework of psychological meaning of products. *Advances in Consumer Research. Association for Consumer Research (U. S.)*, *13*(1), 338–342.

Gallarza, M. G., Saura, I. G., & García, H. C. (2002). Destination image: Towards a conceptual framework. *Annals of Tourism Research*, *29*(1), 56–78. doi:10.1016/S0160-7383(01)00031-7

Galloway, G., Mitchell, R., Getz, D., Crouch, G., & Ong, B. (2008). Sensation seeking and the prediction of attitudes and behaviors of wine tourists. *Tourism Management*, *29*(5), 950–966. doi:10.1016/j.tourman.2007.11.006

Gartner, W. C. (1993). Image formation process. *Journal of Travel & Tourism Marketing*, *2*(2/3), 191–215.

Gartner, W. C. (1996). *Tourism development: Principles, processes, and policies*. New York: Van Nostram Reinhold.

Getz, D., & Brown, G. (2006). Critical success factors for wine tourism regions: A demand analysis. *Tourism Management*, *27*(1), 146–158. doi:10.1016/j.tourman.2004.08.002

Gnoth, J. (2002). Leveraging export brands through a tourism destination brand. *Journal of Brand Management*, *9*(4/5), 262–280. doi:10.1057/palgrave.bm.2540077

González, M. E. A., Comesaña, L. R., & Brea, J. A. F. (2007). Assessing tourist behavioral intentions through perceived service quality and customer satisfaction. *Journal of Business Research*, *60*(2), 153–160. doi:10.1016/j.jbusres.2006.10.014

Goodall, B. (1990). How tourists choose their holidays: An analytical framework. In B. Goodall & G. Ashworth (Eds.), *Marketing in the tourism industry: The promotion of destination regions* (pp. 1–17). London: Routledge.

Gross, M. J., & Brown, G. (2008). An empirical structural model of tourists and places: Progressing involvement and place attachment into tourism. *Tourism Management*, *29*(6), 1141–1151. doi:10.1016/j.tourman.2008.02.009

Haber, S., & Lerner, M. (1998). Correlates of tourist satisfaction. *Annals of Tourism Research*, *25*(4), 197–201.

Hair, J., Anderson, R., Tatham, R., & Black, W. (2006). *Multivariate data analysis* (6th ed.). New Jersey: Prentice Hall.

Halstead, D., Hartman, D., & Schmidt, L. S. (1994). Multi source effects on the satisfaction formation process. *Journal of the Academy of Marketing Science*, *22*(2), 114–129. doi:10.1177/0092070394222002

Hankinson, G. (2004). Relational network brands: Towards a conceptual model of place brands. *Journal of Vacation Marketing*, *10*(2), 109–121. doi:10.1177/135676670401000202

Hankinson, G. (2005). Destination brand images: A business tourism perspective. *Journal of Services Marketing*, *19*(1), 24–32. doi:10.1108/08876040510579361

Henderson, J. C. (2009). Food tourism reviewed. *British Food Journal*, *111*(4), 317–326. doi:10.1108/00070700910951470

Hjalager, A.-M., & Corigliano, M. A. (2000). Food for tourists - determinants of an image. *International Journal of Tourism Research*, *2*(4), 281–293. doi:10.1002/1522-1970(200007/08)2:4<281::AID-JTR228>3.0.CO;2-Y

Holbrook, M. B. (1978). Beyond attitude structure: Toward the informational determinants of attitude. *JMR, Journal of Marketing Research, 15*(4), 545–556. doi:10.2307/3150624

Hunt, J. D. (1975). Image as a factor in tourism development. *Journal of Travel Research, 13*(3), 1–7. doi:10.1177/004728757501300301

Husbands, W. (1989). Social status and perception of tourism in Zambia. *Annals of Tourism Research, 16*(2), 237–253. doi:10.1016/0160-7383(89)90070-4

Hutton, W. (2005). *Authentic Recipes from Malaysia*. Singapore: Periplus Edition.

Hwang, L.-J. J., van Westering, J., & Chen, H.-H. (2004). Exploration of the linkages between gastronomy and heritage of Tainan City, Taiwan. In J. Chen (Ed.), *Advances in Hospitality and Leisure* (Vol. 1, pp. 223–235). Bingley, West Yorkshire: Emerald Group Publishing Limited. doi:10.1016/S1745-3542(04)01015-X

Iso-Ahola, S. E. (1982). Toward a social psychological theory of tourism motivation: A rejoinder. *Annals of Tourism Research, 9*(2), 256–262. doi:10.1016/0160-7383(82)90049-4

Jalis, M. H., Zahari, M. S., Izzat, M., & Othman, Z. (2009). Western tourists' perception of Malaysian gastronomic products. *Asian Social Science, 5*(1), 25–36. doi:10.5539/ass.v5n1p25

Jankowicz, A. D. (2000). *Business Research Projects* (3rd ed.). London: Thompson Learning.

Jenkins, O. H. (1999). Understanding and measuring tourist destination image. *International Journal of Tourism Research, 1*(1), 1–15. doi:10.1002/(SICI)1522-1970(199901/02)1:1<1::AID-JTR143>3.0.CO;2-L

Jensen, O., & Korneliussen, T. (2002). Discriminating perceptions of a peripheral "Nordic Destination" among European tourists. *Tourism and Hospitality Research, 3*(4), 319–330.

Keller, K. L. (1993). Conceptualizing, measuring, and managing customer-based brand equity. *Journal of Marketing, 57*(1), 1–22. doi:10.2307/1252054

Khor, N. J. K. (2006). Nonya flavors: A complete guide to Penang Straits Chinese cuisine. Kuala Lumpur: Star Publications (M) Berhad.

Kim, Y. G., Eves, A., & Scarles, C. (2009). Building a model of local food consumption on trips and holidays: A grounded theory approach. *International Journal of Hospitality Management, 28*(3), 423–431. doi:10.1016/j.ijhm.2008.11.005

Kivela, J., & Crotts, J. C. (2006). Tourism and gastronomy: Gastronomy's influence on how tourists experience a destination. *Journal of Hospitality & Tourism Research (Washington, D.C.), 30*(3), 354–377. doi:10.1177/1096348006286797

Kotler, P., Bowen, J., & Makens, J. (2003). *Marketing for Hospitality and Tourism* (3rd ed.). Upper Saddle River, NJ: Pearson Education, Inc.

Kozak, M., & Rimmington, M. (2000). Tourist satisfaction with Mallorca, Spain, as an off-season holiday destination. *Journal of Travel Research, 38*(3), 260–269. doi:10.1177/004728750003800308

Lee, C., Lee, Y., & Lee, B. (2005). Korea's destination image formed by the 2002 world cup. *Annals of Tourism Research, 32*(4), 839–858. doi:10.1016/j.annals.2004.11.006

Lee, C. K., Yoon, Y. S., & Lee, S. K. (2007). Investigating the relationships among perceived value, satisfaction, and recommendations: The case of the Korean DMZ. *Tourism Management, 28*(1), 204–214. doi:10.1016/j.tourman.2005.12.017

Malaysian Tourism Promotional Board. (2009). *Best Country Brand: Malaysia, Top 10 Value-For-Money Destinations*. Retrieved from Tourism Malaysia website: http://corporate.tourism.gov.my/mediacentre.asp?page=news_desk&news_id=393&subpags=archive

Manderson, L. (1981). Traditional food beliefs and critical life events in Peninsular Malaysia. *Social Sciences Information. Information Sur les Sciences Sociales, 20*(6), 947–975. doi:10.1177/053901848102000606

Mayo, E. J., & Jarvis, L. P. (1981). *The Psychology of Leisure Travel*. Boston: CBI Publishing.

McArthur, A. M. (1962). *Malaya 12, Assignment Report June 1958-November 1959*. Kuala Lumpur: World Health Organization, Regional Office for the Western Pacific.

McFarlane, T., & Pliner, P. (1997). Increasing willingness to taste novel foods: Effects of nutrition and taste information. *Appetite, 28*(3), 227–238. doi:10.1006/appe.1996.0075 PMID:9218096

Meler, M., & Cerović, Z. (2003). Food marketing in the function of tourist product development. *British Food Journal, 105*(3), 175–192. doi:10.1108/00070700310477121

Mill, R. C., & Morrison, A. M. (1992). *The tourism system: An introductory text*. Englewood Cliffs, NJ: Prentice Hall.

Moutinho, L. (1987). Consumer behavior in tourism. *European Journal of Marketing, 21*(10), 5–44. doi:10.1108/EUM0000000004718

Mowle, J., & Merrilees, B. (2005). A functional and symbolic perspective to branding Australian SME wineries. *Journal of Product and Brand Management, 14*(4), 220–227. doi:10.1108/10610420510609221

National Institute of Public Administration. Malaysia (2003). Malaysia Kita. Kuala Lumpur: National Institute of Public Administration.

Okumus, B., Okumus, F., & McKercher, B. (2007). Incorporating local and international cuisines in the marketing of tourism destinations: The cases of Hong Kong and Turkey. *Tourism Management, 28*(1), 253–261. doi:10.1016/j.tourman.2005.12.020

Orth, U. R., & De Marchi, R. (2007). Understanding the relationships between functional, symbolic and experiential brand beliefs, product experiential attributes, and product schema: Advertising-trial interactions revisited. *Journal of Marketing Theory and Practice, 15*(3), 219–233. doi:10.2753/MTP1069-6679150303

Park, W. C., Jaworski, B. J., & MacInnis, D. J. (1986). Strategic brand concept-image management. *Journal of Marketing, 50*(4), 135–145. doi:10.2307/1251291

Parker, C., & Mathews, B. P. (2001). Customer satisfaction: Contrasting academic and consumers' interpretations. *Marketing Intelligence & Planning, 19*(1), 38–44. doi:10.1108/02634500110363790

Prescott, J., Young, O., O'Neill, L., Yau, N. J. N., & Stevens, R. (2002). Motives for food choice: A comparison of consumers from Japan, Taiwan, Malaysia and New Zealand. *Food Quality and Preference, 13*(7-8), 489–495. doi:10.1016/S0950-3293(02)00010-1

Quan, S., & Wang, N. (2004). Towards a structural model of tourist experience: An illustration from food experiences in tourism. *Tourism Management, 25*(3), 297–305. doi:10.1016/S0261-5177(03)00130-4

Riaz, M. N., & Chaudry, M. M. (2004). *Halal food production*. Boca Raton, FL: CRC Press.

Rittichainuwat, B. N., Qu, H., & Brown, T. J. (2001). Thailand's international travel image: Mostly favorable. *The Cornell Hotel and Restaurant Administration Quarterly, 42*(2), 82–95.

Robinson, J. P., Shaver, P. R., & Wrightsman, L. S. (1991). Measures of Personality and Social Psychological Attitudes (ed.). San Diego, CA: Academic Press.

Rogers, P. J. (1996). Food choice, mood and mental performance: some examples and some mechanisms. In H. Meiselman & H. J. H. MacFie (Eds.), *Food choice, acceptance and consumption* (pp. 319–345). London: Blackie. doi:10.1007/978-1-4613-1221-5_9

Rozin, P. (1996). The socio-cultural context of eating and food choice. In H. Meiselman & H. J. H. MacFie (Eds.), *Food choice, acceptance and consumption* (pp. 83–104). London: Blackie. doi:10.1007/978-1-4613-1221-5_2

Ryan, C. (1997). *The tourist experience: The new introduction*. London: Cassell.

Ryan, N. J. (1976). *A history of Malaysia and Singapore*. Kuala Lumpur: Oxford University Press.

Ryu, K., & Jang, S. C. (2006). Intention to experience local cuisine in a travel destination: The modified theory of reasoned action. *Journal of Hospitality & Tourism Research (Washington, D.C.)*, *30*(4), 507–516. doi:10.1177/1096348006287163

Saw, B. (2009). *The Complete Malaysian Cookbook*. Singapore: Marshall Cavendish Cuisine.

Scarpato, R. (2002). Gastronomy as a tourist product: The perspective of gastronomy studies. In A. M. Hjalager & G. Richards (Eds.), *Tourism and gastronomy* (pp. 51–70). London: Routledge.

Scott, N. (2002). Branding the Gold Coast for domestic and international tourism markets. In E. Laws (Ed.), *Tourism Marketing Quality and Service Management Perspectives* (pp. 197–211). London: Continuum.

Selwood, J. (2003). The lure of food: Food as an attraction in destination marketing in Manitoba, Canada. In C. M. Hall, L. Sharples, N. M. Mitchell, & B. Cambourne (Eds.), *Food tourism around the world: Development, management and markets* (pp. 178–191). Oxford: Butterworth Heinemann. doi:10.1016/B978-0-7506-5503-3.50013-0

Shepherd, R. (1989). Factors influencing food preferences and choice. In R. Shepherd (Ed.), *Handbook of the psychophysiology of human eating* (pp. 3–24). Chichester: Wiley.

Sheth, J. N. (1983). An integrative theory of patronage preference and behavior. In W. R. Darden & R. F. Lusch (Eds.), *Patronage Behavior and Retail Management* (pp. 11–27). New York: Elsevier Science.

Sparks, B. (2007). Planning a wine tourism vacation? Factors that help to predict tourist behavioral intentions. *Tourism Management*, *28*(5), 1180–1192. doi:10.1016/j.tourman.2006.11.003

Stabler, M. J. (1990). The image of destinations regions: Theoretical and empirical aspects. In B. Goodall & G. Ashworth (Eds.), *Marketing in the tourism industry: The promotion of destination regions* (pp. 133–161). London: Routledge.

Stern, E., & Krakover, S. (1993). The formation of a composite urban image. *Geographical Analysis*, *25*(2), 130–146. doi:10.1111/j.1538-4632.1993.tb00285.x

Telfer, D. J., & Wall, G. (1996). Linkages between tourism and food production. *Annals of Tourism Research*, *23*(3), 635–653. doi:10.1016/0160-7383(95)00087-9

Tellström, R., Gustafsson, I., & Mossberg, L. (2006). Consuming heritage: The use of local food culture in branding. *Place Branding*, *2*(2), 130–143. doi:10.1057/palgrave.pb.5990051

Tikkanen, I. (2007). Maslow's hierarchy and food tourism in Finland: Five cases. *British Food Journal*, *109*(9), 721–734. doi:10.1108/00070700710780698

Tuorila, H., Meiselman, H. L., Bell, R., Cardello, A. V., & Johnson, W. (1994). Role of sensory and cognitive information in the enhancement of certainty and liking for novel and familiar foods. *Appetite*, *23*(3), 231–246. doi:10.1006/appe.1994.1056 PMID:7726542

Um, S. (1993). Pleasure travel destination choice. In M. Khan, M. Olsen, & T. Var (Eds.), *VNR's Encyclopedia of Hospitality and Tourism* (pp. 811–821). New York: Van Nostrand Reinhold.

Um, S., & Crompton, J. L. (1990). Attitude determinants in tourism destination choice. *Annals of Travel Research*, *17*(3), 432–448. doi:10.1016/0160-7383(90)90008-F

Uysal, M., & Hagan, L. A. R. (1993). Motivation of pleasure travel and tourism. In M. Khan, M. Olsen, & T. Var (Eds.), *VNR's Encyclopedia of Hospitality and Tourism* (pp. 798–810). New York: Van Nostrand Reinhold.

Vickers, Z. M. (1993). Incorporating tasting into a conjoint analysis of taste, health claim, price and brand for purchasing strawberry yogurt. *Journal of Sensory Studies*, *8*(4), 341–352. doi:10.1111/j.1745-459X.1993.tb00224.x

Walmsley, D. J., & Jenkins, J. M. (1993). Appraisive images of tourist areas: Application of personal construct. *The Australian Geographer*, *24*(2), 1–13. doi:10.1080/00049189308703083

Weaver, P. A., McCleary, K. W., Lepisto, L., & Damonte, L. T. (1994). The relationship of destination selection attributes to psychological, behavioral and demographic variables. *Journal of Hospitality & Leisure Marketing*, *2*(2), 93–109. doi:10.1300/J150v02n02_07

Wilson, C. S. (1970). *Food beliefs and practices of Malay fishermen: An ethnographic study of diet on the East Coast of Malaya.* (Unpublished doctoral dissertation). University of California, Berkeley, CA.

Woodside, A. G., & Lysonski, S. (1989). A general model of traveler destination choice. *Journal of Travel Research*, *27*(4), 8–14. doi:10.1177/004728758902700402

Yuan, S., & McDonald, C. (1990). Motivational determinants of international pleasure time. *Journal of Tourism Research*, *6*(3), 42–44.

## KEY TERMS AND DEFINITIONS

**Behavioral Intention:** The likeliness of a person having a recurrent plan or decision.

**Experiential Values:** The sensual and cognitive characteristics that can be experienced through consumption.

**Food Tourism:** A tourism activity that revolves around visiting restaurants and tasting food in a destination of interest. Food related activities is the main reason for a person's travel.

**Food Image:** Food image is the visual information, either tangible or intangible in nature to illustrate food.

**Functional Values:** The core characteristics of goods that could fulfill a person's practical needs.

**Perceived Image:** An individual's subjective perceptions of image.

**Satisfaction:** The extent of overall pleasure or contentment resulting from the contra between and individual's expectation and the experience encountered.

**Symbolic Values:** The intangible feelings and symbolic benefits obtained from goods or services to satisfy a person's self-expression needs.

# Chapter 22

# The Impact of Integrated Marketing Communications on Hotel Brand Equity:
## Does National Culture Matter?

**Maja Šerić**
*University of Valencia, Spain*

**Irene Gil-Saura**
*University of Valencia, Spain*

**Alejandro Mollá-Descals**
*University of Valencia, Spain*

## ABSTRACT

*The Integrated Marketing Communications (IMC) approach appeared as a response to the need for more sophisticated marketing communication discipline in a confusing tourism marketing environment. This chapter examines the impact of IMC on the hotel brand equity dimensions, i.e. brand image, perceived quality, and brand loyalty. Moreover, it estimates the moderating effect of national culture on the relationships examined. The study is approached from the customer perspective and uses survey methodology to assess guests' perception of IMC and brand equity in the hotel contexts. In particular, 335 hotel guests participated in the empirical investigation while staying in high-quality hotels in Rome, Italy. The findings reveal that IMC exerts a positive impact on hotel brand equity. Furthermore, the inter-relationship exists between the three dimensions of hotel brand equity. In general, national culture does not exert a significant impact within the posited model.*

## INTRODUCTION

During the last decade the Integrated Marketing Communications (IMC) approach has received a great interest within the marketing and branding literature (Delgado-Ballester, Navarro, & Sicilia, 2012). The advocates of IMC believe that the concept is "*the major communications development*

DOI: 10.4018/978-1-4666-8606-9.ch022

*of the last decade of the 20th century*" (Kitchen, Brignell, Li, & Jones, 2004a, p. 20), "*absolutely imperative for success*" (Shimp, 2003, p. 6) that "*evidently, is here to stay*" (Kitchen et al., 2004a, p. 19). Undoubtedly, the IMC acceptance is growing rapidly (Kitchen & Schultz, 2009) since both academics and researchers have recognized significant challenges in its future (Fitzpatrick, 2005) and competitive advantages it can provide.

However, further contributions are needed to consolidate this new approach (McGrath, 2005). The IMC literature suggested that future research should concentrate on business practice (Kitchen, Schultz, Kim, Han, & Li, 2004b), that is, in organizations themselves, rather than in the agencies which service their needs (e.g. Eagle, Kitchen, & Balmer, 2007). In particular, there is little empirical evidence on IMC in hotel companies (Šerić & Gil-Saura, 2011), where the need for integration has proven to be as necessary as in other industries (Hudson, 2008). In addition, it seems that consumers' perceptions of marketing communications are often forgotten in IMC research (Gould, 2004), as a considerable amount of literature has centered on managers opinions regarding the IMC implementation, rather than on customer perception of integration (Šerić & Gil-Saura, 2012b). This is why we decide to examine IMC in the hotel context, while adopting a consumer-centric approach.

Moreover, academics and practitioners in the field of marketing and branding have supported the notion that IMC plays an important role in building and maintaining stakeholder relationships, and in leveraging these relationships to create customer-brand equity (Keller, 1993; Duncan & Moriarty, 1998; Duncan, 2002; Anantachart, 2004; Madhavaram, Badrinarayanan, & McDonald, 2005; Baidya & Maity, 2010; Delgado-Ballester et al., 2012; Šerić & Gil-Saura, 2012b). The most recent literature suggests that further research is

necessary to show a greater alignment between the brand and IMC when generating customer loyalty (Kitchen & Schultz, 2009). Besides, there is a need to consider the impact of message consistency on brand equity creation in a specific context (Delgado-Ballester et al., 2012).

If we centre on the hotel environment, we observe that previous studies into marketing communication effects on brand equity have mainly focused on the impact of advertising (e.g. Israeli, Alder, Mehrez, & Sundali, 2000; Daun & Klinger, 2006). Although these contributions are important, we believe that considering communication effects only in terms of advertising is limited as it is usually not the only marketing communication tool which can create and manage brand equity, nor the most important one (Keller, 2009). Therefore, we believe that the holistic view of IMC should be taken when examining how marketing communications affect brand equity and its dimensions.

In addition, a great body of literature showed that differences between national cultures exist and that they have a considerable impact on customer behavior. However, a meticulous research on culture in the hotel context carried by Chen, Cheung, and Law (2012) reveals that there is hardly any empirical evidence on the culture issues in the marketing field in general and regarding the constructs studied in this chapter in particular.

Thereby, the purpose of this study is to fill the existing gap in the literature by assessing guests' perceptions of IMC and brand equity and testing the impact of perceived IMC on the dimensions of customer-based brand equity that were found significant within the hotel context. In addition, it intends to examine the role of national culture on this impact, as well as the differences that might exist in guests' evaluations according to their national culture.

## BACKGROUND

### Integrated Marketing Communications: Conceptualization and Basic Principles

IMC definition remains the main topic in the academic research (Kliatchko, 2009), due to the lack of general agreement on its conceptualization (Kitchen et al., 2004a; Holm, 2006; Kitchen & Schultz, 2009). After reviewing a great number of different IMC definitions proposed in the literature, we consider necessary to develop a new conceptualization that gathers key elements of previous proposals, providing thus a better understanding of the concept. As our proposal relies on seven basic principles of IMC that have been discussed by a number of authors, we will first list and briefly explain them below:

(1). *IMC as a tactical and strategic process.* Nowak and Phelps (1994) suggested that IMC can occur at both tactical (i.e. incorporating a variety of communication devices within a specific type of promotional tool such as advertising, according to the "one voice" principle) and strategic level (i.e. integrating an entire promotional campaign through the use of multiple promotional tools which focus on imparting a unified message). However, one of the major challenges of IMC is to move from tactics to strategy (Holm, 2006). Accordingly, Kliatchko (2008) suggested that *"IMC is an audience-driven business process of strategically managing stakeholders, content, channels, and results of brand communication programs"* (p. 140).

(2). *Coordination and synergies of different communication tools and channels.* Thorson and Moore (1996) defined IMC as *"the strategic coordination of multiple communication voices"*, aiming to optimize the impact of communication *"by coordinating such elements of the marketing mix as advertising, public relations, promotions, direct marketing, and package design"* (p. 1). Thereby, under the IMC process, the rigid tra-ditional above- and below-the-line divide has switched into the 'through-the-line' approach (Hartley & Pickton, 1999; Schultz, 1999), where each communication tool is combined with others to maximize its strengths and minimize its weaknesses (Anantachart, 2004).

(3). *Message clarity and consistency.* IMC is considered as *"the concept under which a company carefully integrates and coordinates its many communications channels to deliver a clear, consistent, and compelling message about the organization and its products"* (Kotler & Armstrong, 1997, p. 450). As Delgado-Ballester et al. (2012) suggested, consistency among all communication messages refers to the existence of a common brand meaning shared by the customers (Keller, 1996) and is essential to gather the right brand-knowledge structure (Reid, Luxton, & Mavondo, 2005). In order to respond efficiently to market requirements and integrate its communications at the same time, a company must try to balance its many voices with the efforts to ensure clarity and consistency in its global expression (Christensen, Firat, & Torp, 2008). The ideal of consistency does not necessarily imply that all the messages have to be identical, but complementary and non-contradictory (Torp, 2009).

(4). *Communication centred on advanced ICT and database management.* Advanced ICT and the Internet have fundamentally changed the ways of interaction and communication (Keller, 2009) and enabled the integration of marketing communications through customer data management (Duncan, 2002; Kitchen et al., 2004a). New electronic medias such as the World Wide Web, e-mail, and interactive television altered the way in which advertisers view marketing communications (Peltier, Schibrowsky, & Schultz, 2003), especially as they affect IMC (Low, 2000). In particular, the unique ability of the advanced technology to provide two-way, customized, one-to-one, database-driven communication programs enabled firms to move towards the IMC paradigm (Kim, Han, & Schultz, 2004). Accordingly, Schultz

(1999) stated that IMC "*appears to be the natural evolution of traditional mass-media advertising, which has been changed, adjusted, and redefined as a result of new technologies*" (p. 337). In fact, IMC could not appear before because it was not achievable without new technologies (Duncan, 2002). Thus, owing to advanced technology solutions, IMC programs are able to capture precise data on customers. This means that database management is of crucial importance for the IMC approach, as it centers on a well-defined target (Kliatchko, 2005).

(5). *Customer-centric communication.* As suggested by Schultz (1993a), "*the IMC process starts with the customer or prospect and then works back to determine and define the forms and methods through which persuasive communications programs should be developed*" (p. 17). Therefore, IMC advocates for an "outside-in" approach, that is, first looking at the integration from the customer or prospect view, rather than a traditional inside-out perspective (Schultz, 1993b; Anantachart, 2004). In fact, the great change in the communication process refers to the fact that the consumers are currently taking control of it, as they decide whether and when to receive the message (Gurău, 2008; Kliatchko, 2008, 2009; Keller, 2009; Kitchen & Schultz, 2009). Likewise, they go through the integration process as they make sense of the messages they receive (Kliatchko, 2009). Moreover, instead of accepting the message that a communicator tries to "push" them, they rather "pull" the information according to their interests (Gurău, 2008; Kitchen & Schultz, 2009).

(6). *IMC as a component of the relationship approach.* The IMC process implies that marketing communications are not limited to the field of advertising, but transcend to the field of relationship marketing. Thereby, one of the objectives of IMC is to develop profitable relationships with the stakeholders and to improve consumer attitudes towards the brand (Duncan & Moriarty, 1998).

Several authors argued that relationship marketing changed the conception of the role of marketing communications (e.g. Duncan & Moriarty, 1998; Eagle & Kitchen, 2000; Reid, 2005; Gurău, 2008). Accordingly, in 1994, Duncan defined IMC as "*the process of strategically controlling or influencing all messages and encouraging purposeful dialogue to create and nourish profitable relationships with customers and other stakeholders*" (Duncan & Caywood, 1996, p. 18).

(7). *IMC as a component of brand equity strategy.* The IMC supporters consider the concept as a revolution meant to enhance marketing efforts and create brand equity (McGrath, 2005). IMC therefore refers to the process of managing customer relationships which drive brand equity (Duncan, 2002). In particular, Mulder (2007) stated that IMC "*supports a targeted, integrated, consistent brand communication strategy for the purpose of building positive lifetime relationships through data-driven techniques, by customer-conscious employees ultimately giving an organisation a competitive advantage and brand equity*" (p. 12). As noted by Keller (1993), a commonly held conception in the marketing and branding literature is that customer-based brand equity creation requires consistent meaning of the brand upheld by the integration of marketing communications over time (Delgado-Ballester et al., 2012).

Thereby, after reviewing the basic principles of IMC, we provide the new definition of the concept: "*The Integrated Marketing Communication (IMC) is a tactical and strategic consumer-centric business process, boosted by advances in Information and Communication Technology (ICT) which, on the basis of information obtained from customers databases, delivers a clear and consistent message throughout the coordination and synergies of different communications tools and channels, in order to nourish long-lasting profitable relationships with customers and other stakeholders and create and maintain brand equity*".

## INTEGRATED MARKETING COMMUNICATIONS IN TOURISM AND HOSPITALITY

Tourism markets and the media have grown more fragmented in the last decade (Hudson, 2008). The consumers find themselves with incomplete media images in a confusing marketing environment, which is why tourism marketers must coordinate all communication messages and sources in order to deliver a consistent, unified message through their promotional activities.

However, researcher on IMC in the tourism and hospitality industry remains rather neglected. After reviewing 60 empirical studies on IMC published since 2000 until 213 we found only a few of them applied in the tourism sector in general, (e.g. Skinner, 2005; Elliott & Boshoff, 2008; Wang, Wu, & Yuan, 2009; Dinnie, Melewar, Seidenfuss, & Musa, 2010) and in the hospitality context in particular (e.g. Kulluvaara & Tornberg, 2003; Šerić & Gil-Saura, 2011, 2012a, 2012b).

Thus, Skinner (2005) examined promotion of Wales as a tourist destination, finding the nation's key stakeholders sent inconsistent messages through websites and key documents. In this sense, "one-voice" principle of IMC was not respected, as different images and weak messages were delivered to customers.

Elliott and Boshoff (2008) analyzed the impact of different business orientations on IMC in small tourism enterprises in South Africa. The results showed a positive impact of: (a) market orientation; (b) entrepreneurial orientation; and (c) pro-active competitor orientation on IMC implementation.

Moreover, Wang et al. (2009) examined the role of IMC on selection of a heritage destination in Taiwan. The authors identified three factors of IMC: (a) public relations; (b) advertisement; and (c) direct sale & promotion, and showed that the influence of each factor changed within different demographic groups.

In addition, Dinnie et al. (2010) studied the principle of coordination that characterizes the IMC approach in the key organizations engaged in nation branding activities (i.e. promotion organizations, investment agencies, national tourism organizations, and embassies). Seven key dimensions of inter-organizational coordination emerged from their findings (i.e. sector, organization domicile, mode, strategy, formulation, nature, frequency, and target audience).

On the other hand, the study of Kulluvaara and Tornberg (2003) analyzed IMC in the hotel context, but was limited to a case study of Icehotel (i.e. a hotel built of ice and snow and a Swedish tourist attraction) and a description of its successful implementation of IMC strategy.

However, the IMC research within the hospitality industry was initiated by Šerić and Gil-Saura (2011, 2012a, 2012b), in particular, in their investigation in high-quality hotels in Dalmatia, the largest region on the coast of Croatia. They first investigated the level of implementation of IMC and ICT from the managers' point of view. The findings demonstrated a high degree of IMC and ICT implementation in high-quality hotels in Dalmatia, the largest region on the coast of Croatia. However, surprisingly, the ICT application increased with the hotel category, whereas the IMC implementation decreased (Šerić & Gil-Saura, 2011). In addition, the authors compared managers' and guests' perceptions of IMC, finding small but significant differences between the two compared groups. They concluded that managers believed that the IMC implementation was greater than the hotel guests actually perceived it (Šerić & Gil-Saura, 2012a). Finally, they tested the relationships among ICT, IMC, and brand equity from the customer perspective (Šerić & Gil-Saura, 2012b). The findings revealed positive relationships between the studied variables. Still, the authors did not analyze the inter-relationship among brand equity dimensions. Moreover, no attempt was made to examine the moderating role of national culture on the IMC impact.

## Customer-Based Brand Equity: Conceptualization and Evaluation

The literature has emphasized the importance of research of brand equity concept due to its strong association with marketing strategy and competitive advantage (Keller, 2003, 2009; Pappu, Quester, & Cooksey, 2005; Hsu T., Hung, & Tang, 2012). Keller (1993, 2003) and Aaker (1991, 1996) provided the main brand equity conceptualizations approaching the construct from the customer perspective. Thus, Keller (1993) defined brand equity as "*the differential effect of brand knowledge on consumer response to the marketing of the brand*" (p. 8). He suggested evaluating the concept through two dimensions of brand knowledge, i.e. brand awareness and brand image.

On the other hand, according to Aaker (1991), brand equity is "*a set of brand assets and liabilities linked to a brand, its name and symbol that adds to or subtracts from the value provided by a product or service to a firm and/or to that firm's customers*" (p. 15). Aaker (1991, 1996) identified the following five brand equity components: (a) brand loyalty; (b) perceived quality; (c) brand associations (referred to as brand image in the hotel environment); (d) brand awareness; and (e) other proprietary brand assets (comprising patents, trademarks, and channel relationships). Yoo and Donthu (2001) suggested that the last dimension of this proposal is not relevant to consumer perception, due to the fact that customer-based brand equity represents the assessment of cognitive and behavioral brand equity through a consumer survey. Therefore, only brand loyalty, perceived quality, brand associations, and brand awareness should be considered as the components of customer-based brand equity.

From a consumer-based behavioral perspective, Yoo and Donthu (2001) defined brand equity as "*consumers' different response between a focal brand and an unbranded product when both have the same level of marketing stimuli and product attributes*" (p. 1). On the basis of Aaker's (1991, 1996) and Keller's (1993) conceptualizations, the authors suggested a three-dimension brand equity model, comprising: (a) brand loyalty; (b) perceived quality; and (c) brand awareness/associations, combined into one dimension. In addition to these dimensions, Ha, Janda, and Muthaly (2010) considered satisfaction as another component of brand equity, showing its mediating role in the impact of perceived quality on brand equity. Moreover, Kim, Jin-Sun, and Kim (2008) employed the scale of Yoo and Donthu (2001) in their study on the impact of multidimensional customer-based brand equity on guests' perceived value and revisit intention in American midscale hotels. However, the authors noted that the adopted scale should be refined and validated in future research, due to the general skepticism among academics on combining brand awareness and brand associations into one brand equity dimension. This might be the reason why brand awareness is ceasing to be considered as the antecedent of customer-based brand equity (Lee, Lee, & Wu, 2011). In this sense, Round and Roper (2012) argued whether brand awareness is generating value for a consumer, as it tends to centre on what a company is doing rather than what consumers are actually getting.

## Hotel Brand Equity

Hotel brand equity represents "*the value that consumers and hotel property owners associate with a hotel brand, and the impact of these associations on their behavior and the subsequent financial performance of the brand*" (Bailey & Ball, 2006, p. 34).

In their proposal of a numerical brand equity index, Prasad and Dev (2000) suggested that brand equity in the hotel context is considered as "*the favorable or unfavorable attitudes and percep-*

*tions that are formed and influence a customer to book at a hotel brand*" (p. 24). In addition, Xu and Chan (2010) provided a conceptual framework for understanding hospitality brand equity, categorizing the concept into its attitudinal (i.e. brand knowledge - divided into brand awareness, brand associations, and quality of experience) and behavioral aspects (i.e. brand loyalty). According to this conceptualization, three brand knowledge dimensions are critical in determining brand equity and overall brand loyalty. However, it is questionable whether the brand associations and the quality of experience are indeed distinct and separable concepts, which is why further research is necessary to corroborate this proposal.

Regarding brand equity evaluation, on the basis of review of 30 empirical studies on brand equity within the tourism and hospitality context, we observe that the conceptualization provided by Aaker (1991, 1996) has been the most frequently applied (e.g. Kim, Kim, & An, 2003; Kim & Kim, 2004, 2005; Kim et al., 2008; Kayaman & Arasli, 2007; Lee & Kim, 2009; Nel, North, Mybur, & Hern, 2009; Hyun & Kim, 2011; Malik & Naeem, 2011). In addition, some authors employed different versions of this proposal. Thus, Cobb-Walgren, Ruble, and Donthu (1995) used only perceptual components (i.e. awareness, brand associations, and perceived quality) when examining the effect of brand equity on consumer preferences and purchase intentions among two set of brands; one from service category (i.e. hotels) and one from product category (i.e. household cleansers). Similarly, Hsu T. et al. (2012) excluded brand loyalty in their proposal of the service-based brand equity category in hospitality and centered only on brand awareness, brand associations, and perceived quality. They have justified this decision by the purpose of their study, which was creating service-based brand equity rather than examining consumer behavior. However, as Aaker (1991) suggested, the reason for including brand loyalty as a dimension of consumer-based brand equity

comes from the relevance of customer satisfaction in brand development. If customers are not satisfied with a brand, they will not be loyal and will switch to another (Kim & Kim, 2005).

On the other hand, some authors incorporated other variables in Aaker's (1991, 1996) and Keller's (2003) brand equity framework. Thus, Denizci and Tasci (2010) proposed value as the fifth component of brand equity of a tourism product (i.e. hotel, restaurant, resort or destination). In addition, Hsu C., Oh, and Assaf (2012) considered management trust and brand reliability as two additional components of brand equity in the luxury hotel environment and relatively new concepts to the brand equity literature.

Furthermore, we observe that the role of awareness in brand equity creation in the hospitality context is rather questionable. In this sense, several studies revealed that it is not a significant dimension of hotel brand equity (e.g. Kim et al., 2003; Kim & Kim; 2004, 2005; Bailey & Ball, 2006; Kayaman & Arasli, 2007; So & King, 2010). In their study on meanings of hotel brand equity, Bailey and Ball (2006) suggested that this might be explained by the fact that there are many well-known hotel brands that are inconsistent in their offer, and therefore, suffer from poor perceptions of service quality among hotel guests. Thereby, a brand name only will not guarantee the success within the hospitality industry (Olsen, West, & Tse, 1998). When providing a measure of hotel brand equity from the customer perspective, So and King (2010) explained this by the fact that experience-based perceptions, rather than brand awareness, affect customer behavior. Therefore, in this chapter we consider brand equity as a construct composed of three dimensions, i.e.: a) brand image, defined as "*consumer perceptions of and preferences for a brand, as reflected by the various types of brand associations held in consumers' memory*" (Keller, 2009, p. 143); b) perceived quality, considered as "*the evaluation that a consumer makes about the excellence or superiority of a product"* (Zeithaml, 1988, p. 3); and c) brand loyalty, understood as *"the attachment that a customer has to a brand"* (Aaker, 1991, p. 39).

## Integrated Marketing Communications and Customer-Based Brand Equity

From the literature review we can observe that scholars have paid hardly any attention to the role that IMC might play in the creation brand equity from the customer perspective (e.g. Delgado-Ballester et al., 2012; Šerić & Gil-Saura, 2012b).

Firstly, Delgado-Ballester et al. (2012) examined the impact of message consistency on brand knowledge, considered as an important antecedent of brand equity. They also analyzed the moderating role of brand familiarity on this influence. The findings showed that brand familiarity moderates the relationship between IMC and brand knowledge since, for familiar brands, moderately consistent messages improved their recall, enhanced their network of associations, and created more favorable responses and brand attitudes. For unfamiliar brands, the authors found no significant differences between high and moderate levels of consistency, except for brand recall, being higher in the case of highly consistent messages. However, due to the fact that this study used an experimental methodology, as the same authors reported, it was not able to truly capture other dynamic processes.

Secondly, Šerić and Gil-Saura (2012b) approached the relationship among IMC and brand equity dimensions in the hospitality context. Although the results suggested that IMC influences positively and significantly hotel brand equity and its dimensions, this impact might have been influenced by technology advancements, which were considered as an antecedent of IMC. In addition, the model was tested within a small sample size, which is why the authors suggested reconsidering

the perception of IMC and its role in brand equity creation among a greater number of respondents, approaching, moreover, the countries with more developed hotel sectors.

Thereby, as suggested by Anantachart (2004), the integration of marketing communications can influence brand equity through the encouragement of positive evaluations and attitudes and the impact on a consumer's memory structure for a brand. A number of studies on hotel brand equity suggested that hospitality firms should consider brand image, perceived quality, and brand loyalty if they want to establish brand equity (e.g. Kim et al., 2003; Kim & Kim, 2005; Kayaman & Arasli, 2007). Therefore, we will discuss the relationships between IMC and these three dimensions.

The branding literature suggests that the integration of marketing communication programs can form consumer perceptions of the product or service and help to create different attributes of brand image (Keller, 1993, 2009; Anantachart, 2004). Marketing communications can influence and control the meanings linked with the brand, and create and reflect the brand image, thus influencing the way consumers perceive the product (Cobb-Walgren et al., 1995). Due to the fact that brand image is shaped in the consumers' memory through brand associations, the consumer links the brand to both favorable and unfavorable concepts (Keller, 2003). The strength of brand associations from communication effects will actually depend on the integration of brand identities (i.e. brand name, logo, and symbol) within the supporting marketing campaigns (Keller, 1993). Moreover, consistent message may create a stronger image suggestion in consumers' memory than a message that delivers conflicting or not highly consistent information (McGrath, 2005). Specifically, in their study on the role of image in the hotel industry, Kandampully and Suhartanto (2000, 2003) suggested that, together with other marketing variables, communication can directly affect the hotel's image. Thereby, we can conclude that customers will perceive a strong brand image when they perceive a consistent message through different communication tools (Keller, 2003; Madhavaram et al., 2005).

In addition, Israeli et al. (2000) stated that repetition in marketing communications could be a signal of quality. In this sense, different studies carried out in hotel companies found that communication is an important indicator of perceived quality (e.g. Kim et al., 2003; Kim & Kim, 2005; Ladhari, 2012). However, these contributions were mainly focused on communication activities provided by hotel employees, rather than marketing communications perception.

Finally, according to Keller (2009), IMC can stimulate intense and active consumer-brand loyalty relationships by facilitating a strong connection between customers and the brand. Thereby, if customers are exposed to consistent brand messages, these messages can help maintain brand loyalty (McGrath, 2005). When focusing on this relationship in the hotel context, Imrie and Fyall (2000) suggested that hotel's promotional mix strategies can ensure customer retention and loyalty. Thereby, we conclude that, from an individual customer perspective, one of the most important goals of IMC is to effectively generate and maintain brand equity through encouragement and reinforcement of brand relationships with the customers and prospects (Anantachart, 2004).

## National Culture in Hospitality

Culture is a social phenomenon of a multidimensional nature (Donthu & Yoo, 1998). Although the culture can be classified in different typologies, such as, national, industrial, occupational, corporate, and organizational (Pizam, 1993), there is a general agreement in the literature to consider national culture as a criteria of measurement in cross-cultural research, as it is a completely objective and easily observable variable. Furthermore, with regard to the cross-cultural research in Europe, there is a tendency to consider Europe as a whole quite homogeneous in cultural terms (e.g. Welzel, Inglehart, Klingemann, 2003).

Within the hotel industry, a number of studies considered national culture when comparing different social groups (e.g. Mattila, 1999, 2000; Tsaur, Lin, & Wu, 2005; Yuksel, Kilinc, & Yuksel, 2006; Ngai, Heung, Wong, & Chan, 2007; Fisher, McPhail, & Menghetti, 2010; Chathoth, Mak, Sim, Jauhari, & Manaktola, 2011; Hsu C. et al., 2012). In this sense, Chen et al. (2012), in their review paper on the development of research on culture in the hotel management field, found that research themes relating to national culture have received the most attention.

With respect to subject areas examined, Chen et al. (2012) found that some studies approached the marketing area (mainly from the cross-cultural perspective) and were centered on the following topics: a) client satisfaction (e.g. Manzur & Jogaratnam, 2006); b) service quality (e.g. Armstrong, Mok, Go, & Chan, 1997; Siguaw & Enz, 1999; Davidson, 2003); c) relationship marketing (e.g. Lockwood & Jones, 1989; Gilbert & Tsao, 2000; Jones & McCleary, 2007; Osman, Hemmington, & Bowie, 2009); d) pricing strategies (e.g. Choi & Mattila, 2006; Mattila & Choi, 2006; Beldona & Kwansa, 2008; Magnini, 2009); e) behavior (e.g. Mattila, 2000; Hsieh & Chang, 2005; Hsieh & Tsai, 2009); and f) international marketing (e.g. Penn & Mooney, 1986; Jones & McCleary, 2004).

From these findings we can conclude that there is hardly any empirical evidence on the constructs studied in this chapter within the research on national culture in the hotel context. While no studies approached IMC in this sense, only few considered some dimensions of brand equity, i.e. quality (e.g. Armstrong et al., 1997; Siguaw & Enz, 1999; Davidson, 2003), and loyalty (e.g. Osman et al., 2009). However, these constructs were mainly approached form the organizational culture perspective. In fact, only Armstrong et al. (1997) compared service quality among different national cultures.

# EMPIRICAL RESEARCH IN HIGH-QUALITY HOTELS IN ITALY

## Research Hypotheses

The objective of this chapter is to examine the impact of Integrated Marketing Communication (IMC) on brand equity dimensions and to empirically test these relationships within the hotel industry. In this section we will propose and justify research hypotheses, which will be tested on data gathered in empirical research conducted in Italian hotels.

A considerable amount of literature suggested that IMC can affect brand equity and that further empirical evidence is necessary to corroborate this impact (e.g. Anantachart, 2004; Madhavaram et al., 2005; Delgado-Ballester et al., 2012; Šerić & Gil-Saura, 2012b). Moreover, a number of studies found that three dimensions of brand equity are significant in the hotel context, i.e. brand image, perceived quality, and brand loyalty (e.g. Kim et al., 2003; Kim & Kim, 2005; Kayaman & Arasli, 2007). Therefore, we posit the following hypotheses:

H1: IMC perception among hotel guests positively and significantly impacts hotel brand image.
H2: IMC perception among hotel guests positively and significantly impacts hotel perceived quality.
H3: IMC perception among hotel guests positively and significantly impacts hotel brand loyalty.

In addition, the inter-relationship existing between the three brand equity components should not be overlooked. The hospitality marketing literature showed that perceived quality can influence brand image (e.g. Kandampully & Hu, 2007; Kayaman & Arasli, 2007; Malik & Naeem, 2011) and customer loyalty. The impact of perceived quality on customer loyalty is both direct (e.g. Kandampully & Hu, 2007; Kayaman & Arasli, 2007; Hyun & Kim, 2011; Malik &

Naeem, 2011; Hsu, C. et al., 2012) and mediated by hotel image (e.g. Kandampully & Hu, 2007). In addition, numerous studies confirmed a positive influence of brand image on brand loyalty within the hospitality industry (e.g. Kandampully & Suhartanto, 2000, 2003; Kandampully & Hu, 2007; Hyun & Kim, 2011; Hsu, C. et al., 2012). On the basis of these considerations, we propose the following hypotheses:

H4: Hotel perceived quality positively and significantly impacts hotel brand image.
H5: Hotel perceived quality positively and significantly impacts hotel brand loyalty.
H6: Hotel brand image positively and significantly impacts hotel brand loyalty.

Finally, national culture is a frequently used criterion in the cross-cultural research within the hotel industry (Chen et al., 2012). In line with previous findings, we believe that national culture will exert a moderating effect on the above proposed relationships and will influence the guest evaluation of the studied variables. Accordingly, we propose the last two hypotheses:

H7: National culture exerts a statistically significant moderating effect on the causal relationships between the studied constructs.
H8: There are statistically significant differences in the guests' evaluation of the studied constructs, according to their national culture.

All the posited hypotheses are gathered in the causal research model, illustrated in Figure 1.

## Research Methodology

### Data Collection and Sample

The data were collected through a structured questionnaire, which consisted of closed questions measured by 5-point Likert type scales. The questionnaire was written in English, Italian, and

*Figure 1. Casual research model.*

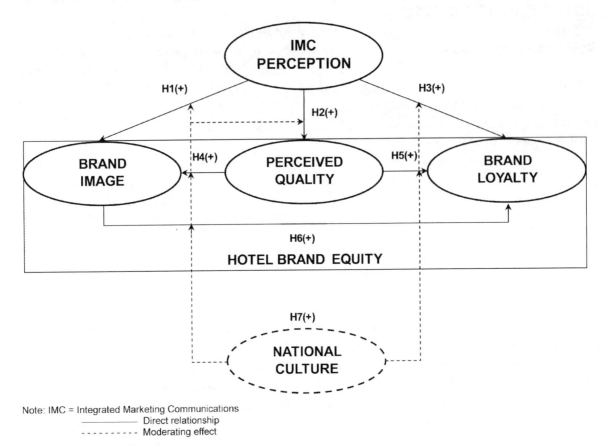

Note: IMC = Integrated Marketing Communications
————————— Direct relationship
- - - - - - - - - Moderating effect

Spanish by experts fluent in Italian and English and native in Spanish. Some adjustments were made to adapt each version of the questionnaire to the respective culture, preserving coherency throughout all three of them. It was mainly administered through personal interviews, while in several cases it was self-administered.

We conducted the empirical research in high-quality hotels located in Rome, Italy. After obtaining the permission from hotel managers to interview the guests, we carried out semi-structured interviews in hotel lobbies. We selected the respondents on the basis of their availability and willingness to participate in the research, approaching a total of 335 guests while staying in eight five- and 12 four-star hotels. As presented in Table 1, most of the respondents were Italians

(32.8%), while foreign guests (67.2%) were mainly from United States (21.2%), Spain (6.9%), France (6.6%), Germany (5.7%), Norway (4.8), United Kingdom (4.2%), and so on.

## Construct Measurement

To measure IMC perception, we adopted the first dimension of Lee and Park's (2007) scale, named "unified communications for consistent message and image". These authors proposed a scale that represents improvements over the previous IMC scales, as it was designed specifically for the development of IMC evaluation and not for another purpose, its procedures are more rigorous in methodology, and it is more comprehensive than other scales. In addition, the authors suggested

*Table 1. Respondents' national culture*

| National culture | Frequency (N=335) | % |
|---|---|---|
| Italian | 110 | 32.8 |
| United States | 71 | 21.2 |
| Spanish | 23 | 6.9 |
| French | 22 | 6.6 |
| German | 19 | 5.7 |
| Norway | 16 | 4.8 |
| British | 14 | 4.2 |
| Australia | 11 | 3.3 |
| Holland | 10 | 3.0 |
| Belgium | 9 | 2.7 |
| Brazil | 6 | 1.8 |
| Argentina | 5 | 1.5 |
| Canada | 5 | 1.5 |
| New Zealand | 5 | 1.5 |
| Hong Kong | 3 | 0.9 |
| India | 2 | 0.6 |
| Israel | 2 | 0.6 |
| Uruguay | 2 | 0.6 |

being comfortable, high level of service, cleanliness, being luxury, suitable place for high-class, feeling special by visiting the hotel, differentiated image), seven to measure perceived quality (i.e. making customers feel special and valued, well-mannered staff, providing services at promised time, effective customer complaints handling, active communication with customers, knowledge and confidence of the staff, anticipated service for special customer needs), and four to assess brand loyalty (i.e. intention to return, satisfaction, intention to recommend, non-intention to change).

## Data Analysis and Results

To confirm the validity of the proposed conceptual framework, a covariance structure analysis or the estimation of a structural equation model was carried out, following the two-step procedure recommended by Anderson and Gerbing (1988). In particular, we first performed a confirmatory factor analysis, followed by estimation of the structural, theoretical, or causal model that allowed obtaining information about the posited hypotheses.

As depicted in Table 2, the confirmatory factor analysis provided acceptable values for the reliability, measured through the composite reliability (CR) and the Cronbach's coefficient alpha for all the constructs. In particular, all the estimated indices were above the threshold of 0.6 for CR (Bagozzi & Yi, 1988) and 0.7 for Cronbach's alpha (Nunnally & Bernstein, 1994), which showed good internal consistency of scales. In addition, we obtained acceptable values for the extracted variances, being all the standardized factor loadings statistically significant for all the items. Moreover, as all AVE values were greater than 0.5, we concluded that more than 50% of variance of a construct was due to its indicators (Fornell & Larcker, 1981). All this allowed us to confirm the convergent validity of the model.

Additionally, in order to test the discriminant validity, we used Fornell and Larcker's (1981) criterion, since it is considered as the most strin

testing this proposal in the European context. We decided to employ the first dimension of the scale as, according to our opinion, it can be easily evaluated by the customer. This is because it primarily focuses on influencing product's recognition, image, consumer's preferences, and attitudes. In fact, this dimension is considered to be a fundamental aspect of IMC and has been identified at the early beginning of its evolution (Lee & Park, 2007). Thereby, we measured the following five aspects of IMC: (a) consistency through communication tools and channels, (b) visual consistency of message, (c) linguistic consistency of message, (d) brand image consistency, and (e) long-term consistency.

On the other hand, the three dimensions of brand equity were measured using the scale of Kim et al. (2003) and Kim and Kim (2005). Seven items were retained to evaluate brand image, (i.e.

451

*Table 2. Confirmatory factor analysis and descriptive statistics results*

| Construct | Item | St. Loading Factor (St. Error) | t | Cronbach's α | Composite Reliability | Average Variance Extracted | Total Sample | | Italian Guests | | Foreign Guests | | U Test |
|---|---|---|---|---|---|---|---|---|---|---|---|---|---|
| | | | | | | | Mean | SD | Mean | SD | Mean | SD | Sig. |
| IMC | Communication tools and channels consistency | 0.823 | - | 0.922 | 0.922 | 0.705 | 3.87 | 0.821 | 3.77 | 0.935 | 3.91 | 0.757 | 0.304 |
| | Visual consistency | 0.816 | 17.234 | | | | 3.92 | 0.762 | 3.88 | 0.810 | 3.94 | 0.739 | 0.554 |
| | Linguistic consistency | 0.880 | 14.854 | | | | 3.93 | 0.759 | 3.88 | 0.810 | 3.95 | 0.733 | 0.504 |
| | Brand image consistency | 0.874 | 16.730 | | | | 3.94 | 0.758 | 3.91 | 0.852 | 3.95 | 0.709 | 0.867 |
| | Long term consistency | 0.802 | 15.566 | | | | 3.88 | 0.750 | 3.76 | 0.908 | 3.93 | 0.688 | 0.228 |
| Brand Image | Comfortable | 0.766 | - | 0.934 | 0.937 | 0.682 | 3.99 | 0.973 | 3.85 | 1.082 | 4.06 | 0.909 | 0.154 |
| | High level of service | 0.853 | 19.870 | | | | 3.66 | 1.992 | 3.60 | 1.294 | 3.69 | 1.141 | 0.701 |
| | Cleanliness | 0.713 | 14.075 | | | | 4.05 | 0.997 | 3.93 | 1.186 | 4.11 | 0.887 | 0.481 |
| | Luxury | 0.888 | 16.929 | | | | 3.15 | 1.437 | 3.19 | 1.594 | 3.13 | 1.356 | 0.629 |
| | Suitable place for high-class | 0.898 | 17.245 | | | | 3.00 | 1.470 | 3.06 | 1.504 | 2.97 | 1.456 | 0.579 |
| | Feeling special | 0.864 | 16.007 | | | | 2.75 | 1.424 | 2.84 | 1.385 | 2.70 | 1.444 | 0.382 |
| | Differentiated image | 0.780 | 14.499 | | | | 3.00 | 1.279 | 3.03 | 1.274 | 2.99 | 1.283 | 0.782 |
| Perceived Quality | Special and valued customer | 0.875 | - | 0.955 | 0.957 | 0.759 | 3.83 | 1.224 | 3.76 | 1.340 | 3.87 | 1.165 | 0.877 |
| | Well-mannered staff | 0.880 | 23.019 | | | | 4.30 | 0.976 | 4.26 | .955 | 4.32 | 0.988 | 0.425 |
| | Services at promised time | 0.884 | 23.014 | | | | 4.07 | 1.086 | 3.92 | 1.076 | 4.15 | 1.086 | 0.025* |
| | Effective complaint handling | 0.861 | 17.375 | | | | 4.02 | 1.032 | 3.95 | 1.065 | 4.05 | 1.016 | 0.363 |
| | Active communication | 0.835 | 21.162 | | | | 4.09 | 1.006 | 4.11 | .952 | 4.08 | 1.034 | 0.975 |
| | Staff knowledge and confidence | 0.892 | 24.142 | | | | 4.02 | 1.018 | 3.95 | 1.091 | 4.06 | 0.980 | 0.462 |
| | Anticipated service for special needs | 0.870 | 32.372 | | | | 3.95 | 1.149 | 3.85 | 1.175 | 4.00 | 1.136 | 0.201 |
| Brand Loyalty | Intention to return | 0.879 | - | 0.940 | 0.943 | 0.805 | 3.68 | 1.243 | 3.55 | 1.359 | 3.75 | 1.180 | 0.309 |
| | Satisfaction | 0.869 | 20.073 | | | | 4.09 | 1.031 | 3.92 | 1.150 | 4.17 | 0.960 | 0.080 |
| | Intention to recommend | 0.937 | 35.095 | | | | 3.95 | 1.230 | 3.75 | 1.342 | 4.05 | 1.162 | 0.093 |
| | Non-intention to change | 0.903 | 31.532 | | | | 3.71 | 1.302 | 3.44 | 1.351 | 3.85 | 1.259 | 0.005* |

Note: * Significant, $p < 0.05$; IMC = Integrated Marketing Communications; Chi-square Satorra-Bentler: 677.12; Degrees of freedom: 224; CFI: 0.928; IFI: 0.929; Bentler-Bonett NNFI: 0.919; RMSEA: 0.078.

*Table 3. Discriminant validity of measurement scales*

| Construct | Correlations | | | |
|---|---|---|---|---|
| | F1 | F2 | F3 | F4 |
| F1. IMC | **0.839** | | | |
| F2. Brand Image | 0.650 | **0.825** | | |
| F3. Perceived Quality | 0.464 | 0.746 | **0.871** | |
| F4. Brand Loyalty | 0.546 | 0.762 | 0.845 | **0.897** |

Note: IMC = Integrated Marketing Communications; Diagonal values in bold are square roots of AVE and others (off-diagonal) are correlations between variables.

gent one (Farrell, 2010). This method requires a construct's extracted variance to be higher than the squared correlation of this construct with another construct. As shown in Table 3, all square roots of AVE were higher than the correlations between constructs. Therefore, the discriminant validity was also confirmed.

Once we verified the reliability and validity of the measurement scales, we estimated the structural equation model for the total sample. As presented in Table 4, we found support for the first six hypotheses. In particular, the results

suggest that the guests' perception of IMC exerts a positive and significant impact on all brand equity dimensions. In addition, positive and significant relationships are found between the three brand equity dimensions, more specifically between: (a) perceived quality and brand image, (b) perceived quality and brand loyalty, and (c) brand image and brand loyalty. These results are consistent with previous literature reporting that IMC positively influences brand equity creation and that the inter-relationship exists between the brand equity components.

*Table 4. Structural equation model results*

| Total sample | | | | | Multisample analysis | | | |
|---|---|---|---|---|---|---|---|---|
| Relationship | Stand. Parameter | Stand. Error | $t$ | Hypothesis | Italian Guests (N=110) | Foreign Guests (N=225) | Chi² Diff. | p-Value |
| IMC → Brand image | 0.387 | 0.053 | 8.073** | H1 supported | 0.417 | 0.379 | 0.300 | 0.584 |
| IMC → Perceived quality | 0.464 | 0.083 | 8.869** | H2 supported | 0.519 | 0.432 | 3.167 | 0.075 |
| IMC → Brand loyalty | 0.110 | 0.069 | 2.576* | H3 supported | 0.112 | 0.093 | 3.207 | 0.073 |
| Perceived quality → Brand image | 0.567 | 0.039 | 10.209** | H4 supported | 0.533 | 0.582 | 0.898 | 0.343 |
| Perceived quality → Brand loyalty | 0.629 | 0.069 | 9.242** | H5 supported | 0.610 | 0.611 | 0.146 | 0.702 |
| Brand image → Brand loyalty | 0.221 | 0.106 | 3.074** | H6 supported | 0.265 | 0.243 | 7.922 | 0.005 |
| Chi-square Satorra-Bentler: 677.14; Degrees of freedom: 224; CFI: 0.928; IFI: 0.929; Bentler-Bonett NNFI: 0.919; RMSEA: 0.078. | | | | | Chi-square Satorra-Bentler: 1055.17; Degrees of freedom: 454; CFI: 0.912; IFI: 0913; Bentler-Bonett NNFI: 0.902; RMSEA: 0.063. | | | |

Finally, a multisample structural equation model was estimated in order to assess the moderating role of national construct on the relationships among the different constructs. To perform this analysis, EQS (version 6.1.) and SPSS (version 19) were used as statistical software. In order to estimate the moderating effect of national culture on the established relationships, we divided the sample in two subsamples, one composed of domestic Italian and another composed of foreign guests, obtaining thus two additional structural models. Although we had to deal with a small subsample of Italian travelers (N=110), a review of applications of structural equation modeling confirms that studies with samples of around 100 individuals are not an unusual practice (Bentler, 2004).

Once we have assured that the constructs were measured in the same way in both models (Hair, Black, Babin, Anderson, & Tatham, 2006), we corroborated that the two models show good measurement scale validity and reliability. The model estimation results indicate that the relationships between IMC and brand equity dimensions are stronger for domestic travelers than for foreign ones. Thus, for Italian guests the path coefficients for the relationships between IMC and brand image, perceived quality, and brand loyalty are 0.417, 0.519, and 0.112, respectively, while for foreign guests they descend 0.379, 0.432, and 0.093, respectively. Nevertheless, these differences are not statistically significant (p>0.05). On the other hand, when testing the role of national culture on the relationships between the brand equity dimensions, we observe that path coefficients from perceived quality and brand image ($\beta$=0.582) and perceived quality and brand loyalty ($\beta$=0.611) are slightly stronger in the structural model for foreign guests than the corresponding path coefficients in the structural model for Italian guests ($\beta$=0.533; $\beta$=0.610). Still, once again, these differences are statistically insignificant (p>0.05). The results show that national culture has a significant moderating effect only on the relationship between brand image and brand loyalty, showing stronger impact among Italian guests (p<0.05). Therefore, H7, which hypothesized the existence of a statistically significant moderating effect of national culture within the proposed model, can only be supported partially.

Regarding the last hypothesis, descriptive statistics and nonparametric test were performed to assess the guest perception of the constructs. When comparing the evaluations of Italian and foreign guests, the Kolmogorov-Smirnov test was first conducted to check the normality of data distribution. As the results showed that the data were not normally distributed, the Mann-Whitney U test was completed, comparing two independent samples, as it is a nonparametric method that should be implemented when data do not show normal distribution. This test was used to determine whether the obtained differences between the two compared subsamples are statistically significant (see Table 2).

The results revealed a relatively high perception of IMC, obtaining brand image consistency the highest mean value (M=3.94) and communications tools and channels consistency the lowest (M=3.87). When comparing two delimited subsamples, we found that foreign guests evaluated all the IMC items better. However, according to the Mann-Whitney U test, these differences are not statistically significant, as all *p* values of IMC items are higher than .05.

On the other hand, the findings showed a more moderate degree of brand image perception, as several items did not reach high levels, e.g. feeling special by visiting the hotel (M=2.75), suitable place for high-class (M=3.00), and differentiated image (M=3.00). In general, the items of these constructs (i.e. being luxury, suitable place for high class, feeling special, differentiated image) reached greater scores among Italian guests. Once again, differences between Italian and foreign guests' evaluations are statistically insignificant.

Regarding perceived quality, the items of this construct obtained relatively high scores, especially those that measured well-mannered staff (M=4.30), active communication with customers (M=4.09), services at promised time (M=4.07), effective customer complaints handling (M=4.02), and knowledge and confidence of the staff (M=4.02). The nonparametric test showed that foreign guests evaluated with higher score all the items, except the one that assessed active communication with guests, which was better scored among Italian respondents. However, only the item that examined whether the hotel provides services at promised time showed statistically significant differences among the two subsamples (p=0.025).

With respect to brand loyalty, guests showed high satisfaction (M=4.09) and intention to recommend the hotel (M=3.95) and slightly lower intention to return (M=3.68) and non-intention to change (M=3.71). When comparing the two subsamples, surprisingly, all the items reached higher scores among foreign guests, while only the evaluation of "non-intention to change" was statistically significant (p=0.005).

To conclude, as *p* values of almost all items are higher than the level of significance .05, we cannot accept the hypothesis H8, which posited statistically significant differences in guest evaluations, according to their national culture.

## SOLUTIONS AND RECOMMENDATIONS

The results of this study confirm a positive and significant relationship between IMC and customer-based hotel brand equity, specifically between perceived unified communications for consistent message and image and: (a) brand image, (b) perceived quality, and (c) brand loyalty. These results suggest that high level of hotel implementation of IMC, and its subsequent guest perception can increase brand equity and provide the hotel with competitive advantages. More specifically, from a customer-based brand equity perspective, our

and maintain strong and favorable associations to the brand image, enhance hotel perceived quality, and encourage brand loyalty.

The practical recommendations and implications of this work are widespread across the hospitality industry. We believe that IMC will certainly lead a new world in the hotel sector, which is why managers should conceive it as an important factor of their marketing strategy. First of all, they need to understand how their marketing communication activities affect consumer perceptions. Then, they need to address the IMC implementation to build and maintain hotel brand equity. As brand equity implies satisfied and loyal customers, the final purpose of implementing IMC in businesses should be to create satisfied and loyal customers.

Moreover, hypotheses predicting positive relationships between the three customer-based brand equity dimensions are supported, showing that perceived quality significantly predicts both brand image and brand loyalty. This is another important implication for hotel managers, who consistently need to provide high-quality services to their guests. In particular, managers of Italian hotels should do their best in making customers feel special and valued and in anticipating services for their special needs, as these items reached lower mean values.

In addition, this study demonstrates that brand loyalty is also influenced by brand image. The recommendation is that hotel companies should do their best in creating a favorable brand image, ensuring comfort, cleanliness, and high-level of service. Specifically, hotels managers should be able to create a differentiated image, making sure that their guests feel special during their stay in the hotel. By doing so, hotels will obtain satisfied customers, who will be willing to return and make positive recommendations about the hotel. Italian high-quality hotels should focus their attention on improving these aspects, as according to the results of our study, brand image perception did not reach high levels, especially among foreign

Finally, national culture does not seem to moderate the relationship examined, nor to exert a significant role in guest evaluations, as Italian and foreign guests assessed the constructs similarly. This result is surprising and it might be related to the delimitation of the sample. Although covering both domestic and foreign guests was critical to increasing generalizability of the findings, different results might have been achieved if the sample was divided in two or more specific national cultures, rather than in Italian and foreign guests.

## FUTURE RESEARCH DIRECTIONS

This study contains some limitations that should be surmounted in future research. First, our findings are limited to the hotel context, in particular, Italian high-quality hotels. To obtain more generalizable results and for comparison purpose, it would be interesting to reconsider the perception of IMC and its role in creation of brand equity not only in lower hotel categories, but also in other tourism and hospitality companies, such as travel agencies and restaurants.

Moreover, some other variables could be included in the model. We did not analyze brand awareness, as previous research showed that it is not a significant dimension of hotel brand equity. However, future studies should consider this variable as one of brand equity dimensions, due to its high importance in brand knowledge creation. Besides, as awareness is assured throughout different marketing communications, the direct relationship between IMC and brand awareness needs to be empirically tested. In addition, brand familiarity could be examined, as it was found to have a moderating role on the relationship between IMC and brand equity.

Finally, the effect of national culture should be reconsidered, approaching a greater number of guests to obtain more representative subsamples. It is surprising the lack of the moderating effect of national culture tested in this work, as it does not

seem to support the idea that companies should consider cultural differences when making their business strategies. Therefore, in future research a representative number of respondents belonging to a specific national culture needs to be approached to re-examine the role of this variable in brand equity creation.

## CONCLUSION

Integration of marketing communications has taken on a new imperative and urgency in recent years. This new communication practice adopts the holistic view of marketing communications in order to deliver a consistent message and achieve a greater impact through the integration of all elements of promotional mix. Considered among many academics and practitioners as the major marketing communications development, we agree that its emergence and expansion is both necessary and acceptable. Nevertheless, some recent voices called for further empirical evidence to consolidate the concept. In addition, the enhancement of brand equity is critical to successful brand management within hotel companies, which is why further research on this construct is necessary in this specific area (Bailey & Ball, 2006).

The marketing literature also suggested that customer insights need further research, which is why this work aims to understand the relationships between IMC and brand equity from the customer perspective. More specifically, we consider that IMC needs to be examined from the customer point of view, following the outside-in approach, which is one of the basic principles of the integration approach. In addition, from a marketing perspective, brand equity is referred to as customer-based brand equity. Conceptualizing brand equity from the customer perspective is useful as it provides both specific guidelines for marketing strategies and areas where research can be convenient in assisting decision making process in management (Keller, 1993). In addition, national culture is another aspect that does not remain neglected when examining customer behavior. However, there is no any empirical evidence on its role when approaching IMC and brand equity building.

This work contributes to existing knowledge on IMC by providing the empirical evidence on its impact on brand equity building. In particular, the following conclusions can be drawn from the present study. First, IMC positively impacts three major hotel brand equity dimensions, i.e. brand image, perceived quality, and brand loyalty, exerting the strongest influence on perceived quality ($\beta$=0.464) and the weakest on brand loyalty ($\beta$=0.110). The second major finding is that the three brand equity dimensions are inter-related, showing the strongest relationship between perceived quality and brand loyalty ($\beta$=0.629). Finally, after dividing the sample into Italian and foreign hotel guests, this research has shown that national culture does not moderate the above mentioned relationships, except the one established between brand image and brand loyalty. In addition, it does not seem to affect guest evaluations of IMC and brand equity dimensions, as similar scores are obtained when the two delimitated subsamples were compared.

To conclude, this chapter makes several original and valuable contributions, thus filling the existing gap in the literature. First, whereas most of the research centered on the IMC implementation in advertising and PR agencies, our study examines the IMC concept in companies themselves. In particular, IMC is studied in a new specific context, i.e. the hotel sector, where the need for integration has proven to be as necessary as in other industries. Second, we have empirically examined the relationship between IMC and brand equity, an issue that, according to the most recent literature, needs empirical evidence. Third, while a considerable amount of literature has been published on the mangers' opinions regarding integration of marketing communications, we

decided to test our research model from the guest perceptive, confirming thus the importance of customer opinions and perceptions as an integral part of business and marketing strategies. Fourth, the role of national culture is examined, an effort which is original both in the IMC and brand equity literature.

## ACKNOWLEDGMENT

The authors are thankful for the support of the projects ECO2010/17475 and ECO2013-43353-R of the Spanish Ministry of Economy and Competitiveness.

## REFERENCES

Aaker, D. A. (1991). *Managing brand equity*. New York, NY: Free Press.

Aaker, D. A. (1996). Measuring brand equity across products and markets. *California Management Review*, 38(3), 102–120. doi:10.2307/41165845

Anantachart, S. (2004). Integrated marketing communications and market planning: Their implications to brand equity building. *Journal of Promotion Management*, 11(1), 101–125. doi:10.1300/J057v11n01_07

Anderson, J. C., & Gerbing, D. W. (1988). Structural equation modelling in practice: A review and recommended two-step approach. *Psychological Bulletin*, 103(3), 411–423. doi:10.1037/0033-2909.103.3.411

Armstrong, R. W., Mok, C., Go, F. M., & Chan, A. (1997). The importance of cross-cultural expectations in the measurement of service quality perceptions in the hotel industry. *International Journal of Hospitality Management*, 16(2), 181–190. doi:10.1016/S0278-4319(97)00004-2

Bagozzi, R. P., & Yi, Y. (1988). On the evaluation of structural equation models. *Journal of the Academy of Marketing Science*, *16*(1), 74–94. doi:10.1007/BF02723327

Baidya, M., & Maity, B. (2010). Effectiveness of integrated marketing communications: Empirical analysis of two brands in India. *Journal of Indian Business Research*, *2*(1), 23–31. doi:10.1108/17554191011032929

Bailey, R., & Ball, S. (2006). An exploration of the meanings of hotel brand equity. *Service Industries Journal*, *26*(1), 15–38. doi:10.1080/02642060500358761

Beldona, S., & Kwansa, F. (2008). The impact of cultural orientation on perceived fairness over demand-based pricing. *International Journal of Hospitality Management*, *27*(4), 594–603. doi:10.1016/j.ijhm.2007.07.024

Bentler, P. M. (2004). *EQS 6 Structural equations program manual*. Encino, CA: Multivariate Software, Inc.

Chathoth, P. K., Mak, B., Sim, J., Jauhari, V., & Manaktola, K. (2011). Assessing dimensions of organizational trust across cultures: A comparative analysis of U.S. and Indian full service hotels. *International Journal of Hospitality Management*, *30*(2), 233–242. doi:10.1016/j.ijhm.2010.09.004

Chen, R. X. Y., Cheung, C., & Law, R. (2012). A review of the literature on culture in hotel management research: What is the future? *International Journal of Hospitality Management*, *31*(1), 52–65. doi:10.1016/j.ijhm.2011.06.010

Choi, S., & Mattila, A. S. (2006). The role of disclosure in variable hotel pricing: A cross-cultural comparison of customers' fairness. *The Cornell Hotel and Restaurant Administration Quarterly*, *47*(1), 27–35. doi:10.1177/0010880405281681

Christensen, L. T., Firat, A. F., & Torp, S. (2008). The organization of integrated communications: Toward flexible integration. *European Journal of Marketing*, *42*(3/4), 423–452. doi:10.1108/03090560810853002

Cobb-Walgren, C. J., Ruble, C. A., & Donthu, N. (1995). Brand equity, brand preference and purchase intent. *Journal of Advertising*, *24*(3), 25–40. doi:10.1080/00913367.1995.10673481

Daun, W., & Klinger, R. (2006). Delivering the message. How premium hotel brands struggle to communicate their value proposition. *International Journal of Contemporary Hospitality Management*, *18*(3), 246–252. doi:10.1108/09596110610658643

Davidson, M. C. (2003). Does organizational climate add to service quality in hotels? *International Journal of Contemporary Hospitality Management*, *15*(4), 206–213. doi:10.1108/09596110310475658

Delgado-Ballester, E., Navarro, A., & Sicilia, M. (2012). Revitalising brands through communication messages: The role of brand familiarity. *European Journal of Marketing*, *46*(1), 31–51. doi:10.1108/03090561211189220

Denizci, B., & Tasci, A. D. A. (2010). Modeling the commonly-assumed relationship between human capital and brand equity in tourism. *Journal of Hospitality Marketing & Management*, *19*(6), 610–628. doi:10.1080/19368623.2010.493073

Dinnie, K., Melewar, T. C., Seidenfuss, K. U., & Musa, G. (2010). Nation branding and integrated marketing communications: An ASEAN perspective. *International Marketing Review*, *27*(4), 388–403. doi:10.1108/02651331011058572

Donthu, N., & Yoo, B. (1998). Cultural influences on service quality expectations. *Journal of Service Research*, *1*(2), 178–186. doi:10.1177/109467059800100207

Duncan, T., & Moriarty, S. E. (1998). A communication-based marketing model for managing relationships. *Journal of Marketing, 62*(2), 1–13. doi:10.2307/1252157

Duncan, T. R. (2002). *IMC: Using advertising and promotion to build brands* (International Edition). New York, NY: The McGraw-Hill Companies, Inc.

Duncan, T. R., & Caywood, C. (1996). The concept, process, and evolution of integrated marketing communications. In E. Thorson & J. Moore (Eds.), *Integrated communication: Synergy of persuasive voices* (pp. 13–34). Mahwah, NJ: Lawrence Erlbaum Associates.

Eagle, L., & Kitchen, P. J. (2000). IMC, brand communications, and corporate cultures. Client/advertising agency co-ordination and cohesion. *European Journal of Marketing, 34*(5/6), 667–686. doi:10.1108/03090560010321983

Eagle, L., Kitchen, P. J., & Bulmer, S. (2007). Insights into interpreting integrated marketing communications. A two-nation qualitative comparison. *European Journal of Marketing, 41*(7/8), 956–970. doi:10.1108/03090560710752474

Elliott, R., & Boshoff, C. (2008). The influence of business orientations in small tourism businesses on the success of integrated marketing communication. *Management Dynamics, 17*(4), 32–46.

Farrell, A. M. (2010). Insufficient discriminant validity: A comment on Bove, Pervan, Beatty and Shiu (2009). *Journal of Business Research, 63*(3), 324–327. doi:10.1016/j.jbusres.2009.05.003

Fisher, R., McPhail, R., & Menghetti, G. (2010). Linking employee attitudes and behaviors with business performance: A comparative analysis of hotels in Mexico and China. *International Journal of Hospitality Management, 29*(3), 397–404. doi:10.1016/j.ijhm.2009.10.021

Fitzpatrick, K. R. (2005). The legal challenge of integrated marketing communication (IMC): Integrating commercial and political speech. *Journal of Advertising, 34*(4), 93–102. doi:10.1080/00913367.2005.10639205

Fornell, C., & Larcker, D. F. (1981). Evaluating structural equation models with unobservable variables and measurement error. *JMR, Journal of Marketing Research, 18*(1), 39–50. doi:10.2307/3151312

Gilbert, D., & Tsao, J. (2000). Exploring Chinese cultural influences and hospitality marketing relationships. *International Journal of Contemporary Hospitality Management, 12*(1), 45–54. doi:10.1108/09596110010305037

Gould, S. J. (2004). IMC as theory and as a poststructural set of practices and discourses: A continuously evolving paradigm shift. *Journal of Advertising Research, 44*(1), 66–70. doi:10.1017/S002184990404019X

Gurău, C. (2008). Integrated online marketing communication: Implementation and management. *Journal of Communication Management, 12*(2), 169–184. doi:10.1108/13632540810881974

Ha, H. Y., Janda, S., & Muthaly, S. (2010). Development of brand equity: Evaluation of four alternative models. *Service Industries Journal, 30*(6), 911–928. doi:10.1080/02642060802320253

Hair, J. F., Black, W. C., Babin, B. J., Anderson, R. E., & Tatham, R. L. (2006). *Multivariate data analysis* (6th ed.). New Jersey, NJ: Prentice-Hall International.

Hartley, B., & Pickton, D. (1999). Integrated marketing communications requires a new way of thinking. *Journal of Marketing Communications, 5*(2), 97–106. doi:10.1080/135272699345699

Holm, O. (2006). Integrated marketing communication: From tactics to strategy. *Corporate Communications: An International Journal, 11*(1), 23–33. doi:10.1108/13563280610643525

Hsieh, A. T., & Chang, J. (2005). The different response to hotels' endorsement advertising by Taiwanese and American tourists. *Journal of Travel & Tourism Marketing, 19*(4), 41–54. doi:10.1300/J073v19n04_04

Hsieh, A. T., & Tsai, C. W. (2009). Does national culture really matter? Hotel service perceptions by Taiwan and American tourists. *International Journal of Culture. Tourism and Hospitality Research, 3*(1), 54–69.

Hsu, C. H. C., Oh, H., & Assaf, A. G. (2012). A customer-based brand equity model for upscale hotels. *Journal of Travel Research, 51*(1), 81–93. doi:10.1177/0047287510394195

Hsu, T. H., Hung, L. C., & Tang, J. W. (2012). An analytical model for building brand equity in hospitality firms. *Annals of Operations Research, 195*(1), 355–378. doi:10.1007/s10479-011-0990-4

Hudson, S. (2008). *Marketing for tourism and hospitality. A global perspective* (2nd ed.). London, UK: Sage. doi:10.4135/9781446280140

Hyun, S. S., & Kim, W. (2011). Dimensions of brand equity in the chain restaurant industry. *Cornell Hospitality Quarterly, 52*(4), 429–437. doi:10.1177/1938965510397533

Imrie, R., & Fyall, A. (2000). Customer retention and loyalty in the independent mid-market hotel sector. *Journal of Hospitality Marketing & Management, 7*(3), 39–54. doi:10.1300/J150v07n03_04

Israeli, A. A., Adler, N., Mehrez, A., & Sundali, J. A. (2000). Investigating the use of advertising for communicating a hotel's strategic assets. *Journal of Hospitality Marketing & Management, 7*(3), 23–37. doi:10.1300/J150v07n03_03

Jones, D. L., & McCleary, K. W. (2004). A model for assessing cultural impacts on inter- national buyer-seller relationships for key accounts of hotel companies. *Journal of Hospitality & Tourism Research (Washington, D.C.), 28*(4), 425–443. doi:10.1177/1096348004265026

Jones, D. L., & McCleary, K. W. (2007). Expectations of working relationships in inter- national buyer-seller relationships: Development of a relationship continuum scale. *Asia Pacific Journal of Tourism Research, 12*(3), 181–202. doi:10.1080/10941660701416747

Kandampully, J., & Hu, H. H. (2007). Do hoteliers need to manage image to retain loyal customers? *International Journal of Contemporary Hospitality Management, 19*(6), 435–443. doi:10.1108/09596110710775101

Kandampully, J., & Suhartanto, D. (2000). Customer loyalty in the hotel industry: The role of customer satisfaction and image. *International Journal of Contemporary Hospitality Management, 12*(6), 346–351. doi:10.1108/09596110010342559

Kandampully, J., & Suhartanto, D. (2003). The role of customer satisfaction and image in gaining customer loyalty in the hotel industry. *Journal of Hospitality Marketing & Management, 10*(1/2), 3–25. doi:10.1300/J150v10n01_02

Kayaman, R., & Arasli, H. (2007). Customer based brand equity: Evidence from the hotel industry. *Managing Service Quality, 17*(1), 92–109. doi:10.1108/09604520710720692

Keller, K. L. (1993). Conceptualizing, measuring, and managing customer-based brand equity. *Journal of Marketing, 57*(1), 1–22. doi:10.2307/1252054

Keller, K. L. (1996). Integrated marketing communications and brand equity. In J. Moore & E. Thorson (Eds.), *Integrated Marketing Communications* (pp. 103–132). Mahwah, NJ: Lawrence Erlbaum Associates.

Keller, K. L. (2003). *Strategic brand management: Building, measuring, and managing brand equity* (2nd ed.). Upper Saddle River, NJ: Prentice Hall.

Keller, K. L. (2009). Building strong brands in a modern marketing communications environment. *Journal of Marketing Communications*, *15*(2/3), 139–155. doi:10.1080/13527260902757530

Kim, H. B., & Kim, W. G. (2005). The relationship between brand equity and firms' performance in luxury hotels and restaurants. *Tourism Management*, *26*(4), 549–560. doi:10.1016/j.tourman.2004.03.010

Kim, H. B., Kim, W. G., & An, J. A. (2003). The effect of customer-based brand equity on firms' financial performance. *Journal of Customer Marketing*, *20*(4), 335–351. doi:10.1108/07363760310483694

Kim, I., Han, D., & Schultz, D. E. (2004). Understanding the diffusion of integrated marketing communication. *Journal of Advertising Research*, *44*(1), 31–45. doi:10.1017/S0021849904040024

Kim, W. G., Jin-Sun, B., & Kim, H. J. (2008). Multidimensional customer-based brand equity and its consequences in midpriced hotels. *Journal of Hospitality & Tourism Research (Washington, D.C.)*, *32*(2), 235–254. doi:10.1177/1096348007313265

Kim, W. G., & Kim, H. B. (2004). Measuring customer-based restaurant brand equity: Investigating the relationship between brand equity and firms' performance. *The Cornell Hotel and Restaurant Administration Quarterly*, *45*(2), 115–131. doi:10.1177/0010880404264507

Kitchen, P. J., Brignell, J., Li, T., & Jones, G. S. (2004a). The emergence of IMC: A theoretical perspective. *Journal of Advertising Research*, *44*(1), 19–30. doi:10.1017/S0021849904040048

Kitchen, P. J., & Schultz, D. E. (2009). IMC: New horizon/false dawn for a marketplace in turmoil? *Journal of Marketing Communications*, *15*(2/3), 197–204. doi:10.1080/13527260903003793

Kitchen, P. J., Schultz, D. E., Kim, I., Han, D., & Li, T. (2004b). Will agencies ever "get" (or understand) IMC? *European Journal of Marketing*, *38*(11/12), 1417–1436. doi:10.1108/03090560410560173

Kliatchko, J. (2005). Towards a new definition of integrated marketing communications (IMC). *International Journal of Advertising*, *24*(1), 7–34.

Kliatchko, J. (2008). Revisiting the IMC construct: A revised definition and four pillars. *International Journal of Advertising*, *27*(1), 133–160.

Kliatchko, J. (2009). IMC 20 years after: A second look at IMC definitions. International. *Journal of Integrated Marketing Communications*, *1*(2), 7–12.

Kotler, P., & Armstrong, G. (1997). *Marketing: An introduction* (4th ed.). Upper Saddle River, NJ: Prentice-Hall.

Kulluvaara, C., & Tornberg, J. (2003). *Integrated marketing communication and tourism. A case study of Icehotel.* (Bachelor's thesis). Retrieved from http://epubl.ltu.se/1404-5508/2003/138/LTU-SHU-EX-03138-SE.pdf

Ladhari, R. (2012). The lodging quality index: An independent assessment of validity and dimensions. *International Journal of Contemporary Hospitality Management*, *24*(4), 628–652. doi:10.1108/09596111211217914

Lee, D. H., & Park, C. W. (2007). Conceptualization and measurement of multidimensionality of integrated marketing communications. *Journal of Advertising Research, 47*(3), 222–236. doi:10.2501/S0021849907070274

Lee, H. M., Lee, C. C., & Wu, C. C. (2011). Brand image strategy affects brand equity after M&A. *European Journal of Marketing, 45*(7/8), 1091–1111. doi:10.1108/03090561111137624

Lee, J. W., & Kim, H. B. (2009). Impacts of perception to alliance companies on hotel's brand equity according to the types of vertical integration. *International Journal of Tourism Sciences, 9*(2), 1–21. doi:10.1080/15980634.2009.11434611

Lockwood, A., & Jones, P. (1989). Creating positive service encounters. *The Cornell Hotel and Restaurant Administration Quarterly, 29*(4), 44–50. doi:10.1177/001088048902900411

Low, G. S. (2000). Correlates of integrated marketing communications. *Journal of Advertising Research, 40*(3), 27–39.

Madhavaram, S., Badrinarayanan, V., & McDonald, R. E. (2005). Integrated marketing communication (IMC) and brand identity as critical components of brand equity strategy: A conceptual framework and research propositions. *Journal of Advertising, 34*(4), 69–80. doi:10.1080/00913367.2005.10639213

Magnini, V. P. (2009). The influence of national culture on the strategic use of salesperson pricing authority: A cross-country study within the hotel industry. *International Journal of Hospitality Management, 28*(1), 173–176. doi:10.1016/j.ijhm.2008.06.002

Malik, M. E., & Naeem, B. (2011). Interrelationship between customer based brand equity constructs: Empirical evidence from hotel industry of Pakistan. Interdisciplinary. *Journal of Contemporary Research in Business, 3*(4), 795–804.

Manzur, L., & Jogaratnam, G. (2006). Impression management and the hospitality service encounter: Ross-cultural differences. *Journal of Travel & Tourism Marketing, 20*(3/4), 21–32.

Mattila, A., & Choi, S. (2006). A cross-cultural comparison of perceived fairness and satisfaction in the context of hotel room pricing. *International Journal of Hospitality Management, 25*(1), 146–153. doi:10.1016/j.ijhm.2004.12.003

Mattila, A. S. (1999). The role of culture in the service evaluation process. *Journal of Service Research, 1*(3), 250–261. doi:10.1177/109467059913006

Mattila, A. S. (2000). The impact of culture and gender on customer evaluations of service encounters. *Journal of Hospitality & Tourism Research (Washington, D.C.), 24*(2), 263–273. doi:10.1177/109634800002400209

McGrath, J. M. (2005). A pilot study testing aspects of the integrated marketing communications concept. *Journal of Marketing Communications, 11*(3), 191–214. doi:10.1080/1352726042000333199

Mulder, D. (2007). *Driving integrated marketing communication home for organizational effectiveness.* Paper presented at the meeting Communications, Civics, Industry of Australian New Zealand Communication Association National Conference (ANZCA), Melbourne, Australia.

Nel, J. D. W., North, E. J., Mybur, T., & Hern, L. (2009). A comparative study of customer-based brand equity across selected South African hotels. *International Retail and Marketing Review, 5*(1), 15–24.

Ngai, E. W. T., Heung, V. C. S., Wong, Y. H., & Chan, K. Y. (2007). Consumer complaint behavior of Asians and non-Asians about hotel services. An empirical analyses. *European Journal of Marketing, 41*(11/12), 1375–1391. doi:10.1108/03090560710821224

Nowak, G., & Phelps, J. (1994). Conceptualizing the integrated marketing communication's phenomenon: An examination of its impact on advertising and its implications for advertising research. *Journal of Current Issues and Research in Advertising, 16*(1), 49–66. doi:10.1080/10641734.1994.10505012

Nunnally, J. C., & Bernstein, I. H. (1994). *Psychometric theory* (3rd ed.). New York, NY: McGraw Hill.

Olsen, M. D., West, J., & Tse, E. (1998). *Strategic management in the hospitality industry* (2nd ed.). New York, NY: John Wiley & Sons.

Osman, H., Hemmington, N., & Bowie, D. (2009). A transactional approach to customer loyalty in the hotel industry. *International Journal of Contemporary Hospitality Management, 21*(3), 239–250. doi:10.1108/09596110910948279

Pappu, R., Quester, P. G., & Cooksey, R. W. (2005). Consumer-based brand equity: Improving the measurement-empirical evidence. *Journal of Product and Brand Management, 14*(3), 143–154. doi:10.1108/10610420510601012

Peltier, J., Schibrowsky, J., & Schultz, D. E. (2003). Interactive integrated marketing communication: Combining the power of IMC, the new media and database marketing. *International Journal of Advertising, 22*(1), 93–115.

Penn, J. M., & Mooney, S. (1986). Cross-cultural negotiations in the hospitality industry: The Japanese market. *International Journal of Hospitality Management, 5*(4), 205–208. doi:10.1016/0278-4319(86)90022-8

Pizam, A. (1993). *Managing cross-cultural hospitality enterprises. The international hospitality industry: Organizational and operational issues.* New York, NY: John Wiley.

Prasad, K., & Dev, C. S. (2000). Managing hotel brand equity: A customer-centric framework for assessing performance. *The Cornell Hotel and Restaurant Administration Quarterly, 41*(3), 22–31. doi:10.1177/001088040004100314

Reid, M. (2005). Performance auditing of integrated marketing communications (IMC) actions and outcomes. *Journal of Advertising, 34*(4), 41–54. doi:10.1080/00913367.2005.10639208

Reid, M., Luxton, S., & Mavondo, F. (2005). The relationship between integrated marketing communication, market orientation, and brand orientation. *Journal of Advertising, 34*(4), 11–23. doi:10.1080/00913367.2005.10639210

Round, D., & Roper, S. (2012). Exploring consumer brand name equity: Gaining insight through the investigation of response to name change. *European Journal of Marketing, 46*(7/8), 938–951. doi:10.1108/03090561211230115

Schultz, D. E. (1993a). Integrated marketing communications: Maybe definition is in the point of view. *Marketing News, 27*(2), 17.

Schultz, D. E. (1993b). Integration helps you plan communications from outside-in. *Marketing News, 27*(6), 12.

Schultz, D. E. (1999). Integrated marketing communications and how it relates to traditional media advertising. In J. P. Jones (Ed.), *The advertising business: Operations, creativity, media planning, integrated communications* (pp. 325–338). London, UK: Sage. doi:10.4135/9781452231440.n34

Šerić, M., & Gil-Saura, I. (2011). Integrated marketing communications and information and communication technology in the hotel sector: An analysis of their use and development in Dalmatian first-class and luxury hotels. *Journal of Retail & Leisure Property, 9*(5), 401–414. doi:10.1057/rlp.2011.4

Šerić, M., & Gil-Saura, I. (2012a). Integrated marketing communications in high-quality hotels of Central and South Dalmatia: A study from managers' and guests' perspectives. *Tržište-Market, 24*(1), 67–83.

Šerić, M., & Gil-Saura, I. (2012b). ICT, IMC, and brand equity in high-quality hotels of Dalmatia: An analysis from guest perceptions. *Journal of Hospitality Marketing & Management, 21*(8), 821–851. doi:10.1080/19368623.2012.633211

Shimp, T. A. (2003). *Advertising, promotion and supplemental aspects of integrated marketing communications* (6th ed.). Cincinnati, OH: South-Western, Thomson Learning.

Siguaw, J. A., & Enz, C. A. (1999). Best practices in information technology. *The Cornell Hotel and Restaurant Administration Quarterly, 40*(5), 58–71. doi:10.1177/001088049904000510

Skinner, H. (2005). Wish you were here? Some problems associated with integrating marketing communications when promoting place brands. *Place Branding, 1*(3), 299–315. doi:10.1057/palgrave.pb.5990030

So, K. K. G., & King, C. (2010). When experience matters: Building and measuring hotel brand equity. The customers' perspective. *International Journal of Contemporary Hospitality Management, 22*(5), 589–608. doi:10.1108/95961191080000538

Thorson, E., & Moore, J. (1996). *Integrated communication: Synergy of persuasive voices*. Mahwah, NJ: Lawrence Erlbaum Associates.

Torp, S. (2009). Integrated communications: From one look to normative consistency. *Corporate Communications: An International Journal, 14*(2), 190–206. doi:10.1108/13563280910953861

Tsaur, S. H., Lin, C. T., & Wu, C. S. (2005). Cultural differences of service quality and behavioral intention in tourist hotels. *Journal of Hospitality Marketing & Management, 13*(1), 41–63. doi:10.1300/J150v13n01_04

Wang, Y. J., Wu, C., & Yuan, J. (2009). The role of integrated marketing communications (IMC) on heritage destination visitations. *Journal of Quality Assurance in Hospitality & Tourism, 10*(3), 218–231. doi:10.1080/15280080902988048

Welzel, C., Inglehart, R., & Klingemann, H. D. (2003). The theory of human development: A cross-cultural analysis. *European Journal of Political Research, 42*(3), 341–379. doi:10.1111/1475-6765.00086

Xu, J. B., & Chan, A. (2010). A conceptual framework of hotel experience and customer-based brand equity. Some research questions and implications. *International Journal of Contemporary Hospitality Management, 22*(2), 174–193. doi:10.1108/09596111011018179

Yoo, B., & Donthu, N. (2001). Developing and validating a multidimensional consumer-based brand equity scale. *Journal of Business Research, 52*(1), 1–14. doi:10.1016/S0148-2963(99)00098-3

Yuksel, A., Kilinc, U. K., & Yuksel, F. (2006). Cross-national analysis of hotel customers' attitudes toward complaining and their complaining behaviours. *Tourism Management, 27*(1), 11–24. doi:10.1016/j.tourman.2004.07.007

Zeithaml, V. A. (1988). Consumer perceptions of price, quality and value: A means-end model and synthesis of evidence. *Journal of Marketing, 52*(3), 2–22. doi:10.2307/1251446

## ADDITIONAL READING

Atilgan, E., Aksoy, S., & Akinci, S. (2005). Determinants of the brand equity: A verification approach in the beverage industry in Turkey. *Marketing Intelligence & Planning*, 23(3), 237–248. doi:10.1108/02634500510597283

Bambauer-Sachse, S., & Mangold, S. (2011). Brand equity dilution through negative online word-of-mouth communication. *Journal of Retailing and Consumer Services*, 18(1), 38–45. doi:10.1016/j.jretconser.2010.09.003

Christensen, L. T., Firat, A. F., & Cornelissen, J. (2009). New tensions and challenges in integrated communications. *Corporate Communications: An International Journal*, 14(2), 207–219. doi:10.1108/13563280910953870

Crotts, J. C., & Erdmann, R. (2000). Does national culture influence consumer's evaluation of travel services? A test of Hofstede's model of cross-cultural differences. *Managing Service Quality*, 10(6), 410–419. doi:10.1108/09604520010351167

Dewhirst, T., & Davis, B. (2005). Brand strategy and integrated marketing communications (IMC). A case study of player's cigarette brand marketing. *Journal of Advertising*, 34(4), 81–92. doi:10.1080/00913367.2005.10639211

Dioko, L., & So, S. I. A. (2012). Branding destinations versus branding hotels in a gaming destination - examining the nature and significance of co-branding effects in the case study of Macao. *International Journal of Hospitality Management*, 31(2), 554–563. doi:10.1016/j.ijhm.2011.07.015

Duncan, T. R., & Everett, S. E. (1993). Client perceptions of integrated marketing communications. *Journal of Advertising Research*, 33(3), 30–39.

Duncan, T. R., & Moriarty, S. E. (1997). *Driving brand value. Using integrated marketing to manage profitable stakeholder relationships*. New York, NY: McGraw-Hill.

Ehrenberg, A. S. C., Barnard, N., Kennedy, R., & Bloom, H. (2002). Brand advertising as creative publicity. *Journal of Advertising Research*, 42(4), 7–18.

Gabrielli, V., & Balboni, B. (2010). SME practice towards integrated marketing communications. *Marketing Intelligence & Planning*, 28(3), 275–290. doi:10.1108/02634501011041426

Hall, E., & Hall, M. (1990). *Understanding cultural differences*. Yarmouth, MA: Intercultural Press.

Hennessey, S. M., Yun, D., MacDonald, R., & MacEachern, M. (2010). The effects of advertising awareness and media form on travel intentions. *Journal of Hospitality Marketing & Management*, 19(3), 217–243. doi:10.1080/19368621003591335

Hofstede, G. (2001). *Culture's consequences: Comparing values, behaviors, institutions and organizations across nations* (2nd ed.). Thousand Oaks, CA: SAGE Publications, Inc.

Hope, C. A. (2004). The impact of national culture on the transfer of "best practice operations management" in hotels in St. Lucia. *Tourism Management*, 25(1), 45–59. doi:10.1016/S0261-5177(03)00059-1

Hung, J. Y., Lin, F. L., & Yang, W. G. (2012). Developing experience-based luxury brand equity in the luxury resorts hotel industry. *Global Journal of Business Research*, 6(4), 45–58.

Hyun, S. S.Sunghyup Sean Hyun. (2010). Predictors of relationship quality and loyalty in the chain restaurant industry. *Cornell Hospitality Quarterly*, 51(2), 251–267. doi:10.1177/1938965510363264

Kerr, G., & Drennan, J. (2010). Same but different – Perceptions of integrated marketing communications among marketing communication partners in Australia. *Journal of Promotion Management*, 16(1), 6–24. doi:10.1080/10496490903571233

Kim, J., & Hardin, A. (2010). The impact of virtual worlds on word-of-mouth: Improving social networking and servicescape in the hospitality industry. *Journal of Hospitality Marketing & Management, 19*(7), 735–753. doi:10.1080/19368623.2010.508005

Korda, A. P. (2011). Hotel image and guests satisfaction as a source of sustainable competitive advantage. *International Journal of Sustainable Economy, 3*(1), 92–106. doi:10.1504/IJSE.2011.037722

Laurie, S., & Mortimer, K. (2011). IMC is dead. Long live IMC: Academics' versus practitioners' views. *Journal of Marketing Management, 27*(13/14), 1464–1478. doi:10.1080/0267257X.2011.627367

Lee, S. C., Barker, S., & Kandampully, J. (2003). Technology, service quality, and customer loyalty in hotels: Australian managerial perspectives. *Managing Service Quality, 13*(5), 423–432. doi:10.1108/09604520310495886

Mohsin, A., & Lockyer, T. (2010). Customer perceptions of service quality in luxury hotels in New Delhi, India: An exploratory study. *International Journal of Contemporary Hospitality Management, 22*(2), 160–173. doi:10.1108/09596111011018160

Motameni, R., & Shahrokhi, M. (1998). Brand equity valuation: A global perspective. *Journal of Product and Brand Management, 7*(4), 275–290. doi:10.1108/10610429810229799

Mulhern, F. (2009). Integrated marketing communications: From media channels to digital connectivity. *Journal of Marketing Communications, 15*(2/3), 85–101. doi:10.1080/13527260902757506

Oak, S., & Dalbor, M. C. (2010). Do institutional investors favor firms with greater brand equity? An empirical investigation of investments in US lodging firms. *International Journal of Contemporary Hospitality Management, 22*(1), 24–40. doi:10.1108/09596111011013453

Schultz, D. E. (2003). Evolving marketing and marketing communication into the twenty-first century. In D. Iacobucci & B. Calder (Eds.), *Kellogg on integrated marketing* (pp. VII–XXI). New Jersey, NJ: Willey.

Seddighi, H. R., Nutall, M. W., & Theocharous, A. L. (2001). Does cultural background of tourist influence the destination choice? An empirical study with special reference to political instability. *Tourism Management, 22*(2), 181–191. doi:10.1016/S0261-5177(00)00046-7

Smith, B. G. (2012). Communication integration: An analysis of context and conditions. *Public Relations Review, 38*(4), 600–608. doi:10.1016/j.pubrev.2012.06.003

Tanford, S., Raab, C., & Kim, Y. S. (2012). Determinants of customer loyalty and purchasing behavior for full-service and limited-service hotels. *International Journal of Hospitality Management, 31*(2), 319–328. doi:10.1016/j.ijhm.2011.04.006

Tasci, A. D. A., & Denizci Guillet, B. (2011). It affects, it affects not: A quasi-experiment on the transfer effect of co-branding on consumer-based brand equity of hospitality products. *International Journal of Hospitality Management, 30*(4), 774–782. doi:10.1016/j.ijhm.2010.12.009

Wang, Y. C., Hsu, K. C., Hsu, S. H., & Hsieh, P. A. J. J. (2011). Constructing an index for brand equity: A hospital example. *Service Industries Journal, 31*(2), 311–322. doi:10.1080/02642060902759145

## KEY TERMS AND DEFINITIONS

**Brand Image:** Consumer perceptions of and preferences for a brand.

**Brand Loyalty:** The attachment that a customer has to a brand, expressed through repeat purchase and intention to recommend.

**Customer-Based Brand Equity:** A consumers' different response between a branded and an unbranded product when both have the same product features and are exposed to the same level of marketing stimuli.

**Hotel Brand Equity:** The value that consumers and hotel property owners associate with a hotel brand.

**Integrated Marketing Communications:** A tactical and strategic consumer-centric business process, boosted by advances in Information and Communication Technology (ICT) which, on the basis of information obtained from customers databases, delivers a clear and consistent message throughout the coordination and synergies of different communications tools and channels, in order to nourish long-lasting profitable relationships with customers and other stakeholders and create and maintain brand equity.

**National Culture:** The set of norms, behaviors, beliefs, customs, and values shared by the population of a sovereign nation.

**Perceived Quality:** The evaluation that a consumer makes about the excellence or superiority of a product.

# Chapter 23

# Expatriate Selection and Retention:
## Identifying and Assessing the Other Characteristics beyond Knowledge, Skills, and Abilities

**Ben Tran**
*Alliant International University, USA*

## ABSTRACT

*Many international hotel chains (IHCs) have sent their employees, their expatriates, overseas to maintain corporate standards, fill skills gaps, and transfer technology and corporate culture in their worldwide properties. The workforce is the backbone of any organization, and IHCs should pay careful attention to trends as well as published research to reduce failures that will ultimately affect its financial state as well as the organization as a whole. This chapter will be on the hotel industry in China. Hence, the focus of this chapter is on the matter that when IHCs are selecting expatriates to send to China, IHRM and IHCs need to identify and assess these expatriates' other characteristics (O). These O characteristics are: (1) desire to prematurely terminate an expatriate's assignment; (2) stable competencies; and (3) intercultural/international business communication.*

## INTRODUCTION

Much research on expatriates' competences derive from the study of sojourners, people who go to live and work in another culture on a temporary basis, but often for an extended period of time (Ho, 2012). Sojourner groups include business personnel, military personnel, foreign students, international development advisors, diplomats, emergency relief workers and international peacekeepers. Two major challenges, according to Tran (2008), confront all people making an international transition (please refer to Tran's study for details regarding Tran's research methods). The first challenges has to do with the person's capacity to become well-adjusted and personally satisfied in the new culture. The second challenge has to do with the person's potential to function and work

DOI: 10.4018/978-1-4666-8606-9.ch023

effectively in the new environment. Accordingly, by definition, a competent expatriate is someone who is able to live contentedly and work successfully in another culture (Vulpe, Kealey, Protheroe, & MacDonald, 2001). Further, research has found that what predicts the ability to live contentedly in a new culture, often differs from what is needed to achieve professional success (Kealey, 1989).

Managers and multinational corporations (MNCs) face challenges of expatriation process anytime expatriates from one culture interacts with employees outside one's home country. Littarell, Salas, Hess, Paley, and Riedel (2006) define expatriates as individuals who relocate from one country to another (Tran, 2008) for at least one year. Expatriate management is required when corporations experience shortages of local skilled management (Kaye & Taylor, 1997), when corporations wish to broaden specific individual's experience by giving new ventures by entering new territories (Torbiorn, 1994). Edstrom and Galbraith (1977) identify three general corporation motives for making this type of transfer to fill positions, management development, and organization development.

As such, the purpose of this chapter is the third phase of the expatriate selection, identifying and assessing the expatriate candidate's characteristics, also known as the other characteristics (O), beyond the knowledge, skills, and abilities (KSAs) (Ho, 2012; Kravetz, 2008; Tran, 2008). These O characteristics are (Ghafoor, Khan, Idrees, Javed, & Ahmed, 2011; Ho, 2012; Hsieh, Lin, & Lee, 2012; Joshua-Gojer, 2012; Ko & Yang, 2011; Rozkwitalska, 2012; Tran, 2008; Vojinic, Matic, & Becic, 2013):

1.  Desire to prematurely terminate an expatriate's assignment
    a.  Extroversion
    b.  Agreeableness
    c.  Conscientiousness
    d.  Emotional Stability
    e.  Openness

2.  Stable competencies
    a.  Self-Maintenance Dimension
    b.  Relation Dimension
    c.  Perceptual Dimension
3.  Intercultural/international business communication
    a.  Different-Language Zones
    b.  Same-Language Zones

If corporations are able to appropriately identify and successfully assess these O characteristics, productively harness their strengths, and effectively implement their purposes, then corporations are able to avoid expatriates' failures, therefore, establish, build, and expand these corporations' reputations, and increase the corporations' return-on-investment (ROI). For corporations that are not able to appropriately identify and successfully assess these O characteristics, according to Tran (2008), have been plagued with financial and nonfinancial negative consequences. However, if done successfully, corporations are able to gain and possess a competitive advantage over other corporations who are less successful with their expatriate ventures. Hence, the focus of this chapter is on China, specifically on the hotel industry there. However, the need of identifying and assessing the other characteristics beyond knowledge, skills, and abilities in the expatriate selection process and for the purpose of retention, the other characteristics (O), the O factor, remains the same for the IHCs industry.

## BACKGROUND: MULTINATIONAL CORPORATIONS (MNCS)

Multinational Corporations (MNCs), when expanding overseas, have to determine the staffing configuration in their multinational subsidiaries. As practice has proven, MNCs typically, in the initial period of a subsidiary operation, delegate their management, usually to a trusted parent country national (PCN) or which is common to a third country national (TCN)—an expatriate (Chen, Wang, & Chu, 2011; Collings, Doherty, Luethy, & Osborn, 2011; Gong, 2003; Okoroafo, Koh, Liu, Lin, & Jin, 2010; Rozkwitalska, 2012). Here, expatriates refer to individuals who have been selected for a foreign assignment and will be sent abroad to a host country on behalf of their headquarter company. While the concept of expatriates is well known to MNCs, expatriates and their work is complex and has a very high rate of failure in the MNCs (Tran, 2008) and in the international hotel chains (IHCs) industry (Adler & Rigg, 2012; Chen et al., 2011; Ghafoor et al., 2011; Joshua-Gojer, 2012; Ko & Yang, 2011; Okoroafo et al., 2010; Tadmor, 2006; Tsai, Zeng, Lan, & Fang, 2012; Webb & Wright, 1996).

One dimension of failure is the enormous price that MNCs pay due to selecting inappropriate expatriates (Tung, 1981). According to Tran (2008), research estimates that US firms lose $2 billion annually in direct costs associated with failed overseas assignments. The direct costs of expatriate problems include loss of business and company reputation, failed negotiations, expatriate depression and loss of self-esteem, and family dysfunction (Black, 1988; Borstorff, Harris, Field, & Giles, 1997). Direct costs of returning a failed expatriate home and finding a replacement range between $50,000USD and $200,000USD (Black & Mendenhall, 1990). Some claim the cost is even higher ranging from $55,000USD to $250,000USD (Copeland & Briggs, 1985; Tung, 1982; Wederspahn, 1992; Zeira & Banai, 1985).

MNCs used here, also encompasses international hotel chains (IHCs), for IHCs are MNCs. Many international hotel chains (IHCs) have sent their employees, their expatriates, overseas to maintain corporate standards, fill skills gaps, and transfer technology and corporate culture in their worldwide properties (Chen et al., 2011; Lomax, 2001; Okoroafo et al., 2010). Although hotel expatriates may live and work in popular tourist destinations or major cities around the world and receive attractive compensation packages, lives of

hotel expatriates are not always full of glamour and excitement (Ho, 2012; Tsai, Zeng, Lan, & Fang, 2012). They may be assigned to underdeveloped or still-developing countries, where cultures, living standards, and business practices significantly differ from those of their home countries (Ghafoor et al., 2011; Okpara & Kabongo, 2011; Tran, 2008). Failure to make cultural adjustment may result in expatriates' incompletion of their international assignments and returning to their home countries prematurely (Ghafoor et al., 2011; Tadmor, 2006; Tran, 2008; Tsai, Zeng, Lan, & Fang, 2012; Webb & Wright, 1996).

In previous studies across different industries researchers have reported expatriates' assignments incompletion rates of approximately 25 to 40 percent (Black, Gregersen, Mendenhall, & Storch, 1999; Chen et al., 2011; Forster, 1997; Harrison, 1994; Okoroafo et al., 2010). The incompletion of overseas assignments has cost MNCs between $50,000 and $150,000 financially to reassign and remunerate their expatriates (Chen et al., 2011; Feng & Pearson, 1999; Okoroafo et al., 2010; Shay & Tracey, 1997; Tran, 2008). Other costs may include lost sales and a fragile corporate image to international corporations (Tran, 2008). For expatriates themselves, they may return to their home country with low self-esteem and become less confident for future assignments. Therefore, understanding what keeps hotel expatriates remaining in their overseas assignment, is an essential component of recruitment and retention strategies for IHCs.

## HOTEL INDUSTRY: CHINA

According to Hollows and Lewis (1995), the China context is different from other business environments for two reasons: the special nature of Chinese culture and the fact that China is in transition from a command economy to a market economy. One of the key features of the China context that Hollows and Lewis described was its *hierarchical structure*, a structure that has characterized Chinese social structure and culture for thousands of years and still has a strong impact on the functioning of organizations. The Confucian ethic of seeing authority as based "more on morality than expertise" probably affects the values of Chinese employees (Burke, Jeng, Koyuncu, & Fiksenbau, 2011; Chen et al., 2011; Davies, Leung, Luk, & Wong, 1995; Okoroafo et al., 2010; Tran, 2014a; Wong & Chan, 2010, p. 438). Another Chinese characteristics is the strength of personal relationship or *guanxi* (關係) (Chen et al., 2011; Davies, Leung, Luk, & Wong, 1995; Okoroafo et al., 2010; Tran, 2014a; Yu & Huimin, 2005).

Since the hotel industry in China has been opened up to international hotel chains, hotels have had to become more competitive, particularly those hotels in the state-owned and privately owned categories (Burke et al., 2011; Mak, 2008; Okoroafo et al., 2010; Wong & Chan, 2010; Yu, 1992). Hotels ownership in China is very complicated. Prior to 1978 there was no international hotel presence in China (Okoroafo et al., 2010; Wong & Chan, 2010). In 1982, the first joint venture hotel was built ownership, as defined by the China National Tourism Administration: state-owned, joint ownership, foreign investment, joint venture, contractual agreement, collectively owned, and privately owned (Burke et al., 2011; Mak, 2008; Okoroafo et al., 2010; Yu, 1992). The issue of which form of hotel ownership is the most desirable is still an important issue in China today. Pine (2000, p. 63) commented: "After 20 years of development, China's hotel industry is characterized by a ship and management systems, and geographically imbalanced distribution." In short, the more complex the ownership, the more difficult it is for expatriates and managers (leaders) to exercise their power, authority, and influence over their subordinates (followers) and therefore conflicts arise (Mwaura, Sutton, & Roberts, 1998; Okoroafo et al., 2010; Yu & Goh, 1995).

## Hospitality Industry in China: Theoretical Framework

The conceptual framework that links structure, strategy and performance is Porter's national competitiveness of a nations' theory, popularly referred to as Porter's Diamond. According to Bakan and Doğan (2012), Basu and Media (2014), and Smit (2010), Michael Porter offered a model that allows examining why some states are more competitive and why some industries with states are more competitive than others are. In this way, Porter's diamond model of national competitiveness was detected as a model with which to assess the sources of competitive advantages of an industry in a particular country and it can help realize the competitive status of a nation in global competition. This model consists of four national determinants of competitive advantage: factor conditions, demand conditions, related and supporting industries, and firm's strategy, structure and rivalry. The Porter's theory is that these factors interact with each other to form conditions where innovation and competitiveness occurs (Bakan & Doğan, 2012; Basu & Media, 2014; Smit, 2010). Hence, according to Porter (1990), national competitiveness will anchored along four dimensions-a nation's factor conditions; demand conditions; firm strategy, structure, and rivalry and related and supporting industries (Bakan & Doğan, 2012; Basu & Media, 2014; Porter, 1990; Smit, 2010). This study focuses on the anchor pertaining to firm structure, strategy, and rivalry. According to Bakan and Doğan (2012) and Smit (2010), there is rich literature on this model (Barragan, 2005; Mehrizi & Pakneiat, 2008; Sun, Fan, Zhou, & Shi, 2010; Watchravesringkan, Karpova, Hodges, & Copeland, 2010). Most studies (e. g. Stone & Ranchlod, 2006) have addressed the macro aspect of his model. For instance, Mohan Kathuria (2008) used Porter's model to investigate the competitiveness of Indians' export industry. One study that has linked the two is Jackson (2006) that linked regional tourism in China to China's socialist economy.

**Leadership Categorization.** Cognitive categorization is defined as "the cognitive process of identifying a particular stimulus as a member of a certain class of stimuli" (Rush & Russell, 1988). Categorization is also considered a process for matching the similarity of a stimulus to a prototype; a prototype is a particular type of person schema representing typical traits (Pennington, 2000). Scholars of the categorization-prototype leadership approach have identified a range of contextual factors that may have impacts on leadership perceptions (Lord, Brown, Harvey, & Hall, 2001) and these factors are: (1) national culture; (2) organizational constraints; (3) leader, follower, and task characteristics; and (4) hierarchical leader levels (Wong & Chan, 2010). How leadership prototypes have evolved in the particular context of the hotel industry in China and the possible impacts that national culture, industry characteristics and culture, and hierarchical levels in an organization have on leadership perceptions are of major interest to this study.

**National Culture and Leadership.** Research has indicated that the leadership prototype varies with national cultures in various dimensions and clusters (House, Hanges, Ruiz-Quintanilla, Dorfman, Javidan, Dickson, & Gupta, 1999). Gerstner and Day (1994) produced one of the earliest and most widely cited studies focusing on cross-cultural comparisons of leadership prototypes. They found significant differences in leadership perceptions, along a set of cultural dimensions initiated by Hofstede (1980), among participants from various countries. In particular, the leadership perceptions had rank order correlation in the *power distance*, *uncertainty avoidance*, and *individualism dimensions*. In the field of the hospitality industry, Testa (2002, 2007) has contributed studies on leadership and cultural congruency in the cruise line industry settings. Testa found that national culture systematically

affected how subordinates evaluated and felt about their leaders. Testa further found that leadership in a multicultural environment was a complex issue and had a significant impact on employees' relationships with their leaders.

**National Settings Characteristics and Leadership.** The hospitality/hotel industry has many unique features. The industry operates in settings where there are frequent interactions between people and it focuses on providing high-quality services to customers. It has its own culture, set of values and practices, and industry characteristics (Guerrier, 1999; Pizam, 1993). These constitute the different contextual and situational variables that may influence perceptions of leadership. Brownell (2008) indicated in a recent review that the leadership skills and attributes needed in service environments are different from those in other types of work environment, and these leadership skills and attributes are effective communication skills and interpersonal competences, which are especially important in the hospitality environment.

**Leadership in Different Hierarchical Levels of an Organization.** Leadership scholars argue that high-level and low-level leaders demonstrate the qualitative aspects of their behavior differently (Antonakis & Atwater, 2002; Hunt, 1991; Lord et al., 2001). Hunt (1991), for example, suggested that, while higher level leadership focuses on mapping out the strategy or vision for an organization, the lower levels could be characterized as more task or technically focused. Epitropaki and Martin (2004) found that there was a statistically significant difference between managerial-supervisory and non-managerial employees in the dimension of *dynamism*. In addition, scholars and practitioners in the hospitality industry have recognized a particular feature of the traditional hierarchical structure in many hospitality organizations, namely that the distance between expatriate and local employees is great (Sutton, 1996).

## Hospitality Industry in China: Foreign-Owned Hotels

To capitalize on the growth, many multinational hotel chains (MHCs) and IHCs have expanded to China. Among the World's top 300 corporate chains ranked by Hotels magazine (Gale, 2009), about 10% have entered China [e.g. Hilton, Hyatt-USA, Changri-la-Hong Kong, Marriott-USA, Accor-France, and some mega-chains like Starwood and InterContinental Hotels-UK (Chen et al., 2011)]. Starwood, whose brands include Sheraton, Westin, St. Regis and W, has thirty-five hotels in China. According to Zhang, Pine, and Lam (2005), Marriott, whose brands include Ritz-Carlton, has twenty-four hotels open on mainland in China, and six more under construction. Carlson operates five hotels, all Radissons, in China, and is building five more, including the five-star Regent International. InterContienental Hotels, which owns the Holiday Inn and Crowned Plaza brands, has twenty hotels on the mainland (Chen et al., 2011).

Many of the foreign-owned hotels have located near the major cities such as Beijing and Shanghai. However, even small cities such as Ningbo (宁波), Hangzhou (杭州), and Nanjin (南京), where populations exceed four million, have drawn development interest. For instance, according to Okoroafo et al. (2010), Carlson is building a Regent International in Ningbo, 100 miles south of Shanghai. But they have stayed away from smaller cities (less than four million people). Foreign-owned hotels entered China using several growth strategies—joint venture, acquisition, mergers, and franchising (Zhang et al., 2005). For example, according to Okoroaf et al. (2010), Marriot-USA enhanced its presence in China after acquisition of Renaissance, which had five mid-priced Ramada hotels in the Chinese cities of Wuhan, Qingdao, Guanzhou, Beijing, and seven upscale New World hotels. Starwood now has a very strong position in China's hotel industry after acquiring Sheraton and Westin.

Suzhou International Hotel joined the InterContinental Hotels groups and became the Holiday Inn Crown Plaza Hotel. Accor entered a joint venture with Zenith Hotels International in 2001, which is a Hong Kong-based firm that operates eight hotels in key Chinese cities and has another four under development. Cendant opened twenty-eight franchised Days Inn brand hotels in China in 2006. Holiday Inn became the biggest hotel operator in China, with twenty-six hotels under their management. Their choices are sometimes designed to appease investors (Graf, 2009).

Generally, foreign-owned hotels in China prefer the *whole ownership first, franchise later* strategy (Zhang et al., 2005). Since foreign-owned hotels think it is risky to franchise in China without first establishing a strong presence and gaining experience there. However, the recent downturn is forcing some foreign operators to use franchise arrangements immediately. For example, the InterContienental Hotels Group, PLC has begun franchising its Holiday Inn Express hotels in China (Chao, 2008). Management contacts allow for tighter control of hotel operation than franchising. Thus, management can assure the quality of hotel service and enhance its goodwill. Initially, hotel chains establish their brand and independently manage their operations. Subsequently, after establishing their standards of operation and creating a mechanism for service support, quality control, and trademark protection, they begin to initiate franchising or licensing to local hotels (Pine, Zhang, & Qi, 2000).

**Managerial Implications and Prospects of Hotel Industry in China: For Chinese Operators.** Since most of the foreign-owned hotels in China have targeted the four and five star segments, local operators can focus on lower star segments. After all, the higher star segments target mostly customers that are overseas travelers and tourists who are familiar with and prefer the home brand names. Another opportunity lies in going after foreign tourists. Marketing research, according to Okoroafo et al. (2010), can be used to further segment and understand the needs of the *value*, not business, or tourist customers. Opportunities do exist in the expanding of the upper-and-middle class Chinese domestic tourists particularly with the recent economic slowdowns. Total number of domestic tourist rose from U.S. $639 million in 1996 to U.S. $870 million in 2003 and revenue from domestic travelers increased from U.S. $42.44 billion in 1996 to U.S. $46.72 billion in 2002 [China National Tourism Administration (CNTA), 2003].

**Managerial Implications and Prospects of Hotel Industry in China: For Foreign Operators.** It is essential for foreign-owned hotels considering entering or expanding in China to fully appreciate the political, social, and cultural differences they will encounter, which make all aspect of *normal* business practices irrelevant to some degree (Okoroafo et al., 2010). *Guanxi* or networked relationships, particularly, is a concept that is difficult for foreigners to understand, and even foreign companies with a history of working in China still encounter frustration in their efforts to do business (Chen et al., 2011; Davies, Leung, Luk, & Wong, 1995; Okoroafo et al., 2010; Tran, 2014a; Yu & Huimin, 2005) in China.

**Hilton's Performance Management Model:** As for the management of personnel, Hilton hotels in the China hotel industry has been experiencing difficulty with its performance management evaluation of *soft skills* (factors) (Hsieh et al., 2012; Tran, 2013; Tran 2014a, 2014b, 2014c; 2014d), where Hilton's performance management is a systemic project that consists of: (1) inspectors; (2) performance assessment; (3) performance management system design from six yards of management; (4) career development; (5) and other supporting staffs of the perfect system (Chen et al., 2011). Hilton, utilized here as an example, is because Hilton is openly willing to admit its challenges, as well as their acceptance of the importance of *soft skills*.

**Hilton's Identification of Soft Skills:** Hilton's assessment results of soft skills will not only assist Hilton with the determination of staff salaries, but will also be used in staff training, promotion, and career development. The results derived from the Hilton's performance of soft skills are divided into four types: (1) selection, (2) training and developing the potential staff, (3) resignation, and (4) promotion and rewards (Chen et al., 2011).

## Success and Failure of Expatriates in Hospitality

A crucial issue in the consideration of cross-cultural training (CCT) is the definition of success and failure (Adler & Rigg, 2012; Chen et al., 2011; Joshua-Gojer, 2012; Ko & Yang, 2011; Okoroafo et al., 2010). Expatriate failure, presently estimated to cost organizations in the range of US $250,000-US $1,000,000 (Chen et al., 2011; Okoroafo et al. 2010; Varner & Palmer, 2002; Tran, 2008), was initially defined by organizations and International Human Resource Management (IHRM) literature as being the measurable financial costs of early return of expatriates and disruption to international operations, or as expatriates who are not retained by their organization following completion of an international assignment (Chen et al., 2011; Garonzik, Brockner, & Siegel, 2000; Okoroafo et al., 2010). The definition was later expanded to include the less measurable financial costs of expatriates who may complete international assignments but who contribute to the loss of business confidence and damaged relations to the host country market through committal of cultural faux pas (Harzing, 2002; Selmer, 2002). Most studies regarding premature repatriation as the one and only measure of failure either with or without listing reasons.

Others use *expatriate failure* as a term encompassing a broad range of themes such as premature repatriation, low performance, and adjustment problems. Many other terms, such as expatriate turnover, expatriate transfer (Adler & Rigg, 2012; Naumann, 1992), and expatriate recall rates (Tung, 1981), are also used interchangeably. Even articles dealing with other areas of expatriate management routinely refer to (high levels of) expatriate failure to frame their arguments. Some authors do question the validity of the understanding, but they do not offer alternatives (Harzing, 1995; Forster, 2000).

In other words, the established understanding of the term *expatriate failure* consists of a core of the categories of 'premature end to an international assignment' and 'premature end caused by a reason' (Joshua-Gojer, 2012, p. 52). An understanding of expatriate failure as "underperformance, or similar, during the assignment" (Chen et al., 2011; Joshua-Gojer, 2012, p. 52; Okoroafo et al., 2010) is also unfolding, and some contributions include repatriate turnover and repatriation problems. However, the literature has been missing a critical, systematic and integrated approach to summarize these various definitions. According to studies by Adler and Rigg (2012), Chen et al. (2011), Ho (2012), Joshua-Gojer (2012), Ko and Yang (2011), Okoroafo et al. (2010), and Tran (2008), in summary, expatriates' failures (in the hospitality industry) is a result of a lack of competencies in stable competencies, communication/language (intercultural/international business communication), and personal characteristics (desire to prematurely terminate an expatriate's assignment).

## Competency of Expatriates in Hospitality

Early in the 1970s, David McClelland (1973), a professor at Harvard University, proposed the idea of competency as a term used to challenge traditional criteria of assessment which had emphasized intelligence evaluation in the higher education system. McClelland's theme provided a conceptual framework that led to many subsequent studies in other fields such as teacher education, vocational education business management, and human resource management (Spencer & Spencer, 1993). To better understand international trade competencies, this section began by defining and grouping competency, followed by introducing the

competency models, then discussing competency in Taiwan and the paradigm shift on competency. A competency was defined in the literature from various perspectives. The American Heritage Dictionary of the English Language (2000) provided a general description as "the state or quality of being properly or well qualified" (p. 376). Numerous scholars have attempted to pin down a definition for competency. Quinn, Faerman, Thompson, and McGrath (1990) indicated that competencies were associated with knowledge and skills for implementing certain assignments or projects effectively. To be effective in a particular competency, one must be able to accomplish the desired results of a job with specific qualifications and personal attributes. Burgoyue (1993) employed a functional perspective to define a competency as how the goals of organizations were best achieved by improving members' performance.

Hoffmann (1999) analyzed past literature and summarized three key points in defining a competency: (a) underlying qualification and attributes of a person, (b) observable behaviors, and (c) standard of individual performance outcomes. The most general and detailed definition was proposed by Parry. Parry's definition has been accepted by numerous scholars (Lucia & Lepsinger, 1999, p. 5):

*A competency is a cluster of related knowledge, skills, and attitudes that affects a major part of one's job (a role or responsibility), that correlates with performance on the job, that can be measure against well-accepted standards, and that can be improved via training and development.*

Likewise, there is a distinction between competencies and knowledge, skills, and abilities (KSAs). Knowledge refers to a body of information about the theoretical and practical understanding of a subject, acquired by a person through experience or education. Skills refer to the application of data or information with manual, verbal, or mental profi-

accomplish something, especially the physical and mental quality to perform activities (Hsieh, Lin, & Lee, 2012; Schneider & Schmitt, 1986; Tran, 2008). In brief, each competency requires several KSAs. While KSAs may underlie competencies just as personal traits may underlie competencies, the KSAs are not the exact competencies. In other words, looking beyond KSAs, and identifying and assessing the other characteristics (O), the O factor is paramount (Ho, 2012; Tran, 2008). That is to say, having the KSAs does not automatically mean that one has a certain competency (Kravetz, 2008; Tran, 2008): one may know how to do a certain task without being able to complete the task proficiently.

Wood and Payne (1998) proposed 11 items as basic criteria for competency-based recruitment and selection: communication, flexibility, achievement orientation, developing others, customer orientation, problem solving, teamwork, analytical thinking, leadership relationship building, planning skills, and organizational skills. In 2001, the European Union identified eight key competencies as the development of indicators which can be used to monitor and evaluate education and training progress across the European Union (Hsieh, Lin, & Lee, 2012): (a) native language proficiency; (b) foreign language proficiency (Ho, 2012; Joshua-Gojer, 2012; Ko & Yang, 2011; Tran, 2008); (c) ability to apply basic math and science; (d) ability to learn by digital function; (e) abilities to learn skills such as time-management, problem-solving, information seeking and applying; (f) social commitment; (g) entrepreneurship such as creativity, planning, achievement motivation; and (h) ability to appreciate culture such as art, music, and literature.

## IDENTIFYING AND ASSESSING THE OTHER CHARACTERSITCS

IHCs often contribute to the issue of expatriates' failures by selecting expatriates based on the misusage of the term *competencies*. According to Marx (1999), most expatriates were appointed by their IHCs based on their technical competency without any consideration of their ability to work overseas. However, expatriates with good performance records in the domestic operation do not necessarily fulfill the responsibilities of their overseas' assignment (Marquardt & Engel, 1993). Expatriation is often characterized by high levels of stress because expatriates need to move through the process of relocation and cultural adjustment (Furnham, 1999). Researchers had found that expatriates' inability to cope with the stress from their assignment would likely set off their disengagement with the assignment, which may result in a premature return to their home countries, due to their poor job performance in the current assignment (Caligiuri, 2000a; Huang, Chi, & Lawler, 2005).

There have been many research efforts in establishing management competencies and skills across different industries. The most frequently identified expatriates' competencies are adaptability, flexibility, communication skills, cultural sensitivity, and leadership skills (Bueno & Tubbs, 2004; Chung-Herrera, Enz, & Lankau, 2003; Engholm & Rowland, 1996; Heames & Harvey, 2006; Hurn, 2006; Kriegl, 2000; Whitfield, 1995). Ho (2012) finds that three competencies of hotel expatriates are—leadership, adaptability, and cultural sensitivity—consistent with the previous literature (i.e. Tran, 2008). These three competencies are evident in helping hotel expatriates make better adjustments in foreign countries and remain at their overseas assignments.

In addition, Ho (2012) uncovered two other important competencies that hotel expatriates are required to be equipped with in order to conquer their challenges from overseas assignments: diplomacy and globalization (Ho, 2012, p. 18). Participants in Ho's (2012) study were competent in being diplomatic among local hotel owners and between local owners and IHCs (please refer to Ho's study for details regarding Ho's research methods). With the diplomatic skill, hotel expatriates are more likely to find a balance to meet both IHCs operation standards requirements and needs of local owners, thus maximize the welfare of all parties. How IHCs and local hotel owners satisfy hotel expatriates' performance may determine whether expatriates may remain in their assignments or not. Studies by Hsieh, Lin, and Lee (2012), Joshua-Gojer (2012), Ko and Yang (2011), and Tran (2008) yielded congruent results.

## Selection of Expatriates in International Hotel Chains

The process of expatriation is most commonly described by selection, training and preparation, transfer and adjustment, monitoring and performance management, and finally repatriation of the individual. Important factors of survival of international corporations in a global market is selecting and posting the right personnel (also known as the right expatriate) which will be successful in pursuing the corporation's goals. Success in the global market is considered to be highly dependent on the quality of international management (Mitrev & Culpepper, 2012). Therefore, appointing proper expatriates abroad is a challenge and a vital task for corporations in order to meet the requirements of international operations and in order to avoid the cost of expatriate failure. There are three interrelated phases in expatriate selection (Harvey & Novicevic, 2002): 1) critical environment issues, 2) organizational issues, and 3) expatriate candidate characteristics.

Models of expatriate selection may vary across the nationality of organization but the principal concepts in early studies have focused on functional capabilities and personal characteristics of potential candidates as main determinants of expatriate success or failure (Caligiuri, 2000b). In order to successfully operate in a global market, an expatriate must possess a complex set of technical, functional, cultural, social and political

skills (Fish, 1999). Harvey and Novicevic (2002) suggest that two additional dynamic abilities of potential expatriate should be integrated into the selection criteria: intuition and creativity. Moreover, experience-based decision making and ability to develop unique solutions to complex problems in a short time period augment expatriate's ability to manage in chaotic rapidly changing environments and should be incorporated into the selection criteria.

Tsai, Zeng, Lan, and Fang (2012) primarily started analyzing two criteria for selecting expatriates: professional skills and the willingness to live abroad (please refer to Tsai et al.'s study for details regarding their research methods). Congruent to Tsai et al. (2012), and Tran (2008), other authors included an additional important element in selection process, and that would be adaptability of spouse and family members. According to their findings, first, most important criteria are professional skills of candidates, and second criterion is adaptability of spouse and family members. This aspect is important due the fact that percentage of relocating spouses in U.S. corporations is about 70% (Lin, Lu, & Lin, 2012). Finally, willingness to work abroad is not so important, according to Tsai et al. (2012).

## Training of Expatriates in International Hotel Chains

Selection process is followed by training, familiarizing the selected expatriate with the country if one's assignment including general awareness of the culture and basic language skills in order to educate the expatriate to interact effectively with members of another culture (Joshua-Gojer, 2012; Ko & Yang, 2011). Training is considered to be important because it could influence an expatriate's adjustment to a new environment (Okpara & Kabongo, 2011) and an expatriate's performance (Caliguri, Phillips, Lazarova, Tarique, & Burgi, 2001). Brislin's model, according to Okpara and

Kabongo (2011), includes three techniques that can be used in cross-cultural training: cognitive (dissemination of information on a foreign cultural environment), affective (learning to deal with cultural incidents), and behavioral (improving ability to adapt to host country's communication style) (Please refer to Okpara and Kabongo's article for the discussion of Brislin's model). Tran (2008) identified these techniques, congruent to Tung's (1981) five (three of the five) basic training programs of cross-cultural training, as: 1) desire to prematurely terminate an expatriate's assignment, 2) stable competencies, and 3) intercultural/international business communication.

Expatriate training has become crucially important and researchers and HR practitioners recognized that cross cultural training (Ghafoor et al., 2011), or expatriate selection and training (Tran, 2008), play an extremely important role in facilitating expatriate's success (Tran, 2008; Waxin & Panaccio, 2005). According to Ghafoor et al. (2011, p. 335), Forster (2000) stated that "Cross cultural training also defined as a procedure intends to increase an individual's ability to cope and work in a foreign environment" (Forster, 2000). "Cross-cultural training (CCT) has long been advocated as a means of facilitating effective cross-cultural interactions" (Black & Mendenhall, 1990, p. 114). Training develops expatriate's learning orientation and helps them to understand the culture of overseas destinations (Porter & Tansky, 1999). Even of its importance, many studies show that companies do not provide or give very limited cross cultural training to expatriates and families because of time constrains, and of high cost (Black, Mendenhall, & Oddou, 1991; Britt, 2002; Desphande & Viswesvaran, 1992; Forster, 2000; Ghafoor et al., 2011; Hsieh, Lin, & Lee, 2012; Ho, 2012; Joshua-Gojer, 2012; Selmer, 2001; Tran, 2008; Tung, 1988; Zakaria, 2000).

## FUTURE RESEARCH AND DIRECTIONS

Since David McClelland (1973) used the term competency as a criterion of assessment in higher education systems, many subsequent studies about competency have made its appearance in other fields such as teacher education, vocational education, business management, and human resource management (Ho, 2012; Hsieh et al., 2012). Comparing the term job descriptions and KSAs, competencies are viewed more broadly and more behavior-based. Each competency requires several KSAs. Competencies included many factors that influence job success but are not included in the job description (Tran, 2008). Three key points in defining a competency are underlying qualification and attributes of a person, observable behaviors, and standards of individual performance outcomes. Thus, the purpose of identifying competencies is to provide a well-trained workforce that will work for organizational goals effectively and efficiently.

Even competencies have been categorized in literature from various perspectives, conceptual capacity, behavior, and knowledge/skills competencies are common groups (Ho, 2012). On the one hand, according to the iceberg model (Hsieh et al., 2012), knowledge and skills were visible and appeared at the top of the iceberg. They were relatively easily developed and improved through education and job training. On the other hand, motives and traits appeared at the base of the iceberg, because both were more likely to be hidden and comprised the innermost part of an individual's personality. Therefore, they were more difficult to develop and reform through school education and job training.

Hard skills usually include professional knowledge and task-oriented skills. Soft skills are those skills associated with the behavior necessary for successful interpersonal interaction (Chen et al., 2011). Comparing soft skills to hard skills requires more intellectual thought processes which factors in a person's intelligence quotient (IQ) (Hsieh et al., 2012; Tran, 2013; Tran, 2014a, 2014b, 2014c). On the other hand, soft skills were mainly related to the emotional quotient (EQ) (Hsieh et al., 2012; Tran, 2013; Tran 2014a, 2014b, 2014c) and cultural intelligence (CQ) (Tran, 2014d). According to Ng, Tan, and Ang (2012), intercultural capabilities are captured by the construct of cultural intelligence [CQ (Ang & Inkpen, 2008; Ang & Van Dyne, 2008)]—defined as a "person's capability for successful adaptation to new cultural settings, that is, for unfamiliar settings attributable to cultural context" (Earley & Ang, 2003, p. 9). CQ, defined as an individual's capability to function and manage effectively in culturally diverse settings (Earley & Ang, 2003), is consistent with Schmidt and Hunter's (2000, p. 3) definition of *general intelligence* (IQ) as "the ability to grasp and reason correctly with abstractions and solve problems." It is built on the growing interest in real-world intelligence, which has yielded several types of intelligence that focus on specific content domains, such as social intelligence (Thorndike & Stein, 1937), EQ (Mayer & Salvoey, 1993), and practical intelligence (Sternberg, 1997), CQ contributes to this research by emphasizing the specific domain of intercultural settings, which has not been examined in prior research despite the practical realities of globalization.

In comparison to the idea of the iceberg model, hard skills tend to refer to visible competencies, and soft skills are similar to hidden ones in the iceberg model (Hsieh, Lin, & Lee, 2012). As there is an overlap between hard and soft skills, it is difficult to precisely categorized and itemize visible and hidden competencies because of a lack of exact definitions in the literature. Currently, several paradigm shifts in the conception and application of competency are occurring. First, companies have moved towards a performance-based pay

system, differentiating employee rewards in accordance with performance. Second, more and more research has emphasized the importance of soft skills (Chen et al., 2011) when the global business environment becomes increasingly knowledge-oriented and keeps changing quickly (Hsieh et al., 2012; Tran, 2008; Tran, 2013; Tran, 2014b, 2014c). Third, to succeed under the market trends in the global economy, future employees need to employ international perspectives to the concept of competency.

Thus, it defines or rather, redefines the focus of attention of the IHCs' expatriate selection and retention process. It brings to light certain solutions that will make identifying and assessing expatriates' other characteristics beyond knowledge, skills, and abilities (KSAs) more effective. It also highlights certain factors that IHCs' trainers need to pay attention to. The workforce is the backbone of any organization, and IHCs should pay careful attention to trends as well as published research to reduce failures that will ultimately affect its financial state as well as the organization as a whole.

MNCs and IHCs are aware of the detrimental result at hand, and there are selection and training programs available, of which, Ghafoor et al. (2011) suggested a synthesized version consisting of four stages: (1) pre-departure training (Avril & Magnini, 2007; Mendenhall, 1999); (2) pre-departure visit (Black & Gregerson, 1991; Sims & Schraeder, 2004); (3) post-departure training (Mendenhall & Wiley, 1994; Sims & Schraeder, 2004; Suutari & Burch, 2001; Vance & Paik, 2002); and (4) training methods and types (Shen, 2005; Waxin & Panaccio, 2005). Tran (2008, 2013), on the other hand, suggested a more detailed and elaborated version, with four stages: (1) selection (self-selection and recruitment); (2) pre-departure [quantitative (O factor) and qualitative (interviewed by current/retried expatriates, direct supervisor, international human resource representative personnel, an expert, and host supervisor) assessments]; (3) post-departure; and (4) expatriate mentor(ship). In implementing Tran's (2008) *Expatriate Selection and Retention Handbook*, IHRM and IHCs, when selecting expatriates, can more effectively identify and assess the expatriate candidates' O characteristics, also known as the other characteristics (O), beyond the knowledge, skills, and abilities (KSAs) (Ho, 2012; Kravetz, 2008; Tran, 2008). These O characteristics are (Ghafoor et al., 2011; Ho, 2012; Hsieh et al., 2012; Joshua-Gojer, 2012; Ko & Yang, 2011; Rozkwitalska, 2012; Tran, 2008; Vojinic et al., 2013): (1) Desire to prematurely terminate an expatriate's assignment; (2) stable competencies; and (3) intercultural/international business communication.

## CONCLUSION

The competitive global business environment makes expatriate assignment a necessary but risky proposition (Stage, 2005). There is a competitive advantage to be gained from expatriate who performances effectively. Hotel companies operating internationally (IHCs) employ expatriates for three main reason: (1) to provide an element of control and coordination in the local operating unit, (2) to provide management development opportunities to senior staff in the organization, and (3) to facilitate the transfer of knowledge (Tran, 2009; Tran, 2014d), skills, and abilities (KSAs) across global borders (Ozdemir & Cizel, 2007). Expatriates are conceptualized as those who are not nationals of the country where they are working, but they are employed because of their employing organization (Adler & Rigg, 2012). When expatriates are assigned to a host country, they are coming into a new business and cultural environment. Adaption to the new cultural environment in the host country is perceived as a major challenge expatriates face on their international assignments and may lead to ineffectiveness or even business failure (Black, 1988; Fisher & Hartel, 2003; Ghafoor et al., 2011; Li, 1996; Shay & Tracey, 1997; Tadmor, 2006; Tsai, Zeng, Lan, & Fang, 2012; Webb & Wright, 1996; Withiam, 1997).

Thus, as IHCs activities increase, staffing of their organizations involves more strategic concerns. As IHCs create more overseas assignments, differences between expatriate assignments and traditional assignments become more apparent. Dissatisfaction with the host country can impact expatriate failure (Chen, Tzeng, & Tang, 2005; Tran 2008). Working in a foreign environment with different political, cultural and economic characteristics, expatriates are faced with job-related and personal problems (Li, 1996; Tran, 2008), as well as it could also be an expensive undertaking to send expatriates overseas. Research suggests that approximately 40% of individuals who undertake an expatriate assignment fail, at a cost to their employer of two to four times their annual salary (Black, Gregersen, Mendenhall, & Storch, 1999; Chen et al., 2011; Feng & Pearson, 1999; Forster, 1997; Harrison, 1994; Lewis, 2006; Okoroafo et al., 2010; Shay & Tracey, 1997; Tran, 2008). Cross-industry studies have estimated American expatriate failure at between 25% and 40% when the expatriate is assigned to a developing country (Shay & Tracey, 1997; Tran, 2008). Avril and Magnini (2007) indicated that in the hotel industry, a large portion of expatriate manager assignments end in failure (Adler & Rigg, 2012; Chen et al., 2011; Okoroafo, 2010).

Expatriate failure or *turnover* occurs when expatriates either quit or return to their home country prior to the completion of their overseas tour (Adler & Rigg, 2012; Magnini & Honeycutt, 2003; Naumann, 1992). The opt six reasons for expatriate failures include: (1) expatriates inability to adapt to the new environment, (2) not achieving family acceptance and assimilation, (3) lack of support from the head office, (4) not having an open mindset, (5) lack of willingness to learn, and (6) expatriate lack of technical competence (Adler & Rigg, 2012; Chen et al., 2011; Ho, 2012; Joshua-Gojer, 2012; Ko & Yang, 2011; Lee, 2007; Tran, 2008; Okoroafo et al., 2010). Expatriates are said to be successful when they meet their IHCs' objectives and maintain management standards at an overseas property for the duration of their assignment (Magnini & Honeycutt, 2003; Vulpe, Kealey, Protheroe, & MacDonald, 2001). Successful expatriates exhibit the following characteristics: adaptability, flexibility, open-mindedness, cross-functional flexibility, sociability, cultural sensitivity, consideration or others, visionary and strategic thinking, leadership skills, and non-authoritarian control (Chien, 2012; Hogan & Goodson, 1990; Jayawardena & Haywood, 2003; Shay & Tracey, 1997).

Yooyanyong and Muenjohn (2010) described expatriates leadership as one of the major factors which contribute to the success of an expatriate and that is should be considered global competency. Expatriates also seem to experience success when they have pro-active attitudes, energy, drive, and determination (Withiam, 1997). Ozdemir and Cizel (2007) identified a list of skills for an effective expatriate: able to develop and use global strategic skills, deal with change and transition, cope with cultural training, handle flexible organizational structures, work with others and in teams, and communicate transferred knowledge (Tran, 2009; Tran, 2014d). Cross cultural training provided to expatriates is critical for success (Erbacher, D'Netto, & Espana, 2006; Forster, 2000; Ghafoor et al., 2011; Tran, 2008). As such, IHRM and IHCs, when selecting expatriates, need to identify and assess the expatriate candidate's characteristics, also known as the other characteristics (O), beyond the knowledge, skills, and abilities (KSAs) (Ho, 2012; Kravetz, 2008; Tran, 2008). These O characteristics are (Ghafoor et al., 2011; Ho, 2012; Hsieh et al., 2012; Joshua-Gojer, 2012; Ko & Yang, 2011; Rozkwitalska, 2012; Tran, 2008; Vojinic et al., 2013): (1) Desire to prematurely terminate an expatriate's assignment; (2) stable competencies; and (3) intercultural/international business communication.

## REFERENCES

Adler, H., & Rigg, J. (2012). Expatriate hotel general managers in Jamaica: Perceptions of human resource, organizational, and operational challenges. *Hotel & Business Management, 1*(1), 1–9.

Ang, S., & Inkpen, A. C. (2008). Cultural intelligence and offshore outsourcing success: A framework of firm-level intercultural capability. *Decision Sciences, 39*(3), 337–358. doi:10.1111/j.1540-5915.2008.00195.x

Ang, S., & Van Dyne, L. (2008). *Handbook of cultural intelligence: Theory, measurement, and application*. New York: M. E. Sharpe.

Antonakis, J., & Atwater, L. (2002). Distance and leadership: A review and a proposed theory. *The Leadership Quarterly, 13*(6), 673–704. doi:10.1016/S1048-9843(02)00155-8

Avrill, A. B., & Magnini, V. P. (2007). A holistic approach to expatriate success. *International Journal of Contemporary Hospitality Management, 19*(1), 53–64. doi:10.1108/09596110710724161

Bakan, İ., & Doğan, İ. F. (2012). Competitiveness of the industries based on the Porter's diamond model: An empirical study. *International Journal of Research and Reviews in Applied Sciences, 11*(3), 441–455.

Barragan, S. (2005). *Assessing the power of Porter's diamond model in the automobile industry in Mexico after ten years of Nafta. Master of Science in Management*. Alberta, Canada: Faculty of Management, University of Lethbridge.

Basu, C., & Media, D. (2014). *The importance of Porter's diamond & Porter's five forces in business*. Retrieved from, November 11, 2014, http://smallbusiness.chron.com/importance-porters-diamond-porters-five-forces-business-33891.html

Black, J. S. (1988). Work role transitions: A study of American expatriate managers in Japan. *Journal of International Business Studies, 19*(2), 277–294. doi:10.1057/palgrave.jibs.8490383

Black, J. S., & Gregersen, H. B. (1991). The other half of the picture: Antecedents of spouse cross cultural adjustment. *Journal of International Business Studies, 22*(3), 461–477. doi:10.1057/palgrave.jibs.8490311

Black, J. S., Gregersen, H. B., Mendenhall, M. E., & Stroch, L. D. (1999). *Global assignments: Expatriating and repatriating international managers*. San Francisco, CA: Jossey-Bass.

Black, J. S., & Medenhall, M. E. (1990). Cross-cultural training effectiveness: A review and a theoretical framework for future research. *Academy of Management Review, 1*(1), 113–136.

Black, J. S., Mendenhall, M. E., & Oddou, G. (1991). Toward a comprehensive model of international adjustment: An integration of multiple theoretical perspectives. *Academy of Management Review, 16*(2), 291–317.

Borstorff, P. C., Harris, S. G., Field, H. S., & Giles, W. F. (1997). Who'll go? A Review of Factors Associated with Employee Willingness to Work Overseas. *Human Resources Planning, 20*(3), 29–40.

Britt, J. (2002). Expatriates want more support from home. *HRMagazine, 47*(4), 21–22.

Brownell, J. (2008). Leading on land and sea: Competencies and context. *International Journal of Hospitality Management, 27*(2), 137–150. doi:10.1016/j.ijhm.2007.11.003

Bueno, C. M., & Tubbs, S. L. (2004). Identifying global leadership competencies: An exploratory study. *Journal of American Academy of Business, 5*(1/2), 80–87.

Burgoyue, J. (1993). The competence movement: Issues, stakeholders and prospects. *Personnel Review, 22*(6), 6–13. doi:10.1108/EUM0000000000812

Burke, R. J., Jeng, W., Koyuncu, M., & Fiksenbau, L. (2011). Work motivations, satisfaction and well-being among hotel managers in China: Passion versus addiction. *Interdisciplinary Journal of Research in Business, 1*(1), 21–34. doi:10.1016/S0148-2963(73)80028-1

Caliguri, P., Phillips, J., Lazarova, M., Tarique, I., & Burgi, P. (2001). The theory of met expectations applied to expatriate adjustment: The role of cross-cultural training (vol. 12). *International Journal of Human Resource Management, 12*(3), 357–372. doi:10.1080/09585190121711

Caligiuri, P. M. (2000a). The big five personality characteristics as predictors of expatriates' desire to terminate the assignment and supervisor-rated performance. *Personnel Psychology, 53*(1), 67–88. doi:10.1111/j.1744-6570.2000.tb00194.x

Caligiuri, P. M. (2000b). Selecting expatriates for personality characteristics: A moderating effect on personality on the relationship between host national contact and cross-cultural adjustment. *Management International Review, 40*(1), 61–80.

Chao, L. (2008). IHG to franchise hotels in China. *Wall Street Journal—Eastern Edition, 251*(23), D5.

Chen, Y. C., Wang, W. C., & Chu, Y. C. (2011). A case study on the business performance management of Hilton hotels corp. *International Business Research, 4*(2), 213–218. doi:10.5539/ibr.v4n2p213

Chien, T. C. (2012). Intercultural training for Taiwanese business expatriates. *Industrial and Commercial Training, 44*(3), 164–170. doi:10.1108/00197851211216772

Chung-Herrera, B. G., Enz, C. A., & Lankau, M. J. (2003). Grooming future hospitality leaders: A competencies model. *The Cornell Hotel and Restaurant Administration Quarterly, 44*(3), 17–25.

CNTA. (2003). *Total number of domestic tourism from 1996-2003.* Retrieved from, March 11, 2014, http://www.chinatour.com

Collings, D. G., Doherty, N., Luethy, M., & Osborn, D. (2011). Understanding and supporting the career implications of international assignments. *Journal of Vocational Behavior, 78*(3), 361–371. doi:10.1016/j.jvb.2011.03.010

Copeland, L., & Griggs, L. (1985). *Going International.* New York: Random House.

Davies, H., Leung, K. P., Luk, T. K., & Wong, Y. H. (1995). The benefits of guanxi: The value of relationships in developing the Chinese market. *Industrial Marketing Management, 24*(3), 207–214. doi:10.1016/0019-8501(94)00079-C

Deshpande, S. P., & Viswesvaran, C. (1992). Is cross-cultural training of expatriate managers effective: A meta-analysis. *International Journal of Intercultural Relations, 16*(3), 295–310. doi:10.1016/0147-1767(92)90054-X

Earley, P. C., & Ang, S. (2003). *Cultural intelligence: Individual interactions across cultures.* Palo Alto, CA: Stanford University Press.

Edstrom, A., & Galbraith, J. R. (1977). Transfer of managers: A comparison of documentary and interpersonal methods. *Academy of Management Journal, 30*(4), 514–539.

Engholm, C., & Rowland, D. (1996). *International excellence: Seven breakthrough strategies for personal and professional success.* New York, NY: Kodansha America.

Epitropaki, O., & Martin, R. (2004). Implicit leadership theories in applied settings: Factor structure, generalizability, and stability over time. *The Journal of Applied Psychology, 89*(2), 293–310. doi:10.1037/0021-9010.89.2.293 PMID:15065976

Erbacher, D., D'Netto, B., & Espana, J. (2006). Expatriate success in China: Impact of personal and situational factors. *The Journal of American Academy of Business, 9*(2), 183–188.

Feng, F., & Pearson, T. E. (1999). Hotel expatriate managers in China: Selection criteria, important skills and knowledge, repatriation concerns, and causes of failure. *Hospital Management, 18*(3), 309–321. doi:10.1016/S0278-4319(99)00031-6

Fish, A. (1999). Selecting managers for cross-border assignments: Building value into process. *International Journal of Management Reviews, 1*(4), 461–483. doi:10.1111/1468-2370.00023

Fisher, G. B., & Hartel, I. Z. (2003). Cross-cultural effectiveness of western expatriate-Thai client interactions: Lessons learned for IHRM research and theory. *Cross Cultural Management, 10*(4), 4–28. doi:10.1108/13527600310797667

Forster, N. (1997). The persistent myth of high expatriate failure rates: A reappraisal. *International Journal of Human Resource Management, 8*(4), 414–433. doi:10.1080/095851997341531

Forster, N. (2000). Expatriates and the impact of cross-cultural training. *Human Resource Management Journal, 10*(3), 63–78. doi:10.1111/j.1748-8583.2000.tb00027.x

Furnham, A. (1990). Expatriate stress: The problems of living abroad. In S. Fisher & C. Cooper (Eds.), *On the move: The psychology of change and transition* (pp. 236–254). Chichester, UK: John Wiley & Sons.

Gale, D. (2009). *World's largest hotel companies: Corporate 300 chart.* Retrieved from, March 11, 2014, http://www.hotelsmag.com/index.asp?lay out=articlePrint&articleID=CA6667503&artic le_prefix=CA&article_id=6667503

Garonzik, R., Brockner, J., & Siegel, P. A. (2000). Identifying international assignees at risk for premature departure: The interactive effect of outcome favorability and procedural fairness. *The Journal of Applied Psychology, 85*(1), 13–20. doi:10.1037/0021-9010.85.1.13 PMID:10740952

Gerstner, C. R., & Day, D. V. (1994). Cross-cultural comparison of leadership prototypes. *The Leadership Quarterly, 5*(2), 121–134. doi:10.1016/1048-9843(94)90024-8

Ghafoor, S., Khan, U. F., Idrees, F., Javed, B., & Ahmed, F. (2011). Evaluation of expatriates performance and their training on international assignments. *Interdisciplinary Journal of Contemporary Research in Business, September, 3*(5), 335-351.

Gong, Y. (2003). Subsidiary staffing in multinational enterprises: Agency, resources and performance. *Academy of Management Journal, 46*(4), 728–739.

Graf, N. (2009). Stock market reactions to entry mode choices of multinational hotel firms. *International Journal of Hospitality Management, 28*(2), 236–244. doi:10.1016/j.ijhm.2008.08.002

Guerrier, Y. (1999). *Organizational behavior in hotels and restaurants: An international perspective.* Chichester, England: Wiley.

Harrison, J. K. (1994). Developing successful expatriate managers: A framework for the structural design and strategic alignment of cross-cultural training programs. *Human Resource Planning, 17*(3), 17–35.

Harvey, M., & Novicevic, M. M. (2002). The hypercompetitive global marketplace: The importance of intuition and creativity in expatriate managers. *Journal of World Business, 37*(2), 127–138. doi:10.1016/S1090-9516(02)00072-X

Harzing, A. W. K. (1995). The persistent myth of high expatriate failure rates. *International Journal of Human Resource Management, 6*(2), 457–475. doi:10.1080/09585199500000028

Harzing, A. W. K. (2002). Are our referencing errors undermining our scholarship and credibility? The case of expatriate failure rates. *Journal of Organizational Behavior, 23*(1), 127–148. doi:10.1002/job.125

Heames, J. T., & Harvey, M. (2006). The evolution of the concept of the executive from the 20th century managers to the 21st century global leader. *Journal of Leadership & Organizational Studies, 13*(2), 20–41.

Ho, Z. J. Y. (2012). What makes hotel expatriates remain in their overseas assignments: A grounded theory study. *Qualitative Report, 17*(51), 1–22.

Hoffmann, T. (1999). The meanings of competency. *Journal of European Industrial Training, 23*(6), 275–285. doi:10.1108/03090599910284650

Hofstede, G. (1980). Motivation, leadership, and organization: Do American theories apply abroad? *Organizational Dynamics, 9*(1), 42–63. doi:10.1016/0090-2616(80)90013-3

Hogan, G. W., & Goodson, J. R. (1990). The key to expatriate success: An analysis of overseas managerial assignments. *Training and Development Journal, 44*(1), 50–52.

Hollows, J., & Lewis, J. (1995). Managing human resources in the Chinese context: The experience of a major multinational. In H. Davis (Ed.), *China business: Context and issues* (pp. 269–285). Hong Kong: Longman.

House, R. J., Hanges, P. J., Ruiz-Quintanilla, S. A., Dorfman, P. W., Javidan, M., Dickson, M., & Gupta, V. (1999). Cultural influences on leadership and organizations. In W. F. Mobley, M. J. Gessner, & V. Arnold (Eds.), *Advances in global leadership* (Vol. 1, pp. 171–233). Stanford, CT: JAI Press.

Hsieh, S. C., Lin, J. S., & Lee, H. C. (2012). Analysis on literature review of competency. *International Review of Business and Economics, 2*, 25–50.

Huang, T., Chi, S., & Lawler, S. J. (2005). The relationship between expatriates' personality traits and their adjustment to international assignments. *International Journal of Human Resource Management, 16*(9), 16–56. doi:10.1080/09585190500239325

Hunt, J. G. (1991). *The leadership: A new synthesis*. Newbury Park, CA: Sage Publications.

Hurn, B. J. (2006). The selection of international business managers: Part 1. *Industrial and Commercial Training, 38*(6), 279–286. doi:10.1108/00197850610685581

Jack, D., & Stage, V. (2005). Success strategies for expats. *American Society for Training and Development, 59*, 48–54.

Jackson, J. (2006). Developing regional tourism in China: The potential for activating business clusters in a socialist market economy. *Tourism Management, 27*(4), 695–706. doi:10.1016/j.tourman.2005.02.007

Jayawardena, C., & Haywood, K. M. (2003). International hotel managers and key Caribbean challenges. *International Journal of Contemporary Hospitability Management, 15*(3), 195–198. doi:10.1108/09596110310470284

Joshua-Gojer, A. E. (2012). Cross-cultural training and success versus failure of expatriates. *Learning and Performance Quarterly, 1*(2), 47–62.

Kaye, M., & Taylor, W. G. K. (1997). Expatriate failure: An interview. *International Journal of Management, 24*(3), 403–413.

Kealey, D. (1989). A study of cross-cultural effectiveness: Theoretical issues, practical applications. *International Journal of Intercultural Relations, 13*(3), 387–428. doi:10.1016/0147-1767(89)90019-9

Ko, H. C., & Yang, M. L. (2011). The effects of cross-cultural training on expatriate assignments. *Intercultural Communication Studies, 20*(1), 158–174.

Kravetz, D. J. (2008). *Building a job competency database: What the leaders do*. Retrieved from, February 26, 2014, http://www.kravetz.com/art2/art2pl.html

Kriegl, U. (2000). International hospitality management: Identifying important skills and effective training. *The Cornell Hotel and Restaurant Administration Quarterly, 41*(2), 64–71. doi:10.1177/001088040004100218

Lee, H. W. (2007). Factors that influence expatriate failure: An interview study. *International Journal of Management, 24*(3), 403–414.

Lewis, B. (2005). Send the right people to the right places. *People Management, 12*, 85.

Li, I. (1996). Predictions of expatriate hotel manager satisfaction in Asian Pacific countries. *International Journal of Hospitality Management, 15*(4), 363–372. doi:10.1016/S0278-4319(96)00038-2

Lin, C. Y., Lu, T. C., & Lin, H. W. (2012). A different perspective of expatriate management. *Human Resource Management Review, 22*(3), 189–207. doi:10.1016/j.hrmr.2012.02.003

Littarell, L. N., Salas, E., Hess, K. P., Paley, M., & Riedel, S. (2006). Expatriate preparation: A critical analysis of 25 years of cross-cultural training research. *Human Resource Development Review, 3*(3), 355–388. doi:10.1177/1534484306290106

Lomax, S. (2001). *Best practices for managers and expatriates: A guide on selection, hiring, and compensation.* New York, NY: Wiley.

Lord, R. G., Brown, D. J., Harvey, J. L., & Hall, R. J. (2001). Contextual constraints on prototype generation and their multilevel consequences for leadership perceptions. *The Leadership Quarterly, 12*(3), 311–338. doi:10.1016/S1048-9843(01)00081-9

Lucia, A. D., & Lepsinger, R. (1999). *The art and science of competency models: Pinpointing critical success factors in organizations.* San Francisco, CA: Jossey-Bass.

Magnini, V. P., & Noneycutt, E. D. Jr. (2003). Learning orientation and the hotel expatriate manager experience. *International Journal of Hospitality Management, 22*(3), 267–280. doi:10.1016/S0278-4319(03)00023-9

Mak, B. (2008). The future of the state-owned hotels in China: Stay or go? *International Journal of Hospitality Management, 27*(3), 355–367. doi:10.1016/j.ijhm.2007.10.003

Marquardt, M. J., & Engel, D. W. (1993). HRD competencies for a shrinking world. *Training and Developing, 46*(5), 59–65.

Marx, E. (1999). *Breaking through cultural shock.* London: Nicolas Brealey.

Mayer, J. D., & Salovey, P. (1993). The intelligence of emotional intelligence. *Intelligence, 17*(4), 433–442. doi:10.1016/0160-2896(93)90010-3

McClelland, D. C. (1973). Testing for competence rather than intelligence. *The American Psychologist, 28*(1), 22–26. doi:10.1037/h0034092 PMID:4684069

Mehrizi, M. H. R., & Pakneiat, M. (2008). Comparative analyses of sectoral innovation system and diamond model: The case of telecom sector of Iran. *Journal of Technology Management & Innovation, 3*(3), 78–90.

Mendenhall, M. (1999). On the need for paradigmatic integration in international human resource management. *Management International Review, 39*(3), 65–87.

Mendenhall, M., & Wiley, C. (1994). Strangers in a strange land. *The American Behavioral Scientist, 37*(5), 605–621. doi:10.1177/0002764294037005003

Mitrev, S., & Culpepper, R. (2012). Expatriation in Europe: Factors and insights. *Journal of International Management Studies, 7*(1), 158–167.

Mohan, K. L. (2008). An analysis of competitiveness of Indian clothing export sector using Porter's model. *Journal of International Business, 3*(4), 39–46.

Mwaura, G., Sutton, J., & Roberts, D. (1998). Corporate and national culture: An irreconcilable dilemma for the hospitality manager? *International Journal of Contemporary Hospitality Management, 10*(6), 212–220. doi:10.1108/09596119810232211

Naumann, E. (1992). A conceptual model of expatriate turnover. *Journal of International Business Studies, 23*(3), 499–531. doi:10.1057/palgrave.jibs.8490277

Ng, K. Y., Tan, M. L., & Ang, S. (2012). Culture capital and cosmopolitan human capital: The impact of global mindset and organizational routines on developing cultural intelligence & international experiences in organizations. In A. Burton-Hones & J. C. Spender (Eds.), *The Oxford handbook of human capital.* Oxford University Press. Retrieved from, November 9, 2014, http://culturalq.com/docs/Ng,%20Tan,%20Ang%20Human%20Capital%202009.pdf

Okoroafo, S. C., Koh, A., Liu, L., & Jin, X. (2010). Hotels in China: A comparison of indigenous and subsidiaries strategies. *Journal of Management Research, 2*(1), 1-10.

Okpara, J. O., & Kabongo, J. D. (2011). Cross-cultural training and expatriate adjustment: A study of western expatriate in Nigeria. *Journal of World Business*, *46*(1), 22–30. doi:10.1016/j.jwb.2010.05.014

Porter, G., & Tansky, J. (1999). Expatriate success may depend on a 'learning orientation': Considerations for selection and training. *Human Resource Management*, *38*(1), 47–60. doi:10.1002/(SICI)1099-050X(199921)38:1<47::AID-HRM5>3.0.CO;2-1

Pennington, D. C. (2000). *Social cognition*. London: Routledge.

Quin, E. R., Faerman, R. S., Thompson, P. M., & McGrath, R. M. (1990). *Becoming a master manager: A competency framework*. John Wiley & Sons.

Ozdemir, B., & Cizel, R. B. (2007). International hotel manager as an emerging concept: A review of expatriate management literature and a model proposal. *Journal of Hospitality and Tourism Management*, *14*(2), 170–187. doi:10.1375/jhtm.14.2.170

Pine, R. (2002). China's hotel industry: Serving a massive market. *The Cornell Hotel and Restaurant Administration Quarterly*, *43*(3), 61–70.

Pine, R., Zhang, H., & Qi, P. (2000). The challenge and opportunities of franchising in China's hotel industry. *International Journal of Contemporary Hospitality Management*, *12*(5), 300–307. doi:10.1108/09596110010339670

Pizam, A. (1993). Managing cross-cultural hospitality enterprises. In P. Jones & A. Pizam (Eds.), *The international hospitality industry: Organizational and operational issues* (pp. 205–225). New York: John Wiley & Sons.

Porter, M. (1990). *The competitiveness advantage of nations*. New York: Free Press.

Rozkwitalska, M. (2012). Staffing top management positions in multinational subsidiaries—a local perspective on expatriate management. *Journal of Global Science & Technology Forum (GSTF). Business Review (Federal Reserve Bank of Philadelphia)*, *2*(2), 50–56.

Rush, M. C., & Russell, J. E. A. (1988). Leader prototypes and prototype-contingent consensus in leader behavior description. *Journal of Experimental Social Psychology*, *24*(1), 88–104. doi:10.1016/0022-1031(88)90045-5

Schmidt, F. L., & Hunter, J. E. (2000). Select on intelligence. In E. A. Locke (Ed.), *The Blackwell handbook of organizational principles* (pp. 3–14). Oxford, England: Blackwell.

Schneider, B., & Schmitt, N. (1986). *Staffing organizations* (2nd ed.). HarperCollins Publishers, Inc.

Selmer, J. (2001). The preference for pre-departure or post-arrival cross-cultural training: An exploratory approach. *Journal of Managerial Psychology*, *16*(1), 50–58. doi:10.1108/02683940110366560

Selmer, J. (2002). Practice makes perfect? International experience and expatriate adjustment. *Management International Review*, *42*(1), 71–87.

Shay, J., & Tracey, J. (1997). Expatriate managers. *The Cornell Hotel and Restaurant Administration Quarterly*, *38*(1), 30–35. doi:10.1177/001088049703800116

Shen, J. (2005). International training and management development: Theory and reality. *Journal of Management Development*, *24*(7), 656–666. doi:10.1108/02621710510608786

Sims, R., & Schraeder, M. (2004). *An examination of salient factor affecting expatriate culture shock*. Retrieved from, March 12, 2014, http://www.highbeam.com/doc/1P3-650634311.html

Smit, A. J. (2010). The competitive advantage of nations: Is Porter's diamond framework a new theory that explains the international competitiveness of countries? *Southern African Business Review, 14*(1), 105–130.

Spencer, L., & Spencer, M. (1993). *Competence at work: Models for superior performance.* NY: John Wiley & Sons.

Sternberg, R. J. (1997). *Successful intelligence: How practical and creative intelligence determine success in life.* New York, NY: Plume.

Stone, H., & Ranchlod, A. (2006). Competitive advantage of a nation in the global arena: A quantitative advancement to Porter's diamond applied to the UK, USA, and BRIC nations. *Strategic Change, 15*(6), 283–284. doi:10.1002/jsc.770

Sun, H., Fan, Z., Zhou, Y., & Shi, Y. (2010). Empirical research on competitiveness factors analysis of real estate industry of Beijing and Tianjin. *Engineering, Construction, and Architectural Management, 17*(3), 240–251. doi:10.1108/09699981011038042

Sutton, J. (1996). A profile of expatriate managers in China's international joint venture hotels. *Asian Journal of Business & Information Systems, 1*(2), 175–190.

Suutari, V., & Burch, D. (2001). The role of on site training and support in expatriation. *Career Development International, 6*(6), 298–311. doi:10.1108/EUM0000000005985

Tadmor, C. T. (2006). Acculturation strategies and integrative complexity as predictors of overseas success. Paper presented at the *Annual Meeting of the Academy of Management* in Atlanta, Georgia. doi:10.5465/AMBPP.2006.27163802

Testa, M. R. (2002). Leadership dyads in the cruise industry: The impact of cultural congruency. *International Journal of Hospitality Management, 21*(4), 425–441. doi:10.1016/S0278-4319(02)00036-1

Testa, M. R. (2007). A deeper look at national culture and leadership in the hospitality industry. *International Journal of Hospitality Management, 26*(2), 468–484. doi:10.1016/j.ijhm.2006.11.001

Thorndike, R., & Stein, S. (1937). An evaluation of the attempts to measure social intelligence. *Psychological Bulletin, 34*(5), 275–285. doi:10.1037/h0053850

Torbiorn, I. (1994). Operative and strategic use of expatriates in new organizations and market structure. *International Studies of Management & Organization, 24*(3), 5–17.

Tran, B. (2008). *Expatriate selection and retention.* Doctoral dissertation. California School of Professional Psychology at Alliant International University, San Francisco, California, United States of America.

Tran, B. (2009). Knowledge management: The construction of knowledge in organizations. In D. Jemielniak & J. Kociatkiewicz (Eds.), *Handbook of research on knowledge-intensive organizations* (pp. 512–528). Hersey, PA: Information Science Reference/ IGI Global. doi:10.4018/978-1-60566-176-6.ch031

Tran, B. (2013). Industrial and organizational (I/O) psychology: The roles and purposes of I/O practitioners in global businesses. In B. Christiansen, E. Turkina, & N. Williams (Eds.), *Cultural and technological influences on global business* (pp. 175–219). Hershey, PA: Premier Reference Sources/IGI Global.

Tran, B. (2014a). Ethos, pathos, and logos of doing business abroad: Geert Hofstede's five dimensions of national culture on transcultural marketing. In B. Christiansen, S. Yildiz, & E. Yildiz (Eds.), *Transcultural marketing for incremental and radical innovation* (pp. 255–280). Hershey, PA: Premier Reference Source.

Tran, B. (2014b). The human elements of the knowledge worker: Identifying, managing, and protecting the intellectual capital within the knowledge management. In M. A. Chilton & J. M. Bloodgood (Eds.), *Knowledge management and competitive advantage: Issues and potential solutions* (pp. 281–303). Hershey, PA: Premier Reference Source/IGI Global. doi:10.4018/978-1-4666-4679-7.ch017

Tran, B. (2014c). Rhetoric of play: Utilizing the gamer factor in selecting and training employees. In T. M. Connolly, T. Hainey, E. Boyle, G. Baxter, & P. Moreno-Ger (Eds.), *Psychology, pedagogy, and assessment in serious Games* (pp. 175–203). Hershey, PA: Premier Refeence Source/IGI Global. doi:10.4018/978-1-4666-4773-2.ch009

Tran, B. (2014d). The foundation of cultural intelligence: Human capital. In B. Christiansen, S. Yıldız, & E. Yıldız (Eds.), *Effective Marketing in contemporary globalism*. Hershey, PA: Premier Reference Source/IGI Global. doi:10.4018/978-1-4666-6220-9.ch020

Tsai, H. L., Zeng, S. Y., Lan, C. H., & Fang, R. J. (2012). The impacts of expatriate selection criteria on organizational performance in subsidiaries of transnational corporate. Recent Researches in Applied Computers and Computational Science. In *Proceedings of the 11th WSEAS International Conference on Applied Computer and Applied Computational Science*. WSEAS.

Tung, R. L. (1981). Selection and training of personnel for overseas assignment. *The Columbia Journal of World Business, 16*(1), 68–78.

Tung, R. L. (1982). Selection and training procedures of United States, European, and Japanese multinationals. *California Management Review, 25*(1), 57–71. doi:10.2307/41164993

Tung, R. L. (1988). *The new expatriates*. Cambridge, MA: Ballinger Publishers.

Vance, C., & Paik, Y. (2002). One size fits all in expatriate pre-departure training? *Journal of Management Development, 21*(7), 557–571. doi:10.1108/02621710210434665

Varner, I. I., & Palmer, T. M. (2002). Successful expatriation and organizational strategies. *Review of Business, 23*(2), 8–11.

Vojinic, P., Matic, M., & Becic, M. (2013). Challenges of expatriation process. In *Proceedings of the 1st International Conference on Management, Marketing, Tourism, Retail, Finance and Computer Applications: Recent Advances in Business Management & Marketing*. Dobrovnik, Croatia: Academic Press.

Vulpe, T., Kealey, D., Protheroe, D., & MacDonald, D. (2001). *A profile of the interculturally effective person*. Center for Intercultural Learning, Canadian Foreign Service Institute.

Watchravesringkan, K., Karpova, E., Hodges, N. N., & Copeland, R. (2010). The competitive position of Thailand's apparel industry challenges and opportunities for globalization. *Journal of Fashion Marketing and Management, 14*(4), 576–597. doi:10.1108/13612021011081751

Waxin, M., & Panaccio, A. (2005). Cross-cultural training to facilitate expatriate adjustment: It works. *Personnel Review, 34*(1), 51–67. doi:10.1108/00483480510571879

Webb, A., & Wright, P. C. (1996). The expatriate experience: Implications for career cusses. *Career Development International, 1*(5), 38–44. doi:10.1108/13620439610130632

Wederspahn, G. (1992). Costing Failures in Expatriate Human Resource Management. *Human Resource Planning, 15*(3), 27–35.

Whitfield, M. (1995). High-flyer hazards. *People Management, 1*(24), 9.

Withiam, G. (1997). The best expatriate managers. *The Cornell Hotel and Restaurant Administration Quarterly, 38*(6), 15. doi:10.1177/001088049703800608

Wong, A., & Chan, A. (2010). Understanding the leadership perceptions of staff in China's hotel industry: Integrating the macro- and micro-aspects of leadership contexts. *International Journal of Hospitality Management, 29*(3), 437–447. doi:10.1016/j.ijhm.2010.01.003

Wood, R., & Payne, T. (1998). *Competency-based recruitment and selection.* New York: John Wiley & Sons.

Yooyanyong, P., & Muenjohn, N. (2010). Leadership styles of expatriate managers: A comparison between American and Japanese expatriates. *The Journal of American Academy of Business, 15*(2), 161–167.

Yu, L. (1992). Hotel development and structures in China. *International Journal of Hospitality Management, 11*(2), 99–110. doi:10.1016/0278-4319(92)90004-F

Yu, L., & Goh, S. H. (1995). Perceptions of management difficulty factors by expatriate hotel professionals in China. *International Journal of Hospitality Management, 14*(3/4), 375–388. doi:10.1016/0278-4319(95)00044-5

Yu, L., & Huimin, G. (2005). Hotel reform in China: A SWOT analysis. *Cornell Hotel and Restaurant Quarterly, 46*(2), 153–169. doi:10.1177/0010880404273892

Zakaria, N. (2000). The effects of cross-cultural training on the acculturation process of the global workforce. *International Journal of Manpower, 21*(6), 492–510. doi:10.1108/01437720010377837

Zeira, Y., & Banai, M. (1985). Selection of Expatriate-Managers in Multinational Corporations: The host environment point of view. *International Studies of Management & Organization, 15*(1), 33–51.

Zhang, H., Pine, R., & Lam, T. (2005). *Tourism and hotel development in China.* New York, NY: The Haworth Hospitality Press and International Business Press.

## ADDITIONAL READING

Cerimagic, S., & Smith, J. (2011). Cross-cultural training: The importance of investing in people. *COBRA 2011: RICS Construction and Property Conference,* 667-675.

Collings, D. G., Doherty, N., Luethy, M., & Osborn, D. (2011). Understanding and supporting the career implications of international assignments. *Journal of Vocational Behavior, 78*(3), 361–371. doi:10.1016/j.jvb.2011.03.010

Crawley, E., Swailes, S., & Walsh, D. (2013). *Introduction to international human resource management.* Oxford University Press.

Dickmann, M., & Baruch, Y. (2010). *Global Careers.* Global HRM.

Fenton, M. G. (7th ed.). (2011). *A study of selection, training, and host country cultural adaption experiences of expatriate faculty from United States AASCU universities.* ProQuest: UMI Dissertation Publishing

Fitzsimmons, S. R., Miska, C., & Stahl, G. (2011). Multicultural employees: Global business' untapped resource. *Organizational Dynamics, 40*(3), 199–206. doi:10.1016/j.orgdyn.2011.04.007

Gai, S., Sumner, K., Bragger, J., & Nooner, K. (2011). Understanding experiences of Indian expatriates in the United States: Stress, satisfaction, social support, and general health. *International Journal of Strategic Management, 11*(3), 158–167.

Halim, H., Rahman, N. A. A., & Mohamad, B. (2013). OES vs SIES: Exploring the cross-cultural adjustment of hotel expatriates in a multicultural society. *International Conference on Communication, Media, Technology and Design, 2(4)*, 413-419.

Hindman, H. (2013). *Mediating the global: Expatria's forms and consequences in Kathmandu.* Stanford University Press. doi:10.11126/stanford/9780804786515.001.0001

Jenkins, E. M., & Mockaitis, A. I. (2010). You're from where? The influence of distance factors on New Zealand expatriates' cross-cultural adjustment. *International Journal of Human Resource Management, 21*(15), 2694–2715. doi:10.1080/09585192.2010.528653

Kuhlmann, T., & Hutchings, K. (2010). Expatriate assignments vs localization of management in China: Staffing choices of Australian and German companies. *Career Development International, 15*(1), 20–38. doi:10.1108/13620431011020871

Landy, F. J., & Conte, J. M. (2012). *Work in the 21st century: An introduction to industrial and organizational psychology* (4th ed.). Wiley.

Lundby, K., Jolton, J., & Kraut, A. I. (2010). *Going global: Practical applications and recommendations for HR and OD professionals in the global workplace.* Pfeiffer.

Masadeh, M. (2013). Out-of-country training for hotel middle managers in Jordan: Selection criteria and implications. *European Journal of Tourism. Hospitality and Recreation, 4*(1), 105–122.

McDonnell, A., Lamare, R., Gunnigle, P., & Lavelle, J. (2010). Developing tomorrow's leaders—evidence of global talent management in multinational enterprises. *Journal of World Business, 45*(2), 150–160. doi:10.1016/j.jwb.2009.09.015

Messner, W. (2013). *Intercultural communication competence: A toolkit for acquiring effective and appropriate intercultural communication and collaboration skills.* CreateSpace Independent Publishing Platform.

Morschett, D., Schramm-Klein, H., & Zentes, J. (2010). *Strategic international management: Tex and cases* (2nd ed.). Gabler Verlag. doi:10.1007/978-3-8349-6331-4

Moulik, S. R., & Mazumdar, S. (2012). Expatriate satisfaction in international assignments: Perspectives from Indian IT professionals working in the US. *International Journal of Human Resource Studies, 2*(3), 59–79.

Noe, R. A. (2010). *Employee training and development* (5th rev. ed.). McGraw Hill Higher Education.

Ross, R. C., Ramalu, S. S., Uli, J., & Kumar, N. (2010). Expatriate performance in international assignments: The role of cultural intelligence as dynamic intercultural competency. *International Journal of Business and Management, 5*(8), 76–85.

Rozkwitalska, M. (2012). Expatriate versus host country manager—who should run a foreign subsidiary? *Journal of Intercultural Management, 4*(4), 39–50.

Kramar, R., & Syed, J. (2012). *Human resource management in a global context: A critical approach.* Palgrave Macmillan.

Selmer, J. (2004). Psychological barriers to adjustment if western business expatriates in China: Newcomers vs long stayers. *International Journal of Human Resource Management, 15*(4), 794–813. doi:10.1080/0958519042000192951

Tornikoski, C. (2011). Fostering expatriate affective commitment: A total reward perspective. *Cross Cultural Management: An International Journal, 18*(2), 214–235. doi:10.1108/13527601111126030

Wankel, C., & Malleck, S. (2011). *Ethical models and applications of globalization: Cultural, sociopolitical and economic perspectives.* Hersey, PA: IGI Global.

White, D. W., Absher, K. R., & Huggins, K. A. (2010). The effects of hardiness and cultural distance on sociocultural adaptation in an expatriate sales manager population. *Journal of Personal Selling & Sales Management, 31*(3), 325–337. doi:10.2753/PSS0885-3134310309

## KEY TERMS AND DEFINITIONS

**Ability:** means the sufficiency of strength to accomplish something, especially the physical and mental quality to perform activities.

**Competency:** the state or quality of being properly or well qualified.

**Competent Expatriate:** A competency is a cluster of related knowledge, skills, and attitudes that affects a major part of one's job (a role or responsibility), that correlates with performance on the job, that can be measure against well-accepted standards, and that can be improved via training and development.

**Cultural Intelligence (CQ):** defined as an individual's capability to function and manage effectively in culturally diverse settings.

**Emotional Quotient (EQ):** is the social intelligence.

**Expatriate:** an individual who relocate from one country to another (Tran, 2008) for at least one year.

**Expatriate Failure:** as a term encompassing a broad range of themes such as premature repatriation, low performance, and adjustment problems. Many other terms, such as expatriate turnover, expatriate transfer, and expatriate recall rates, are also used interchangeably.

**Expatriate Turnover:** occurs when expatriates wither quite or return to their home country prior to the completion of their overseas tour.

**Expatriation:** is most commonly described by selection, training and preparation, transfer and adjustment, monitoring and performance management, and finally, repatriation of the individual.

**Guanxi:** Chinese characteristics of the strength of personal relations.

**Hard Skills:** usually include professional knowledge and task-oriented skills.

**IHCs:** International Hotel Chains.

**Intelligence Quotient [General Intelligence (IQ)]:** the ability to grasp and reason correctly with abstractions and solve problems.

**Intercultural Capabilities:** is captured by the construct of cultural intelligence (CQ), which is defined as a "person's capability for successful adaptation to new cultural settings, that is, for unfamiliar settings attributable to cultural context.

**MNCs:** Multinational Corporations.

**Knowledge:** refers to a body of information about the theoretical and practical understanding of a subject, acquired by a person through experience or education.

**Other Characteristics (O):** congruent to Tung's five basic training programs of cross-cultural training, as: 1) desire to prematurely terminate an expatriate's assignment, 2) stable competencies, and 3) intercultural/international business communication.

**PCN:** Parent Country National.

**Repatriation:** is the process of returning an expatriate back to the home country where the company's headquarter is based.

**ROI:** Return-on-Investment.

**Skills:** refer to the application of data or information with manual, verbal, or mental proficiency.

**Soft Skills:** are those skills associated with the behavior necessary for successful interpersonal interaction.

**TCN:** Third Country National.

# Chapter 24
# Best "Experience" Practices in Medical Tourism

**Mengyu Li**
*The University of Delaware, USA*

**Frederick J. DeMicco**
*The University of Delaware, USA*

## ABSTRACT

*The principal objective of this paper is to demonstrate the best practices in the rising trend of H2H and Medical Tourism. The concept of "Experience Economy" expedites the merging process of hospitality and hospitals: patients are also travelers now whose needs are not merely commodity type of medical care anymore but a memorable wellbeing experience. Moreover, H2H optimizes the process of realizing excellent care, which serves as the fundamental reason for tourism industry. In the section of "Best Practices in Medical Tourism, Christiana Care Way, Starwood Five Human Truths, and H2H packages in Switzerland are selected to show how patient/guest experience can be made more interactive and less transactional. Therefore, although H2H demands the considerable collaboration from all parties involved in order to ultimately present the excellent care that customers, tourists, and patients want, H2H indeed carries tremendous opportunity for hospitals, hotels, Spa, restaurants, transportation, and more.*

## CURRENT TREND

With the development of technology, transportation and global economy, many tourists have begun traveling to other destinations for medical or health and wellness services. This process is called "medical tourism," also known as healthcare tourism, or wellness tourism (Medical Tourism Association). In 2007, an estimated 750,000 Americans traveled abroad for medical care with $2.1 billion spent overseas for care (Deloitte, 2009). According to the results of an online Survey of more than 3,000 Health Care Consumers conducted by Deloitte Center for Health Solutions (2009), almost 39% said they would go abroad for an elective procedure if they could save half the cost and be assured quality was comparable. 88% said they would consider going out of their community or local areas to get care/treatment for a condition if they knew the outcomes were better and the costs were no higher there.

DOI: 10.4018/978-1-4666-8606-9.ch024

In 2008, more than 400,000 non-US residents sought medical care in the United States and spent almost $5 billion for health services. Inbound tourists are primarily from the Middle East, South America and Canada. The most common treatments sought by inbound medical tourists included oncology (31.69%), cardiology (14.17%), and neurology (11.75%), followed by "other" specialties (Stackpole & Associates, 2010). In the research titled as Asia Medical Tourism Analysis and Forecast to 2015, Asian medical tourist number of arrivals is expected to cross the figure of 10 Million by 2015 and the market value in 2011 is expected to double by 2015; 3 countries – India, Thailand, Singapore – are expected to control more than 80% market share in 2015. Many other countries in Asia like Malaysia, Philippines, and South Korea are all keen to make traveling abroad for medical treatment a growth industry within their own economies (Renub Research, 2012).

## MACRO ENVIRONMENT: THE EXPERIENCE ECONOMY

In the modern world, an increasing number of businesses are moving away from the traditional commodity, goods and service model but are becoming more experience-driven. B. Joseph Pine II and James H. Gilmore first introduced "The Experience Economy" in 1999. What many hospitals fail to realize is that patients are also customers, and these customers are charged for the wellbeing they get by being engaged in an experience economy (Pine, B. J., & Gilmore, J. H., 2011). The medical care institutions are expected to offer travel, lodging, spa care and even fitness classes in order to cater to their patients' needs. The goal for the process of the medical care is evolving from transactional care to a transformational experience in which customers/patients receive health benefits, not limited to medical care.

## GOAL OF H2H: EXCELLENT CARE

What are the key components of a fond healthcare experience? When it comes to medical tourism, the success of medical care obviously is one crucial determinant. Unfortunately, the patients and customers will not credit the well-done treatment coming with unpleasant customer service as excellent source of care. Moreover, as one of the most distinctive icons in the service industry, Disney has provided a convincing list summarized by Dr. Lee in his book "If Disney Ran Your Hospital": initiative, teamwork, empathy, courtesy, and communication (Dr. Lee, 2004). Based on the Disney model, six major factors should be considered necessary for realization of excellent care in medical care settings. To be more illustrative, the graphic model for medical care can be created as below:

Successful medical treatment serves as the primary goal of medical tourism. It is the core competency of hospitals while a hospitality team has expertise in customer care. Both teams have competitive methods to reinforce their core competence and enhance their strengths. However, the greater success in medical tourism is to align these two core competencies from both parties. Productivity and efficiency can be maximized by the alignment. Also, success in medical treatment and memorable customer care are compensating each other to deliver excellent medical tourism experience.

For example, the majority of patients will not highly praise their healthcare experiences simply because the health institution is able to deliver successful medical treatments. It is likely that there are a handful of possible other institutions that can achieve the same result. However, H2H that is composed with medical staff, hoteliers, spa staff, personal trainers, and other wellbeing facilitators can significantly differentiate the healthcare institution from conventional ones.

*Figure 1. Dr. Lee's Disney Model on Excellent Care*

Since the expertise of customer care can complete and strengthen the circle of true care for patients' overall wellbeing, having a strong hospitality team inside the health care organization is a substantial competitive advantage. This H2H process bridges the gap between the successful medical treatment and excellent care perceived and experienced by patients. As an expert and pioneer in the field of bringing hospitality to hospitals, Dr. Lee summarized the rest of the five factors that define the excellent care performed by Disney (Dr. Lee, 2004).

## BEST PRACTICES IN MEDICAL TOURISM

### Christiana Care Way

Christiana Care has been recruiting a team of volunteers who act as Ambassadors and Greeters during recent years. In orientation training, Rose Wessells, a Volunteer Services manager at Christiana Care Health System, told a memorable personal story that explicitly demonstrates the excellent care Christiana Care provided to her

*Table 1. Explanation of Disney Model by Dr. Lee*

| Initiative | Sense people's needs before they ask. |
|---|---|
| Teamwork | Help each other out. |
| Empathy | Acknowledge people's feelings. |
| Courtesy | Respect the dignity and privacy of everyone. |
| Communication | Explain what's happening. |

family. This story also carries a promise that is the Christiana Care Way: "We serve our neighbors as respectful, expert, caring partners in their health. We do this by creating innovative, effective, affordable systems of care that our neighbors value" (Christiana Care).

When her mother was very ill, a lovely nurse was taking care of her in Christiana Care hospital. When Ms. Wessells first met the nurse, she was soon impressed by her attentiveness and thoughtfulness. The nurse would ask questions about how would her mother like her to leave the door. She was always taking initiative and showing courtesy to Ms. Wessells' mother and her. There were days that the daughter was so worried about her mother's condition. However, after one event had taken place, the daughter became confident that her mother was going to recover from the illness with the help of the excellent care team onsite.

On that day, she had a pleasant conversation with her mother's nurse and was comforted by her kind words and excellent care. After visiting her mother, Ms. Wessells went to the cafeteria to have lunch. While she was taking her dishes, the nurse suddenly ran to her and anxiously explained to her: "I am taking my lunch break now for about ten minutes, and my colleague Nancy is taking good care of your mother as we speak. I saw you are having lunch here. I want you to know that your mother is taken care of, and you do not have to worry when you see me here." Ms. Wessells was grateful for the communication initiated by the nurse. She felt that there was a team providing excellent care for her mother not just one nurse. When one nurse is occupied, there are more team members to take initiative and ensure the coverage for the patients' needs. The nurse showed her great empathy by anticipating her being worried before Ms. Wessells even saw her.

## Starwood Five Human Truths

In this touching story, the nurse has demonstrated what excellent care should be. Her kind words exemplified the Five Human Truths developed by Starwood and practiced in their hotels as the graph demonstrated below:

The nurse showed Ms. Wessells that she is understood by her anticipatory empathy. The explanation that the nurse gave made the patient's family feel special that the patient's wellbeing was important to the care providers. Because of that, both parties can still have more control over their lives when battling with diseases. Consequently, the success rate of medical care can increase, and the patients can better reach their potentials. In the long run, the excellent care will be the reason for patients to come back to enhance their wellbeing; they feel belong to a particular medical institution among all other options.

## H2H Package

The diversity of patients is obvious at Christiana Care that they receive guests not only from the local area, but also other countries. Christiana Care seeks talent with diverse background, including multi-lingual ability. These multi-lingual Ambassadors/Greeters can assist patients with translation and direction. Patients arrive this medical facility and feel understood. Also, the hospital has gift shop named "Glass Box" available for the convenience of visitors and patients' families. Christiana Care demonstrates the other trend of H2H that hotels offer special rates for the patient family or visitors during hospital stays. There are a variety of hotels for them to choose from: Embassy Suites Newark, Courtyard by Marriott, Sheraton, Blue Hen Bed and Breakfast, Days Inn, etc. Most of

*Figure 2. Starwood Five Human Truths*

these accommodations provide complimentary transportation services to their guests if they need to come to the hospital. The documents from the hospital can reduce the cost of their stay by 10-15%. These guests are welcomed to enjoy the spa, swimming pool, gym, and in-room dinning facilities during their hotel stay as well.

## REFLECTION BASED ON H2H WORK EXPERIENCE

This experience of working at a hospital provides me with a different perspective on medical tourism. When patients arrive medical care institutions, especially from overseas, they are much more vulnerable and sensitive than a regular hotel guest. Instead of taking a vacation with their loved ones at a hotel, they are at the risk

of losing everything they have in a hospital. For patients who need extensive care, they are likely to feel losing control of their own bodies, health, life and even dignity. Having a bed, a restroom, a door, a group of doctors and nurses, a collection of needles and medicines is the fundamentals that a patient needs. The questions are: How could one medical facility become more desirable for patients? Can these basic medical accommodations make a difference for a patient's in-house experience? Is it possible for care providers to complete a memorable experience by merely having operational skills?

The answer to these questions is clearly no. Without doing the fundamental basics right, patients are disappointed from the start, and their experience is on a wrong track to become memorable. The best experience practices are relying on fundamental basics to become memorable. These basics are undoubtedly the core competency of medical care. However, patients are looking for a deeper human connection with their caregivers. This connection is not transactional but interactive. Some patients may have to be assisted to complete the essential functions of living, such as conversing, dining, sleeping and bathing. These are the essential expertise of hospitality. Therefore, as the trend of H2H indicated, excellent care should be provided by all the involved parties, such as hospital staff, hotel employees, Spa therapists, restaurant servers and so on. When everyone in this circle focuses on their core competency, patients are going to receive a better experience during their medical treatment.

Unfortunately, the patient's families tend to be left out of the loop; nevertheless, due to the tremendous pressure and anxiety, sometimes they are the ones who need excellent care and great attention the most. Switzerland has been one of the most popular destinations for medical tourism for decades. Patients and their family members are feeling more engaged when they come here for wellbeing treatment. The local hospitals offer packages that include medical treatments, personalized care, hotel stays, medical spas, sightseeing, shopping and nightlife activities. This greatly eases anxiety and concerns for patients and their families because they perceived the medical care package as a well-arranged plan for them and their families. The key concentration for medical tourism is the overall wellbeing where medical care is playing an important role. It incorporates many more service providers in a larger scope. The realization of medical tourism carries significant opportunities, not limited to hospitals, hotels, spas, restaurants, and transportation (Cetron, DeMicco & Davies, 2010).

See: http://www.udel.edu/udaily/2013/jul/hotels-health-care-071612.html

And http://www.udel.edu/udaily/2014/aug/swiss-medical-tourism-080713.html

## CONCLUSION

Under the umbrella of the current experience economy, medical tourism represents a golden opportunity: hospital's operation model can transform from service business to experience business where patients are no longer charged for the medical treatment performed by doctors and nurses. Instead, customers are paying for their own wellbeing benefits and receiving excellent care. The process of H2H demands the considerable collaboration from all parties in order to ultimately present the excellent care that customers, tourists, and patients are looking for. Furthermore, the fond experience of wellness tourism is rewarded with lifetime loyal visitors. They offer positive reviews and feedbacks to their care providers that can attract an increasing number of tourists. As a result, these care-providing entities are capable of creating unique competitive advantages that generates tremendous profits for businesses.

## REFERENCES

Cetron, M., DeMicco, F., & Davies, O. (2010). *Hospitality and Travel 2015*. Orlando, FL: The American Hotel and Lodging Association Educational Institute.

Christiana Care Health System. (n.d.). *About Christiana Care Care*. Retrieved from http://www.christianacare.org/way

Deloitte, L. L. P. (2009). *Medical tourism: Update and implications*. [Report]. Retrieved from www.deloitte.com

Lee, F. (2004). *If Disney ran your hospital: 9 1/2 things you would do differently*. Bozeman, MT: Second River Healthcare Press.

Medical Tourism Association. (n.d.). *Medical Tourism FAQ's*. Retrieved from http://www.medicaltourismassociation.com/en/medical-tourism-faq-s.html

Pine, B. J., & Gilmore, J. H. (2011). The experience economy (Updated ed.). Boston: Harvard Business Review Press.

Renub Resarch. (2012). *Asia Medical Tourism Analysis and Forecast to 2015*. Retrieved from http://www.marketresearch.com/Renub-Research-v3619/Asia-Medical-Tourism-Forecast-7174680/

Stackpole, & Associates. (2010). *Inbound Medical Tourism: Survey of US International Patient Departments*. Retrieved from http://www.stackpoleassociates.com/

## KEY TERMS AND DEFINITIONS

**Experience Practices:** Implementations of focusing on creating captivating experiences rather than only completing necessary medical procedures.

**H2H:** A rising trend that hospitals are bringing in hospitality talent to optimize customer service for their patients.

**Medical Tourism:** An increase tendency that patients are going overseas as tourists to receive wellbeing treatments, health therapies, or medical surgeries.

**Experience Economy:** A current trend of global economy that consumers are purchasing memorable experiences instead of only physical commodities.

**Core Competency:** A unique and vital expertise that an entity possesses while most its competitors do not.

**Competitive Advantage:** An element that renders business superiority over its competitors such as a team of unique talent, a cutting-edge technology, and a special geographical location. This superiority enables the business a better chance of winning in a competition.

## APPENDIX

**Teaching Notes**

1.  In the article, what is the ultimate goal of H2H? Do you agree? Why?
2.  Based on the current trend and the macro environment of medical tourism, please conduct a SWOT analysis (SWOT: Strength, Weakness, Opportunity and Threat).
3.  Does the goal of H2H, or say "Hotels Bridging Hospitals", co-align with the PESTEL (PESTEL: Political, Economic. Social, Technological, Environmental, Legal) environment of medical tourism? If yes, how?
4.  "Balanced score cards" is a widely used assessment tool to analyze the effectiveness of a company. It measures four aspects of business: financial performance, guest satisfaction, employee scores for managers, as well as sustainability. According to Dr. Lee, how does Disney's five factors play a role in achieving balanced score cards?
5.  In the story of Ms Wessells, how did she interpret the nurse's explanation? What effects did the nurse have on Ms Wessells's perception of Christiana Care?
6.  Will Starwood Five Human Truths possess similar effects if applied in a hospital setting, like Christiana Care? Why or why not?
7.  If you were given an opportunity to redesign a creative H2H plan for hospitals, like Christiana Care, what would you like to do?
8.  Do you think that H2H and medical tourism is inevitable or dispensable? Why?
9.  What are some concerns you have regarding medical tourism or H2H? Please explain.
10. Have you observed or experienced good practices in medical tourism? What have they done to make you feel special?

# Chapter 25

# Explaining Consumer Behavior in the Hospitality Industry:
## CSR Associations and Corporate Image

**Patricia Martínez**
*University of Cantabria, Spain*

**Ignacio Rodríguez del Bosque**
*University of Cantabria, Spain*

## ABSTRACT

*The aim of this chapter is to explore how Corporate Social Responsibility (CSR) associations and corporate image influence customers´ behavior. Specifically, a model is proposed in which CSR and corporate image positively condition customer loyalty. It also proposes that the company´ social responsible initiatives influence customer satisfaction. In order to test this model structural equation modelling is employed on a sample of 382 Spanish hotel customers. This study finds that both corporate image and customer satisfaction contribute to achieve customer loyalty, also proving the roles of corporate image as a mediating variable. Additionally, our results show that CSR influences customer satisfaction. Finally, although we did not corroborate that CSR associations increase customer loyalty CSR associations have an indirect effect on loyalty through corporate image. As the results of studies concerning loyalty will depend on the services or products examined other business areas should be considered to find out about the generalization of these results. Second, other relevant variables could be included in further research.*

## INTRODUCTION

These days, the hospitality industry copes with a number of opportunities and menaces as a result of the current worldwide financial and economic crisis (Tandford et al., 2011). Within Europe, Spain is one of the countries that have suffered most from the crisis because of its severe housing

bubble (Álvarez, 2008). As extant studies corroborate, the service sector is the central sector of the Spanish economy given its contribution to the gross domestic product (GDP) (Alonso-Almeida & Bremser, 2013). In 2010, services represented approximately 72% of the GDP (Instituto Nacional de Estadística, 2011). Moreover, tourism companies are an important element of the Spanish

DOI: 10.4018/978-1-4666-8606-9.ch025

service sector and accounted for nearly 13% in 2010. Within Europe, Spain has the highest number of hotels and restaurants (Alonso-Almeida & Bremser, 2013). Despite the fact that hospitality industry is of major importance for the Spanish economy, as a result of the recession subsequent to the economic crisis, international tourism to Spain deteriorated and spending by international and national tourists declined (Instituto de Estudios Turísticos, 2010).

In order to mitigate the negative impact of the crisis, some tactics allow firms to rebound more rapidly from a critical situation. In the hospitality setting, many companies are developing a loyal customer base (Mason et al., 2006; Tandford et al., 2011) since it is demonstrated that loyal customers buy more, tend to be less price-sensitive than others customers, spend a larger share of their income at the supplier and spread positive word-of-mouth (Williams & Naumann, 2001). As Alonso-Almeida and Bremser (2013, p. 146) state "in crisis periods, loyal customers remain satisfied with their hotel of choice and do not downgrade or switch to other offers". Consequently, maintain customer loyalty is a critical mission not only for hospitality managers, but also for strategic management and marketing research. With this increased interest in customer relationships, it has become increasingly obvious that hospitality theory and practice must include customer loyalty as a central construct in relationships and must also incorporate its antecedents (Mason et al., 2006; Martínez & Rodríguez del Bosque, 2013; Tandford et al., 2011).

To explain customer loyalty, previous studies mainly focus on the analysis of key marketing variables acting as customer loyalty antecedents such as customer satisfaction (Bravo et al., 2012; Clemes et al., 2011) and customer commitment (Botha & Van Der Waldt, 2012; Mattila, 2006). However, corporate social responsibility (CSR) associations have recently been incorporated into traditional models. CSR associations reflect the organization´s status and activities with respect to its perceived societal obligations (Brown & Dacin, 1997). In marketing-based CSR research to identify the channel and process of the effect of CSR associations on consumer behavior and responses is a key issue (Brown & Dacin, 1997; He & Li, 2011; Luo & Bhattacharya, 2006; Marin et al., 2009). Actually, an increasing stream of research proposes to study the influence of CSR associations on consumer attitudes and behaviors (Bravo et al., 2012; Marin et al., 2009; Pérez et al., 2012; Romani et al., 2013). Nevertheless, little attention has been paid to analyze how responsible strategies may influence consumer behavior in the hospitality context (Martínez & Rodríguez del Bosque, 2013). Although a growing number of hospitality companies have implemented a number of socially responsible practices to show their commitment toward this notion (e.g., Meliá Hotels International, NH Hotels or Marriot International), there is still a gap in the literature regarding the effect of these actions on customer behavior in the hospitality setting. In fact, little research has provided a conceptual model to understand how CSR influences hotel customer loyalty formation process (Mason et al., 2006). In line with Chan´s (2011, p. 5) call for research into "a CSR orientation for companies in the hospitality sector to minimize the negative impacts of their activities on natural, cultural and social environments", scholars acknowledge for analyzing how different social and environmental decisions influence customers attitudes and behaviors (Martínez & Rodríguez del Bosque, 2013). Previous studies responding to this call present varied and mixed findings about the effects of CSR on customer outcomes (Pérez et al., 2012; Vlachos et al., 2009). Such ambiguous findings may appear because extant studies neglect relevant mediator variables in CSR-customer outcome relationships (Walsh & Bartikowski, 2013) or because previous studies utilize experimental or artificial settings (Lacey & Kennett-Hensel, 2010).

Therefore, this chapter expands classical consumer behavior paradigms considering CSR in hospitality business as a relevant element that contributes to influence customer´s evaluations and perceptions towards a firm. Specifically, this chapter analyses how CSR and customer satisfaction contribute to retaining customer loyalty through corporate image, a concept usually viewed as a mediating factor between customer perceptions and future intentions (Back, 2005; Bravo et al., 2012; Nguyen & Leblanc, 2001). In this sense, although corporate image is crucial to the success of companies in the hospitality setting, academic studies regarding this topic have been a topic rarely discussed in favor of other perspectives, such as quality, requiring further research on the corporate image of hospitality companies (Moreno-Gil et al., 2012).

This study overcomes several gaps identified in the academic literature. First, a reduced number of studies in CSR associations introduce customer satisfaction within a nomological net of antecedents and consequences (Walsh & Bartikowski, 2013). Although previous research builds on the mediating role of satisfaction to predict behavioral outcomes from corporate ability associations (Caruana, 2002), little research apply satisfaction to clarify the effect of CSR associations on customer behaviors. Second, customer loyalty has been broadly analyzed in relation to customer satisfaction. However, corporate image has received much less attention in relation to customer loyalty (Brunner et al., 2008) despite the importance of this concept in the service sector due to the intangible nature of hospitality operations and the subjective perception of the quality of the hotel services (Christou, 2003). Therefore, the study of these relationships is considered a contributing source to the hospitality literature.

To address these issues, first, this chapter reviews the literature on the antecedents of loyalty and proposes a research model specifically in the hospitality sector. Second, an empirical study validates the model with data from Spanish

customers of hotels, using a structural equation modeling (SEM) approach. Then, the methodology and results are described. Finally, the findings are discussed and their implications for future research are explored.

## BACKGROUND

## Significance of Customer Loyalty

Consumer loyalty toward a firm is defined by Oliver (1997, p. 392) as: "a deeply held commitment to re-buy or re-patronize a preferred product/service consistently in the future, thereby causing repetitive same-brand or same brand-set purchasing, despite situational influences and marketing efforts having the potential to cause switching behavior". Given that clients perceive a greater risk in the choice of service, this notion has become a strategic objective and is of particular importance in the service sector (Polo et al., 2013). Academic literature suggests that loyal customers´ visit frequency is higher and make more purchase than non-loyal customers do. They are also less likely to switch to a competitor brand just because of price and other special promotions and bring in new customers through positive word-of-mouth (Yoo & Bai, 2013).

One of the basic theories of loyalty marketing is that a small increase in the number of loyal customers can lead to a significant increase in profitability (Reichheld, 1993; Reichheld & Sasser, 1990). In their study in the service sector, Reichheld and Sasser (1990) found that a 5% increase in customer retention resulted up to a 125% increase in profits. Moreover, it has been demonstrated that it is six times more expensive to plan marketing strategies to attract new customers than it is to retain existing customers (Petrick, 2004). On the whole, customer loyalty is recognized as a major source of competitive advantage for firms due to its powerful impact on performance (Yoo & Bai, 2013).

*Figure 1. Conceptual model*

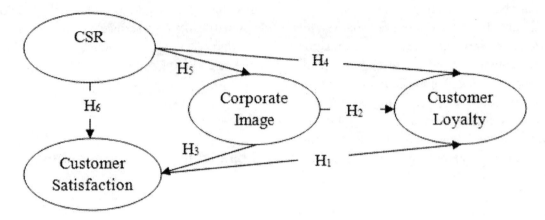

Regarding the construct of customer loyalty, many researchers define loyalty on the basis of not only behavioral but also attitudinal aspects (Back, 2005; Han et al., 2011), since the simple repeat purchase may be due to inertia, indifference or change costs. The behavioral component of customer loyalty is related to repeated transactions made from the consumer in a specific period of time. However, repurchase behavior can be due to satisfaction, a lack of alternatives, or convenience or habit (Pérez et al., 2012). Therefore, it is thought that this approach can lead to identifying as loyalty some behaviors that have been usually described as "spurious loyalty" or "no loyalty", which happen when the repurchase takes place even if the organization has a negative image in the market (Dick & Basu, 1994, p. 100).

A more complete understanding of loyalty, supported in this study, refers to consumer loyalty as a step further. Attitudinal loyalty involves that a positive assessment of the company is made together with the existence of an emotional link between the consumer and the organization that creates a real loyalty (Pérez et al., 2012). This type is linked to active loyalty, which not only means repurchase but also a positive word of mouth. Therefore, some hospitality researchers assessed customer loyalty only employing an attitudinal perspective (Back, 2005; Han & Back, 2008).

However, a customer´s favorable attitude toward a particular product or brand may not assure repeat patronage or repurchase frequency (Dick & Basu, 1994; Oliver, 1997). Thus, hospitality researchers insist and agree that measuring both attitudinal and behavioral aspects is essential to assess customer loyalty precisely (Back, 2005; Han et al., 2011; Martínez & Rodríguez del Bosque, 2013; Petrick, 2004). As a final point, below are the antecedents of loyalty that act as study variables in this research (Figure 1).

## Customer Satisfaction as an Antecedent of Customer Loyalty

Improving customer satisfaction is extensively recognized as an important factor leading to the success of companies (Clemes et al., 2011). The social exchange theory states that satisfaction is one of the focal consequences of exchange partners´ relationship management behaviors (Botha & Van Der Waldt, 2012). In the extremely competitive hotel industry homogenous products and services are offered so hoteliers must find ways to make their offer to stand out among their rivals. As Choi and Chu state (2001, p. 278) "hoteliers need to understand their customers´ needs and meet or exceed these needs". Consequently, customer satisfaction is indispensable for hospitality companies´ survival and profit-earning capacity (Polo et al., 2013).

The services marketing literature presents different definitions of customer satisfaction. However, in the hospitality context, there are two common conceptualizations of satisfaction: (1) transient (transaction-specific) and (2) overall (or cumulative) satisfaction (Ekinci et al., 2006). As these authors explain, transient satisfaction comes from the assessment of events and behaviors taking place during a single interaction whereas overall satisfaction is viewed as a function of multiple transient satisfactions with the services when perceived performance is compared to one or multiple subjective comparison standards. Therefore, overall satisfaction is a post-choice evaluative judgment of a specific purchase occasion (Bitner & Hubbert, 1994). It must be highlighted that behavioral academics such as Oliver (1980) have focused on the antecedents (e.g., comparison standards) and consequences (e.g., behavioral intentions) of this type of satisfaction. However, most recently, hospitality academics have gone beyond these cognitive models to recognize the affective nature of satisfaction (Choi & Chu, 2001). This approach is summarized in Oliver´s (1997, p. 13) definition which states that "satisfaction is the consumer´s fulfillment response. It is a judgment that a product or service feature, or the product or service itself provided (or is providing) a pleasure level of consumption-related fulfillment, including levels of under or over-fulfillment". Here, in this study we follow Oliver (1997) and understand satisfaction as a customer´s overall affective and emotional response to the whole service experience for a single transaction at the post-purchasing point. This view seems most appropriate for the evaluation of hospitality services because they are intangible and a customer´s affective response to hospitality services can be captured after consumption (Ekinci et al., 2006).

Although satisfaction does not guarantee loyalty, academic literature has demonstrated that loyal customers are satisfied (Jones & Sasser

1995). Consequently, loyalty and satisfaction are closely related constructs in the services marketing literature (Cronin et al., 2000). Overall, academics accept that satisfaction influences loyalty (Cronin et al., 2000; Hur et al., 2013). The literature focusing on the hospitality field also includes studies that positively relate customer satisfaction to loyalty (Clemes et al., 2011; Evanschitzky & Wunderlich, 2006). In light of the above, we propose that:

**H₁**: Customer satisfaction will positively influence on customer loyalty

## Corporate Image as a Precursor of Customer Satisfaction and Loyalty

A number of studies have analyzed customer loyalty in relation to customer satisfaction. However, corporate image has received much less attention (Brunner et al., 2008). Corporate image has been suggested as a crucial aspect to the success of hospitality companies (Moreno-Gil et al., 2012) and is defined as perceptions of an organization reflected in the associations held in consumer memory (Keller, 1993). In order to emphasize the relevance of understanding image development, several researchers have attempted to identify the driving forces of this construct and to determine its impact on buying behaviors (Han et al., 2011; Moreno-Gil et al., 2012). Previous studies have proposed that for complex and infrequently used services (e.g., hospitality services) corporate image rather than satisfaction may be the main predictor of loyalty (Andreasssen & Lindestad, 1998). Actually, given the present competitive environment and the growing importance of hospitality organizations in international markets, the importance of corporate image has become a common agenda in hospitality organizations in order to gain competitive advantage (Kandampully & Hu, 2007). In this context, corporate image plays a major role in the process of selecting a hotel by the customer (Chen & Hsu, 2000) and this factor is even more critical in the case of resort hotels (Dubé & Renaghan, 2000). At the same time, corporate image provides a certain quality to the market and reduces the risk of selection by customers (Mangan & Collins, 2002).

Studies on Image Theory propose that an individual´s behavior is based on a psychological representation of reality existing in people´s mind (Martineau, 1958). Consequently, individuals´ behaviors are determined in a greater extent by an image than by reality (Martineau, 1958). In the case of hospitality services that are categorized as experience products whose quality can only be evaluated after consumption, and due to their intangibility, corporate image can be used as an effective mean of predicting the result of the service process (Christou, 2003). In this line of thought several academics consider that corporate image is one of the most consistent and reliable signals which show the ability of hotels to satisfy customers´ needs (Kandampully & Hu, 2007). However, there is no consensus among researchers whether corporate image directly or indirectly influences customer loyalty. For instance, Kandampully and Suhartanto (2000) propose a model in which corporate image and customer satisfaction have direct impacts on customer loyalty. These authors found that hotel image and customer satisfaction with reception, housekeeping, food and beverage and price are positively related to customer loyalty. On the other hand, Chi and Qu (2008) claim that image indirectly influence customer loyalty. Overall, the existing literature suggests a positive association between corporate image and behavioral intentions.

Regarding the relationship between corporate image and satisfaction, several authors (Back, 2005; Bigné et al., 2001; Minkiewicz & Evans, 2011) suggest that image perceptions affect satisfaction because they mold customers´ expectations before the visit and because satisfaction depends on the comparison between those expectations and the service performance (Brunner et al., 2008). According to Andreassen and Lindestad (1998, p. 10) "corporate image is believed to create a halo

effect on customers´ satisfaction judgment [...] when customers are satisfied with the services rendered, their attitude toward the company is improved. This attitude will then affect the consumers´ satisfaction with the company". Additionally, Nguyen and Leblanc (2002, p. 244) state that "a favorable image is a powerful tool [...] for improving [...] levels of satisfaction toward the company". Consequently, it is hypothesized that:

**H₂**: Corporate image will positively influence on customer loyalty

$H_2$: Corporate image will positively influence on customer loyalty

$H_3$: Corporate image will positively influence on customer satisfaction

## CSR Associations and Customer Loyalty

CSR associations are a particular category of corporate associations. Brown and Dacin (1997) use this concept for categorizing the different types of cognitive associations that consumers hold about a corporate brand. Corporate associations are a generic label for all the information about a company that individuals hold. Corporate associations may include inferences, perceptions, beliefs, knowledge of prior behavior about the company, moods and emotions experienced with respect to the company, and evaluations (specific or overall) of the company and its perceived attributes (Brown & Dacin, 1997). In the academic literature several types of corporate associations have been described. However, two categories are considered of particular relevance to the company´s stakeholders, especially for consumers. First, corporate ability associations are related to the company´s expertise in producing and delivering its outputs. On the other hand, CSR associations reflect the organization´s status and activities with respect to its perceived societal obligations (Brown & Dacin, 1997).

An increasing stream of research proposes to study the effects of CSR associations on consumer attitudes and behaviors. Concerning the direct effects of CSR associations on loyalty, Brown and Dacin (1997) argue that CSR influences behavioral outcomes through multiple paths, whether directly or mediated by overall corporate evaluation. Recent studies propose that CSR directly generates customer loyalty, without the necessity of mediating variables (García de los Salmones et al., 2005; Mandhachitara & Poolthong, 2009). According to these studies, CSR is such a significant attribute of corporate image that it is able to mechanically attract the consumer. An alternative explanation proposes that CSR engagements enable firms to understand customer in a better way improving customer-specific knowledge (Sen & Bhattacharya, 2001). In a similar way, Gardberg and Fombrun (2006) propose that positive effects of CSR practices create goodwill reservoirs that encourage customers to act as firm advocates and adjust their behaviors accordingly. Therefore, CSR associations are predicted to directly influence customers´ loyalty intentions.

$H_4$: CSR associations will positively influence on customer loyalty

## CSR Associations and Corporate Image

The role of CSR as a competitive differentiation tool (Du et al., 2007), is motivating the emergence of strategies attempting to project a socially responsible corporate image (Bigné et al., 2010). Previous studies point out that a good CSR strategy may generate a favorable image that positively influences customers´ responses and attitudes toward the firm (Bravo et al., 2012; Loureiro et al., 2012). Following this line of research, some authors have recently started to highlight the importance of aligning corporate image with social behavior in order to create positive associations in the customers mind (Heikkurinen, 2010; Martínez et al., 2014). Moreover, given the growth of the competitive intensity in the hospitality sector and the intangible nature of hospitality services

that leads consumers to perceive no differences between offers, CSR is one the main routes to create a solid and credible corporate image since it is considered as an expression of corporate behavior that allows organizations to be differentiated from the rest of competitors (Balmer et al., 2007; Heikkurinen, 2010) helping companies to position their images towards external and internal stakeholders.

Hospitality businesses have realized the role of corporate image as a powerful source of sustainable competitive advantage (Kandampully & Hu, 2007), and the important role of CSR as a highly effective attribute for a strategy of differentiation and positioning (Heikkurinen, 2010; Martínez et al., 2014). Actually, many hotel managers spend time and resources in advertising the hotel and its CSR initiatives to create a strong and impressive corporate image (Heikkurinen, 2010). Previous studies highlight that among the characteristics of hotels that are perceived as the most important in influencing consumers´ decisions is the image of the organization (Christou, 2003). Therefore, from a hotel´s point of view, it is important to investigate how CSR can be used as a tool for corporate image building.

$H_5$: CSR associations will positively influence on corporate image

## CSR Associations and Customer Satisfaction

Luo and Bhattacharya (2006) underline the importance of considering customer satisfaction as an evaluative consequence of CSR that helps to explain the equivocal link between CSR and a firm´s market value. Extant empirical studies in the service context have suggested that CSR can influence customer satisfaction (Bravo et al., 2012; He & Li, 2011; Martínez & Rodríguez del Bosque, 2013; Walsh & Bartikowski, 2013). Nevertheless, previous studies testing the relationship between CSR and consumer satisfaction have based their analysis on economic criteria. Consequently, the study of this relationship not focusing on economic criteria is considered a contributing source to the hospitality literature.

CSR create a favorable context around the company stimulating the emission of more favorable judgments about the service experience (Brown & Dacin, 1997). Therefore, customers are more understanding to failures in the service delivery improving customer satisfaction. Luo and Bhattacharya (2006, p. 3) articulate three reasons for what they name "the CSR activities-customer satisfaction effect". Firstly, as Maignan, Ferrell and Ferrell (2005) suggest, company´s customers can be potential stakeholders who cares about not only the economic performance of organizations but also to the overall standing (including social performance) of the company. Thus, customers are likely to be more satisfied if services or products providers develop CSR initiatives and present a socially responsible behavior towards society (He & Li, 2011). Secondly, a strong record of CSR creates a favorable image that positively enhances consumers´ evaluations of the firm and their attitude towards it (Sen & Bhattacharya, 2001). Moreover, CSR initiatives are a key element of corporate identity that can lead customers to identify with the company and these customers are more likely to be satisfied with firm´s offerings (Bhattacharya & Sen, 2003). Three, Mithas, Krishnan and Fornell (2005) empirically demonstrate that perceived value is a key antecedent to promoting customer satisfaction. Customers are more likely to derive better perceived value and, consequently, higher satisfaction from a product that is made by a socially responsible company (Luo & Bhattacharya, 2006). Following this line of thought, this chapter argues that CSR associations have an effect on customer satisfaction. Thus, we hypothesize:

**H$_6$**: CSR associations will positively influence on customer satisfaction

# METHODOLOGY

## Sample and Procedure

The data was collected from hotel customers located in Spain for two key reasons. Spain is considered to be amongst the leading countries internationally in the field of tourism and hospitality (Polo et al., 2013; UNMTO, 2012), in which hotels occupy an important position (Instituto Nacional de Estadística, 2011). Furthermore, Spanish hotels operate within an extremely competitive market. Consequently, customers are able to choose their level of loyalty to hotels, such that if they are dissatisfied with a firm, they can cease to deal with it as there are many alternatives. Given that they can identify better offers from competing firms (Bigné et al., 2000), this emphasizes the importance to hospitality companies of carrying out activities that contribute to winning customer loyalty in the sector.

The data collection procedure was conducted in April 4-25, 2011 through personal surveys carried out by students of the University of Cantabria coursing their last academic year. A total of 382 valid questionnaires were obtained after removing incomplete or inaccurate surveys. A non-probability sampling procedure was chosen (Trespalacios et al., 2005) to design the research sample. To ensure greater representation of the data, a multistage sampling by quotas was made by characterizing the population according to two criteria relevant to the investigation: the sex and the age of the respondent. Table 1 summarizes the sample´s description.

## Measurement Instrument

To measure CSR, customer satisfaction, corporate image and customer loyalty, scales validated by the literature were used. Table 2 shows the scales used for each factor. CSR associations were measured following the model provided by Brown and Dacin (1997). Customer satisfaction was

*Table 1. Respondents´ profile*

| | N | % | | N | % |
|---|---|---|---|---|---|
| **Gender** | | | **Age** | | |
| Male | 190 | 49.8 | From 18 to 24 years | 38 | 10 |
| Female | 192 | 50.2 | From 25 to 34 years | 76 | 19.9 |
| | | | From 35 to 44 years | 72 | 18.8 |
| | | | From 45 to 54 years | 72 | 18.9 |
| | | | From 55 to 64 years | 53 | 13.8 |
| | | | Over 65 Years | 71 | 18.6 |
| **Occupation** | | | **Education** | | |
| Student | 54 | 14.1 | No education | 31 | 8.1 |
| Self-employed | 52 | 13.7 | Basic/Elementary/Secondary | 87 | 22.9 |
| Worker | 151 | 39.4 | Baccalaureate/FP/COU/BUP | 114 | 29.8 |
| Retired/Pensioner | 67 | 17.5 | Associate degree | 78 | 20.3 |
| Unemployed | 21 | 5.6 | Higher university | 72 | 18.9 |
| Housework | 37 | 9.7 | | | |

measured following the scale provided by Cronin et al. (2000). Corporate image was measured using the scale validated by Carrasco et al. (2008). Finally, customer loyalty measure was drawn from extant services literature (Sirdeshmuhk et al., 2002; Zeithaml et al., 1996) and included items measuring both the attitudinal and behavioral components of loyalty.

## RESULTS

To analyze the data and test the proposed hypothesis this study employs a two-stage procedure of structural equation modeling (Anderson & Gerbing, 1988). Firstly, the goodness of the measurement instrument´s psychometric properties was analyzed by a Confirmatory Factor Analysis (CFA) and secondly, the structural relations among the theoretically proposed latent variables were analyzed through a Structural Equation Model (SEM). First, the psychometric properties of the CFA undertaken for the proposed scales were estimated using the maximum likelihood method. The Satorra-Bentler test was significant ($\chi^2SB=442.25$; df=142; p=0.00). However, it cannot be considered a reliable indicator of the goodness of fit of the confirmatory analysis because of its

sensitivity in samples exceeding 200 units (Bollen, 1989). Therefore we reviewed other indicators that showed that the overall fit of the model was acceptable [normed fit index (NFI)=0.90; non-normed fit index (NNFI) (or TLI)=0.91; incremental fit index (IFI)=0.92; confirmatory fit index (CFI)=0.92].

So as to verify that all the items used were adequate measures of their respective latent constructs, their reliability and validity were confirmed. This was achieved by analyzing the standardized lambda coefficient of each item, Cronbach´s alpha coefficient and average variance extracted (AVE) (Hair et al., 2010) (Table 3). The individual reliability show a value greater than the minimum acceptable limit which is 0.5 (Hair et al., 2010). Furthermore, Cronbach´s alpha coefficient and AVE were above to the reference value, at 0.70 and 0.50, respectively. These results led us to conclude that the dimensions proposed to measure the set of constructs were valid.

In internal consistency of the scales and the discriminant validity results allow for the estimation of the structural model. The proposed model was estimated using path analysis and maximum likelihood. Again, the Chi-square was significant, due to being sensitive to sample size. The incremental fit measures [confirmatory fit index (CFI)

*Table 2. Measurement scales*

| Ident. | Item |
|---|---|
| **CSR associations** | |
| CSR1 | This company protects the environment |
| CSR2 | This company shows its committed towards society by improving the welfare of the communities in which it operates |
| CSR3 | This company directs part of its budget to donations to social causes |
| CSR4 | This company recycles |
| **Customer Satisfaction** | |
| SAT1 | It is nice to stay in a hotel belonging to brand $X$ |
| SAT2 | I like staying in a hotel belonging to brand $X$ |
| SAT3 | Staying in a hotel of brand $X$ is great |
| **Corporate Image** | |
| IMA1 | Services offered by this company are of high quality |
| IMA2 | Services offered by this company have better features that those of competitors |
| IMA3 | This company arouses sympathy |
| IMA4 | This company transmits a personality that differentiate itself from competitors |
| **Customer Loyalty** | |
| LOY1 | I usually use this hotel company as my first choice compared to other hotel brands |
| LOY2 | It would be costly in terms of money, time and effort to end the relationship with this company |
| LOY3 | I shall continue considering this one as my main hotel brand in the next few years |
| LOY4 | I would recommend this hotel if somebody asked my advice |

=0.92; incremental fit index (IFI)=0.92; normed fit index (NFI)=0.90] were also acceptable. In its totality, the fit of the model can be said to be acceptable (Table 4). Regarding the structural equations, H1 and H2 examine the impact of customer satisfaction and corporate image on customer loyalty. The estimation results of the model (Table 4) reveal that customer satisfaction ($\beta = 0.643*$) and corporate image ($\beta = 0.235*$) have positive effect on customer loyalty. Thus, H1 and H2 are supported. However CSR associations have not a direct effect on customer loyalty ($\beta = 0.058$), so H4 is not supported. The greater power of customer satisfaction when determining customer loyalty is demonstrated, making this variable the main predictor of hotel customer loyalty. We turn next to the indirect antecedents of loyalty. The results show that CSR associations have positive direct effects on customer satisfaction ($\beta = 0.632*$) and corporate image ($\beta = 0.537*$) in support of H6 and H5. In addition, corporate image is positively related to customer satisfaction ($\beta = 0.718*$), which supports H3.

## FUTURE RESEARCH DIRECTIONS

As the results of studies concerning loyalty will depend on the services or products examined other hospitality areas should be considered to find out about the generalization of these results. A reliable image as well as customer satisfaction emerges only for continuously provided services (Brunner et al., 2008). As these authors state for nonrecurring or infrequently services, different processes may be at work. Second, other relevant

*Table 3. Confirmatory factor analysis of the final model*

| Ident. | Item |
|---|---|
| **CSR associations** | |
| CSR1 | This company protects the environment |
| CSR2 | This company shows its committed towards society by improving the welfare of the communities in which it operates |
| CSR3 | This company directs part of its budget to donations to social causes |
| CSR4 | This company recycles |
| **Customer Satisfaction** | |
| SAT1 | It is nice to stay in a hotel belonging to brand $X$ |
| SAT2 | I like staying in a hotel belonging to brand $X$ |
| SAT3 | Staying in a hotel of brand $X$ is great |
| **Corporate Image** | |
| IMA1 | Services offered by this company are of high quality |
| IMA2 | Services offered by this company have better features that those of competitors |
| IMA3 | This company arouses sympathy |
| IMA4 | This company transmits a personality that differentiate itself from competitors |
| **Customer Loyalty** | |
| LOY1 | I usually use this hotel company as my first choice compared to other hotel brands |
| LOY2 | It would be costly in terms of money, time and effort to end the relationship with this company |
| LOY3 | I shall continue considering this one as my main hotel brand in the next few years |
| LOY4 | I would recommend this hotel if somebody asked my advice |

*Table 4. Structural equation model results*

| Hypotheses | Structural relationship | Std. coefficient (Robust t-value) | Contrast |
|---|---|---|---|
| $H_1$ | Satisfaction → Loyalty | 0.643 (10.028)* | Accepted |
| $H_2$ | Image → Loyalty | 0.235 (3.315)* | Accepted |
| $H_3$ | Image → Satisfaction | 0.718 (10.662)* | Accepted |
| $H_4$ | CSR → Loyalty | 0.058 (1.172)* | Rejected |
| $H_5$ | CSR → Image | 0.537 (8.190)* | Accepted |
| $H_6$ | CSR → Satisfaction | 0.632 (10.112)* | Accepted |
| NFI=0.90 | TLI=0.91 CFI=0.92 IFI=0.92 | RMSEA=0.06 | |
| | $\chi^2 = 427.763$, $df = 146$ (p=0.000) | | |

*Figure 2. Structural model estimation*

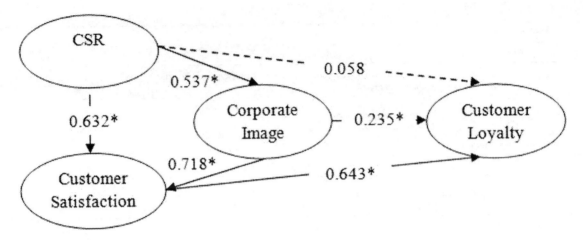

variables could be included in further research. Customer trust, commitment or corporate image dimensions may be tested for their mediating effects. Finally, in this study CSR was measured following the model provided by Brown and Dacin (1997). Future studies may analyze the proposed model in this study by using different conceptual frameworks such as the Carroll's pyramid or the sustainable development-based model in order to provide a more comprehensive model.

## CONCLUSION

Achieving greater customer loyalty is a key strategic objective for hospitality companies given the current time of economic crisis. Relationships between CSR associations, customer satisfaction, corporate image and loyalty in a hotel setting were examined in this study. In the light of the results obtained, some important conclusions can be extracted.

First, it is demonstrated that CSR associations influence hotel corporate image and that corporate image influence customer satisfaction, both enhancing customer loyalty. Consequently, the key to customer loyalty appears to be through developing a favorable and strong corporate

image of the hotel (Kandampully & Hu, 2007). Additionally, we found that CSR associations have direct impact on customer satisfaction. Thus, when a hotel is perceived as socially responsible, customers feel more satisfied. Therefore, respect to investing in CSR, hospitality firms do not need to rely exclusively on corporate image in their efforts to influence customer outcomes positively. The strong CSR-satisfaction link demonstrates that customers value socially responsible firms. Hospitality firms engaging in CSR initiatives can increase customer´s psychological attachment to the company, which translates into higher levels of satisfaction (Walsh & Bartikowski, 2013). Our research expands the conventional vision of CSR influence on consumer behavior and suggests that CSR associations not only affect product and brand evaluations (Brown & Dacin, 1997), but also customer satisfaction. Furthermore, this study extends Luo and Bhattacharya´s (2006) model of customer satisfaction as a path that links CSR to firm financial performance. Similarly, as CSR associations influence corporate image, the benefits of a strong corporate image based on CSR may lead to enhancing customer loyalty. This is particularly relevant in a sector which has experienced drops in occupancy, average daily rate and revenue per available room (Alonso-Almeida &

Bremser, 2013). Although we did not find evidence that CSR associations will result in loyalty, CSR associations have an indirect effect on customer loyalty via corporate image. Therefore, corporate image mediates the effects of CSR associations on customer loyalty.

Our results confirm that consumer perceptions of CSR have an indirect impact on consumer attitudes and behavior towards the hospitality company. In this relationship between CSR and the outcome of customer loyalty, it is important to highlight the mediating factor of corporate image. Therefore, hotels should carefully manage these activities and communicate them properly in order to retain their customers. With regard to this, hoteliers and marketers should develop a positive corporate image and enhance customers´ perceptions of CSR and satisfaction. In particular, they should emphasize the importance of socially responsible issues to customers by promoting CSR campaigns. Moreover, it is highly recommended that hoteliers develop an integrated communication strategy with multiple sources of information to present the specific CSR attributes of hotels. For instance, hotels should use public relations and advertising in order to communicate their socially responsible image to customers. Specifically, by actively participating in social, cultural and environmental forums and events, and using in-house advertising (e.g., in-house magazines and television channels aimed at customers) hotels can develop a favorable corporate image based on CSR aspects.

Results obtained in this study are in line with previous research in other sectors, where this mediating role has already been evidenced (Brown & Dacin, 1997; García de los Salmones et al., 2005). Moreover, hospitality firms should properly integrate their CSR initiatives into their corporate identity programs in order to develop a positive corporate image and gain credibility among customers. In this sense, Heikkurinen

(2010) and Martínez et al. (2014), in their studies based on the growing body of research on the identity-defining nature of organizations´ CSR actions, state that by engaging in CSR activities, hospitality companies will be able to communicate to their relevant stakeholders the valuable characteristics of their corporate identity, thereby building an attractive corporate image and developing customer credibility and trust.

## ACKNOWLEDGMENT

This research was funded by the FPU Scholarship Program provided by the Spanish Ministry of Education, Culture and Sports.

## REFERENCES

Alonso-Almeida, M. M., & Bremser, K. (2013). Strategic responses of the Spanish hospitality sector to the financial crisis. *International Journal of Hospitality Management*, *32*, 141–148. doi:10.1016/j.ijhm.2012.05.004

Álvarez, J. A. (2008). La banca española ante la actual crisis financiera. *Revista de Estabilidad Financiera*, *13*, 23–38.

Anderson, J. C., & Gerbing, D. W. (1988). Structural equation modelling in practice: A review and recommended two-step approach. *Psychological Bulletin*, *103*(3), 411–423. doi:10.1037/0033-2909.103.3.411

Andreassen, T., & Lindestad, B. (1998). Customer loyalty and complex services. *International Journal of Service Industry Management*, *9*(1), 7–23. doi:10.1108/09564239810199923

Back, K. J. (2005). The effects of image congruence on customers´ brand loyalty in the upper middle-class hotel industry. *Journal of Hospitality & Tourism Research (Washington, D.C.), 29*(4), 448–467. doi:10.1177/1096348005276497

Balmer, J. M. T., Fukukawa, K., & Gray, E. R. (2007). The nature and management of ethical corporate identity: A commentary on corporate identity, corporate social responsibility and ethics. *Journal of Business Ethics, 76*(7), 7–15. doi:10.1007/s10551-006-9278-z

Bhattacharya, C. B., & Sen, S. (2003). Consumer-company identification: A framework for understanding consumers´ relationships with companies. *Journal of Marketing, 67*(2), 76–88. doi:10.1509/jmkg.67.2.76.18609

Bigné, J. E., Chumpitaz, R., & Currás, R. (2010). Alliances between brands and social causes: The influence of company credibility on social responsible image. *Journal of Business Ethics, 96*(2), 169–186. doi:10.1007/s10551-010-0461-x

Bigné, J. E., Moliner, M. A., & Callarisa, L. J. (2000). El valor y la fidelización de clientes: Propuesta de modelo dinámico de comportamiento. *Revista Europea de Dirección y Economía de la Empresa, 9*(3), 65–78.

Bigné, J. E., Sánchez, M. I., & Sánchez, J. (2001). Tourism image, evaluation variables and after purchase behaviour: Inter-relationship. *Tourism Management, 22*(6), 607–616. doi:10.1016/S0261-5177(01)00035-8

Bitner, M. J., & Hubbert, A. (1994). Encounter satisfaction versus overall satisfaction versus quality. In Service Quality: New directions in theory and practice (pp. 241-268). Sage.

Bollen, K. A. (1989). *Structural equations with latent variables*. New York: Wiley. doi:10.1002/9781118619179

Botha, E., & Van Der Waldt, D. L. R. (2011). Relationship outcomes as measurement criteria to assist communication strategists to manage organizational relationships. *Revista Innovar, 21*(40), 5–16.

Bravo, R., Matute, J., & Pina, J. M. (2012). Corporate social responsibility as a vehicle to reveal the corporate identity: A study focused on the websites of Spanish financial entities. *Journal of Business Ethics, 107*(2), 129–146. doi:10.1007/s10551-011-1027-2

Brown, T. J., & Dacin, P. A. (1997). The company and the product: Corporate association and consumer product responses. *Journal of Marketing, 61*(1), 68–84. doi:10.2307/1252190

Brunner, T., Stöcklin, M., & Opwis, K. (2007). Satisfaction, image and loyalty: New versus experienced customers. *European Journal of Marketing, 42*(9/10), 1095–1105. doi:10.1108/03090560810891163

Carrasco, I. B., Salinas, E. M., & Pérez, J. (2008). Extensiones de marca en bienes y servicios: Evaluación y efectos sobre la imagen de marca. *Revista Española de Investigación de Mercados ESIC, 12*(2), 25–43.

Caruana, A. (2002). Service loyalty: The effects of service quality and the mediating role of customer satisfaction. *European Journal of Marketing, 36*(7), 811–828. doi:10.1108/03090560210430818

Chen, J. S., & Hsu, C. H. (2000). Measurement of Korean tourists´ perceived images of overseas destinations. *Journal of Travel Research, 38*(4), 411–416. doi:10.1177/004728750003800410

Chi, C. G. Q., & Qu, H. (2008). Examining the structural relationships of destination image, tourist satisfaction and destination loyalty: An integrated approach. *Tourism Management, 29*(4), 624–636. doi:10.1016/j.tourman.2007.06.007

Choi, T. Y., & Chu, R. (2001). Determinants of hotel guests' satisfaction and repeat patronage in the Hong Kong hotel industry. *International Journal of Hospitality Management, 20*(3), 277–297. doi:10.1016/S0278-4319(01)00006-8

Christou, E. (2010). Relationship marketing practices for retention of corporate customers in hospitality contract catering. *Tourism and Hospitality Management, 16*, 1–10.

Clemes, M., Gan, C., & Ren, M. (2011). Synthesizing the effects of service quality, value and customer satisfaction on behavioral intentions in the motel industry: An empirical analysis. *Journal of Hospitality & Tourism Research (Washington, D.C.), 35*(4), 530–568. doi:10.1177/1096348010382239

Cronin, J. J. Jr, Brady, M. K., & Hult, G. T. M. (2000). Assessing the effects of quality, value, and customer satisfaction on customer behavioral intentions in service environments. *Journal of Retailing, 76*(2), 193–218. doi:10.1016/S0022-4359(00)00028-2

Dick, A., & Basu, K. (1994). Customer loyalty: Towards an integrated framework. *Journal of the Academy of Marketing Science, 22*(2), 99–113. doi:10.1177/0092070394222001

Du, S., Bhattacharya, C. B., & Sen, S. (2007). Reaping relational rewards from corporate social responsibility: The role of competitive positioning. *International Journal of Research in Marketing, 24*(3), 224–241. doi:10.1016/j.ijresmar.2007.01.001

Dubé, L., & Renaghan, L. M. (2000). Creating visible customer value: How customers view best–practice champions. *The Cornell Hotel and Restaurant Administration Quarterly, 41*(1), 62–72. doi:10.1177/001088040004100124

Ekinci, Y., Dawes, P., & Massey, G. (2008). An extended model of the antecedents and consequences of customer satisfaction for hospitality services. *European Journal of Marketing, 42*(1/2), 35–68. doi:10.1108/03090560810840907

Evanschitzky, H., & Wunderlich, M. (2006). An examination of moderator effects in the four stage loyalty model. *Journal of Service Research, 8*(4), 330–340. doi:10.1177/1094670506286325

García de los Salmones, M. M., Herrero, A., & Rodríguez del Bosque, I. (2005). Influence of corporate social responsibility on loyalty and valuation of services. *Journal of Business Ethics, 61*(4), 369–385. doi:10.1007/s10551-005-5841-2

Gardberg, N. A., & Fombrun, C. J. (2006). Corporate citizenship: Creating intangible assets across institutional environments. *Academy of Management Review, 31*(2), 329–346. doi:10.5465/AMR.2006.20208684

Hair, J. F., Black, W. C., Babin, B. J., & Anderson, R. E. (2010). *Multivariate Data Analysis.* Upper Saddle River: Pearson Prentice-Hall.

Han, H., & Back, K. (2008). Relationships among image congruence, consumption emotions, and customer loyalty in the lodging industry. *Journal of Hospitality & Tourism Research (Washington, D.C.), 32*(4), 467–490. doi:10.1177/1096348008321666

Han, H., Kimb, Y., & Kima, E. (2011). Cognitive, affective, conative, and action loyalty: Testing the impact of inertia. *International Journal of Hospitality Management, 30*(4), 1108–1119. doi:10.1016/j.ijhm.2011.03.006

He, H., & Li, Y. (2011). CSR and service brand: The mediating effect of brand identification and moderating effect of service quality. *Journal of Business Ethics, 100*(4), 673–688. doi:10.1007/s10551-010-0703-y

Heikkurinen, P. (2010). Image differentiation with corporate environmental responsibility. *Corporate Social Responsibility and Environmental Management, 17*(3), 142–152. doi:10.1002/csr.225

Hur, W. M., Kim, Y., & Park, K. (2013). Assessing the effects of perceived value and satisfaction on customer loyalty: A "Green" Perspective. *Corporate Social Responsibility and Environmental Management, 20*(3), 146–156. doi:10.1002/csr.1280

Instituto de Estudios Turísticos (2011). Balance del Turismo. Año 2010.

Instituto Nacional de Estadística (2010). *España en cifras 2010*. Author.

Instituto Nacional de Estadística. (2011). *Encuesta de ocupación hotelera*. Retrieved June 20, 2013, from: http://www.ine.es/jaxi/menu.do?type=pcaxis&path=%2Ft11%2Fe162eoh&filenebase

Jones, T. O., & Sasser, W. E. (1995). Why satisfied customers defect. *Harvard Business Review, 73*(6), 89–99.

Kandampully, J., & Hu, H. H. (2007). Do hoteliers need to manage image to retain loyal customers? *International Journal of Contemporary Hospitality Management, 19*(6), 435–443. doi:10.1108/09596110710775101

Kandampully, J., & Suhartanto, D. (2000). Customer loyalty in the hotel industry: The role of customer satisfaction and image. *International Journal of Contemporary Hospitality Management, 12*(6), 346–351. doi:10.1108/09596110010342559

Keller, K. L. (1993). Conceptualizing, measuring and managing customer-based brand equity. *Journal of Marketing, 57*(1), 1–22. doi:10.2307/1252054

Lacey, R., & Kennett-Hensel, P. A. (2010). Longitudinal effects of corporate social responsibility on customer relationships. *Journal of Business Ethics, 97*(4), 581–597. doi:10.1007/s10551-010-0526-x

Loureiro, S., Dias, I. M., & Reijnders, L. (2012). The effect of corporate social responsibility on consumer satisfaction and perceived value: The case of the automobile industry sector in Portugal. *Journal of Cleaner Production, 37*, 172–178. doi:10.1016/j.jclepro.2012.07.003

Luo, X., & Bhattacharya, C. B. (2006). Corporate social responsibility, customer satisfaction and market value. *Journal of Marketing, 70*(4), 1–18. doi:10.1509/jmkg.70.4.1

Maignan, I., Ferrell, O. C., & Ferrell, L. (2005). A stakeholder model for implementing social responsibility in marketing. *European Journal of Marketing, 39*(9/10), 956–977. doi:10.1108/03090560510610662

Mandhachitara, R., & Poolthong, Y. (2011). A model of customer loyalty and corporate social responsibility. *Journal of Services Marketing, 25*(2), 122–133. doi:10.1108/08876041111119840

Mangan, E., & Collins, A. (2002). Threats to brand integrity in the hospitality sector: Evidence from a tourist brand. *International Journal of Contemporary Hospitality Management, 14*(6), 286–293. doi:10.1108/09596110210436823

Marin, L., Ruiz, S., & Rubio, A. (2009). The role of identity salience in the effects of corporate social responsibility on consumer behavior. *Journal of Business Ethics, 84*(1), 65–78. doi:10.1007/s10551-008-9673-8

Martineau, P. (1958). The personality of the retail store. *Harvard Business Review, 36*, 47–55.

Martínez, P., Pérez, A., & Rodríguez del Bosque, I. (2014). Exploring the role of CSR in the organizational identity of hospitality companies: A case from the Spanish tourism industry. *Journal of Business Ethics, 124*(1), 47–66. doi:10.1007/s10551-013-1857-1

Martínez, P., & Rodríguez del Bosque, I. (2013). CSR and customer loyalty: The roles of trust, customer identification with the company and satisfaction. *International Journal of Hospitality Management, 35,* 89–99. doi:10.1016/j.ijhm.2013.05.009

Mason, D., Tideswell, C., & Roberts, E. (2006). Guest perceptions of hotel loyalty. *Journal of Hospitality & Tourism Research (Washington, D.C.), 30*(2), 191–206. doi:10.1177/1096348006286364

Mattila, A. S. (2006). How affective commitment boosts guest loyalty (and promotes frequent guest programs). *The Cornell Hotel and Restaurant Administration Quarterly, 47*(2), 174–181. doi:10.1177/0010880405283943

Minkiewicz, J., Evans, J., Bridson, K., & Mavondo, F. (2011). Corporate image in the leisure services sector. *Journal of Services Marketing, 25*(3), 190–201. doi:10.1108/08876041111129173

Mithas, S., Krishnan, M. S., & Fornell, C. (2005). Why do customer relationship management applications affect customer satisfaction? *Journal of Marketing, 69*(4), 201–209. doi:10.1509/jmkg.2005.69.4.201

Moreno-Gil, S., Martín-Santana, J. D., & De León-Ledesma, J. (2012). Factores determinantes del éxito para entender la imagen de un alojamiento turístico. Un estudio empírico en Islas Canarias. *Revista Innovar, 22*(44), 139–152.

Nguyen, N., & Leblanc, G. (2002). Contact personnel, physical environment and the perceived corporate image of intangible services by new clients. *International Journal of Service Industry Management, 13*(3), 242–262. doi:10.1108/09564230210431965

Oliver, R. L. (1980). A cognitive model of the antecedents and consequences of satisfaction decisions. *JMR, Journal of Marketing Research, 17*(4), 460–469. doi:10.2307/3150499

Oliver, R. L. (1997). *Satisfaction: A behavioral perspective on the consumer.* New York: McGraw-Hill.

Perez, A., García de los Salmones, M. M., & Rodríguez del Bosque, I. (2012). The effect of corporate associations on consumer behavior. *European Journal of Marketing, 47*(1), 218–238.

Petrick, J. F. (2004). Are loyal visitors desired visitors? *Tourism Management, 25*(4), 463–470. doi:10.1016/S0261-5177(03)00116-X

Polo, A. I., Frías, D. M., & Rodríguez, M. A. (2013). Antecedents of loyalty toward rural hospitality enterprises: The moderating effect of the customer's previous experience. *International Journal of Hospitality Management, 34,* 127–137. doi:10.1016/j.ijhm.2013.02.011

Reichheld, F. F. (1993). Loyalty-based management. *Harvard Business Review,* (March/April): 64–73. PMID:10124634

Reichheld, F. F., & Sasser, E. W. (1990). Zero defections: Quality comes to services. *Harvard Business Review, 68*(5), 105–116. PMID:10107082

Romani, S., Grappi, S., & Bagozzi, R. P. (2013). Explaining consumer reactions to corporate social responsibility: The role of gratitude and altruistic values. *Journal of Business Ethics, 114*(2), 193–206. doi:10.1007/s10551-012-1337-z

Sen, S., & Bhattacharya, C. B. (2001). Does doing good always lead to doing better? Consumer reactions to corporate social responsibility. *JMR, Journal of Marketing Research, 38*(2), 225–243. doi:10.1509/jmkr.38.2.225.18838

Sirdeshmukh, D., Japdig, S., & Berry, S. (2002). Customer trust, value, and loyalty in relational exchanges. *Journal of Marketing, 66*(1), 15–37. doi:10.1509/jmkg.66.1.15.18449

Tanford, S., Carola, R., & Kimb, Y. S. (2011). The influence of reward program membership and commitment on hotel loyalty. *Journal of Hospitality & Tourism Research (Washington, D.C.)*, *31*, 319–328.

Trespalacios, J. A., Vázquez, R., & Bello, L. (2005). *Investigación de Mercados*. Madrid: Thompson.

United Nations World Tourism Organization. (2012). *Panorama OMT del turismo internacional*. Retrieved July 11, 2013, from: http://dtxtq4w60xqpw.cloudfront.net/sites/all/files/pdf/unwto_highlights12_sp_hr.pdf

Vlachos, P. A., Tsamakos, A., Vrechopoulos, A. P., & Avramadis, P. K. (2009). Corporate social responsibility: Attributions, loyalty and mediating role of trust. *Journal of the Academy of Marketing Science*, *37*(2), 170–180. doi:10.1007/s11747-008-0117-x

Walsh, G., & Bartikowski, B. (2013). Exploring corporate ability and social responsibility associations as antecedents of customer satisfaction cross-culturally. *Journal of Business Research*, *66*(8), 989–995. doi:10.1016/j.jbusres.2011.12.022

Williams, P., & Naumann, E. (2011). Customer satisfaction and business performance: A firm-level analysis. *Journal of Services Marketing*, *25*(1), 20–32. doi:10.1108/08876041111107032

Yoo, M., & Bai, B. (2013). Customer loyalty marketing research: A comparative approach between Hospitality and Business journals. *International Journal of Hospitality Management*, *33*, 166–177. doi:10.1016/j.ijhm.2012.07.009

Zeithaml, V. A., Berry, L. L., & Parasuraman, A. (1996). The behavioral consequences of service quality. *Journal of Marketing*, *60*(2), 31–46. doi:10.2307/1251929

## ADDITIONAL READING

Bramwell, B., Lane, B., McCabe, S., Mosedale, J., & Scarles, C. (2008). Research perspectives on responsible tourism. *Journal of Sustainable Tourism*, *16*(3), 253–257. doi:10.1080/09669580802208201

De Grosbois, D. (2012). Corporate social responsibility reporting by the global hotel industry: Commitment, initiatives and performance. *International Journal of Hospitality Management*, *31*(3), 896–905. doi:10.1016/j.ijhm.2011.10.008

Holcomb, J. L., Upchurch, R. S., & Okumus, F. (2007). Corporate social responsibility: What are top hotel companies reporting? *International Journal of Contemporary Hospitality Management*, *19*(6), 461–475. doi:10.1108/09596110710775129

Holloway, C. J. (2004). *Marketing for Tourism*. Harlow: Prentice Hall.

Martínez, P., & Rodríguez del Bosque, I. (2014). *Corporate marketing: A new marketing paradigm*. Saarbrücken: LAP Lambert Academic Publishing.

Piper, D. L. A. (2013). DLA Piper 2013 Europe Hospitality Outlook Survey. Retrieved 11, November, 2014 from: http://files.dlapiper.com/files/upload/Hospitality-Leisure-Survey-Report-2013.pdf

Tanford, S., Carola, R., & Kimb, Y. S. (2012). Determinants of customer loyalty and purchasing behavior for full-service and limited-service hotels. *International Journal of Hospitality Management*, *31*(2), 319–328. doi:10.1016/j.ijhm.2011.04.006

## KEY TERMS AND DEFINITIONS

**Consumer Behavior:** It is the study of individuals and groups and the processes they use to select and dispose of products, services, experiences or ideas to satisfy needs and the impacts that these processes have on the consumer and society.

**Corporate Image:** Mental picture that springs up at the mention of a company´s name. It is a composite psychological impression that continually changes with the firm´s circumstances, media coverage, performance, pronouncements, etc... Similar to corporate reputation it is the public perception of the firm rather than a reflection of its actual state or position. It is the result of multiple and diverse messages that, accumulated in the collective memory, draw a global meaningful concept able to affect and predict individuals´ behavior.

**Corporate Social Responsibility (CSR):** CSR is about how companies manage the business processes to produce an overall positive impact on society. CSR goes beyond compliance and engages in actions that appear to further some social good, beyond the interests of the firm and that which is required by law (e.g., waste and pollution reduction processes, educational and social programs...).

**Customer Loyalty:** It is a consumer´s preference for a particular company and a commitment to repeatedly purchase that brand in the face of other choices.

**Customer Satisfaction:** Customer satisfaction measures how well the expectations of a customer concerning a product/service provided by a company have been met. Customer satisfaction is an abstract concept and involves such factors as the quality of the product/service provided, the atmosphere of the location where the product/service is purchased and the price of the product/service.

**Hospitality Industry:** It is a broad category of fields within the service industry that includes lodging, event planning, theme parks, transportation, cruise line and additional fields within the tourism industry. The hospitality industry is a several billion dollar industry that mostly depends on the availability of leisure time and disposable income.

**Structural Equation Modelling:** It is a statistical technique for testing and estimating causal relations using a combination of statistical data and qualitative causal assumptions.

# Chapter 26
# Staff Turnover at the Crossboarder Hotel Company:
## A Strategic–Longitudinal Investigation, Part A

**Angelo Camillo**
*Woodbury University, USA*

**Francesca Di Virgilio**
*University of Molise, Italy*

**Loredana Di Pietro**
*University of Molise, Italy*

## ABSTRACT

*This chapter endeavors to draw attention to staff turnover in the hospitality industry by analyzing a company, which will be referred to as "Crossboarder Hotel Company". The actual name has been disguised to maintain the company's confidentiality. The chapter discusses the causes and effects of employee turnover and ways to prevent turnover. Turnover is divided into three categories: job dissatisfaction, errors in employee selection, and poor management. The common cause of turnover however; is job dissatisfaction which affects employees well-being. A survey instrument that included measures of job satisfaction, and demographic information was used to collect information from hotel employees of an American Hotel Chain we refer to as the "Crossboarder Hotel Company", geographically dispersed in Georgia, Alabama, California, North Carolina, Arizona, Texas, Utah, and Indiana. Data from 78 respondents were collected over a three-year period. The results show that favouritism, nepotism, lack of responsibility and accountability, lack of training and improper communication negatively contributed to job satisfaction.*

## INTRODUCTION

The growing hospitality industry always had high staff turnover caused by different contributing factors. The industry is vastly driven by service, and little regard is given to those providing the service. The hospitality industry makes up approximately eight percent of the total workforce in the United

DOI: 10.4018/978-1-4666-8606-9.ch026

States. With an increasing rate of employment, little concern is provided to the needs of employees. The industry is characterized as being part time, low wage, and unstable (Haynes & Fryer, 1999; Bernhardt, Dresser & Hatton, 2003). Even with low wages, employees are required to provide the utter best customer service to all guests for continual business (Grandey, 2003; Lashley, 2001).

According to practitioners in the field, the main cause of turnover is derived from poor management skills. Although, poor management skills are not always management's fault however; the fault reflects on poor training (Sheehan, 1995; White, 1995). The lack of adequate employee training is also a contributing factor for turnover, which includes the training of management. The lack of adequate training results in managers not oriented to deal with and prevent certain situations, which causes management to miss the signs and warnings creating personnel management problems within the company (Laser, 1980). Studies conducted by Wasmuth & Davis (1983b) suggest that immediate supervisor or managers have a significant impact on the levels of staff turnover. If managers demonstrate trust, belief, and assist employees when needed, they will experience a lower level of turnover.

Supervisors lack problem solving skills and leadership skills to properly deal with employee relations also negatively contributes to job satisfaction. This can cause employee dissatisfaction, which leads to employee turnover. Lack of communication skills can also lead to turnover. An important factor is poor communication with employees. Communicating with employees establishes comfort, which allows employees to express their thoughts and concerns, which may not be apparent through body language. Hiring employees without the proper assessment is another reason for the high turnover in hospitality. When there is a high vacancy rate for a position such as housekeeping associate, it is important to promptly fill the positions to ensure the utmost

ees should start the position before clearance from the Human Resources department however, lack of succession planning can contribute to turnover by new employees as well.

This study examines the determinants of employee turnover at the Crossboarder Hotel Company, which employs about 600 staff. This study analyzes the data collected over a 3-year period, from 2007 to 2010, using time series and repeated measure techniques hospitality firm in a 3-year panel spanning from January 2011 to December 2013. In addition, the study addresses the specific positions that have the highest turnover rate. Staff turnover has become a major concern for businesses in general and especially in the hospitality industry. The cost of employee turnover is taking a great toll on organization as well as productivity. Having high turnover can be very injurious for companies especially in upper management in hospitality if employees leave to work for a competing company. It takes time and money to train new employees, but it costs more to replace them.

## LITERATURE REVIEW

Over the years, researchers have conducted extensive research for employee turnover however, but the findings are inconsistent due to the vast diversity in organizations. Organizations are overlooking employees who are loyal, productive and hard working by not realizing that employees are an asset to the organization. Bowden (1952) suggests that solving the problem to staff turnover is by paying the employees more than the competition. This seems like a good idea, only if turnover was solely based on monetary compensation. There are several other contributing factors to staff turnover, which some are not even work related. Hom & Kinicki (2001) suggest that job dissatisfaction can also result from problems arising from work, family, community

in organizations that have instability. Employees favor working for organizations where there is job stability in a predictable work environment (Zuber, 2001). When employees do not find job stability in an organization, their status with the company becomes temporary. Employees will solely remain with an organization, which does not have a predictable work environment until they move to the next job. Other employees may leave the job instantly after dissatisfaction to avoid incurring stress (Griffeth & Hom, 2001). The cause of turnover has evolved to companies dedicating precious time and money in the development of employment procedures and hiring efforts. The efforts to find the ideal candidate have created certain standards the company is looking for (Bowden, 1952). This is more than requirements, in addition to attaining the most qualified available employees, establishing standards for recruiting assists in being consistent and maintaining an above par hiring procedure. It also allows for a better match of company and the employee (Coleman, 1989).

Giffeth & Hom (2001) argue that organization must offer competitive pay and benefits to keep employees satisfied and reduce turnover (Giffeth & Hom, 2001). By offering competitive pay and benefits, it will increase employee morale and productivity. In relation to benefits, it is crucial to allow employees to voice their opinion in the organization. Employees will perform a task more efficiently when they are given appropriate authority for basic decision making, with respect to their working atmosphere (Magner et al. 1996). When an employee shares the vision of the company, extrinsic rewards may not weigh so heavily with the employee. Employees must also have intrinsic motivation to continue performing the job adequately.

There are many other factors that contribute to employee turnover e.g.: poor hiring practices, management style, lack of recognition, and as already mentioned, lack of competitive compensation (Abassi, 2000). The recruitment process is a key step in reducing employee turnover by selecting the employee who best fits the criteria of the job. Practitioners agree that the main key to hiring qualified candidates for the job is to make sure job descriptions are explained and are relevant to the specific job. The job description must also contain a list of skills required to complete the job. They also agree that a job description does not mean they will not do any work outside their described duties, and may need to perform in areas outside their daily routine. Practitioners also agree that if the job description offers no defining, consistent sense of purpose, employers will find it very difficult to attract top talent who will perform well over an extended period of time. Employees should be tested in order to determine their job qualification (Roseman, 1981). Age can also be a factor in employee turnover. The hospitality industry consists of many high schools students who work part time during the summer. It is clear that the younger employees will not stay in the organization for long and only work during the summer as a temporary employee (Mobley, 1982).

Furthermore, stress can also be a leading cause of employee turnover as well as health problems (Caplan, Cobb, French, Harrison, & Pinneau, 1975; Spector, 2003). Cartwright & Cooper (1997) suggest the following to be the leading cause of stress:

- Intrinsic to the job
- Role in the organization
- Relationships at work
- Career development
- Organizational structure and climate
- Non-work Factors

Cartwright and Cooper (1997) also suggest that the effects of these leading causes of stress are:

- High absenteeism
- High labor turnover
- Industrial Relations Difficulties
- Poor Quality Control

The cost of employee turnover is expensive for the organization and time consuming. The organization not only wastes money and time when an employee leaves, they must also spend money and time to retrain new employees. Hinkin & Tracey (2000) have developed a model for turnover cost categories which consist of the following:

- Separation cost
- Recruiting and attracting cost
- Selection cost
- Hiring cost
- Lost-productivity cost

## Purpose of the Study

To identify the factors that contribute to the high staff turnover at Crossboarder Hotel Company. Specifically, the study aims at identifying the sub-factors that may derive from known factors such as job dissatisfaction, lack of management leadership, lack of training and employee recognition, and other unknown factors.

## Methodology

The study analyzes published literature and applies qualitative research method using face – to face interviews, third party investigation and self-reporting questionnaires.

## Sample

The sample consisted of 78 hourly paid company employees not employed at managerial level. The sample was geographically dispersed in Georgia, Alabama, California, North Carolina, Arizona, Texas, Utah, and Indiana

## Instruments

To collect the data the we used a used a multipart self-reporting questionnaire, which consisted of open ended questions, yes and no, and multiple

choices and scaled questions. The survey was administered by an anonymous third party company, which was outsourced by the Crossboarder Hotel Company.

## Data Collection

The data was collected from a convenience sample over a 3 year period from January 2011 to December 2013. A total of 78 questionnaires were received which represented a 100% response rate. Because the survey was anonymous, specific demographics data could not be collected.

## Data Analysis

Qualitative data was analyzed using content analysis technique, coding, frequency, and cross-referencing to eliminate duplication. The raw data from the self-reporting questionnaires was analyzed, tested for errors and missing values. The clean data was rechecked for accuracy, summarized and synthesized.

## Findings

According to the qualitative data analyzed the results show employees' concerns for the lack of management skills and motivation to help them succeed and stay with the company. Table 1 above demonstrates that there are more negative than positive contributing factors to job satisfaction. One of the main concerns from employees was lack of policy implementation, and pay inequality. The positive factors only consisted of "holding everyone to same standards", "involved in everyday tasks and "good listening skills." Table 2 shows the results of the qualitative face-to-face interview. Accordingly, the highest mean is 4.5 on a scale of 1 to 5, 1 being the lowest to 5 being the highest. This indicates that *"I always do my work to the highest standard"* is the main concerning factor respondents had for their job and existence with the company.

*Table 1. Summary of factors that contribute to staff turnover*

| Positive Factors | Negative Factors |
|---|---|
| Hold everyone to same standards | Lack of confidentiality |
| Involved in everyday tasks | Lack of policy implementation |
| Good listening skills | Lack of visible management |
| | Employee nepotism |
| | Pay inequality |
| | Lack of leadership skills |
| | Lack of communication skill/miscommunication |
| | Lack of task assignment and monitoring |
| | Lack of equitable treatment |
| | Biased management |
| | Lack of problem solving skills |
| | Lack of recognition |
| | Lack of motivation |
| | Not following company rules and procedures |
| | Favoritism |
| | Lack of confidence and skills in the job |

## Summary of Qualitative Results

The results of open-ended questions were analyzed and synthesized using coding and frequency. After analyzing the open-ended questions, a trend was appearing amongst all employees and their dissatisfaction for management. Employees felt uncomfortable addressing issues with management due to previous experience of breach of confidentiality. Employees also felt there was favoritism in the workplace, and management lack of policy implementation for certain individuals. Nepotism played a big role in two of the hotels, which causes problems and job dissatisfaction amongst employees. In property A, the positions of General Manager and Assistant General Manager were held by a brother and sister. In property B, the positions of General Manager, Maintenance Supervisor, and Front Desk Agent were held by a wife, husband, and son respectively. Other issues that have arisen from the survey include pay inequality amongst employees, which also takes part in favoritism.

Employees felt that management was lacking leadership skills needed to assign task and monitor them or accuracy. Problems were addressed during reviews and not when they occur. There were no procedures set for employee training and consideration of team building. Management lacks visibility in the day to day tasks by only staying in the office, which makes employees' feel unenthusiastic to do their job. Employee complaints are also concerning lack of responsibility and accountability. The analysis shows managers lack problem solving skills and lack of confidence to do their job. It was also concluded that money is not always the number one motivational factor for employees to do good, but rather recognition and motivation.

After analyzing the survey, we interviewed the Regional Manager who will be referred to as "Mary" who was based on the high survey score of

*Table 2. Summary of Survey Results for All Properties*

| | Synthesis of the Survey Results for All Properties | |
|---|---|---|
| | 1=Strongly Disagree 2=Disagree 3=Neutral 4=Agree 5=Strongly Agree | |
| | **Questions** | **Average** |
| 1 | I enjoy performing the actual day-to-day activities of my job | 4.3 |
| 2 | My General Manager shows confidence and trust in my | 4.4 |
| 3 | My department consistently performs to a high standard | 3.9 |
| 4 | Persons in my Department encourage each other to work together | 3.7 |
| 5 | Everyone in my Department works to maintain high standards of performance | 3.7 |
| 6 | I received adequate feedback on my performance | 3.9 |
| 7 | I always do my work to the highest standard | 4.5 |
| 8 | I believe I received adequate training to perform my job well | 4.1 |
| 9 | I am comfortable asking for more training when I feel I need it | 4.4 |
| 10 | Other departments consistently cooperate and provide assistance in our hotel | 3.8 |
| 11 | I believe there is good communication between departments in our hotel | 3.6 |
| 12 | I feel my efforts are appreciated | 3.9 |
| 13 | I feel like I have an opportunity to grow with this company | 3.2 |
| 14 | I feel I have job security | 3.4 |
| 15 | I feel like this organization values me as an employee | 3.7 |
| 16 | I enjoy pleasing my General Manager | 4.3 |
| 17 | I trust my co-workers | 3.5 |
| 18 | Employees treat other employees like customers | 3.4 |
| 19 | I am proud to work for my company | 4.0 |
| 20 | I have a healthy relationship with co-workers | 4.0 |
| 21 | The workload in my department is equitably distributed | 3.6 |
| 22 | I get the information I need to coordinate my work with others | 3.8 |
| 23 | I am involved in making decisions that affect my job | 3.8 |
| 24 | Communication within my department is good | 3.8 |
| 25 | I feel like I received adequate recognition for good work | 3.7 |
| 26 | Overall, I am satisfied with my job | 3.9 |
| 27 | I feel like there is a great deal I can learn from my General Manager | 4.0 |
| 28 | My General Manager consistently promotes and follows the Company standards he/she expects me to | 4.0 |
| 29 | My General Manager spends more time walking the hotel and interacting with guests than in his/her office | 3.2 |
| 30 | My General Manager is willing to listen to my issues and concerns | 4.2 |
| 31 | My General Manager encourages persons in our department to work as a team | 4.2 |
| 32 | My General Manager is a good role model when it comes to demonstrating and performing my job responsibilities | 4.1 |
| 33 | My General Manager consistently provides help, training and guidance so that I can improve my performance | 4.1 |
| 34 | My General Manager models good skills for getting along with others | 4.0 |
| 35 | My General Manager demonstrates excellent skills for handling difficult or problem guests | 4.2 |
| 36 | My General Manager stays informed about how our department members see and feel about things | 3.9 |

*continued on following page*

*Table 2. Continued*

| | Synthesis of the Survey Results for All Properties | |
|---|---|---|
| | 1=Strongly Disagree 2=Disagree 3=Neutral 4=Agree 5=Strongly Agree | |
| | Questions | Average |
| 37 | My General Manager shows an interest and concern for department members | 4.1 |
| 38 | I have confidence and trust in my General Manager | 4.2 |
| 39 | My General Manager is effective | 4.3 |
| 40 | My General Manager listens and responds to my concerns | 4.1 |
| 41 | Management in general has high degree of honesty | 4.1 |
| 42 | My General Manager is focused on solutions rather than blame | 4.0 |
| 43 | My company's policies are administered fairly | 3.8 |
| 44 | My General Manager consistently and fairly holds employees accountable for their performance | 3.9 |
| 45 | My General Manager seeks out and asks for my input when making decisions that affect my job responsibilities | 4.0 |
| 46 | My General Manager provides clear and concise directions when assigning tasks and/or responsibilities | 4.1 |
| 47 | My General Manager is a good motivator | 4.0 |
| 48 | My General Manager cares about maintaining good morale | 4.1 |
| 49 | Overall, I am satisfied with my General Manager | 4.3 |
| | | |
| | Mean (Average) | 3.9 |
| | Standard Division | 0.3 |

her employees. We asked about implementation of integrity, she responded by stating how her company has policies and procedures in place, and the company's Senior Management team shares their policies with Junior Management whom in return discusses with the staff. Mary strongly believes managers should be portraying high standards to line level employees, constantly communicating all expectations and sharing the outcome as it happens. She added that to turn around employee dissatisfaction and shared meaning must be achieved by making sure all staff is involved with what goals are set or met. Listening to employees' recommendation can be beneficial by providing their input on what can be done differently as a team to become stronger. Mary also believes that sensitivity is an important factor in keeping her staff happy, however not in the decisions made. Sensitivity can be interpreted in many ways such as being sensitive to the person's family life, emotions, and stress. When asked about the company

vision, Mary replied by stating the vision is to have successful hotels with happy employees. She stated, "When the staff takes ownership in their position, you do not have to micro-manage them as an employee". Employees need to be motivated and believe in the company vision to perform satisfactorily. Treating employees respectfully will demonstrate to the employee how the company truly cares about them as an individual.

The following are two extraordinary incidents identified in the investigation. These types of incidents are key contributing factors to employees' dissatisfaction. They clearly show actions of favoritism and nepotism at workplace; concerning factors for all stakeholders.

## 1. Extraordinary Case (Sexual Harassment)

An anonymous complaint was filed for property A regarding sexual harassment with the top management. The complainant wanted to express how he felt uncomfortable doing his job while his co-workers were looking at pornography on the computer next to him. Due to the circumstance that the call was anonymous, further details could not be provided to help resolve the investigation. In an interview with the Human Resources director, who will be referred to as "Stacy", we asked a series of questions to understand the incident. We learned that even though it is not direct contact with the person, watching pornography at work can make another co-worker feel sexually harassed. Both employees were given an employee handbook that outlines sexual harassment and the company's zero tolerance for it. Under section I - Unlawful Harassment, the handbook states, "in accordance with applicable law, the company prohibits unlawful harassment because of sex, race, color, origin, ancestry, religion, creed, physical or mental…" (Employee handbook, 2003). The handbook further clarifies the details of sexual harassment under Section I -1. Other types of harassment is also listed and defined in Section I-2. Nevertheless, the policy was violated. In this instance only one of the two employees participated in the situation willingly, while the other felt harassed. The end result of the situation led to termination of the employee who was watching pornography at work and causing the rest of his co-workers anxiety coming to work.

## 2. Extraordinary Case (Marriage)

Another extraordinary incident that has taken place is marriage in the workplace. Employees feel it is unethical to allow a husband/wife to be direct supervisors of their spouse. It is also against company policy to hire relatives. By hiring relatives, it can create potential conflict of interest in the employment setting, especially where one relative supervises another. The company gives employees who marry, and become related, or engage in an intimate relationship an option to

change positions. The employees have 30 days to decide which individual will remain in his/her current position. If no other position is available, the employees will have 30 days to decide which employee will remain with the company. This incident addresses a specific case of the maintenance supervisor who got married to the General Manager. The employees were currently employed with the company and did not have to change positions or leave the company. This decision was unethical because it set all other employees apart. This decision made a statement to all employees that they do not need to follow policy or procedure. The faith and trust employees had in the company was broken, which will cause them to act unethically themselves. The wife, who was the general manager, showed favoritism to the husband, the maintenance supervisor. Numerous complaints were filed by employees working side by side with the two married couple. Employees state that the husband leaves work and does not clock out, and the wife does not address the issue. Employees also complain that the husband was paid overtime, but does not getting the job done in time. This was a serious issue because the wife was not keeping information confidential about the employees. Employees threatened to address issues with the manager regarding the husband. In resolving the case, the company decided to transfer her husband to another property

## DISCUSSION AND RECOMMENDATIONS

The finding of this case further supports the existing literature. Employee turnover for a business is destructive for the company financially as well as operationally. Companies take different paths to evade turnover by offering employee benefits, bonuses, and competitive salaries. This may be the perfect case for some employees, but for other employees, expectations are much higher than monetary pay. Employers need to incorporate showing support, appreciation, and acknowledging their employees in the daily activities. Staying at a job can have different stimulants, and organizations should observe the employees to uncover the underlying reasons.

The key to employee and employer satisfaction is trust. Employers must allow employees to make choices on their own. Micromanaging an employee is not the best way of invigorating an employee to be productive. The way employees are treated at work will result in their actions and performance. Ensuring managers to acknowledge employees when a task is satisfactorily completed will employee increase morale. In order to stop employee turnover, managers must make sure the candidates are qualified for the position before starting them on the job. This includes clearance of the drug screen test and background check. Another option would be to motivate employees by offering them an incentive such as a bonus for performance. Most importantly, choosing the right candidate for the position by not rushing through the selection process can reduce turnover. After interviewing employees from different hotels, it was concluded that employees would like more attention for their personal needs and more flexibility for telecommuting, schedules, and contributing for day care pay.

Organizations often times overlook the importance of a positive work environment for their employees, but recognition and praise can stimulate the employee to work harder. Companies should set in place employee award, and recognition programs to make sure their employees are happy and productive. Aside from praise, employees must be given a clear path to where they stand with the company. Employees always want to move up the corporate ladder, and they want to know where they could be headed and how they can get there. Encouraging employees to address the managers with any issues and concerns makes the employee comfortable with their job and more dedicated.

Based on the survey conducted, it is important to understand turnover and reduce the high rates in turnover by placing a high emphasis in the following areas:

- Respect
- Transparent policies and procedures
- Recognition of performance
- Training programs
- Discuss career paths
- Make yourself approachable
- Analyze turnover
- Conduct employee surveys
- Make working fun

## IMPLICATIONS FOR MANAGEMENT

Keeping staff turnover low is important. It requires being aware of the current state of the practical working environment, which includes choosing appropriate new hires, providing them with proper training, and talking to staff members to solve problems, as they become known. Management should do all they can to provide superior leadership in all practice by keeping communication lines open with an open door policy and support the entire staff. This will help to create and maintain a place where people want to work and stay.

Importance needs to be stressed on evaluating each position in the company to help identify problems areas, which may need to be restructured. An effective method of position evaluation can be by asking staff members directly. Staff members are the experts in their job and know the flaws, which would allow them to make suggestions on how to better the position. This can be done continually in one-on-one meetings and staff meetings. It will allow managers to be more intact and hands on with their staff. At the same time, it will allow them to acquire feedback on what is working, what is no working, what's changed and where improvements may be needed. Allowing staff to

528

give feedback will improve job productivity and satisfaction by showing their thoughts are valued.

Evaluation of the positions can also be done through observation. Many times employees might feel uncomfortable telling a manager what it is they are doing wrong. The flaws can be assessed through observation of an employee to see what tasks he or she takes on and under what conditions. Manager should ask the following questions specific to the position being observed to find out why there is a high turnover and what needs to be done to reduce turnover:

- Am I creating a desirable work setting?
- Am I assigning tasks appropriately to be performed?
- Am I hiring appropriate staff and training them adequately?
- Am I offering effective ways for staff to communicate?
- Are staff members supporting each other?

It is also very important to be conducting exit interviews to determine the cause of employee turnover. Mangers could ask the following questions to staff members who are leaving their job to determine the causes of staff turnover and how you can prevent it:

- What can we do to make this position better for the next employee?
- What could we have done differently so that you might have wanted to stay with the practice?
- If you could define our practice philosophy in one sentence, what would you say?
- How did our management do at treating you and other employees as our first customers?
- Have we been fair and consistent in our dealings with employees?
- What can our physician(s) do to better express their loyalty to staff and to gain loyalty from staff?

## LIMITATIONS

The limitation preventing further research for staff turnover is the willingness by employees to participate in honest surveys and tests to get accurate results. The survey used for this study is relatively small and only consisted of a fraction of the entire company's workforce. The survey was conducted by a third party company, therefore the accuracy and reliability of the data rests with those who collected it.

## FUTURE RESEARCH

Future research relating to turnover in the hospitality industry may compare the degree of job satisfaction and organizational commitment of leavers versus those who stay. This research may be replicated to all over the United States, and categorized by state to find the contributing factor of turnover by the specific demographic. The results of this multi States study could be subjected to more precise and advanced statistical tools to verify whether the same conclusions will be supported.

## CONCLUSION

Turnover can have a damaging effect on an organization and its employees if nothing is done by the company to stop it. In most cases, turnover is used widely as a performance indicator. Although it is impossible to eliminate turnover altogether, but learning the preventative methods can help reduce the high number in turnover. In addition, the company must be well prepared to take all necessary actions required after a turnover such as job analysis, screening for new candidates, and making sure the candidate is the right fit. There needs to be more effort enforced focusing on maintaining employee job satisfaction and managing controllable causes of turnover since turnover has an immediate effect, particularly in the hospitality industry. In conclusion, it is extremely crucial to evaluate and appraise the job and overall work environment by providing feedback to in order to maintain a healthy work environment.

## REFERENCES

Abassi, S. M., & Hollman, K. W. (2000). Turnover: The real bottom line. *Public Personnel Management, 2*(3), 333–342.

Bowden, G.T. (1952). The Problem of Employee Turnover. *Harvard Business Review, 30*(5), 72-82.

Caplan, R. D., Cobb, S., French, J. R. P., Harrison, R. V., & Pinneau, S. R. J. (1975). *Job demands and worker health.* Washington, DC: H. E.W. Publication.

Cartwright, S., & Cooper, C. L. (1997). *Managing workplace stress.* Thousand Oaks, CA: Sage.

Coleman, L. G. (1989, December 4). Sales force turnover has managers wondering why. *Marketing News, 23*(25), 6–7.

Crossboarder Hotel Company. (2003). *Employee Handbook.* Los Angeles, CA: Author.

Grandey, A. A. (2003). When "the show must go on": Surface acting and deep acting as determinants of emotional exhaustion and peer-rated service delivery. *Academy of Management Journal, 46*(1), 86–96. doi:10.2307/30040678

Griffeth, R. W., & Hom, P. W. (2001). *Retaining valued employees.* Thousand Oaks, CA: Sage Publications Inc.

Hinkin, T. R., & Tracey, J. B. (2000). The cost of turnover: Putting a price on the learning curve. *The Cornell Hotel and Restaurant Administration Quarterly, 41*(3), 14–21. doi:10.1177/001088040004100313

Hom, P. W., & Kinicki, A. J. (2001, October). Toward a greater understanding of how dissatisfaction drives employee turnover. *Academy of Management Journal, 4*, 277–286.

Laser, S. A. (1980). winter). Dealing with the problem of employee turnover. *Human Resource Management, 19*(4), 17–21. doi:10.1002/hrm.3930190404 PMID:10250668

Lashley, C. (2001). *Empowerment: HR strategies for service excellence.* Oxford, UK: Butterworth-Heinemann.

Magner, N., Welker, R., & Johnson, G. (1996). The interactive effects of participation and outcome favorability in performance appraisal on turnover intentions and evaluations of supervisors. *Journal of Occupational and Organizational Psychology, 69*, 135–143. doi:10.1111/j.2044-8325.1996.tb00605.x

Mobley, W. H. (1982). *Employee turnover, causes, consequences, and control.* Manila, Philippines: Addison-Wesley Publishing Company.

Roseman, E. (1981). *Managing employee turnover.* New York, NY: Amacom.

Sheehan, E. P. (1995, February). Affective responses to employee turnover. *The Journal of Social Psychology, 135*(1), 63–69. doi:10.1080/00224545.1995.9711403

Staw, B. M. (1980). The Consequences of Turnover. *Journal of Occupational Behaviour, 1*(4), 253–273.

Wasmuth, W.J., & S.W. Davis, (1983b). Strategies for Managing Employee Turnover. *The Cornell H. R. A. Quarterly, 24*(2), 65-75

Wayne, F. (2000). *Cascio, Costing Human Resources* (4th ed.). Boston: Kent Publishing Company.

White, G. L. (1995, January). Employee turnover: The hidden drain on profits. *HRFocus*, *72*(1), 15–17.

Zuber, A. (2001). A career in food service cons: High turnover. *Nations Restaurant News*, *35*(21), 147–148.

## KEY TERMS AND DEFINITIONS

**Biased Management:** Management inclination or preference that influences judgment from being balanced or even-handed. Prejudice is bias in pejorative sense.

**Coaching:** A training method in which a more experienced or skilled individual provides an employee with advice and guidance intended to help him or her develop skills, improve performance and enhance the quality of his or her career.

**Competencies:** The knowledge, skills and abilities required to perform a specific task or function.

**Emotional Intelligence:** Describes the mental ability an individual possesses enabling him or her to be sensitive and understanding to the emotions of others, as well as to manage his or her own emotions and impulses.

**Employee Favoritism:** Examples of favoritism in the workplace include the management of assigning responsibility or giving promotions based on specific employees' preferences or soliciting sexual favors for job advancement, etc. Other forms of favoritism include nepotism and cronyism.

**Employee Motivation:** Motivation is an employee's intrinsic enthusiasm about and drive to accomplish activities related to work. Motivation is that internal drive that causes an individual to decide to take action.

**Employee Nepotism:** Nepotism is a form of discrimination in which family members or friends are hired for reasons that are note related to their experience, knowledge or skills. It occurs frequently in family-owned businesses, nonprofit organizations, small companies and the performing arts. Additional example of nepotism is to create job specifications that are precisely tailored to the qualifications of only one person -- the friend the employer wants to hire.

**Employee Recognition:** Employee recognition means rewarding a few or all employees who have been identified to have done something exceptional either for the organization or for the employees, or customers, or for the community, or a combination of several activities. Effective recognition systems include activities based on three dimensions: day-to-day, informal, and formal.

**Employee Retention:** An effort by a business to maintain a working environment, which supports current staff in remaining with the company. Many employee retention policies are aimed at addressing the various needs of employees to enhance their job satisfaction and reduce the substantial costs involved in hiring and training new staff.

**Equitable Treatment:** The primary assumptions in the applications of equity theory include: 1. Employees expect a fair return for what they contribute to their jobs, a concept referred to as the "equity norm". 2. Employees determine what their equitable return should be after comparing their inputs and outcomes with those of their coworkers. This concept is referred to as "social comparison". 3. Employees who perceive themselves as being in an inequitable situation will seek to reduce the inequity either by distorting inputs and/or outcomes in their own minds ("cognitive distortion"), by directly altering inputs and/or outputs, or by leaving the organization.

# Compilation of References

AAD. (2014). Associazione Alberghi Diffusi, Italy. www.alberghidiffusi.it

Aaker, D. A. (1991). *Managing brand equity*. New York, NY: Free Press.

Aaker, D. A. (1996). Measuring brand equity across products and markets. *California Management Review*, *38*(3), 102–120. doi:10.2307/41165845

Abassi, S. M., & Hollman, K. W. (2000). Turnover: The real bottom line. *Public Personnel Management*, *2*(3), 333–342.

Abdelhamied, H. H. S. (2013). The Effect of Sales Promotions on Post Promotion Behaviors and Preferences in Fast Food Restaurants. *Tourismos: An International Multidisciplinary Journal of Tourism*, *8*(1), 93–113.

Abernathy, W. J., & Clark, K. B. (1985). Innovation: Mapping the winds of creative destruction. *Research Policy*, *14*(1), 3–22. doi:10.1016/0048-7333(85)90021-6

Aboulnaga, I. A. (1998). Integrating quality and environmental management as competitive business strategy for the twenty-first century. *Environmental Management and Health*, *9*(2), 65–71. doi:10.1108/09566169810211168

*About Six Senses-Six Senses Hotels Resorts Spas-Luxury Resorts*. (n.d.). Retrieved May 20, 2014, from http://www.sixsenses.com/about-us/about-us

Ackfeldt, A. L., & Coote, L. V. (2005). A study of organizational citizenship behavior in a retail setting. *Journal of Business Research*, *58*(2), 151–159. doi:10.1016/S0148-2963(03)00110-3

Act, E. (2010). *Equality Act 2010*. The Equality Act.

Adams, J. S. (1965). *Inequity in Social Exchange*. In L. Berkowitz (Ed.), Advances in Experimental Social Psychology (Vol. 2, pp. 267–299). Academic Press.

Adler, N., & Smilowitz, K. (2007). Hub-and-Spoke Network Alliances and Mergers: Price-Location Competition in the Airline Industry. *Transportation Research: Part B: Methodological*, *41*(4), 394-409. Retrieved from http://www.elsevier.com/wps/find/journaldescription.cws_home/548/description#description

Adler, R. P. (2007). *Next-generation media: The global shift*. Aspen Institute. Retrieved March 10, 2014, from http: www.aspeninstitute.org/atf/cf/%7BDEB6F227-659B-4EC8-8F84 8DF23CA704F5%7D/NEXTGENERATION.PDF

Adler, H., & Rigg, J. (2012). Expatriate hotel general managers in Jamaica: Perceptions of human resource, organizational, and operational challenges. *Hotel & Business Management*, *1*(1), 1–9.

Adler, N. J. (1997a). Global leaders: A dialogue with future history. *International Management*, *1*(2), 21–33.

Adler, N. J., & Bartholomew, S. (1992). Managing globally competent people. *The Academy of Management Executive*, *6*(3), 52–65. doi:10.5465/AME.1992.4274189

Affisco, J. F., Nasri, F., & Paknejad, M. J. (1997). Environmental versus quality standards – an overview and comparison. *International Journal of Quality Science*, *2*(1), 5–23. doi:10.1108/13598539710159059

African Development Bank. (2012). *Lesotho Economic Outlook*. Retrieved April 23, 2014, from http://www.africanexonomicoutlook.org

African Development Bank. (2014). *Tunisia Country Strategy Paper: General Framework for Development.* Retrieved May 7 from http://www.afdb.org/fileadmin/uploads/afdb/Documents/Project-and-Operations/2014-2015_-_Tunisia_Interim_Country_Strategy_Paper.pdf

*Afriski Ski and Mountain Resort website.* (n.d.). Retrieved July 17, 2013, from http://www.afriski.net

AHLA. (2014). 2014 LODGING INDUSTRY PROFILE. AHLA Press room Annual Report. Retrieved May 25, 2015 from https://www.ahla.com/press.aspx

Ahlstrom, D. (2010). Publishing in the Asia Pacific Journal of Management. *Asia Pacific Journal of Management, 27*(1), 1–8. doi:10.1007/s10490-009-9181-0

Ahuvia, A. C. (2005). Beyond extended self: Loved objects and consumers' role identity narratives. *The Journal of Consumer Research, 32*(June), 171–184. doi:10.1086/429607

Aiello, G., Donvito, R., Godey, B., Pederzoli, D., Wiedman, K., Hennings, N., & Siebels, A. (2008). *Luxury brand and country of origin effect: results of an international empirical study.* Paper presented at the International Congress Marketing Trends, Venezia, Italy.

Ajiferuke, M., & Boddewyn, J. J. (1970). Culture and other explanatory variables in comparative management studies. *Academy of Management Journal, 13*(2), 153–163. doi:10.2307/255102

Akgun, E., Dayan, M., & Di Benedetto, A. (2008). New product development team intelligence: Antecedents and consequences. *Information & Management, 45*(4), 221–226. doi:10.1016/j.im.2008.02.004

Aksu, & Özdemir. (2005). Individual learning and organization culture in learning organizations. Five star hotels in the Antalya region of Turkey. *Managerial Auditing Journal, 20*(4), 422–441.

Albrecht, J. N. (2010). Challenges in tourism strategy implementation in peripheral destinations- The case of Stewart Island, New Zealand. *Tourism and Hospitality Planning & Development, 7*(2), 91–110. doi:10.1080/14790531003737102

Allen, L. (1988). Working better with Japanese managers. *Academy of Management Review, 77*(11), 32–49.

Allen, L., O'Toole, W., Harrison, D., & McDonnell, I. (2011). *Festival & special event management* (5th ed.). Milton, Queensland: John Wiley & Sons, Australia, Ltd.

Allen, M. J., & Yen, W. M. (1979). *Introduction to Measurement Theory.* Long Grave, IL: Waveland Press.

Alon, I. (Ed.). (2003). *Chinese Culture, organizational behavior, and international business management.* Westport, Connecticut: Praeger Publishers.

Alonso, A. D., & Ogle, A. (2010). Tourism and hospitality small and medium enterprises and environmental sustainability. *Management Research Review, 33*(8), 818–826. doi:10.1108/01409171011065626

Alonso-Almeida, M. M., & Bremser, K. (2013). Strategic responses of the Spanish hospitality sector to the financial crisis. *International Journal of Hospitality Management, 32*, 141–148. doi:10.1016/j.ijhm.2012.05.004

Alper, A. (2008). Türkiye'de Ekonomik Büyüme ve Turizm İlişkisi Üzerine Ekonometrik Analiz. *Sosyal Bilimler Enstitüsü Dergisi, 24*, 1–11.

AlSayyad, N. (Ed.). (2013). *Consuming tradition, manufacturing heritage: global norms and urban forms in the age of tourism.* Routledge.

Altman, Y., & Iles, P. (1998). Learning, leadership, teams: Corporate learning and organizational change. *Journal of Management Development, 17*(1), 44–55. doi:10.1108/02621719810368682

Álvarez Gil, M. J., Burgos Jimenez, J., & Cespedes Lorente, J. J. (2001). An analysis of environmental management, organizational context and performance of Spanish hotels. *Omega, 29*(6), 457–471. doi:10.1016/S0305-0483(01)00033-0

Álvarez, J. A. (2008). La banca española ante la actual crisis financiera. *Revista de Estabilidad Financiera, 13*, 23–38.

Amankwah-Amoah, J., & Debrah, Y. A. (2011). The evolution of alliances in the global airline industry: A review of the African experience. *Thunderbird International Business Review, 53*(1), 37–50. doi:10.1002/tie.20388

Ambrosini, V., & Bowman, C. (2009). What are dynamic capabilities and are they a useful construct in strategic management? *International Journal of Management Reviews, 11*(1), 29–49. doi:10.1111/j.1468-2370.2008.00251.x

Ambrosini, V., Bowman, C., & Collier, N. (2009). Dynamic capabilities: An exploration of how firms renew their resource base. *British Journal of Management, 20*(1), 9–24. doi:10.1111/j.1467-8551.2008.00610.x

*American Hotel and Lodging Association website.* (n.d.). Retrieved July 16, 2013, from http://www.ahla.com/content.aspx?id=34706

Amit, R., & Schoemaker, P. J. (1993). Strategic assets and organizational rent. *Strategic Management Journal, 14*(1), 33–46. doi:10.1002/smj.4250140105

Anantachart, S. (2004). Integrated marketing communications and market planning: Their implications to brand equity building. *Journal of Promotion Management, 11*(1), 101–125. doi:10.1300/J057v11n01_07

Andaleeb, S. S., & Conway, C. (2006). Customer satisfaction in the restaurant industry: An examination of the transaction-specific model. *Journal of Services Marketing, 20*(1), 3–11. doi:10.1108/08876040610646536

Anderson, J. C., & Gerbing, D. W. (1988). Structural equation modelling in practice: A review and recommended two-step approach. *Psychological Bulletin, 103*(3), 411–423. doi:10.1037/0033-2909.103.3.411

Andreassen, T., & Lindestad, B. (1998). Customer loyalty and complex services. *International Journal of Service Industry Management, 9*(1), 7–23. doi:10.1108/09564239810199923

Ang, S., & Inkpen, A. C. (2008). Cultural intelligence and offshore outsourcing success: A framework of firm-level intercultural capability. *Decision Sciences, 39*(3), 337–358. doi:10.1111/j.1540-5915.2008.00195.x

Ang, S., & Van Dyne, L. (2008). *Handbook of cultural intelligence: Theory, measurement, and application.* New York: M. E. Sharpe.

Anholt, S. (2006). *Competitive identity: The new brand management for nations, cities, and regions.* Palgrave Macmillan. doi:10.1057/9780230627727

Anholt, S. (2009). *Places: Identity, image, and reputation.* Great Britain: Palgrave Macmillan. doi:10.1057/9780230251281

Anjum, A. (2011). *Social Media Marketing.* GRIN.

Antonakis, J., & Atwater, L. (2002). Distance and leadership: A review and a proposed theory. *The Leadership Quarterly, 13*(6), 673–704. doi:10.1016/S1048-9843(02)00155-8

Apostolopoulos, Y., Leivadi, S., & Yiannakis, A. (Eds.). (2013). *The sociology of tourism: theoretical and empirical investigations, 1.* Routledge.

Appadurai, A. (1988). *The social life of things. Commodities in cultural perspective.* Cambridge: Cambridge University Press.

Appadurai, A. (1996). *Modernity al large: cultural dimensions of globalization* (Vol. 1). U of Minnesota Press.

Ardichvili, A., Page, V., & Wentling, T. (2003). Motivation and barriers to participation in virtual knowledge-sharing communities of practice. *Journal of Knowledge Management, 7*(1), 64–77. doi:10.1108/13673270310463626

Arezki, R., Cherif, R., & Piotrowski, J. (2009). Tourism Specialization and Economic Development: Evidence from the UNESCO World Heritage List. *IMF Working Paper 176*

Armstrong, A., & Foley, P. (2003). Foundations of a learning organization: Organization learning mechanisms. *The Learning Organization, 10*(2), 74–82. doi:10.1108/09696470910462085

Armstrong, J. S., & Overton, T. S. (1977). Estimating nonresponse bias in mail surveys. *JMR, Journal of Marketing Research, 14*(3), 396–402. doi:10.2307/3150783

Armstrong, R. W., Mok, C., Go, F. M., & Chan, A. (1997). The importance of cross-cultural expectations in the measurement of service quality perceptions in the hotel industry. *International Journal of Hospitality Management, 16*(2), 181–190. doi:10.1016/S0278-4319(97)00004-2

Armstrong, R. W., & Seng, T. B. (2000). Corporate-Customer satisfaction in the banking industry of Singapore. *International Journal of Bank Marketing, 18*(2/3), 97–111. doi:10.1108/02652320010339617

Aschkenasy, J. (1997). Culture shock: Expatriate benefits are getting squeezed as companies tighten their belts. *International business, 10*(2), 20-27.

Ashford, S. J., Rothbard, N. P., Piderit, S. K., & Dutton, J. E. (1998). Out on a limb: The role of context and impression management in selling gender-equity issues. *Administrative Science Quarterly, 43*(1), 23–57. doi:10.2307/2393590

Ashley, C., De Brine, P., Lehr, A., & Wilde, H. (2007). The Role of Tourism Sector in Expanding Economic Opportunity. *Economic Opportunity Series*, John F. Kennedy School of Government, Overseas Development Institute and International Business Leaders Forum. Retrieved May 7, 2014, from http://www.hks.harvard.edu/m-rcbg/CSRI/publications/report_23_EO%20Tourism%20Final.pdf

Ashworth, G., & Goodall, B. (1988). Tourist images: Marketing considerations. In B. Goodall & G. Ashworth (Eds.), *Marketing in the tourism industry: The promotion of destination regions* (pp. 213–238). USA: Croom Helm.

Aslan, A. (2008). Türkiye' de Ekonomik Büyüme ve Turizm İlişkisi Üzerine Ekonometrik Analiz. *Sosyal Bilimler Enstitüsü Dergisi,* Say:24 Yıl:2008/1, 1-11.

Assaf, A. G., & Josiassen, A. (2012). European vs. U.S. airlines: Performance comparison in a dynamic market. *Tourism Management, 33*(2), 317–326. doi:10.1016/j.tourman.2011.03.012

Atkinson, A. (1988). Answering the eternal question: What does the customer want? *The Cornell Hotel and Restaurant Administration Quarterly, 29*(2), 12–13. doi:10.1177/001088048802900209

Augier, M., & Teece, D. J. (2009). Dynamic capabilities and the role of managers in business strategy and economic performance. *Organization Science, 20*(4), 410–421. doi:10.1287/orsc.1090.0424

Au, L., & Law, R. (2002). Categorical classification of tourism dining. *Annals of Tourism Research, 29*(3), 819–833. doi:10.1016/S0160-7383(01)00078-0

Avrill, A. B., & Magnini, V. P. (2007). A holistic approach to expatriate success. *International Journal of Contemporary Hospitality Management, 19*(1), 53–64. doi:10.1108/09596110710724161

Axelrod, R. (1984). *The Evolution of Cooperation.* New York: Basic Books.

Axelrod, R. (1984). *The evolution or cooperation.* New York: Basic Books.

Ayuso, S. (2006). Adoption of voluntary environmental tools for sustainable tourism: Analyzing the experience of Spanish hotels. *Environmental Management, 13,* 207–220.

Ayuso, S. (2007). Comparing Voluntary Policy Instruments for Sustainable Tourism: The Experience of the Spanish Hotel Sector. *Journal of Sustainable Tourism, 15*(2), 144–159. doi:10.2167/jost617.0

Babbie, E. (1989). *The practice of social research.* Belmont, CA: Wadsworth.

Back, K. J. (2005). The effects of image congruence on customers´ brand loyalty in the upper middle-class hotel industry. *Journal of Hospitality & Tourism Research (Washington, D.C.), 29*(4), 448–467. doi:10.1177/1096348005276497

Baggio, R., Scott, N., & Cooper, C. (2011). Design of Tourism Governance Networks. In E. Laws (Ed.), *Tourist Destination Governance: practice, theory and issues* (pp. 159–172). CABI Publishing. doi:10.1079/9781845937942.0159

Bagozzi, R. P., & Yi, Y. (1988). On the evaluation of structural equation models. *Journal of the Academy of Marketing Science, 16*(1), 74–94. doi:10.1007/BF02723327

Bahar, O. (2006). Turizm Sektörünün Türkiye'nin Ekonomik Büyümesi Üzerindeki Etkisi: VAR Analizi Yaklaşımı. *C.B.Ü. Yönetim ve Ekonomi Dergisi, 13*(2), 137–150.

Baidya, M., & Maity, B. (2010). Effectiveness of integrated marketing communications: Empirical analysis of two brands in India. *Journal of Indian Business Research, 2*(1), 23–31. doi:10.1108/17554191011032929

Bailey, R., & Ball, S. (2006). An exploration of the meanings of hotel brand equity. *Service Industries Journal, 26*(1), 15–38. doi:10.1080/02642060500358761

Bakan, İ., & Doğan, İ. F. (2012). Competitiveness of the industries based on the Porter's diamond model: An empirical study. *International Journal of Research and Reviews in Applied Sciences, 11*(3), 441–455.

Baker, T. L., Hunt, T. G., & Andrews, M. C. (2005). Promoting ethical behavior and organizational citizenship behaviors: The influence of corporate ethical values. *Journal of Business Research*, *59*(7), 849–857. doi:10.1016/j.jbusres.2006.02.004

Bakker, M. (2005). Luxury and tailor-made holidays. *Journal of Travel and Tourism Analyst, 20*, 1–47.

Balmer, J. M. T., Fukukawa, K., & Gray, E. R. (2007). The nature and management of ethical corporate identity: A commentary on corporate identity, corporate social responsibility and ethics. *Journal of Business Ethics*, *76*(7), 7–15. doi:10.1007/s10551-006-9278-z

Baloglu, S. (1997). The relationship between destination images and sociodemographic and trip characteristics of international travelers. *Journal of Vacation Marketing*, *3*(3), 221–233. doi:10.1177/135676679700300304

Baloglu, S., & Assante, L. M. (1999). A content analysis of subject areas and research methods used in five hospitality management journals. *Journal of Hospitality & Tourism Research (Washington, D.C.)*, *23*(1), 53–70. doi:10.1177/109634809902300105

Baloglu, S., & McCleary, K. W. (1999). A model of destination image formation. *Annals of Tourism Research*, *26*(4), 868–897. doi:10.1016/S0160-7383(99)00030-4

*Banyantree Global Foundation*. (2014). Retrieved May 5, 2014, from http://www.banyantreeglobalfoundation.com/about_us/CSRPublications

Barber, N., & Pittaway, L. (2000). Expatriate recruitment in South East Asia: Dilemma or opportunity? *International Journal of Contemporary Hospitality*, *12*(6), 352–359. doi:10.1108/09596110010343530

Barbini, F. M., & Presutti, M. (2013). Tourist experience as an enabler for the development of tourism destinations. In Skills and Tools and Cultural Heritage and Cultural Tourism Management (pp. 59-74). Edizioni D'Errico.

Barbini, F. M., & Presutti, M. (2014). Transforming a peripheral area in an emerging tourism destination. *Tourism Geographies, An International Journal of Tourism Space. Place and Environment*, *16*(2), 190–206.

Barefoot, D., & Szabo, J. (2010). *Friends with Benefits: A Social Media Marketing*. Handbook, California: No Starch Press Inc.

Barla, P., & Constantatos, C. (2006). On the Choice between Strategic Alliance and Merger in the Airline Sector: The Role of Strategic Effects. *Journal of Transport Economics and Policy*, *40*(3), 409–424.

Barling, J., & Gallagher, D. G. (1996). Part-time employment. In C. L. Cooper & I. T. Robertson (Eds.), *International Review of Industrial and Organizational Psychology* (Vol. 11, pp. 241–277). Chichester: Wiley.

Barnard, C. J. (1938). *The functions of the executive*. Cambridge: Harvard University Press.

Barnes, P.E. (1996). Green Standards. *B & E Review, October-December*, 24-28.

Barnett, T., & Kellermanns, F. W. (2006). Are we Family and are we treated as Family? Nonfamily employees' perception of justice in the Family Firm. *Entrepreneurship Theory and Practice*, *30*(6), 837–854. doi:10.1111/j.1540-6520.2006.00155.x

Barney, J. B. (1986a). Strategic factor markets: Expectations, luck, and business strategy. *Management Science*, *32*(10), 1231–1241. doi:10.1287/mnsc.32.10.1231

Barney, J. B. (1986b). Organizational culture: Can it be a source of sustained competitive advantage? *Academy of Management Review*, *11*(3), 656–665. doi:10.5465/AMR.1986.4306261

Barney, J. B. (1991). Firm resources and sustained competitive advantage. *Journal of Management*, *17*(1), 99–120. doi:10.1177/014920639101700108

Barney, J. B. (1996). *Gaining And Sustaining Competitive Advantage*. Reading, MA: Addison Wesley Publishing Company.

Barragan, S. (2005). *Assessing the power of Porter's diamond model in the automobile industry in Mexico after ten years of Nafta. Master of Science in Management*. Alberta, Canada: Faculty of Management, University of Lethbridge.

Barros, C. P., & Peypoch, N. (2009). An evaluation of European airlines' operational performance. *International Journal of Production Economics*, *122*(2), 525–533. doi:10.1016/j.ijpe.2009.04.016

Barrows, C. W. (2008). Food and beverage management. In R. C. Wood & B. Brotherton (Eds.), *The SAGE handbook of hospitality management*. London: Sage. doi:10.4135/9781849200417.n20

Basala, L. S., & Klenosky, D. B. (2001). Travel style preferences for visiting a novel destination: A conjoint investigation across the novelty familiarity continuum. *Journal of Travel Research*, *40*(16), 172–182. doi:10.1177/004728750104000208

Basu, C., & Media, D. (2014). *The importance of Porter's diamond & Porter's five forces in business.* Retrieved from, November 11, 2014, http://smallbusiness.chron.com/ importance-porters-diamond-porters-five-forces-business-33891.html

Bateman, T. S., & Organ, D. W. (1983). Job satisfaction and the good soldier: The relationship between affect and employee citizenship. *Academy of Management Journal*, *26*(4), 587–595. doi:10.2307/255908

Batonda, G., & Perry, C. (2003). Influence of culture on relationship development processes in overseas Chinese/Australian networks. *European Journal of Marketing*, *37*(11/12), 1548–1574. doi:10.1108/03090560310495357

Bauer, I. L. (2014). Romance tourism or female sex tourism? *Travel Medicine and Infectious Disease*, *12*(1), 20–28. doi:10.1016/j.tmaid.2013.09.003 PMID:24332659

Baum, J. A. C., Calabrese, T., & Silverman, B. S. (2000). Don't go it alone: Alliance network composition and startups' performance in Canadian biotechnology. *Strategic Management Journal*, *21*(3), 267–294. doi:10.1002/(SICI)1097-0266(200003)21:3<267::AID-SMJ89>3.0.CO;2-8

Baum, T. (2006). *Human resource management for tourism, hospitality and leisure: an international perspective*. London: Thomson.

Baweh, I. A., Lo, C., Snow, B., & Werner, J. (2011). *An analysis of the policy framework for investment in infrastructure of the Kingdom of Lesotho and its impact on tourism-related infrastructure.* (Unpublished Master Thesis). Sciences Po, Paris.

Bayraktaroglu, S., & Kutanis, R. O. (2003). Transforming hotels into learning organizations: A new strategy for going global. *Tourism Management*, *24*(2), 149–154. doi:10.1016/S0261-5177(02)00061-4

Beard, J. G., & Raghep, M. G. (1983). Measuring leisure motivation. *Journal of Leisure Research*, *15*(3), 219–228.

Becken, S., & Job, H. (2014). Protected areas in an era of global–local change. *Journal of Sustainable Tourism*, *22*(4), 507–527. doi:10.1080/09669582.2013.877913

Becker, G. S. (1964). *Human capital*. New York: Columbia University Press.

Beerli, A., & Martin, J. D. (2004). Factors influencing destination image. *Annals of Tourism Research*, *31*(3), 657–681. doi:10.1016/j.annals.2004.01.010

Beer, S. (1979). *The Heart of Enterprise*. New York, NY: Wiley.

Beldona, S., & Kwansa, F. (2008). The impact of cultural orientation on perceived fairness over demand-based pricing. *International Journal of Hospitality Management*, *27*(4), 594–603. doi:10.1016/j.ijhm.2007.07.024

Belk, R. W. (1988). Possessions and the extended self. *The Journal of Consumer Research*, *15*(September), 139–167. doi:10.1086/209154

Bell, D., & Valentine, G. (1997). *Consuming Geographies: We Are Where We Eat*. London: Routledge.

Belliveau, J. (2006). *Romance on the road*. Baltimore: Beau Monde.

Belloumi, M. (2010). The relationship between tourism receipts, real effective exchange rate and economic growth in Tunisia. *International Journal of Tourism Research*, *12*, 550–560.

Bender, K., & Furman, R. (2004). The implications of sex tourism on men's social, psychological, and physical health. *Qualitative Report*, *9*(2), 176–191.

Bentler, P. M. (2004). *EQS 6 Structural equations program manual*. Encino, CA: Multivariate Software, Inc.

Beritelli, P. (2011). Cooperation among prominent actors in a tourist destination. *Annals of Tourism Research*, *38*(2), 607–629. doi:10.1016/j.annals.2010.11.015

Bernama (2014, June 14). Malaysia bags destination award. *The Star*, Nation, pp. 20.

Bernhardt, A. L., Dresser, & Hatton, E. (2003). The coffee pot wars: Unions and firm restructuring in the hotel industry. In E. Appelbaum, A. Bernhardt, & R. Murnane, (Eds.), Low-wage America: How Employers are Reshaping Opportunity in the Workplace. New York: Russell Sage Foundation

Bertagnoli, L. (2000). Goin' green. *Restaurants & Institutions*, *110*(19), 45–48.

Bharwani, S., & Butt, N. (2012). Challenges for the global hospitality industry: An HR perspective. *Worldwide Hospitality and Tourism Themes*, *4*(2), 150–162. doi:10.1108/17554211211217325

Bhat, S., & Reddy, S. K. (1998). Symbolic and functional positioning of brands. *The Journal of Consumer Marketing, Santa Barbara*, *15*(1), 32–43. doi:10.1108/07363769810202664

Bhattacharya, C. B., & Sen, S. (2003). Consumer-company identification: A framework for understanding consumers' relationships with companies. *Journal of Marketing*, *67*(2), 76–88. doi:10.1509/jmkg.67.2.76.18609

Bhatt, G. D. (2000). Organizing knowledge in the knowledge development cycle. *Journal of Knowledge Management*, *4*(1), 15–26. doi:10.1108/13673270010315371

Bigné, J. E., Chumpitaz, R., & Currás, R. (2010). Alliances between brands and social causes: The influence of company credibility on social responsible image. *Journal of Business Ethics*, *96*(2), 169–186. doi:10.1007/s10551-010-0461-x

Bigné, J. E., Moliner, M. A., & Callarisa, L. J. (2000). El valor y la fidelización de clientes: Propuesta de modelo dinámico de comportamiento. *Revista Europea de Dirección y Economía de la Empresa*, *9*(3), 65–78.

Bigné, J. E., Sánchez, M. I., & Sánchez, J. (2001). Tourism image, evaluation variables and after purchase behavior: Inter-relationship. *Tourism Management*, *22*(6), 607–616. doi:10.1016/S0261-5177(01)00035-8

Bilotkach, V. (2005). Price competition between international airline alliances. *Journal of Transport Economics and Policy*, *39*(2), 167–189.

Bilotkach, V. (2007a). Airline Partnerships and Schedule Coordination. *Journal of Transport Economics and Policy*, *41*(3), 413.

Bilotkach, V. (2007b). Price effects of airline consolidation: Evidence from a sample of transatlantic markets. *Empirical Economics*, *33*(3), 427–448. doi:10.1007/s00181-006-0108-z

Bishop, R., & Robinson, L. S. (1998). *Night market: Sexual cultures and the Thai economic miracle*. London, New York: Routledge.

Bitner, M. J., & Hubbert, A. (1994). Encounter satisfaction versus overall satisfaction versus quality. In Service Quality: New directions in theory and practice (pp. 241-268). Sage.

Bitzer, M. (2012). *Social Media ROI and Why Your Hotel May Be Focussing on the Wrong Turn*. Available at http://www.bluemagnetinteractive.com/blog/117-social-media-roi-and-why-your-hotel-may-be-focusing-on-the-wrong-return.html

Black, J. S. (1988). Work role transitions: A study of American expatriate managers in Japan. *Journal of International Business Studies*, *19*(2), 277–294. doi:10.1057/palgrave.jibs.8490383

Black, J. S., & Gregersen, H. B. (1991). The other half of the picture: Antecedents of spouse cross cultural adjustment. *Journal of International Business Studies*, *22*(3), 461–477. doi:10.1057/palgrave.jibs.8490311

Black, J. S., Gregersen, H. B., & Mendenhall, M. (1992b). Toward a theoretical framework of repatriation adjustment. *Journal of International Business Studies*, *23*(4), 737–760. doi:10.1057/palgrave.jibs.8490286

Black, J. S., Gregersen, H. B., & Mendenhall, M. E. (1992a). *Global assignments: Successfully expatriating and repatriating international managers*. San Francisco, CA: Jossey-Bass.

Black, J. S., Gregersen, H. B., Mendenhall, M. E., & Stroch, L. D. (1999). *Global assignments: Expatriating and repatriating international managers*. San Francisco, CA: Jossey-Bass.

Black, J. S., Gregersen, H. B., Mendenhall, M. E., & Stroh, L. K. (1999). *Globalizing people through international assignments*. New York, NY: Addison-Wesley Longman.

Black, J. S., & Medenhall, M. E. (1990). Cross-cultural training effectiveness: A review and a theoretical framework for future research. *Academy of Management Review, 1*(1), 113–136.

Black, J. S., Mendenhall, M. E., & Oddou, G. (1991). Toward a comprehensive model of international adjustment: An integration of multiple theoretical perspectives. *Academy of Management Review, 16*(2), 291–317.

Blanchard, A., & Horan, T. (1998). Social capital and virtual communities. *Social Science Computer Review, 16*, 293–307. doi:10.1177/089443939801600306

Blau, P. M. (1964). *Exchange and Power in Social Life.* New York: John Wiley & Sons.

Body, W. D. S. (2012). *Annual Report.* Retrieved November, 17, 2011, from www.wto.org

*Boeing Company website.* (n.d.). Retrieved June 28, 2013, from http://www.boeing.com

Bohdanowicz, P. (2005). European hoteliers' environmental attitudes: Greening the business. *The Cornell Hotel and Restaurant Administration Quarterly, 46*(2), 188–204. doi:10.1177/0010880404273891

Bohdanowicz, P., & Martinac, I. (2003). Attitudes towards sustainability in chain hotels- Results of a European survey. *International conference on smart and sustainable built environment, 19*(21), 1-10.

Bollen, K. A. (1989). *Structural equations with latent variables.* New York: Wiley. doi:10.1002/9781118619179

Bolotaeva, V. A. (2011). Marketing Opportunities with Social Networks. *Journal of Internet Social Networking and Virtual Communities.*

Bonabeau, E., Dorigo, M., & Theraulaz, G. (1999). *Swarm intelligence: From natural to artificial Systems.* New York, NY: Oxford University Press.

Bond, M. H. (2002). Reclaiming the individual from Hofstede's ecological analysis: a 20-year odyssey: Comment on Oyserman et al. (2002). *Psychological Bulletin, 128*(1), 73–77. doi:10.1037/0033-2909.128.1.73 PMID:11843548

Bonel, E. (2011). La vendita di prodotti turistici: Internet versus agenzia? Un'analisi dal punto di vista della domanda. *Sinergie rivista di studi e ricerche, 5*(66), 213-236.

Bonsu, S. K. (2009). Colonial images in global times: Consumer interpretations of Africa and Africans in advertising. *Consumption Markets & Culture, 12*(1), 1–25. doi:10.1080/10253860802560789

Booz, Allen, & Hamilton. (1968). *Management of new product.* New York, NY: Booz, Allen and Hamilton Inc.

Booz, Allen, & Hamilton. (1982). *New product management for the 1980s.* New York, NY: Booz, Allen and Hamilton Inc.

Borgan, C. (2010). *Social Media 101.* New Jersey: John Wiley and Sons. doi:10.1002/9781118256138

Bornhorst, T., Brent Ritchie, J. R., & Sheehan, L. (2010). Determinants of tourism success for DMOs & destinations: An empirical examination of stakeholders' perspectives. *Tourism Management, 31*(5), 572–589. doi:10.1016/j.tourman.2009.06.008

Borstorff, P. C., Harris, S. G., Field, H. S., & Giles, W. F. (1997). Who'll go? A Review of Factors Associated with Employee Willingness to Work Overseas. *Human Resources Planning, 20*(3), 29–40.

Botha, E., & Van Der Waldt, D. L. R. (2011). Relationship outcomes as measurement criteria to assist communication strategists to manage organizational relationships. *Revista Innovar, 21*(40), 5–16.

Bowden, G. T. (1952). The Problem of Employee Turnover. *Harvard Business Review, 30*(5), 72-82.

Bowen, J. T., & Chen, S. L. (2001). The relationship between customer loyalty and customer satisfaction. *International Journal of Contemporary Hospitality Management, 13*(5), 213–217. doi:10.1108/09596110110395893

Bowers, C., Pharmer, J. A., & Salas, E. (2000). When member homogeneity is needed in work teams: A meta-analysis. *Small Group Research, 31*(3), 305–327. doi:10.1177/104649640003100303

Boyacigiller, N. (1990). The role of expatriates in the management of interdependence, complexity and risk in multinational corporations. *Journal of International Business Studies*, *21*(3), 357–381. doi:10.1057/palgrave.jibs.8490825

Bramwell, B., & Alletorp, L. (2001). Attitudes in the Danish tourism industry to the roles of business and government in sustainable tourism. *International Journal of Tourism Research*, *3*(2), 91–103. doi:10.1002/jtr.242

Bravo, R., Matute, J., & Pina, J. M. (2012). Corporate social responsibility as a vehicle to reveal the corporate identity: A study focused on the websites of Spanish financial entities. *Journal of Business Ethics*, *107*(2), 129–146. doi:10.1007/s10551-011-1027-2

Bright, S., & Johnson, K. (1985). Training for hospitality. *Journal of European Industrial Training*, *9*(7), 27–31. doi:10.1108/eb014229

Britt, J. (2002). Expatriates want more support from home. *HRMagazine*, *47*(4), 21–22.

Brokaw, S. C. (1990). *An Investigation of Jewellery Store Image Structure*. Unpublished doctoral dissertation, Florida State University: Tallahassee.

Brondoni, S. M. (2007). Prefazione. In S. M. Brondoni (Ed.), *Market-Driven Management, concorrenza e mercati globali* (pp. XI–XIV). Torino: Giappichelli.

Brooks, C. (2008). *Introductory Econometrics for Finance* (2nd ed.). Cambridge, UK: Cambridge University Press. doi:10.1017/CBO9780511841644

Brophy, M. (1996). Environmental policies. In: Chan, E.S.W., & Hawkins, R. (2010), Attitude towards EMSs in an international hotel: and exploratory case study. *International Journal of Hospitality Management*, *29*(4), 641–651.

Brotherton, B. (1999). Towards a definitive view of the nature of hospitality and hospitality management. *International Journal of Contemporary Hospitality Management*, *11*(4), 165–173. doi:10.1108/09596119910263568

Brotherton, B. (2002). Finding the hospitality industry (A response to Paul Slattery). *Journal of Hospitality, Sport, and Tourism Education*, *1*(2), 75–77.

Brotherton, B., & Wood, R. C. (2008). The nature and meanings of hospitality. In R. C. Wood & B. Brotherton (Eds.), *The SAGE handbook of hospitality management*. London: Sage. doi:10.4135/9781849200417.n2

Brouder, P., & Eriksson, R. (2013). Tourism evolution: On the synergies of tourism studies and evolutionary economic geography. *Annals of Tourism Research*, *43*, 370–389. doi:10.1016/j.annals.2013.07.001

Brownell, J. (2008). Leading on land and sea: Competencies and context. *International Journal of Hospitality Management*, *27*(2), 137–150. doi:10.1016/j.ijhm.2007.11.003

Brown, J. S., & Duguid, P. (1991). Organizational learning and communities of practice: Toward a unified view of working, learning and innovation. *Organization Science*, *2*(1), 40–57. doi:10.1287/orsc.2.1.40

Brown, M. (1996). Environmental policy in the hotel sector; "green" strategy or stratagem? *International Journal of Contemporary Management*, *8*(3), 18–23.

Brown, S. P. (1996). A meta-analysis and review of organizational research on job involvement. *Psychological Bulletin*, *120*(2), 235–255. doi:10.1037/0033-2909.120.2.235

Brown, S., Squire, B., & Lewis, M. (2010). The impact of inclusive and fragmented operations strategy processes on operational performance. *International Journal of Production Research*, *48*(14), 4179–4198. doi:10.1080/00207540902942883

Brown, T. J., & Dacin, P. A. (1997). The company and the product: Corporate association and consumer product responses. *Journal of Marketing*, *61*(1), 68–84. doi:10.2307/1252190

Bruch, H., & Sattelberger, T. (2001). Lufthansa's transformation marathon: Process of liberating and focusing change energy. *Human Resource Management*, *40*(3), 249–259. doi:10.1002/hrm.1015

Brueckner, J. (2001). The economics of international codesharing: An analysis of airline alliances. *International Journal of Industrial Organization*, *19*(10), 1475–1498. doi:10.1016/S0167-7187(00)00068-0

Brueckner, J., & Whalen, T. (2000). The Price Effects of International Airline Alliances. *The Journal of Law & Economics*, *43*(2), 503–546. doi:10.1086/467464

Bruner, L. J., & Burns, M. J. (1998). The ISO 14000 Series: Business-friendly environmentalism. *Environmental Regulation and Permitting*, 7(3), 17–19.

Brunner, T., Stöcklin, M., & Opwis, K. (2007). Satisfaction, image and loyalty: New versus experienced customers. *European Journal of Marketing*, 42(9/10), 1095–1105. doi:10.1108/03090560810891163

Bryan, D. (2013). *Small business advertising and brand promotion using Facebook Ads*. Retrieved June 20, 2014 from OpaceWeb: http://www.opace.co.uk/blog/social-media-ppc-facebook-ads-vs-linkedin-ads-vs-google-adwords-which-would-you-choose

Bueno, C. M., & Tubbs, S. L. (2004). Identifying global leadership competencies: An exploratory study. *Journal of American Academy of Business*, 5(1/2), 80–87.

Buhalis, D., & Law, R. (2008). Progress in information technology and tourism management: 20 years on and 10 years after the Internet - The state of e-Tourism research. *Tourism Management*, 29(4), 609–623. doi:10.1016/j.tourman.2008.01.005

Buonocore, F. (2010). Contingent work in the hospitality industry: A mediating model of organizational attitudes. *Tourism Management*, 31(3), 378–385. doi:10.1016/j.tourman.2009.04.005

Burgan, M. (2002). *Marco Polo: Marco Polo and the silk road to China*. Mankato: Compass.

Burgess, J. A. (1978). *Image and Identity* (Occasional Papers in Geography, 23). Hull, UK: University of Hull Publication.

Burgoyue, J. (1993). The competence movement: Issues, stakeholders and prospects. *Personnel Review*, 22(6), 6–13. doi:10.1108/EUM0000000000812

Burke, R. J., Jeng, W., Koyuncu, M., & Fiksenbau, L. (2011). Work motivations, satisfaction and well-being among hotel managers in China: Passion versus addiction. *Interdisciplinary Journal of Research in Business*, 1(1), 21–34. doi:10.1016/S0148-2963(73)80028-1

Burns, P.M. (2006). Innovation, creativity and competitiveness. *Tourism Management Dynamics-trends, management and tools*, 97-107.

Burns, P. M. (1997). Tourism's workforce: Characteristics and inter-cultural perspectives. *Tourism Recreation Research*, 22(1), 48–54. doi:10.1080/02508281.1997.11014785

Butler, R. (1980). The concept of a tourist area life cycle of evolution: Implications for management of resources. *Canadian Geographer*, 24(1), 5–12. doi:10.1111/j.1541-0064.1980.tb00970.x

Cairns, R. D., & Galbraith, J. W. (1990). Artificial Compatibility, Barriers to Entry, and Frequent-Flyer Programs. *The Canadian Journal of Economics. Revue Canadienne d'Economique*, 23(4), 807–816. doi:10.2307/135563

Calantone, R., Garcia, R., & Dröge, C. (2003). The effects of environmental turbulence on new product development strategy planning. *Journal of Product Innovation Management*, 20(2), 90–103. doi:10.1111/1540-5885.2002003

Caligiuri, P. M. (2000a). The big five personality characteristics as predictors of expatriates' desire to terminate the assignment and supervisor-rated performance. *Personnel Psychology*, 53(1), 67–88. doi:10.1111/j.1744-6570.2000.tb00194.x

Caliguri, P. M. (2000b). Selecting expatriates for personality characteristics: A moderating effect on personality on the relationship between host national contact and cross-cultural adjustment. *Management International Review*, 40(1), 61–80.

Caliguri, P., Phillips, J., Lazarova, M., Tarique, I., & Burgi, P. (2001). The theory of met expectations applied to expatriate adjustment: The role of cross-cultural training (vol. 12). *International Journal of Human Resource Management*, 12(3), 357–372. doi:10.1080/09585190121711

Calvert, G., Mobley, S., & Marshall, L. (1994). Grasping the learning organization. *Training & Development*, 48(6), 38–43.

Camillo, A. A., & Di Pietro, L. (2014). An investigation on cultural cuisine of mainland China. Management implications for restaurant operators. In A. A. Camillo (Ed.), Handbook of Research on Global Hospitality and Tourism Management. IGI Global.

Camillo, A., Kim, W. G., Ryan, B., & Moreo, P. (2005). *Trend Forecasting Model of Ethnic Cuisine in America, Using the Italian Cuisine as an Example.* (Unpublished PhD Thesis). University of Michigan, USA.

Camillo, A., Connolly, D., & Kim, W. G.Woo Gon Kim. (2008). Success and Failure in Northern California. Critical Success Factors for Independent Restaurants. *Cornell Hospitality Quarterly, 49*(4), 363–380. doi:10.1177/1938965508317712

Camillo, A., Minguzzi, A., Presenza, A., & Holt, S. (in press). Natural Environmental Sustainability and Micro-Tourism Destinations. *The Case of Southern Italy.*

Campbell, A. (2010, Jan 21). *Social Media — A Definition.* Retrieved June 16, 2014 from Amy Cambell's Web log: https://blogs.law.harvard.edu/amy/2010/01/21/social-media-a-definition/

Campbell, T., & Cairns, H. (1994). Developing and measuring the learning organization: From buzz words to behaviors. *Industrial and Commercial Training, 26*(7), 10–15. doi:10.1108/00197859410064583

Candela, G., & Figini, P. (2003). *Economia del turismo: principi micro e macro economici.* McGraw-Hill.

Capatti, A., & Montanari, M. (2003). *Italian Cuisine: a Cultural History.* New York: Columbia University Press.

Caplan, R. D., Cobb, S., French, J. R. P., Harrison, R. V., & Pinneau, S. R. J. (1975). *Job demands and worker health.* Washington, DC: H. E.W. Publication.

Cappelli, P., & Sherer, P. D. (1991). The missing role of context in OB: The need for a meso-level approach. *Research in Organizational Behavior, 13*, 55–110.

Cappel, S. D., Pearson, T. R., & Romero, E. J. (2003). Strategic group performance in the commercial airline industry. *Journal of Management Research, 3*(2), 53–60.

Carbery, R., Garavan, T., O'Brien, F., & McDonnell, J. (2003). Predicting hotel managers' turnover cognitions. *Journal of Managerial Psychology, 18*(7), 649–679. doi:10.1108/02683940310502377

Carmer, J. C., & Rouzer, D. L. (1974). Healthy functioning from the Gestalt perspective. *The Counseling Psychologist, 4*(4), 20–23. doi:10.1177/001100007400400408

Carrasco, I. B., Salinas, E. M., & Pérez, J. (2008). Extensiones de marca en bienes y servicios: Evaluación y efectos sobre la imagen de marca. *Revista Española de Investigación de Mercados ESIC, 12*(2), 25–43.

Carrig, K. (1997). Reshaping Human Resources for the Next Century: Lessons from a High Flying Airline. *Human Resource Management, 36*(2), 277–289. doi:10.1002/(SICI)1099-050X(199722)36:2<277::AID-HRM8>3.0.CO;2-U

Carter, R. W. (2004). Implications of sporadic tourism growth: Extrapolation from the case of Boracay Island, The Philippines. *Asia Pacific Journal of Tourism Research, 9*, 383–404. doi:10.1080/1094166042000311264

Cartwright, S., & Cooper, C. L. (1997). *Managing workplace stress.* Thousand Oaks, CA: Sage.

Caruana, A. (2002). Service loyalty: The effects of service quality and the mediating role of customer satisfaction. *European Journal of Marketing, 36*(7/8), 811–828. doi:10.1108/03090560210430818

Casanueva, C., Gallego, Á., & Sancho, M. (2013). Network resources and social capital in airline alliance portfolios. *Tourism Management, 36*, 441–453. doi:10.1016/j.tourman.2012.09.014

Casarin, F. (1996). *Il marketing dei prodotti turistici. Specificità e varietà.* Torino: Giappichelli.

Cassee, E. H., & Reuland, R. (1983). Hospitality in hospitals. In E. H. Cassee & R. Reuland (Eds.), *The Management of hospitality.* Oxford: Pergamon.

Cassidy, F. (2012, June 20). *Local Residents' Perceptions on Tourism: An Espiritu Santo and Tangoa Islands, A Vanuatu Study.* Paper presented at the Regional Development: connectedness, business and learning, Springfield, Qld.

Cassidy, F., & Pegg, S. (2011). *The Outer Islands of Vanuatu: Is there a synergy between tourists and locals?* Paper presented at the 4th International Colloquium on Business & Management (ICBM), Bangkok, Thailand.

Cassidy, F. (2002). *A Study of the Potential for Future Tourism Development of the Outer Islands of Vanuatu from the Visitor and Resident Perspective.* Ipswich: The University of Queensland.

Cassidy, F., & Brown, L. (2010). Determinants of small Pacific Island tourism: A Vanuatu study. *Asia Pacific Journal of Tourism Research, 15*(2), 143–153. doi:10.1080/10941661003629953

Caudron, S. (1997). World-class execs. *Industry Week, 246*(22), 60–66.

Caulkin, S. (2001). The Time is Now. *People Management, 7*(17), 32–34.

Causin, G. G. (2007). *A Study to Examine the Preparation and Training of Hospitality Expatriate Executives.* Oklahoma State University. DAI Theses and Dissertations. Retrieved from http://dc.library.okstate.edu/utils/getfile/collection/Dissert/id/73340/filename/74031.pdf

Cavusgil, E., Seggie, S. H., & Talai, M. B. (2007). Dynamic capabilities view: Foundations and research agenda. *Journal of Marketing Theory and Practice, 15*(2), 159–166. doi:10.2753/MTP1069-6679150205

CBI Ministry of Foreign Affairs. (2014). *CBI product factsheet: Wellness tourism from France, Germany, Italy and the UK to Latin America.* Retrieved on June 1, 2014, from http://www.cbi.eu/system/files/marketintel_documents/2014_pfs_wellness_tourism_from_france_germany_italy_and_the_uk_to_latin_america_0.pdf

Central Bank of Lesotho. (2012). *CBL Economic Review.* May, No.142. Retrieved May 7, 2014, from http://www.centralbank.org.ls/publications/MonthlyEconomicReviews/2012/May%202012%20ER.pdf

*Central Bank of Turkish Republic.* (n.d.). Retrieved from http://www.tcmb.gov.tr

Centre for Socio-EcoNomic Development. (2011). Mainstreaming Tourism Development in Least Developed Countries: Coherence and Complimentarity of Policy Instruments. *CSEND Policy Study,* Geneva. Retrieved April 23, 2014, from http://www.csend.org/publications/csend-policy/studies

Çetintaş, H., & Bektaş, Ç. (2008). Türkiye'de Turizm ve Ekonomik Büyüme Arasındaki Kısa ve Uzun Dönemli İlişkiler. *Anatolia, 19*(1), 1–8.

Cetron, M., DeMicco, F., & Davies, O. (2010). *Hospitality and Travel 2015.* Orlando, FL: The American Hotel and Lodging Association Educational Institute.

Chakravarthy, B. A. (1997). A new strategy framework for coping with turbulence. *Sloan Management Review, 38*(2), 69–82.

Chambers, S., Lobb, A., Butler, L., Harvey, K., & Traill, W. B. (2007). Local, national and imported foods: A qualitative study. *Appetite, 49*(1), 208–213. doi:10.1016/j.appet.2007.02.003

Chan, E. S. W., & Hawkins, R. (2010). Attitude towards EMSs in an international hotel: And exploratory case study. *International Journal of Hospitality Management, 29*(4), 641–651. doi:10.1016/j.ijhm.2009.12.002

Chan, E. S. W., & Hawkins, R. (2011). Application of EMSs in a hotel context: A case study. *International Journal of Hospitality Management.*

Chan, J. K. L., & Baum, T. (2007). Motivation factors of ecotourists in ecolodge accommodation: The push and pull factors. *Asia Pacific Journal of Tourism Research, 12*(4), 349–364. doi:10.1080/10941660701761027

Chan, S.-L., & Huang, S.-L. (2004). A systems approach for the development of a sustainable community - the application of the sensitivity model (SM). *Journal of Environmental Management, 72*(3), 133–147. doi:10.1016/j.jenvman.2004.04.003 PMID:15251220

Chao, L. (2008). IHG to franchise hotels in China. *Wall Street Journal—Eastern Edition, 251*(23), D5.

Chaperon, S., & Bramwell, B. (2013). Dependency and agency in peripheral tourism development. *Annals of Tourism Research, 40,* 132–154. doi:10.1016/j.annals.2012.08.003

Chapman, M. (1997). Preface: Social anthropology, business studies, and cultural issues. *International Studies of Management & Organization, 26*(4), 3–29.

Chathoth, P. K., Mak, B., Sim, J., Jauhari, V., & Manaktola, K. (2011). Assessing dimensions of organizational trust across cultures: A comparative analysis of U.S. and Indian full service hotels. *International Journal of Hospitality Management, 30*(2), 233–242. doi:10.1016/j.ijhm.2010.09.004

Chen, G. M. (1993). *A Chinese perspective of communication competence*. Paper presented at the annual convention of the Speech Communication Association, San Antonio, Texas.

Chen, G.-M. (1997). *An examination of PRC business negotiating behaviors.ChicagoERIC Document reproduction service* (No. ED422594). Paper presented at the annual meeting of the national communication association.

Chen, G.-M. (2001, July 11). From Sorry to Apology: Understanding the Chinese. *Chinese Community Forum, 27*.

Chen, C.-F., & Tsai, D. C. (2007). How destination image and evaluative factors affect behavioral intentions? *Tourism Management, 28*(4), 1115–1122. doi:10.1016/j.tourman.2006.07.007

Chen, F., & Chen, C. (2003). The effects of strategic alliances and risk pooling on the load factors of international airline operations. *Transportation Research Part E, Logistics and Transportation Review, 39*(1), 19–34. doi:10.1016/S1366-5545(02)00025-X

Chen, G.-M., & Starosta, W. J. (1998). Chinese conflict management and resolution: Overview and implications. *Intercultural Communication Studies, 7*(1), 1–16.

Chen, J. S., & Hsu, C. H. (2000). Measurement of Korean tourists´ perceived images of overseas destinations. *Journal of Travel Research, 38*(4), 411–416. doi:10.1177/004728750003800410

Chen, R. X. Y., Cheung, C., & Law, R. (2012). A review of the literature on culture in hotel management research: What is the future? *International Journal of Hospitality Management, 31*(1), 52–65. doi:10.1016/j.ijhm.2011.06.010

Chen, R.-S., & Hsiang, C.-H. (2007). A study on the critical success factors for corporations embarking on knowledge community-based e-learning. *Information Sciences, 177*(2), 570–586. doi:10.1016/j.ins.2006.06.005

Chen, X. P., & Peng, S. (2008). Guanxi dynamics: Shiftsi N the Closeness of Ties between Chinese Coworkers. *Management and Organization Review, 4*(1), 63–80. doi:10.1111/j.1740-8784.2007.00078.x

Chen, Y. C., Wang, W. C., & Chu, Y. C. (2011). A case study on the business performance management of Hilton hotels corp. *International Business Research, 4*(2), 213–218. doi:10.5539/ibr.v4n2p213

Chen, Z. X., & Francesco, A. M. (2000). Employee demography, organizational commitment, and turnover intentions in China: Do cultural differences matter? *Human Relations, 53*(6), 869–887. doi:10.1177/0018726700536005

Chen, Z., & Ross, T. (2003). Cooperating upstream while competing downstream: A theory of input joint ventures. *International Journal of Industrial Organization, 21*(3), 381–397. doi:10.1016/S0167-7187(02)00058-9

Chi, C. G. Q., & Qu, H. (2008). Examining the structural relationships of destination image, tourist satisfaction and destination loyalty: An integrated approach. *Tourism Management, 29*(4), 624–636. doi:10.1016/j.tourman.2007.06.007

Chien, T. C. (2012). Intercultural training for Taiwanese business expatriates. *Industrial and Commercial Training, 44*(3), 164–170. doi:10.1108/00197851211216772

Child, J., & Lu, Y. (1996). Introduction: China and international enterprise. In J. Child & L. Yuan (Eds.), *Management issues in China: International enterprises*. London: Routledge. doi:10.1093/0198236255.003.0001

China, F. H. C. (2009). *13th International Exhibition for the Food, Drink, Hospitality, Foodservice, bakery and Retail Industries*. Retrieved December 18, 2009 from www.fhcchina.com and http://www.fhcchina.com/en/index1_2.asp

*China-Italy Chamber of Commerce CICC*. (2009). Retrieved July 18, 2009 from http://www.cameraitacina.com/

Chin, W. (1988). The partial least squares approach for structural equation modeling. In G. A. Marcoulides (Ed.), *Modern methods for business research* (pp. 295–336). New Jersey, NJ: Lawrence Erlbaum Associates.

Chin, W. W. (2010). How to write up and report PLS analyses. In V. Esposito Vinzi, W. W. Chin, J. Henseler, & H. Wang (Eds.), *Handbook of partial least squares: Concepts, methods and applications in marketing and related fields* (pp. 645–689). New York, NY: Springer. doi:10.1007/978-3-540-32827-8_29

Choi, S., & Mattila, A. S. (2006). The role of disclosure in variable hotel pricing: A cross-cultural comparison of customers' fairness. *The Cornell Hotel and Restaurant Administration Quarterly, 47*(1), 27–35. doi:10.1177/0010880405281681

Choi, T. Y., & Chu, R. (2001). Determinants of hotel guests' satisfaction and repeat patronage in the Hong Kong hotel industry. *International Journal of Hospitality Management, 20*(3), 277–297. doi:10.1016/S0278-4319(01)00006-8

Choi, W. M., Chan, A., & Wu, J. (1999). A qualitative and quantitative assessment of Hong Kong's image as a tourist destination. *Tourism Management, 20*(3), 361–365. doi:10.1016/S0261-5177(98)00116-2

Chon, K. S. (1991). Tourism destination modification process: Marketing implications. *Tourism Management, 12*(1), 68–72. doi:10.1016/0261-5177(91)90030-W

Chon, K. S. (1992). The role of destination image in tourism: An extension. *The Tourist Review, 47*(1), 2–8. doi:10.1108/eb058086

Chonko, L. B., & Hunt, S. D. (1985). Ethics and marketing management: An empirical examination. *Journal of Business Research, 13*(4), 339–359. doi:10.1016/0148-2963(85)90006-2

Cho, S., & Johanson, M. (2008). Organizational citizenship behavior and employee performance: Moderating effect of work status in restaurant employees. *Journal of Hospitality & Tourism Research (Washington, D.C.), 32*(3), 307–326. doi:10.1177/1096348008317390

Christensen, L. T., Firat, A. F., & Torp, S. (2008). The organization of integrated communications: Toward flexible integration. *European Journal of Marketing, 42*(3/4), 423–452. doi:10.1108/03090560810853002

Christiana Care Health System. (n.d.). *About Christiana Care Care.* Retrieved from http://www.christianacare.org/way

Christou, E. (2010). Relationship marketing practices for retention of corporate customers in hospitality contract catering. *Tourism and Hospitality Management, 16*, 1–10.

Chua, C. L., Kew, H., & Yong, J. (2005). Airline Code-Share Alliances and Costs: Imposing Concavity on Translog Cost Function Estimation. *Review of Industrial Organization, 26*(4), 461-487. doi: http://www.springerlink.com/link.asp?id=100336

Chung-Herrera, B. G., Enz, C. A., & Lankau, M. J. (2003). Grooming future hospitality leaders: A competencies model. *The Cornell Hotel and Restaurant Administration Quarterly, 44*(3), 17–25.

Churchill, G. A. (1979). A paradigm for developing better measures of marketing constructs. *JMR, Journal of Marketing Research, 16*(1), 64–74. doi:10.2307/3150876

Chutikul, S. (n.d.) *Who are the clients: The exploiters?* http://www.cwa.tnet.co.th/Vol12-1&2/Saisuree.htm

CIA. (2009). *The world factbook.* Retrieved from http://www.cia.gov/cia/publications/factbook

Ciffolilli, A. (2003). Phantom authority, self–selective recruitment and retention of members in virtual communities: The case of Wikipedia. *First Monday, 8*(12[REMOVED HYPERLINK FIELD]). doi:10.5210/fm.v8i12.1108

Clark, J. (November 26, 2007). Older white women join Kenya's sex tourists. *Reuters.* Retrieved March 20, 2012 from http://www.reuters.com/articlePrint?articleId=USN2638979720071126

Clarke, J. (2000). Tourism brands: An exploratory study of the brands box model. *Journal of Vacation Marketing, 6*(4), 329–345. doi:10.1177/135676670000600404

Clemes, M., Gan, C., & Ren, M. (2011). Synthesizing the effects of service quality, value and customer satisfaction on behavioral intentions in the motel industry: An empirical analysis. *Journal of Hospitality & Tourism Research (Washington, D.C.), 35*(4), 530–568. doi:10.1177/1096348010382239

CNTA. (2003). *Total number of domestic tourism from 1996-2003.* Retrieved from, March 11, 2014, http://www.chinatour.com

Coakes, S. J., Steed, L., & Price, J. (2008). *SPSS Version 15.0 for Windows: Analysis without Anguish.* Australia: John Wiley & Sons.

Cobbenhagen, J. (2000). *Successful innovation: Towards a new theory for the management of small and medium-sized enterprises*. Cheltenham, UK: Edward Elgar Publishing Limited.

Cobb-Walgren, C. J., Ruble, C. A., & Donthu, N. (1995). Brand equity, brand preference and purchase intent. *Journal of Advertising, 24*(3), 25–40. doi:10.1080/0091 3367.1995.10673481

Cohen, E. (1972). Towards a sociology of international tourism. *Social Research, 6,* 164–182.

Cohen, E., & Avieli, N. (2004). Food in tourism (Attraction and Impediment). *Annals of Tourism Research, 31*(4), 755–778. doi:10.1016/j.annals.2004.02.003

Cohen, J. (1988). *Statistical power analysis for behavioral sciences*. Hillsdale: Erlbaum.

Cohen, J. (1988). *Statistical power analysis for the behavioral sciences* (2nd ed.). Hillsdale, NJ: Lawrence Erlbaum Associates.

Cohen, M., & Bodeker, G. (2008). *Understanding the global spa industry*. New York, NY: Routledge.

Cohen, W. M., & Levinthal, D. A. (1990). Absorptive capacity: A new perspective on learning and innovation. *Administrative Science Quarterly, 35*(1), 128–152. doi:10.2307/2393553

Coleman, L. G. (1989, December4). Sales force turnover has managers wondering why. *Marketing News, 23*(25), 6–7.

Collesei, U., Casarin, F., & Vescovi, T. (2001). Internet e i cambiamenti nei comportamenti di acquisto del consumatore. *Micro and Macro marketing, 10*(1), 33-50.

Collings, D. G., Doherty, N., Luethy, M., & Osborn, D. (2011). Understanding and supporting the career implications of international assignments. *Journal of Vocational Behavior, 78*(3), 361–371. doi:10.1016/j.jvb.2011.03.010

Comrey, A. L., & Lee, H. B. (1992). *A first course in factor analysis* (2nd ed.). Hillsdale, NJ: Lawrence Eribaum.

Confessore, S. J. (1997). Building a learning organization: Communities of practice, self-directed learning, and continuing medical education. *The Journal of Continuing Education in the Health Professions, 17*(1), 5–11. doi:10.1002/chp.4750170101

Connelly, C. E., & Gallagher, D. G. (2004). Emerging trends in contingent work research. *Journal of Management, 30*(6), 959–983. doi:10.1016/j.jm.2004.06.008

Conner, K. R., & Prahalad, C. K. (1996). A resource-based theory of the firm: Knowledge versus opportunism. *Organization Science, 7*(5), 477–501. doi:10.1287/orsc.7.5.477

Conrad, J. (2010). *Guerrilla Social Media Marketing*. Entrepreneur Media Inc.

Constantin, J. A., & Lusch, R. F. (1994). *Understanding resource management: How to deploy your people, products, and processes for maximum productivity*. Oxford, OH: Planning Forum.

Converse, P. D. (1921). *Marketing methods and politics*. New York: Prentice Hall.

Cook, A., & Glass, C. (2009). Between a rock and a hard place: Managing diversity in a shareholder society. *Human Resource Management Journal, 19*(4), 393–412. doi:10.1111/j.1748-8583.2009.00100.x

Cooper, C. J., Fletcher, S., Wanhill, Gilbert, D., & Shepherd, R. (1998). Tourism Principles and Practice. Essex, UK: Pearson Education.

Cooper, C., & Wahab, S. (Eds.). (2005). *Tourism in the Age of Globalisation*. Routledge.

Cooper, R. G. (1988). The new product process: A decision guide for management. *Journal of Marketing Management, 3*(3), 238–255. doi:10.1080/0267257X.1988.9964044

Cooper, R. G., & Kleinschmidt, E. (2000). New product performance: What distinguishes the star products. *Australian. Journal of Management, 25*(1), 17–45.

Coopey, J. P. (1995). The learning organization: Power, politics, and ideology. *Management Learning, 26*(2), 193–213. doi:10.1177/1350507769502600204

Copeland, L., & Griggs, L. (1985). *Going International*. New York: Random House.

Corbetta, G., & Salvato, C. A. (2004). The board of director in family firms: One size fits all? *Family Business Review, 17*(2), 119–134. doi:10.1111/j.1741-6248.2004.00008.x

Corbin, J., & Strauss, A. (1990). Grounded theory research: Procedures, canons, and evaluative criteria. *Qualitative Sociology, 13*(1), 3–21. doi:10.1007/BF00988593

Corstjens, M, & Umblijs, A. (2012). The Power of Evil: The Damage of Negative Social Media Strongly Outweigh Positive Contributions. *Journal of Advertising Research, 52*(4), 433-449.

Cotton, B. (2007). We must find a balance of sustainability. *Caterer & Hotelkeeper, 197*(4498), 32–33.

Crandall, R. (1980). Motivations for leisure. *Journal of Leisure Research, 12*(1), 45–54.

Crawford-Welch, S., & McCleary, K. W. (1992). An identification of the subject areas and research techniques used in five hospitality-related journals. *International Journal of Hospitality Management, 11*(2), 155–167. doi:10.1016/0278-4319(92)90008-J

Creswell, J. W. (2005). *Educational research: Planning, conducting, and evaluating quantitative and qualitative research* (2nd ed.). Upper Saddle River, NJ: Pearson Education.

Crompton, J. (1979). Motivations for pleasure vacation. *Annals of Tourism Research, 6*(4), 408–424. doi:10.1016/0160-7383(79)90004-5

Crompton, J. L. (1979). An assessment of the image of Mexico as a vacation destination and the influence of geographical location upon the image. *Journal of Travel Research, 18*(4), 18–23. doi:10.1177/004728757901700404

Cronin, J. J. Jr, Brady, M. K., & Hult, G. T. M. (2000). Assessing the effects of quality, value, and customer satisfaction on customer behavioral intentions in service environments. *Journal of Retailing, 76*(2), 193–218. doi:10.1016/S0022-4359(00)00028-2

Cronin, J. J., & Taylor, S. A. (1992). Measuring service quality: A re-examination and extension. *Journal of Marketing, 56*(3), 55–68. doi:10.2307/1252296

Cropanzano, R., & Mitchell, M. S. (2005). Social exchange theory: An interdisciplinary review. *Journal of Management, 31*(6), 874–900. doi:10.1177/0149206305279602

Crossboarder Hotel Company. (2003). *Employee Handbook*. Los Angeles, CA: Author.

Crouch, G. I. (1994). The Study of International Tourism Demand: A Review of Findings. *Journal of Travel Research, 33*(1), 12–23. doi:10.1177/004728759403300102

CSEND. (2010). *Inter-ministerial Coordination and Stakeholder Consultation of Trade Policy Making*. Presented at CSEND-CUTS Book Vernissage, Geneva. Retrieved May 7, 2014, from http://www.csend.org/images/articles/files/20100730-PresentationBookVernissage7.pdf

CSEND. (2011). Mainstreaming Tourism Development in Least Developed Countries: Coherence and Complimentarity of Policy Instruments. *CSEND Policy Study*. Retrieved May 7, 2014, from http://www.csend.org/images/articles/files/2011%2008%2029_Mainstreaming%20Tourism%20Development_Full%20Report.pdf

Culinary Institute of America. (2009). *Italian cuisine. An introduction to the principles o planning, preparation, and presentation of the foods of Italy*. Retrieved 14 September 2009 from http://www.ciachef.edu/

Cunha, M. P., & Gomes, J. F. (2003). Order and disorder in product innovation models. *Creativity and Innovation Management, 12*(3), 174–187. doi:10.1111/1467-8691.00280

Cyert, R., & March, J. G. (1963). *A behavioral theory of the firm*. Englewood Cliffs, NJ: Prentice-Hall.

Czerny, A. I. (2009). Code-Sharing, Price Discrimination and Welfare Losses.[doi: http://www.bath.ac.uk/e-journals/jtep/]. *Journal of Transport Economics and Policy, 43*(2), 193–212.

D'Andrade, R. G. (1984). Cultural meaning systems. In R. A. Shweder & R. A. LeVine (Eds.), *Cultural theory: Essays on mind, self, and emotion* (pp. 88–119). Cambridge: Cambridge University Press.

*Da Marco Group*. (2009). Retrieved December 17, 2009, from http://www.damarco.com.cn/

Daft, R. (1996). *Organizational performance*. New York: Wiley.

Daft, R. L. (2001). *Organization theory and design* (7th ed.). Cincinnati, Ohio: South Western College Publishing.

Daft, R., & Marcic, D. (1998). *Understanding management*. Forth Worth, TX: Dryden Press.

Dall'Ara, G. & Morandi, F. (2010). *Il turismo nei borghi; la normativa, il marketing e i casi di eccellenza. (Tourism in Hamlets; law, marketing and the best practices)*. Matelica (MC), Italy: Nuova giuridica.

Dall'Ara, G., & Esposito, M. (2005). (Il fenomeno degli alberghi diffusi in Italia), Palladino Editor, Campobasso, Italy, 2005.

Dall'Ara, G. (2010). *Manuale dell'Albergo Diffuso; l'idea, la gestione, il marketing dell'ospitalità. (Albergo Diffuso's practice, idea, management, marketing of hospitality)*. Milano, Italy: Franco Angeli.

Dall'Ara, G. (Ed.). (2010). *PMI nel turismo. Un'opportunità per lo sviluppo*. Milano: Franco Angeli.

Daniels, J. D., & Radebaugh, L. H. (1994). *International Business: Environments and operations*. Reading, MA: Addison-Wesley Publishing Company.

Dann, G. (1977). Anomie, Ego-enhancement and Tourism. *Annals of Tourism Research*, 4(4), 184–194. doi:10.1016/0160-7383(77)90037-8

Dann, G. (1996). *The language of tourism: A sociolinguistic perspective*. Oxford: CAB International.

Dash, S., Bruning, E., & Acharya, M. (2009). The effect of power distance and individualism on service quality expectations in banking. *International Journal of Bank Marketing*, 27(5), 336–358. doi:10.1108/02652320910979870

Das, T. K., & Teng, B.-S. (2000). A Resource-Based Theory of Strategic Alliances. *Journal of Management*, 26(1), 31–61. doi:10.1177/014920630002600105

Das, T. K., & Teng, B.-S. (2002). Alliance Constellations: A Social Exchange Perspective. *Academy of Management Review*, 27(3), 445–456. doi:10.2307/4134389

Daun, W., & Klinger, R. (2006). Delivering the message. How premium hotel brands struggle to communicate their value proposition. *International Journal of Contemporary Hospitality Management*, 18(3), 246–252. doi:10.1108/09596110610658643

Davidson, M. C. (2003). Does organizational climate add to service quality in hotels? *International Journal of Contemporary Hospitality Management*, 15(4), 206–213. doi:10.1108/09596110310475658

Davies, H., Leung, K. P., Luk, T. K., & Wong, Y. H. (1995). The benefits of guanxi: The value of relationships in developing the Chinese market. *Industrial Marketing Management*, 24(3), 207–214. doi:10.1016/0019-8501(94)00079-C

Davison, L., & Ryley, T. (2010). Tourism destination preferences of low-cost airline users in the East Midlands. *Journal of Transport Geography*, 18(3), 458–465. doi:10.1016/j.jtrangeo.2009.07.004

Day, G. S. (1994). The Capabilities of Market-Driven Organizations. *Journal of Marketing*, 58(4), 37–52. doi:10.2307/1251915

de Chernatony, L., & Segal-Horn, S. (2001). Building on services' characteristics to develop successful services brands. *Journal of Marketing Management*, 17(7-8), 645–670. doi:10.1362/026725701323366773

de la Barre, S., & Brouder, P. (2013). Consuming stories: Placing food in the Arctic tourism experience. *Journal of Heritage Tourism*, 8(2-3), 213–223. doi:10.1080/1743873X.2013.767811

De Mooij, M. (2004). *Consumer behavior and culture: Consequences for global marketing and advertising*. Thousand Oaks, CA: Sage.

De Mooij, M., & Hofstede, G. (2002). Convergence and divergence in consumer behavior: Implications for international retailing. *Journal of Retailing*, 78(1), 61–69. doi:10.1016/S0022-4359(01)00067-7

De Mooij, M., & Hofstede, G. (2011). Cross-cultural consumer behavior: A review of research findings. *Journal of International Consumer Marketing*, 23(3-4), 181–192.

De Vierville, J. P. (2003). Spa industry, culture and evolution: Time, temperature, touch and truth. *Massage and Bodywork*, 18, 20–31.

Decidedlysocial. (2012). *13 Types of Social Media Platforms and Counting*. Retrieved June 20, 2014 from Decidedlysocial: http://decidedlysocial.com/13-types-of-social-media-platforms-and-counting/

Deighton, J. K. (2007, Sept 26). *Digital Interactivity: Unanticipated Consequences for Markets, Marketing, and Consumers*. Retrieved June 20, 2014 from HBS. edu: http://www.hbs.edu/faculty/Publication%20Files/08-017_1903b556-786c-49fb-8e95-ab9976da8b4b.pdf

Del Conte, A. (2004). *The Concise Gastronomy of Italy*. Barnes and Nobles Books.

Delgado-Ballester, E., Navarro, A., & Sicilia, M. (2012). Revitalising brands through communication messages: The role of brand familiarity. *European Journal of Marketing, 46*(1), 31–51. doi:10.1108/03090561211189220

Della Corte, V., & Sciarelli, M. (2003). Evoluzione del marketing nella filiera turistica: Il ruolo dell'Information and Communication Technology. Proceedings of Congresso Internazionale "Le tendenze del marketing 2003, 11, 28-29.

Della Corte, V. (2000). *La gestione dei sistemi locali di offerta turistica*. Padova: Cedam.

Della Corte, V. (2009). *Imprese e Sistemi Turistici. Il management*. Milano: Egea.

Delmas, M. A., & Terlaak, A. K. (2001). A framework for analyzing environmental voluntary agreements. *California Management Review, 43*(3), 44–63. doi:10.2307/41166088

Deloitte, L. L. P. (2009). *Medical tourism: Update and implications*. [Report]. Retrieved from www.deloitte.com

Demirel, B., Bozdağ, E. G., & Inci, A. G. (2008). *Döviz Kurlarındaki Dalgalanmaların Gelen Turist Sayısına Etkisi: Türkiye Örnegi*. Retrieved from: http://www.deu.edu.tr/userweb/iibf_kongre/dosyalar/demirel.pdf

Demopoulos, P., Futch, J., & Pisello, T. (2008). *The Importance of measuring ROI: the Indicators of Business and IT performance*. An Alinean White Paper.

Denizci, B., & Tasci, A. D. A. (2010). Modeling the commonly-assumed relationship between human capital and brand equity in tourism. *Journal of Hospitality Marketing & Management, 19*(6), 610–628. doi:10.1080/19368623.2010.493073

Department of Statistics Malaysia. (2013). *Population projection, Malaysia 2010-2040*. Retrieved from Department of Statistics Malaysia website: http://www.statistics.gov.my/portal/images/stories/files/LatestReleases/population/Ringkasan_Penemuan-Summary_Findings_2010-2040.pdf

Deresky, H. (1994). *International management: Managing across borders and cultures*. New York: Harper Collins College Publishers.

Deshpandé, R., Farley, J. U., & Webster, F. E. Jr. (1993). Corporate Culture, Customer Orientation, and Innovativeness in Japanese Firms: A Quadrad Analysis. *Journal of Marketing, 57*(1), 23–37. doi:10.2307/1252055

Deshpandé, R., & Webster, F. E. Jr. (1989). Organizational Culture and Marketing: Defining the Research Agenda. *Journal of Marketing, 53*(1), 3–15. doi:10.2307/1251521

Deshpande, S. P., & Viswesvaran, C. (1992). Is cross-cultural training of expatriate managers effective: A meta-analysis. *International Journal of Intercultural Relations, 16*(3), 295–310. doi:10.1016/0147-1767(92)90054-X

Dess, G. G., & Davis, P. S. (1984). Porter's generic strategies as determinants of strategic group membership and organizational performance. *Academy of Management Journal, 27*(3), 467–488. doi:10.2307/256040

Dev, C. S. (2012). *Hospitality branding*. Ithaca, NY: Cornell University Press.

Dewey, C. (2013). Tourism goes mobile and social. The Business Newspaper, 31(18).

Dhaliwal, N. S. (2006). *Tourism*. Vintage Books.

Di Vittorio, A. (2003). E-Tourism. Le nuove forme di comunicazione nel settore turistico. *Micro and Macro Marketing, 12*(1), 59–84.

Dick, A., & Basu, K. (1994). Customer loyalty: Towards an integrated framework. *Journal of the Academy of Marketing Science, 22*(2), 99–113. doi:10.1177/0092070394222001

Diedrich, A., & Garcia-Buades, E. (2009). Local perceptions of tourism as indicators of destination decline. *Tourism Management, 30*(4), 512–521. doi:10.1016/j.tourman.2008.10.009

Dierickx, I., & Cool, K. (1989). Asset stock accumulation and sustainability of competitive advantage. *Management Science, 35*(12), 1504–1511. doi:10.1287/mnsc.35.12.1504

Dinnie, K., Melewar, T. C., Seidenfuss, K. U., & Musa, G. (2010). Nation branding and integrated marketing communications: An ASEAN perspective. *International Marketing Review, 27*(4), 388–403. doi:10.1108/02651331011058572

Dodd, O. A. (1997). An insight into the development and implementation of the international environmental management system ISO 14001. In R. Hillary (Ed.), *Environmental Management Systems and Cleaner Production*. Toronto, Canada: Wiley.

Dodds, R. (2012). Sustainable tourism: A hope or a necessity? The case of Tofino, British Columbia, Canada. *Journal of Sustainable Development, 5*(5), 54–64. doi:10.5539/jsd.v5n5p54

Domestic Statistic. (2010). *Trade and food services activity*. Taiwan: Department of Statistics, Ministry of Economic Affairs.

Donald, M. (1993). *Origins of the modern mind: Three Stages in the Evolution of Culture and Cognition*. Boston: Harvard University Press.

Donthu, N., & Yoo, B. (1998). Cultural influences on service quality expectations. *Journal of Service Research, 1*(2), 178–186. doi:10.1177/109467059800100207

Doran, D. M. (2003). *Nursing-Sensitive Outcomes: State of the Science*. Sudbury, MA: Jones and Bartlett.

Dotlich, D. L., & Noel, J. L. (1998). *Action learning: How the world's top companies are recreating their leaders and themselves*. San Francisco: Jossey-Bass.

Dowling, P., Schuler, R., & Welch, D. (1994). *International dimensions of human resources management* (2nd ed.). Belmont, CA: Wadsworth.

Dowling, P., & Welch, D. (1988). International human resource management: An Australian perspective. *Asia Pacific Journal of Management, 6*(1), 39–65. doi:10.1007/BF01732250

Doxey, G. (1975, 8-11 September). *A causation theory of visitor-resident irritants: Methodology and Research Inferences*. Paper presented at the Travel and Tourism Research Association Sixth Annual Conference, San Diego, California, U.S.A.

Dreachlin, J. L., Hunt, P. L., & Sprainer, E. (1999). Communication patterns and group composition: Implications for patient-centred care team effectiveness. *Journal of Healthcare Management, 44*(4), 252–268. PMID:10539199

Dreachslin, J. L. (2007). Diversity Management and Cultural Competence: Research, Practice, and the Business Case. *Journal of Healthcare Management, 52*(2), 79–86. PMID:17447535

Dritsakis, N. (2008). Immigration and Economic Growth: Further Evidence for Greece. *Applied Economics and Policy Analysis, 2*(1), 207–213.

Drucker, P. F. (1954). *The Practice of Management*. New York: Harper and Row Publishers.

Dubé, L., & Renaghan, L. M. (2000). Creating visible customer value: How customers view best-practice champions. *The Cornell Hotel and Restaurant Administration Quarterly, 41*(1), 62–72. doi:10.1177/001088040004100124

Dubin, R., Champoux, J. E., & Porter, L. W. (1975). Central Life Interests and Organizational Commitment of Blue Collar and Clerical Workers. *Administrative Science Quarterly, 20*(3), 411–421. doi:10.2307/2392000

Duggan, M. S. (2013, Dec 30). *Social Media Update 2013*. Retrieved June 25, 2014 from Pew Internet Reserch: http://www.pewinternet.org/2013/12/30/social-media-update-2013/

Duncan, T. R. (2002). *IMC: Using advertising and promotion to build brands* (International Edition). New York, NY: The McGraw-Hill Companies, Inc.

Duncan, T. R., & Caywood, C. (1996). The concept, process, and evolution of integrated marketing communications. In E. Thorson & J. Moore (Eds.), *Integrated communication: Synergy of persuasive voices* (pp. 13–34). Mahwah, NJ: Lawrence Erlbaum Associates.

Duncan, T., & Moriarty, S. E. (1998). A communication-based marketing model for managing relationships. *Journal of Marketing, 62*(2), 1–13. doi:10.2307/1252157

Dunlap, R. E., Gallup, G. H. Jr, & Gallup, A. M. (1993). Of global concern: Results of the health of the planet survey. *Environment, 35*(9), 7–15, 33–40. doi:10.1080/00139157.1993.9929122

Du, S., Bhattacharya, C. B., & Sen, S. (2007). Reaping relational rewards from corporate social responsibility: The role of competitive positioning. *International Journal of Research in Marketing, 24*(3), 224–241. doi:10.1016/j.ijresmar.2007.01.001

Dussauge, P., & Garrette, B. (1995). Determinants of Success in International Strategic Alliances: Evidence from the Global Aerospace Industry. *Journal of International Business Studies, 26*(3), 505–530. doi:10.1057/palgrave.jibs.8490848

Dyer, J. H., & Singh, H. (1998). The relational view: Cooperative strategy and sources of interorganizational competitive advantage. *Academy of Management Review, 23*(4), 660–679.

Eade, J. (Ed.). (2003). *Living the global city: Globalization as local process.* Routledge.

Eagle, L., & Kitchen, P. J. (2000). IMC, brand communications, and corporate cultures. Client/advertising agency co-ordination and cohesion. *European Journal of Marketing, 34*(5/6), 667–686. doi:10.1108/03090560010321983

Eagle, L., Kitchen, P. J., & Bulmer, S. (2007). Insights into interpreting integrated marketing communications. A two-nation qualitative comparison. *European Journal of Marketing, 41*(7/8), 956–970. doi:10.1108/03090560710752474

Earley, P. C., & Ang, S. (2003). *Cultural intelligence: Individual interactions across cultures.* Palo Alto, CA: Stanford University Press.

EbizMBA. (2014, June). *Top 15 Most Popular Social Networking Sites | June 2014.* Retrieved June 25, 2014 from EbizMBA: http://www.ebizmba.com/articles/social-networking-websites

Echtner, C. M., & Ritchie, J. R. B. (1993). The measurement of destination image: An empirical assessment. *Journal of Travel Research, 31*(3), 3–13. doi:10.1177/004728759303100402

Echtner, C. M., & Ritchie, J. R. B. (2003). The meaning and measurement of destination image. *Journal of Tourism Studies, 14*(1), 37–48.

Edelman, J. B. (2007). *Distributed Influence: Quantifying the Impacts of Social Media.* Available at http://technobabble2dot0.files.wordpress.com/2008/01/edelman-white-paper-distributed-influence-quantifying-the-impact-of-social-media.pdf

Edgell, D. L., & Swanson, J. R. (2013). *Tourism policy and planning: yesterday, today and tomorrow* (2nd ed.). New York: Routledge.

Edmondson, A., & Moingeon, B. (1998). From organizational learning to the learning organization. *Management Learning, 29*(1), 5–20. doi:10.1177/1350507698291001

Edstrom, A., & Galbraith, J. R. (1977). Transfer of managers: A comparison of documentary and interpersonal methods. *Academy of Management Journal, 30*(4), 514–539.

Edwards, A. (2005). *The sustainability revolution.* Gabriola Island, BC, Canada: New Society.

Eisenberger, R., Huntington, R., Hutchinson, S., & Sowa, D. (1986). Perceived organizational support. *The Journal of Applied Psychology, 71*(3), 500–507. doi:10.1037/0021-9010.71.3.500

Eisenhardt, K. M., & Graebner, M. E. (2007). Theory Building from Cases: Opportunities and challenges. *Academy of Management Journal, 50*(1), 25–32. doi:10.5465/AMJ.2007.24160888

Ekeh, P. P. (1974). *Social exchange theory: The two traditions.* Cambridge, MA: Harvard University Press.

Ekinci, Y., Dawes, P., & Massey, G. (2008). An extended model of the antecedents and consequences of customer satisfaction for hospitality services. *European Journal of Marketing, 42*(1/2), 35–68. doi:10.1108/03090560810840907

Elanain, H. M. A. (2007, Summer). The Five-factor model of personality and organizational citizenship behavior in United Arab Emirates. *SAM Advanced Management Journal.*

Elis, S. (2009, February 15). Our rich 'food' heritage. *New Straits Times.*

Elliott, R., & Boshoff, C. (2008). The influence of business orientations in small tourism businesses on the success of integrated marketing communication. *Management Dynamics, 17*(4), 32–46.

Ely, R. J., & Thomas, D. A. (2001). Cultural diversity at work: The effects of diversity perspectives on work group processes and outcomes. *Administrative Science Quarterly, 46*(2), 229–273. doi:10.2307/2667087

Emerson, R. M. (1972). Exchange Theory: Part II: exchange relations and networks. In J. Berger, M. Zelditch, & B. Anderson (Eds.), Sociological theories in progress (vol. 2, pp. 58-87). Boston: Houghton Mifflin.

Emerson, R. M. (1976). Social exchange theory. *Annual Review of Sociology, 2*(1), 335–362. doi:10.1146/annurev.so.02.080176.002003

Engholm, C., & Rowland, D. (1996). *International excellence: Seven breakthrough strategies for personal and professional success.* New York, NY: Kodansha America.

Enloe, C. (2002). *Maneuvers: the international politics of militarising women's lives.* Los Angeles: University of California Press.

Enloe, C. (2014). *Bananas, beaches and bases: Making feminist sense of international politics.* London: Pandora.

Enz, C. A. (2010). *Hospitality strategic management: concepts and cases* (2nd ed.). New York, NY: Wileys.

Epitropaki, O., & Martin, R. (2004). Implicit leadership theories in applied settings: Factor structure, generalizability, and stability over time. *The Journal of Applied Psychology, 89*(2), 293–310. doi:10.1037/0021-9010.89.2.293 PMID:15065976

Erbacher, D., D'Netto, B., & Espana, J. (2006). Expatriate success in China: Impact of personal and situational factors. *The Journal of American Academy of Business, 9*(2), 183–188.

Ernestad V., H. R. (2010). *Social media marketing from a bottom-up perspective - the social media transition.* Retrieved March 28, 2014 from http://www.carphone-warehouse.com

Ernst & Young. (2014). Effectively implementing your tourism strategy. *Global Hospitality Insights: Top Thoughts for 2014.* Retrieved May 7, 2014, from http://www.ey.com/Publication/vwLUAssets/EY_-_Global_hospitality_insights_2014/$FILE/EY-Global-hospitality-insights-2014.pdf

Etlinger, S. (2011). *A Framework for Social Analytics: Six Use Cases for Social media Measurement.* Altimeter Group Publication.

Ettlie, J. E., Bridges, W. P., & O'Keefe, R. D. (1984). Organization strategy and structural differences for radical versus incremental innovation. *Management Science, 30*(6), 682–695. doi:10.1287/mnsc.30.6.682

Ettlie, J. E., & Subramaniam, M. (2004). Changing strategies and tactics for new product development. *Journal of Product Innovation Management, 21*(2), 95–109. doi:10.1111/j.0737-6782.2004.00060.x

Eugenio-Martin, J. L., Morales, N. M., & Scarpa, R. (2004). Tourism and Economic Growth in Latin American Countries: A Panel Data Approach. *Nota di Lavoro, 26.*

Euromonitor International. (2004). *Consumer food service industry in Malaysia.* Chicago, IL: Euromonitor International.

Euromonitor International. (2013). *World Travel Market Global Trend Report.* Retrieved from http://www.wtm-london.com/files/wtm_global_trends_2013.pdf

European Commission. (2003). *The costs and benefits of the costs and benefits of diversity. A study on methods and indicators a study on methods and indicators to measure the cost-effectiveness to measure the cost-effectiveness of diversity policies in enterprises of diversity policies in enterprises.* [Online]. Available at: http://ec.europa.eu/social/BlobServlet?docId=1440&langId=en (Accessed: 16 May 2014).

European Commission. (2010). *Small and medium sized enterprises- craft and micro enterprises.* Available at: http://ec.europa.eu/enterprise/policies/sme/promoting-entrepreneurship/crafts-micro-enterprises/

Evanschitzky, H., & Wunderlich, M. (2006). An examination of moderator effects in the four stage loyalty model. *Journal of Service Research, 8*(4), 330–340. doi:10.1177/1094670506286325

Evans, D. (2012). *Social Media Marketing* (2nd ed.). Indiana: Wiley Publshing.

Evans, M., Cossi, G., & D'Onghia, P. (2000). *World Food Italy*. London, UK: CA, Lonely Planet Publications Pty Ltd.

Evans, N. (2001). Collaborative strategy: An analysis of the changing world of international airline alliances. *Tourism Management*, *22*(3), 229–243. doi:10.1016/S0261-5177(01)00024-3

Fakeye, P. C., & Crompton, J. L. (1991). Image differences between prospective, first-time and repeat visitors to the Lower Rio Grande Valley. *Journal of Travel Research*, *30*(2), 10–16. doi:10.1177/004728759103000202

Fan, D., & Hsu, C. (2014). Potential mainland Chinese cruise travellers' expectations, motivations, and intentions. *Journal of Travel & Tourism Marketing*, *31*(4), 522–535. doi:10.1080/10548408.2014.883948

Fang, T. (2010). Asian management research needs more self-confidence: Reflection on Hofstede (2007) and beyond. *Asia Pacific Journal of Management*, *27*(1), 155–170. doi:10.1007/s10490-009-9134-7

Fan, T. P. C. (2009). Determinants of de novo new entrant survival in the liberalized intra-European scheduled passenger airline industry. *Transportation Research Part E, Logistics and Transportation Review*, *45*(2), 293–306. doi:10.1016/j.tre.2008.09.009

Farrell, A. M. (2010). Insufficient discriminant validity: A comment on Bove, Pervan, Beatty and Shiu (2009). *Journal of Business Research*, *63*(3), 324–327. doi:10.1016/j.jbusres.2009.05.003

Farrell, B., & Twining-Ward, L. (2005). Seven steps towards sustainability: Tourism in the context of new knowledge. *Journal of Sustainable Tourism*, *13*(2), 109–122. doi:10.1080/09669580508668481

Faulkner, B. (2002). Rejuvenating the Gold Coast. *Current Issues in Tourism*, *5*, 472–520. doi:10.1080/13683500208667938

Faulkner, B., & Tideswell, C. (1997). A framework for monitoring community impacts of tourism. *Journal of Sustainable Tourism*, *5*(1), 3–28. doi:10.1080/09669589708667273

Federalberghi. (2010). *Report about the Italian hotel system*. Available at http://www.federalberghicatania.it/allegati/allegato%20circ125.pdf

Federalberghi. (2010). *Sesto rapporto sul sistema alberghiero in Italia 2010*. Roma: Edizioni Ista.

Federalberghi. (2013a). *Relazione sull'attività di Federalberghi nell'anno 2012*. Roma: Edizioni Ista.

Federalberghi. (2013b). *Datatour 2013: Trend e statistiche sull'economia del turismo*. Roma: Edizioni Ista.

Feltenstein, T. (1986). New-product development in food service: A structured approach. *The Cornell Hotel and Restaurant Administration Quarterly*, *27*(3), 63–71. doi:10.1177/001088048602700314

Feng, F., & Pearson, T. E. (1999). Hotel expatriate managers in China: Selection criteria, important skills and knowledge, repatriation concerns, and causes of failure. *Hospital Management*, *18*(3), 309–321. doi:10.1016/S0278-4319(99)00031-6

Feng, R., & Cai, L. A. (2013). Information Search Behavior and Tourist Characteristics: The Internet vis-à-vis. Other Information Sources. In J. E. Mills & R. Law (Eds.), *Handbook of Consumer Behavior Tourism and the Internet*. Routledge.

Ferrari, S., & Adamo, G.E. (2011). Autenticità e risorse locali come attrattive turistiche: il caso della Calabria. *Sinergie rivista di studi e ricerche*, *5*(66), 79-112.

Fesenmaier D.R., Leppers A.W., & O'Leary J.T. (1999). Developing a Knowledge-Based Tourism Marketing Information System. *Information Technology and Tourism, 2*(1).

Field, A. (2005). *Discovering statistics using SPSS: and sex, drugs and rock 'n' roll* (2nd ed.). London: Sage.

Fiji Bureau of Statistics. (2011, October18). 2012.). *Fiji National Census of Population, 2007*, 2014.

Fiji Bureau of Statistics. (2014). Visitor Arrivals: Number by country of residence, 2014

Fiol, M. C., & Lyles, M. A. (1985). Organizational learning. *Academy of Management Review*, *10*(4), 803–813.

Fish, A. (1999). Selecting managers for cross-border assignments: Building value into process. *International Journal of Management Reviews, 1*(4), 461–483. doi:10.1111/1468-2370.00023

Fisher, G. B., & Hartel, I. Z. (2003). Cross-cultural effectiveness of western expatriate-Thai client interactions: Lessons learned for IHRM research and theory. *Cross Cultural Management, 10*(4), 4–28. doi:10.1108/13527600310797667

Fisher, R., McPhail, R., & Menghetti, G. (2010). Linking employee attitudes and behaviors with business performance: A comparative analysis of hotels in Mexico and China. *International Journal of Hospitality Management, 29*(3), 397–404. doi:10.1016/j.ijhm.2009.10.021

Fish, M. (1984). Controlling sex sales to tourists: Commenting on Graburn and Cohen. *Annals of Tourism Research, 11*(4), 615–617. doi:10.1016/0160-7383(84)90055-0

Fitchett, J. A. (2004). The fantasies, orders and roles of sadistic consumption: Game shows and the service encounter. *Consumption Markets & Culture, 7*(4), 285–306. doi:10.1080/1025386042000316298

Fitzpatrick, K. R. (2005). The legal challenge of integrated marketing communication (IMC): Integrating commercial and political speech. *Journal of Advertising, 34*(4), 93–102. doi:10.1080/00913367.2005.10639205

Flores-Fillol, R. (2010). Congested Hubs. *Transportation Research: Part B: Methodological, 44*(3), 358-370. doi: http://www.elsevier.com/wps/find/journaldescription.cws_home/548/description#description

Food and Tourism is Interrelated. (2009, December 19). *Nan Yang Press*, pp. A12.

Ford, R. C., & Richardson, W. D. (1994). Ethical decision making: A review of the empirical Literature. *Journal of Business Ethics, 13*(3), 205–221. doi:10.1007/BF02074820

Fornell, C., & Larcker, D. F. (1981). Evaluating structural equation models with unobservable variables and measurement error. *JMR, Journal of Marketing Research, 18*(1), 39–50. doi:10.2307/3151312

Forster, N. (1997). The persistent myth of high expatriate failure rates: A reappraisal. *International Journal of Human Resource Management, 8*(4), 414–433. doi:10.1080/095851997341531

Forster, N. (2000). Expatriates and the impact of cross-cultural training. *Human Resource Management Journal, 10*(3), 63–78. doi:10.1111/j.1748-8583.2000.tb00027.x

Foss, N. J. (1996). Knowledge-based approaches to the theory of the firm: Some critical comments. *Organization Science, 7*(5), 470–476. doi:10.1287/orsc.7.5.470

Foster, S. (2014). *Spa business trends in Asia and their impact on the global spa industry.* Bangkok, Thailand: Destination Spa Management Ltd. Retrieved June 30, 2014, from http://www.itb-kongress.de/media/itbk/itbk_media/itbk_pdf/praesentationen_2014/ wellness_forum/Spa_Business_Trends_in_Asia-ITB-2014.pdf

Foxall, G. (1990). *Consumer Psychology in Behavioural Perspective.* New York: Rutledge.

Fox, R. (2007). Reinventing the gastronomic identity of Croatian tourist destinations. *Hospital Management, 26*(3), 546–559. doi:10.1016/j.ijhm.2006.03.001

Franco, M., & Estevao, C. (2010). The role of tourism public-private partnerships in regional development: a conceptual model proposal. *Cadernos EBAPE.Br, 8*(4), 600-612.

Franek, M., & Vecera, J. (2008). Personal characteristics and job satisfaction. *E+M Ekonomie A Management, 4*, 63-75.

Freeman, R. E., Pierce, J., & Dodd, R. (2000). *Environmentalism and the new logic of business: How firms can be profitable and leave our children a living planet.* New York, NY: Oxford University Press.

Friedmann, R., & Lessig, V. P. (1986). A framework of psychological meaning of products. *Advances in Consumer Research. Association for Consumer Research (U. S.), 13*(1), 338–342.

Frith, S. W. (1981). *The expatriate dilemma.* Chicago, IL: Nelson-Hall, Inc.

Fuller, W. G. (1994). *New food product development from concept to the market place.* Boca Rotan, FL: CRC Press.

554

Fung, A. (2002). Women's magazines: Construction of identities and cultural consumption in Hong Kong. *Consumption Markets & Culture, 5*(4), 321–336. doi:10.1080/1025386022000001460

Furnham, A. (1990). Expatriate stress: The problems of living abroad. In S. Fisher & C. Cooper (Eds.), *On the move: The psychology of change and transition* (pp. 236–254). Chichester, UK: John Wiley & Sons.

Furrer, O., Liu, B. S.-C., & Sudharshan, D. (2000). The relationships between culture and service quality perceptions: Basis for cross-cultural market segmentation and resource allocation. *Journal of Service Research, 2*(4), 355–371. doi:10.1177/109467050024004

Gale, D. (2009). *World's largest hotel companies: Corporate 300 chart*. Retrieved from, March 11, 2014, http://www.hotelsmag.com/index.asp?layout=articlePrint&articleID=CA6667503&article_prefix=CA&article_id=6667503

Gallaghar, D. R., Andrews, R. N. L., Chandracai, A., & Rohitratana, K. (2004). Environmental Management System in US and Thailand. *Greener Management International, 46*(46), 41–56. doi:10.9774/GLEAF.3062.2004.su.00006

Gallagher, D. G., & McLean Parks, J. (2001). I pledge thee my troth contingently. Commitment and the contingent work relationship. *Human Resource Management Review, 11*(3), 181–208. doi:10.1016/S1053-4822(00)00048-6

Gallarza, M. G., Saura, I. G., & García, H. C. (2002). Destination image: Towards a conceptual framework. *Annals of Tourism Research, 29*(1), 56–78. doi:10.1016/S0160-7383(01)00031-7

Gallego, M. S., Ledesma-Rodriguez, F. J., & Perez- Rodriguez, J. V. (2007). *On the Impact of Exchange Rate Regimes on Tourism*. Retrieved from: http://www.aeefi.com/RePEc/pdf/defi07-07-final

Galloway, G., Mitchell, R., Getz, D., Crouch, G., & Ong, B. (2008). Sensation seeking and the prediction of attitudes and behaviors of wine tourists. *Tourism Management, 29*(5), 950–966. doi:10.1016/j.tourman.2007.11.006

García de los Salmones, M. M., Herrero, A., & Rodríguez del Bosque, I. (2005). Influence of corporate social responsibility on loyalty and valuation of services. *Journal of Business Ethics, 61*(4), 369–385. doi:10.1007/s10551-005-5841-2

Gardberg, N. A., & Fombrun, C. J. (2006). Corporate citizenship: Creating intangible assets across institutional environments. *Academy of Management Review, 31*(2), 329–346. doi:10.5465/AMR.2006.20208684

Garonzik, R., Brockner, J., & Siegel, P. A. (2000). Identifying international assignees at risk for premature departure: The interactive effect of outcome favorability and procedural fairness. *The Journal of Applied Psychology, 85*(1), 13–20. doi:10.1037/0021-9010.85.1.13 PMID:10740952

Gartner, W. (2004). Rural tourism development in the USA. *International Journal of Tourism Research, 6*(3), 151–164. doi:10.1002/jtr.481

Gartner, W. C. (1993). Image formation process. *Journal of Travel & Tourism Marketing, 2*(2/3), 191–215.

Gartner, W. C. (1996). *Tourism development: Principles, processes, and policies*. New York: Van Nostram Reinhold.

Garvin, D. A. (1993). Building learning organizations. *Harvard Business Review, 71*, 78–91. PMID:10127041

Garvin, D. A., Edmondson, A. C., & Gino, F. (2008). Is yours a learning organization? *Harvard Business Review*, 1–11. PMID:18411968

Gayle, P. G. (2008). An empirical analysis of the competitive effects of the Delta/Continental/Northwest codeshare alliance. *The Journal of Law & Economics, 51*(4), 743–775. doi:10.1086/595865

Geber, B. (1992). The care and breeding of global managers. *Training (New York, N.Y.), 29*(7), 32–37.

Geels, F. W., & Kemp, R. (2007). Dynamics in sociotechnical systems: Typology of change processes and contrasting case studies. *Technology in Society, 29*(4), 441–455. doi:10.1016/j.techsoc.2007.08.009

George, J. M., & Brief, A. P. (1992). Feeling good-doing good: A conceptual analysis of the mood at work organizational spontaneity relationship. *Psychological Bulletin, 112*(2), 310–329. doi:10.1037/0033-2909.112.2.310 PMID:1454897

Gernet, J. (1962). Daily Life in China on the Eve of the Mongol Invasion. Stanford, CA: Stanford University Press.

Geron, T. (2013). Airbnb and the unstoppable rise of the share economy. *Forbes, 11*(Feb). Retrieved from http://www.forbes.com/sites/tomiogeron/2013/01/23/airbnb-and-the-unstoppable-rise-of-the-share-economy/

Gerstner, C. R., & Day, D. V. (1994). Cross-cultural comparison of leadership prototypes. *The Leadership Quarterly, 5*(2), 121–134. doi:10.1016/1048-9843(94)90024-8

Gertsen, M. (1990). Intercultural competence and expatriates. *International Journal of Human Resource Management, 1*(3), 341–362. doi:10.1080/09585199000000054

Getz, D. (2008). Event tourism: Definition, evolution, and research. *Tourism Management, 29*(3), 403–428. doi:10.1016/j.tourman.2007.07.017

Getz, D., & Brown, G. (2006). Critical success factors for wine tourism regions: A demand analysis. *Tourism Management, 27*(1), 146–158. doi:10.1016/j.tourman.2004.08.002

Ghafoor, S., Khan, U. F., Idrees, F., Javed, B., & Ahmed, F. (2011). Evaluation of expatriates performance and their training on international assignments. *Interdisciplinary Journal of Contemporary Research in Business, September, 3*(5), 335-351.

Gibson, H. (1998). Sport tourism: A critical analysis of research. *Sport Management Review, 1*(1), 45–76. doi:10.1016/S1441-3523(98)70099-3

Gilbert, D., & Tsao, J. (2000). Exploring Chinese cultural influences and hospitality marketing relationships. *International Journal of Contemporary Hospitality Management, 12*(1), 45–53. doi:10.1108/09596110010305037

Gillen, D., Harris, R., & Oum, T. (2002). Measuring the economic effects of bilateral liberalization air transport. *Transportation Research Part E, Logistics and Transportation Review, 38*(3–4), 155–174. doi:10.1016/S1366-5545(02)00003-0

Gilmore, J. H., & Pine, I. I. J. (2007). *Authenticity*. Boston, MA: Harvard Business Press.

Gilmore, J. H., & Pine, I. I. J. II. (2002). Customer experience places: The new offering frontier. *Strategy and Leadership, 30*(4), 4–11. doi:10.1108/10878570210435306

Gimeno, J. (2004). Competition within and between Networks: The Contingent Effect of Competitive Embeddedness on Alliance Formation. *Academy of Management Journal, 47*(6), 820–842. doi:10.2307/20159625

*Gino's Pasta.* (2009). Retrieved December 17, 2009 from www.gino.com.cn

Ginsberg, A., & Venkatraman, N. (1985). Contingency Perspectives of Organizational Strategy: A Critical Review of the Empirical Research. *Academy of Management Review, 10*(3), 421–434. doi:10.2307/258125

Giordana, F. (2004). *La comunicazione del turismo tra immagine, immaginario e immaginazione, 42*. Milano: Franco Angeli.

Gittinger, T., & Fisher, A. (2004). LBJ champions the Civil Rights Act of 1964. *Prologue-Quarterly Of The National Archives And Records Administration, 36*(2), 10–19.

Glaser, B., & Strauss, A. (1967). *The discovery of grounded theory*. Chicago: Aldine.

Glaser, R., & Weiss, A. M. (1993). Marketing in turbulence environments: Decision processes and the time-sensitivity of information. *JMR, Journal of Marketing Research, 30*(4), 431–453.

Gliatis, N. (1992). *The management of expatriate executives in international hotel companies*. Doctoral dissertation. University of Surrey, Guildford.

Gnoth, J. (2002). Leveraging export brands through a tourism destination brand. *Journal of Brand Management, 9*(4/5), 262–280. doi:10.1057/palgrave.bm.2540077

Goetze, D. (1994). Comparing prisoner's dilemma, commons dilemma, and public goods. provision in the laboratory. *The Journal of Conflict Resolution, 38*(1), 56–86. doi:10.1177/0022002794038001004

Goffman, E. (1955). On facework. *Psychiatry, 18*, 213–231. PMID:13254953

Goldner, C. R., & Ritchie, J. R. B. (2011). *Tourism: Principles, practices, philosophies* (12th ed.). New York: Wiley.

Gong, Y. (2003). Subsidiary staffing in multinational enterprises: Agency, resources and performance. *Academy of Management Journal, 46*(4), 728–739.

Gonzalez, J. V., & Garazo, T. G. (2006). Structural relationships between organizational service orientation, contact employee job satisfaction and citizenship behavior. *International Journal of Service Industry Management, 17*(1), 23–50. doi:10.1108/09564230610651561

González, M. E. A., Comesaña, L. R., & Brea, J. A. F. (2007). Assessing tourist behavioral intentions through perceived service quality and customer satisfaction. *Journal of Business Research, 60*(2), 153–160. doi:10.1016/j.jbusres.2006.10.014

Goodall, B. (1990). How tourists choose their holidays: An analytical framework. In B. Goodall & G. Ashworth (Eds.), *Marketing in the tourism industry: The promotion of destination regions* (pp. 1–17). London: Routledge.

Goodman, A. (2000). Implementing sustainability in service operations at Scandic Hotels. *Interfaces, 30*(3), 202–214. doi:10.1287/inte.30.3.202.11653

Goss-Turner, S. (1996). The accommodation sector. In P. Jones (Ed.), *Introduction to Hospitality Operations* (pp. 21–35). London: Cassell.

Gouldner, A. W. (1960). The norm of reciprocity: A preliminary statement. *American Sociological Review, 25*(2), 161–178. doi:10.2307/2092623

Gould, S. J. (2004). IMC as theory and as a poststructural set of practices and discourses: A continuously evolving paradigm shift. *Journal of Advertising Research, 44*(1), 66–70. doi:10.1017/S002184990404019X

Government of Lesotho. (2012). *Growth and Development Strategic Framework "Towards an accelerated and sustainable economic and social transformation*, pp. 88-91. Retrieved May 7, 2014, from http://www.gov.ls/documents/NSDP%20FINAL%20PRINT%20VERSION%2013%2001%202013[1].pdf

Graen, G. (1976). Role-making processes within complex organizations. In M. D. Dunnette (Ed.), *Handbook of Industrial/Organizational Psychology* (pp. 1210–1259). Chicago: Rand McNally.

Graf, E., & Saguy, S. L. (1991). *Food product development from concept to the market place*. London, UK: Chapman and Hull.

Graf, N. (2009). Stock market reactions to entry mode choices of multinational hotel firms. *International Journal of Hospitality Management, 28*(2), 236–244. doi:10.1016/j.ijhm.2008.08.002

Graham, J. W. (1989). *Organizational Citizenship Behavior: Construct redefinition, operationalization, and validation.* Unpublished working paper, Loyola University of Chicago.

Graham, J. W. (1986). Principled organizational dissent: A theoretical essay. In B. M. Staw & L. L. Cummings (Eds.), *Research in organizational behavior* (Vol. 8, pp. 1–52). Greenwich, CT: JAI Press.

Graham, J. W. (1991). An essay on organizational citizenship behavior. *Employee Responsibilities and Rights Journal, 4*(4), 249–270. doi:10.1007/BF01385031

Grandey, A. A. (2003). When the show must go on: Surface acting and deep acting as determinants of emotional exhaustion and peer-rated service delivery. *Academy of Management Journal, 46*(1), 86–96. doi:10.2307/30040678

Grant, M. (2014). The road to health and wellness tourism: Trends and prospects across the globe. *The Pulse of the Montana State Nurses' Association, 24*(3), 26–31.

Grant, R. M. (1996). Toward a Knowledge-Based Theory of the firm. *Strategic Management Journal, 17*(S2), 109–122. doi:10.1002/smj.4250171110

Grbich, C. (2013). *Qualitative data analysis: An introduction* (2nd ed.). Thousand Oaks, CA: Sage Publication Ltd.

Grest, V. (2004). Mass customization: Consumer trends drive menu innovation at top 400 chains. *Restaurants & Institutions, 112*(15), 26–38.

Gretzel, U. (2011). Intelligent systems in tourism: A social science perspective. *Annals of Tourism Research, 38*(3), 757–779. doi:10.1016/j.annals.2011.04.014

Griffeth, R. W., & Hom, P. W. (2001). *Retaining valued employees*. Thousand Oaks, CA: Sage Publications Inc.

Griffin, R. W. (2005). *Management* (8th ed.). New York: Houghton Mifflin Company.

Gross, M. J., & Brown, G. (2008). An empirical structural model of tourists and places: Progressing involvement and place attachment into tourism. *Tourism Management*, *29*(6), 1141–1151. doi:10.1016/j.tourman.2008.02.009

Gudmundsson, S. V., & Rhoades, D. L. (2001). Airline alliance survival analysis: Typology, strategy and duration. *Transport Policy*, *8*(3), 209–218. doi:10.1016/S0967-070X(01)00016-6

Guerrero, L., Guardia, M. D., Xicola, J., Verbeke, W., Vanhonacker, F., & Zakowska, B. S. (2009). Consumer-driven definition of traditional food products and innovation in traditional foods. A qualitative cross-cultural study. *Appetite*, *52*(2), 345–354. doi:10.1016/j.appet.2008.11.008

Guerrier, Y. (1999). *Organizational behavior in hotels and restaurants: An international perspective*. Chichester, England: Wiley.

Gulati, R. (2007). *Managing network resources: alliances, affiliations and other relational assets*. Oxford: Oxford University Press.

Gunelius, S. (2011). *30 Minute Social Media Marketing*. Ontario: McGraw Hill.

Gurău, C. (2008). Integrated online marketing communication: Implementation and management. *Journal of Communication Management*, *12*(2), 169–184. doi:10.1108/13632540810881974

Gursoy, D., & McCleary, K. W. (2004). An integrative model of tourists' information search behavior. *Annals of Tourism Research*, *31*(2), 353–373. doi:10.1016/j.annals.2003.12.004

Haber, S., & Lerner, M. (1998). Correlates of tourist satisfaction. *Annals of Tourism Research*, *25*(4), 197–201.

Ha, H. Y., Janda, S., & Muthaly, S. (2010). Development of brand equity: Evaluation of four alternative models. *Service Industries Journal*, *30*(6), 911–928. doi:10.1080/02642060802320253

Hair, J. F., Black, W. C., Babin, B. J., & Anderson, R. E. (2010). *Multivariate data analysis* (7th ed.). Englewood Cliffs, NJ: Prentice Hall.

Hair, J. F., Sarstedt, M., Ringle, C. M., & Mena, J. A. (2012). An assessment of the use of partial least squares structural equation modelling in marketing research. *Journal of the Academy of Marketing Science*, *40*(3), 414–433. doi:10.1007/s11747-011-0261-6

Hair, J.F., Hult, G.T., & Ringle, C.M. & Sarstedt. (2014). *A primer on partial least squares structural equation modeling (PLS-SEM)*. Thousand Oaks, CA. Sage (Atlanta, Ga.).

Hajir, K. (2012). *Your Social Media Marketing Plan*. Available at: http://yoursocialmediamarketingplan.com/

Hall, C. (2008). *Tourism planning: Policies, processes and relationships*. Prentice Hall.

Hall, E. (1966). *The hidden dimension*. New York, NY: Anchor Books.

Hall, E. T. (1966). *The hidden dimension: Man's use of space in public and private. London: Bodley Head. Hall, E. T. (1976). Beyond culture*. Garden City: Anchor Press/Doubleday.

Hall, E. T. (1976). *Beyond culture*. Garden City, New York: Doubleday.

Halligan, B., & Shah, D. (2010). Inbound Marketing. New Jersey: Wiley Publishing.

Hallin, C. A., & Marnburg, E. (2008). Knowledge management in the hospitality industry: A review of empirical research. *Tourism Management*, *29*(2), 366–381. doi:10.1016/j.tourman.2007.02.019

Halstead, D., Hartman, D., & Schmidt, L. S. (1994). Multi source effects on the satisfaction formation process. *Journal of the Academy of Marketing Science*, *22*(2), 114–129. doi:10.1177/0092070394222002

Hamel, G., & Prahalad, C. K. (1994). *Competing for the Future*. Boston: Harvard Business School Press.

Hamill, J. (1993). Competitive strategies in the world airline industry. *European Management Journal*, *11*(3), 332–341. doi:10.1016/0263-2373(93)90059-Q

Handy, L., & Barham, K. (1990). International management development in the 1990's. *Journal of European Industrial Training*, *14*(6), 28–31.

Han, H., & Back, K. (2008). Relationships among image congruence, consumption emotions, and customer loyalty in the lodging industry. *Journal of Hospitality & Tourism Research (Washington, D.C.)*, *32*(4), 467–490. doi:10.1177/1096348008321666

Han, H., Kimb, Y., & Kima, E. (2011). Cognitive, affective, conative, and action loyalty: Testing the impact of inertia. *International Journal of Hospitality Management*, *30*(4), 1108–1119. doi:10.1016/j.ijhm.2011.03.006

Hankinson, G. (2004). Relational network brands: Towards a conceptual model of place brands. *Journal of Vacation Marketing*, *10*(2), 109–121. doi:10.1177/135676670401000202

Hankinson, G. (2005). Destination brand images: A business tourism perspective. *Journal of Services Marketing*, *19*(1), 24–32. doi:10.1108/08876040510579361

Hannam, R., & Jimmieson, N. (2002). *The relationship between extra-role behaviors and job burnout for primary school teachers: A Preliminary model and development of an OCB scale*. Retrieved 19 September 2007 from http://www.aare.edu.au/02pap/han02173.htm

Hanna, R., Rohm, A., & Crittenden, V. L. (2011). *We're all connected: The power of the social media ecosystem Kelley School of Business, 54* (pp. 265–273). Elsevier.

Hannum, A. B. (2002). Sex tourism in Latin America. *ReVista: Harvard Review of Latin America*. Winter. Retrieved March 25, 2014 from http://revista.drclas.harvard.edu/book/sex-tourism-latin-america

Harnett, M. (2005). Exotic tastes becoming favorites. *Frozen Food Age*, *53*(8), 24–28.

Harris, M., & Ross, E. B. (1987). *Food and Evolution: Toward a Theory of Human Food Habits*. Temple University Press.

Harrison, D. A., Price, K. H., Gavin, J. H., & Florey, A. T. (2002). Time, teams, and task performance: Changing effects of surface-and deep-level diversity on group functioning. *Academy of Management Journal*, *45*(5), 1029–1045. doi:10.2307/3069328

Harrison, D. A., & Sin, H. S. (2006). What is diversity and how should it be measured? In A. M. Konrad, P. Prasad, & J. K. Pringle (Eds.), *Handbook of workplace diversity* (pp. 191–216). Newbury Park, CA: Sage Publications. doi:10.4135/9781848608092.n9

Harrison, J. K. (1994). Developing successful expatriate managers: A framework for the structural design and strategic alignment of cross-cultural training programs. *Human Resource Planning*, *17*(3), 17–35.

Harris, W., & Moran, R. (1996). *Managing cultural differences: Leadership strategies for a new world* (4th ed.). Houston, TX: Gulf Publishing.

Hartley, B., & Pickton, D. (1999). Integrated marketing communications requires a new way of thinking. *Journal of Marketing Communications*, *5*(2), 97–106. doi:10.1080/135272699345699

Hart, P. M., Wearing, A. J., Conn, M., Carter, N. L., & Dingle, R. K. (2000). Development of the school organizational health questionnaire: A measure for assessing teacher morale and school organizational climate. *Brain Education Psychology*, *70*, 211–228. PMID:10900779

Harvey, M. (1997). Focusing the international personnel performance appraisal process. *Human Resource Development Quarterly*, *8*(1), 41–62. doi:10.1002/hrdq.3920080106

Harvey, M., & Novicevic, M. M. (2002). The hyper-competitive global marketplace: The importance of intuition and creativity in expatriate managers. *Journal of World Business*, *37*(2), 127–138. doi:10.1016/S1090-9516(02)00072-X

Harzing, A. W. K. (1995). The persistent myth of high expatriate failure rates. *International Journal of Human Resource Management*, *6*(2), 457–475. doi:10.1080/09585199500000028

Harzing, A. W. K. (2002). Are our referencing errors undermining our scholarship and credibility? The case of expatriate failure rates. *Journal of Organizational Behavior*, *23*(1), 127–148. doi:10.1002/job.125

Hashimoto, K. (2003). Product life cycle theory: A quantitative application for casino courses in higher education. *International Journal of Hospitality Management*, *22*(2), 177–195. doi:10.1016/S0278-4319(03)00017-3

Hassin, O., & Shy, O. (2004). Code-sharing agreements and interconnections in markets for international flights. *Review of International Economics, 12*(3), 337–352. doi:10.1111/j.1467-9396.2004.00453.x

Hayes, D. K., & Ninemeier, J. D. (2009). *Study Guide To Accompany Human Resources Management in the Hospitality Industry*. New Jersey: John Wiley & Sons.

Hazari, B. R., & Sgro, P. M. (1995). Tourism and growth in a dynamic model of trade. *The Journal of International Trade & Economic Development, 4*(2), 143–252.

Heames, J. T., & Harvey, M. (2006). The evolution of the concept of the executive from the 20th century managers to the 21st century global leader. *Journal of Leadership & Organizational Studies, 13*(2), 20–41.

Heckathorn, D. (1993). Collective action and group heterogeneity: Voluntary provision versus selective incentives. *American Sociological Review, 58*(3), 329–350. doi:10.2307/2095904

He, H., & Li, Y. (2011). CSR and service brand: The mediating effect of brand identification and moderating effect of service quality. *Journal of Business Ethics, 100*(4), 673–688. doi:10.1007/s10551-010-0703-y

Heikkurinen, P. (2010). Image differentiation with corporate environmental responsibility. *Corporate Social Responsibility and Environmental Management, 17*(3), 142–152. doi:10.1002/csr.225

Hein, W. (1997). *Tourism and Sustainable Development*. Hamburg.

Helm, S., Eggert, A., & Garnefeld, I. (2010). Modeling the impact of corporate reputation on customer satisfaction and loyalty using partial least squares. In Vinzi V.E, Chin, W.W., Henseler, J., & Wang, H. (Eds.). Handbook of partial least squares. Concepts, methods and applications in marketing and related fields (pp. 515-534). New York, NY: Springer. doi:10.1007/978-3-540-32827-8_23

Henderson, J. C. (2009). Food tourism reviewed. *British Food Journal, 111*(4), 317–326. doi:10.1108/00070700910951470

Hendricks, J. (2010). *The 21st Century Media Industry*. Lexington Books.

Hendry, C. (1994). *Human resource strategies for international growth*. London: Routledge.

He, Y., Lai, K. K., & Lu, Y. (2011). Linking organizational support to employee commitment: Evidence from hotel industry of China. *International Journal of Human Resource Management, 22*(1), 197–217. doi:10.1080/09585192.2011.538983

Heylighen, F. (1999). Collective intelligence and its implementation on the web: Algorithms to develop a collective mental map. *Computational & Mathematical Organization Theory, 5*(3), 253–280. doi:10.1023/A:1009690407292

Heylighen, F. (2007). Why is open access development so successful? Stigmergic organization and the economics of Information. In B. Lutterbeck, M. Bärwolff, & R. A. Gehring (Eds.), *Open source*. Lehmanns Media.

Hicks-Clarke, D., & Iles, P. (2000). Climate for diversity and its effects on career and organisational attitudes and perceptions. *Personnel Review, 29*(3), 324–345. doi:10.1108/00483480010324689

Higgins-Desbiolles, F. (2006). More than an "industry": The forgotten power of tourism as a social force. *Tourism Management, 27*(6), 1192–1208. doi:10.1016/j.tourman.2005.05.020

Higley, C. J., Leveque, F., & Convery, F. (2001). Environmental Voluntary Approaches: Research Insights for policy - makers.

Hilson, G., & Nayee, V. (2002). Environmental management system implementation in the mining industry: A key to achieving cleaner production. *International Journal of Mineral Processing, 64*(1), 19–41. doi:10.1016/S0301-7516(01)00071-0

Hilton Hotel and Resorts Blue Paper. (2012). *Emerging global spa trends*. Retrieved May 22, 2014, from http://news.hilton.com

Hinch, T., & Higham, J. (2011). *Sport tourism development* (2nd ed.). Channel View Publications.

Hinkin, T. R., & Tracey, J. B. (2000). The cost of turnover: Putting a price on the learning curve. *The Cornell Hotel and Restaurant Administration Quarterly, 41*(3), 14–21. doi:10.1177/001088040004100313

Hipple, S. (1998). Contingent work: Results from the second survey. *Monthly Labor Review, 121*(11), 22–35.

Hirschman, A. O. (1970). *Exit, voice, and loyalty: Responses to decline in firms, organizations, and states.* Cambridge, MA: Harvard University Press.

Hjalager, A. (1997). Innovation patterns in sustainable tourism: An analytical typology. *Tourism Management, 18*(1), 35–41. doi:10.1016/S0261-5177(96)00096-9

Hjalager, A. M. (2007). Stages in the economic globalization of tourism. *Annals of Tourism Research, 34*(2), 437–457. doi:10.1016/j.annals.2006.10.006

Hjalager, A.-M., & Corigliano, M. A. (2000). Food for tourists - determinants of an image. *International Journal of Tourism Research, 2*(4), 281–293. doi:10.1002/1522-1970(200007/08)2:4<281::AID-JTR228>3.0.CO;2-Y

Hoare, R. J., & Butcher, K. (2008). Do Chinese cultural values affect customer satisfaction/loyalty? *International Journal of Contemporary Hospitality Management, 20*(2), 156–171. doi:10.1108/09596110810852140

Hoffman, D. L., & Fodor, M. (2010). Can you measure the ROI of your social media marketing? *MIT Sloan Management Review, 52*(1), 41–49.

Hoffmann, T. (1999). The meanings of competency. *Journal of European Industrial Training, 23*(6), 275–285. doi:10.1108/03090599910284650

Hofstede, G. (1997). The Archimedes effect. Working at the interface of cultures: 18 lives in social science (pp.47-61). M.H. Bond. London: Routledge.

Hofstede, G. 2009. *Geert Hofstede Cultural Dimensions.* Retrieved July 14, 2009 from http://www.geert-hofstede.com/hofstede_dimensions.php

Hofstede, G. (1980). *Culture's consequences: International differences in work related values.* Beverly Hills, CA: Sage.

Hofstede, G. (1980). Motivation, leadership, and organization: Do American theories apply abroad? *Organizational Dynamics, 9*(1), 42–63. doi:10.1016/0090-2616(80)90013-3

Hofstede, G. (1991). *Cultures and organizations: software of the mind.* London: McGraw-Hill.

Hofstede, G. (1997). *Culture and organizations: Software of the mind.* New York: The McGraw Hill Companies, Inc.

Hofstede, G. (2001). *Culture's consequences: Comparing values, behaviors, institutions, and organisations across nations.* CA: Sage Publications.

Hofstede, G., & Bond, M. (1984). Hofstede's cultural dimensions: An independent validation using Rokeach's value survey. *Journal of Cross-Cultural Psychology, 15*(4), 417–433. doi:10.1177/0022002184015004003

Hogan, G. W., & Goodson, J. R. (1990). The key to expatriate success: An analysis of overseas managerial assignments. *Training and Development Journal, 44*(1), 50–52.

Holbrook, M. B. (1978). Beyond attitude structure: Toward the informational determinants of attitude. *JMR, Journal of Marketing Research, 15*(4), 545–556. doi:10.2307/3150624

Holling, C. S. (Ed.). (1978). *Adaptive environmental assessment and management.* Chichester, UK: Wiley.

Hollows, J., & Lewis, J. (1995). Managing human resources in the Chinese context: The experience of a major multinational. In H. Davis (Ed.), *China business: Context and issues* (pp. 269–285). Hong Kong: Longman.

Holm, O. (2006). Integrated marketing communication: From tactics to strategy. *Corporate Communications: An International Journal, 11*(1), 23–33. doi:10.1108/13563280610643525

Homans, G. (1958). *Social Exchange Theory.* Retrieved from http://www.fsc.yorku.ca/york/istheory/wiki/index.php/Social_exchange_theory

Homans, G. (1961). *Social behavior: Its elementary forms.* New York: Harcourt, Brace & World.

Homans, G. (1964). Bringing men back in. *American Sociological Review, 29*(6), 809–818. doi:10.2307/2090864

Hom, P. W., & Kinicki, A. J. (2001, October). Toward a greater understanding of how dissatisfaction drives employee turnover. *Academy of Management Journal, 4,* 277–286.

Honeck, D. (2011). ´Expect the Unexpected´? LDC GATS Commitments as Internationally Credible Policy Indicators? The Example of Mali., *WTO Staff Working Paper*, ERSD-2011-07. Retrieved May 7, 2014, from http://www.wto.org/english/res_e/reser_e/ersd201107_e.pdf, International Union for Conservation of Nature website. Retrieved May 7, 2014, from http://data.iucn.org/dbtw-wpd/html/tourism/section7.html

Hooley, G. J., Greenley, G. E., Cadogan, J. W., & Fahy, J. (2005). The performance impact of marketing resources. *Journal of Business Research*, *58*(1), 18–27. doi:10.1016/S0148-2963(03)00109-7

Horwitz, S. K. (2005). The compositional impact of team diversity on performance: Theoretical consideration. *Human Resource Development Review*, *4*(2), 219–245. doi:10.1177/1534484305275847

Hotelexpo. (2011). *The 20th Shanghai International Hospitality Equipment and Supply Expo*. Retrieved December 17, 2009 from http://www.hotelex.cn/

Houdre, H. (2008). Sustainable Development in the Hotel Industry. *Cornell Industry Perspectives*, *2*, 5–20.

House, R. J., Hanges, P. J., Ruiz-Quintanilla, S. A., Dorfman, P. W., Javidan, M., Dickson, M., & Gupta, V. (1999). Cultural influences on leadership and organizations. In W. F. Mobley, M. J. Gessner, & V. Arnold (Eds.), *Advances in global leadership* (Vol. 1, pp. 171–233). Stanford, CT: JAI Press.

Ho, Z. J. Y. (2012). What makes hotel expatriates remain in their overseas assignments: A grounded theory study. *Qualitative Report*, *17*(51), 1–22.

Hsieh, A. T., & Chang, J. (2005). The different response to hotels' endorsement advertising by Taiwanese and American tourists. *Journal of Travel & Tourism Marketing*, *19*(4), 41–54. doi:10.1300/J073v19n04_04

Hsieh, A. T., & Tsai, C. W. (2009). Does national culture really matter? Hotel service perceptions by Taiwan and American tourists. *International Journal of Culture. Tourism and Hospitality Research*, *3*(1), 54–69.

Hsieh, S. C., Lin, J. S., & Lee, H. C. (2012). Analysis on literature review of competency. *International Review of Business and Economics*, *2*, 25–50.

Hsu, C. H. C., Oh, H., & Assaf, A. G. (2012). A customer-based brand equity model for upscale hotels. *Journal of Travel Research*, *51*(1), 81–93. doi:10.1177/0047287510394195

Hsu, C. H., & Huang, S. S. (2008). Travel motivation: a critical review of the concept's development. In A. G. Woodside & A. Martin (Eds.), *Tourism Management: Analysis, behaviour and strategy* (pp. 14–27). Wallingford: CABI. doi:10.1079/9781845933234.0014

Hsu, T. H., Hung, L. C., & Tang, J. W. (2012). An analytical model for building brand equity in hospitality firms. *Annals of Operations Research*, *195*(1), 355–378. doi:10.1007/s10479-011-0990-4

Huang, S.-L., Wong, J.-H., & Chen, T.-C. (1998). A framework of indicator system for measuring Taipei's urban sustainability. *Landscape and Urban Planning*, *42*(1), 15–27. doi:10.1016/S0169-2046(98)00054-1

Huang, T., Chi, S., & Lawler, S. J. (2005). The relationship between expatriates' personality traits and their adjustment to international assignments. *International Journal of Human Resource Management*, *16*(9), 16–56. doi:10.1080/09585190500239325

Hudson, S. (2008). *Marketing for tourism and hospitality. A global perspective* (2nd ed.). London, UK: Sage. doi:10.4135/9781446280140

Hui, M. K., & Au, K. (2001). Justice Perceptions of Complaints-Handling: A Cross-Cultural Comparison between PRC and Canadian Customers. *Journal of Business Research*, *52*(2), 161–173. doi:10.1016/S0148-2963(99)00068-5

Huliyeti, H., Marchesini, S., & Canavari, M. (2008). Chinese distribution practitioners' Attitudes towards Italian quality foods. *Journal of Chinese Economic and Foreign Trade Studies*, *1*(3), 214–231. doi:10.1108/17544400810912374

Hulland, J. (1999). Use of partial least squares (PLS) in strategic management research: A review of four recent studies. *Strategic Management Journal*, *20*(2), 195–204. doi:10.1002/(SICI)1097-0266(199902)20:2<195::AID-SMJ13>3.0.CO;2-7

Hult, G. T. M., & Ketchen, D. J. Jr. (2001). Does Market Orientation Matter?: A Test of the Relationship between Positional Advantage and Performance. *Strategic Management Journal*, 22(9), 899–906. doi:10.1002/smj.197

Hume, M. (2008). Understanding core and peripheral service quality in customer repurchase of the performing arts. *Managing Service Quality*, 18(4), 349–369. doi:10.1108/09604520810885608

Hunt, J. D. (1975). Image as a factor in tourism development. *Journal of Travel Research*, 13(3), 1–7. doi:10.1177/004728757501300301

Hunt, J. G. (1991). *The leadership: A new synthesis*. Newbury Park, CA: Sage Publications.

Hurn, B. J. (2006). The selection of international business managers: Part 1. *Industrial and Commercial Training*, 38(6), 279–286. doi:10.1108/00197850610685581

Hur, W. M., Kim, Y., & Park, K. (2013). Assessing the effects of perceived value and satisfaction on customer loyalty: A "Green" Perspective. *Corporate Social Responsibility and Environmental Management*, 20(3), 146–156. doi:10.1002/csr.1280

Husbands, W. (1989). Social status and perception of tourism in Zambia. *Annals of Tourism Research*, 16(2), 237–253. doi:10.1016/0160-7383(89)90070-4

Hutton, W. (2005). *Authentic Recipes from Malaysia*. Singapore: Periplus Edition.

Hu, X., Caldentey, R., & Vulcano, G. (2013). Revenue sharing in airline alliances. *Management Science*, 59(5), 1177–1195. doi:10.1287/mnsc.1120.1591

Hwang, K. K. (1987). Face and favor: The Chinese power game. *American Journal of Sociology*, 92(4), 944–974. doi:10.1086/228588

Hwang, K.-K. (1998). Guanxi and Mientze: Conflict resolution in Chinese society. *Intercultural Communication Studies*, 7(1), 17–39.

Hwang, L.-J. J., van Westering, J., & Chen, H.-H. (2004). Exploration of the linkages between gastronomy and heritage of Tainan City, Taiwan. In J. Chen (Ed.), *Advances in Hospitality and Leisure* (Vol. 1, pp. 223–235). Bingley, West Yorkshire: Emerald Group Publishing Limited. doi:10.1016/S1745-3542(04)01015-X

Hyun, S. S., & Kim, W. (2011). Dimensions of brand equity in the chain restaurant industry. *Cornell Hospitality Quarterly*, 52(4), 429–437. doi:10.1177/1938965510397533

Iacobucci, D., & Duhachek, A. (2003). Mediation analysis. Paper presented at the round table at the *Association for Consumer Research Conference (ACR)*, Toronto, Canada.

Iansiti, M. (1995). Shooting the rapids: Managing product development in turbulent environment. *California Management Review*, 38(1), 37–58. doi:10.2307/41165820

Ilies, R., Nahrgang, J. D., & Morgeson, F. P. (2007). Leader-member exchange and citizenship behaviors: A meta-analysis. *The Journal of Applied Psychology*, 92(1), 269–277. doi:10.1037/0021-9010.92.1.269 PMID:17227168

IMF. (2013). *World Economic Outlook: a survey by the staff of the International Monetary Fund*. International Monetary Fund Publications Services.

Imrie, R., & Fyall, A. (2000). Customer retention and loyalty in the independent mid-market hotel sector. *Journal of Hospitality Marketing & Management*, 7(3), 39–54. doi:10.1300/J150v07n03_04

Inkpen, A. C. (1995). *The Management of International Joint Ventures: An Organizational Learning Perspective*. London: Routledge.

Institut Statistique de Polynesie Francaise. (2012). *Visitor arrivals*. Retrieved 05 July 2014, 2014, from http://www.ispf.pf/

Instituto de Estudios Turísticos (2011). Balance del Turismo. Año 2010.

Instituto Nacional de Estadística (2010). *España en cifras 2010*. Author.

Instituto Nacional de Estadística. (2011). *Encuesta de ocupación hotelera*. Retrieved June 20, 2013, from: http://www.ine.es/jaxi/menu.do?type=pcaxis&path=%2Ft11%2Fe162eoh&filenebase

563

International Labour Organization. (2010). Developments and challenges in the hospitality and tourism sector. *Issues paper for discussion at the Global Dialogue Forum for the Hotels, Catering, Tourism Sector.* Retrieved April 23, 2014, from http://www.ilo.org/wcmsp5/groups/public/---ed_dialogue/---sector/documents/meetingdocument/wcms_162202.pdf

International Spa Association (ISPA). (2014). *Spa industry reports.* Lexington, KY: ISPA.

*Invitalia.* (2014). Retrieved from http://www.invitalia.it/site/eng/home/investment-opportunities/tourism/what.html

Ioannou, L. (1995). Unnatural selection. *International Business, 8*(7), 53–57.

Islam, N. (2012). New age orientalism: Ayurvedic 'wellness and spa culture'. *Health Sociology Review, 21*(2), 220–231. doi:10.5172/hesr.2012.21.2.220

Ismert, M., & Petrick, F. (2004). Indicators and standards of quality related to contingent employment in the ski industry. *Journal of Travel Research, 43*(1), 46–56. doi:10.1177/0047287504265512

Iso-Ahola, S. E. (1982). Toward a social psychological theory of tourism motivation: A rejoinder. *Annals of Tourism Research, 9*(2), 256–262. doi:10.1016/0160-7383(82)90049-4

Israeli, A. A., Adler, N., Mehrez, A., & Sundali, J. A. (2000). Investigating the use of advertising for communicating a hotel's strategic assets. *Journal of Hospitality Marketing & Management, 7*(3), 23–37. doi:10.1300/J150v07n03_03

ISTAT. (2014). Capacity and occupancy of tourist accommodation establishments. *Short-term economic statistics.* Directorate of the Italian National Institute of Statistics. Retrieved May 25, 2015 from http://dati.istat.it/?lang=en

Istituto Nazionale di Statistica, I. S. T. A. T. (2008). *Italian Institute of Statistics.* Retrieved July 9, 2019 from www.istat.it

Istituto per il Commercio Estero ICE. (2010). *Italian Foreign Commerce Institute.* Retrieved May 10, 2010, from http://www.ice.it/paesi/asia/cina/index.htm

Italian National Institute of Statistics - Istat. (2014). *Viaggi e vacanze in Italia e all'estero (Travel and Vacations in Italy and abroad).* Available at http://www.istat.it/it/archivio/turismo

*Italian Trade Commission ITC.* (2009). Retrieved July 9, 2019 from http://www.ice.it/paesi/asia/cina/ufficio4.htm?sede

Ivanovic, Z., & Baldigara, T. (2007). Logistics processes in a tourism destination. *Tourism and Hospitality Management, 13,* 595–606.

Jack, D., & Stage, V. (2005). Success strategies for expats. *American Society for Training and Development, 59,* 48–54.

Jackson, G. A. M., & Weed, M. E. (2003). The sport tourism interrelationship. In B. Houlihan (Ed.), *Sport in society: A student introduction* (pp. 235–251). London: Sage.

Jackson, J. (2006). Developing regional tourism in China: The potential for activating business clusters in a socialist market economy. *Tourism Management, 27*(4), 695–706. doi:10.1016/j.tourman.2005.02.007

Jackson, S. E. (1996). The consequences of diversity in multidisciplinary work teams. In M. A. West (Ed.), *Handbook of Work Group Psychology* (pp. 53–76). Chichester, UK: Wiley.

Jacob, N. (2005). Cross-cultural investigations: Emerging concepts. *Journal of Organizational Change Management, 18*(5), 514–528. doi:10.1108/09534810510614986

Jalis, M. H., Zahari, M. S., Izzat, M., & Othman, Z. (2009). Western tourists' perception of Malaysian gastronomic products. *Asian Social Science, 5*(1), 25–36. doi:10.5539/ass.v5n1p25

Jamal, T. B., & Getz, D. (1995). Collaboration theory and community tourism planning. *Annals of Tourism Research, 22*(1), 186–204. doi:10.1016/0160-7383(94)00067-3

Jankowicz, A. D. (2000). *Business Research Projects* (3rd ed.). London: Thompson Learning.

Jashapara, A. (1993). The competitive learning organization: A quest for the Holy Grail. *Management Decision, 31*(8), 52–62. doi:10.1108/00251749310047160

Jashapara, A. (2003). Cognition, Culture and Competition: An Empirical Test of the Learning Organisation. *The Learning Organization*, *10*(1), 31–50. doi:10.1108/09696470310457487

Jaworski, B. J., & Kohli, A. K. (1993). Market Orientation: Antecedents and Consequences. *Journal of Marketing*, *57*(3), 53–70. doi:10.2307/1251854

Jaworski, B., Kohli, A. K., & Sahay, A. (2000). Market-Driven Versus Driving Markets. *Journal of the Academy of Marketing Science*, *28*(1), 45–54. doi:10.1177/0092070300281005

Jayawardena, C., & Haywood, K. M. (2003). International hotel managers and key Caribbean challenges. *International Journal of Contemporary Hospitability Management*, *15*(3), 195–198. doi:10.1108/09596110310470284

Jeffreys, S. (1998). Child versus adult prostitution: A false distinction. In S. Jeffreys (Ed.), *Fight against child sex tourism: Participants' speeches and contributions* (pp. 65–71). Brussels: European Commission.

Jenkins, O. H. (1999). Understanding and measuring tourist destination image. *International Journal of Tourism Research*, *1*(1), 1–15. doi:10.1002/(SICI)1522-1970(199901/02)1:1<1::AID-JTR143>3.0.CO;2-L

Jensen, O., & Korneliussen, T. (2002). Discriminating perceptions of a peripheral "Nordic Destination" among European tourists. *Tourism and Hospitality Research*, *3*(4), 319–330.

Jeong, S. (2004). Sharing information and cultivating knowledge in virtual setting: Increasing social capital in online community of tourism. *e-Review of Tourism Research*, *2*(3). Retrieved from http://ertr.tamu.edu/pdfs/a-64.pdf

Jia, W. (1997-8). Facework as a Chinese conflict-preventive mechanism- a cultural/discourse analysis. *Intercultural Communication Studies*, *7*, 43-58.

Jogaratnam, G., McCleary, K. W., Mena, M., & Yoo, J. J. (2005). An analysis of hospitality and tourism research: Institutional contributions. *Journal of Hospitality & Tourism Research (Washington, D.C.)*, *29*(3), 356–370. doi:10.1177/1096348005276929

Johannessen, J. A., Olsen, B., & Olaisen, J. (1997). Organizing for innovation. *Long Range Planning*, *30*(1), 96–109. doi:10.1016/S0024-6301(96)00101-X

Johnson, A. S., & Ashforth, E. B. (2008). Externalization of employment in a service environment: The role of organizational and customer identification. *Journal of Organizational Behavior*, *29*(3), 287–309. doi:10.1002/job.477

Johnson, C., & Vanetti, M. (2005). Locational strategies of international hotel chains. *Annals of Tourism Research*, *32*(4), 1077–1099. doi:10.1016/j.annals.2005.03.003

Johnson, E. M., & Redman, B. M. (2008). *Spa: a comprehensive introduction*. Lexington, Kentucky: International SPA Association Foundation and American Hotel and Lodging Educational Institute.

Johnson, P., Kikora, R., & Kantner, M. (1990). *TQM Team- Building and Problem Solving*. Southfield, MI: Perry Johnson, Inc.

Johnson, R. B., & Christensen, L. B. (2004). *Educational research: Quantitative, qualitative, and mixed approaches*. Boston: Allyn and Bacon.

Jones, M. L. (2007). *Hofstede- culturally questionable?* Retrieved March 3, 2014, from Http: http://ro.uow.edu.au/cgi/viewcontent.cgi?article=1389&context=comm papers

Jones, D. L., & McCleary, K. W. (2004). A model for assessing cultural impacts on inter- national buyer-seller relationships for key accounts of hotel companies. *Journal of Hospitality & Tourism Research (Washington, D.C.)*, *28*(4), 425–443. doi:10.1177/1096348004265026

Jones, D. L., & McCleary, K. W. (2007). Expectations of working relationships in inter- national buyer-seller relationships: Development of a relationship continuum scale. *Asia Pacific Journal of Tourism Research*, *12*(3), 181–202. doi:10.1080/10941660701416747

Jones, M. T. (2002). Globalization and organizational restructuring: A strategic perspective. *Thunderbird International Business Review*, *44*(3), 325–351. doi:10.1002/tie.10024

Jones, P. (1996). Managing hospitality innovation. *The Cornell Hotel and Restaurant Administration Quarterly, 37*(5), 86–95. doi:10.1177/001088049603700528

Jones, P. (1996). The hospitality industry. In P. Jones (Ed.), *Introduction to hospitality operations.* London: Cassell.

Jones, P., & Wan, L. (1992). Innovation in the UK food-service industry. *International Journal of Contemporary Hospitality Management, 4*(4), 1–3.

Jones, T. O., & Sasser, W. E. (1995). Why satisfied customers defect. *Harvard Business Review, 73*(6), 89–99.

Jorgensen, S. (1997). *Integration of Ecosystem Theories: A Pattern, 2nd.* London: Kluwer Academic Publisher. doi:10.1007/978-94-011-5748-3

Joshua-Gojer, A. E. (2012). Cross-cultural training and success versus failure of expatriates. *Learning and Performance Quarterly, 1*(2), 47–62.

Josiam, B.M., Foster, C.R., & Bahulkar, G. (2012). For Whom The Menu Informs: a Market Segmentation Approach to Nutritional Information on Restaurant Menus. *Tourismos: An International Multidisciplinary Journal of Tourism, 7*(2), 237-259.

Josiam, B. M., & Monteiro, P. A. (2004). Tandoori tastes: Perceptions of Indian restaurants in America. *International Journal of Contemporary Hospitality Management, 16*(1), 18–26. doi:10.1108/09596110410516525

Juvan, E., & Dolnicar, S. (2014). The attitude-behaviour gap in sustainable tourism. *Journal of Tourism Research, 48*, 76–95. doi:10.1016/j.annals.2014.05.012

Kabani, S., & Brogan, C. (2010). *The Zen of Social Media Marketing.* Dallas, TX: Barbell Books.

Kale, P., Dyer, J. H., & Singh, H. (2002). Alliance capability, stock market response, and long-term alliance success: The role of the alliance function. *Strategic Management Journal, 23*(8), 747–767. doi:10.1002/smj.248

Kale, S. H., & Weir, K. M. (1986). Marketing third world countries to the western traveller: The case of India. *Journal of Travel Research, 25*(2), 2–7. doi:10.1177/004728758602500201

Kalleberg, A. L., & Schmidt, K. (1996). Contingent Employment in Organizations: Part-Time, Temporary, and Subcontracting Relations. In A. L. Kalleberg, D. Knoke, P. Marsden, & J. L. Spaeth (Eds.), *Organizations in America; Analyzing Their Structures and Human Resource Practices* (pp. 253–275). Thousand Oaks, CA: Sage Publications.

Kandampully, J. A. (2003). *Services Management: the new paradigm in hospitality.* Prentice Hall.

Kandampully, J., & Hu, H. H. (2007). Do hoteliers need to manage image to retain loyal customers? *International Journal of Contemporary Hospitality Management, 19*(6), 435–443. doi:10.1108/09596110710775101

Kandampully, J., & Suhartanto, D. (2000). Customer loyalty in the hotel industry: The role of customer satisfaction and image. *International Journal of Contemporary Hospitality Management, 12*(6), 346–351. doi:10.1108/09596110010342559

Kandampully, J., & Suhartanto, D. (2003). The role of customer satisfaction and image in gaining customer loyalty in the hotel industry. *Journal of Hospitality Marketing & Management, 10*(1/2), 3–25. doi:10.1300/J150v10n01_02

Kaplan, A. M., & Haenlein, M. (2010). *'Users of the world, unite! The challenges and opportunities of Social Media', Kelley School of Business, 53* (pp. 59–68). Elsevier.

Kaplinsky, R. (2004). Spreading the gains from globalization: What can be learnt from value-chain analysis. *Problems of Economic Transition, 47*(2), 74–115.

Karatepe, O. E., Beirami, E., Bouzari, M., & Safavi, H. P. (2014). Does work engagement mediate the effects of challenge stressors on job outcomes? Evidence from the hotel industry. *International Journal of Hospitality Management, 36*, 14–22. doi:10.1016/j.ijhm.2013.08.003

Kasimu, A. B., Zaiton, S., & Hassan, H. (2012). Hotels involvement in sustainable tourism practices in Klang Valley, Malaysia. *International Journal of Economics and Management, 6*(1), 21–34.

Katz, D., & Kahn, R. L. (1978). *The social psychology of organizations.* New York: Wiley.

Kayaman, R., & Arasli, H. (2007). Customer based brand equity: Evidence from the hotel industry. *Managing Service Quality, 17*(1), 92–109. doi:10.1108/09604520710720692

Kaye, M., & Taylor, W. G. K. (1997). Expatriate failure: An interview. *International Journal of Management, 24*(3), 403–413.

Kealey, D. (1989). A study of cross-cultural effectiveness: Theoretical issues, practical applications. *International Journal of Intercultural Relations, 13*(3), 387–428. doi:10.1016/0147-1767(89)90019-9

Kearney, J., & Zuber-Skerritt, O. (2012). From learning organization to learning community sustainability through lifelong learning. *The Learning Organization, 19*(5), 400–413. doi:10.1108/09696471211239703

Kearney, M. (1995). The local and the global: The anthropology of globalization and transnationalism. *Annual Review of Anthropology, 24*(1), 547–565. doi:10.1146/annurev.an.24.100195.002555

Keillor, B. D., Hult, G. T. M., & Kandemir, D. (2004). A study of the service encounter in eight countries. *Journal of International Marketing, 12*(1), 9–35. doi:10.1509/jimk.12.1.9.25649

Keller, K. L. (1993). Conceptualizing, measuring, and managing customer-based brand equity. *Journal of Marketing, 57*(1), 1–22. doi:10.2307/1252054

Keller, K. L. (1996). Integrated marketing communications and brand equity. In J. Moore & E. Thorson (Eds.), *Integrated Marketing Communications* (pp. 103–132). Mahwah, NJ: Lawrence Erlbaum Associates.

Keller, K. L. (2003). *Strategic brand management: Building, measuring, and managing brand equity* (2nd ed.). Upper Saddle River, NJ: Prentice Hall.

Keller, K. L. (2009). Building strong brands in a modern marketing communications environment. *Journal of Marketing Communications, 15*(2/3), 139–155. doi:10.1080/13527260902757530

Kelly, I. (2002). Australian regional tourism handbook; industry solutions, 2002.

Kelly, C., & Smith, M. (2009). Holistic tourism: integrating body, mind, spirit. In R. Bushell & P. S. Sheldon (Eds.), *Wellness and tourism: Mind, body, spirit, place* (pp. 127–143). New York, NY: Cognizant Communication Corporation.

Khalilzadeh, J., Chiappa, G. D., Jafari, J., & Borujeni, H. Z. (2013). Methodological approaches to job satisfaction measurement in hospitality firms. *International Journal of Contemporary Hospitality Management, 25*(6), 865–882. doi:10.1108/IJCHM-05-2012-0067

Khare, P. (2012). *Social Media Marketing Elearing Kit for Dummies*. New Jersey: John Wiley and Sons.

Khor, N. J. K. (2006). Nonya flavors: A complete guide to Penang Straits Chinese cuisine. Kuala Lumpur: Star Publications (M) Berhad.

Kimbarovsky, R. (2009). *10 Small Business Social Media Marketing Tips*. Available at: http://mashable.com/2009/10/28/small-business-marketing/

Kim, H. B., & Kim, W. G. (2005). The relationship between brand equity and firms' performance in luxury hotels and restaurants. *Tourism Management, 26*(4), 549–560. doi:10.1016/j.tourman.2004.03.010

Kim, H. B., Kim, W. G., & An, J. A. (2003). The effect of customer-based brand equity on firms' financial performance. *Journal of Customer Marketing, 20*(4), 335–351. doi:10.1108/07363760310483694

Kim, I., Han, D., & Schultz, D. E. (2004). Understanding the diffusion of integrated marketing communication. *Journal of Advertising Research, 44*(1), 31–45. doi:10.1017/S0021849904040024

Kimms, A., & Cetiner, D. (2012). Approximate nucleolus-based revenue sharing in airline alliances. *European Journal of Operational Research, 220*(2), 510–521. doi:10.1016/j.ejor.2012.01.057

Kim, W. G., Jin-Sun, B., & Kim, H. J. (2008). Multidimensional customer-based brand equity and its consequences in midpriced hotels. *Journal of Hospitality & Tourism Research (Washington, D.C.), 32*(2), 235–254. doi:10.1177/1096348007313265

Kim, W. G., & Kim, H. B. (2004). Measuring customer-based restaurant brand equity: Investigating the relationship between brand equity and firms' performance. *The Cornell Hotel and Restaurant Administration Quarterly, 45*(2), 115–131. doi:10.1177/0010880404264507

Kim, Y. G., Eves, A., & Scarles, C. (2009). Building a model of local food consumption on trips and holidays: A grounded theory approach. *International Journal of Hospitality Management, 28*(3), 423–431. doi:10.1016/j.ijhm.2008.11.005

Kinlaw, D. (1991). *Developing Superior Work teams: building quality and the competitive edge*. Lexington, MA: Lexington Books.

Kinnear, T. C., & Taylor, J. R. (1996). *Marketing research: an applied approach* (5th ed.). Australia: McGraw-Hill.

Kirk, D. (1995). Environmental management in hotels. *International Journal of Contemporary Hospitality Management, 7*(6), 3–8. doi:10.1108/09596119510095325

Kirkman, B. L., Lowe, K. B., & Gibson, C. B. (2006). A quarter century of "Culture's Consequences": A review of empirical research incorporating Hofstede's cultural values framework. *Journal of International Business Studies, 37*(3), 285–320. doi:10.1057/palgrave.jibs.8400202

Kitchen, P. J., Brignell, J., Li, T., & Jones, G. S. (2004a). The emergence of IMC: A theoretical perspective. *Journal of Advertising Research, 44*(1), 19–30. doi:10.1017/S0021849904040048

Kitchen, P. J., & Schultz, D. E. (2009). IMC: New horizon/false dawn for a marketplace in turmoil? *Journal of Marketing Communications, 15*(2/3), 197–204. doi:10.1080/13527260903003793

Kitchen, P. J., Schultz, D. E., Kim, I., Han, D., & Li, T. (2004b). Will agencies ever "get" (or understand) IMC? *European Journal of Marketing, 38*(11/12), 1417–1436. doi:10.1108/03090560410560173

Kivela, J., & Crotts, J. C. (2006). Tourism and gastronomy: Gastronomy's influence on how tourists experience a destination. *Journal of Hospitality & Tourism Research (Washington, D.C.), 30*(3), 354–377. doi:10.1177/1096348006286797

Kliatchko, J. (2005). Towards a new definition of integrated marketing communications (IMC). *International Journal of Advertising, 24*(1), 7–34.

Kliatchko, J. (2008). Revisiting the IMC construct: A revised definition and four pillars. *International Journal of Advertising, 27*(1), 133–160.

Kliatchko, J. (2009). IMC 20 years after: A second look at IMC definitions. International. *Journal of Integrated Marketing Communications, 1*(2), 7–12.

Kline, R. B. (2005). *Principles and practice of structural equation modelling* (2nd ed.). New York, NY: The Guilford Press.

Kogut, B. (1989). The Stability of Joint Ventures: Reciprocity and Competitive Rivalry. *The Journal of Industrial Economics, 38*(2), 183–198. doi:10.2307/2098529

Kogut, B., Shan, W., & Walker, G. (1992). The make-or-cooperate decision in the context of an industry network. In N. Nohria & R. Eccles (Eds.), *Networks and Organizations: Structure, Form and Action* (pp. 348–365). Boston: Harvard Business School Press.

Ko, H. C., & Yang, M. L. (2011). The effects of cross-cultural training on expatriate assignments. *Intercultural Communication Studies, 20*(1), 158–174.

Kohli, A. K., & Jaworski, B. J. (1990). Market orientation: The construct, research propositions, and managerial implications. *Journal of Marketing, 54*(2), 1–18. doi:10.2307/1251866

Kolpan, S., Smith, B. H., & Weiss, M. A. (2001). Exploring Wine: The Culinary Institute of America's Complete Guide to Wines of the World. Wiley, John and Sons, Incorporated.

Konovsky, M. A., & Organ, D. W. (1996). Dispositional and contextual determinants of organizational citizenship behavior. *Journal of Organizational Behavior, 17*(3), 253–266. doi:10.1002/(SICI)1099-1379(199605)17:3<253::AID-JOB747>3.0.CO;2-Q

Korjala, V. (2012). *Cultural Diversity In Hospitality Management. How to improve cultural diversity workforce* (Bachelor's thesis). Turku University of Applied Science, Finland.

Kotler, P., & Armstrong, G. (1996). *Principles of marketing* (8th ed.). Englewood Cliffs, NJ: Prentice-Hall.

Kotler, P., & Armstrong, G. (1997). *Marketing: An introduction* (4th ed.). Upper Saddle River, NJ: Prentice-Hall.

Kotler, P., Bowen, J., & Makens, J. (2003). *Marketing for Hospitality and Tourism* (3rd ed.). Upper Saddle River, NJ: Pearson Education, Inc.

Kotlinski, W. (2004). The government's role in stimulating national tourism development: The case of Poland. In D. Hall (Ed.), *Tourism and transition: Governance, transformation and development* (pp. 65–72). Wallingford, CT: CABI. doi:10.1079/9780851997483.0065

Kotter, J. (2012). *The key to changing organizational culture*. Retrieved from http://www.forbes.com/johnkotter/2012/09/27/the-key-to-changing-organizational-culture/

Kowalski, R. M. (1996). Complaints and complaining: Functions, antecedents, and consequences. *Psychological Bulletin*, *119*(2), 179–196. doi:10.1037/0033-2909.119.2.179 PMID:8851274

Kozak, M. (2002). Destination benchmarking. *Annals of Tourism Research*, *29*(2), 497–519. doi:10.1016/S0160-7383(01)00072-X

Kozak, M., & Rimmington, M. (1998). Benchmarking: Destination attractiveness and small hospitality business performance. *International Journal of Contemporary Hospitality Management*, *10*(5), 184–188. doi:10.1108/09596119810227767

Kozak, M., & Rimmington, M. (2000). Tourist satisfaction with Mallorca, Spain, as an off-season holiday destination. *Journal of Travel Research*, *38*(3), 260–269. doi:10.1177/004728750003800308

Krakover, S. (2000). Partitioning contingent employment in the hospitality industry. *Tourism Management*, *21*(5), 461–471. doi:10.1016/S0261-5177(99)00101-6

Kravetz, D. J. (2008). *Building a job competency database: What the leaders do*. Retrieved from, February 26, 2014, http://www.kravetz.com/art2/art2pl.html

Kriegl, U. (2000). International hospitality management: Identifying important skills and effective training. *The Cornell Hotel and Restaurant Administration Quarterly*, *41*(2), 64–71. doi:10.1177/001088040004100218

Krishna, A. (2010). *Sensory marketing*. New York, NY: Routledge Taylor and Francis Group.

Kruger, S., Saayman, M., & Ellis, S. (2014). The influence of travel motives on visitor happiness attending a wedding expo. *Journal of Travel & Tourism Marketing*, *31*(5), 649–665. doi:10.1080/10548408.2014.883955

Ku, E. C. S., & Fan, Y. W. (2009). Knowledge sharing and customer relationship management in the travel service alliances. *Total Quality Management & Business Excellence*, *20*(12), 1407–1421. doi:10.1080/14783360903248880

Kulluvaara, C., & Tornberg, J. (2003). *Integrated marketing communication and tourism. A case study of Icehotel.* (Bachelor's thesis). Retrieved from http://epubl.ltu.se/1404-5508/2003/138/LTU-SHU-EX-03138-SE.pdf

Kyriakopoulos, K. (2011). Improvisation in product innovation: The contingent role of market information sources and memory types. *Organization Studies*, *32*(8), 1051–1078. doi:10.1177/0170840611410833

Lacey, R., & Kennett-Hensel, P. A. (2010). Longitudinal effects of corporate social responsibility on customer relationships. *Journal of Business Ethics*, *97*(4), 581–597. doi:10.1007/s10551-010-0526-x

Lacher, R. G., & Oh, C.-O. (2012). Is tourism a low-income industry? Evidence from three coastal regions. *Journal of Travel Research*, *51*(4), 464–472. doi:10.1177/0047287511426342

Ladhari, R. (2012). The lodging quality index: An independent assessment of validity and dimensions. *International Journal of Contemporary Hospitality Management*, *24*(4), 628–652. doi:10.1108/09596111211217914

Lai, K. (2006). *Learning from Chinese philosophies: Ethics of interdependent and contextualised self*. Hampshire: Ashgate.

Lambin, J. J. (2000). *Market-Driven Management*. London: McMillan Business.

Lambin, J. J. (2007). La nuova complessità del mercato globale. In S. M. Brondoni (Ed.), *Market-Driven Management concorrenza e mercati globali* (pp. 65–86). Torino: Giappichelli.

Landau, R. (1991). How competitiveness can be achieved: fostering economic growth and productivity. In R. Landau (Ed.), *Technology and economics: papers commemorating Ralph Landau's service to the National Academy of Engineering*. Washington: National Academy Press.

Landor's top 10 brand trends for 2014. (2014, January). *Marketing News*, p. 4.

Larsen, G. R., & Guiver, J. W. (2013). Understanding tourists' perceptions of distance: A key to reducing the environmental impacts of tourism mobility. *Journal of Sustainable Tourism, 21*(7), 968–981. doi:10.1080/096 69582.2013.819878

Laser, S. A. (1980). winter). Dealing with the problem of employee turnover. *Human Resource Management, 19*(4), 17–21. doi:10.1002/hrm.3930190404 PMID:10250668

Lashley, C. (2001). *Empowerment: HR strategies for service excellence*. Oxford: Butterworth-Heinemann.

Lassiter, J. E. (2000). African culture and personality: Bad social science, effective social activism, or a call to reinvent ethnology. *African Studies Quarterly, 3*(3), 1–20.

Latkova, P., & Vogt, C. A. (2012). Residents' attitudes towards existing and future tourism development in rural communities. *Journal of Travel Research, 51*(1), 50–67. doi:10.1177/0047287510394193

Lavie, D. (2008). Network Resources: Toward a New Social Network Perspective. *Academy of Management Review, 33*(2), 546–550. doi:10.5465/AMR.2008.31193585

Law, R., Leung, D., & Cheung, C. (2012). A Systematic Review, Analysis, and Evaluation of Research Articles in the *Cornell Hospitality Quarterly*. *Cornell Hospitality Quarterly, 5*(4), 365–382. doi:10.1177/1938965512457458

Lawrence, L., Andrews, D., Ralph, B., & France, C. (2002). Identifying and assessing environmental impacts: Investigating ISO 14001 approaches. *The TQM Magazine, 14*(1), 43–50. doi:10.1108/09544780210413237

Laws, E., Richins, H., Agrusa, J. F., & Scott, N. (2011). *Tourist Destination Governance: Practice, Theory and Issues*. CABI International Publishing. doi:10.1079/9781845937942.0000

Lazzarini, S. (2007). The impact of membership in competing alliance constellations: Evidence on the operational performance of global airlines. *Strategic Management Journal, 28*(4), 345–368. doi:10.1002/smj.587

Lee, C. K., Yoon, Y. S., & Lee, S. K. (2007). Investigating the relationships among perceived value, satisfaction, and recommendations: The case of the Korean DMZ. *Tourism Management, 28*(1), 204–214. doi:10.1016/j.tourman.2005.12.017

Lee, C., Lee, Y., & Lee, B. (2005). Korea's destination image formed by the 2002 world cup. *Annals of Tourism Research, 32*(4), 839–858. doi:10.1016/j.annals.2004.11.006

Lee, D. H., & Park, C. W. (2007). Conceptualization and measurement of multidimensionality of integrated marketing communications. *Journal of Advertising Research, 47*(3), 222–236. doi:10.2501/S0021849907070274

Lee, D. Y., & Dawes, P. L. (2005). Guanxi, trust and long-term in orientations in Chinese business markets. *Journal of International Marketing, 13*(2), 30–56. doi:10.1509/jimk.13.2.28.64860

Lee, D.-J., Pae, J. H., & Wong, Y. H. (2001). A model of close business relationships in China (Guanxi). *European Journal of Marketing, 35*(1/2), 51–69. doi:10.1108/03090560110363346

Lee, F. (2004). *If Disney ran your hospital: 9 1/2 things you would do differently*. Bozeman, MT: Second River Healthcare Press.

Lee, H. M., Lee, C. C., & Wu, C. C. (2011). Brand image strategy affects brand equity after M&A. *European Journal of Marketing, 45*(7/8), 1091–1111. doi:10.1108/03090561111137624

Lee, H. W. (2007). Factors that influence expatriate failure: An interview study. *International Journal of Management, 24*(3), 403–414.

Lee, J. W., & Kim, H. B. (2009). Impacts of perception to alliance companies on hotel's brand equity according to the types of vertical integration. *International Journal of Tourism Sciences, 9*(2), 1–21. doi:10.1080/15980634 .2009.11434611

Lee, K. F. (2001). Sustainable tourism destinations: The importance of cleaner production. *Journal of Cleaner Production, 9*(4), 313–323. doi:10.1016/S0959-6526(00)00071-8

Lee, S., Jeon, S., & Kim, D. (2011). The impact of tour quality and tourist satisfaction on tourist loyalty: The case of Chinese tourists in Korea. *Tourism Management, 32*(5), 1115–1124. doi:10.1016/j.tourman.2010.09.016

Leonardi, M. H., Huysman, M., & Steinfield, C. (2013). Enterprise Social Media: Definition, History, and Prospects for the Study of Social Technologies in Organizations. *Journal of Computer-Mediated Communication, 19*(1), 1–19. doi:10.1111/jcc4.12029

Leotta, N. (2005). *Approcci visuali di turismo urbano: il tempo del viaggio, il tempo dello sguardo.* Milano: Hoepli.

LePine, J. A., Erez, A., & Johnson, D. E. (2002). The nature and dimensionality of organizational citizenship behavior: A critical review and meta-analysis. *The Journal of Applied Psychology, 87*(1), 52–65. doi:10.1037/0021-9010.87.1.52 PMID:11916216

LePine, J. A., & Van Dyne, L. (1998). Predicting voice behavior in work groups. *The Journal of Applied Psychology, 83*(6), 853–868. doi:10.1037/0021-9010.83.6.853

Lesotho Department of Research and Development. (2011). *Arrival Statistical Report.* Maseru.

Lesotho Tourism Development Corporation website. Retrieved May 7, 2014, from, http://www.ltdc.org.ls/organisation.php

*Lesotho Tourism Development Corporation.* (2011). Maseru: Lesotho Accommodation Statistics.

Lesotho's Ministry of Finance and Development Planning. (2010). *Lesotho Statistical Yearbook,* Maseru. Retrieved April 23, 2014, from http://liportal.giz.de/fileadmin/user_upload/oeffentlich/Lesotho/10_ueberblick/Statistical_Yearbook_2010.pdf

Levinthal, D. A., & March, J. G. (1993). The myopia of learning. *Strategic Management Journal, 14*(S2), 95–112. doi:10.1002/smj.4250141009

Lewis, B. (2005). Send the right people to the right places. *People Management, 12,* 85.

Lewis-Cameron, A., & Roberts, S. (2010). *Marketing Island Destinations: Concepts and Cases.* London, UK: Elsevier.

Li, L. (1995). *Antecedents and consequences of expatriate satisfaction: An empirical investigation of hotel managers in Pacific Asian countries.* (Doctoral dissertation). Virginia Polytechnic Institute and State University, USA.

Lichtenthaler, U. (2009). Absorptive capacity, environmental turbulence, and the complementarity of organizational learning processes. *Academy of Management Journal, 52*(4), 822–846. doi:10.5465/AMJ.2009.43670902

Li, I. (1996). Predictions of expatriate hotel manager satisfaction in Asian Pacific countries. *International Journal of Hospitality Management, 15*(4), 363–372. doi:10.1016/S0278-4319(96)00038-2

Lim, S. T., & Lee, J. S. (2006). Host population perceptions of the impact of mega-events. *Asia Pacific Journal of Tourism Research, 11*(4), 407–421. doi:10.1080/10941660600931259

Lin, C. Y., Lu, T. C., & Lin, H. W. (2012). A different perspective of expatriate management. *Human Resource Management Review, 22*(3), 189–207. doi:10.1016/j.hrmr.2012.02.003

Lin, I. Y. (2010). The interactive effect of Gestalt situations and arousal seeking tendency on customers' emotional responses: Matching color and music to specific servicescapes. *Journal of Services Marketing, 24*(4), 294–304. doi:10.1108/08876041011053006

Lin, I. Y., & Worthley, R. (2012). Servicescape moderation on personality traits, emotions, satisfaction, and behaviors. *International Journal of Hospitality Management, 31*(1), 31–42. doi:10.1016/j.ijhm.2011.05.009

Lin, M. H. (2008). Airline alliances and entry deterrence. *Transportation Research Part E, Logistics and Transportation Review, 44*(4), 637–652. doi:10.1016/j.tre.2007.05.003

Littarell, L. N., Salas, E., Hess, K. P., Paley, M., & Riedel, S. (2006). Expatriate preparation: A critical analysis of 25 years of cross-cultural training research. *Human Resource Development Review, 3*(3), 355–388. doi:10.1177/1534484306290106

Littrell, L. N., & Salas, E. (2005). A review of cross-cultural training: Best practices, guidelines, and research needs. *Human Resource Development Review, 4*(3), 305–334. doi:10.1177/1534484305278348

Litvin, S. W., Goldsmith, R. E., & Pan, B. (2008). Electronic word-of-mouth in hospitality and tourism management. *Tourism Management, 29*(3), 458–468. doi:10.1016/j.tourman.2007.05.011

Liu, B. S.-C., Furrer, O., & Sudharshan, D. (2001). The relationships between culture and behavioral intentions toward services. *Journal of Service Research*, *4*(2), 118–129. doi:10.1177/109467050142004

Li, Z.-C., Lam, W. H. K., Wong, S. C., & Fu, X. (2010). Optimal route allocation in a liberalizing airline market. *Transportation Research Part B: Methodological*, *44*(7), 886–902. doi:10.1016/j.trb.2009.12.013

Lockwood, A., & Jones, P. (1989). Creating positive service encounters. *The Cornell Hotel and Restaurant Administration Quarterly*, *29*(4), 44–50. doi:10.1177/001088048902900411

Lockwood, A., & Medlik, S. (2001). *Tourism and Hospitality in the 21ˢᵗ Century*. Oxford: Elsevier.

Lockyer, T., & Tsai, M. (2004). Dimensions of Chinese culture values in relation to the hotel dining experience. *Journal of Hospitality and Tourism Management*, *11*(1), 13–29.

Lodahl, T. M., & Kejner, M. (1965). The definition and measurement of job involvement. *The Journal of Applied Psychology*, *49*(1), 24–33. doi:10.1037/h0021692 PMID:14279757

Loermans, J. (2002). Synergizing the learning organization and knowledge management. *Journal of Knowledge Management*, *6*(3), 285–294. doi:10.1108/13673270210434386

Loh, M. (2008). The spa industry in Asia. In M. Cohen & G. Bodeker (Eds.), *Understanding the global spa industry: Spa management* (pp. 41–52). New York, NY: Routledge. doi:10.1016/B978-0-7506-8464-4.00003-5

Lohmöller, J. B. (1989). *Latent variable path modeling with partial least squares*. Heidelberg, Germany: Physica-Verlag. doi:10.1007/978-3-642-52512-4

Lomax, S. (2001). *Best practices for managers and expatriates: A guide on selection, hiring, and compensation*. New York, NY: Wiley.

Lord, R. G., Brown, D. J., Harvey, J. L., & Hall, R. J. (2001). Contextual constraints on prototype generation and their multilevel consequences for leadership perceptions. *The Leadership Quarterly*, *12*(3), 311–338. doi:10.1016/S1048-9843(01)00081-9

Loureiro, S., Dias, I. M., & Reijnders, L. (2012). The effect of corporate social responsibility on consumer satisfaction and perceived value: The case of the automobile industry sector in Portugal. *Journal of Cleaner Production*, *37*, 172–178. doi:10.1016/j.jclepro.2012.07.003

Lovett, J. (2011). *Social Media Metrics Secrets*. Indianapolis: John Wiley and Sons.

Low, G. S. (2000). Correlates of integrated marketing communications. *Journal of Advertising Research*, *40*(3), 27–39.

Lucia, A. D., & Lepsinger, R. (1999). *The art and science of competency models: Pinpointing critical success factors in organizations*. San Francisco, CA: Jossey-Bass.

Luo, X., & Bhattacharya, C. B. (2006). Corporate social responsibility, customer satisfaction and market value. *Journal of Marketing*, *70*(4), 1–18. doi:10.1509/jmkg.70.4.1

Luo, Y. (2007). A coopetition perspective of global competition. *Journal of World Business*, *42*(2), 129–144. doi:10.1016/j.jwb.2006.08.007

Maccioni, S. (2002) Pasta primavera, Le Cirque 2000. New York, NY.

MacFie, H. (1994). Computer assisted product development. *World of Ingredient*, *8*, 45–49.

MacKenzie, S. B., Podsakoff, P. M., & Podsakoff, N. P. (2011). Construct measurement and validation procedures in MIS and behavioral research: Integrating new and existing techniques. *Management Information Systems Quarterly*, *35*(2), 293–334.

Madhavaram, S., Badrinarayanan, V., & McDonald, R. E. (2005). Integrated marketing communication (IMC) and brand identity as critical components of brand equity strategy: A conceptual framework and research propositions. *Journal of Advertising*, *34*(4), 69–80. doi:10.1080/00913367.2005.10639213

Magazine, D. (2008 November 19). *Roof of Africa Rally*. Ezilon Maps website. Retrieved July 17, 2013, from http://www.ezilon.com/maps/africa/lesotho-maps.html

Maggi, B. (2003). *De l'agir organisationnel. Un point de vue sur le travail, le bien-etre, l'apprentissage*. Toulouse: Octarès Editions.

Magner, N., Welker, R., & Johnson, G. (1996). The interactive effects of participation and outcome favorability in performance appraisal on turnover intentions and evaluations of supervisors. *Journal of Occupational and Organizational Psychology*, *69*, 135–143. doi:10.1111/j.2044-8325.1996.tb00605.x

Magnini, V. P. (2009). The influence of national culture on the strategic use of salesperson pricing authority: A cross-country study within the hotel industry. *International Journal of Hospitality Management*, *28*(1), 173–176. doi:10.1016/j.ijhm.2008.06.002

Magnini, V. P., & Noneycutt, E. D. Jr. (2003). Learning orientation and the hotel expatriate manager experience. *International Journal of Hospitality Management*, *22*(3), 267–280. doi:10.1016/S0278-4319(03)00023-9

Maignan, I., Ferrell, O. C., & Ferrell, L. (2005). A stakeholder model for implementing social responsibility in marketing. *European Journal of Marketing*, *39*(9/10), 956–977. doi:10.1108/03090560510610662

Mak, A. H. N., Wong, K. F., & Chang, R. C. Y. (2009). Health or self-indulgence? The motivations and characteristics of spa-goers. *International Journal of Tourism Research*, *11*(2), 185–199. doi:10.1002/jtr.703

Mak, B. (2008). The future of the state-owned hotels in China: Stay or go? *International Journal of Hospitality Management*, *27*(3), 355–367. doi:10.1016/j.ijhm.2007.10.003

Mak, B., & Go, F. (1995). Matching global competition: Cooperation among Asian airlines. *Tourism Management*, *16*(1), 61–65. doi:10.1016/0261-5177(94)00008-X

Malaysian Tourism Promotional Board. (2009). *Best Country Brand: Malaysia, Top 10 Value-For-Money Destinations*. Retrieved from Tourism Malaysia website: http://corporate.tourism.gov.my/mediacentre.asp?page=news_desk&news_id=393&subpags=archive

Malhotra, N. K. (1996). *Marketing research: An applied orientation*. Upper Saddle River, NJ: Prentice Hall.

Malhotra, N. K., Ulgado, F. M., Agarwal, J., & Lan Wu, S. (2005). Dimensions of service quality in developed and developing economies: Multi-country cross-cultural comparisons. *International Marketing Review*, *22*(3), 256–278. doi:10.1108/02651330510602204

Malik, M. E., & Naeem, B. (2011). Interrelationship between customer based brand equity constructs: Empirical evidence from hotel industry of Pakistan. Interdisciplinary. *Journal of Contemporary Research in Business*, *3*(4), 795–804.

Malinowski, B. (1939/1944). The functional theory. In *A scientific theory of culture and other essays*. Chapel Hill, NC: University of North Carolina Press.

Man, A.-P., Roijakkers, N., & Graauw, H. (2010). Managing dynamics through robust alliance governance structures: The case of KLM and Northwest Airlines. *European Management Journal*, *28*(3), 171–181. doi:10.1016/j.emj.2009.11.001

Manacap-Johnson, M. (2014, May). A snapshot of spa destinations across the globe. *The Pulse of the Montana State Nurses' Association*, 36–40.

Manacap-Johnson, M., & Menrisky, A. (2014, May). Medical spa: Leading tourists at the crossroads between medical spa and wellness. *The Pulse of the Montana State Nurses' Association*, 32–34.

Manap KhairulHilmi, A. A. N. (2013). *The Role of User Generated Content (UGC) in Social Media for Tourism Sector*. Retrieved March 28, 2014 from http://www.westeastinstitute.com/wp-content/uploads/2013/07/Khairul-Hilmi-A-Manap.pdf

Manap, K. A. (2013). The Role of User Generated Content (UGC) in Social Media for Tourism Sector. *International Academic Conference Proceedings*, 11-78.

Manderson, L. (1981). Traditional food beliefs and critical life events in Peninsular Malaysia. *Social Sciences Information. Information Sur les Sciences Sociales*, *20*(6), 947–975. doi:10.1177/053901848102000606

Mandhachitara, R., & Lockshin, L. (2004). Fast moving luxury goods: Positioning strategies for scotch whisky in Thai department stores. *International Journal of Retail & Distribution Management*, *32*(6), 312–319. doi:10.1108/09590550410538015

Mandhachitara, R., & Poolthong, Y. (2011). A model of customer loyalty and corporate social responsibility. *Journal of Services Marketing*, *25*(2), 122–133. doi:10.1108/08876041111119840

Mangaliso, M. P. (2001). Building competitive advantage from Ubuntu: Management lessons from South Africa. *The Academy of Management Executive, 15*(3), 23–33. doi:10.5465/AME.2001.5229453

Mangan, E., & Collins, A. (2002). Threats to brand integrity in the hospitality sector: Evidence from a tourist brand. *International Journal of Contemporary Hospitality Management, 14*(6), 286–293. doi:10.1108/09596110210436823

Manzur, L., & Jogaratnam, G. (2006). Impression management and the hospitality service encounter: Ross-cultural differences. *Journal of Travel & Tourism Marketing, 20*(3/4), 21–32.

March, S. J. (1991). Exploration and exploitation in organizational learning. *Organization Science, 2*(1), 71–87. doi:10.1287/orsc.2.1.71

Mariani, M., & Baggio, R. (2012). Special issue: Managing tourism in a changing world: issues and cases. Anatolia. *Journal of Destination Marketing & Management, 2*, 269–272. doi:10.1016/j.jdmm.2013.11.003

Marin, L., Ruiz, S., & Rubio, A. (2009). The role of identity salience in the effects of corporate social responsibility on consumer behavior. *Journal of Business Ethics, 84*(1), 65–78. doi:10.1007/s10551-008-9673-8

Marín, P. L. (1998). Productivity differences in the airline industry: Partial deregulation versus short run protection. *International Journal of Industrial Organization, 16*(4), 395–414. doi:10.1016/S0167-7187(96)01058-2

Marquardt, M. (1999). *The global advantage: How to improve performance through globalization.* Houston, TX: Gulf Publishing.

Marquardt, M. J., & Engel, D. W. (1993). HRD competencies for a shrinking world. *Training and Developing, 46*(5), 59–65.

Marquardt, M., & Snyder, N. (1997). How companies go global: The role of the global integrators and the global mindset. *International Journal of Training and Development, 1*(2), 104–117. doi:10.1111/1468-2419.00011

Marriott (2013). Green Events, inspired by the environment. Zürich Marriott Hotel, Neumühlequai 42, CH-8001 Zürich.+ 41 (0)44. 360.7070. Retrieved from: http://www.marriott.com/hotelwebsites/us/z/zrhdt/zrhdt_pdf/zurich_marriott_hotel_green_events.pdf, November 15, 2013.

Martin, L. (July 23, 2006). Sex, sand, and sugar mummies in a Caribbean beach fantasy. *The Guardian.* Retrieved August 11, 2013 from http://www.theguardian.com/travel/2006/jul/23/jamaica.theatre.theobserver

Martineau, P. (1958). The personality of the retail store. *Harvard Business Review, 36*, 47–55.

Martínez, P., Pérez, A., & Rodríguez del Bosque, I. (2014). Exploring the role of CSR in the organizational identity of hospitality companies: A case from the Spanish tourism industry. *Journal of Business Ethics, 124*(1), 47–66. doi:10.1007/s10551-013-1857-1

Martínez, P., & Rodríguez del Bosque, I. (2013). CSR and customer loyalty: The roles of trust, customer identification with the company and satisfaction. *International Journal of Hospitality Management, 35*, 89–99. doi:10.1016/j.ijhm.2013.05.009

Martini, U. (2000), L'impatto di Internet sulla struttura del mercato turistico *leisure. Technical Report DISA, 36.*

Martini, U. (2013). Introduzione. Approccio alla sostenibilità, *governance* e competitività delle destinazioni turistiche: stato dell'arte e prospettive. In M. Franch & U. Martini (Eds.), *Management per la sostenibilità dello sviluppo turistico e la competitività delle destinazioni* (pp. 17–63). Bologna: Il Mulino.

Marwell, G., & Oliver, P. (1993). *The critical mass in collective action: A micro-social theory.* Cambridge, UK: Cambridge University Press. doi:10.1017/CBO9780511663765

Marx, E. (1999). *Breaking through cultural shock.* London: Nicolas Brealey.

Maslow, A. H. (1943). A theory of human motivation. *Psychological Review, 50*(4), 370–396. doi:10.1037/h0054346

Mason, D., Tideswell, C., & Roberts, E. (2006). Guest perceptions of hotel loyalty. *Journal of Hospitality & Tourism Research (Washington, D.C.)*, *30*(2), 191–206. doi:10.1177/1096348006286364

Mateos-Garcia, J., & Steinmueller, W. E. (2003). *Dynamic features of open source development communities and community processes*. Open Source Movement Research INK Working paper no. 3. Brighton: SPRU-Science and Technology Policy Studies

Mattila, A. S. (1999). The role of culture in the service evaluation process. *Journal of Service Research*, *1*(3), 250–261. doi:10.1177/109467059913006

Mattila, A. S. (2000). The impact of culture and gender on customer evaluations of service encounters. *Journal of Hospitality & Tourism Research (Washington, D.C.)*, *24*(2), 263–273. doi:10.1177/109634800002400209

Mattila, A. S. (2006). How affective commitment boosts guest loyalty (and promotes frequent guest programs). *The Cornell Hotel and Restaurant Administration Quarterly*, *47*(2), 174–181. doi:10.1177/0010880405283943

Mattila, A. S., & Patterson, P. G. (2004). The impact of culture on consumers' perceptions of service recovery efforts. *Journal of Retailing*, *80*(3), 196–206. doi:10.1016/j.jretai.2004.08.001

Mattila, A. S., & Wirtz, J. (2001). Congruency of scent and music as a driver for in-store evaluations and behavior. *Journal of Retailing*, *77*(2), 273–389. doi:10.1016/S0022-4359(01)00042-2

Mattila, A., & Choi, S. (2006). A cross-cultural comparison of perceived fairness and satisfaction in the context of hotel room pricing. *International Journal of Hospitality Management*, *25*(1), 146–153. doi:10.1016/j.ijhm.2004.12.003

Mayer, J. D., & Salovey, P. (1993). The intelligence of emotional intelligence. *Intelligence*, *17*(4), 433–442. doi:10.1016/0160-2896(93)90010-3

Mayo, E. J., & Jarvis, L. P. (1981). *The Psychology of Leisure Travel*. Boston: CBI Publishing.

McArthur, A. M. (1962). *Malaya 12, Assignment Report June 1958-November 1959*. Kuala Lumpur: World Health Organization, Regional Office for the Western Pacific.

McCall, M. W., & Hollenbeck, G. P. (2002). *Developing global executives: The lessons of international experience*. Boston, MA: Harvard Business School Press.

McClelland, D. C. (1973). Testing for competence rather than intelligence. *The American Psychologist*, *28*(1), 22–26. doi:10.1037/h0034092 PMID:4684069

McCombs, E. (1988). Ticket to ride. *BUST*, April/May, 70-73.

McCracken, G. (1988). *Culture and consumption: New approaches to the symbolic character of consumer goods and activities*. Indianapolis, IN: University Press.

McEvily, B., & Zaheer, A. (1999). Bridging ties: A source of firm heterogeneity in competitive capabilities. *Strategic Management Journal*, *20*(12), 1133–1156. doi:10.1002/(SICI)1097-0266(199912)20:12<1133::AID-SMJ74>3.0.CO;2-7

McFarlane, T., & Pliner, P. (1997). Increasing willingness to taste novel foods: Effects of nutrition and taste information. *Appetite*, *28*(3), 227–238. doi:10.1006/appe.1996.0075 PMID:9218096

McGehee, N., & Wattanakamolchai, S. (2009). Corporate Social Responsibility within the U.S. Lodging Industry: An Exploratory Study. *Journal of Hospitality & Tourism Research (Washington, D.C.)*, *33*(3), 417–437. doi:10.1177/1096348009338532

McGill, M. E., Slocum, J. W. Jr, & Lei, D. (1992). Management practices in learning organizations. *Organizational Dynamics*, *21*(1), 5–17. doi:10.1016/0090-2616(92)90082-X

McGrath-Champ, S., & Yang, X. (2002). Cross cultural training, expatriate quality of life and venture performance. *Management Research News*, *25*(8-10), 135.

McGrath, J. M. (2005). A pilot study testing aspects of the integrated marketing communications concept. *Journal of Marketing Communications*, *11*(3), 191–214. doi:10.1080/1352726042000333199

Mcilheney, C. (2013, September). U.S. spa industry returns to growth. *The Pulse of the Montana State Nurses' Association*, 32–35.

McKeeman, J., & Zachary, R. (2007). *Private Sector Competitiveness Project*. Washington: World Bank.

McLean Parks, J., Kidder, D. L., & Gallagher, D. G. (1998). Fitting Square Pegs into round holes: Mapping the Domain of Contingent Work Arrangements onto the psychological contract. *Journal of Organizational Behavior, 19*(S1), 697–730. doi:10.1002/(SICI)1099-1379(1998)19:1+<697::AID-JOB974>3.0.CO;2-I

McLennan, C., Ruhanen, L., Ritchie, B., & Pham, T. (2012). Dynamics of destination development: Investigating the application of transformation theory. *Journal of Hospitality & Tourism Research (Washington, D.C.), 36*(2), 164–190. doi:10.1177/1096348010390816

McPhee, D. (2014). Sex offending and sex tourism: Problems, policy and challenges. *Responding to Sexual Offending: Perceptions, Risk Management and Public Protection,* 93.

Mcsweeney, B. (2002). Hofstede's model of national cultural differences and their consequences: A triumph of faith – a failure of analysis. *Human Relations, 55*(1), 89–118. doi:10.1177/0018726702055001602

Mead, M. (1953). *Cultural patterns and technical change.* New York, NY: UNESCO.

Meadows, D. H., Randers, J., & Meadows, D. L. (2004). *The Limits to Growth: The 30-Year Update.* Chelsea Green: White River Junction, VT. Saarinen, J. (2004). Destinations in change: The transformation process of tourist destinations. *Tourist Studies, 4,* 161–179.

Medical Tourism Association. (n.d.). *Medical Tourism FAQ's.* Retrieved from http://www.medicaltourismassociation.com/en/medical-tourism-faq-s.html

Mehrabian, A., & Russell, J. (1974). *An approach to environmental psychology.* Cambridge, MA: MIT Press.

Mehrizi, M. H. R., & Pakneiat, M. (2008). Comparative analyses of sectoral innovation system and diamond model: The case of telecom sector of Iran. *Journal of Technology Management & Innovation, 3*(3), 78–90.

Meigs, A. (1997). Food as Cultural Construction. In C. Counihan & P. Van Esterik (Eds.), *Food and Culture: A Reader* (pp. 95–106). London: Routledge.

Melendez, J. (2007). *The concept of 'Face' in Chinese culture.* Retrieved April 15, 2010, from http://www4.associatedcontent.com/article/391443/the_concept_of_face_in_chinese_culture.html?cat=9 10/6/2009

Meler, M., & Cerović, Z. (2003). Food marketing in the function of tourist product development. *British Food Journal, 105*(3), 175–192. doi:10.1108/00070700310477121

Melis, A. R. (1991). Society, food, and feudalism. In J. L. Flandrin, M. Montanari, & A. Sonnenfeld (Eds.), *Food: A culinary history from antiquity to the present* (pp. 251–267). New York, NY: Columbia University Press.

Mendenhall, M. E. (1999). On the need for paradigmatic integration in international human resource management. *Management International Review, 39*(2), 1–23.

Mendenhall, M. E. (2000). New perspectives on expatriate adjustment and its relationship to global leadership development. In M. E. Mendenhall, T. M. Kuhlmann, & G. K. Stahl (Eds.), *Developing global leaders: Policies, processes, and innovations.* Westport, CT: Quorum Books.

Mendenhall, M. E., & Oddou, G. R. (1985). The dimensions of expatriate acculturation: A review. *Academy of Management Review, 10,* 39–47.

Mendenhall, M., & Wiley, C. (1994). Strangers in a strange land. *The American Behavioral Scientist, 37*(5), 605–621. doi:10.1177/0002764294037005003

Mente, B. D. (2000). *The Chinese have a word for it: The complete guide to Chinese thought and culture.* Lincolnwood, IL: McGraw-Hill Professional.

Menzies, J. L., & Nguyen, S. N. (2012). An exploration of the motivation to attend for spectators of the Lexmark Indy 300 champ car event, Gold Coast. *Journal of Sport & Tourism, 17*(3), 183–200. doi:10.1080/14775085.2012.734059

Meyer, K. E. (2006). Asian management research needs more self-confidence. *Asia Pacific Journal of Management, 23*(2), 119–137. doi:10.1007/s10490-006-7160-2

Miceli, M. E., & Near, J. E. (1992). *Blowing the whistle: The organizational and legal implications for companies and employees.* New York: Lexington Books.

Middleton, V. T. C. (2001). *Marketing in travel and Tourism* (3rd ed.). Oxford: Butterworth – Heinemann.

Mifli, M. (2004). Managing menu innovation. Paper presented at the 3rd Asia-Pacific Forum for Graduate Student Research in Tourism, Beijing, China.

Miles, R. E., & Snow, C. C. (1978). *Organizational strategy, structure and process.* New York, NY: McGraw-Hill.

Milfelner, B., Gabrijan, V., & Snoj, B. (2008). Can Marketing resources contribute to company performance? *Organizacija, 41*(2), 3–13.

Miller, D., & Friesen, P. H. (1982). Innovation in conservative and entrepreneurial firms: Two models of strategic momentum. *Strategic Management Journal, 3*(1), 1–25. doi:10.1002/smj.4250030102

Miller, J. (2011). Beach boys or sexually exploited children? Competing narratives of sex tourism and their impact on young men in Sri Lanka's informal tourist economy. *Crime, Law, and Social Change, 56*(5), 485–508. doi:10.1007/s10611-011-9330-5

Milliken, F. J., Morrison, E. W., & Hewlin, P. F. (2003). An exploratory study of employee silence: Issues that employees don't communicate upward and why. *Journal of Management Studies, 40*(6), 1453–1476. doi:10.1111/1467-6486.00387

Mill, R. C., & Morrison, A. M. (1992). *The tourism system: An introductory text.* Englewood Cliffs, NJ: Prentice Hall.

Mills, J. E., & Law, R. (Eds.). (2013). *Handbook of Consumer Behavior Tourism and the Internet.* Routledge.

Minghetti, V., & Buhalis, D. (2010). Digital divide in Tourism. *Journal of Travel Research, 49*(3), 267–281.

Ministry of Tourism Republic of Fiji. (2012). Article. *Tourism Performance, 2012,* 2014.

Min, J., & Mitsuhashi, H. (2012). Dynamics of Unclosed Triangles in Alliance Networks: Disappearance of Brokerage Positions and Performance Consequences. *Journal of Management Studies, 49*(6), 1078–1108. doi:10.1111/j.1467-6486.2011.01035.x

Minkiewicz, J., Evans, J., Bridson, K., & Mavondo, F. (2011). Corporate image in the leisure services sector. *Journal of Services Marketing, 25*(3), 190–201. doi:10.1108/08876041111129173

Mistilis, N., & Tolar, M. (2000). *Impact of Macroeconomic Issues on Fiji's Hidden Paradise.* Paper presented at the Council for Australian University Tourism and Hospitality Education (CAUTHE), Mt. Buller, Australia.

Mithas, S., Krishnan, M. S., & Fornell, C. (2005). Why do customer relationship management applications affect customer satisfaction? *Journal of Marketing, 69*(4), 201–209. doi:10.1509/jmkg.2005.69.4.201

Mitrev, S., & Culpepper, R. (2012). Expatriation in Europe: Factors and insights. *Journal of International Management Studies, 7*(1), 158–167.

Mobley, W. H. (1982). *Employee turnover, causes, consequences, and control.* Manila, Philippines: Addison-Wesley Publishing Company.

Mohan, K. L. (2008). An analysis of competitiveness of Indian clothing export sector using Porter's model. *Journal of International Business, 3*(4), 39–46.

Molapo, M. (2013). *Mainstreaming IPoA into National Development Strategies: The Case of Lesotho.* Presented at the Ministry of Development Planning, Lesotho. Retrieved May 7 from http://unohrlls.org/custom-content/uploads/2013/11/Lesotho-Presentation.pdf

Monteson, P. A., & Singer, J. (2004). Marketing a resort-based spa. *Journal of Vacation Marketing, 10*(3), 282–287. doi:10.1177/1356766704010000307

Montoya-Wess, M. M., & Calantone, R. J. (1994). Determinant of new product performance: A review and meta-analysis. *Journal of Product Innovation Management, 11*(5), 397–417. doi:10.1016/0737-6782(94)90029-9

Mooney, S. (1994). Planning and designing the menu. In P. Jones & P. Merricks (Eds.), *The management of foodservice operations* (pp. 45–58). London, UK: Cassell.

Moorman, R. H. (1991). Relationship between organizational justice and organizational citizenship behaviors: Do fairness perceptions influence employee citizenship? *The Journal of Applied Psychology, 76*(6), 845–855. doi:10.1037/0021-9010.76.6.845

Moorman, R. H., & Blakely, G. L. (1995). Individualism collectivism as an individual difference predictor of organizational citizenship behavior. *Journal of Organizational Behavior, 16*(2), 127–142. doi:10.1002/job.4030160204

Moran, P., & Ghoshal, S. (1999). Markets, firms, and the process of economic development. *Academy of Management Review, 24*(3), 390–412.

Moreno-Gil, S., Martín-Santana, J. D., & De León-Ledesma, J. (2012). Factores determinantes del éxito para entender la imagen de un alojamiento turístico. Un estudio empírico en Islas Canarias. *Revista Innovar*, *22*(44), 139–152.

Morosan, C. (2012). Theoretical and Empirical Considerations of Guests' Perceptions of Biometric Systems in Hotels: Extending the Technology Acceptance Model. *Journal of Hospitality & Tourism Research (Washington, D.C.)*, *36*(1), 52–84. doi:10.1177/1096348010380601

Morris, H., Harvey, C., & Kelly, A. (2009). Journal rankings and the ABS journal quality guide. *Management Decision*, *47*(9), 1441–1451. doi:10.1108/00251740910995648

Morrison, A., & O'Gorman, K. (2006). Hospitality studies: Liberating the power of the mind. In P. A. Whitelaw & O. G. Barry (Eds.), *CAUTHE 2006: To the city and beyond* (pp. 453–465). Footscray, Vic.: Victoria University, School of Hospitality, Tourism and Marketing.

Morrison, A., & Teixeira, R. (2004). Small business performance: A tourism sector focus. *Journal of Small Business and Enterprise Development*, *11*(2), 166–173. doi:10.1108/14626000410537100

Moscadeo, G. (2011). Exploring social representations of tourism planning: Issues for governance. *Journal of Sustainable Tourism*, *19*(4-5), 423–436. doi:10.1080/09669582.2011.558625

Motocross News blog. (2008, May 7). *Motocross* [Web log comment] Retrieved July 16, 2013, from http://www.mxnewsfeed.com/article.php?artid=2164

Motowidlo, S. J., & Van Scooter, J. R. (1994). Evidence that Task Performance should be Distinguished from Contextual Performance. *The Journal of Applied Psychology*, *79*(4), 475–480. doi:10.1037/0021-9010.79.4.475

Moutinho, L. (1987). Consumer behavior in tourism. *European Journal of Marketing*, *21*(10), 5–44. doi:10.1108/EUM0000000004718

Moutinho, L. (Ed.). (2011). *Strategic management in tourism*. New York: CABI Publishing. doi:10.1079/9781845935887.0000

Mowday, R. T., & Sutton, R. I. (1993). Organizational behavior: Linking individuals and groups to organizational contexts. *Annual Review of Psychology*, *44*(1), 195–229. doi:10.1146/annurev.ps.44.020193.001211 PMID:19090760

Mowle, J., & Merrilees, B. (2005). A functional and symbolic perspective to branding Australian SME wineries. *Journal of Product and Brand Management*, *14*(4), 220–227. doi:10.1108/10610420510609221

Mrnjavac, E., & Ivanovic, S. (2007). Logistics and logistics processes in a tourism destination. *Tourism and Hospitality Management*, *13*, 531–546.

Mulder, D. (2007). *Driving integrated marketing communication home for organizational effectiveness.* Paper presented at the meeting Communications, Civics, Industry of Australian New Zealand Communication Association National Conference (ANZCA), Melbourne, Australia.

Müller, C. (1999). Networks of 'personal communities' and 'group communities' in different online communication services. In *Proceedings of the Exploring Cyber Society: Social, Political, Economic and Cultural Issues* (Vol. 2). Newcastle, UK: University of Northumberland. Retrieved from: http://www.soz.unibe.ch/ii/virt/newcastle.html

Murdy, S., & Pike, S. (2012). Perceptions of visitor relationship marketing opportunities by destination marketers: An importance-performance analysis. *Tourism Management*, *33*(5), 1281–1285. doi:10.1016/j.tourman.2011.11.024

Murphy, P. (2014). Potential Synergies for the Short-Break Holiday and Rural Tourism Markets: Evidence from a National Australian Survey. *Tourism Planning and Development*, 1-14.

Mwaura, G., Sutton, J., & Roberts, D. (1998). Corporate and national culture: An irreconcilable dilemma for the hospitality manager? *International Journal of Contemporary Hospitality Management*, *10*(6), 212–220. doi:10.1108/09596119810232211

Nadeau, J., Heslop, L., O'Rielly, N. O., & Luk, P. (2008). Destination in a country image context. *Annals of Tourism Research*, *35*(1), 84–106. doi:10.1016/j.annals.2007.06.012

Nagel, J. (2003). *Race, ethnicity, and sexuality: Intimate intersections, forbidden frontiers*. New York: Oxford University Press.

Nahapiet, J., & Ghoshal, S. (1998). Social capital, intellectual capital, and the organizational advantage. *Academy of Management Review, 23*(2), 242–266.

Namasivayam, K., & Lin, I. Y. (2008). The servicescape. In P. Jones & A. Pizam (Eds.), *Handbook of hospitality operations and IT* (pp. 43–62). Burlington, MA: Butterworth-Heinemann. doi:10.1016/B978-0-7506-8753-9.50007-X

Narayan, P. K. (2003). Tourism Demand Modelling: Some Issues Regarding Unit Roots, Co-integration and Diagnostic Tests. *International Journal of Tourism Research, 5*(5), 369–380. doi:10.1002/jtr.440

Narver, J. C., Slater, S. F., & Maclachlan, D. L. (2004). Responsive and proactive market orientation and new-product success. *Journal of Product Innovation Management, 21*(5), 334–347. doi:10.1111/j.0737-6782.2004.00086.x

Nash, D., & Smith, V. L. (1991). Anthropology and tourism. *Annals of Tourism Research, 18*(1), 12–25. doi:10.1016/0160-7383(91)90036-B

*Nashoba Valley Ski Resort website*. (n.d.). Retrieved July 17, 2013, from http//www.skinashoba.com

Nasurdin, A. M., Ahmad, N. H., & Tan, C. L. (2014). *Cultivating service-oriented citizenship behavior among hotel employees: the instrumental roles of training and compensation*. Springer.

National Institute of Public Administration. Malaysia (2003). Malaysia Kita. Kuala Lumpur: National Institute of Public Administration.

National Statistical Office of Papua New Guinea. *Visitor Arrivals Summary Papua New Guinea*. Papua New Guinea: Papua New Guinea Tourism Promotion Authority Retrieved from http://www.tpa.papuanewguinea.travel/Papua-New-Guinea-Tourism-Promotions-Authority/Annual-Visitor-Arrivals-Reports_IDL=42_IDT=328_ID=1806_.html

National Statistical. (2009). *National statistics, Republic of China (Taiwan)*. Retrieved March 9, 2009, from http://eng.stat.gov.tw/mp.asp?mp=5

Naumann, E. (1992). A conceptual model of expatriate turnover. *Journal of International Business Studies, 23*(3), 499–531. doi:10.1057/palgrave.jibs.8490277

Near, J. E., & Miceli, M. E. (1996). Whistle-blowing: Myth and reality. *Journal of Management, 22*(3), 507–526. doi:10.1177/014920639602200306

Nel, J. D. W., North, E. J., Mybur, T., & Hern, L. (2009). A comparative study of customer-based brand equity across selected South African hotels. *International Retail and Marketing Review, 5*(1), 15–24.

Nelson, E. M. (1999). *Internationally-focused managerial behaviors of executives working in large U.S. multinational corporations*. (Doctoral dissertation). University of Illinois at Urbana-Champaign.

Nelson, R. R., & Winter, S. G. (1982). *An evolutionary theory of economic changes*. Cambridge: Belknap Press of Harvard University Press.

Nemeth, C. J., & Staw, B. M. (1989). *The tradeo Vs of social control and innovation in small groups and organizations*. In L. Berkowitz (Ed.), Advances in experimental social psychology (Vol. 22, pp. 175–210). New York: Academic Press.

Nepal, S. K. (2007). Tourism and rural settlements: Nepal's Annapurna region. *Annals of Tourism Research, 34*(4), 855–875. doi:10.1016/j.annals.2007.03.012

Nerker, A., & Roberts, P. W. (2004). Technological and product-market experience and the success of new product introductions in the pharmaceutical industry. *Strategic Management Journal, 25*(89), 779–799. doi:10.1002/smj.417

Nero, G. (1996). A structural model of intra European Union duopoly airline competition. *Journal of Transport Economics and Policy, 30*(2), 137.

Ness, H., Aarstad, J., Haugland, S., & Gronseth, B. (2013). Destination Development: The role of interdestination bridge ties. *Journal of Travel Research, 53*(2), 183–195. doi:10.1177/0047287513491332

Netessine, S., & Shumsky, R. A. (2005). Revenue management games: Horizontal and vertical competition. *Management Science, 51*(5), 813–831. doi:10.1287/mnsc.1040.0356

Nevis, E. C., DiBella, A. J., & Gould, J. M. (1995). Understanding Organizations as Learning Systems. *Sloan Management Review, 36*(2), 73–85.

Ng, K. Y., Tan, M. L., & Ang, S. (2012). Culture capital and cosmopolitan human capital: The impact of global mindset and organizational routines on developing cultural intelligence & international experiences in organizations. In A. Burton-Hones & J. C. Spender (Eds.), *The Oxford handbook of human capital.* Oxford University Press. Retrieved from, November 9, 2014, http://culturalq.com/docs/Ng,%20Tan,%20Ang%20Human%20Capital%202009.pdf

Ngai, E. W. T., Heung, V. C. S., Wong, Y. H., & Chan, K. Y. (2007). Consumer complaint behavior of Asians and non-Asians about hotel services. An empirical analyses. *European Journal of Marketing, 41*(11/12), 1375–1391. doi:10.1108/03090560710821224

Nguyen, N., & Leblanc, G. (2002). Contact personnel, physical environment and the perceived corporate image of intangible services by new clients. *International Journal of Service Industry Management, 13*(3), 242–262. doi:10.1108/09564230210431965

Nickson, D. (2007). *Human Resource Management for the Hospitality and Tourism Industries.* Oxford, UK: Elsevier.

Nicu, I. E. (2012). Human resources motivation - an important factor in the development of business performance. *Annals of the University of Oradea. Economic Science Series, 21*(1), 1039–1045.

Nielsen Global Online Survey. (2009). *Global diners want familiar foods and fair prices.* Retrieved July 7, 2010, from http://tw.en.nielsen.com/site/news20090409e.shmtl.shtml

Nieves, J. A., & Haller, S. (2014). Building dynamic capabilities through knowledge resources. *Tourism Management, 40*, 224–232. doi:10.1016/j.tourman.2013.06.010

Novelli, M., Schmitz, B., & Spencer, T. (2006). Networks, clusters and innovation in tourism: A UK experience. *Tourism Management, 27*(6), 1141–1152. doi:10.1016/j.tourman.2005.11.011

Nowak, G., & Phelps, J. (1994). Conceptualizing the integrated marketing communication's phenomenon: An examination of its impact on advertising and its implications for advertising research. *Journal of Current Issues and Research in Advertising, 16*(1), 49–66. doi:10.1080/10641734.1994.10505012

Nunez, T. (1989). Touristic studies in anthropological perspective. *Hosts and guests: The anthropology of tourism, 2*, 265-279.

Núñez-Serrano, J. A., Turrión, J., & Velázquez, F. J. (2014). Are stars a good indicator of hotel quality? Assymetric information and regulatory heterogeneity in Spain. *Tourism Management, 42*, 77–87. doi:10.1016/j.tourman.2013.10.004

Nunkoo, R., & Ramkissoon, H. (2010). Small island urban tourism: A residents' perspective. *Current Issues in Tourism, 13*(1), 37–60. doi:10.1080/13683500802499414

Nunnally, J. C. (1978). *Psychometric Theory* (2nd ed.). New York, NY: McGraw-Hill.

Nunnally, J. C., & Bernstein, I. H. (1994). *Psychometric theory* (3rd ed.). New York, NY: McGraw Hill.

Nuryanti, W. (1996). Heritage and postmodern tourism. *Annals of Tourism Research, 23*(2), 249–260. doi:10.1016/0160-7383(95)00062-3

O'Connell Davidson, J., & Sanchez Taylor, J. (1999). Fantasy islands: Exploring the demand for sex tourism. *Sun, sex, and gold: Tourism and sex work in the Caribbean*, 37-54.

O'Dell, T. (2010). *Spas: the cultural economy of hospitality, magic and the senses.* Sweden: Nordic Academic Press.

OECD. (2011). *Studies on Tourism. Italy: Review Of Issues And Policies.* OECD Publishing. doi:10.1787/9789264114258-en

Okoroafo, S. C., Koh, A., Liu, L., & Jin, X. (2010). Hotels in China: A comparison of indigenous and subsidiaries strategies. *Journal of Management Research, 2*(1), 1-10.

Okoro, E., & Washington, M. (2012). Workforce diversity and organizational communication: Analysis of human capital performance and productivity. *Journal of Diversity Management, 7*(1), 57–62.

Okpara, J. O., & Kabongo, J. D. (2011). Cross-cultural training and expatriate adjustment: A study of western expatriate in Nigeria. *Journal of World Business, 46*(1), 22–30. doi:10.1016/j.jwb.2010.05.014

Okumus, B., Okumus, F., & McKercher, B. (2007). Incorporating local and international cuisines in the marketing of tourism destinations: The cases of Hong Kong and Turkey. *Tourism Management, 28*(1), 253–261. doi:10.1016/j.tourman.2005.12.020

Olaisen, J., & Revang, Ø. (1991). Information management as the main component in the strategy for the 1990s in Scandinavian airline system (SAS). *International Journal of Information Management, 11*(3), 185–202. doi:10.1016/0268-4012(91)90032-8

Olensky, S. (2014, March 3). *Social Media And Branding: A One On One With A Harvard Business Professor.* Retrieved June 24, 2014 from Forbes: http://www.forbes.com/sites/steveolenski/2014/03/17/social-media-and-branding-a-one-on-one-with-a-harvard-business-professor/

Oliver, R. L. (1980). A cognitive model of the antecedents and consequences of satisfaction decisions. *JMR, Journal of Marketing Research, 17*(4), 460–469. doi:10.2307/3150499

Oliver, R. L. (1997). *Satisfaction: A behavioral perspective on the consumer.* New York: McGraw-Hill.

Olsen, M. D., West, J., & Tse, E. (1998). *Strategic management in the hospitality industry* (2nd ed.). New York, NY: John Wiley & Sons.

Olson, M. (1965). *The logic of collective action.* Cambridge, MA: Harvard University Press.

Omondi, R. K. (2003). Gender and the political economy of sex tourism in Kenya's coastal resorts. Paper presented at International Symposium/Doctorial Course on Feminist Perspective on Global Economic and Political Systems and Women's Struggle for Global Justice, September 24-26 2003, in Tromso, Norway.

Orfila-Sintes, F., Crespi-Cladera, R., & Martinez-Ros, E. (2005). Innovation activity in the hotel industry: Evidence from Balearic Islands. *Tourism Management, 26*(6), 851–865. doi:10.1016/j.tourman.2004.05.005

Organ, D. W. (1988). *Organizational Citizenship Behavior: The good soldier syndrome.* Lexington, MA: Lexington Books.

Ortenblad, A. (2002). A typology of the idea of learning organization. *Management Learning, 33*(2), 213–230. doi:10.1177/1350507602332004

Ortenblad, A. (2004). The learning organization: Towards an integrated model. *The Learning Organization, 11*(2), 129–144. doi:10.1108/09696470410521592

Orth, U. R., & De Marchi, R. (2007). Understanding the relationships between functional, symbolic and experiential brand beliefs, product experiential attributes, and product schema: Advertising-trial interactions revisited. *Journal of Marketing Theory and Practice, 15*(3), 219–233. doi:10.2753/MTP1069-6679150303

Osman, H., Hemmington, N., & Bowie, D. (2009). A transactional approach to customer loyalty in the hotel industry. *International Journal of Contemporary Hospitality Management, 21*(3), 239–250. doi:10.1108/09596110910948279

Otfinoski, S. (2003). *Marco Polo: to China and back.* New York: Benchmark Books.

Ottenbacher, M. C., & Harrington, R. J. (2007). The Innovation development process of michelin-starred chefs. *International Journal of Contemporary Hospitality Management, 19*(6), 444–460. doi:10.1108/09596110710775110

Ottenbacher, M. C., & Harrington, R. J. (2008). The product innovation process of quick-service restaurant chains. *International Journal of Contemporary Hospitality Management, 21*(5), 523–541. doi:10.1108/09596110910967782

Oum, T., & Park, J.-H. (1997). Airline alliances: Current status, policy issues, and future directions. *Journal of Air Transport Management, 3*(3), 133–144. doi:10.1016/S0969-6997(97)00021-5

Oum, T., Park, J.-H., Kim, K., & Yu, C. (2004). The effect of horizontal alliances on firm productivity and profitability: Evidence from the global airline industry. *Journal of Business Research, 57*(8), 844–853. doi:10.1016/S0148-2963(02)00484-8

Oum, T., Park, J.-H., & Zhang, A. (1996). The effects of airline code sharing agreements on firm conduct and international air fares. *Journal of Transport Economics and Policy, 30*, 187–202.

Oxford Dictionaries Online. (2010). In *Oxford Dictionaries Online: English dictionary and language reference.* Retrieved August 3, 2010, from http://oxforddictionaries.com/?attempted=true

Ozdemir, B., & Cizel, R. B. (2007). International hotel manager as an emerging concept: A review of expatriate management literature and a model proposal. *Journal of Hospitality and Tourism Management, 14*(2), 170–187. doi:10.1375/jhtm.14.2.170

Paine, K. D. (2011). *Measuring What matters: online Tools for Understanding Customers, Social Media, Engagement and Key Relationships.* Indianapolis: John Wiley and Sons.

Pan, B. C. J. (2011). *Theoretical Models of Social Media, Marketing Implications, and Future Research Directions.* Retrieved March 25, 2014 from Theoretical Models of Social Media, Marketing Implications, and Future Research Directions: https://www.google.co.uk/search?q=Theoretical+Models+of+Social+Media%2C+Marketing+Implications%2C+and+Future+Research+Directions&rlz=1C5CHFA_enGB513GB513&oq=Theoretical+Models+of+Social+Media%2C+Marketing+Implications%2C+and+Future+Research+Directions&aqs=chrome.69i57j0.1765j0j4&sourceid=chrome&espv=2&es_sm=91&ie=UTF-8

Panaccio, A. J., & Waxin, M. F. (2010). HRM case study: diversity management: facilitating diversity through the recruitment, selection and integration of diverse employees in a Quebec bank. *Journal of the International Academy for Case Studies, 16*(4), 53–66.

Pappu, R., Quester, P. G., & Cooksey, R. W. (2005). Consumer-based brand equity: Improving the measurement-empirical evidence. *Journal of Product and Brand Management, 14*(3), 143–154. doi:10.1108/10610420510601012

Parasuraman, A., Zeithaml, V. A., & Berry, L. L. (1985). A conceptual model of service quality and its implication. *Journal of Marketing, 49*(Fall), 41–50. doi:10.2307/1251430

Parasuraman, A., Zeithaml, V. A., & Berry, L. L. (1988). SERVQUAL: A multiple-item scale for measuring consumer perceptions of service quality. *Journal of Retailing, 64*(1), 12–40.

Parker, B., Zeira, Y., & Hatem, T. (1996). International joint venture managers: Factors affecting personal success and organizational performance. *Journal of International Management, 2*(1), 1–29.

Parker, C., & Mathews, B. P. (2001). Customer satisfaction: Contrasting academic and consumers' interpretations. *Marketing Intelligence & Planning, 19*(1), 38–44. doi:10.1108/02634500110363790

Parkhe, A. (1993). Strategic Alliance Structuring: A Game Theoretic and Transaction Cost Examination of Interfirm Cooperation. *Academy of Management Journal, 36*(4), 794–829. doi:10.2307/256759

Park, J. (1997). The effects of airline alliances on markets and economic welfare. *Transportation Research Part E, Logistics and Transportation Review, 33*(3), 181–195. doi:10.1016/S1366-5545(97)00013-6

Park, J., Park, N., & Zhang, A. (2003). The impact of international alliances on rival firm value: A study of the British Airways/USAir Alliance. *Transportation Research Part E, Logistics and Transportation Review, 39*(1), 1–18. doi:10.1016/S1366-5545(02)00023-6

Park, J., & Zhang, A. (2000). An Empirical Analysis of Global Airline Alliances: Cases in North Atlantic Markets. *Review of Industrial Organization, 16*(4), 367–384. doi:10.1023/A:1007888821999

Park, J., Zhang, A., & Zhang, Y. (2001). Analytical models of international alliances in the airline industry. *Transportation Research Part B: Methodological, 35*(9), 865–886. doi:10.1016/S0191-2615(00)00027-8

Park, S., & Russo, M. (1996). When Competition Eclipses Cooperation: An Event History Analysis of Joint Venture Failure. *Management Science, 42*(6), 875–890. doi:10.1287/mnsc.42.6.875

Park, W. C., Jaworski, B. J., & MacInnis, D. J. (1986). Strategic brand concept-image management. *Journal of Marketing, 50*(4), 135–145. doi:10.2307/1251291

Pasta Fresca Da Salvatore, P. F. D. S. (2009). *Pasta Fresca Restaurant*. Retrieved 17 December 2009 from http://www.pastafresca.com/AboutUS.html

Patterson, P. G., & Smith, T. (2003). A cross-cultural study of switching barriers and propensity to stay with service providers. *Journal of Retailing*, 79(2), 107–120. doi:10.1016/S0022-4359(03)00009-5

Paullay, I. M., Alliger, G. M., & Stone-Romero, E. F. (1994). Construct validation of two instruments designed to measure job involvement and work centrality. *The Journal of Applied Psychology*, 79(2), 224–228. doi:10.1037/0021-9010.79.2.224

Pavlovich, K. (2003). The evolution and transformation of a tourism destination network: The Waitomo caves, New Zealand. *Tourism Management*, 24(2), 203–216. doi:10.1016/S0261-5177(02)00056-0

Pearce, D. G., & Butler, R. (Eds.). (1993). *Fundamentals of Tourist Motivation*. London: Routledge.

Pearce, P. L. (1982). *The social psychology of tourist behavior*. Pergamon Press.

Pearce, P. L. (2011). In Y. Wang & A. Pizman (Eds.), *Destination marketing and management: Theories and applications* (pp. 39–52). Wallingford: CABI. doi:10.1079/9781845937621.0039

Pechlaner, H., & Volgger, M. (2012). How to promote cooperation in the hospitality industry. *International Journal of Contemporary Hospitality Management*, 24(6), 925–945. doi:10.1108/09596111211247245

Pedler, M., Burgoyne, J., & Boydell, T. (1991). *The learning company: A strategy for sustainable development*. New York: McGraw-Hill.

Peltier, J., Schibrowsky, J., & Schultz, D. E. (2003). Interactive integrated marketing communication: Combining the power of IMC, the new media and database marketing. *International Journal of Advertising*, 22(1), 93–115.

Peng, M. W. (2008). *Global Strategy*. Dallas: University of Texas.

Pennington, D. C. (2000). *Social cognition*. London: Routledge.

Penn, J. M., & Mooney, S. (1986). Cross-cultural negotiations in the hospitality industry: The Japanese market. *International Journal of Hospitality Management*, 5(4), 205–208. doi:10.1016/0278-4319(86)90022-8

Penny, W. Y. K. (2007). The use of environmental management as a facilities management tool in the Macao hotel sector. *Emerald Group Publishing Limited*, 25(7/8), 286–295.

Penrose, E. T. (1959). *The Theory of the Growth of the Firm*. Oxford: Oxford University Press.

Perez, A., García de los Salmones, M. M., & Rodríguez del Bosque, I. (2012). The effect of corporate associations on consumer behavior. *European Journal of Marketing*, 47(1), 218–238.

Peteraf, M. A. (1993). The cornerstones of competitive advantage: A resource-based view. *Strategic Management Journal*, 14(3), 179–191. doi:10.1002/smj.4250140303

Peteraf, M. A., & Barney, J. B. (2003). Unraveling the Resource-based tangle. *Managerial and Decision Economics*, 24(4), 309–323. doi:10.1002/mde.1126

Peteraf, M. A., & Bergen, M. E. (2003). Scanning dynamic competitive landscapes: A market-based and resource-based framework. *Strategic Management Journal*, 24(10), 1027–1041. doi:10.1002/smj.325

Petrick, J. F. (2004). Are loyal visitors desired visitors? *Tourism Management*, 25(4), 463–470. doi:10.1016/S0261-5177(03)00116-X

Petrini, C. (2011). *Slow food and slow fish. Our guiding principles*. Slow Food.

Petrini, C., & Padovani, G. (2005). Slow Food Revolution. Da Arcigola a Terra Madre. Una nuova cultura del cibo e della vita. Milan, Rizzoli Editor, Italy.

Phau, I., & Leng, Y. S. (2008). Attitudes toward domestic and foreign luxury brand apparel, A comparison between status and non status seeking teenagers. *Journal of Fashion Marketing and Management*, 12(1), 68–89. doi:10.1108/13612020810857952

583

Phillip, J. L. (1999). Tourist-oriented prostitution in Barbados: The case of the beach boy and the white female tourist. In K. Kempadoo (Ed.), *Sun, sex and gold – Tourism and sex work in the Caribbean* (pp. 183–200). Lanham, MD: Rowman and Littlefield.

Pieniak, Z., Verbeke, W., Vanhonacker, F., Guerrero, L., & Hersleth, M. (2009). Association between traditional food consumption and motives for food choice in six European countries. *Appetite*, *53*(1), 101–108. doi:10.1016/j.appet.2009.05.019

Pierce, J. L., Kostova, T., & Dirks, K. T. (2001). Toward a theory of psychological ownership. *Academy of Management Review*, *26*(2), 298–310.

Pigg, K. E., & Crank, L. D. (2004). Building community social capital: The potential and promise of information and communications technologies. *The Journal of Community Informatics*, *1*(1), 58–73.

Pike, S. (2002). Destination image analysis-a review of 142 papers from 1973 to 2000. *Tourism Management*, *23*(5), 541–549. doi:10.1016/S0261-5177(02)00005-5

Pike, S. (2004). *Destination Marketing Organizations*. Amsterdam: Elsevier.

Pınar, İ. (2005). İzmir İli İçin Turizmin Yeri ve Geliştirme Örneği. *Yönetim ve Ekonomi*, *12*(1), 47–60.

Pine, B. J., & Gilmore, J. H. (2011). The experience economy (Updated ed.). Boston: Harvard Business Review Press.

Pine, J., & Gilmore, J. H. (1998). Welcome to the Experience Economy. *Harvard Business Review*, *76*, 97–106. PMID:10181589

Pine, R. (2002). China's hotel industry: Serving a massive market. *The Cornell Hotel and Restaurant Administration Quarterly*, *43*(3), 61–70.

Pine, R., Zhang, H., & Qi, P. (2000). The challenge and opportunities of franchising in China's hotel industry. *International Journal of Contemporary Hospitality Management*, *12*(5), 300–307. doi:10.1108/09596110010339670

Pisano, G., Shuen, A., & Teece, D. (1997). Dynamic capabilities and strategic management. *Strategic Management Journal*, *18*(7), 509–533. doi:10.1002/(SICI)1097-0266(199708)18:7<509::AID-SMJ882>3.0.CO;2-Z

Piskorski, M. (2012). *Networks as covers: Evidence from business and social on-line networks.* Retrieved June 20, 2014 from HBS. Edu: http://www.people.hbs.edu/mpiskorski/papers/FA-Platforms.pdf

Piskorski, M. (2014). *A Social Strategy: How We Profit from Social Media.* http://www.amazon.com/Social-Strategy-How-Profit-Media/dp/0691153396

Pizam, A. (1993). *Managing cross-cultural hospitality enterprises. The international hospitality industry: Organizational and operational issues.* New York, NY: John Wiley.

Plog, S. (1974). Why destination areas rise and fall in popularity. *The Cornell Hotel and Restaurant Administration Quarterly*, *14*(4), 55–58. doi:10.1177/001088047401400409

Plog, S. C. (1987). Understanding psychographics in tourism research. In J. R. B. Ritchie & C. R. Goeldner (Eds.), *Travel, tourism, and hospitality research. A handbook for managers and researchers* (pp. 203–213). New York: Wiley.

Podsakoff, P. M., Ahearne, M., & MacKenzie, S. B. (1997). Organizational Citizenship Behavior and the Quantity and Quality of Work Group Performance. *The Journal of Applied Psychology*, *82*(2), 262–270. doi:10.1037/0021-9010.82.2.262 PMID:9109284

Podsakoff, P. M., MacKenzie, S. B., Bachrach, D. G., & Podsakoff, N. P. (2005). The influence of management journals in the 1980s and 1990s. *Strategic Management Journal*, *26*(5), 473–488. doi:10.1002/smj.454

Podsakoff, P. M., MacKenzie, S. B., Moorman, R. H., & Fetter, R. (1990). Transformational leader behaviors and their effects on followers' trust in leader, satisfaction, and organizational citizenship behaviors. *The Leadership Quarterly*, *1*(2), 107–142. doi:10.1016/1048-9843(90)90009-7

Podsakoff, P. M., MacKenzie, S. B., Paine, J. B., & Bachrach, D. G. (2000). Organizational citizenship behaviors: A critical review of the theoretical and empirical literature and suggestions for future research. *Journal of Management*, *26*(3), 513–563. doi:10.1177/014920630002600307

Polo, A. I., Frías, D. M., & Rodríguez, M. A. (2013). Antecedents of loyalty toward rural hospitality enterprises: The moderating effect of the customer's previous experience. *International Journal of Hospitality Management, 34*, 127–137. doi:10.1016/j.ijhm.2013.02.011

Pomykalski, A. (2001). *Zarządzanie innowacjami.* Warszawa, Łódź: Wydawnictwo Naukowe PWN.

Poon, A. (1993). *Tourism, Technology and Competitive Strategies.* UK: CAB International.

Popesku, J., & Hall, D. (2004). Sustainability as the basis for future tourism development in Serbia. In D. Hall (Ed.), *Tourism and transition: Governance, transformation and development* (pp. 95–104). Wallingford, CT: CABI. doi:10.1079/9780851997483.0095

Porter, G., & Tansky, J. (1999). Expatriate success may depend on a 'learning orientation': Considerations for selection and training. *Human Resource Management, 38*(1), 47–60. doi:10.1002/(SICI)1099-050X(199921)38:1<47::AID-HRM5>3.0.CO;2-1

Porter, M. (1990). *The competitiveness advantage of nations.* New York: Free Press.

Porter, M. E. (1980). *Competitive strategy: Techniques for analyzing industries and competitors.* New York, NY: John Wiley & Sons, Inc.

Porter, M. E. (1985). Technology and competitive advantage. *The Journal of Business Strategy, 5*(3), 60–79. doi:10.1108/eb039075

Porter, M. E. (Ed.). (1986). *Competition in global industries.* Boston, MA: Harvard Business School Press.

Porth, S., McCall, J., & Bausch, T. A. (1999). Spiritual themes of the learning organization. *Journal of Organizational Change Management, 12*(3), 211–220. doi:10.1108/09534819910273883

Powers, T. F. (1992). Managing international hospitality. *FIU Hospitality Journal, 2*, 25–34.

Prahalad, C., & Hamel, G. (1990). The Core Competence of the Corporation. *Harvard Business Review, 68*(3), 79–91.

Prasad, K., & Dev, C. S. (2000). Managing hotel brand equity: A customer-centric framework for assessing performance. *The Cornell Hotel and Restaurant Administration Quarterly, 41*(3), 22–31. doi:10.1177/001088040004100314

Prayag, G., & Ryan, C. (2011). The relationship between the 'push' and 'pull' factors of a tourist destination: The role of nationality - an analytical qualitative research approach. *Current Issues in Tourism, 14*(2), 121–143. doi:10.1080/13683501003623802

Prescott, J., Young, O., O'Neill, L., Yau, N. J. N., & Stevens, R. (2002). Motives for food choice: A comparison of consumers from Japan, Taiwan, Malaysia and New Zealand. *Food Quality and Preference, 13*(7-8), 489–495. doi:10.1016/S0950-3293(02)00010-1

Presutti, M., Boari, C., & Fratocchi, L. (2007). Knowledge acquisition and the foreign development of high-tech start-ups: A social capital approach. *International Business Review, 16*(1), 23–46. doi:10.1016/j.ibusrev.2006.12.004

PriceWaterhouseCoopers. (2013), *Hospitality Outlook.* Retrieved July 17, 2013, from http://www.pwc.co.za/en_ZA/za/assets/pdf/hospitality-outlook-june-2013.pdf

Prideaux, B. (2000). The resort development spectrum: A new approach to modelling resort development. *Tourism Management, 21*(3), 225–240. doi:10.1016/S0261-5177(99)00055-2

Prieto, I. M., Revilla, E., & Rodríguez-Prado, B. (2009). Building dynamic capabilities in product development: How do contextual antecedents matter? *Scandinavian Journal of Management, 25*(3), 313–326. doi:10.1016/j.scaman.2009.05.005

Province of Rimini. (2012). *Osservatorio sul turismo.* Retrieved from http://www.provincia.rimini.it/informa/statistiche/turismo/2012_report/index.html

Province of Trapani. (2013). *Rapporto sul turismo nella Provincia di Trapani periodo 2012/2013.* Retrieved from: http://www.provincia.trapani.it/Sito/servizi/Avvisi/doc/report%202012.pdf

Province of Trento. (2005). *Destination management.* Retrieved from http://www.turismo.provincia.tn.it/binary/pat_turismo_new/presentazioni_materiale_interni/Marketing_territoriale_e_destination_management_13_03_05_.1203518817.pdf

Pruitt, D., & La Font, S. (1995). For love and money: Romance tourism in Jamaica. *Annals of Tourism Research, 22*(2), 419–440. doi:10.1016/0160-7383(94)00084-0

Pun, K., Hui, I., Lau, H. C. W., Law, H., & Lewis, W. G. (2002). Development of an EMS planning framework for environmental management practices. *International Journal of Quality & Reliability Management, 19*(6), 688–709. doi:10.1108/02656710210429573

PWC website. Retrieved from, http://www.pwc.com/us/en/asset-management/hospitality-leisure/travel-and-tourism.jhtml

Qian, W., Razzaque, M. A., & Keng, K. A. (2007). Chinese cultural values and gift-giving behavior. *Journal of Consumer Marketing, 24*(4), 214–228. doi:10.1108/07363760710756002

Quan, S., & Wang, N. (2004). Towards a structural model of tourist experience: An illustration from food experiences in tourism. *Tourism Management, 25*(3), 297–305. doi:10.1016/S0261-5177(03)00130-4

Quazi, H. A., Khoo, Y. K., Tan, C. M., & Wong, P. S. (2001). Motivation for ISO 14000 certification: Development of a predictive model, Omega. *International Journal of Management Sciences, 29*, 525–542.

Qu, H., Lo, L. H., & Im, H. H. (2011). A model of destination branding: Integrating concepts of branding and destination image. *Tourism Management, 32*(3), 465–476. doi:10.1016/j.tourman.2010.03.014

Quin, E. R., Faerman, R. S., Thompson, P. M., & McGrath, R. M. (1990). *Becoming a master manager: A competency framework.* John Wiley & Sons.

Ramaseshan, B., Yip, L. S., & Pae, J. H. (2006). Power, satisfaction and relationship commitment in Chinese store-tenant relationship and their impact on performance. *Journal of Retailing, 82*(1), 63–70. doi:10.1016/j.jretai.2005.11.004

Ramirez, G. A. (2012). Sustainable development: Paradoxes, misunderstandings and learning organizations. *The Learning Organization, 19*(1), 58–76. doi:10.1108/09696471211190365

Rappaport, A., & Chammah, A. M. (1965). *Prisoner's Dilemma.* Ann Arbor: University of Michigan Press.

Reed, R., & De Fillippi, R. J. (1990). Causal ambiguity, barriers to imitation, and sustainable competitive advantage. *Academy of Management Review, 15*(1), 88–102.

Reggiani, A., Nijkamp, P., & Cento, A. (2010). Connectivity and concentration in airline networks: A complexity analysis of Lufthansa's network. *European Journal of Information Systems, 19*(4), 449–461. doi:10.1057/ejis.2010.11

Reichheld, F. F. (1993). Loyalty-based management. *Harvard Business Review,* (March/April): 64–73. PMID:10124634

Reichheld, F. F., & Sasser, E. W. (1990). Zero defections: Quality comes to services. *Harvard Business Review, 68*(5), 105–116. PMID:10107082

Reid, M. (2005). Performance auditing of integrated marketing communications (IMC) actions and outcomes. *Journal of Advertising, 34*(4), 41–54. doi:10.1080/00913367.2005.10639208

Reid, M., Luxton, S., & Mavondo, F. (2005). The relationship between integrated marketing communication, market orientation, and brand orientation. *Journal of Advertising, 34*(4), 11–23. doi:10.1080/00913367.2005.10639210

Reid, R. D., & Sandler, M. (1992). The use of technology to improve service quality. *Cornell Hotel and Restaurant Quarterly, 33*(3), 68–73. doi:10.1016/0010-8804(92)90123-M

Reimann, M., Lunemann, U. F., & Chase, R. B. (2008). Uncertainty avoidance as a moderator of the relationship between perceived service quality and customer satisfaction. *Journal of Service Research, 11*(1), 63–73. doi:10.1177/1094670508319093

Reimer, A., & Kuehn, R. (2005). The impact of servicescape on quality perception. *European Journal of Marketing, 38*(7/8), 785–808. doi:10.1108/03090560510601761

Reinl, L., & Kelliher, F. (2014). The social dynamics of micro-firm learning in an evolving learning community. *Tourism Management, 40*, 117–125. doi:10.1016/j.tourman.2013.05.012

Reisinger, Y. (2009). *International Tourism: Cultures and Behaviors*. New York: Butterworth- Heinemann.

Reisinger, Y., & Turner, L. W. (2002). Cultural differences between Asian tourist markets and Australian hosts: Part 1. *Journal of Travel Research, 40*(3), 295–315. doi:10.1177/0047287502040003008

Renub Resarch. (2012). *Asia Medical Tourism Analysis and Forecast to 2015*. Retrieved from http://www.marketresearch.com/Renub-Research-v3619/Asia-Medical-Tourism-Forecast-7174680/

*Republic Of Turkey Ministry Of Culture And Tourism*. (n.d.). Retrieved from http: //www.turizm.gov.tr

Research reveals how the world views wellness and health. (2014, January/February). *Pulse*, 12.

Review, L. (2013). *Tourism*. Maseru: Wade Publications, n.d. Retrieved April 23, 2014, from http://www.lesothoreview.com/tourism.htm

Revilla, G., Dodd, T. H., & Hoover, C. (2001). Environmental tactics used by hotel companies in Mexico. *International Journal of Hospitality & Tourism Administration, 1*(3), 111–127. doi:10.1300/J149v01n03_07

Reynolds, R. A., Woods, R., & Baker, J. D. (2007). *Handbook of research on electronic surveys and measurements*. Hershey, PA: Idea Group Reference/IGI Global. doi:10.4018/978-1-59140-792-8

Rheingold, H. (1993). *The online community: Homesteading on the electronic frontier*. New York: Harper Perennial.

Rheingold, H. (2003). *Smart mobs: the next social revolution*. Cambridge, MA: Basic Books.

Rhodes, L., & Eisenberger, R. (2002). Perceived organizational support: A review of the literature. *The Journal of Applied Psychology, 87*(4), 698–714. doi:10.1037/0021-9010.87.4.698 PMID:12184574

Riaz, M. N., & Chaudry, M. M. (2004). *Halal food production*. Boca Raton, FL: CRC Press.

Richards, C. A., & Rundle, A. G. (2011). Business travel and self-rated health, obesity, and cardiovascular disease risk factors. *Journal of Occupational and Environmental Medicine, 53*(4), 358–363. doi:10.1097/JOM.0b013e3182143e77 PMID:21436731

Richter, L. K. (1998). Exploring the political role of gender in tourism research. In W. F. Theobald (Ed.), *Global tourism in the next decade*. Oxford, Woburn: Butterworth Heinemann.

Rifai, T. (2013), *Tourism and Value Chains*. Presentation at, Aid for Trade 4th Annual Review, 8th July, Geneva. Star Alliance website. Retrieved June 30, 2013, from http//www.staralliance.com

Rispoli, M., & Tamma, M. (1995). *Risposte strategiche alla complessità: le forme di offerta dei prodotti alberghieri*. Torino: Giappichelli.

Rispoli, M., & Tamma, M. (1996). *Le imprese alberghiere nell'industria dei viaggi e del turismo*. Padova: CEDAM.

Ritchie, B., & Adair, D. (2002). The growing recognition of sport tourism. *Current Issues in Tourism, 5*(1), 1–6. doi:10.1080/13683500208667903

Ritchie, I., & Hayes, W. (1998). *A guide to implementation of ISO14000 series on environmental management*. Englewood Cliffs, NJ: Prentice-Hall.

Ritchie, J. R. B. (1984). Assessing the impact of hallmark events: Conceptual and research issues. *Journal of Travel Research, 23*(1), 2–11. doi:10.1177/004728758402300101

Ritchie, J. R. B., & Crouch, G. I. (2003). *The Competitive Destination: A Sustainable Tourism Perspective*. Wallingford: CABI Publishing. doi:10.1079/9780851996646.0000

Rittichainuwat, B. N., Qu, H., & Brown, T. J. (2001). Thailand's international travel image: Mostly favorable. *The Cornell Hotel and Restaurant Administration Quarterly, 42*(2), 82–95.

Rivera, M. A., & Upchurch, R. (2008). The role of research in the hospitality industry: A content analysis of the IJHM between 2000 and 2005. *International Journal of Hospitality Management, 27*(4), 632–640. doi:10.1016/j.ijhm.2007.08.008

Roberson, Q. M., & Park, H. J.Hyeon Jeong Park. (2007). Examining the link between diversity and performance: The effects of diversity reputation and leader racial diversity. *Group & Organization Management, 32*(5), 548–568. doi:10.1177/1059601106291124

Robichaud, R., & Khan, M. A. (1988). Responding to market changes: The fast-food experience. *The Cornell Hotel and Restaurant Administration Quarterly, 29*(3), 46–49. doi:10.1177/001088048802900315

Robinson, J. P., Shaver, P. R., & Wrightsman, L. S. (1991). Measures of Personality and Social Psychological Attitudes (ed.). San Diego, CA: Academic Press.

Robock, S. H., & Simmonds, K. (1983). *International business and multinational enterprises*. Homewood, IL: Richard D. Irwin, Inc.

Rogers, P. J. (1996). Food choice, mood and mental performance: some examples and some mechanisms. In H. Meiselman & H. J. H. MacFie (Eds.), *Food choice, acceptance and consumption* (pp. 319–345). London: Blackie. doi:10.1007/978-1-4613-1221-5_9

Rojas, D. S., & Turner, E. (2011). Spam and Pop-Tarts? Joint Response to Anthropology and Tourism. *Anthropology News, 52*(3), 4–4. doi:10.1111/j.1556-3502.2011.52304.x

Romani, S., Grappi, S., & Bagozzi, R. P. (2013). Explaining consumer reactions to corporate social responsibility: The role of gratitude and altruistic values. *Journal of Business Ethics, 114*(2), 193–206. doi:10.1007/s10551-012-1337-z

Ronald, J. L. (1996). Impressions bout the Learning Organization: Looking to see what is behind the curtain. *Human Resource Development Quarterly, 6*(2), 119–122.

Ronnenberg, S. K., Graham, M. E., & Mahmoodi, F. (2011). The important role of change management in environmental management system implementation. *International Journal of Operations & Production Management, 3*(6), 631–647. doi:10.1108/01443571111131971

Roseman, E. (1981). *Managing employee turnover*. New York, NY: Amacom.

Rosenberg, M. J. (2001). *E-learning: Strategies for Delivering Knowledge in the Digital Age*. New York: McGraw-Hill.

Rothwell, W., & Kazanas, H. (1992). *Mastering the instructional design process: A systematic approach*. San Francisco: Jossey-Bass.

Round, D., & Roper, S. (2012). Exploring consumer brand name equity: Gaining insight through the investigation of response to name change. *European Journal of Marketing, 46*(7/8), 938–951. doi:10.1108/03090561211230115

Rousseau, D. M. (1989). Psychological and implied contracts in organizations. *Employee Responsibilities and Rights Journal, 2*(2), 121–139. doi:10.1007/BF01384942

Rousseau, D. M., & Tijoriwala, S. A. (1998). Assessing Psychological Contracts: Issues, Alternatives and Measures. *Journal of Organizational Behavior, 19*(S1), 679–695. doi:10.1002/(SICI)1099-1379(1998)19:1+<679::AID-JOB971>3.0.CO;2-N

Rowley, T., Behrens, D., & Krackhardt, D. (2000). Redundant governance structures: An analysis of structural and relational embeddedness in the steel and semiconductor industries. *Strategic Management Journal, 21*(3), 369–386. doi:10.1002/(SICI)1097-0266(200003)21:3<369::AID-SMJ93>3.0.CO;2-M

Rozin, P. (1996). The socio-cultural context of eating and food choice. In H. Meiselman & H. J. H. MacFie (Eds.), *Food choice, acceptance and consumption* (pp. 83–104). London: Blackie. doi:10.1007/978-1-4613-1221-5_2

Rozkwitalska, M. (2012). Staffing top management positions in multinational subsidiaries—a local perspective on expatriate management. *Journal of Global Science & Technology Forum (GSTF). Business Review (Federal Reserve Bank of Philadelphia), 2*(2), 50–56.

Ruddy, J. (1991). Patterns of hotel management development in South East Asia. *Hospitality Research Journal, 3*, 349–361.

Rumelt, R. P. (1984). Towards a Strategic Theory of the Firm. In R.B. Lamb (Ed.), Competitive Strategic Management (pp. 556-570). Englewood Cliffs, NJ: Prentice-Hall.

Rush, M. C., & Russell, J. E. A. (1988). Leader prototypes and prototype-contingent consensus in leader behavior description. *Journal of Experimental Social Psychology, 24*(1), 88–104. doi:10.1016/0022-1031(88)90045-5

Ryan, C. (1997). *The tourist experience: The new introduction*. London: Cassell.

Ryan, C., & Hall, C. M. (2001). *Sex tourism: Marginal people and liminalities*. London, New York: Routledge.

Ryan, N. J. (1976). *A history of Malaysia and Singapore*. Kuala Lumpur: Oxford University Press.

Ryu, K., & Jang, S. C. (2006). Intention to experience local cuisine in a travel destination: The modified theory of reasoned action. *Journal of Hospitality & Tourism Research (Washington, D.C.)*, *30*(4), 507–516. doi:10.1177/1096348006287163

Saarinen, J., & Kask, T. (2008). Transforming tourism spaces in changing socio-political contexts: The case of Parnu, Estonia, as a tourist destination. *Tourism Geographies*, *10*(4), 452–473. doi:10.1080/14616680802434072

Saarinen, J., Rogerson, C., & Manwa, H. (2011). *Tourism and Millennium Development Goals: tourism for global development?* Routledge.

Sackmann, S. A., Eggenhofer-Rehart, P. M., & Friesl, M. (2009). Sustainable change: Long-term efforts toward developing a learning organization. *The Journal of Applied Behavioral Science*, *45*(4), 521–549. doi:10.1177/0021886309346001

Sadi, M. A., & Henderson, J. C. (2000). The Asian economic crisis and the aviation industry: Impacts and response strategies. *Transport Reviews*, *20*(3), 347–367. doi:10.1080/014416400412841

Safko, L. (2010). *The Social Media Bible*. New Jersey: John Wiley and Sons.

Salavou, H., & Lioukas, S. (2003). Radical product innovations in SMEs: The dominance of entrepreneurial orientation. *Creativity and Innovation Management*, *12*(2), 94–108. doi:10.1111/1467-8691.00272

Salazar, N. B. (2005). Tourism and glocalization "local" tour guiding. *Annals of Tourism Research*, *32*(3), 628–646. doi:10.1016/j.annals.2004.10.012

Salzmann, O., Ionescu-Somers, A., & Steger, U. (2005). The business case for corporate sustainability: Literature review and research options. *European Management Journal*, *23*(1), 27–36. doi:10.1016/j.emj.2004.12.007

Sambasivan, M., & Fei, N. Y. (2008). Evaluation of critical success factors of implementation of ISo 14001 using analytic hierarchy process (AHP): A case study from Malaysia. *Journal of Cleaner Production*, *16*(13), 1424–1433. doi:10.1016/j.jclepro.2007.08.003

Samırkaş, M., & Bahar, O. (2013). *Turizm, Yoksulluk ve Bölgesel Gelişmişlik Farklılıkları*. Ankara, Turkey: Detay Yayıncılık.

Saner, R. (2010). *Trade Policy Governance through Inter-Ministerial Coordination: A Source Book for Trade Officials and Development Experts*. Dordrecht: Republic of Letters Publishing.

Sankar, Y. (2003). Designing the learning organization as an information-processing system: Some design principles from the systems paradigm and cybernetics. *International Journal of Organization Theory and Behavior*, *6*(4), 501–521.

Santos, M. (2011). CSR in SMEs: Strategies, practices, motivations and obstacles. *Social Responsibility Journal*, *7*(3), 490–508. doi:10.1108/17471111111154581

Saw, B. (2009). *The Complete Malaysian Cookbook*. Singapore: Marshall Cavendish Cuisine.

Scarpato, R. (2002). Gastronomy as a tourist product: The perspective of gastronomy studies. In A. M. Hjalager & G. Richards (Eds.), *Tourism and gastronomy* (pp. 51–70). London: Routledge.

Schein, E. H. (1968). Organizational socialization and the profession of management. *Industrial Management Review*, *9*, 1–16.

Scheyvens, R., & Russell, M. (2012). Tourism and poverty alleviation in Fiji: Comparing the impacts of small - and large-scale tourism enterprises. *Journal of Sustainable Tourism*, *20*(3), 417–436. doi:10.1080/09669582.2011.629049

Schianetz, K., Jones, T., Kavanagh, L., Walker, P. A., Lockington, D., & Wood, D. (2009). The practicalities of a learning tourism destination: A case study of the Ningaloo Coast. *International Journal of Tourism Research*, *11*(6), 567–581. doi:10.1002/jtr.729

Schianetz, K., Kavanagh, L., & Lockington, D. (2007). The learning tourism destination: The potential of a learning organisation approach for improving the sustainability of tourism destinations. *Tourism Management, 28*(6), 1485–1496. doi:10.1016/j.tourman.2007.01.012

Schiffman, H. R. (2001). *Sensation and perception*. New York, NY: Wiley & Sons.

Schlinke, J., & Crain, S. (2013). Social Media from an Integrated Marketing and Compliance Perspective. *Journal of Financial Service Professionals, 67*(2), 85-92.

Schlüter, R. G. (2011). Anthropological Roots of Rural Development: A Culinary Tourism Case Study In Argentina. *Tourismos: An International Multidisciplinary Journal of Tourism, 6*(3), 77–91.

Schmallegger, D., & Carson, D. (2010). Is tourism just another staple? A new perspective on tourism in remote regions. *Current Issues in Tourism, 13*(3), 201–221. doi:10.1080/13683500903359152

Schmidt, F. L., & Hunter, J. E. (2000). Select on intelligence. In E. A. Locke (Ed.), *The Blackwell handbook of organizational principles* (pp. 3–14). Oxford, England: Blackwell.

Schmitt, B. (1999). *Experiential marketing*. New York, NY: The Free Press.

Schneider, B., & Schmitt, N. (1986). *Staffing organizations* (2nd ed.). HarperCollins Publishers, Inc.

Schuler, R., Fulkerson, J., & Dowling, P. (1992). An integrative framework of strategic international human resource management. *Human Resource Management, 30*(3), 365–392. doi:10.1002/hrm.3930300305

Schultz, D. E. (1993a). Integrated marketing communications: Maybe definition is in the point of view. *Marketing News, 27*(2), 17.

Schultz, D. E. (1993b). Integration helps you plan communications from outside-in. *Marketing News, 27*(6), 12.

Schultz, D. E. (1999). Integrated marketing communications and how it relates to traditional media advertising. In J. P. Jones (Ed.), *The advertising business: Operations, creativity, media planning, integrated communications* (pp. 325–338). London, UK: Sage. doi:10.4135/9781452231440.n34

Schwandt, D. R., & Marquardt, M. J. (2000). *Organizational learning from world-class theories to global best practices*. Washington, D. C.: St. Lucie Press.

Schwartz, S. H. (1992). In M. P. Zanna (Ed.), *Universals in the content and structure of values: Theoretical advances and empirical tests in 20 countries* (pp. 1–65). Advances in Experimental Social PsychologySan Diego: Academic Press, Inc.

Sciarelli, M. (2008). Resource-Based Theory e Market-Driven Management. *Symphonya, 2*.

Sciarelli, M. (1996). *Processo decisionale e valutazione strategica, la formulazione degli accordi tra imprese*. Padova: Cedam.

Sciarelli, S. (2007). *Il management dei sistemi turistici locali. Strategie e strumenti per la governance*. Torino: Giappichelli.

Scott, N. (2002). Branding the Gold Coast for domestic and international tourism markets. In E. Laws (Ed.), *Tourism Marketing Quality and Service Management Perspectives* (pp. 197–211). London: Continuum.

Scullion, H. (1991). Why companies prefer to use expatriates. *Human Resource Management, 23*, 41–44.

Seaton, A. V., & Alford, P. (2005). The effects of globalisation on tourism promotion. In C. Cooper & S. Wahab (Eds.), *Tourism in the Age of Globalisation* (pp. 97–122). Routledge.

Seetanah, B. (2011). Assessing the dynamic economic impact of tourism for island economy. *Annals of Tourism Research, 38*(1), 291–308. doi:10.1016/j.annals.2010.08.009

Seidl, U. (2012). *Paradies: Liebe* [Paradise: Love]. Austria: Ulrich Seidl Filmproduktion.

Sekaran, U. (2000). *Research methods for business: A skill-building approach* (3rd ed.). New York, NY: John Wiley & Sons, Inc.

Seliger, B. (2002). Toward a more general theory of transformation. *Eastern European Economics, 40*, 36–62.

Selmer, J. (2001). The preference for pre-departure or post-arrival cross-cultural training: An exploratory approach. *Journal of Managerial Psychology, 16*(1), 50–58. doi:10.1108/02683940110366560

Selmer, J. (2002). Practice makes perfect? International experience and expatriate adjustment. *Management International Review, 42*(1), 71–87.

Selwood, J. (2003). The lure of food: Food as an attraction in destination marketing in Manitoba, Canada. In C. M. Hall, L. Sharples, N. M. Mitchell, & B. Cambourne (Eds.), *Food tourism around the world: Development, management and markets* (pp. 178–191). Oxford: Butterworth Heinemann. doi:10.1016/B978-0-7506-5503-3.50013-0

Senge, P. M. (1990). *The fifth discipline: The art and practice of the learning organization.* New York: Currency Doubleday.

Senge, P. M., Kleiner, A., Roberts, C., Ross, R. B., Roth, G., & Smith, B. S. (1999). *The dance of change: The challenge of sustaining momentum in learning organizations.* New York: Currency Doubleday.

Sen, S., & Bhattacharya, C. B. (2001). Does doing good always lead to doing better? Consumer reactions to corporate social responsibility. *JMR, Journal of Marketing Research, 38*(2), 225–243. doi:10.1509/jmkr.38.2.225.18838

SEOPressor. (2012). *Social Media Marketing.* Retrieved June 20, 2014 from Seopressor: http://seopressor.com/social-media-marketing/

Sergeyev, A., & Moscardini, A. (2006). Governance of economic transitions: A case study of Ukraine. *Kybernetes, 35*(1/2), 90–107. doi:10.1108/03684920610640254

Šerić, M., & Gil-Saura, I. (2011). Integrated marketing communications and information and communication technology in the hotel sector: An analysis of their use and development in Dalmatian first-class and luxury hotels. *Journal of Retail & Leisure Property, 9*(5), 401–414. doi:10.1057/rlp.2011.4

Šerić, M., & Gil-Saura, I. (2012a). Integrated marketing communications in high-quality hotels of Central and South Dalmatia: A study from managers' and guests' perspectives. *Tržište-Market, 24*(1), 67–83.

Šerić, M., & Gil-Saura, I. (2012b). ICT, IMC, and brand equity in high-quality hotels of Dalmatia: An analysis from guest perceptions. *Journal of Hospitality Marketing & Management, 21*(8), 821–851. doi:10.1080/19368623.2012.633211

Settoon, R. P., Bennett, N., & Liden, R. C. (1996). Social exchange in organizations: Perceived organizational support, leader-member exchange, and employee reciprocity. *The Journal of Applied Psychology, 81*(3), 219–227. doi:10.1037/0021-9010.81.3.219

Shabbir, S. (2009). Supportive learning environment – a basic ingredient of learning organization. *Proceedings from the 2nd CBRC Conference*, Lahore, Pakistan.

Shanka, T., & Phau, I. Y. (2008). Tourism destination attributes: What the non-visitors say - higher education students' perceptions. *Asia Pacific Journal of Tourism Research, 13*(1), 81–94. doi:10.1080/10941660701883383

Shapiro, B. P. (1988). What the Hell Is 'Market Oriented'? *Harvard Business Review, 66*(6), 119–125.

Shapiro, D. L., Young Von Glinow, M. A., & Cheng, J. L. C. (2005). *Managing multinational teams: global perspectives.* Oxford: Elsevier.

Sharpley, R. (2009). *Tourism Development and the Environment: Beyond Sustainability.* London: Earthscan.

Sharpley, R., & Ussi, M. (2014). Tourism and governance in Small Island Developing States (SIDA): The case of Zanzibar. *International Journal of Tourism Research, 16*(1), 87–96. doi:10.1002/jtr.1904

Shay, J., & Tracey, J. (1997). Expatriate managers. *The Cornell Hotel and Restaurant Administration Quarterly, 38*(1), 30–35. doi:10.1177/001088049703800116

Sheehan, E. P. (1995, February). Affective responses to employee turnover. *The Journal of Social Psychology, 135*(1), 63–69. doi:10.1080/00224545.1995.9711403

Sheehan, L. R., & Brent Ritchie, J. R. (2005). Destination Stakeholders: Exploring Identity and Salience. *Annals of Tourism Research, 32*(3), 711–734. doi:10.1016/j.annals.2004.10.013

Sheehan, L., Brent Ritchie, J. R., & Hudson, S. (2007). The Destination Promotion Triad: Understanding Asymmetric Stakeholder Interdependencies Among the City, Hotels, and DMO. *Journal of Travel Research, 46*(1), 64–74. doi:10.1177/0047287507302383

591

Sheldon, P. S., & Bushell, R. (2009). Introduction to wellness and tourism. In R. Bushell & P. Sheldon (Eds.), *Wellness and tourism: Mind, body, spirit, place* (pp. 3–18). New York, NY: Cognizant Communication Corporation.

Shen, J. (2005). International training and management development: Theory and reality. *Journal of Management Development*, 24(7), 656–666. doi:10.1108/02621710510608786

Shepherd, R. (1989). Factors influencing food preferences and choice. In R. Shepherd (Ed.), *Handbook of the psychophysiology of human eating* (pp. 3–24). Chichester: Wiley.

Sherriff, T. K., Lorna, F., & Stephen, C. Y. (1999). Managing direct selling activities in China - A cultural explanation. *Journal of Business Research*, 45(3), 257–266. doi:10.1016/S0148-2963(97)00237-3

Sherzer, D. (1996). Race matters and matters of race: Interracial relationships in colonial and postcolonial films. *Cinema, Colonialism, Postcolonialism: Perspectives from the French and Francophone World*, 229-248.

Sheth, J. N. (1983). An integrative theory of patronage preference and behavior. In W. R. Darden & R. F. Lusch (Eds.), *Patronage Behavior and Retail Management* (pp. 11–27). New York: Elsevier Science.

Shimp, T. A. (2003). *Advertising, promotion and supplemental aspects of integrated marketing communications* (6th ed.). Cincinnati, OH: South-Western, Thomson Learning.

Shore, L. M., & Tetrick, L. E. (1991). A construct validity study of the survey of perceived organizational support. *The Journal of Applied Psychology*, 76(5), 637–643. doi:10.1037/0021-9010.76.5.637

Siguaw, J. A., & Enz, C. A. (1999). Best practices in information technology. *The Cornell Hotel and Restaurant Administration Quarterly*, 40(5), 58–71. doi:10.1177/001088049904000510

Simon, H. A. (1947). *Administrative behavior*. New York: MacMillan.

Sims, R., & Schraeder, M. (2004). *An examination of salient factor affecting expatriate culture shock.* Retrieved from, March 12, 2014, http://www.highbeam.com/doc/1P3-650634311.html

Singh, R., & Mangat, N. S. (1996). *Elements of Survey Sampling.* Dordrecht, The Netherlands: Kluwer Academic Publishers. doi:10.1007/978-94-017-1404-4

Singh, S. (2008). *Social Media Marketing for Dummies.* John Wiley and Sons.

Sirdeshmukh, D., Japdig, S., & Berry, S. (2002). Customer trust, value, and loyalty in relational exchanges. *Journal of Marketing*, 66(1), 15–37. doi:10.1509/jmkg.66.1.15.18449

SISAD. (2015). International School Specializing in Albergo Diffuso. Retrieved May 25, 2015 from http://www.sisad.it/en/home_page

Skinner, H. (2005). Wish you were here? Some problems associated with integrating marketing communications when promoting place brands. *Place Branding*, 1(3), 299–315. doi:10.1057/palgrave.pb.5990030

Slater, S. F., & Narver, J. C. (1995). Market Orientation and the Learning Organisation. *Journal of Marketing*, 59(3), 63–74. doi:10.2307/1252120

*Slowfood Movement.* (2011). Retrieved July 10, 20111 from http://www.slowfood.com/

Smit, A. J. (2010). The competitive advantage of nations: Is Porter's diamond framework a new theory that explains the international competitiveness of countries? *Southern African Business Review*, 14(1), 105–130.

Smith, N. C. (2003). The new corporate philanthropy. In Harvard Business School Press (Eds.), Harvard Business Review on corporate social responsibility (pp. 157-188). Boston: Harvard Business School Press.

Smith, A. K., & Bolton, R. N. (1998). An experimental investigation of service failure and recovery: Paradox or peril? *Journal of Service Research*, 1(1), 65–81. doi:10.1177/109467059800100106

Smith, A. K., & Bolton, R. N. (2002). The effect of customers' emotional responses to service failures on their recovery effort evaluations and satisfaction judgments. *Journal of the Academy of Marketing Science*, 30(1), 5–23. doi:10.1177/03079450094298

Smith, A. K., Bolton, R. N., & Wagner, J. (1999). A model of customer satisfaction with service encounters involving failure and recovery. *JMR, Journal of Marketing Research, 34*(August), 356–372. doi:10.2307/3152082

Smith, A., & Reynolds, N. (2009). Affect and cognition as predictors of behavioral intentions towards services. *International Marketing Review, 26*(6), 580–600. doi:10.1108/02651330911001305

Smith, C. A., Organ, D. W., & Near, J. P. (1983). Organizational citizenship behavior: Its nature and antecedents. *The Journal of Applied Psychology, 68*(4), 653–663. doi:10.1037/0021-9010.68.4.653

Smith, V. L. (Ed.). (2012). *Hosts and guests: The anthropology of tourism*. University of Pennsylvania Press.

So, K. K. G., & King, C. (2010). When experience matters: Building and measuring hotel brand equity. The customers' perspective. *International Journal of Contemporary Hospitality Management, 22*(5), 589–608. doi:10.1108/95961191080000538

Solomon, M. (2004). *Consumer behavior: Buying, having and being* (6th ed.). Upper Saddle River, NJ: Prentice-Hall.

Soltani, E., & Wilkinson, A. (2010). Stuck in the middle with you: The effects of incongruency of senior and middle managers' orientations on TQM programmes. *International Journal of Operations & Production Management, 30*(4), 365–397. doi:10.1108/01443571011029976

Sorenson, T., & Epps, R. (2003). The role of tourism in the economic transformation of the Central West Queensland Economy. *The Australian Geographer, 34*(1), 73–89. doi:10.1080/00049180320000066164

South Pacific Tourism Organisation. (2014). *Pacific Regional Tourism Strategy 2015-2019*. South Pacific Tourism Organisation.

Spa Finder Wellness 365. (2014). *2014 trends report: Top 10 global spa and wellness trends forecast*. Retrieved May 5, 2014, from http://www.spafinder.com/trends2014.htm

Spa Finder Wellness 365. (2014). *Healthy hotels 2.0*. Retrieved May 5, 2014, from http://www.spafinder.com/trends/2014/healthy-hotels.htm

*Spa Finder's Top Ten European Spa Trends*. (2006, August 27). Retrieved June 20, 2014, from http://www.americanspacom/spa-news/spa-finders-top-ten-european-spa-trends.

Spark, B., Bowen, J., & Klag, S. (2003). Restaurant and the tourist market. *International Journal of Contemporary Hospitality Management, 15*(1), 6–13. doi:10.1108/09596110310458936

Sparks, B. (2007). Planning a wine tourism vacation? Factors that help to predict tourist behavioral intentions. *Tourism Management, 28*(5), 1180–1192. doi:10.1016/j.tourman.2006.11.003

Spencer, L., & Spencer, M. (1993). *Competence at work: Models for superior performance*. NY: John Wiley & Sons.

Spinelli, M. A., & Canavos, G. C. (2000). Investigating the Relationship between Employee Satisfaction and Guest Satisfaction. *The Cornell Hotel and Restaurant Administration Quarterly, 41*(6), 29–33.

Squalli, J. (2013). Airline Passenger Traffic Openness and the Performance of Emirates Airline. *The Quarterly Review of Economics and Finance*, (0). doi:10.1016/j.qref.2013.07.010

Sroufe, R. (2000). Environmental management systems: implications for operations management and firm performance. Ph.D. Dissertation, Michigan State University, Michigan.

Stabler, M. J. (1990). The image of destinations regions: Theoretical and empirical aspects. In B. Goodall & G. Ashworth (Eds.), *Marketing in the tourism industry: The promotion of destination regions* (pp. 133–161). London: Routledge.

Stackpole, & Associates. (2010). *Inbound Medical Tourism: Survey of US International Patient Departments*. Retrieved from http://www.stackpoleassociates.com/

Stanley, D. (2011). *Moon Handbooks Fiji* (9th ed.). Avalon Travel Publishing.

Staw, B. M. (1980). The Consequences of Turnover. *Journal of Occupational Behaviour, 1*(4), 253–273.

Steiner, D. (1972). *Group process and productivity*. New York: Academic Press.

Steinmueller, W. 2002. Virtual communities and the new economy. In: R. Mansell (Ed.), Inside the communication revolution: Evolving patterns of social and technical interaction. Oxford: Oxford University Press doi:10.1093/acprof:oso/9780198296553.003.0002

Stelzner, M. (2011). *2011 Social Media Marketing Industry Report How Marketers Are Using Social Media To Grow Their Businesses*. Retrieved March 16, 2014 From 2011 Social Media Marketing Industry Report: http://www.socialmediaexaminer.com/SocialMediaMarketingReport2011.pdf

Sterman, J. D. (2000). *Business Dynamics: Systems Thinking and Modeling for a Complex World*. Boston: Irwin McGraw-Hill.

Sternberg, R. J. (1997). *Successful intelligence: How practical and creative intelligence determine success in life*. New York, NY: Plume.

Sterne, J. (2010). Social Media Metrics. New Jersey: John Wiley and Sons

Stern, E., & Krakover, S. (1993). The formation of a composite urban image. *Geographical Analysis*, 25(2), 130–146. doi:10.1111/j.1538-4632.1993.tb00285.x

Steven, A. B., Dong, Y., & Dresner, M. (2012). Linkages between customer service, customer satisfaction and performance in the airline industry: Investigation of non-linearities and moderating effects. *Transportation Research Part E, Logistics and Transportation Review*, 48(4), 743–754. doi:10.1016/j.tre.2011.12.006

Stipanuk, D. M. (1993). Tourism and technology: Interactions and implications. *Tourism Management*, 14(4), 267–278. doi:10.1016/0261-5177(93)90061-O

Stone, H., & Ranchlod, A. (2006). Competitive advantage of a nation in the global arena: A quantitative advancement to Porter's diamond applied to the UK, USA, and BRIC nations. *Strategic Change*, 15(6), 283–284. doi:10.1002/jsc.770

Stone, M. (1974). Cross-validatory choice and assessment of statistical predictions. *Journal of the Royal Statistical Society. Series A (General)*, 36(2), 111–147.

Storey, J. (1992). *Developments in the management of human resources*. Cambridge, MA: Blackwell Publications.

Strauss, B., & Mang, P. (1999). Culture shocks in intercultural service encounters? *Journal of Services Marketing*, 13(3/4), 329–346. doi:10.1108/08876049910282583

Sudharatna, Y., & Li, L. (2004). Learning organization characteristics contributed to its readiness-to-change: A study of the mobile phone service industry. *Managing Global Transitions*, 2(2), 163–178.

Sulek, J. M., & Hensley, R. L. (2004). The relative importance of food, atmosphere, and fairness of wait: The case of a full-service restaurant. *The Cornell Hotel and Restaurant Administration Quarterly*, 45(3), 235–247. doi:10.1177/0010880404265345

Sun, H., Fan, Z., Zhou, Y., & Shi, Y. (2010). Empirical research on competitiveness factors analysis of real estate industry of Beijing and Tianjin. *Engineering, Construction, and Architectural Management*, 17(3), 240–251. doi:10.1108/09699981011038042

Susi, T., & Ziemke, T. (2001). Social cognition, artifacts, and stigmergy. *Cognitive Systems Research*, 2(4), 273–290. doi:10.1016/S1389-0417(01)00053-5

Sutton, J. (1996). A profile of expatriate managers in China's international joint venture hotels. *Asian Journal of Business & Information Systems*, 1(2), 175–190.

Suutari, V., & Burch, D. (2001). The role of on site training and support in expatriation. *Career Development International*, 6(6), 298–311. doi:10.1108/EUM0000000005985

Swieringa, J., & Wierdsma, A. (1992). *Becoming a learning organization: Beyond the learning curve*. Reading, MA: Addison-Wesley.

Tabacchi, M. H. (2010). Current research and events in the spa industry. *Cornell Hospitality Quarterly*, 51(1), 102–117. doi:10.1177/1938965509356684

Tabachnick, B. G., & Fidell, L. S. (2001). *Using multivariate statistics* (4th ed.). Boston, MA: Allyn and Bacon.

Tadmor, C. T. (2006). Acculturation strategies and integrative complexity as predictors of overseas success. Paper presented at the *Annual Meeting of the Academy of Management* in Atlanta, Georgia. doi:10.5465/AMBPP.2006.27163802

Tanford, S., Carola, R., & Kimb, Y. S. (2011). The influence of reward program membership and commitment on hotel loyalty. *Journal of Hospitality & Tourism Research (Washington, D.C.)*, *31*, 319–328.

Tanzania's Ministry of natrual Resources and Tourism (2012). *Tourism Master Plan – Strategy and Actions*, p.68. Retrieved May 7, 2014, from http://www.tzonline.org/pdf/tourismmasterplan.pdf

Tao, T., & Wall, G. (2009). A livelihood approach to sustainability. *Asia Pacific Journal of Tourism Research*, *14*(2), 137–152. doi:10.1080/10941660902847187

Tate, S. (2011). Heading South: Love/Sex, necropolitics, and decolonial romance. *Small Axe*, *15*(2), 43–58. doi:10.1215/07990537-1334230

Tayeb, M. (2001). Conducting research across cultures: Overcoming drawbacks and obstacles. *International Journal of Cross Cultural Management*, *1*(1), 91–108. doi:10.1177/147059580111009

Taylor, E., & Riklan, D. (2009).*Mastering the world of Marketing*. New Jersey: Wiley and Sons.

Taylor, H. L. Jr, & McGlynn, L. (2009). International tourism in Cuba: Can capitalism be used to save socialism? *Futures*, *41*(6), 405–413. doi:10.1016/j.futures.2008.11.018

Taylor, J. S. (2001). Dollars are a girl's best friend? Female tourists' sexual behaviour in the Caribbean. *Sociology*, *35*(3), 749–764. doi:10.1177/S0038038501000384

Taylor, M., & Singleton, S. G. (1993). The communal-resource: Transaction costs and the solution ofcollective action problems. *Political Science (Wellington, N.Z.)*, *21*, 95–215.

Taylor, S. J., & Bogdan, R. (1998). *Introduction to qualitative research methods: A guidebook and resource*. New York: Wiley.

Teas, R. K., & Agarwal, S. (2000). The Effects of Extrinsic Product Cues on Consumers' Perceptions of Quality, Sacrifice, and Value. *Journal of the Academy of Marketing Science*, *28*(2), 278–290. doi:10.1177/0092070300282008

Telfer, D. J., & Wall, G. (1996). Linkages between tourism and food production. *Annals of Tourism Research*, *23*(3), 635–653. doi:10.1016/0160-7383(95)00087-9

Tellström, R., Gustafsson, I., & Mossberg, L. (2006). Consuming heritage: The use of local food culture in branding. *Place Branding*, *2*(2), 130–143. doi:10.1057/palgrave.pb.5990051

Tenenhaus, M., Vinzi, V. E., Chatelin, Y.-M., & Lauro, C. (2005). PLS path modeling. *Computational Statistics & Data Analysis*, *48*(1), 159–205. doi:10.1016/j.csda.2004.03.005

Testa, M. R. (2002). Leadership dyads in the cruise industry: The impact of cultural congruency. *International Journal of Hospitality Management*, *21*(4), 425–441. doi:10.1016/S0278-4319(02)00036-1

Testa, M. R. (2007). A deeper look at national culture and leadership in the hospitality industry. *International Journal of Hospitality Management*, *26*(2), 468–484. doi:10.1016/j.ijhm.2006.11.001

The Economist. (1997). The world in figures: The world in 1998. *Economist Publications*, 95-98.

The Equity Kicker. (2012). *More on the future of TV*. Retrieved March 20, 2014 from http://www.carphone-warehouse.com

The Travel Foundation. (2002). *Tourism supply chains*. Retrieved May 7, 2014, from, http://www.thetravelfoundation.org.uk/images/media/5._Tourism_supply_chains.pdf

The Westin Beijing. (2009). *Westin Hotel Beijing*. Retrieved 17 December 2009 from, http://www.starwoodhotels.com/westin/property/area/destinations/overview.html?destination=78andpropertyID=1704

Thomas, M. (2000). Exploring the contexts and meanings of women's experiences of sexual intercourse on holiday. In Tourism and sex: Culture, commerce and coercion (pp. 45-66). New York: Pinter.

Thomases, H. (2010). *Twitter Marketing: An Hour a Day*. Indiana: Wiley Publishing Inc.

Thompson, A. A., & Strickland, A. J. (1996). *Strategic management: concepts and cases* (9th ed.). Chicago, IL: Irwin Truss.

Thorndike, R., & Stein, S. (1937). An evaluation of the attempts to measure social intelligence. *Psychological Bulletin*, *34*(5), 275–285. doi:10.1037/h0053850

Thorson, E., & Moore, J. (1996). *Integrated communication: Synergy of persuasive voices*. Mahwah, NJ: Lawrence Erlbaum Associates.

Tibor, T., & Feldman, I. (1996). *ISO 14000: a guide to the new environmental management standards*. Chicago, IL: Irwin Professional Publishing.

Tideman, M. C. (1983). External influences on the hospitality industry. In E. H. Cassee & E. Reuland (Eds.), *The management of hospitality*. Oxford: Pergamon.

*Tifindell Ski Resort website*. (n.d.). Retrieved July 17, 2013, from http://www.tiffindell.co.za

Tikkanen, I. (2007). Maslow's hierarchy and food tourism in Finland: Five cases. *British Food Journal*, *109*(9), 721–734. doi:10.1108/00070700710780698

Tilley, F. (1999). The gap between the environmental attitudes and the environmental behavior of small firms. *Business Strategy and the Environment*, *8*(4), 238–248. doi:10.1002/(SICI)1099-0836(199907/08)8:4<238::AID-BSE197>3.0.CO;2-M

Tippins, M. J., & Sohi, R. S. (2003). IT competency and firm performance: Is organizational learning a missing link? *Strategic Management Journal*, *24*(8), 745–761. doi:10.1002/smj.337

Torbiorn, I. (1994). Operative and strategic use of expatriates in new organizations and market structure. *International Studies of Management & Organization*, *24*(3), 5–17.

Torp, S. (2009). Integrated communications: From one look to normative consistency. *Corporate Communications: An International Journal*, *14*(2), 190–206. doi:10.1108/13563280910953861

Torres, E. N., & Kline, S. (2013). From customer satisfaction to customer delight: Creating a new standard of service for the hotel industry. *International Journal of Contemporary Hospitality Management*, *25*(5), 642–659. doi:10.1108/IJCHM-Dec-2011-0228

Tosun, C. (1999). An Analysis of the Economic Contribution of Inbound International Tourism in Turkey. *Tourism Economics*, *5*(3), 217–250.

Tran, B. (2008). *Expatriate selection and retention*. Doctoral dissertation. California School of Professional Psychology at Alliant International University, San Francisco, California, United States of America.

Tran, B. (2009). Knowledge management: The construction of knowledge in organizations. In D. Jemielniak & J. Kociatkiewicz (Eds.), *Handbook of research on knowledge-intensive organizations* (pp. 512–528). Hersey, PA: Information Science Reference/ IGI Global. doi:10.4018/978-1-60566-176-6.ch031

Tran, B. (2013). Industrial and organizational (I/O) psychology: The roles and purposes of I/O practitioners in global businesses. In B. Christiansen, E. Turkina, & N. Williams (Eds.), *Cultural and technological influences on global business* (pp. 175–219). Hershey, PA: Premier Reference Sources/IGI Global.

Tran, B. (2014a). Ethos, pathos, and logos of doing business abroad: Geert Hofstede's five dimensions of national culture on transcultural marketing. In B. Christiansen, S. Yildiz, & E. Yildiz (Eds.), *Transcultural marketing for incremental and radical innovation* (pp. 255–280). Hershey, PA: Premier Reference Source.

Tran, B. (2014b). The human elements of the knowledge worker: Identifying, managing, and protecting the intellectual capital within the knowledge management. In M. A. Chilton & J. M. Bloodgood (Eds.), *Knowledge management and competitive advantage: Issues and potential solutions* (pp. 281–303). Hershey, PA: Premier Reference Source/IGI Global. doi:10.4018/978-1-4666-4679-7.ch017

Tran, B. (2014c). Rhetoric of play: Utilizing the gamer factor in selecting and training employees. In T. M. Connolly, T. Hainey, E. Boyle, G. Baxter, & P. Moreno-Ger (Eds.), *Psychology, pedagogy, and assessment in serious Games* (pp. 175–203). Hershey, PA: Premier Refeence Source/ IGI Global. doi:10.4018/978-1-4666-4773-2.ch009

Tran, B. (2014d). The foundation of cultural intelligence: Human capital. In B. Christiansen, S. Yıldız, & E. Yıldız (Eds.), *Effective Marketing in contemporary globalism*. Hershey, PA: Premier Reference Source/IGI Global. doi:10.4018/978-1-4666-6220-9.ch020

Tranfield, D., Denyer, D., & Smart, P. (2003). Towards a Methodology for Developing Evidence-Informed Management Knowledge by Means of Systematic Review. *British Journal of Management, 14*(3), 207–222. doi:10.1111/1467-8551.00375

Treadway, C., & Smith, M. (2010). *Facebook Marketing: An hour a Day*. Indiana: Wiley Publishing.

Trespalacios, J. A., Vázquez, R., & Bello, L. (2005). *Investigación de Mercados*. Madrid: Thompson.

Tretheway, M. (1990). Globalization of the Airline Industry and Implications for Canada. *Logistics and Transportation Review, 26*(4), 357.

Tretheway, M., & Oum, T. (1992). *Airline Economics: Foundations for Strategy and Policy*. Vancouver: University of British Columbia.

Tribe, J., Font, X., Griffiths, N., Vickery, R., & Yale, K. (2000). *Environmental Management of Rural Tourism and Recreation*. London, UK: Cassell.

Trip Advisor. (2015). Reviews and advice on hotels, resorts, flights, vacation rentals, travel packages, and lots more! Retrieved May 25, 2015 from http://www.tripadvisor.com/Hotel_Review-g194930-d633424-Reviews-Residenza_Sveva-Termoli_Province_of_Campobasso_Molise.html

Tsai, H. L., Zeng, S. Y., Lan, C. H., & Fang, R. J. (2012). The impacts of expatriate selection criteria on organizational performance in subsidiaries of transnational corporate. Recent Researches in Applied Computers and Computational Science. In *Proceedings of the 11th WSEAS International Conference on Applied Computer and Applied Computational Science*. WSEAS.

Tsaur, S. H., Lin, C. T., & Wu, C. S. (2005). Cultural differences of service quality and behavioral intention in tourist hotels. *Journal of Hospitality Marketing & Management, 13*(1), 41–63. doi:10.1300/J150v13n01_04

Tsoukatos, E., & Rand, G. K. (2007). Cultural influences on service quality and customer satisfaction: Evidence from Greek insurance. *Managing Service Quality, 17*(4), 467–485. doi:10.1108/09604520710760571

Tsui, A. S., Pearce, J. L., Porter, L. W., & Tripoli, A. M. (1997). Alternative approaches to the employee-organization relationship: Does investment in employees pay off? *Academy of Management Journal, 40*(5), 1089–1121. doi:10.2307/256928

Tsui, A. S., & Wu, J. B. (2005). The employment relationship versus the mutual investment approach: Implications for human resource management. *Human Resource Management, 44*(2), 115–121. doi:10.1002/hrm.20052

Tubergen, A. V., & Van der Linden, S. (2001). A brief history of spa therapy. *Annals of the Rheumatic Diseases, 61*(3), 273–275. doi:10.1136/ard.61.3.273 PMID:11830439

Tung, R. L. (1981). Selection and training of personnel for overseas assignments. *The Columbia Journal of World Business, 16*, 68–78.

Tung, R. L. (1982). Selection and training procedures of United States, European, and Japanese multinationals. *California Management Review, 25*(1), 57–71. doi:10.2307/41164993

Tung, R. L. (1984). Strategic management of human resources in the multi-national enterprise. *Human Resource Management, 23*(2), 129–144. doi:10.1002/hrm.3930230204

Tung, R. L. (1987). Expatriate assignments: Enhancing success and minimizing failure. *The Academy of Management Executive, 1*(2), 117–125. doi:10.5465/AME.1987.4275826

Tung, R. L. (1988). *The new expatriates: Managing human resources abroad*. Cambridge, MA: Ballinger.

Tung, R. L., & Worm, V. (2001). Network capitalism: The role of human Resources in penetrating the China market. *International Journal of Human Resource Management, 12*(4), 517–534. doi:10.1080/713769653

Tuorila, H., Meiselman, H. L., Bell, R., Cardello, A. V., & Johnson, W. (1994). Role of sensory and cognitive information in the enhancement of certainty and liking for novel and familiar foods. *Appetite, 23*(3), 231–246. doi:10.1006/appe.1994.1056 PMID:7726542

*Turkish Statistical Institute*. (n.d.). Retrieved from http://www.tuik.gov.tr

Turner, J., & Shah, R. (2011). *How to Make Money with Social Media*. New Jersey: FT Press.

Tuten, T. (2008). *Advertising 2.0: Social Media Marketing*. Westport: Greenwood Publishing.

Uğuz, S. Ç., & Topbaş, F. (2011). *Döviz Kuru Oynaklığı Turizm Talebi İlişkisi: 1990-2010 Türkiye Örneği*. Paper presented at EconAnadolu 2011: Anadolu International Conference in Economics II, Eskisehir, Turkey.

Ulrich, D. 1998. Six practices for creating communities of value, not proximity. In F. Hesselbein, M. Goldsmith, R. Beckhard, & R. Schubert (Eds.), The community of the future. San Francisco, CA: Jossey-Bass Publishers.

Um, S. (1993). Pleasure travel destination choice. In M. Khan, M. Olsen, & T. Var (Eds.), *VNR's Encyclopedia of Hospitality and Tourism* (pp. 811–821). New York: Van Nostrand Reinhold.

Um, S., & Crompton, J. L. (1990). Attitude determinants in tourism destination choice. *Annals of Travel Research*, *17*(3), 432–448. doi:10.1016/0160-7383(90)90008-F

UNEP & IH&RA, (2001). Environmental Good Practice in Hotels in Enz & Siguaw, *Best Hotel Environmental Practices*, 72-7.

UnionCamere. (2013). *Impresa Turismo, Report about tourism economy in Italy*. Available at http://www.ontit.it/opencms/export/sites/default/ont/it/riservativip/files/impresa_turismo_2013.pdf

United Nations Economic Commission for Africa. (2008). *Sustainable Development Report on Africa*. Retrieved May 7, 2014, from http://www.uneca.org/eca_resources/publications/books/sdra/SDRAfull.pdf

United Nations Environment Programme website. Retrieved from http://www.unep.org/resourceefficiency/Business/SectoralActivities/Tourism/FactsandFiguresaboutTourism/ImpactsofTourism/EconomicImpactsofTourism/NegativeEconomicImpactsofTourism/tabid/78784/Default.aspx

United Nations World Tourism Organization website. Sustainable Tourism – Eliminating Poverty (ST-EP) Programme Retrieved May 7, 2014, from http://www.unwtostep.org/

United Nations World Tourism Organization. (2006). *Support to Institutional and Capacity Strengthen of the Tourism Sector*. Madrid.

United Nations World Tourism Organization. (2010). *Tourism Highlights*. Retrieved May 7, 2014, from http://www.unwto.org/facts/eng/pdf/highlights/UNWTO_Highlights10_en_HR.pdf

United Nations World Tourism Organization. (2012). *Panorama OMT del turismo internacional*. Retrieved July 11, 2013, from: http://dtxtq4w60xqpw.cloudfront.net/sites/all/files/pdf/unwto_highlights12_sp_hr.pdf

United Nations. (2000). *World marriage patterns 2000*. Retrieved February 26, 2012 from http://www.un.org/esa/population/publications/worldmarriage/worldmarriagepatterns2000.pdf

UNTWO. (2003). *Cooperation and partnerships in tourism: a global perspective*. Madrid: World Tourism Organization.

UNWTO. (2000a). *Millennium Development Goals*. Retrieved from http://www.unmillenniumproject.org/goals/

UNWTO. (2000b). *Public-Private Sector Cooperation: Enhancing Tourism Competiveness*. Madrid: World Tourism Organization.

UNWTO. (2007). *A practical guide to tourism destination management*. Madrid: World Tourism Organization.

UNWTO. (2013). *Tourism Highlights 2013 Edition*. Madrid: World Tourism Organization.

UNWTO. (2013). *Tourism Highlights*. Available at www.unwto.org

UNWTO. (2013). *Tourism Highlights*. Madrid, Spain: UNWTO.

Urban, G. L., & Hauser, J. R. (1993). *Design and marketing of new products* (2nd ed.). New Jersey, NJ: Prentice Hall.

Uriely, N. (2005). The tourist experience: Conceptual developments. *Annals of Tourism Research*, *32*(1), 199–216. doi:10.1016/j.annals.2004.07.008

Uysal, M., & Hagan, L. A. R. (1993). Motivation of pleasure travel and tourism. In M. Khan, M. Olsen, & T. Var (Eds.), *VNR's Encyclopedia of Hospitality and Tourism* (pp. 798–810). New York: Van Nostrand Reinhold.

Van de Ven, A. H., & Polley, D. (1992). Learning While Innovating. *Organization Science*, *3*(1), 92–116. doi:10.1287/orsc.3.1.92

Van den Belt, M. (2004). *Mediated Modeling: A System Dynamics Approach to Environmental Consensus Building*. Washington, DC: Island Press.

Van den Bergh, J. C. J. M. (1991). *Dynamic models for sustainable development*. Amsterdam: Thesis Tinbergen Institute.

Van Dyne, L., Cummings, L., & McLean Parks, J. (1995). Extra-role behaviors: In pursuit of construct and definitional clarity (a bridge over muddied waters). *Research in Organizational Behavior*, *17*, 215–285.

Van Dyne, L., Graham, J. W., & Dienesch, R. M. (1994). Organizational citizenship behavior: Construct redefinition, measurement, and validation. *Academy of Management Journal*, *37*(4), 765–802. doi:10.2307/256600

Van Dyne, L., & LePine, J. A. (1998). Helping and voice extra-role behavior: Evidence of construct and predictive validity. *Academy of Management Journal*, *41*(1), 108–119. doi:10.2307/256902

Van Scotter, J. R., & Motowidlo, S. J. (1996). Interpersonal Facilitation and Job Dedication as Separate Facets of Contextual Performance. *The Journal of Applied Psychology*, *81*(5), 525–531. doi:10.1037/0021-9010.81.5.525

Vance, C., & Paik, Y. (2002). One size fits all in expatriate pre-departure training? *Journal of Management Development*, *21*(7), 557–571. doi:10.1108/02621710210434665

Vargo, S. L., & Lusch, R. F. (2004). Evolving to a new dominant logic for marketing. *Journal of Marketing*, *68*(1), 1–17. doi:10.1509/jmkg.68.1.1.24036

Varner, I. I., & Palmer, T. M. (2002). Successful expatriation and organizational strategies. *Review of Business*, *23*(2), 8–11.

Veblen, T. (1902). *The theory of the leisure class: An economic study of institutions*. New York: Macmillan.

Veeck, A., & Burns, A. C. (2005). Changing tastes: The adoption of new food choices in post-reform China. *Journal of Business Research*, *58*(5), 644–652. doi:10.1016/j.jbusres.2003.08.009

Vellas, F. (2012), *The indirect impact of tourism: an economic analysis*. Retrieved April, 23, 2012, from www2.unwto.org/agora/indirect-impact-tourism-economic-analysis

Vernon, J., Essex, S., Pinder, D., & Curry, K. (2003). The 'greening' of tourism microbusinesses: Outcomes of focus group investigations in South East Cornwall. *Business Strategy and the Environment*, *12*(1), 49–69. doi:10.1002/bse.348

Verona, G., & Ravasi, D. (2003). Unbundling dynamic capabilities: An exploratory study of continuous product innovation. *Industrial and Corporate Change*, *12*(3), 577–606. doi:10.1093/icc/12.3.577

Vester, F., & Hesler, A. (1982). *Sensitivity Model*. Frankfurt: Main, Umlandverband Frankfurt.

Vickers, Z. M. (1993). Incorporating tasting into a conjoint analysis of taste, health claim, price and brand for purchasing strawberry yogurt. *Journal of Sensory Studies*, *8*(4), 341–352. doi:10.1111/j.1745-459X.1993.tb00224.x

Vidal González, M. (2008). Intangible heritage tourism and identity. *Tourism Management*, *29*(4), 807–810. doi:10.1016/j.tourman.2007.07.003

Vigoda–Gadot, E., Shoam, A., Schwabsky, N., & Ruvio, A. (2008). Public Sector Innovation for Europe: A Multinational Eight–Country Exploration of Citizens' Perspectives. *Public Administration*, *2*(2), 307–329. doi:10.1111/j.1467-9299.2008.00731.x

Vlachos, P. A., Tsamakos, A., Vrechopoulos, A. P., & Avramadis, P. K. (2009). Corporate social responsibility: Attributions, loyalty and mediating role of trust. *Journal of the Academy of Marketing Science*, *37*(2), 170–180. doi:10.1007/s11747-008-0117-x

Voigt, C., Brown, G., & Howat, G. (2011). Wellness tourists: In search of transformation. *Tourism Review*, *66*(1/2), 16–30. doi:10.1108/16605371111127206

Vojinic, P., Matic, M., & Becic, M. (2013). Challenges of expatriation process. In *Proceedings of the 1st International Conference on Management, Marketing, Tourism, Retail, Finance and Computer Applications: Recent Advances in Business Management & Marketing*. Dobrovnik, Croatia: Academic Press.

Volgger, M., & Pechlaner, H. (2014). Requirements for destination management organizations in destination governance: Understanding DMO success. *Tourism Management, 41*(9), 64–75. doi:10.1016/j.tourman.2013.09.001

Vorhies, D. W., & Harker, M. (2000). The Capabilities and Performance Advantages of Market-Driven Firms: An Empirical Investigation. *Australian Journal of Management, 25*(2), 145–173. doi:10.1177/031289620002500203

Voss, C. A., Roth, A. V., Rosenzweig, E. D., Blackmon, K., & Chase, R. B. (2004). A tale of two countries' conservatism, service quality and feedback on customer satisfaction. *Journal of Service Research, 6*(3), 212–230. doi:10.1177/1094670503260120

Vulpe, T., Kealey, D., Protheroe, D., & MacDonald, D. (2001). *A profile of the interculturally effective person.* Center for Intercultural Learning, Canadian Foreign Service Institute.

Wagner, C. M., Huber, B., Sweeney, E., & Smyth, A. (2005). B2B e-marketplaces in the airline industry: Process drivers and performance indicators. *International Journal of Logistics: Research & Applications, 8*(4), 283–297. doi:10.1080/13675560500407390

Walker, P. A., Greiner, R., McDonald, D., & Lyne, V. (1999). The tourism futures simulator: A systems thinking approach. *Environmental Modelling & Software, 14*(1), 59–67. doi:10.1016/S1364-8152(98)00033-4

Wallerstein, I. (1990). Culture as the ideological battleground of the modern world-system. *Theory, Culture & Society, 7*(2-3), 31–55. doi:10.1177/026327690007002003

Walmsley, D. J., & Jenkins, J. M. (1993). Appraisive images of tourist areas: Application of personal construct. *The Australian Geographer, 24*(2), 1–13. doi:10.1080/00049189308703083

Walsh, G., & Bartikowski, B. (2013). Exploring corporate ability and social responsibility associations as antecedents of customer satisfaction cross-culturally. *Journal of Business Research, 66*(8), 989–995. doi:10.1016/j.jbusres.2011.12.022

Wang, C. L., & Ahmed, P. K. (2007). Dynamic capabilities: A review and research agenda. *International Journal of Management Reviews, 9*(1), 31–51. doi:10.1111/j.1468-2370.2007.00201.x

Wang, Y. J., Wu, C., & Yuan, J. (2009). The role of integrated marketing communications (IMC) on heritage destination visitations. *Journal of Quality Assurance in Hospitality & Tourism, 10*(3), 218–231. doi:10.1080/15280080902988048

Wang, Y., & Fesenmaier, D. R. (2007). Collaborative destination marketing: A case study of Elkhart County, Indiana. *Tourism Management, 28*(3), 863–875. doi:10.1016/j.tourman.2006.02.007

Wang, Y., & Krakover, S. (2008). Destination marketing: Competition, cooperation or coopetition? *International Journal of Contemporary Hospitality Management, 20*(2), 126–141. doi:10.1108/09596110810852122

Wang, Y., & Pizam, A. (2011). *Destination marketing and management: theories and applications.* CABI International Publishing. doi:10.1079/9781845937621.0000

Wang, Y., Vela, M. R., & Tyler, K. (2008). Cultural perspectives: Chinese perceptions of UK hotel service quality. *International Journal of Culture. Tourism and Hospitality Research, 2*(4), 312–329.

Wang, Z. (1982). *Han Civilization.* New Haven, CT: Yale University Press.

Wang, Z. H., Evans, M., & Turner, L. (2004). Effects of strategic airline alliances on air transport market competition: An empirical analysis. *Tourism Economics, 10*(1), 23–44. doi:10.5367/000000004773166501

Wasko, M. M., Teigland, R., & Faraj, S. (2009). The provision of online public goods: Examining social structure in an electronic network of practice. *Decision Support Systems, 47*(3), 254–265. doi:10.1016/j.dss.2009.02.012

Wasmuth, W.J., & S.W. Davis, (1983b). Strategies for Managing Employee Turnover. *The Cornell H. R. A. Quarterly, 24*(2), 65-75

Wassmer, U., Dussauge, P., & Planellas, M. (2010). How to Manage Alliances Better Than One at a Time. *MIT Sloan Management Review, 51*(3), 77–84.

Watchravesringkan, K., Karpova, E., Hodges, N. N., & Copeland, R. (2010). The competitive position of Thailand's apparel industry challenges and opportunities for globalization. *Journal of Fashion Marketing and Management, 14*(4), 576–597. doi:10.1108/13612021011081751

Watkins, M. (2013). *What is organizational culture?* Retrieved from http://blogs.hbr.org/2013/05/what-is-organizational-culture?

Watkins, K. E., & Marsick, V. J. (1993). *Sculpting the Learning Organization*. San Francisco: Jossey-Bass.

Waxin, M., & Panaccio, A. (2005). Cross-cultural training to facilitate expatriate adjustment: It works. *Personnel Review, 34*(1), 51–67. doi:10.1108/00483480510571879

Wayne, F. (2000). *Cascio, Costing Human Resources* (4th ed.). Boston: Kent Publishing Company.

Weaver, D. B. (2001). Ecotourism in the Context of Other Tourism Types. In D. B. Weaver (Ed.), *The encyclopedia of ecotourism* (pp. 73–84). New York: CABI Publishing.

Weaver, D., & Lawton, L. (2012). *Tourism Management* (4th ed.). Australia: John Wiley & Sons.

Weaver, P. A., McCleary, K. W., Lepisto, L., & Damonte, L. T. (1994). The relationship of destination selection attributes to psychological, behavioral and demographic variables. *Journal of Hospitality & Leisure Marketing, 2*(2), 93–109. doi:10.1300/J150v02n02_07

Webb, A., & Wright, P. C. (1996). The expatriate experience: Implications for career cusses. *Career Development International, 1*(5), 38–44. doi:10.1108/13620439610130632

Webb, D., Webster, C., & Krepapa, A. (2000). An Exploration of The Meaning and Outcomes of a Customer-Defined Market Orientation. *Journal of Business Research, 48*(2), 101–112. doi:10.1016/S0148-2963(98)00114-3

Weber, K. (2005). Travelers' Perceptions of Airline Alliance Benefits and Performance. *Journal of Travel Research, 43*(3), 257–265. doi:10.1177/0047287504272029

Weber, K., & Sparks, B. (2009). The effect of preconsumption mood and service recovery measures on customer evaluations and behavior in a strategic alliance setting. *Journal of Hospitality & Tourism Research (Washington, D.C.), 33*(1), 106–125. doi:10.1177/1096348008329863

Weber, K., & Sparks, B. A. (2006). Social Identity's Impact on Service Recovery Evaluations in Alliances. *Annals of Tourism Research, 33*(3), 859–863. doi:10.1016/j.annals.2006.03.003

Wederspahn, G. (1992). Costing Failures in Expatriate Human Resource Management. *Human Resource Planning, 15*(3), 27–35.

Weichselbaumer, D. (2012). Sex, romance and the carnivalesque between female tourists and Caribbean men. *Tourism Management, 33*(5), 1220–1229. doi:10.1016/j.tourman.2011.11.009

Welch, D. (1990). *The personnel variable in international business operations: A study of expatriate management in Australian companies.* (Doctoral dissertation). Monash University, Melbourne, Australia.

Wellman, B., Chen, W., & Dong, W. (2002). Networking Guanxi. In T. Gold, D. Guthrie, & D. Wank (Eds.), *Social connections in China: Institutions, culture, and the changing nature of Guanxi.* Cambridge: Cambridge University Press. doi:10.1017/CBO9780511499579.013

Welzel, C., Inglehart, R., & Klingemann, H. D. (2003). The theory of human development: A cross-cultural analysis. *European Journal of Political Research, 42*(3), 341–379. doi:10.1111/1475-6765.00086

Wentling, R., & Palma-Rivas, N. (1997). *Diversity in the workplace series report #2: Current status and future trends of diversity initiatives in the workplace: Diversity expert's perspective.* Berkeley, CA: National Center for Research in Vocational Education.

Wen, Y.-H., & Hsu, C.-I. (2006). Interactive multiobjective programming in airline network design for international airline code-share alliance. *European Journal of Operational Research, 174*(1), 404–426. doi:10.1016/j.ejor.2005.02.040

Wernerfelt, B. (1984). A resource-based view of the firm. *Strategic Management Journal, 5*(2), 171–180. doi:10.1002/smj.4250050207

West, J. B. (1996). Prediction of barometric pressures at high altitude with the use of model atmospheres. *Journal of Applied Physiology (Bethesda, Md.), 81*(4), 1850–1854. Retrieved from http://www.ncbi.nlm.nih.gov/pubmed/8904608 PMID:8904608

West, R., & Turner, L. H. (2004). *Introducing communication theory: Analysis and application* (2nd ed.). USA: McGraw-Hill Companies.

West, S. H. (1997). Playing With Food: Performance, Food, and the Aesthetics of Artificiality in the Sung and Yuan. *Harvard Journal of Asiatic Studies, 57*(1), 67–106. doi:10.2307/2719361

Wetzels, M., Schroder, G. O., & Oppen, V. C. (2009). Using PLS path modeling for assessing hierarchical construct models: Guidelines and empirical illustration. *Management Information Systems Quarterly, 33*(1), 177–195.

White, G. L. (1995, January). Employee turnover: The hidden drain on profits. *HRFocus, 72*(1), 15–17.

White, S. (2002). Rigor and relevance in avian management research: Where are we and where can we go? *Asia Pacific Journal of Management, 19*(2/3), 287–352. doi:10.1023/A:1016295803623

Whitfield, M. (1995). High-flyer hazards. *People Management, 1*(24), 9.

Whitla, P., Walters, P. G., & Davies, H. (2007). Global strategies in the international hotel industry. *International Journal of Hospitality Management, 26*(4), 777–792. doi:10.1016/j.ijhm.2006.08.001

Who's the average male spa-goer? (2014, January/February). *Pulse*, 36-37.

Williams, L. J., & Anderson, S. E. (1991). Job satisfaction and organizational commitment as predictors of organizational citizenship and in-role behaviors. *Journal of Management, 17*(3), 601–617. doi:10.1177/014920639101700305

Williamson, O. E. (1981). The Economics of Organization: The Transaction Cost Approach. *American Journal of Sociology, 87*(3), 548–577. doi:10.1086/227496

Williams, P., & Naumann, E. (2011). Customer satisfaction and business performance: A firm-level analysis. *Journal of Services Marketing, 25*(1), 20–32. doi:10.1108/08876041111107032

Wilson, C. S. (1970). *Food beliefs and practices of Malay fishermen: An ethnographic study of diet on the East Coast of Malaya*. (Unpublished doctoral dissertation). University of California, Berkeley, CA.

Wimmer, R. D., & Dominick, J. R. (2003). Mass media research: An introduction. Belmont, CA: Thomson/Wadsworth.

Winsted, K. F. (1997). The service experience in two cultures: A behavioral perspective. *Journal of Retailing, 73*(3), 337–360. doi:10.1016/S0022-4359(97)90022-1

Wiranatha, A. S. (2001). *A systems model for regional planning towards sustainable development in Bali, Indonesia*. (Unpublished Ph.D. thesis). University of Queensland, St. Lucia, Australia.

Withey, M. J., & Cooper, W. H. (1989). Predicting exit, voice, loyalty, and neglect. *Administrative Science Quarterly, 34*(4), 521–539. doi:10.2307/2393565

Withiam, G. (1997). The best expatriate managers. *The Cornell Hotel and Restaurant Administration Quarterly, 38*(6), 15. doi:10.1177/001088049703800608

Wodecka-Hyjek, A. (2014). A learning public organization as the condition for innovations Adaptation. *Procedia: Social and Behavioral Sciences, 110*(24), 148–155. doi:10.1016/j.sbspro.2013.12.857

Woisetschläger, D. M., Michaelis, M., & Backhaus, C. (2007). The "Dark Side" of Brand Alliances: How the Exit of Alliance Members Affects Consumer Perceptions. *Advances in Consumer Research. Association for Consumer Research (U. S.), 35*, 483.

Wolak, R., Kalafatis, S., & Harris, P. (1998). An investigation into four characteristics of services. *Journal of Empirical Generalizations in Marketing Science, 3*, 22–43.

Wold, H. (1982). Soft modeling: The basic design and some extensions. In K. G. Jöreskog & H. Wold (Eds.), *Systems under indirect observation: Causality, structure, prediction* (Vol. 2, pp. 1–54). Amsterdam, Holland: North Holland.

Wong, A., & Chan, A. (2010). Understanding the leadership perceptions of staff in China's hotel industry: Integrating the macro- and micro-aspects of leadership contexts. *International Journal of Hospitality Management, 29*(3), 437–447. doi:10.1016/j.ijhm.2010.01.003

Wong, N. Y. (2004). The role of culture in the perception of service recovery. *Journal of Business Research, 57*(9), 957–963. doi:10.1016/S0148-2963(03)00002-X

Wood, R., & Payne, T. (1998). *Competency-based recruitment and selection*. New York: John Wiley & Sons.

Woodside, A. G., & Lysonski, S. (1989). A general model of traveler destination choice. *Journal of Travel Research*, *27*(4), 8–14. doi:10.1177/004728758902700402

Wood, V. R., & Robertson, K. R. (1997). Strategic orientation and export success: An empirical study. *International Marketing Review*, *14*(6), 424–444. doi:10.1108/02651339710192975

*World Bank website*. (n.d.). Retrieved July 16, 2013, from http://siteresources.worldbank.org

World Economic Forum. (2013). *The Africa Competitiveness Report*. Retrieved May 7, 2014, from http://www3.weforum.org/docs/WEF_Africa_Competitiveness_Report_2013.pdf

World Economic Forum. (2013). *The Travel & Tourism Competitiveness Report 2013*. Geneva: Author.

World Tourism Organization. (2014), *World Tourism Barometer, 12*. Madrid: UNWTO, Retrieved Dicember, 2014 from www.unwto.org/facts/eng/barometer.htm

World Trade Organization, United Nations World Tourism Organization and Organization for Economic Cooperation and Development. (2013). Tourism and Value Chains. *Aid for Trade 4th Annual Review*. Retrieved July 17, 2013, from http://www.wto.org/english/tratop_e/devel_e/a4t_e/global_review13prog_e/tourism_28june.pdf

World Trade Organization. (2013). *Aid for Trade 4th Annual Review Programme*. Retrieved July 17, 2013, from http://www.wto.org/english/tratop_e/devel_e/a4t_e/aid4trade_e.htm

World Trade Organization. United Nations World Tourism Organization & Organization for Economic Cooperation and Development (2013). *Aid for Trade and Value Chains in Tourism*. Retrieved May 7, 2014, from http://www.wto.org/english/tratop_e/devel_e/a4t_e/global_review13prog_e/tourism_28june.pdf, **World Bank (2011, October 27). Should we be promoting tourism sector investment? [Web log comment]. Retrieved May 7, 2014, from**http://blogs.worldbank.org/psd/should-we-be-promoting-tourism-sector-investment

World Travel & Tourism Council (WTTC). (2013). *Travel & Tourism Economic Impact 2013 – Italy*. Available at http:// www. ontit.it/ opencms/ export/sites/ default/ ont/ it/ documenti/files/ ONT_2013-07-12_02986.pdf

World Travel & Tourism Council. (2012), *Travel and Tourism Economic Impact*. London: WTTC. Retrieved from www.wttc.org/site_media/uploads/downloads/world2012.pdf

World Travel and Tourism Council. (2010). *Progress and Priorities Report*. Retrieved May 7, 2014, from http://www.wttc.org/bin/pdf/original_pdf_file/pandp_final2_low_res.pdf

World Travel and Tourism Council. (2013). *Travel & Tourism Economic Impact*. Retrieved May 7, 2014, from http://www.wttc.org/site_media/uploads/downloads/world2013_1.pdf

Wright, B. E., & Davis, B. S. (2003). Job satisfaction in the public sector – the role of the work environment. *American Review of Public Administration*, *33*(1), 70–90. doi:10.1177/0275074002250254

Wright, C. P., Groenevelt, H., & Shumsky, R. A. (2010). Dynamic revenue management in airline alliances. *Transportation Science*, *44*(1), 15–37. doi:10.1287/trsc.1090.0300

WTTC. (2013). *China-World Travel & Tourism Council*. Retrieved March 15 2014, from http: http://www.google.com.hk/url?sa=t&rct=j&q=&esrc=s&source=web&cd=1&ved=0CB0QFjAA&url=http%3A%2F%2Fwww.wttc.org%2F~%2Fmedia%2Ffiles%2Freports%2Fbenchmark%2520reports%2Fcountry%2520results%2Fchina%2520benchmarking%25202013.ashx&ei=CL5oVPCMHtCxacKEgsgE&usg=AFQjCNGIvcWEUvLOoPAdAqzJ3gX_7xo5wA

Xiang, Z., & Gretzel, U. (2010). *'Role of social media in online travel information search'*, *Tourism Management*, *31* (pp. 179–188). Elsevier.

Xu, J. B., & Chan, A. (2010). A conceptual framework of hotel experience and customer-based brand equity. Some research questions and implications. *International Journal of Contemporary Hospitality Management*, *22*(2), 174–193. doi:10.1108/09596111011018179

Yang, X., Gu, C., & Wang, Q. (2011). Study on the driving force of tourist flows. *Geographical Research, 1*.

Yang, B., Watkins, K. E., & Marsick, V. J. (2004). The construct of the learning organization: Dimensions, measurement, and validation. *Human Resource Development Quarterly, 15*(1), 31–55. doi:10.1002/hrdq.1086

Yang, J. T. (2004). Qualitative knowledge capturing and organizational learning: Two case studies in Taiwan hotels. *Tourism Management, 25*(4), 421–428. doi:10.1016/S0261-5177(03)00114-6

Yang, J. T. (2010). Antecedents and consequences of knowledge sharing in international tourist hotels. *International Journal of Hospitality Management, 29*(1), 42–52. doi:10.1016/j.ijhm.2009.05.004

Yang, J. T., & Wan, C. (2004). Advancing organizational effectiveness and knowledge management implementation. *Tourism Management, 25*(5), 593–601. doi:10.1016/j.tourman.2003.08.002

Yang, J.-Y., & Liu, A. (2003). Frequent Flyer Program: A case study of China airline's marketing initiative—Dynasty Flyer Program. *Tourism Management, 24*(5), 587–595. doi:10.1016/S0261-5177(03)00007-4

Yan, S., & Chen, C.-. (2008). Optimal flight scheduling models for cargo airlines under alliances. *Journal of Scheduling, 11*(3), 175–186. doi:10.1007/s10951-007-0020-1

Yap, G. C. L. (2012). An Examination of the Effects of Exchange Rates on Australia's Inbound Tourism Growth: A Multivariate Conditional Volatility Approach. *International Journal of Business Studies, 20*(1), 111-132.

Yee, L. (2002a). Stepping up. *Restaurants & Institutions, 112*(16), 28–34.

Yee, L. (2002b). Tailoring trends. *Restaurants & Institutions, 112*(21), 26–44.

Yeoman, I., & McMahon-Beattie, U. (2006). Luxury markets and premium pricing. *Journal of Revenue and Pricing Management, 4*(4), 319–328. doi:10.1057/palgrave.rpm.5170155

Yeo, R. K. (2006). Learning Institution to Learning Organization: Kudos to reflective Practitioners. *ICFAI Journal of European Industrial Training, 30*(5), 396–419. doi:10.1108/03090590610677944

Yeung, O., Johnston, K., & Chan, N. (2014). *The global wellness tourism economy 2013*. New York, NY: Global Wellness Institute.

Yin, R. (2003). *Case Study Research: Design and Methods*. SAGE Publications.

Yin, R. K. (1994). *Case Study Research. Design and Methods*. Newbury Park, CA: Sage Publications.

Yin, X., Wu, J., & Tsai, W. (2012). When Unconnected Others Connect: Does Degree of Brokerage Persist After the Formation of a Multipartner Alliance? *Organization Science, 23*(6), 1682–1699. doi:10.1287/orsc.1110.0711

Yip, G. S. (1992). *Total global strategy: Managing for worldwide competitive advantage*. Englewood Cliffs, NJ: Prentice Hall.

Yoo, B., & Donthu, N. (2001). Developing and validating a multidimensional consumer-based brand equity scale. *Journal of Business Research, 52*(1), 1–14. doi:10.1016/S0148-2963(99)00098-3

Yoo, M., & Bai, B. (2013). Customer loyalty marketing research: A comparative approach between Hospitality and Business journals. *International Journal of Hospitality Management, 33*, 166–177. doi:10.1016/j.ijhm.2012.07.009

Yoon, M. H., & Suh, J. (2003). Organizational citizenship behaviours and service quality as external effectiveness of contact employees. *Journal of Business Research, 56*(8), 597–611. doi:10.1016/S0148-2963(01)00290-9

Yooyanyong, P., & Muenjohn, N. (2010). Leadership styles of expatriate managers: A comparison between American and Japanese expatriates. *The Journal of American Academy of Business, 15*(2), 161–167.

Youssef, W., & Hansen, M. (1994). Consequences of strategic alliances between international airlines: The case of Swissair and SAS. *Transportation Research Part A, Policy and Practice, 28*(5), 415–431. doi:10.1016/0965-8564(94)90024-8

Yuan, S., & McDonald, C. (1990). Motivational determinants of international pleasure time. *Journal of Tourism Research, 6*(3), 42–44.

Yúdice, G. (2003). *The expediency of culture: Uses of culture in the global era*. Duke University Press.

Yuksel, A., Kilinc, U. K., & Yuksel, F. (2006). Cross-national analysis of hotel customers' attitudes toward complaining and their complaining behaviours. *Tourism Management*, 27(1), 11–24. doi:10.1016/j.tourman.2004.07.007

Yu, L. (1992). Hotel development and structures in China. *International Journal of Hospitality Management*, 11(2), 99–110. doi:10.1016/0278-4319(92)90004-F

Yu, L., & Goh, S. H. (1995). Perceptions of management difficulty factors by expatriate hotel professionals in China. *International Journal of Hospitality Management*, 14(3/4), 375–388. doi:10.1016/0278-4319(95)00044-5

Yu, L., & Huimin, G. (2005). Hotel reform in China: A SWOT analysis. *Cornell Hotel and Restaurant Quarterly*, 46(2), 153–169. doi:10.1177/0010880404273892

Yule, H., & Cordier, H. (1923). *The Travels of Marco Polo*. Dover Publications.

Yurtseven, R. H., & Kaya, O. (2011). Local Food In Local Menus: The Case Of Gokceada. *Tourismos: An International Multidisciplinary Journal of Tourism*, 6(2), 263–275.

Zakaria, N. (2000). The effects of cross-cultural training on the acculturation process of the global workforce. *International Journal of Manpower*, 21(6), 492–510. doi:10.1108/01437720010377837

Zarrella, D. (2009). *The Social Media Marketing Book*. Sebastopol, CA: O`Reilly Books.

Zeira, Y., & Banai, M. (1985). Selection of Expatriate-Managers in Multinational Corporations: The host environment point of view. *International Studies of Management & Organization*, 15(1), 33–51.

Zeithaml, V. A. (1988). Consumer perceptions of price, quality and value: A means-end model and synthesis of evidence. *Journal of Marketing*, 52(3), 2–22. doi:10.2307/1251446

Zeithaml, V. A., Berry, L. L., & Parasuraman, A. (1996). The behavioral consequences of service quality. *Journal of Marketing*, 60(2), 31–46. doi:10.2307/1251929

Zeithaml, V. A., Bitner, M. J., & Gremler, D. D. (2006). *Services marketing: integrating customer focus across the firm*. New York: McGrawhill.

Zeithaml, V. A., Parasuraman, A., & Berry, L. L. (1990). *Delivering Quality Service; Balancing Customer Perceptions and Expectations*. New York: Free Press.

Zhang, A., & Zhang, Y. (2006). Rivalry between strategic alliances. *International Journal of Industrial Organization*, 24(2), 287–301. doi:10.1016/j.ijindorg.2005.04.005

Zhang, H., Pine, R., & Lam, T. (2005). *Tourism and hotel development in China*. New York, NY: The Haworth Hospitality Press and International Business Press.

Zhang, J., Beatty, S. E., & Walsh, G. (2008). Review and future directions of cross-cultural consumer services research. *Journal of Business Research*, 61(3), 211–224. doi:10.1016/j.jbusres.2007.06.003

Zhao, D., & Lin, I. Y. (2014). Understanding tourists' perception and evaluation of inter-cultural service encounters: A holistic mental model process. *International Journal of Culture, Tourism, and Hospitality Research*.

Zhong, L., Deng, J., & Xiang, B. (2007). Tourism development and the tourism area life-cycle model: A case study of Zhangjiajie National Forest Park, China. *Tourism Management*, 29(5), 841–856. doi:10.1016/j.tourman.2007.10.002

Zikmund, W. G., Babin, W. G., Carr, J. C., & Griffin, M. (2013). *Business research methods* (9th ed.). Mason, OH: South-Western Cengage Learning.

Zollo, M., & Winter, S. G. (2002). Deliberate learning and the evolution of dynamics capabilities. *Organization Science*, 13(3), 339–351. doi:10.1287/orsc.13.3.339.2780

Zubair, S., Bowen, D., & Elwin, J. (2011). Not quite paradise: Inadequacies of environmental impact assessment in the Maldives. *Tourism Management*, 32(2), 225–234. doi:10.1016/j.tourman.2009.12.007

Zuber, A. (2001). A career in food service cons: High turnover. *Nations Restaurant News*, 35(21), 147–148.

# About the Contributors

**Angelo A. Camillo**, PhD, is Associate Professor of Strategic Management at Woodbury University in Burbank California, USA. He has over 35 years of international hospitality industry management experience and has worked and lived in ten countries and four continents. He holds a degree from Heidelberg Hotel Management School Germany, a MBA from San Francisco State University, and a PhD from Oklahoma State University. He teaches courses in Strategic Management, Global Enterprise Management, Business Ethics, Organizational Behavior, and special topics in Hospitality Entrepreneurship and Business Development. He is also hospitality business consultant to major international corporations.

\* \* \*

**Raphaël K. Akamavi** (PhD, The University of Leeds) is a Lecturer in Marketing at The Hull University Business School, The University of Hull, UK. His research interests include product / service innovation with co-creation/co-production, service quality with customer experience, customer relationship management, social capital, and organizational performance. Various refereed papers have been published in a wide range of national and international peer-reviewed outlets (e.g. European Journal of Marketing, Journal of Services Marketing, International Journal of Business Studies, Journal of Financial Services Marketing, Tourism Management etc). His research has achieved award recognition: Award for Best Paper at the 6th International Services Management Conference in Cyprus 2013.

**Francesco Maria Barbini**, Ph.D., is assistant professor of organizational behavior at the Department of Management of the University of Bologna, where he teaches organization theory, organization of tourism enterprises, and human resource management in tourism enterprises. He participates in the research activities of the Center for Advanced Studies on Tourism of the University of Bologna. His main research interests are related to the subjects of organizational change, disaster management, and organization in tourism and cultural heritage industry.

**Jennifer R. Calhoun**, over the past 20 years Jennifer has held various operational and academic positions in the hospitality industry and is also an academic and corporate educator working with a wide range of clients in hospitality including individual properties, brands, management companies and associations. She is currently a PhD Candidate in the Department of Nutrition, Dietetics, and Hospitality Management at Auburn University. Her area of research interests is the sustainable relationships among employers, employees and customers in the hospitality and tourism industry. She is especially interested in the influence of human resource practices on hospitality workers overall success and the influences of processional development initiatives on the hospitality workforce as a means of obtaining a sustained competitive advantage. Among her recognition and awards are: In 2014 she was awarded the Graduate Teaching Assistant Program (GTAP) Fellowship; 2013, awarded the President's Graduate Opportunity Program Fellowship and the Lee and Bob Cannon Endowment for Scholarship in Nutrition and the NDHM: Competitive Graduate Research Fellowship. In 2012, she was awarded the AH&LEF Graduate Scholarship and the Anamerle Arant Memorial Scholarship. In 2010, she received "The Lamp of Knowledge Award for United States Educator" from the American Hotel and Lodging Educational Institute (AH&LEI). Jennifer is also the former Director of the Hospitality and Tourism Institute at a community college and former Director of Seminar Programs at AH&LA Educational Institute. She travels extensively to pursue a variety of professional enrichment and industry/academic liaison activities. She holds various professional certifications including the Certified Hospitality Educator (CHE), and is a Master Instructor for this certification as well as a certified facilitator in "Skills for an Empowered Workforce" by Development Dimensions International (DDI). She is also a consultant with AH&LEI on USAID international projects to build capacity, partnerships, and to improve tourism and hospitality education within organizations and destinations. Projects have included counties such as Grenada, Armenia, Albania and Serbia. Her research has been published in the Journal of Human Resources in Hospitality & Tourism and a book chapter under review with IGI Global. She serves on various industry and professional associations that include a former member of the Nomination Committee for the International Council for Hotels, Restaurants and Institutional Educators (ICHRIE) and currently serves on the ICHRIE Strategic Planning Committee, the Industry Committee, and the Professional Development Committee, as well as, a member of the Alabama Hotel Association, and a Founding Member of Hospitality Educators: www.hospitalityeducators.com. A member of the National Association for Female Executives (NAFE) and a member of the Eta Sigma Delta, Gamma Sigma Delta, Kappa Omicron Nu, and HonorSociety.org.

**Frances Cassidy** is a lecturer in tourism and marketing and has extensive research in the area of small island tourism in developing countries. Frances has given presentations on the travel and tourism industry to visiting international travel agents. She has travelled extensively and is a CTM and member of AFTA, PATA and QTIC.

**Gina Fe G. Causin** has more than 20 years of experience in meeting and event operation and hospitality education. She has taught in Introduction to the Event Industry, Advanced Event Operations, Special Events/Convention Sales, Introduction to Lodging, Advanced Lodging Operations, Housekeeping, Facilities and Design and other hospitality and tourism courses. She has published in the Journal of Family and Consumer Sciences, International Journal of Contemporary Hospitality Management, International Journal of Hospitality Management, and Electronic Journal of Hospitality Legal, Safety and Security Research. Her research interests are sustainability of cultural festivals using the triple bottom line approach, expatriation, culture and socialization, green meetings, events and lodging.

**Sumesh S. Dadwal** is a Senior Lecturer and Programme Leader (MBA), University of Glyndwr, London Campus, London, UK. Dr Dadwal has 15-years of experience in business academic research, teaching, e-Learning, quality assurances and in wide range of business, tourism and Healthcare subjects. He is actively engaged in postgraduate and PhD research supervision. His core areas include International

Marketing & Globalisation, contemporary and technological trends in the marketing, Strategic & technological innovation Management. Besides this, he is also a freelance consultant (business analysis) for emerging markets and also a Member of Advisory and Editorial Board of Academics at some journals of repute.

**Fred DeMicco** is Professor and ARAMARK Endowed Chair in the Department of Hotel, Restaurant and Institutional Management at the University of Delaware. Formerly, he was Associate Director in the School of Hotel, Restaurant and Recreation Management at Penn State University, where he was Professor-in-Charge of the HRIM undergraduate program (and the Master of Science and PhD graduate program for five years), and presently is a Conti Distinguished Professor at the Pennsylvania State University's School of Hotel, Restaurant and Recreation Management. He has worked in Healthcare at the Massachusetts General Hospital, Boston and at Walt Disney World in hotel and restaurant management. Dr. DeMicco's scholarly interests are in; International Strategic Management, Medical Tourism, Wine & Beverage Management and Innovation. He has worked on projects with ARAMARK at four Summer Olympic Games (living in Atlanta, Australia, Athens and Beijing) and has taught and lead dozens of Study@Sea cruise ship management courses around the world. Since 2007, Dr. DeMicco has been supported and is working with the Foundation of the Bank of Volterra to open a new campus in the center of Tuscany for business management and students in the Arts & Sciences. He completed his Ph.D. in Hotel, Restaurant and Institutional Management at Virginia Polytechnic Institute and State University under the direction of Dr. Michael D. Olsen. In 1996, he worked in Hotel Management at Walt Disney World, Florida. Dr. DeMicco also obtained his Ducktorate Degree from Disney University. Dr. DeMicco also served as the Chief Dietitian and Associate Director of Dining and Technology responsible for all menu planning, technology and nutrition in the Virginia Tech Dining Services for five years. He has also been employed by Aramark, Marriott Vacation Club International and several healthcare operations including assisted living facilities. He has authored or co-authored nearly 100 refereed articles in the area of hospitality management and he has co-authored several books including *Restaurant Management: A Best Practices Approach* with Kendall-Hunt Publishers (2015) and *Hospitality 2015: The Future of Hospitality & Travel (2010)* with the Educational Institute of the American Hotel and Lodging Association. Dr. DeMicco is on the Editorial Advisory Board of the Journal of Hospitality & Tourism Research and several other notable research journals.

**Loredana Di Pietro**, PhD, is an Assistant Professor of Organizational Studies in the department of Human and Social Sciences, University of Molise. She teaches courses in Event Management, Business Organization, and Organizational Behavior. She has been involved in researching the organizational consumer behavior, business organization, team-based organization and, organizational conflict resolution.

**Francesca Di Virgilio**, PhD, is Assistant Professor of Organizational Studies in the Department of Economics, Management, Society and Institutions at the University of Molise, Italy. She received her Ph.D. degree in Organization, Technology and Development of Human Resources from the University of Molise, Italy. She was Visiting Researcher at Research Center of Industrial Relations & Organizational Behavior (IROB), Warwick Business School, Warwick, UK. She has been teaching courses at undergraduate and graduate levels including international master programs in several universities on topics such as organization design, organizational behavior, knowledge management and human resources management. She has taught in some of the national Public Administration involved in tailored training program on topics such as job design and organizational analysis, leadership, team building and organizational change. Over the years the results of her research activities have been enriched with the collaboration of peers both nationally and internationally with research articles and publications. She has presented research papers at international conferences: Athens Institute for Education and Research, Athens, Greece, Universidad de Malaga, EIASM (European Institute for Advanced Studies in Management, Belgium), Excellence in Services: Paisley Scotland (United Kingdom), Research School SOM -University of Groningen (NETHERLANDS), Universit de Biarritz, (Francia), Universit du Sud Tolulon-Var (Francia), Universit de Toulouse (Francia). She received a prestigious national award, Roberto Marrama - In search of Research Talent. She is Editor for the International Journal of Digital Content Technology and its Applications, Editor and reviewer for the Journal of Computer Science, Technology and Application. Her research interests and publications focus on human knowledge management, groups' knowledge, social network, e-wom, groups' dynamic, conflict and job stress.

**Alecia C. Douglas** is currently an associate professor at Auburn University in Auburn, Alabama who has served the Hotel and Restaurant Management Program since August 2008. She earned her Ph.D. in Hospitality and Tourism Management from Purdue University in December 2008 and her MSc. in Hospitality Information Technology Management from the University of Delaware in May 2004. Her teaching responsibilities at Auburn University include both undergraduate and graduate core and elective courses. Over the last decade, she has numerous research manuscripts published in some of the top hospitality and tourism journals and refereed papers presented at national and international research conferences. Alecia has a strong record of scholarly achievements in academic research with over 40 journal publications and conference proceedings that have garnered more than 700 citations per Google Scholar Citation Index. She has amassed a culturally diverse work experience in a variety of hotel and restaurant positions in the Caribbean, North America, and Europe.

**Mario Filadoro** (Programme Officer, CSEND) graduated in International Relations from the San Andres University in Argentina. He also has an MA in International Relations and Negotiations from the Latin American Faculty of Social Sciences in Argentina (FLACSO) and an MA in EU International Relations and Diplomacy from the College of Europe in Belgium. Before joining CSEND, he was at the World Trade Organization where he was involved in the development and delivery of online courses on topics related to the multilateral trade system for government officials from least developed and developing countries. Mr. Filadoro's main topics of interest are: trade agreements, EU & Latin America, regionalism and multilateralism, sustainability and tourism.

**Andri Georgiadou** is a Lecturer in Human Resource Management at Hertfordshire Business School. She has completed her Doctorate in managing cultural diversity in Cyprus at London Metropolitan University. Andri's research interests span areas of human resource management including equality and diversity, international HRM and cross-cultural management.

**Irene Gil-Saura** is a full professor in marketing and chair holder in the Marketing Department at the University of Valencia. Her investigation is focused on services marketing, consumer behavior, and retailing. Her articles have appeared in many journals, such as: Tourism Management, Industrial Marketing Management, The Service Industries Journal, Annals of Tourism Research, International Journal of Hospitality Management, Journal of Hospitality Marketing & Management, Journal of Vacation Marketing, International Journal of Contemporary Hospitality Management, etc. She has had conferences papers in the Annual Conference at the European Marketing Academy – EMAC, Conference of the European Association for Education and Research in the Commercial Distribution (EAERCD), International Marketing Trends Conference, and so on.

**Hanafi Hamzah** has 17 years of industrial experience with international airlines and private university. Hanafi graduated with specialization in Tourism and Hospitality Management and is currently pursuing a PhD. from Universiti Putra Malaysia and one of the panels for the Malaysian Qualification Agency in Tourism and Hospitality programme.

**Rahmat Hashim** is an Associate Professor in the Department of Culinary Arts and Gastronomy at the Faculty of Hotel & Tourism Management, Uiniversiti Teknologi MARA Malaysia. He earned his PhD (Food and Leisure) at Sheffield Hallam University. His research interests cover a range of topics in competence management and cognitive skills.

**Svetlana Holt**, Ed. D., has been teaching Management, Leadership, Organizational Behavior, and Strategy undergraduate and graduate courses at Woodbury University School of Business since 2004. Before joining Woodbury community of educators, Svetlana Holt worked as an editor/producer of European business publications, a Russian/English court interpreter, a quality controller for movie editing companies, a store manager for a retail coffee company, a sales manager for industrial chemicals distributor, an office manager for a health center, a service director at LAXCS for United Airlines, and a writing lab supervisor at Los Angeles Community College District. She has fifteen years' experience in corporate training for performance improvement, quality control, small business administration, database management, student support, and new curricula design and evaluation. Dr. Holt is a registered practitioner for Yale's Mayer-Salovey-Caruso emotional intelligence model of organizational development. Her research and publications topics include empathy in leadership, leadership in multicultural settings, emotional intelligence as it relates to organizational performance, international marketing and entrepreneurship, leading the millennial generation, and academic achievement in higher education. Dr. Holt holds a Bachelor's degree in Germanic Philology, TESL and Interpreting from State University of St. Petersburg, Russia, a Master's degree in Business Administration from Woodbury University, a Doctorate in Organizational Leadership from Pepperdine University, and a Post-doctoral Certification in Management and Marketing from Tulane University. She is a member of Delta Mu Delta National Honor Society in Business Administration, member of Phi Delta Kappa International Honor Society for Educators, and a member of the International Society for Performance Improvement.

**Margee Hume** is a Professor in the School of Business and Law at the University of Central Queensland. She researches in innovation in health, professional services, process mapping and service innovation. She has extensive skills in business operations/marketing strategy, interactive technology and strategic marketing. She has an impressive and extensive list of publications in prestigious journals and outlets. Her teaching interest includes service strategy, innovation and digital technology in particular healthcare interactive/digital technology. She specialises in novel methods including application of operations management techniques in a services paradigm.

**Chryso Iasonos** studied Economics at the University of Cyprus and Marketing Management at the Cyprus Institute of Marketing. She has continued her professional studies doing the ACCA and completing the MBA from London South Bank University. She has worked in several Audit Firms as a Chartered Accountant and is currently working as a Golf Membership and Marketing Executive at Aphrodite Hills Resort, Cyprus.

**Sunny (Seonhee) Jeong** is Assistant Professor of Business, Ph.D. in Recreation, Sport and Tourism at the University of Illinois at Urbana-Champaign. Dr. Sunny Jeong joined the faculty at the Business Department of the Wittenberg University in 2012. Before Wittenberg, she worked at the business college at the University of Illinois at Urbana-Champaign. She received her Ph.D. and M.S. (Library Information Science) from the University of Illinois at Urbana-Champaign. Her teaching area is International Business, Business in East Asia, and Global Social Entrepreneurship. Her research interests are social and spiritual capital in management and in international business. She has consulted small-medium companies of USA, Korea, and China. She also advises new social venture development (L3C, 501(C)3 corporation).

**Shahrim Karim** is an Associate Professor and Head of Department of Food Service and Management, Faculty of Food Science and Technology, Universiti Putra Malaysia. His research interests include food and culture, culinary tourism, food habits, and consumer behavior. He has more than 20 years of experience in culinary arts and the hospitality industry. In addition, he travels to promote Malaysia's Heritage food to the world. Shahrim enjoys gardening and writing everything about food.

**Marcus Raphael Lee** graduated in International Relations and History from Boston University and also has a Masters of Business Administration – Hospitality and Tourism from The George Washington University. Marcus was a research assistant at CSEND in 2013. Before joining CSEND, he worked at Four Seasons Hotel in Washington D.C. as Food and Beverage Coordinator/Host.

**Quee-Ling Leong** has a M.Sc. in Food Management from the Universiti Putra Malaysia. Currently, she is pursuing her Doctoral Degree in the area of gastronomic culture and tourism. Her research interests revolves around gastronomy, heritage food, tourism, tourist's behavior and destination marketing.

**Mengyu Li** is going to attend University of Delaware (UD) as a graduate student majoring in Information System & Technology Management in the fall, 2015. She will also be working as a Graduate Assistant to provide any technical support and customer service to faculty members on campus. Mengyu served the St. Regis Monarch Beach Resort & Spa as Human Resources Administrative Assistant for one year. She received Honors Bachelor's Degree from the Hotel, Restaurant and Institutional Management program at UD in Spring 2014. She had worked and been trained at several other hospitality entities, including the St. Regis Aspen, Borgata Water Club, Courtyard Marriott at UD, and Vita Nova restaurant. In addition, Mengyu has passion for community services. She volunteered at Christiana Care Health as their Guest Service Concierge. She embraced the spirit of hospitality and the strong culture at Christiana Care. She was inspired to observe and exercise the best experience practices in bring hospitality to hospitals, or "H2H."

**Yingying Liao** is an Assistant Professor of Quality Management at Hamdan Bin Mohammed Smart University in UAE. Prior to her current appointment, she worked at the International Business School Suzhou (IBSS), Xi'an Jiaotong-Liverpool University, China. Her research interest inlcluding service quality, the dynamics of Chinese cultural values and service quality dimensions of hospitality industry, and managing human resources in services. She published papaer in TQM & Business Excellence, International Journal of Production Research, European Business Review, Journal of Business Ethics and Service Industries Journal and presented papers in several national and international conferences.

**Ingrid Y. Lin** is an Associate Professor of the School of Travel Industry Management at University of Hawai'i at Mānoa. Her area of expertise includes services/hospitality marketing. Her research interests fall within areas of services marketing, consumer behavior, Human Resources Management, and Hotel/Resort and Spa Management. Research topics studied include servicescapes, customer switching behavior, cross-cultural studies, restaurant tipping systems, inter-cultural service encounter, and luxury spa experience. She has published in Journal of Services Marketing, Journal of Hospitality and Tourism Research, International Journal of Hospitality Management, International Journal of Contemporary Hospitality Management, and Journal of Hospitality Marketing and Management. She received her Ph.D. in hotel, restaurant, and institutional management from Pennsylvania State University; Master of Science in hospitality industry studies from New York University; and Bachelor of Science in hospitality administration from Boston University. She has academic/teaching experience both in the U.S. (Saint Xavier University in Chicago, IL; Penn State University in State College, PA) and in Taiwan (Tunghai University and Providence University in Taichung, Taiwan).

**Patricia Martinez** is a PhD candidate at the University of Cantabria (Spain). Her current research interests include corporate social responsibility, consumer behavior and corporate marketing. Her research focuses on theoretical and empirical studies in the tourism sector. Patricia's works have been published in journals of international impact such as International Journal of Hospitality Management, Journal of Business Ethics, Journal of Travel and Tourism Marketing and Service Business. She is also author of two chapters in several collective works and one book. She regularly participates in prestigious international and national conferences, such as those organized by EMAC, AEMARK and ACEDE.

**Mazalan Mifli** is Senior Lecturer in Hotel Management Programme in the Faculty of Business, Economics and Accountancy at Universiti Malaysia Sabah in Kota Kinabalu, Sabah, Malaysia. After seven years' experience in the hospitality industry locally and abroad, he joined the academic field as a tutor. Having graduated with a Master's Degree from the University of Surrey, his specialist interest is in menu development in the food service industry. Currently, both his Ph.D. thesis and recent publications have focused on new menu development in the chain restaurants, particularly in relation to the adoption of strategic product innovation orientation along with market orientation in a mature consumer food service market.

**Hrisa Mitreva** is a Business Travel Consultant in BCD Travel, Kingston upon Hull office. Prior to this position she has worked as Event Manager in Paracyn Ltd, Bulgaria and Operational Manager in Elly Express Ltd, Bulgaria. She holds Cambridge International Diploma in Travel and Tourism, IATA/UFTAA Stepping into Management Diploma, IATA/UFTAA Level Consultant Diploma, IATA/UFTAA foundation and & EBT course diploma, IATA/UFTAA Agent-GDS Amadeus certificate. She finished her bachelor degree at the Hull University Business School. Her research interest focuses on business travel and airline industry alliances.

**Alejandro Mollá-Descals** is a full professor in marketing and chair holder in the Marketing Department at the University of Valencia. His investigation is focused on retail distribution and consumer behavior. His articles have been published in many journals, such as Management Decision, The Service Industries Journal, Journal of Relationship Marketing, Decision Support Systems, Journal of Product & Brand Management, The International Review of Retail, Distribution and Consumer Research, etc. He has had conferences papers in the Annual Conference at the European Marketing Academy – EMAC, Conference of the European Association for Education and Research in the Commercial Distribution (EAERCD), International Marketing Trends Conference, and so on.

**Dirisa Mulindwa** is a Senior lecturer at the University of Sunderland, at the University's London Campus, UK. His research centers on the use of new technologies in tourism and hospitality, particularly how the ROI of these technologies can be evaluated. His doctoral studies focused on the issues of participation, Poverty alleviation and local development using community tourism as the engine for development. Currently, he is teaching on a number of modules including etourism and Hospitality management Studies.

**Vipin Nadda** is a competent, conscientious, reliable and motivated academic professional driven with well organized team spirit and goal oriented approach. He is currently serving as Programme Manager (Postgraduate-Tourism & Hospitality) with University of Sunderland, London Campus. A science graduate with MBA (Marketing), MTA (Tourism) and PhD, he has more than fifteen years of Experience in academics and Industry. Besides this, he has also published two books and presented papers in various international seminars and Global conferences. Dr. Nadda also freelances as 'Education development consultant' for Global Examination Board, University of East London, and 'Associate lecturer' with the Glyndwr University/BPP University/Anglia Ruskin University, Director of studies for PhD with Cardiff Metropolitan University UK, as 'Member of Academic Council' and Chief Examiner for Confederation of Tourism and Hospitality (CTH), London. As an experienced academician, he has been Lecturing a variety of courses ranging from Marketing, HR in 'Business and Management' to 'International Tourism and Hospitality Management' in the UK as well as overseas. With a wide range of industry experience, he has served as 'Product development Manager in the 'Tourism Industry' and 'Marketing Manager' in the 'Pharmaceutical industry' developing tour packages for domestic as well as International customers alongwith the formulation and implementation of business development and marketing strategies overseas. As a consultant to the industry, he was actively involved in the employee's recruitment, development and delivery of training programmes for many companies.

**Charito G. Ngwenya** was the Dean Emeriti of the School of Business Administration of San Isidro College in Malaybalay, Philippines. She has a Bachelor of Science in Business Management from Xavier University, Cagayan de Oro, Philippines and a Graduate degree, MBA School from Cagayan de Oro, Philippines. Currently, she is the COO of BE Meeting Services.

**Ornella Papaluca** is a Research Fellow at the University of Naples Federico II. She received a PhD in Tourism Management in 2011, defending a thesis on La relazione tra Coordinamento e Sistema di Risorse nei prodotti di turismo sostenibile: uno studio attraverso il: Multiple Case Study (The relationship between coordination and resources in sustainable tourism products: a multiple case study). Ornella Papaluca's main research topics are: Resource-Based Theory, Stakeholder Management Theory, Sustainable Development and Sustainable Tourism, Tourism Management, Social Enterprises, Social Innovation and Social Network Analysis. She is a member of Sistur (Societ Italiana di Scienze del Turismo). She has published several chapters in books and has presented several papers in national and international congresses and conferences. She got an award as Best Paper from Young Researchers in the XXXIII Convegno AIDEA. Some of her papers have been published as chapters in books or they have been selected for being published in a selection of conference proceedings.

**Angelo Presenza**, PhD, (University "G. D'Annunzio" of Chieti-Pescara) is Assistant Professor of Business Organization and Tourism Management. He holds a PhD in Organization studies and a Master in Tourism Management. His main research areas of interest are Destination Governance and Management, Event management, Gastronomy and Food, Innovation, and Entrepreneurship. Some of his main recent articles are Presenza et al. (2014), Stakeholder e-involvement and participatory tourism planning: analysis of an Italian case study, International Journal of Knowledge-Based Development, 5(3),311-328; Presenza and Del Chiappa (2013), Entrepreneurial strategies in leveraging food as a tourist resource: a cross-regional analysis in Italy, Journal of Heritage Tourism, 8(2-3),182-192; Presenza and Sheehan (2013), Planning tourism through sporting events, International Journal of Event and Festival Management, 4(2),125-139.

**Manuela Presutti** is an Associate Professor of Management at the Department of Management of Bologna. In 2003, she took a Ph.D in General Management at the University of Bologna – Rimini branch, where she teaches Management of Tourism and Tourism Management. From 2005 to 2010 she was an Assistant Professor at the Department of Management of Bologna. She participates in the research activities of the Advanced School of Tourism Sciences - Rimini Campus of the University of Bologna. Manuela Presutti's main research activity was originally focused on small firms and internationalisation process. During the last years, her research interests have included the analysis of social networks, entrepreneurship, and tourism management.

**Ignacio Rodriguez del Bosque** is Professor of Marketing at the University of Cantabria (Spain). His areas of research include tourism, business communication, relationship marketing and distribution channels. His papers have been published in several international journals, such as Annals of Tourism Research, Tourism Management, Journal of Retailing and Consumer Services, and Industrial Marketing Management.

**Meryem Samirkas** (Assist. Prof. Dr) was born in Mersin/Turkey in 1979. She graduated from Mersin University, Faculty of Economics and Administrative Sciences, Department of Economics in 2001. She got master degree from Mersin University, Institute of Social Sciences, Public Management, Department of Management Sciences and received her PhD degree from Mugla University, Institute of Social Sciences, Department of Economics in 2011. Between 2012 and 2013 she carried out her academic research about tourism economics and macroeconomics at Surrey University in Tourism Management in the Faculty of Business, Economics and Law in the UK. Meryem Samirkaş is still serving as an Assist Prof. in Department of Economics in the Faculty of Economics and Administrative Science in Yuzuncu Yil University.

**Mustafa Can Samirkas** (Lecturer) was born in Mersin/Turkey in 1984. He graduated from Çukurova University, Faculty of Economics and Administrative Sciences, Department of Business Administrative in 2006. He got Business Administrative Sciences master degree from Çukurova University, Institute of Social Sciences and is studying for a PhD on finance, at Çukurova University. He worked at a Participation Bank between 2007-2010 in Turkey as a financial analyst. His research interests focus on banking, financial management, financial analysing and international finance. Mustafa Can Samirkaş is still serving as a lecturer at Department of Finance, Banking and Insurance in Erdemli Vocational School in Mersin University.

**Raymond Saner** is Titular Professor in International Relations and International Management (University of Basle) where he teaches negotiations and dispute settlement at WTO. He also teaches at Sciences Po, Paris in the Master of Public Affairs programme (in partnership with LSE and SIPA-Columbia University) and teaches negotiations in a multi-stakeholder context at the Centre for Sustainability (CSM), Leuphana University in Lüneburg, Germany. He is the co-founder of CSEND, a Geneva based NGRDO (non-governmental research and development organisation (since 1993) and the director of CSEND's Diplomacy Dialogue branch. His research and consulting focuses on conflict studies and international negotiations at bilateral, plurilateral and multilateral levels in the field of trade (WTO), employment and poverty reduction (ILO, PRSP), trade and development (WTO, UNCTAD, EIF), human and social capital development in the educational sector (GATS/ES/WTO and OECD) and trade, investment and climate change (UNCTAD). Raymond Saner pioneered the field of business diplomacy and contributes to the study of multi-stakeholder diplomacy within the field of diplomacy and teaches at Diplomatic Academies and Schools in Europe and North America. He is a reviewer of the Journal of Applied Behaviour (JABS), the Journal of Managerial Psychology, and the Public Organization Review. He has published 14 books, 17 book chapters and 42 refereed journal articles and is reviewer of the Journal of Behavioural Sciences, Public Organization Review and the Journal of Managerial Psychology.

**Maja Šerić** is an assistant professor in the Marketing Department at the University of Valencia. She received Ph.D. Degree in Marketing and her investigation is focused on integrated marketing communications, brand equity, and hospitality marketing. Her papers have been published in several journals, such as: International Journal of Hospitality Management, International Journal of Contemporary Hospitality Management, Journal of Hospitality Marketing & Management, Journal of Relationship Marketing, etc. She has had conference papers in the Annual Conference at the European Marketing Academy – EMAC, Conference of the European Association for Education and Research in the Commercial Distribution (EAERCD), International Marketing Trends Conference, and so on.

**Lorn Sheehan** is Professor of Strategy and Associate Director of the School of Business Administration in the Faculty of Management at Dalhousie University. He is also cross appointed to the School of Resource and Environmental Studies in the Faculty of Management. He also holds a faculty appointment at the University Bayreuth, Germany. Lorn teaches in the areas of strategic management and tourism management. His research is related to tourism destination management, stakeholder management, and entrepreneurship. He has delivered numerous conference presentations and published numerous articles in leading peer-reviewed journals in the tourism field.

**Brent Smith** is Associate Professor of Marketing in the Erivan K. Haub School of Business at Saint Joseph's University. His primary interests include marketing strategy, international marketing, cultural values, marketing ethics, and marketing analytics. His scholarly research appears in Psychology & Marketing, Journal of Business Ethics, Advances in International Management, Marketing Education Review, Journal of Business-to-Business Marketing, Sport Management Education Journal, and other outlets.

**Ebrahim Soltani** (PhD – University of Strathclyde, UK) is a professor of Quality Management at Hamdan Bin Mohammed Smart University (HBMSU), Dubai, United Arab Emirates (UAE). Prior to his appointment, he was a professor of Operations Management at the University of Kent Business School, UK. Ebrahim's research has considered the management of quality in different economic sectors, factors influencing the efficacy of quality and productivity initiatives, human resources issue related to quality management, the management of supply chain and quality in an era of globalisation, and the peculiarities of management mind-set towards operations improvement initiatives. He has recently been working on an Economic and Social Research Council (ESRC)-funded research project which aims to examine 'the dynamics of contextual forces, management's orientations and change management practices in the banking and financial institutions'. He has written widely on managing operations improvement initiatives in a wide range of publications including: British Journal of Management, International Journal of Operations and Production Management, International Journal of Production Research, Production Planning and Control, International Journal of Human Resource Management, Journal of World Business, and Total Quality Management. Ebrahim is an academic member of the ESRC peer review college in the UK and editorial review board Member of several peer-reviewed international journals.

**Mario Tani** is a Research Fellow at the University of Naples Federico II. He received a PhD in Business administration defending a thesis on Knowledge Flows in Short Food Supply Chains in February 2010. He has taught Business Management at the University of Salerno. His main research topics are focused on Stakeholder Management, Alliances and Agreements, Innovation and Social Innovation, Social Enterprises (mostly related to Fair Trade Organizations). He uses Social Network Analysis and Structural Equations Models and has been twice at the Essex University's Summer School on SSDA. He has published some articles in scientific journals and some chapters in book (Italian and International as well). He has attended many conferences presenting papers that have been several times selected to be published as chapters in books or in special issues of scientific journals. He has got the award of Best Paper from Young Researchers" in the XXXIII Convegno AIDEA.

**Ben Tran** received his Doctor of Psychology (Psy.D) in Organizational Consulting/Organizational Psychology from California School of Professional Psychology at Alliant International University in San Francisco, California, United States of America. Dr. Tran's research interests include domestic and expatriate recruitment, selection, retention, evaluation, & training, CSR, business and organizational ethics, organizational/international organizational behavior, knowledge management, and minorities in multinational corporations. Dr. Tran has presented articles on topics of business and management ethics, expatriate, and gender and minorities in multinational corporations at the Academy of Management, Society for the Advancement of Management, and International Standing Conference on Organizational Symbolism. Dr. Tran has also published articles and book chapters with the Social Responsibility Journal, Journal of International Trade Law and Policy, Journal of Economics, Finance and Administrative Science, Financial Management Institute of Canada, and IGI Global.

**Rubina Vieira** is a Lecturer of Tourism Management and has been lecturing at independent colleges and universities for several years. She has a degree in International Relations from Universidade de Lisboa. Rubina completed an MA in Tourism Management at the University of Westminster. She has worked as an associate lecturer for the University of Sunderland and Anglia Ruskin University and is now undertaking PhD research on 'Tourism, Diaspora and Mobilities' at Leeds Beckett University.

**Wei-Yuan Wang** is the Dean of Research and Development Office, and Associate Professor of Department of Business Administration at the Shih Chien University, Taiwan, R.O.C. She received her Ph.D. from the National Chengchi University, Taiwan. Her major research interests include strategies management of corporations and consumer behavior. She has published papers in prestigious journals, such as Canadian Journal of Administrative Sciences, Total Quality Management & Business Excellence, the Journal of Grey System Notice, and others.

**Yue Xu** (PhD, Crandfield School of Management) is a Lecturer in International Business and Strategy at The Hull University Business School, UK. Her research interests focus on the internationalization of different types of firms, in particular firms from the emerging market. She adopts cross disciplinary approach to explore issues regarding innovation and institutions in different sectors, especially the service sectors. She published on European Journal of Marketing, Tourism Management, etc. She has a number of working papers in progresses on the internationalisation of airline companies.

**Lichia Yiu** is President and co-founder of the Centre for Socio-Eco-Nomic Development in Geneva, Switzerland, an independent think tank with special consultative status of the UN. Her current research focuses on aid effectiveness, cross-sector alliances for socio-economic development and on human capital development. She was the originator of the policyscape for tourism development mapping which was published in the report on "Mainstreaming Tourism Development: Policy Coherence and Complementarity" (2011). Presently she is working on the CSEND project developing a participatory monitoring and large data methodology for the implementation of the 2016-2030 UN Sustainable Development Goals. Besides policy research and consulting, she continues to give guest lecturing around the world and visiting professorships in leading Asian universities.

# Index